WRITERS, READERS, AND REPUTATIONS

WRITERS, READERS, AND REPUTATIONS

Literary Life in Britain 1870–1918

PHILIP WALLER

OXFORD
UNIVERSITY PRESS

OXFORD

UNIVERSITY PRESS

Great Clarendon Street, Oxford OX2 6DP

Oxford University Press is a department of the University of Oxford.
It furthers the University's objective of excellence in research, scholarship,
and education by publishing worldwide in

Oxford New York

Auckland Cape Town Dar es Salaam Hong Kong Karachi
Kuala Lumpur Madrid Melbourne Mexico City Nairobi
New Delhi Shanghai Taipei Toronto

With offices in

Argentina Austria Brazil Chile Czech Republic France Greece
Guatemala Hungary Italy Japan Poland Portugal Singapore
South Korea Switzerland Thailand Turkey Ukraine Vietnam

Oxford is a registered trade mark of Oxford University Press
in the UK and in certain other countries

Published in the United States
by Oxford University Press Inc., New York

© Philip Waller 2006

The moral rights of the author have been asserted
Database right Oxford University Press (maker)

First published 2006
Reprinted 2006

British Library Cataloguing in Publication Data

Data available

Library of Congress Cataloging in Publication Data

Data available

Typeset by Newgen Imaging Systems (P) Ltd., Chennai, India
Printed in Great Britain
on acid-free paper by
Antony Rowe Ltd., Chippenham, Wiltshire

ISBN 0–19–820677–1   978–0–19–820677–4

3 5 7 9 10 8 6 4 2

To Matthew, Amy, and Joe,
who grew up with this party going on around them

PREFACE

This book conjures up aspects of literary life in late nineteenth- and early twentieth-century England. It was then that a genuine mass market for literature arose, and with it the phenomenon of the best-seller. Authors' behaviour and standing, the public's responses, and the images created, are the uniting themes of what follows.

The book was conceived, I blush to admit, in the early 1980s, and the material in it has been compiled systematically, though too often desultorily, over the years. Other commissions and duties have supervened: 'The life of the tutor of a college is so incessantly disturbed, so minutely subdivided, that it is difficult indeed for him to produce the least example of a work of "long breath".' That was written a century ago by Edmund Gosse about the bishop and ecclesiastical historian Mandell Creighton, who, curiously, had also been a Fellow of Merton and (founding) editor of the *English Historical Review*. Spells as Senior Tutor and Sub-Warden have slowed the production of this work; yet the College has also provided support and stimulation, and the secretarial help given by Clare Bass, by Julie Gerhardi, and above all by Judith Kirby has been invaluable. The encouragement of Tony Morris, Ruth Parr, and Anne Gelling at the Oxford University Press is likewise much appreciated; and Laurien Berkeley's help has been especially important in the final stages. I must also thank the Radcliffe Trust for appointing me to a History Fellowship, which relieved me of tutorial teaching for the academic year 1997–8. The University of Oxford's Modern History Faculty Board assisted in the preparation of the typescript for publication by equipping me with the services of Jeff New, whom I wish particularly to thank. He went through the entire text, which, extensive though it remains, was once much longer still; accordingly, considerable areas have been truncated or excluded altogether—among them, authors' involvement in the theatre, their relations with the literature of other countries, and their explorations in the realm of unorthodox religion—which can be examined in a succeeding volume.

When this study was started, the subject was eccentric to most concerns, certainly in history faculties, largely in literature faculties too, both seized with sundry '-isms'. Since then it has stealthily become fashionable. It is now enveloped as 'Life Writing', characteristically sonorous jargon that signifies a new academic specialism (aka a professional job creation scheme), though it risks simultaneously throttling public interest. This book is designed to entertain as well as inform.

P.W.

Merton College, Oxford

CONTENTS

IV. WRITERS AND THE PUBLIC: PENMEN AS PUNDITS

LIST OF ILLUSTRATIONS

LIST OF ABBREVIATIONS

BOP	*Boy's Own Paper*
DNB	*Dictionary of National Biography*
GOP	*Girl's Own Paper*
M.A.P.	*Mainly About People*
Oxford DNB	*Oxford Dictionary of National Biography* (2004)
PP	*Parliamentary Papers*
TLS	*Times Literary Supplement*

I

THE READING WORLD

We shall not busy ourselves with what men ought to have admired, what they ought to have written, what they ought to have thought, but with what they did think, write, admire.

(George Saintsbury, *A History of Criticism and Literary Taste in Europe* (1900))

There are three adjectives that have had a devastating effect on English life during the last generation: *new; quick; cheap*.

(Henry Hadow 20 July 1913, in *John Bailey, 1864–1931: Letter and Diaries*, ed. Mrs S. K. Bailey (1935))

Every day we can see the art of literature being more securely harnessed to the chariot of commerce (or should it be the other way round?).

(Michael Joseph, *The Commercial Side of Literature* (1925))

... nothing one reads is ever really lost even if it is apparently forgotten, some impression must have been left, other ideas produced—in fact most books are keynotes.

(Mary Gladstone in *Mary Gladstone (Mrs. Drew): Her Diaries and Letters*, ed. Lucy Masterman (1930))

1

Back to the Future: Authors at the Movies

The late Victorian period ushered in an unprecedented phenomenon, a mass reading public. We may now want to add that this was both the first and the *only* mass literary age. By the time of the Great War, and the development of cinema, telephone, and wireless, audio-visual communication was ready to fetter the written word and to contest its supremacy over the imagination.[1] The *New Statesman* in 1914 was alert in noticing in the press 'one of the most significant paragraphs that have appeared for some time—significant at least to the social historian'; namely,

the announcement that during the past year fewer books had been borrowed from the public libraries in Edinburgh. The significance lies in the fact, not that this happened in Edinburgh, but that it is said to have happened as a result of the popularity of the cinematograph. There is no question that the invention of the cinematograph has made a more radical change in the habits of civilised and partially civilised peoples than anything since the invention of steam.[2]

The *New Statesman* was right to think that the experience of Edinburgh was not unique. The same was reported about Nottingham, where the cinema was blamed for more than a decline in the number of library books borrowed: there gangs of boys, 'fired by the cowboy drama', were charging about the streets 'armed with pistols'.[3] In Glasgow a teenage gang called the Anderston Redskins terrorized its neighbourhood, and in Manchester the Ancoats Napoo was famed for slicing off womens' plaits on the streets and trams in imitation of the scalping techniques of cinematic Red Indians.[4] The wave of school strikes in 1911, when

---

[1] See Viscount Grey's address to the Royal Society of Literature, 'The Pleasure of Reading', May 1924, rep. in Viscount Grey, *Falloden Papers* (1928), esp. 12–14. Grey also blamed the increasing frequency of motor travel for the post-war decline in the reading habit: 'a long railway-journey affords a first-rate opportunity for reading', but a car journey did not.

[2] *New Statesman*, 10 Jan. 1914, 424.

[3] Quoted in Harry Hendrick, *Images of Youth: Age, Class, and the Male Youth Problem 1880–1920* (Oxford, 1990), 133.

[4] Stephen Humphries, *Hooligans or Rebels? An Oral History of Working-Class Childhood and Youth 1889–1939* (Oxford, 1981), 189, 191.

children agitated for a reduction in the use of corporal punishment and detention, and for shorter school hours, longer holidays, and 'no homework', was also attributed in part to the influence of the cinema showing newsreels of the widespread adult strike disturbances of the time.[5] Delinquency was thus encouraged by the cinema presenting before 'these children's greedy eyes with heartless indiscrimination horrors unimaginable...night by night...terrific massacres, horrible catastrophes, motor-car smashes, public hangings, lynchings'. So it was said in 1913; and magistrates could always be found to trace the origins of a criminal career to the same malign source.[6]

To assuage concerns that films were sapping the nation's moral fibre during the Great War, the government commissioned an inquiry under the chairmanship of the Bishop of Birmingham, Charles Gore. Sceptics on this question were included among the membership, such as Marie Stopes and, representing the Society of Authors, an exasperated Edgar Jepson, who described it as

as footling a business as ever I had to do with, and at the end the Stationery Office published a thick volume of its proceedings with the evidence of every busy-body in England, who had insisted on obtaining publicity by appearing before it. What it cost...goodness knows! And at a time when all the money was needed for shells for Passchendaele. All I remember of it is the Canon of the Church of England, a scion of a fine old clerical family, who came to tell us with earnest horror that a medical friend of his had told him that the moving pictures had advanced the age of puberty among the young girls of Lambeth by one year. What could one do with a cleric like that, I ask you?[7]

When the National Council for Public Morals reported in 1917, it tempered the fear that the cinema caused criminality or was responsible for the increase in juvenile crime, having received submissions from chief constables that scotched the idea; but it held fast to the suspicion of sinister influences, stressing 'the moral dangers of darkness' and how films were 'familiarizing the minds of young people with loose ideas of the relations between the sexes'.[8] Schoolteachers especially continued to deplore the effects of the cinema on children. Edward Lyttleton, headmaster of Eton and a resolute hand while administering corporal punishment, was a frequent letter-writer to the press in support of libraries' refusals to stock sensational novels such as Compton Mackenzie's first volume of *Sinister Street* (1913), averring that 'sanity and upright manliness are destroyed, not only by the reading of obscene stuff, but by a premature interest in sex matters'.[9] In 1917 he advocated the exclusion from cinemas of all under 18 years of age, although

---

[5] *The Times*, 13 Sept. 1911. Probably, it was the adult example that exercised the greater influence; for example, there were also school strikes in 1889, coinciding with the Great Docks Strike, when there were no cinema pictures. See *The Times*, 11 Oct. 1889.

[6] Geoffrey Pearson, *Hooligan: A History of Respectable Fears* (1983), 63–4.

[7] Edgar Jepson, *Memories of an Edwardian and Neo-Georgian* (1937), 207.

[8] Quoted in Pearson, *Hooligan*, 32, and in Hendrick, *Images of Youth*, 133.

[9] Letter to *The Times*, in Compton Mackenzie, *My Life and Times: Octave Four 1907–1915* (1965), 197. It was not clear whether Lyttleton had actually read *Sinister Street*.

the impressionable young might be shown films in the schoolroom under supervision. He argued that 'the effects of cinema pictures upon children might be bad, although the pictures were good . . . Children having failed to do things right in school, and seeing films in the cinemas where outwitted policemen, petty larcenies etc. were made to appear simple, saw a field where they might excel if they tried.'[10] In fact, action had been taken already in several towns, in Manchester, Liverpool, and elsewhere, before the Great War to prohibit young persons apparently under 16 (in some cases 14) years of age from attending the later evening performances, unless accompanied by an adult. But even where such supervision existed and where the films shown were 'excellent and instructive' and contained no 'outrage against social order',[11] it still was open to argue that cinemas had ill side-effects. The flickering light caused eye-strain and the stuffy atmosphere damaged health; and the 'vulgarity and silliness, and the distorted, unreal, Americanized (in the worst sense) view of life presented must have a deteriorating effect, and lead, at the best, to the formation of false ideals'.[12]

Less censorious, even sympathetic accounts can be found. C. B. Hawkins's social survey of Norwich, published in 1910, noted the market advantage held by the cinema over the music hall in that city:

Best clothes are a *sine qua non* for the music hall, whereas the cinematograph may be visited without this formality. It is also rather cheaper. Admission is only 2*d.*, whereas the Hippodrome is at least 3*d.*, and if you have reached the stage of 'walking out', it is *de rigueur* to go to the pit, which costs 6*d.*

Hawkins further added:

The popularity of the cinematograph is one of the remarkable phenomena of modern times. But it is after all the most primitive and the simplest of all forms of expression— pictures which tell a story. Here again the morality is always good. The stories which are thrown on the screen, invariably with a musical accompaniment, are either unspeakably sentimental, or crammed with the most thrilling horrors—but it is virtue which triumphs, and the villain never fails to get his proper reward, and innocence always comes by its own. To understand the fascination of such things it is only necessary to realise the endless monotony of industrial life. The average under-educated factory operative who has been cramped for six days in the week at one mechanical operation, demands the

---

[10] *Oxford Times*, 24 Feb. 1917.   [11] Charles E. B. Russell, *Social Problems of the North* (1913), 97–8.
[12] Charles E. B. Russell, *The Problems of Juvenile Crime* (1917), 6, quoted in Pearson, *Hooligan*, 31. The studios of the pre-war British film industry were centred in the East London suburbs: see Margaret O'Brien and Julia Holland, ' "Picture Shows": The Early British Film Industry in Walthamstow', *History Today*, Feb. 1987, 9–15. About a quarter of the films exhibited in Britain in 1914 were British-made, a proportion that fell to 5 per cent by 1926. The disruption of the Great War apart, one explanation for the decline was the greater size of the American domestic market, which enabled the US film industry to recover its costs quicker. As early as 1910 there were 10,000 cinemas in the United States attracting audiences of 30 million per week (Richard Maltby (ed.), *Dreams for Sale: Popular Culture in the 20th Century* (1989), 37). The revolution involved distribution as well as production: most cinemas in Britain, like most pubs, became tied houses in exclusive networks.

wildest and most thrilling adventures by way of compensation. It is a natural reaction, and is better satisfied in this way than in the public-house.[13]

This very lightness of the cinema's appeal was what troubled others who did not condemn its morality. The popularity of the cinema was judged 'only another sign of the restless spirit of the age', 'pandering to the taste for sensation' and adding to that category of modern entertainments which 'makes no demand upon any sustained thought'. Its precursor, the music hall, had also been condemned for the rapidity with which 'turns' followed each other: 'serious succeeded by comic, and sentimental by tragic'. The 'same inability to concentrate attention' was expressed in the preference for reading ' "tit-bits" or any collection of snippets to the long-drawn-out tales of former days'.[14] Thus addressed the cinema was but one aspect of the debate about modern culture. Much of it was focused as a particular issue concerning young working-class males. The period 1880–1920 is distinguished for the 'discovery' of special psychological and behavioural characteristics governing masculine adolescence. This led to the labelling of a host of economic, social, and moral 'problems' that required the attention of State legislators, teachers, and philanthropists if the nation's youth were to become capable citizens.[15]

There can be little doubt that some adolescents did take to the cinema in a big way. Pat O'Mara recalled spending his tuppences on 'regular twelve-hour Saturday vigils in the Palais de Luxe Cinema' in pre-war Liverpool.[16] But O'Mara and other male youths hardly constituted the entire clientele. The Christian Social Union worker Charles Russell, who was also city councillor for 'a very poor ward' in Manchester, acknowledged the 'fascination which the films possess for many older persons'; and he explained this by their wanting a change of scene from the home. This was especially true for women: widows escaping loneliness and mothers who were fugitives from domestic drudgery. The cinema was thus much like the cleaned-up music hall, to be praised for contributing 'no little of the decrease in drunkenness'; and it was 'the cheapest of all forms of entertainment, since for a penny or two a couple of hours' amusement may be enjoyed, as well as rest in a comfortable chair'. Hence 'the coming of the kinematograph theatre has been in many ways a great boon'. The pity was that 'its management caters as a rule only for the less serious tastes of the audience, neglecting the instructive possibilities of photographic films'. In sum: 'It is to be feared that purely silly and sensational amusements are coming to play a much larger part in the general life of the community.'[17]

This discussion of the cinema as a social and cultural problem is relatively familiar. Less well emphasized by historians are the responses of writers and

[13] C. B. Hawkins, *Norwich: A Social Study* (1910), 310–11.   [14] Russell, *Social Problems*, 96–7.

[15] See Hendrick, *Images of Youth*; and, generally, Donald J. Shoemaker, *Theories of Delinquency: An Examination of Explanations of Delinquent Behaviour* (Oxford, 1990).

[16] Pat O'Mara, *The Autobiography of a Liverpool Irish Slummy* (1934), 97.

[17] Russell, *Social Problems*, 7, 94–8.

publishers. It was in America that the first magazines appeared devoted entirely to the new medium. Among the pioneers was the *Motion Picture Magazine*, followed in 1915 by the *Picture-Play Weekly*, which emanated from the largest publisher of popular fiction, Street & Smith. These magazines featured film reviews and film-star news, short stories based upon films, and a section of 'Hints for Scenario Writers'.[18] They generated a large circulation and correspondence which signalled the emergence of the film fan and budding screenwriter. In Britain a similar set of reactions was evident.[19] Authors took note of the cinema's seductions and its commercial potential. Henry James may have been fated to craft only 'invincibly unsaleable' books, as he deprecatingly defined them; but he 'quite revelled' in a cinematograph exhibition that pictured the heavyweight boxing match in Carson City, Nevada, in 1897 when the American 'Gentleman' James Corbett lost his world title to the British-born Bob Fitzsimmons, who felled him with a solar-plexus punch.[20] And in the short story 'Crapy Cornelia' (1909) James described a 'little sparsely feathered black hat' as an object 'that grew and grew, that came nearer and nearer, while it met his eyes, after the manner of images in the cinematograph'.[21] A similar comparison previously occurred to Edith Nesbit in *The Railway Children* (1906): 'when the train passed the fence where the three children were, newspapers and hands and handkerchiefs were waved madly, till all that side of the train was fluttery with white like the pictures of the King's Coronation in the biograph at Maskelyne and Cook's'.[22] But the supreme moment when cinema was married with literature had been provided by Kipling in 'Mrs Bathurst' (1904). Here he told the story of the unsettling effect on four men who happen to see the moving image of a woman they think they recognize among a crowd filmed at a station. The station is Paddington in London, the newsreel is shown at a cinema in Cape Town in South Africa, and the woman is a sailors' boarding-house keeper at Hauraki near Auckland in New Zealand: the world is now a parish linked in snapshot. Within a few years the cinema show was an urban fixture. Always up to date, Arnold Bennett described in *The Price of Love* (1914) how the Five Towns of the Potteries could boast of 'picture-palaces in dozens' as well as theatres and music halls. In chapter 8, 'The Cinema', Louis Fores takes Rachel Fleckring to the Imperial Cinema de Luxe:

The Imperial had set out to be the most gorgeous cinema in the Five Towns; and it simply was. Its advertisements read: 'There is always room at the top'. There was. Over the ceiling of its foyer enormous crimson peonies expanded like tropic blooms, and the

---

[18] Quentin Reynolds, *The Fiction Factory* (New York, 1955), 169–70. The cover of the first issue of *Picture-Play Weekly*, 4 Sept. 1915, pictured Charlie Chaplin in a scene from his latest film, *In the Park*.

[19] David Robinson, *World Cinema: A Short History*, (rev. edn. 1981), 31.

[20] Leon Edel, *The Life of Henry James*, ii (Harmondsworth, 1977), 230.

[21] Leon Edel (ed.), *The Complete Tales of Henry James*, xii: 1903–1910 (1964), 343.

[22] E. Nesbit, *The Railway Children* (Oxford, 1991), 178. Maskelyne and Cook's Hall of Magic was in Piccadilly.

heart of each peony was a sixteen-candle-power electric lamp. No other two cinemas in the Five Towns, it was reported, consumed together as much current as the Imperial de Luxe; and nobody could deny that the degree of excellence of a cinema is finally settled by its consumption of electricity.[23]

Welcomed at the cinema entrance by a commissionaire 'dressed not less glitteringly than an Admiral of the Fleet in full uniform', Rachel is transported into a 'crystal dream'.

Authors wrote about the cinema; they soon wrote for the cinema and like the cinema. This last was Douglas Goldring's tart assessment in 1920 of Compton Mackenzie's development as a novelist, from *The Passionate Elopement* (1911), *Carnival* (1912), *Sinister Street* (1913–14), and *Guy and Pauline* (1915), through to *Sylvia Scarlett* (1918), *Sylvia and Michael* (1919), and *Poor Relations* (1919). It was a matter of Mackenzie coming to realize, thought Goldring, that he had no talent for psychology or characterization. The novels all suffered from spiritual emptiness, the people in them lacking sincerity or depth of feeling. Mackenzie could only describe people, places, and situations externally; but he did that with brilliance, showing that he 'had little to learn about cameras . . . when he wrote of the appearance of a street, or of the outside of a house, the amazed reader felt that that street or that house must actually have been before his eyes at that time'. Goldring contended that Mackenzie progressively came to terms with his deficiency as a novelist and decided to take on the cinema at its own level, concealing 'his inability to describe the real emotions and experiences of real people by diverting his readers with a series of vivid pictures'. He thus 'found himself—not as a serious novelist, but as that very valuable thing, an entertainer'.[24] None of this was particularly surprising: Mackenzie hailed from a theatrical family and was brother to the stage and film star Fay Compton. *Carnival*, about a ballet dancer and stage life, sold nearly half a million copies and was immediately adapted for the theatre; afterwards it was made into a radio play and both silent and sound films.[25]

In 1915 Walter de la Mare mocked the silent cinema, calling it the 'unsubjective Academy of the deaf mute'. This was his response to the press reporting the brazen declaration of Hall Caine, one of the country's best-selling authors, that were he starting his career now he would produce films, not novels.[26] The special circumstances of the war years, when Caine was involved in propaganda, had whetted his interest; and cinematic adaptations of his stories were already under way.[27] E. Phillips Oppenheim, assigned to the Ministry of Information, recalled that 'Hall Caine, with a portfolio of war films under his arm, was a *constant*

---

[23] Arnold Bennett, *The Price of Love* (1914), ch. 8.   [24] Douglas Goldring, *Reputations* (1920), 42–51.

[25] Donald Brook, *Writers' Gallery* (1970), 84. *Carnival* was first filmed in 1921, *Sinister Street* in 1922.

[26] Walter de la Mare, *Westminster Gazette*, 2 Oct. 1915, in Norman Sherry (ed.), *Conrad: The Critical Heritage* (1973), 292.

[27] Vivian Allen, *Hall Caine: Portrait of a Victorian Romancer* (Sheffield, 1997), 360 ff., for the film associations.

visitor.'[28] The effectiveness of film as propaganda was now more widely appreciated, as were its commercial possibilities for the writer. Oppenheim himself was not slow to spot this. He was living as a tax exile on the Riviera in 1925 when Sidney Dark wrote of him that 'perhaps more than any other English novelist he has discovered (and exploited) the financial possibilities of the cinema'.[29] Oppenheim's thrillers were set in grand hotels, casinos, and foreign embassies, with a cast of rich and titled characters travelling to exotic and mysterious locations via luxury liners and transcontinental trains. These ingredients naturally served cinema spectacle, although prudent film-makers with an eye to an international audience needed to show caution about identifying foreign villainy. William Le Queux's fictional exercise in Germanophobia *The Invasion of 1910* (1906) attracted the Gaumont Cinematograph Company in 1912. It not only planned to change the title, updating it to *The Raid of 1915*, it also intended to shoot two endings, one with Britain as the winner, the other Germany. *Punch* mischievously recommended showing Britain victorious in Germany, and Germany victorious in Britain.[30] Finished in 1913, the film was held up by the new British Board of Film Censors and, when eventually released in October 1914, three months after the start of the Great War, it had been retitled again, appearing as *If England were Invaded*. Le Queux estimated that his contract was worth more than £3,000, no small matter for an author who was facing bankruptcy proceedings in 1913.[31]

Book, play, and film were not discrete. The first film of an Arnold Bennett work, *The Great Adventurer* (1915), was adapted from his successful play with that title (1913), which itself had been adapted from his novel *Buried Alive* (1908). Bennett wrote of the film: 'Of course it was tremendously vulgarized, but it was certainly not so bad as I expected. It contained some ideas that would have been in the play if I had thought of them.'[32] *Milestones* (play, 1912) became a film in 1916; but Bennett was yet to be convinced that the financial terms were attractive enough. Early in 1917 he discussed with his agent, J. B. Pinker, 'the whole question of cinematograph rights, which I regard as a swindle on the author'.[33] One particularly thorny matter was brought into focus by Baroness Orczy, whose *Scarlet Pimpernel* (1905) was both a best-seller and a long-running stage success. The contract for the play had been drawn up between the authors (Orczy and her husband, Montagu Barstow) and the producers (Fred Terry and his wife,

[28] E. Phillips Oppenheim, *Pool of Memory* (1941), 41. Caine scripted the film *Victory and Peace* (1918), involving Ellen Terry and Ben Greet.   [29] Sidney Dark, *Mainly about Other People* (1925), 219.

[30] *Punch*, 1 May 1912.

[31] The Official Receiver judged this estimate exaggerated, however; see Roger T. Stearn, 'The Mysterious Mr Le Queux: War Novelist, Defence Publicist and Counterspy', *Soldiers of the Queen: The Journal of the Victorian Military Society*, 70 (Sept. 1992), 21. Dr Stearn kindly gave me a copy of his article.

[32] Arnold Bennett to Septimus Bennett, 11 July 1916, in James Hepburn (ed.), *Letters of Arnold Bennett*, iv: *Family Letters* (Oxford, 1986), 162.

[33] Newman Flower (ed.), *The Journals of Arnold Bennett*, ii: *1911–1921* (1932), 184 (24 Jan. 1917). See also pp. 267, 269 (29 Apr., 3 July 1920) for further conversations with Pinker about film contracts.

Julia Neilson, who also played the leads); but, while Orczy was keen to strike a deal for a cinema version, 'Fred Terry was an avowed and bitter enemy of the films, which he looked upon as successful rivals of theatrical enterprise.' Not being able to budge Terry, Orczy went to law, whereupon stalemate became solidified by a ruling that, 'whereas the copyright in the book was indisputably mine, the rights in the play were equally indisputably the Terrys'. Neither side would be allowed to negotiate cinematograph rights without the consent of the other.'[34] An American adaptation of *The Scarlet Pimpernel* was made in 1917; but, essentially, Orczy remained frustrated until Terry's death in 1932 freed her to negotiate with Alexander Korda and London Film Productions. Their celebrated film version, starring Leslie Howard, Merle Oberon, and Raymond Massey, finally reached the screens in 1934.

Frances Hodgson Burnett found herself confronted with a different, albeit related, issue—whether the film of a story might drain away custom from a play production and thus leave the author little better off. She was conscious of having several lucrative assets, especially her best-seller *Little Lord Fauntleroy* (1886), from which she had carved a profitable stage version in 1888. In 1911 she received an offer from the Vitagraph company, but her agent advised against her selling the rights. She commented, 'I already know that the motion pictures are said to greatly influence the theatres and as *Fauntleroy* is continually played still, I feel sure that Mr Edwards is right.'[35] A year later she reviewed the position, having been approached by the Kinemacolor company, 'which is rich and respectable and whose process is by far the most interesting'. She was beginning to reckon that 'Moving Picture rights . . . are likely to represent definite income in the future'; and in October 1913 Kinemacolor cabled its offer: 'Guarantee $8,000 Minimum For First Two Years', for films of *The Dawn of a Tomorrow* (1906) and of *Esmeralda*, which she had written in the 1870s and made into a popular play with William Gillette in 1881. On returning to New York, she finalized contracts for these and for four other films of her books: *Fauntleroy, The Pretty Sister of José* (1889), *A Lady of Quality* (1896), and *The Little Princess* (1905). She also contemplated writing 'an original story for the cinematograph'. Mary Pickford was to star in several of these films—*The Dawn of a Tomorrow* and *Esmeralda*, made in 1915—and when she appeared in the lavish production of *Little Lord Fauntleroy* in 1921, playing both the little Lord and his mother (a more fitting part for a no longer slender 27-year-old), it was screened in some 8,000 cinemas in North America and countless more worldwide.[36]

'We have had a great excitement this week—great to us, who live so soberly & remotely.' This was Florence Dugdale, soon-to-be wife of the septuagenarian

---

[34] Baroness Orczy, *Links in the Chain of Life* (1947), 164–6.

[35] Ann Thwaite, *Waiting for the Party: The Life of Frances Hodgson Burnett, 1849–1924* (1994), 231. Vitagraph annoyed Hall Caine by making an unauthorized version of his best-seller *The Christian* (1897) in 1914, and reissuing it in 1917, five years before he was a party to a production (Allen, *Caine*, 360).

[36] Thwaite, *Burnett*, 231–2, 237, 245–6.

novelist and poet Thomas Hardy, writing from deepest Dorset in 1913. For the Herkomer Film Company had come to Dorchester, to present a private showing of their films for Hardy and to select scenes for *Far from the Madding Crowd*. Their film of this novel was never in fact made; but Hardy was the better off by Herkomer's purchase of the film rights.[37] That the sums involved were now fast rising can be evidenced by J. M. Barrie. He was offered £2,000 'in advance of royalties' by Hollywood for the film rights to *Peter Pan* in 1912, and a £20,000 advance by the French in 1918.[38] Barrie's fascination with the new medium was illustrated by his organizing a 'Cinema Supper' at the Savoy Theatre on 3 July 1914, a month before the outbreak of the Great War. This comprised a banquet (the guests included the Prime Minister, Asquith) and a series of sketches, all recorded on film. It was Barrie's intention to include movie shots of his guests, arriving, eating, and drinking, as a scene in his revue. Asquith disallowed this, properly guarding his relaxation; still, Barrie seemed set on making a film—or on humiliating his friends—and he transferred his film crew to the wastes of Essex, where, with Granville Barker as co-director, he staged a western sketch involving Lord Howard de Walden (an ancestor had foiled the Gunpowder Plot), the Ibsenite critic William Archer, and G. K. Chesterton and Bernard Shaw, all dressed as cowboys.[39] These antics apart, the first of Barrie's work to be filmed was *The Admirable Crichton* (1902), which appeared, mangled in title and most else, first as *Shipwrecked* in 1913, then as *Male and Female* in 1919. The latter was directed by Cecil B. DeMille and starred Gloria Swanson as the spoilt Lady Mary Lasenby. It was scripted by Jeanie Macpherson: Barrie 'had nothing to do with this, except to take his very large fee, and was pretty well disgusted by what he eventually saw'.[40] Films of Barrie plays or stories came tumbling out: nine between 1913 and 1918, and a further seven between 1919 and 1922. When an American production of *Peter Pan*, directed by Herbert Brenon, emerged in 1924, Barrie 'thought decidedly more favourably of it' because Brenon's cutting followed his instructions; but, Barrie added, 'so far it is only repeating what is done on the stage, and the only reason for a film should be that it does the things the stage can't do'.[41]

Liberated from money worries, Barrie could afford to give consideration to the artistic question. For penurious authors the cinema's principal attraction was the

---

[37] Florence Dugdale to Rebekah Owen, 10 Dec. 1913, in Michael Millgate (ed.), *Letters of Emma and Florence Hardy* (Oxford, 1996), 90. On Sir Hubert von Herkomer, who had died in 1914 and is best known as a painter, see *DNB*. *Far from the Madding Crowd* eventually appeared on film, directed by Laurence Trimble, in 1915. The first Hardy story to be filmed, *Tess of the D'Urbervilles*, in 1913, was an American production. [38] Viola Meynell (ed.), *Letters of J. M. Barrie* (1942), 60–1.

[39] G. K. Chesterton, *Autobiography* (1936), 237–41 (including a photograph of Barrie and his four 'cowboys' opposite p. 240). *Rosy Rapture*, a film sequence written by Barrie and directed by Percy Nash for a revue at the Duke of York Theatre in 1914, included Chesterton and Shaw. The latter, together with Barrie himself, also appeared in *Masks and Faces* (1918), based on the novel (1854) by Charles Reade, who had adapted it for the stage with Tom Taylor.

[40] Denis Mackail, *The Story of J.M.B.* (1941), 468–70, 554–5, 588–90; and Meynell (ed.), *Barrie Letters*, 104–5.

[41] Barrie to Lady Cynthia Asquith, 14 Nov. 1924, in Meynell (ed.), *Barrie Letters*, 201. Barrie's keen interest in the cinema can be followed in the diaries of Lady Cynthia Asquith, who became Barrie's secretary in 1918: see *Diaries 1915–1918* (1987), 153–4, 361–2, 368–71, 452.

revenue it might yield. Lady Cynthia Asquith recorded in her diary in 1917 a conversation involving Charles Whibley and D. H. Lawrence: 'We talked a lot about the cinema and agreed all to try and make our fortunes by writing plays for it—I said I would get hold of a manuscript of a "scenario" to ascertain the technique.'[42] This was a pipe-dream, and no film was made of a Lawrence story before 1950. Generally, the author whose name was established as a public favourite stood more chance of exploiting the film medium; and, in his lifetime at least, Lawrence was not in that category. In 1925 the literary agent Michael Joseph wrote, 'Mention film rights to the inexperienced author and his eye lights up at once.' He then added damply, 'This optimistic attitude is not justified by the facts.' Joseph reckoned that the 'average price for an ordinary "five-reeler" where the author is not very well known is about £200 in this country', in America about double. Joseph, however, knew of £5,000 being paid recently by an English company; and in America '$50,000 [over £10,000] is by no means a top price'.[43]

Authors whose names and stories already struck a chord with the public were the ones who commanded the higher fee. Rider Haggard was perhaps the country's best-paid writer between 1887 and 1894, when his earnings exceeded £10,000 annually. Between 1905 and 1909 these had fallen to a third. Still, about £3,500 constituted a handsome income and cheap editions of his adventures were selling strongly: *She* (1887) had sold half a million copies in its first penny edition in 1903. By the middle of the Great War Haggard's income had bounced back: he was receiving £9,000 from cinema royalties. The film rights to six of his novels had been bought. His comforts thereafter derived as much from this source as from book sales. A new film version of *She* opened in England in February 1916. By June nearly 2 million people had paid to see it. Haggard himself viewed it in October, noting tersely: 'It is fair, considering all things, though somewhat distressing to an author.'[44] Anthony Hope too enjoyed a cinematic windfall. After *The Prisoner of Zenda* (1894) launched him into the top bracket of author–earners, he aggregated £70,000 from his work over the next decade. Like Haggard's, his income then tailed off. Hope considered his boom well and truly over by 1909; he was receiving smaller advances and selling few copies of new stories, although sevenpenny editions of his 1890s favourites were popular. In 1913 *The Prisoner of Zenda* was first filmed. Hope saw it at Twickenham—'interesting, queer, and slightly ridiculous', he thought. *The Prisoner*'s sequel, *Rupert of Hentzau* (1898), was also soon destined for celluloid conversion. The decade 1913–23 brought Hope

[42] Cynthia Asquith, *Diaries*, 372 (27 Nov. 1917).

[43] Michael Joseph, *The Commercial Side of Literature* (n.d. [1925]), 184–90.

[44] D. S. Higgins, *Rider Haggard: The Great Storyteller* (1981), chs. 5–9; id. (ed.), *The Private Diaries of Sir Henry Rider Haggard 1914–1925* (1980), entries for 5 June, 2 Oct. 1916. The six novels to which film rights were bought in 1915–16 were, with original publication in brackets: *Dawn* (1884), *King Solomon's Mines* (1885), *Allan Quatermain* (1887), *She* (1887), *Montezuma's Daughter* (1893), and *Queen Sheba's Ring* (1910). *She* had been filmed twice before, in 1908 and 1911.

£10,000 from film rights. Wisely, in 1922 he refused an offer of £2,000 to part with all future cinema rights in *The Prisoner* and *Rupert*; shortly afterwards, he received the same sum just for eight years' interest in *Rupert*.[45]

The emerging film industry had challenged theatres and especially the variety houses and music halls most directly, though it was through music halls, as well as fairgrounds and travelling showmen, that films were first projected. In 1904 a 'Daily Bioscope' opened in Bishopsgate, London. Soon, several music halls and theatres such as the Balham Empire were given over to film shows.[46] The first purpose-built cinema in Britain was the Central Hall in Colne, Lancashire, in 1908.[47] London had ninety cinemas in 1909, 400 in 1912; Manchester had over 100 in 1913, and there were 3,500 altogether in Britain in 1914. By 1917 there were 3.5 million filmgoers per day in Britain, and half the acting profession was exclusively engaged in film work. One, Charlie Chaplin, so 'projected his personality over the globe' as to become 'the most celebrated man the world has ever known'. Born in Walworth in 1889, the son of music-hall performers, Chaplin made his debut as a clog-dancer at the Theatre Royal, Manchester, in 1898 before progressing to Hollywood in 1913, contracted to the Keystone Film Company at $150 (about £30) per week. The first Chaplin films were released in Britain in June 1914. During the war Chaplin's waif–tramp became a universal figure, the apotheosis of the common man, whose 'theme is the triumph of the humble and meek over the embattled tyrannies of the world'.[48] More prosaically, there were Chaplin dolls, toys and figurines, picture postcards, newspaper cartoons and comic-strip magazines, music sheets, dances and songs, and other spin-off merchandise.[49] In 1921, when Chaplin called on J. M. Barrie—a meeting between the world's best-known and richest actor and the country's best-known and richest dramatist—a police escort was required for the film star; and, naturally, all these policemen, Barrie observed, produced 'their own autograph books for him [Chaplin] to sign'.[50]

In 1917 Chaplin had signed the famous 'million-dollar contract' with First National; but the question then that most concerned the critic A. R. Orage was 'whether the cinema can ever command the attention of the intelligent as a form of art'. He was doubtful: 'The programme is designed to amuse, to thrill, to interest, but never to instruct.' This was beneficial for the theatre and for

[45] Sir Charles Mallet, *Anthony Hope and his Books* (1935), 182, 184, 214, 248–9. Films of *The Prisoner* were released in 1913, 1915, and 1922; and of *Rupert* in 1916 and 1923.

[46] The first of London's principal theatres to put on films was Drury Lane when managed by Arthur Collins. This was on 22 March 1916, when D. W. Griffith's *The Birth of a Nation* was shown: 'It ran for eighty-seven performances at ordinary theatre prices, and was revived the next year, when it ran for another twenty-six performances. *Intolerance*, another of Griffith's films, was shown on April 7, 1917, and ran for eighty-six performances' (Horace Collins, *My Best Riches* (1941), 86). For the relationship of the nascent film industry to the world of theatres and music halls, see Allardyce Nicoll, *English Drama, 1900–1930* (Cambridge, 1973), 40–8.   [47] Robinson, *World Cinema*, 27.

[48] A. G. Gardiner, 'Charles Chaplin', in Gardiner, *Certain People of Importance* (1929), 186–91.

[49] David Robinson, *Chaplin: His Life and Art* (1985), 142–54.

[50] Meynell (ed.), *Barrie Letters*, 194. Chaplin stayed until two in the morning with Barrie, who found him intelligent, forceful, and likeable, and was amused when he called stage drama the 'Speakies'.

literature. Just as journals of ideas not only coexisted but flourished alongside picture-papers, so drama and the novel might profit if the cinema drew off 'those elements that are actually superfluous in those arts'. Chiefly, this meant mere sense-impression, Orage noting that before the cinema came, too many play productions emphasized the picturesque. Beerbohm Tree's staging of Shakespeare at Her/His Majesty's Theatre had involved extravagant tableaux: Alma-Tadema marble, real trees and terraces, gondolas, fountains, and livestock. Tree was 'a cinema-artiste before his time', Orage concluded; but, now that the cinema was developing, 'the play of character, of psychology, and of the spoken word may come to be written again'.[51]

A similar assessment had been made by the *New Statesman* in 1914. Because films were silent (and remained so until 1927), it predicted that 'literature and drama will survive even the most ingenious cinematograph. It is the rival of the painter rather than of the poet and the novelist. The painter has always laboured under the handicap that he could not portray, but only suggest, movement . . . Perhaps the Titians and Corots of the future will be film-painters. Certainly the Friths will be.'[52] Somerset Maugham put the relationship between film and literature differently in 1921, predicting that 'in the long run it will be found futile to adapt stories for the screen from novels or from plays, and that any advance in this form of entertainment which may eventually lead to something artistic, lies in the story written directly for projection on the white screen'.[53] At this embryonic stage, the advantage lay with the established author, preferably one who was dead and who therefore could not protest about the travesty made of his work. Saki was exceptional in this as in many things. Dead since 1916, he had his wishes protected by a surviving sister, who still in 1937 rejected requests from America to film an adaptation of *The Unbearable Bassington* (1912). Recollecting his 'detestation of that country's commercialism', she stated that Saki would never sanction any adaptation by another hand 'and as he did not care for films, no mention of film rights was ever made in the [publisher's] agreements. So in refusing permission I am doing what he would have done himself. Judging by the vulgarization of some British authors' works when filmed, I can imagine what

---

[51] *The New Age*, 21 (1917), 488–9, repr. in Wallace Martin (ed.), *Orage as Critic* (1974), 106–7. Presumably, Orage knew that Tree had become a film actor, appearing in *Henry VIII* in 1911, *Trilby* in 1914, and *The Old Folks at Home* and *Macbeth* in 1916. He even appeared as an uncredited extra in D. W. Griffith's *Intolerance* (1916). Lady Cynthia Asquith saw Tree's *Macbeth* and judged it comically awful; see her *Diaries*, 182 (29 June 1916), and Hesketh Pearson, *Beerbohm Tree* (1988), 225. The world's first film sequence of Shakespeare, in 1899, featured Tree in a tableau of King John signing Magna Carta. It was filmed on the Victoria Embankment. (The National Film Theatre included it in a Silent Shakespeare Season in 1994; see *The Times*, 4 Aug. 1994, 31.) Tree was early aware of the challenge represented by the new medium, predicting in 1905: 'the theatre will go under if the Kinematograph plays are improved, as they threaten to be' (R. D. Blumenfeld, *R.D.B.'s Diary 1887–1914* (1930), 199–200 (4 July 1905)). On the *film d'art* trend, see Robinson, *World Cinema*, 50–5.   [52] *New Statesman*, 10 Jan. 1914, 426.

[53] Ted Morgan, *Somerset Maugham* (1980), 248.

a hash would be made of Saki's stories.'[54] But having sat through an 'original' film and finding it intolerable, *The Times*'s critic in 1920 had been in no doubt that 'the better-class film' would continue to draw inspiration from past novels and plays; whereupon he welcomed an advertisement by the Ideal Film Company that it had in preparation films of novels such as Dickens's *Pickwick Papers* (1837), Walter Besant's *All Sorts and Conditions of Men* (1882), and George Gissing's *Demos* (1886), and of plays such as Walter Howard's *The Prince and the Beggar-Maid* (1908), Dion Clayton Calthorp's *The Old Country* (1916), and H. F. Maltby's *The Rotters* (1916). He had recently seen a film of Pinero's, *The Gay Lord Quex* (1899), which 'takes no liberties with the text; and altogether is an example of how this kind of thing should be done'. The benefits were twofold: to a past novel or play of quality that was given a new lease of life, and to the cinema itself, which, like a nouveau riche, was raised by following an aristocratic model.[55] But practice regularly deviated from this code. Somerset Maugham's initial experience of his works being filmed—his novel *The Explorer* (1907) was filmed in 1915, his plays *Smith* (1909) and *The Land of Promise* (1913–14) in 1917—was 'horror mitigated only by the fifteen thousand dollars'.[56]

After the Great War it became commonplace for best-selling authors to be hired to write film scenarios, adapting their own or another's work, or commissioned to produce a new story for the screen. The producer Jesse Lasky, who in 1912 had gone into partnership with Sam Goldfish (later Goldwyn) and Cecil B. DeMille, was keen to contract such authors, instruct them in the technical peculiarities of film production, and get them to write screen scenarios. This was in 1920, and among those who accepted his invitation were Maugham, Sir Gilbert Parker, Edward Knoblock, Maurice Maeterlinck, and Elinor Glyn. Glyn moved to Hollywood for seven years and was paid $10,000 (over £2,000) per picture, plus travelling expenses. She was credited with introducing to Hollywood more authentic costuming, settings, and staging of historical and High Society drama, and also with instructing stars such as Rudolph Valentino and Gloria Swanson about 'the art of making love before a camera in a way which would carry conviction'. Still, she did not disguise the cavalier way with which studios handled an author's work:

All authors, living or dead, famous or obscure, shared the same fate. Their stories were re-written and completely altered either by the stenographers and continuity girls of the scenario department, or by the Assistant Director and his lady-love, or by the leading lady, or by anyone else who happened to pass through the studio; and even when at last after infinite struggle a scene was shot which bore some resemblance to the original story it was certain to be left out in the cutting-room or pared away to such an extent that all meaning which it might once have had was lost.[57]

---

[54] A. J. Langguth, *Saki: A Life of Hector Hugh Munro* (Oxford, 1982), 323.
[55] *The Times*, 7 June 1920.   [56] Morgan, *Maugham*, 144, 157, 249.
[57] Elinor Glyn, *Romantic Adventure* (1936), chs. xxvii, xxix; Robinson, *World Cinema*, 110.

Such disillusionment notwithstanding, authors continued to accept the cheques. Hugh Walpole was one of many so engaged. He even appeared in a film, acting the part of the Vicar of Blunderstone in his own adaptation of Dickens's *David Copperfield* for MGM in 1935.[58] G. K. A. Bell's remark to Arthur Benson in 1915, when he styled Walpole as a member of the '*Cinematograph* school' of authors, now appeared less of a slight than a prophecy.[59]

[58] Rupert Hart-Davis, *Hugh Walpole* (1952), 348–51. See also James Agate, *A Shorter Ego* (1946), 58 (2 Nov. 1934), for disparaging comments on this. Walpole was not the first famous author to act on film: Mark Twain appeared in *A Curious Dream* (1907) and *The Prince and the Pauper* (1909), and Conan Doyle in *The $5,000,000 Counterfeiting Plot* (1914) and *The Lost World* (1925).

[59] David Newsome, *On the Edge of Paradise: A. C. Benson, The Diarist* (1980), 326. Bell was then Chaplain to the Archbishop of Canterbury.

2

Consenting and Dissenting Bibliophiles in Public and Private

These working men put us men of leisure to horrible shame by the amount they manage to read.

(John Bailey, Feb. 1917, *Letters and Diaries*, ed. Mrs S. K. Bailey (1935)).[1]

Spectacle aside, whether theatrical, cinematic, or sporting, reading still held pride of place among pre-1914 entertainments. Max Beerbohm's eponymous heroine Zuleika Dobson (1911) was fantastic not just for her beauty but for the size of her library. It comprised two books, *Bradshaw's Railway Timetable* and the *A.B.C. Guide*.[2] By contrast, a real-life romantic, Frances Stevenson, born in 1888, recollected that from childhood she

read greedily. Books then were not so easily come by as they are now, and were much more precious. In those days we read our books over and over again, and loved them none the less for doing so. As children we had to be content with those already on our bookshelves and any that were given us. I formed an early acquaintance with Dickens, weeping copiously over Little Dorrit and Little Nell; and I knew by heart many of the passages in the *Ingoldsby Legends*, a volume that had been given me as a Christmas present when I was ten years old! The poems fascinated and horrified me, as did also the Cruikshank illustrations to the book. I wept over the 'Wide, Wide World' and 'Home Influence', but I lost myself in a magical world while reading the poems of Scott. I think

---

[1] Bailey (1864–1931) took a weekly class in literature at Toynbee Hall and, later, at the Working Men's College. His remark was provoked by having had lunch with Frederick Rockell, of the Co-operative Wholesale Society. He had formed a friendship with Rockell from mutual love of literature, on 10 March 1906 recording how Rockell 'pleased me when we were looking at some ship pictures by quoting Bridges' "Whither O Splendid Ship". No one who hasn't a real turn for poetry quotes or cares for that. I hardly know a better test of imagination' (Mrs S. K. Bailey (ed.), *John Bailey, 1864–1931: Letters and Diaries* (1935), 102).
[2] In real life Frank Harris claimed to have heard of an 'English millionaire, ennobled for his wealth, boast that he had only two books in his house: one "the guid book" meaning the Bible that he never opened, and the other his cheque book' (Frank Harris, *My Life and Loves* (1966), 279). Against this has to be set Beerbohm's opinion that Harris told the truth only when his invention flagged (David Cecil, *Max* (1964), 164). Beerbohm was himself guilty of the same, declaring to Will Rothenstein that he had read nothing—only Thackeray's *The Four Georges* (1860) and Lear's *Book of Nonsense* (1846), though lately he had sampled Wilde's *Intentions* (1891). See William Rothenstein, *Men and Memories, 1872–1900* (1934), 146.

I read them all during one summer holiday, in a special spot in our garden; my mother reproving me for being a 'bookworm', and unwilling to give her help when needed.

Even before my teens my reading entered upon the romantic stage. I read *Quo Vadis* and longed to be a Christian martyr; I read Rider Haggard's *She* and wished for nothing so much as to be 'the World's Desire' then *Robert Ellesmere* [sic] and I knew that the most wonderful thing in the world would be to marry a *good* man—preferably a clergyman—and to devote my life to good works.[3]

Stevenson fell perhaps marginally short of this ideal by becoming Lloyd George's secretary and mistress; still, books provided dreams to invoke and models to imitate. This sometimes had its pretentious side. Saxon Sydney-Turner manufactured himself into such a specimen from a suburban villa at Hove. He communicated to friends by letters written in Ciceronian Latin, and moved in the sort of circles where people asked each other: 'What did you mean, Virginia, when you said, about three years ago, that your view of life was that of a Henry James novel, and mine of a George Meredith?'[4] In 1914, writing about the 'New Novel', James himself argued that critical awareness on the part of readers constituted 'the very education of our imaginative life'; earlier, in his 'London Notes' in 1897, he had been more concerned to examine how novelists were able to weave 'the spell of the magician'. In part, it required an act of willing surrender by readers; but 'the note of sincerity in the artist is what most matters, what most reaches and touches'. Novelists' spellbinding effects 'offer us another world', a common denominator of otherwise dissimilarities such as Jane Austen, Charlotte Brontë, Dumas *père*, Dostoevsky, and Marie Corelli.[5]

It was indisputable that so many readers were animated by literature. This was especially true of provincial England, thought the editor (1853–60) of the *Quarterly Review*, the Revd Whitwell Elwin. Thackeray agreed with him; when stuck in 'a dismal dirty inn at Halifax' in Yorkshire during his lecture tour in 1857, he made himself comfortable by reading and 'pleasant talk about books' with people he met. 'It is the quiet country-folks who read books,' he reckoned, 'not we busy Londoners whose life is a scramble of clubs and parties. Books are aeras in these people's lives, and such as give them pleasure are remembered for years and years.'[6]

The serial publication of stories in newspapers, magazines, and periodicals sustained the temptation to live in the excitement of books. In their auto-biographies both Mark Tellar and Archibald Marshall remembered as boys seizing on *The Graphic* for its serialization of Rider Haggard's *She* (1886–7), with illustrations by Maurice Greiffenhagen. Later, when Marshall was at Cambridge,

---

[3] Frances Lloyd George, *The Years that are Past* (1967), 19–20.

[4] Virginia Stephen (later Woolf) to her sister Vanessa Bell, 19 Aug. 1909, in Nigel Nicolson and Joanne Trautmann Banks (eds.), *The Flight of the Mind: The Letters of Virginia Woolf*, i: *1888–1912* (1993), 409.

[5] James E. Miller, Jr. (ed.), *Theory of Fiction: Henry James* (Lincoln, Nebr., 1972), 321–2, 325–6.

[6] Letter to Mrs Thomas Frederick Elliot and Kate Perry, 21–2 Feb. 1857, in Edgar F. Harden (ed.), *Selected Letters of William Makepeace Thackeray* (1996), 315–16.

gossip had it that the Dean of King's and the University Registrar cut a service in chapel in order to be the first at high table to discover the denouement of *The Hound of the Baskervilles* (1902). The book publication of Doyle's story was timed just to precede its last instalment in the *Strand Magazine*.[7]

Bibliophily rising to bibliomania was common. Many aristocratic great collections had been built up irregularly, along with hoards of paintings, porcelain, and furniture. Even so, there were some abnormal accumulations, the result of genuine erudition or addiction on the part of individual noblemen. In 1892 financial need caused the fifth Earl Spencer to sell the bulk of the Althorp Collection of 43,000 volumes to the widow of a cotton magnate, Enriquetta Rylands. This formed the basis of the John Rylands Library, which was opened to the public on 1 January 1900.[8] Previously, in 1882–3, the great Sunderland Library at Blenheim Palace had been sold off for nearly £60,000 by the seventh Duke of Marlborough, a forced economy following his predecessors' reckless spending;[9] and in 1887 the twenty-sixth Earl of Crawford, also in financial straits, sold a substantial portion of the Bibliotheca Lindesiana. But this earl, like his predecessor and successor, was a scholar–collector who continued to add as well as divest. His heir (as Lord Balcarres) formed a friendship across the party and class divide with John Burns from mutual love of books. The first working-class Cabinet minister (in 1906), Burns used his salary to enlarge his own library: he bought 'a third folio of Shakespeare for £12—a good bargain if the volume is perfect'.[10] He also retained habits formed during his artisan days, when money was tighter and the choice was between another book and food on the table. He told Arnold Bennett in 1915 how his conscience still gave him trouble over this: 'when he had been buying a book too many he would leave it at the [National Liberal] club and then take it home last thing at night, after his wife was in bed, and hide it'.[11]

Many another impressive library was built up by individuals in the period. Sidney and Beatrice Webb's collection of social-science literature and government publications, which ultimately went to the London School of Economics, is among the best known of the utilitarian kind. In contrast, the Birmingham businessman W. T. Smedley assembled a collection of incunabula and Elizabethan literature described by *The Times* in 1921 as 'unique' and one of the finest libraries in England. A benefactor of many institutions, Smedley was also fired by

---

[7] Archibald Marshall, *Out and About* (1933), 5, 158; Mark Tellar, *A Young Man's Passage* (1952), 46.

[8] On Mrs Rylands, see *Review of Reviews* (Sept. 1892), 253.

[9] Randolph S. Churchill, *Winston S. Churchill*, i: *Youth 1874–1900* (1966), 96.

[10] John Vincent (ed.), *The Crawford Papers: The Journals of David Lindsay, Twenty-Seventh Earl of Crawford and the Tenth Earl of Balcarres* (Manchester, 1984), 6–7, 69, 103.

[11] Flower (ed.), *Bennett Journals*, ii. 145 (2 Oct. 1915). After 1919 Burns was relieved of money worries, being the beneficiary of an annual pension of £1,000 bequeathed in the will of Andrew Carnegie. As a trade unionist, Burns had previously denounced the steel magnate's ruthlessness; but Carnegie, the founder of a peace fund in 1910, admired Burns's stand against the Great War. See Francis W. Hirst, *In the Golden Days* (1947), 237.

a conviction that Bacon wrote Shakespeare. He offered his collection to the University of London on condition that it provide the basis of a Francis Bacon Memorial Library, though eventually his library found its way to America because the University could not afford to erect a building to house it.[12] Literature was already being marked as an investment. In the 1890s, Maurice Baring recalled, 'second-hand booksellers were speculating in the first editions of the new poets' and 'always urging us to buy them on the plea that they would go up' in value. That turned out true for those who bought their Yeats then, or the first and second Rhymers' Club anthologies. Baring himself, at Cambridge in 1893, was one of the few to buy Francis Thompson's first published book of verse.[13] A decade earlier the bookworm barrister Augustine Birrell cited the catalogues of second-hand booksellers as proof that 'never were so many private libraries in course of growth as there are today'. Not only were such catalogues plentiful, they exhibited both a substantial rise and 'hateful uniformity of prices' as country booksellers even in remote regions were guided by the London auctions and conducted a postal trade.[14] Yet Birrell, who started life in modest circumstances, was able to build up a library of nearly 10,000 volumes;[15] and a country gentleman book-collector such as Siegfried Sassoon, who did not suffer the same pinch, was still able to gloat about 'what wonderful bargains were to be discovered in the catalogues of second-hand booksellers at Birmingham!' Among them was Pope's *Homer*: 'Six folio volumes, first edition, and they had only cost fifteen bob plus the postage'.[16] That paled beside Thomas Hardy's astonishment at finding a first edition of Hobbes's *Leviathan* (1651) for 6d. in a shop in Bath in 1902: 'I did not know it was a 1st ed. when I bought it, or I shd. hardly have had the conscience to take it.'[17] This confession, darkly triumphal, was characteristic Hardy; equally, George Gissing's misfortune, related in *The Private Papers of Henry Ryecroft* (1903), was typical of the tyranny of fate which clasped him. There he told how he had come across a first edition of Gibbon's *Decline and Fall* (1776–88) in a bookshop near Portland Road Station at the absurdly low price of 1s. per volume, and how, having no money, 'to possess those clean-paged quartos I would have sold my

---

[12] Constance Smedley, *Crusaders* (1929), 48, 90–1. On the Bacon controversy, see below, Ch. 6.

[13] Maurice Baring, *The Puppet Show of Memory* (1922), 147, 150. *Punch*, 13 Oct. 1894, 177, was scathing about such speculation, publishing a prospectus for 'The O'er-rated Bosh Company (Limited). Caterers by (self) appointment to the Yellow-book, the Rhymers' Club, and Nobody Else in Particular'.

[14] Augustine Birrell, 'Bookbuying', in Birrell, *Obiter Dicta* (1884), repr. in Ernest Rhys and Lloyd Vaughan (eds.), *A Century of English Essays* (1913), 434–5. See also James Clegg, *The Directory of Second-Hand Booksellers* (1891). One second-hand bookseller, whose postal business Birrell used in the early 1890s, was the future novelist, Arnold Bennett. Apparently, Birrell neglected to send the money for his purchase (Reginald Pound, *Arnold Bennett* (1952), 80).

[15] Augustine Birrell, *Things Past Redress* (1937), 53–6, 237–9, 263–76, for his library and literary tastes; and Sir Charles Tennyson, *Stars and Markets* (1957), ch. 5 for reminiscences of Birrell, his stepfather. On Birrell, who was later Chief Secretary for Ireland, see *DNB 1931–1940*, 80–3. Modern novels were the main exception to Birrell's catholic love of literature, though in later life he took to them too.

[16] Siegfried Sassoon, *Memoirs of a Fox-Hunting Man* (1965), 88–9.

[17] Hardy to Florence Henniker, 28 Nov. 1902, in Richard Little Purdy and Michael Millgate (eds.), *The Collected Letters of Thomas Hardy*, iii. *1902–1908* (Oxford, 1982), 40.

coat'. He made an arrangement with the bookseller, walked the miles home to his Islington lodgings, raised the cash, then walked back again, repeating the journey twice more until he had portered all six volumes, at the end collapsing on his chair, 'perspiring, flaccid, aching—exultant!' Like every Gissing story, the happiness did not last: 'Years after, I sold my first edition of Gibbon for even less than it cost me; it went with a great many other fine books in folio and quarto, which I could not drag about with me in my constant removals; the man who bought them spoke of them as "tombstones".'[18]

Revelling in perverseness, Samuel Butler liked to proclaim that he had 'the smallest library of any man in London who is by way of being literary'; but this was because he considered the British Museum, where he did his reading, 'my private library'.[19] Book possession for pleasure and self-improvement was more characteristic and, for the historian, more significant for what it discloses about the age. Reading was not just a solitary pursuit. The habit of husbands and wives reading together is a marked feature of memoirs of the period. The family constituted a reading unit, children as well as adults. 'Reading aloud in the family circle was an established custom until the children had grown up and left home,' wrote Geraldine Hodgson about the upbringing of the poet James Elroy (Roy) Flecker in the 1880s and 1890s: 'Thus, by a very early age, Roy had listened to large parts of Dickens, Longfellow, and Tennyson, and to much of Thackeray, George Eliot, Carlyle, and Browning.'[20] Such occasions, when the father was involved, do much to soften our image of a distant and stern Victorian paterfamilias. So Charles Reilly remembered about his father, an architect–surveyor who worked a good deal at home, where the rule was that he was not to be disturbed and, at meals, not addressed unless he spoke first. But there was always a delightful exception, on Saturday evenings, when

we all assembled round the fire to hear him read Dickens, generally, so it seems to me, scenes from *Pickwick Papers*. He read very well and we loved listening. We had our favourite scenes and would beg for them time after time. I feel now his own kindly nature, hidden in those days under a false idea of what a father should be like, came out through the humanity of Dickens.[21]

Such readings were not only from books. The weekly magazine or monthly periodical, with poems, short stories, and serializations as well as essays and articles, provided supplementary fare. Implicit was a guarantee of standards for the family circle. Thus the prevalence of bowdlerism can be correlated with the rise of a mass reading market where the propriety of the published product was

[18] George Gissing, *The Private Papers of Henry Ryecroft* (Brighton, 1982), 39–41, 233.
[19] Letter to Robert Bridges, 6 Feb. 1900, in Henry Festing Jones, *Samuel Butler, Author of Erewhon (1835–1902): A Memoir* (1919), ii. 320.
[20] Geraldine Hodgson, *The Life of James Elroy Flecker* (Oxford, 1925), 22. Extracts from all of these authors and more were anthologized by the popular publisher Pearson at the turn of the century, prefaced by advice on 'How to Recite'; see *Pearson's New Reciter and Reader* (1904), pp. vii–xiii.
[21] C. H. Reilly, *Scaffolding in the Sky* (1938), 8–9.

assured and indelicacy banished from Bible and Shakespeare as well as from mortal literature.[22]

The habit of reading and collecting books was not confined to the comfortable and leisured classes, though plainly opportunities were unequal and professional interests influenced a bias towards books. Consider the case of William Robertson Nicoll, born in 1851 in an Aberdeenshire manse. His father, on an annual stipend of under £200, was an omnivorous reader who built up a library of 17,000 volumes. Though naturally abundant in theology, ecclesiastical history, and classics, the collection represented most branches of literature. Young Nicoll's boyhood reading included Scott, Disraeli, the Brontës, Bulwer Lytton, Shelley, Johnson, Addison, Steele, Goldsmith, Emerson, Lowell, Longfellow, and umpteen lesser-known authors. He afterwards graduated from the ministry to religious journal editor, literary critic, anthologist, and publisher's reader; and, settling in Hampstead in 1892, he built up his own library of 25,000 volumes. It contained few rare books and testified to his appreciation of the range of English literature, with a cheerfully unapologetic 'love for those unfortunate beings known as the minor poets'.[23]

Nicoll was a truly heroic reader, a two-book-a-day man who (said his friend J. M. Barrie) considered the next best thing to a good book was a bad book. He devoured even more newspapers than books; and though later he took up golf, his preferred exercise was reading, accompanied by pipe or cigarettes.[24] He was an exaggeration of a type: the Scots' democratic appetite for book-reading and education was a source of pride to compatriots. Barrie's plays such as *What Every Woman Knows* (1908) and *Mary Rose* (1920) contain many a glancing reference to this, not surprisingly, since Barrie shared that appetite. R. B. Haldane, who represented Haddingtonshire for twenty-five years before taking a peerage in 1911, remembered the agricultural labourers of that constituency as 'great, burly, strong fellows, well educated, and with wives as keen as they were; the cottages without a speck of dirt among the furniture, and an abundance of books'.[25] It will

---

[22] Noele Perrin, *Dr Bowdler's Legacy: A History of Expurgated Books in England and America* (Boston, 1992) gives a largely jocular case history. One example of magazine censorship may be given here. Wilkie Collins's *The Law and the Lady* (1875) was initially serialized in the illustrated weekly *The Graphic* from September 1874 until the editor objected to a passage where the crippled Miserrimus Dexter tries to kiss Valerie Macallam as 'an attempted violation of the heroine', adding that 'You distinctly told me before the story began that as it was the autobiography of a young lady there would certainly be nothing coarse or improper in it; whereas, in my opinion, and in the opinion of a good many other people too, there is a disagreeable flavour pervading the story generally.' Collins consulted his lawyers, but *The Graphic* publicly repudiated the serialization—'the story is not one which we should have voluntarily selected to place before our readers'—and Collins could only relieve his feelings by planting in *The World* through its editor, his friend Edmund Yates, a denunciation of *The Graphic*'s conduct. See Catherine Peters, *The King of Inventors: A Life of Wilkie Collins* (1991), 371. See also below, pp. 997–8

[23] T. H. Darlow, *William Robertson Nicoll: Life and Letters* (1925), 149.

[24] Harry Preston, *Memories* (1929), 205–7.

[25] Liberal Education Department, *National Education: Three Speeches on the Education Question* (1913), 20. See also Lord Rosebery, 'The Formation of the Scottish Character' (1908), in Rosebery, *Miscellanies, Literary and Historical* (1921), ii. 134–51.

be noticed that Haldane included women along with men in his panegyric. There were other testimonies to this. The wife of the artist Sir Arthur Clay—they had an estate at Ardmeallie in Banffshire—told Sir Mountstuart Grant Duff in 1898 about 'a Scotch-woman of the peasant class . . . [who] knew reams of Tennyson by heart, and her great pleasure was to repeat his poetry to a visitor while she herded her cow'.[26] 'How universally the people read,' Harriet Beecher Stowe had noted about Scottish villages, following her tour of Britain in 1853, when she was acclaimed as the author of *Uncle Tom's Cabin* (1852). This sold a million and a half copies in its first year, three times the quantity in the United States.[27]

This love of literature among many ordinary folk was not a phenomenon confined to Scotland. Literature was commonly classed as a luxury, and publishers were apt to lament how book-buying suffered more acutely than most trades during economic recessions; as Methuen's house magazine quaintly expressed it in the 1890s, 'a straitened income is felt in the library sooner than in the stables or the cellar'.[28] Yet many poor people made extraordinary sacrifices to equip themselves with books, presumably because they failed to appreciate the superiority of acquiring champion racehorses or vintage claret. The dockers' leader Ben Tillett went hungry in order to buy books. The exchange rate, calculated Conan Doyle, who mooched about second-hand bookshops in Edinburgh as a poor medical student, was a twopenny book or lunch of mutton pie.[29] Tillett thereby struggled through the literary classics, as well as works on evolution by Darwin, Spencer, and Huxley, famished and exhausted after his day's work in the warehouse. He gained access to more books when he became librarian for his Congregationalist chapel in Bethnal Green. He also tried to teach himself Latin and Greek with the ambition of becoming a barrister.[30] Tillett was typical of the working-class autodidact, a familiar figure in the annals of nineteenth-century social progress, whose mid-century incarnation can be found in one of the first trade union MPs, Thomas Burt. Burt was nicknamed the pitman philosopher. It was characteristic that, in his presidential address to the Trades Union Congress in 1891, he should underpin a call for the redistribution of wealth by reciting Browning:

> Make no more giants, God,
> But elevate the race at once![31]

The parliamentary reporter Alexander Mackintosh noted that Burt's friendship with Sir Edward Grey at Westminster stemmed from their ability to quote poetry

[26] Sir Mountstuart Grant Duff, *Notes from a Diary, 1896 to January 23, 1901* (1905), i. 306 (24 Feb. 1898).

[27] Joan D. Hedrick, *Harriet Beecher Stowe* (Oxford, 1995), 233, 442.

[28] Maureen Duffy, *A Thousand Capricious Chances: A History of the Methuen List* (1989), 26.

[29] Martin Booth, *The Doctor, The Detective and Arthur Conan Doyle: A Biography of Arthur Conan Doyle* (1997), 53.

[30] Ben Tillett, *Memories and Reflections* (1931), 88 ff.; Jonathan Schneer, *Ben Tillett* (1982), 24.

[31] *Report of the Proceedings of the Twenty-Fourth Annual Trades Union Congress*, held at Newcastle, 1891, 34–5.

to each other, Wordsworth being a favourite of both.[32] Burt's distinction was extolled by *The Miner* in February 1887:

From his boyhood he had sought to 'improve the moments as they fly' and had subjected himself to a course of reading, including the choicest literary productions of the English language. The poetry of Milton, Shakespeare, Tennyson, Wordsworth, Longfellow, Shelley and Burns; the philosophy of Adam Smith, J. S. Mill, Bastiat, Professor Fawcett, Thornton, Emerson, Carlyle, and Channing; the eloquence of Burke, Grattan, and Curran; the fiction of Scott, Thackeray, Dickens, George Eliot, and the history of Macaulay, Gibbon and Hume. How many of our young men know even the names here mentioned! He also, with the aid of a Popular Educator, mastered, to some degree at least, the propositions of Euclid, and the mysteries of shorthand, while French and German came in for a share of attention.[33]

The exceptional extent of Burt's self-education was stressed;[34] but the historian may in addition explore how this literature came within reach of a poor boy growing up in the 1850s in a north-east colliery village, and how he made his selections. Newcastle Free Library was not opened until 1880, when Burt, at the inauguration, recalled how he spent the first eighteen pence he earned as a pit-lad on a book. Repeatedly thereafter, any spare pocket money went on book purchase, Burt walking the 16-mile round trip between Seaton Delaval and Newcastle. Modifying the claims of *The Miner*, Burt's first biographer reported that Burt 'read no fiction, nor has he read much fiction to this day. Even the great Sir Walter [Scott] does not seem to have attracted him until later life, when he read nearly all that "the wizard" wrote.'[35]

Seriousness had determined Burt's initial selections, as did price. The educational mission of the university extension movement, which was active among the north-east pitmen from 1879, had begun with a course of political economy before progressing to moral philosophy and scientific and technical subjects. This work was hampered always by financial problems. Fees alone could not cover the cost of courses; but the miners were unwilling to concede to employers and other middle-class people a greater say on the extension committees in exchange for donations. Moreover, even as hard times enveloped the coal trade in the mid-1880s and a bid to get the miners' union to subsidize the extension movement was dashed, the local demand for further education was unabated. Studies sparked by the extension courses continued outside its formal supervision, sustained by a strong sense of collective self-improvement; and literature was included among

---

[32] Sir Alexander Mackintosh, *Echoes of Big Ben: A Journalist's Parliamentary Diary (1881–1940)* (n.d.), 30.

[33] Quoted in Joyce M. Bellamy and John Saville (eds.), *Dictionary of Labour Biography*, i (1972), 61. Burt also tried to teach himself Latin and Greek.

[34] Exceptional but not unique: R. A. S. Redmayne, *Men, Mines and Memories* (1942), 31, recalls a miner at Seaton Delaval with a passion for literature: in 'his cottage he had the works of many of the English classics in prose and poetry, three hundred volumes in all' (quoted in Alon Kadish, 'University Extension and the Working Classes: The Case of the Northumberland Miners', *Historical Research* (June 1987), 198).

[35] Aaron Watson, *A Great Labour Leader, Being a Life of the Right Hon. Thomas Burt M.P.* (1908), 62.

the syllabuses. In 1890, following a lecture series on Shakespeare to the Students' Association at one pit village, Backworth in Northumberland, a Classical Novel-Reading Union was formed. 'Backworth read fiction,' one of its organizers reported, but 'it was not fiction of the best class, and there was no systematic study of the best works of the best authors, and scanty knowledge of the great classics of fiction which are among life's best textbooks'. The Union involved an active membership of eighty-three out of a total village population of 2,000. An entrance fee of 1s. was charged; its secretary was required to seek the advice of 'competent literary authorities' about recommended reading; and in 'the course of four years, twenty novels were read and thirty-four meetings held at which books were discussed, and fifty-four papers were read on a variety of literary, moral, social and political issues raised by the books'.[36]

The case of the Backworth miners is not at variance with the overall picture of the university extension movement. Out of fifty-seven courses put on by Cambridge University extension lecturers in the winter of 1886, ten were on literature; and for the London Society the sum was seven out of thirty-one. This proportion, about 20 per cent of all courses being devoted to literature, was not thought unreasonable or surprising. G. J. Goschen, one-time president of the Local Government Board, identified three motives that might incline ordinary people towards higher education. The primary was to improve breadwinning capacity. Hence, technical and commercial instruction was most popular, a trend abetted by the authorities' concern that Britain keep its industrial pre-eminence. Allied to this was the intellectual excitement generated by the physical sciences, whose discoveries and advances dominated the news and seemed to relegate other activities to the realm of indulgence or sentiment. Second in popularity were courses in history and political economy, because these informed people about the government and society of their day. This reflected the prevailing rationalist and utilitarian ideology. Third came literature. This had no obvious function except as 'a luxury to brighten life and kindle thought'. Yet through literature the reader 'explores the strange voyages of man's moral reason, the impulses of the human heart, the chances and changes that have overtaken human ideals of virtue and happiness, of conduct and manners, and the shifting fortunes of great conceptions of truth and virtue'. Such books 'awaken within us the diviner mind, and rouse us to a consciousness of what is best in others and ourselves'.[37] These were the words of John Morley, justifying the study of literature in an address to the London Society for the Extension of University Teaching, in 1887. What was wanted to fulfil this ideal, he averred, was discipline; and he argued that

it requires no praeterhuman force of will in any young man or woman—unless household circumstances are more than usually vexatious and unfavourable—to get at least half an hour out of a solid busy day for good and disinterested reading . . . Now, in half an

---

[36] Kadish, 'University Extension', 206.
[37] John Morley, 'On the Study of Literature' (1887), in Morley *Studies in Literature* (1907), 202, 218.

hour I fancy you can read fifteen or twenty pages of Burke; or you can read one of Wordworth's masterpieces—say the lines on Tintern; or say, one third—if a scholar, in the original, and if not, in a translation—of a book of the Iliad or the Æneid. But try for yourselves what you can read in half an hour. Then multiply the half-hour by 365, and consider what treasures you might have laid by at the end of the year; and what happiness, fortitude, and wisdom they would have given you during all the days of your life.[38]

This raised the question of book selection and acquisition. Mark Pattison, Rector of Lincoln College, Oxford (1861–84) during Morley's time as an undergraduate, once deplored as shamefully small the annual amount expended on books by the middle classes. He advocated as a minimum a shilling in the pound (5 per cent of income) and reckoned that no self-respecting individual ought to possess fewer than a thousand books. These could be stored in a bookcase 13 feet by 10 feet, a space available to everyone, he thought. Morley demurred: what was ideal for the £1,000 p.a. family was unreasonable to expect of the £200, still less of 'a workman who earns a quarter of that sum'. Anyway, 'a man does not really need to have a great many books'—an atlas, dictionary, and encyclopedia, certainly, but beyond that Morley would not be drawn except to advise that 'most books worth reading once are worth reading twice, and—what is most important of all—the masterpieces of literature are worth reading a thousand times'.[39] Such discrimination was ideal. Morley himself did not practise biblio-abstinence. 'I have collected some nine or ten thousand volumes,' he told Lady Battersea in 1905. 'Of these I have read only two thousand, and I've only three or four years in which to read the remaining seven or eight thousand!! Think how busy I must be.'[40]

The choice of books was governed by both price and accessibility. It was Sir Walter Scott—together with Robert Cadell, his new publisher after the collapse of Constable-Ballantyne—who made publishing history by bringing out a relatively cheap (5s. per volume) complete edition of the Waverley Novels from 1829;[41] but quality new fiction largely remained price-restricted, inhibiting popular sales, until the last decade of the nineteenth century. The standard price, 10s. 6d. per volume, or 31s. 6d. per three-decker novel, put most new fiction out of general circulation except via borrowing through the commercial and (after mid-century) free public libraries, although a cheaper one-volume reprint might follow after an agreed number of years. Bentley's series of Standard Novels and Romances ran successfully for two decades from 1834, being mostly 6s. one-volume reprints; and Routledge's Railway Library, started in 1848, pushed its

---

[38] John Morley, *Studies in Literature*, 207.   [39] Ibid. 204–5, 209.

[40] Morley to Lady Battersea, 16 Aug. 1905, in Lucy Cohen, *Lady Rothschild and her Daughters, 1821–1931* (1935), 226. In fact, Morley had another eighteen years left to him, dying in 1923 in his eighty-fifth year.

[41] Jane Millgate, *Scott's Last Edition: A Study in Publishing History* (Edinburgh, 1989). This experiment in cheap novel publication was ironic because it was Scott's *Kenilworth* (1821) that was the first novel to be issued in what became the standard price of one and a half guineas per three volumes, which held for most of the rest of the century.

prices down to 1s. and extended its list to over 1,200 titles. The success of the series, and of the firm generally—in part from marketing a cheap pirated edition of *Uncle Tom's Cabin* (1852), which sold over half a million copies—enabled Routledge's to pay Bulwer Lytton the staggering sum of £25,000 for the rights to reprint all his thirty-five works, in 1853–4.[42] In 1891 Thomas Hardy told Lytton's son, the former Viceroy of India, who published poetry under the name of Owen Meredith, how much he had appreciated his father's promotion of cheap editions of his books:

I have just been led to think that the true evidence of being known as a writer is after all the sight of one's works scattered about bookstalls in ridiculously cheap editions, e.g.: I was walking along that end of the Strand where the discount booksellers have their shops, when I saw Owen Meredith's poems in a popular series—nicely bound square little books published at only a shilling. The numbers of people who buy these books must be enormous, since the publishers say that it is only the large sale which enables them to set such a low price on volumes of so good an appearance. Among the poems I found some I had not before known. I have often been struck with the way in which the late Lord Lytton forestalled recent ideas on this matter of cheapness: at a time when it was almost risky to sell at a low price he was one of the few who saw that there lay the secret of the future in wide literary fame, & abolished prohibitiveness as between himself & the mass of the thinking public—the poorer class of thinkers—by consenting to paper covers at 2s/-. Had it not been for this I for one should never as a boy have wept over his heroines—living as I did live in a lonely place where borrowing was impracticable.[43]

As well as Routledge's cut-price Lytton, there were other passing enterprises whose popular purpose was caught in their series titles—the Parlour Library, published by Simms & McIntyre, and the Run and Read Library, published by Burton of Ipswich[44]—culminating in the famous yellowbacks (priced at 2s. or 2s. 6d.), which Chapman & Hall distributed through W. H. Smith's station trade from the late 1850s.[45] The same publisher had previously brought out a popular edition of Dickens, at $1\frac{1}{2}$ d. a part; but among the best-known pioneers of cheap book publication was Henry Bohn, whose Standard Library started issuing classics in 1846 at 3s. 6d. per volume.[46] Bohn was also a profiteer from piracy

---

[42] John Sutherland, *The Longman Companion to Victorian Fiction* (1988), 519, 545–6; Eveleigh Nash, *I Liked the Life I Lived* (1941), 38–9.

[43] Hardy to Lord Lytton, 15 July 1891, in Richard Little Purdy and Michael Millgate (eds.), *The Collected Letters of Thomas Hardy*, i: *1840–1892* (Oxford, 1978), 240. Equally fond memories were held for Lytton's novels by members of the more privileged classes; see Grant Duff, *Diary, 1896 to 1901*, i. 20–1 (18 Feb. 1896) for a conversation at The Club between himself, Field Marshal Lord Wolseley, and the Conservative leader, Arthur Balfour.

[44] Joseph Shaylor, *The Fascination of Books with Other Papers on Books and Bookselling* (1912), 87–99.

[45] Sutherland, *Companion*, 685. William Morris did not have a great library (until he began collecting early printed books), nor was he a particularly devoted reader though he was a fast one; but 'his shelves were half filled with a strange collection of the yellow-backed novels which he had bought on railway journeys' (J. W. Mackail, *The Life of William Morris* (Oxford, 1950), i. 225).

[46] Peter Keating, *The Haunted Study: A Social History of the English Novel 1875–1914* (1989), 22–6, 432–6. On Henry Bohn (1796–1884), see *DNB*. By 1903 Bohn's Library series included 760 volumes, price 3s. 6d. or 5s. with few exceptions (see the full-page advertisement in *T.P.'s Weekly*, 24 Apr. 1903, 763); but this was the

of American fiction, in his case exploiting Fenimore Cooper and Nathaniel Hawthorne; but, altogether, his various 'libraries' comprised several hundred volumes and included historical, theological, and philosophical works as well as classic English and foreign (in translation) literature. Thomas Burt's acquisition of Gibbon and Milton was in Bohn's edition; he also found cheap issues of Cowper, Pope, Wordsworth, and Longfellow.

Had Burt been beginning his self-education later in the century he would have found an even more extensive series of popular editions of literary classics. Chandos Classics, published by Frederick Warne & Co., sold 3.5 million volumes between 1868 and 1884,[47] and 5 million before Frederick Warne himself retired in the 1890s. Eveleigh Nash, who worked for Warne's between 1896 and 1898, wrote that 'the firm, with its wide range of publications, did business in practically every town in the United Kingdom. Even in the Rhondda Valley one could find Warne's publications in shops unknown to the majority of London publishers.'[48] Burt also bought knowledge by instalments, through periodicals such as Cassell's *Popular Educator* and *Educational Course*. John Cassell was a Christian temperance lecturer who had moved into the tea trade—Thomas Hardy's mother always bought Cassell's tea—and progressed into publishing as an offshoot of printing his tea labels. His first independent publishing venture was to reproduce the Bible in penny parts. It sold over a million copies. He pursued the evangel of education in the same spirit. The *Popular Educator*, begun on 8 April 1853, became known as the working man's university. Burt was one of thousands to seize its opportunities. Thomas Hardy taught himself German by this means.[49] The firm did not escape financial crises; but in the year of his death, 1865, Cassell wrote to the champion free trader Richard Cobden about his aspiration of 'something higher than mere commercial success, namely of the moral and intellectual advancement of the people'.[50] The consequences of this philosophy were not always liberal. All mention of alcohol or adultery, and any strong language—the common but culpable 'damn'—were habitually excised from stories serialized in Cassell's family magazines. This created friction with authors such as Charles Reade and Wilkie Collins.[51] The same firm started the Library of English Literature (five volumes) in 1875, which sold 20,000 copies, and was reissued in sevenpenny monthly parts in 1883–7. There followed (1886–90) the National Library (214 volumes), selling at 3*d.* or 6*d.* each, and with a circulation of 50,000–100,000 per

---

vestige of the name, because Bohn had sold his copyrights and plates to Chatto & Windus in 1874 for £20,000, and his stock ten years before for £40,000. See Sutherland, *Companion*. 74.

[47] Richard. D. Altick, *The English Common Reader: A Social History of the Mass Reading Public 1800–1900* (Chicago, 1957, 1963), 243.   [48] Nash, *Life*, 28–9.

[49] Florence Emily Hardy, *The Life of Thomas Hardy 1840–1928* (1972), 25.

[50] Cassell to Cobden, Mar. 1865, in Newman Flower, *Just as it Happened* (1950), 58.

[51] Flower, *Just as it Happened*, 74–5, cites correspondence between the firm and Collins and Reade about this. Reade's *A Terrible Temptation* (1871), serialized in *Cassell's Magazine*, brought about a collapse in sales, and the directors even contemplated suing Reade for damages. The book version was published by Chapman & Hall.

volume. Both Cassell's series were edited and introduced by Henry Morley, who also initiated Routledge's Universal Library (1883–88), sixty-three volumes selling at 1s. or 1s. 6d. each.[52]

Morley was akin to Cassell in conceiving of the propagation of literature as a religious as well as patriotic duty. Born in 1822 and brought up as a strict Anglican, he converted to Unitarianism and thenceforward sought to promote Christian cooperation rather than sectarianism. Love of literature was a lifelong passion and, though initially he followed his father and qualified and practised as a doctor, he set up as a schoolteacher, then joined Dickens's staff on *Household Words* and later edited *The Examiner*. In 1857 he started teaching literature to evening classes at King's College London; in 1865 he advanced to the chair of English Language and Literature at University College, London. Morley was a pioneer in the causes of university extension and higher education for women, an indefatigable lecturer throughout the country, and a dedicated missioner to bring knowledge of English literature within reach of the many. In an obituary ode in 1894 *Punch* saluted Morley thus: 'He made Good Letters Cheap!'[53] As well as introducing hundreds of classics, he had also set himself to tell the story of English literature from its beginnings. His *English Writers*, started in 1867, struggled to reach the age of Shakespeare, after ten volumes, by the time of his death. It was a work of Teutonic earnestness and pedestrianism but its popular offshoot, *A First Sketch of English Literature* (1873), approached sales of 40,000 by 1900. Preacher as much as teacher, Morley traced the path of English literature as if holy ground, 'a natural corrective to the materialist tendencies of the age, as an embodiment of the religious life of England in every shape . . .'. Believing that 'the chief use . . . of a study of English literature is to sustain the spiritual side of life',[54] he dwelt on this genius in succeeding generations of writers, making an exception of only two, Sterne and Byron, whom he condemned in his very last lecture at University College 'as having wilfully perverted their talents to the harm of their fellow-men'.[55]

This high-mindedness frequently distorted authors' actual purposes and overlooked their interests. Writers, even such as Wilkie Collins who had several best-selling titles, were ambivalent about cheap books. It was all very well for the glorious dead to be reissued for a song, but the living needed to watch the pounds, shillings, and pence. In a royalty system it was equally attractive to contemplate *raising* the cover price in order to enlarge the profit on each sale. Publishers invariably held out tempting options to established authors, none of which involved lower prices: illustrated editions, de luxe editions, cabinet editions, and all manner of uniform editions for the collector. New and emerging

---

[52] Henry Shaen Solly, *The Life of Henry Morley, LL.D.* (1898), 305, 355–7. See also *Punch*, 25 Jan. 1896, 41, for its salute to cheap reprint series.   [53] *Punch*, 26 May 1894, 251.

[54] Morley to H. R. Fox Bourne, 15 July 1881, in Solly, *Morley*, 330.

[55] 'One who knew him well' (quoted ibid. 369).

authors, indeed all who had a restricted or uncertain market, were best projected by limited editions, as the Bodley Head (established in 1887) press understood. During the first years of its operation practically its entire list consisted of limited editions, notably of poets such as Richard Le Gallienne, John Davidson, John Gray, and Francis Thompson, with art nouveau lettering and layouts by Charles Rickets, C. H. Shannon, and Aubrey Beardsley. The 'first edition mania' that this excited incurred both wrath and ridicule, the *Fortnightly Review* observing that 'First editions of Dickens and Thackeray are no longer the rage of the collecting public . . . [while] every ephemeral and often rubbishy tract by living authors is being eagerly bought.' The *Pall Mall Gazette* specifically condemned the publishers Elkin Mathews and John Lane at the Bodley Head, who 'issue nearly all their books on the principle that rarity, not excellence, involves a speedy rise in price'. Where the work had a risqué reputation, the limited-edition strategy worked particularly well, and Lane was clearly thinking along these lines in 1892 when he aired the possibility of publishing Bernard Shaw's *Widowers' Houses*. 'Were you serious about publishing a play of mine?', the flabbergasted oracle queried. 'I am not sure that it would be a very gorgeous investment,' he added modestly, before recovering his poise to add, 'but I suppose a limited edition at a high price would be bought by a certain number of idiots who would not buy anything of mien for a penny or a shilling'.[56] In his case, Lane soon thought better of it; yet many perfectly respectable authors, such as the future Poet Laureate Robert Bridges, cannily exploited the private or limited-edition market.

To advocate cheaper books was thus to gamble on a vast volume of sales; and, when the operation faltered, authors tended to blame the publisher, as George Eliot upbraided Blackwood in 1862 about poor publicity for a cheap edition of her works.[57] Still more courses existed, both to serialize a novel in weekly 'penny numbers' and to reduce the period between the original three-volume publication and the issue of an inexpensive one-volume edition. Wilkie Collins's move to a new publisher, Chatto & Windus, in 1874–5, and his adoption of A. P. Watt as his literary agent in 1881, were designed to effect these last strategies.[58] All this was predicated on the assumption that the three-volume novel would remain the standard. Too many authors were set in this style. In 1886 Collins did experiment

---

[56] J. W. Lambert and Michael Ratcliffe, *The Bodley Head 1887–1987*, (1987) 75, 102.

[57] Timothy Hands, *A George Eliot Chronology* (1989), 80.

[58] A previous publisher, Bentley's, had considered using Collins's *Basil: A Story of Modern Life* (1852) as a spearhead to cut the price of a new publication to 10s. 6d. See Jenny Bourne Taylor, *In the Secret Theatre of Home: Wilkie Collins, Sensation Narrative, and Nineteenth-Century Psychology* (1988), 209, 280; also Peters, *Collins*, 368–70. Enquiring whether Collins's quitting Smith, Elder & Co. and moving to Chatto's satisfied his desire to have cheaper books, Robertson Scott was told by Chatto & Windus that 'with fourteen of Collins' books they did not get lower than six shillings, and afterwards in "illustrated boards", two shillings' (J. W. Robertson Scott, *The Story of the Pall Mall Gazette, of its First Editor Frederick Greenwood, and of its Founder George Murray Smith* (New York, 1971), 83–4). However, following Collins's death in 1889, Chatto published a sixpenny paperback of *The Woman in White* (1860), which apparently sold 300,000 copies (Peters, *Collins*, 434).

by writing a 133-page novel for the Bristol publisher J. W. Arrowsmith, *The Guilty River*, which was issued as a shilling paperback in a large edition; but the story was poor, and Arrowsmith bewailed the 25,000 surplus copies unsold when Collins died in 1889.[59] That, coincidentally, was the year when Arrowsmith published his most famous book: Jerome K. Jerome's *Three Men in a Boat*, in one volume, priced 3s. 6d. This sold 202,000 copies up to August 1909, when another imprint of 5,000 was released. In a new preface at the twenty-year mark, Jerome recorded that an American pirate had sold over a million copies; also that it had been translated into all European languages and some Asian.[60] Arrowsmith was a maverick publisher. Keble Howard's first book, a shilling volume of 'Social Jester' articles he had written as 'Chicot' for the *Sketch*, was published by Arrowsmith in 1901; and Howard described Arrowsmith's operation:

He had a little office on the [Bristol] quayside, and personally read all the manuscripts that came to the office. He was a printer as well as a publisher, and did not bother to publish all the year round. He just waited until something came his way that seemed likely to hit the taste of the public, and then he published it. Not very much money was spent in advertising the book. It had to sink or swim according to its merits and the taste of the public.[61]

Arrowsmith made mistakes. In 1886 he turned down the first Sherlock Holmes novella, *A Study in Scarlet*, which Ward, Lock & Co. eventually published in one volume in 1887 after pressing the impecunious author, Conan Doyle, to part with the copyright for £25.[62] But the acuteness with which Arrowsmith's instinct worked on occasion was evidenced by the best-sellers on his list. This included the Bristolian Hugh Conway's *Called Back* (1884), a sensational murder story which Arrowsmith first published in his *Christmas Annual* for 1883 and then in shilling paperback. *Called Back* sold 400,000 copies over the next fifteen years, partly, it was said, because of a review in *Truth* by Henry Labouchere, who declared that 'Wilkie Collins never penned a more enthralling story,' but also on the back of a successful stage adaptation.[63] A decade later Arrowsmith hit the jackpot again, with Anthony Hope (Hawkins), *The Prisoner of Zenda* (1894), another one-volume best-seller; but it was *Three Men in a Boat* of which Arrowsmith was most bemusedly proud, saying, 'I pay Jerome so much in royalties

[59] Peters, *Collins*, 418–19.   [60] *The Bookman* (Aug. 1909), 199–200.

[61] Keble Howard, *My Motley Life* (1927), 159–60.

[62] Booth, *Conan Doyle*, 109–10. Arrowsmith did eventually obtain Conan Doyle for his list, including as volume xvi in his 3s. 6d. series the two stories *Beyond the City* (1891), Conan Doyle's essayed satire on suburban New Women, and *The Great Shadow* (1892), a Napoleonic saga.

[63] On Hugh Conway (F. J. Fargus, 1847–85), see Sutherland, *Companion*, 100–1, 222–3. Altick, *Common Reader*, 386, citing the *Publishers' Circular*, 12 Nov. 1898, gives sales of 400,000 to that date. See also Mark Tellar, *A Young Man's Passage* (1950), 58, for him confessing to his prep-school teacher that during the holidays he had read Conway's *Called Back*, together with Fergus Hume's *The Mystery of the Hansom Cab* (1887) and stories by Miss M. E. Braddon, Mrs Henry Wood, and Ouida. His teacher wrote back, 'Dear Tellar, you have fallen into bad company. If you have not already read them, try *The Mill on the Floss, Jane Eyre* and *Vanity Fair*.'

every year. I can't imagine what becomes of all the copies of that book I issue. I often think the public must eat them.'[64]

Arrowsmith in the 1880s was anticipating that revolution in book-publishing which would become practically universal from the mid-1890s, the switch from the triple-decker to the single-volume format. The three-volume novel was geared to the circulating library market dominated by Mudie's and W. H. Smith's. The consequences for authors of that commercial stranglehold were spelled out for the American journalist R. D. Blumenfeld in 1887 by Walter Besant, founder of the Society of Authors (1884):

Mr Besant astonished me by telling me that the novel *The Golden Butterfly*, which he and the late Mr Rice wrote in partnership, did not have so great a sale as the later book, *The World Went Very Well Then*, and that the American circulation of the latter was greater than the British. The trouble in this country is that average people do not buy books, but subscribe to the pernicious library system. They seem to be prepared to wait weeks for their turn at a new volume.[65]

Grant Duff similarly became acquainted with the realities of publishing when he joined the committee of the Literary Fund, which dispensed pensions and charitable assistance to indigent authors. Coming away from a committee meeting with the historian W. E. H. Lecky in June 1889, he recorded in his diary that Lecky had been told by the publisher Charles Longman that 'most books just about paid their expenses'.[66]

Besant's overall assessment of the literary profession in 1892 was not much more rosy. While perhaps a hundred novelists were able to live by their work, and fifty could be classed as a thousand-pounds-a-year author, the vast majority struggled. Publishers generally paid novelists from £50 to £100 for the copyright, and made for themselves about £100 to £200 on each book.[67] Young authors on the rise, such as J. M. Barrie, began to denounce the three-volume norm in the early 1890s. 'The bane of British literature at present is its bulk,' Barrie declared in 'A Plea for Smaller Books': 'Our literature lies crushed beneath its load of "padding".' There were few exceptions. The most notable was Robert Louis Stevenson, all of whose best-selling stories in the 1880s—*Treasure Island* (1883), *Dr Jekyll and Mr Hyde* (1886), *Kidnapped* (1886), *The Black Arrow* (1888) and *The Master of Ballantrae* (1889)—were published in one-volume format from the start.

---

[64] Howard, *Motley Life*, 160. As an indication of the importance of *Three Men in a Boat* to Arrowsmith, it was designated number 1 in his 3s. 6d. series. *The Prisoner of Zenda* was 18. On Arrowsmith's, see the essay by John R. Turner in Patricia J. Anderson and Jonathan Rose (eds.), *British Literary Publishing Houses 1820–1880* (1991), 11–14; Arrowsmith also published the Grossmiths' *Diary of a Nobody* (1892), Andrew Lang's *My Own Fairy Book* (1895), and G. K. Chesterton's *The Man who was Thursday* (1908). Following his schooling at Clifton in the late 1870s and early 1880s, where he edited the school magazine, Q formed a lifelong friendship with Arrowsmith: see Sir Arthur Quiller-Couch, *Memories and Opinions: An Unfinished Autobiography*, ed. S. C. Roberts (Cambridge, 1944), 67. Arrowsmith became a benefactor of Bristol University.

[65] Blumenfeld, *R.D.B.'s Diary*, 17 (27 June 1887). *The Golden Butterfly* was published in 1876.

[66] Sir Mount Stuart E. Grant Duff, *Notes from a Diary (1901) 1889–1891*, i. 92–3 (19 June 1889).

[67] Walter Besant, 'Literature as a Career', *Forum* (Aug. 1892), *Review of Reviews*, 6 (Sept. 1892), 258.

Several imitators and rivals of Stevenson in the adventure and historical-romance school, such as Rider Haggard with *King Solomon's Mines* (1885) and *She* (1887) and Conan Doyle with *Micah Clarke* (1889), were also issued in one volume. However, there appeared to be no set policy or consistency about this: Doyle's second essay in historical fiction, *The White Company* (1891), was published in three volumes. Barrie instanced as 'one of the fine things to remember about George Eliot . . . that she was offered a tempting sum to lengthen one of her books, and declined it'. This was *Silas Marner* (issued in one volume, 1861); yet she had not sustained this discipline, and *Romola* (1863) and *Felix Holt* (1866) were each first published in three volumes and *Middlemarch* (1872) and *Daniel Deronda* (1876) in four. At the time Barrie made his assessment, the only contemporary novelists—Stevenson and his imitators apart—who resisted the inducements to stretch out their work, like 'paper bags blown out with wind', were the writers of 'the shilling novels, now so popular'; but these, 'being mostly refuse, need not be considered'. Everyone else seemed trapped by the system—'The public blames the author, the author the publisher, the publisher the public'—but the issue was really very simple, 'a commercial question'. This was that

the publisher's appeal is to the library, which prefers books to be in several volumes, thus tempting the public to become heavy subscribers. The publisher flourishes moderately without much risk under this arrangement, for the libraries take as many copies of an average book as will at least secure him against a loss. He also bears in mind that a twenty-shilling book's cost of production may be little more than that of a six-shilling book. To appeal direct to the public with cheap single volumes might mean a much greater sale, but it would be more risky. The gain to literature would be certain. Many books which now get a library circulation would never be printed, and the better books would drop the ballast that now keeps them trailing to earth, for padding would be at a discount. As it is, books of merit, when offered, years after their first publication, in one volume, have a considerable sale, which would doubtless have been much greater had they been published originally at the same price, and without their superfluous chapters.

This call for sanity was all very well from Barrie, who was being boomed as 'the Dickens of Scotland' and who could expect to profit from popularity.[68] The fear was that novel-buying was a relatively inelastic, not an infinitely expansive, habit, and that best-sellers did not add to the total of novels purchased so much as draw off customers from buying less well-publicized books. The economic and social forces behind this theory were explained by the philosopher Herbert Spencer, in response to a suggestion that books might become even cheaper and sell hugely if copyright was abolished: 'No doubt that might be the case with some books, as with a great many other articles; but however much you lowered the price of cod-liver oil, you would not largely increase the number of purchasers.' He added drily, 'most people would much rather take a spoonful of cod-liver oil every day,

---

[68] J. M. Barrie, *Two of Them* (New York, 1893), 192–6. The depiction of Barrie as 'the Dickens of Scotland' is taken from the advertisements of his works, contained in the end pages of *Two of Them*.

than read one of my books'.[69] The actual state of affairs was not dissimilar, so W. T. Stead remarked in March 1892, in summary of the last year's literary trends. 'Seldom has there been a season so given up to the three volume novel,' he noted. 'First we had Mr J. M. Barrie's "The Little Minister", then Mr Hardy's "Tess of the D'Urbervilles", and now everyone is reading Mrs Humphry Ward's "The History of David Grieve"... and the booksellers tell me that the whole book-selling trade, as far as novels are concerned, suffers in due proportion.'[70] The rate at which *The Little Minister* sold in its different formats was revealing. The original three-volume, 31s. 6d. edition was published in September 1891 and reprinted in November, but it had sold only 1,000 copies by December 1892, evidently mostly to the circulating libraries. The one-volume, 7s. 6d. edition, published on 5 February 1892 and reprinted on 23 February and again in March, April, June, July, August, and September, sold 10,000 by December; and the 6s. edition, published in October 1892, sold 6,000 by that same December. An illustrated edition first appeared in July 1893 and, by December of that year, the total sales of the one-volume editions were over 35,000.[71] Barrie never again published a triple-decker.

When from the mid-1890s the triple-decker novel was superseded as the norm by the single-volume novel selling for 6s., the position that many writers of modest to average sales had dreaded came into being. A habitually glum George Gissing was made even glummer, recording in his diary on 9 August 1894:

Read Hall Caine's 'The Manxman', which has just appeared in 1 vol., instead of 3.—a result of the recent Mudie revolution . . . The publishers seem disposed to give up the 3-vol. publication altogether, and the Authors' Society has passed a resolution to the same effect. My own interests in the matter are entirely dubious.—Caine's book very poor.[72]

Likewise Ford Madox Ford, who embarked on a literary career in the 1890s, was starting out at the wrong time for a writer of his kind:

As he, on several occasions, pointed out, in the 'three decker' period of the last century, a novelist who regularly sold from three to six thousand copies of his books, at a guinea and a half, could enjoy a life of dignity and comfort on the proceeds. When novels came down to six shillings and sales continued at the old level, the results for esteemed but non-commercial authors, were cataclysmic. Hence the rapid growth of gangs and rackets, the

---

[69] Grant Duff, *Diary, 1896 to 1901*, i. 186–7.

[70] *Review of Reviews* (Mar. 1892), 306. The same journal in April 1892 (p. 417) contained a further recommendation of Barrie's *Little Minister*, after it had been reissued in one volume, price 7s. 6d.: 'Most novels it is perhaps best to borrow; this, now that it is in its one volume form, should be bought.' The *Little Minister*, along with Hall Caine's *The Scapegoat* (1891), were recommended as novels which 'may be read by all, man and woman, boy and girl'.

[71] Simon Nowell-Smith, *The House of Cassell, 1848–1958* (1958), 189; other information from the May 1898 edition, styled the 'Fifty-ninth Thousand', of J. M. Barrie, *The Little Minister*, with nine illustrations by W. Hole RSA.

[72] Pierre Coustillas (ed.), *London and the Life of Literature in Late Victorian England: The Diary of George Gissing, Novelist* (Hassocks, 1978), 343.

cut-throat competition for publicity and the recurring crises of those who had no skill in marketing their produce.[73]

But the pre-1890 book trade had been no arcadia for most authors, who tended to be squeezed between publishers and booksellers when both competed to offer large discounts to customers. The 'odd copy' convention was practically standard, by which publishers included twenty-four books in every order of twenty-five; moreover, publishers offered booksellers other financial inducements to settle their bills quickly, while booksellers in turn undersold each other in order to avoid keeping dormant stocks. Lewis Carroll protested about these practices in 1875, having seen the consequences for his profits.[74] He was better qualified than most authors to clarify the position: first because he was a mathematician and secondly because he undertook all the production costs of his own books, from printing and illustrating to advertising, and he contracted the publisher Macmillan's to distribute them for a 10 per cent commission on sales. Having done his *Alice* accounts, Carroll reached 'some startling conclusions', informing Macmillan's that 'On every 1000 copies sold, your profit is £20.16.8, mine is £56.5.0, the bookseller's £70.16.8. This seems to me altogether unfair . . . His profits should be the least of the three, not the *greatest*.' Macmillan fobbed him off with a defence of the trade, including the booksellers, whose costs in rent, rates, and wages he described; but Carroll made his stand in 1883 when he dictated the terms on which his books would be supplied, this notice appearing in all his books: 'In selling Mr Lewis Carroll's books to the Trade, Messrs. Macmillan and Co. will abate 2*d* in the shilling (no odd copies), and allow 5 per cent discount within six months, and 10 per cent for cash. In selling them to the Public (for cash only) they will allow 10 per cent discount.' These were hardly draconian terms and, though some booksellers howled, he succeeded in selling his books under such conditions thereafter.[75] Carroll could exploit his advantage as a best-seller, whereas ordinary writers continued to suffer from publishers' and booksellers' cut-throat discounting.

---

[73] Douglas Goldring, *South Lodge* (1943), 232.

[74] The situation is not dissimilar today, though now aggravated by the intervention of supermarkets into bookselling: see, the letter to *The Times*, 6 Mar. 2004, on behalf of the Royal Society of Literature from Michael Holroyd (president), Victoria Glendinning, David Hughes, P. D. James, Claire Tomalin (vice-presidents), and Maggie Gee (chair): 'we believe the proposal to remove the recommended retail price (the jacket price) from books would be a catastrophic blow to literature in this country. Supermarket booksellers might benefit, but the publishing industry and the book-loving public would suffer. At the moment, authors' royalty payments are based on a percentage of the jacket price; if they came to be based on discounted point-of-sale prices, they would fall dramatically. Already, the earnings of the average writer in this country are less than £20,000 per annum. Many writers would simply be pushed out of business. Publishers would be forced to kowtow to the demands from supermarket chains for pre-packaged bestsellers and larger and larger discounts on books. They could no longer take vital risks on new authors and interesting but unpredictable books. The book-buying public would have less and less choice; and small booksellers, unable to offer large discounts, would be impossibly squeezed.'

[75] Stuart Dodgson Collingwood, *The Life and Letters of Lewis Carroll*, (n.d), 188–90; and Morton N. Cohen, *Lewis Carroll: A Biography* (New York, 1996), 304, 429–30.

Matters might have deteriorated further for the little author had not the market been restabilized by the Net Book Agreement, under which booksellers pledged to disallow discounting on books published net. The publisher Frederick Macmillan was its architect and, when he later came to write a history of the campaign, it was significant that the very first words of his account were: 'The evils of underselling . . .'.[76] Macmillan pioneered the net book in 1890, initially against opposition from the trade; but most booksellers came round to the idea, recognizing it as a mechanism to stop their being ground down by anarchic underselling to the point where they could not survive by bookselling alone but must stock their shops with miscellaneous wares or else go out of business. Both *The Bookseller* and the *Publishers' Circular* in the late 1880s were opening each issue with a page or more of notices of dissolutions, bankruptcies, and winding-up auctions, the former journal stating that the 'spreading custom of giving 25% discount off the published price of books is fast ruining the bookselling business as an independent trade'.[77] Whether the public had actually benefited from rampant discounting was doubtful. The discount itself was often an illusion because publishers, cognizant of the general practice, kept their book prices artificially high so as to accommodate this toll. The first book launched as a net book by Macmillan was, appropriately enough, Alfred Marshall's *The Principles of Economics* (1890). Macmillan told the Cambridge professor,

Our theory is that the proper thing to do is only to allow the retail bookseller such a discount from the published price as will give him a fair profit if he gets the full price for a book. This of course would enable publishers to make books, nominally, cheaper . . . Our idea would be to make the price [of *Principles of Economics*] 12*s*. 6*d. net* instead of 16*s*., and the trade price would be 10*s*. 5*d*. with a further discount at settlement averaging 5 per cent. We shall also abolish the 'odd copy'—i.e. 25 books will not be charged as 24 or 13 as 12$\frac{1}{2}$.[78]

Macmillan's published another fifteen books at net in 1890, and progressively enlarged this output with a further 708 between 1891 and 1898. Other publishers followed suit, although still the 'great mass of popular literature', that is, fiction, was offered at a discount of 25 per cent (threepence in the shilling).[79]

The Net Book Agreement was formally universalized in 1899. The publishers, led again by Macmillan's, then fought off a challenge from the *Times* Book Club in 1906–8, which they charged with undermining their selling price by offering new books at a discount price to subscribers. This was not strictly correct: the books being offered at discount were generally weeks or months old, had been read by two or more subscribers, and, therefore, were properly classified as used or second-hand. As such, the general manager of *The Times*, C. F. Moberly Bell,

---

[76] Sir Frederick Macmillan, *The Net Book Agreement 1899 and the Book War 1906–1908* (1924), 1.
[77] Quoted in Lambert and Ratcliffe, *Bodley Head*, 21.
[78] Macmillan to Marshall, 15 Apr. 1890, in Macmillan, *Net Book Agreement*, 14–15; also in Simon Nowell-Smith (ed.), *Letters to Macmillan* (1967), 220.   [79] Macmillan, *Net Book Agreement*, 17–18.

argued that he was not breaching the terms of the Net Book Agreement. Several of *The Times*'s promotions appeared (to their subscribers) mouthwatering and (to the publishers and booksellers) heart-stopping bargains: Winston Churchill's Life of his father, Lord Randolph, published at 36s., was offered at 7s.; and six-shilling novels were reduced to 9d. or 11d. pence. Moberly Bell's motives were not foremost altruistic. Selling for threepence, *The Times* was in financial difficulties, losing ground to other papers which undercut it. Moberly Bell sought to increase circulation by making *The Times* more attractive rather than cheaper. Among other strategies, he explored the option of adding supplements—the Literary Supplement; the Financial and Commercial Supplement—without charge, but, though welcomed by existing readers, these did not notably raise circulation. The launch of a Book Club fitted the bill better and, to be fair to Moberly Bell, he believed that he was pursuing a public good as well as furthering the interest of *The Times* by taking this action. Obliging booksellers not to offer books at bargain prices appeared antipathetic to free trade and a monopoly conspiracy against the public; moreover, it offended against a legal judgment pronounced in 1852, when publishers had endeavoured to strangle the discount bookselling firm of Bickers & Bush by refusing supplies. The judicial ruling then was that although an owner such as a publisher might set what price he wished on any article offered for sale, once it had been purchased it derogated from the rights of ownership for the original seller to dictate terms under which the article could be resold.[80] In any case, Moberly Bell stoutly maintained, practice in the real world was at variance with the Net Book Agreement. Not only did many individuals sell books as second-hand within a few weeks of purchase, there also existed booksellers who sold new net books at below net price; moreover, publishers themselves sold off new books at half price or less within a few months, classifying these as remainders. Publishers had long tolerated the large circulating libraries, Mudie's and W. H. Smith's, which sold off stock when and how they wished; indeed, publishers did not just turn a blind eye to this, they conspired in it because Mudie's and Smith's were such large purchasers that their orders for books guaranteed for publishers a comfortable market at a certain level without requiring further effort on their part.

Moberly Bell forged ahead, therefore. The Book Club required of publishers that they should sell to it books at the lowest price they sold to anyone else. Moberly Bell believed that thereby the market for books would expand; demand had been artificially curbed and neither publishers nor booksellers had cause for anxiety. It did not turn out this way. When *The Times* sent out 700,000

---

[80] For Macmillan's denunciation of the free trade 'fetish' and its inapplicability to bookselling, see ibid. 1–4, 24, 34–5, 65. The Booksellers' Association dissolved under the impact of the 1852 ruling; a new association was founded in 1895 in support of the net system. Several famous names had backed the 1852 decision; predictably Gladstone, Cobden, and John Stuart Mill, but among authors, Dickens, Carlyle, and Tom Taylor. Opinion gradually turned against an unfettered free trade in books with the advance of legislation providing copyright protection.

prospectuses and catalogues to its subscribers, and aimed to maintain a stock of 25,000 volumes, continuously replenished, a battle royal commenced. In July 1906 the Publishers' Association resolved to cut off supplies and to withdraw their advertisements from *The Times* unless it undertook not to resell books until six months after publication. The threat to *The Times*'s advertising revenue was a sharp weapon. Moberly Bell had hoped to persuade publishers to spend on advertising 15 to 20 per cent of the value of the books that the Book Club bought; further, the Publishers' Association resolution that a net book should not be sold as second-hand, or a non-net book sold for less than 75 per cent of published price, within six months, represented a stiffening of the 1899 Net Book Agreement. Moberly Bell would not submit to this restriction, and attempted to court writers directly. An invitation to Kipling to undertake an inquiry into the issues involved was rejected. Kipling would not take sides against Macmillan, whose star author he was. Still more grievously misjudged was the approach made to Conan Doyle. Having been refused by Smith, Elder & Co. a large order at trade prices of the historical romance *Sir Nigel* (1906), the *Times* Book Club applied to Doyle to exercise his author's right of acquiring these: 'we should be glad, if you see no objection, to obtain direct from you 1950 copies, as 1800, upon the usual trade terms, provided that we can obtain them at once'.[81] *The Times* thus sought to divide and rule, by exploiting authors' privileges of special terms; but Doyle was outraged and divulged *The Times*'s ploy in a letter to the *Standard*: 'When you consider that this provision in the contract is a traditional courtesy for the convenience of the author in supplying his friends with copies it seems hard to find a word which would express the meanness involved in using it as a weapon—or suggesting it as one—against the publisher himself.'[82]

Rival newspapers were eager to publicize *The Times*'s embarrassment, but Moberly Bell's conviction that he had public support seemed well founded as the Book Club during the first 500 days of its operation (to 30 April 1907) sold 650,000 new and second-hand books. Relations deteriorated further when *The Times* carried a series of advertisements, supplemented with articles by the economist Arthur Shadwell, purporting to expose practices in the publishing and bookselling industry as the operations of a cosy cartel which planned to cheat the public and amass gross profits. Book Club subscribers were also circularized with a request that, in their other capacity as individual purchasers or as library users, they should boycott the publications of Macmillan, Constable, Edward Arnold, Smith, Elder & Co., and such publishers as were prominent in blacklisting the Book Club. In autumn 1907 *The Times* targeted John Murray, who refused supplies of *The Letters of Queen Victoria*, edited by Arthur Benson and Viscount Esher and

---

[81] The 1,950 copies would be achieved by an order of 150 dozen batches (a nominal 1,800 copies), with an extra copy included free in each dozen.

[82] Letter to the *Standard*, 20 Nov. 1906, enclosing a letter from the *Times* Book Club, 16 Nov. 1906, in John Michael Gibson and Roger Lancelyn Green (eds.), *The Unknown Conan Doyle: Letters to the Press* (1986), 123.

published in three volumes at 3 guineas. This was the kind of book in which *The Times*'s subscribers could be expected to show avid interest, and the Book Club was therefore especially frustrated by the embargo. In an otherwise laudatory review, the *Times Literary Supplement* criticized the pricing of the book, and *The Times* itself carried letters alleging that Murray could have realized a reasonable profit by issuing the book for a pound and was thus practising 'simple extortion'—language which the discerning attributed to Moberly Bell and his Book Club agent, the American Horace Hooper.[83] A libel action ensued and Murray was awarded £7,500 damages against *The Times* in May 1908. It was not, however, this particular case that sank Moberly Bell and his Book Club. Its popularity was plain. There were 27,000 members; and the Conservative MP J. Henniker Heaton, who was celebrated for his championship of the Imperial Penny Postage system, which had been introduced in 1898, organized a petition in support of the Book Club that attracted 10,000 signatures. Yet its operating costs were unsupportable. Faced with the publishers' ban on supplying it at concessionary rates, a ban which the publishers also succeeded in enforcing on the book wholesalers Simpkin's, *The Times* was incurring losses of £800 a week. This aggravated the financial crisis at *The Times*, which passed into new ownership, that of Lord Northcliffe (the former Alfred Harmsworth) during 1908. The struggle was discontinued and the Publishers' Association emerged with the Net Book Agreement now stronger than ever.[84]

Significantly, the Society of Authors took the publishers' side during the 'Book War'. This decision of its management committee did not go uncontested. Bernard Shaw, a member of both the Society's council and its management committee, deplored the way in which the Publishers' Association had taken up arms against *The Times* without first consulting authors, and was forfeiting substantial business by refusing to supply the Book Club. Shaw was also impressed by *The Times*'s contention that the Net Book Agreement kept prices artificially high, and he was unconvinced by the publishers' and booksellers' record:

As to all this pious horror about throwing new books at scrap price on the market, pray how many books do we see every year produced by publishers who, too languid to

---

[83] See the account by Edward Bell, of the Publishers' Association, in Macmillan, *Net Book Agreement*, 58–60. Evidence given by Murray in the trial provided some explanation for the volumes' high price, especially the outlay involved in paying £950 to the amanuensis of the letters and a staggering £5,592 14s. 2d. to the 'authors' (the editors Esher and Benson). Arnold Bennett, who reported this in his column for the *New Age*, 16 May 1908, scoffed that Murray's sense of business was farcical, albeit revealing for its disclosures about the parasitic mandarinism operating in undemocratic Britain (Bennett, *Books and Persons: Being Comments on a Past Epoch 1908–1911* (1917) 11–16). By the end of the year the three volumes were available for 6s.—'a cost that may seem to be almost a gift', wrote George Meredith, who added in a puff for the *Times* Book Club: 'The book of Queen Victoria's Letters is one for every household having a bookshelf' (letter to the manager of the *Times* Book Club, 24 Nov. 1908, in C. L. Cline (ed.), *The Letters of George Meredith* (Oxford, 1970), iii. 1678–9).

[84] This account of the book war is based upon E. H. C. Moberly Bell, *The Life and Letters of C. F. Moberly Bell* (1927), ch. xii, Macmillan, *Net Book Agreement*, and Charles Morgan, *The House of Macmillan (1843–1943)* (1943), ch. 11.

sustain interest in them, too poor to advertise them, and too incapable to distribute them, 'remainder' them at a few pence per copy, and leave the author penniless or out of pocket whilst the bookseller sells off the stock with a very fair profit at a large reduction on the published price?[85]

In August 1907 Shaw authorized a special edition of 500 copies of his plays for the *Times* Book Club. Likewise, G. M. Trevelyan instructed his publisher, Longman, to issue his *Garibaldi's Defence of the Roman Republic* (1907) at 6s. 6d., about 40 or 50 per cent cheaper than normal. 'These experiments proved most successful, and shortly afterwards Chatto & Windus reduced 6s novels to 2s 6d net,' wrote Moberly Bell's daughter, who added that her father 'received every day offers of books of all sorts from authors, and was generally able to introduce them to a publisher who would issue them cheaply'.[86]

It never took much to sour relations between publishers and authors, or to incite authors to turn on each other. There were no undisputed leaders of the profession in whom absolute confidence was vested. It was clearly a mistake for *The Times* to alienate Conan Doyle, whose probity was widely respected; equally clearly, no triumph to attract Bernard Shaw. The support of a self-promoting socialist loudmouth and oddball was the sort that each party wished given to its enemy. Moberly Bell had imagined that the Book Club would advance by winning the best-sellers' favour, but the jealousies and divisions that these authors excited probably did more damage. The best-sellers were a notoriously individualistic, not to say egotistical, bunch, and fellow authors were apt to interpret their statements of public interest as self-interest. The two outstanding best-sellers of the day, Hall Caine and Marie Corelli, were both members of the Society of Authors; indeed, Caine had represented the Society in copyright negotiations with the United States and Canada in the previous decade. However, by 1906 each was isolated by success and judged almost mad with vanity. That they also hated each other and should now take different sides almost went without saying. Caine declared his hand on 10 October 1906 in a letter to the *Daily Mail* which he duly published separately as a pamphlet, blaming the Net Book Agreement for keeping up prices against the interest of authors and readers. Accordingly, he determined to issue cheaply one of his own works, his stage adaptation of *The Bondman*, and to make public its sales. This roused A. E. W. Mason to write to the *Daily Mail*, 'It needed a Mr Hall Caine to seize upon the most serious crisis in which the fortunes of authors have been for many years involved to apply it to advertising himself and his play.' Cartoons of Caine appeared in other papers: one displayed him banging a drum, his coat papered with banknotes, and another depicted him flying his own kite, with the motto 'Ill blows the wind that profits nobody'. When *The Bondman* play was published, under the auspices of the *Daily Mail*, at price 2s., Caine's critics felt vindicated: a fraction of the length of a normal

[85] Letter to *The Times*, 17 Nov. 1906, in Victor Bonham-Carter, *Authors by Profession* (1978), 197.
[86] Bell, *Moberly Bell*, 272.

novel, it did not substantiate the case that book prices in general were unfair. In November Caine retired from the fray, telling a Bexhill banquet that the Book War was likely to persist until Judgement Day.[87]

That same month Marie Corelli hoisted her colours. Even 'the most unsophisticated lover of bargains', she declared in the *Rapid Review*, could identify the better deal: a subscription to the *Times* Book Club, costing £3 18s., 'with the unnecessary Times forced upon the subscriber', versus a subscription to the circulating libraries of Mudie's or W. H. Smith's, costing £2. 2s. for three or four volumes, in town or country, 'inclusive of the appreciated privilege of doing *without* the Times altogether'. While predictable that she would take the opposite side to Caine, Corelli was consistent in her distaste for being sold cheaply, whether it was indirectly through free public libraries or directly in cut-price format. She was confident about retaining her massive slice of the existing market and considered herself worth every penny of the standard 6s. at which she sold. To her literary agent A. P. Watt she had denounced the *Times* Book Club in July as 'a Yankee scheme for "cornering" the book-selling and publishing trade', adding: 'With authors who do not "hold" the public they can succeed,—and sell books published at 6/- for 2/6d. But I do not want this to be done with *me*!'[88]

By contrast, American methods of bookselling—bulk discounting and through mail order—appealed to a third best-seller of the day, Mrs Humphry Ward, who happened also to be another of Corelli's *bêtes noires*. Mrs Ward was struck by the volume of sales her novels achieved in America compared with Britain; moreover, her husband was a friend of Moberly Bell and employed by *The Times* as art critic, though his position was increasingly precarious. The need to maximize her own earnings pressed on Mrs Ward. She faced particularly heavy demands at this time, financing her son's parliamentary ambitions and funding a network of child play centres. She was thus torn when her publisher, Reginald Smith of Smith, Elder & Co., emerged as one of the doughty champions of the Publishers' Association. Smith was angered by the *Times* Book Club's promotion of Mrs Ward's *The Marriage of William Ashe* (1905) at 11d., a novel that he was then selling for 2s. 6d.; and he refused the Club any copies of her latest story, *Fenwick's Career*, when that was published in May 1906. To buy off Mrs Ward, Smith made her an ex gratia payment for forfeited sales, reckoned as 2,000 copies; and, when he otherwise stood firm, Mrs Ward's essayed mediation between the two sides in November 1906 evaporated.[89]

These differences reverberated at the Society of Authors' annual general meeting in 1907 when a resolution criticizing the management committee's support of the publishers was debated. It was proposed by Sidney Lee, the

[87] Allen, *Caine*, 316; *Punch*, 24 Oct. 1906, 296, 304, and 7 Nov. 1906, 329, 334, on the Caine and Corelli interventions. [88] Teresa Ransom, *The Mysterious Miss Marie Corelli* (Stroud, 1999), 158.
[89] John Sutherland, *Mrs Humphry Ward: Eminent Victorian, Pre-eminent Edwardian* (Oxford, 1990), 262–3, 271, 274–5.

Shakespearean scholar; he was also editor of the *Dictionary of National Biography*, which was the flagship of Smith, Elder & Co.'s publishing list. Lee received support from many sorts of authors: the zoologist Professor Ray Lankester, the Indian governor, poet, and historian Sir Alfred Lyall, and the story-writer, Zionist, and militant supporter of women's suffrage Israel Zangwill. The last-named, true to his firebrand character, launched himself against both the committee's decision and Bernard Shaw's dissentient action. Lee's motion fell by some fifty votes to thirty-six, but the dispute caused the Society to reform its constitution in order to make the executive more accountable to the wider membership.[90]

Thomas Hardy was a member of the Society of Authors' council at this time. He endorsed its position though he had taken no part in its formulation. 'Poor literature', he moaned, 'cuts a sorry figure' in this wrangle between publishers and distributors. He believed that the commercialization of literature had gone far enough: the author of quality needed the protection of the Net Book Agreement against the '500,000-copy men', the best-sellers, who were the only writers who stood to gain from aggressive marketing and discounting.[91] His instinct was justified according to calculations made by Moberly Bell when planning purchases by the Book Club: 'A novel of Mrs Humphry Ward might require 5000 copies, a novel by an unknown we should buy as we were asked for it only.'[92] Hardy, who stopped writing novels after *Jude the Obscure* (1895), had a particular interest in this dispute, being concerned for the sales of a cheap Pocket Edition of his works which his publisher, Macmillan's, had recently launched, at price 2s. 6d.[93] Hardy well understood the perilous economics associated with cheap editions, even for a highly regarded and successful, but not best-selling, author. In 1900 the London branch of his American publisher, Harper's, had produced a sixpenny edition of his most popular novel, *Tess of the D'Urbervilles* (1891); and the entire run of 100,000 copies was sold within twelve months. At a royalty of a penny a copy, this brought Hardy less than £420; by comparison, the apparently meagre sale which the six-shilling edition of this and all the rest of his fourteen books achieved, about 3,000 combined, yielded about £225 for the same period. An author such as Hardy could not afford to be offered at knock-down prices for too long, for fear of exhausting his market and of damaging ordinary sales. Hardy noted that the experiment of publishing *Tess* in a sixpenny edition 'may have suggested to the public that they were all going to be cheapened—the 6/- edition suffered'.[94] Accordingly, neither he nor Macmillan's was enthusiastic about an approach from the Oxford University Press in 1907, seeking permission to include one of Hardy's Wessex novels in the World's Classics series of shilling reprints. They were sceptical of the claim made by Henry Frowde on behalf of

[90] Bonham-Carter, *Authors by Profession*, 197–8.
[91] Hardy to Henry Newbolt, 4 Nov. 1906, in Purdy and Millgate (eds.), *Hardy Letters* iii., 233–4.
[92] Letter to a friend in India, 2 June 1905, in Bell, *Moberly Bell*, 252.
[93] Hardy to Edmund Gosse, 21 Nov. 1906, in Purdy and Millgate (eds.), *Hardy Letters*, iii, 236.
[94] Hardy to Frederick Macmillan, 22 Mar. 1906, ibid. 13.

the Press that 'experience shows that the sale of a book in The World's Classics does not injure but help, the sale in a more expensive edition'.[95] That was a gamble they were not prepared to take. The 2*s*. 6*d*. Pocket Edition was their Plimsoll line; indeed, Hardy encouraged Macmillan to

keep the 6/- edition with illustrations well alive. Some of the better class of buyers tell me that it is their favourite, & I think that the nearer you keep it to its original appearance the better they like it. I fancy the demand will ultimately resolve itself into one for that edition & the 2/6. Some day perhaps we could better make it worth the higher price by an extra illustration or two, a larger map, etc.[96]

Hardy even let it be known that, rather than entertain the idea of appearing in the World's Classics, 'I should . . . be more interested in an *edition de luxe*'.[97] Hardy's shrewdness in these things was learned by others only after painful experience. Theodore Watts-Dunton, author of *Aylwin* (1898), which had met with a large initial success, told Douglas Goldring in 1909 that 'from the financial standpoint he regretted bitterly having allowed it to appear in "The World's Classics" '.[98] It was during that year that the Society of Authors circulated its members, together with booksellers and publishers, asking first, whether new novels should be priced at less than 6*s*. in pursuit of increased sales and, ideally, bigger profits to the trade and larger returns to the writer; and secondly, whether writers would authorize cheap editions within a period shorter than the usual two years from first publication. The majority answered in the negative to both questions. To make even £75 from a new novel, the first question postulated sales of 3,000 copies, on which the author received 10 per cent royalty; as for the second, it was assumed that authors would be forced to accept a smaller royalty on cheaper-priced books or, if not, need to achieve sales of 9,000–12,000 copies for a 2*s*. book, or 8,000 copies at 2*s*. 6*d*. and 6,000 copies at 3*s*., to yield equivalent returns.[99] Such sales were beyond the expectation of most authors. These economics were spelled out by the journalist-turned-literary agent (and eventual publisher) Michael Joseph in the mid-1920s, when the effects of the cheap books revolution had worked through. Inflation in manufacturing and distribution costs during the Great War had increased publishers' expenses two or three times, while the standard price for a new novel had risen only from 6*s*. to 7*s*. 6*d*. Joseph stated: 'An averagely successful novel sells from about two to three thousand copies. The sales of many novels do not exceed 1,000 copies, and a considerable number sell no more than a few hundred copies.'[100] Only if the first edition at the standard price had sold out completely was it reasonable for a publisher to contemplate cheaper editions. Such editions incurred no new compositors' costs and thus

[95] Hardy to Frederick Macmillan, 23 Jan. 1907, ibid. 246.
[96] Hardy to Frederick Macmillan, 27 Sept. 1907, ibid. 274.
[97] Hardy to Frederick Macmillan, 25 Jan. 1907, ibid. 246.
[98] Goldring, *Reputations*, 222; id., *Life Interests* (1948), 195.
[99] Bonham-Carter, *Authors by Profession*, 211.   [100] Joseph, *Commercial Side of Literature*, 179.

publishers' profit margins expanded; however, few authors' books reached this stage and, if they did, proportionately their royalty revenue shrank.

The original advocates of cheap books had not been intending to deluge the public with popular fiction. The most eccentric instance was R. H. Horne issuing the first editions of *Orion* (1843) at a farthing as a protest 'to mark the public contempt into which epic poetry had fallen'.[101] Matthew Arnold was another protagonist in the cause. Having attended a farewell banquet for Dickens, who was about to embark for America in 1867, Arnold brooded about his own reputation, telling Bulwer Lytton: 'I have had very little success with the general public, and I sincerely think that it is a fault in an author not to succeed with his general public, and that the great authors are those who do succeed with it'.[102] In 1883 Arnold declared himself pleased that a book of his poems had for some time been in circulation 'at a comparatively cheap price', and that he had 'long had the wish to try the experiment of bringing out one of my prose books at a price yet cheaper'. This was fulfilled with a popular condensed edition in that year of *Literature and Dogma: An Essay towards a Better Apprehension of the Bible*. He explained that he did

not, however, choose for the experiment of a popular edition this book, merely because it admits of being shortened, or because it has been much in demand. I choose it far more for the reason that I think it, of all my books in prose, the one most important (if I may say so) and most capable of being useful.

It had been misrepresented, he added, in the ten years since its initial publication, as an attack either on Christianity itself or on the errors of popular Christianity, whereas his object was 'to re-assure those who feel attachment to Christianity, to the Bible, but who recognise the growing discredit befalling miracles and the supernatural. Such persons are to be re-assured, not by disguising or extenuating the discredit which has befallen miracles and the supernatural, but by insisting on the natural truth of Christianity.'[103]

Campaigners for cheap books did, nonetheless, also press for inexpensive reprints of standard literature. A leading advocate was William Laird Clowes, who was editor of Cassell's *Miniature Encyclopaedia* (1898) and advisory editor of the Unit Library (1901).[104] Clowes did not give an unalloyed welcome to Cassell's

---

[101] On Horne (1802–84), see Edmund Gosse, *Portraits and Sketches* (1912), 97–115, where it is noted: 'Elizabeth Barrett sent out to the nearest bookshop for a shilling's worth, but was refused her four dozen copies. Purchasers had to produce their brass farthings for each "Orion", and no change was given . . . Everybody talked about Mr Horne's "farthing" poem, and after some editions had run out the price was cautiously raised. But when the tenth edition appeared, at a cost of seven shillings, the public perceived that its leg was being pulled, and it purchased "Orion" no more.' Horne's *Orion* is now remembered, if at all, for the line 'Tis always morning somewhere in the world'. For this tenth edition, price 7*s*, see Chatto & Windus catalogue (Nov. 1886), 13.

[102] Arnold to Lytton, 4 Nov. 1867, in Earl of Lytton, *The Life of Edward Bulwer First Lord Lytton* (1913), ii. 444.

[103] Matthew Arnold, Preface, 1883, to Arnold, *Literature and Dogma* (1897), pp. v–vii.

[104] On Clowes (1856–1905), the naval correspondent of several newspapers, including *The Times*, and a principal in the agitation to re-equip and expand the Navy in the late 1880s, historian and writer of historical romances about the Navy, knighted in 1902, see *DNB Supplement 1901–1911*, i. 374–5.

efforts. Some reissues were, he wrote, if not bowdlerized, then 'Cassellized, or subjected to a cruel and procrustean docking, that they might fit the limits of the volumes in which they were embedded'.[105] The editor of the best-known Cassell's classic reprint series in the 1880s, Henry Morley, readily admitted both charges. Rabelais's works and Boccaccio's *Decameron* had been censored for decency's sake, and others abbreviated for reasons of space; but in the first case, it was better to have the half than the whole, and in the second to have the half than none.[106] Clowes indeed acknowledged Cassell's useful service, as that of Joseph Dent's Temple Classics (1896) and the even humbler penny libraries of poetry and (abridged) novels launched by George Newnes and W. T. Stead. Newnes— publisher of *Tit-Bits*, which was selling 671,000 copies a week by 1897—and Stead had been partners in the *Review of Reviews*, which Stead edited from its inception in 1890. Their partnership dissolved after a few months, but both men were enthusiastic popularizers. In the mid-1890s Newnes issued his Penny Library of Famous Books, each with 80–120 pages of tiny type that tried the eyesight and was flimsy in construction; but these brought to the humblest homes unabridged works of Goldsmith, Scott, Poe, Dickens, Marryat, Mayne Reid, and many others, including translations of Dumas, Eugène Sue, and Mérimée. The more spacious novels appeared in several parts. Altogether, the first forty-four of Newnes's penny novels sold about 4.25 million; but even this achievement was surpassed by Stead when he launched the Penny Popular Novels series from the *Review of Reviews* office in January 1896. Predictably hailed by *Punch* as 'Penny Steadfuls',[107] these began with an abridged version of Rider Haggard's *She*; by the end of the year 7.2 million copies of the Penny Popular Novels had been snapped up, and the series continued production until 1900. Stead also devised a Penny Poets series. Issuing a volume per week, up to 2 million copies were sold in 1895–6. Then there was his Books for the Bairns series, containing children's classics, nursery rhymes and other tales. These were paperbacks, more expensive at 3*d.*, but well illustrated, and 228 titles were issued by 1920.[108]

The late Victorian and Edwardian period was a great age of cheap reprints. In part copyright law facilitated this: the 1842 Act had established copyright for a period of forty-two years from first publication date or seven years after the author's death, whichever was the longer. Thus many of the early and mid-Victorian classics were entering the public domain and, with a large potential readership and improved printing technology, publishers raced to compete for the market.[109] 'We are now living in an age of handsome reprints,' wrote

[105] William Laird Clowes, 'The Cheapening of Useful Books', *Fortnightly Review* (July 1901), 88–98.
[106] Solly, *Morley*, 356.   [107] *Punch*, 18 Jan. 1896, 30.
[108] Ann Parry, 'George Newnes Limited', and J. O. Baylen, 'Review of Reviews Office', in Jonathan Rose and Patricia J. Anderson (eds.), *British Literary Publishing Houses, 1881–1965* (1991), 228, 270–1.
[109] Publishers also aimed to saturate the market with cheap editions of an author just *before* copyright expired. Thus Macmillan's in 1889 produced monthly volumes of Charles Kingsley in sixpenny editions: 2 million were printed, including half a million of *Westward Ho!* (1855). See Morgan, *Macmillan*, 136. Copyright law was altered again in 1911. The period was increased to the life of the author and fifty years

Augustine Birrell in 1894. He added, 'It is possible to publish a good-sized book on good paper and sell it at a profit for four-pence halfpenny.' Such a business operation depended on one proviso, that the author had breathed his last: 'dead authors are amazingly cheap. Not merely Shakespeare and Milton, Bunyan and Burns, but Scott and Macaulay, Thackeray and Dickens . . . You may buy twenty books by dead men at the price of one work by a living man.' As Birrell rattled off the names of series after series of reprints now available—the Camelot Classics, the Carisbrooke Library, the Chandos Classics, the Canterbury Poets, etc.—he was moved to reflect that the scales were so heavily weighted against new work by living authors that 'of all the odd crazes, the craze to be for ever reading new books is one of the oddest'.[110] There was an element of brazenness in the way in which publishers seized on works as they fell out of copyright, none more shameless than Routledge's advertisement of its Universal Ruskin at 1s. per volume in 1907, which made it appear that Ruskin himself, by arranging to publish his own books from 1871 and fixing their prices from 1882, had ripped off the public to the tune of £4,000 per year.[111] That Ruskin had been trying to circumvent the publishers' and booksellers' rings and cut-throat discounting at the authors' expense was conveniently misconstrued.[112]

'The Progress of the Working Classes in the Last Half Century' was the title of a famous essay by a senior official at the Board of Trade, Robert Giffen, and delivered as his presidential address to the Statistical Society on 20 November 1883. It was a subject frequently debated by Victorians, one on which politicians, economists, religious leaders, and multifarious philosophers and moralizers regularly gave voice. The Victorian period was, in the words of the Liberal statesman Gladstone, 'an agitated and expectant age'.[113] The Statistical Society had kept the question under review ever since its foundation in 1833 and, in the Society's jubilee year, Giffen aimed to settle it once and for all. He documented the case for a substantial growth in working-class real incomes through an increase in wages and reduction in prices for many common articles not offset by any rise in house rents and rates. This rosy picture was glossed by evidence of improved life expectancy, widening educational opportunity, and a decline in levels of pauperism and criminal activity; and it was completed with the audacious claim that

---

after death; there were other important conditions governing posthumous work and extracts for use in schools. See Sir Frank Mackinnon, 'Notes on the History of English Copyright', app. II in Margaret Drabble (ed.), *The Oxford Companion to English Literature*, 5th edn. (1985). The situation remained largely unchanged until 1995, when a European Union directive extended copyright from fifty to seventy years after an author's death, thus bringing back into copyright the work of many authors. See *TLS*, 18 Feb. 1994, 5 Jan. 1996.

[110] Augustine Birrell, 'Books Old and New', in Birrell, *Essays about Men, Women and Books* (1907), 134–46.

[111] *T.P.'s Weekly*, 8 Feb. 1907, 181.

[112] E. T. Cook, *The Life of John Ruskin* (1912), ii. 330–1. Cf. Edward Bell of the Publishers' Association in 1910: 'That the author or his assignee has a right to fix the price of his book cannot be disputed, as was exemplified years ago when Ruskin, probably to his own disadvantage, refused to issue cheap editions of his books' (quoted in Macmillan, *Net Book Agreement*, 65).

[113] Quoted in Mary Drew, *Catherine Gladstone* (1919), 47.

'almost the whole of the great material improvement of the last fifty years has gone to the masses'.[114] The tendentiousness of this thesis was plain: Giffen sought to vindicate the fiscal policy of free trade and the social policy of laissez-faire, implying that the free market naturally contained within itself mechanisms for greater overall prosperity and more equitable redistribution of wealth, so that no state socialism or any other radical restructuring of the system was required. Such confidence was less commonly echoed after the 1880s as a stubborn and sub-merged mass of poverty was exposed, as agricultural and business profits were hit by foreign competition, as the insecurity of employment was highlighted, and as relations between the classes became contested. The debate about the standard of living was too serious to be left to statisticians, whose fetish for quantification tended to disregard or make facile assumptions about the quality of life. Nevertheless, for all the disquiet that surfaced from the late nineteenth century, there were also signs of continued betterment. The New Liberal Charles Mas-terman was not one who was content to uphold the status quo; still, he accepted that substantial progress had taken place, and in 1906 he identified two recent causes of increased popular comfort: the electric tram and the gas stove. Mas-terman commented mordantly: 'The combined energies of statesmen and phi-lanthropists in half a century have created no such desirable change as has been wrought by these absurd mechanical inventions.'[115] Trams facilitated migrations to new dormitory suburbs away from inner-city slums; and, Parliament having at last consented to allow trams across Westminster Bridge, Masterman reckoned workingmen living south of the Thames thereby saved an hour daily in com-muting. Social life thus benefited from extended leisure; and Masterman even painted an image of 'trams, brilliantly lighted, in which reading is a pleasure'. On crowded journeys this was probably fanciful; but the installation of pre-payment slot meters in working-class homes from the 1890s had caused on increase in the use of gas for lighting as well as for cooking. Its spread was not uniform throughout urban areas and in the Yorkshire West Riding it remained con-spicuously inadequate before the Great War. Still, the trend was unmistakably one of rapid diffusion: in Manchester 32.5 per cent, in Birmingham 38.2 per cent, in Liverpool 39.3 per cent, in Newcastle and Gateshead 43.9 per cent, in Leicester 54.3 per cent, and in London about 60 per cent of all consumers enjoyed this advantage by 1906.[116] Elsewhere, without the incandescent mantle, illumination was now generally provided by paraffin lamp rather than by candles; and the price of both gas and paraffin had fallen progressively between the early 1870s and mid-1890s. The point hardly needs emphasis that the enhancement in domestic lighting for many ordinary people provided more opportunity for reading. At the

---

[114] 'The Progress of the Working Classes in the Last Half Century' (1883), repr. in Sir Robert Giffen, *Economic Inquiries and Studies* (1904), vol. i, ch. x, p. 417. On Giffen (1837–1910), see *DNB Supplement 1901–1911*, ii. 103–5.   [115] Lucy Masterman, *C. F. G. Masterman* (1968), 83.
[116] See M. J. Daunton, *House and Home in the Victorian City: Working-Class Housing 1850–1914* (1983), ch. 10, esp. table 10.1; also J. S. Hurt, *Elementary Schooling and the Working Classes 1860–1918* (1979), 186–7, 228.

same time, improved methods of printing and distribution were bringing more books, journals, and newspapers within the range of the working class.

The possibilities opened by this new publishing technology animated Gladstone, when taking tea with the fifteenth Earl of Derby in June 1889: 'he said [it] would revolutionize literature by cheapening books, to an extent which we could not now foresee: he talked about this in a vehement, excited tone, which rather startled his audience'.[117] Though almost incessantly burdened by public duties, Gladstone strove to find time for books which, though he claimed to be a slow reader, he disciplined himself to devour at every opportunity. He was, he said, a five-minutes reader:

> He never waits for anybody or anything. If there is an interval between his being dressed for dinner or a drive or walk and the need for leaving his room, he spends it, however short, in his book. In an instant he is deep in it; in an instant he is clean out of it. He reads the moment he is up and dressed, and he reads a good while after he has put on his dressing-gown for bed. . . . He keeps no one waiting, but never, if he can help it, allows himself to wait. All the time thus saved goes towards reading.[118]

By these means, Gladstone accumulated 'two or three hours for general reading' each day. His own library at Hawarden, which contained 10,000 books, he called the Temple of Peace.[119] In 1890 he returned to the subject of cheaper books on receiving a deputation from the bookbinding firm Hazell, Watson & Viney, who presented him with a set of Ruskin's *Modern Painters*. Gladstone recommended that the costs of bookbinding in leather be reduced by labour-saving machinery, as this particular process alone had not shared in the general cheapening of book production which characterized their generation.[120] Nor was Gladstone content to leave matters there, for the March edition of the *Nineteenth Century* carried his article 'On Books and the Housing of Them'. Here the great man got down to the

---

[117] John Vincent (ed.), *The Later Derby Diaries* (Bristol, 1981), 130 (26 June 1889).

[118] Lord Rendel, *Personal Papers* (1931), 80, 98 (8 June 1891, 29 Feb. 1892). See also 'The Home Life of Mr Gladstone', *Young Man* (Jan. 1892), in which his reading habits were described. He was most particular, it said, in maintaining variation in his reading and, during the previous summer, had on hand Dr Langer's Roman History (in German) for morning reading, Virgil for the afternoon, and a novel in the evening. He still considered Scott the king of novelists but, among modern novels that had struck him, he placed *Mehalah* (1880), Sabine Baring-Gould's most reprinted work, 'very high for force and originality', and Paul Bourget's *Le Disciple* 'as a psychological study' (*Review of Reviews* (Jan. 1892), 41). Gladstone's daughter lists the books read during her parents' honeymoon; she also records that her mother used to tell her that 'it was something of a shock' to her and her sister Mary Glynne, who married Lord Lyttelton, 'when, after marriage, any little waiting time, as at the railway station, which during their engagement would have been spent in love-making, was now spent in reading—both husbands carrying the inevitable little classic in their pockets. Out it would come and quickly engross the owner. Lord Lyttelton was to be seen at cricket matches in the playing field at Eton, lying on his front, reading between the overs, but never missing a ball' (Drew, *Gladstone*, 32, 36–7).

[119] Viscount Gladstone, *After Thirty Years* (1928), 5, 10. See also Lord Rosebery's presidential address to the Edinburgh Philosophical Institution, 25 Nov. 1898, 'Statesmen and Bookmen', in which he said of Gladstone, 'no one ever attained so much eminence as a statesmen who was essentially so bookish a man' (Lord Rosebery, *Miscellanies, Literary and Historical* (1921), ii. 208–28).

[120] *Review of Reviews* (June 1890), 522.

detail of building a personal library: apparently, the best method was shelving in sections 3 feet long, 1 foot deep, and 9 feet high, by which means the cost of a bookcase need not exceed 1d. per volume, and 20,000 volumes of all sizes could be stored in a library 40 feet long by 20 feet broad without making the room resemble a warehouse. He also made suggestions for mounting bookcases on sliding trays. By this stage, Gladstone had parted company with most readers and been left with an audience of one, his friend the historian Lord Acton, with his famed collection of some 60,000 volumes.[121] More modest in ambition was the author of an article in the *Girl's Own Paper* in 1891 who instructed readers about how to convert a broken piano into a bookcase, the upper part making three shelves, the keyboard a writing-desk, and the lower part a cupboard for magazines and papers;[122] or Augustine Birrell, who in an essay of 1897 thought to encourage library formation by informing the world that 'a bicycle takes more room than 1,000 books'.[123] But Mr Gladstone was no more utopian than a Mr Macnaghten, the author of a new Licensing Bill, who, in the *National Review*, outlined his scheme to promote temperance: bars should be abolished in every pub, which additionally he would require to provide three large rooms (dining, smoking, non-smoking), equipped with at least three daily papers, two weeklies, and two magazines, and a library of a hundred books whose selection would be determined by a competent board.[124] However idiosyncratic Mr Gladstone and Mr Macnaghten were in their different ways, both represented that widespread wish to encourage popular access to books. And Gladstone did implement his ideal, spending £30,000 on founding a hostel and library for the pursuit of divine learning: this was St Deiniol's at Hawarden, Flintshire (Clwyd), where he had his own home.[125] Seeing it under construction and describing it as 'a terrible building of corrugated iron overlooking the Sands of Dee', Wilfrid Blunt nevertheless allowed that it was 'conveniently arranged, and must be an advantage to the inhabitants'.[126]

To widen the availability of books and to diffuse the habit and joy of reading was a key mission in the late nineteenth century. It involved extending the library

---

[121] *Review of Reviews* (Mar. 1890), 217–18, says 100,000 volumes; the *DNB Supplement 1901–1911*, i. 8–12, says 59,000 volumes. Grant Duff visited Acton's library, which he depicted as a 'vast warehouse of books, but few people could read in it with any comfort. Everything like beauty or convenience has been advisedly sacrificed' (Grant Duff, *Diary, 1896 to 1901*, i. 259 (19 Aug. 1897)). The collection was housed at Aldenham, the Shropshire country house that Acton inherited. After Acton's death in 1902 it was bought by Andrew Carnegie, who presented it to John Morley, who in turn donated it to the University of Cambridge. See also David Mathew, *Acton: The Formative Years* (1946), p. iii, ch. ii, for the Aldenham library.   [122] *Review of Reviews* (Nov. 1891), 483.
[123] Augustine Birrell, 'The Johnsonian Legend' (1897), in Birrell, *Self-Selected Essays: A Second Series* (1916), 88.   [124] *Review of Reviews* (Feb. 1890), 136.
[125] John Morley, *The Life of William Ewart Gladstone* (1911), ii. 660, 761.
[126] Wilfrid Scawen Blunt, *My Diaries, Being a Personal Narrative of Events 1888–1914* (New York, 1980), i. 73 (2 Sept. 1892). Blunt's account was jaundiced against Gladstone for two reasons, political and poetical. As for the first, Blunt had been alienated by Gladstone's Egyptian policy and by 1892, apart from agreeing about Irish Home Rule, shared little common ground. As for the second, on perusing the shelves of Gladstone's own library, Blunt came across a copy of *Sonnets of Proteus* which Blunt had given him in 1884, with the leaves still uncut. The present St Deiniol's Library building was built as the national memorial to Gladstone.

system as well as marketing cheaper books. Mudie's and W. H. Smith's subscription libraries were the best-known and largest commercial operations, catering for a middle-class clientele for the most part; but there were umpteen smaller counterparts, even ordinary shops in industrial and market towns which, while principally selling other wares, might contain a couple of shelves of books for lending or circulation at a tiny subscription. Robert Blatchford, growing up in Halifax in the 1860s, read from the penny library there Defoe's *Robinson Crusoe*, Southey's *Life of Nelson*, Dickens's *The Old Curiosity Shop*, and novels by Captain Marryat, the Brontës, and Miss M. E. Braddon.[127] Public free libraries developed from Ewart's Act in 1850. This permitted municipal councils to expend the yield of a halfpenny (from 1855, a penny) rate on free library and equivalent services, such as museums and galleries. The expansion of the system was irregular but persistent. By 1885 about 25 per cent of England's population was covered by a public library; by 1914, 62 per cent. The great majority was in towns: a report in 1913–14 reckoned that 79 per cent of the urban population had access to a public library, and this figure included Ireland. Over a third of the libraries functioning by 1914 had emerged since 1900, over two-thirds since 1890. At the war's end in 1918 there were 456 library authorities in England, compared with 107 in 1886: the periods of fastest expansion had been 1892–6, with an annual average of almost twenty starting a service, and 1905–7, with an annual average of over thirty.[128] Ratepayer resistance was far from routed; vital to the growth were philanthropic donations. Many were local: Preston benefited from the bequest of a town's solicitor, Edmund Robert Harris; Barnsley from the enterprise of a linen-draper, Charles Harvey; and Hull from the generosity of the mustard manufacturer James Reckitt. The sugar-refiner Henry Tate, best known now for his foundation of the Tate Gallery, spent over £30,000 on public library benefaction in Streatham (where he lived), Balham, Brixton, and Lambeth; and the Edinburgh-based publisher Thomas Nelson bequeathed £50,000 towards four public libraries there.[129] Even so, Tate, Nelson, and all were eclipsed by the grants made by John Passmore Edwards and Andrew Carnegie. Edwards, born in 1823, made his fortune from magazine and newspaper ownership, particularly the *Echo*, the capital's original halfpenny daily, which he bought and edited from 1876 and sold in 1896. A Cobdenite pacifist and one-time Liberal MP, Edwards became a conspicuous benefactor and, in his final entry in *Who's Who*—he died in 1911—he recorded that he had founded over seventy institutions including convalescent homes and hospitals, 'erected eleven drinking fountains, and placed thirty-two marble busts of eminent men by eminent artists in public buildings'. Twenty-five free libraries were associated with his name—fifteen in the poorer areas of London and eight in his native Cornwall—and he presented over 80,000 books not only to libraries but

[127] Robert Blatchford, *My Eighty Years* (1931), 44.

[128] Thomas Kelly, *A History of Public Libraries in Great Britain, 1845–1975*, rev. edn. (1977), 122–4, 188.

[129] Ibid. 119–20; Charles Geake (ed.), *Appreciations and Addresses Delivered by Lord Rosebery* (1899), 220–31, for Rosebery's address at the opening of the first of the Nelson-donated public libraries, on 10 May 1897.

to hospitals, reading rooms, and other institutions.[130] The Dunfermline-born Pittsburgh steel magnate Carnegie eventually outstripped Edwards. Carnegie's first grant towards a library in England was £10,000 for Keighley in Yorkshire, in 1899. Rural areas were generally the most thinly provided but, where local initiative arose, Carnegie's aid could be attracted. Such was the case in Hereford diocese, where the bishop, John Percival, a former headmaster at Clifton and Rugby and President of Trinity College, Oxford, in 1906, devised a circulation of boxes 'of fifty books of standard literature (history, biography, science, fiction, etc.)' to schools in the region, 'exchanged quarterly [for] a small annual sub-scription covering the cost of carriage and management'.[131] After five years there were seventy-eight schools involved in the scheme, and over 40,000 books in circulation. A parallel system of boxes of books for adults in villages was also thriving. Percival himself 'took great pains over the choice of books. Some were to be books of a general religious interest, but not those written with an obvious religious "moral"; some were to be books on agriculture; some novels by the great writers were always included'.[132] It was Carnegie, to whom Percival appealed, who defrayed outstanding costs. By the time the Carnegie United Kingdom Trust was created with capital of £2 million. in 1913, Carnegie had already disbursed donations of £1.75 million. in aid of public libraries and made promises that brought the total to nearly £2 million. The Trust now operated stricter rules, generally making grants for buildings and fixtures, not books. Thus, the receiving authority had to provide a site and to levy a rate for maintenance; but when Carnegie died in 1919, approaching half the library authorities in England had obtained some assistance from him.[133]

Information about the occupations and class of reader exists. Parliamentary returns for 1876–7 record such details for thirty-seven libraries and indicate that the overwhelming majority were working-class. Leeds's lending library placed 19 per cent of readers in the professional and middle classes, 81 per cent in the working classes. These figures concerned ticket not book issues, and evidence about comparative use is more difficult to obtain; but a striking feature of these library reports was the information about age and sex, suggesting that between 30 and 40 per cent of readers were aged under 21 and possibly 20 per cent female. Subsequent surveys reflected the broad changes taking place in economy and society: readers who were classified as 'mechanics' and factory workers fell in representation as clerks and those in commercial occupations rose; and by the middle of the Edwardian period estimates of the proportion of female readers

---

[130] Kelly, *Public Libraries* 120–1; *Who Was Who, 1897–1916*, 221. Edwards refused a knighthood from both Queen Victoria and King Edward VII.

[131] Letter from Canon Bannister to *The Times*, 6 Sept. 1912, in William Temple, *The Life of Bishop Percival* (1921), 289.

[132] Temple, *Percival*, 290. Controversy arose in 1913 about whether a permanent rather than circulating library system was preferable, to which Percival replied that the ideal was both.

[133] Kelly, *Public Libraries*, 116–17.

were as high at 41 per cent, with almost half of all readers being put at under 20 and nearly three-quarters aged under 40.[134] Still, it was the great variety of borrowers' occupations that stood out in the individual accounts. The City of Westminster could be reckoned among the most exceptional of places, containing as it did the seat of Parliament and government departments; yet a report setting out the occupations of borrowers newly enrolled at its public libraries between 1 April 1905 and 31 March 1906 proved that even there ordinary folk and the downright humble were making use of its facilities. Groups with the largest representation were, respectively, clerks, scholars, civil servants, domestic servants, dressmakers, and assistants; there were also milk-carriers, messenger boys, charwomen, office boys, window cleaners, hawkers, omnibus drivers, farriers, and bricklayers along with the august sort—MPs, army officers, lawyers, and clergy.[135]

The constraints on public library provision were not just ones of cost. Their management excited debate, particularly about the sorts of books to be stocked—whether fiction should be excluded altogether or at least under-represented compared with so-called serious literature—theology, history, biography, science and technical works, and reference and vocational literature; and whether open-shelf access should be allowed. There was thus disgruntlement that readers were being entertained rather than edified at public expense. Statistics supplied by Birmingham, Liverpool, and Manchester libraries in 1894 indicated that about 77 per cent of all lending involved fiction, including possibly 10 per cent classified as juvenile literature; and much the same was reckoned nationally in the mid-Edwardian period, the figure being almost 80 per cent, of which 15 per cent was juvenile literature.[136] The former editor of the *Fortnightly Review* and *Pall Mall Gazette* and Liberal minister John Morley expressed his concern in an address to students of the London Society for the Extension of University Teaching in 1887. He too had seen reports disclosing that in one big northern town fiction comprised 76 per cent of all books lent, in another 82 per cent, and in yet another 84 per cent and he compared the position unfavourably with Scotland, where 'there is a larger demand for books called serious than in England'. He suspected the reason to be that 'in the Scotch universities there are what we have not in England—well-attended chairs of literature, systematically and methodically studied'. But, he added,

Do not let it be supposed that I at all underrate the value of fiction. On the contrary, when a man has done a hard day's work, what can he do better than fall to and read the novels of Walter Scott, or the Brontës, or Mrs Gaskell, or some of our living writers. I am rather a voracious reader of fiction myself. I do not, therefore, point to it as a reproach or as a source of discouragement, that fiction takes so large a place in the objects of literary interest. I only suggest that it is much too large, and we should be better pleased if it

---

[134] Kelly, *Public Libraries*, 82–4, 191–2.   [135] *Gentlemen's Magazine*, 301 (Sept. 1906), 306.
[136] Kelly, *Public Libraries*, 192–3.

sank to about 40 per cent, and what is classified as general literature rose from 13 to 25 per cent.[137]

Morley tried to avoid appearing censorious. Others were unabashed about identifying what they regarded as pernicious. Following inquiries he made in 1907, Dr Ernest Baker, then librarian of Woolwich's public libraries and later director of the Library School at University College London, found that an average of twenty-eight copies of William Le Queux's thrillers was stocked at each of twenty-one public libraries. Such books he deplored as 'decidedly below the standard admissible in a rate-supported library' and 'furnishing the means for intellectual debauchery, or brain-sedatives for the idle and infirm';[138] and he pleaded for librarians to discriminate between 'classical' and 'ephemeral' fiction. Resolutions at that year's Library Association conference stated that 'the function of a Public Lending Library is to provide good literature', by which was meant books of 'literary or educational value'. Thus 'every library should be supplied with fiction that has attained the position of classical literature; and . . . the purchase of mere ephemeral fiction of no literary or moral value, even if without offence, is not within their proper province'.[139] Such resolutions were not binding; they were also unnecessarily alarmist. Certain libraries published records of books taken out by individuals; and, while historians will acknowledge the random character of such evidence and qualify it further by recognizing that book choice was in part dictated by availability, these data do not provide support for the proposition that the lowest orders of society subsisted off the lowest class of literature. The annual report for 1887 for Portsmouth Public Library included lists of works borrowed during the previous year by two individuals:

A Labourer	A Domestic Servant
[J. R.] Green's	*East Lynne*, by [Mrs Henry] Wood [1861]
Short History of the English People [1874]	[E. C. Dawson], *The History and Life of*
[Frederick] Greenwood's	*Bishop Hannington* [1887]
Little Ragamuffins [1886]	[Miss M. E. Braddon], *Lady Audley's*
The Graphic and *Illustrated London News*	*Secret* [1862]
[Charles Dickens'], *Dombey and*	*Look Before You Leap*, by [Mrs H.]
Son [1848]	Alexander [1865]
[Charles Dickens'], *Old Curiosity*	*Canadian Pictures* by Marquis of
Shop [1841]	Lorne [1884]
[Charles Dickens'], *Tale of Two Cities*	*Girl of the Period*, by [E. Lynn]
[1859]	Linton [1869]

---

[137] Morley, 'On the Study of Literature' (1887), in Morley, *Studies in Literature*, 203–4.

[138] Ernest A. Baker, 'The Standard of Fiction in Public Libraries', *Library Association Record*, 9 (1907), quoted in Roger T. Stearn, 'Mysterious Mr. Le Queux', 9. News that fiction comprised only 16.3 per cent of the books stocked by the public libraries of Stoke Newington, north London, and that there had been a decrease of nearly 2.5 per cent in the number of fiction titles borrowed in the previous year, caused *Punch*, 8 July 1908, 34–5, to imagine a military insurrection of popular novelists there generalled by Le Queux.

[139] Kelly, *Public Libraries*, 195.

[Walter Besants'], *All Sorts and Conditions of Men* [1882]

[Walter Besant and James Rice], *By Celia's Arbour* [3 vols., 1878]

Ireland, its Scenery, Character, etc., 3 vols.

Tales from Blackwood

Reminiscences of Abraham Lincoln [edited by A. T. Rice, 1886]

Harry Richmond, by [George] Meredith [1871][140]

She, by [Rider] Haggard [1887]

[Gustave Louis M. Strauss], *Dishes and Drinks, or Philosophies in the Kitchen* [1887]

[Mrs Fenwick Miller], *Life of Harriet Martineau* [1884]

[George Eliot], *Mill on the Floss* [1860]

Her World against a Lie, by [Florence] Marryat [3 vols., 1879]

Carnegie himself had confidently declared in 1891, 'They who begin with fiction, generally end with solid literature.'[141] Even if that confidence was misplaced, the argument that fiction-reading caused mental and moral debilitation was not sustainable; nor did fiction-reading want for defenders. Novelists fervently protested their good intentions and their beneficent influence against those inclined to follow Carlyle in thinking 'how perilous and close a cousinship it [fiction] has with lying'. At the banquet to honour Dickens before his departure for America in 1868, Anthony Trollope had affirmed that 'we who write fiction have taught purity of life, nobility of action, and self denial, and have taught those lessons with allurements to both the old and the young which no other teacher of the present day can reach, and which no prophet can teach'.[142] In 1883 the respected editor of the *Liverpool Mercury*, John Lovell, told the Library Association that

though a work of fiction may be fictitious in form, though its sequences and its circumstantialities may be pure inventions, it may nevertheless be most veracious in its substance. It may enlarge the reader's knowledge, supply him with food for thought, furnish him with rules of conduct, help to form his character, and give him a wider and more intelligent outlook upon life than he ever had before.

Lovell roundly concluded that 'it is no part of the function of the Managers of Free Libraries to decide what kinds of literature the public shall or shall not read'.[143] As it happened, it was then that Lovell was giving the afterwards bestselling novelist Hall Caine his start in journalism. The son of a shipwright, Caine had been largely dependent on public sources to satisfy his appetite for knowledge and to feed his imagination: 'The Free Library at Liverpool was my great hunting-ground in those days', he would later reminisce. He simply roamed the shelves and took down and took in anything and everything, fiction, poetry, history, theology; in this way he encountered Coleridge, a formative influence. Caine was therefore educated, he said, courtesy of the public library system.[144]

The former prime minister Lord Rosebery was equally keen to squash the notion that they had endowed 'nothing but a sort of gratuitous circulating library

---

[140] Kelly, *Public Libraries*, 87–8. Information in square brackets has been added. [141] Ibid. 194.

[142] K. J. Fielding (ed.), *The Speeches of Charles Dickens* (Oxford, 1960), 374.

[143] Kelly, *Public Libraries*, 86. [144] Allen, *Caine*, 21, 23, 149.

of all the sensational novels that come out'. This was a canard, he declared at the formal opening of a Passmore Edwards library at Uxbridge Road in London on 25 June 1896: 'I do not believe that is the experience of free public libraries.' There was plentiful evidence of 'the artisan class', men, women, and children, 'thirsting for knowledge'. In any case, he reflected, 'a man had better read a sensational novel than read nothing'. Here Rosebery's animus as a disenchanted politician asserted itself: it was the press, not novels, that constituted 'one of the greatest enemies of independent thinking'. Newspaper sensationalism confused or deadened the brain; and Rosebery lauded the free public libraries as a counter to the press by furnishing inducement 'to come to some temple of reading and of thought where they can form their conclusions and their convictions'.

Yet Rosebery also acknowledged that 'every free public library requires a taster in the shape of a librarian . . . a taster to guide the student as to what he wants'.[145] Librarianship was a new profession, and its practitioners were anxious to assert their credentials. The *Review of Reviews* declared in 1891, 'it is little use for Mr Carnegie or other benefactors to dump truck loads of books in a town unless they also supply a luminous and instructed custodian to lend them out'.[146] The Library Association published from 1889 its own journal, *The Library*;[147] and Thomas Greenwood's *Free Public Libraries* (1886) was a key tract giving advice about how to organize new foundations. The atmosphere was not always welcoming. When Constance Smedley visited the United States, she was struck by the contrast; particularly, as a writer of children's books she noticed the greater access allowed there for children to browse. She also praised the bright pictures on walls, flowers in vases, and the college students working at the desks who were always ready to help: 'all this was the antithesis of the red tape, ugliness, and drabness of many of our Free Libraries'.[148] There was much room for improvement, therefore; nonetheless, that was under way. While the urban system was still patchy by 1890, rural areas were entirely forlorn before the setting up of county councils in 1888–9 and the reform of parish councils in 1893–4 produced an enabling structure. There was a larger ideological purpose here, to arrest the advance of urbanization, which, many argued, was proceeding at too great a pace in England. Those who sought to revivify country life understood that rural depopulation derived not just from changes in methods of agriculture which employed fewer people on the land, but also from want of amenities—among these, inferior domestic sanitation and lighting, and a shortage of recreational opportunities which led many to migrate to towns in pursuit of excitement as well as work and higher wages.[149] The machinery now existed to correct this, it was

---

[145] Lord Rosebery, 'The Work of Public Libraries' (1896), in Geake (ed.), *Appreciations and Addresses*, 235–43.   [146] *Review of Reviews* (Oct. 1891), 333.
[147] From 1899 *The Library* became an independent journal, absorbing in 1920 the *Transactions of the Bibliographical Society* (est. 1892–3).   [148] Smedley, *Crusaders*, 227.
[149] On this debate, P. J. Waller, *Town, City and Nation: England 1850–1914* (Oxford, 1981), ch. 5.

argued: county councils should establish a free central library in every shire, coordinated with reading rooms in every village, where books for exchange could be deposited and collected weekly. There was no need to build special reading rooms: the village school could serve. And, to circumvent the funding problem, it was proposed through the *Daily News* in 1891 that an association should be started to supply such libraries 'free with the best literature and periodicals'.[150] In 1907 it was estimated that 15 per cent of books, and 41 per cent of periodicals, in public libraries resulted from donations;[151] and this remained an important supplement of the ratepayers' provision for many years. Some wealthy and public-spirited authors abetted this; for example, when Douglas Sladen gave up his Richmond home, The Avenue House, in 1923, he presented his library of 13,000 volumes, together with bookcases, to the Borough of Richmond Library.[152]

The expansion of the free library system was not universally welcomed by authors. Where the displacement of the guinea-and-a-half three-decker novel by the six-shilling single-volume novel caused financial anxiety for authors of limited sales, so the extension of the free library network alarmed the best-sellers. The Society of Authors received a complaint in 1913 that one town librarian had introduced a short-term borrowing rule for a popular novel. This was done to accelerate its circulation among readers; as a result its sales were snuffed out at local bookshops.[153] Worse was proved against other librarians, that they sought out review copies, remainders, and even stolen books, and that they bullied booksellers into selling at prices in breach of the Net Book Agreement.[154] During the fuss generated by H. G. Wells's *Ann Veronica* (1909), which was banned by many public libraries, T. W. Hand, the Leeds Librarian, admitted that the reason it had not appeared in any of his city's libraries was 'not the character of the book, but the fact that we never purchase our novels until they have become cheaper'.[155] The best-seller Marie Corelli held no brief for H. G. Wells; rather, she hated the whole idea of public libraries, which she denounced as

extremely detrimental to the prosperity of authors. A popular author would have good reason to rejoice if his works were excluded from Free Libraries, inasmuch as his sales would be twice, perhaps three times as large. If a Free Library takes a dozen copies of a book, that dozen copies has probably to serve for five or six hundred people, who get it in turn individually. But if the book could not possibly be obtained for gratuitous reading in this fashion, and could only be secured by purchase, then it follows that five or six hundred copies would be sold instead of twelve. This applies only to authors whose works the public clamour for, and insist on reading; with the more select 'unpopular' geniuses the plan, of course, would not meet with approval.[156]

[150] *Review of Reviews* (Oct. 1891), 334.   [151] Kelly, *Public Libraries*, 188.

[152] Douglas Sladen, *My Long Life: Anecdotes and Adventures* (1939), 307.

[153] Bonham-Carter, *Authors by Profession*, 211.

[154] Sir Stanley Unwin, *The Truth about Publishing*, rev. edn. (1946), 209.

[155] *New Age*, 24 Feb. 1910, in Bennett, *Books and Persons*, 189.

[156] Marie Corelli, 'The Vulgarity of Wealth', in Corelli, *Free Opinions* (1905), 108.

Here was the Authors' Lending Rights campaign in embryo. Corelli pressed her case with two additional arguments. One was an *ad hominem* attack on Carnegie's munificence as vanity patronage of the working classes. The libraries were 'brick and mortar advertisements of his own great wealth and unfailing liberality'. His money would be better spent providing employment by reviving 'the spinning and silk-weaving industries in England'. But Carnegie's indifference to the real welfare of the working classes was only to be expected if it was remembered 'how Carnegie made his millions, and how he sanctioned the action of the Pinkerton police force in firing on his men when they "struck" for higher wages'. Corelli's second argument was an appeal to personal dignity and public health:

The true lover of books will never want to peruse volumes that are thumbed and soiled by hundreds of other hands—he or she will manage to buy them and keep them as friends in the private household. Any book, save the most expensive 'édition de luxe', can be purchased for a few shillings,—a little saving on drugged beer and betting would enable the most ordinary mechanic to stock himself with a very decent library of his own. To borrow one's mental fare from Free Libraries is a dirty habit to begin with. It is rather like picking up eatables dropped by some one else in the road, and making one's dinner off another's leavings. One book, clean and fresh from the bookseller's counter, is worth half a dozen of the soiled and messy knock-about volumes, which many of our medical men assure us carry disease-germs in their too-frequently fingered pages. Free Libraries are undoubtedly very useful resorts for betting men. They can run in, glance at the newspapers for the latest 'Sporting Items' and run out again. But why ratepayers should support such houses of call for these gentry remains a mystery which one would have to pierce through all the Wool and Wobble of Municipal Corporations to solve.[157]

Corelli pressed her case in and out of season. In *The Sorrows of Satan* (1895) the novelist Geoffrey Tempest, having unexpectedly inherited £5 million, laughs at the idea that he might found a free library, 'for these institutions, besides becoming centres for infectious diseases, generally get presided over by a committee of local grocers who presume to consider themselves judges of literature'.[158] And in 1903, in Stratford upon Avon, where Corelli resided, she led the opposition to the town council's decision to establish a free library endowed with Carnegie money, although the nub of the controversy here was its situation in Henley Street, which would involve an act of municipal vandalism, the demolition of old cottages close to Shakespeare's birthplace.[159] Arnold Bennett never went so far as to oppose free libraries, yet he too deplored the state of their books, especially novels. Each one passed through thirty to a hundred homes a year and was 'repulsively foul, greasy, sticky, black . . . Can you wonder that it should carry deposits of jam, egg, butter, coffee, and personal dirt? You cannot. But you are entitled to wonder why the Municipal Sanitary Inspector does not inspect it and

---

[157] Corelli, 'A Vital Point of Education', in Corelli, *Free Opinions*, 9–10.
[158] Marie Corelli, *The Sorrows of Satan* (Oxford, 1996), 48–9.   [159] Ransom, *Corelli*, ch. 7.

order it to be destroyed.' But Bennett's principal objection was that 'few new novels' got into such libraries, and those that did had to be ' "innocuous", that is, devoid of original ideas'. A municipal library's fiction was, therefore, usually a quarter-century out of date, which was fine for followers of Charlotte M. Yonge or Charles Kingsley. Otherwise, its presiding committee's policy was determined by the goal of supplying 'women old and young with outmoded, viciously respectable, viciously sentimental fiction'. This harsh verdict Bennett tempered only in a degree, conceding that a 'fraction of its activity' was beneficial, to the artisan as well as to the lower-middle classes.[160]

These animadversions notwithstanding, the free library network grew; and alongside it the subscription libraries of Mudie's and W. H. Smith's continued, joined in the early twentieth century by, fleetingly, the *Times* Book Club and, more comprehensively, by Boots. The last was an ancillary to the multiple-branch chemists and, if Arnold Bennett was correctly informed, it was run almost as a loss-leader, since Boots haemorrhaged 10,000 books a year and tolerated this as a means of advertising the shops' other wares. Bennett marvelled at Boot's generosity: 'If you desire a book which he has not got in stock he will buy it and lend it to you for twopence.' Accordingly, for the lower-middle classes, with an annual average family income of £200, in many towns their 'sole point of contact with living literature is the chemist's shop'. Bennett made two observations about its libraries' clients: 'One is that they are usually women, and the other is that they hire their books at haphazard, nearly in the dark, with no previous knowledge of what is good and what is bad.'[161] For the majority of authors this was just as well. Without such libraries, both free and subscription, 'there would be no market for at least 75 per cent of the novels which are now published', stated Michael Joseph in 1925.[162]

Meanwhile, publishers were competing to bring the best literature within the reach of readers of modest means. The year 1900 opened with Nelson's New Century Library, closely followed by Grant Richards's World's Classics in 1901, Collins's Pocket Classics in 1903, and Dent's Everyman Library in 1906. Dent's aimed to produce 'a thousand volumes of the world's most famous books' at the 'democratic price of one shilling';[163] but Everyman and World's Classics (which sold for the same price) were only the two most outstanding for quality of some eighty series of cheap reprinted classics in the early 1900s.[164] Though

---

[160] *New Age*, 18 Feb. 1909, in Bennett, *Books and Persons*, 104–5.   [161] Ibid. 106–7.

[162] Joseph, *Commercial Side of Literature*, 182.

[163] It did so after half a century. See William Haley, 'The Way of the Popularizer', *TLS*, 24 Mar. 1978, 353–4.

[164] The first ten titles in the World's Classics were: C. Brontë, *Jane Eyre*; Lamb, *Essays of Elia*; Tennyson, *Poems 1830–65*; Goldsmith, *The Vicar of Wakefield*; Hazlitt, *Table Talk*; Emerson, *Essays*; Keats, *Poems*; Dickens, *Oliver Twist*; Barham, *Ingoldsby Legends*; E. Brontë, *Wuthering Heights*. Having reached number 66, Borrow's *Lavengro*, Richards was bankrupt and the series was bought in 1905–6 by Oxford University Press, which followed with A. Brontë, *The Tenant of Wildfell Hall*, Thoreau's *Walden*, and Gibbon's fourth volume of *Decline and Fall*, and so on to 620 volumes by 1970. See Peter Sutcliffe, *The Oxford University Press: An Informal History* (Oxford, 1978), 140–4.

Mr Gladstone was now dead, his rule was apparently being widely adopted, namely, 'that no exertion spent upon any of the classics of the world, and attended with any amount of real result, is thrown away'.[165] The success of Everyman was extraordinary. Started in 1906, it comprised 213 volumes by February 1907, when its advertisements proclaimed, 'Nearly 2,000,000 volumes sold in less than Twelve Months'.[166] A year later, when the 300th volume was issued, Everyman's advertisements boasted the 'remarkable sale of nearly $3\frac{1}{2}$ million volumes in two years'.[167] Oxford University Press, which had taken over the World's Classics, was more bemused than bumptious; but its message was the same. 'Who reads and buys *The World's Classics?*', the question was posed in its house magazine, *The Periodical*, in 1907: 'We do not profess to know, but the fact remains that nearly two million copies have been sold.' It was a reasonable guess that they included the literate young of the lower-middle and aspiring professional classes.[168] Derek Hudson, born in 1911, recalled the books he discovered on his father's shelves, mostly 'bought by him from his modest resources as a young law-student and solicitor in the years before 1914 ... The classic writers were properly represented, often in the early volumes of the Everyman Library.'[169] Those further down in the social order should not be excluded from the reckoning too. Just like Thomas Burt or Ben Tillett before him, Thomas Burke now measured his book purchases as a teenager in the early 1900s in terms of meals forfeited. Every volume of the World's Classics, Canterbury Poets, or Scott Library series meant the missing of at least two meals, and George Newnes's Thin Paper Classics four meals. The last, though more expensive, were his favourite because, issued on the then new India paper, they contained more words in compact form—the whole of Lamb, Milton, Burns, Coleridge, or Marlowe, or all Peacock's novels, in one volume. Burke would also acquire 'a few rakings' from Paternoster Row and Farringdon Road second-hand bookshops, 'paid for by walking home from the City, four miles, instead of taking bus or tram'.[170] In the North there was Neville Cardus, who was born illegitimate. He left board school at the age of 13 for a succession of dead-end jobs as messenger boy and pilot of a carpenter's handcart before finding a clerical post in a marine insurance company; yet he had larger ambitions to become a writer and he attended free lectures at Manchester University, where he was baffled by Bernard Bosanquet's exposition of Hegelianism. In 1912 Cardus travelled to Shrewsbury School to take up an appointment as assistant cricket professional, bearing with him his belongings in a battered tin box, secured with rope in lieu of a lock.

---

[165] Quoted by William Robertson Nicoll, Preface to *The Problem of 'Edwin Drood'* (1912), in Darlow, *Nicoll*, 226. [166] *T.P.'s Weekly*, 8 Feb. 1907.

[167] Ibid., 14 Feb. 1908.

[168] Styled by Arnold Bennett in his *New Age* column, 22 Aug. 1908, thus: 'Franklinish and self-improving young men (and conceivably women)'. He added spikily: 'Such volumes are to be found in many refined and strenuous homes—oftener unopened than opened—but still there!' (*Books and Persons*, 33–4). [169] Derek Hudson, *The Forgotten King and Other Essays* (1960), 237.

[170] Thomas Burke, *Son of London* (1948), 162–3. On Burke (1886–1945), see *Who Was Who, 1941–1950*, 164.

The box contained, together with a few clothes, about a hundred books, mainly of the Everyman and Home University Library kind: Grote's *History of Greece*, Descartes's *Discourse on Method*, Bagehot's *Literary Studies*, Milton's *Paradise Lost*, and the like. It was when reading Gilbert Murray's rendering of Euripides' *Medea*, by the side of the cricket field, that Cardus was noticed by the headmaster, C. A. Alington, who invited him to be his secretary after the start of the Great War.[171]

Such accounts raise for the historian familiar questions about representativeness. While such questions are ultimately intractable, they are susceptible to pessimistic or optimistic impression. Each case was argued at the time. Pessimism came naturally to George Gissing, the Victorians' antidote to Samuel Smiles. Whatever critical success came to him for his 'realist' novels about the miseries of working- and middle-class life and the literary marketplace, he was rarely rewarded by popular acclaim and sales; and his personal life was a disaster area. In his final reflections, *The Private Papers of Henry Ryecroft* (1903), he candidly declared: 'I am no friend of the people... Every instinct of my being is anti-democratic, and I dread to think of what our England may become when Demos rules irresistibly.'[172] That established, he considered the case for public improvement:

I see a great many publishing-houses zealously active in putting forth every kind of book, new and old... To the multitude is offered a long succession of classic authors, in beautiful form, at a minimum cost... Surely one must take for granted that throughout the land, in town and country, private libraries are growing apace; that by the people at large a great deal of time is devoted to reading...

Two things must be remembered. However considerable this literary traffic, regarded by itself, it is relatively of small extent. And, in the second place, literary activity is by no means an invariable proof of that mental attitude which marks the truly civilized man.

Lay aside the 'literary organ,' which appears once a week, and take up the newspaper, which comes forth every day, morning and evening. Here you get the true proportion of things... It may be that a few books are 'noticed'; granting that the 'notice' is in any way noticeable, compare the space it occupies with that devoted to the material interests of life: you have a gauge of the real importance of intellectual endeavour to the people at large. No, the public which reads, in any sense of the word worth considering, is very, very small; the public which would feel no lack if all book-printing ceased to-morrow, is enormous...

I am told that their semi-education will be integrated. We are in a transition stage, between the bad old time when only a few had academic privileges, and that happy future which will see all men liberally instructed. Unfortunately for this argument, education is a thing of which only the few are capable; teach as you will, only a small percentage will profit by your most zealous energy. On an ungenerous soil it is vain to look for rich crops.[173]

---

[171] Neville Cardus, *Autobiography* (1947), 60–1, 67, 80–1.   [172] Gissing, *Ryecroft*, 47.
[173] Ibid. 64–71.

Thus consumed by anti-democratic anxiety, Gissing advanced three propositions: that there were fewer readers than many supposed, that serious readers were even rarer, and that reading did not make better citizens.

The optimistic position, equally naturally, was taken by John Buchan. He climbed in social class and prospered while Gissing fell and struggled. Buchan chose the titles for Nelson's Sixpenny and Sevenpenny Libraries as well as for the 1s. 6d. non-fiction Notable Books and General Literature series, which together sold in millions. Buchan believed that an entirely new reading public had been created. In 1907 he argued:

The philosophy of the reprint is that people are made to read who did not read before, and to buy who before only read. A demand is created by forcing a particular supply on the world . . . the reprint, appearing in myriads and covering bookstalls and shop counters with attractive colours, pushed itself from very numbers. Instead of hiding shyly, like most books, on a shelf, it clamoured to be bought. Accordingly, for almost the first time in the history of literature, we find books selling as freely and widely as, say, soap or bootlaces. There is no loss of dignity in the comparison. In a properly constituted community books are as much a necessity to all as tobacco, and are bought and sold in the same way.[174]

This last was a common enough prediction. The former editor of the *Pall Mall Gazette* and *St James's Gazette* Frederick Greenwood contemplated writing about this in his 'Looker-On' column for *Blackwood's Magazine* in 1898: 'The probability that novels will become ordinary commodities, & be sold at the drapers, & with pounds of tea . . .'.[175] Greenwood was apprehensive that this multiplying literature would contain no intellectual or spiritual nourishment; but Buchan, in an unpublished address of 1910, further argued that

the better the work is the better it sells. We have tried experiments, and occasionally included a book of only trivial interest which has been a great success at a high price. But the comfortably-off people who subscribe to the big circulating libraries are not a good guide to the tastes of the people who are only able to afford a few pence for a book, and want to buy rather than to borrow . . . Books of serious value which have failed with the middle class public have often had an enormous success in these cheap libraries and trivial books which have delighted that better-off public have been neglected . . . The new reading public, which has grown up in the last twenty years and is a thousand times larger than any reading public before in the world's history, is an intelligent public, a serious public, a public which, if I were a great writer, I would far rather write for than for the bored ladies who get a weekly box from the library.[176]

Packaged in a series format the novice reader thus received some guidance towards literature of quality, even though the term 'classic' was sometimes

---

[174] Janet Adam Smith, *John Buchan* (Oxford, 1985), 169.

[175] Robertson Scott, *Pall Mall Gazette*, 300.

[176] Smith, *Buchan*, 170. In his autobiography Buchan claimed that by the eve of the Great War Nelson's was one of the world's largest publishers of cheap books: *Memory Hold-the-Door* (1940), 140.

stretched. Methuen's, one of the new publishers of the 1890s, launched its sixpenny Standard Library series, under the general editorship of Sidney Lee, editor of the *Dictionary of National Biography*, in 1904–5. An ex-schoolteacher and active Liberal, Methuen proclaimed that 'when fifty volumes have been published, you will have a shelf-full of the finest literature of the world for under thirty shillings. Here is indeed the Poor Man's University.' Methuen had taken an even more radical initiative in 1899 with his Library of Fiction, which also sold for 6*d*. and by 1902 comprised thirty-two titles. Some were reprints but most were new and, Methuen boomed, 'in no case has the work of an author of high repute been published in the first instance at that price'. The new fiction included stories by E. W. Hornung, Robert Barr, Cutliffe Hyne, and Sabine Baring-Gould, and was

published simultaneously both at sixpence and at a higher price. Messrs Methuen recognise the inevitable tendencies of an age of cheap literature. The theatre has its stalls and its pit, the railway its first and its third classes; so the novelist may well have a double audience, and while the wealthy will still pay six shillings for their novels, those of limited means may be able to purchase the same book in a decent but less luxurious form.

Methuen repeated his message with a Sixpenny Library series in 1902, which included 'great and popular books of past years', such as Mrs Gaskell's *Cranford* (1853), George Eliot's *The Mill on the Floss* (1860), and Lew Wallace's *Ben Hur* (1880): there was 'a large class of readers who are somewhat weary of the average magazine, who cannot buy a six-shilling novel or subscribe to a library, and who enjoy a healthy story full of incident or pathos or humour'.[177] By 1909, however, Methuen appeared to have developed cold feet about including new fiction reprints in such format, because he joined a conclave of publishers—including Hutchinson, Longman, Macmillan, and Reginald Smith—who sought to panic authors by their assertion that 'Any author allowing a novel to be sold at sevenpence will find the sales of his next book at 6*s*. suffering a considerable decrease.' An inquiry made for the Authors' Society by Bernard Shaw, Maurice Hewlett, and Anthony Hope was unimpressed. So was Arnold Bennett, as Jacob Tonson in his *New Age* column. Told that Nelson's alone were then selling 20,000 such books each week, he reported that W. H. Smith's, 'now the largest buyers of 6*s*. novels in England', and their competitors Wyman's 'do not find that the sevenpenny has interfered with the 6*s*. novel'.[178]

There were also anthologies designed to shape tastes and, quite simply, to make available literature which was otherwise inaccessible or unvalued. One of the most popular was *A Thousand and One Gems of English Poetry* (1867), compiled by Charles Mackay, a former editor of the *Illustrated London News*.[179] Flora Thompson

[177] Quotations from Duffy, *Methuen*, 15–16, 32.

[178] *New Age*, 18 Feb. and 29 Apr. 1909, in Bennett, *Books and Persons*, 107, 130–3.

[179] Mackay (1814–89) was also the author of songs such as 'The Good Time Coming', which would earn him a place in anthologies and dictionaries of quotations; in addition, he was the nominal stepfather (possible natural father or grandfather) of the best-seller Marie Corelli, on whom, see Ch. 22. Sutherland, *Companion*, 397; Sladen, *Long Life*, 347.

recollected young Willie, whose family were village carpenters, being fond of reading, including poetry: 'somehow he had got possession of an old shattered copy of an anthology called *A Thousand and One Gems*', which he read aloud with her, sitting under nut trees at the bottom of the garden, in the 1890s.[180] Quiller-Couch's *Oxford Book of English Verse* (1900) remains now among the best known, his publishers utilizing thin India paper to produce a volume of over 1,000 pages. Reprinted twelve times before 1918, some half a million copies were sold by the time of Quiller-Couch's death in 1944. Discriminating critics quarrelled with his selection from the start;[181] but Q—as Quiller-Couch was already known—was a name that carried popular appeal, because of his own stories written in Robert Louis Stevenson style. When the *Westminster Gazette* polled public libraries in 1896 about what boys read, Q had run a close second to G. A. Henty, quite an achievement when it is reckoned that 'Henty the Great' (J. M. Barrie's designation) had authored scores of books compared with Q's handful at that date.[182] Nor was it the case that Q's *Dead Man's Rock* (1887) or *The Splendid Spur* (1889) were popular with boys only: his Cornish romances, *Troy Town* (1888), *The Ship of Stars* (1899), and the rest, were adult favourites too. This meant that the affixing of Q's name to the Oxford anthology practically guaranteed broad sales. He was not the sole occupant of the field. In his Preface Q acknowledged a debt to other recent anthologists, H. C. Beeching, A. H. Bullen, Churton Collins, W. E. Henley, Frederick Locker-Lampson, Archbishop Trench, W. B. Yeats, and more. Above all, there was F. T. Palgrave's *Golden Treasury of Best Songs and Lyrical Poems in the English Language*. This was originally compiled after a Cornish holiday and conversations with Tennyson, the painters Holman Hunt and Val Prinsep, and the poet–sculptor Thomas Woolner. Again, eyebrows were raised about Palgrave's rations and omissions, Wordsworth clocking up forty-one pieces to Shakespeare's thirty-two and Shelley's twenty-two, and William Blake excluded altogether.[183] But the *Golden Treasury* was reprinted many times since first publication in 1861, to which was added a second series in 1897, the year of the anthologist's death. In its obituary notice *The Times* observed that Palgrave, 'while not himself a great poet, had done more than anyone else of his time, with the exception of Mr Matthew Arnold, to guide the public taste to what is best in poetic literature'.[184]

---

[180] Flora Thompson, *Lark Rise to Candleford* (Oxford, 1947), 466.

[181] Thomas Hardy, for example, 'was much disappointed: the selected names are a good & fairly exhaustive list, but the specimens chosen show a narrow judgment & a bias in favour of particular views of life which make the book second-rate of its class' (Hardy to Florence Henniker, 24 Dec. 1900, in Purdy and Millgate (eds.), *Hardy Letters*, ii. 277). In an interview with Henry Nevinson in 1906 Hardy explained: 'He thought badly of the *Oxford Book of Verse* for its love of tags and morals in the mid-Victorian manner'. (Henry W. Nevinson, *More Changes, More Chances* (1925), 179–80). But in his preface to the new edition, written as the clouds of war were gathering again and dated Whitsun 1939, Q defended this dominant note of 'valiancy—of the old Roman "virtue" mated with cheerfulness . . . It is indigenous, proper to our native spirit, and it will endure'. [182] Letter to Q, 19 Jan. 1896, in Meynell (ed.), *Barrie Letters*, 9.

[183] See F. T. Palgrave's 'Personal Recollections', in Hallam Tennyson, *Alfred Lord Tennyson* (1899), 842–8; Sir Edward Cook, *More Literary Recreations* (1919), 14–17.

[184] *The Times*, 26 Oct. 1897. Formerly Assistant Secretary of the Education Office, Palgrave had been Professor of Poetry at Oxford (1885–95). The success of the *Golden Treasury* formula encouraged the

Henry and Grace Hadow attempted to fulfil the same office with their *Oxford Treasury of English Literature*, in three volumes, 1906–8. There is evidence of these reaching working-class homes. Richard Garnett's *International Library of Famous Literature*, promoted by the *Standard* newspaper, appeared in 1899 in twenty volumes. This was 'regarded with a reverence amounting to awe' by D. H. Lawrence, according to Jessie Chambers, a view confirmed by the editor of his letters, who notices the many quotations and allusions that derived from it.[185] Of course, public admiration and critical estimation frequently parted company. The 'strange and unique position in literature' of the verse and moral essays of Martin Tupper, whose *Proverbial Philosophy* (1838–76, in four series) sold over 100,000 copies in Britain and nearly half a million in America by the time of his death in 1889, caused *The Times* to remark: 'This is a tribute to the British heart rather than to its intellect.'[186] The appetite for knowledge was, however, real and persistent. The *Encyclopaedia Britannica* won the blue ribbon of the breed. The ninth edition, published by Adam Black and edited by Spencer Baynes and William Robertson Smith, appeared in twenty-four volumes between 1875 and 1888. Bernard Shaw was one who ploughed his way through most of it, albeit skirting around the more intractable science, during his self-education in the Reading Room of the British Museum in the 1880s.[187] Almost as remorseless—it is impossible to conceive an equally or more remorseless creature than Shaw—was Bruce Cummings, better known subsequently as W. N. P. Barbellion, who treated the world to his *Journal of a Disappointed Man* (1919). Cummings did not avoid the science, which was a twin passion with literature in his life; but his method of gorging on the *Encyclopaedia Britannica* was less systematic than Shaw's. He would simply think of a word, any word—'pins, nutmegs, Wallaby'—look it up, and read the 'learned articles till my eyes ached and my head swam. The sight of those huge tomes made me tremble with a lover's impatience . . . I winced at nothing. I rejected nothing.'[188] The *Encyclopaedia Britannica* was, therefore, revered, and not solely as a repository of wisdom: Robin Baily, born in 1885, as a boy 'found these volumes exactly what I needed to build tunnels for my toy train'.[189] The ninth edition sold nearly half a million copies—'including American and pirated

publisher Macmillan to follow it up with a *Children's Treasury* and *Treasury of English Sacred Poetry* (Palgrave was a hymnodist as well as poet). The *Golden Treasury* was a favourite vade mecum for soldiers in the Great War. Fearing court martial after protesting about the continuance of the war in 1917, Siegfried Sassoon applied his mind to the *Golden Treasury*: 'I was learning by heart as many poems as possible, my idea being that they would be a help to me in prison, where, I imagined, no books would be allowed' (Siegfried Sassoon, *Memoirs of an Infantry Officer* (1965), 228).

[185] James T. Boulton (ed.), *The Letters of D. H. Lawrence*, i: Sept. 1901-May 1913 (Cambridge, 1979), 4–6; John Worthen, *D. H. Lawrence: The Early Years, 1885–1912* (Cambridge, 1991), 111.

[186] *The Times*, 30 Nov. 1889; see also Derek Hudson, *Martin Tupper: His Rise and Fall* (1949).

[187] Michael Holroyd, *Bernard Shaw* (1988–91), i. 84.

[188] W. N. P. Barbellion, *Enjoying Life and Other Literary Remains* (1919), 12–13 (journal, July 1914).

[189] R. E. H. Baily (ed.), *Ruth Bourne Diaries: A Victorian Memoir* (Colchester, 1973), 57. The *Encyclopaedia Britannica* came into his mother's gentry family as a present from the grandfather in 1884, in seventeen volumes, then having been published up to the letter O.

editions'—and was twice reprinted in 1894 and 1896. In 1898 *The Times* began a promotion of yet another reissue. This was sold at about half the original price, with a revolving bookcase in which to store it. The stereotype plates of the work had been bought up by an American speculator, Horace E. Hooper, partner in a publishing firm, Hooper & Jackson; and it was he who persuaded *The Times's* manager, Moberly Bell, to join forces. The *Britannica* was delivered to subscribers on payment to *The Times* of 1 guinea, with a promise to pay a further 14 guineas in monthly instalments. *The Times* boomed the promotion and took the initial guinea and responsibility for the delivery, while Hooper accepted the risk of collecting the outstanding sum. The advertising campaign hoodwinked the unwary into thinking that what was on offer was a new edition of the *Britannica*, not one with articles now ten years and more out of date; but Moberly Bell defended their action. Advertisements clearly stated that it was the ninth edition that was being sold and, he maintained, complainants were generally released from their contract, though these were few: eleven out of 4,300 in the second month of the sale.[190] Still, their hard sell upset many traditional readers of *The Times*, 'scaring invalids in their beds, and [becoming] the source of alarm to many innocent people', wrote Max Pemberton.[191] Undeterred, *The Times* went on to commission an eleven-volume supplement, which, incorporated with the previous twenty-four volumes, comprised the tenth edition in 1902–3; and Hooper was given virtual charge of the advertising department of *The Times* in 1904, on a contract which gave him a half-share in profits (or loss) over the previous year's revenue.[192]

The refined expressed contempt. The assistant editor of *The Spectator*, Charles L. Graves, collaborated with the assistant editor of *Punch*, E. V. Lucas, in a 'series of skits, *Wisdom While You Wait, Signs of the Times, Hustled History*, and so on, directed mostly against the Americanisation of publishing methods of the proprietors of the *Encyclopaedia Britannica* and other works demanding a large public'.[193] Lucas's disdain was gratuitous: among Hooper's other promotions was *Fifty Years of Punch*. Hooper also pushed a dictionary and atlas; and it was he who had masterminded the sale of the twenty-volume *International Library of Famous Literature*. Rivals in the advertising trade expressed unbounded admiration. John Morgan Richards, a fellow American, domiciled in England since 1867 and now owner of *The Academy*, reckoned that £500,000 was spent on advertising these works, that public libraries and private subscribers had expended over £2.5 million on buying them, and that the profits were enormous. 'In all my advertising experience', he wrote in 1905,

I have never seen better use made of position, space and type than that firm [Hooper & Jackson] achieved for themselves in the announcement of their books . . . The terms upon which the purchase was made—that of monthly or deferred payments—was a startling

[190] Bell, *Moberly Bell*, 243–4.   [191] Max Pemberton, *Lord Northcliffe: A Memoir* (n.d.), 131.
[192] Bell, *Moberly Bell*, 248.   [193] Eric Parker, *Memory Looks Forward* (n.d), 151.

proposition to the book-buyer; and the tempting bait thus held out accomplished the object in view, and secured subscriptions; and I have been assured that the defaulters in connection with the different payments were modest in the extreme.

Richards acknowledged that the *Encyclopaedia Britannica* was the most difficult challenge, because it involved so many volumes and the subscriber might take on an ultimate responsibility for between £28 and £48, according to the different bindings; consequently, it was 'the greatest triumph'.[194] Several on the receiving end were not so celebratory. The lawyer and literary man J. H. Balfour Browne in his memoirs in 1917 still harboured some bitterness about it. 'I was the dupe of one of the greatest literary tricks of the age,' he wrote; that is, having bought *The Times*'s version of the ninth edition he had felt compelled to buy the supplement in order 'to bring the colossal information up to date'.[195] Worse, the production line did not halt there. One of the editors of the supplement, Hugh Chisholm, formerly of the *St James's Gazette*, became editor of an entirely revised eleventh edition in twenty-nine volumes, which Cambridge University Press published in 1910–11.[196]

The publisher William Heinemann, talking to the critic William Archer in December 1901, reckoned that the whole strategy of the subscription edition, so successful in America, was discredited in England by the *Britannica* scam, because it entailed 'a set of books that nobody really wanted . . . [and] when people had got the books, they found they were out of date'.[197] In America the subscription edition—standard sets in supposedly superior bindings or with illustrations that were not the same as editions sold in ordinary bookshops—were hawked by travelling salesmen; and this was not the method generally adopted in Britain, which was promotion through newspapers and magazines. The brickbats fired at *The Times* were in part caused by shock that a paper of its reputation should stoop to these tactics, not that it was the sole practitioner. In spite of the aggressive marketing, the *Britannica* did not occupy the field. Reaching more readers were the Harmsworth and the Chambers encyclopedias, which were also purchasable in instalments. Harmsworth started the 'part works' department of his press in 1897, and this flourished in the Edwardian period. A considerable cause was the output of Arthur Mee, who personified the working-class quest for knowledge. The second of ten children born to a Nottinghamshire railway fireman and his wife, who were devout Baptists, Mee worked for Newnes's *Tit-Bits* before joining Harmsworth's *Daily Mail*; and it was there that he came to Harmsworth's notice, having constructed a 'system of 250,000 cross-indexed press-cuttings'. Harmsworth commissioned Mee to produce the *Self-Educator* between 1905 and

---

[194] John Morgan Richards, *With John Bull and Jonathan* (1905), 235–6.
[195] J. H. Balfour Browne, *Recollections Literary and Political* (1917), 152.
[196] See the prefatory note to the 11th edition of the *Encyclopaedia Britannica*, vol. i, pp. viii–ix; and *DNB 1922–1930*, 183–4, for Chisholm (1866–1924). The assistant editor of the 11th edition, Ronald McNeill, was also a former editor of the *St James's Gazette* (1900–4); he subsequently became an MP and a leading advocate of Ulster's resistance to Irish Home Rule.   [197] William Archer, *Real Conversations* (1904), 194.

1907, and the *Children's Encyclopaedia* in fortnightly parts from 1908. 'Few men in England have such power in their hands for good as you,' Harmsworth (now Lord Northcliffe) wrote to Mee in 1910; and this 'book of my heart', as Mee called it, sold 52 million volumes across the world by 1946.[198] The new edition of *Chambers's Encyclopaedia* (1888–92) should also be remembered. Henry Morley contributed the article 'The History and Genius of English Literature'.[199] The 1906 illustrated edition was strongly pushed by *T.P.'s Weekly*; but G. K. Chesterton, who was born in 1874, did not need the incentive of illustrations. An omnivorous reader, Chesterton had already 'read whole volumes of *Chambers' Encyclopaedia* . . . It was the sort of pleasure that a cow must have in grazing all day long.'[200]

---

[198] Reginald Pound and Geoffrey Harmsworth, *Northcliffe* (1959), 294–5, 398; *DNB 1941–1950*, 584–5, for Mee (1875–1943).   [199] Solly, *Morley*, 369.

[200] Maisie Ward, *Return to Chesterton* (1952), 15. An assistant editor of *Chambers's Encyclopaedia* was Thomas Davidson (1856–1923), who later served as Presbyterian chaplain at Vienna, Brussels, and Karlsbad until the outbreak of the Great War; see *Who Was Who, 1916–1928*, 267. Another was the Romany scholar Francis Hindes Groome (1851–1902), on whom, see the appreciation in Theodore Watts-Dunton, *Old Familiar Faces* (1916), 277–303. See also the advertisements for *Chambers's Encyclopaedia* in *T.P.'s Weekly*, 1, 8, 29 Nov. 1907.

3

Literary Advice and Advisers

I

As the nineteenth century progressed, there was no shortage of advice to the callow reader. That which attracted most attention was 'The Choice of Books', first delivered as a lecture to the Working Men's College in Great Ormond Street, London, in 1885 by Sir John Lubbock, the banker MP for London University and later Lord Avebury.[1] Lubbock's name survives today principally as the originator of the Bank Holiday (1871) and promoter of legislation to preserve ancient monuments (1882). An experimental biologist, he also played his violin to bees in order to demonstrate their deafness. Enormous interest was generated by his lecture, which listed 100 items and soon became known as the 'best 100 books'; and it was sustained by Lubbock's article on books in the *Contemporary Review*, February 1886. Naturally, Oscar Wilde followed with a different classification: books to read, books to reread, and books not to read at all. The last he recommended to the university extension movement as an urgent mission: 'Whoever will select out of the chaos of our modern curricula "The Worst Hundred Books" . . . will confer on the rising generation a real and lasting benefit.'[2] Wilde's advice notwithstanding, the hundred best were included in Lubbock's *Pleasures of Life* (first series 1887; second series 1889) and reissued (slightly revised) as a pamphlet by the *Pall Mall Gazette* in 1891, and again by Harmsworth in 1898. By 1914, *The Pleasures of Life, Part I*, was in its 262nd thousand and *Part II* in its 232nd thousand, and there were over thirty foreign editions.[3] Lubbock's imprimatur also gave a fillip to the sales of the books on his list. All the titles were

---

[1] Thackeray had been one client of the bank, Lubbock, Forster & Co. On Lubbock (1834–1914), see *DNB* and Horace G. Hutchinson, *Life of Sir John Lubbock* (1914).

[2] Letter in *Pall Mall Gazette*, 8 Feb. 1886, repr. in Rupert Hart-Davis (ed.), *Selected Letters of Oscar Wilde* (Oxford, 1979), 65–6. Henry James declined the *Pall Mall Gazette*'s invitation to itemize his best hundred, declaring that 'the reading of the newspapers is *the* pernicious habit and the father of all idleness and laxity' (quoted in J. Saxon Mills, *Sir Edward Cook K.B.E.* (1921), 75, where 'laxity' is given as 'levity'). James's correspondence with Cook is republished in Leon Edel (ed.), *Henry James Letters*, iii: *1883–1895* (1984), 108–9. Cook, the editor of the *Pall Mall Gazette*, published as the *Best Hundred Books Extra* the letters and contributions from well-known figures on this question, including Arnold and Ruskin.

[3] The two parts, published by Macmillan, were also available in one volume in various formats, priced from 6d. to 3s. See also Hutchinson, *Lubbock*, i. 245–8, for appreciative letters from working men; ii. 55–7, for Frederic Harrison's alternatives, ii. 91–5, for Lubbock's further reflections; Grant Duff, *Diary, 1896*

reprinted in a series by Routledge's, one per fortnight, starting in 1892 and finishing in 1896.[4]

Critics heaped comminations on Lubbock's head. ' "The Best Hundred Books" notion is, of course, an absurdity,' wrote George Saintsbury; 'if it ever had been accepted (as it never was) by "Victorians" who "counted" in the slightest degree, Victorianism would deserve the worst that has been, or could be said of it . . . In one sense there may be ten best books, in another ten thousand; but attempting to number them deserves worse curses than those from which King David had to choose.'[5] It is true that the Lubbock Hundred had its ludicrous aspect. It included the whole of Homer, Hesiod, Virgil, Horace, Livy, Epictetus, Herodotus, and Thucydides, and particular works of Xenophon, Aristotle, Æschylus, Sophocles, Euripides, Aristophanes, Plato, Plutarch, Tacitus, Demosthenes, Cicero, Marcus Aurelius, and so on. Even conversant classicists quailed—or else upbraided him for his omissions: where was Ovid, Juvenal . . . ? But when Lubbock left the Mediterranean and headed east, taking in a large slice of the Koran, the Persian epic *Shahnamah*, the Hindu *Sakuntala, Ramayana* and *Mahabharata*, before arriving at Confucius, even the most erudite felt destined to plough this examination.[6] And all this preceded Lubbock's encounter with Europe. But there is no need to elaborate: it was a stiff test by any measure. Lubbock was unrepentant

to 1901, i. 25 (13 June 1898), for Lubbock having told him that 'his little book on *The Pleasures of Life* has just been translated into Mahratti—a curious sign of the times'. The essence of Lubbock's advice was distilled in his other popular manual *The Use of Life* (1894), which sold 50,000 copies by 1900 and was in its 186th thousand by 1913. Books, he asserted, 'must read for improvement rather than for amusement. Light and entertaining books are valuable, just as sugar is an important article of food, especially for children, but we cannot live upon it. Some novels are excellent, but too much devotion to them greatly diminishes the pleasure which may be derived from reading. Moreover, there are books which are no books, and to read which is mere waste of time; while there are others so bad, that we cannot read them without pollution; if they were men we should kick them into the street. There are cases in which it is well to be warned against the temptations and dangers of life, but anything which familiarises us with evil, is itself an evil. So also there are other books, happily many others, which no one can read without being the better for them. By useful literature we do not mean that only which will help a man in his business or profession. That is useful, no doubt, but by no means the highest use of books. The best books elevate us into a region of disinterested thought where personal objects fade into insignificance, and the trouble and the anxieties of the world are almost forgotten'. (Lord Avebury [Sir John Lubbock], *The Use of Life* (1900), 91).

[4] Carried away by this success, the Routledge sons paid themselves annual salaries of £10,000, and drove the firm to bankruptcy: James J. Barnes and Patience P. Barnes, 'George Routledge and Sons' in Anderson and Rose (eds.), *British Literary Publishing Houses*, 265.   [5] George Saintsbury, *Scrap Book* (1922), 213.

[6] Translations were available, though not thereby always accessible until the Routledge's Hundred Best Books series was launched. Famously, Kalidasa's *Sakuntala* had appeared in Sir William Jones's translation, *The Lost Ring* (1789), and was reissued in Sir Monies Monier-Williams's new edition in the late 19th century; the *Mahabharata* was translated into English by Protap Chandra Roy in 1883, and the *Ramayana* appeared in five volumes, translated by R. T. H Griffith, 1870–5. An English version of part of Firdausi's *Shahnamah* was edited by James Atkinson in 1832, and was reissued in a new edition in 1892. The Elizabethan Stage Society put on an adaptation of *Sakuntala* in the Conservatory of the Botanical Gardens in Regent's Park in 1899, translated by Laurence Binyon and produced by William Poel, with lyrics by Arthur Symons and music by Arnold Dolmetsch. This involved Indian actors, but also a stuffed tiger and antelope, which the audience regarded as risible. It nonetheless impressed W. B Yeats. See Karl Beckson, *Arthur Symons* (Oxford, 1987), 183; John Kelly and Ronald Schuchard (eds.), *The Collected Letters of W. B. Yeats*, iii (Oxford, 1994), 179.

and, following a minor revision of his list, in 1890 reiterated his overall purpose: 'I drew up the list, not as that of the hundred best books, but, which is very different, of those which have been most frequently recommended as best worth reading.' As an instance, he cited Confucius' *Sheking* and *Analects*: 'I must humbly confess that I do not greatly admire either; but I recommended them because they are held in the most profound veneration by the Chinese race, containing 400,000,000 of our fellow men.' Moreover, he added sweetly, 'both works are quite short'.[7]

Lubbock's list was organized by category: religion, philosophy, ethics, logic, the epic, history, political economy, travel, natural history, essays, poetry, drama, biography, and so forth. He had been chary about admitting science, not because he doubted its importance—'to many minds it is the most fruitful and interesting subject of all'—but because 'science is so rapidly progressive'. Nonetheless, Bacon's *Novum Organum* and Darwin's *Origin of Species* and *Naturalist's Voyage* could not be ignored. Firmly upheld was the omission of works by living authors, 'though from many of them I have myself derived the keenest enjoyment.'[8] The Laureate's demise in 1892 would eventually allow Lubbock to tag Tennyson's 'Idylls and Smaller Poems' onto a revised list of 'best' poets which ran through Chaucer, Shakespeare, Milton, Dante, Spencer, Scott, Wordsworth ('Mr Arnold's selection'), Pope, Burns, Byron, and Gray. Still, the list was, his critics politely noted, rather light on light literature. Lubbock was not disconcerted. He could always cite lists even more forbidding, notably that produced two years earlier by Lord Acton, who later was made Regius Professor of Modern History at Cambridge. Acton had no time for Shakespeare, Milton, Scott, Thackeray, Dickens, Tennyson. These ended up in a dustbin of classic rejects, together with Homer, Seneca, Cicero, Plutarch, Tacitus, Livy, Xenophon, Thucydides, Bacon, Descartes, Molière, Thomas à Kempis, and all Eastern literature. 'Some of the omissions in Lord Acton's list must surely have been accidental,' Lubbock speculated generously; yet he did not allow Acton to escape unscathed. 'Life is short; we have none of us too much leisure,' Lubbock observed magisterially, as only great men do when delivering a platitude; 'and, except for those who are making a special study of such subjects, I can hardly imagine it could be worth while to read such books as, for instance, Mignet's *Négotiations*, or Carte's *Histoire de Mouvements Religieux dans le Canton de Vaud*, or Rousseau's *Considérations sur la Pologne*.'[9] What Lubbock termed 'Literature and Fiction' had been almost entirely absent from Acton's list.

A similar abstemiousness about imaginative literature characterized the Home Ruler R. Barry O'Brien's essay 'The Best Hundred Irish Books', which he published first in the *Freeman's Journal* and then as a pamphlet in 1886 under the

---

[7] Preface to the Twentieth Edition, Aug. 1890, Avebury, *The Pleasures of Life, Part I* (1913), pp. xiv–xv.
[8] Avebury, *Pleasures of Life, Part I*, 76.
[9] Preface to the Forty-First English Edition, Avebury, *Pleasures of Life, Part I*, pp. v–vii.

pseudonym Historicus. His aim was to raise national consciousness by a regimen of reading about Ireland's history; accordingly, he valued 'the faculty of research' and 'an inherent love of justice' above 'style' and the 'picturesque'. The result was as enticing as a banquet of dry biscuits, the grim ultimate in liberal rationalism. In any event, the exercise was rendered mostly useless so far as popular enlightenment was concerned, because fewer than ten of the recommendations were not priced out of reach or otherwise rare, noted a despairing Sir Gavan Duffy, the erstwhile Young Irelander who had devised the Library of Ireland series of Irish biography, poetry and criticism, available for a shilling apiece. O'Brien's list also, perversely, failed the test of Irishness when applied by a later band of Gaelic purists, because he included a quantity of non-Irish authors.[10]

Lubbock, meanwhile, had rearranged his own menu. He discarded Jane Austen from a revised list in favour of Schiller's *William Tell* 'because English novelists were somewhat over-represented'[11]—yet there remained Swift's *Gulliver's Travels*, Defoe's *Robinson Crusoe*, Goldsmith's *Vicar of Wakefield*, and, from the nineteenth century, Thackeray's *Vanity Fair* and *Pendennis*, Lytton's *Last Days of Pompeii*, George Eliot's *Adam Bede*, and Kingsley's *Westward Ho!* Dickens was admitted with *Pickwick* and *David Copperfield*, and the entire novels of Scott were smuggled in as one item. From many perspectives, such lists, whether by Lubbock, Acton, or whomever, all seemed a chronic exercise in futility, Operation Omniscience for some imagined world citizen—except that there is evidence of their being treated seriously. Police Sergeant Hewitt of Finsbury Park and Fulham, who prided himself on being a cut above the artisan class, regularly pondered Lubbock's list and kept it by him into the Edwardian period, although his actual reading (certainly, the reading he enjoyed) was stories by Rider Haggard, Marie Corelli, Stanley Weyman, Anthony Hope, W. J. Locke, and the rising stars Jeffrey Farnol and Edgar Wallace. Hewitt's son noted wryly about the Lubbock century, that it 'included nearly all the books one didn't want to read, or gave up if one tried . . . For the most part they were the books which, it seemed, you should expect to find in every intelligent man's private library; with, in most such libraries, their leaves uncut'.[12]

The Lubbock Hundred appeared better suited for veneration than as a practical course of reading; but the fundamental idea was too popular to pass over, and it found many supporters. It was a variant on standard Victorian parlour games— what books to take (the Bible and Shakespeare usually given) when marooned on a desert island, when travelling by train, when exploring darkest Africa, when climbing the Alps, when waging war, or when incarcerated in gaol. Practical circumstances affected choice in these instances: as the editor of the *Pall Mall Gazette* put it, 'It is easy to say that one prefers Tennyson to Browning or *vice*

---

[10] Ian Sheehy, 'Irish Journalists and Litterateurs in Late Victorian London c.1870–1910,' D.Phil. thesis (Oxford, 2003), 211–14, 249–50.

[11] Preface to the Twentieth Edition, Avebury, *Pleasures of Life, Part I*, p. xvi.

[12] C. H. Rolph [C. R. Hewitt], *London Particulars* (Oxford, 1982), 83–4.

versa; it is more difficult to be quite sure, in packing a small valise, that either volume will prove itself preferable to an extra pair of socks or shoes.'[13] The idea of a Best Hundred allowed for greater spaciousness and, with it, more serious-ness. Its most resolute advocates were to be found in the Positivist community, presided over by Frederic Harrison, whose own choice of books was published in the same year as Lubbock's Hundred. Comte's calendars of great men and great works had been an obvious inspiration for Lubbock's initiative; indeed, one version of Lubbock's list included Comte's *Catechism*. Harrison, who taught at the Working Men's College, was keen to exercise judicial authority at 'the great assize of letters', as a force for the public good and the Religion of Humanity.[14] When staying with Lady Russell at Pembroke Lodge in 1888, Harrison lectured on the great books of the world at a little school in nearby Petersham in Surrey. Again, there was some querulousness on the part of those who had some qua-lification to assess its worth. Sir Mountstuart Grant Duff wrote, 'Most of the judgments which he enunciated were such as I should have expected as being in accordance with what I know of his opinions, and of his vast literary knowledge, but he put *Quentin Durward* strangely high, and considered that it and *Faust*— what a conjunction!—were the two last great books of the world of the kind about which he is speaking.'[15] Still, in one respect the greater usefulness of Harrison's over Lubbock's choice of books was evident from his giving infor-mation about editions and translations. This was helpful for public as well as personal library constitution. Harrison himself was involved in the book-buying policy of the select London Library. Following Lubbock's and Harrison's lead, a wave of advice manuals now washed over the public. Among the new publica-tions in July 1891, for instance, were *A Guide Book to Books* edited by E. B. Sargant and Bernhard Whishaw, and Arthur Acland MP's *A Guide to the Choice of Books*. The first, priced 5s. for 340 pages, collated the recommendations of over 150 specialists, advising both student and general reader about essential reading for an understanding of particular subjects; the second, priced 3s. 6d. for 128 pages, aimed to list the 'standard works in every department of literature which shall prove useful to those who are forming parish libraries, etc.'.[16]

II

Such earnestness was sure to provoke a reaction. 'The Hundred Best Soporifics' was an alternative title proposed by one iconoclastic correspondent to the *Pall Mall Gazette*.[17] The Conservative leader and author of a treatise on philo-sophical doubt, Arthur Balfour, also naturally dissented from the formulaic. In his

---

[13] Sir Edward Cooke, *More Literary Recreations* (1919), 3.

[14] Martha S. Vogeler, *Frederic Harrison: The Vocations of a Positivist* (Oxford, 1984), ch. 8.

[15] Sir Mountstuart Grant Duff, *Notes from a Diary, 1886–1888* (1900), ii. 172 (23 Oct. 1888).

[16] *Review of Reviews* (July 1891), 98.

[17] C. L. Cline (ed.), *The Letters of George Meredith* (Oxford, 1970), iii. 1503 n., which also gives Meredith's letter to the *Pall Mall Gazette* (June 1904), commenting on the best hundred books.

rectorial address at St Andrews University he encouraged students simply to read what they most enjoyed. Where Harrison had issued doleful warnings against 'gorging and enfeebling' the mind by stuffing it with ill-chosen literature, Balfour was all in favour of idle curiosity, adding with a barely disguised swipe at Harrison, 'True dullness is seldom acquired. It is a natural grace, the manifestations of which, however modified by education, remain in substance the same.'[18] Probably ever since reading existed, certainly since the Renaissance and right through to our own day, the world has been full of guides convinced that readers are impressionable creatures and that without their advice readers will go to the dogs and civil society be damned. This torrent of homily and instruction has been subject to seasonal swells over the years, as the flow has been directed to a particular category of reader: to all children, sometimes specifically boys or specifically girls; to adolescents, spinsters, and bachelors; to working-class wives, middle-class matrons, aristocratic ladies, and princesses; to horny-handed labourers, skilled artisans, captains of industry, independent gentlemen, courtiers, statesmen, and proconsuls; in fact, everyone from Aunt Sally to Uncle Tom Cobbleigh. And not just ordained ministers of God have assumed the missionary position. The appointed advisers of the nation's reading have included schoolteachers, medical authorities, civil servants, librarians, and the like, also authors themselves, publishers, editors, journalists; indeed anyone who has been blessed with a wagging finger on one hand and with a pen in the other. The evaluation of their strictures and of how readers fared has much occupied the erudite in recent years.[19] Yet less consideration has been given to how far such advice was, at the time, judged so much huff and puff, the flapping and flatulence of so many busybodies, bores, and humbugs. Walter Raleigh, Professor of English Literature at Oxford and, therefore, ostensibly in the intellectual counselling business himself, in 1905 conceived of founding a Shock Society 'to give a healthier, firmer tone to morals'. 'Anyone is eligible who is shocked at things,' he gravely explained, adding, 'To disapprove *will not do*, you must be shocked.' There was a further catch: 'When the original list is complete, only those who are shocked at something which no existing member is shocked at will be eligible.'[20]

Historians should not so emphasize the serious in Victorian England as to ignore the comic. It is true that a good deal of humour, particularly the horseplay,

[18] Blanche E. C. Dugdale, *Arthur James Balfour* (1936), i. 189–90; and Lucy Masterman (ed.), *Mary Gladstone (Mrs. Drew): Her Diaries and Letters* (1930), 296 (diary, 23 Oct. 1883), for how Balfour 'sharply and rather pettishly criticised' Lord Acton's hundred best. John Morley, a friend of Harrison and fellow Positivist, evidently disliked the whole notion of 'the best books'; he too was concerned about the prigs who might now stalk the land after dipping into 'a hundred parcels of heterogeneous scraps'. Nonetheless, he loyally commended Harrison's *Choice of Books*: 'You will find there as much wise thought, eloquently and brilliantly put, as in any volume of its size and on its subject, whether it be in the list of a hundred or not.' See Morley, 'Aphorisms' (1887) and 'On the Study of Literature' (1887), in Morley, *Studies in Literature*, 56, 211–2.

[19] The most thorough is Kate Flint, *The Woman Reader, 1837–1914* (Oxford, 1995).

[20] Raleigh to Mrs Dowdall, 7 Aug. 1905, in Lady Raleigh (ed.), *The Letters of Sir Walter Raleigh (1879–1922)* (1926), ii. 280.

ragging, and practical jokes, fashionable among the public-school and country-house set, was not very funny. Hubert Henry Davies nicely acknowledged this in his comedy drama *A Single Man* (1910), when the distinguished author Robin Worthington is spotted playing the fool with a group of well-bred hearties:

LOUISE. A man of *his* ability ought not to have been so much amused when Miss Sims stuck her thumb in the strawberry jam.

LADY COTTRELL. *I* was exceedingly amused. It was a thoroughly characteristic example of British wit and humour.[21]

It is also true that there was a serious side to Victorian comedy. 'One excellent test of the civilization of a country', argued George Meredith with some solemnity, 'I take to be the flourishing of the Comic idea and Comedy; and the test of true Comedy is that it shall awaken thoughtful laughter.'[22] Famously, in the late Victorian and Edwardian theatre and in countless street-corner orations and letters to the press, Bernard Shaw sought to make thinking fun. Wilde had also once prospered by combining philosophy and wit. Perhaps, the philosophy was pseudo because, as Wilde told Conan Doyle, 'I throw probability out of the window for the sake of a phrase, and the chance of an epigram makes me desert truth.'[23] Wilde brazenly recycled jokes from essay to play and from play to play; and he generally stuck to the clichéd formula of a guilty secret before he brilliantly parodied the whole genre in *The Importance of Being Earnest* (1895). Even his inferior work *A Woman of No Importance* (1893) and *An Ideal Husband* (1895) contained that shimmering dialogue, replete with topical twists, which brought the fashionable dinner party to the stage: smart hits about contemporary culture and taste, education and politics, the dual standard of morality in marriage for the two sexes, and the aristocratic penchant for colonial wealth, company promotion, and philanthropy. Of course, as Henry James put it tartly (and with not a little envy), Wilde's plays contained 'absolutely no characterization and all the people talk equally strained Oscar'; but there was

so much drollery—that is, 'cheeky' paradoxical wit of dialogue, and the pit and the gallery are so pleased at finding themselves clever enough to 'catch on' to four or five of the ingenious—too ingenious—*mots* in the dozen, that it makes them feel quite '*décadent*' and '*raffiné*' and they enjoy the sensation as a change from the stodgy. Moreover they think they are hearing the talk of the *grand monde* (poor old *grand monde*), and altogether feel privileged and modern.[24]

---

[21] Hubert Henry Davies, *Plays* (1921), ii. 97.

[22] George Meredith, 'On the Idea of Comedy and of the Uses of the Comic Spirit' (1877), 46. The essay, originally delivered as a lecture at the London Institution, 1 February 1877, was reprinted in the Surrey Edition of the Collected Works, 1912, together with *The Tragic Comedians* and *The House on the Beach*.

[23] Wilde to Conan Doyle (Apr. 1891), in Hart-Davis (ed.), *Wilde's Letters*, 95. Robert Hichens in *The Green Carnation* (1949), 55, has his Lord Alfred Douglas character, Lord Reggie Hastings, deliver the nice line 'Poor Oscar! He is terribly truthful. He reminds me so much of George Washington.'

[24] To Mrs Hugh Bell, 23 Feb. 1892, in Edel (ed.), *James Letters*, iii. 372–3. James was reporting on *Lady Windermere's Fan*.

Wilde, as also Shaw, followed in W. S. Gilbert's wake. Their comic spirit was Gilbert with a difference, reason without rhyme. 'Gilbert is simply a paradoxically humorous cynic,' wrote Shaw. 'He accepts the conventional ideals implicitly, but observes that people do not really live up to them. This he regards as a failure on their part at which he mocks bitterly.' Neither Shaw nor Wilde sustained conventional ideals. Shaw had read Marx's *Das Kapital* (in French translation) and he was converted to socialism; rather, to be more consistent with Shaw's own description, he was subverted. *Das Kapital* was 'the only book that ever turned me upside down', he said, to the glee of Max Beerbohm, who reckoned that Shaw remained upside down for the rest of his life. 'My method is to take the utmost trouble to find the right thing to say, and then say it with the utmost levity,' declared Shaw. 'And all the time the real joke is that I am in earnest.'[25] Wilde did not burden himself with such obviously heavy ideological baggage; but there was an aesthetic socialism beating beneath his surface wit, and he too liked to make his audiences a little uncomfortable in their amusement. *Lady Windermere's Fan* (1892), which initiated his dramatic career, Wilde subtitled 'A Play about a Good Woman', a teasing allusion to Hardy's *Tess*, which had roused passions in the previous year.

Shaw and, less strenuously, Wilde endeavoured to create laughter and to point lessons at the same time. They did not monopolize the art of humour. There was a new comedy that contained no sermon. Saki (Hector Munro) agreed with Wilde about the necessity of embellishing truth: 'A little inaccuracy sometimes saves tons of explanation.' Saki also combined comedy with cruelty: ' "Waldo is one of those people who would be enormously improved by death", said Clovis.' To *The Unbearable Bassington* (1912) he appended a characteristic note: 'This story has no moral. If it points out an evil at any rate it suggests no remedy.'[26] Saki was not *sui generis*. It was said of Bret Harte when he died in 1902, having spent his last twenty years in Britain, that 'he made no parade of his moral aims; he did not think it his business to instruct the world in matters of politics, theology or science . . . Nobody was less conscious of a "mission".' He was simply a humorist, therefore without 'the owl-like seriousness of our gloomy young geniuses'.[27] Then there was Max Beerbohm, whose parodies and caricatures were spiced by malice and absurdity. The comedy of his only novel, *Zuleika Dobson* (1911), was thought by many, from Arnold Bennett to Edmund Gosse, spoiled by its callous conclusion, the universal suicide of Zuleika's undergraduate beaux.

Amoral humour was a feature of this period. It is commonly associated with the dandified aestheticism of the 1880s and the 1890s, a flaunting of convention. In fact, it had a much more popular currency and, if a firm provenance is wanted, it can be said to have originated with *The Idle Thoughts of an Idle Fellow* (1886), which the author dedicated to his pipe. Following the dedication came an explanatory preface: 'What readers ask now-a-days in a book is that it should improve,

[25] Holroyd, *Shaw*, i. 130, 133, 304. [26] Langguth, *Saki*, 208. [27] *TLS*, 9 May 1902, 129.

instruct, and elevate. This book wouldn't elevate a cow. I cannot conscientiously recommend it for any useful purposes whatever. All I can suggest is, that when you get tired of reading "the best hundred books", you may take this up for half an hour. It will be a change.'[28] It was written by a former railway clerk and commission agent who had been orphaned in his early teens, and who was now in his mid-twenties trying to supplement a modest wage as a solicitor's clerk by penny-a-lining for cheap magazines: Jerome K. Jerome. *Idle Thoughts* sold 23,000 copies in Britain in its first year; and in America which (he said) paid him the compliment of pirating the book, it sold by the hundred thousand. Richer, therefore, only from his domestic royalties of twopence-halfpenny a copy, Jerome in 1889 issued his masterpiece, *Three Men in a Boat*. Here the Victorian work ethic was dished once and for all: 'I like work; it fascinates me. I can sit and look at it for hours.'

Jerome inaugurated a revolution in humour.[29] For this he was reviled. He recalled, 'I think I may claim to have been, for the first twenty years of my career, the best abused author in England. *Punch* invariably referred to me as "'Arry K. Arry", and would then proceed to solemnly lecture me on the sin of mistaking vulgarity for humour and impertinence for wit.'[30] The split infinitive here was likely deliberate. *Punch* was actually tickled by some of Jerome's performances, such as his digs at dramatic conventions which were collected as *Stage-land* (1890); but *Three Men in a Boat* it persisted in regarding as pernicious. The source of this humour was identified as 'Yankee-land', filtered through the *Sporting Times*.[31] The

---

[28] Jerome K. Jerome, *The Idle Thoughts of an Idle Fellow: A Book for an Idle Holiday* (1886), preface.

[29] Jerome himself modestly ceded first place to his friend Barry Pain, declaring that it was to him 'the reproach "new humorist" was first applied. It began with a sketch of his in the *Granta*—a simple little thing entitled "The Love Story of a Sardine" ' (Jerome K. Jerome, *My Life and Times* (1983), 143.) Pain was writing for *Granta* when up at Cambridge in 1884–6; but his first book, *In a Canadian Canoe*, compiled from these contributions to *Granta*, was not published until 1891, two years after Jerome's *Three Men in a Boat* and five years after his *Idle Thoughts*. Pain followed this with *Stories and Interludes* (1892), which, as with Jerome, contained sly digs at Victorian earnestness, referring, for example, to 'a room where he never did any work, and which was consequently called his study'. Pain became a regular contributor to *Punch*, and was connected by marriage to the influential R. C. Lehmann, on whom, see below. *Punch*, 29 Aug. 1891, 99, contains a review of *In a Canadian Canoe*, which readers were enjoined to buy for its 'piquant savour and quaint originality of style'.

[30] Jerome, *Life and Times*, 57–8. The Cockney 'Arry was the invention of the *Punch* journalist E. J. Milliken (*c*.1839–1897), who contributed to *The 'Arry Papers* (1874–97); see Sir Francis C. Burnand, *Records and Reminiscences, Personal and General* (1904), ii. 258–9; Sutherland, *Companion*, 435. For an example of others' use of this snobbish term, see the entry for 18 Sept. 1892 in the diary of Ruth Bourne, a prep-school proprietor's wife: 'We went to London by the 10.5 and spent an "Arrysh" sort of day. We got on a steamer at Charing Cross and went up river to Kew; the company was not aristocratic—but certainly well behaved only very smelly.' Mrs Bourne did, however, read *Three Men in a Boat* to pupils at her school (diary, 30 Jan. 1893). See Baily (ed.), *Ruth Bourne Diaries*, 153, 171; and, generally on the question of speech snobbery, P. J. Waller (ed.), *Politics and Social Change in Modern Britain* (Hassocks, 1987), ch. 1.

[31] *Punch*, 1 Feb. 1890, 57; also *Punch*, 4 Oct. 1890, 157, for the parody *One Man in a Coat* by 'Arry O.K. Arry, 'Author of "Stige Fices", "Cheap Words of a Chippy Chappie", etsetterer', to which was attached the prefatory note that the 'Novel was carefully wrapped up in some odd leaves of Mark Twain's *Innocents Abroad*'. Jerome's sequels to *Three Men in a Boat* received equally poor reviews from *Punch*: see 16 May 1891, 239, for the review of *The Diary of a Pilgrimage*, dismissed as "'Arry Abroad'. *Punch* continued to target Jerome thereafter, linking his work to the fashion for low-life tales, which it considered intellectually

alleged American influence was sufficiently damning for many purists. This amused Harold Frederic, the *New York Times* London correspondent and a novelist himself. Seated at dinner next to Jerome he questioned him—'Where's your flint hammer? Left it in the cloak-room?'[32]—as if he were a neanderthal. It was the author's and his characters' social class and style—lower-middle class, slapdash, and spontaneous—that upset most reviewers. 'Colloquial clerk's English', sneered the *Saturday Review*, 5 October 1889, adding that, while it was a 'tour de force in fun of a certain kind', 'the life it describes and the humour that it records are poor and limited and decidedly vulgar.'[33] The book's immense popularity, running into millions of sales in Britain, America, and Europe, was proof of the power of a new mass reading public, enjoying their Bank Holiday jaunts much like the three boatmen ('to say nothing of the dog'), and revelling in their Saturday half-day sprees much like the singular George: 'George goes to sleep at a bank from ten to four each day, except Saturdays, when they wake him up and put him outside at two.'

Jerome was not only the groundlings' favourite. Surveying his own profession of literary criticism with habitual periodic disdain, Walter Raleigh reckoned that 'Jerome K. Jerome is in some ways a far decenter writer than Brunetière or Saintsbury or any of the professed critics. He goes and begets a brat for himself, and doesn't pule about other people's amours. If I write an autobiography it shall be called "Confessions of a Pimp".'[34] Jerome, however, did not follow through the revolution in humour. He was susceptible to the fashionable pantheism and pretty writing about nature. He also could not contain a maudlin streak, although that did little apparent harm to his popularity. On the strength of his reputation as a humorist, he was invited to co-edit (with Robert Barr) a new monthly magazine, *The Idler*, in 1892. This set itself to rival both the well-established *Punch* and the recently founded *Strand Magazine* by combining comedy, short-story fiction, and celebrity interviews. It attracted talented writers, some established, others on the rise: Americans, Mark Twain, Stephen Crane, Bret Harte, Oliver Wendell Holmes; and British, Conan Doyle, Kipling, H. G. Wells, W. W. Jacobs, Eden Phillpotts, Israel Zangwill. There was a characteristic Jerome note to the first issue: the advice, 'it is always the best policy to speak the truth—unless, of course, you are an exceptionally good liar'.[35] The *Review of Reviews*, which initially welcomed *The Idler*, was soon expressing concern: of the third issue, it observed, '*The Idler* is in danger of becoming somewhat vulgar, with a vulgarity of the music hall.'[36] But the atmosphere of a jolly club (with membership available to all, price sixpence) which was prevalent in *The Idler* was not violently subversive and *The*

---

dishonest: see *Punch*, 16 Oct. 1897, 169, for the parody interview of 'Mr. Sloggington Blowfrog', author of *Three Monkeys in the Dusthole*.

[32] Jerome, *Life and Times*, 58.   [33] Joseph Connolly, *Jerome K. Jerome* (1982), 75.

[34] Raleigh to John Sampson, 31 Dec. 1904, in Raleigh (ed.), *Raleigh Letters*, 268–9. Brunetière was Ferdinand Brunetière, leading French literary scholar and member of the Académie Française since 1893; as for Saintsbury, see below.   [35] Connolly, *Jerome*, 87.

[36] *Review of Reviews* (Feb. 1892), 188, (Apr. 1892), 395.

Spectator noted, 'There is obviously a danger that the New Humorists may form themselves into a close coterie, and may commit the mistake of thinking that the public are much more interested than they actually are, in the jokes they make at each other's expense.'[37]

The New Humour, then, quickly became formularized. It was a social rung lower than *Punch* (established in 1841), which progressively shed its radical and bohemian character and, after 1880, was steered by a predominantly public-school, Cambridge clique: Francis Burnand, Owen Seaman, Anstey Guthrie, E. V. Lucas, and R. C. Lehmann.[38] *Punch* was not only successful but increasingly so: its sales rose from 58,000 in 1902, to 80,000 in 1908 and 110,000 in 1913.[39] All 'the Shires, the Vicarages, and the Messes of England',[40] which were assumed by *Punch*'s editorial board to be its natural constituency, did not add up to 100,000, so historians must reckon on there being a further unaccounted readership. E. M. Forster, writing in 1920, had no doubt where this other readership was located:

Turn over the pages of *Punch*. There is neither wit, laughter, nor satire in our national jester—only the snigger of a suburban householder who can understand nothing that does not resemble himself. Week after week, under Mr. Punch's supervision, a man falls off his horse, or a colonel misses a golf ball, or a little girl makes a mistake in her prayers. Week after week ladies show not too much of their legs, foreigners are deprecated, originality condemned. Week after week a bricklayer does not do as much work as he ought and a futurist does more than he need. It is all supposed to be so good-tempered and clean; it is also supposed to be funny. It is actually an outstanding example of our attitude towards criticism: the middle-class Englishman, with a smile on his clean-shaven lips, is engaged in admiring himself and ignoring the rest of mankind.[41]

Forster was probably right to associate *Punch* with suburbia, though his belittlement betrayed inhibitions of his own.

Henry Lucy had been offered the editorship of *Punch* in 1897. He regarded the post as 'the blue riband of British journalism', by dint of 'its historical associations, its world-wide influence, and its personal distinction'; indeed, 'I would rather have been Editor of *Punch* than Emperor of India.'[42] Such superiority made *Punch*

---

[37] *The Spectator*, 6 Feb. 1892. See also the *Times* obituary, 15 June 1927; and the *DNB* notice of Jerome (*DNB 1922–1930*, 454–5) by his friend and associate George Burgin.

[38] The odd man out was Lucas, who went neither to public school nor to Oxbridge. The Cambridge *Granta*, which was co-founded in 1889 and then owned by Rudie Lehmann, acted as a feeder for *Punch*. Lehmann (1856–1929) was for a time editor of the *Daily News* (in which he invested £10,000) and a Liberal MP for Leicestershire, Harborough 1906–10 (Stephen Koss, *Fleet Street Radical* (1973), 41–2; Marshall, *Out and About* I, 28, 69–75, 87–9). Burnand, Seaman, and Guthrie all received notices in the *DNB*.

[39] These figures were print orders, actual sales being perhaps a thousand fewer; see Derek Hudson, 'Reading', in Simon Nowell-Smith (ed.), *Edwardian England 1901–1914* (Oxford, 1964), 325. For the first decade of *Punch*'s existence, see R. D. Altick, *Punch: The Lively Youth of a British Institution, 1841–1851* (Columbus, Ohio, 1996). [40] A. A. Milne, *Autobiography* (1939), 237.

[41] E. M. Forster, 'Notes on the English Character' (1920), in Forster, *Abinger Harvest* (1945), 9.

[42] Sir Henry Lucy, *Diary of a Journalist* (1920), 324; Ann Thwaite, *A. A. Milne: His Life* (1990), 103. He nonetheless turned down the editorship, from loyalty to the long-serving Burnand. Lucy wrote the parliamentary notes 'The Diary of Toby M.P.' for *Punch* from 1881 to 1916. The proprietors of *Punch* were William Bradbury (of the London printing firm) and Sir William Agnew (of the art dealers), who were brothers-in-law.

itself a target. When W. S. Gilbert met Burnand, *Punch*'s editor for twenty-six years from 1880, he remarked that he supposed *Punch* received hundreds of jokes sent in every week. On Burnand assenting, Gilbert asked why he never put any of them in.[43] Yet it would be wrong to conclude from Gilbert's gibe then or Forster's later that *Punch* invariably missed the mark. What *Punch* specialized in was artful burlesque and ingenious parody of ancient and modern authors. This was a favourite Victorian recreation. The most prodigious exercise in the genre was achieved by Walter Hamilton, fellow of the Royal Geographical and Royal Historical societies. He edited six volumes of *Parodies of the Works of English and American Authors* (1884–9); and he dealt brusquely with eminences who forbade their originals to be republished alongside the parodies. Robert Browning was hooted at by Hamilton when he withheld his permission in 1888.[44] Parody, therefore, provided a counterpoint to the Hundred Best Books homiletics although, paradoxically, parody required an anthologist's expertise fully to appreciate the joke. *Punch*'s social observation was sharp, even viperous on occasion, as in R. C. Lehmann's series 'Modern Types', which ran through 1890–1;[45] and literary fashions from aestheticism to Ibsenism were guyed unmercifully. This exposed *Punch* to a charge of conservatism; and it is the case that its iconoclasm tended to be acerbic when directed against progressive cults and affectionate when aimed at conventional tastes. Still, *Punch* performed salutary public service with its cock-a-snook series such as 'Prize Novels'—also written by R. C. Lehmann—which deflated an entire library of best-selling or celebrated contemporary authors: not just its favourite *bête noire* Jerome K. Jerome, but J. M. Barrie, Walter Besant, R. D. Blackmore, Marie Corelli, Hall Caine, Rider Haggard, Rudyard Kipling, Edna Lyall, George Meredith, Olive Schreiner, Robert Louis Stevenson, Jules Verne, Mrs Humphry Ward, and Zola.[46]

When A. A. Milne joined *Punch* in 1906—again from an apprenticeship on *Granta* at Cambridge—he added a whimsical humour all of his own. The last point he was sensitive about: he denied that he was copying J. M. Barrie's peculiar (and highly profitable) whimsy.[47] Milne found in the new editor, Seaman, a future model for Eeyore. Seaman was also an outstanding snob and dyed-in-the-wool Tory, but several Liberals provided balance at *Punch*'s Table, including Lehmann,

---

[43] Douglas Jerrold, *Georgian Adventure* (1938), 288. The joke gained extra bite because Burnand believed that he was better qualified to be Sullivan's librettist; see Jane W. Stedman's notice of Burnand, *Oxford DNB*.

[44] William Clyde DeVane and Kenneth Leslie Knickerbocker (eds.), *New Letters of Robert Browning* (1951), 364–5.

[45] The series started with 'The Dull Roysterer' on 22 Feb. 1890, 89. See *Punch*, 18 July 1891, 5, for the identification of Lehmann as the author of this series.

[46] The series began on 4 Oct. 1890. Lehmann issued the parodies in book form, *Mr Punch's Prize Novels*, in 1893.

[47] Milne, *Autobiography*, 235. Milne further noted about himself that one of his few lapses into unconventionality was 'a notorious distaste for lavatory jokes . . . In this respect I only differed from my contemporaries by thinking that the first necessity of a joke was that it should be funny; smuttiness was not enough' (ibid. 154). For his extreme dislike of being termed 'whimsical', Thwaite, *Milne*, 97, 158, 347.

who was an MP, and Milne himself, who canvassed in the December 1910 general election and converted to pacifism on reading Norman Angell's *The Great Illusion* (1910).[48] It was easy to suppose *Punch* to be enveloped in the Establishment when the editor's annual salary in the Edwardian period was £1,300, and both Burnand and Seaman were knighted. Yet Burnand's irregularity showed itself early on, as he became a Roman Catholic convert and was drawn to the stage. True, his humorous wink was too often arch, according to Milne's estimate:

This was a time when 'humorists' were not only labelled as such, but were qualified inevitably as 'genial'. To be genial, in fact, was almost enough. For the rest, italics and exclamation-marks were recognised badges of wit, periphrasis was in itself jocular, and an appropriate quotation from Dickens was proof to the most sceptical that the writer was a jolly good fellow. In this school the pun naturally held high esteem. There was no mistaking a pun; it was, from the fact of its being there, a genial contribution to the entertainment. Burnand contributed much in this line; and if a great deal of it was no more than a formal acknowledgement of his reputation as a humorist, there were to be found here and there real flashes of brilliance. One much-quoted saying of his was in answer to the charge that *Punch*, in his time, was not so good as it used to be—'It never was.'[49]

Punch thus appeared even to its own contributors periodically to exhibit those sclerotic symptoms that went with a status as National Institution. But Burnand both played up to a cultivated elite and entertained the popular market. On the one hand he serialized in *Punch* the Grossmiths' *Diary of a Nobody* (1892)—it was Burnand himself who suggested the title—and on the other hand he was author of some 120 farces, including *Black Eye'd Susan* (1866) and *The Colonel* (1881), which were still being staged when he wrote his memoirs in 1904.[50] Burnand also contributed to more than one Christmas pantomime at Drury Lane.[51] Frank Harris noted about Burnand's *Blue Beard* that as a play it was 'worse than absurd, incredibly trivial'; but it included such 'a rain of the most terrible puns and verbal acrobatics ever heard on any stage' that made Harris estimate Burnand as an extraordinary talent.[52]

   The historian, therefore, should not fail to acknowledge a strengthening band of humorists, operating in theatre and music hall, in book and magazine, who pricked at the solemnities of their morally urgent contemporaries. One of the qualities that made J. M. Barrie the highest-paid dramatist of his generation was this pervasive sense of fun. He did not spare the Calvinism that inspired so much achievement and humourlessness in his fellow Scots. In *What Every Woman Knows*

---

[48] Thwaite, *Milne*, 146, 160, 460, where it is noted that Milne voted Conservative for the first time in 1945.

[49] *DNB 1912–1921*, 78. The joke about *Punch* being famous for not being as funny as it used to be was Max Beerbohm's, although Barrie says much the same at the start of Act III of *Mary Rose* (1920).

[50] Burnand, *Records*, ii. 164.   [51] Blumenfeld, *R.D.B.'s Diary*, 168 (16 Dec. 1901).

[52] Harris, *Life and Loves*, 368–9. George Meredith once described Burnand as 'reeking puns from every pore' (quoted in Siegfried Sassoon, *Meredith* (1948), 63).

(1908) John Shand has risen from lowly origins to become an MP, a Radical with a driving purpose to promote progress, women's suffrage, and all. He is dour in the extreme; it is his wife, Maggie, whose touches make his speeches the hits they are. John is quite unconscious of this service, indeed unconscious both of her wit and of wit altogether:

MAGGIE. You've worked so hard, you've had none of the fun that comes to most men long before they're your age.
JOHN. I never was one for fun. I cannot call to mind, Maggie, ever having laughed in my life.
MAGGIE. You have no sense of humour.
JOHN. Not a spark.
MAGGIE. I've sometimes thought that if you had, it might make you fonder of me. I think one needs a sense of humour to be fond of me.
JOHN. I remember reading of some one that said it needed a surgical operation to get a joke into a Scotsman's head.
MAGGIE. Yes, that's been said.
JOHN. What beats me, Maggie, is how you could insert a joke with an operation.

[He considers this and gives it up.]⁵³

At the climax of the play Maggie patiently explains,

> Every man who is high up loves to think that he has done it all himself; and the wife smiles, and lets it go at that. It's our only joke. Every woman knows that. [*He stares at her in hopeless perplexity.*] Oh, John, if only you could laugh at me.
> JOHN. I can't laugh, Maggie.
> [*But as he continues to stare at her a strange disorder appears in his face.* MAGGIE *feels that it is to be now or never.*]
> MAGGIE. Laugh, John, laugh. Watch me; see how easy it is.
> [*A terrible struggle is taking place within him. He creaks. Something that may be mirth forces a passage, at first painfully, no more joy in it than in the discoloured water from a spring that has long been dry. Soon, however, he laughs loud and long. The spring water is become clear.* MAGGIE *claps her hands. He is saved.*]⁵⁴

III

Salvation was not normally thought of in this still-pious age as being attained through laughter. While the humorists won a considerable following, the earnest improvers had no intention of beating a retreat. In 1900 the Liberal *Daily News*—recently bought by the Quaker George Cadbury, who rigidly excluded racing and betting—held a poll on the Best Hundred books for children, with the object of influencing the establishment of a children's library at West Ham. *Punch* despaired: noting the omission of Mark Twain's *Adventures of Tom Sawyer* (1876) and

---

⁵³ Barrie, *Plays*, 344–5.   ⁵⁴ Ibid. 389–90.

Huckleberry Finn (1884), and of Mayne Reid's exciting prairie tales such as *The Rifle Rangers* (1849) and *The Scalp Hunters* (1851), all dumped in favour of 'moral powder stories' such as Charlotte M. Yonge's *The Daisy Chain* (1856) and F. W. Farrar's *Eric; or, Little By Little* (1858), it versified the want of judgement thus:

> For many in this 'little list'
> Bear titles ominous with warning;
> O Plebiscite, why thus insist
> On books provocative of yawning![55]

The idea of the best books was nevertheless sustained with little loss of appetite by the Edwardians. The versatile editor Clement Shorter gave a new twist to the game when he issued his Best Hundred in *Immortal Memories* (1907), arguing, 'There are great books that can be read only by the few, but surely the very greatest appeal alike to the educated and the illiterate, to the man of rich intellectual endowment and to the man to whom all processes of reasoning are incomprehensible.' Almost before this apparently absurd notion could sink in, that an unlettered idiot might ever be found closely perusing some masterpiece, Shorter struck with the example of *Hamlet*: 'It "holds the boards" at the small provincial theatre, it is enacted by Mr Crummles to an illiterate peasantry, and it is performed by the greatest actor to the most select city audience. It is made the subject of study by learned commentators. It is world-embracing.' Accordingly, Shorter designed his list to appeal both to scholars and to ordinary people—'for English boys and girls just growing into manhood and womanhood, or for those who have had no educational advantages in early years'. Given this criterion, it comes as rather a shock to the twenty-first century reader to find the majority of Lubbock's Hundred and even of the ascetic Acton's upheld. In fact, there were only fifteen items on Shorter's list which did not appear in these two predecessors': Balzac's *Père Goriot*, Catullus, Crabbe's *Tales of the Hall*, Madame D'Arblay's *Diary*, Dumas's *Three Musketeers*, Hogg's *Life of Shelley*, Howell's *Familiar Letters*, Johnson's *Rasselas*, Landor's *Imaginary Conversations*, Lever's *Charles O'Malley*, Morier's *Hajji Baba*, Peacock's *Nightmare Abbey*, Reade's *Cloister and the Hearth*, Richardson's *Clarissa Harlowe*, and Sime's *Life of Lessing*. Shorter also found a place for Rousseau's *Confessions*, Boccaccio, and Fielding's *Tom Jones*, which no doubt caused Lubbock's stern verdict that his list was 'too light, too merely amusing'.[56] Yet the popular literary paper *T.P.'s Weekly* commented that, while disagreement with particular inclusions was unavoidable, the list 'has one great advantage; it contains no single volume that would not be found *interesting* by the ordinary reader.'[57]

---

[55] *Punch*, 21 Mar. 1900, 206.

[56] Preface to the Forty-First English Edition, Avebury, *Pleasures of Life*, pp. v–ix.

[57] See the editorial comments on the list in *T.P.'s Weekly*, 15 Nov. 1907, 641. On Shorter, editor of the *Illustrated London News, Sphere, Tatler, Album*, and *Pick-Me-Up*, see *DNB 1922–1930*, 771–2. Douglas Sladen, *Twenty Years off my Life* (1914), 196, called him 'one of the pioneers of modern journalism'; and Flower, *Just as it Happened*, 232–3, also paid tribute to his brilliance and knowledge, though spoiled by his egoism and

This judgement about the cerebral and concentrative capacity of the ordinary reader by *T.P.'s Weekly* is deserving of our respect, even if it leads us also to meditate how differently constituted was the ordinary reader of 1907 from that of 2006. Incontestably, *T.P.'s Weekly* aimed at, and thought it knew, the new reading public. It took its title from the initials of the forenames of the founding editor, Thomas Power (Tay Pay[58]) O'Connor, who kept the controlling interest until bought out by the Pearson newspaper group in 1908. O'Connor's is one of those names that crops up in British history in three quite different contexts—as a champion of Irish Home Rule, as a prototypical modern journalist, and as first president of the British Board of Film Censors—but he remains still a shadowy figure, and measurement of his influence is pregnant with difficulty. For over forty years, from 1885 to 1929, he represented the Liverpool Scotland constituency as an Irish Nationalist, the only one ever to capture an English seat.[59] He ended his days as Father of the House, a repository of parliamentary tradition: one of the last to wear his hat in the Commons and one of a dwindling band of snuff addicts.[60] This was a far cry from when his denunciation of Joseph Chamberlain as 'Judas' during the debate on the second Home Rule Bill in 1893 resulted in what *The Times*'s reporter called 'a really serious fisticuff encounter' between Irish Nationalist and Unionist MPs.[61] That breach of parliamentary etiquette apart, O'Connor was widely admired; as Robert Farquharson, a Liberal MP from 1880 to 1906, put it:

Few of the House speakers can equal—it would be almost hopeless to excel—'Tay Pay', as his many friends delight to call him, for he has all the Irish faculty for success: a fine voice, a rich and copious vocabulary, and the debating power which enables him at a moment's notice to follow opponents with damaging success, have made him a real power.[62]

O'Connor's main political role was as fixer for the Parnellite party and fundraiser for the Nationalist cause, especially in America. O'Connor remained always something of the bachelor bookman in appearance and habits, in his 'black frock-coat, nigger-brown with snuff and still more snuff from that continual snuff-box';[63] but in 1885 he had married Elisabeth (Bess) Howard (*née* Paschal), who

---

hustling tactlessness. Arnold Bennett did not think much of his prose style: 'the sea', he once wrote, was 'as flat as a page of Clement Shorter' (Bennett, *Things that have Interested Me* (1923), 7). George Meredith also delivered a back-handed compliment: 'Shorter, the type of literary man who would print a famous writer's blotting pad in a limited edition if he could get hold of it, though, according to his lights and limitations, he did his best to further the appreciation of good literature' (quoted in Scott, *Pall Mall Gazette*, 430, and in Sassoon, *Meredith*, 230).

[58] The nickname, according to Bernard Shaw, was coined by Edmund Yates, editor of *The World*; J. W. Robertson Scott, *'We' and Me* (1956), 166.

[59] On this, see L. W. Brady, *T. P. O'Connor and the Liverpool Irish* (1983); P. J. Waller, *Democracy and Sectarianism: A Political and Social History of Liverpool 1868-1939* (Liverpool, 1981).

[60] Mackintosh, *Echoes of Big Ben*, 86, 144.   [61] *The Times*, 28 July 1893.

[62] Robert Farquharson, *In and Out of Parliament* (1911), 329.

[63] Flower, *Just as it Happened*, 228. Reminiscing in 1917, O'Connor 'said that he had been the most trustful and easily deceived man imaginable. It was all very well he said, but the connections of a simple

possessed, according to the 'New Woman' journalist and novelist Ella Hepworth Dixon, 'the longest eye lashes I have ever seen, save those of Mr Max Beerbohm'.[64] The new Mrs O'Connor was the daughter of a Texan judge who had supported the Union cause in the civil war, and she came equipped with a 10 year-old son and social and literary ambitions.[65] For a time, when O'Connor was editor of the *Star*, they lived over the shop in a luxurious flat, on the top floor of the *Star* building;[66] then they began to live and entertain in some style in Queen Anne's Gate, over-looking St James's Park, before moving again in 1891 to Oakley Lodge in Upper Cheyne Row, Chelsea. They also kept a house in Brighton until their marriage faltered after 1905. O'Connor was always moaning about money but he was not too short of it to give up his rounds of golf[67] or his turn of the fashionable Continental resorts and spas.[68] He could be seen too at Society occasions, such as Lady Jeune's receptions.[69] When Mrs Hodgson Burnett first met him, it was at a country-house party in 1896 at Fryston Hall, home of the Earl of Crewe, the former Lord Lieutenant of Ireland; and when she returned to England in 1900, she included O'Connor in one of her own dinner parties at a house she rented from Lord Burghclere in Charles Street, off Berkeley Square. The wheeler-dealer side of O'Connor was again evident on this occasion. Discussing with Mrs Burnett the prospects of her son Vivian entering publishing after leaving Harvard, O'Connor told her, 'If he wants to come here, I could get him in with the Harmsworths directly.'[70] O'Connor himself had a reputation as a popular political commentator and biographer, dubbed by a derisive colleague 'the modern Plutarch at £10 a week'.[71] He published instant studies of *Disraeli* (1878, 1879), *Gladstone's House of Commons* (1885), *The Parnell Movement* (1886), *Parnell* (1891), *Napoleon* (1896), and *Campbell-Bannerman* (1908). Above all, as a prominent newspaper editor, O'Connor was influential in developing new features and wider markets.

man with women were apt to have "pecuniary endings" ' ((Flower (ed.), *Bennett Journals*, ii. 199 (1 June 1917)).

[64] Thwaite, *Waiting for the Party*, 262.

[65] See her reminiscences: Mrs T. P. O'Connor, *I Myself* (1910). She was president of the Society for Women Journalists in 1905. She also appeared on the stage and wrote plays, which flopped until she teamed up with the designer Graham Robertson and the light composer Frederick Norton to present *Pinkie and the Fairies* (1908). She further stated that, as soon as she began to work for her living, she became a suffragist (p. 152).

[66] The flat cost £700 to establish, a sizeable sum in those days; and this expenditure was held against O'Connor by the paper's board of directors, among other more serious differences, when he was ousted form the editorial chair; see T. P. O'Connor, *Memoirs of an Old Parliamentarian* (1929), ii. 268.

[67] O'Connor enjoyed playing golf with the cricketer W. G. Grace, according to Sladen, *Twenty Years*, 198. He listed cycling as well as golf under his recreations in *Who's Who* (1905), 1207.

[68] Douglas Sladen, who first met O'Connor in Boston in 1888–9, when O'Connor was on an American fundraising tour for the Irish Nationalist Party, recorded that 'He showed his friendship by the enthu-siastic way in which he backed everything I wrote or did, and by the many hours of his delightful society which he launched on me at Monte Carlo, when I was free to drop in to tea with him at the Hôtel de Paris without invitation or notice. Though, if I let him know that I was coming he would try to get some person of interest who was staying in the hotel to meet me' (Sladen, *Long Life*, 86, 224).

[69] See Coventry Patmore's surprise at meeting him there—Sir Francis and Lady Jeune were Con-servatives; Derek Patmore, *The Life and Times of Coventry Patmore* (1949), 227.

[70] Thwaite, *Burnett*, 197.   [71] Sir Patrick O'Brien, quoted in Brady, *O'Connor*, 98.

The debate about who has the best claim to be considered the originator of what Matthew Arnold termed the New Journalism—T. P. O'Connor, Henry Labouchere, W. T. Stead, Alfred Harmsworth, Kennedy Jones, and all—is inconclusive because it involves such a miscellany of considerations, typeface and layout as well as content, style, and methods: interviews and profiles, exposés and investigations, personal sidelines and gossip, sensation and 'human interest' stories, and shorter but sharper (and more partisan) political news.[72] The question is further complicated by having to weigh the transmission of recent American practices against the evolution of British journalistic habits from 1855, when the repeal of the stamp duty saw the start of penny national and provincial dailies. O'Connor began his series of editorships in January 1888 with the *Star*, a halfpenny London evening paper floated with a capital of £40,000 raised from various sources, including wealthy Liberal MPs, the chemicals industrialist J. T. Brunner, the Yorkshire woollens manufacturer Isaac Holden, and the mustard magnate J. J. Colman. The Radical MP and editor of *Truth* Henry Labouchere brokered these contacts; and Wilfrid Blunt, the ex-diplomat and poet recently imprisoned in Ireland for incitement during landlord–tenant clashes, was another shareholder. Told that 'circulation was a thing of slow growth, and if I managed to get to thirty thousand a day in the first month I ought to be fully satisfied', O'Connor was understandably 'triumphant' when the *Star* started with sales of 142,600, rising to average daily sales of 162,866 by June when, it was claimed, it was selling each week a quarter of a million more copies than any previous London evening paper. The opportunity of promoting a union of hearts between the British and Irish democracies was amply seized by O'Connor. His editorials pressed the cause of Irish Home Rule together with a Radical programme of land taxation and housing reform which was carried forward by the Progressives' victory on the new London County Council, first elected in January 1889.[73] The talent involved in the *Star* is well known: H.W. Massingham, Robert Donald, Thomas Marlowe, Ernest Parke, Sidney Webb, Bernard Shaw and, in the literary columns, Clement Shorter, Richard Le Gallienne, and A. B. Walkley.[74]

Besides writing leaders, O'Connor contributed a gossip column, 'Mainly about People'. It would be unwise for historians to underestimate this—or the

---

[72] O'Connor's manifesto for the *Star*, that it should be 'animated, readable and stirring', and his article 'The New Journalism', *New Review* (Oct. 1889), are extensively quoted in *The History of The Times*, iii: *The Twentieth Century Test 1884–1912* (1947), 96–7, 780–1. Matthew Arnold coined the phrase 'the New Journalism' in an article in the *Nineteenth Century* (May 1887), referring to Stead's editorship of the *Pall Mall Gazette*. [73] O'Connor, *Memoirs*, vol. ii, ch. xiv; and Sheehy, 'Irish Journalists', ch. 4. [74] It was Massingham who brought Shaw to the *Star*. Shaw was then working for *The World* as art critic and for the *Pall Mall Gazette*, where he had been increasingly frustrated in his work as a book reviewer. He was to be no more content at the *Star*. O'Connor claimed that he had never heard of him or of Webb and was shocked to discover they were both socialists rather than radicals. Shaw was soon shunted from assistant leader-writer to music critic and, when Shaw also smuggled social criticism into his music column, O'Connor 'almost literally starved him out' by paying him meanly. See O'Connor, *Memoirs*, ii. 256, 265–7; Holroyd, *Shaw*, i. 214–15, 234–7.

popularity of its racing tipster Captain Coe (Charles Mitchell)[75] and the reporting of divorce and murder cases—in weighing the causes of the *Star*'s success. Robert Hichens, in *The Green Carnation* (1894), has his Oscar Wilde character Esmé Amarinth remark that the *Star* 'circulates chiefly among members of the Conservative party who desire to know what the aristocracy are doing'[76]—a sly dig at the *Star*'s Radical credentials, but a paradox that also hit the mark. 'Mainly about People' was a title which O'Connor subsequently carried over as *M.A.P.*, the penny weekly magazine he founded and edited, 1898–1909. *M.A.P.* was designed, O'Connor told Francis Gribble, who worked for him, as 'a sort of a penny *Truth* with a dash of *Modern Society*'.[77] O'Connor's reputation both as a publicist and as a man of reforming instincts and wide tolerance was such that the pariah Wilde considered inviting him to write the introduction to a cheap shilling edition of *The Ballad of Reading Gaol* (1898).[78] The assistant editor of the *Star*, Massingham, further accounted O'Connor as 'the fastest descriptive writer I ever knew';[79] but it was Massingham who displaced O'Connor from the editorial chair and was himself ousted in 1890–1, a rapid succession explained in large part by political disagreements with the paper's financial directors. Other criticisms of O'Connor involved cronyism. This was as commonplace in Fleet Street as in the rest of the world, including the Government, where Lord Salisbury's habit of packing the ministry with relations caused the Cabinet to be nicknamed the Hotel Cecil; but O'Connor had appointed his brother-in-law William O'Malley secretary and then manager of the *Star* and given a start to many an ambitious young journalist of Irish origins much like his own. This patronage did him no good now, when it was seized on by his detractors in the boardroom, or in the long run, when W. P. Ryan and D. P. Moran later repaid his kindliness by scathing remarks about his lifestyle as an Anglicized rather than 'true' Irishman. Shown the door, O'Connor, whose salary had been £1,200, received 'the unheard-of sum' of £15,000 or more in compensation, on condition that he must not start another London evening paper for three years.[80]

---

[75] Scott, '*We*' *and Me*, 174, for his importance to the *Star*'s fortunes.   [76] Hichens, *Green Carnation*, 77.

[77] Francis Gribble, *Seen in Passing* (1929), 172–3. *M. A. P.*'s subtitle was 'A Popular Penny Weekly of Pleasant Gossip, Personal Portraits and Social News'. *M. A. P.* mixed profiles and tittle-tattle about celebrities in all walks of life—literature, theatre, law, Church, politics, armed services—with news about social engagements. There were, in addition, women's pages; a short story or serial; a City page; a bridge column and competition (from the 12 Dec. 1903 issue); and, invariably, some clever and original feature, e.g. The Book of the Week Reviewed by the Author, which could be a very revealing exercise about how a popular author saw his or her purpose and market and responded to critical reviews. The editorial in *M. A. P.*, 11 June 1904, 659, boasted of the magazine's success in the colonies and United States, as well as in Britain. *M. A. P.* also encouraged support for good causes: see 20 Aug. 1904, 232, recording nearly £350 raised by readers towards the Fresh Air Fund, designed to organize country holidays for children from slum homes. *M. A. P.* was published by Arthur Pearson's, which gradually took it over and eventually sidelined O'Connor; see Hamilton Fyfe, *T. P. O'Connor* (1934), 189–92. *Punch* styled it *P. A. P.*: see *Punch*, 15 Oct. 1913, 324.

[78] Wilde to Leonard Smithers, *c*.4 May 1898, in Hart-Davis (ed.), *Wilde Letters*, 340.

[79] Quoted in Brady, *O'Connor*, 101.

[80] The 'unheard-of sum' is from R. D. Blumenfeld, *All in a Lifetime* (1931), 227, who says it was £17,000. O'Connor himself (*Memoirs*, ii. 270) gave £15,000 as the sum, and his first biographer, Hamilton Fyfe, who knew him personally, follows him (Fyfe, *O'Connor*, 155) as does Brady, *O'Connor*, 116. According to

Some of this money O'Connor put into the *Sunday Sun*, which he started in May 1891. Two years later, in 1893, it metamorphosed into the *Weekly Sun*, issued unusually on both Saturdays and Sundays, a move that raised the circulation from 20,000 to 100,000; at the same time he brought out the *Sun* as a halfpenny evening paper. Again, O'Connor's talent-spotting was in evidence when he drew from Birmingham the aggressive and ambitious Kennedy Jones and put him in charge of the newsroom.[81] He also invited J. L. Garvin, then a cub journalist on the *Newcastle Daily Chronicle*, to join the *Evening Sun* as leader-writer.[82] Garvin was not yet drawn to London; but O'Connor's *Suns* directed their beam to those locations where popular interest was hottest. The law courts were one, and Kennedy Jones 'sent boy after boy to the Court to carry off "copy" as fast as it could be produced'. O'Connor even had the idea that 'murder trials and other *causes célèbres* ought not to be baldly reported by stenographers, but to be described picturesquely by writers of fiction'. This proved 'more ingenious than practical',[83] but O'Connor's *Suns* contained other innovative features, including columns of supposed women's interest and, more importantly from our point of view, conspicuous attention to literature. In the eight-page *Sunday Sun* O'Connor's 'Book of the Week' article stood out. It appeared on the front page, although, his most recent biographer mordantly notes, it was 'in many ways the forerunner of that type of literary criticism that is so personalized that it has very little to say about the book in question.'[84] O'Connor had been advised against offering any sort of literary fare to his readers, but he maintained the belief that 'literature pays even with the most democratic audience'.[85] Less viable was the *Sun*'s financial base. O'Connor admitted, 'I started it with insufficient capital'; yet the *Sun* grew monstrously and O'Connor compared himself to Frankenstein, wrestling to control its movement.[86] Equally O'Connor struggled to apportion his energies between politics and journalism, at a time when Parnell's disgrace and death brought turmoil to the Irish Nationalist cause; and ultimately he was glad to have the journals taken over.[87] But he was not done with popular

O'Connor, at the time of the disagreements with the *Star*'s directors, 'I had only one friend on the board, the late Mr Wilfrid Blunt; but he was futile.' In addition, Fyfe stated that, while putting part of the £15,000 into the *Sun*, O'Connor invested the rest in South African mining shares which collapsed during the Boer War when he was forced to sell them 'for one-fifth of what he paid for them'. O'Connor reckoned that, had he stayed with the *Star*, 'I might have had something like twenty or twenty-five thousand a year out of it'—though how these sums were arrived at is not specified. O'Connor also lost money by investing in a Virginia tobacco and cotton speculation, recommended to him by Thomas Nelson Page, who was Virginia-born, an author of Southern stories and eventually US Ambassador to Italy. At his death in 1929 O'Connor's effects were probated at a relatively meagre £1,248 15s. 3d.

[81] On Kennedy Jones (1865–1921), see *Who Was Who, 1916–1928*, 565, and Pound and Harmsworth, *Northcliffe*, 168–74. He became editor of the *Evening News* (1894–1900) and, because of his close association with Alfred Harmsworth (later Lord Northcliffe), liked to style himself joint founder of the *Daily Mail* and *Daily Mirror*. He entered Parliament as Unionist MP for Middlesex (Hornsey) in 1916.

[82] J. L. Garvin to Wilfrid Meynell, 27 Mar. 1894, in Viola Meynell, *Francis Thompson and Wilfrid Meynell* (1952), 100–1. Garvin was later editor of the *Pall Mall Gazette* and, most famously, of the *Observer*. See also David Ayerst, *Garvin of the Observer* (1985), 27.   [83] Gribble, *Seen in Passing*, 155.

[84] Brady, *O'Connor*, 128.   [85] Fyfe, *O'Connor*, 164.   [86] O'Connor, *Memoirs*, ii. 270.

[87] An unsympathetic portrait of a disenchanted O'Connor during his *Sun* period, as the character Theobald Cunningham, editor of the evening *Gleam* and *Sunday Gleam*, was sketched by W. P. Ryan in his

journalism. He still had *M.A.P.* when on 14 November 1902 he started *T.P.'s Weekly*, a penny journal of some thirty-six to forty pages.

What matters about *T.P.'s Weekly* is not just the welcome it received from noted authors—George Meredith, Arnold Bennett, G. K. Chesterton, Joseph Conrad, Thomas Hardy, and H. G. Wells—or the financial returns it brought O'Connor.[88] The significant point is that it was considered feasible, not lunatic, to launch a literary paper for the masses, a proposition that would be both intellectually and commercially inconceivable in our own day. George Meredith celebrated this in the second issue, which reported that 200,000 copies of the first number were sold on the first day: 'We have entered upon the period of Democracy in Literature.'[89] After six weeks the circulation was stated settled at a figure approaching a quarter of million; and, whereas 20–25 per cent 'returns' (unsold copies) was standard for new papers, *T.P.'s Weekly* boasted that its had been under 9 per cent on all issues.[90] *T.P.'s Weekly* aimed, according to its prospectus, 'to bring to many thousands a love of letters'. It was devoted almost entirely to literary topics and, though it also gave space to books about history, philosophy, religion, popular science, and medicine, its chief focus was on fiction and poetry. The prevailing tone was light but the ethic unmistakably one of serious self-improvement. Moreover, as the correspondence column evidenced, its readership was female and male, and reached down to the lowest levels of the working class as well as up and across the seriated levels of the lower- and middle-middle classes. In 1932 Thomas Burke paid tribute to *T.P.'s Weekly* for having fired his imagination and given direction to his life. Burke's later friendship with Charlie Chaplin stemmed in part from their discovery that as teenagers in the Edwardian period, unknown to each other,

each of us was recoiling from the drab, draggled Kennington in which we lived; each of us, in a crude, undirected way, was yearning towards the things of decency and the things of the mind, and each of us was hopeless of ever attaining them. I discovered literature by picking up a copy of *T.P.'s Weekly* in a tea-shop; he [Chaplin] discovered the inwardness of music on hearing a man playing a clarinet outside a Kennington pub—playing *The Honeysuckle and the Bee!*[91]

Dwellers in the expanding working-class and lower-middle-class dormitory suburbs were the chief sorts of reader to whom *T.P.'s Weekly* was aimed, to judge by the pitch of several articles in the early issues. One contained tips to City clerks

novel *Daisy Darley; or, The Fairy Gold of Fleet Street* (1913). Ryan had worked on O'Connor's *Sun* in the early 1890s. Sheehy, 'Irish Journalists', ch. 7.

[88] About this there is only speculation. According to Brady, *O'Connor*, 132, O'Connor was said to be earning 'either £6,000 or £10,000 a year', though Brady thinks this 'probably an exaggeration' by his political enemies.

[89] *T.P.'s Weekly*, 21 Nov. 1902, 58. O'Connor had become a passionate Meredithian after first reading *Beauchamp's Career* (1875) on a train; Fyfe, *O'Connor*, 137–8.   [90] *T.P.'s Weekly*, 26 Dec. 1902, 211.

[91] Thomas Burke, quoted in Robinson, *Chaplin*, 287. Burke (1886–1945) achieved fame with *Limehouse Nights* (1916), his short stories about London's Chinatown. One of these, 'The Chink and the Child', was bought by Chaplin and made into a film, *Broken Blossoms*, directed by D. W. Griffith, in 1919.

about where and how to lunch;[92] another, on 'The Real Suburbs', rebutted the familiar sneer that suburbanites all lived in the same houses, all furnished their homes in the same style, all commuted to work on the same trains, all gathered in the evenings about the same pianos; in sum, were all identical, anxious, hard-up, and unimaginative. *T.P.'s Weekly* wanted to dispel the gloom from the lower-middle classes which Gissing's fiction had cast around it. There was an intolerable inability to seize life's opportunities for enjoyment in Gissing's pathetic characters, who pursued their seedy existences without hope and humour. Their dreadful self-pity seemed a 'diseased vanity and egomania', as if, Douglas Goldring exclaimed, they 'bore the motto "please kick me" suspended round their servile necks . . . Gissing's people are chained far more by their own idiotic sense of possession (the "little home", the "few choice books"), and by their Victorian respectability, than they are by their poverty'. Such delimited horizons were detestable, because books were to be valued not as a trinket betokening 'education' or 'social position' but in order to 'send the reader back to life refreshed and stimulated'.[93] Arnold Bennett knew the strengths as well as the shortcomings of this class better than most, as a former solicitor's clerk himself and through the friends he made in London when he was starting off as a writer. In 1897 he described an evening with a 'typical respectable Clerk and his wife', both in their thirties. When their talk turned to books, he found the wife well able to reel off titles and preferences from the works of authors such as Charlotte Brontë and George Eliot. Having mentioned Mrs Henry Wood, she again specified what she thought 'the best of *hers*', whereupon the clerk interjected that he had not only not read that, he had read nothing by Mrs Henry Wood. 'I don't think *you'd* care for them,' said the wife, showing respect for her husband's taste: 'There isn't much *in* them, you know.' Bennett found the couple 'skilful, experienced, alive, in the things which lay within their own segment of life's circle' and, though apt to feel 'lost and awed' when they strayed outside it, they were not unadventurous or uninquisitive. They knew all about the programmes at the Empire and the Alhambra; and, the clerk having registered that he had 'read Lamb, and had a distant interest in Stevenson, he asked, "What is this *Yellow Book*, Mr Bennett?" as if he were inquiring into the nature of the differential calculus or bimetallism'.[94]

T.P.'s Weekly endorsed that philosophy, holding out to this expanding social class the rich possibilities of life and literature; and it robustly defended suburbanites as individuals. It acknowledged that they faced pressures to follow routines, but the message was that they should feel no need to justify their

---

[92] *T.P.'s Weekly*, 28 Nov. 1902, 83.

[93] Goldring, *Reputations*, 125–32. After reading *New Grub Street* (1891) for the first time during the Great War, Goldring fled to the nearest cinema looking to Charlie Chaplin to dispel his depression.

[94] Flower (ed.), *Bennett Journals*, i. 30–1 (30 Jan. 1897). Bennett contributed to the *Yellow Book* (July 1895), a short story called 'A Letter Home', just before he quit the solicitor's office for journalism. On the *Yellow Book*, which ran for thirteen issues, quarterly, between 1894 and 1897, see Sutherland, *Companion*, 685.

existence: 'it is irritating to hear of a label such as "suburbanism" so lightly attached to countless human beings . . . to explain some millions by a phrase'.[95] Readers' responses to this were interesting. A clerk's wife did indeed raise a heart-rending cry about 'the pitifulness of our lives in the scrape, scrape, eternal scrape of it to make the two ends meet, those two ends!' But she, too, endorsed that vindication of ordinary suburbanites which was *T.P.'s Weekly's* theme.[96] Other correspondents suggested that an indictment of suburbia might be better directed against the wealthier villadom 'where the prevailing ideal is no mere respect-ability, but gentility: where the man with three hundred a year won't know the man with two hundred and fifty; and where the little girls when they go to school ask other little girls "How many servants do you keep at your house?" ' The writer of this particular letter wrote from his own experience as a resident for nearly two years past 'in a "superior" suburb' of Streatham. It had many attractive features, he stated; but, denominating himself 'a loving disciple of that great saint of the last century, Mr Matthew Arnold', and endeavouring to follow Arnold's creed and to live for culture, he was oppressed by 'the hopeless Phi-listinism of the place . . . the low, vulgar views of life; the sordid content; the ignoble scorn of art and literature; the childish ignorance of all that is best in the intellectual life of to-day; and the pitiful clergy-ridden attitude assumed in social life; the dressing and the dining'. It was, therefore, suburbans of this superior class who were the complacent vulgarians—'fat, foolish, flat-footed Philistines, everyone of them'—rather than the scraping and pinched, but also inquisitive and improving, suburbans of the popular class.[97] Perhaps this was overdoing it, but perhaps not. In 1899 the Fabians Hubert Bland and his wife, Edith Nesbit, moved to a substantial eighteenth-century house with Tudor outbuildings, Well Hall in Eltham, chiefly on the strength of Edith's earnings as an author of children's stories. They revelled in their new-found fortune but, during the Edwardian years, rows of new houses began to creep closer to theirs. Bland was furious. So was Edith Nesbit, though prepared to allow, when it was pointed out to her, the incongruity of her feeling this when, as professed socialists, they had long called for improved working-class housing. Still, Nesbit vented those feelings by con-structing cardboard and brown-paper models of factories, suburban villas, and terraced houses which, at parties for her friends, she incinerated in her garden at sunset. E. M. Forster was an assistant at one such bonfire. This was Nesbit's protest against industrialization and jerry-building. At the end of the decade her royalties and journalistic earnings fell off and money became tight once more. To supplement her income, she set up a stall by the front gate to sell vegetables and flowers from the garden.[98] Working- and lower-middle class neighbours thus proved useful after all, if only as consumers with pennies to spend. What local shopkeepers thought of Nesbit's undercutting is not recorded.

[95] *T.P.'s Weekly*, 16 Jan. 1903, 296.   [96] Ibid., 30 Jan. 1903, 374–5.
[97] Ibid., 20 Feb. 1903, 470, 472.
[98] Doris Langley Moore, *E. Nesbit: A Biography* (Philadelphia, 1966), 250–2.

The opening issue of *T.P.'s Weekly* started with the first of a two-part review of George Eliot, based upon J. W. Cross's *Life and Letters* (1885) and Leslie Stephen's *George Eliot* (1902) in the Men of Letters series. This was followed by a profile of Rider Haggard as a prelude to the serialization of his latest, *Stella Fregelius*. A series of 'Short, Powerful and Romantic Stories' was inaugurated by Silas K. Hocking's 'The Adventures of Latimer Field, Curate'; there was also a focus column on Maeterlinck, and extracts from classics by De Quincey, Macaulay, Newman, and Froude. These almost incongruous juxtapositions were the essence of *T.P.'s Weekly*: its spirit was a cheerful eclecticism, premissed on the conviction that there was no reason why readers should not enjoy equally Conrad and Conan Doyle and their interest range across all literature from Samuel Butler to Miss Braddon. An article in 1903 advising readers how to establish and run book clubs among their circles of friends—the ideal number was thought to lie between one and two dozen people—emphasized that the committee should fairly represent diverse tastes: 'If the committee is too bookish, too narrow and too superior in its predilections—if, for example, it happens to have a mania for the works of Mr Henry James and Mr W. B. Yeats to the exclusion of Mrs Humphry Ward and Mr Benjamin Kidd—there will soon be a row in that club and wigs on the club-green.'[99] A series of articles, 'The Savoir-Faire Papers' by Arnold Bennett using the sobriquet 'The Man Who Does', also gave advice, without condescension, to readers about how to plan their reading and how to discover the best bargains: an article recommending new series of cheap classics, an article on foreign novels, another on reference books, and so on. How much this was appreciated by readers is evident from the correspondence it drew.[100]

The modern critic may easily disparage these articles as cheapjack wisdom, cobbled together pell-mell style by hack journalists thumbing through reference literature. Philip Gibbs wrote such a series under the pen-name 'Self-Help' in the early 1900s. These were then published as a book, *Knowledge is Power*, in 1903. At the time he conceived of the articles, Gibbs was in his early twenties, recently married, and finding it hard to manage on his pay working for Tillotson's, the proprietors of the *Bolton Evening News*, who had developed the country's principal organization for the syndication of serialized fiction among provincial newspapers. Gibbs afterwards confessed that

my knowledge was not always more than a week old, being based on books which I had devoured the week before, as a pupil-teacher keeps in advance of his class. But all the

---

[99] *T.P.'s Weekly*, 21 Aug. 1903, 370.

[100] Ibid., 26 Dec. 1902, 211; 9 Jan. 1903, 275; 16 Jan. 1903, 307; 30 Jan. 1903, 365; 6 Feb. 1903, 398; 20 Feb. 1903, 467; 20 Mar. 1903, 595. Bennett's column (retitled A Novelist's Notebook from Nov. 1903) was discontinued by the acting editor, Whitten, in the spring of 1904, allegedly as an economy measure. The crisis had evidently passed by January 1906, when Bennett was rehired to do another series, the Savoir Vivre Papers, together with the novelist Eden Phillpotts, with whom Bennett also collaborated in writing plays. For the Savoir Faire Papers and Novelist's Notebook, Bennett received £165 a year; the new contract was for £450. Bennett continued to write for *T.P.'s Weekly*, beginning a new series of articles in October 1909. See Flower (ed.), *Bennett Journals*, i. 120–1, 125–6, 162, 166, 224–6, 330, 337.

reading I had done as a boy, all my youthful enthusiasm for Shakespeare, Milton, Scott, Thackeray, Dickens, George Eliot, and Hardy, and the great masters, all my study of history—not very deep but fairly wide—was a great source of supply now when I sat down to write about great books, and the wisdom of the ages, and the love of poetry and art and drama and all beauty. These articles of mine had a surprising success, far beyond the British Isles, for *The Weekly Scotsman* in which they appeared among other papers . . . went to far outposts wherever a Scot had established himself, and I had letters from all parts of the world discussing the subjects with which I had dealt, and finding pleasure in my essays on books and writers.[101]

Thus, for all their hasty composition and spurious authority, Gibbs's articles did convey an infectious idealism about books. According to *T.P.'s Weekly*, Gibbs's articles drew nearly 3,000 letters, and it commended his sentiment about wanting 'to act as a guide . . . to self-taught students who will proceed with me along the Pilgrim's Way' towards the acquisition of culture.[102] This was the mood of the age, although Kipling put a cruder construction on it in a talk on 'The Uses of Reading' at Wellington College in May 1912: 'over and above all the help we can get from our ordinary training, association with our betters, and our very limited experience, we can pick up from Literature a few general and fundamental ideas as to how the great game of life has been played by the best players'.[103]

O'Connor was the inspiration behind *T.P.'s Weekly* and a regular contributor of reviews and features, but his political career and other newspaper interests meant that the practical editorship devolved to others.[104] Three, Wilfred Whitten, J. A. T. Lloyd, and Holbrook Jackson, stood out. Whitten, who wrote under the pseudonym John O'London, served as acting editor from the magazine's foundation in 1902 to 1911. Whitten had been assistant editor of *The Academy* between 1896 and 1902, responsible with the editor Lewis Hind for enlivening a literary journal which had become conventional and even stale. Under Hind and Whitten, *The Academy* introduced readers' competitions ('choose appropriate literary mottoes for the various rooms of one's house'), published lists of best-selling books derived from metropolitan and provincial bookshops, and inaugurated annual awards to emerging authors.[105] The proclaimed aim was 'to encourage, to seek for promise, sincerity, and thoroughness in literary art rather than to acknowledge fulfilment'; so the citation read on 14 January 1899, when Joseph Conrad was dowered with 50 guineas for *Tales of Unrest* (1898).[106] The magazine

---

[101] Philip Gibbs, *The Pageant of the Years* (1946), 32–3, 59.

[102] *T.P.'s Weekly*, 20 Nov. 1903, 793.

[103] Rudyard Kipling, 'The Uses of Reading' (1912), in Kipling, *A Book of Words* (1928), 96.

[104] O'Connor relinquished all connection with *T.P.'s Weekly* just before the Great War; see *Punch*, 24 June 1914, 481.

[105] *The Academy* had been bought in 1896 by the American patent-medicine advertiser John Morgan Richards, father of Pearl Craigie (who wrote as John Oliver Hobbes). See Alvin Sullivan (ed.), *British Literary Magazines: The Victorian and Edwardian Age, 1837–1913* (1984), 4–5.

[106] The award came as a shock to the penurious Conrad: 'When I opened the letter I thought it was a mistake,' he told Edward Garnett; but it had been Garnett who had puffed the book and its author in *The Academy* three months earlier. Sherry (ed.), *Conrad*, 14, 104–10.

simultaneously awarded a prize to Maurice Hewlett for *The Forest Lovers* (1898). Thus, *The Academy* shrewdly divined the literary market, identifying in Hewlett an immediate best-seller and in Conrad a long-term winner. At *T.P.'s Weekly* Whitten was given freer rein to his talent for popularizing literature; later he joined the *Daily Mail*, 1916–19, before moving on to found and edit *John O'London's Weekly*, 1919–36. This last enterprise, financed by Newnes, remained consistent with Whitten's mission: he told Neville Cardus, then making his first visit to London and applying for the job of sub-editor, that *John O'London's Weekly* was intended as a literary paper 'for readers not "high-brow", but eager to know their way amongst the masterpieces'. Cardus 'liked the look of Whitten's mild face and spectacles'; he also appreciated his whispered advice not to chuck in his prospects of rising on the *Manchester Guardian* when a Newnes manager was inveigling him to sign a contract.[107] Sidney Dark eventually joined Whitten on *John O'London's Weekly* after returning from Paris, where he had been reporting the Peace Conference. Before the War Dark contributed theatre and book reviews to the *Daily Mail* and *Daily Express*, but he regarded working with Whitten as special. He was 'one of the most attractive men of letters whom I have ever known', he remarked in 1925, and 'certainly among the half-dozen best writers of English now living'. Whitten talked just as well, most happily about books, and was 'a sound scholar with a vast amount of out-of-the-way information'. Moreover, though he found office work tiresome and was unpredictable in timekeeping, he was 'a master of accuracy, and no journalist was ever more careful to check his references'. Whitten was also modest in habits; it was certain, thought Dark, that he never had 'the slightest desire to dine at the Ritz'.[108]

J. A. T. Lloyd, who served as assistant editor of *T.P.'s Weekly*, 1903–8, was an unexpected complement to Whitten. From well-to-do Irish stock, Lloyd was schooled at Rugby and took a law degree from Trinity College, Dublin, but was otherwise unorthodox, having begun his journalist career in Canada with the *Toronto Week*. In the Edwardian period he cultivated a knowledge of continental European literature, publishing several books on Russian authors and translations from French. His second wife, whom he married in 1917, was the granddaughter of the Marquis de Peyronny.[109] Succeeding Whitten as acting editor of *T.P.'s Weekly* in 1911 was Holbrook Jackson. Possibly, it was his Liverpool upbringing that brought him into contact with O'Connor; otherwise, it was his adherence to *T.P.'s Weekly*'s belief in the magic of books. As a teenager he had been transported from Merseyside to the South Sea Islands. The vessel that bore him

---

[107] Cardus, *Autobiography*, 269–71.

[108] Dark, *Other People*, 214–16. Dark left *John O'London's Weekly* in 1924 to edit the *Church Times*. Whitten died in 1942. He had written a biography of Daniel Defoe but his main publications before the Great War reflected his love of the capital: *London Stories* (1911) and *A Londoner's London* (1913). In the 1905 *Who's Who* he gave 'perambulating London' as a recreation. Arnold Bennett also lauded Whitten as 'one of the finest prose writers now writing in English', in his *New Age* column, 4 Apr. 1908; *Books and Persons*, 3–7.   [109] Lloyd died in 1956: see *Who Was Who, 1951–1960*, 667.

was imagination in the form of a 'musty copy' of Herman Melville's *Typee* (1846), bought for 3*d*. from a second-hand bookstall by the Liverpool docks. Jackson was conscious that 'modern life is becoming too rapid for overmuch dalliance with books, and it becomes increasingly more difficult for bookish persons to catch up with the lost reading of yesterday'. Still, he affirmed, 'it is good to have dreams, and the dream of a holiday in a library is a very pleasant one'.[110]

It was Jackson's collaboration with A. R. Orage that was actually the making of him as a man of letters. Orage, born in 1873, was the older by two years. An elementary teacher in Leeds, he had been co-founder of a branch of the Independent Labour Party there in 1894; he contributed a book column for the *Labour Leader*, and lectured both for the ILP and for the Theosophical Society. Jackson also proclaimed himself a socialist, and it was he who introduced Orage to Nietzsche's writings at a time when Orage's thinking contained a volatile brew of Hindu mysticism and Neoplatonism. Their first meeting in 1900 was recalled by Jackson seven years later: 'You [Orage] left behind you that night, or rather the next morning, for we had talked the night away, a translation of the *Bhagavad Gita*; and you carried under your arm my copy of the first English version of *Thus Spake Zarathustra*.'[111] Jackson and Orage founded the Leeds Arts Club in 1902 as a forum for philosophical and cultural discussion; but in 1905 they moved to London, where they joined the Fabian Society and aimed to live by their pens. Within two years they were entitled to call themselves joint editors of a weekly, although that bald statement suggests a greater station than was the case. The weekly was the insolvent *New Age*, which Orage and Jackson rescued in 1907 on the strength of two donations of £500 each from Bernard Shaw and a sympathetic banker. Shaw had been attracted by Orage's expositions of Nietzsche—*Friedrich Nietzsche, the Dionysian Spirit of the Age*, and *Nietzsche in Outline and Aphorism*—and by Jackson's study of Shaw himself, published in 1907. The *New Age* was kept afloat only by inviting literary, artistic, and political controversialists to contribute articles free, because Orage and Jackson could not afford to pay contributors.[112] Orage's specified aim had been to turn the *New Age* into a 'socialist *Spectator*', but the open door meant accepting articles such as G. K. Chesterton's 'Why I am not a Socialist', published in the issue for 4 January 1908. Shaw himself was a regular—it was in the *New Age* dated 15 February 1908 that he defined the distinguishing marks of that newly discovered quadruped the 'Chesterbelloc'—and Wells and Bennett, and, later, Pound, Yeats, T. E. Hulme, and many lesser-known species of 'social reformers, economic wizards, votaries of philosophy, bores and cranks'[113] found space in the *New Age*'s columns. It made for liveliness, not coherence; but by now Jackson had relinquished his joint editorship and Orage was in sole charge. Jackson remained a steady Fabian, active in provincial

---

[110] Holbrook Jackson, *Southward Ho! And Other Essays* (1914), 5–16, 37.
[111] Holbrook Jackson, *Bernard Shaw* (1907), 12; quoted in Martin (ed.), *Orage*, 9.
[112] Michael Holroyd, *Bernard Shaw*, ii: *1898–1918* (1989), 192.
[113] Quoted in Sullivan (ed.), *Literary Magazines 1837–1913*, 251.

lecturing, whereas Orage spun away, seized by the possibilities of Guild Socialism and Social Credit.[114]

Jackson's assumption of the acting editorship of *T.P.'s Weekly* in 1911 represented that paper's highwater mark. Few journals establish themselves as permanent fixtures without effective management and renewed investment; and O'Connor's interest in his paper was now much diminished. According to Cecil Roberts, who had it from Jackson, with whom he became friendly from 1917, O'Connor 'was lazy and extravagant in his later years and left the running of the paper to Holbrook Jackson'; and this was no sinecure because 'O'Connor mercilessly milked his paper and there were recurrent crises when the printers refused to go to press unless their bills were settled.' Jackson himself had considerable business acumen, as his subsequent management of the National Trade Press showed: 'He presided ably over Board meetings, planning campaigns for advertising textiles, etc. His editorship of mammoth trade magazines showed his flair for lay-out, his high technical expertise in illustration and typography'.[115] This enterprise he combined with a passion for books, as collector and critic; and his permanent reputation as a literary historian was made by his study *The Eighteen Nineties* (1913). From 1914 *T.P.'s Weekly* was entirely in Jackson's hands as editor, and it was he who in 1916 changed its name to *To-day*, the title once used for the weekly founded by Jerome K. Jerome in 1893. The spirit of the new *To-day* was an astute combination of the two, updated for a cinema-going, gossipmongering, and fashion-conscious as well as reading public, being advertised as:

Books, Drama, Music, Picture-Plays, Poetry, Men and Women in politics, science and society. High-class fiction. The best short story weekly. Modes for both sexes. Cartoons by the world's best artists. The Chestnut Tree for after-dinner stories. Exposure of Shams, attacks on abuses. Virility without vulgarity. Jest, humour, fun and wisdom.[116]

Soon after, Jackson entirely refounded *To-day* as a new literary journal, both an outlet and review of contemporary letters. In this way the final curtain was brought down on *T.P.'s Weekly*. It had, however, occupied an important role in the diffusion of literary taste and culture over the previous fifteen years, and its contribution should be marked by historians.

IV

The standard format of *T.P.'s Weekly* included: a two-page 'Book of the Week' review, 'T.P. and his Anecdotage' (about literary-cum-historical curiosities), 'Books and their Writers' (extracts from new publications), 'Novel Notes' (short reviews of popular fiction), 'T.P.'s Bookshelf' (further brief notices of, usually,

---

[114] Martin (ed.), *Orage*, 7; A. M. McBriar, *Fabian Socialism and English Politics 1884–1918* (Cambridge, 1962), 182. [115] Cecil Roberts, *The Years of Promise* (1968), 202–4.
[116] Quoted in Charlotte C. Watkins, 'To-day', in Sullivan (ed.), *Literary Magazines 1837–1913*, 417.

anthologies, literary biographies, and memoirs), 'Literary Gossip' (combining book recommendations from other journals and what seem suspiciously like publishers' puffs), an editorial page of literary musing, a 'Books and Prints Values' column (answering readers' queries about the market worth of their possessions), 'Notes, Questions, and Answers' columns (where readers corresponded with each other about literary matters), 'Literary Help' columns (where readers' own literary efforts were, for a fee, appraised),[117] and 'T.P.'s Letter Box' (correspondence arising from previously featured articles). The articles numbered ten or a dozen per issue and, taking at random an issue five years from its inception, that for 1 November 1907 dealt with 'The Poetry of the 19th Century' (being the fifth of a series of twelve), 'English Influence on French Literature', 'The Spell of the Stuarts' (about Jacobitism), 'Some Popular Fallacies' (about medicine, animals, and the law), 'The Farthing Epic' (about Horne's *Orion*), 'Cameos from the Classics' (an extract from Bulwer Lytton's *Last Days of Pompeii*), 'The Woman's Wage' (the sixth of a series dealing with women's opportunities for employment, this on the Post Office and Civil Service), 'The Wisdom of Nietzsche' ('a quite alien theory of volition'), 'The Real Inventor of the Steamship', 'Five O'Clock Tea Talk' (about female dress), and 'Friends in Council' (life as a lady typist in Paris).

The feminine slant of several articles is striking. It was an emphasis of this period, eventually receiving the imprimatur of *The Times* on 1 October 1910, when it published (until Christmas) a weekly *Woman's Supplement*. Originally intended to be launched in early summer, it had been postponed out of deference to the mourning ritual imposed by the death of Edward VII. *The Times* then endeavoured to recover the momentum by booming its initiative:

It is intended that the *Woman's Supplement* shall deal with all the interests and activities of women, from politics and public work to domestic life and dress, and shall give expression to the aims and achievements in many fields by which the women of to-day are making the present age remarkable. Every educated woman nowadays reads her newspaper, and reads in it just those items of general information which her husband or father reads. For all that, she is often heard to complain that the interests of men alone, or of both sexes together, seem to fill the paper, and that there is little or no space left for the many events and topics which interest women alone.

That these events and topics are not confined to amusement and dress no one needs to be reminded; nor is there any call for a new journal devoted exclusively to that side of female life. At the same time, the day of the 'mannish' woman is over; and the best work, in the home and in the world, is being done by women who have no mind to unsex themselves and think it no sacrifice of self-respect to be agreeable company or to wear a becoming hat. The *Woman's Supplement* will be issued with *The Times* every Saturday. Its shape and size will be the same as those of the *Literary Supplement*, and its contributors will include writers and workers of both sexes.[118]

---

[117] For a parody, 'More Literary Help', see *Punch*, 21 Aug. 1907, 133.
[118] *The Times*, 19 Sept. 1910.

The Times was indeed making up for lost ground: in 1910 it was among the last, not the first, of papers to recognize the importance of its female audience. This step had been repeatedly urged on *The Times*'s manager. Always he had refused because he would not admit any difference between 'the reading requirements of an intelligent woman and an intelligent man. What are the subjects that appeal exclusively to women, and cannot come in the columns of *The Times*? I know of none but women's dress. I can see no reason why intelligent people should be divided according to sex than according to their height or the colour of their hair.'[119] This dignified position was wanting in business sense. In 1891, when invited by *Sell's Price Guide* to define the criteria for starting a successful halfpenny daily in London, W. T. Stead included these instructions among his editorial 'Ten Commandments': '5. Interest the women and elder children. From an advertising point of view the women are invaluable. The ordinary daily paper seldom touches the domestic side of life . . . 7. Publish a short story every other day, alternating possibly with a ballad or poem on a subject of the day.'[120] Stead was frank about the commercial advantages of securing a female readership. What he said soon became the common experience in the trade. Helena Swanwick had her eyes opened when she became managing editor of the female suffrage journal the *Common Cause* in 1909. She was straight away approached by an agent wanting to place advertisements for women's clothes and cosmetics. He intimated that the *Common Cause* should 'do something to help' through its editorials. Coldly explaining that theirs was a journal to promote women's concerns in politics and social reform, Swanwick rejected any arrangement, but their 'little talk made it clear to me why the "Women's Page" in most newspapers is so largely concerned with matters dealing with purchasable articles, even when the names of those articles are withheld'. Subsequently, she pondered the injurious consequences for women journalists that stemmed from these developments:

The segregation of men and women in journalism is as bad as it is elsewhere. The establishing by many newspapers of repute of a 'Woman's Page' has been a disaster for women who can write about other than the dedicated 'Women's subjects'. I know two distinguished woman journalists who complain bitterly that, whereas fifteen years or so ago, their articles were printed along with other 'Specials', since their paper had started a 'Women's Page', they were liable to be shoved in there, in company with antimacassars, and lip-stick and bead mats.[121]

It would be naive, therefore, to ignore the revenue motive in this bid for a female readership, yet wrong to suppose that no motive other than the mercenary was involved. Arthur Machen, whose supernatural tales appeared in magazine as well as book form in the 1890s, was told by one journalist: 'Always remember that we appeal not to the cabman, but to the cabman's wife.'[122] When introducing the

---

[119] Bell, *Moberly Bell*, 250.   [120] *Review of Reviews*, (Oct. 1891), 415.
[121] H. M. Swanwick, *I have been Young* (1935), 195–6, 234.
[122] Aidan Reynolds and William Charlton, *Arthur Machen* (Philadelphia, 1964), 40.

Star in 1888, O'Connor had proclaimed:

The charwoman that lives in St Giles, the seamstress that is sweated in Whitechapel, the labourer that stands begging for work outside the dockyard gate in St George's-in-the-East—these are the persons by whose condition we shall judge the policy of the different political parties, and as it relieves or injures or leaves unhelped their position, shall that policy by us be praised or condemned, helped or resisted.[123]

It was one thing to hold these groups' interests in mind, it was another altogether to include them in the readership; but this is what O'Connor also aimed to do with his *Sun* stable in the late 1890s.[124] One of the pioneer 'New Woman' novels, *The Story of a Modern Woman* (1894) by Ella Hepworth Dixon, was accorded the entire front page by O'Connor.[125] The clarion sounded by the heroine, Mary Erle, was a protestation of female mutualism: 'I can't, I won't, deliberately injure another woman,' she declares to the unworthy Vincent Hemming, who is trying to persuade her to elope to France, after he has contracted a loveless marriage to a vulgar heiress. 'All we modern women mean to help each other now. If we were united, we could lead the world,' she exclaims, choosing the course of unmarried independence, like the author herself, who identified this as the 'keynote of her book', 'a plea for a kind of moral and social trades-unionism among women'.[126] *T.P.'s Weekly* was generally pitched at that class of women who possessed some education and ambition of professional employment and independence. It did not neglect the plight of those in 'trade'— factories, shops, and domestic industry and service—and it sought 'to turn the attention of the sympathetic public to the increasing ranks of women forced into employment without adequate training, physique, or just conditions of work and wage';[127] but it was principally the aspiring class of New Woman which *T.P.'s Weekly* aimed to include in its constituency. Their growing presence in the workforce evidently brightened the lives of many men, authors included—at least, the successful ones who could afford their services. Barrie, in an aside in *What Every Woman Knows* (1908), describes Maggie Shann as being 'as neat as if she were one of the army of typists (who are quite the nicest kind of women)'.[128] That generic 'army' suggested a problem, however: there was rather a lot of them and they tended to be stuck in the ranks, not raised to officer class. Kate, the heroine of *The Twelve-Pound Look* (1910), is taunted by her former husband, the rich businessman Harry Sims: when he first knew her, she was a 'penniless parson's daughter' and now she was a 'typist at eighteen shillings a week!' 'Not a bit of it, Harry,' she retorts proudly, 'I double that'; but it is not the amount that

---

[123] O'Connor, *Memoirs*, ii. 255.   [124] Fyfe, *O'Connor*, 163.

[125] Thwaite, *Burnett*, 159, where this is cited, states that the paper was O'Connor's *Weekly News*, which I take to be a misidentification of his *Weekly Sun*. On Ella Hepworth Dixon, daughter of William Hepworth Dixon, the editor of the *Athenaeum* (1853–69), see Sutherland, *Companion*, 189–90, 606–7. She edited *The Englishwoman* until 1895.   [126] Quoted in Flint, *The Woman Reader*, 310.

[127] *T.P.'s Weekly*, 8 Nov. 1907, 610, referring to Edward Cadbury, M. Cécile Matheson, and George Shann, *Women's Work and Wages* (1906).   [128] Barrie, *Plays*, 377.

justifies her pride, rather that it is money she has earned. In their marriage she had felt her spirit crushed by his contempt for everyone and everything that was not measurable by his material standard. His idea of a wife was as a trophy doll bedecked with pearls whose only animation was to chorus his success. Kate eventually rebelled against ornamental uselessness and determined to prove her own worth:

It took me nearly six months; but I earned it fairly. [*She presses her hand on the typewriter as lovingly as many a woman has pressed a rose.*] I learned this. I hired it and taught myself. I got some work through a friend, and with my first twelve pounds I paid for my machine. Then I considered that I was free to go, and I went.

When she left him, Harry of course suspected all his male acquaintances. It was inconceivable that she had not left him for another man; and the symmetry of this crafted one-act play by Barrie is completed by the closing dialogue between Sims and his second wife. Kate has been sent by an agency to type replies to the letters of congratulation Sims expects to receive when his knighthood is conferred in a few days time; but Sims gets rid of her. He has not disclosed their relationship to his current wife. 'The person doesn't suit,' he says airily, adding, 'What a different existence yours is from that poor lonely wretch's':

LADY SIMS. Yes, but she has a very contented face.
SIR HARRY. [*with a stamp of his foot*]. All put on. What?
LADY SIMS. [*timidly*]. I didn't say anything.
SIR HARRY. [*snapping*]. One would think you envied her.
LADY SIMS. Envied? Oh no—but I thought she looked so alive. It was while she was working the machine.
SIR HARRY. Alive? That's no life. It's you that are alive. [Curtly] I'm busy, Emmy.
[*He sits at his writing table.*]
LADY SIMS. [*dutifully*]. I'm sorry I'll go, Harry. [*Inconsequentially*] Are they very expensive?
SIR HARRY. What?
LADY SIMS. Those machines?
[*When she has gone the possible meaning of her question startles him. The curtain hides him from us, but we may be sure that he will soon be bland again. We have a comfortable feeling, you and I, that there is nothing of* HARRY SIMS *in us.*][129]

The typewriter, apparently such a routine instrument, had become a symbol of feminist independence, and the clatter of its keys was to its operators akin to the sweetest notes produced by a virtuoso playing a Stradivarius. *T.P.'s Weekly* understood this, while not shielding women from the darker economic context. In 1907 it invited typists to consider bettering their prospects by secretarial work in Paris: 'Yesterday, the lady was practically non-existent in the world of business. Today, she not only is a reality, but, unfortunately, in most of our home markets,

[129] Barrie, *Plays*, 719–36.

she is nothing more or less than a drug. That is why girls of an enterprising and energetic turn look abroad . . . for the means of livelihood it is so very difficult for them to obtain at home.'[130] It recommended acquiring the Pitman's shorthand system, adapted to French.

The encouragement to learn foreign languages was pressed broadly by *T.P.'s Weekly* and not addressed only to these female readers. There was a regular pen pals' column, effecting contacts between readers for this purpose. Their zealousness was impressive, sometimes painful. *Punch* in 1906 seized on this from *T.P.'s Weekly* personal column: 'GERMAN, LATIN, and FRENCH.—P.V. would like to communicate with natives speaking the above languages.'[131] The paper also carried advertisements from firms offering foreign-language courses, by post, in small classes, and privately: Hugo's Language Schools, Rosenblum's Language Institute ('two free trial lessons in French, German, Italian, Spanish or Russian to any person mentioning *T.P.'s Weekly*',[132]) and the Swan–Bétis course. The co-author of the last, Howard Swan, contributed a two-part article on 'The Self Study of French', which recommended that, when the student was sufficiently advanced to tackle a novel, the best author to begin with was Dumas *père*.[133] The issue for 1 November 1907 contained an extract from Flaubert, in the original French.

T.P.'s Weekly, like many another magazine and journal of the day, carried advertisements of competitions, offering money and other prizes, in order to attract a readership. Periodically, it held a competition of its own. One sought the best explanation of some lines of Wordsworth, quoted in its series of articles on nineteenth-century poetry. The winner of the 1-guinea first prize on this occasion personified the self-improvement disposition: Norman (later Lord) Birkett, subsequently a Liberal MP, barrister, and judge. At this time Birkett had just entered Emmanuel College, Cambridge, at the advanced age for an undergraduate of 24, having left school at 15, served an apprenticeship in his father's drapery business at Ulverston, Lancashire, and studied at home with a view to joining the Methodist ministry.[134] Competitions involving some literary skill were widespread. The fiercest was found in the Saturday edition of the *Westminster Gazette*, which every fortnight for twenty years under J. A. Spender's editorship (from 1895) offered a 2-guinea prize for turning a selected extract of English poetry into Latin or Greek metre. Spender was a former Balliol classicist; the competition was set by

[130] *T.P.'s Weekly*, 1 Nov. 1907, 588.   [131] *Punch*, 21 Nov. 1906, 375.

[132] *T.P.'s Weekly*, 22 Nov. 1907, 678.

[133] Ibid., 6 Dec. 1907, 740, 752, and 20 Dec. 1907, 822, for further plugs of the Swan-Bétis courses. The issues for 24 and 31 January 1908, 108, 148, followed with a two-part article, 'Some Pitfalls in French'. O'Connor himself was fluent in French and German, an asset recognized by the *Daily Telegraph*, which employed him as sub-editor dealing with war news during the Franco-Prussian War of 1870 (see *DNB 1922–1930*, 643). He remained eager to acquire languages; for instance, before embarking on a trip to Scandinavia with his wife, during which they met Ibsen and the composer Grieg, he arranged for a Norwegian teacher to give him lessons; O'Connor, *I Myself*, 227.

[134] *T.P.'s Weekly*, 22 Nov. 1907, 668, for the winning entries to the competition; and *DNB 1961–1970*, 110–12, on Birkett.

a Brasenose tutor, H. F. Fox; and it was most frequently won by the Warden of All Souls, F. W. Pember. If this did not appear discouraging enough, the Saturday *Westminster* also ran other regular competitions, requiring original verse or prose to fit various models or metres, epigrams and epitaphs, aphorisms and parodies, all judged by Naomi Royde-Smith, the paper's uncompromising literary editor for a decade from 1912. Yet there were always sufficient contributions to occupy a page or two of the paper and, Spender commented, 'the English are supposed to be unliterary, but the impression I got was that there never could in any country at any time have been a cleverer group of young people'.[135]

At the other end of the competition quality scale were the many publications of Arthur Pearson, the Harmsworth brothers, and George Newnes, who, according to R. D. Blumenfeld in 1892, 'all base their fortunes' on the missing-word style of guessing game as a means of 'weekly circulation getting'. The prizes (and the publishers' gains) were funded by requiring each entry to be accompanied by a shilling postal order; and, Blumenfeld reported, 'Pearson says at one time the replies came in so thick and fast with shilling postal orders enclosed that it was impossible to keep control. Office boys were found with their pockets stuffed with postal orders. Those that were crossed they shoved down the drains and choked them up.'[136] The young Arnold Bennett and his family were enthusiastic (and successful) players of these games. When in 1893 missing-word competitions and their like were pronounced illegal as constituting a lottery and thereby inviting national degeneration, this judgement brought 'indignation and affliction into tens of thousands of respectable homes', according to Bennett's ringing declaration in *These Twain* (1916).[137] Perhaps it was just as well that a halt was called to the competition craze. *Punch* in 1890 thought that saturation point had been reached already:

This age has been called an Age of Progress, an Age of Reform, an Age of Intellect, an Age of Shams; everything in fact except it is destined to be chiefly remembered. The humble but frantic solver of Acrostics has had his turn, the correct expounder of the law of Hard Cases has by this time established a complete code of etiquette; the doll-dresser, the epigram-maker, the teller of witty stories, the calculator who can discover by an instinct the number of letters in a given page of print, all have displayed their ingenuity, and have been magnificently rewarded by prizes varying in value from the mere publication of their names, up to a policy of life insurance, or a completely furnished mansion in Peckham Rye. In fact, it has been calculated by competent actuaries that taking a generation at about thirty-three years, and making every reasonable allowance for errors of postage, stoppage *in transitu*, fraudulent bankruptcies and unauthorised conversions,

---

[135] J. A. Spender, *Life, Journalism and Politics* (1927), ii. 145–7.

[136] Blumenfeld, *R.D.B.'s Diary*, 61 (13 Dec. 1892). Blumenfeld later joined Pearson as editor of his *Daily Express* from 1904. See also Pound and Harmsworth, *Northcliffe*, 84–7, 94–9, 106–13, 140–5, on 'missing word' competitions and other prizes. Apparently, the 'greatest ever' competition, to guess the amount of gold coin in the Bank of England on an appointed day in 1889, elicited 718,218 postcards to the Harmsworths' *Answers*. [137] Pound, *Bennett*, 71, 76.

120 per cent, of all persons alive in Great Britain and Ireland in any given day of twenty-four hours, must have received a prize of some sort.[138]

Not all competitions had been organized by newspapermen. Jerome K. Jerome recalled how a 'wave of intellectuality' had washed across England in the late 1880s: 'A popular form of entertainment was the Spelling-Bee. The competitors sat in rows upon the platform, while the body of the hall would be filled with an excited audience, armed with dictionaries.'[139] *T.P.'s Weekly* also deployed gimmickry to rouse a readership, including inducements to buy particular publications. O'Connor himself plainly had commercial links to publishing firms. A popular fiction series was marketed under the generic title of *T.P.'s Sixpennies*; and articles in *T.P.'s Weekly* on nineteenth-century poetry, contributed by Laurie Magnus, did not disclose that its author was joint managing director of Routledge's.[140] But none of this detracts from the ethos of *T.P.'s Weekly*, which was that literature, and improving the mind, was fun as well as functional. Characteristic was the Christmas number for 1907, which contained 'A Scheme of Reading for 1908' by G. K. Chesterton,[141] and 'Mental Stock-Taking' by Arnold Bennett. The classics were made alluring, not forbidding, although the term 'classics' was sometimes generous: the Cameos from the Classics series between November 1907 and February 1908, for instance, contained extracts from Bulwer Lytton, Plutarch, Mrs Craik, William Maginn, Thomas Hughes, Longfellow, Thackeray, Richter, Gray, Napier, Carlyle, and Macaulay. Not having to pay royalties on most such books, publishers were now issuing them in cheap profusion. These were the days, Frank Swinnerton remarked, when Aristotle's *Poetics* was offered at 3d. Production costs were low, and sales high. In his influential articles, first published in *T.P.'s Weekly*, then issued as a working men's education pamphlet entitled *Literary Taste: How to Form It* (1909), Arnold Bennett gave 'detailed instructions for collecting a complete library of English Literature'. It comprised 204 authors in 352 volumes at prices ranging from 6d. to 7s. 6d. The total cost of this library was £26 14s. 7d., although it was understood that the thrifty working man could always pare down this sum by scouring street market stalls and barrows for second-hand copies.[142]

The variety of books then available is not always easy for us to grasp. Wilfred Whitten recalled once trying to get a second-hand bookseller to admit that he

---

[138] *Punch*, 4 Oct. 1890, 157.   [139] Jerome, *Life and Times*, 76.

[140] See the accompanying advertisements for the *Illustrated Chambers's Encyclopaedia* and for the Routledge list. On Magnus, who was formerly general editor of John Murray's educational publications, see *Who's Who* (1905), 1056. His son was Sir Philip Magnus, the historian.

[141] See Maise Ward, *Gilbert Keith Chesterton* (1944), 170, 186.

[142] See, for example, the reference to the book barrows at the pavement market between Farringdon Road Station and the Clerkenwell Road in London, *The Academy*, 1 May 1897, 478–9. In his regular books column in *The Speaker*, 31 Mar. 1902, Quiller-Couch extolled the Charing Cross Road bookseller Bertram Dobell: 'it was he who took arms the other day against the Westminster City Council in defence of the out-of-door stall, the "classic sixpenny-box"—and brought off a drawn battle' (repr. in Sir Arthur Quiller-Couch, *Adventures in Criticism* (Cambridge, 1924), 29).

could not sell some of the books displayed on his outside shelf. Whitten identified several likely candidates: obsolete multi-volume works such as Sir Paul Rycaut's *History of the Turkish Empire* (1679) or James Hervey's *Meditations and Contemplations* (1746-7), which 'seemed to be excellent for pressing trousers, but not otherwise useful'. But no; though the bookseller did not claim they would sell easily, sell them he would. Before 1914 there was no such thing as a dead book. Yet, Whitten added, a change would come about during the war when 'millions of old books went to the pulping mill. In the irony of Fate they were sacrificed when they were seen to be worth the paper on which they were printed.'[143] Whitten, whose hobby was walking London and scouring its bookstalls, was familiar with the trade. So was Arnold Bennett. While working as a solicitor's clerk, he had operated a postal business in second-hand books from his London lodgings.[144] And it remained a favourite subject, to which he frequently returned; in 1907, for instance, contributing to the *Evening News* articles on buying a library, and in 1909 for the *Reader's Review* on 'How to Use a Public Library'.[145]

Good books, Bennett observed, could be roughly divided into the inspiring and the informative; but his object was 'to encourage catholic taste, not exclusive taste'. Above all, to impress that Literature was Life:

Literature, instead of being an accessory, is the fundamental *sine qua non* of complete living. I am extremely anxious to avoid rhetorical exaggerations. I do not think I am guilty of one in asserting that he who has not been 'presented to the freedom' of literature has not wakened up out of his prenatal sleep. He is merely not born. He can't see; he can't hear; he can't feel, in any full sense. . . . The aim of literary study is not to amuse the hours of leisure; it is to awake oneself, it is to be alive, to intensify one's capacity for pleasure, for sympathy, and for comprehension. It is not to affect one hour, but twenty-four hours. It is to change utterly one's relations with the world. People who don't want to live, people who would sooner hibernate than feel intensely, will be wise to eschew literature. They had better, to quote from the finest passage in a fine poem, 'sit around and eat blackberries'. The sight of a 'common bush afire with God' might upset their nerves.[146]

Central to the Bennett brief were the classics: '*Your taste has to pass before the bar of the classics. That is the point. If you differ with a classic, it is you who are wrong, and not the book. If you differ with a modern work, you may be wrong or you may be right, but no judge is authoritative enough to decide.*'[147] This command about the classics was potentially alarming. A decade before, when some seven months short of his thirtieth birthday, Bennett had agonized about his own shortcomings:

The appearance to-day of the first volume of a new edition of Boswell's 'Johnson', edited by Augustine Birrell, reminds me once again that I have read but little of that work. Does

---

[143] John O'London, *Unposted Letters concerning Life and Literature* (1924), 152-4.
[144] Pound, *Bennett*, 80.   [145] Flowers (ed.) *Bennett Journals*, i. 237, 326 (20 July 1907, 29 Sept. 1909).
[146] Arnold Bennett, *Literary Taste*, ed. Frank Swinnerton (1938), 15-21. Bennett was quoting (actually misquoting) from Elizabeth Barrett Browning's *Aurora Leigh* (1856).   [147] Ibid. 50-1.

there, I wonder, exist a being who has read all, or approximately all, that the person of average culture is supposed to have read, and that not to have read is a social sin? If such a being does exist, surely he is an old, a very old man, who has read steadily that which he ought to have read sixteen hours a day, from early infancy. I cannot recall a single author of whom I have read everything—even of Jane Austen. I have never seen 'Susan' and 'The Watsons', one of which I have been told is superlatively good. Then there are large tracts of Shakespeare, Bacon, Spenser, nearly all Chaucer, Congreve, Dryden, Pope, Swift, Sterne, Johnson, Scott, Coleridge, Shelley, Byron, Edgeworth, Ferrier, Lamb, Leigh Hunt, Wordsworth (nearly all), Tennyson, Swinburne, the Brontës, George Eliot, W. Morris, George Meredith, Thomas Hardy, Savage Landor, Thackeray, Carlyle—in fact every classical author and most good modern authors, which I have never even over-looked. A list of the masterpieces I have *not* read would fill a volume. With only one author can I call myself familiar, Jane Austen. With Keats and Stevenson, I have an acquaintance. So far of English. Of foreign authors I am familiar with de Maupassant and the de Goncourts. I have yet to finish Don Quixote!

   Nevertheless I cannot accuse myself of default. I have been extremely fond of reading since I was 20, and since I was 20 I have read practically nothing (save professionally, as a literary critic) but what was 'right'. My leisure has been moderate, my desire strong and steady, my taste in selection certainly above the average, and yet in ten years I seem scarcely to have made an impression upon the intolerable multitude of volumes which 'everyone is supposed to have read'.[148]

Yet, in *Literary Taste* Bennett remained unrelenting. If the working classes were to acquire sophistication of thought and expression in order to better themselves and to take on the more privileged classes, not just as equals but as superiors, the classics were unavoidable. In making his selection, Bennett dispensed with the limitation of the hundred and confined his recommendations to *English* literature. Over a half of his recommended authors, and nearly 60 per cent of the recommended titles, were drawn from the nineteenth century. He stopped short of evaluating any living author: his list closed with George Gissing, who had died in 1903, recommending *Thyrza* (1887) and *The Private Papers of Henry Ryecroft* (1903) but not *New Grub Street* (1891). Thus Meredith, Swinburne, Hardy, Conrad, James, Kipling, Moore, Shaw, Barrie, Wells, Galsworthy, and Bennett himself, all were denied by the bar. Lubbock's original Best Hundred and most others' exercised the same restraint; but all such inhibitions were finally brushed aside by J. M. Robertson, who produced a series of articles, 'The Best Hundred Books of Today', for *T.P.'s Weekly* in 1908. This was in response to an appeal made by Richard Whiteing in an address delivered at the 'Tribune' Rendezvous, when he had startled the literary world by proposing, *inter alia*, that all books should be published for a penny.[149]

   That these two men, Robertson and Whiteing, should encourage popular intellectual body-building was highly appropriate. Both were examples of the self-educated who rose to public recognition, although their names may be little

---

[148] Flower (ed.), *Bennett Journals*, i. 18–19 (15 Oct. 1896).
[149] *Punch*, 18 Dec. 1907, 438–9, for a spoof discussion of authors' horrified reactions to this.

remembered today. Whiteing, the younger by sixteen years, was born in 1840, the son of a clerk in the Stamp Office. Motherless from infancy, he lived with foster parents and served a seven-year apprenticeship as a seal-engraver, attending also evening art classes and the Working Men's College in Great Ormond Street. Not prospering in trade, he went to Paris as secretary of an Anglo-French working-class exhibition in 1866. He later recalled that he travelled 'without a word of French, but with plentiful pigeon-German' acquired from another seal-engraver; but he soon did acquire French and began a career as journalist, becoming Paris correspondent for the London and New York editors of *World*, with a commission to rove and report from Europe's principal capitals. The *Manchester Guardian* also employed his services, and he remained based in Paris until 1886, when he joined the *Daily News* in London. He retired from journalism in 1899, the year he published his best-known work, *No. 5 John Street*, a condition-of-England novel in the form of a report to the Pitcairn Islands on the inhabitants of a London tenement, modelled after Swift and Carlyle. Whiteing wrote other books, a previous novel, *The Island* (1888), in which the Pitcairn fantasy formula was first etched; more novels, autobiographical recollections, a history of Napoleon's invasion of Russia, miscellaneous essays, and introductions to the work of Emerson and Thoreau. When Bennett came to know Whiteing in 1909 he found him 'old, deafish, a good quiet talker', still imbued with a passion for literature. Indeed, 'he had a sort of startled enthusiasm for "The O.W.T." [Bennett's *The Old Wives' Tale*, 1908]. He was half-way through it, and it appeared to have knocked him over quite.'[150] Whiteing's was a genuine, if not surpassing, achievement, all made possible by the world of letters; and he was incorporated into the *Dictionary of National Biography* following his death in 1928.[151]

Robertson was recognized in the same way. Born on the Isle of Arran in 1856, he left school at 13 and also graduated to journalism; but, unlike Whiteing, Robertson at the age of 50 became an MP and rose to junior ministerial level in the Asquith governments. More than that, Robertson was a controversialist, the successor to Charles Bradlaugh as leader of the British secularist and rationalist neo-Malthusian movements.[152] He was also a stalwart of the South Place Ethical Society and of the Rainbow Circle discussion group of philosophical radicals and progressives.[153] He wrote a substantial history of freethinking in 1899, and much

---

[150] Flower (ed.), *Bennett Journals*, i. 345 (21 Dec. 1909). The editor of the *Daily News*, A. G. Gardiner, ranked Whiteing, along with Augustine Birrell and John Morley, as one of the three best conversationalists, Whiteing because of 'the deep love of his kind that warms the generous current of his talk' (A. G. Gardiner, *Leaves in the Wind* (1920), 63–4).

[151] *DNB 1922–1930*, 907; also Sutherland, *Companion*, 671, and *M.A.P.*, 20 Feb. 1904, 213. He left effects probated at £1,302 9s. 7d. He was then resident at 35a High Street, Hampstead.

[152] Robertson wrote a substantial part of the official life of Bradlaugh, in collaboration with Bradlaugh's daughter Hypatia Bonner in 1894, dealing with his parliamentary struggles over the oath, his philosophy, and secular propaganda.

[153] See Michael Freeden (ed.), *Minutes of the Rainbow Circle, 1894–1924*, Camden 4th ser., 38 (1989). Robertson read twenty-two papers to the Rainbow Circle between 1899 and 1923, a total not exceeded by any other member.

else, which his admirer Professor Harold Laski evaluated in the highest terms:

He was recognized as one of the leading Shakespearean scholars of his time. He was a literary critic of distinction, and his *Modern Humanists* (1891) contains some of the best work done in Great Britain since Matthew Arnold . . . He did work of great importance in social science; his studies of H. T. Buckle, of the evolution of states, of German racial theories, of free trade, and thrift, are all remarkable alike for their insight and learning. It is, indeed, difficult to know what field of humanistic studies was outside his competence.

Having 'a certain irritated bluntness of manner', and holding no formal academic post, Robertson was not appreciated as he should have been, thought Laski; but, he predicted, 'his intellectual position will be much higher in the next generation than it was during his lifetime'.[154]

Robertson was thus well qualified to pronounce for *T.P.'s Weekly* on the Best Hundred Books of Today, given both his intellectual assertiveness and personal experience of that urge to acquire literary discrimination which motivated its readership. He had no snobbish animosity against the best-seller either, and once surprised Lucy Masterman by the manner in which he 'poured praise on *Sanders of the River*'.[155] Robertson remained, however, wary of giving an impression that the contemporary was to be preferred to the past:

we are faced by the fact that some old books are still powerful forces. To say nothing of the ancients, Montaigne, for instance, is still a cherished companion, influential on thought and conduct; Spinoza still deeply influences thought; and one of the prime favourites of our British generation, Omar Khayyám, dates in the original from the Middle Ages. We must allow ourselves a certain latitude, and we must recognize at the start that our set of a 'hundred living modern books' does not really compete with any 'hundred best books'.

In the same way, he added, many nineteenth-century authors, now dead, such as Goethe, Shelley, and Keats, 'are still truly modern'. There was yet another difficulty, the growth of academic specialization, a particular problem in the sciences: his list, therefore, 'must cater for the thoughtful "general reader", not for the specialist', and since this general reader was English, the foreign books must be available in translation. For the rest, the rule obtained that the scientific and philosophical books should be really important, not necessarily 'true' in regard to findings or doctrine but 'dynamic'—'those which stand for originality and stir or modify movements of opinion'. For it was the case, he argued, that the 'provinces in which our age was most notably innovated are those of physics, biology, and sociology'. The ructions these had made had left a lasting imprint on Britain's culture, so much so that 'the "modern" age has had to think out afresh its ethics, its metaphysical philosophy, its views on historical religion, and its views on

---

[154] *DNB 1931–1940*, 736–7. For a modern assessment, G. A. Wells (ed.), *J. M. Robertson: Liberal, Rationalist, and Scholar* (1987).

[155] Masterman, *Masterman*, 364. Edgar Wallace was the author of *Sanders of the River*, (1911).

education'. All these forces in turn meant that the modern age 'has had to prove its artistic vitality by renewing its poetry, its literary "criticism of life", its fiction and its drama'.[156]

There was an infectious confidence about Robertson's rationalist school that enthused rather than daunted the unqualified. Youngsters in Edwardian Britain who had little formal schooling but limitless curiosity really did feel fired by his example to enlarge their compass of understanding and to better their station. Neville Cardus, who was already beginning to teach himself about music, in his late teens compiled for himself 'a cultural scheme':

so many hours a week to that subject, so many hours to this. I decided that as knowledge was one and indivisible, each subject would need to be studied in relation to all or most others; Synthesis (said I to myself) was the thing. I came upon the works of J. M. Robertson, also once a poor boy who by self-education had made himself informed and critical far beyond the scope of most of the dons at the universities. Possibly in his Scottish zeal he went too far; he took all knowledge for his province, and in the course of a mortally-spanned life achieved two unprecedented feats of criticism. He attacked and exposed, by deductive and inductive reasoning, the historical authenticity of

(a) Jesus Christ

and

(b) Shakespeare

But he was stimulating, and his books served as my encyclopaedia . . . My Schema was drawn up so comprehensively that it involved metaphysics, with ethics and aesthetics correlated; sociology, economics, comparative religion and all literature.

Eventually, Cardus came to his senses:

I did not keep rigorously to the Schema, for one day I picked up a copy of Samuel Butler's Note Books and read the following: 'Never try to learn anything until the not knowing it has come to be a nuisance to you for some time . . . A boy should never be made to learn anything until it is obvious that he cannot get on without it . . . ' I have ever since acted more or less upon that wise saying. The older I grow the more it seems to me that miscellaneous education for the young is dangerous; it merely clutters up the untrained mind with information. Information can always be found in reference books.[157]

V

Less demanding pastoral duties were undertaken by Robertson Nicoll's pamphlet of October 1917, *A Library for Five Pounds*, advising how to make a cheap collection of the best books. It was Nicoll who had launched the sixpenny monthly *The*

---

[156] *T.P.'s Weekly*, 10 Jan. 1908, 41. The same, of course, applied to the other arts, painting, sculpture, architecture, and music; but these were excluded by the scheme, which was limited to books.

[157] Cardus, *Autobiography*, 54–6.

Bookman: A Magazine for Bookreaders, Bookbuyers, and Booksellers, on 25 September 1891, the first issue of which sold some 20,000 copies.[158] As editor of the *British Weekly*, the most influential Nonconformist periodical, Nicoll viewed *The Bookman* as an extension of his mission to rid religious Dissent of that reputation for philistine hostility to the world of culture and imaginative literature which the Puritan Commonwealth had won originally and which Matthew Arnold in *Culture and Anarchy* (1869) recently confirmed.[159] Nicoll believed that 'much more might be done in the way of uniting religion with literature';[160] and he had a high opinion of the role to be played in this by journalism. Nicoll was a counterpart to T. P. O'Connor in reckoning the journalists' power to shape opinion, a generation after the *Daily Telegraph* had transformed the market as the first major diurnal to sell for one penny. By the 1880s it claimed the 'largest circulation in the world', an average 'excess of half a million copies weekly over any other morning paper'.[161] Its impact was saluted in the melodrama *The Silver King* (1882), by Henry Arthur Jones and Henry Herman. 'That is all very well, but the Psalms and the *Daily Telegraph* are not the same thing!' says one devotee to another, who wants to read aloud a report from the paper as he does the Scriptures in church. Henry Nevinson, at the premiere, happened to be seated close to Matthew Arnold: 'It was all his own criticism in brief. How he laughed!'[162]

The rising influence of newspapermen was now reflected in the number of proprietors returned as MPs: an average of twenty-four at every general election between 1880 and the Great War, compared with an average of four in each parliament between 1832 and 1880.[163] They were joined by an average of thirty-one journalist MPs in every parliament after 1880.[163] In other respects too their prestige was being recognized. The first non-theological work that Nicoll published under his own name was *James Macdonell, Journalist* (1890). It was, he claimed, the first life of a journalist pure and simple ever written.[164] In this, as in much else, Nicoll showed his percipience, although journalists did not always treat each other with respect, let alone always act in ways that earned them public respect. In 1890 *Punch*'s cartoonist Harry Furniss clearly thought England's practitioners less gentlemanly than their French counterparts for the manner in

---

[158] Claude A. Prance, 'The Bookman', in Sullivan (ed.), *Literary Magazines 1837–1913*, 43–9.

[159] Darlow, *Nicoll*, 153–4, 165–6, 323–4.

[160] Valentine Cunningham, *Everywhere Spoken Against: Dissent in the Victorian Novel* (Oxford, 1975), 62.

[161] Viscount Camrose, *British Newspapers and their Controllers* (1947), 27.

[162] Nevinson's reminiscence, written in December 1922 on the centenary of Arnold's birth, reprinted in Evelyn Sharp (ed.), *Henry Nevinson: Visions and Memories* (Oxford, 1944), 32.

[163] Alan J. Lee, *The Origins of the Popular Press in England, 1855–1914* (1976), 294, 296.

[164] *Review of Reviews* (Jan. 1890), 77. Nicoll had just published a study of Tennyson in 1884, under the pseudonym Walter E. Wace. Macdonell died in 1879 at the age of 37; he had been a journalist with the *Aberdeen Free Press* and *Edinburgh Daily Review*, and editor of the *Northern Daily Express* before moving on to the *Daily Telegraph* and *The Times*. Nicoll claimed to have written the first biography of a journalist; Philip Gibbs, correspondingly, claimed to have written 'the first novel about Fleet Street behind the scenes'—a reference to *The Street of Adventure* (1909)—although his pride and royalties were dented when its authentic atmosphere generated libel actions; see Gibbs, *Pageant*, 68–70.

JOURNALISM IN FRANCE. JOURNALISM IN ENGLAND.
(A CONTRAST.)

FIG. 3.1. Harry Furniss spotlights subtle cross-Channel distinctions in journalists' styles of argument. *Source*: *Punch*, 4 October 1890

which they settled their differences (see Figure 3.1) 'Articles on journalists are becoming more and more the feature in the magazines,' noted the *Review of Reviews* in 1892, as it summarized currently running series on newspaper editors and leading columnists. The same was observed in 1900 by the Liberal politician and man of letters Herbert Paul: 'journalists have acquired a habit of talking about each other. Twenty years, or even ten years, ago, they were as little inclined to blow the trumpet of their profession—occupation they would have called it then—as the permanent members of the Civil Service, who, as the late Lord Farrer so admirably said, prefer power to fame'.[165] This was hardly surprising in view of the power of opinion formation they were believed to wield; and their salaries reflected this enhanced station. In the early 1890s the editor of a provincial daily, the *Yorkshire Post*, was paid £1,200 a year;[166] but regional dignity

---

[165] Herbert Paul, 'The Prince of Journalists', *Nineteenth Century* (Jan. 1900), repr. in Herbert Paul, *Men and Letters* (1901), 261–83. Paul's essay was chiefly about Jonathan Swift. For a snapshot of the editors of the leading dailies and periodicals in the mid-1880s, [T. H. S. Escott], *Society in London*, rev. edn. (1886), 139–44. [166] *Review of Reviews* (Apr. 1892), 372–3.

was rapidly being rivalled, even overtaken, by the ranks of feature journalists working for the popular press, as instanced by two members of Edward Hulton's team, who in 1891 were to join forces as co-founders of the Socialist *Clarion*: Robert Blatchford and Alex M. Thompson. In 1885, when Hulton bought *Bell's Life in London*, Blatchford was taken on at £4 a week to write a daily column of 'Notes on News', for which he adopted his afterwards celebrated pen-name 'Nunquam Dormio'; six years later, he was receiving £1,000 per year. *Bell's Life* was soon merged with Hulton's main paper, the *Sporting Chronicle*, and Blatchford became the principal writer on its sabbath stablemate, the *Sunday Chronicle*, which Hulton founded in 1886. Thompson, meanwhile, was contributing the 'Echoes of the Day' column to the *Sporting Chronicle*. Initially on £6 per week, Thompson was on £900 per annum before his thirtieth birthday. Blatchford recalled:

There was not a public-school man, nor a properly trained journalist among us, but because we belonged to the crowd and understood the crowd we knew how to amuse and interest them, and the paper sold like hot cakes. We had a splashy, jolly, colloquial style, an intimate style, which the strictly proper journals considered bad form. Our work was not so cheap as it seemed, though, and it suited our readers and our purpose; it had at least two merits: it was easy to read and easy to understand.[167]

With the advent of the New Journalism, commanding large sales, a revolution in some journalists' pay occurred. Sidney Dark, who worked for both Alfred Harmsworth's *Daily Mail* (established in 1896) and Arthur Pearson's *Daily Express* (established in 1900), reckoned that 'between the years of the founding of the *Daily Mail* and the Great War, Fleet Street salaries . . . must have increased by at least fifty per cent'.[168] The best-paid editor in 1900 was the *Daily Mail*'s, on £5,000 per year; ten years later over £10,000 was the norm for him and other successful editors. Misery aplenty existed: 2,100 out of 3,600 members of the National Union of Journalists in 1913 received less than £160 per year (the threshold at which income tax started), and there were many worse-paid casuals outside the union.[169] Journalists enjoyed little security or, putting it another way, greater mobility of talent between papers. The speed at which a man rose could be spectacular. According to R. D. Blumenfeld in 1901, Kennedy Jones, who ran the Harmsworth newspaper empire, had 'an income of at least £25,000 a year'. When Blumenfeld first knew him in the early 1890s, Jones considered himself 'prosperous on seven or eight pounds a week' working for T. P. O'Connor's evening *Sun*.[170] In 1909 Viscount Esher, the *éminence grise* of Edwardian court politics,

---

[167] Blatchford, *My Eighty Years*, 169–93; Alex M. Thompson, *Here I Lie* (1937), 40, 55, 62.

[168] Dark, *Other People*, 11–12.

[169] Lee, *Popular Press*, 109, 112. See also Clement J. Bundock, *The National Union of Journalists: A Jubilee History 1907–1957* (Oxford, 1957). The NUJ started with about 1,000 members in 1907, mostly men, though it admitted women. The cardinal qualification was three years' regular work as a journalist; and it specifically excluded newspaper proprietors, managers, and directors who, having been members of the Institute of Journalists (formed in 1890), had previously inhibited journalists' collective bargaining.

[170] Blumenfeld, *Diary*, 142 (2 Dec. 1901).

involved him in a campaign to pressure the Liberal Cabinet to build more Dreadnoughts. Jones, Esher wrote, 'was a compositor once. He is now worth several millions. He sees few people, but wields all the power of Harmsworth's papers.'[171]

It was a populist power wielded with an eye to the balance sheet. Janet Hogarth resigned as the *Times* Book Club's librarian in 1909, when Jones engineered a combination of all the circulating libraries, designing to appease the purity movement by banning or restricting certain novels that trespassed against conventional morality. 'Think of Kennedy Jones and the purity of literature,' Hogarth said scornfully to Horace Hooper, whom Jones had ousted from *The Times* after the Northcliffe takeover. 'Think of Kennedy Jones and literature, let alone purity!' was Hooper's even more scornful reply.[172] Jones himself exuded a machismo pride in this revolution. He told John Morley, 'You left journalism a profession, we have made it a branch of commerce.'[173] Until the advent of a cheap popular press with mass circulation, Morley had been one of the greatest journalist stars: editor of the *Fortnightly Review* (1867–82) and *Pall Mall Gazette* (1881–3), in which latter capacity he was paid £2,000 per year. He was also editor of the English Men of Letters series, and a famed biographer or exegetist of Burke (1867 and 1879), Voltaire (1872), Rousseau (1873), Diderot and the Encyclopedists (1878), Cromwell (1900), and Gladstone (1903). In his valedictory upon leaving the *Fortnightly*, Morley reported a fellow review editor telling him that 'he regarded himself as equal in importance to seventy-five Members of Parliament'.[174] Morley himself did not just rival political leaders, he became one. He was pitchforked into the Cabinet as Chief Secretary for Ireland in 1886, served in the same office in 1892–5, returned as Secretary of State for India in 1905–10, and became Lord President of the Council in 1910–14, complete with peerage. It was journalism that made both his reputation and fortune. In 1881, the year he published his life of Richard Cobden, Morley told the drama critic Joseph Knight, who had known him in his struggling days when he had used the pawnshop, that his previous year's income was £5,000; that is, equivalent to the Prime Minister's salary.[175] Less grandly, Charles Masterman became Parliamentary Secretary to the Local Government Board in 1908. His wife wrote: 'Financially the change was

---

[171] Maurice V. Brett (ed.), *Journals and Letters of Reginald, Viscount Esher* (1934–8), ii: *1903–1910*, 379 (31 Mar. 1909). See also Flower (ed.), *Bennett Journals*, ii. 222, for Jones's declaration that '*he* was really the parent of the new journalism'; and Bell, *Moberly Bell*, 304, for Moberly Bell's assessment in 1909 that 'Jones . . . had got his influence over Northcliffe by being always right in matters of finance.' The manager of *The Times* since 1890, Moberly Bell found himself eased out by Jones after Lord Northcliffe (the former Alfred Harmsworth) took over the paper in 1908. For vignettes of Jones's pugnacity and rags-to-riches ruthlessness, driving himself as hard as he did others, see Preston, *Memories*, 77–82, 212–13, 281.

[172] Janet E. Courtney, *Recollected in Tranquillity* (1926), 211.   [173] Lee, *Popular Press*, 104.

[174] John Morley, 'Valedictory' (1882), in Morley, *Studies in Literature*, 335–6. Morley himself thought that British journalists still exercised less influence than their counterparts in France.

[175] Gribble, *Seen in Passing*, 123. Cf. Morley's remark to R. D. Blumenfeld that 'a journalist's life is to be preferred to any other' (*R.D.B.'s Diary*, 120 (30 Oct. 1900)). For a profile of Morley by his one-time assistant on the *Pall Mall Gazette*, W. T. Stead, see *Review of Reviews* (Nov. 1890), 423–37.

negligible. He was making quite the £1,500 a year in journalism': this was as leader-writer for the *Daily News*, and contributor to *The Speaker* (later *The Nation*), *Independent Review*, *Albany Review*, *Athenaeum*, and more.[176] Robertson Nicoll himself did so well out of journalism that *Punch* paid him the backhanded compliment of dubbing him 'the most successful Christian of his time'.[177]

Nicoll's *British Weekly* had first appeared on 5 November 1886, subtitled 'A Journal of Social and Christian Progress'. From the start Nicoll included a literary section and in January 1887 initiated a series of articles by celebrities, among them Robert Louis Stevenson and Walter Besant on 'Books which have Influenced Me'. The *British Weekly* also published short stories and serialized fiction. Clement Shorter reckoned that Nicoll possessed 'perhaps the keenest scent for a book that will sell of any man in the book business'.[178] Heading Nicoll's list of literary discoveries was J. M. Barrie. He became a lifelong friend and described Nicoll as 'one of the few men I think I could travel with without wanting to push him over a cliff'.[179] Nicoll was proud too of his promotion of Ian Maclaren and S. R. Crockett, ordained ministers both, and principals in the 'kaleyard' (cabbage-patch) school of sentimental stories about Scottish small-town life, which enjoyed great vogue.[180] Nicoll's nose for talent reached beyond the obvious. He invited W. B. Yeats, as a 'distinguished poet', to advise readers of *The Bookman* about the disposition of the laureateship in 1892 at a time when Yeats's reputation was barely formed; and he encouraged Hodder & Stoughton to publish Yeats's play *The Shadowy Waters*.[181] 'He was a curious mixture of the practical, the ruthless, the devout, and even the mystical,' wrote the Revd R. J. Campbell on

---

[176] Masterman, *Masterman*, 104.

[177] Gardiner, *People of Importance*, 234. Success was Nicoll's chief measure of a man's character. Failure he attributed to want of brains or industry; and this attitude made him enemies. See the testimony of his elder daughter and nephew, in Darlow, *Nicoll*, 420–1.

[178] Darlow, *Nicoll*, 331.

[179] Barrie to Maarten Maartens, 17 Dec. 1893, in Meynell (ed.), *Barrie Letters*, 29. Barrie's first publication in a London paper was in the *St James's Gazette*, 17 Nov. 1884, and this encouraged him to move to London and try his luck as a freelance. The *St James's* editor, Frederick Greenwood, subsequently accepted about seventy articles from Barrie, about half of his total pieces published, over the next two years; and, at a retirement dinner for Greenwood in 1907, Barrie declared 'He invented me. I owe almost everything to him.' But all these articles were anonymous. Barrie's big breakthrough came when his articles were published under his name and these were for Robertson Nicoll, beginning on 1 July 1887. He afterwards wrote fifty or sixty articles for the *British Weekly*. 'Nicoll also set me to the writing of books and got them published, and for the rest of his life was the wisest and kindest of counsellors . . .' (J. M. Barrie, *The Greenwood Hat* (1937), 270, 284).

[180] And excited critical contempt, not just from metropolitan critics but from the Scottish realist school, epitomized by George Douglas, *The House with the Green Shutters* (1901). Douglas (George Douglas Brown (1869–1902); see *DNB Supplement 1901–1911*, i. 236) was a former Balliol man; and the question was judged sufficiently important to attract Oxford Union debate, R. C. K. Ensor defending the merits of the kaleyard school against the onslaught of John Buchan; see Smith, *Buchan*, 86–7. Also, Islay Murray Donaldson, *The Life and Work of Samuel Rutherford Crockett* (Aberdeen, 1989); William Robertson Nicoll, *'Ian Maclaren': The Life of the Rev. John Watson* (1908). Maclaren's best-seller *Beside the Bonnie Brier Bush* (1894) was published by Hodder & Stoughton, for whom Nicoll was publisher's reader. By the time of Maclaren's death in 1907 the sales amounted to 256,000 copies in Britain and 484,000 in America, 'exclusive of an incomplete pirated edition which was circulated in enormous numbers at a low price'; Nicoll, *Maclaren*, 168.   [181] Alan Wade (ed.), *The Letters of W. B. Yeats* (1954), 218, 322.

Nicoll's death in 1923.[182] Nicoll's worldliness was plain to those who had dealings with him. Keble Howard recalled his advice, following lunch at the Devonshire Club: 'Ye'll never have a great success with a book until ye kill a baby.'[183] Publicly, Nicoll's literary judgement was guided by ethical considerations. Thus H. G. Wells's *Tono-Bungay* (1909) excited his disapproval by its supposed sexual licence;[184] and he was loathe to recommend 'realist' novels except where their revelation of sin underlined the need for redemption. He was untroubled by the charge levelled against his friend Ian Maclaren's books, that their presentation of life was idyllic. They were so, he maintained, from clear choice and good purpose, not from ignorance of actual circumstances. They sought to expose 'the hidden beauty of the soul . . . the perennial nobleness and heroism of the homeliest human nature'. And, though they were religious in tone, Nicoll approved their undogmatic stance, showing most sympathy for Presbyterian Moderates and little liking for the narrower forms of sectarianism, whether extreme Evangelicalism, high Calvinism, revivalism and Plymouthism, or Modernism. 'Conduct, character—these were the great results and tests of true religion,' Nicoll proclaimed.[185] This critical standpoint erected no bar between editor and reader. The *British Weekly*'s readership, predominantly Nonconformist, included umpteen ordinary souls, such as a former naval rating-turned-postman whose Somerset village contained no library and whose wage would not stretch to buying new books. He therefore valued the *British Weekly* the more. Equally grateful was the Lancashire man who started reading the *British Weekly* as a newspaper boy, which 'gave me the taste for forming my own library, and also led me on later to read contributions by writers in the press you referred to. You were my Shepherd as far as reading matter is concerned. My actual education was very scanty, and I can safely say, without exaggeration, that I went to the *British Weekly* school.'[186]

All Nicoll's journalism was of a piece in the belief that 'in the great extension of reading and half-education among young men and many young women, there is a special necessity for knowing the books of the time'.[187] *The Bookman* supplied a classification of books published each month, articles, poems, reviews, brief notes, and features.[188] The first issue included a guide to Thomas Hardy's

---

[182] Darlow, *Nicoll*, 424.   [183] Howard, *Motley Life*, 254.

[184] Arnold Bennett ridiculed Nicoll's review in the *New Age* 4 Mar. 1909; *Books and Persons*, 114–16. Wells's dislike of Nicoll was expressed by his nicknaming him Dr Tomlinson Keyhole: Stephen Koss, *Nonconformity in Modern British Politics* (1975), 41.

[185] Nicoll, *Maclaren*, 179–80. Nicoll's 'Claudius Clear' column in the *British Weekly*, with its homilies and faux omniscience, earned him the spoof in *Punch*, 15 July 1903, 25: 'The Correspondence of Claudius Drear. Letters to British Weaklings'.

[186] Darlow, *Nicoll*, 425–6. Lloyd George always liked to keep in touch with Nonconformist popular opinion by reading the *British Weekly*. See Masterman, *Masterman*, 138, for her diary account of how, during the 1909 Budget crisis, Lloyd George motored around the Brighton suburban newsagents and failed to find a copy of the *British Weekly*, ending up with *John Bull*, *Sportsman*, and *Comic Cuts*.

[187] Letter from Nicoll to Dr James Denney, 1 Jan. 1897, in Darlow, *Nicoll*, 154.

[188] List of distinguished contributors, in Darlow, *Nicoll*, 101. *The Bookman* gave G. K. Chesterton his start in journalism, as a reviewer of art books when he was coming to terms with his inadequacy as

Wessex, an estimate of Kipling, recollections of the Carlyles and their circle, an account of Richard Burton at Damascus, an article on the provincial dailies, and an engraving of Tennyson as a young man. The second issue, for November 1891, continued the recollections of the Carlyles; and other features included the Brontës (with portraits) and Robert Louis Stevenson. It was an attractive mix and, for Thomas Burke, a teenager without many prospects but with secret desires of becoming a writer himself, it was the most thrilling of publications

I lived through each month for it; after each issue I was looking impatiently for the next. It was my only peep-hole into my own world—the world where I was at home, and from which, by my lack of this and that, I was as cut off as if that world were beyond the moon. In its gossip, its reviews, its portraits and other illustrations, its studies of the figures of English literature, and its publishers' advertisements, it was my Magic Lantern.

The walls of his bedroom in the first-floor lodgings which his parents rented in Geneva Road, Brixton, were hung with 'presentation plates from the *Bookman* of Lamb, Keats, Shelley, Coleridge, Milton, FitzGerald, Blake and Goethe'; and in the last year of his life, 1945, Burke could still recall particular issues—the Lamb number in March 1903 or the Hawthorne number in July 1904—and 'I know at once on what evening or morning I bought it, and what the weather was, what the events of the time, what was happening in the unquiet corners of my mind, what books I was reading, what story I was trying to write.'[189]

Nicoll had hit on a winning formula, and *The Bookman*'s fortunes were undisturbed when an apparent rival appeared in the shape of the *Times Literary Supplement*. The *TLS* actually catered for a different audience: the editor, Bruce Richmond, told one of his young reviewers, Virginia Stephen, in 1905 that it was 'an academic paper, and treats books in the academic spirit'.[190] Later it would style itself 'A medium of literary intelligence'. The *TLS* grew as a marsupial from the *Times* 'Books of the Week' section, edited from 1891 by James Thursfield, who gave way to Richmond after 1902.[191] Pressure upon space (particularly acute during the Boer War) and the incentive of publishers' advertising caused this development. In 1901 *The Times* had devoted 260 columns to book reviews,

---

an artist at the Slade: 'I need not say that, having entirely failed to learn how to draw or paint, I tossed off easily enough some criticisms of the weaker points of Rubens or the misdirected talents of Tintoretto. I had discovered the easiest of all professions; which I have pursued ever since' (Chesterton, *Autobiography*, 96–7).

[189] Burke, *Son of London*, 160–2. Bruce Cummings (W. N. P. Barbellion) was another regular reader of the *Bookman*; see Barbellion, *Enjoying Life*, 60.

[190] Virginia Stephen to Violet Dickinson, in Nicolson and Banks (eds.), *Flight of the Mind*, 188.

[191] Both were Oxford Greats men, Thursfield indeed a former don. Though the cloak of anonymity concealed most *TLS* reviewers' names (until 1974), university men from the start exercised considerable sway over the *TLS*; See *DNB* 1922–1930, 843–4 (Thursfield); 1941–1950, 307–9 (Gordon); 1961–1970, 881–2 (Richmond); and John Gross, *The Rise and Fall of the Man of Letters*, (1969) 326. Until his editorship of the *TLS* made growing demands on his time, Richmond was in the habit of dining weekly with old university friends when they would read together Greek and Latin authors. See Bailey (ed.), *Bailey Letters and Diaries*, 10–11, 53.

fifty-five of these to novels.[192] It could keep pace with the expanding literary market only at the cost of sacrificing its reputation as a journal of record; for instance, by trimming its parliamentary reports, and this it was not prepared to do. The *TLS* was issued free with *The Times* from 17 January 1902, and published separately, price one penny, from 19 March 1914, whereupon the cost of *The Times* also fell to a penny. The initial number of the autonomous *TLS* opened with the first instalment of Henry James's survey of the prospects for the novel, 'The Younger Generation'; and sales figures were given as 35,539. After ten issues (21 May 1914) these had risen to 45,000 but already, by the start of the Great War, they had dropped back to 43,000 and, by 30 December 1915, had returned to base, at 35,586. When the editor, Richmond, 'commanded . . . as by a sacred charge' George Gordon to write an article for the *TLS* about the *Essays of Elia* (1823, 1828, 1833) in 1920, he told him that 'Lamb is the only great English writer on whom . . . the Supplement had never had its say'—a mark then of its extensive coverage.[193] The *TLS* was belatedly endeavouring to bring academic authority and discipline to an exercise that had been, if not always in democratic hands, infused with a democratic purpose for the past thirty years; that is, a mission to furnish the mass of ordinary people with a critical appreciation of literature.

---

[192] Adolf Wood, 'A Paper and its Editors', *TLS*, 17 Jan. 1982. Also Derwent May, *Critical Times: The History of the Times Literary Supplement* (2001).

[193] Gordon to Florence Nixon, 17 Sept. 1920, in Mary C. Gordon (ed.), *The Letters of George S. Gordon, 1902–1942* (Oxford, 1943), 139. Gordon was then Professor of English Literature at Leeds; he succeeded Raleigh as Merton Professor of English Literature at Oxford in 1922, and became President of Magdalen College, Oxford, in 1928.

4

Reviews and Reviewers

The literary critic has become a man of mark on the newspaper to-day. He counts. He is no longer the cricket-reporter in disguise. He does not certainly gain the ambassadorial salary of the writer of the financial article. But he counts. He disports himself over three columns or so each morning. Of course, he is chiefly a critic of novels. It is useless for serious persons to gird against the 'tyranny' of the novel, to refer to it as light trash, to regret its vogue. If the novel is on top it has earned its place. It didn't fall up there by the force of gravity. It climbed there.

(Arnold Bennett, *The Tribune*, 6 Aug. 1906)

I

The Bookman and the *Times Literary Supplement* were purpose-built to review past and present literature; but even the most heterodox journals were conformist in conceding generous space to literature. The first issue of *The Anarchist*, 18 March 1894, trumpeted its master plan to destroy 'a corrupt and rotten society' by refusal of rent and universal strike, yet it also contained the serialization of a novel, albeit a turgidly didactic specimen by Henry Mackay. Several Bernard Shaw novels, *An Unsocial Socialist*, *Cashel Byron's Profession*, *The Irrational Knot*, and *Love among the Artists*, were serialized in socialist magazines between 1884 and 1888, after accumulating rejection slips from commercial publishers;[1] and the revolutionary communism of the Socialist League's journal, *Commonweal*, was made less minatory by the pre-publication serialization of William Morris's *Dream of John Ball* (1888) and *News from Nowhere* (1891). As for Keir Hardie's *Labour Leader*, that was positively bracing with A. R. Orage's weekly book column (1895–7); likewise Robert Blatchford's breezy *Clarion* was famous for entwining socialism with literature and other entertainment.[2] Ordinary newspapers were no less attentive.

---

[1] Holroyd, *Shaw*, i. 120.

[2] Circulation of these socialist papers was mostly small. That of *Commonweal* was about 2,800 in 1888 and entirely uneconomic. Morris subsidized it and the Socialist League to the tune of £500 p.a.; its end was foreshadowed in 1890 when Morris needed to retrench his expenditure by a half (letter to Bruce Glasier, 19 Mar. 1890, in Philip Henderson (ed.), *The Letters of William Morris to his Family and Friends* (1950), 321–2).

Henry Nevinson recalled of his time as literary editor of the *Daily Chronicle*, 1899–1903, that

in those fortunate days for literature it was a rather important position. Three whole columns of the paper were nearly always given to review or other literary subjects every day, and hundreds of thousands of people took the *Chronicle* for those columns and nothing else, to such a pitch of excellence had the page been raised by [H. W.] Massingham, its first editor, and by [Henry] Norman in succession.[3]

Much the same can be said of the *Daily News* when Archibald Marshall, Charles Masterman, R. A. Scott-James, and Robert Lynd were the literary editors.[4] Not that their position was sheltered from political waves. Both the *Daily Chronicle* and the *Daily News* were subject to changes of ownership as a consequence of the Liberal Party's divisions about the Boer War and direction of policy; and literary editors came and went with the tide.

The advent of the reviewer as a power in literature can be dated fairly precisely, correlated with emergence of the monthly periodicals the *Edinburgh Review* (1802) and the *Quarterly Review* (1807). R. C. K. Ensor, surveying 'the channels by which a public opinion has been formed about books', noted that in the eighteenth century 'the fate of books was not decided by reviewers'. Most books then were published by subscription. These circulated among a restricted class and were puffed by patrons of good standing, aristocratic, prelatical, and political. The poet William Cowper, in his letters from 1782, signalled the arrival of reviewers of new books but paid no regard to their opinions. Things had changed by 1819 when 'the *Quarterly Review* published the article [by J. W. Croker] which was widely supposed to have killed Keats. It makes no difference for our purpose that he in fact died from other causes; what is relevant is that so many of his friends (including Shelley) believed that a review could kill an author—a notion hardly conceivable in Cowper's day.'[5] Reviewing grew in scale thereafter, *pari passu* with the expanding market for novels and other literature, and with the introduction of weekly journals such as the *Athenaeum* (1828). By the late nineteenth century the review had become ubiquitous, in the daily press and magazine alike.

This quantity is easy to recognize, but the importance and quality of book reviews and literary essays are difficult to appraise. In 1917 Arnold Bennett

---

The exception was the *Clarion*, started in 1891, which enjoyed a weekly circulation of about 34,000, shooting up to 60,000 and more with the success of Blatchford's articles on socialism. These were printed separately in 1893 as *Merrie England*; the penny edition, published in 1894, sold over 2 million copies in Britain, America, and elsewhere in translation. See R. C. K. Ensor's notice of Blatchford in *DNB 1941–1950*, 86–7; Blatchford, *My Eighty Years*, 196–7; and Thompson, *Here I Lie*, 100–4, 116.

[3] Henry W. Nevinson, *Fire of Life* (1935), 82. Philip Gibbs, who at the age of 16 (in 1893) had his first article published by the *Daily Chronicle* and who afterwards worked for the paper, described it as 'then the most literary newspaper in London' (Gibbs, *Pageant*, 16).

[4] Marshall, *Out and About*, chs. v–vi; also *DNB 1941–1950*, 542–3 (for Lynd), and *DNB 1951–1960*, 872–3 (for Scott-James); Masterman, *Masterman*, 50; Koss, *Fleet Street Radical*, 57–60.

[5] R. C. K. Ensor, 'The Diffusion of Ideas', in G. F. J. Cumberlege (ed.), *Essays Mainly on the Nineteenth Century Presented to Sir Humphrey Milford* (Oxford, 1948), 83.

nominated the *Manchester Guardian* as the newspaper that 'publishes the most fastidious and judicious literary criticism in Britain'; but this verdict was given as part of a promotion for his friend Frank Swinnerton, who combined novel-writing with reviewing for the *Manchester Guardian* and work as publisher's reader for Chatto & Windus.[6] In any case, the most discriminating criticism was not necessarily the most influential. The one-time editor of the *Daily Mail's* literary supplement Archibald Marshall set 'apart altogether from the serious critics...men like T. P. O'Connor and Robertson Nicoll and Clement Shorter, who long ago discovered the news value of books; their names were known, and they did well out of their discovery'.[7] Though none made a lasting mark in the annals of literary criticism, it would be a serious neglect if historians ignored their influence. In 1950 the publisher Newman Flower specifically recalled O'Connor's significance, noting that he 'must have reviewed nearly as many books as there are stars in the sky. In the years of his powers—and I am now writing about those times when he edited *M.A.P.* at the beginning of this century, T.P. was a great critic. He could then make a book.'[8] In their respective periodicals—O'Connor in *T.P.'s Weekly* and *M.A.P.*, Nicoll in the *British Weekly* and *The Bookman*, Shorter in the *Sphere*, *Sketch*, or *Illustrated London News*—it was their huckster's style in booming the Book of the Week, Book of the Month, or Novel of the Season, as much as their literary 'misjudgements', which so offended the sensitive.[9] Not that the rest of the press had shunned this format. In *Punch* in 1888 George Du Maurier cartooned 'A Slave of Fashion', in which a lady subscriber to a circulating library asks the dumbstruck assistant, 'What kind of books are read this season?'[10] Arnold Bennett remembered the late 1890s, 'when it was part of my duty as a serious journalist to finish at Christmas a two-thousand word article, full of discrimination as fine as Irish lace, about the fiction of the year; and other terrifying specialists were engaged to deal amply with the remaining branches of literature.' Gradually, such spaciousness was trimmed and, by the New Year 1911, 'many newspapers dismissed the entire fiction of 1910 in a single paragraph', the literary critics operating like racing tipsters, simply listing this or that title as being among the likely books of the year. Usually, these were books published during the

---

[6] Frank Swinnerton, *Arnold Bennett: A Last Word* (New York, 1978), 114. Bennett did not, of course, always approve of the *Manchester Guardian's* judgements, for instance, objecting to its puffery of A. F. Wedgwood's *The Shadow of a Titan* (1910) and, most of all, to the prominence it gave to Mrs Humphry Ward's *Diana Mallory* (1908) by reviewing it on the leader page. But, then, Mrs Ward was a novelist whom Bennett loved to hate. *New Age*, 3 Oct. 1908 and 25 Aug. 1910, in Bennett, *Books and Persons*, 47–52, 237–8.

[7] Marshall, *Out and About*, 328.

[8] Flower, *Just as it Happened*, 228. Cf. Arnold Bennett's verdict after O'Connor dined with him in Paris: 'We came back here and went through a lot of my books. He proved himself at once a fairly accomplished bookman. But late in the evening when we were talking about religion, Malthusianism, etc. I discovered that in some matters his ideas were a strange mixture of crudity and fineness' (Flower (ed.), *Bennett Journals*, i. 229–30 (20 Feb. 1906)).

[9] 'The Novel of the Season', *New Age*, 11 July 1908, in Bennett, *Books and Persons*, 26–9. Shorter's style of reviewing was parodied in Max Beerbohm, *A Christmas Garland* (1912), with introd. by N. John Hall (New Haven, 1993), 65.   [10] *Punch*, 24 Nov. 1888, 250.

autumn season, the critic careless that earlier in the year he had pronounced 'several books as being "great", "masterly", "unforgettable", "genius"'. Bennett added tartly: 'No author, and particularly no novelist who wishes to go down to posterity, should publish during the spring season; it is fatal.' In any case, newspapers were now more interested in nominating the motor car rather than the novel of the year.[11]

At the New Vagabonds Club in 1897, in a speech responding to a dinner in his honour, H. G. Wells had taken on the reviewers with all the confidence of a 30-year-old who had become famous overnight with the publication of *The Time Machine* (1895). He developed a horticultural metaphor. After comparing new authors to seedlings, he classified reviewers as: slug-reviewers, who preyed on the first tender leaves of authors; bird-reviewers, who pecked damagingly here and there; and heavy-reviewers, who crushed with their boots whole beds of shoots. Wells further complained of reviewers' habits of irrigation: some drenched writers with flattery so copious as to rot their roots, while colleagues so withheld encouragement that plants dried up. Others too observed that not all was right in Literature's herbaceous borders. The paying public now had admission to this market garden and influenced what was displayed and deemed fine. In particular, the public had an eye for the tawdry and indecent, its prurience excited by reviews that attacked books for their supposed immorality. Thomas Hardy, though hurt by what he regarded as misrepresentations of *Tess of the D'Urbervilles* (1891) by reviewers in the *Saturday Review, The Spectator*, and the *New Review*, benefited by increased sales because of the attention drawn to his questionable ethics.[12] When he repeated the exercise with *Jude the Obscure* (1895) and was execrated as an advocate of free love, 'the unexpected result . . . is that I am overwhelmed with requests for stories to an extent that I have never before experienced—though I had imagined before publishing it that it wd. considerably lower my commercial value'.[13]

Carlyle had exercised his power of prophecy about this in 1856. He wrote wrathfully to the poet Coventry Patmore, who shared his forebodings about a democratic degradation of literary standards:

The Public of readers, now that everybody has taken to read, and whosoever has twopence in his pocket to pay into a Circulating Library, whether he have any fraction of wit in his head or not, is a sovereign Rhadamanthus of Books for the time being, has become more astonishing than ever! Probably, there never was such a *Plebs* before, entitled to hold up its thumb with *vivat* or *pereat* to the poor fencers in the Literary Ring. The only remedy is, not to mind them; to set one's face against them like a flint: for they cannot kill one, after all, though they think they do it . . . Unhappily the reviewer too is

[11] *New Age*, 12 Jan. 1911, in Bennett, *Books and Persons*, 289–90.

[12] See Hardy's letter to Tillotson & Son, 18 Jan. 1892, remarking on 'the unexpected success of my new novel', and to Edward Clodd, 4 Feb. 1892, noting that 'there is no check to the sale of the book. Mudie keeps ordering more and more—and others *pari passu*' (Purdy and Millgate (eds.), *Hardy Letters*, ii. 253, 257).

[13] Hardy to Florence Henniker, 1 June 1896, in Purdy and Millgate (eds.), *Hardy Letters*, ii. 122.

generally in the exact ratio of the readers, a dark blockhead with braggartism superadded; probably the supreme blockhead of blockheads, being a vocal one withal, and conscious of being *wise*. Him we must also leave to his fate: an inevitable phenomenon ('like people, like priest'), yet a transitory one, he too.[14]

In 1902 John Galsworthy, meditating about Andrew Lang's recently published essay 'Literature in the Nineteenth Century', thought that the best point he made about the reviewer's role was that 'a Critic can only say what pleases him personally'. Galsworthy therefore believed that 'bitterness in attack' was uncalled for.[15] This raises questions of personal interest and of how books were allocated for review. In his autobiography Anthony Trollope averred that 'much of the literary criticism which we now have is very bad indeed;—so bad as to be open to the charge both of dishonesty and incapacity. Books are criticised without being read,—are criticised by favour,—and are trusted by editors to the criticism of the incompetent.' Trollope advocated signed articles and reviews. He initiated this practice as a co-founder of the *Fortnightly Review* in 1865, in this following *Macmillan's Magazine*, of which David Masson was first editor (1859–68).[16] The same rule was adopted in 1877 by the founding editor of the *Nineteenth Century*, James Knowles, who over the next twenty-five years allowed only four pseudonyms, one, to his chagrin, being William Sharp masquerading as Fiona Macleod.[17] Anonymity was anathema to those who liked the sound of their own voice; and in the Edwardian period G. K. Chesterton was megaphonic. A robust populist, he liked to frighten readers with the threat to democracy inherent in a 'secret society' of anonymous journalism. He was prepared to allow it for leading articles, otherwise not; moreover, he insisted that 'the name of the proprietor as well as the editor should be printed upon every paper' and, where the paper was corporately owned, a list of the shareholders published, so that readers could see whose interest was being served.[18] There were, however, drawbacks attending this principle of openness. Trollope understood that the 'ordinary reader would not care to have his books recommended to him by Jones'. The attractiveness of anonymous reviewing was that 'the recommendation of the great unknown comes to him with all the weight of *The Times*, the *Spectator*, or the *Saturday*'.[19] When the reviewer of a book or writer of an article went unnamed, the self was suppressed and the duty of serving a higher public authority and upholding

---

[14] Carlyle to Patmore, 9 Aug. 1856, in Basil Champneys, *Memoirs and Correspondence of Coventry Patmore* (1900), ii. 312–13. Previously, in 1831, Carlyle had deplored 'the prevalence of Reviewing' as disclosing 'the diseased self-conscious state of Literature'. Then, he was tilting against the prestige of reviews such as the *Edinburgh, Quarterly*, and *Blackwood's*, and also against Romantic introspection. See Thomas Carlyle, *Critical and Miscellaneous Essays* (1872), iv. 21–2; and, for the context, Gross, *Man of Letters*, chs. 1–2.

[15] Galsworthy to Garnett, 11 May 1902, in Edward Garnett (ed.), *Letters from John Galsworthy 1900–1932* (1934), 39. Lang made a similar declaration in *Adventures among Books* (1905), 4: 'In literature, as in love, one can only speak for himself.'   [16] Sullivan, *British Literary Magazines 1837–1913*, 215–19.

[17] Priscilla Metcalf, *James Knowles: Victorian Editor and Architect* (Oxford, 1980), 284.

[18] G. K. Chesterton, *All Things Considered* (1908), 7, 164–6.

[19] Anthony Trollope, *An Autobiography* (1946), 175.

ethical standards and artistic canons was more easily fulfilled; that at any rate was the ideal of literary critics who perceived their function as a Coleridgean clerisy. There were other justifications; for example, the impersonal rule provided cover for contributions from public leaders such as politicians and churchmen, and from experts in various fields—scientists, doctors, architects, and civil servants—who otherwise would be bound to silence by professional etiquette.[20] Less nobly, the anonymous and pseudonymous system licensed personal attacks and permitted mercenaries to review the same work in different publications.

John Morley pondered these questions as departing editor of the *Fortnightly* in 1882. He had not been so insistent as his predecessor, George Henry Lewes, in applying the rule of signed articles. While admitting the moral superiority of attribution, Morley noted that 'one indirect effect . . . [of] the new system is its tendency to narrow the openings' for unknown writers. Faced with 'two articles of equal merit an editor would naturally choose the one which should carry the additional recommendation of a name of recognised authority'. Editors would have no inducement to discover new talent, rather 'to find as many authors as possible whom the public has already discovered and accepted for itself'. There were other considerations. Under the anonymous system, editors intervened more, amending, even mutilating articles because it was the journal itself, not individual authors, whose reputation was at stake. Moreover, habit and temper varied greatly: 'Some men write best when they sign what they write; they find impersonality a mystification and an incumbrance; anonymity makes them stiff, pompous, and over-magisterial. With others, however, the effect is just the reverse. If they sign, they become self-conscious, stilted, and even pretentious; it is only when they are anonymous that they recover simplicity and ease.' In any case, Morley reckoned, 'it is impossible for a writer of real distinction to remain anonymous. If a writer in a periodical interests the public, they are sure to find out who he is.'[21]

These arguments and animadversions were pitched at too high a level so far as most novelists were concerned. The risible incompetence of reviewers constituted one feature of a semi-autobiographical story by J. M. Barrie, 'Four-in-Hand Novelists', in 1893;[22] but it was the corruption of the system that most exercised others. A good many reviewers, it was alleged, were simply publishers' salesmen in disguise. In 1884 Edmund Gosse privately denounced 'the undignified modern system of arranging beforehand for the review of books'; later he fell out with Northcliffe, for whom he had been editing *Books*, the *Daily Mail*'s halfpenny, four-page literary supplement, because, he maintained, the reviewing was superficial and venal, dictated by commercial puffery at the behest of particular

---

[20] David Vincent, *The Culture of Secrecy: Britain, 1832–1998* (Oxford, 1998), 65–6, sets the issue in the wider context.
[21] Morley, 'Memorials of a Man of Letters' (1878) and 'Valedictory' (1882), in Morley, *Studies in Literature*, 300–8, 328–34. [22] Barrie, *Two of Them*, 255–62.

publishers.[23] In his memoirs the novelist Archibald Marshall, who was Gosse's assistant editor on *Books* and who briefly took it over after Gosse's departure, presented Gosse's disagreement with Northcliffe more as an upmarket–downmarket confrontation than as a question of ethics.[24] Yet, Marshall also observed that Northcliffe was friendly with the publisher Heinemann and that publishers paid a lower advertising rate in a large circulation paper such as the *Daily Mail*. In 1907 the decision was taken to close *Books* (which was costing Northcliffe £20,000 a year) when 'it had been proved to be not worth while to sell them [publishers] space that could be used to bring in more money'.[25] In his resignation letter Gosse gave Northcliffe reasons other than a troubled conscience as causing his decision to quit: 'In a less depressed time of the publishing trade, and when there are fewer distracting and depressing influences abroad, I am sure that our experiment would have had a commercial success. In younger hands than mine, it may have.'[26] Scribes also protested their innocence. Sidney Dark, who wrote theatre criticism and book reviews for the *Daily Mail* (and for the *Daily Express*), denied that he was ever given editorial or proprietorial directions about what to write.[27] Still, it is not difficult to cite an instance of Northcliffe exercising arbitrary authority. In 1913 he took against Keble Howard's *Lord London*, a novel based on Northcliffe's career, which Chapman & Hall published. The *Daily Mail's* former drama critic, Howard specialized in writing light sketches. He disclaimed any intent to disparage Northcliffe, but Northcliffe was furious at what he considered an insulting portrayal of his father. He instructed his newspapers, which now included *The Times*, to ostracize all Chapman & Hall publications. Their books were not even listed, let alone reviewed, and their advertisements were refused. Chapman & Hall submitted. *Lord London* was suppressed and Howard, after threatening legal action, was bought off for £150.[28]

[23] Ann Thwaite, *Edmund Gosse: A Literary Landscape 1849–1928* (Oxford, 1985), 428–30, 533. The first issue of *Books* appeared on 27 October 1906.
[24] Marshall aimed to employ more popular reviewers and columnists, Ford Madox Hueffer [Ford], Barry Pain, and G. K. Chesterton; yet, the evidence is not conclusive that Gosse courted the recherché. Robbie Ross was one of his contributors (Maureen Borland, *Wilde's Devoted Friend: A Life of Robert Ross, 1869–1918* (Oxford, 1990), 114, 117), but Gosse rejected Arthur Symons's poem 'Japan', to Symons's great disgust (Beckson, *Symons*, 281–2). Thomas Hardy's poem 'Autumn in My Lord's Park', was published by Gosse in the 17 November 1906 issue; subsequently, Hardy tried to interest Marshall in publishing work by Florence Dugdale, whom Hardy was to marry in 1914; Purdy and Millgate (eds.), *Hardy Letters*, iii. 232–3, 235, 261–2.
[25] Marshall, *Out and About*, chs. ix–xi, for his account of *Books*; and Sandra Kemp, Charlotte Mitchell, and David Trotter (eds.), *Edwardian Fiction* (Oxford, 1997), 268–9, for Marshall (1866–1934).
[26] Pound and Harmsworth, *Northcliffe*, 300.   [27] Dark, *Mainly about Other People*, 20.
[28] J. Don Vann, 'Chapman and Hall', in Anderson and Rose (eds.), *British Literary Publishing Houses*, 107–8; and Pound and Harmsworth, *Northcliffe*, 450. Keble Howard's account in *My Motley Life*, 185–8, is strange. His aim in writing the novel was, he attested, to provide 'a true and sympathetic picture' of a man whom the envious decried as 'tyrannical, ignorant, mean, and so forth'; and he cited reviews from the *Standard* and the *Guardian* praising *Lord London* as a self-help guide for young men to acquire wealth and power. Howard blamed Northcliffe's acolytes for misrepresenting his story in a cable to their chief while he was in America, whereupon Northcliffe acted to block it. When Northcliffe actually read *Lord London*, he was not offended, Howard maintained: 'I have a letter from him in which he says "I am not a bit cross

As founder and leading light of the Society of Authors, Walter Besant might be thought to have been in the know about what went on. He made outspoken criticisms of the reviewing trade in his posthumously published autobiography in 1902. He deplored how too many 'trashy novels' were noticed. Space instead should have been allocated to a serious appreciation of 'a work of art' by a reviewer cognizant of 'what the canons of criticism mean'. Worse was the practice among editors of ignoring the 'personal element' which swayed reviewing: 'He allows the log-roller to praise his own friends and the spiteful and envious failure to abuse his enemies.'[29] The poet–novelist Richard Le Gallienne was considered generous to a fault as a reviewer in the 1890s; but at least he was funny—or brass-necked—about it, having adopted 'Log Roller' as his nom de plume. He combined reviewing with acting as literary adviser to Elkin Mathews and John Lane at the Bodley Head. Examples of sterling probity could be cited in counterbalance, albeit more easily from the past than current. When the poet T. K. Hervey, who edited the *Athenaeum* (1846–53), invited David Masson to become a reviewer, it was his absolute independence that he emphasized: 'If I send you a book by my own brother, and you do not like it, you are to say so frankly.'[30] The question is, which was the common practice? On Besant's death in 1901, his Hampstead neighbour Robertson Nicoll wrote: 'He hated the clique system which is still a considerable evil in London literary life, though it seems to me that it is diminishing. Sir Walter Besant did not think it was diminishing, however; in fact the last time I saw him he said he feared it was increasing.'[31] Umpiring this difference is a difficult job. Nicoll himself was both a publisher's reader and a spider in the reviewing web; and Besant's complaint may have been a touch too autobiographical. Shan Bullock, brooding in late life about his own failure to make much reputation or money by his stories, recalled that 'Sir Walter Besant who succeeded well in his heyday lived to see his books hawked from publisher to publisher & himself in penury.'[32] That was to paint the transition in strong colours; but it was true that Besant's novels passed out of popularity, and this probably affected his judgement about the ascendancy of 'trashy novels'. The intellectual content of Besant's own work was not obvious. The poet Ernest Dowson, whose ideal novelists were George Meredith and Henry James ('the Master'), together with Turgenev and assorted French models, Balzac, Stendhal, Flaubert, Maupassant, and Zola, disparaged Besant and his once regular co-author James Rice as 'Besant and Rice pudding'. 'How my soul abhors the blatant good-humoured self-satisfaction of Besant and his school,' he exclaimed in 1889.[33]

about it", and a copy of another letter in which he writes that he would be quite willing for the book to be re-published with a few lines expunged.' The last words of that sentence rather give the lie to the rest.

[29] Sir Walter Besant, *Autobiography*, ed. S. Squire Sprigge (1902), 194–5.

[30] W. Robertson Nicoll, *A Bookman's Letters* (1913), 81.   [31] Ibid. 152.

[32] Shan Bullock to Sir Horace Plunkett, 8 Aug. 1921, Plunkett Foundation for Co-operative Studies archives, Long Hanborough, Oxfordshire.

[33] To Arthur Moore, 1–2 Apr., 29 Dec. 1889, 8 June 1890, in Desmond Flower and Henry Maas (eds.), *The Letters of Ernest Dowson* (1967), 60, 122–3, 151.

Other young authors such a Rudyard Kipling regarded Besant more fondly, as a dispenser of wise advice. Meeting Besant at the Savile in the 1890s, he was told to steer clear of the critics whom he might hear airing their views and intriguing at the club, for if he fell 'in with one lot', he would be knifed by the other. They were 'like a girls' school where they stick out their tongues at each other when they pass', said Besant.[34] He was far from alone in his conspiracy theory. Robert Bridges gave similar indications in his warning to Arthur Benson in 1897, when Benson contemplated quitting his post at Eton for a career as a professional author: he 'talked very interestingly about the horrible logrolling atmosphere of London literary circles—being asked to meet reviewers; having it hinted that if you will be civil to so and so he will give you a good review and so forth'.[35]

In 1898, in *The Author*, the house magazine of the Society of Authors, Besant gave his verdict that 'the reputation of the reviewer and the influence of the review' seemed likely 'to decay and die altogether'. This prospect inspired *Punch* to proffer advice to the budding critic. 'Never "slate" a book, for its writer may one day review a volume of your own. When in doubt, keep it vague,' and so on; but if the critic was inclined to venture on a eulogy, it helpfully supplied specimens of the Cultured Style as favoured in the literary weekly—'It is a little more difficult to manage than the Pompous, but you can win a reputation by it for "rare distinction in criticism" '—and of the Egotistic Style, which was essentially chit-chat about the reviewer and was 'very popular just now . . . Its special advantage is that it relieves you from the troublesome necessity of reading a single page of the volume.'[36] And only a few months earlier *Punch* had taken its cue from *As You Like It*, sketching 'The Seven Stages of Literature', a cycle whereby the author could expect to be transported by capricious critics first to stardom and finally to the remainders shelf.[37] All this rather bore out Besant's complaint. Perhaps naively, Besant thought that American journals exhibited a higher standard than the English. John Morgan Richards, the American advertiser who bought *The Academy*, would not admit to having acquired a debased currency: 'During my proprietorship of *The Academy*, I had often the pleasure of hearing American authors express high appreciation of English literary criticism.'[38] Henry James was not one of them. 'It is long since I looked at an English review,' he informed Charles Eliot Norton in 1893; 'I was "choked off", in past years, by their strange mediocrity and commonness.'[39] The uncharitable, however, could always explain James's abstention as a reaction to his own market

---

[34] Rudyard Kipling, *Something of Myself*, ed. Thomas Pinney (Cambridge, 1991), 51. Kipling claimed, 'For that reason, I have never directly or indirectly criticized any fellow craftsman's output'; yet he did win praise from the critics Edmund Gosse and Andrew Lang, who were fellow Savileans, and he was particularly cultivated by the *Saturday Review*'s editor, Walter Pollock, and his assistant, George Saintsbury, also Savileans, with whom he would breakfast. Saintsbury became a lifelong friend, and 'I learned to rely on Saintsbury's judgment in the weightier matters of the Laws of Literature' (ibid. 52).

[35] Newsome, *Edge of Paradise*, 90.   [36] *Punch*, 5 Mar. 1898, 102.   [37] *Punch*, 9 Oct. 1897, 160–1.

[38] Richards, *With John Bull and Jonathan*, 264–5.

[39] 15 Nov. 1893, in Edel (ed.), *James Letters*, iii. 440.

failure. 'Tell it not in Samoa—or at least not in Tahiti,' he whispered to Robert Louis Stevenson; 'but I *don't* sell ten copies! and neither editors nor publishers will have anything whatever to say to me.'[40] Thomas Hardy saw only convergence. Pondering the reception of *The Dynasts* (1904–8), he 'mentioned the entire futility of American criticism, which always waits to see what English critics say before it dares express an opinion'.[41] Gosse too considered American reviewing much deteriorated when he confided in Austin Dobson in 1917:

The reviews of the American edition of my *Life of Swinburne* are now pouring in; and there is not one which would not disgrace an English provincial newspaper! Such ignorance, such absence of literary feeling, such vulgarity! It is really very serious for the Americans to possess such a contemptible press. Praise and blame alike, what they say is as worthless as the blame or praise of a boy scout would be. It surely was not so 30 years ago when we had so much to do with the U.S.A., you and I?[42]

II

Authors were not without means to influence the reception of their work, although Trollope's Lady Carbury, by sleeping with a reviewer, in *The Way We Live Now* (1875), must be considered extreme. The complimentary copy system was increasingly favoured. The Society hostess Lady Dorothy Nevill, who had known Bulwer Lytton in his best-selling prime, noted in 1906: 'I always feel sorry that he never gave me his novels; in those days authors were not nearly so generous as they are to-day, when books are showered in all directions—more given than read.'[43] Robert Sherard recalled about Oscar Wilde: 'He was not disdainful of the indispensable arts for fostering social advancement.' He deployed the strategy abroad as well as at home: 'On his arrival in Paris he had sent copies of his volume of poems, with letters, to various artists and authors,' thus to gain notice and entry into salons.[44] Wilde was flamboyant but even a lawyer, J. H. Balfour Browne, felt little hesitation about approaching Carlyle for permission to dedicate a novel to him, or about sending another to Disraeli in the hope of gaining an endorsement.[45] In 1858 an East India Company officer, Captain G. F. Atkinson, had gone further, both dedicating his book about India (*Curry and Rice*) to Thackeray and also suggesting that Thackeray might suborn *The Times*; but Thackeray warned him about 'The Thunderer's' jealous independence and terrible power:

As for that little hint about Printing House Square, I know the Editors and most of the writers; and, knowing, never think of asking a favour for myself or any mortal man. They

---

[40] 5 Aug. 1893, ibid. 428.   [41] Nevinson, *More Changes*, 165 (26 Apr. 1906).

[42] Thwaite, *Gosse*, 479.

[43] Ralph Nevill (ed.), The *Reminiscences of Lady Dorothy Nevill* (n.d. [1910]), 75.

[44] Robert H. Sherard, *Oscar Wilde: The Story of an Unhappy Friendship* (1908), 70.

[45] Balfour Browne, *Recollections*, 180–2. His novels were published in the early 1870s under the pseudonym Hamilton Marshall.

are awful and inscrutable, and a request for a notice might bring a slasher down upon you, such as I once had in the Times for one of my own books (Esmond) of wh. the sale was absolutely stopped by a Times article.[46]

Responding to an author's complaint about a reviewer's misjudgement, Moberly Bell, manager of *The Times* in its pre-Northcliffe period, was still boasting about its ironclad integrity in 1905. He noted how other papers, if not exactly corrupt, were 'disagreeably tainted' by allowing a need for advertising revenue to affect their reviews. Accordingly, 'every novel and every play is declared to be worthy of Thackeray or of Shakespeare . . . but I am glad to see that we don't go into this hysterical gush about any one, and the result is that you hardly ever see us quoted in advertisements'.[47] This was a private communication; but in 1890 *Punch*'s reviewer 'The Baron de Book-Worms' had gone public about the approaches made to him: 'So many persons have sent in touching requests to the Baron only to notice their books with one little word, that his library table groans under their weight. To about a hundred of them that one little word might be "Bosh!"—but even then they'd be pleased.'[48]

That attempts to influence reviewers or other writers might backfire did not halt the practice. Edith Nesbit was a particularly energetic exponent throughout her life, sending copies of her books to fellow authors and celebrities both 'known or unknown to her . . . in the hope of eliciting their favourable attention'.[49] Thus Swinburne, Wilde, and Rider Haggard were on the receiving end of her first book of verses, *Lays and Legends* (1886). Perhaps there was justifiable cause in her case. She was the principal breadwinner after her wayward husband, Hubert Bland, fell victim to embezzlement by his business partner. But Nesbit clearly lusted after praise of her work and did not take kindly to criticism:

Her friends record a quite alarming sensitiveness in this respect and her letters themselves occasionally contain a hint of it. Mr [Laurence] Housman remembered with some embarrassment after long years how hurt she was when she wanted him to say that, of modern women poets, she came about next to Christina Rossetti, and he insisted that Alice Meynell and Mrs Marriott-Watson, to name no others, were her betters.[50]

Henry James was treated like a literary assay office. Mrs Belloc Lowndes once put it to him that this explained their friendship: she was the sole writer of his acquaintance who never sent him her work. He replied, ' "You are the

---

[46] Thackeray to Captain Atkinson, 27 Dec. 1858, in Harden (ed.), *Thackeray Letters*, 334, where it is noted that the damaging review of *Henry Esmond* was written by Samuel Phillips and appeared in *The Times*, 22 Dec. 1852.

[47] Letter, 30 June 1905, in John Morgan Richards, *The Life of John Oliver Hobbes, Told in her Correspondence with Numerous Friends* (1911), 311.

[48] *Punch*, 6 Sept. 1890, 113. The designation Baron de Book-Worms was a playful reference to the junior minister Baron de Worms (1840–1903), who, while British-born and -bred, had inherited this hereditary title of the Austrian Empire. The joke lost currency in 1895, when Worms was raised to the British peerage as Lord Pirbright.   [49] Moore, *Nesbit*, 94.

[50] Ibid., 175–6.

only human being who has ever guessed—shall I say, ah me, what the coming of those parcels—those kind, those generous, those gracious gifts—means to their grateful, their often embarrassed, their sometimes perplexed, recipient"—and then his voice died away.' His surviving correspondence disclosed 'the painstaking and sometimes the painful efforts' James made to say something 'at once laudatory and memorable, if not sincere, concerning novels which, given his peculiar type of imagination, and his theories as to creative work, were bound to have bored and exasperated him'.[51] This well-nigh universal practice was full of unexpected comic opportunities. Particularly rich was Thomas Hardy's struggle to respond to Mrs Humphry Ward's *Marriage of William Ashe* (1905);[52] but he moved into top form when Violet Hunt sent her *White Rose of Withered Leaf* (1908):

Why should you have wasted a nice copy of your new book upon me—a recluse who does not read a novel a twelvemonth nowadays. I am reading yours, however, &, so far as I have got, think that Amy had not much to complain of in the way the world used her; she was oddly lucky in getting just the places that she wanted. However there may be something coming that I wot not of, which justifies her 'wearyleaf'ness . . .

You are quite up-to-date in motor-car traveling, I see. It is a disagreeable way of getting about the country I think, & always gives me the back-ache next day . . . You are a bit slip-shod in your English in the early pages, by the way, but get more facile & masterly as you get on.[53]

The previous summer Hunt had invited Hardy to a garden party. His reply comprised two sentences: 'I could not come. I had toothache, for one thing, & I am too gloomy for garden parties.'[54]

Authors recommended authors to each other or to the public at large, by word of mouth, by epistolary advertisement, and by acting as reviewers. One best-seller would even plug another best-seller in the course of a story, as C. N. and A. M. Williamson did for Guy Boothby in *The Lightning Conductor* (1902), where a character tells a friend: 'I pretended to be reading an awfully exciting book of Guy Boothby's—really *great*!'[55] But it would be wrong to suppose, when reviewers puffed books by authors who were their friends, that the friendship was paramount over the test of literature. Quite likely, it was some agreement about what constituted good literature which caused the friendship, and reviewers were keen to inform the world about qualities they had discerned in their friends. From the mid-1880s Robert Louis Stevenson generally could do no wrong for reviewers, and his foreign residence made their hearts beat fonder still. *Punch* in 1890 produced a parody of a Stevenson novel—*A Buccaneer's Blood-Bath* by

---

[51] Mrs Belloc Lowndes, *The Merry Wives of Westminster* (1946), 187.
[52] Hardy to Mrs Humphry Ward, 24 Mar. 1905, in Purdy and Millgate (eds.), *Hardy Letters*, iii. 163.
[53] Hardy to Violet Hunt, [Mar. 1908?], ibid. 300–1.
[54] Hardy to Violet Hunt, [summer 1907?], ibid. 257.
[55] C. N. and A. M. Williamson, *The Lightning Conductor* (n.d.), 117. On Boothby and the Williamsons, see below.

L. S. Deevenson—to which it attached an editorial prolegomenon:

For some weeks before this Novel actually arrived, we received by every post an immense consignment of paragraphs, notices, and newspaper cuttings, all referring to it in glowing terms. 'This', observed the *Bi-Weekly Boomer*, 'is, perhaps, the most brilliant effort of the brilliant and versatile Author's genius. Humour and pathos are inextricably blended in it. He sweeps with confident finger over the whole gamut of human emotions, and moves us equally to terror and to pity. Of the style, it is sufficient to say that it is Mr Deevenson's.'[56]

Stevenson was already a public favourite. The championship of George Meredith and Joseph Conrad was a more uphill business. Meredith's genius went unrecognized too long, for some twenty or thirty years in the opinion of his devotees, whereupon a conclave of them, including Grant Allen, W. E. Henley, William Minto, and George Saintsbury, resolved to manufacture a vogue. 'The result of the gathering', so the bookman Robertson Nicoll remembered, 'was that Meredith *was* boomed.'[57] Not that Meredith was without influence in the publishing world. On the contrary, he received £150 a year as publisher's reader for Chapman & Hall, admittedly a morsel compared to John Morley's £1,000 for fulfilling the same gatekeeper function for Macmillan's, if the gossip about their salaries heard by George Gissing at the Savile Club in 1896 was accurate.[58] Conrad's reviewers were frequently also his friends; but they made little headway against the generality of newspapers and journals, which, while gradually understanding that 'the proper thing is to praise Mr. Conrad's work', damned it with faint praise and always drew attention to its unnatural and difficult English prose style.[59] Until the launching of *Chance* in 1913, 'the general indifference to his novels looked like being permanent', wrote the literary agent-turned-publisher Eveleigh Nash. *Chance*, then as now, was not considered the finest of Conrad's products, yet it was promoted by concerted effort and, as Nash put it, 'through a splendid conspiracy among the leading editors and reviewers in Great Britain and America', it became 'a great and immediate success . . . *Chance* changed the popular estimate of him as a writer. Readers began to inquire for every book he had written, and collected editions were issued in London and New York. Conrad, from a material point of view, was a made man at last.'[60]

Authors were sometimes recipients of unwanted encomiums from those close to them. In the foreword to *Pot-boilers* (1918) Clive Bell wrote of 'our three best living novelists—Hardy, Conrad and Virginia Woolf'. This was an embarrassing elevation for Virginia Woolf, author of but one published novel, *The Voyage Out*

---

[56] *Punch*, 22 Nov. 1890, 244.

[57] Nicoll, *Bookman's Letters*, 4. See also below, pp. 892–5 on this. For William Minto (1845–93), editor of the *Examiner*, 1874–6, novelist, and Professor of English at Aberdeen from 1880 (Sutherland, *Companion*, 436–7).   [58] Coustillas (ed.), *Gissing's Diary*, 400 (11 Jan. 1896).

[59] *New Age*, 18 Sept. 1908, for Arnold Bennett taking the *Athenaeum*'s reviewer to task over this: Bennett, *Books and Persons*, 36–40.

[60] Nash, *Life*, 172–3. The jacket design also made for *Chance*'s success.

(1915); she was also Bell's sister-in-law. To her credit, she responded that Bell 'seems to have little natural insight into literature'.[61] Arnold Bennett's grievance in 1904 was different, though it came to the same point in the end. He complained to the editor of the *Pall Mall Gazette*, Sir Douglas Straight, that the reviewer of *A Great Man* (1904) had plainly not read it properly, he had so 'grossly misrepresented the plot'. The upshot was that Straight ordered a second review to appear, this time a very favourable one which acknowledged the superficiality of the first. Bennett owned that this was 'decidedly handsome'; but he was troubled that 'many people will think I am a friend of Straight's and that the first review slipped in without his knowledge'.[62] Editors did indeed sometimes intervene to preserve their standing with the famous and influential. George Saintsbury recalled the first editor of *The Academy*, Charles Appleton, 'begging me to modify and mollify *slightly* (to do him justice he wanted no discreditable "transaction") a review of *Daniel Deronda*. "You see", he said, "the *Academy's* one of the very few papers George Lewes lets her see, and it would be a pity if she were quite choked off". '[63]

Evidence about authors and publishers endeavouring to arrange friendly or prominent notices of their books is not difficult to gather. After fuming for years against reviewers—'the whole sty of grunters', the 'gooseys and ganders', the 'verminous tribe', and 'those night-men who are always emptying their cart at my door'—Robert Browning resolved 'to rub their noses in their own filth' by writing *Pacchiarotto and How he Worked in Distemper* (1876); more constructively and with far more beneficial consequences for his income and reputation, he developed the habit of sending proofs of his forthcoming publications to known allies and presumed favourable critics to review. For the last decade of his life he also had the assistance of the Browning Society (established in 1881) in promulgating his message and chorusing his virtue.[64] Then there is Eric Parker's journal for 13 October 1910: 'Cook [Theodore Cook, editor of *The Field*] read letter from Kipling and asked me to do the job Kipling had suggested. Asked me to review *Rewards and Fairies*.' It would be preposterous for historians to infer that a notice in *The Field* might make much difference to Kipling's standing and sales by 1910 or at any time; still, it confirms how authors habitually pulled strings where possible, in this case Kipling directing his book towards one who had been an admirer for over a decade, and who was an influential journalist in county circles among the shooting and fishing fraternity.[65] Hugh Walpole was, however, supreme

---

[61] Ann Olivier Bell (ed.), *The Diary of Virginia Woolf*, i (1979), 151 (28 May 1918).

[62] Flower (ed.) *Bennett Journals*, i. 180 (14 June 1904).

[63] George Saintsbury, *A Last Scrap Book* (1924), 270–1. *Daniel Deronda* (1876) turned out to be George Eliot's last novel.

[64] DeVane and Knickerbocker (eds.), *New Letters of Browning*, 93, 97, 160, 309–11; Michael Millgate, *Testamentary Acts: Browning, Tennyson, James, Hardy* (Oxford, 1995), 14, 211.

[65] Parker, *Memory Looks Forward*, 96. Parker, ex-Eton and Oxford, started his journalist career on the *St James's Gazette* in 1899, then wrote for *The Spectator* before editing the *Country Gentleman*, *Gamekeeper*, and *The Field*. He was also joint editor of the Lonsdale Library of sporting literature.

champion for the systematic way in which he cultivated favour, undeterred by the prospect of humiliation. While still an undergraduate at Cambridge, he wrote two novels and made a beeline to Arthur Benson: 'He confessed he had for years made a kind of hero of me! from a photograph, and as E.W.B.'s son: then from books.'[66] Walpole's overture suggested personal as well as literary intent. This unnerved Benson, who was a repressed homosexual and hated demonstrativeness. Walpole persisted, and not just in pursuit of Benson. His first novel he sent

with a pleasant letter to all the leading writers of the day, and in this he told each one how greatly he admired his works, how much he had learned from his study of them, and how ardently he aspired to follow, albeit at a humble distance, the trail his correspondent had blazed. He laid his book at the feet of a great artist as a tribute of a young man entering upon the profession of letters to one whom he would always look up to as his master. Deprecatingly fully conscious of his audacity in asking so busy a man to waste his time on a neophyte's puny effort, he begged for criticism and guidance. Few of the replies were perfunctory. The authors he wrote to, flattered by his praise, answered at length . . . Here, they felt, was someone worth taking a little trouble over.

This was Somerset Maugham's revenge on Walpole, whom he caricatured as Alroy (Roy) Kear in *Cakes and Ale* (1930); but, then, Maugham had been a target of letters from Walpole, as had Max Beerbohm, Arnold Bennett, E. M. Forster, Edmund Gosse, Thomas Hardy, Henry James, Rudyard Kipling, Robert Ross, Howard Sturgis, H. G. Wells, Virginia Woolf, *et omnes*. Moreover, Walpole did not stop at fellow authors but included reviewers. To the hostile critic,

he writes a long letter . . . telling him that he is very sorry he thought his book bad, but his review was so interesting in itself, and if he might venture to say so, showed so much critical sense and so much feeling for words, that he felt bound to write to him. No one is more anxious to improve himself than he, and he hopes he is still capable of learning. He does not want to be a bore, but if the critic has nothing to do on Wednesday or Friday will he come and lunch at the Savoy and tell him why exactly he thought his book so bad? No one can order a lunch better than Roy, and generally by the time the critic has eaten half a dozen oysters and a cut from a saddle of baby lamb, he has eaten his words too. It is only poetic justice that when Roy's next novel comes out the critic should see in the new work a very great advance.[67]

Francis Gribble, who joined T. P. O'Connor's *Sun* in 1893, was quite candid about how the reviewing racket operated. He was commissioned to produce four articles a week, signed or unsigned, on subjects of his choice. Mostly, he spotlighted what took his interest, from Toynbee Hall to the New English Art Club, and he liked to get out and about, making weekend excursions to Bournemouth

[66] Newsome, *Edge of Paradise*, 177. E.W.B. is Edward White Benson, Arthur's father, late Archbishop of Canterbury. Walpole, whose father was Bishop of Edinburgh (1910–29), at this time was considering entering the Church as well as a writing career.

[67] W. Somerset Maugham, *Cakes and Ale; or, The Skeleton in the Cupboard* (1979), 19–20. Also Robin Maugham, *Somerset and All the Maughams* (1966), 131–2; Hart-Davis, *Walpole*, 45, 316–17. For Walpole's courting Henry James: Edel, *James*, ii. 686–97. Maugham and Walpole had attended the same school, King's Canterbury, which gave the satire added bite.

or Boulogne, Clacton or Paris. 'Another way of providing myself with subjects', he wrote, 'was to help such of my friends as needed publicity by interviewing them, or reviewing their books.' He protested the correctness of his practice:

I liked advertising my friends in that way; but I also liked to maintain my detached point of view, and had no idea of allowing myself to be made use of by novelists who looked to journalists to persuade a hesitating world to accept them at their own valuation, as a certain number of them were disposed to do, inviting the journalists to stay with them, deadening their critical sense with hospitality, and loading them up to the Plimsoll mark with their epoch-making aphorisms and their tit-bits of personal gossip.

No doubt, it was with entire impartiality on Gribble's part and with entire innocence on the part of the publisher John Lane, a friend of Gribble, that Lane 'supplied me with material for a series of articles on "the junior Muses" '—that is, the new or upcoming poets, Richard Le Gallienne, Arthur Symons, Norman Gale, and Alice Meynell, all of whom happened to be published by Lane. And it was also by chance that

he came to see me, one day, in my chambers, carrying in his hand a little prose work, very artistically got up . . . It was a most remarkable book, he said—unique—outspoken—modern—quite sure to attract attention. It could probably be T.P.'s 'book of the week' in the *Weekly Sun*. It would make an equally good subject for an article in the *Sun*. Would I read it, and, if I were sufficiently interested, etc. . . . ?[68]

The book was *Keynotes* (1893) by George Egerton, with a frontispiece designed by Aubrey Beardsley. T. P. O'Connor did afterwards promote it as his Book of the Week in the *Weekly Sun*, where he reviewed it 'at great length in the manner of a man whose heartstrings were torn by its pathos'; and Gribble wrote about it for the *Sun*, albeit it in a serio-comic style which was taken for a parody. A landmark book was thereby launched: an inspirational text that triggered the 'New Woman' school of fiction and a best-selling fillip for a new publishing house which went on to create a series around it, comprising thirty-three *Keynotes* titles.[69]

Such practices were commonplace and not judged too irregular. Even Conan Doyle, whose probity was considered unimpeachable, 'once begged Lacon Watson to review his poems for *The Bookman*';[70] but it was Doyle who publicly berated two breaches of literary etiquette in letters to the *Daily Chronicle* in 1897 and 1899: first Hall Caine's strategem of whipping up pre-publication interest by feeding the press with accounts of authorial problems manfully overcome in bringing a colossal work to a brilliant conclusion; secondly, Robertson Nicoll's

[68] Gribble, *Seen in Passing*, 164, 169–71.

[69] Sutherland, *Companion*, 209–10, 350–1, 361; Lambert and Ratcliffe, *Bodley Head*, 38, 84–6, 98–100. Lane's approaching Gribble is in part explained by Egerton's resistance to personal publicity (on which, see below, p. 417); but his confidence in *Keynotes* was not evident at the outset when only 500 of the first print run of 1,100 copies were issued. After fourteen months 6,071 had been marketed; by 1899 it was in its 8th edition.

[70] Hesketh Pearson, *Conan Doyle* (1987), 154. Conan Doyle was no great poet, in quality or quantity. Presumably, the poems in this instance were *Songs of Action* (1898). E. H. Lacon Watson (1865–1948) was a poet and comic writer, who contributed to *Punch* and was at this time on the staff of *Literature*.

habit of multiple reviewing under noms de plume in various journals which he edited when he was also salaried adviser to an important publisher (Hodder & Stoughton).[71] Perhaps, this deserved sympathy more than scorn: Rebecca West compared reviewing a novel twice to being sick off an empty stomach.[72] It was not a trait singular to Nicoll or to novel-reviewers. Edward Graham's biography of the headmaster of Harrow, Montagu Butler, was reviewed three times, in the *Times Literary Supplement, Edinburgh Review*, and *Saturday Review*, by Walter Sichel. A pupil at Harrow in the 1860s, Sichel was keen to express 'admiring affection' for 'my dear Dr Butler'.[73]

In the round, these practices disturbed the scrupulous; and the call went out that standards had to be upheld if the profession of authorship and the business of publishing and reviewing were to command respect. Whether this was generally heeded may be doubted. Unable to eradicate malpractice, a later generation made humour out of it. In 1932 a mock trial of literary critics took place in the theatre of the London School of Economics, in aid of the London Hospital Fund. Four well-known authors and reviewers, J. B. Priestley, Sylvia Lynd, Ralph Straus, and Rebecca West, agreed to participate, as 'defendants' arraigned on a charge of 'not reading books'. One accusation was that reviewers had caused a 'steady debasement of the critical currency'; as a result, 'the word masterpiece had come to be devoid of any meaning, especially on Sundays'. Defending himself with simulated indignation, Straus declared that 'he doubted if the public wanted criticism, and that editors certainly only wanted a story of the author's social connexions. He had only once used the word "masterpiece", and this was in reviewing a book of which he was both the publisher and (under another name) the author.' Mrs Lynd, too, had a defence. Firstly, she did sometimes read the books sent to her for review, especially in traffic jams; secondly, if she did not read them, 'it was the fault of the authors for not compelling her'; finally, 'it was on the whole fortunate for the authors if their books were not read. In her experience, they preferred to be praised'.[74] This last was also George Moore's verdict: 'The trouble with the book trade is not that there are too many books so much as too many masterpieces. Nowadays a publisher is very unlucky if he does not handle at least thirty-six masterpieces during the season.'[75]

Perhaps it was this very quantity of encomiums that made authors bristle when they were dealt something less. The experience of J. A. Spender, editor for

---

[71] Letters, 7 Aug. 1897, 16, 18 May 1899; in Gibson and Green (eds.), *Unknown Conan Doyle*, 52–7; Pearson, *Conan Doyle*, 125–6, 155–7; and Booth, *Conan Doyle*, 219–20. Hall Caine's habit of self-advertisement (but really, Shaw thought, envy on the part of others at his success) led to his being blackballed when proposed for membership of the Dramatists' Club in 1909. For Shaw's curious relationship with Hall Caine, see Dan H. Laurence (ed.), *Bernard Shaw: Collected Letters 1898–1910* (New York, 1972), 865–6, 884–8, 910–13.   [72] Agate, *Shorter Ego*, 65.

[73] Walter Sichel, *The Sands of Time* (1923), 83.

[74] *The Times*, 4 May 1932. Sylvia Lynd (d. 1952) was a novelist and poet, involved in the Book Society and married to Robert Lynd, literary editor of the *Daily News/News Chronicle*; Ralph Straus (1882–1950) was a novelist, who also issued privately printed books from his own press.

[75] Geraint Goodwin, *Conversations with George Moore* (1940), 240.

twenty-nine years (from 1895) of the *Westminster Gazette*, was that authors—and actors—were far more prickly about criticism than 'all the politicians put together'.[76] Writers who were bruised by fierce criticism more than once fought back, literally so in the case of the Hon. Grantley Berkeley, who organized a gang to horsewhip the proprietor of *Fraser's Magazine* after a review of his novel *Berkeley Castle* in 1836.[77] George Meredith later saluted him as the Hon. Everard Romfrey, the 'fighting earl', in *Beauchamp's Career* (1875).[78] Archdeacon F. W. Farrar, author of the *Life of Christ* (1874) and the school story *Eric; or, Little by Little* (1858), also enjoyed himself towards the end of his life by publicizing past misjudgements of his, by then acknowledged, 'great' works.[79]

The most interesting reaction came from Hall Caine, when Routledge's reissued his *Cobwebs of Criticism* in 1907.[80] This was first published in 1883, the year following D. G. Rossetti's death. An intimate of Rossetti's failing years, Caine took his cue from the celebrated explosion in the early 1870s when Robert Buchanan denigrated Rossetti's poetry in 'The Fleshly School of Poetry', to which Rossetti retaliated with 'The Stealthy School of Criticism'. Caine's 1883 book began as a lecture series in Liverpool, and their purpose was to expose misjudgements of Byron, Coleridge, Leigh Hunt, Keats, Shelley, Southey, and Wordsworth, made by reviewers of their day. Caine had not published any fiction in 1883, whereas in 1907 he was among the most highly paid and—in his view—maligned novelists of the age. A new preface to *Cobwebs of Criticism* provided the ideal vehicle to respond to his critics, because he could not be convicted of pleading his own cause when he first wrote the essays. He began by reiterating their theme, to collate

the fatuous invectives and jeremiads with which . . . the accepted critics of the time had received works of literature which are now established as masterpieces in the opinion of the world. The doltish objurgations of the pretentious dunces who told Wordsworth that he 'would not do', and the Boeotian booings of the mooncalves who advised Keats to 'go back to his ointment boxes', were not so much serious things to me then as ridiculous witnesses to the perpetual presence of the egregious ass. But I have since thought that these curiosities of criticism have a certain philosophical value as evidences of the operation of laws of the human mind, which are probably as active now as they were a hundred years ago.[81]

---

[76] Spender, *Life, Journalism and Politics*, ii. 151–2.

[77] The review was by the editor William Maginn, whose authorship Fraser did not disclose to Berkeley but who then challenged Berkeley to a duel. Two law suits followed, Fraser suing Berkeley for assault and Berkeley counter-suing for slander: Fraser was awarded a substantial £100, Berkeley a miserable £2; Sutherland, *Companion*, 59. 'Fraser's behaviour appeared nobler than the others', thought Thackeray, to whom Fraser owed money and was careless about repaying, though 'perhaps Grantley Berkely [*sic*] was not so very wrong in beating him' (Thackeray to Mrs Henry Carmichael-Smyth, 30 July 1840, in Harden (ed.), *Thackeray's Letters*, 66).

[78] Lionel Stevenson, *The Ordeal of George Meredith* (New York, 1967), 199–200.

[79] *Review of Reviews* (May 1890), 518.

[80] It was given wide notice, being quoted, for example, in *T.P.'s Weekly*, 29 Nov. 1907, 693.

[81] T. H. Hall Caine, *Cobwebs of Criticism* (1908), new preface, dated Oct. 1907, p. ix.

This supplied an opening for further speculation: 'I think it would have been interesting at the present hour to see the first contemptuous treatment of comparatively recent works which are now cited as masterpieces of literature and held up to the shame and disgrace of the degenerate authors of our own time.' Instead Caine contented himself with general observations about the current state of criticism. His principal charge was that it was 'in too many cases an unjust and arbitary power, acting to the injury of literature and the misleading of the public. Indeed, I should say broadly, that the worst tyranny in the world at this hour . . . is the tyranny of the critic.' The critic was nearly always at odds with the public; and he cited his own novels and plays—those which the critics most disliked were most popular with the public. Why was this? Many critics, Caine stated, were writers themselves, though usually not poets or novelists: they were authors of 'serious' books—history, biography, and the like—and unversed in imaginative literature. Equally widespread was contempt for the public: critics assumed that if a book was popular, it must be bad. This was patently untrue, argued Caine, because 'Shakespeare and Scott, Dickens and George Eliot, when published at prices that are within the reach of the public, are the best selling books in the language.' Critics were, therefore, jealous of the sales enjoyed by popular writers, and encouraged to be vindictive under cover of anonymity. Caine concluded his indictment by saying that,

while much that I have written in this prefatory note comes out of the experience of my twenty-five years as an author, and is intended to express my calm conviction that criticism during the past hundred years, has on the whole done little for literature except to discourage and to blacken it, I am hardly conscious that anything I have said has had a personal reference to, or has derived its origin from any literary troubles of mine.[82]

Caine's disclaimer transgressed the bounds of credulity. His overall judgement now, about the tyranny of the critic and the critic's contempt for the public, was in plain contradiction to his previous preface, written in 1882 before he became a novelist. There he argued that, compared with the first quarter of the nineteenth century, 'rancorous abuse' was no longer the dominant note; rather, too much modern criticism was 'mincing in tone', displaying a 'disposition towards universal applause'. Morals possibly remained suspect: Caine pointed to the coterie character of much criticism, expecting reciprocal compliments. Altogether, however, Caine argued in 1882 that 'criticism is less powerful now than it was eighty years ago . . . Notwithstanding the multiplicity of literary guides . . . criticism seems to lose ground in England, and to look more than ever to the popular judgment to give hint as to the way it should go.'[83] The irony should be noted that, shortly after composing the original remarks in 1882, Caine became a reviewer of the hack kind, mostly for the *Liverpool Mercury* but also for the *Athenaeum* and *The Academy*, when he would 'review sixteen books a

---

[82] T. H. Hall Caine, *Cobwebs of Criticism* (1908), new preface, dated Oct. 1907, pp. xii–xxvii.
[83] Ibid., pp. xxxvii–xxxviii.

week...and be paid thirty shillings a column for the reviews'.[84] Perhaps this experience strengthened rather than weakened his later arguments; and there was enough weight of opinion, from other writers and from critics themselves, to lend substance to them. But, at bottom, what he seemed to be objecting to in 1907 was his treatment by metropolitan critics for the quality reviews and by the academic establishment; above all, objecting to any criticism, that his every novel was not instantly and universally acclaimed as a classic.

Caine's habit of giving interviews to the press prior to a forthcoming publication, about which Conan Doyle complained in 1897, was a device plainly designed to sway reviewers. *Punch* mercilessly hounded him for this, concocting a parody of his style as Eminent Author, a 'simple, unassuming man' who 'refuse[s] to be interviewed by any journalist who devotes less than two columns to his description of my house and his eulogy of myself'. When the interviewer protests that the copy Caine is dictating to him has 'been published already within the last month in a dozen papers', the Eminent Author is upset: ' "In a dozen?" he exclaimed, angrily. "In thirty at the very least! In a dozen, indeed! What do you take me for? Do you think I am a miserable second-rate writer who is only interviewed once a week or so?" ' At the end, the Eminent Author again proclaims his hatred of being interviewed—he wants to be 'alone—alone with the mighty thoughts that crowd upon my master-mind, thoughts which will delight thousands of readers and make my name immortal'. And so the interviewer is dismissed—but not before he is showered with 'photographs of myself, and some views of my house'.[85]

Caine actually fared very well at the hands of reviewers, in the provincial press especially but far from exclusively there—a circumstance perhaps explained also by his practice of 'sending out five hundred presentation copies of a book, all carefully inscribed', if the clubland gossip picked up by Arthur Benson had truth in it.[86] Certainly Edmund Gosse, to his own later embarrassment, lauded Caine in 1894 for having made a decided 'contribution to literature' with *The Manxman* (1894);[87] yet, according to the trade itself, it was not usually one particularly puffing review but 'a concatenation of good ones at about the same time' that moved sales.[88] Both quality and quantity distinguished Caine's publisher Heinemann's promotional advertisements, as these extracts show:

Hall Caine reaches heights attained only by the greatest masters of fiction. He belongs to that small minority of the great elect of literature. (T. P. O'Connor)

The author prepares to be great, really means to be great, and, in my judgment, always succeeds in being great. (Joseph Parker)

The author has respected, and that deeply, his message, his art and his readers. (Robertson Nicoll, *British Weekly*)

[84] Flower, *Just as it Happened*, 222.   [85] *Punch*, 18 Sept. 1897, 122.
[86] Newsome, *Edge of Paradise*, 90.   [87] See below, p. 729.
[88] Rupert Hart-Davis (ed.), *The Lyttelton Hart-Davis Letters: Correspondence of George Lyttelton and Rupert Hart-Davis*, i and ii: *1955–57* (1985), 293.

The novel is a great effort, splendid in emotion and vitality, a noble inspiration carried to noble issues, an honour to Hall Caine and to English fiction. (Joseph Cowen, *Newcastle Chronicle*)

A great and impressive work, a work of might and a work of high purpose. (J. Cuming Walters, *Manchester City News*)

A great book, great in conception and execution; a strong book, strong in situation and character; and a human book, human in its pathos, its terror and its passion. (Sir Walter Besant)

Hailed as a masterpiece, alike for its poetic beauty and realistic grandeur. (*Glasgow Herald*)

It is not too much to say that it is the most powerful story that has been written in the present generation. It is a work of genius. (*The Scotsman*)

Hall Caine stands apart among his novelistic brethren, though reminding one somewhat of Victor Hugo. (*The World*)

Heinemann was even able to parade plaudits from the former Prime Minister, Gladstone, albeit in characteristically labyrinthine manner.[89] Still, whether flattering reviews existed or not, authors and their media collaborators banged the drum regardless. In 1907 *Punch* found this announcement beyond satire, *The Illustrated Mail*'s heralding a new production from the pen of the thriller-writer William Le Queux: 'We can honestly say it is the best story that has ever appeared in our pages. We have Mr. Le Queux's permission to say so.'[90]

III

Less heat and more light were transmitted by Augustine Birrell, who in turn irritated Henry James by 'a self-satisfied smile after he speaks'.[91] In 'Authors and Critics' (1894), Birrell dilated on the tendency among contemporary authors to resent criticism. Their position appeared to be that it was the public's duty to appreciate them, rather than their responsibility to please the public. Such an attitude was not just fallacious, it was futile. 'Reading is a democratic pursuit,' Birrell reminded authors; 'the volume of unprinted criticism is immense, and its force amazing.'[92] The reading public could not be prevented from talking about authors and books. This it did freely, in railway carriages and smoking rooms, at meal tables and at work, wherever people were inclined. Compared with this vast, natural constituency of outspoken and unlicensed criticism, the attempted manufacture of opinion by the press was unimportant. Arnold Bennett, in his critic's column for *The Tribune* in 1906, echoed this: personal recommendations by one reader to another sold more books than did reviews. This verdict outraged 'A Young Author' from Bloomsbury, whose novel-writing for four or five years

---

[89] Frontispiece to Hall Caine, *The Deemster* (1887; collected edn., 1921).   [90] *Punch*, 23 Jan. 1907, 67.
[91] To Mr and Mrs William James, 28 May 1894, in Edel (ed.), *James Letters*, iii. 480.
[92] Birrell, *Men, Women, and Books*, 216, 221–2.

had passed unnoticed. For him, there was 'only one remedy: the reviewers on our daily and weekly Press should be increased'.[93] Bennett was unmoved and, after *The Tribune* had folded and he transferred to the *New Age* he reiterated the case, thinking it especially true for a particular class of novel which became a 'book of the year' by virtue of being talked about by 'the right people'. These constituted the metropolitan elite, numbering 12,055 persons (Bennett enjoyed giving them a spurious precision), who dined out three times a week in the West End and who were '"in the know", politically, socially, and intellectually'. It was by their agency—or as Bennett preferred to sniff, 'their refined and judicial twittering'— that E. M. Forster's *Howards End* achieved such salience in 1910.[94]

The American owner of the literary periodical *The Academy* John Morgan Richards, was well placed to adjudicate this question—and for two additional reasons: firstly, because he had made his fortune as an advertiser; secondly, because he was the father (and biographer) of a celebrity author, Pearl Craigie (John Oliver Hobbes). Recounting how she achieved a hit with her first novel, *Some Emotions and a Moral* (1891), he noted that she was pleased by the laudatory reviews, especially from T. P. O'Connor in the *Sunday Sun* and from his own friend the minister at the City Temple Dr Joseph Parker in the *British Weekly*; and displeased by the hostile reviews, especially those in *The Athenaeum* and the *Manchester Guardian*. But, Richards added, while authors naturally brooded over their reviews, 'as is always the case, at least with fiction, it was the gossip of the clubs and dinner-tables' that made a book popular.[95] In his daughter's case, it was Society whispers surrounding the collapse of her marriage—a theme sensationally pursued in the story—before the press reporting of her subsequent divorce suit brought her circumstances to the notice of a wider public.

Applying a lawyer's forensic science to the question, Augustine Birrell was even sceptical whether bad reviews at all damaged an author: 'The reading community owes no allegiance, and pays no obedience, to the critical journals, who, if they really want to injure an author, and deprive him of his little meed of contemporary praise and profit, should leave him severely alone. To refer to him is to advertise him.'[96] Continuing to administer a healthy dose of realism, Birrell reckoned that the problem was not good or bad reviewing but too much reviewing. Overproduction of books was responsible, a point underscored by *Punch*'s reviewer in 1890 when he asked, 'Why doesn't some publisher bring out *The Utterbosh Series*, for, upon my word . . . the greater part of the books sent in for "notice" are simply beneath it.'[97] Birrell, too, accepted that nine out of ten books scarcely merited review. Why then had the reviewing habit become so general? 'It is a trade thing,' Birrell answered: a newspaper or periodical 'gets the books, and it gets the advertisements, and then it does the best it can for itself and its

---

[93] *The Tribune*, 6 (Bennett) and 7 ('A Young Author') Aug. 1906.
[94] *New Age*, 12 Jan. 1911, in Bennett, *Books and Persons*, 291–1.
[95] Richards, *John Oliver Hobbes*, 63, 69.   [96] Birrell, *Men, Women, and Books*, 225.
[97] *Punch*, 20 Sept. 1890, 137.

readers by distributing the former amongst its contributors with the request that they will make as lively "copy" as they can'. Authors, therefore, needed to understand that their books were almost incidental to the business of reviewing. Books primarily served as vehicles to show off the reviewers' prejudices, which Birrell (following Ecclesiastes) likened to the crackling of thorns under a pot. Moreover, readers approached reviews in the same spirit: 'The review is not written for those who have read or intend to read the book, but for a crowd of people who do not mean to read it, but who want to be amused or interested by a so-called review of it, which must therefore be an independent, substantive literary production.' There was no point in authors bewailing the absence of reviewers of incorruptible integrity and unerring judgement. If a charge was to be brought, it was that reviewers were too free, not grudging, with praise. Were they to do less hack work, they might be more fastidious. Still, not all was desolation. No critic worth the label could disguise elation when, after sacrificing years to reviewing so much derivative work, he encountered 'some Stevenson, some Barrie, some Kipling—[who] had actually written something which was not only in form but in fact a new book'.[98]

Birrell's sanguine forecast depended on reviewers not becoming so deadened by drudgery that they failed to spot originality. A common complaint of authors concerned critics lazily typecasting them. Shan Bullock was one increasingly frustrated that his singularity was passing unnoticed. Born in 1865 of Fermanagh farming stock, he settled in England at the age of 18 and pursued a writing career while holding minor positions in the Civil Service. Sketches and short stories formed his first publication, *The Awkward Squads* (1893), which was followed by another nine titles, including several novels, before 1906. Usually set in the Ulster border region, they dealt with the quirky relationships of Protestant and Catholic provincial life. Their simple humour, pastoralism, pathos, and modest charm drew a warm response from reviewers; yet they invariably pigeonholed Bullock as a Northern Irish imitator of the Scottish kaleyard school of S. R. Crockett, Ian Maclaren and the younger J. M. Barrie. Bullock responded: *The Squireen* (1903) was 'sombre in tone' and 'strikes out a somewhat original line', noted the *Times Literary Supplement*; but it was unimpressed by this tale of degeneration and criticized inconsistencies in the melodramatic plotting.[99] Bullock's school story *The Cubs* (1906) was better received but the problem of stereotyping recurred anew. The common verdict was that this was a mongrel cross between *Tom Brown's Schooldays* and *Stalky & Co.*, and that Bullock fell short of both Hughes and Kipling. Certainly, he did not enjoy their popularity and sales. Hence, Bullock chose to tackle a different subject, the struggles of the suburban lower-middle classes. *Robert Thorne: The Story of a London Clerk* (1907) is now recognized by social historians in terms used by the *Daily Express* at the time: 'a remarkable

[98] Birrell, *Men, Women, and Books*, 210–33.   [99] *TLS*, 6 Mar. 1903, 73.

work, worthy indeed to be described as a human document'.[100] Its air of authenticity was unsurprising because Bullock lived the life he fictionalized and, just prior to *Robert Thorne*'s publication, he was one of seven signatories to an open letter to the *Fortnightly Review* which detailed the dissatisfactions of his class.[101] Again, however, the special merit of Bullock's storytelling tended to get lost in an invocation of more celebrated names. Reviewing *Robert Thorne* in the *Daily News*, C. F. G. Masterman acknowledged its 'sense of reality . . . a more accurate and less indignant interpretation of lower middle-class life in London than the novels of George Gissing; a companion to the draper's assistant or scientific student of Mr. H. G. Wells'. But Masterman did not leave it there. Having been promoted to a junior ministerial post in Asquith's Government, Masterman issued his own tract for the times, *The Condition of England* (1909), in which he singled out Bullock's *Robert Thorne* as a measure of the suburbans' 'communal poverty of interest and ideal'.[102]

Slapped down as a shallow suburban, Bullock resumed his first line of work, writing stories of Ulster life; but he now had reason to hope that his distinctive contribution might be recognized. For he had acquired a patron, Sir Horace Plunkett, with whose mission to disseminate ideals of agrarian cooperatives and to avoid the partition of Ireland under Home Rule he was closely associated for the next decade.[103] When the manuscript of *Hetty: The Story of an Ulster Family* (1911) was finished, he wrote to Plunkett: 'I can never write anything better . . . and as I have tried so hard, and as I owe you so much, and as Ireland owes you so much',[104] he wished to dedicate the story to him. Plunkett consented, but Bullock was not content to leave its promotion there. He approached Clement Shorter, then editor of the *Sphere* and omnibus literary operator, whose wife was the Irish poet Dora Sigerson. Bullock was upset that the English reviewers' typecasting of Irish writing had left no place for him:

My dear Shorter,

I have asked Laurie [the publisher T. Werner Laurie] to send you a personal copy of my new book 'Hetty'. If you can will you read it, and if you think it good enough may I ask you to help it.

I hate writing like this & troubling one who has been always so good to me; but I have worked so hard over this book & put such a lot into it, & it represents middle class Ulster life so closely as I see it, that I want to see if I can by means of it attain some definitive

---

[100] Two pages of extracts from reviews of *Robert Thorne* (1907) preface the title page of Bullock's *Master John* (1909).

[101] 'The Burden of the Middle Classes', *Fortnightly Review* (Sept. 1906), 411–20. For the context, see Philip Waller, 'Altercation over Civil Society: The Bitter Cry of the Edwardian Middle Classes', in Jose Harris (ed.), *Civil Society in British History: Ideas, Identities, Institutions* (Oxford, 2003), ch. 6.

[102] C.F.G. Masterman, *The Condition of England* (1911), 70–2.

[103] Bullock's correspondence with Plunkett (fifty-four letters) is preserved in the archives of the Plunkett Foundation for Co-operative Studies, Long Hanborough, Oxfordshire. Bullock served on the secretariat of the Irish Convention, chaired by Plunkett in 1917–18.

[104] Bullock to Plunkett, 19 Apr. 1911.

place as an Irish writer. I think I deserve at least the recognition given to Birmingham & Miss Lawless and Miss Barlow & the 'Irish R.M.' writers—& I think Yeats & his school have had a long turn of it in the front of things. Surely prose as well as poetry & the drama has claims. Anyhow, I do wish you would use your great influence to help me in any direction you can—always assuming you find the book worthy. I am hoping Laurie to [*sic*] send copies to Justin McCarthy, John Redmond, Wm. O'Brien, Birrell, T.P. and others—but of course the ultimate criticism will be literary & it is that I look for most. I *should* like a definitive place as an Ulster novelist—for that is all I ever can be.

Forgive this trumpeting of myself—it's the first & last time.

> Yours ever,
> Shan F. Bullock[105]

Bullock's hopes were not realized. Whatever Shorter's string-pulling, it proved impossible to generate substantial sales and popularity for an author of Ulster life. The reputation of the province for dourness and belligerence was against it, and a Liberal agnostic Ulsterman like Bullock appeared almost a contradiction in terms. Disappointed, and approaching 50 by the outbreak of the Great War, Bullock thereafter published intermittently: a novelette to assist recruiting in Ireland, *The Making of a Soldier; or, How the Lad Went Away* (1916), which bid farewell to its hero at the Dardanelles; another adventure in the City clerk genre, *Mr. Ruby Jumps the Traces* (1917), modelled on H. G. Wells's *History of Mr. Polly* (1910); some reflective poetry, *Mors et Vita* (1923), following the death of his wife; and a nostalgic last tale of the Ulster farming class in *The Loughsiders* (1924), dedicated 'To my brother Willie. This story of the Ireland we remember and love and hope to see again'. Ironically, this was saluted as Bullock's finest story, but he had already quit the race. In 1921 he told Plunkett how he was contemplating writing

a book on the philosophy of failure. Is success better than failure, I mean from the personal point of view? Given a certain minimum of money & comfort, I think the happiest men are what the world calls failures. The cost of maintaining success is tremendous & racks both body & mind . . . I have had great ambitions and once thought I might succeed. I worked hard & tried hard. All has come to nothing. Yet I don't fret, but feel on the whole relieved to have a competence, good health, & no burden of reputation to maintain.[106]

Plunkett endeavoured to argue Bullock out of it, but the autumnal mood was on him: 'Stevenson once wrote that to journey hopefully is better than to arrive, & surely he was right.'[107]

---

[105] Bullock to Shorter, 3 Aug. 1911, Brotherton Library, Leeds, Clement Shorter Correspondence. For the individuals mentioned in this letter, see Sutherland, *Companion*, 258, 364–5, for Emily Lawless (1845–1913), and Kemp *et al.*, *Edwardian Fiction*, 18–19, 32–3, for Jane Barlow (1857–1917) and George A. Birmingham (James Owen Hannay, 1865–1950). The 'Irish R.M.' authors were Somerville and Ross (ibid. 367–8); McCarthy, Redmond, O'Brien were all leading Irish Nationalist politicians; the belletrist Birrell was now Cabinet Chief Secretary for Ireland; 'T.P.' was T. P. O'Connor.

[106] Bullock to Plunkett, 8 Aug. 1921.   [107] Bullock to Plunkett, 12 Aug. 1921.

Bullock never got out of the writers' third division, in his lifetime or since. It was different for Samuel Butler, whose fate at the hands of reviewers and in the marketplace affords a nice comparison with Bullock's. Butler was the author of several 'new' books, yet reviewers generally (or those who were thought to carry weight) did not respond to his originality as Augustine Birrell had supposed. Some exceptions existed, of course. Bernard Shaw, reviewing for the *Pall Mall Gazette*, was impressed by *Luck or Cunning* (1886),[108] one of Butler's tilts at the tyranny of natural selection; but, though Butler was to exercise considerable influence on Shaw, and Shaw was to play a significant part in the promotion of Butler's posthumous reputation, Shaw's recommendation at the time was practically worthless, coming as it did from a failed novelist and a columnist of pontifical perversity. With umpteen publications, from *Erewhon* (1872) and *The Fair Haven* (1873), *Life and Habit* (1877) and *Evolution Old and New* (1899), through to *The Authoress of the Odyssey* (1897) and *Shakespeare's Sonnets Reconsidered* (1899), Butler succeeded only in alienating the clerical, scientific, classical, and literary establishments. He was thus subjected to 'the long course of practical boycott . . . or, if not boycott, of sneer, snarl and misrepresentation'. In 1899, three years before his death, he calculated that he had *lost* £960 17s. 6d. on having his work published. The only one to have made money, under £70, was *Erewhon*, which sold 3,842 copies across a quarter-century; none other sold more than 640 copies and eight sold fewer than 300. Having financial independence, Butler could afford to indulge himself: 'I am so intent upon pleasing myself that I have not time to cater for the public.' Yet, 'I confess I should like my books to pay their expenses and put me a little in pocket besides.'[109] He sought advice from the Society of Authors, while feeling that 'very likely they can do nothing for me'. He also recalled once asking Charles Darwin—with whom he quarrelled intellectually and personally—what it is that sells a book; to which Darwin replied, 'he did not believe it was reviews or advertisements, but simply "being talked about"'. Butler was inclined to concur, while adding,

but surely a good flaming review helps to get a book talked about. I have often inquired at my publishers' after a review and I never found one that made any perceptible increase or decrease of sale, and the same with advertisements. I think, however, that the review of *Erewhon* in the *Spectator* did sell a few copies of *Erewhon*, but then it was such a very strong one and the anonymousness of the book stimulated curiosity.[110]

Contemplating the question further, Butler concluded that it was the author's own intent, his choice of subject and style, that mattered most; above all, whether he was playing for immediate popularity or lasting credit. 'The supposition that the world is ever in league to put a man down is childish. Hardly less childish is it for an author to lay the blame on reviewers.' He acknowledged that 'a *mot d'ordre*

[108] Holroyd, *Shaw*, i. 212–13.
[109] Henry Festing Jones (ed.), *The Notebooks of Samuel Butler* (1985), 368–77.   [110] Ibid. 161.

given by a few wire-pullers can, for a time, make or mar any man's success';[111] but a permanent name was claimed by different means. Butler prided himself on his independence of fashion and militant unorthodoxy, and he (rightly) thought that he had planned a waiting game: his posthumously published novel *The Way of All Flesh* (1903) and a selection of his *Notebooks* (edited by Festing Jones, 1912) did much to shape twentieth-century writers' images of the Victorian family and religion, its oppressiveness and hypocrisies. Butler consoled himself that 'there can be no greater misfortune for a man of letters or of contemplation than to be recognised in his own lifetime'; but he was also candid enough to regret that he was denied opportunities to reach a wider public. When publishers brought out new magazines, he was not invited to contribute, his name carrying no commercial clout. 'Heaven forbid that I should blame them for doing exactly what I should do myself in their place,' he wrote. And he mused, 'Perhaps it is better that I should not have a chance of becoming a hack-writer, for I should grasp it at once if it were offered me.'[112]

Butler's ruminations about the operations of the literary market are revealing, yet need to be discounted as by an author who, in his lifetime, was reckoned a peculiar of limited appeal. The trade view was enunciated by Michael Joseph in 1925: 'The experience of most publishers is that good reviews will help a good book enormously (a "good" book in the sense of a saleable book) and that although good reviews will slightly benefit a "bad" book they cannot be expected to sell it if it proves to be the kind of book the public will not buy.' Why the public went for one thing rather than another always involved a 'huge element of chance'. Especially this was so for a first book by an unknown; likewise, a work by a modestly established author, 'whose loyal public may be safely estimated to within a few thousands', might suddenly take. Quality was no guide: 'Good books'— Joseph was now using 'good' as a mark of literary and intellectual merit—'don't sell, bad books do, and very often. Public taste is absolutely mystifying.'[113]

Of some significance in this context is the case of Marie Corelli, like Hall Caine a monster best-seller. During the Great War she told a fan, who later wrote a biography of her, that she had forbidden the sending-out of her books for review after

I discovered that reviewing was always done 'by favour'—either by personally knowing the critics—entertaining them to dinner—and (sometimes) paying them for a favourable notice. When I had learned this *beyond all doubt*, I would *have none of it*—it seemed so worthless and *dishonest*. I determined to trust myself to the public; and so far my trust has not been misplaced . . . I belong to no 'clique' of press-organizers, and literary folks who 'write up each other!' I stand *alone*, wishful to keep myself and my work such as it is, *clean* from any sort of humbug!—and the approval I have had from some of the world's *greatest* men, has been quite *unsought* and *unexpected*.[114]

[111] Henry Festing Jones (ed.), *The Notebooks of Samuel Butler* (1985), 180–1.   [112] Ibid. 167, 367.
[113] Joseph, *Commercial Side of Literature*, 173, 220–1.
[114] Undated letter, c.1916, in William Stuart Scott, *Marie Corelli* (1955), 61–2.

The last remark radiated disingenuousness, and the rest a certain amount of paranoia; yet, she raised questions that require answering. One of her most famous stories, *The Sorrows of Satan* (1895), exposed the various corrupt practices operating in the literary market. Publishers habitually created booms by falsification of sales. A common trick is described to the bemused author in the story:

I shall only issue two hundred and fifty copies at first . . . All these two hundred and fifty will be *given away* by me in the proper quarters on the day of publication . . . in order to be able to announce at once in all the papers that *'The first large edition of the new novel by Geoffrey Tempest being exhausted on the day of publication, a second is in rapid preparation.'* You see we thus hoodwink the public, who of course are not in our secrets, and are not to know whether an edition is two hundred or two thousand. The second edition will of course be ready behind the scenes, and will consist of another two hundred and fifty . . . [This] second edition will be sent off 'on sale or return' to provincial booksellers, and then we shall announce—*'In consequence of the enormous demand for the new novel by Geoffrey Tempest, the large second edition is out of print. A third will be issued in the course of next week.'* And so on, and so on . . . It is only a question of diplomacy and a little dextrous humbugging of the trade.[115]

Not many authors were likely to object to such manipulation, or to this publisher's style of advertising to make a novel fly. It involved placing in the newspapers a

paragraph of about some seventy lines or so, describing the book in a vague sort of way as *'likely to create a new era of thought'*—or, *'ere long everybody who is anybody will be compelled to read this remarkable work'*—or, *'as something that must be welcome to all who would understand the drift of one of the most delicate and burning questions of the time'*. These are all stock phrases, used over and over again by the reviewers—there's no copyright in them. And the last one always 'tells' wonderfully, considering how old it is, and how often it has been made to do duty, because any allusion to a *'delicate and burning question'* makes a number of people think the novel must be improper, and they send for it at once![116]

Authors could do their own booming by employing a literary agent to feed newspaper gossip columns with tit-bits of how sought-after they were by Society; or by splashing money about, they could be seen at the best places—Cowes Week, the Derby, even royal levées. Corelli added, 'for the benefit of the public, who are sadly uninstructed on these matters, I may here state as a very plain unvarnished truth, that for forty pounds, a well-known "agency" will guarantee the insertion of *any* paragraph, provided it is not libellous, in no less than four hundred newspapers'.[117] This softening-up process was aimed at suborning reviewers:

There are only six leading men who do all the reviews, and between them they cover all the English magazines, and some of the American too, as well as the London

---

[115] Marie Corelli, *The Sorrows of Satan* (1895; Oxford, 1996), 79–80; also pp. 65, 170, for other accounts of this malpractice. [116] Ibid. 78–9.

[117] Ibid., 54–9.

papers . . . The man at the head of the list, David McWhing, is the most formidable of the lot . . . If you can secure McWhing, you need not trouble so much about the others, as he generally gives the 'lead', and has his own way with the editors. He is one of the 'personal friends' of the editor of the *Nineteenth Century* for example and you would be sure to get a notice there, which would otherwise be impossible. No reviewer *can* review anything for that magazine unless he *is* one of the editor's friends. You must manage McWhing, or he might, just for the sake of 'showing off', cut you up rather roughly.[118]

Corelli even attached a footnote to the penultimate sentence of this outburst: 'The author has Mr. Knowles's own written authority for this fact,' reference to James Knowles, editor of the *Nineteenth Century*. In 1895, the same year as the publication of *The Sorrows of Satan*, Corelli complained in an article in *The Idler* magazine that Knowles had spurned the offer of a review of her previous best-seller, *Barabbas* (1893), by Canon Wilberforce, with the sweeping declaration that no work of hers would ever be noticed in the *Nineteenth Century*.[119]

'McWhing' is subsequently managed in Corelli's story, the multi-millionaire author Geoffrey Tempest contriving, through his devilish agent, to donate £500 to 'a charity of which Mr McWhing is chief patron'.[120] Accordingly, Tempest figures as McWhing's 'discovery' and 'genius of the day'. McWhing makes the novel his Book of the Month, because of its 'extraordinary brilliancy and pro-mise'. Tempest himself feels more annoyance than disgust when none of this booming or 'the applause of cultured journalism' inflates his sales, which remain meagre. This outcome is contrasted with the runaway success of a novel by Mavis Clare, published at the same time. Tempest has even tried to nobble its progress by writing anonymously a damning review, another common tactic, Corelli implies. Clare's novel 'has been literally cut to pieces whenever it has been noticed at all—and yet the public go for her and don't go for you', Tempest's publisher patiently explains: 'You see people have got Compulsory Education now, and I'm afraid they begin to mistrust criticism, preferring to form their own independent opinions . . .'. What counts is that a work is undertaken with 'a high and unselfish intent' and 'nobly' performed.[121] Tempest begins to understand this when finally he meets Clare, who is 'personified truth!' There is a dovecote in her garden, and he finds that she has named the birds after particular papers: the Saturday Review (a 'strutting' and 'quarrelsome' creature); the Speaker ('a fat fussy fantail' who 'fancies he's important, you know, but he isn't'); the Sketch ('not at all a well-bred bird'); the Illustrated London News ('that bland old grey thing'), and so on, through the entire periodical and newspaper flock, until she addresses a 'spiteful-looking' owl, who looks wise but is 'just as stupid as ever he can be. That is why I call him the "Athenaeum"!' And over in the corner,

---

[118] Marie Corelli, *The Sorrows of Satan* (1895; Oxford, 1996), 81–2.
[119] Scott, *Corelli*, 170. Canon Wilberforce was A. B. O. Wilberforce (1841–1916), Canon of Westminster, 1894–1900.   [120] Corelli, *Sorrows of Satan*, 136.
[121] Ibid. 170–2.

'half-asleep on the wall', is Public Opinion. Clare explains to Tempest the purpose of her elaborate joke:

I used to worry a good deal over my work, and wonder why it was that the press people were so unnecessarily hard upon me, when they showed so much leniency and encouragement to far worse writers—but after a little serious consideration, finding that critical opinion carried no sort of conviction whatever to the public, I determined to trouble no more about it—except in the way of doves!

To which she added, pityingly, 'I suppose I help to feed them . . . they get something from their editors for "slashing" my work—and they probably make a little more out of selling their "review copies".'[122]

It was not chance that Mavis Clare and Marie Corelli bore the same initials. Clare is a fictional glorification of Corelli, who, having been habitually mauled by highbrow reviewers, instructed Methuen to insert a notice in *The Sorrows of Satan*: 'NO COPIES OF THIS BOOK ARE SENT OUT FOR REVIEW. Members of the press will therefore obtain it (should they wish to do so) in the usual way with the rest of the public, i.e., through the Booksellers and the Libraries.' This embargo naturally whetted the press's appetite and, perversely, generated publicity. That was accentuated by the sensational content of the novel, whose onslaught against the corrupting power of money was not confined to the venal world of publishing. Corelli railed against an all-pervading 'sensual egotism' in Society, Church, and State. 'New Women' who betray their sex, aristocratic brides who barter their titles in loveless marriages to millionaires, clergy who have ceased to believe in religion, all come under Corelli's lash for having sold their souls to Satan. The Devil himself literally stalks the land. In the climax of the story he is pictured arm-in-arm with 'a well-known Cabinet Minister', together entering Parliament.[123]

The Sorrows of Satan was not, therefore, ignored by the press. It was predictably slated; *Punch* for example, lambasted it as a 'farrago . . . of balderdash and vanity', yet it required a column and a half of commentary to reach this conclusion.[124] One of *The Sorrows'* principal publicists was W. T. Stead, whose hobby-horse too was that 'English society is in such a thoroughly rotten state.' Stead paid his 6s. for the book like any ordinary customer, then gave it a twelve-page splash in the *Review of Reviews*, of which he was editor. Having summarized its plot, he hailed its conception as 'sublime' and its execution as lacking 'restraint of any kind': 'She paints indeed, but it is with a brush as huge as a bill-sticker's. But let no one despise it. It is the supreme example of a popular style; the zenith attained by the Penny Dreadfulesque in the last decade of the nineteenth century.'[125] *The Sorrows of Satan* racked up 200,000 sales by the end of the Great War—if Methuen's advertisement is believed.[126]

At a debate at the Whitefriars Club in 1901 Anthony Hope—author of the bestselling *Prisoner of Zenda* (1894)—'said that every novelist had a certain regard

---

[122] Ibid. 187–9.   [123] Ibid. 390.   [124] *Punch*, 7 Dec. 1895, 269.   [125] Scott, *Corelli*, 171–2.
[126] Methuen's catalogue in 1920 claimed 202,000 copies sold; Ransom, *Corelli*, 201.

and gratitude for Miss Corelli because she had routed the critics on their own ground and sold her books without sending copies to reviewers'. Robertson Nicoll, replying, reminded authors that a literary critic was not like a publisher's reader (though Nicoll was both), who advised principally whether a book would sell. The literary critic

has to decide whether the book is good literature or not. Taken in this way, the victory of the critics has been complete, and Marie Corelli ceasing to send out her books is a striking testimony to that victory, for it means that she knows that wherever the books go and amid all the vicissitudes of the journalistic world she will never get a competent person to say that her works are literature.[127]

Nicoll appeared a little tender on the subject. The McWhing character in *The Sorrows of Satan*, it was suspected, portrayed him, with perhaps a dash of Andrew Lang. Nicoll did not discuss the means by which Corelli could circumvent reviewers and still obtain favourable publicity. She had a literary agent, A. P. Watt; she also exploited the complimentary copy system. Included in this largesse was Nicoll himself. In receipt of one, he wrote to her: 'I have read your book with great pleasure, and will write something about it. It is full of pure wisdom and good feeling.'[128] Corelli and her publishers also fed the press with juicy morsels, about how royalty read her books; she wrote controversial articles for the press, and she made public appearances.[129] *Punch* was decided that, for all her supposed coyness, Corelli was in the front rank of self-advertisers along with Hall Caine or George Sims, the popular melodramatist who marketed his own brand of hair restorer, Tatcho:

The Marie Corelli Circulation Creator,

'Puffo.'

Puffo for Prose Writers.
Puffo for Paragraphists.
Puffo for Pifflers.
Puffo for Philosophers.
Puffo for Princes.
Puffo for Personages.

This mixture is invaluable for ungrammatical middle-class households. Taken internally in large doses of three to a bottle it prevents the patient from being shocked at anything, and makes him or her another man or woman. It is lurid, unconventional, scarlet, effusive, bombastic, and untrammeled. None genuine without the trade-mark, a picture of a patent-leather-booted Devil swallowing one glass of absinthe, with the legend, 'Criticism, that is the enemy!'

---

[127] Robertson Nicoll to Quiller Couch, 24 Feb. 1901, in Darlow, *Nicoll*, 171.
[128] Letter, 3 Nov. 1920, in Darlow, *Nicoll*, 297. The book was *The Love of Long Ago: and Other Stories*.
[129] On this, see above, Ch. 22.

PUFFO has vellumed its way into Windsor Castle!
PUFFO makes you sit up!
PUFFO has the scent of Poppies!

Bad men hate PUFFO.
Good men love PUFFO.
PUFFO is POPULAR.

'I certify that PUFFO is made from my own dear little teeny-weeny receipt, and I don't care a bit what naughty critics say about it. [*Signed*] MARIE CORELLI.'[130]

Corelli could not be convicted of half-measures. *God's Good Men* (1904) contained a prefatory Author's Note:

For all sins, whether of omission or non-omission, of construction or non-construction, of conformity or non-conformity, of crudity or complexity, of diffuseness or dullness, of expression or of method, of inception or conception, of sequence or sequel, of singularity or individuality,—likewise for all errors whether technical and pertaining to the printer, or literary and pertaining to the author, and for everything imaginable or unimaginable that may be found commendable or uncommendable, pleasing or displeasing, aggravating or satisfying in this humble love-story for which no man will be wise and no woman the worse,

GENTLE REVIEWER BE MERCIFUL UNTO ME!

        AND,

From wilful misquotations,—from sentences garbled, and randomly set forth to the public without context, continuation or conclusion, in attempt to do injury to both the story and its writer,—from the novel skimmer's epitome, abridgment, synopsis or running commentary,—and from the objective analysis of literary-clique 'stylists', and other distinguished persons, who, by reason of their superior intellectuality to all the rest of the world, are always able, and more than ready to condemn a book without reading it,

MAY AN HONEST PRESS DELIVER ME!

It should be remarked that this 'humble love-story' contained another self-depiction of Corelli as the unjustly victimized heroine Maryllia and, *inter alia* allowed her to work off animosity against individuals with whom she had been feuding in her home town of Stratford upon Avon, together with comminations against unworthy clergy and sundry social evils such as motor cars and smoking.

Far from causing her to fade into obscurity, therefore, Corelli's rants about reviewers and other talking points of the day ensured that she received extensive coverage in the press. She was a recognized literary star and popular lecturer, whose doings and sayings were news; and her publishers' advertisements were bold and booming. Testimonials, therefore, were available on tap, notably this extract from Claudius Clear's column in the *British Weekly*, employed to promote

---

[130] *Punch*, 6 Nov. 1897, 205. The reference to absinthe is an allusion to Corelli's *Wormwood* (1890), her denunciation of French decadence.

the 'SECOND LARGE EDITION' of *The Treasure of Heaven* (1906):

It seems to me the best and healthiest of all Miss Corelli's books. She is carried along for the greater part of the tale by the current of pure and high feeling, and she reads a most wholesome lesson to a generation much tempted to cynicism—the eternal lesson that love is the prize and wealth of life . . . The story is full of life from beginning to end . . . it will rank high among the author's works alike in merit and in popularity.[131]

Claudius Clear was Robertson Nicoll. How Nicoll was brought on side by Corelli is a nice question; but one factor was the evident enthusiasm for her 'Christian' message shown by the Nonconformist readership of the *British Weekly* and epitomized by Nicoll's friend and Hampstead neighbour Dr Joseph Parker, the influential minister at the City Temple. In 1914 Corelli's latest publication, *Innocent* received a solitary review—in the *British Weekly* from the pen of the now Sir William Robertson Nicoll.[132]

IV

Some reviews still today excite interest, as the incunabula of major writers. Bernard Shaw, H. G. Wells, Henry James, Arnold Bennett, and the like, all served as reviewers and valued the platform and income. H. W. Nevinson later boasted of being the first to give Edward Thomas regular employment as a reviewer. Thomas's poetic reputation blossomed after his death in 1917 in the battle of Arras; therefore, his reviews of Hardy, Swinburne, Yeats, Synge, Pound, Frost, D. H. Lawrence, and W. H. Davies, among many others, now merit notice for the development of his self-consciousness about natural language.[133] The reality was grim. Invariably depressed, sometimes despairing, the 'doomed hack' (as he styled himself) needed opium to pour out his Niagara of words: reviews, intro-ductions, essays, anthologies, and books, about Richard Jefferies or Walter Pater, about Oxford or Windsor Castle, about Beautiful Wales or the Icknield Way ('the Norfolk-jacket school of writing', he called it), about anything that yielded cash to maintain his family. 'Please tell me of some celebrated monarch, poet, prostitute or hero that I can write a book about,' he begged Edward Garnett, ready to undertake any potboiler.[134] In the summer of 1905 Thomas was doing unusually well, making nearly £5 a week from reviewing when *The Academy*, *The Speaker*, and *Outlook*, all converged in requiring his services. But, his friend Norman Douglas observed, this was 'a dog's life'. They dreamed of no longer having to write 'ridiculous articles, but open in some country village a small shop', selling tobacco, chocolate, stationery, and such like, and entertaining

---

[131] Advertisement in *The Tribune*, 14 Sept. 1906, 2.   [132] Scott, *Corelli*, 63.
[133] Edna Longley (ed.), *A Language not to be Betrayed: Selected Prose of Edward Thomas* (1981).
[134] John Moore, *The Life and Letters of Edward Thomas* (1983), 185.

friends at weekends.[135] Douglas would find the capital and Thomas the shop. They never did; instead, in one week Thomas reviewed

> Tchaikowsky's *Life and Letters*.
> A folio Chaucer.
> A new Keats.
> *Thomas Moore*, by Stephen Gervyn.
> *The Grey Brethren*, by Michael Fairless.
> *William Bodham Donne and His Friends*.
> *The Heptameron*.
> *The Decameron*.
> *Peeps Into Nature's Ways*.
> *A Country Diary*.
> *Travels Round Our Village*.
> A German on *The Development of the Feeling for Nature*.
> A Frenchman on Charles Lamb.

In the same week the *Chronicle* suddenly went mad (it seemed) and asked him to submit frequent 'Prose Poems about the Country.' 'O God,' he groaned. 'Prose Poems! A horrible phrase for a horrible thing . . .'

He stole two chapters out of his yet unpublished *Wales* and sent them off guiltily. The *Chronicle* took them, and paid him two guineas, and he was rich.[136]

Such multi-tasking supplied another argument for anonymity, thought the long-serving editor J. A. Spender, who turned out 12,000–15,000 words during every week of his own journalistic life, including leaders, special articles, and book reviews—at one time 'five or six novels a week and a good many other books besides!'[137] Had he signed his name, the public could not have tolerated such 'pontificating, such liberties with other people, such airs', from one individual.[138] As a salaried editor, Spender was one of the fortunates: most book-reviewers were paid by the word. This introduced a breadwinning calculus into the artistic equation: 'if a critic wrote a short review, after putting himself to the trouble of reading a long book, or still more, if he decided it was not worth reviewing at all, he got nothing for his pains'. The *Westminster Gazette*, Spender's paper, aimed to do justice to all parties: the publishers', authors', and readers' desire for sufficient notice, and the reviewers' need for remuneration. Very short reviews were discountenanced; criticisms usually ran 'to at least half a column, and on fit occasions a good deal more'. The consequence of this was that two-thirds of books sent for review were shelved and, 'in spite of the utmost care, there was no denying that books of great merit were over-looked or inadequately handled'. But Spender singled out William Archer, Churton Collins,

---

[135] Norman Douglas, *Looking Back: An Autobiographical Excursion* (1934), 174.
[136] Moore, *Edward Thomas*, 124. Moore noted that Thomas had already written three articles on Lamb in three months. [137] Spender, *Life, Journalism and Politics*, i. 58.
[138] Ibid. ii. 155, 158.

Walter de la Mare, J. D. Beresford, Middleton Murry, and J. A. Blaikie as reviewers for the pre-war *Westminster* who produced first-class work unswayed by their meagre reward: 'These were men whose sense of literary fitness would never let them spin words to make pennies, and I knew absolutely with them the merits of the books were everything.'[139]

This was the ideal. Then there was the real. An account of Wilfrid Meynell, husband of the poet–essayist Alice Meynell, conjures up another picture of journalism's hectic pace. Up to 1895 he was editor of two periodicals, *Merry England* and the *Weekly Register*, writing much of their content himself. *Merry England* ended in that year, and he rid himself of the *Weekly Register* in 1899. Throughout this time and afterwards he was also a freelancer, assisted in the breadth of his operations by that anonymity so prized by Spender: 'he reviewed week in week out for the *Athenaeum* and *The Academy*; paragraphed daily for the *Daily Chronicle*; wrote articles almost monthly for *The Art Journal*; gossiped and commented every week in *The Tablet*, and occasionally in the *Illustrated London News*, though, as a reviewer at large, knowing little or nothing of his subject-matter that was not presented in the book reviewed'. Meynell's two columns of miscellany (entitled 'From the Office Window') for the *Daily Chronicle*, his wife fondly called 'your dear pathetic witty paragraphs'—pathetic because she knew the toil that went into them on top of everything else and how important they were to their income.[140]

The plight of Lady Constance Lytton cannot compare with Wilfrid Meynell's, still less with Edward Thomas's; yet it betrays some of the same practices. She joined the reviewing trade in 1893, when aged 24. It was two years after her father's death: he had been Viceroy of India and Ambassador in Paris, and his family now found their circumstances poorer. Lady Constance sought to make her own way and, her younger sister recorded,

she is at present reading two novels, three volumes each, to be reviewed for the *National Review*, and last night arrived *sixteen* volumes she is to read and write upon for the *Saturday* [*Review*], and having done these sixteen more will be sent. She reads on average one volume a day, and sometimes more. Is life worth living on these terms? . . . I cannot imagine a worse Purgatory. It makes my head ache to see Con reading, reading all day. Betty[141] seems to think it is a far more intellectual employment than darning stockings and says that for that reason Con should be encouraged in it. If she lived with Con she would not say so. While you are darning stockings, your mind is at least free, and your thoughts may be on the grandest subjects. Also you can talk and be agreeable while darning. But surely there can be nothing intellectual in passing your whole day and most of the night in the study of trashy words, which prevent all thought upon higher subjects.

---

[139] Spender, *Life, Journalism and Politics*, ii. 148–9.

[140] Meynell, *Francis Thompson and Wilfrid Meynell*, 140, 191. Samples of Meynell's weekly income for 1902, on pp. 135–6, show him also contributing to the *Pall Mall Gazette* and *Tatler*, and acting as publishers' reader.

[141] The eldest sister, Lady Elizabeth Lytton, married since 1888 to the politician Gerald Balfour.

I can imagine nothing more intellectually lowering, not to mention that as a companion she becomes intolerable.[142]

Most reviewing was of this urgent kind or worse: sham omniscience, masking anxiety, feigning sensibility. It appeared, therefore, almost haphazard whether a reviewer's thumb turned up or down. Pearl Craigie, the author John Oliver Hobbes, and her publisher Fisher Unwin exploited this, Unwin several times implementing her suggestion of placing in his advertisements for her books extracts from favourable and unfavourable reviews in parallel columns, she thinking this 'amusing and a very excellent way of showing up the absurdities of modern criticism'.[143] Still, she did not neglect the business of buttering influential reviewers. Following the publication of *The Gods, Some Mortals, and Lord Wickenham* (1895), she wrote a lavish letter to W. L. Courtney in response to his 'most sympathetic and valuable notice' in the *Daily Telegraph*.[144] She also served as president of the Society for Women Journalists in 1895–6; and in 1896 her father bought the literary periodical *The Academy*. It was Craigie who shoehorned Charles Lewis Hind into the editorial chair. Editor previously of the *Pall Mall Budget*, he had cultivated her socially. Craigie began the new regime at *The Academy* by reviewing an edition of Edward Gibbon's *Autobiographies and Letters*, a harmless enough intellectual exercise; soon afterwards she was receiving angry and abusive missives, some anonymous, from authors who accused her of running *The Academy* as a covert means of slating their work. Upset, she placed a notice in *The Times* as well as in *The Academy*, declaring 'that she does not contribute reviews, articles, or paragraphs to *The Academy*, and that everything she writes is signed either by her name or pseudonym'. Her father too affirmed that 'the books that were sent in for review were never submitted to her for criticism, nor did she read the reviews until they were published'. Yet the suspicion hurt, and he added: 'A long period elapsed before she would again write anything for the paper.'[145]

Desmond MacCarthy later endeavoured to put the whole thing in perspective— which involved lowering expectations. He had slipped into 'literary journalism' upon leaving Cambridge. This was around 1900, when 'criticism was not even a respectable profession otherwise, only slipshod trifling; and certainly discoursing about books and authors can be a very soft job'. Intending to live by his pen, he found the 'readiest way . . . was to comment upon books and plays'. He was not paid more than 30s. a week at first; but he found the work easy and so he continued, never ceasing to regret that 'to live always close to the deafening cataract of books is chilling to literary endeavour. So many good books, let alone the others, are seen to be unnecessary.'[146] Ludicrous combinations of

---

[142] Lady Emily Lytton to the Revd Whitewell Elwin (former editor of the *Quarterly Review*), 15 Dec. 1893, in Lady Emily Lutyens, *A Blessed Girl: Memoirs of a Victorian Girlhood Chronicled in an Exchange of Letters 1887–1896* (1953), 263–4.   [143] Undated letter, c.1891–2, in Richards, *John Oliver Hobbes*, 75–6.
[144] Ibid. 88–9.   [145] Ibid. 124.   [146] Desmond MacCarthy, *Portraits* (1931), 209–10.

assignments were known to everyone in the business. John Morley recollected one 'reviewer on the staff of a famous journal' receiving for 'his week's task, *General Hamley on the Art of War*, a three-volume novel, a work on dainty dishes, and a translation of Pindar'.[147] When H. J. Massingham became assistant editor of *The Athenaeum* in 1913, one of his duties was book-reviewing: 'He produced chiefly "potted" reviews of a dozen lines or so, and recalls with horror the days when he was expected to "review" anything up to fifty books a week!'[148] The novel-a-day man or woman was tame by comparison. In 1906 Arnold Bennett announced, 'I am no longer a reviewer, but in my time I have reviewed considerably over a thousand novels in three years, and I do not suppose that my case was exceptional.'[149] Bennett had then risen, at least in his own estimation, from book-reviewer to literary columnist, a distinction that was not always meaningful to the public.

Virginia Woolf divided the task of reviewing into two operations: 'gutting' (summarizing contents) and 'stamping' (affixing a seal of (dis)approval).[150] She started reviewing in November 1904 as a 22-year-old, buoyed by family connections: her recently deceased father, Sir Leslie Stephen, editor of the *Cornhill Magazine* and the *Dictionary of National Biography*, had known most eminent authors and journal editors. She quickly got into the groove: 'I finished my novel in the train, and wrote my review this morning in 1/2 an hour, and sent it off, so that was pretty quick, I won't say good, work.'[151] After her first year's experience she compared reviewing to sausage manufacture. The *Times Literary Supplement* would send a novel every week, 'which has to be read on Sunday, written on Monday, and printed on Friday'.[152] In addition, she was accepting commissions from *The Academy*, the *National Review*, and the *Guardian*, the last being a High Church journal though the Stephen family was freethinking. 'I write great nonsense,' she told a friend; 'but you will understand that I have to make money to pay my bills.'[153] She complained when editors 'cut out a good half—and altered words on their own account'.[154] This was particularly annoying when the book merited attention, as she thought for Henry James, *The Golden Bowl* (1905), over which she had toiled for five days.[155] The whole business was ridiculous—'The editor of the Guardian . . . has sent me 7 volumes of poetry and tragedy to review!'[156] Worse, she succumbed to the temptation that anonymous reviewing afforded to stab at authors whose success she thought undeserved. She had been reviewing only for a month when she angled for a novel by the best-selling

[147] Morley, 'Valedictory' (1882), in Morley, *Studies in Literature*, 331.
[148] Brook, *Writers' Gallery*, 90.   [149] *The Tribune*, 6 Aug. 1906.
[150] J. A. Sutherland, *Fiction and the Fiction Industry* (1978), 86.
[151] Letter to Madge Vaughan, 30 Nov. 1904, in Nicolson and Banks (eds.), *Flight of the Mind*, 161.
[152] Letter to Lady Robert Cecil, 10 Nov. 1905, ibid. 211–12.
[153] Letter to Violet Dickinson, 9 Nov. 1905, ibid. 210.
[154] Letter to Violet Dickinson, 28 Feb. 1905, ibid. 181.
[155] Letter to Violet Dickinson, mid-Feb. 1905, ibid. 178.
[156] Letter to Violet Dickinson, Jan. 1906, ibid. 217.

Maurice Hewlett, simply in order to give 'that affected Dandy his due! My real delight in reviewing is to say nasty things; and hitherto I have had to [be] respectful'.[157] Her conscience stirred on occasion: 'I know what a humbug I am, and ask myself what right I have to dictate what's good and bad, when I couldn't, probably, do as well myself!'[158] Still, it didn't seem to matter when she let herself go: 'I have reviewed a novel called The Glen O'Weeping [by Marjorie Bowen, 1907]; damned it, and now all the other reviewers are exclaiming, and there is a 2nd edition.'[159]

In 1886 Thomas Hardy had reported to Robert Louis Stevenson the conversation at a Rabelais Club dinner, at which the American essayist Oliver Wendell Holmes was guest. The general wish was expressed that a proper author should 'write something on the art of criticism. [George] Meredith says somebody who has produced creative work ought to do it—so that the critics may get some rudimentary knowledge of the trade they profess'.[160] Flatteringly, Hardy hoped that Stevenson might do it; in fact, it was another diner that night, Henry James, who was to attempt the largest contribution to the critics' education. Hardy himself never reviewed;[161] and his correspondence reads like a marathon moan against the army of reviewers who so little understood or sympathized with his work. The most rewarded authors were no more content. Tennyson would rail about reviewers to anyone who would listen and at the shortest of acquaintance. When Charles Dodgson (Lewis Carroll) first met Tennyson in 1857, he enquired the meaning of two passages in his poems. One concerned *Maud* (1855), upon which Tennyson 'said there had never been a poem so misunderstood by the "ninnies of critics" as "Maud"'.[162] According to a family friend, Tennyson held an 'almost hypersensibility to criticism. He spoke of certain things that had been said of him by men long since dead, and the bitterness of the criticism remained with him.' He was especially contemptuous of critics who denied him originality or imagination: 'They allow me nothing. For instance, "The deep moans around with many voices". "The deep", Byron; "moans", Horace; "many voices", Homer; and so on.'[163] Hardy could match this. He felt particularly strongly against anonymous journalism:

I have suffered terribly at times from reviews—pecuniarily, & still more mentally, & the crown of my bitterness has been my sense of unfairness in such impersonal means of attack, wh. conveys to an unthinking public the idea of an immense weight of opinion

---

[157] Letter to Madge Vaughan, mid-Dec. 1904, ibid. 166–7.
[158] Letter to Lady Robert Cecil, 22 Dec. 1904, ibid. 167.
[159] Letter to Violet Dickinson, May 1907, ibid. 295.
[160] Hardy to Robert Louis Stevenson, 7 June 1886, in Purdy and Millgate (eds.), *Hardy Letters*, i. 147.
[161] Hardy to Arthur Moule, 20 Sept. 1891, in Purdy and Millgate (eds.), *Hardy Letters*, i. 244.
[162] Diary, quoted in Collingwood, *Carroll*, 69.
[163] Canon H. D. Rawnsley, *Memories of the Tennysons* (Glasgow, 1900), 112–13, 139. The critic alluded to was probably John Churton Collins, on whom, see below pp. 158–60.

behind, to which you can only oppose your own little solitary personality: when the truth is that there is only another little solitary personality against yours all the time.[164]

Hardy was not ready to allow that criticism reflected a reasonable difference of opinion. Pretentiousness and triviality, he thought, went hand-in-hand with a deliberate disinclination to appreciate what the author was attempting or had achieved.[165] Abuse was dished out from sheer stupidity and prejudice. Hardy noted about *The Mayor of Casterbridge* (1886) that the *Saturday Review* had 'thrown cold water on it but then the *Saturday* man into whose hands my books are put has always been saying that my stories are dull'.[166] As for the *Quarterly Review*, when it attacked *Tess* in 1892, Hardy dubbed it 'just what the Q. might have been expected to say': that is, 'a mere manufacture, to suit the prejudices of its fossilized subscribers & keep the review alive upon their money'.[167] Hardy made no impression on the editor of *The Spectator*, R. H. Hutton, in 1888 when he sent him a tart two-sentence letter: 'I published "The Woodlanders", & the *Spectator* objected to that story. I publish "Wessex Tales" which are unobjectionable, & the *Spectator* takes no notice of them at all.' Hutton considered Hardy unreasonable: *The Spectator* had treated him not just well but better than any novelist. In fact, Hutton's review of *The Woodlanders* had raised 'serious fault' with Hardy's 'moral standard'; but Hardy was premature in complaining because a favourable review of *Wessex Tales* in *The Spectator* closely followed his letter.[168] This was a drawn match, therefore; but Hardy's chief contention, that many papers adopted a ritual response to an author as a supposed familiarity with his work grew, had considerable force. He told John Addington Symonds in 1889: 'critics . . . appear to think that to call me a pessimist & a pagan is to say all that is necessary for my condemnation'.[169] In 1907, aged 67 and wearied by the unavailing quest to gain universal appreciation, Hardy found solace in grim humour, telling the multifarious editor and critic Clement Shorter:

I endeavour to profit from the opinions of those wonderful youths & maidens, my reviewers, & am laying to heart a few infallible truths taught by them: e.g.,—

> That T.H.'s verse is his only claim to notice.
> That T.H.'s prose is his only real work.
> That T.H.'s early novels are best.
> That T.H.'s later novels are best.
> That T.H.'s novels are good in plot & bad in character.
> That T.H.'s novels are bad in plot & good in charr.
> That T.H.'s philosophy is all that matters.

---

[164] Hardy to Edmund Gosse, 19 Oct. 1886, in Purdy and Millgate (eds.), *Hardy Letters*, i. 154.
[165] Hardy to Alfred Austin, 6 Feb. 1892, ibid. 258.
[166] Hardy to Stevenson, 7 June 1886, and to Edmund Gosse, 24 Dec. 1886, ibid. 147, 159, where the *Saturday*'s reviewer is identified as probably George Saintsbury.
[167] Hardy to Roden Noel, 18 Apr. 1892, and to J. Stanley Little, 22 Apr. 1892, ibid. 264–5.
[168] Hardy to R. H. Hutton, 17 July 1888, ibid. 178.
[169] Hardy to John Addington Symonds, 14 Apr. 1889, ibid. 190.

That T.H.'s writings are good in spite of their bad philosophy.

This is as far as I have got at present, but I struggle gallantly on.[170]

It was a position most authors arrived at eventually. Arnold Bennett got there in 1929 when he reflected

I have written between seventy and eighty books. But also I have only written four: 'The Old Wives' Tale', 'The Card', 'Clayhanger' and 'Riceyman Steps'. All the others are made a reproach to me because they are neither 'The Old Wives' Tale', nor 'The Card', nor 'Clayhanger', nor 'Riceyman Steps'.[171]

V

The lords of the reviewing world before the Great War were the bookmen and belletrists Andrew Lang, Edmund Gosse, and George Saintsbury.[172] Their eminence did not relieve them of the toil that bore so heavily upon Edward Thomas, Wilfrid Meynell, and the rest. On Lang's death in 1912, Gosse wrote that he had been 'worn tired, harassed by the unceasing struggle, the life-long slinging of sentences from that inexhaustible ink-pot'.[173] Lang, a one-time Oxford don, was an omnibus and prolific penman. This was lampooned in a spoof biography, compiled in 1901:

LANG, ANDREW, the Prismatic Fairy King, was born in the Golf Stream in 1844, and shortly after his election as honorary fellow of Sandford and Merton College, emigrated to the Southern Pacific, where he resided for several years, conducting investigations into the primitive culture of the aborigines, his sojourn being commemorated in the touching *chanson,* 'Maori had a little Lang'. Returning from Samoa, where his brindled hair was much admired by Tusitala, Mr Lang established a company at St Andrew's for the promotion of ballades, rondeaus, teetotems, pickles, Rider Haggard, shilling shockers, translations, leaders, criticism, epics and other tropical and Jacobite *bric-à-brac.* In addition to all the daily papers, Mr Lang writes regularly for the following journals: *The Rock, The Economist, The Statist, The Exchange and Mart, Answers, Cricket, Golf Illustrated, The Rod and Gun, Home Chat, Myra's Journal, The Golden Penny, The Broad Arrow,* and *The War Cry.*[174]

There was much sense in this nonsense. Folklorist, anthropologist, psychical researcher, historian, poet, novelist, writer of fairy tales, translator of Homer and of medieval French poets, biographer of the Conservative leader Sir Stafford Northcote as well as of many men of letters, Lang appeared multiform; above all, he was literary pundit for the *Daily News,* in which 'every morning, and I believe

---

[170] Hardy to Clement Shorter, 3 Aug. 1907, in Purdy and Millgate (eds.), *Hardy Letters,* iii. 266.

[171] Arnold Bennett, *Journal, 1929* (1930), 131–2.

[172] Respectively, 1844–1912, 1849–1928, 1845–1933; see *DNB* and John Gross, *The Rise and Fall of the Man of Letters* (1969).

[173] Edmund Gosse, 'Andrew Lang', in Gosse, *Portraits and Sketches,* 205.

[174] Sidney Stephen and Leslie Lee (eds.), *Lives of the 'Lustrious: A Dictionary of Irrational Biography* (1901), 52. Tusitala was Robert Louis Stevenson's Samoan nickname, meaning 'teller of stories'.

in a hundred other places, [he] uses his beautiful thin facility to write everything down to the lowest level of Philistine twaddle—the view of the old lady round the corner or the clever person at the dinner party'.[175] This was Henry James, stung by Lang's imperviousness to his art. Thomas Hardy made much the same response to what he regarded as Lang's pat piety in criticizing *Tess*.[176] In 1916 the second Mrs Hardy expressed perplexity when Edward Clodd, Hardy's old free-thinking friend, declared that he had liked Lang, 'whom of all men, living or dead, I think my husband most detested'; adding how Hardy relished citing George Meredith's verdict that 'Lang had no heart'.[177] Yet, in 1886 Hardy had had no compunction about sucking up to Lang, who was his junior in age by some four years but whose favour might enhance Hardy's standing: 'I have so much admiration for the "infinite variety" of your literary achievements that I venture to take advantage of our slight acquaintance by asking you to accept a copy of my "Mayor of Casterbridge". If you will find a place for it on your shelves it will give me great pleasure.'[178] Hardy was then more furtive than Maurice Hewlett later: *The Queen's Quair* (1904) was dedicated to Lang, Hewlett evidently having decided to go for the double after dedicating *The Life and Death of Richard Yea-and-Nay* (1900) to Lang's rival critic-in-chief Edmund Gosse.[179]

It is easy enough to parade disparaging assessments of Lang, by Max Beerbohm, who was ever ready to deflate the mighty, or by a chippy H. G. Wells, who delivered several pungent attacks on the puerility of Lang's literary tastes.[180] Naturally, authors who did well by Lang took another view. Among them was Anthony Hope: Lang's acclaim of *The Prisoner of Zenda* (1894) at a Royal Academy banquet was reckoned an important stimulus to its sales. For all that, Hope's eulogy of Lang, that he was one of 'a few great men' able to bridge 'the gulf between "esoteric" and "popular" literature', should not be disregarded.[181] Certainly, Lang wielded an influence in the literary marketplace. As well as being a prominent reviewer, Lang was a reader for the publisher Longman's. His distinct partiality in fiction was for adventure and historical romance. It was on his advice that Longman's accepted Conan Doyle's first essay in historical fiction, *Micah Clarke* (1889), after other publishers rejected it. Robert Louis Stevenson was for Lang the best of contemporary novelists, and for whom he supplied some

---

[175] Henry James to R. L. Stevenson, 31 July 1888, in Edel (eds.), *James Letters*, iii. 240. Early James had been appreciated by Lang, but with James's developing complexity Lang fell out of sympathy.

[176] Hardy to Edward Clodd, 4 Feb. 1892, in Purdy and Millgate (eds.), *Hardy Letters*, i. 257; and Michael Millgate, *Thomas Hardy: A Biography* (1985), 320–1. Lang's article on *Tess* appeared in the *New Review* (Feb. 1892). For a defence of Lang's position regarding Hardy, see Roger Lancelyn Green, *Andrew Lang* (Leicester, 1946), 169–70.

[177] Florence Hardy to Edward Clodd, 23 Sept. 1916, in Millgate (ed.), *Letters of Emma and Florence Hardy*, 121.

[178] Hardy to Andrew Lang, 3 June 1886, in Purdy and Millgate (eds.), *Hardy Letters*, i. 146.

[179] Max Beerbohm's parody ('Fond Hearts Askew') of *The Forest Lovers* (1898), Hewlett's first best-seller, is knowingly dedicated to Robertson Nicoll; Beerbohm, *Christmas Garland*, 167.

[180] Cecil, *Max*, 155–6; Patrick Parrinder and Robert Philmus (eds.), *H. G. Wells's Literary Criticism* (Brighton, 1980), 55, 83–7, 157, 160.   [181] Anthony Hope, *Memories and Notes* (1927), 181–2.

research about Scottish history;[182] but his protégé was Rider Haggard, who dedicated both *She* (1887) and *Ayesha* (1905) to him.[183] Lang collaborated with Haggard over several stories; he also championed Haggard against charges of meretriciousness and plagiarism when his startlingly sudden popularity brought critical envy.[184] There is no question who won the public's vote in this quarrel. Lang's taste was its taste: Doyle's *Micah Clarke*, reprinted twelve times in four years, became an approved textbook after serialization in *Longman's School Magazine* in 1894.[185] As for Haggard, 'What a night that was when I read it till four in the morning,' wrote Ernest Raymond about the moment when as a boy he discovered *King Solomon's Mines* (1885). Raymond immediately elevated it to that category of book, along with Captain Marryat's sea stories, which 'when sorrowfully I reached their end I would turn back to their beginning and start again'.[186] Haggard, like Sir Walter Scott and Stevenson, fulfilled Lang's recipe for a good read: 'more claymores, less psychology'.[187] Lang's only regret when hurling Mrs Humphry Ward's *David Grieve* (1892) from the carriage window was fear that the heavy volume might derail the next train.[188]

Edmund Gosse, whom H. G. Wells once called 'the official British man of letters', had also been a great admirer of *She*, which 'thrilled and terrified' him. He thought it placed Haggard 'in the very front rank of imaginative creators. I am aware that these are very strong words and I am not in the habit of flinging such things about.'[189] Although nowadays best known as the author of a masterpiece of autobiographical fiction, *Father and Son* (1907), Gosse first won a reputation as literary critic. In this he had no mean accomplishments and instincts, being among the first to recognize Kipling's genius and to introduce Ibsen and Gide to

---

[182] 'Recollections of R. L. Stevenson', in Lang, *Adventures among Books*, 41–56, in which Lang admitted that 'though we corresponded, not unfrequently, I never was of the inner circle of his friends'.

[183] Lang also promoted (and collaborated with) A. E. W. Mason, now best known for *The Four Feathers* (1902).

[184] The chief assailant of Haggard was James Runciman, 'King Plagiarism and Court', *Fortnightly Review* (Mar. 1890): Haggard was king of the family of plagiarists, with Frances Hodgson Burnett queen and F. Anstey heir, in Runciman's opinion. On Runciman (1852–91), Sutherland, *Companion*, 546–7; for a defence of Haggard, D. S. Higgins, *Rider Haggard: The Great Storyteller* (1981), ch. 6. *Punch*, which normally held no brief for best-sellers, thought that Runciman 'would be unable to sustain [his indictment of plagiarism] in a Court of Common Sense . . . unless it were first laid down as a fixed principle, that a writer of fiction must never have recourse to any narrative of facts whereon to base his Romance' (*Punch*, 15 Mar. 1890), 125. F. Anstey (Thomas Anstey Guthrie) was a regular contributor to *Punch*, which perhaps explains why *Punch* swept aside Runciman's charge. *Punch* remained convinced of Lang's mettle; see the obituary eulogy 'What greater man of letters than Andrew Lang have we known in our time?', 16 Oct. 1912, 323. Haggard's fond recollection of Lang, written in 1912 on hearing of Lang's death, appeared as chapter xv of Sir Henry Rider Haggard, *The Days of my Life: An Autobiography* (1926), ii. 72–82.

[185] Booth, *Conan Doyle*, 128–9; Sutherland, *Companion*, 431–2.

[186] Ernest Raymond, *The Story of my Days: An Autobiography 1888–1922* (1968), 76–7.

[187] Haggard himself, however, was concerned to emphasize that his books were not just action yarns: 'it occurred to me that in *She* herself some readers might find a type of the spirit of intellectual Paganism, or perhaps even of our own modern Agnosticism; of the spirit, at any rate, which looks to earth, and earth alone, for its comforts and rewards' (letter to *The Spectator*, 22 Jan. 1887).

[188] D. S. Higgins (ed.), *The Private Diaries of Sir Henry Rider Haggard 1914–1925* (1980), 12, 190–1.

[189] Gosse's subsequent friendship with Haggard was clouded in 1891 by the death of Haggard's son Jock, left in the Gosses' care when the Haggards were in Mexico; Thwaite, *Gosse*, 334–6; Higgins, *Haggard*, 105.

English readers. His literary friendships with Swinburne, Stevenson, Hardy, Henry James, and more were important. Gosse was not university-educated and never a full-time literary man. He began, aged 17, as a transcriber in the British Museum, working in conditions that a royal commission would condemn as injurious to health. This was the Den, a steel-caged cellar, 'my hell of rotten morocco' where in summer the assistants baked 'like a crumpet'.[190] He then progressed as a civil servant, first a translator at the Board of Trade, ultimately Librarian of the House of Lords.[191] He was skilled at bringing literary people together at parties at his home; and the librarianship enabled him to extend his patronage, for example, inviting Thomas Hardy to take tea with Balfour, the Prime Minister, and Lord Salisbury, son of the previous Prime Minister, on the Terrace of the House of Lords soon after his appointment in 1904.[192] This was Gosse at his most unctuous. Friends such as Arthur Benson recoiled at how he would 'posture pathetically before eminent persons, becoming arch and ingratiating with titled ladies (Lady Londonderry, especially), even pretending a deep interest in golf in order to gain the friendship of Arthur Balfour'.[193]

Gosse's burgeoning literary reputation had brought him offers of professorial chairs from the United States and, from Cambridge, the Clark lectureship, supported by references from Matthew Arnold, Tennyson, and Browning. The Clark he accepted, and he enjoyed five years at Trinity College, until he 'paid, fearfully, the penalty of a false position'.[194] His published lectures, *From Shakespeare to Pope* (1885), dedicated to Tennyson, were castigated as habitually ignorant, the work of a charlatan whose only use was to illustrate 'the manner in which English literature should not be taught'.[195] The author of this slashing attack, which appeared in the *Quarterly Review*, October 1886, was John Churton Collins, a Balliol-educated university extension lecturer, who was disappointed by his rejection for the recently established Oxford professorship that enthroned Language (philology) at the expense of Literature.[196] Collins crusaded for an Oxford

---

[190] Gosse, 'A First Sight of Tennyson', in Gosse, *Portraits and Sketches*, 130–1, 134.

[191] Gosse was one of a group of writers and critics who were or had been civil servants: William Allingham (Customs service), W. J. Courthope (Education Office; Civil Service Commissioner), Austin Dobson (Board of Trade), R. Erskine Childers (Clerk in the House of Commons), H. B. Forman (Post Office), W. S. Gilbert (Education Office), Maurice Hewlett (Land Revenue Records Office), A. E. Housman (Patent Office), W. W. Jacobs (Savings Banks Department), W. M. Rossetti (Inland Revenue), Clement Scott (War Office), Clement Shorter (Exchequer and Audit Department, Somerset House), Bram Stoker (Dublin Castle, Inspector of Petty Sessions), A. B. Walkley (Postmaster-General's Office), William Hale White (Mark Rutherford, Admiralty). Matthew Arnold, an inspector of schools, applied and failed to become Librarian of the House of Commons in 1867.

[192] Hardy to Edmund Gosse, 4 May, 18 June, and 15 July 1904, in Purdy and Millgate (eds.), *Hardy Letters*, iii. 124, 127, 131.   [193] Newsome, *Edge of Paradise*, 90.

[194] Henry James to William Dean Howells, 7 Dec. 1886, in Edel (ed.), *James Letters*, iii. 149. For his sympathetic letter to Gosse, 26 Oct. 1886, ibid. 136–7.   [195] Quoted in Thwaite, *Gosse*, 282.

[196] On Collins (1848–1908), see *DNB*, and Chris Baldick, *The Social Mission of English Criticism 1848–1932* (Oxford, 1983), 64–5, 72–5. The new chair, held with a fellowship at Merton, was designated Language and Literature; its first occupant was A. S. Napier, a German-trained philologist who pluralistically held the Rawlinson Professorship of Anglo-Saxon from 1903. The wishes of Merton College (perhaps influenced by Andrew Lang, a former Fellow) to establish a separate Literature chair had been overruled by the

joint school of Classics and English Literature to promote a humanizing culture with intellectual rigour, the antithesis as he saw it of Gosse's woolly generalities and flowery superficiality. He had subjected Tennyson to a series of critical examinations in the *Cornhill*, afterwards enlarged as *Illustrations of Tennyson* (1891). There Collins traced Tennyson's borrowed ideas to their origins, many from ancient writers. Tennyson especially mirrored Virgil, Collins argued, citing parallel passages from their poetry. This comparative literature method led remorselessly to the conclusion that Tennyson must be dethroned and, at best, 'stand first in the second rank of poets'.[197] Such an exercise 'simply made creative artists laugh', wrote Arnold Bennett, for whom it provided confirmation that professorial literary criticism was 'entirely sterile', proof only that Collins, for all his learning and industry, 'had no artistic feeling'.[198] Collins indeed was habitually seized by enthusiasms: one that entertained *Punch* in 1906 was his defence in the *National Review* of Judge Jeffreys, notorious for the 'bloody assize' in the aftermath of Monmouth's rebellion in 1685.[199] Previously, in the *Pall Mall Gazette*, he had lauded Stephen Phillips's debut *Poems* (1897) as work that 'passed the line which divides talent from genius', although in this he was in good company. *The Academy* awarded Phillips its 100 guineas prize for the year's 'most important contribution to literature'; and William Watson in the *Fortnightly Review*, W. L. Courtney in the *Daily Telegraph*, William Archer in *Outlook*, Richard Le Gallienne in the *Sketch*, and reviewers in *The Times*, the *Daily Chronicle*, *The Spectator*, and *Literature*, all joined in singing (as the *Westminster Gazette* put it) 'a chorus of applause, which recalls the early triumphs of Swinburne and Tennyson'.[200] Collins's onslaught against Gosse, however, was the literary scandal of its time, to be ranked with Macaulay's demolition of Croker and Buchanan's denunciation of Rossetti. Collins's son afterwards wrote: 'When such men as W. E. Gladstone, John Bright, Dr. Benson (then Archbishop of Canterbury), Cardinal Manning, Dr. Fairbairn [Congregationalist divine], Lord Coleridge (the Lord Chief Justice), Prof. Huxley, Matthew Arnold and Lord Lytton (to mention but a few) gave their opinions on the subject, it will be seen how universal was the interest shown.'[201]

university's Hebdomadal Council; but the college persisted and amended its statutes in 1892–3, although not until Sir Walter Raleigh's appointment in 1914 did the reconstituted professorship of English Literature become reality.

[197] *Review of Reviews* (Dec. 1891), 636. Collins later published with Methuen various editions, with introductions and notes, of Tennyson, *Early Poems, In Memoriam, Maud* and *The Princess*. On Tennyson's sensitivity to the charge of plagiarism in this matter of his assimilation of and allusiveness to classical authors, see Cook, *More Literary Recreations*, 179–86, and above, p. 153.

[198] *New Age*, 26 Sept. 1908, in Bennett, *Books and Persons*, 41–2.

[199] See 'More Whitewash', *Punch*, 17 Oct. 1906, 279.

[200] Reviews collated as advertisements by the publisher John Lane, in the end pages of Stephen Phillips, *Herod: A Tragedy* (1901). See also below, p. 1022.

[201] Quoted in Thwaite, *Gosse*, 280. The incident was still being drawn upon fifteen years later when Sidney Stephen and Leslie Lee composed their lampoon curriculum vitae in *Lives of the 'Lustrious*, 35: 'GOSSE, EDMUND, Dictator and Literary Chaperon, was born at Churton-on-Trent in 1849. He entered the Board of Trade at an early age, and has made translations of Ibsen, Obsen, and Dobsen, to the surprise and delight of successive Permanent Secretaries. His latest work is entitled *Hippodromia; or, the Gods in*

Gosse was wounded by Collins's exposure of his carelessness, but not fatally. The vehemence and *ad hominem* style of Collins's attack caused friends to rally around Gosse, among them his fellow sufferer Tennyson, whose opinion that Collins was a 'jackass' Gosse embellished via Smollett into the verdict that Collins was a 'Louse upon the Locks of Literature'.[202] In 1904 Walter Raleigh took the chair of English Language and Literature at Oxford that Collins sought. Raleigh had also been on the receiving end of a Collins review (of *Style*, 1897); he now wrote that 'Collins is rapidly becoming a kind of divinity of pedantry—mothers frighten their children with his name to prevent mistakes in dates.'[203]

In retrospect the Gosse–Collins controversy might appear as the point at which dilettante and professional academic literary criticism began their modern separation. Yet the superiority of the one over the other was never conclusive because the amateur was not always devoid of expertise and the accredited scholar was not always equipped with artistic sensibility or was immune to sloppiness. Certainly, Gosse liked to indulge himself as a dilettante, and he produced a classic of this kind, *Gossip in a Library*, in 1892. This appeared only a year after he had been savaged again, this time in the *Pall Mall Gazette* by William Archer, who blasted his translation of Ibsen's *Hedda Gabler*. 'He *has* a genius for inaccuracy', wrote Henry James ruefully, 'which makes it difficult to dress his wounds.'[204] But Gosse was tough and resilient: his upbringing had seen to that. Chesterton, who rather liked him, wrote that beneath a 'courtly and silken manner' Gosse 'despised all opinions'; and he exuded an 'extraordinary depth of geniality in his impartial cynicism'.[205] What was recognized as 'the general perfidy of Gosse' appeared amusing rather than sinister.[206] It was understood that he had a tendency to tailor views in line with those held by persons of weight and note. Thus, on Lang's death in 1912, he expressed to one correspondent not just

---

Cranbourn Street. Authorities: Collins's *Ephemera Critica* and *Ode to the Passions*.' The *Hippodromia* was a send-up of Gosse's masque *Hypolympia* (1901), which Henry James and Arthur Pinero hailed ecstatically but, Gosse reported, was otherwise treated in the press 'as absolute imbecility and rot unparalleled'. See Thwaite, *Gosse*, 378.

[202] Thwaite, *Gosse*, 295–7; Robert Bernard Martin, *Tennyson:-The Unquiet Heart* (Oxford, 1980), 529; Cecil Y. Lang and Edgar F. Shannon, Jr. (eds.), *The Letters of Alfred Lord Tennyson*, iii: *1871–1892* (Oxford, 1990), 327 n. 1. Hardy too wrote to console Gosse: letters, 19 Oct. and 11 Nov. 1886, in Purdy and Millgate (eds.), *Hardy Letters*, i. 154, 156. But Hardy also later supported a petition to award Collins's widow a Civil List pension; see Hardy to John Lane, 23 Dec. 1908, in Purdy and Millgate (eds.), *Hardy Letters*, iii. 362. Yeats, who had met Collins during a visit to Oxford in 1888, liked him better than other Fellows he dined with: 'a most cheerful, mild, pink and white little man, full of the freshest, the most unreasonablest enthusiasms' (Yeats to Katharine Tynan, 25 Aug. 1888, in Wade (ed.), *Yeats Letters*, 82).

[203] Letter to C. H. Firth, 27 Oct. 1904. Raleigh, again, liked Collins personally, finding him 'very humane, and curiously modest concerning Universities and the way to work them', when he stayed with him in Birmingham in 1903. But with a pen in his hand, Collins was transformed. 'It is the drill sergeant's idea of literature, with Macaulay for the Great Dook,' thought Raleigh. See his letter to D. Nichol Smith, 3 July 1905, Raleigh (ed.), *Raleigh Letters*, i. 265, ii. 279.

[204] To Robert Louis Stevenson, 18 Feb. 1891, in Edel (ed.), *James Letters*, iii. 338.

[205] Chesterton, *Autobiography*, 93.

[206] Cynthia Asquith, *Diaries* (1987), 404 (28 Jan. 1918), reporting a conversation about Gosse between Charles Whibley and Evan Charteris.

the conventional piety that he was shocked to lose his 'old companion and friend of 35 years' but that Lang's was 'the most elegant mind that the English-speaking race has brought forth in our time'; then, writing a few months later to Henry James, whose contempt for Lang as critic Gosse knew, he declared: 'Somehow his memory *irritates* me! . . . His puerility, as you say, was heart-rending.'[207] Gosse's published appraisal of Lang artfully combined these contradictory opinions, though stab marks showed from the stiletto. 'The magnitude and multitude of Lang's performances', Gosse began, 'almost paralyse expression'; but he soon found the words to deny his rival's vaunted versatility. There was in fact no versatility: 'what he liked and admired as a youth he liked and admired as an elderly man', and 'those who speak of his "versatility" should recollect what large tracts of the literature of the world, and even of England, existed outside the dimmest apprehension of Andrew Lang'. Lang's taste was exclusively romantic and 'in the end it must be fatal, to sustain the entire structure of life and thought, on the illusions of romance. But that was what Lang did—he built his house upon the rainbow.' This intellectual superficiality was married to emotional shallowness: 'His nature was slightly inhuman; it was unwise to count upon its sympathy beyond a point which was very easily reached in social intercourse . . . Lang was like an Angora cat, whose gentleness and soft fur, and general aspect of pure amenity, invite to caresses, which are suddenly met by the outspread paw with claws awake.' In sum, Gosse mused: 'I am impatient to see this vast mass of writing reduced to the limits of its author's delicate, true, but somewhat evasive and ephemeral genius . . . Lang's only misfortune was not to be completely in contact with life, and his work will survive exactly where he was most faithful to his innermost illusions.'[208]

This behaviour should not be taken to signify that Gosse was simply poisonous and without opinions of his own or that these were jejune. In 1904 he unburdened himself to Arthur Benson, saying that 'the older he grew the more he felt that personality and individuality were *the* qualities in art; that nothing else mattered much. "I may or may not agree with a man on questions of morals and art, but all I desire is to feel that it is a perfectly *sincere* point of view".'[209] And in 1912, in the preface to *Portraits and Sketches*, essays on British and foreign authors whose work interested him or whom he had known, from Swinburne to Gide, he wrote:

the men discussed in the following pages had the common characteristic of devotion to literature; all were writers, and each had, in his own time and way, a serious and even a passionate conception of the responsibilities of the art of writing. They were all, in their

---

[207] Green, *Lang*, 157, 178. In 1886, attempting to persuade Macmillan's to publish his story *The Unequal Yoke* as a single-volume novel, Gosse had cited Lang's support, saying, 'there are few men whose good word for a work is so well worth having just now as his'. And, with a nice extra touch, he proposed that his authorship be anonymous and the book be dedicated to Henry James, 'which would add a note of mystification' (Simon Nowell-Smith (ed.), *Letters to Macmillan* (1967), 209).

[208] Gosse, 'Andrew Lang', *Portraits and Sketches*, 199–211.

[209] Percy Lubbock (ed.), *The Diary of Arthur Christopher Benson* (1927), 94 (12 Nov. 1904).

various capacities, engaged in keeping bright, and in passing on unquenched, the torch of literary tradition.[210]

Gosse's reputation stood high—in 1913 the poet Flecker, who did not ordinarily lavish praise, called him 'the biggest critic alive'[211]—because he too endeavoured to uphold this commission; moreover, he did not confine his notice to one or another branch of English literature but sought to alert readers to the emerging authors from continental Europe and Scandinavia. Gosse also prevailed because sensibility, intuition, and feeling for style, those indefinable ingredients of 'good taste', remained prized qualities in a literary critic.

Such broad sweep of allusion and assessment continued to characterize much university-based as well as journalistic literary criticism. Thus, George Saintsbury could move to the Regius Chair of Rhetoric and English Literature at Edinburgh in 1895 from the assistant editorship of the *Saturday Review*, after two decades of copious journalism.[212] Saintsbury was a monument of industry, 'a regular Albert Memorial of learning', observed a sarcastic Arnold Bennett, himself no slouch in the productivity stakes.[213] In 1902, during the summer vacation from his own professorial duties at Glasgow, Walter Raleigh confessed: 'I have written about $\frac{1}{3}$ of a small book. This depresses me, for my colleague of Edinburgh has probably written about $1\frac{1}{2}$ books (big ones) in the same number of weeks.'[214] In twenty years of journalism Saintsbury reckoned to have written 'the equivalent of at least a hundred volumes of the "Every Gentleman's Library" type—and probably more'; and never to have repeated a sentence. He was decently proud of this, though he supposed his friend and fellow literary critic H. D. Traill 'must

---

[210] Gosse, *Portraits and Sketches*, pp. vii–viii.   [211] Hodgson, *Flecker*, 198.

[212] Another candidate for the Edinburgh chair was the poet–editor W. E. Henley; John Connell, *W. E. Henley* (1972), 304–6. So was Walter Raleigh, then Professor of Modern Literature at Liverpool; and he wrote to John Sampson, 27 July 1895, facetiously giving a bookie's view of the field:

Henley, Saintsbury, Churton Collins, W. Sharp, Eric Robinson, Vaughan, Herford, McCormick, Me, Lord Balfour's gardener's son (it is believed).

Odds on the course.		
	3 to 1	on the Gardener's son
	4 to 1	against Saintsbury
	25 to 1	against Henley
	1000 to 8	against Me
	1000 to 8	against Churton Collins
	1000 to 8	against Vaughan
	10,000 to 3	against W. Sharp
		E. Robertson
		Herford
		McCormick

Raleigh (ed.), *Raleigh Letters*, i. 186. Vaughan was C. E. Vaughan, then Professor of English Literature at University College, Cardiff; Sharp was William Sharp (a.k.a. Fiona Macleod); Herford was C. H. Herford, then Professor of English Language and Literature at Aberystwyth; McCormick was W. S. McCormick, lecturer in English at Glasgow, and afterwards Professor at St Andrews and secretary to the Carnegie Trust for the Universities of Scotland. The individual variously called Robinson and Robertson is given as Eric S. Robertson in the index of Raleigh (ed.), *Raleigh Letters*, but not otherwise identified.

[213] *New Age*, 26 Sept. 1908, in Bennett, *Books and Persons*, 42.

[214] Raleigh to D. Nichol Smith, Aug. 1902, in Raleigh (ed.), *Raleigh Letters*, i. 241.

have doubled the hundred at least', without sacrifice of quality.[215] But, then, these were the days of prodigious penmen: Roger Lancelyn Green computed Andrew Lang's output at equal to 300 volumes—'even excluding the great amount of Lang's work that is lost to us in the anonymous files of forgotten daily papers'.[216] Like Lang's, Saintsbury's journalism was combined with book-writing, a steady stream of works on English and European literature, critical, historical, and biographical; and these held the field as authorities years after his retirement from the professorial chair in 1915. With one signal exception, there was no kind of literary criticism he did not write, that exception being drama, Saintsbury having 'something of a distaste for the theatre', though he added that 'I have a tolerable familiarity with the whole range of English dramatic literature . . . Also I know my Shakespeare as well as I do the multiplication table.'[217] In his Oxford student days he had turned to history, law, and political economy for a year after reading Greats; but he was told that he lost one fellowship competition by submitting an essay that was considered to subscribe to the controversial theory of 'art for art's sake'. He was never an adherent of this: 'form *without* matter, art *without* life', he wrote, 'are inconceivable'.[218]

Saintsbury was a declared opponent of the tyranny of rules and dogmas in literary criticism. The idea of finality amused him as a vain concept. There was always an infinity of interpretations, although a serious critic must not be cavalier, Saintsbury deploring that 'in the two extensive departments of Biblical and Shakespearean criticism, nothing is commoner than to find practitioners who seem to have no notion of evidence at all'.[219] These precepts may suggest a pedestrian even-handedness about Saintsbury; in fact, he was a boisterous and belligerent High Church and High Tory partisan, whose 'general views on politics and religion' most nearly coincided with those of W. H. Mallock, author of *The New Republic* (1877) and anti-socialist polemicist.[220] Outside of literature, Saintsbury nominated the Tractarian Dr Pusey and Field Marshal Lord Roberts as almost the only Englishmen 'whom I have ever regarded with actual and personal veneration';[221] he was also the Compleat Imbiber, his connoisseurship incorporating wine as well as books. The thread connecting his literary criticism, his politics, his religion, and his cellar was a ripe sense of personal freedom and fulfilment. Nostrums allied to late Victorian Liberalism struck him as killjoy and illiberal, as tending to enhance State power. He particularly loathed teetotalism, and also defended gambling from those who sought to repress or tax it as a sin.[222] Saintsbury fearlessly proclaimed his Toryism—not Conservatism, though that

---

[215] Saintsbury, *Scrap Book*, 129–30. On H. D. Traill (1842–1900), see *DNB*: he published light verse as well as regular reviews and essays, and was first editor of *Literature*, started in 1897.

[216] Green, *Lang*, p. x. Green includes a bibliography of Lang's work at pp. 241–59.

[217] George Saintsbury, *A Second Scrap Book* (1923), 104–5. [218] Saintsbury, *Scrap Book*, 114, 116, 236.

[219] Ibid. 28, 229.

[220] Saintsbury, *Second Scrap Book*, 176–7. On Mallock (1849–1923), *DNB 1922–1930*, 556–7.

[221] Saintsbury, *Scrap Book*, 290–1. [222] Ibid. 120–3; id., *Second Scrap Book*, 136–43, 259–63, 289–91.

designation was preferable to 'Unionist' and infinitely better than Tory Democracy, which he believed fundamentally incompatible.[223]

If Liberalism posed threats to personal liberty—'Liberals have always destroyed'; 'there is not really a constructive measure to their credit on the Statute Book'[224]—then these were mild compared with the menace of socialism. Saintsbury read Marx as an undergraduate and later 'was constantly reviewing (which with me meant reading) books' about Marxist economics. As economics, they 'never had any real existence', being mere 'phantasms, will-o'-the-wisps'; yet, linked to the ideology of socialism and to the power of organized labour, they portended a 'hideous... "proletarian" world, with no variety, no "quality", nothing noble, ancient, memorial in it; but in theory simply a gigantic sty of evenly-fed swine, in practice a den of fratricidal and cannibalic monsters'.[225] The origins of such a creed Saintsbury traced to the malign follies of the French Revolution. Against 'the sentimental pleas of Socialist Democracy', he set the record, namely, 'all attempts to establish Liberty, Equality, and Fraternity have failed more or less disastrously and disgustingly'. In contrast, the principles of Toryism—'Inequality, Individualism, Heredity, Property, etc.'—matched 'the physical and historical *facts* of life', by which he meant that people were not born equal or free, and that conflict was natural and healthy.[226] 'People talk of "class selfishness",' Saintsbury wrote. 'Well, I know something of history, and I have never heard or read of any class—tyrant, aristocrat, capitalist, slave-holder, buccaneer, middle-class shopkeeper—so absolutely and exclusively governed by selfishness as Trades Union "Labour".'[227]

All of a piece with this aboriginal Toryism were Saintsbury's views on education. He blamed the failures of the schools system after 1870 on 'a dissatisfied *intelligentsia*', fixated with social and political engineering. He believed that education 'can "develop" nothing that is not there already, and can rather doubtfully develop some things that are'.[228] He repudiated the former Lord Chancellor R. B. Haldane's statement that 'One of the greatest sources of the unrest and class-consciousness to-day lay in the fact that the working classes found themselves to an enormous extent cut off from the chances of higher education.' Not so, countered Saintsbury:

before the later nineteenth century... any gutter child of the towns might become an archbishop or any hedge-bantling of the country a Lord Chancellor. Parish schools, grammar schools, universities, always have given the right ladder to the real salmon, and

---

[223] Saintsbury, *Second Scrap Book*, 318–26; id., *Last Scrap Book*, 85–6, 143–73. Cf. Saintsbury's proclamation in the Preface to *The Earl of Derby* (1892), p. v, warning readers that he had written it 'from the point of view of a Tory. And as I have heard several persons say that they do not exactly know what a Tory means, I may add that I define a Tory as a person who would, at the respective times and in the respective circumstances, have opposed Catholic Emancipation, Reform, the Repeal of the Corn Laws, and the whole Irish legislation of Mr. Gladstone.'   [224] Saintsbury, *Last Scrap Book*, 283–8.
[225] Saintsbury, *Scrap Book*, 163–5.   [226] Ibid. 44–9.
[227] Ibid. 96; id., *Second Scrap Book*, 249–50, 324.   [228] Saintsbury, *Scrap Book*, 19, 137.

always might have continued to do it on reasonable scales and without overcrowding or disappointment.[229]

What Saintsbury chiefly resisted in the modern system was the salience given to social class. He witheringly rebuked a Board of Education official who regretted that the experience of ascending the educational ladder 'was wont to estrange the climbers from their own class. In other words, *he* wished (if his wish is intelligible) to perpetuate a caste system of the most objectionable kind possible, by giving a continuous primary, secondary, and, I suppose, academic culture to the working classes *by* itself, and so to keep it *to* itself.'[230] Saintsbury instead proposed a radical reactionary programme, which included: the gradual withdrawal of the State from involvement in education, replacing the funding derived from rates and taxes by charitable endowments and payment of fees ('adjusted to the income of the parents'); the restriction of 'scholarships' to 'cases of proved and indubitable *merit*'; and the restoration of clerical control of education, to raise 'the standard of morality, manners, and political atmosphere, as well as religion'. Teachers would benefit by these changes; above all, by being 'freed from what is the greatest curse of the teacher—the unteachable oaf who *has* to be taught'.[231] As for those 'pestilent' so-called democrats who advocated Spelling Reform or Simplification, Saintsbury asked, had they 'ever thought of the *beauty* of words'?[232]

The relationship between Saintsbury's vehement political and social philosophy and the platform he adopted as literary critic yielded interesting results. That his reviewing was forthright and his books about literature bore an individual hallmark is to be expected. He had, he hastened to emphasize, no antipathy to 'labour': how could he when he had 'practised that same nearly all the days of my life, and heartily respected other labourers, from colonels and canons to corporals and carpenters'? What he objected to was class organization and systematization, the capitalization of people and things in the abstract. Thus 'labour' was worthy but 'Labour' abhorrent. In the same way, ' "Science", "Education", "Liberty", and sometimes even, I am afraid, "Literature" ', had, Saintsbury thought, 'a bad effect'.[233] As a literary critic, he sought 'to accentuate the importance of treatment over that of mere subject'. He was not at all hostile to the new and the provocative, still less a Little Englander in taste. He extolled the poetry written by Edgar Allan Poe and Walt Whitman at a time when it was distinctly unfashionable, even in America; and, when writing on Baudelaire, Flaubert, and Gautier in the 1870s, he clearly discerned their remarkable quality.[234] Saintsbury also bestowed praise on compositions whose message he rejected. Thus, nothing

seems to me sillier and more mischievous than that of Mr Swinburne's *Song in Time of Revolution*. Political logic and ethics tell me that revolution in the abstract is nearly always unjustifiable, and political history tells me, more emphatically and unanswerably, that revolutions in the concrete have nearly always done much mischief, and seldom, if ever,

---

[229] Ibid. 138.   [230] Ibid. 139.   [231] Ibid. 267–70.   [232] Saintsbury, *Last Scrap Book*, 96.
[233] Saintsbury, *Scrap Book*, 94.   [234] Ibid. 115.

much good . . . But this does not make me in the least insensible to the *vis superba formae* in the piece—to the rise and rush and roar of the volleying anapaests, the deft and fresh handling of the Biblical language, the rocketing soar of the whole to the final explosion:

> For the breath of the face of the Lord that is felt in the bones of the dead.[235]

Saintsbury maintained that political preferences should have no part to play in judging Swinburne, Shelley, Milton, or any other poet—'No: a poet's opinions, tastes, principles, actions, ideals, character, and so forth, matter absolutely nothing when he is considered as a poet. You may hang him *as a poet* "for his bad verses", but for nothing else.'[236] Hence Saintsbury declared himself 'an unrepentant and immutable Old Swinburnian, as far as his poetry is concerned'.[237]

Saintsbury's leading advice to teachers who wanted to disseminate an appreciation of literature was that they should 'always proceed by familiarizing the *unfamiliar*', that is, the history of previous literary endeavour. He himself little reviewed contemporary literature, and he warned teachers against using it in their classes, first because 'you take away the freshness of the enjoyment that should be in finding out *for oneself* what one's fellows are doing and thinking', and second because 'you abstain from providing the necessary condition of that enjoyment if it is to be intelligent—knowledge of what has gone before'. His own recipe was 'as much catholicity as possible'. 'The religion of literature is a sort of Pantheism,' he added. 'You never know where the presence of the Divine *may* show itself, though you should know where it has shown. And you must never forbid it to show itself, anyhow or anywhere.'[238]

We should acknowledge, therefore, the enlightened influence on an incipient democracy of the literary studies and reviews written by a critic whose politics were unenlightened. Arnold Bennett, who knew a thing or two both about novel-writing and about French literature, was impressed when he picked up Saintsbury's history of the French novel in 1917. Though he found it prolix, 'it shows that he does understand something of the craft of novel-writing. His tracing of the development of the technique of the novel in the 17th century is interesting, and, to me, quite new. The amount of this old man's reading is staggering.'[239] Aside from his literary work, Saintsbury plainly enjoyed playing the curmudgeonly old Tory, for whom modern values and even the modern

---

[235] Saintsbury, *Scrap Book*, 86–7. In *A Second Scrap Book*, 82, he recorded in a footnote that 'all I have ever asked of poet or parson, tutor or tale-teller' was that 'they never brought politics into their proper business'.   [236] Saintsbury, *Second Scrap Book*, 147, and *Last Scrap Book*, 39, 49.

[237] Saintsbury, *Last Scrap Book*, 136.

[238] ibid. 197. Cf. George Saintsbury, *A Short History of English Literature* (1898), 797: 'everyone should be helped and encouraged to acquaint himself in his measure with the subject—to gain some knowledge, as far as concerns his own nation and language, of the grace and the glory of the written word that conquers Time'.

[239] Flower (ed.) *Bennett Journals*, ii. 212 (26 Dec. 1917). Previously, when writing for the *New Age*, 26 Sept. 1908, Bennett had been less appreciative; yet, he admitted that he had found Saintsbury's *Studies of French Literature* 'very useful', applauding also his critical introductions to Dent's editions of Balzac; Bennett, *Books and Persons*, 42–3.

Conservative Party were anaemic and faithless. In 1922 he composed a diatribe against standardization by citing the fate of the sausage. Its current representation was so lacking in personality as to be a travesty of its great forebears, once of admirable constitution and variety. Saintsbury pronounced with solemn precision: the 'last sausage that I remember as worthy of its ancient popularity was produced at Sidmouth' in the early 1880s. This saga of the sausage stood as a metaphor for Saintsbury's defence of individuality, independence, quality, and history. He did the late Victorian reading public no harm 'by teaching the mind not to "shy" at what is strange to it'.[240] And to have the self-confidence to be true to one's beliefs: in politics and religion, 'as in literature and in art, in work and play, in personal relations, and in everything else, I have loved things and persons because *I* loved them, and loathed them because *I* loathed—not because the love or the loathing was fashionable or unfashionable, profitable or unprofitable, orthodox or heretical, customary or eccentric'.[241]

VI

Literary appreciation, then, proliferated in this period, in popular papers, in prestige periodicals, and in formal publications. Standards were being set; in fact, a canon was being debated. In characteristic language, speaking at the Royal Academy in 1906, Kipling declared: 'The Record of the Tribe is its enduring literature.'[242] This sentiment was widely echoed; but the process of selecting the classic and of specifying what should endure seemed to elevate the critic above the author. This puffery annoyed the fastidious H. C. Beeching, whose 'private diary' appeared anonymously in the *Cornhill Magazine* in the late 1890s.[243] Browsing in London's bookshops, observing the Christmas shoppers, he noted:

The great bulk of the new books seemed to be reprints of classic authors, which is a sign at least of healthy taste: but it seems the public will not buy them without a certificate pre-fixed from some modern critic. So Scott is patted on the back by Mr. Lang, Johnson by Mr. Birrell, the rest of the eighteenth century writers by Mr. Dobson, females in general by Mrs. Ritchie, Job by Mr. Jacobs, and the world at large by Professor Saintsbury.[244]

How publishers went about choosing their certificating authority can be instanced by Augustine Birrell. In 1884, when he was aged 34 and a Chancery

---

[240] Saintsbury, *Scrap Book*, 196, 216–7. There was a similar animadversion about the state of the sandwich in *A Second Scrap Book*, 116–24.   [241] Saintsbury, *Scrap Book*, p. ix.

[242] Rudyard Kipling, 'Literature' (1906), in *Kipling Book of Words*, 5.

[243] On Beeching (1859–1919), see *DNB*. At this time a clergyman at Yattendon in Berkshire, Beeching afterwards was Dean of Norwich. His most famous parishioner (and choirmaster) at Yattendon was the future Laureate Robert Bridges, whose niece Beeching married. The two men quarrelled, however, over the order of service. See John St Loe Strachey, *The Adventure of Living: A Subjective Autobiography* (1922), 196–200, for his commissioning Beeching to produce a 'diary' for the *Cornhill*.

[244] [H. C. Beeching], *Pages from a Private Diary* (1898), 138.

lawyer, he had published at his own expense in an edition of 250 a collection of facile essays on literary topics, *Obiter Dicta*. He sent out a dozen copies for review:

Then the unexpected happened. The book, prettily got up, was one (as I now can perceive) very easy to review, for it raised a good many questions, and was composed in a style not yet worn out. The papers all reviewed it quickly and favourably. The *Times*, the *Spectator* (two notices), the *St James's Gazette*, the *World* and many others in town and the provinces.[245]

The original edition soon sold out and was reprinted several times in new editions of 500 each; and Birrell followed it with an article in the *Contemporary Review* on the centenary of the death of Dr Johnson. He thus assumed, however insubstantially, the status of 'man of letters' and, when Thomas Wemyss Reid founded the weekly *Speaker* in 1890, Birrell became a regular contributor of literary articles and occasional reviewer. His 'scribbling propensities' were a natural outgrowth of a love of books and also a solace for the death of his wife and their baby, in childbirth in 1879, after thirteen months of marriage. In 1888 he married again, to a widow with three young children. Birrell acquired more than a new family: Eleanor was the widow of Lionel Tennyson, the Laureate's second son, and she was the daughter of the poet and connoisseur Frederick Locker-Lampson. As things turned out, this tie did not carry Birrell far with Tennyson himself. His son's marriage had been strained, and Tennyson did not approve of Eleanor remarrying or of Birrell's provincial Nonconformist origins and Home Rule politics.[246] But Birrell's literary network now included Robert Browning, who was a godfather (Dean Stanley was the other) of his new wife's eldest son. This strengthened a connection that Birrell had initiated when he sent Browning a complimentary copy of *Obiter Dicta*, containing an essay on Browning's poetry, which elicited an invitation to lunch. Birrell advanced in another direction in 1889 when he became a Liberal MP. Wilde flippantly remarked that Birrell 'deserted the turmoil of literature for the peace of the House of Commons';[247] but these pursuits were not exclusive. Birrell's pen continued activity even as he rose in politics and in the law—he became a QC in 1885 and Quain Professor of Law at London University in 1896. He published a *Life of Charlotte Brontë* in 1885, essays on *Men, Women and Books* in 1894, further literary essays in 1900 and 1901, appreciations of William Hazlitt and Andrew Marvell in the English Men of Letters series in 1902 and 1905, and a life of his colleague the Solicitor-General (and cartoonist) Sir Frank Lockwood, in 1898, as well as legal writings. Moreover, as a member of the Johnson Club, he issued a new edition of Boswell's *Life of Johnson* (1791) in 1897 and thereafter was in demand for introductions to various leavings of the Johnson–Boswell circle. In 1908 he was approached by Frank Sidgwick, who was in the process of establishing the new publishing firm of Sidgwick & Jackson. Birrell's market stock now appeared all the greater as a Cabinet minister

---

[245] Birrell, *Things Past Redress*, 100–1.   [246] Martin, *Tennyson*, 522–3, 566.
[247] Oscar Wilde, 'The Critic as Artist' (1891), in Wilde, *Plays, Prose Writings, and Poems* (1962), 34.

(Education, 1905–7; Ireland, 1907–16), although he was not noticeably successful in that role. Sidgwick was wanting to reissue *Letters of James Boswell to the Rev. W. J. Temple*, originally published in 1857; and his invitation to Birrell to cobble an introduction stressed speed of delivery more than content: 'I don't require of necessity more than 1,000 words, though I should *like* more—up to 3,000. In any case I could offer ten guineas for the copyright thereof. The trouble is that I must issue the book early in the autumn, but could wait till the end of September for your MS.'[248]

Birrell, for once, could not oblige; and his place was filled by the ever-ready Thomas Seccombe. A scratch combination of literary pairings was apparent in other instances. In 1886, having learned that Ernest Rhys was editor-in-charge of the Camelot Series of classics, published by the Walter Scott Company, 21-year-old Arthur Symons inveigled a commission to provide an introduction and notes to the essays of Leigh Hunt. To his former schoolteacher Symons confessed: '*Entre nous*, I have never read a page of Leigh Hunt in my life! Do you know any of his work?'[249] The practice of the great academic presses was not always different. The pool of qualified scholars was limited. Twenty-six-year-old George Gordon, having signalled that he was deserting Greats for English Literature, was sent by Oxford University Press in 1907 'proofs of an edition of Scott's *Legend of Montrose* which wants an introduction, notes and glossary almost by return of post'. It was 'not the sort of work I *crave*', Gordon told his future wife; 'but interesting and worth £15. They are making me, as Chapman puts it, their "17th century man", with a vengeance.' A year later he confessed that it was

my favourite form of hackwork to make glossaries to Scott's novels. I have made five for the Press. It is a kind of anonymous mechanical work which suits me; for I love reading Scott, and I know the Scots dialect, which makes it easy. When I am in low water, and my wits stand still, I take up a novel of Scott's that the Press has not yet reached in its series of his works and make a glossary to it. I have a standing commission for them to do it![250]

By now he had also turned out an introduction to Henry Peacham's *The Compleat Gentleman* (1622) for the Tudor & Stuart Library of the Press, and furnished a preface to John Galt (1779–1839).

Consideration of the role of literary critics arose at a dinner party in 1899 given by R. B. Haldane, Liberal politician and promoter of new universities. One guest, the Clerk to the Privy Council, Sir Almeric FitzRoy, endeavoured to umpire a conversational joust between Mrs Horner, 'who justified my host's description of her as a very clever woman', and Edmund Gosse, 'whose functions as a literary critic she was inclined to rate cheaply'. FitzRoy coolly noted the difference

---

[248] F. Sidgwick to A. Birrell, 27 Aug. 1908, in Bodleian Library, Oxford, Sidgwick & Jackson MSS, Letter-book 2, fo. 240.   [249] Beckson, *Symons*, 32.

[250] Gordon to Mary C. Biggar, 2 Feb. 1907 and 28 Jan. 1908, in Gordon (ed.), *Gordon Letters*, 16, 34. R. W. Chapman was then assistant secretary at Oxford University Press.

between the critical ideal and the inadequate practice:

I was not concerned to defend Mr Gosse's exercise of his privileges, and indeed as a critic
he has encountered more than one disastrous fall; but I did defend more emphatically the
position of criticism as in the first rank of modern literary effort, and illustrated my
argument by an appeal to Anatole France's famous dictum: 'Le bon critique est celui qui
raconte les aventures de son âme au milieu des chefs-d'œuvre'. Mrs Horner refused to
admit that Anatole France's claims to consideration were at all first-rate: Gosse, who
agreed with me as to the supreme position he occupied among modern French writers,
gave away his case in the eyes of the lady by describing him as the Andrew Lang of
French literature, and destroyed my respect for his critical judgement.[251]

The disagreement here had narrowed to the question of whether a literary
critic's particular assessment was 'right'. This was (and is) an ultimately futile
exercise. Being 'wrong' is as intrinsic to a certain type of literary criticism as being
'right': if it is judgemental, a question of establishing taste, marking out frontiers,
and laying down the law, then always contemporaries and posterity will dispute
the fitness of the cuisine, the boundary, and the legislation. In 1916 Max
Beerbohm paid tribute to Dixon Scott, an outstanding critic in his and others'
opinion. Robertson Nicoll, with his eye for talent, had spotted this former bank
clerk's reviews in the *Liverpool Courier* and *Manchester Guardian* and given him a
wider platform by inviting him to contribute to *The Bookman*. Dixon Scott's
achievement was abbreviated when, as a lieutenant in the Royal Field Artillery,
he died of dysentery at Gallipoli in 1915: he was aged 34. The qualities that
Beerbohm admired in Dixon Scott's essays—which, with the exception of those
on Browning and William Morris, practically all concerned authors who were
alive at the time of writing—were 'his imagination and insight, his humour and
wisdom', 'the wide "synthetic sweep" of his mind', and 'the truly exquisite
subtlety he had in analysis', combined with 'verbal felicity'. Being a man of his
age, Dixon Scott delighted in paradox; but there was depth of feeling as well as
cleverness. His reviews were, therefore, stamped in a personal manner; yet,
Beerbohm emphasized, this was not an obtrusive or insistent egotism, because he
was revealing the richness of his understanding of the authors about whom he
wrote. His reviewing was, then, fundamentally an exercise in humility. Dixon
Scott himself thought that his provincialism instilled in him the perspective to
appreciate 'something finer than he has ever experienced'. Beerbohm demurred
at the idea that provincialism necessarily taught this—'I have known provincials

---

[251] Sir Almeric FitzRoy, *Memoirs* (1923), i. 12 (3 Mar. 1899). Mrs Horner (*née* Aimée Isaacson) was a self-
styled 'Femme de Lettres'. Born in Brazil, she was a notable traveller, linguist, and Primrose League
Dame, as well as an authoress. She campaigned against the butchering of birds for female fashion, and
campaigned for 'happy horses': she introduced sunhats for carriage horses in 1899. Her husband,
F. W. Horner, was editor–proprietor of the *Whitehall Review*, and Tory MP for North Lambeth 1899–1906,
his career ending in bankruptcy. He also was a writer (under the name Martyn Field) and described
himself as 'the only Englishman who has ever written a 3-act play in French and successfully produced in
Paris i.e. at the Théâtre de la Renaissance, and which had a "run" there of four months'. See *Who's Who*
(1905), 797.

to be very aggressive, very pragmatical and cocksure'—but he accepted that this gift was what distinguished Dixon Scott as a critic. It marked a departure from a once dominant school of criticism, the magisterial:

Gone are the days when we dared bench ourselves aloft to acquit or condemn, according to a fixed code of laws, the shivering artist in the dock. Many of us, no doubt, would like to go on doing this; but wouldn't the laughter in court be unquenchable if we did? . . . At the coming of the romantic school in literature, at the passing of the classical school, the old criticism had ceased to exist; but it didn't know this; nobody knew this. It was in quite recent times that people, looking back, realized that the current judicial criticism of literature in the nineteenth century had been one long series of awful 'howlers' . . . only now was it generally recognized that . . . the critic was not the superior of the creative artist; that his duty was not to dictate, but to understand and suggest; that he had, in fine, no right to wear a full-bottomed wig and looked very well in a peaked cap with INTER-PRETER round the front of it . . . Long robes and ermine may have been gratifying to their wearers, but were incompatible with any natural freedom of movement, and smothered all individuality. Nowadays the critic is free to be actively himself.[252]

Downplaying or discarding the hanging-judge routine of the reviewers' duties raised as many problems as it solved. What was left, other than self-indulgence? Would not reviewers be better occupied in creative writing? Such doubts about the validity of literary criticism occurred at the very time when English Studies were being formalized in school and university curricula. Notable among the sceptics was Walter Raleigh, who became Professor of English Literature at Oxford in 1904. He chafed under the obligation to churn out studies of great authors, Chaucer, Shakespeare, Milton, Wordsworth, and the like: 'I have always longed to escape from this parasitical kind of literature, and to speak for myself; but my profession makes this kind natural to me, so I suppose I shall die a mere critic.'[253] Having graduated as a historian in 1885, Raleigh had begun by expounding the history of English literature to the students at Aligarh College in India. Illness drove him home in 1887, whereupon he did the rounds of university extension lecturing before taking chairs at Liverpool and Glasgow universities. That career epitomized the second-class status of English studies: suitable for the inferior or unintellectual classes, meaning those denied access to, or incapable of learning, the Greek and Latin languages, literature, and philosophy; in other words, working men and middle-class women, provincials and colonials.

Certain types looked kindly on such developments. One was the novelist and Spencerian evolutionary philosopher Grant Allen. He too was an Oxford gradu-ate, but he had been raised in North America and taught both in schools and at a college for blacks in Jamaica. Allen scorned the sort of education in the classics that obtained in male public schools: 'the boys go on as ever with Musa, Musae, like so many parrots, and are turned out at last, in nine cases out of ten, with just

---

[252] Max Beerbohm, Introduction to Dixon Scott, *Men of Letters* (1916), pp. xiii–xiv.
[253] Raleigh to Macmillan, 2 Sept. 1903, in Nowell-Smith (ed.), *Letters to Macmillan*, 252.

enough smattering of Greek and Latin grammar to have acquired a life-long distaste for Homer and an inconquerable incapacity for understanding Æschylus'. By contrast, girls, 'till lately so very ill-taught', were benefiting from the recent establishment of schools that operated without several traditional constraints: 'Less hampered by professions and examinations than the boys, the girls are beginning to know something of, not indeed of the universe in which they live, its laws and its properties, but of literature and history, and the principal facts of human development.'[254]

The study of English Literature was incorporated into the examination of candidates for the Indian Civil Service.[255] It was a vehicle for transmitting the ascendant cultural heritage to subject peoples—inside as well as outside the British Isles. Having acquired 'culture', they could thereby compete on more equal terms in metropolitan society. That was one reason why English Literature courses generally took hold in Scottish universities earlier than in England itself, having their roots in the Scots' ambitions to cast off their handicapping 'Scotticisms' in order to advance in the dominant country after Union in 1707.[256] Robertson Nicoll and J. M. Barrie were but two who took this route. For the industrial working classes in England, particularly for those attending adult evening classes in mechanics institutes or university extension work, English was thought suitable to provide a humanizing, liberal education to correct an over-emphasis on technical instruction and mechanical science and to complement studies in constitutional history, political economy, and public health. It was 'the poor man's classics'; and, for women, it would quicken their charity while not too greatly taxing their brains. English Studies were also incorporated into syllabuses for those sections of the middle classes not privileged to enter the principal public schools; but the objectives were unclear, whether instruction in rhetoric, grammar, and style, as an exercise in polite taste and moral refinement, or as an adjunct to the history of the nation.

These uncertainties plagued the debates about the establishment of the English School at Oxford. When a professorship of English Language and Literature was established at Merton College in 1885, the Warden was deputed to approach Matthew Arnold to ascertain his availability; but, on Arnold ruling himself out as 'a more or less ornamental lecturer, who might deliver a few well-finished discourses in each year, but who could not undertake the weekly drudgery of teaching', the post was filled by the philologist A. S. Napier, who had held a similar chair at Göttingen and who was disinclined to admit the study of literature beyond the age of Chaucer.[257] There was no thought of dethroning Greats (*Literae Humaniores*,

---

[254] Grant Allen, *Post-Prandial Philosophy* (1894), 128–9; and pp. 18–26 for Allen advocating, not education in science, so much as science in education.

[255] See J. Churton Collins, 'The New Scheme for the Indian Civil Service Examinations', *Contemporary Review* (June 1891), 595: 'At last the study of our national literature, rescued from its degrading thraldom to philology, has again been placed on a proper basis.'

[256] See Robert Crawford (ed.), *The Scottish Invention of English Literature* (Cambridge, 1998).

[257] George Charles Brodrick, *Memories and Impressions, 1831–1900* (1900), 263.

Greek and Latin language, literature, history, and philosophy). The question, rather, was how to make English Literature academically respectable, to promote rigorous standards of scholarship instead of frivolous 'chatter about Shelley'. That was the contemptuous estimation of E. A. Freeman, Regius Professor of Modern History. Schools of English and History had developed at civic universities but intellectual standards were too frequently surrendered to factual cramming and mechanical recitation. Other possibilities were canvassed: to marry English Literature with the Classics (as Churton Collins proposed), to unite it with Modern European Languages, or to invent an English *Literae Humaniores*. Ultimately, the Oxford English undergraduate school which emerged in 1894 bolted English Literature on to the University's pre-existing plant in Anglo-Saxon and philological study; and, being also understaffed, the course proved initially unattractive. When Raleigh became Professor in 1904, the Finals were sat by only five men and fifteen women; at his death in 1922, the contingent had risen to seventy men and forty-six women.[258] Raleigh was not easily converted to the notion that literature and literary sensibility were things that could be taught. In 1906 he reported on a paper read by a student to a research class. It was

empty, magniloquent, abstract, flatulent, pretentious, confused, and sub-human. I could have wept salt tears. But I couldn't do anything else: the young man wanted a clean heart and a new spirit, not a little topdressing. That's my trouble; literature even at its worst, is tremendously expressive: substitute a public uniform, and you get more decency, but you don't increase the amount of the real thing.[259]

The questions of what exactly a course in English Literature was meant to do, and how the professor should go about it, long puzzled Raleigh. When he was teaching at Owen's College, Manchester, in 1889, he had communicated his concerns to Edmund Gosse. If the function of literary criticism was

simply tracing literary cause and effect as history is said to be the tracing of political cause and effect, I do not see why a lover of literature ever should go on to it any more than I see why a lover of painting should study chemistry.

Besides, an annoying author springs up here and there who has read simply nothing, and plays havoc with the influences. My class here has read very little, but it comes to College and religiously learns why Byron wrote as he did—imparted with a certainty that amuses me more than them.

On the other hand, there is the Mrs Jarley function of criticism, which I try to mix with the other.

I like the German scientific notion if it could be worked out, but I do not see that caring for particular books as to their matter, is a help to philosophizing about them. And they cannot demonstrate that Burns could by no possibility have been born in 1700.

I am at a loss for anything consistent, so I go on the beaten track which seems to me inconsistent.[260]

[258] See David Nichol Smith, Preface to Raleigh (ed.), *Raleigh Letters*, vol. i, p.xiv.
[259] Raleigh to George W. Prothero, 23 May 1906, ibid. ii. 298.
[260] Raleigh to Gosse, 16 May 1889, ibid. i. 130. The reference is to Mrs Jarley's waxwork show in Dickens's *Old Curiosity Shop* (1841).

Raleigh's doubts were not dissipated in Oxford. In the civic universities the position was little different; yet the public standing of the subject, and sympathy for its cultivating mission, were perhaps greater in the provinces. As a Fellow by Examination at Magdalen College, Oxford, in 1907, George Gordon was that college's first ever Prize Fellow in English Literature. When he left for the chair of English Literature at Leeds in 1913, he was further buoyed to find the *Yorkshire Post* reporting his inaugural lecture.[261]

[261] Gordon to George Galbraith, 7 Nov. 1913, in Gordon (ed.), *Gordon Letters*, 55.

5

The Great Tradition

ALICE. Are you very studious, Cosmo?
COSMO [*neatly*]. My favourite authors are William Shakespeare and William
    Milton. They are grand, don't you think?
ALICE. I'm only a woman, you see; and I'm afraid they sometimes bore me,
    especially William Milton.
COSMO [*with relief*]. Do they? Me, too.

(J. M. Barrie, *Alice Sit-By-The-Fire* (1905))

I

When the Cambridge literary scholar F. R. Leavis published *The Great Tradition* in
1948, he was adding the coping stone to a structure of Victorian and Edwardian
construction. The discourse was Hellenistic in character and Arnoldian in purpose, positing that English Literature was not primarily designed for amusement
(hence the problem about settling Dickens's place in the Great Tradition[1]) but
about expressing the essential heritage and cultural continuity. The creation of a
literary canon was thus quasi-theological: major authors as prophets, significant
texts as scriptures, interpreted and disseminated by literary critics as priests and
magi. Truly to read a great work was an exceptional experience, an almost
sacramental rite through which emblematic authors transmitted what was deepest in them. There was mysticism here, the pursuit of eternal values. There was
also literary patriotism, the assembly of a storehouse of national treasures. The
impetus towards the creation of a canon grew from disquiet about democracy,
the foreboding that Christian churches, modern science and philosophy, popular

---

[1] F. R. and Q. D. Leavis's fullest assessment is in *Dickens the Novelist* (1970), whose preface stated firmly
'that Dickens was one of the greatest of creative writers; that with the intelligence inherent in creative
genius, he developed a fully conscious devotion to his art, becoming as a popular and fecund, yet
profound, serious and wonderfully resourceful practising novelist, a master of it; and that, as such, he
demands a critical attention he has not had'. The Leavises were particularly pained by 'the trend of
American criticism of Dickens, from Edmund Wilson onwards, as being... essentially ignorant and
misdirecting'; but in *The Great Tradition*, Dickens had been sidelined because, *Hard Times* (1854) apart,
Leavis then decided that his genius was primarily as an entertainer; anyway, Mrs Leavis had previously
pronounced that he was 'emotionally uneducated' and 'immature'; Gross, *Man of Letters*, 286, 294.

education and commercial entertainment, were failing to civilize the masses, instruct them in their duties as subjects, sustain a sense of organic community, and immunize them from socialism or, worse, Bolshevism. The conviction that the traditional governing classes and mercenary middle classes were active conspirators in the cultural debasement and materialist preferences of the masses only drove the missionaries for English Literature more fervently forward. A landmark event in this process was the foundation of the English Association in 1906 'to promote the due recognition of English as an essential element in the national education'.[2]

When Leavis propounded his Great Tradition he distinguished between books that were historically important in the development of the English novel—such as the pioneering work by Defoe, Fielding, Richardson, and Sterne—and what he termed 'the significant few'. He presumed that major authors 'are all very original technically'; accordingly, none was admitted to the Great Tradition from innovation or perfection of form or style alone. The defining characteristic of 'the few really great' was 'that they not only change the possibilities of the art for practitioners and readers, but that they are significant in terms of the human awareness they promote; awareness of the possibilities of life'. For Leavis the Great Tradition began with Jane Austen—'Her work, like the work of all great creative writers, gives a meaning to the past'; moreover, 'without her intense moral preoccupation she wouldn't have been a great novelist'—and it continued through George Eliot, Henry James, Joseph Conrad, and D. H. Lawrence.[3]

Few of the pre-1914 generation of critics would have dissented from these premises. The same agenda had been set by Henry James:

The effect, if not the prime office, of criticism is to make our absorption and our enjoyment of the things that feed the mind as aware of itself as possible, since that awareness quickens the mental demand, which thus in turn wanders further and further for pasture . . . This is the very education of our imaginative life.[4]

The true critic was, therefore, at odds with the prevailing spirit of the age, defined by James as the tendency 'to treat, one manner of book, like one manner of person, as, if not absolutely as good as another, yet good enough for any democratic use'.[5] On the contrary, James argued, it was essential to preserve 'the critical spirit to-day, in presence of the rising tide of prose fiction, a watery waste out of which old standards and landmarks are seen barely to emerge, like chimneys and the tops of trees in a country under flood'.[6] This was a commission

---

[2] Quoted in Baldick, *English Criticism*, 93; see also Robert Colls and Philip Dodd (eds.), *Englishness: Politics and Culture 1880–1920* (1986), 102 ff. President of the Association was the patriotic poet Henry Newbolt, who chaired a government committee on the question, publishing its report as *The Teaching of English in England* (1921). For the Professor of English Literature at Oxford, Walter Raleigh's mordant comments on the inaugural strivings of the English Association, see Raleigh (ed.), *Raleigh Letters*, ii. 299.

[3] F. R. Leavis, *The Great Tradition* (1948), 2–7.

[4] Henry James, 'The New Novel', in James, *Notes on Novelists* (New York, 1969), 315.

[5] Ibid. 317.   [6] Henry James, 'Emile Zola' (1902–3), ibid. 26.

consciously embraced by the journal *Literature*, which made its debut in October 1897. Aspiring to make *Literature*, 'the organ of the literary classes', its editor, H. D. Traill, proclaimed that 'contemporary criticism is running a real danger of neglecting its discriminative function, and of forgetting that the special recognition which it owes to writers of genuine literary merit is necessarily depreciated in value by association with a too liberal complaisance of attention to all writers whatsoever'. Leslie Stephen put the matter more brutally in the sixth issue of *Literature*, in an article entitled 'Perishable Books', when he asked, 'Will our grandchildren have any cause for sorrow if ninety-nine hundredths of all the publications of today should disappear like a bad dream?'[7]

Agreement about the critic's duty did not mean that Dr Leavis's Great Tradition in 1948 echoed his predecessors' in 1914 or 1885. Saintsbury, who boasted of his own 'naughty catholicity', was dismissive of Matthew Arnold's critical judgement, which he reckoned 'so unequal and limited as to be sometimes, in his own word of anathema, simply "capricious"'. Arnold sought 'to "order the universe of literature", so that it should only contain "the chief and principal things" as they seemed to his temperament'. Saintsbury thought this the equivalent of wearing blinkers; further, he derided Arnold's 'fallacy-heresy as to Poetry being "a criticism of life"'. Arnold—and, by extension, Leavis later—committed '*the* Unpardonable Sin of Criticism—the inquiring of a work of art whether it has done, not what the artist meant it, but what the critic wanted it, to do'.[8] The rise and fall of literary reputations according to critical and popular taste interested Saintsbury greatly as a subject. He wrote essays and reviews about this throughout his career, though he never systematically developed the theme: 'the *History of Literary Reputations* is another of the books I should like to have written'.[9]

II

Most Victorian critics put Scott ahead of Austen. From this Dr Leavis later violently dissented, relegating Scott to a footnote as

a kind of inspired folk-lorist . . . Not having the creative writer's interest in literature, he made no serious attempt to work out his own form and break away from the bad tradition of the eighteenth-century romance . . . Out of Scott a bad tradition came . . . And with [Robert Louis] Stevenson it took on 'literary' sophistication and fine writing.[10]

This was not how most Victorians saw it. The former Governor of Canada and of India, afterwards ambassador in several major European capitals, Lord Dufferin

---

[7] Quoted by Carol de Saint Victor in her article on *Literature* in Sullivan (ed.), *Literary Magazines 1837–1913*, 199–201. *Literature* did not long survive the death of its founding editor, Traill, in 1900: it was merged with *The Academy* in 1902 but, Victor argues, its real lineage should be traced through the *Times Literary Supplement*, which was also started in 1902.   [8] Saintsbury, *Last Scrap Book*, 195–8.

[9] Ibid. 37, written on the centenary of Byron's death in 1924.

[10] Leavis, *Great Tradition*, 14 n. 1.

was decided. Aged 70 in 1896, he wrote: 'I love Sir Walter Scott with all my heart; and, my mother excepted, I think he has done more to form my character than any other influence; for he is the soul of purity, chivalry, respect for women and healthy religious feeling.'[11] This was a particularly unfortunate statement in Dufferin's case, because he was about to besmirch his reputation by acting as an unsuspecting front for one of Whitaker Wright's shady companies; still, almost as a matter of course, Sir John Lubbock had included Scott in his entirety, poems as well as novels, in his Best Hundred in 1886. He was astonished when Lord Acton and Clement Shorter did not do the same, and clearly thought this proof of their desiring to shock or being unhinged (Acton also omitted Shakespeare).[12] The term 'Victorian' can be stretched to include, in this context, continental Europeans—Scott's importance to Dumas was obvious—and Americans. The gentry class of the quasi-feudal Southern states predictably revelled in Scott but so, perhaps surprisingly, did Jeffersonian democrats like that apostle of the new America Walt Whitman, who recalled in old age:

How much I am indebted to Scott no one can tell—I couldn't tell it myself—but it has permeated me through and through. If you could reduce the *Leaves* [*of Grass*] to their elements you would see Scott unmistakably active at the roots. I remember the Tales of My Landlord, Ivanhoe, The Fortunes of Nigel—yes, and Kenilworth—its great pageantry— then there's the Heart of Midlothian, which I have read a dozen times or more.

Whitman rejected the notion that he was old-fashioned in this liking for Scott or for one of Scott's American counterparts, James Fenimore Cooper: 'Scott, Cooper, such men, always, perpetually . . . take life forward—take each new generation forward.'[13]

Henry James's first published essay in literary criticism, in 1864, was on Scott and, though he thought him far from immaculate, James's final verdict, given in 1914 after suffering Compton Mackenzie's and H. G. Wells's latest work, was that 'It all makes Walter Scott, him only, readable again.'[14] Most Victorians did not even consider it worth bothering to compare Scott with other writers, still less with their contemporaries. For them, the only interesting question was a comparison of Scott with Scott; as the title of J. M. Barrie's essay phrased it in 1893, 'What is Scott's Best Novel?' The choice of the one-time Chancellor of the Exchequer Robert Lowe had been for *St Ronan's Well* (1824) and that of the Prime Minister, Mr Gladstone, for *Kenilworth* (1821).[15] Barrie's was for *Ivanhoe* (1819), though he acknowledged that many people would pick one of the Scottish

[11] Harold Nicolson, *Helen's Tower* (1937), 41.

[12] Preface to the Forty-First English Edition, Avebury, *Pleasures of Life*, p. viii.

[13] Edgar Lee Masters, *Whitman* (1937), 11–12.

[14] James to Edith Wharton, 9 Nov. 1914, in Lyall H. Powers (ed.), *Henry James and Edith Wharton: Letters 1900–1915* (1990), 316.

[15] Grant Duff, *Diary, 1889–1891*, ii. 125 (7 Apr. 1891); and for Gladstone's love of Scott, see Rendel, *Personal Papers*, 102 (26 Sept. 1894). When Tony Blair, in the run-up to his general election victory in 1997, appeared on the radio programme *Desert Island Discs*, he chose Scott's *Ivanhoe* as his castaway book.

novels, probably *Guy Mannering* (1815) or *The Antiquary* (1816). Another public, mainly theatregoers, might reckon *Rob Roy* (1817) his masterpiece, because it had been the most successfully adapted for the stage, being put on 'nearly every year' by Scottish theatre managers, and 'the piece never fails to attract'.[16] *Rob Roy* was top for George Du Maurier, as also Robertson Nicoll, who reckoned he had read it sixty times. 'I owe more to Scott than to any other writer,' Nicoll stated. 'Every year even in the busiest times I have read over his best stories.'[17] Beyond the Great War, veteran members of the Literary Society still delighted in this challenge of selecting Scott from Scott when, for example, Sidney Colvin nominated *The Bride of Lammermoor* (1819) as the 'greatest of all.'[18]

Scott had travelled to the end of the earth or, at least, to Australia. T. A. Browne, whose father had transported convicts there, grandly retitled his cattle-grazing ground—then grimly called The Swamp—Swattlesea Mere after Sir Roger Wildrake's estate in *Woodstock* (1826); and when he came to write novels himself, Browne took the guise of Rolf Boldrewood from *Marmion* (1808).[19] For Hugh Walpole, who also came up from down under, in his case from New Zealand, Scott was a lifelong passion. *The Talisman* (1825) was the first book he ever bought, at the age of 14 in 1898; and from a subscription library in Durham he proceeded to read all of Scott, who influenced his own first writings. One bonus of his father's promotion to the bishopric of Edinburgh was that they could make the pilgrimage together to Abbotsford. However many times Walpole read Scott, he never failed to be moved, as in 1918, when he 'read a little *Heart of Midlothian* and actually wept, at my age too, over Jeanie's meeting with the Queen, but it's a *perfect* piece of writing'.[20] After the war Walpole set about becoming a collector. His plan was to obtain everything penned by Scott and about Scott, as well as first editions of every significant novel written in English. In time he would expand his net to include other novelists' manuscripts, works published in the 1890s, 'yellowbacks', American novels, and books on the Lake District; and he accumulated nearly 30,000 items before his death in 1941. But his original goal remained the most important, so much so that he liked to dream that in a previous life he had been 'a bowlegged, snuff-taking, spectacled little bookseller' in an Edinburgh back street, into whose shop Scott entered and touched him on the shoulder.[21] Walpole bought the corrected proofs of *Redgauntlet* (1824) in 1919; the manuscript of *Count Robert of Paris* (1831), together with a lock of Scott's hair, in 1920; and the manuscript of *The Fortunes of Nigel*

---

[16] Barrie, *Two of Them*, 272–6; Janet Dunbar, *J. M. Barrie: The Man behind the Image* (Newton Abbot, 1971), 27, for Barrie's discovery of Scott when a schoolboy. Stage adaptations were important in diffusing Scott's popularity: Allardyce Nicoll, *A History of Late Nineteenth Century Drama 1850–1900* (Cambridge, 1946), i. 80, notes eight different versions of *Ivanhoe* and five of *The Heart of Midlothian*, 1850–1900.

[17] Leonée Ormond, *George Du Maurier* (1969), 54; Darlow, *Nicoll*, 419.

[18] Bailey (ed.), *Bailey Letters and Diaries*, 191 (8 Dec. 1919). *The Bride of Lammermoor* was also Swinburne's selection, he telling Arthur Benson in 1903 that it was 'a *perfect* story' (Lubbock, *Benson*, 65).

[19] See P. D. Edward's notice of Browne (1826–1915), *Oxford DNB*.

[20] Hart-Davis, *Walpole*, 172.   [21] Ibid. 180.

(1822), once owned by Ruskin, in 1921. He paid a San Francisco bookseller the enormous sum of $4,000 (£823) for fifty-seven letters of Scott in 1920, which in 1946 would resell at Christie's for only £220; but his greatest coup occurred in 1921, when Scott's descendants sold through Sothebys thirty-two volumes of the Abbotsford Correspondence, containing about 7,000 letters written to Scott, which Walpole secured for £1,500. In his will Walpole left this to the National Library of Scotland. Whatever little agues beset Walpole, there was always a cure in Scott: a cold would send him to bed, where he would happily read the Abbotsford Correspondence or Scott's *Journal* (1890), 'very nearly my favourite book in the world, I think. You can actually hear him speaking through the page.'[22] Or there was the Wilkie drawing of Scott to regard, positioned over his drawing room mantelpiece, which he bought in 1920. For the centenary of Scott's death in 1932 he wrote a 15,000-word preface to a Scott anthology; he prepared numerous articles and speeches; he participated in a dinner at Stirling, a service at Dryburgh, and a procession in Edinburgh; and he topped everything by staying overnight in Abbotsford, where he slept in Scott's bed. Walpole's last reading of Scott was in the month before his death, when he was endeavouring to finish *Katherine Christian* (1944).

John Buchan was similarly possessed. In 1917, just as he was taking over the direction of wartime propaganda in the newly formed Department of Information, he was treated for a duodenal ulcer. Recuperating after the operation, 'he read through a dozen of the Waverley Novels, the Valois and D'Artagnan cycles of Dumas, then Victor Hugo's *Notre Dame* and the immense *Les Misérables*, almost a library in itself, ending up with half a dozen of Balzac; and this in order to consider how Scott stood the test'.[23] Buchan eventually paid his tribute in the centenary year with *Sir Walter Scott* (1932), which G. M. Trevelyan—one of its dedicatees; the other was the Prime Minister, Stanley Baldwin—considered 'not only the best one-volumed book on Scott, but the best one-volumed biography in the language'.[24] That sold 19,000 copies during its first year of publication.[25]

Scott had been a best-seller virtually from the start. Though a first edition of *Waverley* (1814) sold at a London auction for £200 a century later, those who owned first editions of his other novels, as J. H. Balfour Browne did of *Kenilworth* (1821), awoke from dreams of avarice when he saw this advertised in a bookseller's catalogue for a mere 8s.[26] By the late nineteenth century the novels were extensively available—*The Talisman* that Walpole bought in 1898 was in a sixpenny edition—and the ordinary person's familiarity with Scott was widely evident. When Jerome K. Jerome was waiting on Charles Hawtrey, hoping to get him to read a play of his in the mid-1880s, the stage doorman at the Globe

---

[22] Hart-Davis, *Walpole*, 219.   [23] *John Buchan by his Wife and Friends* (1947), 185.
[24] Ibid., Preface, 16.   [25] Smith, *Buchan*, 297.
[26] Balfour Browne, *Recollections*, 150. Cf. Andrew Lang, *The Library* (1892), p. xiv: 'Why Mr. [Robert Louis] Stevenson's first editions should be four or five times as valuable as Sir Walter Scott's is a mystery which, I'm sure, will puzzle and divert the modern author.'

gave him a worn copy of *The Talisman* to pass the time, saying that he judged it
the finest of all Scott's novels.[27] The Dean of Westminster also related that 'when
working men came to be shown round the Abbey, he often tried the experiment
of alluding to one of Scott's novels and asking how many of them had read it,
eliciting, in general, a fairly satisfactory response'.[28] Revealing too, for all its
bathos, was the subject chosen for its monthly prize by the sixpenny girls'
magazine *Atalanta* in 1891: a guinea for the best doll dressed in the costume of any
character from Scott's novels.[29] As for the poet–dramatist who shot to fame with
his own *Atalanta* (1865), Swinburne felt that he was speaking for the world when
he wrote, 'If there is one thing of which a reasonable man might have felt
reasonably confident, it is that nothing could heighten the admiration or deepen
the affection felt by him for the name and memory of Sir Walter Scott.' But this
did happen for Swinburne in 1890, when J. G. Tait published Scott's *Journal* in
three volumes; thus, Swinburne decided, 'the year 1890 must ever be remembered in the history of letters as "Scott's year"'. Though Scott himself, as
Swinburne now discovered, had derided the comparison—'The blockheads talk
of my being like Shakespeare—not fit to tie his brogues' (11 December 1826)—
Swinburne asserted it to be 'true that if there were or could be any man whom it
would not be a monstrous absurdity to compare with Shakespeare as a creator of
men and an inventor of circumstance, that man could be none other than Scott'.[30]
HM Government, at least, seemed content with this comparison when in 1912 it
commissioned a new fleet of warships named after characters in Shakespeare's
and Scott's works.[31]

For a budding writer in the late 1880s, such as the failed accountant Richard Le
Gallienne, the obvious ambition was to dream of becoming a second Scott.[32]
Scott's supremacy had never been in doubt for Robert Louis Stevenson, who
called him 'out and away the king of the romantics'.[33] George Saintsbury, author
of *Sir Walter Scott* (1897), was scarcely less enthusiastic; nor did his enthusiasm
abate with age. In his *Scrap Book* in 1922 he recorded that he was 'reading for the
hundredth time *the* Short Story of the World—Scott's "Wandering Willie's
Tale"'.[34] Andrew Lang was equally certain about Scott, whose books captivated
him as a boy and 'grow better on every fresh reading'.[35] For Lang, who hailed

---

[27] Jerome, *Life and Times*, 101.   [28] Grant Duff, *Diary, 1889–1891*, ii. 165 (6 July 1891).
[29] *Review of Reviews* (Jan. 1891), 67. On *Atalanta* (1887–98), edited by the prolific Lillie Meade (1854–1915),
see Sutherland, *Companion*, 32, 427.
[30] 'The Journal of Sir Walter Scott' (1891), in Algernon Charles Swinburne, *Studies in Prose and Poetry*
(1915), I, 5–6.
[31] *Punch*, 11 Sept. 1912, 213, appreciated the potential for absurdity, proposing, in the interest of feminism, a torpedo boat called *Brontë* and a destroyer named *Jane Eyre*; and, to bring home to the Germans
that the pen is mightier than the sword, threatening to lay down one *Arnold Bennett* for every two *Moltkes*
or *Bismarcks*.
[32] Geoffrey Smerdon and Richard Whittington-Egan, *The Quest of the Golden Boy* (1960).
[33] Robert Louis Stevenson, *Memories & Portraits* (1887), 269.
[34] Saintsbury, *Scrap Book*, 14. John Buchan also nominated 'Wandering Willie's Tale' (from *Redgauntlet*,
1824) 'the best short story in the world'; see Bailey, *Letters and Diaries*, 270 (22 Mar. 1927).
[35] Lang, *Adventures among Books*, 82.

from the Border country, Scott was the *ne plus ultra*, 'his favourite novelist of any age'; and he rated him as a poet too. He wrote introductions and notes, comprising some 430 pages, to the Border Edition of the Waverley Novels (1892–4), as well as a short Life of Scott (1906) and a study of the Border Ballads (1910). Some of Lang's theories excited scorn, particularly his satisfying himself that *Waverley* (1814), which Scott first set aside and finished at a different period, was only partly written by Scott and completed by an inferior bungler.[36] Still, Lang's two-volume *Life and Letters of John Gibson Lockhart* (1896)—about Scott's brother-in-law and original biographer—was acclaimed as one of the finest biographies of the century and Lang's own most scholarly work.[37] This did not displace Lockhart's *Life of Scott* from its throne. Leslie Stephen gave his daughter, the later Virginia Woolf, this as a present on her fifteenth birthday in 1897: 'ten most exquisite little volumes, half bound in purple leather, with gilt scrolls and twirls and thistles everywhere, and a most artistic blue and brown mottling on their other parts'.[38] At the opposite end of the generation scale, in 1917–18, when he was 90, Sir Edward Fry asked his wife and daughters to read Lockhart's *Life of Scott* to him to take his mind off the Great War, which, as a Quaker, he abhorred—'and for many hours every day . . . to all ten volumes . . . he listened in the last winter of his life'.[39]

Andrew Lang also enjoyed Jane Austen and wrote about her; but this was to establish his preference for her over the Brontës. The idea of even attempting a comparison between her stature and Scott's, let alone raising her above Scott, was unthinkable. Austen was not unregarded, of course. She figured in Lubbock's original Best Hundred while falling out of his revised version. George Eliot, who little read light fiction, appreciated Austen as an observer of life. So, famously, did Tennyson, who placed her above Eliot herself.[40] He compared Austen with Shakespeare for being 'so true to [human] nature' in her insights into character. This, Edmund Gosse remarked, was 'a courageous thing to say in Victorian circles fifty years ago'; but Tennyson was using Austen to counter the claims of the philosophical novel, as epitomized by the 'strenuous solemnity', the 'heavy and doctrinaire' tone of the novels Eliot that was producing in her final period.[41] A similar explanation occurred in the 1890s to the critic A. B. Walkley, who was concerned about the lack of esteem then accorded for Austen. The lofty sort, 'who liked big thumping declarations or at least some critical agenda about the world's ills, could not forgive Jane Austen's apparent lack of ideals'. This was the 'jargon nowadays—we talk of Ibsen's ideals and Wagner's and Miss Marie Corelli's—but it was not one of Miss Austen's words'. In fact, Walkley

---

[36] Bailey, *Letters and Diaries*, 222, 256 (13 Feb. 1923, 7 Dec. 1925).

[37] Green, *Lang*, 111–12, 162. In 1911, when the *Cornhill* published a series of 'examination papers' set on one well-known author by another, Lang set that on Scott. See Parker, *Memory Looks Forward*, 105.

[38] Virginia to Thoby Stephen, 1 Feb. 1897, in Nicolson and Banks (eds.), *Flight of the Mind*, 4.

[39] Agnes Fry, *Sir Edward Fry* (Oxford, 1921), 262.

[40] Quoted in Leslie Stephen, *George Eliot* (1902), 192.

[41] 'George Eliot', in Edmund Gosse, *Aspects and Impressions* (1922), 12–15.

maintained, she did have ideals, and they were not a bad lot: 'Truth, I should say, sincerity, quiet scorn of affectation and humbug, a home-keeping modesty, tender sympathy, maidenly reticence, and cheery good humour.' The problem was that her virtues were too discreet for modern tastes: 'In an age of "sensational" head-lines, kinematographs, motor-cars, and boomsters . . . she would never consent to appear at the Women Writers' Dinner.'[42]

Austen's style had admirers in the Victorians' dissident branch. It amused them to nickname 'a Collins' the type of overblown communication employed by the obsequious Revd William Collins in *Pride and Prejudice* (1813). This dislike of cant was also one cause of Arnold Bennett's fondness for Austen. For the rest, Austen did have some popular following, but largely for the wrong reasons, treating her like a Kate Greenaway cut-out. Henry James condemned this cult, indicting 'the body of publishers, editors, illustrators, producers of the pleasant twaddle of magazines; who have found their "dear", our dear, everybody's dear, Jane so infinitely to their material purpose'.[43] Flora Thompson, later known for the *Lark Rise* trilogy (1939–43), made her debut in print in *The Ladies Companion* in 1911, as the winner of a competition for the best essay on Jane Austen.[44] The long-serving editor of the *Westminster Gazette* J. A. Spender could not be convicted of mawkishness; still, his appetite for Austen's novels, which always accompanied him on travels, was primarily an escapist refreshment, for 'the temporary blotting out of worry and vexation'.[45] There was little sustained or developed critical interest in Austen. Professors A. C. Bradley, George Saintsbury, and Walter Raleigh composed incidental aperçus; but the chief focus of books about Austen was biographical, drawing upon the several publications by her kin which culminated in R. A. and W. Austen-Leigh's *Jane Austen: Her Life and Letters* (1913). It was not until the 1920s, when R. W. Chapman published his annotated standard edition of the novels, and an edition of her letters in 1932, that scholarly appreciation of Austen entered upon its modern boom.

Typical of the previous state of Austen studies was Constance Hill, *Jane Austen: Her Homes and Friends* (1902). *A Life of Jane Austen* for the Great Writers series had issued from Goldwin Smith in 1892. This combination could hardly have been more incongruous. A former Regius Professor of History at Oxford, Smith had lived in self-imposed exile in the United States and Canada since 1868. His reputation was as a wild controversialist 'of advanced opinions on all subjects, religious, social and political. He was clever, extremely well-informed, so far as books can make a man knowing, but unable to profit even by that limited

---

[42] A. B. Walkley, *Frames of Mind* (1899), 107–12.

[43] Henry James, 'The Lesson of Balzac' (1905), quoted in Leon Edel, *Henry James: The Master 1901–1916* (New York, 1972), 282.

[44] Gillian Lindsay, *Flora Thompson* (1990), 81. In her own semi-autobiographical account, it is while she is working in the village post office, when she takes out a library ticket at the Mechanics Institute, that she discovers *Pride and Prejudice*. This was her introduction to Jane Austen 'which was to be a precious possession for life' (Thompson, *Lark Rise*, 428). [45] Spender, *Life, Journalism and Politics*, i. 14.

experience of life from a restless vanity and overflowing conceit, which prevented him from ever observing or thinking of anything but himself.'[46] Thus ran Disraeli's sneering assessment of 'the Oxford Professor' in *Lothair* (1870), which predictably goaded Smith into lashing out against Jews in public life.[47] Henry James, who admired Austen's craft and was altogether better qualified to write about it, nevertheless composed no extended appreciation. To a Harvard graduate who completed a dissertation on Austen's novels in 1883, James commented that were he to attempt an evaluation of 'the delightful Jane', 'I could have found it in me to speak more of her genius—of the extraordinary vividness with which she saw what she did see, and of her narrow unconscious perfection of form'. James possessed the acuteness to notice that she conveyed through her heroines 'an impression of "passion" ', unlike most critics, who followed Charlotte Brontë in believing that she delineated only 'the surface of the lives of genteel English people . . . She ruffles her readers by nothing vehement, disturbs him by nothing profound. The passions are perfectly unknown to her . . .'.[48] Otherwise, James held orthodox opinions: about 'the narrowness of Miss Austen's social horizon'; about 'her apparent want of consciousness of nature'; and about 'the want of moral illumination on the part of her heroines, who had undoubtedly small and second-rate minds and were perfect she-Philistines'.[49] It was in fact Saintsbury not James who suspected that she was wrongly charged with being a miniaturist, in his preface to an 1894 edition of *Pride and Prejudice*:

If her world is a microcosm, the cosmic quality of it is at least as eminent as the littleness. She does not touch what she does not feel herself called to paint; I am not so sure that she could not have painted what she did not feel herself called to touch . . . For if her knowledge was not very extended, she knew two things which only genius knows. The one was humanity, and the other was art. On the first head she could not make a mistake; her men, though limited, are true, and her women are, in the old sense, 'absolute'. As to art, if she has never tried idealism, her realism is real to a degree which makes the false realism of our own day look merely dead-alive.[50]

With few exceptions, the conventional Victorian wisdom was that Austen's novels had charm and fineness of form but her world was too exiguous and sterile to warrant significance. It was not an artistry that appealed to the idealism of Alice Meynell, who was an influential essayist as well as poet. She dubbed Austen second-class because of her cynicism: 'Mankind lives by vital relations; and if these are mean, so is the life, so is the art that expresses them because it can express no more. With Miss Austen love, vengeance, devotion, duty, maternity,

---

[46] Benjamin Disraeli, *Lothair* (Oxford, 1975), 77–8.

[47] See Sidney Lee's notice of Goldwin Smith (1823–1910), *DNB Supplement 1901–1911*, iii. 328–40; also Goldwin Smith, *Reminiscences* (1910), 171–2, 182.

[48] Quoted in Mary Lascelles, *Jane Austen and her Art* (Oxford, 1963), 119.

[49] Henry James to George Pellew, 23 June 1883, in Edel (ed.), *James Letters*, ii. 422–3.

[50] 'Pride and Prejudice' (1894), in George Saintsbury, *Prefaces and Essays* (1933), 200–1. To Saintsbury too, however, is owed coinage of the unfortunate term 'Janeites'.

sacrifice, are infinitely trivial.'[51] The critical standpoint was, therefore, rather patronizing, represented at its most vapid by T. P. O'Connor reviewing G. E. Mitton's *Jane Austen and her Times* (1907). The greater part of the review was taken up by quotations illustrating 'the cold disdain of Jane Austen for the clergyman' of the unreformed Anglican Church. Implicit was O'Connor's tilting at the Establishment or, more charitably, the message, how more diligent in performing their office were the professional clergy nowadays. This contrast was made deliberate in respect of the subjection of women: 'The intelligence and position of women were probably much lower in the days of Jane Austen than in ours. It may be that her disposition was keenly and almost cynically observant; but there are very few women in her books, and they are all rather stupid . . . No young lady of the period would be considered to have lived up to the ideas of true respectability if she showed the least desire to choose her own husband.' The review ended by noting, 'The entire amount she received for her books to her death was £700, much less than a popular author would receive to-day for a single book.'[52]

Nor had matters changed much by the end of the Great War. As a summer relaxation in 1920, Thomas Hardy and his wife—he 80 years old, she half his age—moved on to *Emma*, after reading together *Persuasion* and *Northanger Abbey*. At least one chord was struck: 'T.H. is much amused at finding he has *many* characteristics in common with Mr. Woodhouse,' Emma's gloomily valetudinarian father.[53] Among the new generation of novelists, E. M. Forster would admit in 1924 that, all along, he had been captive:

I am a Jane Austenite, and therefore slightly imbecile about Jane Austen. My fatuous expression, and airs of personal immunity—how ill they set on the face, say, of a Stevensonian! But Jane Austen is so different. She is my favourite author! I read and re-read, the mouth open and the mind closed. Shut up in measureless content, I greet her by the name of most kind hostess, while criticism slumbers.[54]

Forster's satire of social manners was a trait he shared with his idol. But his admission of devotion was almost shamefaced and, though Austen's admirers had grown as Scott's and Stevenson's had depleted, the established view remained condescending. It was the initiative of an eccentric Irish Catholic, Percy Fitzgerald, who combined the careers of barrister, Hanoverian and stage historian, and romantic novelist and sculptor, that led to a memorial bust of Austen being placed in the Pump Room at Bath in 1912; and, though now approaching 80,

---

[51] 'The Classic Novelist', in Alice Meynell, *The Second Person Singular and Other Essays* (Oxford, n.d.), 62–7.

[52] *T. P.'s Weekly*, 29 Nov. 1907, 689–90. Accordingly, first editions of Austen, unlike most of Scott, were rare. Virginia Stephen wrote to Violet Dickinson (daughter of a Somerset squire and descended on her mother's side from the third Lord Auckland), 27 Feb. 1910: 'I saw a bookseller the other day who says that first editions of Miss Austen are very valuable. Have you sold yours?' (Nicolson and Banks (eds.), *Flight of the Mind*, 422).

[53] Florence Hardy to Sydney Cockerell, 8 Aug. 1920, in Millgate (ed.), *Emma and Florence Hardy*, 167.

[54] E. M. Forster, 'Jane Austen' (1924), in Forster, *Abinger Harvest*, 145.

Fitzgerald both executed and unveiled the object himself.[55] The centenary of her death, 1917, was marked by a tablet at her Hampshire cottage, whereupon C. W. Brodribb, *The Times*'s assistant editor, commented:

At first sight she lacks so much that on approaching her after Fielding, or Scott, or Dickens, or Meredith, or many another male and female writer of fiction, obviously so much more versed at first hand with the ways of the world and with the manifold gradations of human goodness and badness, one wonders what secret charm an observer so restricted can possess to retain her spell over the fourth and fifth generations of readers after her own day . . . Jane Austen knew her own limitations, and without in the least regretting what she had to forgo she kept her narrow virtues and rather precise, lady-like energies strictly within the bounds in which they could most naturally operate. She stands the test, within a distinctly limited range of absolute sincerity. It is pleasant to think that undeviating faithfulness, albeit in comparatively little, continues to receive, even after one hundred years and in a most distracted period of public taste, the general recognition which it deserves.[56]

III

The crucial test of great writers, according to the belletrist Augustine Birrell, was their ability to weave themselves into the texture of their countrymen's lives, to pass into their proverbial language, to colour their thoughts, and to accompany them wherever they might wander. At the Browning Hall Settlement, Walworth, on 12 December 1897, Birrell advised: 'you must look far beyond the cliques and coteries of a self-conscious culture; you must look out upon the open road and the flagged walks of cities where men and women are living their lives and playing their parts'. The great writer was thus a kind of mystical spirit, animating and elevating Everyman; but the particular *patrie* mattered hugely, and those who dwelt in the same realm were privileged to receive this spirit passing into them most naturally and fully. Great writers could make a great nation just as did men of action. 'The longer I live', Birrell declared, 'I become convinced that the only two things that really count in national existence are a succession of writers of genius and the proud memories of great, noble, and honourable deeds.'[57]

Writers themselves were sensitive to their symbolic importance, even the secluded, such as the Jesuit poet Gerard Manley Hopkins, who informed Robert Bridges that 'a great work by an Englishman is like a great battle won by England'.[58] The Positivist Frederic Harrison was equally patriotic but also had

---

[55] *Annual Register for 1912* (1913), pt. ii, p. 12. On Percy Fitzgerald (1834–1925), see Sutherland, *Companion*, 227; and *Who's Who* (1905), 548. He also executed busts of Carlyle, Dickens, Thackeray, and Lord Leighton, and a tablet to Cardinal Manning.

[56] *The Times*, 18 July 1917. On Brodribb, journalist, literary scholar, and versifier, *DNB 1941–1950*, 107–8.

[57] Augustine Birrell, *Miscellanies* (1901), 179–82.

[58] Quoted by Tom Paulin in *TLS*, 14 Aug. 1987. Hopkins wrote in similar vein to Coventry Patmore in 1886: 'Your poems are a great deed done for the Catholic Church and another for England—for the British

universal designs: he conceived the role of the literary critic as pleading 'before the Supreme Court of the Republic of Letters' or acting as 'judge in the supreme court of equity'.[59] His friend George Henry Lewes further affirmed:

Literature is at once the cause and effect of social progress. It deepens our natural sensibilities and strengthens by exercise our intellectual capacities. It stores up the accumulated experience of the race, connecting Past and Present into a conscious unity; and with this store it feeds successive generations, to be fed in turn by them.

Given that literature was this 'delicate index of social evolution', it was necessary, if improvement was to be sustained, for the unworthy to be exposed and excised:

If many of the novels of today are considerably better than those of twenty or thirty years ago, because they partake in the general advance in culture and its wider diffusion, the vast increase in novels, mostly worthless, is a serious danger to public culture, a danger which becomes more and more imminent, and which can only be arrested by an energetic resolution on behalf of the critics to do their duty with conscientious rigour.[60]

Lewes himself was a versatile performer, author of the standard *Life of Goethe* (1855), first editor of the *Fortnightly Review* (1865), drama critic, student too of physiology, psychology, and philosophy; but one of his primary duties as a member of the critical constabulary was the encouragement and exhibition of George Eliot's literary eminence.[61] This might cast doubt on his credentials as impartial critic, since he and Eliot cohabited; but there was also a close correspondence of their minds.

Literary policing also meant practical censorship. Generally, this involved critics invigilating the morals of fiction set before the public; additionally for Lewes at home, this involved filleting the press, removing any hostile notices of Eliot's work before she could set eyes on them. But its main business was checking an author's credentials for admission to the pantheon. This exercise struck H. G. Wells as farcical:

Literary criticism in those days [the 1890s] had some odd conventions. It was still either scholarly or with scholarly pretensions. It was dominated by the mediaeval assumption that whatever is worth knowing is already known and whatever is worth doing has already been done . . . So it came about that every one of us who started writing in the nineties, was discovered to be a 'a second'—somebody or other. In the course of two or three years I was welcomed as a second Dickens, a second Bulwer Lytton and a second

---

Empire, which now trembles in the balance, held in the hands of unwisdom . . .' (Patmore, *Coventry Patmore*, 212).

[59] Quoted in Vogeler, *Harrison*, 305, 311.

[60] G. H. Lewes, 'The Principles of Success in Literature', *Fortnightly Review* (May 1865), and 'Criticism in Relation to Novels', *Fortnightly Review* (Dec. 1865), quoted in Bourne Taylor, *In the Secret Theatre of Home*, 20–1, 247. Taylor contrasts Lewes and *The Times*'s critic in the 1860s, E. S. Dallas, who was more hopeful about the emergence of a mass readership.

[61] Sir Sidney Colvin, *Memories and Notes of Persons and Places 1852–1912* (1921), 90–2, for an account of Lewes as host at The Priory, the St John's Wood home he shared with Eliot.

Jules Verne. But also I was a second Barrie, though J.M.B. was hardly more than my contemporary, and, when I turned to short stories, I became a second Kipling . . . Later on I figured also as a second Diderot, a second Carlyle and a second Rousseau . . . The influence of the publisher who wanted us to be new but did not want us to be *strange*, worked in the same direction as educated criticism.[62]

But it was not just publishers, literary critics, academics, and all-purpose panjandrums who participated in the manufacture of authorial pedigree. Writer also patronized writer. Sean O'Casey encountered W. B. Yeats in such a mood when he submitted plays for the Abbey Theatre. Interviewed by Yeats, O'Casey was told that he was an Irish Dostoevsky. O'Casey found it difficult to keep a straight face. He happened to know that Yeats was as ignorant of Dostoevsky as he was until only a week before, when Lady Gregory, shocked by Yeats's neglect of the Russian, had given him *The Idiot* and *The Brothers Karamazov* to read. O'Casey allowed the bogus tribute to pass without comment, while vowing to assert his singularity next time—'Some had said he was another Chekhov, others, a Dickens, and another Ben Jonson. He knew himself that he was like Sean O'Casey, and he was determined to be like no-one else . . .'.[63]

The commission of building a canon was conducted with earnestness. We may glimpse the construction by beginning with the response to Dickens's death in 1870. Not anticipating the critical challenge to Dickens's eminence which would follow, *The Times*, once the novelist's adversary, led in insisting that he be buried in Westminster Abbey, which was 'the peculiar resting place of English literary genius; and among those whose sacred dust lies there, or whose names are recorded on the walls, very few are more worthy than Charles Dickens of such a home. Fewer still, we believe, will be regarded with more honour as time passes, and his greatness grows upon us.'[64] The Dean of Westminster, A. P. Stanley, so complied that, while Dickens's wishes for a private funeral were respected, the arrangements which the family had made for his burial at Rochester Cathedral were set aside. A site was chosen next to Handel: 'it pained me', wrote Samuel Butler, who worshipped Handel and composed a cantata after his manner, 'to think that people who could do this could become Deans of Westminster'.[65] For three days the grave in Westminster Abbey was left open, to allow thousands to file past, representatives of a sorrow that was worldwide; but the mourning cannot be said to have been completed until his confidant John Forster published the *Life of Charles Dickens* (1872–4). That itself divided Dickens's former friends. Wilkie Collins observed:

One of the worst vices of the age we live in is the shameless disregard of truth prevalent among friends, writing or speaking in public, of celebrated persons whom they have

---

[62] H. G. Wells, *Experiment in Autobiography*, ii (1969), 507–8.
[63] Sean O'Casey, *Inishfallen, Fare Thee Well* (1949), in O'Casey, *Autobiographies* (1963), 163.
[64] Quoted in Edgar Johnson, *Charles Dickens* (1953), ii. 1155–6.
[65] Jones (ed.), *Notebooks of Samuel Butler*, 134.

survived. Unblushing exaggeration of the merits, position and influence of the dead man seems to be considered as sufficient warrant for a deliberate concealment of his failings and faults—which is nothing less than lying of the passive sort, artfully adapted to its purpose as a pedestal on which the writer or speaker can present himself to the public in a favorable light.[66]

But, it transpired, Collins's animus was directed against Forster's self-promotion in the biography, which he dubbed 'The Life of John Forster, with notices of Dickens'; and Collins was equally prepared to suppress unflattering details of Dickens's life.[67] Reviewers of the biography even held that Forster disclosed too much: 'There is nothing . . . that has so grated on its readers as Dickens's reference to his mother . . . It has threatened disillusionment to more people than anything else written by or about Dickens.'[68] Forster's biography left a number of what he called 'indications' that Dickens had lived a less than exemplary life, but he was far from wanting to undermine Dickens's reputation and he destroyed the majority of letters he used in compiling the *Life*, in this following the start made by Dickens himself.[69] Whatever Forster's shortcomings, for most readers of Dickens these did not matter. Dickens was so secure in public esteem that he was elevated almost to secular sainthood. Newman Flower, later head of Cassell's, used this very metaphor when he wrote, 'In the secret places of my heart there has always been a little altar set up to Charles Dickens. To be able to read and re-read that man has made it worth my while getting born.' In 1901 he left his bed at four in the morning to travel from Croydon to watch the funeral procession of Queen Victoria. He joined the crowd and, to pass hours of waiting, stood reading *Bleak House*. A stir eventually made him look up from his book; alas, the royal section of the cortège had gone.[70] Unconsciously, Flower had paid less respect to the monarch than to the greatest novelist of her reign; but he was hardly alone in this. It was in the same year, 1901, that Ernest Raymond as a teenager first took a Dickens from the shelf: 'By the grace and favour of God, it was *Pickwick Papers* . . . At some stage in the reading I knew with a happy breathless certainty that this was what I wanted to do with my life: to write books like this.'[71] He was lucky: *Oliver Twist* (1838), the first Dickens that A. A. Milne was exposed to, at 9, gave him nightmares.[72] Raymond experienced a turning point in life much as Andrew Lang had done fifty years earlier:

I had minded my lessons, and satisfied my teachers—I know I was reading Pinnock's 'History of Rome' for pleasure—till 'the wicked day of destiny' came, and I felt a 'call',

---

[66] Quoted in Peters, *Collins*, 349.

[67] Collins kept Dickens's letters, while Dickens burnt Collins's. At one time they sampled Paris's brothels together. Dickens's daughter Kate married Collins's artist brother Charles, but the friendship between the two authors cooled as the marriage foundered; and Kate was to remarry another artist, Perugini.   [68] Quoted in Peters, *Collins*, 350.

[69] James A. Davies, *John Forster: A Literary Life* (Leicester, 1983); Ian Hamilton, *Keepers of the Flame: Literary Estates and the Rise of Biography* (1992), ch. 9.

[70] Flower, *Just as it Happened*, 17, 46.   [71] Raymond, *Autobiography*, 77–80.

[72] Thwaite, *Milne*, 41.

and underwent a process which may be described as the opposite of 'conversion'. The 'call' came from Dickens. *Pickwick* was brought into the house. From that hour it was all over, for five or six years, with anything like industry and lesson-books. I read *Pickwick* in convulsions of mirth. I dropped Pinnock's 'Rome' for good.[73]

Others lived with their Dickens until art and reality became intermixed. Of William Morris it was said that

when he was not dreaming of himself as Tristram or Sigurd, he identified himself very closely with two creations of a quite different mould, Joe Gargery and Mr Boffin. Both of these amiable characters he more or less consciously copied, if it be not truer to say more or less naturally resembled, and knew that he resembled. The 'Morning, morning!' of the latter, and the 'Wot larks!' of the former he adopted as his own favourite methods of salutation. And one of the phrases that were most constantly on his lips, which he used indiscriminately to indicate his disapproval of anything from Parliamentary institutions to the architecture of St Paul's Cathedral, was, as all his friends will remember, the last recorded saying of Mr F.'s Aunt, 'Bring him forard, and I'll chuck him out o' winder'.[74]

Nor did Dickens lose anything by translation, if Joseph Conrad's experience was true for his umpteen foreign readers. The first imaginative work by an Englishman he read was *Nicholas Nickleby* (1839): 'It is extraordinary how well Mrs. Nickleby could chatter disconnectedly in Polish and the sinister Ralph rage in that language. As to the Crummles family and the family of the learned Squeers, it seemed as natural to them as their native speech.'[75]

Dickens also mesmerized the public by leaving some unfinished business, *The Mystery of Edwin Drood* (1870). The qualifications for being seized by this were a fixation with puzzle-solving as much as a love of Dickens. Conan Doyle qualified on both counts. When practising as a doctor at Southsea, he treated the Portsmouth Literary and Philosophical Society to his own ending to Dickens's novel; later, when famous as the creator of Sherlock Holmes, he continued his researches into *The Mystery*.[76] Books, notably by Cumming Walters and Andrew Lang in 1905, and a profusion of articles, kept the issue alive of 'who done it'.[77] Robertson Nicoll chipped in with 50,000 words on the subject;[78] and Comyns Carr adapted the novel for the stage.[79] There was even a mock trial of Drood in 1913 at which several writers attempted a solution. Conan Doyle's persistence was

---

[73] Lang, *Adventures among Books*, 10–11.

[74] Mackail, *Morris*, i. 227. Joe Gargery is from *Great Expectations* (1861), Mr Boffin *Our Mutual Friend* (1865), and Mr F.'s aunt *Little Dorrit* (1857). Watts-Dunton, *Old Familiar Faces*, 249, also recalled Morris's high spirits when he read aloud from Dickens.

[75] Joseph Conrad, *A Personal Record*, in Conrad, *Collected Works*, ix. 71.

[76] Booth, *Conan Doyle*, 97–8, 149.   [77] Green, *Lang*, 200; Newsome, *Edge of Paradise*, 251.

[78] In *The Problem of 'Edwin Drood'*, Nicoll, a devotee of Dickens, concluded '(1) that Edwin Drood was actually murdered by Jasper; (2) that Datchery was Helena Landless in disguise' (Darlow, *Nicoll*, 225–6).

[79] Carr's *The Mystery of Edwin Drood* opened at the New Theatre, Cardiff, on 21 Nov. 1907, then transferred to His Majesty's Theatre in the West End on 4 Jan. 1908; but Beerbohm Tree was not a success as Jasper and the play was taken off after a month. Tree previously played Fagin in Carr's adaptation of *Oliver Twist* and that had 'filled the theatre for over three months in the autumn of 1905' (Pearson, *Tree*, 153–4).

particularly commendable. His finest hour came in 1927 when he summoned Dickens at a seance. 'I was sorry to go across before I got him out of his trouble. The poor chap has had a hard time,' Dickens told Doyle, only to add tantalizingly: 'I don't know which is better—to solve your mystery in your notebook or let it remain a mystery.'[80] Alas, he opted for the latter.

A still better guide to the popular absorption of Dickens was the prevalence of public readings. Those who heard Dickens himself felt privileged to the end of their days. The colonial official Sir Robert Herbert told his fellow clubman Sir Mountstuart Grant Duff in 1897 how he had been 'extremely struck' by Dickens's 'great dramatic power' and that nothing since had equalled his reading of the tragic passages in *Oliver Twist*. Grant Duff added sententiously, 'Herbert represents the very expressed essence of the old Eton and Oxford education, which gives his opinion, about a writer like Dickens, a peculiar interest.'[81] Flora Thompson hailed from rustic rather than Varsity Oxford; but she felt the same second-hand from Penny Readings in the 1890s: 'The star turn was given by an old gentleman from a neighbouring village, who, in his youth, had heard Dickens read his own works in public and aimed at reproducing in his own rendering the expression and mannerisms of the master.' These were hugely enjoyed, for country audiences mostly preferred to listen than to read: 'they were waiting, a public ready-made, for the wireless and the cinema'.[82] In the big cities Penny Readings had lost popularity by the 1890s. Redolent of a 'philanthropic, parsonic, patronising attitude' to the poor, 'their purpose was to keep those people from enjoying the impious delights and polluting atmosphere of the theatre and the music-hall', wrote Thomas Burke, who was born in 1886, and who described as 'anaemic' a Penny Reading he attended in Brixton, given by 'Lady Bountiful' Church workers there.[83] First in the repertoire on that occasion was an extract from *A Christmas Carol* (1843). Yet it was in the 1890s that the actor–manager Sir Squire Bancroft raised over £20,000 for charities through public readings of *Christmas Carol*.[84]

A Dickens Fellowship was established in 1902, with branches in many towns and a reach that became international. It aimed to unite his devotees in study and enjoyment, publishing from 1905 the journal *The Dickensian*; it also sought to advance his causes, campaigning against public abuses and social evils and propagating principles of humanity. Fred Kitton, one of its founders, mobilized the Fellowship to press Portsmouth Corporation to acquire Dickens's birthplace, 13 Mile End Terrace, Portsea, as a permanent museum in 1903. Kitton died in 1904, whereupon the Fellowship set about raising a public subscription to keep his

---

[80] Gibson and Green (eds.), *Unknown Conan Doyle*, 324, 356–7.

[81] Grant Duff, *Diary, 1896 to 1901*, i. 242 (5 July 1897). On Sir Robert Herbert (1831–1905), *DNB Supplement 1901–1911*, ii. 253–4.

[82] Thompson, *Lark Rise*, 448–9. There is a similar account for rural Warwickshire in M. K. Ashby, *Joseph Ashby of Tysoe, 1859–1919* (1974), 94.   [83] Burke, *Son of London*, 48–9.

[84] The Bancrofts, *Recollections of Sixty Years* (1909), ch. xiii. For the dramatic quality of these readings, see Sydney Holland [Viscount Knutsford], *In Black and White* (1928), 371.

collection of Dickensiana from being sold to America or broken up.[85] The Guildhall Library agreed to provide a room for this, calling it a National Dickens Library; and the inauguration occurred on 7 February 1908, the ninety-sixth anniversary of Dickens's birth.[86] *T.P.'s Weekly* had taken the lead in publicizing that subscription; four years later, at the centenary, the *Daily Telegraph* sponsored a Sunday evening gala performance at the Coliseum in aid of a Dickens Memorial. This extravaganza of extracts and tableaux from Dickens's works, produced by Seymour Hicks, involved 300 performers, including the Follies' comedian Harry Pélissier as Mr Pickwick. There was a music score by Elgar, and Dame Madge Kendal came out of retirement to recite the poem 'Dickens in Camp'.[87] There followed, during the first year of the Great War, an adaptation of *David Copperfield* which was staged in the West End to maintain public morale.[88] How many people ingested their Dickens by these means rather than by reading him is incalculable, but historians should not ignore the many play versions. Fred Kitton counted sixty by 1886.[89] It was John Martin-Harvey, playing Sidney Carton in *The Only Way* (1899), who popularized the valediction from *A Tale of Two Cities* (1859), 'It is a far, far better thing that I do, than I have ever done.'[90] Soon afterwards the cinema took up Dickens too, *A Tale of Two Cities* first being filmed in 1907.[91]

All the while, literary critics were fighting over the position that Dickens should occupy in the canon of classics. Once Forster's memorial *Life* was digested, Dickens's reputation with critics of the cerebral sort slumped. Andrew Lang did his best in introductions to the multi-volume Gadshill Edition of Dickens, but his personal preference was for Scott and Thackeray above Dickens; and Swinburne, with his usual excess, lambasted Lang's disservice.[92] Another idiosyncratic appreciation was George Gissing's *Charles Dickens: A Critical Study* (1898), published in Blackie's Victorian Era series.[93] In 1899 Gissing also acted as editor, providing introductions to Methuen's series of Dickens's novels that had passed

[85] On F. G. Kitton (1856–1904), see *Oxford DNB*

[86] *T.P.'s Weekly*, 8 Feb. 1907, 177. The paper inaugurated the subscription with a £25 donation. The fund closed with £259 10s. 2d. raised. See *T.P.'s Weekly*, 14 Feb. 1908, 209, for the opening ceremony: speakers included the former Cabinet minister Lord James of Hereford, who was Vice-President of the Dickens Fellowship and President of the Boz Club.

[87] Collins, *My Best Riches*, 180–2; and *The Times*, 8 Jan. 1912.

[88] The adaptation, by Louis Parker, opened at His Majesty's Theatre on Christmas Eve 1914 and ran until April 1915, Beerbohm Tree playing both Micawber and Peggotty; see Pearson, *Tree*, 154–5.

[89] Fred G. Kitton, *Dickensiana*, (1886), 362–82. A later count listed 3,000 adaptations: P. Botton, *Dickens Dramatised* (1987), cited in *Oxford DNB*'s entry on Dickens by Michael Slater.

[90] See Nicholas Butler, *John Martin-Harvey* (Colchester, 1998). In 1912 Martin-Harvey presented a one-act version of the climactic scenes of *A Tale of Two Cities* for the music halls; Nicoll, *English Drama*, 46. The author of *The Only Way* was the Revd Freeman Wills, vicar of St Agatha, Finsbury. His brother W. G. Wills (1828–91) was also famous as a dramatist, notably of *Charles I* (1872), which gave Henry Irving a big success at the Lyceum.

[91] Many films of Dickens's stories were directed and produced by Thomas Bentley, beginning with *Oliver Twist* in 1912; see *The Times*, 21 Sept. 1921, for a tribute to this 'enthusiastic Dickensian', then in the midst of filming *Pickwick* at Elstree Studios.

[92] Green, *Lang*, 163. Swinburne's elegy 'Dickens' was published in *A Century of Roundels* (1883).

[93] See John Spiers and Pierre Coustillas, *The Rediscovery of George Gissing* (1971), 120–3, and John Halperin, *Gissing: A Life in Books* (Oxford, 1982), 269–70, for its reception.

out of copyright; and the same publisher issued G. K. Chesterton's *Charles Dickens* in 1906. It was Chesterton's study, together with his prefaces to the Everyman Dickens, that was the most revealing about Dickens's status among the generation after his death. About his reputation in the world at large Chesterton was in no doubt. His death was mourned 'as no public man has ever been mourned; for prime ministers and princes were private persons compared with Dickens. He had been a great popular king, like a king of some more primal age whom his people could come and see, giving judgment under an oak tree.' About Dickens's reputation in the world of letters there was more dispute. *Inter alia*, Chesterton's *Dickens* was a virtuoso assault on all those intellectual fashions which Chesterton viewed with distaste and which he believed were ephemeral compared to the everlasting Dickens. By combining causes he thereby explained why Dickens had fallen from critical favour. Dickens was discordant with latter-day 'realists' who revelled in a pessimism about human capacity, imprisoned in the new pseudo-science of psychology and cramped by environmentalism. There was nothing scientific, self-conscious, analytical or exact about Dickens: 'exaggeration . . . is entirely the definition of Dickens's art'. Those who sought to copy life as 'realists', Chesterton contended, ultimately depicted only its narrowness, whereas Dickens, with his riotous theatricality and rich colouring of sentiment, exuded 'democratic optimism—a confidence in common men', 'a world that encouraged anybody to be anything'. Dickens was also out of favour with those who sought to elevate fiction to an art form. This was because Dickens 'never talked down to the people'. Moreover, 'Dickens's work is to be reckoned always by characters, sometimes by groups, oftener by episodes, but never by novels.' He was, therefore, 'a mythologist rather than a novelist'. And just as he failed to conform to the expectations of 'realists' and 'artists', so he was far from sharing the decadents' contempt for bourgeois conventions: Dickens expressed 'the romance of the middle classes'. Chesterton scarcely bothered to argue this further, because the decadence of the 1880s and 1890s was gone even as he wrote: 'The hour of absinthe is over.' Where he invested effort was in presenting the healthfulness of Dickens, whose only fault was that he was 'a little too happy'. There was present in Dickens a 'conjunction of common sense with uncommon sensibility':

Even when he raved like a maniac he did not rave like a monomaniac . . . He had no special point of mental pain or repugnance, like Ruskin's horror of steam and iron, or Mr Bernard Shaw's permanent irritation against romantic love. He was annoyed at the ordinary annoyances: only he was more annoyed than was necessary. He did not desire strange delights, blue wine or black women with Baudelaire, or cruel sights east of Suez with Mr Kipling. He wanted what a healthy man wants . . .

Chesterton's final judgement was unqualified:

At a certain period of his contemporary fame, an average Englishman would have said that there were at that moment in England about five or six able and equal novelists. He could have made a list, Dickens, Bulwer Lytton, Thackeray, Charlotte Brontë, George

Eliot, perhaps more. Forty years or more have passed and some of them have slipped to a lower place. Some would now say that the highest platform is left to Thackeray and Dickens; some to Dickens, Thackeray, and George Eliot; some to Dickens, Thackeray, and Charlotte Brontë. I venture to offer the proposition that when more years have passed and more weeding has been effected, Dickens will dominate the whole England of the nineteenth century; he will be left on that platform alone.[94]

It did not matter that Chesterton ignored Dickens's hypocrisies, his brutal ditching of his wife, and the darker side of his work, or that his book was as much Chesterton on Chesterton as Chesterton on Dickens. That was the case with Chesterton whatever his subject. But in this instance he supplied a Dickens which the public—and other populist pundits such as Robertson Nicoll—wanted to believe in.[95] Chesterton kept daily in touch with Dickens: his study contained Dickens's chair.[96] Devoted, too, was the ritual of Gordon Hewart, who rose to become Lord Chief Justice: he read Dickens every night of his life.[97]

No critical carping could unpick Dickens's popularity: 4.24 million copies of his books were sold in the first dozen years following his death.[98] Dickens's principal publishers, Chapman & Hall, had pioneered the cheap imprint of their star author during his lifetime; thereafter, the firm enlarged its investment with the Gadshill Edition in thirty-six volumes (1897–1908), the Biographical Edition in nineteen volumes (1902), the Oxford India Paper Edition in seventeen volumes (1901–2), the National Edition in forty volumes (1906–8), the Centenary Edition in thirty-six volumes (1910–11), and the Universal Edition in twenty-one volumes (1913–14), as well as publishing *The Dickensian* magazine from 1905. 'If it wasn't for Dickens, we might as well put up the shutters tomorrow,' Arthur Waugh was told on joining Chapman & Hall early in the new century;[99] but by now other publishers had got in on the act and even stolen a march on that firm. Macmillan's, for example, acquired Charles Dickens the younger to contribute a biographical and biblio-graphical introduction to its editions in the early 1890s.[100] Soon the market was flooded with cut-price Dickens. His books were everywhere. They even appeared in Reading prison library, at Wilde's request.[101]

---

[94] Quotations from G. K. Chesterton, *Charles Dickens* (1906), 14–18, 87, 106, 126, 128, 237, 290, 296. See also the letter, 6 Sept. 1906, that Chesterton's book drew from Bernard Shaw, who described himself as 'a supersaturated Dickensite' (Ward, *Chesterton*, 156–8).

[95] Nicoll, who, towards the end of his life, wrote, 'You cannot have too much Dickens,' considered Chesterton's *Dickens* 'the ablest literary criticism by any living English writer' (Darlow, *Nicoll*, 225). *Punch*, 12 Sept. 1906, paid its tribute by composing a spoof biography of George Bradshaw (of railway timetable fame) 'somewhat in the manner of Mr. G. K. Chesterton's "Charles Dickens"'.

[96] Ward, *Return to Chesterton*, 151. The most famous representation was the engraving *The Empty Chair, Gad's Hill—Ninth of June 1870*, by Luke Fildes, whom Dickens had commissioned to illustrate *The Mystery of Edwin Drood*. Its reproduction, in *The Graphic* at Christmas 1870, made a great impression on bereaved Dickensians everywhere, among them Vincent van Gogh, who painted his *Chair* in 1888.

[97] Flower, *Just as it Happened*, 250. For Hewart (1870–1943), see *DNB*.

[98] *DNB*, xv (1888), 30, citing the authority of Mowbray Morris in *Fortnightly Review* (Dec. 1882).

[99] J. Don Vann, 'Chapman and Hall', in Anderson and Rose (eds.), *British Literary Publishing Houses*, 106.

[100] *Review of Reviews* (May 1892), 522.   [101] Hart-Davis (ed.), *Wilde's Letters*, 145.

This very popularity suggested an intellectual shallowness which worried the canonically minded. Henry James had started the ball rolling with a devastating review of *Our Mutual Friend* (1865), dubbed 'the poorest of Mr Dickens's works' and 'poor with the poverty not of momentary embarrassment, but of permanent exhaustion'. James being 'convinced that it is one of the chief conditions of his genius not to see beneath the surface of things', he called him 'the greatest of superficial novelists'. Dickens might have been 'a great observer and a great humorist, but he is nothing of a philosopher', and his characters were 'a mere bundle of eccentricities, animated by no principle of nature whatever'.[102] Such reservations were eventually enshrined in the *Dictionary of National Biography*, whose entry on Dickens was compiled by the editor, Leslie Stephen. The *DNB* was commissioned in 1882 by the publisher George Smith, who had profited from Charlotte Brontë, George Eliot, Thackeray, Trollope, Darwin, Ruskin—and from the sale of a mineral water, Apollinaris. He invested £150,000 in the *DNB*, reckoned he might lose £50,000 and eventually settled for losing £70,000—about £5 million today—as sixty-three volumes appeared every quarter from 1885 to 1900. It was, he said with generous understatement, his gift to English literature;[103] but the notion of an establishment thus stamping reputations worried the heretical Samuel Butler, who thought that 'such a work as the *Dictionary of National Biography* adds more terror to death than death of itself could inspire'.[104] The rule followed was that wittily prescribed by Alfred Ainger, 'No flowers, by request'. There were few floral tributes in Stephen's notice: 'If literary fame could be safely measured by popularity with the half-educated, Dickens must claim the highest position among English novelists.' Sheltering behind the pretext of reporting the views of Dickens's 'more severe critics'—James plainly a leader—Stephen contended that Dickens's vivacity 'implies little real depth or tenderness of feeling; and his amazing powers of observation were out of proportion to his powers of reflection'. Hence his books were 'inimitable caricatures of contemporary "humours" rather than the masterpieces of a great observer of human nature. The decision between these and more eulogistic opinions must be left to a future edition of this dictionary.'[105] So Stephen resigned it; but it was plain where his position rested, and this verdict exercised authority over much subsequent literary criticism. The serious-minded, vauntingly philosophical novelist of the late nineteenth century simply shunted Dickens aside. Mrs Humphry Ward dismayed Earl Kimberley in 1897: 'I mentioned Dickens. She did not seem enthusiastic about him. His later works, she said, she had never read.'[106]

---

[102] Miller (ed.), *Theory of Fiction*, 211–14.

[103] Noel Annan, *Leslie Stephen: The Godless Victorian* (New York, 1984), 83–9.

[104] Jones (ed.), *Notebooks of Samuel Butler*, 365.

[105] *DNB*, xv (1888), 20–30, for the full notice. Cf. the equally cool assessment in George Saintsbury, *Corrected Impressions*, 2nd edn. (1895), 117–37.

[106] Angus Hawkins and John Powell (eds.), *The Journal of John Wodehouse First Earl of Kimberley, for 1862–1902*, Camden 5th ser., 9 (1997), 447.

Dickensian redoubts survived aplenty, up and down the land and across social classes. Neville Cardus was born in 1889 in Rusholme, Manchester, the illegitimate offspring of a police constable's daughter and the first violinist of a visiting orchestra. He was a board school pupil who ended his formal education at 13 but, from this difficult childhood, he treasured one great moment:

I discovered Charles Dickens and went crazy. I borrowed *Copperfield* from the Municipal Lending Library and the ordinary universe became unreal, hardly there. I read at meals; I read in the streets; at night I would read under the lamps on my way to anywhere I happened to be going; I would read until I was frozen cold, then run like mad to the next lamp. I read in bed, surreptitiously and against the rules, using a tallow candle. I read myself to an acute state of myopia . . .

Later, as music critic for the *Manchester Guardian*, Cardus came to know the conductor Sir Thomas Beecham. One of their bonds was Dickens, whom they judged 'not only the greatest revealer of English humorous character since Shakespeare, but also the greatest master of the Grotesque in our literature'. Above all, 'we agreed that men who did not like Dickens were not to be trusted'.[107]

Measured by wealth and privilege, the Charteris family, kin of the earls of Elcho, inhabited a different planet from the Cardus family; yet they shared this unswerving loyalty to 'beloved Dickens'. Extracts from Dickens were prescribed bedtime reading for the offspring, and Lady Cynthia Asquith, daughter of the eleventh Earl, not only regularly reread her favourite stories but deployed a love of Dickens as 'my principal touchstone about people'. Duff Cooper and Mark Sykes played this trump card to ensure her friendship when their talk turned into 'a Dickens paean' and they 'seemed to know him verbatim'.[108] Conversely, she declared fiercely that she would never have married Herbert (Beb) Asquith had she realised that he possessed 'this dreadful lacuna' in his make-up, a dim view of Dickens. The admission occurred during a dinner party in 1918, involving Sir Walter Raleigh, Professor of English Literature at Oxford:

The Professor has just re-discovered Dickens—having not touched him for years and approached him critically, he has now found himself caught up in a flame of love and admiration . . . Beb said, with a sort of pride, that at Oxford they had considered Dickens something scarcely to be mentioned, and he accused us of being on the wave of the counter reaction. This annoyed me.

. . . To my joy, the Professor was an eloquent ally and said Dickens was a 'howling swell': that he had suffered from mispraise—which had produced the reaction against him—that by his contemporaries he had been liked for the comic and the sentimental, and that now the tide of true appreciation had thrown him right up amongst the giants . . . To Beb's inquiry he maintained that Sterne was 'thin' beside him, Meredith nowhere, and Thackeray *pour rire*. In fact he said he had 'eternity'.[109]

---

[107] Cardus, *Autobiography*, 22, 236.   [108] Cynthia Asquith, *Diaries*, 238 (23 Nov. 1916).
[109] Ibid. 396–7 (15 Jan. 1918).

But the denigration of Dickens as intellectual lightweight remained fixed. George Moore, who liked to strike unconventional poses, was actually uttering the critical standard when, at another dinner involving Lady Cynthia, he dismissed Dickens as 'a mere buffoon', one of a long line of English novelists, Fielding, Scott, *et omnes*, who were without 'any seriousness of mind'. Such views were now, Lady Cynthia recognized, 'fairly boring blasphemies'.[110] As the original 'best-seller', Dickens was tarred with that brush when, in the generation following his death, the full force of the mass reading public was felt on literature and its taste was judged debased. The poet Roy Flecker declared, 'The whole doctrine of Mr Chesterton is a fraud: his whole argument for democracy in art amounts to this: "Dickens was a good writer and popular: therefore, good writers are popular".'[111] Flecker cited as an instance of the rottenness of public taste Marie Corelli's popularity; but he did not see that the fastidious mind might fall into a similar syllogism: 'Marie Corelli is a bad writer and popular; Dickens was popular, therefore, Dickens was a bad writer.'

IV

No such doubts apparently attended the passing of George Eliot a decade after Dickens. Mary Gladstone, the Prime Minister's daughter, wrote of 'the overwhelming loss to the world'; yet even this seemed meagre compared to Lord Acton's tribute, which was all the more extraordinary given his Catholic faith:

In problems of life and thought wh. baffled Shakespeare disgracefully, her touch was unfailing. No writer ever lived who had anything like her power of manifold but disinterested and impartially observant sympathy. If Sophocles or Cervantes had lived in the light of our culture, if Dante had prospered like Manzoni, Geo. Eliot might have had a rival.[112]

Leslie Stephen once again contributed the *DNB* notice. He recoiled from some of Eliot's didacticism, but there was unmistakable philosophical weight here, and Stephen unhesitatingly placed her in the first rank of fiction.[113] In making this judgement he was antiphonally responding to *The Times*'s anthem, sung when welcoming the publication in 1885 of the biography by John Walter Cross, Eliot's husband for the last months of her life:

George Eliot was a writer by herself . . . She blended the intellectual, the philosophical, and the metaphysical with all that was most simple, most natural and most human.

---

[110] Ibid. 445 (1 June 1918). Cf. Max Beerbohm's parody of Moore's assertiveness and pretentious ignorance in 'Dickens'; *Christmas Garland*, 179–85.

[111] 'The Public as Art Critic', in James Elroy Flecker, *Collected Prose* (1922), 243–50.

[112] Masterman (ed.), *Mary Gladstone*, 213 (1 Jan. 1881).

[113] *DNB*, xiii (1888), 216–22. When Stephen wrote more lengthily on Eliot for the English Men of Letters series, he noted that her works 'have not, at the present day, quite so high a position as was assigned to them by contemporary enthusiasm' (Stephen, *George Eliot*, 206). Thomas Hardy, while admiring her both as novelist and as philosopher, declined an invitation to assess her for Blackwood's Modern English Writers series; letter, 9 Sept. 1901, in Purdy and Millgate (eds.), *Hardy's Letters*, ii. 299.

Profoundly thoughtful herself, she forced her readers to think in spite of themselves, and nevertheless to read on, instead of throwing her volumes aside. Pregnant and deeply suggestive thought softened by touching pathos and brightened by wit, humour, and fancy, was so inextricably mixed up in her scenes, her descriptions, her characters, and her inimitable dialogues, that the one was to be taken with the other, and there was no possibility of 'skipping'. Nevertheless she was universally read—she was read with absorbing interest; and consequently, in our opinion, she did more to raise the standard of English fiction than any writer of the century.[114]

This notion that Eliot was universally read, grotesque as a literal statement, was valid as a normative and prescriptive judgement.[115] It was consistent with the acclaim that heralded *Middlemarch* in 1871–2, the *Daily Telegraph* considering it 'almost profane to speak of ordinary novels in the same breath with George Eliot's'. Consistent too with her own high purpose in writing fiction, 'to make it a contribution to literature, and not a mere addition to the heap of books'; as she put it in 1876, 'my writing is simply a set of experiments in life—an endeavour to see what our thought and emotion may be capable of'.[116] Unmistakably, this had issued a challenge to the notion of literature as romance; and in 1895, fifteen years after Eliot's death, when Blackwood's was bringing out a cheap standard edition of her works, *Punch*'s reviewer questioned whether her popularity was holding up, particularly among younger people. Rereading *The Mill on the Floss* (1860), he experienced the old spell once more—but this was a story written 'before the malign influence of the schoolmaster George Henry Lewes made itself felt'.[117] It was Cross's Life that had shaken others, making it seem as if Dorothea Brooke in *Middlemarch* was less a creation than a self-portrait—'a jelly-like, most impressionable mind, . . . pedantic and priggish . . . a strange mixture of the bluestocking and the gushing woman'. Not only did Eliot appear to have been 'no fun', worse,

---

[114] *The Times*, 27 Jan. 1885. The only hitch to the hallowing of George Eliot came from ecclesiastical authorities. Eliot had wished to be buried in Westminster Abbey, among the literary pantheon; but her friends faced the obvious difficulty, as T. H. Huxley put it, that 'George Eliot is known not only as a great writer, but as a person whose life and opinions were in notorious antagonism to Christian practice in regard to marriage, and Christian theory in regard to dogma.' The Dean of Westminster, A. P. Stanley, made it known that 'strong representations' would be needed to overcome his opposition, and the memorialists backed off. Eliot was buried in an unconsecrated part of Highgate cemetery, close to G. H. Lewes's grave. Gordon S. Haight, *George Eliot: A Biography* (Oxford, 1968), 548–9.

[115] One place where Eliot was not read, or at least not available in the library until the 20th century, was this author's own college. When Andrew Lang was a Fellow in the early 1870s, he 'made a great effort to have the works of George Eliot put in the Merton Library, esteeming her the peer of Shakespeare'; but the motion was defeated by the philosopher F. H. Bradley (Green, *Lang*, 37). Whether Bradley objected on philosophical or literary grounds is not clear. Bradley later struck up an unlikely friendship with the sensational novelist and beauty Elinor Glyn, after a chance meeting on the Riviera in 1910. He appeared as the retired professor, Cheiron, in Glyn's *Halcyone* (1912), having assiduously read the manuscript, corrected her spelling, and supplied Greek quotations; Glyn, *Romantic Adventure*, 213; also Anthony Glyn, *Elinor Glyn* (1955), 195, 201–2, 205.

[116] Quotations from Hands, *George Eliot Chronology*, 125, 139, 144.

[117] *Punch*, 19 Oct. 1895, 185. Cf. George Saintsbury, *Corrected Impressions* (1895), 168: 'I think George Eliot might possibly have occupied a higher place in literary history if she had never met him [G. H. Lewes] at all; but it is rather more probable that she might have occupied none whatever.'

she appeared to have had 'no moral struggles', having shed 'with utmost ease . . . her youthful faiths and beliefs in spite of their intensity'.[118]

The problem of pecking order in the literary canon thus remained a real one. Undergraduates at the Oxford Union in the mid-1860s had debated the motion 'that George Eliot is the greatest English novelist of the present century'—a surprisingly bold resolution, coming as it did before the publication of *Middlemarch* and when Dickens was still alive and Thackeray but recently dead.[119] It sidelined too the claims of Scott, Austen, the Brontës, and more. In such debates several authors, who in the twentieth century would achieve a following as 'eminent Victorians', were automatically excluded from consideration. Anthony Trollope was one. He was widely enjoyed in his day. Probably the last letter he wrote, before his fatal stroke in 1882, was to express pleasure on learning that Cardinal Newman read his novels.[120] But enjoyment was not the same as esteem. Alice Meynell expressed a common opinion about his worth, that Trollope was the ideal novelist for the reader in 'say, the second week of a convalescence'.[121] Gissing speculated whether the posthumous publication of Trollope's autobiography was the cause of his disrepute, because of its revelation of the mechanical method and mercenary purpose by which 'a big, blusterous, genial brute' turned out books, 'so many words every quarter of an hour'. Yet this, Gissing argued with his usual fine contempt for democracy, would be to give too much credit to 'the great big stupid public', by assuming that it was offended by the notion that literary work was a kind of manufacture. Forster's biography of Dickens included similar disclosures about the literary life, that it involved hard bargaining and toil; yet Dickens was loved and revered. Gissing acknowledged that this was right. Trollope was looked down upon, not because of his methods but because of 'an inferiority of mind, of nature'. He remained no better than 'an admirable writer of the pedestrian school'.[122]

Bernard Shaw was an equally devoted Dickensian, seeing him as an apostle of the Life Force philosophy; still, as book reviewer for the *Pall Mall Gazette*, 1885–8, Shaw delighted in contrariness by extolling Trollope in preference to the belletrist and aesthetic schools, the romantic and sensational novelists, or the shock merchants revelling in depictions of low life, who were then in favour:

Society has not yet forgiven that excellent novelist for having worked so many hours a day, like a carpenter or tailor, instead of periodically going mad with inspiration and

---

[118] Masterman (ed.), *Mary Gladstone*, 342–3 (5–6 Feb. 1885).

[119] J. W. Mackail, *James Leigh Strachan-Davidson, Master of Balliol* (Oxford, 1925), 22. The debate is not dated but was probably when Strachan-Davidson was an officer in the Union, following the publication of Eliot's *Felix Holt, The Radical* (1866). Strachan-Davidson supported the motion, though his favourite reading was Scott and Austen.

[120] To Lord Emly, 27 Oct. 1882, in Bradford Allen Booth (ed.), *The Letters of Anthony Trollope* (Oxford, 1951), 494–5.

[121] Quoted in Viola Meynell, *Alice Meynell* (1947), 198.

[122] Gissing, *Ryecroft*, 212–16. Cf. Henry James: 'I have read Trollope's autobiography and regard it as one of the most curious and amazing books in all literature, for its density, blockishness and general thickness and soddenness' (letter to Thomas Sergeant Perry, 25 Nov. 1883, in Edel (ed.), *James Letters*, iii. 14).

hewing Barchester Towers at one frenzied stroke out of chaos, that being the only genuinely artistic method. Yet, if we except the giants of the craft, he is entitled to rank among English writers as the first sincerely naturalistic novelist of our day. He delivered us from the marvels, senseless accidents, and cat's-cradle plots of old romance, and gave us, to the best of his ability, a faithful picture of the daily life of the upper and middle classes. If any contemptuously exclaim here, 'Aha! The upper and middle classes! Why did not the snob give us the daily life of the slum and the gutter, on which all society rests to-day?' the answer is simple and convincing. He, as an honest realist, only told what he knew; and, being a middle class man, he did not and could not know the daily life of the slum and gutter.[123]

Trollope later provided comfort for the likes of Siegfried Sassoon during the horrors of the Great War: 'If only I could wake up and find myself living among the parsons and squires of Trollope's Barsetshire, jogging easily from Christmas to Christmas, and hunting three days a week with the Duke of Omnium's Hounds . . . '.[124] In this reverie he was soon joined by J. M. Barrie and more; as Barrie's secretary wrote, 'One of his great solaces was Anthony Trollope, whom, like many others, he rediscovered after the First World War.'[125] This was at the point when George Eliot's stock had plummeted. Edmund Gosse stated in 1922: 'George Eliot is unduly neglected now, but it is the revenge of time on her for the praise expended on her works in her lifetime.'[126] More than that was involved. Walter Raleigh had seen it coming, and can be considered a founder member of the Trollope appreciation guild. Relishing the part of iconoclast, he wrote in 1905, after lying abed reading Trollope, 'I'm afraid it's no use anyone telling me that Thackeray is a better novelist than Trollope,' throwing in for good measure that Mrs Oliphant was better than George Eliot, for whose 'twopenny meliorism' he had long felt distaste. He explained a little: 'Trollope starts off with ordinary people, that bore you in life and in books, and makes an epic of them because he understands affection, which the others take for granted or are superior about. I wish there were a Trollope movement, it would be so healthy.'[127] What recommended Trollope, and Jane Austen, to many during and after the war was

---

[123] Holroyd, *Shaw*, i. 211.   [124] Sassoon, *Infantry Officer*, 209.

[125] Cynthia Asquith, *Portrait of Barrie* (1954), 57.

[126] Gosse, *Aspects and Impressions*, 15.

[127] Letter to Miss C. A. Kerr, 15 Apr. 1905, in Raleigh (ed.), *Raleigh Letters*, i. 272. For Raleigh's animus against Thackeray, see below, Ch. 6. The jibe about George Eliot's 'twopenny meliorism' is from a letter to his future wife, 21 Apr. 1890, in Raleigh (ed.), *Raleigh Letters*, i. 149. Whether by coincidence or not, Robert Louis Stevenson made exactly the same comparison between Eliot and Oliphant. William Archer wrote of his last meeting with Stevenson in 1887: 'he is one of the heretics who depreciate George Eliot. Of course, it is natural that the leader of the narrative-at-any-price school should have a certain down on her methods, and I knew already that he had; but I was rather taken aback to hear him say that, if Mrs Oliphant had only husbanded her strength, he thought she had more genius than George Eliot' (R. C. Terry (ed.), *Robert Louis Stevenson* (1996), 109). On Mrs Oliphant (1828–97), whose seven-volume 'Chronicles of Carlingford', begun in 1863, had followed the Trollope pattern, see Sutherland, *Companion*, 476–7. Stevenson also enjoyed Trollope—though he was rather shamefaced about it, in a letter to his parents, 21 Feb. 1878 (Sidney Colvin (ed.), *The Letters of Robert Louis Stevenson* (1901), i. 126)—and the circle was complete when Raleigh published his appreciation of Stevenson in 1895.

(as Dorothy Richardson put it) 'their complete non-literariness'.[128] They did not subordinate their instincts in order to produce lifeless 'works of art' or charmless philosophical fiction. Desmond MacCarthy concurred when he too pondered why it was that, following the war, Trollope was 'held in higher estimation than George Eliot, and that not a few consider him a greater *novelist* than Thackeray (against this Trollope himself would loudly protest), though they would admit him to be very inferior to Thackeray as a writer'. The reason was that the later generation no longer accepted the Victorians' conviction that a novel must be

'a work of art' in the same sense that a sonata, a picture, or a poem is a work of art. It is extremely doubtful whether the aim of the novel is to make an aesthetic appeal. Passages in it may do so; but it aims also at satisfying our curiosity about life and engaging our sympathies quite as much as at satisfying the aesthetic sense.

'Trollope', MacCarthy added, 'did not know what the word artist meant'; but he passed all other tests with flying colours. Like Balzac and Hardy, he was a 'world-creating novelist'; but Trollope actually went further, because not only was his Barset 'solidly and consistently imagined' in its topography and society, he also invented 'the device of reintroducing the same characters at different ages and in different connections'. Above all, he appealed by his 'generous and sensible' set of moral values. These 'tallied exactly with the experiences of normal, but not deeply inquiring people'.[129]

V

Trollope was never a candidate for canonization in the estimate of late Victorians, unlike Eliot or Browning and Tennyson. To these last two, serious thought was accorded about their ranking among the illustrious. Both were buried in Westminster Abbey. Browning was the first to die; and Grant Duff, who attended the service, recorded in his diary, 'Half London was there of course.'[130] 'They were really national obsequies,' wrote Henry James, who was compensated for his attendance by reporting the occasion (anonymously) for *The Speaker*.[131] Browning, however, was necessarily judged with one eye on Tennyson. Anticipating this,

---

[128] John Rosenberg, *Dorothy Richardson: The Genius they Forgot* (1973), 50.

[129] MacCarthy, *Portraits*, i. 270–7. In an essay of 1883 Henry James also identified 'this happy, instinctive perception of human varieties' as Trollope's particular genius; likewise argued that 'his perception of character was naturally more just and liberal than that of the naturalists' (Miller (ed.), *Theory of Fiction*, 199, 215). See also George Saintsbury, *A Short History of English Literature* (1898), 751, where Trollope is styled as 'a good deal underrated since [his death], never perhaps rated or likely to be rated by good critics among the first, but sure with such critics, sooner or later, of recognition as interesting and singularly typical'. Saintsbury's own more appreciative 'Trollope Revisited' (1921) is included in his *Collected Essays and Papers* (1923), ii. 312–43, as an upgrade on his original assessment in *Corrected Impressions*, 2nd edn. (1895), 172–7.   [130] Grant Duff, *Diary, 1889–1891*, i. 201 (31 Dec. 1889).

[131] To Katherine De Kay Bronson, 12 Jan. 1890, in Edel (ed.), *James Letters*, iii. 269. James's account was republished in *Essays in London* (1893).

Browning liked to joke that he had already beaten Tennyson in the honours stakes. After a dinner put on by Benjamin Jowett, which both poets attended, Browning remarked: 'They've given Tennyson a peerage, and me a Fellowship of Balliol. I prefer the Fellowship.'[132] Browning's death called for more sober assessment. Note *The Spectator*'s careful eulogy:

In poetic and artistic genius, the Laureate no doubt ranks above him; but in the strength and fertility and vividness of his imaginative and intellectual life, Browning has had no superior during the generation which has lived since the death of Wordsworth. Cosmopolitan in his interests, penetrating in his knowledge of men and women, and marvellously rich in the discernment and appreciation of new moral and intellectual conditions, Browning's poems range over a larger area of genuine human experience and motive than those of any other poet of the century. Moreover, all he has written has been ethically pure and intellectually bracing, marked almost uniformly by both courage and charity.[133]

Other periodicals followed with their own funerary routines. A commemorative ode from Browning's friend Sir Theodore Martin in *Blackwood's Magazine* and another from the Revd H. D. Rawnsley in *Murray's Magazine* were outbid by a couple of sonnets from Aubrey de Vere in *Macmillan's Magazine* and seven from Swinburne in the *Fortnightly Review*. This was a generous ration, especially considering Browning's opinion of 'The Leper' and 'Les Noyades' which he called 'moral mistakes, redeemed by much intellectual ability', a judgement that had caused problems for Swinburne when he sought to publish them in *Poems and Ballads* (1866).[134] The *Quarterly Review* crowned Browning 'our greatest modern seer' and the Revd Stopford Brooke set up the scaffolding for his future study of Browning with an essay in the *Contemporary Review*.[135] Elsewhere, Edmund Gosse defined the characteristics of Browning's talk, incidentally preening himself on his intimacy;[136] and in the *National Review* H. D. Traill adjudged imperishable Browning's services to the country's intellectual and spiritual life. But Browning's best work preceded his popularity, thought Traill; and 'it will have, I fear, to be added that no poet so eminent as Mr Browning has ever left behind him so large a body of brilliant, profound, inspiring literature, wherein the essential characteristics of poetry will be sought in vain'.[137] There were intimations here of Wilde's 'prose Browning', which, like many of Wilde's quips, was a sharpened version

---

[132] Bennett, *Journal 1929*, 6. Browning appears to have been the first Honorary Fellow of Balliol (in 1867), though not an alumnus; John Jones, *Balliol College: A History, 1263–1939* (Oxford, 1988), 206 n. 19.

[133] *The Spectator*, 21 Dec. 1889.

[134] DeVane and Knickerbocker (eds.), *New Letters of Browning*, 150–1, 186. Swinburne's seven sonnets on the death of Browning were republished in his *Astrophel and Other Poems* (1894).

[135] See his 'Browning and Tennyson', chapter 1 of Stopford A. Brooke, *The Poetry of Robert Browning* (1902), 1–56. Brooke was author also of *Tennyson: His Art and Relation to Modern Life* (1894), and of a *Primer of English Literature* (1876), which sold half a million copies by the year of his death, 1916. On Brooke, his heterodox theology and literary work, see *DNB 1912–1921*, 68–9.

[136] Cf. Max Beerbohm's wicked parody of Gosse's style in 'A Recollection', in which Gosse supposedly engineers a meeting between Browning and Ibsen, over turkey and plum pudding, in Venice; *Christmas Garland*, 133–43.   [137] *Review of Reviews* (Jan. 1890), 37–8; (May 1890), 403–4.

of a sentiment already in circulation. Though personally friendly, Tennyson had also remarked that Browning was a great poet 'without the glory of words'.[138] Trollope had been characteristically robust in dispatch of both, in the last year of his life writing to his son: 'Yes; Browning is a stodger. In Milton there are many true things. In Tennyson there are some. In Browning there are a few. His phraseology is as you say sometimes fearful.'[139] Browning offended against Trollope's key principles of good writing, intelligibility, and harmoniousness.[140] These problems did not deter the many from wanting to possess their own share of the shade. Booksellers reported a rush for copies of Browning's works, especially *Asolando*, which Smith, Elder & Co. published only the day before Browning died.[141] Even then Browning could not avoid comparison with Tennyson. Tennyson's *Demeter and Other Poems* was published on the same day, and sold 20,000 copies in its first week.[142]

Browning had not generally matched the commercial success of Tennyson. The popularity of his wife Elizabeth Barrett Browning's poetry also long out-stripped his own. The irony was not lost on Browning himself when in late life novice poets sought his advice about publication: 'It seems strange and almost sad to me that I should be imagined of authority in this kind—I who for years and years could not get a line printed except at my own expense.'[143] From 1848 his publisher was Chapman & Hall, who still had on their hands copies of the first editions of *Christmas-Eve and Easter-Day* (1850) and *Men and Women* (1855) in 1863.[144] His *Collected Poems* (1863) went well, as did a volume of *Selections* chosen by B. W. Procter (Barry Cornwall) and John Forster; yet, when he switched to Smith, Elder & Co. for *The Ring and the Book* (1868–9), the £1,250 he received for five years' publication rights was greater than for any of his previous books.[145] The really big leap in his literary income came only in the last four years of his life; and a sixteen-volume cheap edition of the *Poetical Works* was marketed in 1888.[146] With this new-found popularity went a corresponding rise in the resale value of the early work. Copies of *Bells and Pomegranates* (1841–6) could be found occasionally in booksellers' catalogues, Browning told one inquirer in 1882, 'at an absurd price'; and to a bibliophile in 1888 he expressed himself 'contentedly amused at the fact that a little affair of my own [*Pauline*, 1833], published more than half a century ago at my own expense,—and absolute loss of every

---

[138] Rendel, *Personal Papers*, 77. It was a regular complaint of Tennyson about Browning; e.g. 'He can conceive of grand dramatic situations, but where's the music?' or 'there ought to be some melody in poetry, it should not be all thought' (Rawnsley, *Memories of the Tennysons*, 101, 140).

[139] To Henry Merivale Trollope, 23 Jan. 1882, in Booth (ed.), *Trollope's Letters*, 468.

[140] Trollope, *Autobiography*, 210–11.

[141] The publisher George Murray Smith (1824–1901) was the first in England to hear, by telegram from Venice, of Browning's death; he in turn told George Buckle, the editor of *The Times*, which therefore scooped other papers with the news. Smith arranged the funeral in the Abbey, and acted as a pall-bearer (Robertson Scott, *Pall Mall Gazette*, 41–2).   [142] Martin, *Tennyson*, 571.

[143] To an unidentified correspondent, 9 July 1886, in DeVane and Knickerbocker (eds.), *New Letters of Browning*, 331.   [144] Ibid. 400.

[145] Ibid. 184.   [146] Ibid. 355, 392.

penny,—then selling (were there buyers) at some three shillings and six pence, now is hardly procurable for £25, and has already been reprinted in *facsimile* as a curiosity!'[147]

Browning was in boom, therefore, when he died in 1889. The majority now solemnly murmured about Browning's genius, and private correspondence seemingly echoed the public tributes. 'We have lost a true-hearted poet and a *great thinker in verse*,' Aubrey de Vere wrote;[148] yet, this same Aubrey de Vere had been more often than not mystified by the poems, complaining that they were written in a sort of shorthand. He had once tackled Browning about their obscurity, to which Browning stoutly replied, 'I have heard that criticism before, and have twice gone carefully through them without being able to detect a single obscure expression.'[149] *Sordello* (1840) was notoriously the toughest assignment. When Douglas Jerrold ventured on it while convalescing, he entered a state of panic that his illness had destroyed his reason; then, having passed the book from his bedside to a visiting friend, who also exhibited utter incomprehension, he collapsed relieved on his pillow with a cry of 'Thank God'.[150] Nor had Browning been immediately clarified for the young Rudyard Kipling by having *Men and Women* (1855) hurled at his head by a violent-tempered schoolmaster.[151] Browning himself had hoped to avoid the need for explanations; but 'the trickle of such inquiries began in the middle Sixties, reached a sizeable stream during the Seventies; then in the Eighties, as a logical growth from these beginnings, came the organized curiosity of the Browning societies'.[152] Three hundred girls at the North London Collegiate School were even set an examination on Browning's play *Strafford* (1837), following a term's study in 1883, whereupon the Browning enthusiast Emily Hickey brought out an annotated edition in 1884.[153] The play had failed as a drama under Macready's direction; now it failed as history, damned by the Oxford scholar S. R. Gardiner, who contributed an introduction to Hickey's edition—'Not merely are there frequent minor inaccuracies, but the very roots of the situation are untrue to facts.'[154]

Schoolgirls nonetheless pluckily grasped the nettle. Shortly before his death Browning sent some notes on 'Prospice' in response to a pupil at King Edward VI High School for Girls in Birmingham, who was entering a competition for the best recitation of his poetry. In her memoirs, where this treasured epistle was reproduced, Constance Smedley reflected in commonsensical fashion how Browning's contemporaries 'tried to read occult meanings into everything he wrote and often

---

[147] To C. Butler, 25 June 1888, ibid. 360.   [148] Grant Duff, *Diary, 1889–1891*, i. 238 (24 Mar. 1890).
[149] Ibid. ii. 180 (5 Aug. 1891).
[150] Hart-Davis (ed.), *Lyttleton Hart-Davis Letters*, 377. Cf. Saintsbury, *Corrected Impressions*, 100: 'I have never myself quite understood what people meant and still sometimes seem to mean by the "obscurity", the "difficulty" of "Sordello". It is distinctly breathless and it is unduly affected; but if anybody has got a brain at all, that brain ought not to be very much exercised in following the fortunes of Sordello and Taurello, Alberic and Ezzelin, Adelaide and the rest.'   [151] Kipling, *Something of Myself*, 22.
[152] DeVane and Knickerbocker (eds.), *New Letters of Browning*, 203.
[153] Ibid. 281, 284. Hickey, the Browning Society's first secretary, taught at the North London Collegiate School.   [154] Ibid. 354.

mistook hurried chaotic passages which had not been clearly thought out, mystical depths it was their duty to fathom'.[155] 'On the Alleged Obscurity of Mr Browning's Poetry' had been one of the subjects that Augustine Birrell tackled in *Obiter Dicta* (1884). But when Birrell endeavoured to practise his preaching by then publishing a selection of Browning's poetry, his edition was condemned for the exiguity of its explanatory notes. 'The reader will often be surprised', Birrell had written airily in his introduction, 'how frequently obscurity and difficulty will be dissipated and removed by a careful study of the context.' Sir Edward Cook, leading interpreter of another Victorian sage, Ruskin, was having none of it: 'Any reader who applies this flattering unction to a study of *Aristophanes' Apology* or of *Sordello* or of some parts of *The Ring and the Book* will be sadly disappointed. Mr Birrell's specific is too much like that of faith-healers. Difficulties in an obscure and allusive poet do not vanish by pretending that they are not there.'[156]

Members of the Browning Society (established in 1881), like Birrell himself, seemed to possess this mettlesomeness in abundance. While some almost terrorized the object of their worship, by pestering Browning with enquiries, others such as that odd couple the versifier and children's author Edith Nesbit and her libertine husband, Hubert Bland, carried on regardless. As ardent Browningites, they read the poetry to each other, Hubert apparently possessing the knack of declaiming it 'in a manner that smoothed away all its difficulties'.[157] The Browning Society only just outlasted Browning himself, dissolving in 1891; but its decade of evangelism climaxed with a shilling selection of his work, which appeared in 1890 and cleared 60,000 copies in its first year.[158] It was also responsible for guides to the Browning mysteries. In 1892 F. Mary Wilson's *A Primer on Browning* (Macmillan, 248 pages for 2s. 6d.) was published. This was recommended as being of a more elementary character than Mrs Sutherland Orr's *Handbook* (1885), which had carried Browning's own seal of approval; but, for the really dedicated, there was Edward Berdoe's *The Browning Cyclopaedia* (Sonnenschein, 572 pages for 10s. 6d.), which contained 'copious explanatory notes and references on all difficult passages'.[159] Even Berdoe was stumped on occasion, and his *Cyclopaedia* contained a page of 'unsolved difficulties', about which he appealed to his readers for help in answering.[160] At Browning's death in 1889 a polite façade had been generally maintained about the poems' intelligence and intelligibility; but persistent probing would soon wring out of individuals, even from that mighty brain Mr Gladstone, the admission, 'The worst of it is that I can't read him.'[161]

---

[155] Smedley, *Crusaders*, 10–14.   [156] Cook, *More Literary Recreations*, 163.

[157] Moore, *Nesbit*, 98.

[158] William Benzie, *Dr. F. J. Furnivall* (Norman, Okla., 1983), 230, 243; and Frederick Rogers, *Labour, Life and Literature*, ed. David Rubinstein (Brighton, 1973), 40, 44, 167–8.

[159] *Review of Reviews* (Jan. 1892), 93, 97.

[160] Edward Berdoe, *The Browning Cyclopaedia* (1892), p. xi. For Berdoe, Browning was not a 'mere man', rather a 'Buddha on the highest peak of the Himalayas of thought' (Benzie, *Furnivall*, 221).

[161] Rendel, *Personal Papers*, 77 (7 June 1891). It thus might have disturbed the GOM to learn that in 1881 Dr F. J. Furnivall had called Browning 'the Gladstone of poetry'. Yet that was precisely why Furnivall had

On the religious front, the freethinking fraternity Leslie Stephen and Thomas Hardy progressively disclosed their doubts about Browning, Stephen writing on 'Browning's Casuistry' in the *National Review* in 1902,[162] and Hardy communicating to Gosse in 1899 his conviction that 'the longer I live the more does B's character seem *the* literary puzzle of the 19th century. How could smug Christian optimism worthy of a dissenting grocer find a place inside a man who was so vast a seer & feeler when on neutral ground?' Hardy encouraged Gosse to write an essay that might explain that riddle; as a spur, he offered his own 'theory which you will call horrible—that perceiving he wd. obtain in a stupid nation no hearing as a poet if he gave himself in his entirety, he professed a certain mass of commonplace opinion as a bait to get the rest of him taken'.[163] Browning had been naturally alien too to the author of *The Earthly Paradise* (1868–70), William Morris. The Fabian journalist William Clarke reported in 1891, 'Browning's poetry he [Morris] dislikes *in toto*, and he abuses it in no measured language. Its abruptness, obscurity, theology, introspection, its constant dwelling on sin and probing of the secrets of the hearts are all utterly distasteful . . .'.[164] Understandably, it was the men of religion who dominated the initial discussion of Browning's significance. No communion neglected the opportunity to preach to its congregation. R. H. Hutton temporarily vacated his editorial chair of *The Spectator* to emphasize for the plain Protestant readers of *Good Words* Browning's insights as a religious teacher; the *Church Quarterly* eulogized Browning as a staunch Anglican and anti-papist; the *Presbyterian and Reform Review* averred that Browning held 'an optimism which is consistent with man's total depravity' and the *Primitive Methodist Quarterly* was cheered that Browning, 'so original, so various, so virile, with such plastic gifts, we shall never see its like again', had remained steadfast to his liberal, Nonconformist upbringing. Even the *Jewish Quarterly Review* carried twenty-seven pages about Browning as a religious thinker, acknowledging 'a leader and fellow comrade of all those who seek after God' but faulting his Broad Churchism for 'its vagueness, and its want of touch

---

founded the Browning Society, admitting that, while 'first of our Nation', Browning had 'not the great statesman's fire or clearness', and thus could not 'move the heart of all like Gladstone can' without a band of disciples carrying his message to the people (Benzie, *Furnivall*, 244–5).

[162] On which, see Hardy to Sir George Douglas, 2 Dec. 1902, in Purdy and Millgate (eds.), *Hardy Letters*, iii. 41. Positivists were, however, divided about Browning: Frederic Harrison, while liking him personally, disliked the poetry, yet Cotter Morison and Charles Herford were members of the Browning Society; Vogeler, *Harrison*, 288.

[163] Hardy to Edmund Gosse, 6 Mar. 1899, in Purdy and Millgate (eds.), *Hardy Letters*, ii. 216–17. Yet Hardy had presented Browning with *Wessex Tales* on Browning's seventy-sixth birthday in 1888, together with a deferential note; and in 1901 he noted 'how slowly & surely he [Browning] is overtopping Tennyson' (Hardy to Robert Browning, 7 May 1888, ibid. i. 175–6, and Hardy to Florence Henniker, 25 July 1901, ibid. ii. 293).

[164] William Clarke, 'William Morris', *New England Magazine*, (Feb. 1891), *Review of Reviews* (Mar. 1891), 248. Browning found Morris's and other Pre-Raphaelites' poetry a 'weariness', though he was prepared to support a Morris-inspired campaign, on behalf of the Society for the Protection of Ancient Buildings, to spare City churches from demolition in 1878; DeVane and Knickerbocker (eds.), *New Letters of Browning*, 244.

with the practical religious life'. Nor was the Catholic Church indifferent to Browning's passing, though it was in the style of malediction that comment was made: Father Rickaby spelled out in the *Month* what Catholics ought to think, concluding, 'we fearlessly affirm that there is more true spirituality in the Penny Catechism than in all Browning's poems put together'.[165] It was almost an anti-climax when W. M. Rossetti drew a parallel between Browning's long-sighted-ness in one eye and short-sightedness in the other—though he had forgotten which—and 'the duality of mental vision which is so apparent in Browning's poems' whereupon the book-length biographical and literary studies appeared. Among the first, in April 1890, was a volume in the Walter Scott Co. Great Writers series, by William Sharp, who was not yet fully formed as a dual per-sonality with Fiona Macleod.[166] Then it was over to America, where *Lippincott's Magazine* published the reminiscences of Mrs Bloomfield Moore, 'one of the poet's most intimate friends in his late years', and conveyed the sorrow of Ouida, writing from Florence about the 'irreparable loss' and 'inestimable privilege of his personal acquaintance'.[167]

The debate about Browning's religious views rumbled into 1891 and beyond. A key article was Mrs Sutherland Orr, 'The Religious Opinions of Robert Browning', in the *Contemporary Review*, December 1891. Sister of the artist Lord Leighton, Mrs Orr was Browning's authorized biographer. Now, she admitted that she had underestimated the vital part played by Nonconformism in shaping his faith. Nevertheless, he was no ordinary Dissenter or even Christian,

for he rejected the antithesis of good and evil, on which orthodox christianity rests; he held, in common with Pantheists, though without reference to them, that every form of moral existence is required for a complete human world . . . No man was more capable of healthy moral indignation, or more anxious for the enforcement of human justice in its most stringent forms. But he would have denied eternal damnation under any conception of sin. He spurned the doctrine with his whole being as incompatible with the attributes of God; and, since inexorable divine judgment had no part in his creed, the official Mediator or Redeemer was also excluded from it. He even spoke of the Gospel teaching as valid only for mental states other than his own. But he never ceased to believe in Christ as, mystically or by actual miracle, a manifestation of Divine love.

Mrs Orr concluded that Browning's 'language was, in later years, more habitually that of a Theist than that of a Christian. And, as his abstract Supreme Being was more remote than the God of Christian theology, so was the God of his real life more familiarly near, more anthropomorphic in character than the image of Deity usually reflected by the educated religious mind.'[168]

This attention to Browning's faith as a measure of his poet's station registers how central the question of religious belief and unbelief was in intellectual debate

---

[165] *Review of Reviews* (Feb. 1890), 125; (May 1890), 403–4; (Aug. 1890), 141.
[166] On Sharp (1855–1905), who wrote also as Fiona Macleod after 1894, see Sutherland, *Companion*, 568–9.   [167] *Review of Reviews* (May 1890), 403.
[168] *Review of Reviews* (Dec. 1891), 589.

in the late nineteenth and early twentieth centuries. Few literary evaluations made at that time can now be understood without reckoning on this. What seemed so striking to many contemporary commentators, and to critics of the generation following, was not the peculiar articles of Browning's Christian faith, but rather that he should have held Christian beliefs at all and remained a religious optimist, whereas other (it seemed, most) men of letters revelled in rationalism, rediscovered pagan Nature, were mired in pessimism, or else pursued psychic and mystic substitutes for the received religion. Hence the alacrity with which G. K. Chesterton accepted the invitation to write on Browning for Macmillan's English Men of Letters series (1903). Chesterton, then in his late twenties and reacting against the irreligion of his own upbringing, grasped at Browning as a means of finding spiritual direction:

I will not say that I wrote a book on Browning; but I wrote a book on love, liberty, poetry, my own views on God and religion (highly undeveloped), and various theories of my own about optimism and pessimism and the hope of the world . . . There were very few biographical facts in the book, and those were nearly all wrong.[169]

His idiosyncrasy notwithstanding, Browning remained the favourite poet of many a committed Christian. About *The Ring and the Book* (1868–9) the poet and critic John Bailey wrote in 1899 that it was 'one of the highest utterances of the faith of one of the highest-souled of men. It is Browning's Christianity . . . which alone can come home to us as a way of life.' Reading Browning again at the end of 1909, he wrote to a clergyman friend, 'The "young" critics say Browning is dead. One can only reply—they'll be dead first, if they ever come alive.' There was simply no substitute for his certainty: 'After all, politics play a small part in the whole scheme of life, and the great things, the universal things, sing "God's in His Heaven, all's right with the world". (How the Socialists hate R.B. for those lines: as if they were a philosophical denial of the existence of evil!)'[170] Leading ecclesiastics in the Established Church persistently paid tribute. It was William Boyd Carpenter, the long-serving Bishop of Ripon (1884–1912), whose address occupied primary place during the Browning Centenary in Westminster College Hall on 7 May 1912, following a thanksgiving service in the Abbey.[171] For Mandell Creighton, Bishop of London at the turn of the century, no modern writer expressed so forcibly 'our permanent relation to God';[172] and at Rochester and Southwark, the Bishop, E. S. Talbot, and his wife held Browning readings, which they 'took great trouble to make really valuable by inviting speakers like Canon Scott Holland, Mr G. K. Chesterton, Mr John Bailey, Mrs Benson'. Well into old age, Talbot 'enjoyed bringing out every shade of meaning in his reading of the

---

[169] Chesterton, *Autobiography*, 95.
[170] Quotations respectively from Bailey's diary, 8 Jan. 1899, and letters to the Revd F. G. Ellerton, 1 Jan. 1910 and 28 Apr. 1914, in Bailey, *Letters and Diaries*, 70, 117, 147.
[171] William Knight (ed.), *The Robert Browning Centenary Celebration* (1912).
[172] Letter, 9 Oct. 1899, in Louise Creighton (ed.), *Life and Letters of Mandell Creighton* (1904), ii. 412.

Bible and of great passages of English literature, especially of Browning'.[173] Talbot died in 1934, when, coincidentally, the Bishop of Durham, Hensley Henson, was closing his account of a troubled year for the Church

with the epilogue of Browning's profoundly suggestive poem, 'A Death in the Desert'. Sixty years have passed since first I read it at Oxford, and then it seemed to me convincing and consoling. In the long interval I have read much, thought much, observed much, garnered a harvest of manifold experience. To-day I find myself unable to discover any conclusion better fitted to satisfy Christian thought, or to provide a sure foundation for Christian discipline. It is the rock on which the Christian Church was built, and I know no other foundation on which in a changing world that Church can continue to stand firm.[174]

Suitably, it was a predecessor as Bishop of Durham, Brooke Foss Westcott, a former Regius Professor of Divinity at Cambridge, who preached the sermon at Westminster Abbey for Browning's funeral in 1889. Sir William Richmond, who came to know Westcott after painting his portrait, noted that 'he loved Browning' and thought him 'one of the greatest modern teachers'. Westcott expressed his own position in a paper to the Browning Society at Cambridge: 'He has laid bare what there is in man of sordid, selfish, impure, corrupt, brutish, and he proclaims, in spite of every disappointment and every wound, that he still finds a spiritual power without him, which restores assurance as to the destiny of creation.'[175]

It was now necessary to ring the critical note. The *Manchester Quarterly* pealed loudly, although it may doubted if the sound carried to many outside the North-West. And its article, by James T. Foard, who disparaged 'the preposterous popularity of Browning' as 'the momentary breath of an untutored mind', was not even about Browning. His was a panegyric to another versifier recently dead in 1890, Edwin Waugh. Foard had a point: Waugh was a superstar of the North Country penny-readings circuit, and his dialect poems and stories sold thousands in pamphlet, broadsheet, and ballad form. His loss was felt more by the people of that region than a brace of Brownings.[176] This was not what the critical establishment cared to know. Their minds were focused on what rank Browning should occupy on the classical podium. Nor did they much want to hear from another outsider, Walt Whitman, whose opinions about fellow poets, British and American, were disclosed in the *North American Review* in a piece indecorously titled 'Old Poets'. Here Whitman dealt in a pretty relaxed, not to say off-hand way, with both the barely cold Browning and the barely warm Tennyson. Of Browning, he remarked, 'I don't know enough to say much; he must be studied

---

[173] Gwendolen Stephenson, *Edward Stuart Talbot, 1844–1934* (1936), 178, 204, where it is noted that Talbot's doctrinal mentor, Dean Church, shared this devotion to Browning.

[174] Herbert Hensley Henson, *Retrospect of an Unimportant Life* (Oxford, 1943), ii. 329, where Browning's epilogue addressed to Cerinthus, the traditional opponent of St John, is quoted.

[175] Arthur Westcott, *Life and Letters of Brooke Foss Westcott* (1903), i. 362, ii. 34, 67–8.

[176] *Review of Reviews* (Aug. 1890), 163. On Waugh (1817–90), see Martha Vicinus, *The Industrial Muse* (1974), ch. 5, and Patrick Joyce, *Visions of the People* (Cambridge, 1991), chs. 10–12. Waugh had retired to the seaside in 1886 with a Civil List pension of £90 p.a.

deeply out, too, and quite certainly repays the trouble—but I am old and indolent, and cannot study (and never did).' Not much greater consideration was
accorded Tennyson and his 'flowery' effusions;[177] still, Whitman was at least
proceeding along the right lines, which was to venture some comparison
between Browning and Tennyson, in preparation for the moment when they
both passed into the pantheon. An unsigned piece in the *Edinburgh Review* moved
the business along: 'Tennyson and Browning', the very order in which they were
titled signifying the conclusion that 'Tennyson, from the exquisite finish and
melody of his style, and from the breadth and elevation of his thoughts, not only
stands upon a far higher pinnacle than Mr Browning ever reached, but also will
take a more permanent place hereafter amongst the greatest of English poets.'[178]
And Henry Van Dyke's *The Poetry of Tennyson*, published by Elkin Mathews in
1890, was rhetorical but definite: 'In the future, when men call the roll of the
poets who have given splendour to the name of England, they will begin with
Shakespeare and Milton, and who shall have the third place if it be not Alfred
Tennyson?'[179]

In 1892 Tennyson duly followed Browning to the greater beyond or, as *The
Times* reported it,

On Thursday, October 6, at 1.35 a.m. the great poet breathed his last. Nothing could have
been more striking than the scene during the last few hours. On the bed a figure of
breathing marble, flooded and bathed in the light of the full moon streaming through the
oriel window; his hand clasping the Shakespeare which he had asked for but recently, and
which he had kept by him to the end; the moonlight; the majestic figure as he lay there,
'drawing thicker breath', irresistibly brought to our minds his own 'Passing of King
Arthur'. His last conscious words were words of love addressed to his wife and son—
words too sacred to be written here . . .

The Times's account was less elaborate than many, especially the *Pall Mall
Gazette*, which claimed the scoop in depicting the deathbed scene.[180] The
arrangements had been romantically planned by Tennyson's family, following
the most successful model of the century, Shelley's end in 1822, launched into the
Gulf of Spezia on a pyre by Byron and Leigh Hunt, with *Sophocles* in one pocket
and *Keats* in the other. The courtier Reginald Brett thoroughly approved the
Tennysons' stage management. 'It is a fitting death,' he wrote in his journal,
likening it to General Gordon's, doing his duty to Christ and Empire.[181] Every
paper and journal carried extensive tributes and recollections, with the singular
exception of the *Fortnightly Review*. Its editor, the egregious Frank Harris, considered Tennyson a brainless sentimentalist. He contrasted the adulation for

---

[177] Walt Whitman, 'Old Poets', *North American Review* (Nov. 1890), *Review of Reviews* (Dec. 1890), 580.
The article was reprinted in vol. iii of Whitman's *Complete Works*. See also Masters, *Whitman*, 244–6, 254.
[178] 'Tennyson and Browning', *Edinburgh Review* (Nov. 1890), *Review of Reviews* (Nov. 1890), 471.
[179] *Review of Reviews* (May 1890), 448.
[180] *Review of Reviews* (Nov. 1892), 435–51, for the press coverage; Martin, *Tennyson*, 581–2, for the factual
record.   [181] Brett, *Esher*, i. 163 (7 Oct. 1892).

Tennyson with the fate of James Thomson: *The City of Dreadful Night* (1874) was superior to anything of Tennyson's, yet Thomson had died in penury, virtually unappreciated.[182] Most other people had been preparing their superlatives for years before Tennyson's death. Ruskin, in 1878, styled him, 'after Homer, the greatest painter of Nature'.[183] It was difficult to stand out against this sort of thing, although Samuel Butler's father's love of Tennyson aggravated the offensiveness of all his opinions in his son's mind. Still, Butler allowed that it had taken him much effort to learn to dislike Tennyson (and also Thackeray) as cordially as he did, admitting, 'For how many years did I not almost worship them?'[184]

The Tennyson stock was sustained by his son Hallam's publication of *Alfred Lord Tennyson: A Memoir*, in two volumes in August 1897. The judge Sir Edward Fry spoke for many when he 'said that it was a book that no one could read without being the better for it'.[185] It had been in preparation before the Laureate's demise, and it was dedicated by permission to the Queen. Reprinted three times in quick succession in the original format, in October and November 1897 and in 1898, it was reissued in an edition de luxe in four volumes in 1898 and 1899 and in one-volume popular form in 1899 and 1905. People who had known Tennyson understood that the portrait had been polished. Sir Mountstuart Grant Duff remarked: 'No reasonable person could expect that *The Life of Tennyson* by his son, would have been an actual picture of the man with all his roughness and oddities; but I do not think that posterity would have gained anything by possessing a careful transcript of these.'[186] Instead, disciples clamoured for clarification of the great man's message. Though Tennyson's work had not Browning's black hole of nebulosity, Hallam was 'perpetually receiving letters from all the ends of the earth asking him the meaning of this or that line of his father's'.[187] Hallam had made it plain, especially to his father's friends, that it was to be he and no one else who was charged with this commission. He had in his sights James Knowles, the editor of the *Nineteenth Century*, whose very title was conceived by Tennyson. Knowles was also a poet, though an architect by profession; indeed, he had designed Tennyson's Surrey home, Aldworth. The December issue of the *Nineteenth Century*, following the death, had been suitably reverent, containing seven poems in tribute to Tennyson: by Knowles himself, and by Thomas Hardy, F. W. H. Myers, Roden Noel, F. T. Palgrave, Aubrey de Vere, and Theodore Watts (later Watts-Dunton). The next, in January 1893, included a threnody from

---

[182] Harris, *Life and Loves*, 649–58, 696, 700. Harris's position was not dissimilar from George Meredith's. *Enoch Arden* (1864) had been the point at which Meredith turned away from Tennyson, disgusted by his 'panderings to the depraved sentimentalism of our drawing-rooms'. Correspondingly, Meredith found 'a massive impressiveness' in *The City of Dreadful Night* and, after Thomson's death in 1882, wrote: 'He is one of those personalities who need fear no comparison with their writings.' Thomson, it is only fair to remark, had extolled Meredith's own 'supreme achievements', in reviewing *Beauchamp's Career* (1876). Sassoon, *Meredith*, 84, 103–4, 125–6.   [183] Masterman (ed.), *Mary Gladstone*, 129 (14 Jan. 1878).

[185] Jones, *Notebooks of Samuel Butler*, 183, 188.   [185] Fry, *Sir Edward Fry*, 267.

[186] Grant Duff, *Diary, 1896 to 1901*, i. 297–8 (30 Jan. 1898).   [187] Ibid. 283 (6 Dec. 1897).

Swinburne and 'A Personal Reminiscence' by Knowles, this being the second in a
series of 'Aspects of Tennyson' by various authors which continued in February,
March, May, and October. Knowles's essay elicited a furious response from
Hallam Tennyson, who, now discovering that Knowles had made notes of
Tennyson's occasional explanations of his poems, accused Knowles of 'treachery'
and trespass on the family's copyright property.[188] This squabble was predictable:
Knowles believed that Tennyson had favoured him as official biographer and he
was peeved when Hallam had been anointed.[189] But all Hallam's puffing could
not ensure that criticism was squeezed out. In 1899 Frederic Harrison registered
the Positivists' annoyance with Tennyson's muddled mysticism. He reckoned
that he never 'shook men's minds' as had Byron, Shelley, and Wordsworth. Yet
Harrison like almost everyone was awed by Tennyson's 'unsurpassed melody'
and 'purity of language'; and, come the centenary of Tennyson's birth in 1909,
amid the renewed encomiums, Harrison's verdict was heard placing Tennyson
with the best poets of his age.[190] Hollywood paid its tribute at the same time. The
director D. W. Griffith, now best known for the screen mastery he exhibited in
The Birth of a Nation (1916) and *Intolerance* (1918), twice adapted *Enoch Arden* (1864)
for the cinema, in 1908 (as *After Many Years*) and 1911. The 1911 version was filmed
in two parts and originally shown on successive days until audience demand led
to their being combined as the first two-reeler. It was also 'the first movie without
a chase', an omission that had disturbed the producers at American Biograph,
who questioned how it could succeed. Its juxtapositions of dramatic close-ups and
cutbacks, with Annie Lee awaiting Enoch's return followed by a scene of him on
a desert island, were considered altogether confusing: ' "How can you tell a story
jumping about like that? The people won't know what it's about. "Well," said Mr
Griffith, "doesn"t Dickens write that way?" '[191] Perhaps the moguls thereby
concluded that it was Dickens who had written *Enoch Arden*; but, one way or
another, Tennyson was launched on his film career.

   Crowds at Tennyson's funeral were conspicuously larger than at Browning's.
According to A. J. Munby, who was there, people 'were eagerly buying for a
penny his likeness and Over the Bar'.[192] No member of the royal family was
present. The Prince of Wales was at Newmarket.[193] The Prime Minister absented

[188] Metcalf, *Knowles*, 339–42.   [189] Martin, *Tennyson*, 507.

[190] Vogeler, *Harrison*, 306–7, 310, 316. Harrison's fellow Positivist Leslie Stephen had been even more
severe in 1885, telling his sister-in-law Anne Thackeray Ritchie that she 'set up my bristles by calling that
maudlin Tennyson heroic! of all things. He is pretty enough, but has always the keepsake flavour. The
Idylls are sickening' (letter, 29 May 1885, in Hester Thackeray Fuller and Violet Hammersley (eds.),
Thackeray's Daughter (Dublin, 1951), 157). However, Stephen's daughter Virginia (later Woolf) found
Tennyson an antidote to the disappointments of Society balls: 'She crept miserably into the corner of a
ballroom to read *In Memoriam*, while Vanessa [her elder sister, later Bell] was partnered in every dance'
(Nicolson and Banks (eds.), *Flight of the Mind*, p. xvi).   [191] Robinson, *World Cinema*, 60–1.

[192] Derek Hudson, *Munby: Man of Two Worlds* (1974), 420.

[193] Philip Magnus, *King Edward VII* (1967), 301. The Queen herself, however, was moved by accounts of
the funeral of 'our great poet': see her letter, 15 Oct. 1892, to the empress Frederick of Germany, in Agatha
Ramm (ed.), *Beloved and Darling Child: Last Letters between Queen Victoria and her Eldest Daughter 1886–1901*
(1990), 149.

himself too, although he, Gladstone, having raised Tennyson to the peerage and then fallen out with him, could claim to be preoccupied with the new government he had formed in August. As for the poets, the most notable shirker was Swinburne, who remained holed up in Putney; but the rest of Literature and of those who counted in mankind clocked in. As Henry James put it, 'too many masters of Balliol, too many Deans and Alfred Austins'. The poets were deemed insufficiently grand to serve as pall-bearers, who included a duke (Argyll), pairs of marquesses (Dufferin and Salisbury) and earls (Rosebery and Selborne), a baron (Kelvin) and baronet (Paget), the American Minister in London (White), two historians (Froude and Lecky), and one Master of Balliol (Jowett).[194] The poets hid any disappointment. Their public face was reflected in the *National Observer*, edited by W. E. Henley, which announced that 'the English race shall not outlive his name, nor his work'.[195]

This seemed certain, though it rather surprised Tennyson's admirers in after years how much magic would evaporate from the work. In 1912, at the Digby Hotel in Sherborne, Edmund Gosse and Arthur Benson read Tennyson together in the evening: 'we are determined to work through *In Memoriam*. But we find much of it obscure, pedantic, cold, unemphatic, unpoetical. I am rather horrified to find how it has lost its charm. Gosse says with a profound sigh, "We must never forget that poetry must have *charm*—the one essential." '[196] This mood inspired Gosse to write an essay in which he recalled his first meeting Tennyson in 1871. It began: 'There is a reaction in the popular feeling about Tennyson, and I am told that upon the young he has lost his hold, which was like that of an octopus upon us in my salad days.'[197] By 1917, when he published his *Life of Swinburne* and reflected on the contrast between Tennyson's *Idylls of the King* (1862) and Swinburne's *Poems and Ballads* (1866), Gosse was no more than icily polite as he endeavoured to hold the ring:

It is violent and unjust to sweep away, as some petulant youthful critics are nowadays apt to do, the value of Tennyson's idyllic work. Take even the baldest portions of it, take the sentimental story of 'Dora', and the skill of the verse, the lucidity and directness of the narrative command respect. But the influence of it was deadening, and we see the unquestioned genius of Tennyson in 1862 acting as an upas tree in English poetry, a wide-spreading and highly popular growth beneath whose branches true imagination withered away.[198]

Such deflation was generally unanticipated in 1892. Then *The Times* followed its description of the deathbed with a panegyric of the poet's life and 'great and imperishable work; his name had long been a charmed household word around

---

[194] Martin, *Tennyson*, 582–3; Lang and Shannon (eds.), *Tennyson's Letters*, iii., 449–50, for a list of pall-bearers and distinguished mourners.
[195] *National Observer*, 15 Oct. 1892, quoted in Connell, *Henley*, 258.
[196] Lubbock, *Benson*, 243 (1 Sept. 1912).
[197] Gosse, 'A First Sight of Tennyson', in Gosse, *Portraits and Sketches*, 129–34.
[198] Edmund Gosse, *The Life of Algernon Charles Swinburne* (1917), 135.

the hearths and in the hearts of his admiring countrymen, for he was eminently the poet of the feelings and the affections'. *The Times*'s phraseology was carefully chosen: Tennyson may have been a household name but he had not been a popular poet in the sense of being bought and read by the people. 'Too dear for demos', was W. T. Stead's verdict. He deplored Tennyson's refusal to authorize anything less than a six-shilling volume of his verse during his lifetime. Stead's father was a Nonconformist minister in a Tyneside village who painfully built up his own library out of a meagre stipend of £80 per annum.

The older poets were already on our shelves. I remember buying Shakespeare's plays at two, and sometimes three for a penny, and often finding it difficult to get the penny. I had attained manhood before I had a Tennyson of my own. As a consequence, Tennyson has never been to me what he might have been; and what was true in my case is at this moment true of millions in these islands. In the United States the poor man could have had Tennyson's poems on his shelf. In the United Kingdom he cannot even to this day. He can buy Shakespeare, Scott, Burns, Milton, Byron, Longfellow, at a shilling each, and he will pay for the complete works of all these poets no more than what he would pay for the cheapest collected edition of the poems of Tennyson.

Stead added that Tennyson's aristocratic aloofness meant that he

was never of the people as Burns was of the people. He would have been a greater man if he had but lived in a wider world. He was always the poet of the library, of the drawing-room, and of the boudoir. He was fastidious and almost finicky; sensitive to a degree almost absurd in a man of such splendid physique.[199]

The Times drew a different moral from the life, that genius can run to waste without strength of character. Endowed with natural facility, Tennyson might have heeded only the flatterers of his early poetry and disregarded stern critics; instead, he

meditated and laboured over his gracefully polished work; each melodious line and measured couplet was the deliberate expression of his feelings; he wrote slowly and published leisurely . . . his deepest sentiments were seldom obscure; the loftiest flights of his philosophical mysticism rarely carried him beyond reach of the perceptions of his intelligent worshippers . . . [200]

The critic and artist thus exercised joint responsibility in the choiring of Literature and, from the youngest reader upwards, this canticle found antiphonal response. Newman Flower, born in 1879, was running from the classroom at Weymouth College to his housemaster's in a snowstorm when someone 'banged my arm as he sped past and shouted: "Tennyson's dead!" . . . And in my pocket was a volume of Tennyson's poems, for we had been doing *In Memoriam* that afternoon. I plunged on through the blanket of snow, feeling that a literary god who sat high on an unapproachable Olympus, had passed and left some place which

---

[199] *Review of Reviews* (Nov. 1892), 437. Cheap reprints followed Tennyson's death and the expiry of copyright.   [200] *The Times*, 7 Oct. 1892.

none could fill.'[201] In 1899 the parish church of Haslemere, near Aldworth, where Tennyson died, acquired a stained-glass window, designed by Sir Edward Burne-Jones and depicting Sir Galahad. It was subscribed by local admirers. Keble Howard saluted these bereaved devotees with his gentle comedy *The Smiths of Surbiton* (1906), in which Miss Snow renames her house Locksley Lodge. It was the least a Tennyson 'monomaniac' could do. In the final analysis, lyricism mattered most. In *Adventures among Books* (1905) Andrew Lang, a poet himself, wrote that Browning seemed to have 'more influence, though that influence is vague, on persons who chiefly care for thought, than on those who chiefly care for poetry'. For Tennyson, it was otherwise, and for this reason Lang placed him practically beyond reach: 'I am convinced that we scarcely know how great a poet Lord Tennyson is; use has made him too familiar . . . Truly, the Laureate remains the most various, the sweetest, the most exquisite, the most learned, the most Virgilian of all English poets, and we may pity the lovers of poetry who died before Tennyson came.'[202]

VI

Another part of the critic's responsibility was to gloss over shortcomings or unsavoury aspects in the life of the artist and to accentuate the exemplary spirit of the work. John Ruskin's torments were a case in point. His marriage in 1848 was never consummated and his young bride deserted him for the artist Millais. He then became infatuated with Rose La Touche, a child whom he first met in 1858 and one of whose letters to him, addressed 'Dearest St. Crumpet', he carried wrapped in gold sheets throughout his life.[203] 'I am perhaps one of the most unhappy men in the world just now,' Ruskin disconcertingly remarked to Anne Thackeray at a dinner party in 1860.[204] This was a classic conversation-stopper; but on other occasions Ruskin was impossible to curb once he got going, as Gladstone, not short of stamina himself, learned to his cost. Alfred Lyttelton recalled being 'at Hawarden [Gladstone's home in North Wales] when the prophet came thither. The first day Gladstone held his own in talk fairly well, but on the second Ruskin quite over-powered him.'[205] Hence, Gladstone was fond of recounting a conversation with Ruskin about the Quakers, whom Gladstone faulted for the

baldness of their creed, and their pretension to have discovered as a new feature the supreme importance of the inner life. He pointed out, however, their great claims to respect and gratitude, because Quakers had reformed our prisons, established a peace party, and abolished slavery. To this Ruskin quietly replied that unfortunately these achievements

---

[201] Flower, *Just as it Happened*, 249.   [202] Lang, *Adventures among Books*, 21–2, 26.

[203] J. Howard Whitehouse, *The Solitary Warrior: New Letters by Ruskin* (1929), 14.

[204] Fuller and Hammersley (eds.), *Thackeray's Daughter*, 145.

[205] Grant Duff, *Diary, 1896 to 1901*, ii. 221 (7 May 1900).

were no merit in his eyes. For he thought the prisons ought not to have been reformed, that war was beneficial, and that slavery should not have been abolished.[206]

Gladstone's daughter Mary, privileged to hear this ultra-Tory torrent—it occurred in 1882—noted that Ruskin augmented the account by proposing also 'that punishment of crime shd. be absolute, that the wrong man shd. be executed rather than none, [and] that the idle rich were the worst burden on the nation', this last aperçu crystallizing in 'a plan for imprisoning every idler who had over £5,000 a year'.[207] Such confidences were for private circulation, yet common enough among the Establishment. After reading at the Athenaeum a section of Ruskin's autobiography, *Praeterita*, published in instalments between 1885 and 1889, Grant Duff reflected that it was 'an admirable specimen of its author's merits and defects—striking sentences and remarks, showing much insight and alternating with harum-scarum nonsense'.[208] The judge Sir Edward Fry was entirely 'intolerant of Ruskin, whose obliteration of the line between art and ethics seemed to him wilful confusion'.[209] It was not just Ruskin's mental collapse in his last years, but his previous denunciation of orthodox political economy and the commercial imperative, that posed the challenge to the obituarists (as George Eliot once put it) of 'using his knowledge gratefully, and shutting our ears to his wrathful innuendoes against the whole modern world'.[210] At the death *The Times* dealt with the problem thus:

One of the most prolific brains of this century, most penetrative in analysis, most ingenious in analogy, most delicately acute of perception, and most finely strung to all the harmonies of art and nature, has been finally stayed in its working, over-fretted and outworn . . . It might have been happier for him had his nature allowed him to limit his labour to what for most men is the domain of art . . . But when the field of art widened under his ken till it came to be conterminous with the continent of social economy, his existence grew to be a battle, and a battle that could have but one issue. For the third quarter of his life, in particular, he was like a fierce and feverish swimmer breasting the full force of the tendencies of his time. Like all such swimmers, he went down in the hopeless struggle. We may frame differing judgments on the goals he made for, on the course he shaped, or on the wisdom and utility of such striving; but all who can judge generously must own the heroism of the effort and the nobleness of the nature . . . He spent himself, his fortune, and finally his mental health in what seemed at the time a vain struggle, as many a saint and prophet has spent himself before. Nevertheless in his retirement his countrymen were not forgetful that a great man was still amongst them. On his 80th birthday last year a most distinguished body of signatories, headed by the Prince of Wales, united to present him with an address to show their 'deepest respect and sincerest affection' . . . With all his faults of prolixity, paradox, and want of self-control he stands supreme as a writer of the highest order of prose—with Swift, with Burke, with Goldsmith, with Newman.[211]

[206] Rendel, *Personal Papers*, 69–70 (4 Feb. 1889).
[207] Masterman (ed.), *Mary Gladstone*, 255 (5 July 1882).
[208] Grant Duff, *Diary, 1889–1891*, i. 134 (14 Aug. 1889).   [209] Fry, *Sir Edward Fry*, 267.
[210] 9 June 1880, quoted in Hands, *George Eliot Chronology*, 167.   [211] *The Times*, 22 Jan. 1900.

Much to the amusement of Augustine Birrell, *The Times* 'alternately ridiculed his [Ruskin's] doctrines and demanded his burial in Westminster Abbey'.[212] It got the right result in the end although, to the countless number who called themselves Ruskinians, whatever *The Times's* verdict their faith was unshakeable. First editions of the works had been eagerly sought for decades past: £16 to £20 was standard for *The Stones of Venice* (1851–3) even in 1881.[213] Ruskinians were well supplied by reverent exegeses such as *Studies in Ruskin: Some Aspects of the Work and Teaching of John Ruskin*, by the editor of the *Pall Mall Gazette*, Edward Cook. It was published in 1890, cost 6s., and contained chapter titles such as 'The Gospel according to Ruskin'. 'It seemed to me', wrote Cook humbly in the preface, 'that I might be doing a real service, in these days of Ruskin Societies and Ruskin Reading Guilds, by attempting to set forth what appeared to me to be the main and essential drift of his teaching'.[214]

The Ruskin Society owed its impetus to J. Howard Whitehouse, a graduate of Mason College, Birmingham, who in the Edwardian period was a principal in the settlement movement. He was secretary first of the Carnegie Dunfermline Trust (1902), then of Toynbee Hall (1904–7), and finally Warden of the Manchester University Settlement (1909–10), at which point he became a Liberal MP. Whitehouse edited the Ruskin journal *Saint George*, 1898–1911; he wrote tracts on social and educational reform; and he promoted the boys' club movement as a foundation for healthy citizenship. The mutuality that, in Ruskin's view, a wholesome society should exhibit was enshrined in National Insurance legislation, which Whitehouse, as an assistant to Lloyd George, helped to implement. In 1919 he founded Bembridge School and was its headmaster for thirty-five years, seeking to practise Ruskinian principles. Since he also bought Brantwood, Ruskin's Lake District home, it can be truly said of Whitehouse that he dedicated his long life—he was born in 1873 and died in 1955—in service of Ruskin.[215] Alongside the Ruskin Society was the Ruskin Reading Guild, started in 1887. Its prime mover was William Marwick, and its purpose was to promote the study of Ruskin, together with other visionaries such as Carlyle, Mazzini, and Tolstoy, who exercised such sway over modern Europe. Home-reading circles characterized the Guild's activities.[216] Among the more strenuous Ruskin clubs was that set up by Dr Clifford, the influential Baptist minister of Westbourne

---

[212] Birrell, *Self-Selected Essays*, 199–200.

[213] E. T. Cook to H. F. Fox, autumn 1881, in Mills, *Sir Edward Cook* 31.

[214] *Review of Reviews* (Oct. 1890), 399. A second edition of *Studies in Ruskin* followed in 1891. In 1890 Ruskin's publisher, George Allen, reported Ruskin saying that *Crown of Wild Olive* (1866) would be the book of his which would stand longest, though *Sesame and Lilies* (1865) was then the public's favourite. See Anne Thackeray Ritchie, 'John Ruskin: An Essay', *Harper's Monthly, Review of Reviews* (Mar. 1890), 194.

[215] Jose Harris, 'Ruskin and Social Reform', in Dinah Birch (ed.), *Ruskin and the Dawn of the Modern* (Oxford, 1999), 22–3.

[216] See *Review of Reviews* (Oct. 1891), 391, welcoming the first issue of *World Literature*, a twopenny magazine for use by Ruskin Reading Guilds.

Park Chapel. It began by studying the *Crown of Wild Olive* (1866), in the chapel parlour, between seven and eight o'clock on a weekday morning.[217]

There are grounds for scepticism about the impact of all this. Most members of Ruskin societies and guilds were professional people with swollen social consciences, keen to pursue Marwick's inviting prospectus: 'to look at Literature, Science, Art, Music and Social Philosophy in relation to the progress of the human race'.[218] This constituted a tall order for the fewer working-class members whose time was otherwise consumed by ordinary cares. Marwick's Ruskinian journals, *World Literature* and *Igdrasil* (the latter's title was taken from Carlyle), did not last; and Ruskin's own 'letters to the workmen of Great Britain', *Fors Clavigera*, issued in instalments, 1871–84, did not generally find their designated audience. Yet *Unto this Last* (partly serialized, 1860; book, 1862), Ruskin's ethical indictment of unfettered market economics, began to sell 2,000 copies per annum after it was reissued in 1877; and George Allen's cheap editions in the 1890s further enlarged Ruskin's audience.[219] It was a rare person who boasted about never having read Ruskin. George Moore was one; but he added, 'were I able to draw like him, I should never have troubled to write'.[220] In 1897 Methuen reported that its top-selling non-fiction title was *The Life and Work of John Ruskin* (2 vols., 1893) by W. G. Collingwood, the acolyte who nursed Ruskin at Brantwood;[221] and from the forty-five replies which W. T. Stead received from newly elected Labour and Lib–Lab MPs in 1906, to his invitation to nominate the 'books that have helped me', it became reasonable to argue that Ruskin was the single most influential author to touch the hearts and minds of the British labour movement. Ruskin was mentioned seventeen times (and eight of these particularized *Unto This Last*). This drove the Bible into second place with sixteen nominations, although those respondents who omitted the Holy Scripture perhaps did so because they presumed it such a universal influence. In the strictly secular stakes, Ruskin won at a canter over Carlyle and Dickens (13), Henry George (11), John

---

[217] *Review of Reviews* (Apr. 1892), 381. Clifford would emerge as an architect of the passive resistance movement against the 1902 Education Act, a refusal by members of the Free Churches to pay rates until their grievances were met. Robertson Nicoll reflected: 'No one lives in such ascetic simplicity and does more of the hard underground work of reclamation. When people lose son or daughter in London they write to Clifford and he never neglects them. He is by far the most influential Nonconformist in London, and the only one who has great influence with the artisan class' (Darlow, *Nicoll*, 164). Naturally, Balfour, the Prime Minister and promoter of the 1902 Act, disagreed. Balfour's response, *Dr Clifford on Religious Education*, was rated by Desmond MacCarthy as 'a model of intellectual castigation only just below Newman's reply to Kingsley' (MacCarthy, *Portraits*, 21–2).

[218] The journal *Igdrasil*, edited by Marwick, quoted by Francis O'Forman, 'Ruskin's Science of the 1870s: Science, Education, and the Nation', in Birch (ed.), *Ruskin*, 44.

[219] Lawrence Goldman, 'Ruskin, Oxford, and the British Labour Movement 1880–1914', in Birch (ed.), *Ruskin*, 60. *Unto This Last*, according to Edward Cook, Ruskin believed his best book, 'most pregnant in ideas and most successful in style'; but this had excited such outcry that its serial publication, first in the *Cornhill Magazine*, then in *Fraser's Magazine*, had been discontinued. Allen became Ruskin's publisher only in 1873; previously, Ruskin was with Smith, Elder & Co. See Robertson Scott, *Pall Mall Gazette*, 47–50, 75–8.

[220] Goodwin, *George Moore*, 169.

[221] Duffy, *Methuen*, 24. Collingwood and his family subsequently exercised considerable influence on Arthur Ransome; Hugh Brogan, *The Life of Arthur Ransome* (1984), 42–8.

Stuart Mill, Scott, and Shakespeare (10), Bunyan (8), Robert Burns (6), William Morris (3). Karl Marx trailed with 2.[222]

The most important medium for disseminating Ruskin's teaching among the working class was the university extension movement, in particular, courses given by G. W. Hudson Shaw in northern industrial towns;[223] and the origins of many of these lecturers' and social reformers' discipleship can in turn be traced to Ruskin's lectures at Oxford when he was Slade Professor of Art (1870–9, 1883–4).[224] Henry Nevinson, who was at Christ Church, remembered how Ruskin's 'magical voice held the crowded audience spellbound far beyond the appointed hour. Upon me the humour, the irony, and keen flashes of satire made the deepest impression, but beyond these lay the depth of thought and the passion of indignation which raised his lectures far above the height of religious services.' Nevinson wrote this in 1936 as a tribute to 'one of the noblest spirits ever produced by our country'; later, on hearing that Ruskin was being spoken of as an 'old fraud', he expressed his fury in verse, apostrophizing, 'O Master of the hand, the heart, the head', and answering as Ruskin himself had riposted to critics, 'They wash the dirty linen of their soul.'[225]

Historians are not trained to subscribe to a deus ex machina thesis. It is naive to suppose that the progressive conversion to Ruskin's ethical doctrines, between the 1870s and the early 1900s, was uninfluenced by the context of cyclical industrial unemployment and rural depopulation, the aggravated housing and environmental crises, and the poverty surveys which made many question orthodox economic and social policies and affirm a different value: that the true Wealth is Life. It was thus that Ruskin acted on individuals as well as groups. Through reading *Unto this Last*, with its pounding message 'THERE IS NO WEALTH BUT LIFE', Violet Markham—who was brought up at Tapton House, set in 85 beautiful Derbyshire acres—began to realize that her luxuries were owed to the labour of the filthy, forlorn miners she occasionally caught sight of. Her father was a director of a coal and iron company and, her conscience awakened by Ruskin, she embraced educational and philanthropic work in neighbouring Chesterfield, founding and financing a settlement there in 1902.[226] Bernard Shaw was also a devoted Ruskinian, initially for practical reasons when he functioned as art critic for *The World*, 1886–9. While ignorance never inhibited Shaw from utterance, his qualifications as art critic were exiguous and not improved by a colour-blindness about blues and greens. Ruskin supplied him not only with a formula for judging art but also to see the big picture of art in relation to society, especially that moral dimension which served human

---

[222] Goldman in Birch (ed.), *Ruskin*, 58. The same appeared true among working-class readers generally. According to an 1897 survey of free libraries in twenty-seven medium-size and small towns, Carlyle and Ruskin topped the list of most borrowed in the non-fiction category. Others in demand were Froude, J. R. Green, and Macaulay: Kelly, *Public Libraries*, 193.

[223] The evidence is advanced by Goldman, in Birch (ed.), *Ruskin*, 73 ff.

[224] Harris, 'Ruskin and Social Reform', ibid. 20 ff.   [225] Sharp (ed.), *Nevinson*, 126–9.

[226] Violet Markham, *Return Passage* (Oxford, 1953), 50, 63–7.

progress.[227] Shaw also hero-worshipped William Morris because on Morris, influential in turn, Ruskin's impact had been profound. Morris had jibbed at the fifth volume of *Modern Painters* (1860), calling it 'mostly gammon'; but 'all his serious references to Ruskin showed that he retained towards him the attitude of a scholar to a great teacher and master, not only in matters of art, but throughout the whole sphere of human life'.[228] It was the same for the Positivists. Frederic Harrison assessed Ruskin for the English Men of Letters series and for the *Encyclopaedia Britannica* in 1902. He was uneasy about 'the morbid wanderings of the mind' displayed in *Fors Clavigera*, and about Ruskin's ignorance of elementary scientific principles (Ruskin was antipathetic to Darwinism);[229] but generally he turned a blind eye to this 'wild and foolish' side. Harrison chaired the committee that commissioned Onslow Ford to sculpt the Ruskin memorial in Westminster Abbey, banishing thoughts that Ruskin himself had hated the Abbey walls being cluttered with such objects. Harrison's son recollected that Harrison 'rarely got through a meal' without reference to Ruskin.[230]

Antipathetic types could equally claim paternity from Ruskin. The empire-builder Cecil Rhodes regarded as seminal Ruskin's Inaugural Lecture as Slade Professor in 1870, with its exhortation for England to 'found colonies as fast and as far as she is able', or else perish as a race.[231] On the other hand, J. A. Hobson, whose critique of imperialism influenced Lenin in turn, was also inspired by Ruskin. Hobson's *John Ruskin: Social Reformer* (1898) registered his importance for a cardinal New Liberal social thinker and heretical economist of underconsumption theory.[232] Numerous other writers also attempted to come to terms with Ruskin's multifarious consequences, among them Alice Meynell in Blackwood's Modern English Writers series. The choice of Meynell, a Catholic poet, to write about Ruskin was not inappropriate, because Ruskin had been a great admirer of her verses, although she, like Cardinal Manning, had been overly optimistic that Ruskin too would eventually convert to Rome.[233] As for Edward Cook, his work of discipleship was only begun with *Studies in Ruskin*. He evaluated Ruskin for the *Dictionary of National Biography* in 1901; co-edited (with Alexander Wedderburn) the Library Edition of Ruskin's *Works*, a monumental production of thirty-nine volumes, 1903–12; and wrote a two-volume *Life of John Ruskin* in 1911. Cook's own biographer was surprised by the scant remuneration he received—'Many a person obtains for a second-rate novel as much as Cook for these thirty-nine volumes and the immense labour they represent'—and acknowledged that it 'was in truth a labour of love'. By it, Cook was confirmed in his devotion:

Ruskin wrote about everything—mountains, rivers, lakes and clouds; geology, minerals, flowers, birds and snakes; about architecture, painting, sculpture, music, drawing,

---

[227] Holroyd, *Shaw*, i. 142, 146.   [228] Mackail, *Morris*, i. 226.
[229] Birch (ed.), *Ruskin*, 24, 36, 175.   [230] Vogeler, *Harrison*, 296–7, 307, 316–18.
[231] Richard Symonds, *Oxford and Empire: The Last Lost Cause?* (1896), 25–6, 162.
[232] Birch (ed.), *Ruskin*, 24–5, 71–3.
[233] Helen Gill Viljoen (ed.), *The Brantwood Diary of John Ruskin* (New Haven, 1971), 595, 612.

cookery, political economy, education, poetry, morals, mythology, history, socialism, theology, coins, manuscript. He ranged from Monmouth to Macedon, from Giotto to goose-pie. The index to his works might compete with Mrs Beeton for the title 'Inquire within upon everything'.

Moreover, it was not just a case of logorrhoea. Cook was fond of quoting a German admirer, that Ruskin 'has never written anything worthless or unimportant'.[234]

It was in some distress, therefore, in 1919, when the faithful gathered to mark the centenary of Ruskin's birth, that their lectures as much searched for an explanation of the posthumous slump in his reputation as lauded his lasting influence. The triumphalists' view was that Ruskin was less consulted because his opinions, once judged fanatical and fantastic, were now part of the lexicon of modern progress and accepted almost as minimum standards. His very success in shaping social improvements had thus dulled the distinctiveness of his contribution, although C. F. G. Masterman noted, as some causes of Ruskin's declining reputation, his contempt for popular pleasures such as drinking and gambling, and his supposed anti-urbanism and overestimation of the regenerative powers of agriculture for the country's economy, community spirit, and moral character.[235] More slyly, E. M. Forster had insinuated another explanation for the irrelevance of Ruskin in *Howards End* (1910), where the sad figure of the clerk Leonard Bast is pictured reading *The Stones of Venice* (1851–3) in his basement dwelling of B Block flats at Camellia Road, Vauxhall, close by the roar of the railway:

'Seven miles to the north of Venice —'

How perfectly the famous chapter opens! How supreme its command of admonition and of poetry! The rich man is speaking to us from his gondola . . . Leonard was trying to form his style on Ruskin: he understood him to be the greatest master of English Prose. He read forward steadily, occasionally making a few notes.

'Let us consider a little each of these characters in succession, and first (for of the shafts enough has been said already), what is very peculiar to this church—its luminousness.'

Was there anything to be learnt from this fine sentence? Could he adapt it to the needs of daily life? Could he introduce it, with modifications, when he next wrote a letter to his brother, the lay-reader? For example:

'Let us consider a little each of these characters in succession, and first (for of the absence of ventilation enough has been said already), what is very peculiar to this flat—its obscurity.'

Something told him that the modifications would not do; and that something, had he known it, was the spirit of English Prose. 'My flat is dark as well as stuffy.' Those were the words for him.

And the voice in the gondola rolled on, piping melodiously of Effort and Self-Sacrifice, full of high purpose, full of beauty, full even of sympathy and the love of men, yet

---

[234] Mills, *Cook*, 224–7.

[235] J. Howard Whitehouse (ed.), *Ruskin the Prophet and Other Centenary Studies* (1920). Among the contributors were Lawrence Binyon, John Masefield, and H. W. Nevinson. See also Masterman (ed.), *Masterman*, 314–15; Herbert Read, *The Contrary Experience: Autobiographies* (1973), 273–6; MacCarthy, *Portraits*, i. 234–41.

somehow eluding all that was actual and insistent in Leonard's life. For it was the voice of one who had never been dirty or hungry, and had not guessed successfully what dirt and hunger are.

An afterwards workless, deceived and disillusioned Leonard, when bailiffs have seized his Ruskins and much else, decides that 'the real thing's money, and all the rest is a dream'.[236]

VII

For the obituarist and canonically minded critic, Ruskin's peculiarities were nugatory compared with Swinburne's, whose one-time paganism and republicanism, alcoholism and sado-masochism, developed into full-scale neurosis.[237] The Swinburne of *Poems and Ballads* (1866) had seemed like an avatar, an unrestrained, passionate, immoral genius who defied all intellectual, political, and religious conventions. 'He was not merely a poet, but a flag,' Edmund Gosse wrote; 'and not merely a flag, but the Red Flag incarnate.'[238] At Oxford and Cambridge undergraduates caroused through the streets declaiming from 'Faustine', 'Dolores', or 'A Song in Time of Revolution'.[239] This reputation was still capable of producing converts among the impressionable young in the 1890s. At Cambridge, Charles Masterman and his friends were fired after hearing Frederic Myers lecture on Swinburne and recite from his works in a 'deep impassioned chant . . . From that moment commenced an allegiance which speedily passed into an unfaltering worship . . . The period . . . of intoxication, when we would hurl Swinburnian imprecations upon "whatever gods may be" or, in the interval between a football match and a hearty meal proclaim our thirst for annihilation to the unconscious stars.'[240] Not that the declamatory style swept all along. The decidedly non-revolutionary *Anti-Jacobin*, on 21 March 1891, published a burlesque 'papyrus from Putney' in the Swinburne manner by the poet Lionel Johnson, who, drawn to Catholicism, was a constellation apart.[241] Elsewhere, Swinburne's place in history was being measured more closely. Another young man, lately down from Cambridge and now preparing for the diplomatic, Maurice Baring, was arrested by a discussion at Gosse's literary salon in Delamere Terrace, where Arthur Symons remarked that 'there was a period in everyone's life when one thought Swinburne's poetry not only the best, but the only poetry

---

[236] E. M. Forster, *Howards End* (Harmondsworth 1971), 47–8, 222.

[237] For the problems Edmund Gosse faced in composing his notice for the *DNB* (1912) and in writing the *Life* (1917), see Thwaite, *Gosse*, 474–81, and letter from Gosse, 30 Jan. 1918, in Bailey, *Letters and Diaries*, 181–2.   [238] Gosse, 'Swinburne', in Gosse, *Portraits and Sketches*, 4.

[239] Gosse, *Life of Swinburne*, 160–1, and pp. 136–63 for the context generally, for the publisher's nervousness about printing *Poems and Ballads*, and for the critical reaction.

[240] C. F. G. Masterman, *In Peril of Change* (1905), quoted in Masterman (ed.), *Masterman*, 24.

[241] For Ernest Dowson's delight in the parody, see his letter to Arthur Moore, 20 Mar. 1891, in Flower and Maas (eds.), *Dowson's Letters*, 190.

worth reading. It seemed then to annihilate all other verse.' At this, Gosse, who would write the appraisal in the *Dictionary of National Biography* (1912) and the *Life* (1917), declared that 'he would not be at all surprised, if some day Swinburne's verse were to appear almost unintelligible to future generations. He thought it possible that Swinburne might survive merely as a literary curiosity, like Cowley. He also said that Swinburne in his later manner was like a wheel that spun round and round without any intellectual cog.'[242]

This judgement was not without personal animus. Gosse, close to Swinburne in the 1870s, had become estranged as the poet fell under the wing of Theodore Watts-Dunton and, 'believing that Watts-Dunton had poisoned Swinburne's mind against him, ... he reserved his enthusiasm' for the earlier work.[243] Yet in 1912 Gosse placed on record his verdict that 'Whatever vicissitudes of taste our literature may undergo, one thing appears to me absolutely certain, that Swinburne will end by taking his place as one of the few unchallenged Immortals . . .'.[244]

Twenty-five years after *Poems and Ballads* (1866), Robert Louis Stevenson still recalled the 'spell' of Swinburne's verses, though he evidently cherished less his copy of *The Queen Mother and Rosamund* (1860), which he tried to barter at a railway ticket office for his fare to Edinburgh.[245] That Swinburne's later performances were variable (albeit unremittingly copious) was widely acknowledged, yet devotion to Swinburne did not always fade with maturity. In 1917, during a pause from wartime responsibilities, Masterman paid 'a pilgrimage to Bonchurch churchyard [Isle of Wight] to the grave of Swinburne'.[246] It was here that Thomas Hardy in 1910 composed 'Singer Asleep', being 'vexed' that a cross had been erected over Swinburne's tomb.[247] In 1897 Hardy had told Swinburne how thirty years previously he had been so absorbed in *Poems and Ballads* while 'walking along the crowded London streets, to my imminent risk of being knocked down'.[248] Hardy's admiration for Swinburne's poetry did not entirely explain the sense of kinship. In 1908, to the editor of the *Daily News*, A. G. Gardiner, he reckoned that he had suffered more abuse and misrepresentation from reviewers and the press generally, 'rougher, I suppose, than any living writer, except perhaps my friend Mr Swinburne'.[249] The two thus spiritually linked arms. Swinburne, who praised *Jude the Obscure* (1895), once delightedly told Hardy that

---

[242] Baring, *Puppet Show*, 155. Cf. the paradox contrived in Hichens, *Green Carnation*, 55: 'The writer ... has at least three minds—his Society mind, his writing mind, and his real mind. They are all quite separate and distinct, or they ought to be. When his writing mind and his real mind get mixed up together, he ceases to be an artist. That is why Swinburne has gone off so much. If you want to write really fine erotic poetry, you must live an absolutely rigid and entirely respectable life.'

[243] Rothenstein, *Men and Memories, 1900–1922*, 168. [244] Gosse, *Portraits and Sketches*, p. ix.

[245] H. W. Garrod, 'The Poetry of R. L. Stevenson', in Cumberlege (ed.), *Essays Mainly on the Nineteenth Century*, 44. Lang, *Adventures among Books*, 49–50, gives another version. Stevenson's admiration for Swinburne was not reciprocated; Swinburne, to Gosse's dismay, thought Stevenson talentless; Gosse, *Portraits and Sketches*, 56. [246] Masterman (ed.), *Masterman*, 294.

[247] Florence Hardy to Sydney Cockerell, 6 Dec. 1918, in Millgate (ed.), *Emma and Florence Hardy*, 152.

[248] Hardy to A. C. Swinburne, 1 April 1897, in Purdy and Millgate (eds.), *Hardy Letters*, ii. 158.

[249] Hardy to A. G. Gardiner, 19 Mar. 1908, ibid., iii. 308.

he had seen in a paper 'Swinburne planteth, & Hardy watereth, & Satan giveth the increase.'[250] Swinburne had persisted, unapologetic. When Quiller-Couch was compiling his *Oxford Book of English Verse* (1900) and he approached Swinburne for copyright permissions, Swinburne granted these only on condition that 'Hertha', the pantheistic, anti-Christian poem he had composed in 1868, be included in full.[251]

Swinburne made many an enemy. None was more implacable than Dr F. J. Furnivall, Cambridge don and copious founder of organizations: the Working Men's College, the Early English Text Society, the Chaucer Society, the Wiclif Society, the Ballad Society, the New Shakspere Society, the Shelley Society, and the Browning Society. Famed alike for his magpie erudition and enthusiasm for women's sculling, Furnivall held decided convictions on all manner of subjects. His tactlessness was supreme. Robert Browning sorrowfully reflected about 'poor Furnivall's incontinence of tongue' apropos a libel case in 1888, when Furnivall was ordered to pay £100 damages and costs.[252] Speaking at the inaugural meeting of the English Association in 1906, Furnivall breezily announced, 'William Morris once said to me, Damn the Classics—What do you think, Furnivall?'[253]—not a sentiment that the assembled schoolteachers wished to hear. Furnivall's influence was benign in the case of the secretary to the Bank of England, Kenneth Grahame, whom he advised to abandon poetry for prose;[254] but for the most part Furnivall was a fully paid-up member of the awkward squad. Manliness was one of the highest qualities esteemed by Victorians; but Furnivall took it to a new plane, Bernard Shaw remarking that Furnivall was agnostic because 'he could not forgive Jesus for not putting up a fight in Gethsemane'.[255] Literature was his substitute Christianity. He made a religion of great writers. Hence critics' clashes when Furnivall was involved were like crusaders colliding with infidels, producing plenty of gore. Mercifully, he did not eat meat and consume alcohol or worse might have ensued. It was over different conceptions of Shakespeare that Furnivall quarrelled with Swinburne. Swinburne had his own theories about the dating and provenance of particular plays and about Shakespeare's metrical

---

[250] Hardy to Lady Grove, 11 Aug. 1907, ibid. iii. 268.

[251] The upshot was that 'The compositor at the University Press wrote to Q. asking to be excused from handling this blasphemous item. His scruples were respected.' So Q told A. L. Rowse; see Richard Ollard, *A Man of Contradictions: A Life of A. L. Rowse* (1999), 121. Hertha was dropped from the New Edition which Q issued in 1939. It was first published in Swinburne's *Songs before Sunrise* (1871), which he dedicated to Mazzini.

[252] Letter to Mrs Charles Skirrow, 8 Feb. 1888, in DeVane and Knickerbocker (eds.), *New Letters of Browning*, 356; and Benzie, *Furnivall*, 234–5, for the case.

[253] Professor Sir Walter Raleigh cherished this also for being 'W. Morris's single witticism'; then recollecting Morris's general humourlessness, added, 'I doubt if he meant it' (letter to Percy Simpson, 4 Sept. 1912, in Raleigh (ed.), *Raleigh Letters*, ii. 396).

[254] See Herbert M. Grimsditch's notice of Grahame (1859–1932) in *DNB 1931–1940*, 357. Grahame was secretary of the New Shakspere Society in the early 1880s.

[255] Benzie, *Furnivall*, 195. Shaw participated in three of Furnivall's societies in the 1880s: the Shelley, the New Shakspere, and the Browning, to the last of which 'he had been elected by mistake' (Holroyd, *Shaw*, i. 126).

development, pitting his aestheticism against the textual 'science' of Furnivall and his associates. Ever emotional, Swinburne became seized with a sense of mission to 'massacre the pedants' of the New Shakspere ('Shack-spur', Swinburne sneeringly pronounced it) Society.[256] Relishing a fight in which no blow was ruled too low, Furnivall told him 'to teach his grandmother to suck eggs' and that his ear was 'a poetaster's, hairy, thick and dull'. Name-calling followed mud-slinging. Injecting a dose of philological learning into the fray, Furnivall insisted on styling Swinburne 'Pigsbrook'. To this Swinburne replied in kind by dubbing Furnivall 'Brothel-dyke' or 'Brothelsbank Flunkivall', before descending into the lavatorial by referring to 'Fartiwell & Co' and the 'Shitspeare Society'. To the embarrassment of the friends of each, the demented duo slugged it out by essay, review, pamphlet, and correspondence, over a period of five years. When scholars at home and abroad protested about the undignified wrangle, Furnivall ejected those who were members of the New Shakspere Society, including the Duke of Devonshire, Mandell Creighton, and Professor Jebb, striking out their names with a protestation about 'this present caballing against me', adding for good measure, 'I am now glad to be rid of you.' Miraculously, the Society survived another ten years; but its publications slowed to a trickle and terminated in 1886, and the Swinburne ruction was widely seen as responsible for its collapse.[257]

Swinburne's Francophilia was another peculiarity. Its chief constituents were hatred of Napoleon III and idolization of Victor Hugo. There was also his carolling the poet of decadence, Baudelaire. Swinburne lauded *Les Fleurs du mal* (1857) in the *Spectator* in 1862; and in 1867 he wrote his elegy, 'Ave atque Vale'.[258] Informed by Gosse that Swinburne had composed this in a Turkish bath, Arthur Benson retorted that he was not surprised, because Swinburne's entire work seemed to have been written in that state. 'Of course it's howibly good,' he added.[259] Swinburne's patriotism resurfaced, however, as Anglo-French friction grew. When Will Rothenstein called in 1895 to make a drawing of him, 'Swinburne talked violently against the French, saying he had lost all interest in them, since France had become a Republic, as they are always ready to fly at our throats and would crush us at any moment, if they could.'[260] Worse, from the Radicals' point of view, was to follow on 11 October 1899, when Swinburne's poem 'The Transvaal' was published in *The Times*, rallying the jingoes to dispatch the enemies of England: 'To scourge these dogs, agape with jaws afoam, Down out of life. Strike, England, and strike home.'[261] This militaristic outburst would

---

[256] Gosse, *Portraits and Sketches*, 41–2, 54–5. This also caused a breach between Swinburne and Browning when the latter accepted the presidency of the New Shakspere Society in 1879 (Tennyson having declined it). [257] Benzie, *Furnivall*, 197–208; Gosse, *Life of Swinburne*, 249–51.

[258] Gosse, *Life of Swinburne*, 89–92, 167–8. 'Ave atque Vale' appeared in Swinburne's *Poems and Ballads*, 2nd ser. (1878) and was reprinted as poem no. 814 in Q's *Oxford Book of English Verse* (1900; new edn., 1939).

[259] Maurice Baring's account, quoted in Newsome, *Edge of Paradise*, 88; and Gosse, *Portraits and Sketches*, 5, for Swinburne telling him about the Turkish bath.

[260] Journal, 10 Aug. 1895, in Rothenstein, *Men and Memories, 1872–1900*, 233.

[261] Thomas Hardy, loyal to Swinburne's genius, was first prepared to excuse it. The sonnet, he wrote, 'disappoints me, but probably it was dashed off in a hurry' (Hardy to Florence Henniker, 11 Oct. 1899, in

have appeared less of a contradiction had they known that, on leaving Eton in 1853 and for some twenty years after, Swinburne lusted after a career as cavalry officer. About the Balaklava Charge, he declared: 'To be prepared for such a chance as that was the one dream of my life.'[262] When Arnold Bennett picked up Swinburne in the Tauchnitz edition while living in France, he was astonished at the 'cheap and conceited' patriotism Swinburne was capable of: 'I would not write a thing called "England: an Ode"... I would as soon write "Burslem: an Ode" or "The Bennetts: an Ode". I would treat such a theme ironically, or realistically. But loud, sounding praise, ecstasy—No.'[263] Nevertheless, Swinburne persisted in what George Saintsbury called 'that curious delusion of his that he himself was a Republican',[264] a delusion which the world largely shared.

From 1879 Swinburne was sheltered from that world, watched over at The Pines, Putney, by Theodore Watts-Dunton. A grim account of the ménage was given to the poet Wilfrid Blunt by his cousin George Wyndham, whose visit in 1891 had

ended in Watts reading out his own poems instead of letting Swinburne read his. Watts, George tells me, keeps Swinburne prisoner, as a keeper keeps a lunatic. He had explained to George that some years ago he had found Swinburne in bed, dying of what is called 'drunkard's diarrhoea', and that having got him round, he now considers Swinburne as his own property, and treats him like a naughty boy, 'a case', said George, 'for police interference'.[265]

By 1899, when Max Beerbohm took lunch at Putney, the patient had been dried out, though the hand was 'tremulous' and accompanied by a 'painful longing look at a pint of Bass'.[266] The glass of beer was allowed when Arthur Benson visited in 1903 to talk about the book he was writing on Rossetti; but the occasion was distressing for the way in which Watts-Dunton pushed himself forward: '"Swinburne", he said several times over, "is a mere boy still [he was in his late sixties, Watts-Dunton over 70], and must be treated like one—a simple schoolboy, full of hasty impulses and generous thoughts—like April showers."'[267]

Purdy and Millgate (eds.), *Hardy Letters*, ii. 232). But when George Gissing lambasted Swinburne's militarism in *Review of the Week*, 4 Nov. 1899, Hardy accepted that Gissing had pronounced 'the right word at the right moment' (letter, 5 Nov. 1899, in Purdy and Millgate (eds.), *Hardy Letters*, 235). 'The Transvaal' was published in Swinburne's *A Channel Passage and Other Poems* (1899).

[262] Gosse, *Life of Swinburne*, 28.

[263] Flower (ed.), *Bennett Journals*, i. 285 (3 Apr. 1908). 'England: An Ode' was published in Swinburne's *Astrophel and Other Poems* (1894).   [264] Saintsbury, *Scrap Book*, 278.

[265] Blunt, *Diaries*, i. 55 (7 Aug. 1891). The anti-imperialist Blunt was no sympathetic reader of Swinburne's later poetry, particularly of that 'ridiculous sonnet in favour of the [Boer] war'; still less did he like Watts-Dunton's productions, the most famous being *Aylwin* (1898), which he dubbed 'a thing of the lowest order of childish melodrama'. On Swinburne's death, he judged him 'the greatest lyric poet of the English tongue', albeit 'our worst prose writer'; but his contempt for Watts-Dunton, 'who had used him as an advertisement for his own literary trash', was undimmed (i. 333, 373 (17 Oct. 1899, 6 Nov. 1900), and ii. 242–3 (11 Apr. 1909)). On Watts-Dunton (1832–1914) and *Aylwin*, which sold 16,000 copies shortly after publication; Sutherland, *Companion*, 36, 662.

[266] Quoted in Cecil, *Max*, 208. Beerbohm regarded Swinburne as the modern Catullus, Catullus being the Latin poet whom Swinburne himself most admired; Gosse, *Swinburne*, 25.

[267] Lubbock, *Benson*, 67 (4 Apr. 1903).

But Swinburne had long ceased to act as Ariel, and Watts-Dunton never was a front-runner for the part of Prospero.

Happily, at Swinburne's death all was forgiven. Indeed, the trend was marked in the years before as his collected works were published in 1904–5, the Authors' Society pondered forwarding his name for the Nobel Prize for Literature, and the University of Oxford offered him an honorary degree (which he refused) in 1907. At the death critics rallied to extol him. This proved too much for Thomas Hardy. He was disgusted by blandishments which signalled that the Establishment was determined to wipe the record clean and claim Swinburne as its own: 'The kindly cowardice of many papers is overwhelming him with such toleration, such theological judgments, hypocritical sympathy, and misdirected eulogy that, to use his own words again, "it makes one sick in a corner" ....'.[268] Among the exceptions was Henry Nevinson's 'lamentation over the last of our poets who had unquestioned claim to greatness'. This was published in *The Nation*. Nevinson refused to dwell on common points of agreement—'on the mastery of metre, the new music that he wrought with our language, or the passionate sweetness of his lyrical power'. He also conceded that Swinburne often sacrificed sense to sound. What he was concerned to rebut was the idea that Swinburne was a poet of pleasure and sensual gratification. On the contrary, he was 'our greatest poet of pain ... of yearning pain, of dying joy, of satiety, of desire regretfully fulfilled ... That is the tragedy he sang. In the midst of all this sorrow and delusive hope there is not much remains for mankind'—except 'the indomitable will in the never-ending contest for man's freedom'.[269] More conventional piety came from George Meredith, who had been largely estranged from Swinburne since the 1860s.[270] Meredith now wrote to Watts-Dunton: 'He was the greatest of our lyrical poets—of the world's, I could say, considering what a language he had to wield'. To both Watts-Dunton and *The Times* Meredith declared, 'Song was his natural voice,' the letter to *The Times* concluding, 'Those who follow this great poet to his grave may take to heart that the name of Swinburne is one to shine star-like in English literature—a peer among our noblest.'[271] The tribute was fitting, for Swinburne's death on 10 April 1909 was followed by Meredith's own on 18 May. This made 1909 a black year for literature. So Leslie Stephen's children appreciated. Their father, founding editor of the *Dictionary of National Biography*, had been a friend of Meredith, who based Vernon Whitford in *The Egoist* (1879) on

---

[268] Quoted in Millgate, *Hardy*, 461. In a letter to his daughter Robertson Nicoll boasted, 'Watts-Dunton says that my *Contemporary* article is the only good thing done about Swinburne,' a reference to his assessment in the *Contemporary Review* (June 1909). See Darlow, *Nicoll*, 206.

[269] *The Nation*, 17 Apr. 1909, rep. in Sharp (ed.), *Nevinson*, 47–51.

[270] Swinburne had defended Meredith's *Modern Poems* (1862) against the slashing attack by R. H. Hutton in *The Spectator*, but could not accept his later style ('Browning was born with a stammer, but I fear Meredith has cultivated his stammer'). Meredith equally took exception to Swinburne's extravagances of style—and behaviour—but was sincere in his belief about Swinburne's genius as poet and place among the immortals; Nicoll, *Bookman's Letters*, 14–15.

[271] Meredith to Watts-Dunton, 13 Apr. and to *The Times*, 14 Apr. 1909, in Cline (ed.), *Meredith's Letters*, iii. 1691–2. Cf. an earlier effusion to Watts-Dunton., 6 Nov. 1904, ibid. 1509.

him. Stephen had died in 1904, but his children still reckoned stock according to his measurement, Adrian solemnly remarking to his sister Virginia that '1909 is as disastrous as 1809 was prolific.'[272]

Compared with Swinburne, Meredith's only transparent vice was the opacity of his style. Meredith had this in common with Browning. Not only had they made no concessions to a readership with their esoteric and erudite vocabulary, they actually imposed such severe intellectual demands with their abstruseness and allusiveness of thought that unleisured and untrained readers were bound to suffer anguish. But there was a difference. Sidney Colvin, who knew both, testified that 'Browning's talk had not much intellectual resemblance to his poetry.' In talk he was 'straightforward, plain, emphatic, heartily and agreeably voluble', whereas, with pen in hand, he would

discover a thousand complications and implications and side-issues beneath the surface of the simplest-seeming matters; complications which often he could only express by defying the rules of grammar and discarding half the auxiliary parts of speech, by stitching clause on to clause and packing parenthesis within parenthesis, till the drift of his sentences became dark and their conclusion indiscoverable. (The mere act of writing seemed to have a peculiar effect on him, for I have known him manage to be obscure even in a telegram.)[273]

With Meredith there was less disjunction between speech and writing, possibly because, as a long-time invalid, he had more opportunity to prepare his conversational contortions. Listeners were made conscious that they had been admitted to an occasion, first by Meredith's voice with 'its strong virile *timbre*', then by his overflowing monologues. Colvin disputed whether Meredith's verbal pyrotechnics were simply the actions of a show-off:

The truth is that Meredith cherished an ideal of what the brilliance of everyday social intercourse ought to be which corresponded not at all to the capacities of ordinary persons but to the quite abnormal and super-athletic activities of his own brain. He never fully realised the difference between his own intellect and those of average people. In his novels he will often make characters described as ordinary talk like himself, and they, being his creations, can only do as he bids them. But when in real life he would sometimes try to lift the talk of a commonplace company to his own plane, the result was apt to be that he would be left discoursing alone to auditors silent and gaping, disconcerted or perhaps even annoyed.[274]

Meredithians disputed whether to prefer his novels or his poems. Colvin himself was repelled by some of the poetry which Meredith would read aloud, 'so close-packed and complicated in construction, so dense with thought and imagery'. When Meredith explained his purpose—'Concentration and suggestion, Colvin,

---

[272] Virginia Stephen to her sister Vanessa Bell, 18 May 1909, in Nicolson and Banks (eds.), *Flight of the Mind*, 396. Virginia hoped that the *Quarterly Review* 'would ask me to explain him [Meredith], once and for all!' Tennyson, Edward FitzGerald, and Charles Darwin were all born in 1809.

[273] Colvin, *Memories*, 80–1.   [274] Ibid. 173–5.

concentration and suggestion, those are the things I care for and am always trying for in poetry'—his hostility softened. Colvin thereby understood that what drew admirers, such as G. M. Trevelyan, author of *The Poetry and Philosophy of George Meredith* (1906), was this 'continual athletic play of wit and challenge to mental effort in the reader'. Wilfrid Meynell echoed this: people loved Meredith because of, not in spite of, the difficulty of comprehension—

Readers during the last half of the past century who wanted to be in the company of an intellectual superior filled their need when they took their Meredith volumes to their heads and their hearts. We hear much of his obscurities. But you might nearly as well quarrel with a grape because of its indigestible pips, or buy your grocer's shelled walnuts in order to save the preliminary exercise with the crackers which is necessary to their full enjoyment.[275]

It was this intellectual challenge that provoked the joke in Robert Hichens's *The Green Carnation* (1894), where the Wildean Esmé Amarinth plans to bring out a new edition of Meredith, 'done into English by himself'.[276]

Meredithians were apt to lose their balance in looking up to his summit. John Morley, the rationalist intellectual who occupied editorial chairs and Cabinet seats, was once asked 'who, among the famous men he had known, most corresponded to the general idea of a man of genius, and he answered without hesitation "Meredith" '—before catching himself from falling over, by adding the correction, 'always, of course, saving Mr. Gladstone', in whose Liberal governments he served and whose official biography he wrote.[277] In its obituary (penned, perhaps, by Morley himself), *The Times* allowed itself full rein:

It will long be difficult to believe that that great brain is at rest, that there is no George Meredith in the flesh to spur men to endeavour, or to laugh at them for their good . . . His public he conquered slowly and with difficulty. He never leaped into fame, but climbed to it, with many a setback, along an inhospitable path. Yet in the end he achieved the position of the greatest man of letters of his age, a position disputed, if at all, by the poet whose death we mourned a month ago . . . With George Meredith passes the last of the Victorian giants, and as such his fitting resting place is Westminster Abbey.

For, *The Times* averred, notwithstanding his relatively meagre sales,

Meredith was a prophet, charged with an urgent message. That message was not so much any original interpretation of the past, or any particular process of laying by for the future, as the right use of the present . . . Nature, as he said . . . plays for seasons, not eternities; and man would be well advised to do the same.[278]

---

[275] Meynell, *Francis Thompson and Wilfrid Meynell*, 142.   [276] Hichens, *Green Carnation*, 42.

[277] Spender, *Life, Journalism and Politics*, i. 77. Spender himself nominated Meredith as 'the man of genius of all I have seen'. He also cited Meredith's own shrewd assessment of Morley: 'Cut him open and you will find a clergyman inside.'

[278] *The Times*, 19 May 1909. The identification of Morley's 'prose cadences' is made in Sassoon, *Meredith*, 90. The editor of the *Daily News*, A. G. Gardiner, wrote a comparable eulogy about 'the last of the giants', in *Prophets*, Priests and Kings (1908, 1914), 45–52.

Meredith's nature-worship posed a problem for the ecclesiastical authorities, one resolved in typical Anglican compromise. The Dean of Westminster would not sanction his burial in the Abbey but approved a memorial service. He could do no less. The rank order of greatness had been defined by the Society of Authors. The first president (in 1884) was Tennyson; at his death in 1892 Swinburne and the historian W. E. H. Lecky were shortlisted, but Meredith had been chosen 'almost without debate'.[279]

By common assent Meredith was prodigiously endowed for authorship— 'George Eliot's successor in logical order', as the *Quarterly Review* put it in 1891. Yet, 'despite reviews, a cheap reprint, and American pirates, Mr Meredith still remains Scriptor Ignotus, a treasury of good things which few will be at the trouble of unlocking'. It was thus habitually assumed that Meredith was too complicated a writer for popular consumption, but Helena Swanwick recalled one exception from among the succession of inadequate domestic servants who passed through her household in the 1890s: 'The best I had in those years was a young Welshwoman, who read the novels of Merédith (as she called him) and enjoyed them . . . She was intelligent enough to make her own life and knew what to do with her freedom.'[280] She was not the only female reader inspired by the independence and intelligence that Meredith invested in his fictional women. In 1897, while working as a post office assistant at Grayshott, near Haslemere, Flora Thompson 'became so great an admirer that she could have passed a stiffish examination in the plots and characters of his novels'. She learned by heart 'most of his simpler poems'; but it was Meredith's novels which

revealed a new world to her, a world where women existed in their own right, not merely loved or unloved, as the complement of men . . . She accepted the author's word that there were such women, though she had herself never come in contact with any women half as delightful, and thought of their world as a paradise of the well-born and well-educated, from which she was barred by her birth.[281]

Flora travelled one summer Sunday to Box Hill, hoping to glimpse Meredith at Flint Cottage.

Was Meredith's failure generally to amass a wide readership the fault of the reader or the writer? The *Quarterly*'s critic in 1891 was inclined to spell out the awful truth, that the genius was 'dry and exasperating; tediously brilliant; witty and wise out of season; filling our eyes with diamond dust which is as blinding as sand or steam; not ponderous like his own Dr Middleton, but suffocating; and, in short, if one could say it without incivility, a bore'.[282] Walter Raleigh took much the same view: 'I suppose Meredith is the cleverest novelist that has ever written,' he mused in 1901, 'and no more like a great novelist than I am like Sandow,' he

---

[279] Bonham-Carter, *Authors by Profession*, 154. Thomas Hardy succeeded on Meredith's death.
[280] Swanwick, *I have been Young*, 151–2.
[281] Flora Thompson, *A Country Calendar and Other Writings*, ed. Margaret Lane, (Oxford, 1984), 174.
[282] Anon., 'English Realism and Romance', *Quarterly Review*, Oct. 1891, *Review of Reviews* (Nov. 1891), 500. *Punch*, 31 Oct. 1891, 213, endorsed the *Quarterly*'s verdict.

added, referring to the renowned German body-builder. There was 'no construction' in Meredith's novels; they had 'rotten' plots and, Raleigh thought, 'a strong strain of vulgarity running through them'. Raleigh considered the novels 'much inferior to his poems'.[283] That last grudging appreciation could not appease the Meredithians, for whom no praise was too high to garland his throne. Both Max Beerbohm and G. K. Chesterton made a profession of spiking reputations, but each allowed an exception in Meredith's case and was humbled by his immensity. For Beerbohm, Meredith was first in poetry and philosophy, the greatest English author since Shakespeare,[284] while Chesterton declared, 'Meredith is a whopper.' Characteristically, Chesterton also had some seventeen theories which might account for Meredith's magnitude as poet and novelist.[285] In 1905, when Chesterton and his wife visited, Meredith was in his late seventies, frail, deaf, and crippled; yet, Chesterton found him 'startlingly young' and talking 'like a torrent—not about the books he had written—he was far too much alive for that. He talked about the books he had not written.' He gave Chesterton ideas for a dozen stories and Chesterton was overcome 'with a blurred sensation of the million possibilities of creative literature. I really had the feeling that I had seen the creative quality; which is supernatural.' Elsewhere, he wrote of Meredith as 'the type of a stronger generation, in his mountainous love of liberty, in his large and ambitious scheme of work; in his philosophical sense of human fraternity, and in his child-like gusto for complexities and vanities'.[286] A memorial edition of Meredith's works, in twenty-seven volumes, was issued between 1909 and 1911. The veneration felt for Meredith in literature was as great as that felt for G. F. Watts in art, and his subsequent fall in reputation equally catastrophic.[287]

---

[283] Raleigh to John Sampson, 26 Aug. 1901, in Raleigh (ed.), *Raleigh Letters*, i. 233.

[284] Cecil, *Max*, 209, 214; also Beerbohm, *Chistmas Garland*, 189–97, for 'Euphemia Clashthought', Max's parody of Meredith, which originally appeared in the *Saturday Review* in 1896. With its revision and reissue in 1912, Max included a footnote: 'It were not, as a general rule, well to republish after a man's death the skit you made of his work while he lived. Meredith, however, was so transcendent that such skits must ever be harmless, and so lasting will his fame be that they can never lose what freshness they may have had at first.'

[285] Undated letter to Frances Blogg, whom Chesterton married in 1901, in Ward, *Return to Chesterton*, 40.

[286] Sassoon, *Meredith*, 251–2; Maisie Ward, *Gilbert Keith Chesterton* (1944), 150; and Chesterton, *Autobiography*, 287–8. Meredith also offered plots and story outlines to H. G. Wells.

[287] Rothenstein, *Men and Memories, 1872–1900*, 32. Suitably, Watts had painted Meredith in 1893: see Ch. 8.

6

The Commemoration Movement

I

The Great War raised the literary marmoreal movement to new intensity. Just as Lord Kitchener was promoted to poster grade first-class, so Rupert Brooke was forged into icon. Few could have predicted this. In 1911 his first book of poems was published—the same that was to sell almost 100,000 copies in the next twenty years—to outcries of horror at Rugby, where his father had taught and where Brooke himself was educated and returned as a temporary teacher. A pupil, Gervas Huxley, remembered 'even the liberal-minded Mrs Steel [wife of the housemaster C. G. Steel] expressing at lunch at our House VIth table her sympathy with poor Mrs Brooke for the shame that Rupert had brought on her and the school'.[1] Four years on, in 1915, Brooke was the subject of a splendid panegyric, composed for *The Times* by the First Lord of the Admiralty, Winston Churchill. The possibility that genuine grief moved Churchill is not excluded by observing that news of Brooke's death reached him on the eve of the Gallipoli landings; but Churchill's obituary, and the stricken prefaces to Brooke's posthumous publications by Eddie Marsh (who was Churchill's secretary) and Henry James, combined to fix the representative symbol of the lost generation for the Establishment. And it was extraordinarily effective. Not just for its influence on the Dean of St Paul's, W. R. Inge, who preached on Easter Sunday 1915 about Brooke's 1914 sonnets,[2] but also for its impact on serving soldiers. Ernest Raymond wrote that 'for many of us who, at that time, were young and at war, and had some idealism, especially perhaps those of us on Gallipoli, the five sonnets "caught our youth", and helped us in secret places of the heart'.[3] Images of Brooke were reproduced aplenty, notably the classic profile photographed by Sherril Schell in 1913 which served as frontispiece to *1914 and Other Poems* (1915).

---

[1] Gervas Huxley *Both Hands: An Autobiography* (1970), 52. Cf. the skit in *Punch*, 10 Sept. 1913, 219, which treated Brooke as an emotional, snobbish, and spoiled public schoolboy.

[2] *The Times*, 26 Apr. 1915, Inge declaring that Brooke 'found in his readiness to do his duty a high religious joy'. This did not accord with Brooke's actual position. His attitude was 'If Armageddon is *on*, I suppose one should be there' (quoted in Christopher Hassall, *Rupert Brooke: A Biography* (1964), 459).

[3] Raymond, *My Days*, 130–1. Cf. Vera Brittain's correspondence with her fiancé, Roland Leighton, an aspiring poet, who would be killed on 23 Dec. 1915; letters, 18 May, 29 July, and 2 Aug. 1915, in Alan Bishop and Mark Bostridge (eds.), *Letters from a Lost Generation* (1998).

Brooke the Fabian socialist, Brooke the mocking 'neo-pagan' (Virginia Woolf's designation),[4] and Brooke the adolescent doubter and decadent who lost his virginity in a homosexual tryst in which he was the seducer, all were banished to make way for that flawless image 'with classic symmetry of mind and body'.[5]

Henry James, who prefaced Brooke's *Letters from America* (1916), rightly predicted that 'a wondrous romantic, heroic legend will form'. James first met Brooke in 1909, on a visit to Cambridge. Stunned by his handsomeness, James was reassured when Desmond MacCarthy told him that his poetry was bad: 'Well, I must say I am *relieved*, for with *that* appearance if he had also talent it would be too unfair.'[6] James composed his preface in a different frame of mind. It brought a bonus for James himself, enabling the Prime Minister, Asquith, to brush aside Viscount Morley's opposition and to confer on him the Order of Merit.[7] James's friend Arthur Benson, now Master of Magdalene College, Cambridge, was astonished by 'the growth of the legend before one's eyes':

What nonsense it is, to be sure. H.J. hadn't much to say except that R.B. was a cheerful and high-spirited boy who lived in many ways a normal life, enjoyed himself, was not spoilt, and then wrote some fine bits of poetry . . . After all H.J.'s pontification, dim with incense-smoke, stately, mysterious, R.B.'s robust letters are almost a shock. It is as if one went up to receive a sacrament in a great dark church, and were greeted by shouts of laughter and a shower of chocolate creams.[8]

This verdict was committed to a diary; others too, such as E. M. Forster and Edward Thomas, who were aware of the falseness of the Brooke legend, mostly confined their scepticism to private correspondence.[9] As for D. H. Lawrence, who loathed the war, it was entirely in character when at a lunch in October 1915 he should entertain his hosts, Beb and Lady Cynthia Asquith, by being 'merciless about poor little Eddie [Marsh], giving an excellent imitation of his lamenting Rupert Brooke over his evening whisky'.[10] A public knocking was not on.

---

[4] In a letter to Clive Bell, 18 Apr. 1911, in Nicolson and Banks (eds.), *Flight of the Mind*, 460.

[5] Churchill's obituary, *The Times*, 26 Apr. 1915, repr. in Martin Gilbert, *Winston S. Churchill*, Companion vol. iii/1: *August 1914–April 1915* (1972), 814. See also, Christopher Hassall, *Edward Marsh* (1959), 445–7; Sir Geoffrey Keynes (ed.), *The Letters of Rupert Brooke* (1968); Paul Delany, *The Neo-Pagans: Friendship and Love in the Rupert Brooke Circle* (1987); Hamilton, *Keepers of the Flame* 222–37. The Brooke cult continues to draw: in January 1995 a lock of Brooke's hair, encased in a gold frame, fetched £1,320 at Bloomsbury Book Auctions. Altogether, this collection of Brooke memorabilia fetched £32,000, double the forecast. The purchaser of the lock of hair was Mike Read, a disc jockey. *The Times*, 14 Jan. 1995.

[6] Geoffrey Keynes, *The Gates of Memory* (Oxford, 1983), 73.

[7] Edel, *James: The Master 1901–1916*, 520–1, 539, 555–7.   [8] Newsome, *Edge of Paradise*, 318, 334.

[9] See Forster's letter of 2 Aug. 1915, in P. N. Furbank, *E. M. Forster: A Life* (1979), ii. 18–19, and in Mary Lago and P. N. Furbank (eds.), *Selected Letters of E. M. Forster*, i. *1879–1920* (1985), 227; and Thomas's correspondence with Robert Frost, 13 June 1915 and 19 Oct. 1916, in William Cooke, *Edward Thomas: A Critical Biography, 1878–1917* (1970) 91–2.

[10] Asquith, *Diaries*, 94 (28 Oct. 1915). Her diary records several occasions when, in the family circle or with a romantic companion, Brooke's poems were read aloud; 12 June and 19 Sept. 1915. As for 'poor little Eddie', it is likely that, for all his strong homosexual inclinations, Marsh never consummated a physical relationship, satisfying himself with a boot fetish; James Lees-Milne, *A Mingled Measure: Diaries, 1953–1972* (1994), 59 (22 Apr. 1954).

Virginia Woolf was put into difficulty in July 1918 when offered *The Collected Poems of Rupert Brooke: With a Memoir* for review for the *Times Literary Supplement*. She told the editor, Bruce Richmond, 'I should like to explain Rupert to the public.' Richmond accepted that 'there was much misunderstanding'; but his remark—'He was a very jolly sort of fellow'—hardly seemed the basis for a slashing reassessment. Woolf consulted James and Lytton Strachey. They had known Brooke since prep school and Cambridge, although as pacifists both, not to mention their homosexual partialities, she was plainly entering the enemy camp. Her view of Marsh's memoir was that it was 'a disgraceful sloppy sentimental rhapsody, leaving Rupert rather tarnished'; and, following her conversation with James Strachey, that Brooke was 'jealous, moody, ill-balanced, all of which I knew, but can hardly say in writing'.[11] The punches were pulled, therefore; and it was mostly left to the gossip mill to grind out notes of dissent. Thus Thomas Hardy got to know that Marsh's Memoir 'did not show one side of him—that there was a *hardness* in his character'—only by chance meeting Elliott Felkin, once at Cambridge with Brooke and now in 1918 an officer overseeing the German prisoners of war who were chopping down Hardy's trees.[12] It was still considered bad form when, ten years after the death, the poet-supertramp W. H. Davies wrote roundly, 'Rupert Brooke was not only not a great poet—his work shows not the least sign that he would ever have become one . . . and to talk of a severe loss to English poetry is all sentimental cant and humbug.' It was because of his personal charm and connections that his death was turned into 'the most extraordinary thing in the history of literature. He was made to represent Literature in the Great War.' As a consequence, Davies added with pleasing cynicism, real poets such as himself were asked to read their own work at recitals, for which people 'paid guineas to see and hear them'.[13]

II

If the loss of contemporaries, now eulogized as great writers, was attended with special solemnity, so also were their lustrous predecessors metaphorically exhumed and recommitted with appropriate memorials. It seemed a peculiarly British trait, the *Times Literary Supplement* had observed in 1902 when evaluating Alexandre Dumas's reputation one hundred years after his birth; at any rate, 'France is not so fond of "centenaries" as we are.'[14] The apparent coldness of the French had been noticed by A. B. Walkley in 1899: 'when they celebrated the centenary of Balzac's birth at Tours, the town council declined to contribute to

---

[11] Bell, *Woolf Diaries*, 170–2 (18, 23, 27 July 1918). Brooke's correspondence with James Strachey was largely suppressed by his trustee Geoffrey Keynes: it was published in Keith Hale (ed.), *Friends and Apostles: The Correspondence of Rupert Brooke and James Strachey, 1905–1914* (New Haven, 1998).

[12] Florence Hardy to Sydney Cockerell, 25 Oct. 1918, in Millgate (ed.), *Emma and Florence Hardy*, 148.

[13] W. H. Davies, *Later Days* (1927), 151–3.   [14] *TLS*, 4 July 1902, 193.

the expenses'.[15] This was an unfair measure. Ratepayer niggardliness was not unknown in Britain. Commemorations were initiated by cultists of various sorts and not always from aesthetic motives alone, but with an eye to the commercial main chance or with recherché ideological ends to promote. The distant sound of grinding axes was not, therefore, conducive to the disgorging of public funds. Less contentiousness was evident when the association was with an institution rather than a place. The old-boy syndrome presupposed shared values; and no mythology was more influential than Thomas Hughes's *Tom Brown's Schooldays* (1857), which romanticized the public-school ethos at Thomas Arnold's Rugby. Hughes died in 1896; a year later one of Arnold's successors as headmaster, John Percival, now Bishop of Hereford, endowed the annual award of school prizes of Hughes's books as a memorial to their author.[16]

If the Victorian literary commemoration movement can be said to have had a start, it was launched by the Burns centenary in 1859 and the Shakespeare ter-centenary in 1864. These were names not just precious in their country of origin but figures to whom global homage was paid; as Lord Rosebery styled them, 'that miracle called Shakespeare . . . [and] the miracle called Burns.'[17] Anniversary cults once associated with Christian saints and significant moments in the history of religious congregations were now supplemented, even outnumbered, by com-memorations of secular heroes and decisive events in the history of nations. The two types might still be combined, as they were in 1888, when Liverpool Orangemen celebrated the tercentenary of the defeat of the Spanish Armada as a triumph over Catholic tyranny, although this note was avoided at Plymouth Ho, where the foundation stone of a national memorial was laid by the fifteenth Duke of Norfolk, the country's leading lay Catholic. There the Duke emphasized that their purpose was not to express antipathy to another nation or religion but 'to teach the present generation of Englishmen that they had a glorious history to look back upon and that the duties and responsibilities of that history must be remembered'.[18]

In 1885 the *Pall Mall Gazette* observed 'the present rage for centenaries'.[19] It believed that this was a widespread trend; however, with few exceptions, these celebrations saluted only the greatest figures and major events. Outside special interest groups, they did not usually elicit popular appeal. The scope of the

---

[15] Walkley, *Frames of Mind*, 119. Tours nonetheless remained a magnet for Balzac enthusiasts. Molly Randolph, the American heroine of C. N. and A. M. Williamson's best-seller *The Lightning Conductor* (1902), indulges in a Balzacian binge while visiting the town: 'I never appreciated him as I do here, on his "native heath". I have begged Brown [the Hon. Jack Winston who is masquerading as her chauffeur] to name his master's car "Balzac", because it, too, is a "violent and complicated genius". I've gazed at the house where Balzac was born; I've photographed the Balzac medallion; I've stuffed my trunks with illustrated editions of Balzac's books; and I've gone to see everything I could find, which he ever spoke about' ((n.d.), 48). [16] William Temple, *Life of Bishop Percival* (1921), 156–7.

[17] Geake (ed.), *Appreciations*, 52.

[18] For the controversial Liverpool demonstration, Waller, *Democracy and Sectarianism*, 94; and for the Duke of Norfolk, Roland Quinault, 'The Cult of the Centenary, c.1784–1914', *Historical Research*, Oct. 1998, 315. [19] Quinault, 'Cult of the Centenary', 316.

commemoration movement then so widened that in the Edwardian period Edmund Gosse could state that 'the habit of centenaries had not seized the British public forty years ago'.[20] One sign of this generalized literary memorial mania that gradually took hold in the generation before the Great War had been evident in April 1874, the golden jubilee of the death from fever of Lord Byron at Missolonghi during the War of Greek Independence. A Byron Memorial Committee was formed by Edward Trelawny, then past 80 years of age. He had conducted Shelley's cremation after the poet drowned in the Bay of Spezia. An associate of both poets, Trelawny was famed for his swashbuckling escapades, and for the novel *The Adventures of a Younger Son* (1831) and the *Recollections* (1858) where he wrote about their relationships. He now outraged Swinburne by including his name as a member of the Byron Memorial Committee, without having asked him. This was an understandable error, because Swinburne had published a laudatory introduction to a selection of Byron's poetry in 1866.[21] Trelawny was not to know that Swinburne had turned hostile to the poetry and poet meanwhile; but this was a foretaste of the touchiness and tiffs which dogged the memorial movement in years to come. As it happened, Trelawny was also an outsize liar and fantasist, as ready to dilate about his friendship with Keats (whom he never knew) as about Byron and Shelley and his own heroics.[22] The manufacture of myth, too, would occupy its place in the memorial movement.

Gosse was in attendance at one of the next events, a modest (only in terms of numbers) affair when Swinburne hosted a party of five at a Soho tavern in February 1875, to commemorate the centenary of the births of Walter Savage Landor and Charles Lamb. Gosse commented drily about Swinburne's initiative: 'So far as I know, it was the only time in his life that he ever "organised" anything.'[23] Afterwards, Gosse himself would more than make up this deficit; but, among the literary archaeologists who now busied themselves in devising public memorials, none dug deeper than Canon H. D. Rawnsley. A co-founder of the National Trust (1895), designed to preserve the Lake District as a landscape shrine to the Lake Poets, Rawnsley tirelessly conducted parties of the great and good around the sites, most treasured being Wordsworth's homes Dove Cottage and Rydal Mount.[24] Rawnsley was 'full of ardour and enthusiasm, a creature of fads', wrote Lady Battersea, adding, after one such expedition, 'I was never without Mr Rawnsley all day, and oh, what did I not drink in!'[25] Browning was another poet to elicit Rawnsley's discipleship—Rawnsley composed 'At Browning's Grave' and 'The Poet's Home-Going' for the Centenary Celebration

---

[20] Gosse, *Portraits and Sketches*, 52–4.   [21] Gosse, *Swinburne*, 142–3, 220–1.
[22] David Crane, *Lord Byron's Jackal* (1998).   [23] Gosse, *Portraits and Sketches*, 52–4; id., *Swinburne*, 223–5.
[24] Stopford Brooke and his brother William were other principals in the movement in the early 1890s to preserve Dove Cottage as a national memorial; Lawrence Pearsall Jacks, *Life and Letters of Stopford Brooke* (1917), ii. 457, 459.
[25] Lady Battersea's journal, 14 and 20 Aug. 1895, in Cohen, *Rothschild and her Daughters*, 248. On Rawnsley (1851–1920): *DNB Missing Persons*, 548–9.

at Westminster Abbey on 7 May 1912[26]—but in 1898 he organized perhaps the most unusual memorial of the period, to Caedmon (*fl.* 670), the first English Christian poet. The site chosen was nearby the Abbey ruins at Whitby, where Caedmon supposedly received his vision to write verse.[27] Lord Normanby was prevailed upon to persuade the Poet Laureate, Austin, to unveil Caedmon's cross.[28] During his address Austin observed: 'Memorials and monuments to distinguished forerunners of our race have during the last few years been raised with so much lavishness, and so little discrimination, that a feeling almost of repugnance to their multiplication has been growing up in the public mind; and in that sentiment I must allow, I have had my share.' Austin consented to perform this ceremony only, he maintained, because 'Caedmon, his remote predecessor, was wholly unencumbered with the lumber of learning, and therefore all the more impressionable to the two main earthly sources of poetic inspiration, external nature and the human heart.'[29]

Caedmon easily led in the joint antiquity and obscurity stakes. Then far better known was Charles Dibdin, 'the British Sailor's Poet Laureate', as *Punch* dubbed him. He had died in 1814, but his grave in the cemetery of St Martin's, Pratt Street, in Camden Town, London, which contained lines from 'Tom Bowling' on the headstone, was dilapidated by 1888, whereupon *Punch* cried shame and appealed for a suitable memorial: 'Charles Dibdin "did his duty", in a fashion that laid sea-girt England under an eternal obligation. Now let England do hers!'[30] Still, even where a memorial to a hero existed already, late Victorians insisted on paying their own homage. In 1883 the printers of London had commissioned a stained-glass window for St Margaret's, next to Westminster Abbey, in honour of William Caxton, who was buried in the church; and the window incorporated an epitaph by Tennyson, who judged this the best of all his products in this line, next to that he had composed for the Arctic explorer Sir John Franklin in the Abbey itself.[31] Soon the time would come when authors of whatever reputation would be recognized by some commemorative plaque. This was signalled in 1912–13, when C. H. Herford, who was Professor of English Literature at Manchester University and a Positivist by creed, organized a lecture series and subscription to place a memorial to George Gissing at Owen's College, from where as a student Gissing had been expelled in disgrace.[32] Connections, however tenuous, were now marked. In June 1914 a memorial tablet to William Hale White was unveiled

---

[26] Knight (ed.), *Browning Centenary*, 12–18.

[27] Bram Stoker chose much the same spot for Lucy Westenra's fateful meeting with the undead vampire, in *Dracula*, published in the previous year, 1897.

[28] Normanby, the third Marquess, had his seat at Mulgrave Castle, Whitby. He was an unusual hereditary peer, in that he was a practising clergyman: vicar of St Mark's, Worsley, Manchester, 1872–90, then Canon of St George's Chapel, Windsor.

[29] *The Times*, 22 Sept. 1898; G. F. Browne, *The Recollections of a Bishop* (1915), 213; and *Punch*, 1 Oct. 1898, 150.   [30] *Punch*, 25 Feb. 1888, 89; and *Oxford DNB* for Dibdin (bap. 1745; d. 1814).

[31] Tennyson, *Tennyson*, 647; and Masterman (ed.), *Mary Gladstone*, 289.

[32] Vogeler, *Harrison*, 327. H. G. Wells was a supporter of the Gissing memorial, to be sculpted by Eric Gill. On C. H. Herford (1853–1931), *DNB 1931–1940*, 423–4.

at Hastings by Robertson Nicoll. White's semi-autobiographical novels, written under the pseudonym Mark Rutherford, had registered the spiritual doubts and conflicts that beset Dissent. White died in 1913, aged 81. It was Nicoll's persistent praise of his works in the pages of the *British Weekly* that 'compelled the public to recognise the lonely genius of "Mark Rutherford", and there were few achievements of which he felt more proud'.[33] Yet White had been born in Bedford and lived mostly in London, where he was a civil servant. His residence in Hastings was brief (1892–1900) and in retirement.

Enthusiasts were not deterred from their missions by slightness of link to the object of their worship. In 1896 Passmore Edwards dedicated one of the many public free libraries he founded to the memory of Leigh Hunt and the actor Charles Kean;[34] and Canon Rawnsley followed up the Caedmon commemoration by publishing *Memories of the Tennysons* in 1900. Rawnsley's own encounters with Tennyson were few, but his and Tennyson's fathers had been rectors of neighbouring Lincolnshire parishes, and it was Rawnsley senior who had officiated at the poet's wedding. Rawnsley's account now served to uphold the legend of a great man who, however high he soared, kept loyal to his local roots: 'he told many "Linkishire" stories, he talking in broadest dialect and delightful humour'. What was termed 'the weird side of the work of the Laureate' was admitted but explained by his closeness to ordinary folk and his acute ear for their 'superstitions in matter of boggles and witches and wise men'. Here, then, was an untroubled childhood, unconventional only in so far as the poet's genius was always marked:

What struck me in the district was the way in which Alfred Tennyson's personality had impressed itself on the simple people. There were old folk at Spilsby, at Louth, at Horncastle, who could remember either what 'Mr Halfred', as they called him, was like when a boy, or had heard their mothers and fathers tell them of their remembrances.[35]

There was no hint here of the cursed 'black blood' of the Tennysons which darkened the Laureate's childhood and cast a shadow across his life: his father's murderous rages and the insanity, alcoholism, drug addiction, and poverty that afflicted the family.

III

It was symptomatic of the strength of the memorial movement that the sceptical did not oppose it *tout court*; rather they pleaded for greater discrimination. The services of the former Prime Minister, Lord Rosebery, were much sought after, so much that he was moved to mild protest, at the opening of an exhibition of Thackeray relics to commemorate the centenary of his birth, at the novelist's old

[33] Darlow, *Nicoll*, 231, 332.
[34] This library, in Uxbridge Road, London, was formally opened by Lord Rosebery on 25 June 1896; Geake (ed.), *Appreciations*, 234.   [35] Rawnsley, *Memories of the Tennysons*, 28, 52, 108.

school, Charterhouse, in 1911. His protest was not, as perhaps it should have been, about the incongruity of Thackeray being put on show at a place where he had spent six miserable years and been 'lulled into indolence ... abused into sulkiness and bullied into despair'.[36] Instead, Rosebery took issue with the modern mania for commemorations: 'Celebrations of this kind have become to some extent vulgarized, and they should almost be divided into classes, first, second, third, or the like. For we live in an age of centenaries,' he commented wearily. He advised his audience to exercise more judgement about which commemoration ought to detain them; but he admitted Thackeray's genius and was quite happy to nominate *Vanity Fair* (1848) 'the most full and various novel in the English language'.[37]

Thackeray's daughter Lady Ritchie, now aged 74, was naturally present on this occasion. She was the most solicitous keeper of his flame, retaining a close hold over his papers and discountenancing proposals for a full biography.[38] What little failures she suffered stemmed, as is usual, from close to home. Virginia Stephen, to whom Lady Ritchie was Aunt Anny—reported gleefully to a friend in 1906 that her brother Thoby had 'made £1000. *one thousand pounds* by selling 10 pages of Thackerays [*sic*] Lord Bateman ... to Pierpont Morgan'.[39] Two days after the Charterhouse commemoration—on 18 July, Thackeray's actual centenary day— Lady Ritchie was the toast of a garden party at the Middle Temple, organized by the publisher Reginald Smith to promote the Centenary Edition of Thackeray's works, to which she had written introductions.[40] This new edition ran to twenty-six volumes, double that of the so-called Biographical Edition, which Reginald's father-in-law, George Smith—Thackeray's original publisher and the owner of the copyrights—had issued in 1898; and Lady Ritchie's introductions to the new edition were revised versions of the old. She did extraordinarily well financially from this enterprise, making £8,000 from the Biographical Edition and more from the Centenary Edition, which mitigated her disappointment at the failure of Smith, Elder & Co. to launch, in connection with Harper's of New York, a Standard Edition in 1907. She also contributed an article on her father to a special

---

[36] To Mrs Henry Carmichael-Smyth, 16 Apr. 1829, in Harden (ed.), *Thackeray's Letters*, 5.

[37] Rosebery, *Miscellanies*, i. 59–76. Max Beerbohm also judged *Vanity Fair* the greatest English novel, and he held to this all his life; Cecil, *Max*, 33. George Saintsbury opted for *Henry Esmond* (1852), 'Thackeray's greatest book, and one of the great books of the world for unvarying and all-penetrating grasp of life and for faultless *mimesis* or reconstruction of it'; see Saintsbury, *Second Scrap Book*, 241–9 on the supposed waning of Thackeray's reputation. Saintsbury edited the *Oxford Thackeray*, 17 vols. (1908).

[38] Hamilton, *Keepers of the Flame*, 144–5.

[39] To Violet Dickinson, 22 July 1906, in Nicolson and Banks (eds.), *Flight of the Mind*, 232, where it is explained that *Lord Bateman* was 'an anonymous ballad, embellished by Charles Dickens and George Cruikshank, who published it in 1839. In that same year Thackeray wrote it out and illustrated it, and it was this manuscript which had descended to Thoby through his father'—that is, Leslie Stephen, whose first marriage was to Thackeray's younger daughter. Thoby Stephen did not long enjoy his fortune: he died in November, aged 26. The financier Pierpont Morgan (1837–1913) was one of the richest men in America.

[40] Description of the party in Fuller and Hammersley (eds.), *Thackeray's Daughter*, 173, and in Lowndes, *Merry Wives of Westminster*, 170.

jubilee edition of the *Cornhill Magazine* in January 1910, Thackeray having been its first editor in 1860. Altogether, Lady Ritchie's labours had the effect of giving Thackeray the lead over Dickens in the posthumous race for renown, if Swinburne's assessment in the *Quarterly Review*, July 1902, is followed:

In life Dickens was the more prosperous: Thackeray has had the better fortune after death. To the exquisite genius, the tender devotion, the faultless taste and the unfailing tact of his daughter, we owe the most perfect memorial ever raised to the fame and to the character of any great writer on record by any editor or commentator or writer of prefaces or preludes to his work.[41]

   This did not dislodge Dickens from his treasured place in Swinburne's heart: 'He was so fond of Dickens that he read through the whole of his novels every three years.'[42] Still, it was apparent that Thackerayans were already supplied with devotional scriptures long before Rosebery's stumbling words of salute at the 1911 centenary; indeed, led by the literary critic Thomas Seccombe, they founded the Titmarsh Club in 1906 'for the purpose of bringing together admirers of the writings of William Makepeace Thackeray'.[43] It was, however, an occupational risk of such gatherings that they drew cuckoos into the nest. Professor Walter Raleigh responded to Seccombe's invitation to join the Titmarsh by saying that he was honoured, though possibly held one disqualification in relation to Thackeray; namely,

I rather dislike him. When he speaks of snobs, I cannot abide him. Even his English has, I think, been overpraised. But he made living creatures, so I do not deny that he is a god. In India I believe one is allowed to worship with all sorts of reservations at the shrine of a strange cult. I don't know if this is part of your scheme: many one-man societies exist to bully the infidel.[44]

At a club dinner, when worse for drink, Raleigh ventilated his feelings more strongly still. Afterwards he apologized:

I hate quarrelling about Thackeray, and I mostly always avoid it. I can't bear him, but it's silly and useless to say so. His bogus Queen Anne talk. His *patronage* of Swift. His habit of noticing things that only a valet, or E. F. Benson, would notice, such as that the greengrocer is waiting, in cotton gloves. He's a dreadful man, superior to the last gasp,

---

[41] Winifred Gérin, *Anne Thackeray Ritchie* (Oxford, 1981), 262; also pp. 231–6, 243–52, 263–8, for Lady Ritchie's introductions to Thackeray's works.   [42] Gosse, *Swinburne*, 248.

[43] See Hardy to Thomas Seccombe, 19 Oct. 1907, declining to dine with the Titmarsh Club, meeting at the Mont Blanc restaurant in Soho, with the American Ambassador, Whitelaw Reid, presiding. Hardy also declined to contribute an introduction to a contemplated new complete edition of Thackeray's works: Hardy to Frederic Kitton, 17 Jan. 1902, in Purdy and Millgate (eds.), *Hardy Letters*, iii. 2, 279. On Seccombe (1866–1923), see *DNB* 1922–1930, 755–6: he contributed over 700 notices to the *DNB*, including that for George Meredith. The Titmarsh Club took its name from one of Thackeray's stories, 'The History of Samuel Titmarsh and the Great Hoggarty Diamond', published in *Fraser's Magazine*, Sept.–Dec. 1841. Andrew Lang, who judged Thackeray 'our greatest master of fiction . . . since Scott' and whose favourite Thackeray was *Pendennis* (1850), wrote: 'The best part of the existence of a man of letters is his looking forward to it through the spectacles of Titmarsh' (*Adventures among Books*, 15, 78).

[44] Letter, 25 Sept. 1906, in Raleigh (ed.), *Raleigh Letters*, ii. 305.

and incurably sentimental in what I call a timid way. Also damd moral. He's no use at all to me.[45]

Thackeray's reputation survived with little damage from Raleigh's onslaught, it being the literary equivalent of that adjustment of the sculptor's chisel that Onslow Ford's assistant wielded in 1900 when persuaded by Thackeray's daughter to remove part of the luxuriant whiskers from Marochetti's bust in Westminster Abbey.[46]

Lord Rosebery appeased the Thackerayans in 1911. He also performed at Lichfield in 1909, for the bicentenary of Dr Johnson's birth.[47] There was never any question of Johnson's flame sputtering into extinction. Rosebery had been preceded at Lichfield by Robertson Nicoll in the previous year. He gave an address and unveiled a statue of Boswell there, Nicoll standing in for Churton Collins, recently drowned in Oulton Broad; but this was no false position for Nicoll, whose admiration for Johnson 'hardly fell short of idolatry'.[48] In recent years the flame had been tended most solicitously by the Johnson Club (established in 1884), whose members published their proceedings, and whose one-time 'prior' was the scholar George Birkbeck Hill. Through the Clarendon Press at Oxford, Hill issued some thirteen volumes of Johnsonia: a six-volume edition of Boswell's Life in 1887, two volumes of Letters in 1892, two volumes of Miscellanies in 1897, and three volumes of *Lives of the English Poets* published posthumously in 1905.[49] In 1910 the Johnson Society (Lichfield) was founded, and a proud president of it towards the end of his own life was the novelist–playwright Anthony Hope (Hawkins).[50] The office of popularizer meanwhile was undertaken by Alice Meynell's *Johnson, Extracts*, with an introduction by G. K. Chesterton, in 1911; and by John Bailey, whose *Dr Johnson and his Circle* (1913) for the Home University Library series was widely praised.[51] Yet it needed Cecil Harmsworth, who as one of the fraternal dynasty of popular newspaper magnates seemed an unlikely knight errant, to intervene in 1911 to save the house where Johnson had lived in the 1750s, started *The Rambler* and *The Idler*, and worked on his dictionary. This was 17 Gough Square, off Fleet Street. Much dilapidated, it was due for demolition until bought for the nation by Harmsworth, restored, and opened to the public in 1912.[52]

---

[45] To E. V. Lucas, 8 June 1918, ibid. ii. 484.

[46] Gérin, *Ritchie*, 261–2, and Fuller and Hammersley (eds.), *Thackeray's Daughter*, 169–70.

[47] Rosebery, *Miscellanies*, i. 31–58.

[48] Darlow, *Nicoll*, 198–9. Nicoll was a member of the Johnson Club from 1895 to 1918.

[49] For Dr Birkbeck Hill (1835–1903), *DNB Supplement 1901–1911*, ii. 263–5; and 'The Johnson Legend' (1897) in Birrell, *Self-Selected Essays*, 88–95. How far Birkbeck Hill's labours were appreciated at large is another question; Lang, *Adventures*, 121, reported coming across Hill's edition of Boswell's Life in a public library with the pages still uncut.

[50] Mallet, *Hope*, 276–7, for Hope's speech on assuming the presidency of the society in 1931; also p. 184, for Hope's pilgrimage to Lichfield in 1905.   [51] Bailey (ed.), *Bailey Letters*, 13, 131–3, 140.

[52] Pound and Harmsworth, *Northcliffe*, 397; *The Times*, 5 Oct. 1996, for Betty Gathergood (1916–96), curator of Dr Johnson's House and descendant of the first and second curators, Isabelle Dyble and Phyllis Rowell; and *History Today* (Mar. 2003), 62–3.

Lord Rosebery had done his duty by Dr Johnson in 1909, but his busiest year was 1896, the centenary of Burns's death. For collectors of the literature, the main event was W. E. Henley's and Thomas F. Henderson's four-volume edition of *The Poetry of Robert Burns*, published in Edinburgh in 1896–7, containing in the margins explanations of words and phrases for those readers whose Burns fervour did not run to an understanding of his dialect. Irvine, Ayrshire, where Burns burned down his house after an over-exuberant Hogmanay, drew the Poet Laureate Austin to unveil its statue of the poet on 18 July;[53] but Rosebery gave two lengthy addresses about Burns on the same day, 21 July, at Dumfries & Glasgow, and a third on 26 September at the unveiling of yet another statue to Burns at Paisley.[54] Evidently feeling that he had not satisfied his services to Literature in that year, he then took the lead at a meeting in Edinburgh on 10 December, called to consider the question of a Scottish memorial to Robert Louis Stevenson. Rosebery had instigated the appeal by writing to the press to enquire whether one was being planned. His call was answered, apparently unambiguously: 'a remarkable gathering crammed the Music Hall at four o'clock on an uncongenial winter afternoon', and among them were Stevenson's mother and several of his friends.[55] In fact, the meeting was as stage-managed as a party conference. Prominent on the platform as a 'friend' of Stevenson was J. M. Barrie: he had never actually met Stevenson, though they admired each other's work and Barrie would unveil the eventual memorial. The Stevenson Memorial Committee had also invited two other rising literary stars, Kipling and Quiller-Couch. Neither could attend, but the association of these popular names was important to the cause, and Quiller-Couch would complete Stevenson's unfinished story *St Ives*. 'I really wish you had been here if only to hear the roars of welcome with which your name was greeted', Barrie wrote to Q, enclosing *The Scotsman*'s account of the meeting. Barrie continued:

You don't understand what a public you have here. It is comparatively limited but it is the public that will carry this memorial to success. The 'people' of course are as they always were indifferent to R.L.S. and think this confounded 'art' an absurdity. They were at the meeting because Lord R. was in the chair. There is a fierce enough local opposition to the thing, in influential circles, but they are afraid to speak out because his lordship is about. (I loathe snobbishness so much that I hate to write of it, but there it is.) The papers are really hating the movement but Rosebery sat on a newspaper article of yesterday morning advocating waiting 10 or 20 years, and they sneak behind him to-day. The cultured lot are very enthusiastic and the students and other poor men no less so. But there's no question that Rosebery has done it all . . .[56]

Rosebery's address was artfully conceived, asserting a fastidiousness against the modern commemorative mania:

it will be a source of pride soon to men, women, or children to say that they have never received a testimonial. The minister as he enters and as he quits his manse is hallowed by

---

[53] *Punch*, 11 July 1896, 17, anticipates what Austin might say.
[54] Rosebery, *Miscellanies*, i. 3–30, ii. 3–6.   [55] Geake (ed.), *Appreciations*, 88–90.
[56] To Quiller-Couch, 11 Dec. 1896, in Meynell (ed.), *Barrie Letters*, 11–12.

such presents; the faithful railway porter who has been for five years at his post is honoured in the same way. No man who has lived a blameless life for ten or for twenty years can well avoid the shadow of this persecution. But, for all that, it is not for the sake of Robert Louis Stevenson that I would put up this memorial; it is for our own sakes. I do not, at any rate, wish to belong to a generation of which it shall be said that they had this consummate being living and dying among them and did not recognise his splendour and his merit.[57]

Rosebery proved persuasive; but the question arises, why did Edinburgh's worthies require persuasion? Perhaps it was because of lingering memories of Stevenson's raffish and godless student days and his brushes with local tradesmen, or because his corpus of work was assessed as little better than boys' yarns. Again, his migratory life made tenuous his links with the city. The issue of the Edinburgh Edition of his works in 1894 repaired the connection, but Stevenson's attitude to his native country always involved irreverence. What he called 'the race making'[58] of the Scots fascinated him, and he tackled its symbolic figures, John Knox, David Hume, Robert Burns, Walter Scott, and more, in several essays. He was conscious of wanting to stand in a particular literary tradition, constituting the third member of 'Scotland's three puir Rabbies', following after Robert Burns and Robert Fergusson, each of whom had foreshortened and suffering lives.[59] Yet Stevenson's spirit of worship was not so straight-faced as some Scots might wish. When he first saw the Glasgow memorial to Knox, he recalled 'laughing for an hour'.[60] The recipient of this intelligence, W. Craibe Angus, planned a Burns Exhibition in Glasgow in 1891, and had the idea of sending out to Samoa, Stevenson's home, a precious copy of the *Jolly Beggar* for Stevenson to autograph, which the Exhibition would then display. Stevenson was touched that such effort was contemplated to unite his name with Burns's memory, while firmly discountenancing the project—such a treasure should not be risked on 'the treacherous posts, and the perils of the sea, and the carelessness of authors'.[61]

Stevenson's association with Burns had not always been welcomed. In 1875 he was commissioned to write on Burns for the *Encyclopaedia Britannica*, but his submission 'was thought to convey a view of the poet too frankly critical, and too little in accordance with the accepted Scotch tradition; and the publishers, duly paying him for his labours, transferred the task to Professor Shairp'.[62] Yet Stevenson's offence then was nothing so grievous as W. E. Henley's later, when he lashed the Burns cult in 1897 as a warm-up to lashing the Stevenson cult in 1901. The final volume of Henley's and Henderson's edition of Burns's poetry was irretrievably marred, for the Burns priesthood, by Henley's Terminal Essay, in

---

[57] Rosebery, *Miscellanies*, ii. 22–9, and Geake (ed.), *Appreciations*, 89–102.
[58] Letter to Mrs Sitwell, Jan. 1874, in Colvin (ed.), *Stevenson's Letters*, i. 74.
[59] Quoted in Terry, *Stevenson*, 31.
[60] Letter to W. Craibe Angus, summer 1891, in Colvin (ed.), *Stevenson's Letters*, ii. 233.
[61] Letter to W. Craibe Angus, Apr. 1891, ibid. ii. 222–3.
[62] Ibid. i. 106. Stevenson published a revised and enlarged version of his 'Burns' in the *Cornhill Magazine* and in his *Familiar Studies of Men and Books* (1882).

which he sought to appraise Burns's achievement '*on right grounds*'. This was as a '*man of letters*' only, not 'as Scotsman, as gent of genius, as drunkard, as this, that and the other'. Burns, Henley wrote, 'has been the victim of more ignorant and besotted eulogy than any man that ever lived'. Henley loathed the 'shystering admirers' who revelled in legend and did not trouble to read what Burns wrote; he would be happiest 'if never another mutchkin were drunk, nor ever another haggis carved in his honour'. Henley knew what he was doing and knew what to expect: 'the Howl of Execration'. Worse, he welcomed it and added insult to injury by seeing the Scots in need of English home truths: 'I fancy I'll have the English critics with me—the most of the Scots against me. After all, *we* have a literature, and they have only R.B. Or rather, they have a literature, and have suppressed it in R.B.'s favour. "Instead of which" they see him as he never was, and run wild in the exaltation of an optical illusion.'[63]

What, then, were the tests to decide whether a memorial to a writer was justi-fied? Where strong popular support was manifested, this was naturally deserving of acknowledgement, whether or not it coincided with a significant anniversary and whether or not a place could claim special association with the honorand. Rosebery began his address in St Andrew's Hall, Glasgow, on 21 July 1896, the centenary of Burns's death, by remarking, 'What the direct connection of Burns with Glasgow may be I am not exactly sure.'[64] Still, Glaswegians dutifully congregated around their statue of Burns on that day. The monument itself had been erected in 1877, a year of no particular note, although its unveiling occurred on 25 January, so-called Burns Night, the poet's birthday. Subscriptions had been raised by 'the working classes of Scotland', according to *The Times*; and, while the business was organized by the Lord Provost and a committee, the ceremony

awakened great enthusiasm throughout the country, and advantage was taken of the occasion for a grand demonstration in honour of the memory of Scotland's greatest bard. There was a great trades' procession, which marched through the streets accompanied by instrumental bands playing appropriate music. The city was crowded with visitors, the greatest contingent being from Ayrshire, Burns's native county, and in Glasgow and the neighbouring towns a general holyday was observed.[65]

The statue was unveiled by Lord Houghton, who, in his address, observed that the custom of erecting such monuments derived from great civilizations such as the ancient Greeks and Romans who wanted a means of preserving in the popular mind an image of heroic men and their deeds. It still held true, he argued, in an age of the printed book and mass literacy.

The talismanic position Burns held for Scots was exceptional. Equally extra-ordinary was the latitude allowed to those entitled to be Scots on such occasions. Robert Browning was Camberwell-born but his mother was of German–Scottish extraction, and he was duly invited by the Burns' Monument Committee to

---

[63] Quotations from Henley's letters, 18 May, 17 Aug., and 20 Sept. 1897, in Connell, *Henley*, 317, 320–1.
[64] Geake (ed.), *Appreciations*, 48.   [65] *The Times*, 26 Jan. 1877.

attend the Glasgow unveiling and banquet in 1877. He regretfully declined; but even in the last months of his life, in 1889, he was being sent the works of Burns to autograph.[66] The centenary of Burns's birth, 1859, had been widely celebrated by festivals and dinners. It was also seized upon by entrepreneurs, who issued commemorative pottery and other memorabilia and sponsored competitions and prizes.[67] Burns clubs perpetuated the Immortal Memory, not just throughout Scotland but wherever Scots actual and honorary congregated. The torch passed across generations: the lawyer and literary man J. H. Balfour Browne took pride in recollecting, when he presided at an annual Burns Club dinner in Dumfries, that he followed his father, a doctor, who had been chairman of the 1859 dinner.[68] Politics as well as poetry animated these festivities, for, as Burns had said, 'Liberty's a glorious feast.' This keynote was sounded by Ralph Waldo Emerson at the Burns celebration in Boston, Massachusetts, when he pronounced that 'the songs of Burns were as important in the history of freedom as the American Declaration of Independence or the French Rights of Man'.[69] And it was echoed by Lord Rosebery at Dumfries and Glasgow in 1896. While allowing the Scots' special claim, he emphasized Burns's universal appeal as 'the champion and patron saint of Democracy'.[70]

IV

Civic pride was also summoned in such commemorations, as if the association with an author would add a cubit to the stature of each citizen. While Rosebery as a former prime minister was the most appropriate master of ceremonies for authors of canonical status, Robertson Nicoll was always available to act as impresario at commemorations of minor-league writers, especially those dear to a religious-minded public. Editor of both the *British Weekly* and *The Bookman*, Nicoll united the evangels of Christianity and Literature in his pronouncements. Thus the centenary of William Cowper's death saw Nicoll produce an address on 'The Passion of Cowper' for presentation at Olney, Buckinghamshire, where Cowper had written his popular hymns, 'God moves in a mysterious way' and 'Oh, for a closer walk with God'. As it happened, Nicoll could not deliver his address in person, but he published it in the *British Weekly* on 3 May 1900 and reissued it in *The Lamp of Sacrifice*, his collection of Sermons on Special Occasions.[71] In 1903 Norwich was the venue for a lecture on the centenary of George Borrow's birth, given by Clement Shorter, one of his champions among modern men of letters.[72] Ten years on, in July 1913, Norwich played host to

---

[66] Browning to Gordon Smith, 16 Jan. 1877; and to unidentified correspondents, 9 Mar. 1887 and 25 Apr. 1889, in DeVane and Knickerbocker (eds.), *New Letters of Browning*, 236, 341, 373.

[67] See the notice of Sir Theodore Martin, *DNB Supplement 1901–1911*, ii. 576: he was 'one of the umpires for the prize offered by the Crystal Palace Company'. [68] Balfour Browne, *Recollections*, 171–3.

[69] Quinault, 'Cult of the Centenary', 308. [70] Geake (ed.), *Appreciations*, 34, 45, 58, 63.

[71] Darlow, *Nicoll*, 167. [72] *T.P.'s Weekly*, 25 Dec. 1903, 964.

another festival, this time to celebrate the gift to the city of the house where Borrow grew up. Shorter was again a speaker, together with Augustine Birrell and Robertson Nicoll.[73] Shorter was present too, with Thomas Hardy, at the 150th anniversary celebration of the birth of the poet George Crabbe in 1905 at Aldeburgh, Suffolk, where their mutual friend Edward Clodd lived at Strafford House. It was Clodd, banker, freethinker, and folklorist, who organized that occasion;[74] but a better model for a local commemoration was the Alexander Pope bicentenary in 1888, held at Twickenham, where the poet lived after 1718. The proceedings were organized by a committee involving the critics Edmund Gosse and Austin Dobson, the keeper of printed books at the British Museum Richard Garnett, and the civil servant W. J. Courthope, who completed the standard ten-volume edition of Pope's works (1871–89) begun by Whitwell Elwin. They were supported by the former Governor of Madras, Sir Mountstuart Grant Duff, who, on resettling in England, lived at York House, Twickenham, and was active in the Literary Society. The culmination of their efforts was a week-long exhibition of Pope relics in the Town Hall, introduced in an address by Professor Henry Morley; and when the committee wound up its work, the small profit made was spent on books relating to the Pope period for the Twickenham Free Library.[75]

Such occasions mixed conviviality with civic pride and serious purpose, to rescue neglected names and to restate forgotten philosophies. Commemorations especially appealed to those steeped in the Positivist tradition, with its Religion of Humanity and ethical models. The leader of that school, Frederic Harrison, contributed to a Keats centenary volume in 1895 and was ever ready throughout his long life to pen tributes on suitable anniversaries, international and domestic: his biographer cites 'Dante's sexcentenary, Molière's tercentenary, Smollett's bicentenary, and centenaries of Kingsley and George Eliot'.[76] Thinking scientifically, Positivists preferred to signify the anniversary of death, not birth, because that marked the sum of the subject's achievements; nevertheless, it was not difficult to persuade Harrison to participate in both kinds of commemoration, where he judged the honorand fit. His revised edition of Comte's masterwork *The New Calendar of Great Men* (1892) comprised 538 names. When Grant Duff dined with him in 1897, Harrison was keenly anticipating the millenary of Alfred the Great's death.[77] He had been pipped by

[73] Darlow, *Nicoll*, 227.

[74] Hardy to Edward Clodd, 7 Sept. 1905, in Purdy and Millgate (eds.), *Hardy Letters*, iii. 180.

[75] Grant Duff, *Diary, 1886–1888*, ii. 115, 133, 142–5. On W. J. Courthope (1842–1917), elected Professor of Poetry at Oxford in 1895: *DNB 1912–1921*, 126–7. Grant Duff considered him 'certainly one of the men best read in English poetry'. They were fellow members of The Club (Grant Duff, *Diary, 1896–1901*, i. 19); but the poet Flecker delivered a slashing attack on Courthope's evaluations, in the *English Review* (Feb. 1911): 'He estimates poets by their influence rather than their merit, this is excusable: but to estimate their merit by their influence, to allow direct literary criticism to be coloured by the contemporary importance or posthumous popularity of the poet, is not excusable' (Hodgson, *Flecker*, 160).

[76] Vogeler, *Harrison*, 383.   [77] Grant Duff, *Diary, 1896–1901*, i. 286 (21 Dec. 1897).

the Poet Laureate Austin, who issued *Alfred the Great, England's Darling*, in 1896. This was fulsomely dedicated:

To
Her Royal Highness
Alexandra, Princess of Wales
Daughter of Vanished Vikings
And
Mother of English Kings To Be
I Respectfully Tender
This Inadequate Record
Of
The Greatest of Englishmen[78]

Hoots from *Punch* notwithstanding,[79] *Alfred the Great* found a public. Four editions were produced in January and February 1896 and a fifth in 1901, when the millenary celebrations were centred on Winchester, the ancient Saxon capital, where Alfred was buried. Naturally, Lord Rosebery was on hand to make a speech and to unveil the statue sculpted by Hamo Thornycroft. The actor Sir Henry Irving gave a reading but it was Harrison's lecture that struck the high note. Alfred he defined as 'the embodiment of our civilisation', the founder of the nation, its Navy, diplomacy, law, education, and literature.[80] The year 1909 was, however, regarded by Harrison as the 'annus mirabilis' because of the convergence of the quatercentenary of the birth of Calvin, bicentenary of the birth of Dr Johnson, centenary of the births of Gladstone and Tennyson, and centenary of the death of Thomas Paine. It was also both the centenary of the birth of Charles Darwin and the fiftieth jubilee of *The Origin of Species*. Harrison took part in so many commemorations, he likened himself to Scott's Old Mortality.[81]

Commemorations were frequently disturbed, though, by troublesome doubts and intrusions. Disciplined in the regulation of his own life, Anthony Trollope was ever the man to espy humbug and to resent calls on his time and purse. To his wife he wrote from Rome, on 4 March 1875: 'I do not care twopence about that Kingsley memorial. The folk are very pressing & may wait.'[82] This was a proposed memorial to Charles Kingsley, who died on 23 January, consisting of an expansion to Eversley church, where he was rector, and a bust by Thomas Woolner in Westminster Abbey. Trollope nonetheless contributed, as he also subscribed to other memorials, for Longfellow and, enthusiastically, for Thackeray. Different people held different visions of a writer, and a statue or other rigid

---

[78] Alfred Austin, *Alfred the Great, England's Darling* (1896; 5th edn., 1901). In the preface Austin complained that critics wrongly assumed that he had written this 'narrative poem in dialogue form' for performance on stage.

[79] *Punch*, 8 Feb. 1896, 65; and ibid., 15 Feb. 1896, 81, for a spoof diary in which Austin rewrites *Rule, Britannia!*

[80] The millenary of Alfred's birth was celebrated at Wantage, Berkshire, in 1849. See Quinault, 'Cult of the Centenary', 306–7, 319.　　　　　　　　　　　　　　　[81] Vogeler, *Harrison*, 296–8.

[82] To Rose Trollope, 4 Mar. 1875, in Booth (ed.), *Trollope's Letters*, 336.

effigy often seemed the least satisfactory way of representing multiple meanings. J. M. Barrie expressed this at the unveiling of Eric Kennington's statue to Thomas Hardy at Dorchester in 1931:

I know some things about Hardy that I feel sure cannot be in Mr Kennington's work, and . . . I should like to steal here in a white coat, with a hammer and chisel and chip those little bits in. Perhaps I shall find the statue surrounded by critics, all in white coats, all chipping; each one of us zealous to get in some favourite bit of his own . . .

Hardy proved an exceptionally difficult assignment. That darkness of spirit, which Barrie preferred to style his 'undaunted mind', was not designed to draw revellers. 'There were years certainly when I thought him the most unhappy man I had ever known,' Barrie confessed, before adding: 'but if he had escaped his weird we could not have had our Hardy. And, after all, can one be altogether unhappy, even when ridden by the Furies, if he is producing masterpieces?'[83] Statues did have the virtue of reasonable permanence, a lingering statement of an author's significance, however interpreters disagreed about the message; yet that very solidity all too quickly became a target for those who cared neither one way or another. Only a month after the unveiling Barrie was 'disturbed by hearing that people have been writing their names on the T.H. statue. Perhaps they can be stopped from doing this without putting up a railing but otherwise it should certainly go up . . . What a strange passion this is, writing names on works of art— it seems to be common to the whole world.'[84]

Devotees of authors were also upset at the commercialization of the distinguished dead or their hijacking by the Establishment. Preparations for the centenary of Keats's birth were inaugurated by a memorial service in Hampstead parish church, complete with officiating parson and surpliced choir. The poet W. S. Blunt described the 'curious ceremony':

Gosse, who presided, made a dull, platitudinous oration in the tone of a sermon . . . and the others were even duller. Houghton alone was brief and to the point. The poet's bust was then unveiled, and throughout the only allusion to religion was when one of the speakers enumerated what Keats was not, and included in the list that he was *not* a religious propagandist. When all was over the worthy vicar consoled himself with some prayers and an anthem.[85]

The Houghton who had Blunt's meagre approval was the second Lord Houghton, created Earl of Crewe in this year after serving as Lord Lieutenant of Ireland. He had been married to the daughter of a duke (Somerset) and would shortly remarry to the daughter of a prime minister (Rosebery). He was also president of the Literary Fund, but on this occasion he was in effect representing

---

[83] Address enclosed with letter to Mrs Hardy, 4 Sept. 1931, in Meynell (ed.), *Barrie Letters*, 161–2.
[84] Barrie to Mrs Hardy, 16 Oct. 1931, ibid. 163.
[85] Blunt, *Diaries*, i. 145 (16 July 1894). For a more favourable account of Gosse's oration, Thwaite, *Gosse*, 352.

his father, whose *Life, Letters and Literary Remains of John Keats* (1848) had done much to establish Keats's standing for mid- and late Victorians. The unveiling was preceded by luncheon at the home of Walter Besant, the novelist and founder of the Society of Authors. He also was elevated this year, to a knighthood; and other Hampstead literati, among them George Du Maurier, mingled with the motley celebrities, scholars, and hangers-on: Theodore Watts-Dunton, Sidney Colvin, and the author of *Little Lord Fauntleroy*, Mrs Hodgson Burnett. Israel Zangwill was there too and, when the Gosse children decked the Keats bust with laurels, remarked: 'The irony of it! Just as they did to him then they would do to another today, who had his genius.'[86] This was a reference to the abuse rained on Keats's poetry from contemporary critics such as Lockhart who had scorned the 'Cockney School of Poetry'; but Zangwill did not specify whom he thought was the Keats of his own time. One poignant record of this occasion remains: Walter Sickert's painting of Aubrey Beardsley attending the unveiling. Beardsley would die in 1898 at exactly Keats's age, a mere 25.[87]

There were some gratifying aspects about the Hampstead memorial. Contributions to the endowment of Keats House in Wentworth Place came from round the world, conspicuously from American admirers. Local worthies such as the three-times Mayor of Hampstead, F. Geere Howard, were also involved, moved no doubt by civic loyalty and personal generosity while harbouring ambitions to represent the constituency in Parliament.[88] The disgraced former Cabinet minister Sir Charles Dilke, who was now resuming his own parliamentary career, played a part too. Dilke's grandfather, an Admiralty civil servant who became manager of the *Daily News* and founder of the *Athenaeum* magazine, had been a friend of Keats at Hampstead; and Sir Charles inherited from him various relics, including the only portrait of Keats which Joseph Severn painted from life. These he donated to the Keats House; previously Dilke was instrumental in obtaining a Civil List pension for Keats's sister Mme Llanos, in 1880. But Dilke had been angered to discover in 1878 that his ownership of Keats's love letters to Fanny Brawne, which he and his grandfather bought with a view to preventing publication, was void, and that Fanny's son had the right to sell them to H. Buxton Forman, who edited them for publication.[89] So incensed was Oscar Wilde by the auction of these letters for over £500 that he composed a sonnet protesting at 'so vulgar a sacrilege'.[90] The unethical also branched out into the

---

[86] Thwaite, *Burnett*, 165.   [87] Sickert's painting of Beardsley is in the Tate Gallery.

[88] F. G. Howard was an electrical engineer; he stood as Liberal candidate for Hampstead in January 1910 but failed to win election. His son was co-founder of the publishers Jonathan Cape in 1920. See Michael S. Howard, *Jonathan Cape, Publisher* (1977), 7–8.

[89] Stephen Gwynn and Gertrude M. Tuckwell, *The Life of the Rt. Hon. Sir Charles Dilke, Bart. M.P.* (1917), i. 5, ii. 235, 238, 542–4.

[90] Keats was Wilde's favourite poet. Wilde also composed a sonnet at Keats's graveside, which 'is to me the holiest place in Rome'; and he was delighted when lecturing in the United States to meet Keats's niece, at Louisville in 1882. She gave him the manuscript of 'Sonnet on Blue', which he had framed and which, ironically, was disposed of at the auction of Wilde's own belongings following his disgrace and bankruptcy in the Keats centenary year, 1895; Hart-Davis (ed.), *Wilde Letters*, 16–17, 38, 59, 183 and *More*

criminal. The profitable traffic in literary manuscripts and rare editions was assiduously stimulated by forgers; but the activities of the chief of these, Buxton Forman himself and T. J. Wise, were not exposed until 1934.[91]

V

Centenaries and other anniversaries were occasions for critical reassessment and public education. Browning's devotees showed impatience in this regard, but they invented a plausible justification to restore their idol to the limelight seven years after his death by holding a service in St Marylebone Church to commemorate the jubilee of his romantic runaway marriage to Elizabeth Barrett. The marriage had taken place on 12 September 1846, whereas the 1896 commemoration was held on 12 December, the day Browning died in 1889. Invitations to the service took the form of a facsimile of the entry in the marriage register, portraits of the couple, extracts from their poetry, and a description from Mrs Orr's *Life of Robert Browning* of how Browning had commemorated his marriage whenever he was in London by kissing the pavement in front of the church. The full choral service was led by the Dean of Canterbury, who sermonized about the sacred institution of marriage:

he scarcely knew of another instance so striking—if, indeed, there was any other in human history—of two, who had enriched their century with songs that could not die owing their best of long-continued earthly happiness to their union in holy matrimony. In an age which had so many poets and writers, not indeed ungifted, but of the baser sort who had polluted the world with the realism of moral mud, which had sneered at marriage and endeavoured to paint the gate of hell with Paradise, who had eulogized the bonds of vagrant passions and the weight of chance desires as though freedom consisted in the slavery of our lower nature, it was a precious boon and antidote that these two poets of the supremer class thought it little shame, as did the ancient poet of the Canticles, to glorify a pure and holy love . . .[92]

In 1903 Sidney Colvin married the widowed Mrs Sitwell in St Marylebone because of its association with the Brownings.[93]

The first meeting of the London Browning Society had met on 28 October 1881, drawing 300 people dedicated to 'the manliest, the strongest, the life-fullest, the deepest, the thoughtfullest living poet, the one most needing earnest study, and the one most worthy of it'. So its founder, F. J. Furnivall, had proclaimed, before receiving the poet's own wry observation that it was '300 years too early for a Browning Society'.[94] Browning's name was also attached to a social settlement at

---

Letters, 89–90. It was reported during the bicentenary of Keats's birth that Keats House at Hampstead continues to attract 25,000 visitors each year; *The Times*, 1 Nov. 1995.

[91] *DNB 1931–1940*, 95–17, for Wise; also below, p. 256.   [92] *The Times*, 14 Dec. 1896.

[93] Henry James was a guest: Edel, *James*, ii. 507–8.

[94] DeVane and Knickerbocker (eds.), *Browning's Letters*, 280.

Walworth, one of London's poorest districts, centred on the conventicle where Browning had been baptized. It was opened by the former Liberal Home Secretary and future Prime Minister, Asquith, on 21 November 1895. *Punch's* versifiers considered this a far worthier enterprise than umpteen Browning societies' exegetical explorations:

> Well! It does me truer honour, I protest
>   Than the quest
> Of my minor mystic meanings, cryptic, crude,
>   By the brood
> Of 'disciples' who at meetings Browning-Clubbish
>   Talk such rubbish![95]

And, as if on cue, the Browning Settlement would soon establish its place in the country's history. It was there that the National Committee for Obtaining Old Age Pensions was formed in 1898. Its decade of persistent lobbying brought a boon to millions. The connection with Browning was not only titular, because the committee's organizing secretary, a bookbinder, Frederick Rogers, regarded Browning as one of the three (with Shakespeare and Milton) greatest poets in the language and as a source of perpetual inspiration. Rogers had been responsible for the publication of the first cheap edition of Browning, price 1s., in 1890, so as to diffuse his message among ordinary people.[96]

The centenary of Browning's birth, 1912, brought a ten-volume set of the works, edited by F. G. Kenyon, director of the British Museum. This then appeared good form rather than a response to market demand, so Sir Walter Raleigh implied when he told Edmund Gosse that, from his vantage point as Professor of English Literature at Oxford, 'the young I think are, for the present, not reading Browning much'.[97] Still, the anniversary itself, 7 May, was deployed by the newly formed Academic Committee of the Royal Society of Literature— designed by Gosse as an Anglican equivalent of the Académie française[98]—to show off its intellectual pre-eminence and dignity by staging at Caxton Hall a double address on Browning. Gosse presided, and the principal speakers were the playwright Sir Arthur Pinero, who took as his subject Browning the dramatist, and Henry James, who attended to 'The Novel in *The Ring and the Book*'. It was a major moment for James, now almost 70 years old. During his decades' residence in England, this was the Master's first public lecture and, according to most accounts, the audience was drawn as much to hear James being James as to hear James on Browning. Unfortunately, prolonged pregnancy had done nothing for James's audibility; moreover, the audience was near exhaustion after an over-long and over-passionate panegyric from Pinero. Nevertheless, respect was paid to the

---

[95] *Punch*, 21 Dec. 1895, 298.

[96] Rogers, *Labour, Life and Literature*, ch. xii. Warden of the Browning Settlement was the Congregational minister F. Herbert Stead, brother of the campaigning journalist W. T. Stead.

[97] Raleigh to Gosse, 25 Jan. 1912, in Raleigh (ed.), *Raleigh Letters*, ii. 376. Raleigh added, 'Donne and Crabbe are going strong.' [98] On this, see Ch. 5.

eminent living as to the eminent dead, and when James resumed his seat it appeared 'as if the applause would never cease'.[99]

The Caxton Hall performance was not the only salute to Browning on that day. The main event was a service in Westminster Abbey, followed by a series of addresses in Westminster College Hall, afterwards published as a Festschrift. The model for this was the use of the Abbey and Jerusalem Room by the Wordsworth Society which convened to commemorate its hero in 1883 and 1886, presided over by Matthew Arnold and Lord Selborne respectively. In 1912 the Marquess of Crewe, leader of the House of Lords and author of some lines on Browning in *Stray Verses* (1889), presided; but the organizer was Professor William Knight, who declared that 'more than one thousand letters have reached me from our own and other lands as to this centenary celebration'. As proof, the Festschrift contained a twenty-two-page appendix listing those who had responded to his invitation to join the 'committee of sympathizers'. They included

Men of Letters and of Science, Artists, Actors, Lawyers, Judges, Diplomatists, Statesmen, Ecclesiastics of all denominations, our two Archbishops, more than twenty Anglican Bishops, Nonconformists throughout England and Scotland, with members and officials of the Roman Catholic Church, heads of Houses in Oxford, Cambridge and elsewhere; University professors in England and Scotland, peers and peasants, working men and working women, numerous admirers in America, also Italian and Colonial representatives.[100]

Homilies were judged all the more necessary in the case of classic authors about whose reputation a suspicion of impropriety lingered. Andrew Lang in 1905 recalled his childhood when

Vanity Fair was under a taboo. It is not easy to say why; but Mr Thackeray himself informed a small boy, whom he found reading *Vanity Fair* under the table, that he had better read something else. What harm can the story do to a child? He reads about Waterloo, about fat Jos, about little George and the pony, about little Rawdon and the rat-hunt, and is happy and unharmed.[101]

This was being too innocent. One of Pearl Craigie's teachers had complained to her mother that she 'knew "the whole of" Thackeray, and read him in school-hours, and she did not think Thackeray was an author any girl of thirteen ought to be allowed to read'.[102] Henry Fielding suffered still more: his omission from Lubbock's Best Hundred Books George Meredith suspected was 'in deference to the family circle'.[103] G. K. Chesterton relished denouncing such humbug when

---

[99] Edel, *James*, ii. 739–42; James to Edith Wharton, 12 May 1912, in Powers (ed.), *Letters*, 221. James's lecture on Browning was published in his *Notes on Novelists*, 385–411. The famous comparison-'Shelley, let us say in the connection, is a light and Swinburne, let us say, a sound; Browning alone of them all is a temperature'-is at p. 401.   [100] Knight, *Browning Centenary*, p. xiii.

[101] Lang, *Adventures*, 13.

[102] Richards, *John Oliver Hobbes*, 11. Pearl Craigie (1867–1906), Richards's daughter, wrote under the pseudonym John Oliver Hobbes.

[103] Meredith to the *Pall Mall Gazette*, [June 1904], in Cline (ed.), *Meredith's Letters*, iii. 1503.

the bicentenary of Fielding's birth in 1907 generated a profusion of articles debating whether he was an offensive writer and *Tom Jones* (1749) an immoral book.[104] Thackeray had presented his appreciation of Fielding in *The Times* in 1840, but that had not done the trick.[105] In 1918 Lady Strachey, Lytton's mother, entertained Virginia Woolf by telling her that, when she was 18 in the late 1850s, her father sanctioned her reading *Tom Jones* 'on condition she never said sh'd read it'.[106] In the late nineteenth century it was George Saintsbury who did most to boom Fielding's genius, in introductions to his novels in 1893, when he nominated him, together with Shakespeare, Milton, and Swift, as one of the 'four Atlantes of English verse and prose'.[107] Also finally abandoning shilly-shallying was Andrew Lang, who, while still thinking Scott the premier novelist, declared *Tom Jones* to be the greatest novel in the language.[108] Nonetheless, amid the surge of Fielding reprints in 1907, publishers blithely exploited the risqué (see Fig. 6.1).[109] There was also a comic opera, *Tom Jones*, with music by Edward German and libretto by Alex M. Thompson and Robert Courtneidge. The last named was responsible for the production, which opened in Manchester in March 1907, moved to the West End in April, then was taken to New York.[110]

A different impetus lay behind the movement to raise a statue to Milton in 1903–4. No anniversary was involved here—the poet was born in 1608 and died in 1674—but St Giles, Cripplegate, in whose nave Milton was buried, needed restoration. Opportunity also beckoned to secure an open space in front of the church after several old houses were demolished. Deputy J. J. Baddeley proposed to donate a statue of the poet to stand there, but soaring property prices in the City caused the site to be valued at £3,500. Of that sum, £2,000 was subscribed by St Giles parishioners, and £500 by the Goldsmiths' Company, which left £1,000 still wanted. *T.P.'s Weekly* took the lead in appealing for subscriptions, stressing how desirable it was that these should be 'small and numerous rather than few and large' so that the memorial would genuinely represent the democracy's appreciation. Champions of Milton among the great and good were plentiful. For Frederic Harrison, Milton was a 'lifeboat in the storms of modern literature'.[111] 'Milton!', Tennyson once boomed, 'a name to resound for ages'; and George Eliot called him 'her demi-god'.[112] Moreover, as Commonwealthman and Puritan,

---

[104] 'Tom Jones and Morality', in Chesterton, *All Things*, 259–66.

[105] *The Times*, 2 Sept. 1840, for Thackeray's essay 'Fielding's Works'. See Harden (ed.), *Thackeray's Letters*, 166–7. [106] Bell, *Woolf*, 107 (18 Jan. 1918).

[107] 'Fielding, Introduction' (1893), in Saintsbury, *Prefaces*, 22. [108] Green, *Lang*, 161.

[109] Advertisement in *T.P.'s Weekly*, 8 Feb. 1907, 176. A twelve-volume Library Edition of Fielding's novels had been published by Constable in 1898. Thomas Hardy declined to write an introduction; Edmund Gosse did so, after first submitting his essay to Hardy's scrutiny. For Hardy's mixed opinion of Fielding, see Hardy to Gosse, 20 Nov. 1895, 1 July and 8 Sept. 1898, and Hardy to Archibald Constable & Co., 24 June 1989, in Purdy and Millgate (eds.), *Hardy Letters*, ii. 99, 195–6.

[110] It created a stir in America, in part because the co-author Thompson was unmasked as being also editor of the socialist *Clarion*. Interviewed on the deck of the *Lusitania*, 'Thompson said that he had come over here to work for *Tom Jones*, and would refuse to deliver lectures or write articles on socialism or politics while in America' (Thompson, *Here I Lie*, 297). [111] Vogeler, *Harrison*, 333.

[112] Stephen, *Eliot*, 198. William Morris, by contrast, 'always abused [Milton], though he sometimes betrayed more knowledge of him than he would have been willing to admit' (Mackail, *Morris*, i. 226).

FIG. 6.1. Bicentenary spice: selling the 'Unexpurgated' Henry Fielding.
Source: *T.P.'s Weekly*, 8 February 1907, 176

iconoclast and advocate of press freedom, Milton was a particular hero to Radical Nonconformity and working-class autodidacts. Jerome K. Jerome's younger brother was christened Milton: their father was a Congregationalist preacher.[113] The Quaker politician John Bright's speeches were woven with quotations from Milton.[114] The Erastian Whig politician and one-time Liberal Party leader Sir

It was Milton's puritanism and what he regarded as his false classicism that Morris disliked; *Review of Reviews* (Mar. 1891), 248.

[113] Jerome, *Life and Times*, 11. Milton Jerome died aged 6.

[114] Grant Duff, *Diary, 1896–1901*, i. 304 (17 Feb. 1898); R. Barry O'Brien, *John Bright* (n.d. [1910]), 436–7; Masterman (ed.), *Mary Gladstone*, 86, for her diary account (15 Sept. 1873) of sitting next to Bright at dinner—'Immense enthusiasm for *Paradise Regained*'.

William Harcourt was also a devotee. He never forgave Wilfrid Blunt for sneering at *Paradise Lost* and styling Milton 'a bombastic windbag': 'This was touching a sacred subject to him.'[115] The next generation of poets would divide about this. Still venerating *Paradise Lost*, Siegfried Sassoon was shocked when Robert Graves, at their meeting during the Great War, preferred Samuel Butler.[116] But for many a schoolboy Milton had become simply a handy tag, an all-purpose Great English Poet. The poetry prize for pupils at St Paul's was called the Milton Prize; but G. K. Chesterton, who won it in the early 1890s, did so with a confection that was as incongruously alien to Milton as is possible to conceive, his subject being the Jesuit St Francis Xavier preaching to the Chinese.[117]

The subscription list for a Milton statue in 1903–4 was published in *T.P.'s Weekly*. Heading it were 10 guineas from T. P. O'Connor himself and 5 guineas from Alfred Austin; Conan Doyle, Arnold Bennett and Eden Phillpotts, and Sir Charles Dilke and Justin McCarthy contributed 1 guinea each, George Grossmith £1, Silas K. Hocking half a guinea, and Clement Shorter and Austin Dobson 5s. There was nothing from Andrew Lang, who included *Paradise Lost* among 'Books I have stuck in'.[118] One of the more distinctive contributions was a shilling, anonymously, from 'an actress, yet a student and lover of Milton', and 2s. 6d. from 'one who in childhood saw the funeral of a man whose father was living in the time of Milton'; yet much the greatest number came in tiny sums from ordinary people distinguished only by their esteem for the poet. To stimulate participation, *T.P.'s Weekly* announced that every reader who collected 1 guinea, and who forwarded that sum with the names and addresses of the subscribers, would be sent a souvenir copy of Milton's *Shorter Poems*, published in Methuen's Little Library Series and inscribed with T. P. O'Connor's signature.[119] The subscription ran for twenty-three weeks and closed with almost £300 raised in June 1904, when it was stated that Horace Mountford's bronze had gone to the foundry for casting. The *T.P.'s Weekly* subscription thus fell short—in any case, the original estimate of £1,000 was now closer to £2,000—and the rest was raised from City guilds and corporate donors.[120] Still, enough had been done to merit the claim that this was a popular memorial, although never sufficient to appease Milton idolaters such as the Bishop of Durham, Handley Moule, who complained that Milton now was more 'read about than read'.[121]

This reprimand was issued at the tercentenary of Milton's birth in 1908. By contrast with the movement in 1903, the tercentenary commemoration was led

---

[115] Blunt, *Diaries*, ii. 107 (1 Oct. 1904). The description 'bombastic windbag' was probably too close to the bone, fittingly applied to Harcourt himself.

[116] Jean Moorcroft Wilson, *Siegfried Sassoon: The Making of a War Poet, 1886–1918* (2002), 216.

[117] Chesterton, *Autobiography*, 66.   [118] Green, *Lang*, 162.

[119] *T.P.' s Weekly*, 4 Dec. 1903, 868.

[120] Ibid., 20 Nov. 1903, 801, to 24 June 1904, 834. The sculptor, Mountford, previously cast the statue of Darwin at Shrewsbury.

[121] Article in *The Churchman*, Dec. 1908, in John Battersby Harford and Frederick Charles Macdonald, *Handley Carr Glyn Moule, Bishop of Durham* (n.d. [1922]), 306.

from the summit of the scholarly establishment, the British Academy, which prevailed on George Meredith to compose a tribute. This he did, in forty-six lines of blank verse, which broadcast his own as well as Milton's 'voice for Freedom'.[122] It was the last poem the octogenarian monarch of letters wrote. Thomas Hardy, aged 68 and in the habit of refusing invitations to formal occasions, also stirred. In July he spent two days in Cambridge, where the celebrations were centred on Milton's former college, Christ's; and in December he attended the Milton banquet at the Mansion House, London—'not that I care for banquets, but I felt that I owed such attention to John Milton'.[123] Yet it was in Hereford, not Cambridge or London, that the most imaginative exploitation of Milton's name occurred. There, the Bishop, John Percival, a Liberal appointee, used the Milton tercentenary to advance a long-held ideal, reunion between the Church of England and Nonconformity, by summoning a gathering of

Christians of different denominations for common worship and conference in honour of his [Milton's] great name and in the cause of godly union and concord.

To Milton, as to Bunyan, our religious and literary life, to whatever denomination we belong, owes more than any of us can estimate, and our common indebtedness to such supremely gifted souls should help to lift us above those traditional sectarian barriers which too commonly divide us, stopping the flow of Christian brotherhood and fellowship.[124]

VI

Jealousies rather than harmony had been evident in 1892, when the centenary of Shelley's birth produced a glut of publications and debate about the poet's renown. By 'an undesigned coincidence' (so he maintained), F. S. Ellis, former New Bond Street bookseller and friend of Morris, Rossetti, Ruskin, and Swinburne, concluded a labour of six years, *Lexical Concordance to the Poetical Works of Percy Bysshe Shelley*, in the centenary year. In the preface he contended rather sourly that he had never met 'a single person outside the circle of professed students . . . who could lay claim to have read more than two or three of his most celebrated lyrics'.[125] *The Spectator* took issue with this, defending ordinary readers

---

[122] Sassoon, *Meredith*, 258–9.

[123] Hardy to Florence Henniker, 23 Dec. 1908; also to Emma Hardy, 13 July 1908, in Purdy and Millgate (eds.), *Hardy Letters*, iii. 325, 361.   [124] Temple, *Percival*, 312.

[125] F. S. Ellis, *Lexical Concordance to the Poetical Works of Percy Bysshe Shelley* (1892), pp. vii–viii. Ellis further advised readers to cast aside all biographies because all that was worth knowing about Shelley was his soul, to be discovered by studying the poetry. On Ellis, *DNB Supplement 1901–1911*, i. 625–6. The most important of the recent biographies was Edward Dowden's two-volume *Life*, published in 1886. Shelley's complete works—four volumes of the prose (1880) and four volumes of the poetry (1876) (new editions, 1882 and 1892)—were edited by Harry Buxton Forman (1842–1917), a senior civil servant in the Post Office. Forman's editions still 'constitute a landmark', according to the modern authority; see Neville Rogers (ed.), *The Complete Poetical Works of Percy Bysshe Shelley* (Oxford, 1972), vol. i, p. xxv. Forman also purchased and edited Keats's letters: but there was a darker side to the scholarship, the business of forgery in which Forman collaborated with the bookseller–bibliographer T. J. Wise (1859–1937). The notice of Forman in *DNB 1912–1921*, 192–3, has added piquancy by virtue of Wise being co-author.

from the hauteur of the expert: 'We do not know what a "professed student" is; must he belong to a "Shelley Society", or is he permitted to enjoy the poet in his own study?'[126] This tart reference to the Shelley Society spotlighted another of the rumbustious Dr Furnivall's creations. Trouble came calling early on. In 1885 Robert Browning, beneficiary of Furnivall's associational fecundity when he had founded the Browning Society, refused his invitation to be first president of the Shelley, because he could not countenance Shelley's principles and behaviour: 'I painfully contrast my notions of Shelley the *man* and Shelley, well, even the *poet*, with what they were sixty years ago, when I only had his works, for a certainty, and took his character on trust.'[127] In 1886, when the Shelley Society was at last in being, exception was then taken to an application for membership from Edward Aveling because, while married, he was cohabiting with Eleanor Marx. The committee's chairman, W. M. Rossetti, threatened to resign in sympathy, remarking reasonably enough that Aveling's conduct resembled Shelley's own; and he was supported against the majority by the vegetarian and animal rights' pioneer Henry Salt, who caustically suggested that they rename their body the 'Respectable Society'. The Shelley Society further overreached itself by backing productions of *The Cenci*—banned by the Lord Chamberlain—and *Hellas*; and it dissolved in 1892. It had provided some impetus to scholarly studies of Shelley, and allied branches or reading groups emerged in Oxford and Cambridge, Birmingham, Hackney, and Reading; but altogether its six years' span of activity appeared rather lost on the public.[128]

Shelley's heroic status nevertheless remained high, especially among heterodox fellow poets such as Hardy, who confessed 'that of all men dead whom I should like to meet in the Elysian fields I would choose Shelley, not only for his unearthly, weird, wild appearance & genius, but for his genuineness, earnestness, & enthusiasms on behalf of the oppressed'.[129] Henry Nevinson recalled about the late 1870s, when he was in his twenties and learnt most of *Hellas* by heart: 'in those days we all tried to grow as much like Shelley as possible, though without great success', he added wryly.[130] The Shelley centenary exposed the sanitizing side of the memorial movement. University College, Oxford, which had expelled Shelley in 1811 for circulating *The Necessity of Atheism*, now found a dark corner to display a white marble shrine by Onslow Ford and a dome by Basil Champneys.[131] Ford's monument was originally designed to be placed over Shelley's grave in Rome, but family disagreements blocked that.[132] Oxford thereby benefited, and the University's Bodleian Library was endowed with

---

[126] *The Spectator*, 4 June 1892. [127] Betty Miller, *Robert Browning* (1952), 270.

[128] Benzie, *Furnivall*, 243–52.

[129] Hardy to Florence Henniker, 24 Jan. 1897, in Purdy and Millgate (eds.), *Hardy Letters*, ii. 144.

[130] Sharp (ed.), *Nevinson*, 131.

[131] Edmund Gosse, who was among the gathering of eminent writers and intellectuals at the opening, had lunch beforehand with Walter Pater at Brasenose and was astonished to discover that Pater had not been invited; Logan Pearsall Smith, *Unforgotten Years* (1938), 173–4.

[132] Rogers, *Labour, Life and Literature*, 166.

Shelley manuscripts by the poet's descendants, to which was added in 1898 the guitar that Shelley had given Jane Williams, the subject of 'To a Lady with a Guitar'.[133] At the birthplace, Horsham, the unveiling of a Shelley monument—a fountain—featured an address by Edmund Gosse, who, according to Bernard Shaw, ignored the rebel's antipathy to monarchy, matrimony, and meat.[134]

Perhaps the public too failed to grasp the significance of such ceremonies, if the experience of the Christopher Marlowe Memorial Committee is any guide. Its inspiration did, however, stem from the working-class autodidact tradition, because the original proposal emanated from the Elizabethan Society at the Toynbee Hall settlement in East London. Its vice-president was the bookbinder Frederick Rogers, who later would be a driving force of the movement to obtain old age pensions. Rogers became secretary of a Marlowe Committee, after a fellow enthusiast at Toynbee Hall wrote to the *Standard* on 26 July 1888, deploring the neglect of Marlowe, who 'laid the foundation of English blank verse, which, in its more developed form through the medium of Shakespeare and Milton, has become the life-blood of English literature, and the supreme instrument of tragic poetry'.[135] This stirred a star cast to form the committee, with the Lord Chief Justice, Lord Coleridge, as chairman, and Sidney Lee, the *DNB* editor who was president of the Elizabethan Society, as treasurer; and they boasted among their nominal membership Tennyson, Browning, Swinburne, Alfred Austin, Andrew Lang, Edmund Gosse, Leslie Stephen, H. C. Beeching, A. H. Bullen, Richard Garnett, James Russell Lowell, and several American scholars. Whether they were assisted also by the inclusion of John Addington Symonds's name is an open question, because Marlowe was a supposed sodomite; but this was not the only problem facing the Committee. From the start it met 'obloquy', as Rogers put it, when vociferous secularist societies seized on the Marlowe movement as a vindication of their cause, Marlowe also having had the reputation of an atheist. This was especially distasteful to Rogers himself, a strong Anglo-Catholic Churchman. Progressively, the Committee shook off the association, and their fundraising benefited from public readings by the theatre world's leading couple, Henry Irving and Ellen Terry, and from the support of the popular actor–manager Wilson Barrett. The year 1893 was the tercentenary of Marlowe's death, but the Committee had its scheme in order two years early; prudently too they opted to commemorate Canterbury, his birthplace, rather

[133] *The Times*, 22 June 1898. The guitar was gifted to the Bodleian by the American Shelley collector E. W. Silsbee, who had bought it from Williams's descendants.

[134] For Shelley centenary articles and the memorial at Horsham, *Review of Reviews* (Aug.–Sept. 1892), 150, 167, 261. Horsham residents still decry it: see the letter to *The Times*, 4 Dec. 1996, from John Watson, who noted 'the Shelley memorial fountain is not only unpopular locally for its ugliness and the fact that it does not work, but also because of its inappropriate significance (Shelley died from drowning)'. Shaw celebrated his version of Shelley in several prefaces to his plays, notably *Getting Married* (1908) and *Back to Methuselah* (1921). He also liked to recount how 'at a public meeting of the Shelley Society I scandalized many of the members by saying that I had joined because, like Shelley, I was a Socialist, an atheist, and a vegetarian . . .'. See Preface to *Immaturity* (1930) in G. B. Shaw, *Prefaces* (1934), 632.

[135] Quoted in Rogers, *Labour, Life and Literature*, 160–1.

than the Deptford tavern where Marlowe met his violent end. Irving was lined up to perform the unveiling, because the monument included Irving himself, sculpted by Onslow Ford as Tamburlaine the Great, one of four characters from Marlowe's plays. Behind the scenes all was not well, for Edmund Gosse played a suitably shifty impresario of the bizarre ceremony, which took place in the old Butter Market, Canterbury, on 16 December 1891. Gosse had evaded Irving's request to compose some special verses, countering that it were better for Irving to declaim Swinburne on Marlowe, for which he secured Swinburne's curt permission. Irving preferred caution, choosing instead some lines from Marlowe himself; even more tactful was his failure to disclose that Marlowe was no longer staged. Irving had been altogether sceptical of the thing: 'I don't believe they care a rap about Marlowe at Canterbury.' Rogers, who also gave an address, admitted the same. The Mayor and other officials dutifully attended; but the people of Canterbury 'were not interested, and the crowd came largely from outside'. Still, Irving was elated by drawing a crowd from whatever source; and his pleasure was then heightened by discovering that one person turned up from misapprehension that the monument hailed the public hangman Marwood, author only of the 'long drop'.[136]

VII

The question of how to recognize Marlowe's contemporary, Shakespeare, was another matter. He was in no danger of suffering neglect, though the perpetual interest involved periods of intense enthusiasm. The late 1760s had seen one such surge, associated with Dr Johnson's edition in 1765 and the actor–manager David Garrick's rain-lashed Jubilee Celebration at Stratford in September 1769.[137] The next of any magnitude was a three-day gala on 23–5 April 1827, organized at Stratford by a Shakespeare Club, which proposed thenceforward to hold a Triennial Commemorative Festival. *The Times* described the extravaganza: roads into the town from London, Birmingham, and Warwick thronging with stagecoaches and requisitioned vehicles of every sort; processions, bands, bell-ringing, and cannonades; concerts, shows, and pageants of Shakespearean characters; grand dinners and a mayoral laying of the cornerstone for an intended new theatre. This initiative was chiefly local, and most actors were amateur—'Much surprise is manifested at the absence of London performers,' *The Times* reported[138]—but the combination of civic and national pride, and commercial and theatrical boosterism, betrayed in this episode, was a foretaste of things to come.

The late Victorians' infatuation with Shakespeare was more sustained. Swinburne had a theory that great writers could be divided into two categories:

---

[136] Laurence Irving, *Henry Irving: The Actor and his World* (1989), 539, 541; Thwaite, *Gosse*, 352; Rogers, *Labour, Life and Literature*, 164. On William Marwood (1820–83), see *DNB*; he was a Lincolnshire, not a Kentish, man. [137] Geoffrey Whitworth, *The Making of a National Theatre* (1951), 23–4. [138] *The Times*, 24 Apr. 1827.

gods and giants.[139] This might not find favour with schools of literary criticism today, but it generally accorded with Victorian sentiment that Shakespeare occupied the divine department. Swinburne and his adversary Dr Furnivall could agree about this. Furnivall himself had been keen to mark Shakespeare's 300th birthday in 1864 with celebrations in New York and with the construction of a suitable monument in England. It was the monument part that infuriated Ruskin when Furnivall solicited his support: 'Do you think Shakespeare or anybody else will sleep the sounder because you build more bad Gothic somewhere, in everybody's way?—monument!—isn't this island and the race monuments enough—I won't have anything to do with it.'[140] Spats were thus the order of the day for the National Shakespeare Committee, which was inaugurated in 1863 to coordinate the variety of commemorations. Its secretary was the editor of the *Athenaeum*, William Hepworth Dixon; and, having pitchforked Bulwer Lytton, Dickens, and Tennyson onto the wagon as vice-presidents, he contrived to exclude Thackeray, with whom he had recently quarrelled.[141] The testiness continued long after, as the business of funding and building a Memorial Theatre in Stratford dragged on. Robert Browning sent a two-sentence snorter to Dixon on 27 July 1871, the first of which told him that he would be away, and the second of which ran: 'If you simply want to put my name along with the rest, I need not say you can do so,—for I find that any protest of mine against such a proceeding is supposed to mean nothing at all,—and really the matter is of little importance to anybody—including myself.'[142]

The actual festivities that took place in London in 1864 disgusted *The Times*, which thought they vulgarized Shakespeare's memory and resembled Barnum's circus. The Crystal Palace sported a replica of Shakespeare's Stratford home and redisplayed a Shakespeare monument produced two years before for the International Exhibition. Not just the impression of a circus but a circus in fact processed through Stratford itself. Businessmen, led by the mayor, local brewer Edward Flower, were the moving force behind the eleven-day festival there, which included a sermon by Richard Chevenix Trench, the former Dean of Westminster, recently appointed Archbishop of Dublin. Trench was not unqualified in matters literary. A poet himself, he secured his place in history by proposing in 1857 that the Philological Society embark on compiling a new dictionary, which later emerged as the prodigious *Oxford English Dictionary*; but his sermon on Shakespeare recast him for mid-Victorian tastes, emphasizing his combination of 'the loftiest genius and the most perfect sobermindedness'.[143] The coming of the railway to Stratford in 1860 now boosted the number of visitors; but the Stratford and London committees were competitors rather than partners.[144]

---

[139] Gosse, 'Swinburne', in Gosse, *Portraits and Sketches*, 41.   [140] Benzie, *Furnivall*, 193.
[141] D. J. Taylor, *Thackeray* (2000), 439–42.
[142] DeVane and Knickerbocker (eds.), *New Letters of Browning*, 202.
[143] J. Bromley, *The Man of Ten Talents: A Portrait of Richard Chevenix Trench, 1807–86, Philologist, Poet, Theologian, Archbishop* (1959), 160–1.   [144] Quinault, 'Cult of the Centenary', 310–11.

Still, Shakespeare's plays, or selections from them, were then performed throughout the country.[145]

Both scholarly and unscholarly disputed how best to interpret Shakespeare. Haines remarks in Joyce's *Ulysses* (1922), 'Shakespeare is the happy hunting ground of all minds that have lost their balance.'[146] Baconian theory excited both sapient and plain fools. In 1903 the critics W. W. Greg and W. H. Mallock conducted a furious controversy about 'facts and fancies' in the Bacon–Shakespeare controversy; only the latest instalment. Philip Gibbs lost his position with the *Daily Express* at this time when the owner, Arthur Pearson, wanted him to write articles making it appear convincing that Bacon wrote the plays. Gibbs thought it nonsense and walked out of his job.[147] One who expended extraordinary energy, endeavouring to prove by logarithms that Bacon wrote Shakespeare, was the novelist Edith Nesbit.[148] In this, she was pursuing a line initiated by the egregious Elizabeth Wells Gallup, who in 1899 'proved' by cipher cryptography that Bacon was both the author of the plays and the legitimate offspring of Elizabeth I. Andrew Lang put her and other Baconians to flight in his posthumously published *Shakespeare, Bacon and the Great Unknown* (1912).[149] Professor Sir Walter Raleigh also had no time for Baconians.[150] Chesterton, characteristically contrary, preferred to advocate that Shakespeare wrote Bacon,[151] while Dr Furnivall thought the whole thing so absurd, 'You might just as well say that Gladstone wrote the works of Charles Dickens.' J. M. Barrie was altogether more encouraging. In his rectorial address at St Andrews University in 1922, he advised students to keep up the old topics, such as Bacon having written Shakespeare, adding—'or if he did not he missed the opportunity of his life'.[152] Bacon, by then, had got his own statue, unveiled by the former Prime Minister Arthur Balfour at Gray's Inn—of which Bacon had been treasurer 300 years earlier—on 27 June 1912.

Problems of authorship apart, almost all agreed about the supremacy of Shakespeare's genius. Almost all, because the obvious superior to Shakespeare, according to Bernard Shaw, was Bernard Shaw: 'With the single exception of Homer, there is no eminent writer, not even Sir Walter Scott, whom I can despise so utterly as I despise Shakespeare when I measure my mind against his.' This was the nonsensical drumming of a self-advertising showman but, as A. G. Gardiner acknowledged in the 1920s, having published estimations of Shaw either side of the Great War, there came a time when people no longer laughed when he was mentioned in the same breath as Shakespeare.[153] Moreover, 'If he throws stones

---

[145] Bancroft, *Recollections*, 23.   [146] James Joyce, *Ulysses* (Harmondsworth, 1968), 248.
[147] Gibbs, *Pageant*, 48.   [148] Moore, *Nesbit*, 226–9.
[149] Green, *Lang*, 161. Mrs Gallup, an American, published *Bilateral Cypher of Francis Bacon* in 1899. *Punch* had a field day with her; e.g. 8 Jan. 1902, 19, 21, and 12 Mar. 1902, 196.
[150] Letter to J. W. Wilkinshaw, 20 June 1912, in Raleigh (ed.), *Raleigh Letters*, ii. 380–1.
[151] Chesterton, *Autobiography*, 85.   [152] J. M. Barrie, *Courage* (1922), 41.
[153] Gardiner, *Certain People of Importance*, 210–15. For a cartoon of Man (Shakespeare) and Superman (Shaw), *Punch*, 3 Oct. 1906.

at Shakespeare, it is not because he is so foolish as not to appreciate the greatness of Shakespeare, but because he believes Bardolatry is as deadening as any other idol worship, and because the creative power that kindles us to life must express itself in new forms and new terms.' Shaw knew his Shakespeare as well as the most besotted Bardolater; as a young man, he could recite whole plays, and 'Hamlet and Falstaff were more alive to me than any living politician or even any relative.'[154] Shaw composed *The Dark Lady of the Sonnets* (1910)'for a performance in aid of the funds for the project of establishing a National Theatre as a memorial to Shakespeare';[155] but he refused invitations to Stratford to commemorate Shakespeare anniversaries—'Why should I celebrate Shakespeare's birthday? I do not even celebrate my own.'[156]

'If Shakespeare had not written dramas,' averred Walter Rowley, Fellow of the Society of Antiquaries in 1897, 'he would have been known as the greatest poet of his era.'[157] The Laureate, Tennyson, had acknowledged this in 1868, when, ever conscious about his own place in history, he chose to lay the foundation stone for his new home, Aldworth in Surrey, on Shakespeare's traditional birthday, St George's Day, 23 April.[158] His mood was catching: when Fanny Kemble read Shakespeare after lunching at Aldworth in 1871, she did so 'magnificently, with tears streaming down her cheeks'.[159] As for Tennyson himself, he 'seldom seemed to remember his *own* lines and would always read from the book...but he would repeat from memory pages of Shakespeare without hesitating'.[160] Others displayed similar accomplishments. Benjamin Jowett's erudition was, as befitting the head of Balliol, masterful, though he modestly disclaimed the title occasionally conferred on him, that of being 'a living concordance to Shakespeare'.[161] Even that 'arch-vulgarian' the Prince of Wales recognized Shakespeare's worth, while failing to recognize Sidney Lee, editor of the *Dictionary of National Biography*, in whose honour the publisher George Smith arranged a dinner in 1897: 'And what is your special subject, Mr Lee?' On being told it was Shakespeare, the Prince advised: 'Stick to it, Mr Lee; stick to it. There's money in it.'[162] Beyond this, the Prince's focus wavered. Like many he might at one time have at least been exposed to Charles and Mary Lamb's *Tales from Shakespeare* (1807); but at a Marlborough House dinner in 1900 to celebrate the

[154] Holroyd, *Shaw*, i. 41. See also Laurence (ed.), *Shaw, Collected Letters 1898–1910*, 143, 551–2.
[155] Shaw, *Prefaces*, 722–38.
[156] Christopher St John (ed.), *Ellen Terry and Bernard Shaw: A Correspondence* (1949), 390.
[157] Walter Rowley, 'Shakespearean Ballads and Songs', in J. E. Muddock (ed.), *The Savage Club Papers* (1897), 175.
[158] Tennyson, *Tennyson*, 461. Shakespeare was baptized on 26 April 1564 and died on 23 April 1616, but it is 23 April which is traditionally celebrated as his birthday.   [159] Tennyson, *Tennyson*, 507.
[160] Arthur Lee's journal, 1891, in Alan Clark (ed.), *'A Good Innings': The Private Papers of Viscount Lee of Fareham* (1974), 47.   [161] Geoffrey Faber, *Jowett: A Portrait with Background* (1957), 370.
[162] Quoted in Scott, *Pall Mall Gazette*, 246. Lee subsequently wrote the notice of Edward VII in the *DNB*, which created a stir by scaling down his ability and achievements; see Viscount Esher to Viscount Morley, 16 Aug. 1912, in Brett (ed.), *Esher*. iii. 105–6. Nevertheless, George V invited Lee to undertake the official biography, which he published in two volumes in 1925. It was Henry James who styled Edward 'an arch-vulgarian' (Edel, *James*, ii. 426).

completion of the original *DNB*, when Canon Ainger was introduced to him as a very great authority on Lamb, the Prince's thoughts turned naturally to the lower-case variety, on whose merits, grilled or roast, no glutton was better qualified to pronounce. Still, the Prince's essentialist view of Shakespeare was that also taken by publishers, who tumbled over each other to produce new editions—ordinary or with scholarly annotations and in luxurious facsimile folios. The Cambridge Shakespeare and the Globe edition were timed for the 1864 tercentenary. In 1892 Henry Frowde at Oxford University Press published the complete works, with a preface by W. J. Craig and glossary explaining the obsolete words, in one volume of 1,264 pages for 3s. 6d. He further astonished the world with a companion edition made of the revolutionary Oxford India paper. This weighed under 19 ounces and was only seven-eighths of an inch thick; however, it cost 10s. 6d. and, for all the miracle of technology which produced it, it was not considered a tactful gift for myopes.[163] In 1905 Methuen's catalogue advertised a miniature revolving bookcase at 10s., to go with its Little Quarto Shakespeares.[164]

There was plainly a market here for display. It had been satirized by George and Weedon Grossmith, whose City clerk, Mr Pooter, having been struck by the splendours of red enamel, paints in this colour not only the flowerpots, coal-scuttle, bathtub, washstand, towel-horse, chest of drawers, and servant's bedroom, but also 'the backs of our *Shakespeare*, the binding of which had almost worn out'.[165] Pooter had his counterpart in life. The personal library of the Manchester newspaper magnate Edward Hulton, whose real love was horse racing, was said to contain 'twelve sumptuously bound volumes lettered "Grand National Shakespeare"'.[166] And the Prince of Wales's instinct proved right for J. M. Barrie:

When for a start in life I answered an advertisement for a leader-writer in a provincial newspaper, I was asked to send specimens of my leaders, and I, who had never written (nor read) a leader, sent instead a treatise on King Lear. I was appointed; so it was Shakespeare who got me on to the Press.[167]

At his height as a dramatist, Barrie repaid some of this debt by *Dear Brutus* (1917), his reworking of *A Midsummer Night's Dream* according to the lesson of *Julius Caesar*:

> The fault, dear Brutus, is not in our stars,
> But in ourselves, that we are underlings.

At the humblest level too Shakespeare operated as currency. Norman Hancock, born in 1894, recalled that at his father's drapery shop in Somerset goods were priced in sums ending with three farthings instead of a complete penny or shilling,

---

[163] The Bible was produced in the same way in 1892: 1,566 pages in a volume measuring 3¾ in. by 2⅛ in. by ⅞ in. See *Review of Reviews* (Jan. 1892), 97–8.   [164] Duffy, *Methuen*, 31.

[165] George and Weedon Grossmith, *The Diary of a Nobody* (Harmondsworth, 1968), 42.

[166] Agate, *Shorter Ego*, 113. On Sir Edward Hulton (1869–1925), see *DNB 1922–1930*, 441–2.

[167] Barrie, *Greenwood Hat*, 124. The paper was the *Nottingham Journal*.

to create an illusion of cheapness; hence a farthing change was involved in most transactions, but such coins were regarded as a nuisance by customers and the habit prevailed of offering instead articles such as pencils, hatpins or collar studs: 'One of the favourite farthing changes was a folding card containing six assorted sewing needles. The outside covers of the card were printed in colour and contained a portrait of Shakespeare's house, Anne Hathaway's cottage, and Stratford-on-Avon church.'[168]

A sure mark of Shakespeare's pre-eminence was the reluctance shown by the most esteemed Victorian authors to attempt an assessment. Macmillan's launched its English Men of Letters series in 1878, under the general editorship of John Morley, and for over a quarter-century failed to commission a study of Shakespeare, after both Matthew Arnold and George Eliot refused.[169] It was not until 1903 that an author was found. This was the Professor of English Literature at Oxford, Walter Raleigh. He was conscious that it would be 'impossible to please all his [Shakespeare's] lovers'. He aimed therefore to please himself, gratified that 'I should be given the opportunity of designing a monument for the poet I love best, in the national cathedral church. The *English Men of Letters* is not as other series are.'[170] He asked for three years to do the job, during which the sense of honour wore off. Raleigh struggled, even offering Macmillan '£100 to be shut of my engagement' in 1905. When it was published in 1907, he was relieved as well as elated by the prospect of royalties from large sales.[171]

There was less bashfulness about Frank Harris, whose whisper, Edmund Gosse once remarked to Arthur Symons, 'shakes the table'.[172] Among the most moving tributes to the Bard was that paid by Harris when his booming bass was heard over luncheon at the Café Royal in 1896: ' "Unnatural vice! I know nothing of the joys of unnatural vice. You must ask my friend Oscar about them. But", he went on, with a reverential change of tone, "had Shakespeare asked me, I should have had to submit".'[173] As the hero of an immodest autobiography who had 'no enemy except corsets', Harris is now dismissed as a swaggering libertine or worthless fantasist; but he was an influential editor in his day, and the author of short stories praised by Meredith and other discerning critics.[174] His knowledge of

---

[168] Norman Hancock, *An Innocent Grows Up* (1947), 78.

[169] Morley tried to tempt Frederic Harrison by suggesting that 'you may smuggle the whole religion of Humanity in upon the British public'. See Morley to Harrison, 1 Sept. 1879, in F. W. Hirst, *Early Life and Letters of John Morley* (1927), ii. 82.

[170] Walter Raleigh to George Macmillan, 30 Aug. 1903, in Raleigh (ed.), *Raleigh Letters*, ii. 550.

[171] Raleigh to John Sampson, 7 Nov. 1905, and to W. MacNeile Dixon, 3 Mar. 1907, in Raleigh (ed.), *Raleigh Letters*, ii. 288, 312. See also Darlow, *Nicoll*, 358–9, for Robertson Nicoll's appraisal of Raleigh's *Shakespeare*.   [172] Quoted in Beckson, *Symons*, 231.

[173] Cecil, *Max*, 164. Max Beerbohm was at the luncheon and subsequently cartooned the imagined terrible coupling of Harris and the Bard. The same story is told, with minor differences of detail, in Hugh Kingsmill, *Frank Harris* (1949), 70–1. Kingsmill heard it from Hesketh Pearson, who was told it by Robert Ross.

[174] See the *Fortnightly Review* article 'The Genius of Mr Frank Harris', welcoming his short story 'Elder Conklin'; *Review of Reviews* (June 1892), 592. Meredith, however, refused to allow Harris's publisher to use his puff; Meredith to Grant Richards, 11 Dec. 1900, in Cline (ed.), *Meredith's Letters*, iii. 1379.

Shakespeare was also extensive. In 1898 he sold his interest in the *Saturday Review* and retired to the Riviera, intending, amid business and amorous speculation and the application of his trusty stomach pump, to pursue his Shakespearean studies. The result was *The Man Shakespeare* (1909), which Arnold Bennett judged 'masterful and masterly', a book which would last as long as Shakespeare.[175] Bennett was blustering; yet his own habits testified to the symbolic importance of Shakespeare. He long kept Shakespeare's works by his bedside. But he never read them: 'So in the end I put the Shakespeare volume back on a shelf. It struck me as pretentiously out of place . . . .'.[176]

Bennett's plaudit of Harris's Shakespeare was almost reserved compared to Middleton Murry's, in the avant-garde monthly *Rhythm*, of which he was editor:

To re-create this soul was one of the highest tasks that a great artist could undertake. To achieve where Coleridge and Goethe failed needed a man on a spiritual equality with William Shakespeare, perhaps without the supreme poetic gift, yet for intellect and power of divination his spiritual equal . . . Who is the man who has done this thing? This man is Frank Harris, acknowledged by all the great men of letters of his time to be greater than they; accepted by artists as their superior, unknown to the vast British public, greater than his contemporaries because he is a master of life.[177]

Harris's study involved a contemporary agenda. One purpose was to construct 'a totally new conception' by reading Shakespeare's psychology, thus rescuing him from the 'blindness and stupidity' of academic Bardolaters. Another was to deploy Shakespeare as a missile against Puritanism, the prudery that was 'enfeebling English thought and impoverishing English speech'. Shakespeare may have been a man for all seasons but he was also redefined from season to season. Harris even sought to get his life of Shakespeare filmed.[178]

The Shakespeare academic industry was disparaged by Harris, but there was no doubt it was thriving. George Moore liked to upset these people too. Though he claimed to 'have got more out of [Walter Savage] Landor than out of Shakespeare', Moore understood that Shakespeare was a writer of some significance. The play

---

[175] Flower (ed.), *Bennett Journals*, i. 329–30 (5, 8 Oct. 1909); Bennett to J. B. Pinker, 8 Nov. 1908, in James Hepburn (ed.), *Letters of Arnold Bennett*, i. *Letters to J. B. Pinker* (Oxford, 1966), 106; and Bennett to Harris, 30 Nov. 1908, 30 Oct. 1909, ibid. ii: *1889–1915* (Oxford, 1968), 238–41, 258–9. Bennett had been scathing about Raleigh's *Shakespeare* in his column for the *New Age*, 26 Sept. 1908, thinking that the Professor should have burnt it, along with his book *Style* (1897): 'For they are as hollow as a drum and as unoriginal as a bride-cake: nothing but vacuity with an icing of phrases' (Bennett, *Books and Persons*, 45). Raleigh himself, when wrestling with his own study, had advised Macmillan's to reject Harris's *Shakespeare*: 'Most of what he says has been said before, more delicately. What has not been said before, and is all his own, seems to me wrong' (Raleigh to Frederick Macmillan, 27 Oct. 1906, in Nowell-Smith (ed.), *Letters to Macmillan*, 253–5). See also Beerbohm, *Christmas Garland*, 77–82, for a parody of Harris's. *The Man Shakespeare*.

[176] Bennett, *Journal 1929*, 158–9.

[177] Murry concluded his article by declaring 'Even if *Rhythm* achieves nothing else that is ultimately permanent, it shall be rescued from oblivion by this alone, that it told the truth about Frank Harris' (J. Middleton Murry, 'Who is the Man?', *Rhythm* (July 1912), in Kingsmill, *Harris*, 9, 12). On *Rhythm*, see Sullivan, *Literary Magazines 1837–1913*, 360–5; and F. A. Lea, *The Life of John Middleton Murry* (1959), ch. iii.

[178] Harris, *Life and Loves*, 2, 398, 584, 847, 936–41, 1046–9.

he wrote spoofing Shakespeare was really 'an emetic' against scholarly pedantry and triviality:

> Every week there are columns and columns on whether there was a comma here or whether a sentence was run on there, whether he mentioned this town or that man. The *Times Literary Supplement* never fails, with letters and still more letters. Someone is always discovering something—there are forty-five volumes on the hats he wore (I don't know the exact number), and another twenty on the boots, and fifteen on the flowers he mentions—on and on, without any point or charm of any sort.[179]

VIII

Shakespeare's birthplace, Stratford upon Avon, was assured as a place of literary pilgrimage. It was 'the northern Bethlehem' according to Heine; and Henry James called it 'the Mecca of the English-speaking race' in his short story 'The Birthplace' (1903), a parable about the tourist-infested town and manufacture of legends. From the early 1870s James classified himself as a 'passionate pilgrim' to this 'richest corner of England';[180] yet, revisiting Stratford with John Bailey in 1908, he felt that he was no nearer solving 'the inscrutable mystery of Shakespeare: the works on the one side and, on the other, that dull face, and all the stories we know of the man; "commonplace; commonplace; almost degrading" '.[181] This puzzlement was shared by the townsfolk, if the story told by Henry Irving and J. L. Toole contained any truth. Cross—examining a Stratfordian who was dimly aware that Shakespeare was known 'for summat', they received the intelligence that 'he wrote for the Bible'.[182] In 1879 the Memorial Theatre was formally opened and a summer festival inaugurated, principally endowed by local brewer Charles Flower.[183] His appeal had tested the patience of many, including Anthony Trollope:

> I don't care two pence for the Shakespeare Memorial or Mr. Flower. If there be any one who does not want more memorials than have been already given, it is Shakespeare! Mr. Flower is a worthy old gent,—who wants to go down to posterity hanging on to some distant rag of the hindermost garment of the bard of Avon; but I don't want or care to assist his views. £1000 and a site!! Surely he can hang on to a rag without costing me five guineas! And there seems to be a lot of money. All Stratford-on-Avon seems to be run over with £100's.[184]

[179] Goodwin, *Moore*, 102–3, 241.

[180] Edel, *James*, ii. 472–9. James contributed a preface to *The Tempest* in 1907, in an edition presided over by Sidney Lee.

[181] Bailey (ed.), *Bailey Letters and Diaries*, 112 (13 June 1908). Bailey was the author of *Shakespeare* (1929) in Longman's English Heritage series.					[182] Grant Duff, *Diary, 1886–1888*, i. 91 (23 Apr. 1887).

[183] Charles was the son of Edward Flower, who had organized the 1864 commemoration. £21,000 was raised by Charles Flower; and the opening performance at the Memorial Theatre on 23 April 1879 was *Much Ado about Nothing*, starring Barry Sullivan and Helen Faucit; see Whitworth, *National Theatre*, 37. The London brewers Barclay Perkins also placed a memorial tablet to Shakespeare on the site of the Globe Theatre, Park Street, Southwark, on 9 October 1909, unveiled by Sir Herbert Beerbohm Tree.

[184] To Kate Field, 11 Apr. 1878, in Booth (ed.), *Trollope's Letters*, 392–3.

Trollope felt there were many more deserving causes. The Memorial Theatre nevertheless emerged. Close by the theatre was a more lordly contribution, although even that epithet appears too mean to describe the colossal statue of Shakespeare, complete with four life-size figures at its base. It was sculpted by the Rt. Hon. Lord Ronald Sutherland-Gower, and it is difficult to imagine a tribute from a higher personage. A son of the second Duke and twentieth Earl of Sutherland, Lord Ronald told *Who's Who* that he was also 'uncle and great uncle of the Dukes of Argyll, Sutherland, Leinster, and Westminster, etc.'.[185] The casualness of that 'et cetera' was sublime. After Eton and Cambridge, Lord Ronald had become an MP. That was not a struggle. He represented Sutherland, a county which his family largely owned, and Lord Ronald faced no contest, just like all the family's nominees at every election between 1832 and 1880. Lord Ronald, tiring of political duty, in 1874 yielded the seat to a kinsman and turned to art and literature. He produced a crop of statues, including *Marie Antoinette on her Way to Execution*, and publications, about Michaelangelo, Gainsborough, Romney, and Wilkie. A trustee of the National Portrait Gallery, Lord Ronald was also a trustee of the Birthplace and Memorial Theatre at Stratford. There were few bigger bigwigs to fire a ten-gun salute to Shakespeare.

In spite of the Sutherland–Gower imprimatur, the Memorial Theatre excited repugnance. 'Monstrous', Wilfrid Blunt called it in 1894, 'perhaps the most degraded in architecture of our graceless age'; but his object in visiting Stratford was to complete 'my pilgrimage by reading the Sonnets at the poet's tomb'.[186] Arthur Benson, making the same journey in 1904, had no poems to read, only inspiration to seek. Standing before Shakespeare's tomb, Benson 'prayed with all my might over his head, to do worthily; he is the Father and Head of all our English writing, poetry and prose; and a writer may well pray there for a double portion of that Spirit'.[187] The first Shakespeare Festival attracted 1,500 people; in 1894, over 4,000; and in 1904, some 14,000, as the season was extended to three weeks.[188] Arnold Bennett's ardour cooled accordingly. In 1896 he found Stratford 'a simple, straight-forward, unaffected town—sane and serene like Shakespeare's last plays and last years'. He even thought the Memorial Theatre looked distinguished—'by moonlight'. But, wrote Newman Flower, who edited his journals, 'in later years Bennett reversed his judgment and would not go near Stratford-on-Avon on account of its affectedness'.[189]

---

[185] *Who Was Who, 1916–1928*, 426, for Sutherland-Gower (1845–1916). A homosexual and friend of Wilde, Lord Ronald was a supposed model for Lord Henry Wotton in *The Picture of Dorian Gray* (1891).

[186] Blunt, *Diaries*, 148 (13 Aug. 1894). The Memorial Theatre was destroyed by fire in 1926 and replaced by a new building, opened in 1932. This, designed by Gilbert Scott, was no better liked; *The Times*, 25 Apr. 1932, and Phyllis Hartnoll (ed.), *The Oxford Companion to the Theatre*, 4th edn. (1990), 761.

[187] Newsome, *Edge of Paradise*, 140.

[188] J. A. R. Pimlott, *The Englishman's Holiday: A Social History* (1976), 258. A folk-song and folk-dancing festival and summer school were added after 1909, owing to the promotion of Mary Neale and Cecil Sharp, whose different views about the authenticity of performances divided the Memorial Theatre's governors. See Maud Karpeles, *Cecil Sharp: His Life and Work* (1967), ch. viii.

[189] Flower (ed.), *Bennett Journals*, i. 12–13 (3 Aug. 1896).

Recollecting that Carlyle once called all English-speakers the subjects of King Shakespeare, *The Spectator* sourly observed in 1894 that 'we are hardly literary enough for Shakespeare to-day'.[190] That was true if the repertoire of the Penny Gaffs is considered, when *Hamlet* alternated with *Sweeney Todd* and *The Murder in the Red Barn* and was chopped to forty-five minutes comprising largely sword fights.[191] It was also true if the standard of many a late Victorian or Edwardian 'Shakespeare Reading' is subject to too formal a test. Even their participants were often unimpressed, as organizers of such readings found their group solidarity strained by the wounded pride of those allocated minor rather than plum parts.[192] Seventeen-year-old Ruth Bourne recorded disparaging remarks in her diary about the feeble renderings of *Julius Caesar* and *Macbeth* made by members of her circle in Worcestershire in 1883. There, Shakespeare Readings principally served as social gatherings for local gentry and notables.[193] Few could rival the resources available to Sir Theodore and Lady Martin at Onslow Square. The official biographer of the Prince Consort, Martin was well known also as a writer about the theatre and, from 1889, a trustee of Shakespeare's birthplace. His wife was the actress Helen Faucit and, as the *Dictionary of National Biography* unctuously noted, 'in their London home between 1882 and 1887 they and their friends, including Henry Irving and Canon Ainger, took part in readings of Shakespeare, whose excellence attracted attention'.[194] Previously, in 1874, the ever enthusiastic Dr Furnivall broadcast through the *Daily News* a characteristically batty scheme to counter the dullness of dinner parties by organizing husband and wife teams to declaim Shakespeare's plays—in correct chronological sequence.[195]

Many a working man needed no such trappings, or required instruction in Shakespeare. The Bradford Labour MP Fred Jowett knew several who could recite long passages from Shakespeare;[196] and the same was said about Barney Barnato, who rose from East End pauper to millionaire landlord. Though 'utterly uneducated', Barnato could 'recite from memory whole acts of Shakespeare without a single false pronunciation or emphasis'.[197] There is also cause to notice Tom Mann and the engineers at Thornycroft's in Chiswick, who in 1883 formed a Shakespeare Mutual Improvement Society for discussions about all sorts of topics, literary, scientific, historical, philosophical, astronomical, and physiological.[198] Being Warwickshire-born, Mann always felt pride in Shakespeare, but it was not until he encountered a Scotsman named Jeffries who worked on the lathe next to him at Cubitt's workshop in Gray's Inn Road that this became a passion. Jeffries was Shakespeare-obsessed: 'His one and only recreation was to read Shakespeare, and books that dealt with Shakespeare, plus seeing every

---

[190] *The Spectator*, 1 Sept. 1894.   [191] Jerome, *Life and Times*, 73.   [192] Asquith, *Diaries*, 521–2.
[193] Baily (ed.), *Ruth Bourne Diaries*, 31–2. Ruth Bourne, when married as Mrs Edward Baily, the wife of a prep-school proprietor, continued to participate in Shakespeare Readings; see her diary for 6 Nov. 1891, ibid. 134.   [194] *DNB Supplement 1901–1911*, ii. 578.
[195] Benzie, *Furnivall*, 67.
[196] F. W. Jowett's foreword to Fenner Brockway, *Socialism over 60 Years* (1946), 20.
[197] Flower (ed.), *Bennett Journals*, i. 353–4 (18 Jan. 1910).   [198] Tom Mann, *Memoirs* (1923), 30.

Shakespeare play performed.' Mann was now captivated: 'from that time I was never lonely so long as a volume of Shakespeare was available'. Throughout his career as socialist agitator and revolutionary syndicalist, Mann kept his Shakespeare by him. He insisted that his friends too celebrate Shakespeare's anniversary, and at home he 'instituted "joyous evenings", when everyone had to sing, recite or at least read something of Shakespeare. In hospital after his eighty-first birthday he recited to his fellow patients. Indescribable fire and music would fill his tiny sitting-room in those last years as he strode about it, roaring out his favourite passages . . . .'.[199] A Shakespeare Reading Society likewise flourished at the Working Men's College;[200] and, on being told about the enthusiasm shown for Shakespeare by working men who attended the Toynbee Hall settlement, and about their difficulties in getting hold of reliable texts, the publisher J. M. Dent issued the Temple Shakespeare, forty volumes each priced 1s. between 1894 and 1896. Over the next forty years Dent sold 5 million copies, boasting 'the largest sale made in Shakespeare since the plays were written'.[201]

Radical working men had been prominent in the Shakespeare tercentenary in 1864;[202] but their Shakespearean interest was not unquestioning. The assertiveness of labour involved not only a struggle for political rights and improved conditions of work and living; it also required that society recognize their moral worth and independence. Working men challenged misrepresentations of their character. Shakespeare's treatment of the poor and plebeian element in his plays was hotly debated. The actor–manager Beerbohm Tree was surprised by this when he delivered a Sunday afternoon lecture on 'The Humanity of Shakespeare' to a working-class audience in Poplar Town Hall, under the chairmanship of Will Crooks, who was London's first Labour mayor (of Poplar, 1901) and from 1903 Labour MP for Woolwich. Tree was interrogated—'Did he [Shakespeare], or did he not, ridicule the working classes?'—and much pavement discussion followed the lecture. The editor of *T.P.'s Weekly*, Wilfred Whitten, felt that this line of questioning had been excited more by the political agenda of recent critics than by genuine difficulty about understanding Shakespeare's plays and purpose. He identified 'a little green paper-covered book' published by the Free Age Press in which Bernard Shaw, Tolstoy, and others contended that all low-born characters in Shakespeare were figures of fun or else unimportant and that Shakespeare was unable to conceive of anyone humbler than an aristocrat rising to the dignity of tragedy. This was to misconceive Shakespeare's genius, which was not to try to anticipate the class sensibilities of a later age, to expose abuses, or to preach doctrines of reform, but to fathom human nature.[203]

Enormous exposure was given to Shakespeare with the establishment of Frank Benson's theatrical company at Stratford from 1886, and his and Ben Greet's

---

[199] Dona Torr, *Tom Mann and his Times*, i: *1856–1890* (1956), 67–8.   [200] Benzie, *Furnivall*, 67.
[201] Quoted in Jonathan Rose, 'J. M. Dent and Sons', in Rose and Anderson (eds.), *British Literary Publishing Houses*, 82.   [202] Quinault, 'Cult of the Centenary', 311.
[203] O'London, *Unposted Letters*, 14–18.

IX

Shakespeare's emblematic importance was expressed above all in this movement to establish a national theatre. Advocated episodically from 1848 by Tom Taylor, Matthew Arnold, Sir Theodore Martin, and more,[218] the idea flourished most in the decade after 1905 when Shakespeare memorial committees appealed for funds. The impetus stemmed from a former Stratford man, Richard Badger, who made a fortune from the North Country brewing trade. Now aged 83, he proposed through *The Times* in 1903 to donate £1,000 towards the cost of 'erecting in London and at Stratford-on-Avon, a statue worthy of Shakespeare's fame'.[219] A London Shakespeare League had been formed on 23 April 1902, with Dr Furnivall as its president, and holding three objectives:

1. To extend the recognition of the interest which London possesses as the scene of the lifework of William Shakespeare.
2. To organise an Annual Commemoration of the poet in London.
3. To focus the movement for a Shakespeare Memorial in London.[220]

But the League had not advanced far until Badger's intervention; it was Badger who first approached the London County Council for a suitable site, ideally on the South Bank of the Thames, and Badger who in a further letter to *The Times* offered £2,500 towards the project.[221] A new Shakespeare Memorial Committee now emerged, comprising eight members of the London Shakespeare League with Furnivall as chairman, together with the presidents or directors of the British Academy, Royal Academy, and other august institutions, the chairman of the LCC, and the Lord Mayor of London. But at a public meeting at the Mansion House on 28 February 1905 it was evident that various proposals, many incompatible, were under review, including a statue or other architectural monument, and a small memorial theatre, a national theatre, a Shakespeare House, or a Shakespeare fund. There were also different sites in mind: the new Kingsway and Aldwych, or near

---

[218] The originator of the first concerted attempt to found a National Theatre, 'wherein the works of Shakespeare, the "world's greatest moral teacher", may be constantly performed', was a London publisher, Effingham William Wilson. This was in 1848, and he was inspired by the success of a Shakespeare committee in purchasing Shakespeare's birthplace for the nation in 1847. His idea was taken up by the Shakespeare Committee, led by the scholar, civil servant, and playwright Tom Taylor, and supported by Theodore Martin. Numerous well-known authors and theatre people, including Bulwer Lytton, Dickens, Eliza Cook, Sheridan Knowles, and Charles Kemble, responded, though several were gloomy about its prospects, Dickens stating, 'I wish I could cherish a stronger faith than I have, in the probability of its establishment on a rational footing within fifty years' (Whitworth, *National Theatre*, 26–9). For Martin's case, see 'The Drama in England', *Quarterly Review* (Jan. 1872); for the late Victorian revival of the idea of a National Theatre, see George Barlow, 'Talent and Genius on the Stage', *Contemporary Review* (Sept. 1892), 385–94; and for the idea of a Shakespeare or National Theatre linked to a Royal Academy of Dramatic Art, see Nicoll, *Late Nineteenth Century Drama*, 62–7.
[219] Letter from Richard Badger, *The Times*, 28 May 1903, in Whitworth, *National Theatre*, 40–1.
[220] Quoted in Whitworth, *National Theatre*, 40.
[221] Richard Badger, *The Times*, 12 Aug. 1904, in Whitworth, *National Theatre*, 41–2. In his will Badger increased the provision to £3,500.

Buckingham Palace, as well as the South Bank. The City of London and the LCC were petitioned for a site; and some £100,000 of an estimated £500,000 requirement was collected before the Great War suspended this endeavour.[222]

Such summary statement conceals a complex of quarrels, which were comprehensively sent up in *Punch* by F. Anstey (Thomas Anstey Guthrie), assuming the part of peacemaker. His proposal incorporated everyone's pet plan. First, the site must be as prominent as possible and that meant Campden Hill. The current waterworks and tower would be demolished to make way for a colossal statue of the seated Bard, pensively plotting his finest play with chin supported by the left hand, the whole to be not less than 500 feet high, so as to dominate the entire metropolis, outdo the Great Wheel or the Eiffel Tower and be visible from the seas. This statue should itself be set on a pedestal building, some 150 feet high, in the Elizabethan or Jacobean style, with Renaissance façades, whose interior would house the national theatre. From it, visitors would rise by hydraulic lifts and spiral staircases inside the statue, which, cast in bronze, would be hollow. On the first floor, at waist level, the library was to be placed, 'furnished with a complete collection of all the volumes that have ever been written about him in any language', including, it was to be hoped, 'the original MS. of the late Mr. Curdle's celebrated essay "On the character of *Juliet*'s Nurse's Deceased Husband"'. Electricity would power the lighting here, afforced by windows inset into the buttons on the Bard's doublet. A corridor must run through the outstretched right arm to exit at the palm, which would hold a promenade, open-air restaurant, bandstand, and space for a summer theatre. The floor above, at chest height, must accommodate a School of Elocution for spouting blank verse; finally, inside the skull, a luscious winter garden under a majestic glazed dome, for whose better illumination, inside and out, the head must, unfortunately, be bald. Still, with a shilling charge for admission, pupils' fees, restaurant leases, and takings at bars and sideshows, the whole thing should not only pay for itself but also return a dividend.[223]

This imaginative and unifying scheme aside, it was important not to confuse two central issues, a Shakespeare memorial and a national theatre, though doubtless many at the time were perplexed by bickering committees, petitioners, and counter-petitioners. Thomas Hardy was bewildered when Edmund Gosse and Arthur Pinero invited him to join J. M. Barrie and others in a protest letter to *The Times* criticizing the Shakespeare Memorial Committee, to which Hardy had subscribed. 'Never mind,' Hardy told Pinero: 'W.S.'s reputation is doubtless safe enough, whatever we do.'[224] It did not dawn on Hardy at first that the

---

[222] Nicoll, *English Drama*, 74–7. Also Gibbs, *Pageant*, 49–50; Gibbs was employed by the Shakespeare Memorial Committee to recruit supporters and raise funds, and he tells of enlisting Lord Chief Justice Alverstone and Field Marshal Earl Roberts.

[223] 'My Ideas for a Shakespeare Memorial', *Punch*, 8 Apr. 1908, 260–1.

[224] Hardy to Gosse, 23 Feb. 1905, and to Pinero, 24 Feb. 1905, in Purdy and Millgate (eds.), *Hardy Letters*, iii. 155–7. Other contributors to the letter, which appeared in *The Times* on 27 Feb. 1905, were Professor A. C. Bradley, Lord Carlisle, Sir W. S. Gilbert, Maurice Hewlett, the Earl of Lytton, Gilbert Murray, Lord

Gosse–Pinero party favoured a national theatre as a Shakespeare memorial but, when he had sorted it out, he was clear where he stood. He told Israel Gollancz— who was Professor of English Literature at King's College London, secretary of the British Academy, and secretary also of the Shakespeare Memorial Committee—that naming 'an important *street* or *square* after Shakespeare would seem to be as effectual a means as any of keeping his name on the tongues of citizens, & his personality in their minds'.[225] Hardy did not want a theatre, writing first defensively to the literary editor of the *Daily News*, R. A. Scott-James 'I am so remote from the practical drama . . . Shakespeare in his literary aspect is really all I care about';[226] then more expansively to the editor of the *Daily Chronicle*, Robert Donald:

If I felt at all strongly, or indeed weakly, on the desirability of a memorial to Shakespeare in the shape of a Theatre, I would join the committee. But I do not think that Shakespeare appertains particularly to the theatrical world nowadays, if ever he did. His distinction as a minister of the theatre is infinitesimal beside his distinction as a poet, man of letters, & seer of life, & that his expression of himself was cast in the form of words for actors, & not in the form of books to be read, was an accident of his social circumstances that he himself despised. I would, besides, hazard the guess that he, & all poets of high rank whose works have taken a stage direction, will cease altogether to be acted some day, & be simply studied.

I therefore do not see the good of a memorial Theatre, or for that matter any other material monument to him, & prefer not to join the committee.[227]

The Times also approved of a Shakespeare memorial but was sceptical about a national theatre. This would not engender 'New Drama'. J. T. Grein's Independent Theatre, established in 1891 to do just that, had come and gone; why, therefore, should public endowment succeed where private enterprise failed? There was no point in pouring funds into a theatre which the public would not visit and which had no new worthy plays to produce. Its promoters were beginning at the wrong end: a healthy National Drama was required before a national theatre. The model for *The Times* drama critic A. B. Walkley was to be found in Ireland, building up a national theatre from roots laid in repertory; an

Onslow, Sir Frederick Pollock, A. B. Walkley, and Professor Aldis Wright. They particularly condemned one proposal (apparently favoured by Gollancz), that of erecting as a Shakespeare memorial an institution to serve the humanities as Burlington House served the natural sciences; the signatories averred that 'any museum which could be formed in London would be a rubbish heap of trivialities' (Whitworth, *National Theatre*, 44). Hardy's confusion was understandable. Pinero, for example, opposed William Archer's scheme for a National Theatre when this was mooted in 1904; but he became an advocate of a Shakespeare Memorial Theatre performing this very role, staging classic drama and encouraging new drama of quality, as 'an English Theatre where the whole of our drama can be studied in its best examples'; see his Mansion House speech in 1908 in Hamilton Fyfe, *Sir Arthur Pinero's Plays and Players* (1930), 287. For a spoof of a chaotic Shakespeare Memorial Committee meeting, see *Punch*, 8 Mar. 1905, 164, 167: it features parodies of Sidney Lee, Edmund Gosse, W. S. Gilbert, Bernard Shaw, F. J. Furnivall, Marie Corelli, and Hall Caine.

[225] Hardy to Israel Gollancz, 26 June 1905, in Purdy and Millgate (eds.), *Hardy Letters*, iii. 174.
[226] Hardy to R. A. Scott-James, 5 Apr. 1908, ibid. iii. 310.
[227] Hardy to Robert Donald, 10 May 1908, ibid. iii. 313.

idea adumbrated by the Ibsenite William Archer and the actor–dramatist Harley Granville Barker in 1904, and enlarged in 1907 in their *National Theatre: Scheme and Estimates*.[228] The unstated politics of the thing troubled many. Pinero had remarked to Archer in 1901: 'supposing the funds forthcoming, I have no objection whatever to your ideal theatre, except that I do not see who is to run it. The practical men who might do so are not available, and the faddists and cranks who are available by the score would empty the finest theatre that was ever built.' Pinero then resolutely defended the actor–manager system, instancing the Bancrofts at the Prince of Wales and Irving at the Lyceum: 'this thoroughly English system of private enterprise—of individual endeavour—which you [Archer] are denouncing. It develops character—it gives a personal quality to art—it fills our theatrical history with great figures. Abroad, the man is merged in the institution; here, the institution is the man.'[229] The suspicion was rife that the concept of a national theatre was just another agitation got up by socialists, scheming to extend the State's direction of national life. Continental models were discouraging: the French National Theatre was showing 'every sign of incompetence and disorganization'.[230] This was also argued by Lytton Strachey in *The Spectator* in 1907–8: officialdom would strangle artistic independence and originality.[231] Finally, most withering of all, scorn was expressed about the competence of the thespian class; as Will Rothenstein expostulated, 'a National Shakespeare Theatre! when scarcely an actor or actress can let half a dozen lines of blank verse run off the tongue'.[232]

The proponents of a national theatre redoubled their advocacy in the face of doubt; but the wrangles of theatre and literary people over this issue became a public embarrassment. Senior politicians and other grandees were wheeled out to establish union between the factions. One essayed peacemaker was Viscount Esher, habitual wire-puller in Edwardian high politics. His plan, communicated to the Earl of Plymouth in 1908, was that

we should all of us agree to endeavour to frame a plan for a Theatre to contain a monument of Shakespeare.

Subject to a 'National Theatre' being a practical scheme in its financial aspects, a decision should be come to upon the primary question whether such a theatre should be a subsidised theatre or not, and alternate schemes might be prepared.

This can only, in my opinion, be done by a small committee (not more than six) who would call witnesses and prepare a report *upon evidence* received. Short of this being done, there will be no possibility of approaching any Minister or the Public, with a hope of success.[233]

---

[228] Letter from W. B. Yeats and Lady Gregory to *The Times*, 16 June 1910; *The Times*, 24 Apr. 1913; Dennis Kennedy, *Granville Barker and the Dream of Theatre* (Cambridge, 1986).

[229] Archer, *Real Conversations*, 9, 11.   [230] *TLS*, 21 Feb. 1902, 45–6.

[231] Michael Holroyd, *Lytton Strachey and the Bloomsbury Group: His Work, their Influence* (1971), 112.

[232] Rothenstein, *Men and Memories, 1900–1922*, 68.

[233] Esher to Plymouth, 24 May 1908, in Brett (ed.), *Esher*, ii. 315. The first Earl of Plymouth (1857–1923) had served as First Commissioner of Works, 1902–5. See *Punch*, 18 Mar. 1908, 212–13, for another parody of a Shakespeare memorial meeting involving Esher.

Following more months of committee meetings and private conversations, Esher realized that the protagonists of a national theatre 'have faced none of the real difficulties'.[234] Their forte was making ringing declarations. Thus, supported on the platform by Arthur Pinero and Bernard Shaw, the actor–manager Sir John Hare cited Matthew Arnold:

We are not free from the clamour of those who frankly declare that the state has no concern with those non-marketable forces, like cultivated imagination, wholesome sentiment, high reverence, which tend to build up the character of our citizens by ennobling their thoughts and inspiring their motives. Where these men would have the State do less I would have it do more (Cheers).

Hare added, 'The state of our theatre was still chaotic and ineffective. Month by month, year by year, the work of the theatre was becoming more a trade and less an art, and commercial interests paralysed the aspirations and ambitions of the most artistic and conscientious of our managers.'[235] Any statement from one actor–manager about the condition of the theatre was calculated always to inflame another actor–manager, who inferred that his own work was being slighted. Beerbohm Tree was adamant that he had already given signal service to Shakespeare and to Art, and that his own theatre, His Majesty's, was better run than a committee-managed national theatre would ever be; and he told Esher that 'the National Theatre, in order to live, must adopt the method of the modern theatre, and not seek to cater for "epicures in mediocrity" '.[236] Esher was at the end of his tether by May 1909, recognizing the force of Bernard Shaw's remark 'If you continue to attend the Committee as it now is, and to preside over its babblings and chatterings, you will lose your reason.'[237] Esher stepped down in favour of the former Colonial Secretary Alfred Lyttelton, whose widow later recalled, 'Never were his gifts as an arbitrator more valuable than on the occasions when he took the chair and steered the discussions of one of the most excitable collections of people ever flung together by differing interests.'[238] What theatre people did best was disport themselves theatrically. The social high point of the Coronation year, 1911, was the Shakespeare Ball in the Albert Hall, nominally to raise funds for a national theatre but actually an opportunity to cut a costumed figure.[239]

It was left to the Liberal Unionist MP, former Oxford don, and director of the London School of Economics, Halford Mackinder, to try to combine the Shakespeare memorial and national theatre proposals when, on St George's Day and Shakespeare's traditional birthday, 23 April 1913, he introduced into Parliament a private member's bill for State support of a national theatre 'for the performance of the plays of Shakespeare and other dramas of recognized merit'.

[234] *Journal*, 23 Oct. 1908, in Brett (ed.), *Esher*, ii. 352. This was written following a lunch with J. M. Barrie, Granville Barker, and William Archer. [235] *The Times*, 20 May 1908.
[236] Tree to Esher, 1 Jan. 1909, in Brett (ed.), *Esher*, ii. 354–5.
[237] Shaw to Esher, 4 May 1909, ibid. ii. 386. [238] Edith Lyttelton, *Alfred Lyttelton* (1917), 381.
[239] For J. M. Barrie's part in designing the Duchess of Sutherland's costume, see Dunbar, *Barrie*, 196–7.

As an imperialist, Mackinder hoped this would unite the Empire by providing a place of pilgrimage for colonials visiting London, imbuing them with the common literary heritage.[240] But his motion failed to command sufficient votes and, with the advent of the Great War, all schemes were in abeyance.

There remained only the commission of performing Shakespeare with more force and fervour than ever before. Beerbohm Tree had bid to excite such a patriotic mood by staging *King John* on the day the Boer War was declared, 12 October 1899. The Radical anti-imperialist poet Wilfrid Blunt, who had been brought up in the Catholic faith, attended the theatre, accompanied by his cousin George Wyndham, who, by contrast, was a Conservative minister and strong imperialist. Blunt was disgusted by 'an egregious performance. I never cared about *King John*, and, as acted by Tree, it was a violent piece of ranting. George . . . told me that Tree had chosen the play as being full of Jingo tags and no Popery talk. But the audience was too dull to seize the points.'[241] This last verdict was disputed by Edmund Gosse's recollection: he was sharing a box with the Commander-in-Chief, Lord Wolseley, on 'that memorable evening [when] there were many verses in the play which seemed appropriate to the occasion'.[242] Tree's production of *King John* became the first Shakespeare to be recorded on film.[243] The dissemination of Shakespeare during the Great War was not so sectarian. Pocket Shakespeares were commonly included in a soldier's kit, judged an essential part of the 'active service trousseau', as Lady Cynthia Asquith styled it when planning such for her husband, Beb, who had enlisted in the Royal Field Artillery.[244] The wartime productions of the plays, most concentrated in the tercentenary of Shakespeare's death, 1916, were occasions for declarations of national unity and English genius.[245] Commemorations were held at Westminster Abbey, in churches throughout the land, even at the front and in prisoner-of-war camps; and Benson, who peregrinated the country declaiming *Henry V*, was knighted on stage by King George, following a production of *Julius Caesar*. It was now that the Old Vic gained its reputation as the 'home of Shakespeare'.[246] Under Lilian Baylis's management, every Shakespeare play was performed there between 1914 and 1923.

The last words on the subject should be personal, because the true measure is gauged by the meaning Shakespeare held for individuals throughout their lives or at crucial moments in their lives. 'We all know Shakespeare as it were privately,' wrote the poet Alice Meynell, 'and thus words about him touch our autobiography.' Born in 1847, she remembered as a child her mother taking her and

[240] W. H. Parker, *Mackinder: Geography as an Aid to Statecraft* (Oxford, 1982), 41–2.

[241] Blunt, *Diaries*, i. 332 (12 Oct. 1899). See also Pearson, *Tree*, 127–8.

[242] 'Some Recollections of Lord Wolseley' (1921), in Gosse, *Aspects and Impressions*, 283.

[243] One reel of this survives, according to Robert Shaughnessy (ed.), *Shakespeare on Film* (Basingstoke, 1998), 2, where the production is misdated as 1898.   [244] Asquith, *Diaries*, 7 (19 Apr. 1915).

[245] Colls and Dodd (eds.), *Englishness*, 20, 118–19.

[246] Richard Findlater, *Lilian Baylis: The Lady of the Old Vic* (1975); and *DNB 1931–1940*, 53–4.

her sister to the Stratford birthplace, whereupon her mother 'burst into tears with a fresh love and fresh grief' which she felt for Shakespeare. For Alice too, her own daughter wrote, 'Shakespeare haunted her writing and her life.' It culminated in a poem for the tercentenary in 1916, 'my one, *one* masterpiece' she called it.[247] The impact was no less strong on those charged with the conduct of great affairs, whose change of fortune spurred contemplation. In 1916 the Foreign Secretary, Sir Edward Grey, was deposed from the Cabinet:

When I went out of office after eleven years of it, very tired, and for the time not fit for anything, I spent some weeks alone in the country. During that time I read, or re-read, several of Shakespeare's plays. The impression produced upon me by his incredible power and range was really that of awe; I felt almost afraid to be alone in the room with him—as if I were in the presence of something supernatural.[248]

[247] Meynell, *Alice Meynell*, 203–5, 317.   [248] Grey, *Falloden Papers*, 17.

7

English Literature's Foreign Relations; or, ''E dunno où il est!'*

All three [Bobbie, Peter, and Phyllis] had been *taught* French at school. How deeply they now wished that they had *learned* it!

(Edith Nesbit, *The Railway Children* (1906))

I return in trivial mood to your catalogue, and am surprised to find on page twelve the words *'compagnons de voyage'*. As I am unable to discern any difference between *'compagnons de voyage'* and 'travelling companions', I am full of curiosity to learn if the writer of the catalogue has discovered a distinction in meaning between the French and English phrase. If he has not discovered any, I should like to hear why he prints French words instead of English. True it is that Mr William de Morgan always sprinkled his pages with French. When I asked this eminent writer why he did so, he answered: 'A page of English seems blunt and cheerless without a French word or two. They attract the reader's eye and please him, and they please me, for I am not very well acquainted with the language', an answer that sets me thinking that your catalogue-maker is a belated reader of Mr de Morgan's novels.

(George Moore to Ernest Benn, 26 July 1929)

Speak in French when you can't think of the English for the thing.

(The Red Queen's advice to Alice in Lewis Carroll, *Through the Looking Glass* (1872))

Oh, to acquire culture! Oh, to pronounce foreign names correctly! Oh, to be well informed, discoursing at ease on every subject that a lady started! But it would take one years. With an hour at lunch and a few shattered hours in the evening, how was it possible to catch up with leisured women, who had been reading steadily from childhood! His brain might be full of names, he might

---

*''E dunno où il est!' is the title of a cartoon in *Punch*, 8 Sept. 1894, 119, which features a monocled Englishman in deerstalker cap and matching tweedcheck jacket, leaning out of a railway carriage as it runs into the Gare du Nord, Paris, stabbing a finger in the direction of two grinning porters, and inquiring, 'Oh-er-I say-er-garsong! Kel ay le nomme du set plass?'

have even heard of Monet and Debussy! the trouble was that he could not string them together into a sentence, he could not make them 'tell' . . .

(The culturally aspiring clerk Leonard Bast in E. M. Forster, *Howards End* (1910))

. . . he did not regret not having travelled much, for places rarely came up to the expectations which had been created by his imagination.

(Walter de la Mare in Russell Brain *Tea with Walter de la Mare* (1957))

> For he might have been a Roosian
> A French, or Turk, or Proosian,
> Or perhaps Itali-an!
> But in spite of all temptations,
> To belong to other nations,
> He remains an Englishman!

(W. S. Gilbert, *HMS Pinafore* (1878))

All you gain by travel is the discovery that you have gained nothing, and have done rightly in trusting to your innate ideas—or not done rightly in distrusting them . . .

(Robert Browning in 1845, in Betty Miller. *Robert Browning* (1952))

I

The conventional term is 'English literature', yet it is a remarkable feature of this age how un-English many of its better-known authors were, by birthplace, by parentage, by marriage, or by having spent some influential period abroad. It made for a rare richness and variety in the literature. Another consequence was to raise a question mark about the pursuit of a 'national' culture, by literary patriots of the day and by literary scholars since. Essentially, this was a vain and impossible proceeding because of the continual traffic with 'foreign' cultures. While it appeared, particularly from the nineteenth century, that 'English literature' was achieving an ascendancy throughout the world, the truth was that 'English literature' was perpetually absorbing foreign influences and the hybrid was changing from season to season as from author to author. The witticism about Joseph Conrad, that he didn't have to polish his English so much as english his Polish, was symptomatic; but even this was not quite right since English was Conrad's second foreign language after French, which also left an imprint on the style and structure of his work.[1] John Galsworthy, who first met him in 1893 at Adelaide, Australia,

---

[1] Yves Hervouet, *The French Face of Joseph Conrad* (Cambridge, 1991), for the influence of Flaubert, Maupassant, and Anatole France especially. Douglas Goldring, who was Ford Madox Ford's assistant on the *English Review*, remembered accompanying Ford to visit Conrad in 1909, when Conrad 'talked a queer exciting mixture of French and English' (Goldring, *Reputations*, 217). And when Conrad talked to

when Conrad was a mariner aboard the *Torrens*, wrote that Conrad 'was ever more at home with French literature than with English, spoke that language with less accent, liked Frenchmen, and better understood their clearer thoughts'.[2] According to Ford Madox Ford, who co-authored several novels with him, Conrad actively disliked 'the English mind', thought English defective as a prose medium, and adopted it only because English had no stylists whereas French had plenty.[3]

Perhaps it was also in the nature of a national joke that that paramount English institution *Punch* was for over a quarter-century (1880–1906) edited by a quasi-foreigner. This was Francis Burnand, whose origins on his father's side were French Swiss and Savoyard. His grandmother generally conversed in French and German, and never wrote intelligible English or spoke it without calamitous errors, which may be why Burnand became an incorrigible punster and burlesque-writer.[4] France proper provided a Huguenot ancestry for Maurice Hewlett and a parent for William Le Queux, George Du Maurier, Hilaire and Marie Belloc, and E. M. Delafield. Mrs Henry Wood passed the first twenty years of her married life in France. Anne Thackeray Ritchie likewise was not born in France but spent some formative years there. France was the setting for her first novels;[5] she wrote a life of Mme de Sévigné, relished reading French memoirs and, to keep abreast of French news, 'subscribed to the *Revue des Deux Mondes* and *Le Journal* to the end of her days'.[6] So did Marie Belloc, who was a correspondent on French literary affairs for various weeklies in the late 1880s and early 1890s: 'Even when I was in London, I read all the new French books I could get hold of, and for a time I subscribed to a French circulating library.' She then 'regarded myself as French'; adding in 1944, 'I have remained *toute Française de côeur*.'[7] Swinburne's, fluency in French derived from his grandfather, the sixth baronet Sir John Swinburne, who 'exercised a strong influence over [him]...had been born and brought up in France, and cultivated the memory of Mirabeau. In habits, dress, and modes of thought he was like a French nobleman of the *ancien régime*.'[8] France also provided a birthplace for Violet Paget (Vernon Lee) and Somerset

Henry James about the structure and prospects of the English novel, it was in French that they spoke; likewise, in French that Conrad inscribed his gift to James of *The Nigger of the Narcissus* (1897). Edel, *James*, ii. 392, 396.

[2] Galsworthy, 'Reminiscences of Conrad' (1924), in Galsworthy, *Castles in Spain and Other Screeds* (1927), 79. The dig in that final phrase was prelude to Galsworthy contending that Conrad was *sui generis*: though he admitted his 'admiration for Flaubert, de Maupassant, Turgenev, and Henry James...I can trace no definite influence on him by any writer' (p. 89).

[3] Ford Madox Ford, *Return to Yesterday* (1999), 24, 55, 218, 221.

[4] Burnand, *Records*, i. 28–44. As if to develop the strain of oddity, Burnand converted to Rome in 1858.

[5] These were *The Story of Elizabeth* (1863) and *The Village on the Cliff* (1867), highly praised by the likes of George Moore, Rhoda Broughton, and John Morley. See Fuller and Hammersley (eds.), *Thackeray's Daughter*, 8–9, 100–1, 120; and Sutherland, *Companion*, 537–8, 608.

[6] Fuller and Hammersley (eds.), *Thackeray's Daughter*, 176.

[7] Mrs Belloc Lowndes, *Where Love and Friendship Dwelt* (1944), 158, 186, 243. She contributed 'Paris Notes' and reviews of French books to the *Pall Mall Gazette* and *Review of Reviews*; Susan Lowndes (ed.), *Diaries and Letters of Marie Belloc Lowndes 1911–1947* (1971), 7–16.

[8] Gosse's notice of Swinburne, *DNB Supplement 1901–11*, iv. 456.

Maugham; primary education for W. S. Gilbert; a convent education for Marie
Corelli and Edith Nesbit; a first love affair for Coventry Patmore and asylum for
his bankrupt father; a cultural quest and wife for Arnold Bennett; a refuge for his
imagination and a second wife of French descent for George Meredith; escape
from a second wife and a graveyard for George Gissing. Affectation led Robert
Louis Stevenson and Richard Le Gallienne to Frenchify one part of their names;
and Le Gallienne would die in France, albeit fifty years after *The Quest of the
Golden Girl* (1896) made his reputation. Oscar Wilde had his French connection
too. *Salomé* (1894) was first performed there. Such was his indignation at the Lord
Chamberlain's refusal to license a performance at home that Wilde 'declared his
intention of leaving England and of applying for letters of naturalization as a
French citizen'.[9] Wilde had to settle for exile and burial in France.

It was not just the enduringly famous who absorbed foreign experiences in
their lives. Consider Alex M. Thompson, a name known to historians of
the Labour movement as co-founder of that most English of Socialist papers the
Clarion, in 1891, but largely lost to historians of literature. Thompson was author
or co-author of melodramas, comedies, pantomimes, and musicals, including *The
Arcadians*, which opened at the Shaftesbury Theatre in 1909 and stayed for two
years—the second-longest-running production in the West End, 1900–14.
Thompson was born in Karlsruhe, Baden, in 1861. His parents were English but
his father moved the family there 'because he had many children, because he
believed in foreign experience as a means of education, because it was cheap, and
because it was very pleasant to live in South Germany before Prussian militarism
and industrialism' spoiled it. He uprooted his family again in 1866, when Prussia
and Austria warred for the supremacy of Germany: first to Chelles on the Marne,
then to Paris, where Alex attended a Protestant school before progressing to the
Lycée St Louis. Another upheaval was necessary during the Franco-Prussian war
of 1870–1, when the Thompsons fled to England, then returned to France for the
father to wind up his French *rentes* and invest in new Spanish loans. This proved
to be the last of a series of disastrous misjudgements. The proclamation of a
republic brought about a collapse of Spanish stock in 1873, and a bankrupt
Thompson *père* drowned himself in the river Dee at Chester. Young Alex was
fatherless; he also felt stateless—an Englishman abroad in England. He had never
heard of cricket, drunk tea, or tasted the English apology for bread; even an open
coal fire was strange. 'I was very French,' he recalled in 1937, adding: 'I knew only
a few words of English, and to this day I have not acquired the easy fluency of
perfect assurance in speaking or writing.'[10]

France occupied a secure place in the hearts and minds of several British authors
and artists. The Netherlands was altogether modest in its contribution, although in
Lawrence Alma-Tadema it produced one of late Victorian England's most successful
painters and a brother-in-law for Edmund Gosse. George Du Maurier first met

    [9] Sherard, *Wilde*, 134–5.   [10] Thompson, *Here I Lie*, 3–32.

Alma-Tadema when they were both art students at Antwerp in 1857. He even resembled him and in London was mistaken for him by gushing females who declared how they adored his representation of marble and roses. Seizing their hands, Du Maurier would invite them in a heavy Dutch accent to 'Gom to me on my Chewsdays', and often speculated whether they did.[11] Alma-Tadema lived grandly in St John's Wood; and his scenic skills enlivened the theatres of Henry Irving and Beerbohm Tree.[12] The authorial connection was slighter. Joris-Karl Huysmans was of Dutch extraction, though Paris-born and- based. *A Rebours* (1884) encouraged Aubrey Beardsley and Oscar Wilde further to cultivate artifice. This was the 'yellow book' that Lord Henry Wotton gives Dorian Gray. 'It was a poisonous book,' the fascinated Dorian muses. 'The heavy odour of incense seemed to cling about its pages and to trouble the brain.'[13]

Huysmans aside, the principal Dutch author of the period, so far as the general public was concerned, was Maarten Maartens.[14] He had had an elementary education in England, was most influenced by English literature, and published his novels of Dutch life in English. He was an admirer of Thomas Hardy, and his work echoed that in its animus against established religion and inclination to portray victimized women. Robertson Nicoll developed a friendship with him, and Maartens was so much adopted by the British literary establishment that he was made an Honorary Fellow of the Royal Society of Literature. He also became a member of the General Council of the Authors' Club in 1908, the sole foreign author to be so. There were still more connections. The first wife of the versatile novelist Francis Gribble was Dutch;[15] and in J. T. Grein the Netherlands produced a one-man miscellany. Born in 1862 in Amsterdam, he was educated in the Netherlands, Germany, and Belgium, before settling in London and assuming British nationality in 1895. He was a City businessman, an East India merchant who acted as Consul first for the Congo Free State, then for Liberia. More importantly in the literary context, he served the *Sunday Times* as drama critic. A 'highly excitable person, whose voice sometimes rose to a shriek', Grein felt passionately about the theatre.[16] As co-founder of the Independent Theatre Club in 1891, staging Ibsen, Shaw, and other Continental and native dramatists who were originally shunned by the commercial theatre or the censor, Grein came to occupy an honoured place in the roll of those who advanced the new 'theatre of ideas'.[17] For the same reason he would attract the attentions of the security services and of Pemberton Billing's 'Vigilantes' during the Great War. With the

[11] Ormond, *Du Maurier*, 438.
[12] On Alma-Tadema (1836–1912), see *DNB 1912–1921*, 4–6, and R. J. Barrow, *Lawrence Alma-Tadema* (2002).
[13] Oscar Wilde, *The Picture of Dorian Gray* (1891), in Wilde, *Plays, Prose Writings, and Poems*, 173, 249.
[14] On Maartens (1858–1915), Sutherland, *Companion*, 390–1.
[15] Gribble, *Seen in Passing*, 181. On Gribble (1862–1946), see Kemp *et al.*, *Edwardian Fiction*, 161–2.
[16] Nash, *Life*, 41.
[17] On Grein (1862–1935), see *Who's Who* (1905), 664, *Who Was Who, 1929–1940*, 555, and *Oxford DNB*. For the dinner given by the Critics' Circle to mark Grein's seventieth birthday and fiftieth year as a drama critic, see Agate, *Shorter Ego*, 27–8 (29 Dec. 1932).

fierce syllogism characteristic of the paranoid, they concluded that anyone who was connected with Maud Allan's performance of *Salomé*, had had commercial links with Germany, and bore a German-sounding name must *ipso facto* be a pervert and spy.[18] Grein's significance in London's cultural life was previously registered by a back-handed compliment in *The Green Carnation* (1894), in which Esmé Amarinth—modelled on Oscar Wilde—deplores George Moore's involvement with Grein:

He ought to associate more with educated people, instead of going perpetually to the dependent performances of the independent theatre, whose motto seems to be, 'If I don't shock you, I'm a Dutchman!' How curiously archaic it must feel to be a Dutchman. It must be like having been born in Iceland, or educated at a grammar-school. I would give almost anything to feel really Dutch for half-an-hour.[19]

Among the most itinerant authors was that pioneer New Woman George Egerton, who was born Mary Chavelita Dunne in Australia in 1859 of Welsh–Irish stock. Taking up with a married man, she cohabited for a year in Norway until his partiality for the bottle alienated her. Norway, meanwhile, infected her with literary ambitions. Ibsenism was in the air, and she developed a crush on Knut Hamsun. He found her personally less attractive than her ability to translate his *Hunger* (1890) into English, calculating the potential profits from publication in the 'beef-language'.[20] Rebuffed by Hamsun, she settled in England and Ireland, married and divorced a Canadian, then married the literary agent R. Golding Bright.[21]

By contrast, professional as well as personal reasons explain the migrations of the poet–playwright Roy Flecker. Though eventually buried in Cheltenham, Flecker died at Davos in Switzerland; but the greater part of his short adult life (he died from consumption, aged 30, in 1915) was spent in the consular service, largely in the Middle East. 'I am a violent phil-Hellene,' he told Douglas Goldring; and this love of Greece—he married a Greek—and the French Parnassian school, intermixed with the classics, seemingly much influenced his distinctive writing.[22] However, his friend Francis Birrell (Augustine Birrell's son) reckoned Flecker remained 'three parts the typical Englishman, and considerably less than a quarter the exotic, a pose he adopted more often in verse than in life'. Flecker prided himself on understanding things oriental, yet the more he did the more he disliked them, especially their cruelties. In 1913 he wrote, 'I loathe the East and the Easterns.'[23] Gloucestershire and the Cotswolds principally occupied his heart and

---

[18] Michael Kettle, *Salome's Last Veil: The Libel Case of the Century* (1977), 17–18 and *passim*; and G. R. Searle, *Corruption in British Politics 1895–1930* (Oxford, 1987), 262–3.

[19] Hichens, *Green Carnation*, 120.

[20] Robert Ferguson, *Enigma: The Life of Knut Hamsun* (1987), 117.

[21] On George Egerton (1859–1945), Sutherland, *Companion*, 209–10.

[22] Goldring, *Life Interests*, 56. On Flecker (1884–1915), see *DNB 1912–1921*, 189–90; Hodgson, *Flecker*; Goldring, *Reputations*, 3–35; and the Preface to *The Golden Journey to Samarkand* (1913), repr. in Flecker, *Collected Prose*, 237–41.

[23] Hodgson, *Flecker*, 147, 154–5. Hodgson's epilogue, 'The Development of Flecker's Art', contains a measured assessment of the various influences on his work; ibid. 235–83.

thoughts. Still, he had a flair for foreign languages, learned eight or nine, and had actually seen many of the places to which he alluded in his work. In 1913 a young admirer, Cecil Roberts, sent him a copy of his own recently published work, *Phyllistrata and Other Poems*, to which Flecker responded: 'when I write about Greece I have an advantage—an enormous advantage over other poets—yourself included. I have been there. You talk about the "snow-white porticoes" of the Acropolis. They were rather a lovely golden brown.' He added, 'I think English poets want to get out of England and out of English literature and then to return to discover England.' To that end he advised Roberts, 'Every country in Europe is worth living in but Switzerland,' his objection to Switzerland being founded upon a detestation of fir trees.[24] Staring from the window of a Swiss sanatorium, Flecker drew no pleasure from the snow-laden terrain, which he contemptuously called 'white-wash'.[25]

As a general attitude, this was typical among men of letters. Subtract the scenery, which was loved and hated in turn, and there was little else of Switzerland to remark upon. Swiss culture drew nobody. Alpinists and skiers showed off their athleticism there; otherwise it supported only by the sick. Conan Doyle combined these causes. A vigorous sportsman, he was even a trendsetter when in 1894 he used Norwegian skis for cross-country treks in Switzerland;[26] but another reason for his presence at Davos was his first wife's tubercular condition, from which she would die in 1906. Davos much developed as a resort meanwhile; as Sidney Colvin remarked in 1899, 'to many readers [it] is doubtless familiar, with its railway, its modern shops, its electric lighting, and its crowds of winter sports visitors bent on outdoor and indoor entertainment', altogether transformed from the sparse place which Robert Louis Stevenson had to approach 'by an eight hours' laborious drive' during the two winters he spent there as a consumptive in 1880–1 and where at the same time John Addington Symonds was establishing his chalet home.[27] Robert Bridges spent nine months in Switzerland in 1905–6 because of his wife's health, but the country provided no creative stimulus.[28] All this appeared much as in the days of Sydney Smith. 'I look upon Switzerland as an inferior sort of Scotland,' Smith had written to Lord Holland in 1815. Since Smith regarded Scotland as the 'knuckle-end of England—that land of Calvin, oat-cakes, and sulphur'[29]—this was no great recommendation.

Switzerland and France, and Belgium and Germany, but chiefly Italy, were the locations of Alice Meynell's and L. N. Parker's peripatetic childhoods. Parker is little remembered today, but he was a popular playwright and one-time director of music at Sherborne. There he staged a pageant in 1905 to commemorate the twelfth centenary of the town, its bishopric, and school, the publicity for which

---

[24] Letter from Flecker, 29 Aug. 1913, in Roberts, *Years of Promise*, 49. Roberts's requiem poem 'James Elroy Flecker 1884–1915' is reproduced at pp. 272–3. [25] Hodgson, *Flecker*, 210.
[26] Booth, *Conan Doyle*, 192–3. [27] Colvin, *Stevenson's Letters*, i. 181.
[28] Edward Thompson, *Robert Bridges 1844–1930* (Oxford, 1944), 67.
[29] *Oxford Dictionary of Quotations*, 2nd edn., rev. (1974), 504–5.

inspired a wave of civic and folk celebrations throughout Edwardian England.[30] Parker's forenames, Louis Napoleon, were calculated to make Swinburne froth and foam. A more august choice, Dante, was dowered upon Gabriel Rossetti. He and his sister Christina were the most famous English writers of Italian descent, children of a Neapolitan political exile. According to Watts-Dunton, who knew them, Christina especially was conscious of being by nationality alien and un-English: 'Christina, though she made only one visit to Italy, felt herself to be an Italian, and would smile when any one talked to her of the John Bullism of her brother Gabriel . . . '.[31] The Italian in George Augustus Sala, 'the king of journalists', was less a matter of national loyalty—his Italian father, who taught dancing and deportment, died before his son completed his first year—than a prepotent of his bohemianism. Sala's mother, the daughter of a Demerara plantation owner, was a concert singer, and Sala was schooled in Paris with Dumas *fils*, before embarking on a multifarous career as illustrator and popular novelist, periodical editor, war reporter, and foreign correspondent, traversing the globe, across Europe to Russia, and from Australia to Central and North America, always spending and drinking liberally.[32] Sala's successor as the best-known Anglo-Italian writer was, by some distance, Rafael Sabatini. He was 20 when Sala died in 1895, and his first novel, *The Tavern Knight*, an English civil war saga, was not published until 1904. Born in Italy of an Italian musician father and English mother, Sabatini was schooled in Switzerland and Portugal before he settled in England, marrying an Englishwoman in 1905. He was active in business, a partner in the publishers Martin Secker during the Great War, when he also served in Intelligence; and he became a British citizen in 1918. But it was as an author of historical heroics, involving flashing swordplay and heaving bosoms, that Sabatini's name resounded. He churned out over forty of these, tailor-made for Hollywood adaptation, such as *The Sea Hawk* (1915).[33] The descent was from Scott, via Dumas, spiced by more overt violence and passion.

For the rest, Germany and the Baltic produced a parent for Ford Madox Ford, Max Beerbohm, R. C. Lehmann, Alfred Sutro, Robert Graves, Normal Douglas, and the publisher William Heinemann; a wife for D. H. Lawrence; a schooling for Beatrice Harraden and George Meredith; and experiences, sometimes unsettling and of varying duration, for E. M. Forster, Hugh Walpole, and Katherine Mansfield. Among the more unusual acquisitions from Germany was Hulda Friederichs, who was born at Ronsdorf in Prussia and educated at Cologne and St Andrews in Scotland. At the age of 17 she went to Russia as governess with an English family and, after six years at St Petersburg, settled in England, where, in

---

[30] Waller, *Town, City and Nation*, 314. On Parker (1852–1944), see *DNB*. Thomas Hardy was invited to contribute to the Sherborne Pageant. He declined, though otherwise gave it his support; see Hardy to Louis Parker and H. J. Seymour, 30 Sept. 1904, in Purdy and Millgate (eds.), *Hardy Letters*, iii. 135–6.

[31] Watts–Dunton, *Old Familiar Faces*, 204.

[32] On Sala (1828–95), see *DNB* and Sutherland, *Companion*, 551–2.

[33] On Sabatini (1895–1950) *DNB Missing Persons*, 578; and Kemp *et al.*, *Edwardian Fiction*, 350. Errol Flynn and Flora Robson starred in the 1940 film version of *The Sea Hawk*.

1883, she joined the *Pall Mall Gazette*. Originally private secretary to the editor, W. T. Stead, she contributed to the *Pall Mall Gazette* on 'subjects of interest to women' and, as she proudly told *Who's Who*, she was 'the first woman journalist engaged on exactly the same terms, with regard to work and pay, as male members of the staff'.[34] Not that her relations with them were smooth—they called her 'the Friederichs' and 'the Prussian Governess' and bewared her temper—but among her scoops, she having cultivated Mrs Drew, Gladstone's daughter, was an interview profile of the GOM at home at Hawarden.[35] She remained with the *Pall Mall Gazette* until 1892–3, when it was bought by W. W. Astor, who changed its politics. In common with the then editor, E. T. Cook, and his assistant, J. A. Spender, Friederichs joined the *Westminster Gazette*, founded in 1893 as a Liberal evening paper by George Newnes; and from 1896 to 1905 she edited its offshoot, the sixpenny weekly *Westminster Budget*. Polyglottal, Friederichs translated poetry (into English and German) from Russian, Swedish, Spanish, and French; and she was the author of, among other things, *The Romance of the Salvation Army* (1907) and *The Life of Sir George Newnes* (1911).

Germany also featured strongly in Jerome K. Jerome's life. Though on the scale of things his four years' residence there was not large, it won him a lasting adulation in that country where (he purred in his memoirs) his stock stood higher than in England. Jerome's Europeanism began at home. His wife was the daughter of a Spanish army lieutenant, and his hidden middle name, Klapka, was Hungarian. This was not because Magyar blood ran in the family but because his father, a Nonconformist lay preacher, provided harbour for an exiled Hungarian nationalist of that name in the 1850s. Still, Hungary did later produce a memorable British author, Baroness Orczy, who before she arrived in London at the age of 15 in 1880 knew no English. She then conceived 'a perfect presentation of an English gentleman', Sir Percy Blakeney, *The Scarlet Pimpernel* (1905).[36] From the opposite fringes of Europe, there originated from Denmark a second wife for Richard Le Gallienne and from Portugal Arthur Pinero's father, while, nearer to home, there came from Ireland, Justin McCarthy,[37] George Moore, Bram Stoker, Wilde, Shaw, Yeats, Synge, and Joyce; and from Scotland, Barrie, Buchan, S. R. Crockett, 'Ian Maclaren', John Davidson, Robert Louis Stevenson, and Conan Doyle, though the parents of the last named had Anglo-Irish ancestry.

---

[34] On Friederichs (1856/7–1927), see *Who's Who* (1905), 582–3, *Who Was Who*, 1916–1928, 382, and *Oxford DNB*. [35] J. W. Robertson Scott, *'We' and Me* (1956), 123–5.

[36] Orczy, *Chain of Life*, 7, 25.

[37] Justin McCarthy (1830–1912) was well known in his day as novelist as well as politician and contemporary historian. In *Time* on 'Ireland's Present Influence on Thought and Literature' in 1890, McCarthy lamented that Ireland then was producing nothing to match the sway once exercised in England by Burke, Sheridan, Goldsmith, Thomas Moore, and Maria Edgeworth. Irish talent, he argued, had gone in for politics or journalism, abandoning literary endeavour. McCarthy's objurgation was unfortunate in its timing, just prior to the eruption of Shaw, Wilde, Yeats, Joyce, and the rest. His article was really a plea for Home Rule, prophesying that out of a politically liberated Ireland would emerge a new Irish contribution to English literature. *Review of Reviews* (Apr. 1890), 285. On McCarthy and his fiction, see Sutherland, *Companion*, 392, and *DNB* 1912–1921, 351–2.

The case could be made that the so-called home countries were as strange to each other as any foreign country. Stevenson argued that with respect to Scotland and England in 'The Foreigner at Home'.[38] The same emphatically obtained for Ireland and hardly less for Wales, where, in 1892, three-quarters of Wales's inhabitants rarely used English in their ordinary conversation and chapel communions.[39] Such evidence masked the long-term trend, which was the progress of English-speaking and English usage in Wales as in Ireland; and this would not be reversed in the new century, although its advance would be slowed and bilingualism increase when nationalists in both countries captured the education systems and broadcasting media. England's regional and class dialects could not be legitimized and sustained in the same way against the tide of standard English in book, magazine, and newspaper. In the late nineteenth century, throughout the land, from Edwin Waugh in Lancashire to William Barnes in Dorset, there existed dialect writers of high quality who enjoyed a popular following. Nevertheless, social convention was becoming more exacting in prescribing what was and what was not linguistically acceptable. Just as it was approved for an aristocratic lady to go 'slumming' among the poor in philanthropic work, so it was considered an estimable mark of his manliness, humour, and simplicity that the Poet Laureate Tennyson should cherish his Lincolnshire origins and include dialect pieces such as *The Northern Farmer: Old Style* in *Enoch Arden* (1864). By contrast, a resistance operated against those who were assumed to be trying to step up. The Manxman T. E. Brown felt this strongly. He was a dialect poet by choice, actually a classical scholar who in 1854 won a fellowship of Oriel College, Oxford. For some forty years he taught as a schoolmaster, first at his own former school, King Williams College on the Isle of Man, and then at Clifton College, Bristol. Most of his poetic output, and that for which he remains known, was written in the Anglo-Manx dialect; but he also wrote lyrics in standard English which were not so well received:

How funny it is that so many people are surprised that I can write decent English verses. They have focussed me as a dialect poet, a man of the people, imperfectly educated, and

---

[38] Stevenson, *Memories and Portraits*, 1–23. Also Robert Louis Stevenson, *Familiar Studies of Men and Books* (1925), p. vii, where Scotland was styled 'a country far more essentially different from England than many parts of America'; and his letter to his mother, 28 July 1873, written from Sudbury, Suffolk: 'I cannot get over my astonishment—indeed, it increases every day—at the hopeless gulf that there is between England and Scotland, and English and Scotch. Nothing is the same; and I feel as strange and outlandish here as I do in France and Germany' (Colvin (ed.), *Stevenson's Letters*, i. 49). Other Scots preferred to emphasize the growing convergence of Scotland and England. The once flourishing oral tradition of clannish genealogies, raids, and rebellions, from feudal times to the Jacobites, which Scott, Stevenson, and others had exploited, was fast passing, thought Andrew Lang, who wrote: 'Scotland, or at least Scottish society, is now only English society—a little narrower, a little prouder, sometimes even a little duller' (*Adventures among Books*, 70–1). But perhaps this just evidenced how strange the Scots were to each other; Stevenson, for instance, found Highlanders incomprehensible (letter to his mother, 11 Sept. 1868, in Colvin (ed.), *Stevenson's Letters*, i. 17).

[39] B. G. Evans, 'Welsh Language and Education', *Welsh Review* (Mar. 1892), cited in *Review of Reviews* (Mar. 1892), 294.

so forth; and they seem rather indignant at my writing in a new and more cultivated field. What ought I to do? Shall I put on my next title page—'Late Fellow of Oriel', etc.?, or am I always to abide under the ironic cloak of rusticity?[40]

Robert Louis Stevenson it was, however, who personified the wanderlust that seized so many authors in this period. Beset by pulmonary illnesses, Stevenson spent most of his abbreviated adult life—he died in 1894, aged 44—outside Britain. His first books, *An Inland Voyage* (1878) and *Travels with a Donkey in the Cévennes* (1879), were set in Belgium and France. He returned to live on the Continent, in Switzerland and France, broken by a few years in Bournemouth, before moving to California; and it was eventually Samoa that claimed him.[41] Wilde, however, considered that this dulled his imagination: 'I see that romantic surroundings are the worst surroundings possible for a romantic writer,' he concluded after being bored by the *Vailima Letters* (1895), which he digested in the decidedly unromantic setting of his cell in Reading Gaol. 'In Gower Street Stevenson could have written a new *Trois Mousquetaires*,' he mused. 'In Samoa he wrote letters to *The Times* about Germans.'[42] South Sea islands seemed even less exotic when Rupert Brooke voyaged there in 1913. Though he judged the Samoans and Fijians

stronger, beautifuller, kindlier, more hospitable and courteous, greater lovers of beauty, and even wittier, than average Europeans . . . they are—under our influence—a dying race. We gradually fill their lands with plantations and Indian coolies. The Hawaians, up in the 'Sandwich Islands', have almost altogether gone, and their arts and music with them, and their islands are a replica of America. A cheerful thought, that all these places are to become indistinguishable from Denver and Birmingham and Stuttgart, and the people of dress and behaviour precisely like Herr Schmidt, and Mr Robinson and Hiram O. Guggenheim.[43]

Brooke took full advantage of this fading paradise to father an illegitimate child in Tahiti.[44]

No part of the world now seemed beyond reach. The informal empire in South America, particularly Argentina and Uruguay, where British economic interest

---

[40] Quoted in Samuel Norris, *Two Men of Manxland: Hall Caine, Novelist, T. E. Brown, Poet* (Douglas, 1947), 268–9. Brown did in fact represent himself as 'T. E. Brown, M.A., Late Fellow Oriel College', when his *Fo'c's'le Yarns* (1881) were republished. Among the admirers of the *Yarns* was Henry Sidgwick, who wrote to his sister from Cambridge on 26 March 1881: 'Buy 'em—or persuade friends to' (Arthur and Eleanor Sidgwick, *Henry Sidgwick* (1906), 352). On Brown (1830–97), see *Oxford DNB*.

[41] Stevenson wrote South Seas stories such as *The Beach of Falesá* (1892), and he took an active interest in Samoan political struggles; but he also continued to write stories with a Scottish context, *Catriona* (1893) and more, writing to Sidney Colvin in August 1893: 'Singular that I should fulfil the Scots destiny throughout, and live a voluntary exile, and have my head filled with the blessed, beastly place all the time!' (Sidney Colvin (ed.), *Vailima Letters* (1901), 302). Conspicuous in Stevenson's library in Samoa were books on Scottish history and folklore and also a sizeable collection of French history and fiction: complete editions of Balzac ('which had evidently been read with care', according to Arthur Mahaffy's account in 1895) and of Hugo, plus Daudet, Maupassant, Merimée, and 'a swarm of the more ephemeral novels'. See Neil Macara Brown, 'Le Ona's Library', *Scottish Book Collector*, 4/8 (Dec. 1994–Jan. 1995), 5–8.

[42] To Robert Ross, 6 Apr. 1897, in Hart–Davis (ed.), *Wilde Letters*, 246.

[43] Letter to Violet Asquith, Dec. 1913, in Keynes (ed.), *Brooke Letters*, 543–4.

[44] The child, Alice Rapolo, died in the early 1990s: see *Sunday Times*, 27 Oct. 1996.

waxed, delivered up W. H. Hudson. It also provided a continent of adventure for R. B. Cunninghame Graham, whose maternal grandmother was Spanish and whose wife was born in Chile of a Spanish mother and French father.[45] The formal Empire generated a still more extensive motley. The co-founder of *The Idler* Robert Barr, though born in Glasgow in 1850, was brought up in Canada from 1854 and worked there and in America, not settling in England until 1881.[46] The mother of Henry de Vere Stacpoole, author of *The Blue Lagoon* (1908), was born in Canada, and he travelled extensively with her. Stacpoole himself was born near Dublin—his father was a Church of Ireland clergyman–schoolteacher—but, after graduating in medicine, he then voyaged about the world as a ship's doctor.[47] Even more than Stacpoole, Edith Somerville might appear eternally Irish, but she was born in Corfu, where her colonel father was serving; and even stay-at-home Violet Martin—the other half of 'Somerville and Ross'—had relations who went out to the colonies. This supplied the theme for their first co-authored novel, *An Irish Cousin* (1889), which told the story of a Canadian girl visiting her ancestral home.[48] Canada, more precariously, was the birthplace of Wyndham Lewis in 1882, born on his American father's yacht when it was anchored off Nova Scotia; but W. J. Locke, the son of a banker, outshone this exoticism, born in Barbados in 1863 and brought up in Trinidad.[49] South Africa occupied Rider Haggard, John Buchan, and Edgar Wallace; it also yielded Olive Schreiner, 'the one woman of genius whom South Africa has yet produced', the *Review of Reviews* called her, in reference to *The Story of an African Farm* (1883), which exercised such an influence on feminists and sold some 100,000 copies by 1900.[50] Colonial service in West Africa as a doctor was both the ruin and the remaking of R. Austin Freeman: ruin because the blackwater fever he contracted made him unfit for permanent employment in medicine on returning to England in 1891; remaking because it motivated him to turn to fiction-writing, producing some African adventure stories before creating his celebrated medical hero Dr Thorndyke in *The Red Thumb Mark* (1907). Conan Doyle had also fallen victim

[45] There were an estimated 18,000 Britons in Argentina in 1872, according to the British Consul; Cedric Watts and Laurence Davies, *Cunninghame Graham* (Cambridge, 1979), 36.

[46] On Barr (1850–1912), writer of miscellaneous fiction, see Sutherland, *Companion*, 46. When Arnold Bennett first met Barr in 1898, he regarded him as an American. Barr had kept 'the Yankee accent'. Though he judged him as possessing practically no feeling for literature, he thought him 'an admirable specimen of the man of talent who makes of letters an honest trade'; Flower (ed.), *Bennett Journals*, 69–70, 188 (19 Jan. 1898, 21 July 1904). Cosmo Hamilton, who dramatized Barr's Ruritania–style romance *The Countess Tekla* (1898), again stated in his reminiscences that Barr was an American; Cosmo Hamilton, *People Worth Talking About* (1934), 82.

[47] On Stacpoole (1863–1951), see Kemp *et al.* (eds.), *Edwardian Fiction*, 371–2.

[48] Maurice Collis, *Somerville and Ross* (1968), 28, 61–4.

[49] On Locke (1863–1930), see *DNB. 1922–1930*, 514–15; Sutherland, *Companion*, 380; Kemp *et al.* (eds.), *Edwardian Fiction*, 244.

[50] *Review of Reviews* (Apr. 1890), 266. On Schreiner (1855–1920), see Sutherland, *Companion*, 557–9; and Ruth First and Ann Scott, *Olive Schreiner* (New York, 1980), 120–4, 185, 371, for the reception and sales of *African Farm*. Not all were plaudits; see the savage (and very funny) spoof of Schreiner's allegorical style by R. C. Lehmann, in *Punch*, 16 May 1891, 229.

to fever during his voyage to West Africa as a ship's surgeon in 1881–2. Its climate was as great a contrast as could be imagined from that he experienced on his previous service aboard an Arctic whaler. Doyle was decided in advising all who might be tempted to follow him to West Africa: 'Don't'.[51]

The Empire both old and new shaped the literary career of Morley Roberts, Gissing's friend from college days, who wandered and worked his way through Australia, California, and South Africa, and became one of the highest-paid novelists and short-story writers of the 1890s.[52] Such alchemy did not obtain in every case. Henry Kingsley, Charles Kingsley's dissolute younger brother, spent five hard years in Australia's goldfields without making his fortune, though these experiences illuminated his first novel, *The Recollections of Geoffrey Hamlyn* (1859).[53] Anthony Trollope's son Fred also went out to Australia, to take up farming in the New South Wales bush in 1865. Trollope visited him in 1871–2 and again in 1875 and featured him as the Harry Heathcote character in a short story, 'Malachi's Cave'.[54] Trollope further recorded his impressions in travelogues, but he advised against choosing Australia 'as a scene for a first novel, because readers do not care for a narrow sphere of life'. Still, he added, 'if the Australian novel be good, men will read it,—as they did those of Henry Kingsley'.[55] Poor 'Orion' Horne had turned to a variety of occupations in Australia in the 1860s: gold commissioner, waterworks commissioner, newspaper editor, and cochineal cultivator. He was even credited with being a pioneer of Australian wine-growing; but his writings, such as the choral drama *Prometheus, the Fire-Bringer*, which he composed in Australia, did not revive his flagging reputation and he was dependent on the £50 annual pension dispensed by Disraeli's Government after he returned to England.[56] By contrast, a three-years' spell in Australia after leaving Uppingham School gave E. W. Hornung his start as a novelist with *A Bride from the Bush* (1890); when he published *Under Two Skies* (1892), short stories in which an English setting alternated with an Australian, he was advised that his English stories were the weaker, lacking individuality: 'Mr Hornung evidently knows his Australia well, and if he would only . . . confine himself to Australian matter, he should have a great success.'[57] New Zealand produced Mary Annette Beauchamp (the 'Elizabeth' of *Elizabeth and her German Garden*, 1898), Katherine Mansfield, and Hugh Walpole. New Zealand also provided five years of sheep-farming for Samuel Butler, and its topography featured in his dystopias *Erewhon* (1872) and *Erewhon Revisited* (1901). Gilbert Murray was born in Sydney, New South Wales,

---

[51] Booth, *Conan Doyle*, 74.

[52] On Morley Roberts (1857–1942), see Sutherland, *Companion*, 539–40.

[53] Ibid. 356–7, 525, for Henry Kingsley (1830–76); Nowell–Smith, *Letters to Macmillan*, 40–2.

[54] To Mary Holmes, 15 June 1876, in Booth (ed.), *Trollope's Letters*, 355–6.

[55] To Miss Badham, 9 May 1881, ibid. 454.

[56] Gosse, '"Orion" Horne', in Gosse, *Portraits and Sketches*, 108–12.

[57] *Review of Reviews* (June 1892), 614. Hornung (1866–1921) was born in Middlesbrough, the son of a solicitor. The family was originally Slavonic, with Transylvanian connections. Hornung married Conan Doyle's sister in 1893; see *DNB Missing Persons*, 331.

and Mrs Humphry Ward in Hobart, Tasmania. Equally unlikely, the author of the Dartmoor cycle of novels, Eden Phillpotts, was born in India.[58] And India, once the birthplace of Thackeray, now produced the rarest jewel, Kipling. Burma, meanwhile, dealt a cruel joker in Hector Munro (Saki), whose mother was killed by a rampant cow.

Such a list is not difficult to compile but far from exhaustive. Who now remembers the six and a half years that Walter Besant spent in Mauritius as a professor at the Royal College? Yet this was a period that 'completely changed the whole current of my thoughts—my views of society, order, religion, everything'.[59] Not least, it made him determined to embark on a literary career on returning to England. Much the same applied to Grant Allen. He was born in Canada and brought up there and in the United States, then—after a period in France—he graduated from Oxford to a chair in philosophy at a government-founded college for blacks in Jamaica. That institution failing, he returned to England to become a versatile writer of books on science, philosophy, psychology, and history. He also turned out a variety of fiction, from detective novels to social criticism, including *The Woman Who Did* (1895), which both secured the publishing firm of John Lane and generated a sequence of novels debating the ethics of marriage and the position of women.[60] Allen was the son of Scots–Irish parents,[61] his father being an Irish Church minister who had migrated to Ontario. Imperial missionary service and trade likewise accounted for the birthplace of M. P. Shiel, author of exotic fantasies. He was born in Plymouth, Montserrat, in the West Indies, where his father was both a Methodist lay preacher and merchant-ship owner; the mother was of mixed race.[62] In 1880, when he was 15, his father bizarrely had him made King of Redonda in a coronation conducted by the Bishop of Antigua. Sheill—as the surname was then spelled—senior had spotted this uninhabitable mile-long rocky isle when sailing past; and, being of romantic Irish descent, he had claimed it for the one boy among his nine children. Although HM Government afterwards made Redonda a formal dependency of Antigua, in order to exploit the phosphate found there, Shiel continued to style himself its monarch, King Felipe, until death in 1947, whereupon his friend the poet John Gawsworth (Terence Ian Fytton Armstrong) succeeded him as King Juan. In 1903 *M.A.P.* had nominated Shiel 'the most haunting writer of the day' because of his 'qualities of dazzling imagination, breathlessness, and grip'. Two prime ministers, Gladstone and Rosebery, were counted among the admirers of *Prince Zaleski* (1895) and *The Rajah's Sapphire* (1896); but it was *The Yellow Danger*

[58] Flower (ed.), *Bennett Journals*, i. 72, 76, 81, 97, for Phillpotts's account of his upbringing and how he became a writer.   [59] *The Autobiography of Sir Walter Besant*, ed. S. Squire Sprigge (1902), 148–9.
[60] On Grant Allen (1848–99), see Sutherland, *Companion*, 20–1, and *Oxford DNB*.
[61] Allen liked to call himself a Celt and lauded the Celtic contribution to Britain; indeed, attributed most economic, social, and political progress to this source. But he defined this as an unconquerable spirit of independence rather than as an ethnic group—'Of course, I am not silly enough to believe there is any such thing as a Celtic race' (Allen, *Post–Prandial Philosophy*, ch. xviii).
[62] See Albert R. Vogeler's notice of Shiel (1865–1947), *Oxford DNB*.

(1898), a thriller introducing the first of many oriental villains who aimed at world domination, that made his fortune. Shiel's own favourite among his books and the one that found most readers subsequently was *The Purple Cloud* (1901), an apocalyptic vision about the survivors of volcanic eruptions, releasing a poison gas cloud that wipes out most of mankind. Shiel was now spending over half the year on the Continent, mostly in Spain. His first wife was Spanish; and from his adopted country he fed the British public accounts of his supposed adventures, such as his capture by Gypsies in the Sierra Morena mountains, from whose clutches he escaped with the connivance of the brigand leader's daughter. He also treated readers to his philosophy of inhalation (he listed breathing, along with bicycling and fencing, and mathematics and mountaineering, among his recreations), holding that most people breathe too fast and thereby weaken their health and mind, a theory which he generously ascribed to the Arabs.[63]

Shiel was singular by most standards, and his imperial origin freakish; but other well-known writers might be cited who emerged from the Empire, authentic colonials as it were. One was Gilbert Parker, Canadian by birth and education. He spent a period in Australia as associate editor of the *Sydney Herald* before making a double career in England, as a sensational novelist of the frontier and as a Conservative MP, 1900–18.[64] After his marriage to a rich New Yorker, the feeling arose that 'he had become more impressive than was needful'.[65] Parker's swagger was much commented on, 'the most immaculately dressed man in town', reported R. D. Blumenfeld in 1900. He had been told that Parker's 'book royalties are £7,000 a year, and perhaps more'.[66] These rose higher in the Edwardian period, according to the Unionist Party's chief whip, Lord Balcarres, to whom Parker was anxious to dedicate his latest fiction in 1912: 'He tells me that a novel brings him in £20,000 of which £5,000–£10,000 is to be paid in advance of publication. His sale is enormous.'[67] Nor was Parker all show. He was a promoter of the cause of imperial unity. He organized the first conference of universities of the Empire in 1903, and was chairman of the Imperial South Africa Association, 1903–11. His ambitions of Cabinet office were frustrated by the Unionists' defeat in three successive general elections; but he was an architect of the party's attempts to counter the Liberals' Land Campaign with a programme based on small ownership, land banks, and cooperative purchase and marketing.[68] He also evinced some prescience in understanding the new science of aviation, intervening in the

---

[63] See the profile of Shiel in *M.A.P.*, 17 Oct. 1903, 477; also Sutherland, *Companion*, 573, and Kemp *et al.* (eds.), *Edwardian Fiction*, 360–1, where it is noted, 'He applied to the Royal Literary Fund in 1914, stating that he was going blind, had three children, the youngest four months old, and that his annual income had declined from about £2,000 at the turn of the century to about £150.' The *Oxford DNB* adds that 'In December 1914 Shiel was briefly imprisoned in Wormwood Scrubs for reasons undetermined.' Arthur Ransome dedicated *Bohemia in London* (1907) to him.

[64] On Parker (1862–1932), see *DNB 1931–1940*, 671–2; Sutherland, *Companion*, 490.

[65] Jerome, *Life and Times*, 139.   [66] Blumenfeld, *R.D.B.'s Diary*, 76 (6 Oct. 1900).

[67] Vincent (ed.), *Crawford Papers*, 291 (5 Dec. 1912).

[68] Sir Gilbert Parker, 'Small Ownership, Land Banks, and Co-operation', *Fortnightly Review* (Dec. 1909), 1079–91. On his Cabinet ambitions, Vincent (ed.), *Crawford Papers*, 123 (7 Mar. 1909).

Commons' first debate on aeronautics, on 2 August 1909, to exhort the Government to establish a school to train pilots and to conduct practical experiments.[69] Parker was knighted in 1902, created a baronet in 1915, and made a Privy Councillor in 1916, the last in recognition of his superintendence of allied propaganda towards America.

Equally forgotten now is C. Haddon Chambers, son of an Irish Australian civil servant. Chambers was a bushranger before emigrating to England in 1882. He had a reputation for wildness and made his name as journalist, short-story writer, and playwright. In 1888 'he suddenly took London by storm with his play, *Captain Swift*. Captain Swift was one of the greatest parts which Beerbohm Tree has created, and from that time forward Chambers became one of the dramatists who count.'[70] This was the verdict of Douglas Sladen, who, as editor of *Who's Who*, knew the capital's literary circles. Chambers had apparently pursued Tree into a Turkish bath, where the cornered and perspiring actor–manager was made to listen to *Captain Swift*.[71] Chambers also wrote *The Tyranny of Tears*, which, in Keble Howard's opinion, was 'possibly the best light comedy in our language'. Curiously, Howard thought Chambers 'rather a sad person', though this might have been a consequence of their meeting on a boat to Boulogne.[72] In the Edwardian period Chambers was the subject of many a flattering profile and 'regarded as one of the best dressed men in London', an obvious rival for Gilbert Parker.[73] His Mayfair home was the address of a man who had made it; likewise his clubs, and the recreations listed in *Who's Who*—'swimming, boat-sailing, riding, driving, shooting, boxing, fencing'. At his death in 1921 Anthony Hope hailed him as 'a *very* dexterous playwright'.[74]

It was easy to affect a superciliousness about outposts of empire. Did one come *over* from Australia or come *up*? Oscar Wilde preferred the latter: 'I believe that absurdly shaped country lies right underneath the floor of one's coal-cellar.'[75] As an apprentice decadent, Ernest Dowson too liked to impress fellow undergraduates at Oxford in the late 1880s with his studied ignorance of such unsophisticated regions. He thought it chic to insist that Australia was peopled by pygmies while, on the other hand, he paraded exact knowledge about the bohemian life in Paris.[76] Writers who visited Australia did not always admire what they found. After a lecture tour there D. Christie Murray penned a pair of articles on 'The Antipodeans' for the *Contemporary Review* in 1891. These contained a catalogue of horrors. He identified a resentment of England among Australians and he predicted from this Anglophobia an eventual separatist movement: 'To the next generation England will be a geographical expression,

[69] I owe this reference to Sylvia Adams.

[70] Sladen, *Twenty Years*, 244. See also Pearson, *Tree*, 52–4; Jerome, *Life and Times*, 108; and *Who Was Who, 1916–1928*, 187, for Chambers (1860–1921).   [71] Gribble, *Seen in Passing*, 219.

[72] Howard, *Motley Life*, 257.   [73] *T.P.'s Weekly*, 25 Sept. 1903, 524; and *M.A.P.*, 10 Feb. 1906, 126.

[74] Mallet, *Hope*, 247.

[75] Wilde to Mrs Bernard Beere, Apr. 1894, in Hart-Davis (ed.), *Wilde's Letters*, 118.

[76] Thomas Wright, 'Ernest Dowson at Oxford', *Oxford Magazine*, Eighth Week, Trinity Term, 1999, 14.

and the Empire a myth in imminent danger of becoming a bogey.' Commercially, Australian protectionism was on the rise, together with an antipathy to immigration; but in business Australians were unsound, their rate of insolvencies far outstripping that of England. As for their culture, though formally well educated, Australians were materialist and pagan. Their real religion was 'the worship of athleticism'. Socially, Australians were prone to confound courtesy with servility. Hence their propensity for rudeness and profanity: 'there is more swearing to the square mile [there] than suffices for the crowded millions of Great Britain'. As for Australian slang, 'it is ugly, and good for nothing but to be forgotten'. Murray's opinions naturally created a stir.[77] They ran counter to the ideology of imperial federation and English-speaking union, promoted as a cross-party enthusiasm by many, including W. T. Stead, who in 1892 started an Australian edition of the *Review of Reviews* which incorporated the whole of the British edition together with a sixteen-page extra given over to the life and literature of Australia.[78] That a white Australian ideal of prohibiting coloured immigration should be about the only policy agreed upon by the several states when they federated in 1900 was hardly a bone of contention for the likes of Rider Haggard, who shared their nightmare about a Yellow Peril and who in 1916 visited Australia with a view to facilitating the settlement of ex-soldiers there.[79] Indeed, following Australia's sacrifices of men in the imperial cause in the Boer War and Great War, writers felt even more obliged to enter into a state of denial about the general beastliness of that country and the alien qualities of its people. Barrie's stage directions for *Mary Rose* (1920) introduce a young Australian soldier, a recently familiar sight in any London street: 'In his voice is the Australian tang that became such a friendly sound to us,' Barrie noted, before describing his 'sinewy' physique, 'clear eye', and 'tolerant grin'.[80] As if to underline the union, it turns out that the soldier is originally from Sussex, had run away to Australia at the age of 12, and is now returning to the family manor house to appease his mother's spirit.

Murray's account in 1891 was partial, therefore; moreover, it was possible to observe the same things without reaching such drastic conclusions. Douglas Sladen spent five years in Australia in the early 1880s as the first Professor of

---

[77] Rejoinders included articles by the Hon. John Fortescue and Sir Edward Braddon. The controversy can be followed in *Review of Reviews* (Aug. 1891), 154, (Sept. 1891), 271, (Nov. 1891), 455, (Dec. 1891), 617–18. On D. Christie Murray (1847–1907), see Sutherland, *Companion*, 451–2, and Kemp *et al.* (eds.), *Edwardian Fiction*, 289, where it is noted that Murray in 1893 first applied to the Royal Literary Fund after a nervous collapse and bankruptcy had caused his income to fall from £2,700 to £30 in a year. He had been in the Army, a parliamentary reporter, and foreign and war correspondent, before writing fiction. A strong supporter of Zola's defence of Captain Dreyfus, Christie continued to court controversy, in 1899 declaring: 'The present pessimistic and hopeless kind of fiction, written by a lot of schoolgirls who did not know what life was, was not going to last' (speech at the Article Club, quoted in *Punch*, 18 Jan. 1899, 34). Twice married, and the father of six children (four of them illegitimate), he left only £50 at death; see *Oxford DNB*.

[78] The editor of the Australian edition was the Revd W. H. Fitchett; see *Review of Reviews* (Apr. 1892), 396, (June 1892), 608–10.

[79] A. D. Harvey, 'Old Objectionables', *TLS*, 2 Jan. 2004, for Haggard's report to the Colonial Office on white Australia; and Higgins (ed.), *Haggard's Diaries*, 57–64, for the 1916 visit.

[80] Barrie, *Plays*, 532.

Modern History at the University of Sydney. He also 'discovered that nothing was of any importance in Australia except sport and money'.[81] Nonetheless, Sladen enjoyed the place, married an Australian, and developed an admiration for the talents of Australian or Australia-influenced writers. 'I Owe Everything to Australia' was the title of a chapter in his autobiography, published in 1939. The inspiration for his own poetry was Adam Lindsay Gordon's, and it was through Sladen's championing that a memorial bust was placed in Westminster Abbey in 1934, the year following Gordon's centenary.[82] Sladen compiled two anthologies: *Australian Ballads and Rhymes* (1888) for which Walter Scott & Co. of Newcastle paid him an honorarium of £25 and sold 20,000 copies in its first year; and *A Century of Australian Song* (1888), reviewed by Oscar Wilde as 'as extraordinary collection of mediocrities whom Mr Slader has somewhat ruthlessly, dragged from their modest and well-merited obscurity'. In 1912, when Gordon's poems had fallen out of copyright, Sladen published a collected edition which sold 10,000 copies in its first year, and he co-authored a biography, *Adam Lindsay Gordon and his Friends in England and Australia*.[83] Sladen also devoted a chapter of his first instalment of memoirs in 1914 to Australian authors in London;[84] and the influential publisher's reader Edward Garnett had been so struck by the quality of one Australian writer, Henry Lawson, that he persuaded Fisher Unwin to launch an Over-Seas Library series in 1898.[85] Macmillan's, whose Colonial Library was begun in 1886 for the circulation of standard works and popular fiction in the Empire, occasionally published colonial authors simultaneously both in the Colonial Library and in their 3s. 6d. series in England. One successful instance was the bushranger romance *Robbery under Arms* (1888) by Rolf Boldrewood, otherwise T. A. Browne, a police magistrate in New South Wales;[86] but it was Guy Boothby, having returned to England (where he had been schooled) from Adelaide in 1894, who 'struck oil', as Sladen put it. Boothby's

[81] Sladen, *Twenty Years*, 17.

[82] The bust was sculpted by Kathleen Bruce; Lady Kennet, *Self-Portrait of an Artist* (1949), 296.

[83] Robert Hart-Davis (ed.), *More Letters of Oscar Wilde* (1985), 77; Sladen, *Long Life*, 62–3, 69–70, 80–1, 134–6, 202–3, 330–9, 347. On Gordon (1833–70), see D. C. Browning and John W. Cousin (eds.), *Everyman's Dictionary of Literary Biography* (1950), 270; he was born in the Azores, brought up in Cheltenham (where Sladen also went to school) joined the Australian Mounted Police, entered politics in South Australia, and committed suicide in 1870.

[84] Sladen, *Twenty Years*, 17 and ch. xx. Sladen's uncle Sir Charles Sladen had been Prime Minister of Victoria. When Yeats met Sladen for the first time in 1888, he called him 'the Australian poet' (letter to Katharine Tynan, Sept. 1888, in Wade (ed.), *Yeats's Letters*, 89). See also *M.A.P.*, 14 Nov. 1903, 600, for a feature on Australian novelists now writing in England: these included Louis Becke, Rolf Boldrewood, Guy Boothby, Ada Cambridge, Mrs Campbell Praed, and H. B. Marriott Watson.

[85] Watts and Davies, *Cunninghame Graham*, 169–70. By contrast, Viscount Hampden, on return from serving as Governor of New South Wales (1895–9), told his friend Wilfrid Blunt that he 'found it dull work among people without literature, art, or culture of any kind, except a taste for bad music'. Invited to stay on as Governor-General, he refused. Blunt, *My Diaries*, i. 321 (18 May 1899).

[86] On Boldrewood (1826–1915), see *Oxford DNB*; Sutherland, *Companion*, 74, 538; Kemp *et al.* (eds.), *Edwardian Fiction*, 38; Sladen, *Twenty Years*, 241–2; Nowell-Smith (ed.), *Letters to Macmillan*, 210–14. He was actually born in London but brought up in Australia from the age of 5. In the Preface to *Robbery under Arms* he wrote: 'though presented in the guise of fiction . . . much of the narrative is literally true, as can be verified by official records'.

Dr Nikola mysteries rivalled Doyle's Sherlock Holmes in popularity and, wrote Sladen, 'at one time [he] was making nine thousand a year out of his writing. I remember his chartering an eight hundred ton steam yacht, and he had some wonderful prize dogs at the Manor House, close to the Kempton Park racecourse, in which he lived.'[87] Not all settled so well. Louis Becke won a greater reputation among literary critics than did Boothby for his tales of the Pacific; but he never made the fortune that was predicted and, at the Savage Club in 1900, R. D. Blumenfeld heard him say that 'he felt more lost and lonely in London than he ever did on the loneliest of South Sea Islands'.[88]

II

In 1920 Bernard Shaw saluted the Victorians' 'cosmopolitan intellectualism'.[89] This was prompted by his reviewing a work by Vernon Lee (Violet Paget). Her capacity to strike awe in those who encountered her in Italy, where she would discourse about the Renaissance and all points on the cultural compass, was apparently limitless; and it earned her an honourable mention in Browning's last published poem, *Asolando* (1889). Maurice Baring styled her 'by far the cleverest person I ever met in my life and the person possessed with the widest range of the rarest culture'. Fortunately, this paragon's half-brother was a uniquely horrible egotist who practised invalidism for over twenty years; and Baring recovered his poise by using him as part-model for the unpleasant Prince Guido Roccapalumba in *Cat's Cradle* (1925).[90] As a novelist Lee was markedly unsuccessful. Her romantic disposition was towards her own sex and her intellectual and aesthetic tastes those of Ruskin, Pater, and John Addington Symonds. Their combination in *Miss Brown* (1884) did not impress its dedicatee, Henry James, who called it 'a rather deplorable mistake'.[91] Lee's sustained cerebral energy eventually proved too much for Max Beerbohm, who, on the title page of his copy of her *Gospels of Anarchy* (1908), cartooned her in a bonnet sipping tea, and wrote:

Poor dear dreadful little lady! Always having a crow [*sic*] to pick, ever so coyly, with Nietzsche, or a wee lance to break with Mr Carlyle, or a sweet but sharp little warning to whisper in the ear of Mr H. G. Wells, or Strindberg or Darwin or D'Annunzio! What a dreadful little bore and busybody! How artfully at this moment she must be button-holing Einstein! And Signor Croce—and Mr James Joyce![92]

---

[87] Sladen, *Twenty Years*, 242. On Boothby (1867–1905), see *Oxford DNB*; Sutherland, *Companion*, 76; and Kemp *et al.* (eds.), *Edwardian Fiction*, 39–40.

[88] Blumenfeld, *R.D.B.'s Diary*, 104 (21 Oct. 1900). On Becke (1855–1913), who sunk into alcoholism and returned to die, equally lonely, in Sydney, see Sutherland, *Companion*, 53–4, and Kemp *et al.* (eds.), *Edwardian Fiction*, 22–3.

[89] G. B. Shaw, review of Vernon Lee, *Satan the Waster* (1920), *The Nation*, 18 Sept. 1920, quoted in Peter Gunn, *Vernon Lee: Violet Paget, 1856–1935* (New York, 1975), 2.

[90] Emma Letley, *Maurice Baring: A Citizen of Europe* (1991), 39, 48–9.   [91] Gunn, *Lee*, 104.

[92] Ibid. 3.

Lee published over forty works: fiction, fables, philosophy, psychology, philology, musicology, history, travel, and aesthetics. She is credited with introducing (in 1904) the concept of 'empathy' into the English language and discourse;[93] but the question remains how far she matured from her own youthful self-description as 'a half-baked polyglot scribbler'.[94]

How far Shaw's observation was generally applicable to Victorian authors is another matter. He was one himself; that is, he spent his first forty-five years a Victorian. Shaw's sweep of interests was seemingly global, yet his grindstone of a brain would powder everything into an assimilable order, all rendered with much the same hallmark. His first visit to the Continent had taken him to Antwerp, which he found 'exactly like Limerick, only duller'. This was in April 1889. He crossed the Channel again for the Wagner festival in Bayreuth that summer and, with fellow Fabian Sidney Webb, roamed through Belgium, France, Germany, and Austria in 1890. Webb possessed a cerebral power superior even to Shaw's, according to Shaw's own reckoning, but again it was a brain whose streamline track did not deviate so as to admit inspiration from nature home or abroad. Amid mountain and forest Webb sat down to compose an article about municipal death duties. Shaw himself felt reduced when abroad: 'If there was anything Shaw learnt from bombarding round Europe, it was how travel narrowed the mind. His one weapon, language, broke in his hand and he fell to the conclusion that the only country you could learn more about by going abroad was your own'.[95]

This would appear to raise questions about the vaunted 'cosmopolitan intellectualism' of the Victorians (and Edwardians), suggesting that it would be wrong to emphasize their openness to the influence of foreign ideas. A commonplace mind remained commonplace however far it roamed. So did a repellent spirit. After leaving Oxford in the early 1880s, Edgar Jepson embarked on an ersatz Grand Tour with a Balliol chum, the second Earl Russell. He then fell into teaching classics in prep schools before taking a post at the Lodge School, St John's in Barbados, at £125 per year, double his previous stipend. Reflecting on his four years there, Jepson wrote: 'I could never feel that the actual blacks were quite human, and the Barbadians were sure that they were not. Quadroons were different, and the more white blood there was in the coloured the more human they appeared to be.'[96] On returning to England, determined to become a literary figure, he composed his first novel, *Sibyl Falcon* (1895), a sadistic thriller featuring villainous blacks. Nor did globe-trotting and world-reporting alchemize G. A. Sala and make him more capable of producing work worth reading; rather it manufactured a more monstrous bore. Such was the verdict of Oscar Wilde's circle, whose opinions were mimicked by Robert

---

[93] R. W. Burchfield (ed.), *A Supplement to the Oxford English Dictionary* (Oxford, 1972), i. 936.
[94] Lambert and Ratcliffe, *Bodley Head*, 122.   [95] Holroyd, *Shaw*, i. 218–19.
[96] Jepson, *Memories of a Victorian*, 193.

Hichens in *The Green Carnation*. His Wilde character Esmé Araminth remarks, amid Sunday yawns:

I once wrote an article for a newspaper, but that was before I had met Sala. Ever since then I have been haunted by the fear that if I did it again I might grow like him. I believe he has lived in Mexico. His style always strikes me as decidedly Mexican. I met him at dinner, and he told me facts that I did not previously know, all the time I was trying to eat. Afterwards in the drawing-room he gave a lecture. I rather forget the subject, but I think it was, 'Eggs I have known'. He knew a great many.[97]

Nor is it right to suppose that genius will always grow by foreign experience. On the contrary, the stronger the mind the better able to resist fugitive impressions. Sala's one-time editor Charles Dickens supplies point to this argument. As befitting his status as literary superstar, Dickens was much travelled, voyaging to America and crossing the Channel many times. Among the many attractions of France was that he could move about more openly with his mistress Nelly Ternan.[98] Even prior to this passion he was prolonging his periods abroad. 'J'ai si longtemps demeuré—on the Continent—que j'ais presqu' oublié my native tongue', he wrote with that tongue firmly in cheek.[99] His fondness for France was such that he sent his sons to a boarding school at Boulogne, yet it was a school whose head was an English cleric. Such qualifications bear out G. K. Chesterton, who reckoned that, mentally, Dickens never travelled out of England. Chesterton found no trace, in *Pictures from Italy* (1846), 'that he really felt the great foreign things which lie in wait for us in the south of Europe, the Latin civilization, the Catholic Church, the art of the centre, the endless end of Rome. His travels are not travels in Italy, but travels in Dickensland.' It was characteristic that amid the Italian sunshine he was writing *The Chimes* (1844), the second of his Christmas books, and dreaming of 'fog and snow and hail and happiness'; and that, when in Switzerland in 1846, he bemoaned his inability to get on with *Dombey and Son* (1848) because he was deprived of London's streets: 'My figures seem disposed to stagnate without crowds about them.' Accordingly, Chesterton concluded, 'the Englishman abroad is for all serious purposes, simply the Englishman at home'.[100]

This appeared perversely to underestimate or ignore in British writers a keenness to search for foreign experiences, an alacrity to seize on them, and a willingness to be stimulated by them. Still, the eventual outcome was largely their absorption into, rather than redirection of, the mainstream evolution of British politics, philosophy, religion, social codes, and letters. Anthony Trollope made two world tours, and conscientiously boned up on places he would pass through. In 1875 he read the first volume of his then dead friend Sir James

---

[97] Hichens, *Green Carnation*, 145–6.   [98] Claire Tomalin, *The Invisible Woman* (1991).
[99] Letter to H. K. Browne, 6 July 1853, in Graham Storey, Kathleen Tillotson, and Angus Easson (eds.), *The Letters of Charles Dickens*, vii: *1853–1855* (Oxford, 1993), 111.
[100] Chesterton, *Dickens*, 153–7, 178–9.

Tennent's *Ceylon* (1859), Tennent having been an official both there and in India; yet, Trollope told his wife, 'I almost doubt whether I can get thro the second. Nothing longer or duller ever was written.'[101] Trollope generally paid for his travels by firing off impressions in the form of letters to newspapers, at £15 a time, with another £5 if their syndication appeared in eighteen or more journals;[102] and there was invariably a follow-up travelogue book or a trigger for some fiction to be got out of these excursions. There were also family calls to make, the son in Australia and a niece who was born and lived in Italy; but Trollope was not reconstituted by travel. His partialities remained fixed. He followed his wife to the Continent in August 1879 and met her at Gérardmer, Vosges, 'a most detestable place to my way of thinking', he remarked, 'as are all these places in France. One has to get into Switzerland or South Germany before one finds a pleasant country or a pleasant people'.[103] His last substantial extra-European voyage had been to South Africa in 1877. He was a supporter of the High Commissioner Sir Henry Bartle Frere's expansionist policy there, respecting the Boer and native territories. He held South African stock as part of his shares portfolio, and he marvelled at the great hole from which diamonds were dug; but he had not been twelve hours ashore at Cape Town without feeling it was 'a poor, niggery, yellowfaced, half-bred sort of place, with an ugly Dutch flavour',[104] and nothing he encountered elsewhere disturbed that view. When preparing to be taken to see some beauty spot, he wrote that the 'grandest scenery in the world to me would be Montagu Square'[105]—his home. Even in regard to people and places, such as the United States, for which he felt attraction, Trollope recognized and revelled in his own limitations. To his American friend Kate Field, by whom he was smitten, he mused, while in Waltham, Massachusetts, 'I was thinking to-day that nature intended me for an American rather than an Englishman. I think I should have made a better American. Yet I hold it higher to be a bad Englishman, as I am, than a good American,—as I am not.'[106]

Like Trollope had been, the late Victorian and Edwardian literary classes were inveterate wanderers. Excepting members of the Alpine Club, who exercised among the mountains, most travellers and migrants made for the Mediterranean. Being hallowed by Byron, Shelley, and Keats, and latterly by the Brownings, Italy was the favoured destination; yet, it was necessary to get things into proportion. Reading Mrs Browning's published letters in 1900, Wilfrid Blunt was reminded how much he admired her and her husband's poetry; but he had nothing but contempt for their life in Italy, 'infected with the sentimental vulgarity of the Anglo-American colony, which had its headquarters in Storey's rooms in the Palazzo Barberini, and which so nauseated me thirty and more years ago in Rome'. As for Robert Browning, whom Blunt judged 'a thinker of a very high

---

[101] To Rose Trollope, 17 Mar. 1875, in Booth (ed.), *Trollope's Letters*, 339.
[102] To Nicholas Trübner, 26 Feb. 1875, ibid. 335.   [103] To John Blackwood, 8 Aug. 1879, ibid. 423.
[104] To John Blackwood, 21 July 1877, ibid. 374.
[105] To Henry Merivale Trollope, 9 Oct. 1877, ibid. 381.   [106] To Kate Field, 23 Aug. 1862, ibid. 118.

order, the most intellectual poet we have perhaps ever had', he remembered him in his later years as 'a gossipy diner-out in London and teller of second-rate funny stories'.[107] Subtracting the cruelty from this judgement, there remains no doubt about the strength of Robert Browning's homing instinct. At his wife's funeral in Florence and in the days around, he was subject to heartfelt appeals by a variety of distinguished Italians, including one of Cavour's ministers, not to leave their country; or, if he must, to induce their son Pen to make his career there, because 'we want those who were friends in our ill days to share in our coming good fortunes—every thing will be open to him!' Browning, while suitably moved, was resolute about returning: 'Of course', he asserted, 'Pen is and will be English as I am English and his Mother was pure English to the hatred of all un-English cowardice, vituperation, and lies . . . '.[108] The lived life was thus different from the pretend of poetry. George Meredith also recognized this folly of supposing otherwise, after visiting Venice, where he

followed Byron's and Shelley's footsteps there on the Lido. I have seldom felt melancholy so strongly as when standing there. You know I despise melancholy, but the feeling came. I love both those poets; and with my heart given to them I felt as if I stood in a dead and useless time. So are we played with sometimes![109]

A fashion for the Riviera was growing apace, especially after Queen Victoria's first vacation at Menton in 1882. There was nothing literary about the climate, the yachting, the golfing, and the gaming tables that drew writers such as Grant Allen, Arnold Bennett, R. D. Blumenfeld, Julia Frankau, Frank Harris, E. Phillips Oppenheim, Baroness Orczy, Gilbert Parker, Henry de Vere Stacpoole, and C. N. and A. M. Williamson, who played, recuperated, or settled on the Riviera.[110] For W. J. Locke, however, it appeared a coming home rather than a going away. A tubercular condition, first diagnosed in 1890, finally prompted his move to Cannes in 1921, after a markedly successful twenty years of novel- and playwriting; but his friend Anthony Hope, who admired Locke's connoisseurship of food and wine, and considered he wrote better about France than about England, felt that 'he was *French by nature*'.[111]

Expeditions to the Levant, Egypt, and the Holy Land seemed generally more spiritual, albeit increasingly less adventurous. Some few followed in the tradition of gentleman amateur like Wilfrid Blunt in wandering about Arabia; but, as E. M. Forster put it, with pardonable exaggeration, in his review of Blunt's diaries when these were published after the Great War, 'the age of independent travel, though

---

[107] Blunt, *Diaries*, i. 373 (6 Nov. 1900).

[108] Letter to John Forster, July 1861, in DeVane and Knickerbocker (eds.), *New Letters of Robert Browning*, 140.

[109] Quoted in G. M. Trevelyan, 'George Meredith', in Trevelyan, *Recreations of an Historian* (1919), 96–7.

[110] Allen, *Post-Prandial Philosophy*, ch. xvii ('On the Casino Terrace'); Orczy, *Chain of Life*, esp. chs. xx–xxiv; also *The Times*, 19 Feb. 1913, for an article about the Riviera's golf courses. The Hon. Jack Winston, hero of Williamson and Williamson, *The Lightning Conductor*, declares, 'The Pau links are the best on the Continent' (p. 62).   [111] Mallet, *Hope*, 275.

no one realizes it yet, is drawing to an end'.[112] From the late 1880s the Cook's tour of Egypt and Palestine was the more common experience, attracting some 5,000 or 6,000 annually. Cook's posters depicting the Sphinx and a genie transporting tourists on a magic carpet were familiar sights at railway stations and elsewhere.[113] 'We are going to Egypt,' says Emily Prentice, the glamorous young widow in John Oliver Hobbes (Pearl Craigie's) *The Sinner's Comedy* (1892). She is about to be married to a baronet and is planning her honeymoon: 'Egypt is *newer* than Paris,' she pronounces with panache.[114] When Robert Hichens visited Egypt, it was to recover his health, sapped by London living. Travelling down the Nile, he met E. F. Benson, the Archbishop of Canterbury's son who found fame with *Dodo: A Detail of the Day* (1893). This witty Society novel featured a heroine modelled on Margot Tennant, who would marry a future prime minister, Asquith, in 1894. Even more intriguing for Hichens, he encountered at the Hôtel de Louxor Lord Alfred Douglas and Reggie Turner; and it was on the strength of Benson's example and, through Douglas's introduction, coming to know Oscar Wilde in London that Hichens wrote *The Green Carnation*, his clever *roman-à-clef* about the homosexual aesthetes.[115] Egypt was the accidental spark of this particular fiction, therefore; but, years later, Hichens returned to a North African location (Biskra, the Algerian health resort), which became the source for his bestselling desert romance *The Garden of Allah* (1904).[116] All the while the British presence in Egypt was consolidated. During Lord Cromer's 'Over-Baring' proconsular rule, Cairo came to have its own Social season. So often was it described that Maurice Hewlett reckoned Cairo as 'written out' as Florence was for authors;[117] and when E. M. Forster passed down the Suez Canal en route to India in 1912 and glimpsed Egypt for the first time (he would return there with the Red Cross during the Great War), he felt that he had seen nothing new—'It was like sailing through the Royal Academy.'[118] Conan Doyle spent six months in Egypt in 1895–6, escorting his wife, who was seeking relief from tuberculosis. Membership of the Turf Club occupied some hours, but Doyle always had energy to burn and, when he fictionalized his Egyptian adventures in *The Tragedy of the Korosko* (1898), he drew on his voyage up the Nile by Cook's paddle steamer and on his interlude as war correspondent when the Sudan conflict reignited.[119]

[112] Forster, 'Wilfrid Blunt: The Later Diaries' (1920), in Forster, *Abinger Harvest*, 277.

[113] Nesbit, *Railway Children*, 64, 190. Cook's first tour of Egypt and the Holy Land was in 1869; and, having provided transport for the British Army during the Mahdi's revolt in 1884–5, he commissioned a new fleet of Nile steamers in 1886. Cook rather than Cromer was 'King of Egypt' to most locals; some even thought he was King of England. Cook's tourists were reckoned to spend over £500,000 annually there by the late 1880s and some £2m. by 1905. See Piers Brendon, *Thomas Cook: 150 Years of Popular Tourism* (1991), esp. chs. 7, 10, 12; John Pemble, *The Mediterranean Passion: Victorians and Edwardians in the South* (Oxford, 1987), 46–7.

[114] John Oliver Hobbes, *Some Emotions and a Moral* and 'The Sinner's Comedy' (1905), 182.

[115] See Hichens's Introduction to the 1949 reissue of *The Green Carnation*.

[116] See the Preface to the 24th edition (1914) of Robert Hichens, *The Garden of Allah* (1904).

[117] Maurice Hewlett, *Earthwork out of Tuscany* (1901), 9.

[118] To Florence Barger, [c.17] Oct. 1912, in Lago and Furbank (eds.), *Forster's Letters*, i. 140.

[119] Booth, *Doyle*, 207–11.

Doyle's story involves a party of Cook's tourists on their Nile voyage being seized by Dervishes and then rescued by a detachment of the Indian Camel Corps. Otherwise, it was a regular pattern for members of the British landed and professional classes to journey to Egypt to join friends and relations stationed there in the diplomatic or armed services. Thus, Hubert Henry Davies, in his play *A Single Man* (1910), almost casually mentions, to give verisimilitude to the characters Henry Worthington, a cavalry officer, and his wife, that they have been spending their winters in Egypt.[120] The Worthingtons are strait-laced, but Egypt was also associated with a raffish set. Their appetite for 'the fleshpots of Egypt' provided a convenient handle for novelists such as Marie Corelli (who never set foot in Egypt) to carve a reputation by denouncing the sybaritism of modern Society, to which its shameless members contributed by revelling in their nickname: the Liver Brigade.[121] Violet Markham, in her early twenties, was one socialite who sailed out to Egypt during the season in 1895, when 'the Mahdi still occupied Khartoum and Gordon's death remained unavenged'; nonetheless, 'I plunged headlong into what for me was a fantastic round of gaities . . . [and] danced and rode and flirted with the British officers of the Egyptian Army.'[122] Elinor Glyn was equally enraptured by her experiences, returning to write *The Reflections of Ambrosine* (1902) and including a lavish account of the Khedive's Ball in *His Hour* (1910).[123] Bigger themes, a comparison of British and Egyptian nationalisms and religions, were woven into the blackcloth of Hall Caine's controversial epic *The White Prophet* (1909).

During this period a modest amount of expatriation was caused by various forms of national hatred: fugitives from Britain's fogs, industrial urbanization, and social restraints. The person who chose to settle abroad, wanting to indulge some vice or to escape the past, was a stock figure of literature and based only too often on real models: 'those shiftless Europeans that are a moral eye-sore to the respectability of a foreign colony in almost every exotic part of the world', as Joseph Conrad described them.[124] Max Beerbohm was hardly in this disreputable class, but his talent for surprise was displayed in 1910 when, at the age of 38, he retired to Rapallo. He had discovered Italy four years earlier on an assignment to write articles for the *Daily Mail*. In 1910 he was newly married, disenchanted by London, and drawn to Italy by the economy of living and opportunities for quiet reflection; but it appeared an altogether mysterious removal, which Max sustained for forty-five years, during which he never learned Italian.[125] What has

---

[120] Davies, *Plays*, ii. 70.   [121] Corelli, *Sorrows of Satan*, 36–7.

[122] Markham, *Return Passage*, 45. See also Fanny, Lady Blunt, *My Reminiscences* (1918), ch. xviii; she was in Egypt at the same time, during the 1895–6 winter season, and attended a ball given by the Connaught Rangers in honour of the Duke of Cambridge. It cost, she was told, £2,000.

[123] Glyn, *Romantic Adventure*, ch. x.

[124] Joseph Conrad, *Nostromo* (1963), 49. Cf. Kathleen Bruce, reminiscing about her visit with some other art students to Italy in 1904: 'The joke amongst us was that no one settled in Florence unless he had been ejected from his own country . . .' (Kennet, *Self-Portrait*, 56).

[125] Cecil, *Max*, 290–2, 303–4, 332; S. N. Behrman, *Conversation with Max* (1960), 8, 11, 14, 147–8. At nearby Portofino were (briefly) Beerbohm's friends the artist William Nicholson and the author of *Elizabeth and her German Garden* (1898), Elizabeth von Arnim.

been called 'the British Literary Diaspora, the great flight of writers from England' is properly dated to the 1920s and 1930s.[126] More commonly, before 1914 they were travellers and visitors; yet, contacts were multiplying in the pre-war decade, such as a network of writers' clubs and other associations in the major cities of Europe, America, and the colonies. These benefited women writers as well as men, above all women who were young and single or who wanted to travel independently of husband and family. The architect of the International Association of Lyceum Clubs, Constance Smedley, described the previous position. For the favoured few 'a certain social position ensured introductions to one's embassy and possibilities of meeting foreign society in their own homes. But the girl whose resources were limited never got beyond a "pension" and had no opportunities of making contacts with the educated people of a country.'[127] An absence of connections was not necessarily a handicap. The anonymity of abroad allowed social invention. The poet Wilfred Owen, son of a railway clerk in Birkenhead, taught English at the Berlitz school in Bordeaux in 1913–14, where he pretended to be a baronet's son.[128]

Ill health still remained a principal cause of the compulsion to visit foreign lands, as it had in the case of Stevenson. Stella Benson was only the latest of a long line of British valetudinarians when she spent eighteen months in Switzerland, then in 1912 voyaged to the West Indies, of which she wrote in her first book, *I Pose* (1915). Writing was in the family—her aunt was the novelist Mary Cholmondeley; but social work in Hoxton and involvement in the suffrage movement and Women's Land Army shaped her character quite as much as did her later residence in California and China.[129] Illnesses apart, the main motives for travelling were mixed, in pursuit of cheap living, enchantment, education, and illicit pleasures. As for the first, Francis Gribble spent several years wandering and writing about Europe, chiefly Switzerland; and his memoirs were replete with mouth-watering details about the fantastic cheapness of Continental accommodation and meals in the late 1880s and 1890s.[130] As for the last, the complications of conducting a liaison at home drove many a married woman to Paris, noted Wilfrid Blunt, an experienced adulterer, in the 1860s. In 1890, while enjoying another affair, he recorded: 'English women are astonishing at Paris . . . they seem to have seen and done everything it is possible to see and do and some things which are impossible.'[131] In 1904 Arnold Bennett provided corroboration of this uninhibitedness of the English woman in Paris when he read

---

[126] Paul Fussell, *Abroad: British Literary Travelling between the Wars* (Oxford, 1982), 11.

[127] Smedley, *Crusaders*, 55.   [128] Jon Stallworthy, *Wilfred Owen: (Oxford, 1977)*, 95–6.

[129] On Stella Benson, *née* Anderson (1892–1933), see *DNB 1931–1940*, 13.

[130] Gribble, *Seen in Passing*, chs. xi–xii, esp. pp. 175–6. The cost of living was also a prime cause of expatriation. When Charles Tennyson, grandson of the poet, spent a period studying in Germany between leaving Eton and going up to Cambridge in 1899, he found that in Dresden, 'as in many German cities, there was a fairly numerous colony of British subjects who had retired there in order to make the best of small fixed incomes' (Tennyson, *Stars and Markets*, 80).

[131] Elizabeth Longford, *A Pilgrimage of Passion: The Life of Wilfrid Scawen Blunt* (1982), 62, 281.

about the arrest of an English couple for having, or attempting, sexual intercourse in the place de l'Archeêchê, although in this instance the couple were possibly newly-weds rather than adulterers.[132] Wilkie Collins's first sexual encounter occurred in Paris in the late 1830s, when he was aged 13. Afterwards, he generously placed his experience at the disposal of his friend Charles Dickens, his senior by twelve years, Collins acting as guide and procurer for Dickens's excursions through the Parisian brothel scene.[133] Not that there were no prostitutes in London (contemporaries estimated 80,000 and more);[134] rather, misconduct seemed more practicable and alluring when distance was placed between man and hearth. It was the prostitutes of Paris as well as the casinos of Monte Carlo that drew the composer Arthur Sullivan to make repeated Continental visits.[135]

Homosexuals too showed a marked preference for the Continent's greater freedoms (to express it idealistically) or for its greater distance from the reach of the law and access to catamites at lower cost (to express it pragmatically). When Oscar Wilde was released from prison, assumed the name Sebastian Melmoth and (as Blunt pleasantly put it) 'returned to Paris and to his dog's vomit', he was cheered at the thought of trysts with expatriate homosexuals such as 'dear Reggie Cholmondley, with his large faun's eyes and honey-sweet smile'.[136] Wilde did suffer setbacks. France was not so free and easy. 'A hotel-keeper at Monte Carlo had refused to receive him and his companion,' wrote Robert Sherard of a time *before* Wilde's public disgrace. After it, he was regularly turned away from restaurants and hotels, though at Dieppe this was attributed to the colony of English residents and visitors, who made it clear that they would withdraw their custom if Wilde was served.[137] A study of the seasonal migration patterns of homosexuals would be incomplete without a call at Capri, which it was de rigueur for them to visit. The Villa Cercola, where John Ellingham Brooks lived, was a regular summer haunt of Somerset Maugham and E. F. Benson.[138]

Abroad was the place to end it all when social shame beckoned. The Continental hotel room became the classic location for some of Britain's premier suicides. Major General Sir Hector (Fighting Mac) Macdonald led by example. A hero of the Gordon Highlanders, he had risen from the ranks and served valiantly throughout the Empire; but, rather than face court martial for alleged homosexual relations with native boys in Ceylon, he shot himself at the Hotel Regina in Paris.[139] Less dignified altogether was the fifth Marquess of Anglesey.

---

[132] Flower (ed.), *Bennett Journals*, 177 (31 May 1904).

[133] William M. Clarke, *The Secret Life of Wilkie Collins* (1988).

[134] Steven Marcus, *The Other Victorians: A Study of Sexuality and Pornography in Mid-Nineteenth-Century England* (1969), 8.

[135] Arthur Jacobs, *Arthur Sullivan: A Victorian Musician* (Oxford, 1986), 61, 171, 252, 306, 329.

[136] Blunt, *Diaries*, i. 375 (10 Dec. 1900); Wilde to Lord Alfred Douglas, 2? June 1897, in Hart-Davis (ed.), *Wilde Letters*, 289. Cholmondley (1865–1902), grandson of the first Lord Delamere, lived in Paris.

[137] Sherard, *Wilde*, 121–2, 240.   [138] Mackenzie, *Life and Times*, iv. 233.

[139] For the *Daily Express* report, see James McMillan, *The Way we Were 1900–1914* (1978), 234–5. On Macdonald (1853–1903), *Oxford DNB*.

'Toppy' to his friends, he perished at the Hotel Royale, Monte Carlo, in 1905. A pouting grotesque, in the six years of his marquessate he ran up debts to the tune of £544,000, mostly on self-adornment. His marriage to a cousin had been dissolved for non-consummation.[140] In 1908 Holbrook Jackson nicely summarized the impression which these sorts of British visitors made on their French hosts. He recounted how he had been sitting in a Paris café when he was offered *Le Matin* by a newspaper vendor: ' "No, thanks," I said forgetfully in English. His face lit up intelligently, and he offered me first the *Daily Mail*, then some mildly indecent picture postcards. He recognised my nationality'.[141]

Because the Mediterranean regions were also cradles of classical and Christian civilizations, a pattern of Homeric odyssey and holy mission was recurrent. The historian of these pilgrimages ultimately draws a negative conclusion about their impact: 'Too often their mental horizons contracted as their physical horizons widened, and they returned home settled rather than disturbed in their views about life and art, God and man, good and evil.'[142] *Punch* poked fun at the type of traveller who, after months of voyaging across Europe, was left with only the haziest of recollections of places visited: the man who said, 'Rome—Rome. Wasn't that the place where I bought the shocking bad cigars?'[143] A character in Guy Boothby's best-seller *The Red Rat's Daughter* (1899) complains both about how British tourists can be found everywhere across Europe and about their need for education in foreign cultures, 'so that they should not inquire the French for Eau de Cologne, or ask what sort of vegetable pâté de foie gras is when they encountered it upon their menus'.[144] This was a cruel caricature; yet, probably most tourists were not fluent in other languages and they travelled on the 'Continong' in the certainty that the British way of doing things was best. The Continent was, after all, foreign; and it was wise to be cautious about it. Saki's Reginald advised 'never be flippantly rude to any inoffensive, grey-bearded stranger that you may meet in pine forests or hotel smoking-rooms on the Continent. It always turns out to be the King of Sweden.'[145] Just as alarming, the Continent was teeming with Roman Catholics. Thankfully, a network of Anglican clergymen was in operation to safeguard English Protestant souls. The repertoire of Wilde's friend Reggie Turner, who was a superb mimic, included

---

[140] On Anglesey (1875–1905), see *Who Was Who, 1897–1916*, 18; the Hon. Vicary Gibbs (ed.), *The Complete Peerage* (1910), i. 141; *National Trust Magazine* (Spring 2001), 24.

[141] Holbrook Jackson, 'Immortal Russia' (1908), in Jackson, *Southward Ho!*, 170.

[142] Pemble, *Mediterranean Passion*, 274.

[143] Quoted in Rudyard Kipling, 'Some Aspects of Travel' (1914), in Kipling, *A Book of Words* (1928), 104. George Du Maurier was responsible for many cartoons ridiculing the English abroad: their linguistic incompetence and insular ways. See Ormond, *Du Maurier*, 311.

[144] Guy Boothby, *The Red Rat's Daughter* (1899), 17. The hero, Jack Browne, is heir to a soap millionaire ('Browne's Mimosa Soap, Fragrant and Antiseptic'); he owns a grand yacht and is well travelled, not just through the usual European playgrounds from Norway to Monte Carlo, but also in Egypt, India, Russia, and the Far East—much like the author himself.

[145] 'Reginald on the Academy', *Reginald* (1904), in Hector Hugh Munro, *The Complete Stories of Saki* (Ware, 1993), 11.

impersonating the mannerisms of English clerics aboard Italian railway carriages.[146] During his regular summer excursions to Italy and Switzerland, Samuel Butler plotted to avoid the English-frequented hotels for this reason, to escape the pressure to attend Sunday services. 'People ought to be allowed to leave their cards at church, instead of going inside,' he remarked sardonically.[147] The much-travelled civil servant and drama critic A. B. Walkley bore a similar grudge: 'I discovered that the worst hotels in Europe are in the towns which have an English resident chaplain; and so I became an enemy to the Church of England.'[148] Later he relented after reckoning the chaplain a symptom not the cause. The real explanation for the dire experience of these hotels was the uneatable food: 'that bad, banal old menu' of soup, cod, mutton cutlets, roast chicken, blancmange, and stewed rhubarb which the English clientele appeared to want wherever they went and for which, upon deeper reflection, Walkley blamed migratory flocks of spinsters and old maids rather than the chaplains. *Punch* identified the same culprits in its serialized story 'The Travelling Companions'. The first episode opens with our two heroes, a Somerset House civil servant and a City worker, both in their late twenties, at travel agents, where they overhear an old lady cross-examining the booking clerk 'whether there is an English service at Yodeldorf, and is it held in the hotel, and Evangelical, or High Church, and are the sittings free, and what Hymn-book they use?'[149] Voltaire might have joked long ago that England had seventy religions and only one sauce, but the Victorian lady was confident that that one was quite enough. 'How superior our English cooking is to what we used to get abroad,' reflects Mrs Mervyn in Florence Barclay's story *Guy Mervyn* in 1891.[150]

The intellectual was troubled by different challenges. 'You need not be much of a philologist to remember that travel is the same word as travail,' Walkley groaned, as he recited the usual 'miseries of holiday-making in foreign parts—lost luggage, quarrels with the Custom House, damp sheets, and so forth'. More appalling than the physical discomforts was the way in which the mind seized up:

This is partly caused by your unfamiliarity with a foreign language. You have to say not what you mean, but what you can. Your conversation with your fellow-creatures is not conditioned by your ideas but by your vocabulary. You are bursting with reflections on the eternal verities and the philosophy of the absolute, and all you can say (intelligibly) is 'pass the mustard' or 'two absinthes and a soda split'. But by degrees your ideas become as limited as your language. All the ordinary stimulants upon which, unconsciously, you depend for your intellectual well-being—the newspapers, the reviews, the chatter at the club—are absent, and you feel like Crusoe on his Island, with all the world to begin over

---

[146] S. N. Behrman, *Conversations with Max* (1960), 186.
[147] Jones (ed.), *Notebooks of Samuel Butler*, 342.   [148] Walkley, *Frames of Mind*, 206.
[149] *Punch*, 25 July 1891, 40. Part X of 'The Travelling Companions' features the moment at the Insel Hotel, Constance, when our heroes are confronted by the English chaplain and his wife; *Punch*, 10 Oct. 1891, 172–3. The author was probably the editor, Frank Burnand.
[150] Brandon Roy [Mrs Barclay], *Guy Mervyn* (1891), ii. 205.

again; you have, as it were, to fashion yourself a home-made intellectual equipment out of goat skins and a few articles saved from the wreck. So you are gradually reduced to imbecility. You even forget the rudiments of your own business. At home I am accustomed to review plays. But when I am abroad I cannot exercise the critical faculty, even over a Punch and Judy show. I have sat out the most inept and childish performances, entertainments by fifth-rate conjurors, bad plays by worse strolling players, and I have accepted the enthusiastic comments of the unsophisticated burgesses on either side of me without a murmur. I have become a mere country cousin in the pit.[151]

Still, the physical side could not be disregarded altogether when there was the water and sanitation to worry about. Thackeray, though long used to living on the Continent, especially in Paris, contracted malarial fever in Italy in 1853. This, when superimposed on existing problems he had with 'my hydraulic engine' (urinary disorders exacerbated by venereal disease), ruined his health for the rest of his life.[152] It was thus sensible to show precaution, of which Thomas Hardy was a master. In 1902 he advised Arthur Symons, who was planning to visit Constantinople, to 'take a bottle of quinine in concentrated form (like thin treacle). It kept us free from fever etc., on a Roman visit some years ago.'[153]

III

The number of cross-Channel passengers doubled between 1882 and 1904, from over half a million to over a million.[154] By comparison nowadays, such sums appear trivial;[155] but it is salutary to be reminded of the almost universal parochialness of life before railways and steamships and rising real wages multiplied other possibilities. In 1829, a year after Thomas Arnold took charge of Rugby School and saw the roll of pupils climb above 200, he wrote: 'More than half my boys never saw the sea, and never were in London, and it is surprising how the first of these disadvantages interferes with their understanding much of the ancient poetry, while the other keeps the range of their ideas in an exceedingly narrow compass.'[156] As the London–Birmingham railway was brought to Rugby, Arnold declared, 'I rejoice to see it, and think that feudality is gone for ever.'[157] That was to exaggerate the power of the railway as an engine for social equality; and for many more generations, the great majority of Britons who experienced foreign travel were drawn from the middle classes and above. 'A Social Butterfly' noted in 1904: 'Nowadays we are cosmopolitan, and the modern woman makes her trip to Paris and the Continent as a matter of course. Many of us will spend a fortnight or so at some French watering-place before we are off to

---

[151] Walkley, *Frames of Mind*, 225–6.   [152] Harden (ed.), *Thackeray's Letters*, pp. xxii, 322.
[153] Hardy to Arthur Symons, 18 Aug. 1902, in Purdy and Millgate (eds.), *Hardy Letters*, iii. 31.
[154] Pimlott, *Englishman's Holiday*, chs. xi–xii.
[155] In 1996 43 m. Britons travelled abroad (34.5 m. to western Europe); *The Times*, 6 Mar. 1997.
[156] Letter to J. T. Coleridge, 4 Nov. 1829, in Arthur Penrhyn Stanley, *Life and Correspondence of Thomas Arnold, D.D.* (1846), 147.   [157] Ibid. 507.

Scotland, or settle in the country for the autumn season.'[158] The plus point was apparent in the sartorial improvement of Society women, profiting from a transfer of French chic; the negative was apparent in the 'aristocratic, self-absorbed voices'[159] heard all over Europe from Menton to Malta, and from Paris to Palermo, which were redolent of the English sense of superiority. Browning, a Boanerges himself, had reported from Italy in the years before he settled there: 'As for the travelling English, they are horrible, and at Florence, unbearable . . . their voices in your ear at every turn . . . and such voices!'[160] Disruptions to this Society schedule were keenly felt, therefore. When Balfour tendered his resignation on 4 December 1905, a general election was imminent. The *Daily Express*'s Society columnist reported the consequences on 31 December:

The political situation at home has had a disastrous effect on the season at Cairo and on the Riviera. Earlier in the year arrangements had been made for the usual winter invasion of the south, but all this had been knocked on the head by the events of the last month. Villas at Mentone and San Remo have been placed hurriedly in the agents' hands, with instructions to accept the first offer, while arrangements with Biarritz hotels have had to be cancelled at the last moment.[161]

The patrician sort, with their imperious manners, no longer had the Continent to themselves, however. E. M. Forster was not patrician but he was precious when, aged 27 and touring the chateau country with his mother in 1906, he reported: 'France is full of horrible English.'[162] In February 1908 the Chancellor of the Exchequer and soon-to-be Prime Minister, Asquith, condoled with his daughter Violet, whose first impressions of Montana, Switzerland, where she was recuperating from a lung infection,

were not altogether alluring. I am surprised that there should be such a crowd of the vulgarer class of English encamped there now, when the holidays are or ought to be over. Margot [Asquith's second wife], however, declares that it is just the same at St Moritz where she got her best lessons in skating and other forms of 'winter sport' from bounders and 'trailers' of our own race.

Returning in January 1909, Violet Asquith this time complained that the train to Switzerland was full, with every seat taken; and she and her companions, who included Mrs Humphry Ward's son Arnold, were 'much disconcerted on finding a swarthy stranger was going to spend the night with us' in their salon-lits.[163]

By the Edwardian period it was commonplace for individuals to publish a record of foreign excursions in their curriculum vitae. One prolific writer of potboiler fiction from the 1890s, whose stories were often set in faraway places,

---

[158] *M.A.P.*, 30 July 1904, 127.   [159] Flower (ed.), *Bennett Journals*, i. 300 (14 Dec. 1908).
[160] Miller, *Browning*, 138–9.   [161] Quoted in McMillan, *Way we Were*, 108.
[162] To Edward Joseph Dent, 3 Oct. 1906, in Lago and Furbank (eds.), *Forster's Letters*, i. 85.
[163] H. H. Asquith to Violet Asquith, 5 Feb. 1908; Violet Asquith to Venetia Stanley, 26 Jan. 1909; Violet Asquith's diary, 6 Jan. 1912, in Mark Bonham Carter and Mark Pottle (eds.), *Lantern Slides: The Diaries and Letters of Violet Bonham Carter* (1996), 140, 174–5, 293.

was C. J. Cutcliffe Hyne. In *Who's Who* he styled himself both 'novelist and traveller' and, after summarizing his upbringing—he was born in 1866, the son of a clergyman, and educated at Bradford Grammar School and Clare College, Cambridge—he stated that he had 'travelled in Balearic Islands, Europe, Canary Islands, Congo Free State, Gold Coast, Arctic Sea, Russian Lapland, North America, Mexican Gulf Keys, Algeria, Tunisia, Southern Morocco, etc.; also much at sea; makes a point of covering at least 10,000 miles of new ground every year'.[164] In the same vein, boastful or simply enthusiastic, was the actor–manager Edward Terry. Vanity was consistent with his profession—the theatre he opened in 1887 he called Terry's—but, as well as being the author or adapter of several plays, he wrote about bullfighting in Spain and about Sinhalese theatre and, in *Who's Who*, listed his foreign travel thus: 'visited India, Australia, Ceylon, Mauritius, Egypt, Spain, Russia, Poland, Finland, Lapland, Norway, Spitzbergen, Iceland, Sweden, Denmark, Cape Colony, Natal, Transvaal, Orange River, Morocco, America, Canada, etc.'.[165] As for autobiographies, these automatically contained chapters which recounted impressions of foreign places and peoples. Sir Squire and Lady Bancroft, having retired from the stage in 1885, made regular visits to Continental spas, the Alps, the French Riviera, and Italy; and, though they did not entirely spare readers of their *Recollections* from their holiday notes, they were conscious that by 1909 foreign travel was a less exclusive privilege— 'In these days of easy travel, with such temptations as "A Week in Lovely Lucerne for Five Pounds", there is no need to dwell on trips to Norway or Continental watering-places . . . '.[166] This exhaustion, and from it a search for the still more exotic, had already been anticipated by a terminally bored Edward FitzGerald in 1846:

He [Tennyson] is come back from Switzerland rather disappointed, I am glad to say. How could such herds of gaping idiots come back enchanted if there were much worth going to see? I think that tours in Switzerland and Italy are less often published now than formerly; but there is all Turkey, Greece, and the East to be prostituted also; and I fear we shan't hear the end of it in our lifetimes. Suffolk turnips seem to me so classical compared to all that sort of thing.[167]

Thomas Hardy's first foreign travel was his honeymoon to Paris in 1874. In later years he and his wife, Emma, visited Belgium, the Netherlands, Switzerland, and Italy, and Emma several times popped across to Calais without him. France was 'the country I love most after our own—& the one I shall want to fly to perhaps

---

[164] *Who's Who* (1905), 827. Some of the sea travel had been as ordinary seaman, and some as a ship's doctor (Cutcliffe Hyne had read Natural Science at Cambridge). He listed his recreations thus: 'big game shooting, automobilism, an enthusiastic cave-hunter'. He lived at Kettlewell in North Yorkshire, a district popular with potholing and cave-exploring daredevils. On Hyne (1866–1944), see Sutherland, *Companion*, 315–16; Kemp et al.(eds.), *Edwardian Fiction*, 201.

[165] On Edward Terry (1844–1912), see *Who Was Who, 1897–1916*, 702. He sold his theatre in 1910, which became a cinema in 1912 and was demolished in 1923; Hartnoll (ed.), *Theatre Companion*, 815–16.

[166] The Bancrofts, *Recollections*, 296.

[167] To W. F. Pollock [1846], in J. M. Cohen (ed.), *Letters of Edward FitzGerald* (1960), 59–60.

some day or other when fighting comes on here, or our beautiful free land changes its character', she wrote in anxious assessment of the political situation in 1906.[168] Hardy himself told Lady Grove in 1908 how some young friends of his were now taking day excursions from Weymouth to Cherbourg—thus to 'acquire a smattering acquaintance with France & French scenes at 5s/- a head! It sounds trippy, but after all, they do see a foreign country for a few hours.'[169] When still working as a clerk in the late 1880s, Jerome K. Jerome and a friend from the office—'Arrys personified—'saved up all one winter, and at Easter we took a trip to Antwerp'. The next year they went to Boulogne; then, moving inland off the beaten track, discovered that 'one could spend a holiday abroad much cheaper than in England'.[170] *Punch* never tired of guying ''Arry Abroad', and he was still going strong in 1906, complete with loud check suit, when, in response to his guide who inquires 'Monsieur finds eet a vairy eenteresting old place, ees eet not?', 'Arry ('who *will* speak French') replies, 'Pas demi!'[171] A. B. Walkley was altogether dubious about the foreignness of these Bank Holiday foreign experiences: 'The seductive itineraries put forth in the railway companies' advertisements tempt us out of London only to find ourselves—whether it be at Brighton or on the boulevards at Antwerp or the Hague—among a crown of fellow Londoners.'[172] Still, it was impressive how far people were prepared to travel in order to misbehave. Arnold Bennett was put out during a Baltic cruise in 1913 to discover, on leaving Esbjerg, 'the boat *empesté* by a gang of English girls—probably clerks in some large establishment—doubtless quite decent in their own line. But terribly gauche, ungraceful, and unfeminine and *mal ficelées* by comparison with the Danish.'[173]

There was an evident working-class interest in foreign travel. When Virginia Stephen began to give literature and history classes to working-class women at Morley College in the Waterloo Road, south London, in 1905, she talked to them about Italy and passed around illustrations of places where she had made her own first visit in the previous spring. Thus stimulated, they 'told me about their Aunts who said that there was water in all the streets in Venice, and was it true, and the Clergyman at home (Yorkshire) had been to Rome, and shown them pictures of it'.[174] Writers took account of the comic potential in this. In *The Railway Children* (1906), when the Russian refugee is deposited at the station and the locals are mystified by his language, a figure of authority steps forward: ' "Sounds like French to me", said the Station Master, who had once been to Boulogne for the day.'[175] In *Esther Waters* (1894) the bookmaker William Latch describes to Esther,

---

[168] Emma Hardy to Rebekah Owen, 26 Dec. 1906, in Millgate (ed.), *Emma and Florence Hardy*, 34.

[169] Hardy to Lady Grove, 25 Aug. 1908, in Purdy and Millgate (eds.), *Hardy Letters*, iii. 330.

[170] Jerome, *Life and Times*, 148.

[171] *Punch*, 3 Oct. 1906, 241. Cf. the verses in *Punch*, 17 Aug. 1895, 81, in response to an article in the *Echo* on how 'Harrys' bring discredit to Britain by flaunting their supposed superiority over foreigners when taking trips abroad.   [172] Walkley, *Frames of Mind*, 213.

[173] Flower (ed.) *Bennett Journals*, ii. 67 (29 Aug. 1913).

[174] Letter to Violet Dickinson, Feb. 1905, in Nicolson and Banks (eds.), *Flight of the Mind*, 177.

[175] Nesbit, *Railway Children*, 66.

the illiterate servant-girl by whom he has fathered a child, the progress of his first marriage:

'We first went to Boulogne, that's in France; but every one speaks English there, and there's a nice billiard-room handy, where all the betting men came in of an evening . . . Then we went on to Paris. The race-meetings is very 'andy—I will say that for Paris—half an hour's drive and there you are.'

'Did your wife like Paris?'

'Yes, she liked it pretty well—it is all the place for fashion, and the shops is grand; but she got tired of it too, and we went to Italy.'

'Where's that?'

'That's down south. A beast of a place—nothing but sour wine, and all the cookery done in oil, and nothing to do but seeing picture-galleries. I got that sick of it I could stand it no longer, and I said, ' "I've 'ad enough of this. I want to go home, where I can get a glass of Burton and a cut from the joint, and where there's a 'orse worth looking at." ',[176]

The quantity of lower-middle and working-class travellers taking foreign excursions should not be overlooked, therefore, though it would be discreditable to take Mr and Mrs Latch as typical. The Manchester Society of Arts first arranged for artisans to visit the Paris Exhibition in 1855; and in 1858 Dr F. J. Furnivall, a co-founder of the Working Men's College, had taken a group of working men to Normandy.[177] Such expeditions became more common from the 1880s, when various clubs, usually connected with religious and educational institutions, included working-class people in their parties. Thomas Okey, a basket-maker, was one who benefited: he later rose to become the first Professor of Italian at Cambridge. His original visit to Italy, in 1888, was inspired by a small group—'four or five clerks, schoolmasters, artisans, or shop-assistants'—who met at Toynbee Hall (established in 1884) in Whitechapel to read and talk about the Italian republican Mazzini. Their idea was to make a secular pilgrimage to Mazzini's grave at Genoa; this was then broadened to include Florence and Pisa. Eighty-one men and women formed the party who made this tour, travelling via Antwerp, Brussels, Lucerne, and Milan.[178] From it arose the Toynbee Travellers' Club, with its own constitution: 'The object of the club is not merely to promote pleasant trips, but its aim is educational, and its basis mutual helpfulness.' Subscriptions were 2s. per annum. All were enjoined to attend lectures or to undertake directed reading about the country it was proposed to visit. In 1892 the Club comprised about 200 members. Honorary associates included persons elected for special service to the Club, such as the Italian Minister of Public Instruction, Professor Villari, who had been present at Elizabeth Barrett Browning's funeral in 1861.[179]

---

[176] George Moore, *Esther Waters* (1962), 194.   [177] Benzie, *Furnivall*, 54.

[178] T. Okey, *A Basketful of Memories* (1930), ch. viii; Asa Briggs and Anne Macartney, *Toynbee Hall: The First Hundred Years* (1984), 31–2, which notes in point of fact that the first foreign excursion of 'Toynbee pilgrims' occurred in 1887, when the Warden, the Revd Samuel Barnett, took a party of eight to Belgium.

[179] See Robert Browning's description to John Forster, July 1861, in DeVane and Knickerbocker, *New Letters of Robert Browning*, 137. Pasquale Villari (1827–1917) was awarded the honorary DCL by the

Concessionary rates were negotiated from railway and ferry companies and hotels; and members could reimburse the Club's treasurer in instalments. Extraordinary economies were achieved—£5 per person for a week in Paris; the same for a week in Belgium (Antwerp, Brussels, Waterloo, Ghent, and Bruges); and £9 18s. plus 30s. or £2 incidental expenses for an eighteen-day tour which took in Lucerne, Milan, Verona, Venice, and Lugano, in 1889.[180] Each package included guided visits to galleries, museums, and special sites.

Toynbee was a pioneer in mutual travel. Among its famous imitators was the Workmen's Travelling Club, which offered bargain fares to members of trade unions, cooperative societies, and friendly societies.[181] That was in 1902, by which date example had spread widely. Two members of the Toynbee Travellers' Club—one was Thomas Okey—organized a nineteen-day Italian excursion (including Venice, Verona, Padua, Mantua, Pavia, and Milan) in September 1891 for twenty-seven members of the Art Workers' Guild, painters, sculptors, etchers, brass and iron workers, wood-carvers, and architects, who each paid under £13. Joining them was Bernard Shaw. He was not impressed. He reported to William Morris about 'the fearful solitude created by these 27 men, most of whom have taken up art as the last refuge of general incompetence'; then regretted this sneer—'I doubt if this remark will bear examination: I suppose it is in the nature of such an expedition that we should all appear fools to one another . . . '. Michael Holroyd speculates that Shaw's peevishness was caused by a surfeit of staring at ornate buildings and by his 'having to travel as a devout Catholic under a vow in order to obtain vegetarian meals'.[182] The verdicts of the twenty-seven about what it was like to be bottled up with Shaw for nineteen days are not recorded; and Shaw so far set aside his reservations as to rejoin the Art Workers' Guild in 1894 for an inspection of Florence, Genoa, and Milan.[183]

The Toynbee model also appealed to church organizations, particularly those in which congregational participation was a force. For them the Middle East rather than the Mediterranean beckoned. Cecil Roberts, born in Nottingham in 1892, recalled his local Wesleyan minister annually conducting a month's pilgrimage to Palestine. Roberts's neighbours, the baker Mr Lane and his wife, saved for twenty years to go. On their return, 'they were never quite the same again' and 'whenever anyone spoke of Mr Lane he added "—who's been to the Holy Land" '.[184] Involving still greater numbers were the polytechnics, which by 1903 were organizing foreign holidays for over 10,000 persons annually. It was through the Regent Street secretary, Robert Mitchell, that visits to the Paris Exhibition were first arranged for 2,100 men and 400 women in 1889, costing £2 7s. 6d. each. Polytechnics provided further education for persons mostly aged between 16 and

---

University of Oxford in 1904. He had been involved in the 1848 revolutions in Naples, his birthplace in 1827. A historian, several of his books were published in English translation, on Machiavelli's life and times (1878–83), on Savonarola (1860), and on the history of Florence (1893), where he then lived.

[180] *Review of Reviews* (June 1892), 619–25.   [181] Briggs and Macartney, *Toynbee Hall*, 32.
[182] Holroyd, *Shaw*, i. 219.   [183] Ibid. 314.   [184] Roberts, *Years of Promise*, 16.

25, in ordinary employment; but their travel excursions were not confined to polytechnic students. These aimed to create bonds of fellowship and to stimulate study of foreign cultures more broadly. They also extended the travel outside the European mainland: to Norway, Madeira, Morocco, and, in 1893, to the Chicago World's Fair. The Norwegian trip, in 1891, was the first to involve Henry Simpson Lunn, a former medical missionary in India who, having been invalided home, became a founder of cooperative travel for Free Church ministers and their congregations before establishing an agency in 1909, specializing in Alpine sports holidays.[185]

With these examples before them, newspapers and journals dedicated to encouraging popular self-improvement spread the message further.[186] Robert Roberts remembers his father, a corner-shopkeeper in a Salford slum district, taking *Harmsworth's Self-Educator* in fortnightly instalments and, when not otherwise incapacitated by drink, being particularly drawn to the foreign-language section. This contained parallel columns of words in Latin and their modern European language equivalents, which he would make his family learn and recite.[187] The Robertses never ventured abroad to try out their random vocabulary; but W. T. Stead's *Review of Reviews* had already promoted home exchanges as a means of acquiring foreign languages. The first occurred in 1898, when two French women stayed with a Gloucester family, who in turn visited France in 1899. This scheme expanded when a French schools inspector and a German bookseller began acting as corresponding secretaries; in addition, there developed a more formal system of holiday language courses in Europe, costing between £11 and £12, including travel, board, and lodging, for a month's instruction. *T.P.'s Weekly*, too, offered advice through articles such as 'Continental Holidays: Notes for the Inexperienced—and Experienced'. One correspondent, a shop assistant, wrote: 'My income is 40s. a week. I wish to go abroad with my wife this summer for a ten days' tour. Is it possible to do so?'; to which the paper responded by recommending a visit to Bruges at a cost of £2 16s. per person, all in.[188] A similar sum, £2 12s. 3d., took James Elroy Flecker from London to Chiasso in 1908. He reported home, having advanced further: 'We get rooms for a franc a night, and travel third class, and are having a very extensive and pleasant journey. My itinerary has been Perugia, Assisi, Rome, Viterbo, Orvieto, Siena, San Gemignano, by foot; Volterra, Cecina, Montefescali, Usciano, drive to Monte Olivito, Monte Pulciano, Cortona, Arezzo, whence I write.'[189] In this light, John Middleton Murry and a schoolfriend, both aged 17, were perhaps

---

[185] Ethel M. Hogg, *Quintin Hogg* (1904), 231–5; Pimlott, *Englishman's Holiday*, 169–70, 176.

[186] *Review of Reviews* (Aug. 1891), 181–4, (June 1892), 628–9.

[187] Robert Roberts, *A Ragged Schooling: Growing up in the Classic Slum* (Manchester, 1978), 31–2.

[188] *T.P.'s Weekly*, 24 July 1903, 228; 31 July 1903, 273, 276; 21 Aug. 1903, 372; 4 Mar. 1904, 308; 1 Apr. 1904, 436; 29 Apr. 1904, 567–8; 3 June 1904, 728; 9 Dec. 1910, 767. On the front page of the first issue of the *Daily Mail*, 4 May 1896, Cook's offered a week in Switzerland at Whitsun for 5 guineas, and another agency a weekend in Ostend for 10s. 6d. first class, 8s. 6d. second class; Mackenzie, *Life and Times*, ii. 146.

[189] Hodgson, *Flecker*, 126.

over-budgeting when they saved up £9 between them for a fortnight's walking holiday in Brittany in 1907. This was Murry's first foreign adventure. He, now a scholar at Christ's Hospital, was a former board school pupil from Peckham, the son of a lowly Inland Revenue clerk who had himself begun as a messenger-boy.[190] By contrast, Philip Gibbs's origins were firmly middle-class but, as the fifth child of seven of a Board of Education civil servant, money was not infinite and, when Gibbs married in 1898, his income was £120 per annum 'with perhaps a few extra guineas earned by a fairy tale or an article'. In his autobiography he was 'astonished to remember' that out of that sum he and his wife during their first year of marriage could afford a fortnight in Paris, 'and were so rich at the end of it that we bought presents for our family'.[191]

It is plain, therefore, that from the 1890s a greater diversity of Britons travelled abroad than is generally supposed; and, while the majority never left Britain's shores, foreign places and peoples were made more familiar by travellers' lectures and lantern-slides and, from the Edwardian period, by cinema projection. There were myriad accounts, too, transmitted via relations and friends, from those who served with the armed forces or who had emigrated, although these were generally to extra-European destinations, the British Empire and the Americas foremost.[192] Britain being the workshop of the world, there were a good many firms that dispatched their employees on foreign contracts, and individuals with marketable skills who, either when employment was short at home or through sheer adventure and curiosity, worked their way from country to country. The artisan engineer John Burns wandered from 'Moscow to Madrid' in this way;[193] and it was because of his father working as a civil engineer in Spain that the heart-throb actor Lewis Waller had been born in Bilbao in 1860.

The role played by novelists, poets, and playwrights in the volume and strength of cultural transmissions should not be lost sight of. Writers were in part responsible for the image of Abroad, as a fantasy Ruritania of the kind that Anthony Hope depicted in *The Prisoner of Zenda* (1894), in which a lookalike Englishman gentleman takes the place of the king and not only defeats serpentine intrigue but also gives to the foreign country a demonstration of good government based on upright character and a clear sense of honour and justice.[194] Nor did the real world seem so different when a distinguished line of foreign authors, Turgenev, Hugo, and Zola, who were in conflict with illiberal stances taken by

[190] Lea, *Murry*, 13.   [191] Gibbs, *Pageant*, 27.
[192] The historian A. L. Rowse, (b. 1903) well described in his autobiography the dispersed communities of Cornish miners in America, Canada, South Africa, and Australia, maintaining links with their home villages, by letter and exchange of press cuttings; indeed, he argued, Cornish people often knew what was going on in these parts of the world rather better than what was happening in London and 'up country'; *A Cornish Childhood* (1975), 34–5, 39–40, 62.   [193] *DNB 1941–1950*, 121–4, for Burns (1858–1943).
[194] *The Prisoner of Zenda* was subtitled 'Being the History of Three Months in the Life of an English Gentleman'. The plot against the legitimate king is masterminded by his brother Black Michael, who is eventually killed and superseded as lead villain by Rupert of Hentzau: 'Wicked men I have known in plenty, but Rupert Hentzau remains unique in my experience.' He is left alive at the story's end, conveniently paving the way for a sequel, *Rupert of Hentzau* (1898).

their own governments, found sanctuary in Britain. Following numerous rash constitutional experiments, too many foreigners appeared to settle for regimes that W. S. Gilbert dubbed 'Despotism tempered by Dynamite'.[195] For most Englishmen it was axiomatic that the British political system was envied for its liberties and stability. Commercially and imperially, Britain's star was in the ascendant for the greater part of the century; and, socially, a strong culture had developed around religious toleration and personal freedom. National self-abuse might be practised by an awkward squad of British writers, such as Ernest Dowson, who bemoaned the philistine ascendancy;[196] yet the Briton abroad generally felt no inferiority. Florence Barclay, best-selling author of *The Rosary* (1909), expressed this perfectly. Like her heroine, Mrs Barclay had been to Paris, Switzerland, and the Riviera, had heard the roar of Niagara in North America, climbed the Great Pyramid in Egypt, and wandered throughout Palestine in 'the footsteps of the greatest human life ever lived'. But there was no place like home:

The white cliffs of Dover gradually became more solid and distinct, until at length they rose from the sea, a strong white wall, emblem of the undeniable purity of England, the stainless honour and integrity of her throne, her church, her parliament, her courts of justice, and her dealings at home and abroad, whether with friend or foe. 'Strength and whiteness', thought Jane as she paced the steamer's deck; and after a two years' absence her heart went out to her native land.[197]

Simple- (or single-) minded patriotism was not the preserve of the provincial and uncultured. Fanny, Lady Blunt—wife of Sir John Blunt, one-time Consul-General in the Levant—was born in 1840 in Therapia, a suburb of Constantinople, where her father represented the East India Company; and her mother's family was Persian in origin. She spoke Turkish, considered herself a friend of the country, and wrote a well-received book, *The People of Turkey* (1878); yet she was quite clear about their place and hers in the scheme of things. 'In semi-savage countries like Turkey', she wrote, 'it is generally recognised that the love of honours, decorations, and money earned with the least possible trouble will get the better of the patriotism of the majority.' Lady Blunt preferred 'to stand on the merits of my English nationality, for like all Britishers who are foreign or colonial born, I love the grand old country which has produced the greatest nation of the world, and claim it for my own'.[198] This inherent Little Englander psychology and uncomplicated patriotism would flourish even more intensely during the inter-war period when fascism and communism swept across the Continent. 'Not until I am safely back in England do I ever feel that the world is quite sane,' wrote

---

[195] W. S. Gilbert, 'Utopia Limited; or, The Flowers of Progress' (1893), in Gilbert, *Savoy Operas*, 566.
[196] See Flower and Maas (eds.), *The Letters of Ernest Dowson, passim*.
[197] Florence Barclay, *The Rosary* (1925), 125–6, 138. Cf. Mrs Barclay's letters to her mother, written in 1881 when coming to the end of her tour of Europe and the Holy Land: 'Before we reach England again I shall have been in *fifteen* countries, but I have not seen one which can be compared with our little island' (*The Life of Florence Barclay: A Study in Personality*, by 'one of her daughters' (1921), 87).
[198] Lady Blunt, *Reminiscences*, pp. ix–x, 210.

J. B. Priestley. 'Never once have I arrived in a foreign country and cried "This is the place for me". I would rather spend a holiday in Tuscany than in the Black Country, but if I were compelled to choose between living in West Bromwich or Florence, I should make straight for West Bromwich.'[199] Writing in the *Westminster Gazette* in the 1890s, Grant Allen had ridiculed the Englishman's undifferentiated notion of Abroad and his smug superiority to all contained therein.[200] As a radical rationalist, he had a well-rehearsed litany of faults and follies to reel off, declaiming against the aristocratic land monopoly, hereditary rule through the House of Lords, an unscientific education system, and women's thraldom. 'We have a Moloch in England to whom we sacrifice much,' he averred. 'And his hateful name is Vested Interest.'[201] London, too, he deplored as a 'squalid village', the result of municipal misgovernment;[202] yet, in the final analysis Allen was led by his heart: 'I just *love* England.' He counted Italy's towns as one of the two 'great glories of Europe', but the other was England's countryside. Allen understood Browning's yearning when he too was domiciled in Italy. 'Oh, to be in England now that April's there?'

At Perugia, last spring, through weeks of tramontana, how one yearned for the sight of yellow English primroses! Not love England, indeed! Milton's England, Shelley's England; the England of the skylark, the dog-rose, the honeysuckle! Not love England, forsooth! Why, I love every flower, every blade of grass in it . . . No son of the soil can love England as those love her very stones who have come from newer lands over sea to her ivy-clad church-towers, her mouldering castles, her immemorial elms, the berries on her holly, the may in her hedgerows. Are not all these bound up in our souls with each cherished line of Shakespeare and Wordsworth? Do they not rouse faint echoes of Gray and Goldsmith? Even before I ever set foot in England, how I longed to behold my first cowslip, my first foxglove! And now, I have wandered through the footpaths that run obliquely across English pastures, picking meadowsweet and fritillaries, for half a lifetime, till I have learned by heart every leaf and petal. You think because I dislike one squalid village—'The Wen', stout English William Cobbett delighted to call it—I don't love England. You think because I see some spots on the sun of the English character, I don't love Englishmen. Why, how can any man who speaks the English tongue, and boasts one drop of English blood in his veins, not be proud of England? England, the mother of poets and thinkers; England, that gave us Newton, Darwin, Spencer; England, that holds in her lap Oxford, Salisbury, Durham; England of daisy and heather and pine-wood![203]

All this from one who was Canadian-born and a self-styled Celt! The historian needs to show caution, therefore, about assuming that a writer's foreign experiences and sympathies would erase or count more than an Anglican tradition and loyalty. 'Might a nation go on being great for ever? If so, are *we* that nation?', Allen asked; then answered that 'England stands where she does, because God put her there; and until He invents a new order of things (which

---

[199] J. B. Priestley, *English Journey* (1934), 416.   [200] Allen, *Post–Prandial Philosophy*, 165–72.
[201] Ibid. 103.   [202] *Punch*, 9 Sept. 1893, 113.   [203] Allen, *Post-Prandial Philosophy*, 174–5.

may, of course, happen any day—as, for example, if aerial navigation came in) she must continue . . .'. And that place was at 'the centre of civilisation'.[204]

IV

Familiarity with Europe and its literature, nonetheless, seemed a necessary part of the author's education, if he was to advance from minor to major status and to persuade the critics and cultivated public to take him seriously. This involved more than making an excursion to Dieppe, Boulogne, or other Anglicized resort. Douglas Goldring felt this about Arnold Bennett, that he had been driven 'to prove . . . that he is *not a provincial*'. That was why he first moved to London—

and from London it is but a step to Paris, that paradise of the clever English provincial dissatisfied with his environment, that disastrous finishing school for second-rate minds. Mr Bennett (to judge entirely from his books) got Paris badly; but it had the effect of putting an edge on his technique. When, in a literary sense, he returned to his native province, he did so with a new power of presentation, a new detachment, and a clearer sense of values.[205]

The culture business had not impressed Jerome K. Jerome. Paris, he felt, was 'a much over-rated city, and half the Louvre ought to be cleared out and sent to a rummage sale'. Its streets, he added, 'are much too wide and straight: well adapted, no doubt, to the shooting down of citizens . . . but otherwise uninteresting'. It was the same for languages: 'Of course, if you want to argue, more study is needful; but for all the essentials of a quiet life, a working knowledge of twenty verbs and a hundred nouns, together with just a handful of adjectives and pronouns, can be made to serve.'[206] Jerome omitted several further uses to which a foreign language could be put. One was to make confessions or exchange confidences in the security that the lower orders would not rumble what was going on. Gladstone used Italian when recording in his diary his shame at the feelings aroused in him by reading pornography and by finding attractive the prostitutes he was endeavouring to reform.[207] Likewise, a foreign language was ideal for purveying smut. In 1885 George Du Maurier described to a chum how he had been seated close to Lily Langtry in church when they were guests at a wedding: 'I had a good study of Mrs Langtry, back, front & both profils—neither Poynter nor Millais have done her justice. Si Madame L. était Eve, et moi Adam, je n'aurais pas attendre qu'elle m'offre la pomme . . .'.[208] Barrie makes this trick backfire in *Mary Rose* (1920) when Mary Rose and her husband, Simon, on a

---

[204] Allen, *Post-Prandial Philosophy*, 44–52.
[205] Goldring, *Reputations*, 152–3. Bennett's wife thought much the same: see Marguerite Bennett, *My Arnold Bennett* (1931), 44–5, 53.   [206] Jerome, *Life and Times*, 148–9.
[207] H. C. G. Matthew, *Gladstone 1809–1874* (Oxford, 1986), 92; id. (ed.), *The Gladstone Diaries*, iv–xiii (Oxford, 1974–94) iv: 1848–54, 35–7.
[208] Letter to T. Armstrong, 28 Nov. 1885, quoted in Ormond, *Du Maurier*, 387.

remote Outer Hebridean isle, are trying to manage their boatman Cameron, a 'gawky youth of twenty'. He, while helpful, makes it plain that he is not an inferior, whereupon Mary Rose advises, 'Simon, do be careful. If you want to say anything to me that is dangerous, say it in French.' The following results:

MARY ROSE. *Prenez garde, mon brave!*
SIMON. *Mon Dieu! Qu'il est un drôle!*
MARY ROSE. *Mais moi, je l'aime; il est tellement*—What is the French for an original?
SIMON. That stumps me.
CAMERON. Colloquially *coquin* might be used, though the classic writers would
    probably say simply *un original*.
SIMON [*with a groan*]. Phew, this is serious. What was that book you were reading,
    Cameron, while I was fishing?
CAMERON. It iss a small Euripides I carry in the pocket, Mr Blake.
SIMON. Latin, Mary Rose!
CAMERON. It may be Latin, but in these parts we know no better than to call it Greek.[209]

It emerges that Cameron, a crofter's son, is studying at Aberdeen University; his ambition is to enter the ministry. He turns his hand to anything during vacations to pay for his fees. Barrie conducted this situation with humour but, from his own humble background, he was sensitive to this generally unpleasant habit of deploying a foreign language to assert a superiority over those who had not acquired it. In *What Every Woman Knows* (1908) an ex-railway porter who has worked his way through university to become an MP feels slighted when the Tory toff whom he has just defeated offers his congratulations in French.[210]

Jerome K. Jerome was deliberately deprecating about his own abilities. He could speak and understand foreign languages well enough, yet liked to play up to the vulgarian image his detractors pinned to him. This suited the aesthetic set who cultivated a snob humour about upstart accomplishment. Robert Hichens caught this nicely in *The Green Carnation*, in an exchange between Lord Reggie Hastings (Lord Alfred Douglas) and Esmé Amarinth (Wilde):

[LORD REGGIE]. How horrible this spread of education is!...I am told there is a
    Scotch hairdresser in Bond Street who speaks French like a native.
[ESMÉ]. Of Scotland or France?[211]

The running joke of Somerville and Ross's *In the Vine Country* (1892), based on articles they wrote for the *Lady's Pictorial*, which had covered their expenses of a fortnight in France, is that they upset their hosts by speaking French so atrociously.[212] It was simply not normal for a patriotic Englishman to speak a foreign language fluently, especially French; and P. G. Wodehouse would later depict Monty Bodkin's discomfort on the terrace of the Hotel Magnifique at Cannes when into his face 'there had crept a look of furtive shame, the shifty hangdog

---

[209] Barrie, *Plays*, 561–2.   [210] Ibid. 333.   [211] Hichens, *Green Carnation*, 22.
[212] Collis, *Somerville and Ross*, 93.

look which announces that an Englishman is about to talk French'.[213] Doubtless, there were many writers who resembled H. G. Wells's Mr Polly, for whom the study of French was 'pursued but never satisfactorily overtaken'.[214] Then there were writers who, while schooled in foreign languages, never betrayed the slightest deviation from their native nostrums. Charlotte M. Yonge was educated in French, Spanish, German, Italian, and Greek, all without exciting an intellectual curiosity or subversion of her domestic concerns; indeed, her biographer comments, 'it is odd that this most insular of writers should have had so through a grounding in foreign languages'.[215] Yonge travelled abroad just once. Accompanied by her maid and by her younger brother and his wife, she went in 1869 to Normandy to stay with the octogenarian savant François Guizot, who had been Minister of Education and Prime Minister under Louis-Philippe. The reason was the desire of the statesman's daughter Mme Guizot de Witt to translate Yonge's work into French, a compliment that Yonge would reciprocate by translating hers into English. Guizot himself shared Yonge's enthusiasm of providing moral education for the masses, as a counter-revolutionary strategy, though it is doubtful whether she approved of his having also translated Gibbon into French. Yonge's visit to the Guizots was conditional on one important factor: that their family life adhered to her ideal English model. They were 'Protestants, and devout Protestants at that, who held family prayers every day and Sunday services conducted in Madame de Witt's boudoir. For all her High Church principles and her dislike of Nonconformity, Charlotte could never have felt at her ease in a Papistical household.'[216]

The Continent was thus mostly excommunicated from Yonge's mind. The same can be said for A. C. Benson. It must be counted an egregious example of English eccentricity—or of English snubs to foreigners—that Benson was appointed president of the Modern Languages Association in 1905–6, because his knowledge of foreign languages and interest in foreign countries were strictly limited. 'Words of a foreign language', Benson told Maurice Baring, 'to him were symbols, like the figures of a Noah's Ark, whereas in English every word fired a train of association, and sometimes a single word was enough to redeem a whole page.'[217] A master at Eton before becoming a Cambridge don, Benson had been three or four times to Italy and Spain and, in spite of an antipathy to

---

[213] P. G. Wodehouse, *The Luck of the Bodkins* (1935), ch. 1, quoted in Frances Donaldson, *P. G. Wodehouse: A Biography* (1982), 31.

[214] Wells attributed his difficulties to his schooling at Mr Thomas Morley's Academy in Bromley High Street: 'Old Tommy taught French out of a crammer's textbook, and, in spite of the fact that he had on several occasions visited Boulogne, he was quite unable to talk in that elusive tongue . . . He crippled my French for life.' Nonetheless, Wells relearnt French by reading Voltaire for himself in the early 1880s and through visits to France thereafter, though he always struggled to speak and understand it when spoken. He also acquired traveller's Spanish, Italian, and German, only to forget them as soon as the occasion lapsed. Wells, *Experiment in Autobiography*, i. 30, 91, 137–8.

[215] Georgina Battiscombe, *Charlotte Mary Yonge: The Story of an Uneventful Life* (1943), 54.

[216] Ibid. 129–30. On Guizot (1787–1874) see Douglas Johnson, *Guizot: Aspects of French History, 1787–1874* (1974).   [217] Quoted in Newsome, *On the Edge of Paradise*, 88.

philathleticism, he had climbed in Switzerland; but for the last thirty years of his life, between 1895 and 1925, he went abroad only once more, to Italy under doctor's orders in 1907. His friend Percy Lubbock explained: 'foreign ways disagreed with him, foreign tongues baffled him—he preferred to stay at home'.[218]

There were authors who were neither linguistically incompetent nor culturally blinkered. Henry James was a spectacular specimen. When Mrs Humphry Ward was in his company in Italy,

I realised perhaps more fully than ever before the extraordinary range of his knowledge and sympathies. Roman history and antiquities, Italian art, Renaissance sculpture, the personalities and events of the Risorgimento, all these solid *connaissances* and many more were to be recognised perpetually as rich elements in the general wealth of Mr James's mind.

He was fluent in Italian, of course; and, as for his French, Mrs Ward was given an illustration of its perfection by the novelist Paul Bourget. Bourget, adept at reading and speaking English, had yet been baffled by the technical terms Kipling deployed in 'McAndrew's Hymn' and he could get nowhere with the poem, whereupon James straight away put it into 'vigorous idiomatic French—an extraordinary feat'.[219] Mrs Ward herself knew French, German, Italian, and Spanish; she also had Latin, and in 1886, when her 10-year-old son was grappling with the classics, she 'began seriously to read Greek'. Before she became a novelist, she did a great deal of reviewing of French and Spanish books for the *Pall Mall Gazette* and of other foreign books for *The Times*: 'Three or four volumes of these books a week is about all I can do, and that seems to go no way,' she complained.[220]

Another in the polyglot league was George Eliot, who, in addition to Latin, Greek, and Hebrew, had 'a thorough knowledge of French, German, Italian, and Spanish'. Still, while she 'could talk in each language correctly', this was 'with difficulty',[221] whereas Jerome K. Jerome's German was more than passable after living there for a couple of years. Jerome found much to admire about the German people and way of life. He was well travelled elsewhere, too: in the Low Countries, Scandinavia, Switzerland, Italy, Russia. But he felt it right not to make too big a thing about it, while stressing that the literary establishment who pontificated about an elite of British and Continental authors really did not know the facts. At a time when he was being roundly abused in literary journals at home, he found that abroad he was everywhere hailed. In Germany his *Three Men on the Bummel* (1900) was 'officially adopted as a school reading-book'; and in Russia he was mobbed by fans at St Petersburg station.[222] Of the early 1900s, he recalled, his friend Eden Phillpotts's work was read widely abroad,

especially in Germany and Switzerland. Zangwill was known everywhere in literary circles. Barrie, to my surprise, was almost unknown. I was speaking of him once at a party

[218] Lubbock (ed.), *Benson Diary*, 37, 182.
[219] Mrs Humphry Ward, *A Writer's Recollections* (1919), 325–6.
[220] Janet Penrose Trevelyan, *The Life of Mrs. Humphry Ward* (1923), 37, 46.
[221] Stephen, *George Eliot*, 196–7.   [222] Jerome, *Life and Times*, 85, 151.

Caledonian Market in 1916, Arnold Bennett encountered 'one well-dressed man [who] had never heard of Balzac'.[231] Probably the most read Continental author in Britain in the nineteenth and early twentieth centuries was Alexandre Dumas—Dumas père—with his Musketeers cycle and *Count of Monte Cristo*, written in the 1840s. He had been a formula writer, a true entrepreneur who employed ghosts, euphemistically called secretaries and scribes, to maintain the Dumas output.[232] In some measure, the British success enjoyed by Dumas was a case of a country importing goods manufactured from its own raw materials, because Scott and Shakespeare were obvious sources of Dumas's inspiration.[233] Robert Louis Stevenson, who included *Le Vicomte de Bragelonne* (1848), the last of the Musketeers cycle, among the books that he read again and again, called Dumas 'the great, unblushing French thief'; but the borrowing was not only one-way, Stevenson noting about Thackeray's *Henry Esmond* (1852) that 'the scene at Castlewood is pure Dumas'.[234] Dumas's popularity in Britain was extended by stage adaptations. His heroic leads seemed tailored for handsome actors who specialized in swordplay, although when Arnold Bennett saw Lewis Waller in the *Three Musketeers* he judged it a 'humiliating spectacle'.[235] Salutes to Dumas were numerous. In *Trilby* (1894) the three British art students in Paris are styled the 'three musketeers of the brush': Taffy is Porthos and Athos rolled into one, the Laird is D'Artagnan, and Little Billee is Aramis. Du Maurier mused: 'It will not do to push the simile too far; besides, unlike the good Dumas, one has a conscience.' Dumas, he added, played ducks and drakes with historical facts and personages; yet, 'if Athos, Porthos and Co. are not historical by this time, I should like to know who are!'[236] In the 1890s the foremost British imitator of Dumas was Stanley Weyman, whose best-selling career began with *A Gentleman of France* (1893) and *Under the Red Robe* (1894). Weyman was actually quite as much a conscious follower of Trollope, but he had had his own real-life escapade in France when he and his brother had been seized as supposed spies in 1885;[237] and it was apropos Weyman that Ellen Terry told Bernard Shaw in 1896 that 'crowds of novelists now-a-days fancy they are the dear Musketeers all over again!'[238] Yet

---

[231] Flower (ed.), *Bennett Journals*, ii. 165 (8 June 1916). At this auction, according to Bennett, the books in most demand were those by Kipling, Chesterton, Conrad, and himself.

[232] The story was told of Dumas bumping into a friend and asking him, 'Have you read my new novel?', to which the friend replied, 'No. Have you?' (Flower, *Just as it Happened*, 41).

[233] See George Saintsbury, 'Scott and Dumas', originally in *Fortnightly Review*, 1894, repr. in Saintsbury, *Collected Essays and Papers 1895–1920* (1923), iii. 20–1, in which Dumas is ranked 'second only to Sir Walter himself' in the historical novel department.   [234] Stevenson, *Memories and Portraits*, 230, 259.

[235] Flower (ed.), *Bennett Journals*, i. 41, 315 (12 July 1897, 18 Mar. 1909). Cf. George Lyttelton: 'no one but Lewis Waller ever made a stage-fight look convincing' (letter, 31 Jan. 1957, in Hart-Davis (ed.), *Lyttelton Hart-Davis Letters*, 250). The year 1898 saw some half-a-dozen *Musketeers* adaptations staged; Nicoll, *Late Nineteenth Century Drama*, 210.   [236] George Du Maurier, *Trilby* (1947), 154–5.

[237] See *Oxford DNB* for Weyman (1855–1928).

[238] Terry to Shaw, late Oct. 1896, in St John, *Terry-Shaw Correspondence*, 99. Stanley Weyman made his reputation with *A Gentleman of France* (1893), following this with *The Man in Black* (1894), *The Red Cockade* (1895), and *Count Hannibal* (1901). Stevenson, who read *A Gentleman of France* in his Samoan exile, enthused about it as 'the most exquisite pleasure; a real chivalrous yarn, like the Dumas' and yet unlike' (Colvin

the original was not overtaken, and hearts were warmed by reaquaintance. The last months of 1916 saw Asquith plumb the depths after his eldest son, Raymond, was killed in the war and he was deposed from the premiership. Asquith's partial recovery of spirits was signalled on 21 March 1917: 'I have at last got my books into something like decent order, but I have not yet selected which to re-read: with the exception of "Monte Cristo", which I have not read for thirty years, and of which I take a nightly dose.'[239] It was the same for Sir William Robertson Nicoll, who for over thirty years presided over the *British Weekly*. He was in Bournemouth in 1917 to campaign for further State restrictions of alcohol production and retail, a subject dear to his many Nonconformist readers. The month was February, the weather freezing and Nicoll, suffering the flu, 'got through the time, coughing and reading Dumas. I read the three volumes of "The Three Musketeers", the three volumes of "Twenty Years After", and the four volumes of the "Vicomte de Bagelonne"—every word; and if there be better reading in the world I don't know it.'[240]

This loyalty did not long outlast the Great War. It is true that the cinema sustained *The Three Musketeers* as a swashbuckling drama, with new versions appearing in most decades; but these were increasingly tongue-in-cheek, period parodies, and the book was left behind. James Barrie signalled the passing in 1922:

I have finished the *Three Musketeers* and feel I have now bidden them a final farewell—*adieu* not *au revoir*. Glorious rhodomontade or sublime balderdash, it is on the whole the finest work of fiction in the world; even re-reading when you are old and scared you can see your old self going strong with it. Never was anything else quite so gay, unless the summer you read it first. No 'character-drawing' worth speaking of. Any dull dog of today could go so much deeper in Milady—but hey nonny nonny.[241]

Among the many editions of Dumas available in Britain by the Edwardian period was the sixty-volume set of J. M. Dent & Co., which in 1906–7 reissued a forty-eight-volume edition at the rate of four per month, price 2s. 6d. per volume. The most famous Dumas was also in Dent's Everyman series, price 1s.: *The Three Musketeers* was number 81 in the list. Methuen's versions were cheaper still: it had marketed the entire Dumas in paperback at 6d. per volume in 1904, with the blazoned advertisement 'A Giant of Letters'.[242] This was the note struck by Swinburne's poem 'The Centenary of Alexandre Dumas', published in the *Nineteenth Century and After*, in August 1902; yet for the younger generation of

(ed.), *Vailima Letters*, 273); and, at the famous Jubilee Ball at Devonshire House in 1897, Viscount Esher chose fancy dress as 'A Gentleman of France in 1628' (see the photograph in Brett (ed.), *Esher*, i. 204).

[239] The Earl of Oxford and Asquith, *Memories and Reflections 1852–1927* (1928) ii. 160.

[240] Nicoll to Sir George Riddell, 9 Feb. 1917, in Darlow, *Nicoll*, 260.

[241] Letter to Lady Cynthia Asquith, 21 Nov. 1922, in Meynell (ed.), *Barrie Letters*, 196.

[242] Dent's advertisement in *T.P.'s Weekly*, 8 Feb. 1907, 170; Methuen's in *Pall Mall Gazette*, 21 July 1904, 3. Methuen conceived the idea during the Dumas centenary in 1902. His edition boasted of being a new translation 'by Mr Alfred Allison, whose competence is unquestioned, and he is assisted by a group of able scholars' (Duffy, *Methuen*, 31). Andrew Lang had introduced a shilling paperback edition of *The Three Musketeers* for Methuen in 1903; see the welcome in *Punch*, 28 Oct. 1903, 306.

writers, who were wrapped in new cults of literary art and symbol or wanting to promulgate awareness of the social condition, Dumas was not in the reckoning. The *Times Literary Supplement* was alert to this divide. In 1902 it noted his still unrivalled popularity a hundred years after his birth and some three decades after his death; but it also styled Dumas 'the favourite of the literary "masses", not of the literary "classes" '.[243]

What may be said of other foreign authors? Standard reference works certainly paid them attention, not just the encyclopedias but *Who's Who* where, for instance, in 1905 the curious could find their publications listed and learn that Gorky 'was successively a painter of ikons, pedlar of kvass, scullery-boy, gardener, watchman, and baker's apprentice' and that Maeterlinck's recreations were 'bee-keeping, canoeing, skating, bicycling', and Tolstoy's 'chess, cycling, lawn-tennis, swimming and reading'. The inclusiveness of *Who's Who* was impressive. It suggests a presumption on the part of publisher and editor that foreign authors were part of the English literary commonwealth and that their names would crop up with sufficient regularity in newspapers and periodicals and on playbills and booklists. That there were pockets of genuine interest in Continental literature among British writers and readers in this period is obvious, therefore. These included some quite powerful individual transmissions; but to argue for a pervasive influence would be excessive.

[243] *TLS*, 4 July 1902, 193.

II
WRITERS AND THE PUBLIC:
THE PRICE OF FAME

[Literature] which was once a grave and honourable profession has now degenerated into a noisy, pushing, self-advertising trade; and he who would teach is not always abreast of those whom he undertakes to teach . . . [The] democratic wave has covered the garden of the Hesperides with mud and slime.

(Mrs Lynn Linton, 'Literature Then and Now', *Fortnightly Review*, April 1890)

In these noisy days of literary newspapers and literary interviewers, publishers' puffing catalogues, illustrated with portraits, and communicated paragraphs, it is difficult to avoid knowing perhaps too much about authors.

(Augustine Birrell, reviewing the first supplemental volumes of the *Dictionary of National Biography*, 1901)

The distinguished person is a cult . . . And just as there are people who devote their spare time to collecting ideas which are so new and strange as to have exaggerated importance, so too there are others, and these are the majority, who might be said to collect these exaggerated personalities known as eminent men. The pastime is sometimes called 'lionising' and . . . in some countries, particularly in the United States, it has become shameless convention. Personal distinction of any kind is there received with a rapturous adoration which has small reference to the thing achieved by the adored one. In England it is different; we like to waylay eminent and distinguished persons and to look at them (we will sometimes pay for the privilege), but we nearly always end by laughing at them.

(Holbrook Jackson, *Southward Ho! And Other Essays* (1914))

All great literary men are shy. I am myself though I am told it is hardly noticeable.

(Jerome K. Jerome, *The Idle Thoughts of an Idle Fellow* (1886))

8

Product Advertising and Self-Advertising

I

A writer's canonization was most evident in the obsequies which followed death, death being as Henry James called it 'the Distinguished Thing'.[1] Public recognition also lapped about the living. H. W. Nevinson thought the actual public sceptics: 'though the English people read more in quantity than any other nation, the literary gift is regarded among us as a sign of probable incapacity, and not, as in France and ancient Greece, as an assurance of far-reaching powers'.[2] Perhaps; but authors were a force in advertising. Dickens named particular products in his stories, and enterprising tradesmen and manufacturers used his characters and themes in their merchandising.[3] *Pickwick Papers*, easily his most popular work, gave rise to Pickwick chintzes, canes, coats, hats, and cigars, not to mention Weller corduroy breeches. When Fred Kitton itemized these in 1886, there was also a racehorse named Dickens, and a species of hyacinth; and Boz cabs once plied the streets.[4] Bulwer Lytton had belatedly got in the act with his science fiction story *The Coming Race* (1871), featuring a subterranean civilization equipped with a superior fund of energy, 'vril'.[5] This was appropriated by manufacturers for their brand names Bovril, the beef extract drink and gravy, and Virol, 'a tasty toffee mixture with reputed curative powers, ladled out to children at least until the end of the Second World War'.[6] Bovril's makers seemed avid for further literary accreditation thereafter. When Kipling included a reference to Bovril in a short story, it was hailed as proof of their product's nourishing properties which vitalized Britain's forces in the Boer War.[7] The sickly who resorted to 'Eno's fruit salt' were meanwhile sustained by Tennyson's picture (with lines by Carlyle) in an advertisement in 1886.[8] The tragedian Thomas Hardy was less in the limelight

---

[1] Edel, *James*, ii. 800.   [2] Nevinson, *Fire of Life*, 306.
[3] Gerard Curtis, 'Dickens in the Visual Market', in John O. Jordan and Robert L. Patten (eds.), *Literature in the Marketplace* (Cambridge, 1995), 218–23.   [4] Kitton, *Dickensiana*, pp. xxiii–xxiv.
[5] Sutherland, *Companion*, 143–4. A new edition of Bulwer Lytton's *The Coming Race* (1871), with an introduction by Brian Aldiss, was issued by Broadview Press, Toronto, in 2002.
[6] Letter from Brian Aldiss, *TLS*, 5 Dec. 2003.   [7] McMillan, *Way we Were*, 144–5.
[8] Lang and Shannon (eds.), *Tennyson's Letters*, iii. 340.

but, though the thought is almost too gruesome to contemplate, he unofficially assisted his wife, Emma, to judge (with Lady Conan Doyle) *Tatler*'s competition to find the nation's most photogenic babies in 1904.[9]

These were all authors whose names are generally remembered today. Names less familiar now but well known then also boomed products and services. In the early 1890s Sir Edwin Arnold's poetry featured in a toothpaste advertisement, and Francis Gribble's on a poster promoting the skills of a boxing kangaroo at the Royal Aquarium. Gribble, with an Oxford First in Greats, had been contributing to light entertainment periodicals such as *Arrow*, *Hawk*, *Bat*, *Pick-Me-Up*, *The Idler*, and *Phil May's Annual*. This use of his poetry amused him, whereas Sir Edwin, having pretensions to be Laureate, fired off letters of complaint. Neither had any redress because they had not copyrighted these verses. Gribble drily reflected that the 'commercial branch of the poetical profession' was then unorganized.[10]

The position was fast changing. Poets in the past had aristocratic patrons; why should not modern millionaires endow poets and so achieve immortality, asked Richard Le Gallienne in 1898, thus to incite *Punch* to imagine odes in honour of the grocery knight Lipton—

> (Your health in fragrant tea and fruity!)
> How can you sin against the light
> Who paid the champion cheque for Duty?

—or the company speculator Hooley:

> Big syndicates of Song be floated
> And, by a touch of humour, get
> The Stock Exchange to have 'em quoted![11]

Still, the first literary earnings received by the Nottingham-born Cecil Roberts were from the pharmacy firm Boots, which was based in that city. Boots used his youthful poems for its calendars, paying £3 a poem. Meeting the founder, Roberts was told by Jesse Boot that, when young, he too once won 10s. in a competition to promote Day and Martin's blacking by rhyme.[12] In the Edwardian period

---

[9] Emma Hardy to Clement Shorter, 15 Sept. 1904, in Millgate (ed.), *Emma and Florence Hardy*, 28–30. Gruesome because Hardy wrote what must rank as one of the least consoling letters to a parent grieving for the loss of a child, as Rider Haggard was for the death of his 10-year-old son in 1891: 'Please give my kind regards to Mrs Haggard, & tell her how deeply our sympathy was with you both in your bereavement. Though, to be candid, I think the death of a child is never really to be regretted, when one reflects on what he has escaped' (Hardy to Haggard, May 1891, in Purdy and Millgate (eds.), *Hardy Letters*, i. 325). The second Mrs Hardy, writing to Lady Hoare on 21 April 1918, stated, 'He is genuinely afraid of babies . . .', although to the birth control campaigner Marie Stopes on 14 Sept. 1923 she said that 'he would have welcomed a child when we married first, ten years ago'. Hardy was 73 when he remarried, his second wife, Florence, then 35. Millgate (ed.), *Emma and Florence Hardy*, 141, 203.
[10] Gribble, *Seen in Passing*, 99–101. See also *Punch*, 14 Aug. 1901, 113, for 'A Ballade of Literary Advertisement'.   [11] *Punch*, 15 Jan. 1898.
[12] Cecil Roberts, *The Growing Boy* (1967), 106. Cf. *Punch*, 8 July 1903, 17, citing this appeal in the magazine *Hearth and Home*: 'To POETS.—A Prize of One Guinea is offered for a set of verses . . . Competitors are to take for subject any advertisement appearing in the issues of *Hearth and Home* for July 2, 9, 16, or 23.'

British businessmen were being enjoined to regard advertising as an essential tool of industry like Americans did. This was the message of W. Teignmouth Shore, who replaced Lewis Hind as editor of *The Academy* in 1903. Shore was a marketing and advertising consultant, as well as journalist, novelist, and lecturer.[13] The owner of *The Academy* from 1896 to 1905[14] was John Morgan Richards. An American domiciled in England since 1867, and father of the novelist Pearl Craigie (John Oliver Hobbes), Richards was a rich businessman whose speciality was advertising. He pioneered the sale of American products—cigarettes and patent goods—in England and was 'the first to engage a full advertisement column in a single issue of a London daily, and a whole back page of several London weeklies'. 'After an experience of over fifty years', he wrote in 1905, 'I consider that advertising as a profession is the most fascinating form of speculation.' A mark of his pre-eminence was his election in 1904 as first president of the Sphinx, a peripatetic monthly dining club of some twenty men 'connected with the advertising profession, and their allies', among them publishers and press proprietors. The Sphinx met at venues such as the Hotel Cecil and, following their feasting, held 'important and valuable' debates on advertising philosophies and practice.[15]

The association in the public mind of advertising and things American was strong at this time. Kipling—who had married an American and lived in Vermont—wrote a Boer War short story, 'The Captive', which features an American, Laughton O. Zigler, an advertiser-cum-inventor of a field gun and explosive. By wanting to sell these to both sides in the conflict, he epitomizes the stateless amorality of the free market.[16] Likewise, it was a telling moment in H.G. Wells's *Tono-Bungay* (1909) when the advertiser and sharpster Edward Ponderevo, 'the Napoleon of Commerce', declares that he wishes he had been born American.[17] Not that Britain was or had been an advertising-free Eden awaiting the American serpent. Wells's Ponderevo is in the patent-medicine trade, whose quackery Carlyle long ago ridiculed with his mock apology 'Brothers, I am sorry I have got no Morrison's Pill for curing the maladies of Society'. Carlyle had also scorned what he considered the senseless waste of energy put into advertising, by citing 'The Hatter in the Strand of London, [who] instead of making better felt-hats than

---

[13] W. Teignmouth Shore, 'The Craft of the Advertiser', *Fortnightly Review* (Feb. 1907), 301–10. On Teignmouth Shore (1865–1932), *Who Was Who, 1929–1940*, 1231–2; Kemp *et al.* (eds.), *Edwardian Fiction*, 361. His father had been a clergyman, fashionable among the Mayfair classes; see Escott, *Society in London*, 82.

[14] *Literature*, bought from *The Times*'s stable, was incorporated with *The Academy* in 1902. In February 1905 Richards sold the titles to Sir George Newnes.

[15] Richards, *John Bull and Jonathan*, 47–8, 56, 66, 282–3.

[16] Zigler is also a freemason. 'The Captive' was first published in *Collier's Weekly*, 6 Dec. 1902, and in book form in Kipling, *Traffics and Discoveries* (1904). It is republished in Kipling, *War Stories and Poems*, ed. with introd. Andrew Rutherford (Oxford, 1990). The story is otherwise memorable for the verdict voiced by the British general that the Boer War was most useful for providing new troops with combat experience for greater tests to come: 'It's a first-class dress-parade for Armageddon' (p. 212).

[17] Thomas Richards, *The Commodity Culture of Victorian England* (Stanford, Calif., 1990), 12, 148–55, 184–6.

another, mounts a huge lath-and-plaster Hat, seven-feet high, upon wheels; sends a man to drive it through the streets; hoping to be saved *thereby*'.[18]

Advertising was ubiquitous in the Victorian period, on buildings, omnibuses, cabs, and carts—and on the person, as the mobile sandwich-board man testified. Advertisers' manuals and directories were plentiful too; and authors did not neglect it as a subject for fiction. Trollope understood it as intrinsic to *The Way We Live Now* (1875); and George Gissing made it central in *In the Year of the Jubilee* (1894), having in *The Nether World* (1889), classicist that he was, compared mass culture to a Roman saturnalia. In 1893 *Punch* applauded a report in the *Saturday Review* that a 'Society had been formed to deliver us from hideous advertisements'.[19] The style of Victorian advertising owed much to the theatre, with its fashion for spectacle and sensation; but the appeals made were characteristic of a commodity-based society, preying on consumers' susceptibility to concerns about their status, health, and attractiveness to the opposite sex. The American dimension to this expanding trade was to give it much greater institutional form, with emergent specialist advertising companies employing a new professional order of copywriters and designers; and associated with this was a dramatic increase in the media output.

The truly remarkable development in the United States was the rising circulation of monthly magazines from perhaps 4 million at the end of the civil war to about 18 million in 1890 and 64 million in 1905, whereupon three copies existed for every four people and four issues found their way to every household. During the period of most startling increase, 1890–1905, the issue of newspapers and weeklies rose from 36 to 57 million, fewer, therefore, than the monthlies whose market leaders were the newcomers, *Cosmopolitan, Ladies' Home Journal, McClure's Magazine*, and *Munsey's Magazine*. 'Do you know why the Americans have half-a-dozen first-rate illustrated magazines, while we have only one—the *Pall Mall*?', the publisher William Heinemann asked the critic William Archer in December 1901. He answered his own question: 'It is simply because of the facilities for distribution offered by the Post Office.' In America books and magazines enjoyed a postal rate of 1 cent per pound weight; in Britain, the equivalent was 4*d*., or eight times as expensive.[20] The new American monthlies differed from predecessors such as the *Century* or *Harper's Magazine*, by selling for a dime (10 cents) rather than a quarter (25 cents); and their content was dominated by 'human interest' and entertainment features and by light fiction. Above all, they were replete with advertisements. *Harper's* traditionally carried sedate publishers' advertisements of new books and, being mostly *Harper's* own, they produced no substantial outside revenue; but the new magazines were awash with 'lifestyle' advertisements of goods such as bicycles, cameras, pens, watches, fashionable

---

[18] Thomas Carlyle, *Past and Present* (n.d.), 17, 100.   [19] *Punch*, 8 Apr. 1893, 161.
[20] Archer, *Real Conversations*, 192.

clothes, cutlery, furniture, patent medicines and insurance, soaps and packaged drinks, cereals and biscuits. These were illustrated by the latest photo-engraving technology and targeted at the multiplying clerical and skilled labour forces of the cities.[21] Nor was this just a matter of selling more beans than before. There was an institutional purpose, the creation of friendly corporate images by a nascent public relations sector, to counter campaigns waged against big business by anti-trust legislation, by trade unions, and by muckraking journalists.[22]

Authors in Britain as well as in America responded by finding nothing degrading about singing the praises of a commodity or company if a fee was attached. Edgar Wallace would later reckon to earn £25 for a magazine story and £200 from a manufacturer whose product he prominently named in the course of the story. The pre-war master of this device was rumoured to be the popular playwright George R. Sims.[23] Of course, such brand identification might be innocent, the result of an author's quest for realism and authenticity. None suspected the prim Marie Corelli of designing to join the distillery's payroll when, in *Thelma* (1887), she referred to a character Sandy Macfarlane's 'flask of Glenlivet'.[24] Still, it struck the *Athenaeum's* reviewer of Rider Haggard's *She* (1887) as suspicious to be 'dragged down suddenly from the heights of the supernatural, the immortal and the divinely fair, by the . . . superfluous mention of Gladstone bags, shooting boots, and Bryant & May's matches', as if Haggard had been designing an 'advertisement for the Army and Navy Store'.[25] Helena Swanwick, editor (1909–14) of the suffragist paper the *Common Cause*, stated that disguised advertising was rife in the Women's Pages of newspapers and in women's magazines.[26] That approaches were made to writers is clear from a collection of Kipling's papers retained by his secretary Miss K. E. Parker between 1902 and 1904. This included an offer of a 6 h.p. Lanchester if only Kipling would 'immortalize' his benefactor in a story. Keen motorist though he was, Kipling politely declined.[27]

---

[21] Richard Ohmann, *Selling Culture: Magazines, Markets and Class at the Turn of the Century* (1996).

[22] Roland Marchand, *Creating the Corporate Soul: The Rise of Public Relations and Corporate Imagery in American Big Business* (1998). Stephen Fox, writing in the 1980s, 'concluded that advertising gathered power early in the century, reached a peak of influence in the 1920s, and since then—despite consistent gains in volume and omnipresence—has steadily lost influence over American life'. He sought to explain this paradox through two forces: increasing regulation and restriction of what advertisers were allowed to claim, and increasing sophistication and scepticism on the part of the public. Stephen Fox, *The Mirror Makers: A History of American Advertising and its Creators* (New York, 1985), 8, 328–9.

[23] Margaret Lane, *Edgar Wallace: The Biography of a Phenomenon* (1938), 245–6. Cf. the publisher Rupert Hart–Davis reporting the gossip about Ian Fleming's James Bond stories on 28 April 1957: 'that when Ian Fleming mentions any particular food, clothing or cigarettes in his books, the makers reward him with presents in kind: "in fact", said my friend, "Ian's are the only modern thrillers with built–in commercials"' (Hart–Davis (ed.), *Lyttelton Hart–Davis Letters*, 290).

[24] Marie Corelli, *Thelma: A Norwegian Princess* (1896), 114.

[25] *Athenaeum*, 15 Jan. 1887, quoted in Richards, *Commodity Culture*, 118.

[26] Swanwick, *I have been Young*, 195–7.   [27] *The Times*, 30 Oct. 1996.

FIG. 8.1. Female authors fight nerves: advertisements for Phosferine tonic. *Sources*: *M.A.P.*, 6 January 1905, 15, and 20 January 1906, 67. Reference (Shelfmark) N. 2289c.8. © Bodleian Library

GREAT LIMERICK COMPETITION.

£500 FIRST PRIZE.

GREATEST CASH PRIZES EVER OFFERED.
Competent Staff of Judges.

2nd Prize, £50; 3rd, £25; 4th, £15; 5th, £10; and 100 Consolation Prizes.

NO ENTRANCE FEE.

CLOSES FEB. 26.

YOUR LAST CHANCE!

This is the first occasion on record when a firm of genuine Tobacco Manufacturers have supplied their goods direct to the public. Messrs. E. D. Gerard & Co., Ltd., 8, Lambeth Palace Road, London, S.E., have inaugurated this Competition for the sole purpose of further introducing to discerning smokers their latest success, "Hall Caine" Cigarettes, Turkish and Virginian.

THE PRICE. "Hall Caine" Cigarettes have always, and are now, being sold throughout the United Kingdom at 5s. per 100, but as a huge advertisement, to all Competitors in this great Limerick, **the Cigarettes will be sold at THREE SHILLINGS per 100, post paid.**

THE PRIZES are absolutely guaranteed by the firm of Messrs. E. D. Gerard & Co., Ltd., and **will be given independently of the number of Cigarettes sold, whether 500 or 5,000,000.** The whole scheme is purely and simply an advertisement, the cash prizes offered being considered part of the advertising expenditure.

CONDITIONS. Simply fill up the last line of the Limerick printed below, and forward to us with P.O. for 3s., crossed "& Co." with order for 100 "Hall Caine" Cigarettes. State whether Turkish or Virginian are required.

IMPORTANT NOTICE. 1. Competitors are requested to send in their last lines as early as possible as the closing date is Feb. 26th, and it is impossible to judge them all fairly in one week. 2. Prize money will be posted to winners within one week of the result being made public. 3. No member of the firm, employee, or friend of any member or employee, is eligible to compete. 4. Any number of last lines may be sent, but for each further 100 "Hall Caine" Cigarettes must be purchased, and the price thereof, 3s. including postage, remitted. **Send immediately, as this advertisement may not appear again.**

Whitehall Court, S.W.
Dec., 1905.

I find the Cigarettes most excellent and feel proud of being their sponsor. I wish you every possible success with them.

Hall Caine

ENTRY COUPON.

CUT OUT THIS COUPON AND FILL UP CAREFULLY.

GENTLEMEN.—Kindly send post paid a box of Turkish (Virginian) Cigarettes, for which I enclose P.O. for 3s. If from any cause you do not execute this order, you are at liberty to return my money, and by so doing I entirely waive my right to be considered a Competitor. If Virginian are required strike out Turkish and vice versa.

Full Name...(Please write clearly).

Postal Address...

Town...County...

I agree to accept the Committee's decision as final, and enter the Competition on that distinct understanding.

If more than one last line is sent, write same with name and address on a separate sheet of plain paper and pin to the Entry Coupon. Only one attempt must be made on each sheet, and for each line 100 "Hall Caine" Cigarettes must be purchased at 3s., including postage. Additional Entry Coupons sent on receipt of stamped addressed envelope.

Address Envelope:
The Limerick Committee.................190
E. D. Gerard & Co., Ltd.,
8, Lambeth Palace Road, London, S.E.

There's a Cigarette called the Hall Caine
Once tried, always asked for again,
In flavour and zest,
It excels all the rest,

....

FIG. 8.2. A best-selling puff: 'Hall Caine' cigarettes.
Source: *T.P.'s Weekly*, 14 February 1908

puffed was his own brand of cigarettes. The amount spent by smokers was now rising significantly, and literary and other celebrities cheerfully joined in the promotion. 'Tobacco is the sister of Literature,' pronounced Professor Sir Walter Raleigh, true to his namesake, who introduced the habit.[38] In 1883 A. Arthur Reade—compiler of the advice manuals *Literary Success* and *How to Write English*—issued *Study and Stimulants*, which included this testimonial from Anthony Trollope:

I have been a smoker nearly all my life. Five years ago, I found it certainly was hurting me, causing my hand to shake and producing somnolence. I gave it up for two years. A doctor told me I had smoked too much (three large cigars daily). Two years since, I took it up again, and now smoke three small cigars (very small), and, so far as I can tell, without any effect.[39]

Trollope died from a stroke nine months later. He was an asthmatic, not the ideal condition to combine with smoking; still, he had been convinced, as he once told his publisher John Blackwood, 'of the glories of tobacco'.[40] The advice given to Trollope notwithstanding, the medical profession had not yet generally declared against smoking. Far from it: the *British Medical Journal*, edited by Ernest Hart, a tobacco addict himself, argued that smoking in moderation 'cheered and lightened the working hours'. Those who suspected that smoking caused cancer were decried as ignoramuses or faddists.[41]

Smoking was a sure sign of the 'modern woman'. Gissing's *In the Year of Jubilee* (1894) features Beatrice French, aged 26 and running the South London Fashionable Dress Supply Association, a racket designed to exploit gullible and pretentious members of her sex. At her new flat in Brixton she seeks to impress Nancy Lord by offering her a cigarette from a box in her drawing room, saying 'It's expected of a sensible woman nowadays. I've got to like it. Better try; no need to make yourself uncomfortable. Just keep the smoke in your mouth for half-a-minute, and blow it out prettily. I buy these in the Haymarket; special brand for women.'[42] The author of *Little Lord Fauntleroy* (1886), Mrs Hodgson Burnett, maintained that Turkish cigarettes, inhaled between nibbles of peppermint creams, warded off 'neuritis';[43] and Virginia Stephen, whose mind was periodically unhinged, in 1904 took up pipe-smoking, 'which the doctor thinks an excellent thing, and I find it very soothing'.[44] The one-time queen of flamboyant fiction Ouida had smoked cigars. The high-spirited heroine of her desert romance *Under Two Flags* (1867), who dies for love, was resplendently

---

[38] Quoted in Gardiner, *Leaves in the Wind*, 46. Gardiner, editor of the *Daily News*, was struggling to give up smoking at that time.   [39] Letter, 11 Feb. 1882, in Booth (ed.), *Trollope's Letters*, 472.

[40] Letter, 6 Jan. 1875, ibid. 330.

[41] P. W. J. Bartrip, *Mirror of Medicine: A History of the British Medical Journal* (Oxford, 1990), 162. On E. A. Hart (1835–98), see *DNB*. His brother-in-law was Canon Barnett, first Warden of Toynbee Hall; and Hart was a power in the publishing firm Smith, Elder & Co.

[42] George Gissing, *In the Year of Jubilee* (1895), 300.   [43] Thwaite, *Burnett*, 158, 163, 229.

[44] Letter to Violet Dickinson, 30 Sept. 1904, in Nicolson and Banks (eds.), *Flight of the Mind*, 144.

named Cigarette:

She was pretty, she was insolent, she was intolerably coquettish, she was mischievous as a marmoset, she would swear if need be like a Zowave, she could fire galloping, she could toss off her brandy or her vermout like a trooper, she would on occasion clench her little brown hand and deal a blow that the recipient would not covet twice, she was an *enfant de Paris*, and had all its wickedness at her fingers, she would sing you *guinguette* songs till you were suffocated with laughter, and she would dance the cancan at the Salle de Mars . . . [45]

All this plus 'a thousand lovers'; still, Cigarette also found time to inhale the eponymous weed. Otherwise, it was the male who was expected to cut the dashing figure, and the cigarette became his glamorous accessory. Manners deteriorated accordingly. Lord Frederic Hamilton, a heavy smoker himself, deplored the post-Victorian smart set who casually flicked ash about Society drawing rooms and stubbed out fag-ends on fine carpets and furniture.[46]

The poseur found in the cigarette a new stage prop. Oscar Wilde was distressed to learn that his feckless brother Willie—briefly married to an American widow—was smoking American cigarettes: 'You really must not do anything so horrid. Charming people should smoke gold-tipped cigarettes or die . . .'.[47] Wilde himself favoured the Parascho brand and bought them by the thousand. Robert Sherard witnessed him in his Tite Street home carrying, 'as he moved from one room to another, a box of cigarettes of the size of a large biscuit-tin'.[48] Even for a chain-smoker, as Wilde was in his pre-convict period, this was overdoing things. Romantic heroes naturally smoked exotic brands. Mrs Barclay showed some humour about this. The heroes of *The Rosary* (1909) and *Through the Postern Gate* (1912) smoke Zenith Marcovitch cigarettes, whose distinctive aroma cannot be bettered 'for drawing-room and garden purposes'. The smell, which 'mingles with the flowers', apparently proves fatal to black beetles indoors and to unwanted insects outdoors; moreover, the cigarettes come 'packed in jolly green boxes, twelve shillings a hundred! I must remember in case I want to give him a Christmas present', declares the heroine of *The Rosary* thoughtfully.[49] The tobacco industry had reason to be most grateful for J. M. Barrie's set of smoking-club stories, *My Lady Nicotine* (1890). Later he pretended that 'part of it . . . was written before I had ever smoked' yet, he was a persistent pipe and cigar man in the 1880s as well as after, in spite of bronchial ailments. His convulsive hacking cough was instantly recognizable. Still, as he gently remarked in *Alice Sit-by-the-Fire* (1905), 'no real villain smokes a pipe'.[50] The auction for Barrie's endorsement

---

[45] Ouida, *Under Two Flags: A Story of the Household of the Desert* (Oxford, 1995), 175.

[46] Lord Frederic Hamilton, *The Days before Yesterday* (n.d. [1920]), 90–1. Also Farquharson, *In and Out of Parliament*, 107–8, for further objurgations about Society smoking habits. Farquharson was a doctor, but his disapproval of smoking was on aesthetic not medical grounds.

[47] To William Wilde, c.10 July 1893, in Hart-Davis (ed.), *Wilde's Letters*, 113.   [48] Sherard, *Wilde*, 53–4.

[49] Barclay, *The Rosary*, 88, 222; id., *Through the Postern Gate* (n.d. [156th thousand]), 78–9, 118.

[50] Barrie, *Plays*, 271.

was won by Carreras, which produced the Craven brand—'What I call the "Arcadia" in *My Lady Nicotine* is the Craven mixture and no other' was Barrie's message in Carreras's advertisements.[51] Neat also was the way in which the Ardath Tobacco Company (established in 1896) benefited from the association with Marie Corelli's best-seller *Ardath* (1889), though this story of the occult was as far removed from commercial as any other reality. In fact, Corelli was belligerently hostile to smoking. The hero of *God's Good Man* (1904), the Revd John Walden, articulates her views when he tells Maryllia Vancourt that he has 'a strong prejudice against smoking women'. (Having a shaky grasp of grammar and no humour, Corelli did not consider if the last two words may have been better reversed.) Smoking degrades women in men's eyes, Walden believes; and, when Maryllia asserts that women should be able to smoke as men smoke, he retorts

'Men—a very large majority of them too—habitually get drunk. Do you think it justifiable for women to get drunk by way of following the men's example?'

  'Why no, of course not!'—she answered quickly—'But drunkenness is a vice —'

  'So is smoking! And it is quite as unhealthy as all vices are. There have been more addle-pated statesmen and politicians in England since smoking became a daily necessity with them than were ever known before. I don't believe in any human being who turns his brain into a chimney.'[52]

Corelli was in good company: the anti-smoking lobby included Queen Victoria, Cardinal Manning, the Bishop of Hereford (John Percival), Bernard Shaw, Thomas Hardy, and Tolstoy;[53] but Carlyle, a smoker from the age of 11, had been among the confirmed addicts, likewise Charles Kingsley, Coventry Patmore, and Tennyson. Even the Nonconformists' favourite fabler, Silas K. Hocking, admitted to the *Review of Reviews* in 1908, 'I now smoke half-a-dozen cigarettes a day— *sometimes more*': the italics being contributed by *Punch*, which exclaimed, 'Oh, Silas, you profligate!'[54] Sinner on a much greater scale was the children's author Edith Nesbit, 'one of the earliest of the chain-smokers', recalled Edgar Jepson.[55] She rolled her own cigarettes; probably this, rather than that Nesbit happened also to be a Fabian Socialist, explains why she was not sought out by advertisers.

[51] See advertisement in *M.A.P.*, 20 May 1905, 2; and Blumenfeld, *R.D.B.'s Diary*, 209 (6 Feb. 1908). Also Barrie to J. J. Carreras, 18 Jan. 1897, in Meynell (ed.), *Letters*, 34; Flower (ed.), *Bennett Journals*, ii. 239 (31 Oct. 1918); Dunbar, *Barrie*, 62, 86–7; Asquith, *Barrie*, 22–4. *Punch* was particularly scathing about Barrie's prostitution. R. C. Lehmann's spoof story—'Thrums on the Auld String' by 'J. Muir Kirrie, Author of "A Door on Thumbs", "Eight Bald Fiddlers", "When a Man Sees Double", "My Gentleman Meerschaum", etc.,'—came 'enclosed in a wrapper labelled "Arcadia Mixture. Strength and Aroma combined. Sold in six-shilling cases. Special terms for Southrons. Liberal allowance for returned empties" ' (*Punch*, 15 Nov. 1890, 229). George Meredith and the music-hall comedian Dan Leno also smoked the 'Arcadia' mixture; Walkley, *Frames of Mind*, 76.

[52] Marie Corelli, *God's Good Man: A Simple Love Story* (1904), 438–9; and *M.A.P.*, 20 Aug. 1904, 215, for the Ardath Tobacco Co.

[53] Tolstoy's tirade against tobacco was published in the *Contemporary Review* in 1891. It inspired a scornfully comic ode in *Punch*, 21 Feb. 1891, 85. For Hardy's detestation, Florence Hardy to Paul Lemperly, 8 Apr. 1925, in Millgate (ed.), *Emma and Florence Hardy*, 222.   [54] *Punch*, 25 Mar. 1908, 226.

[55] Jepson, *Memories of an Edwardian and Neo-Georgian*, 23; Moore, *Nesbit*, 82.

Holding subversive opinions did not alienate the industry if the author was reckoned to carry clout with consumers. The weekly circulation of the Socialist *Clarion*, which rose from 40,000–50,000 in 1892 to 90,000 by 1914, was sufficient to induce a firm of tobacco manufacturers to introduce Dangle's Mixture, named after the paper's co-founder and columnist 'Dangle', alias Alex M. Thompson, who happened also to be a popular playwright.[56] Manufacturers of the Marsuma brand of Havana cigar recruited several satisfied customers from the literary and artistic world in their advertisements: the actor–manager Sir Henry Irving, the cartoonist Carruthers Gould, and 'our greatest dramatist' Arthur Pinero.[57] The actor–manager Gerald Du Maurier even 'bestowed his distinguished name'[58] on the Du Maurier brand of cigarette, in part as a tribute to his father, George, the author of *Trilby* (1894) and a notoriously heavy smoker. Similarly, it is a measure of Charles Reade's persisting fame that, though he died in 1884, an advertisement for Player's Navy Mixture was still using a head-and-shoulder drawing of him, with quotation, in 1906.[59] Fictional characters too were seized upon where these were equally well or better known than their creators. Thus, the pensive pipeman Sherlock Holmes featured in advertisements for Cope's 'Bond of Union' Smoking Mixture.[60]

The merchandising of goods associated with a best-seller was keenly exploited. The hat was only the most famous accessory arising out of *Trilby*. According to John Masefield, there were also 'boots, shoes, collars, toothpastes, coats, songs and dances named after *Trilby*'.[61] Du Maurier himself was asked to authorize the patent of a Trilby kitchen range.[62] In Yorkshire he came across a village sweet-shop which advertised 'Trilby Drops'; alas, the girl behind the counter had no idea what 'Trilby' signified.[63] *Trilby* was, however, turned into a successful play by Paul Potter. It was staged first in the United States—where a town was named Trilby—and afterwards at the Haymarket in London by Beerbohm Tree, who played the mesmerist–musician Svengali. Tree dubbed the melodrama 'hog-wash'; but it played for six months and made him such profits that he built a new theatre, Her Majesty's, on the proceeds.[64]

Children as well as adults were targeted by trades battening on the popularity of books by Lewis Carroll, Kate Greenaway, and Beatrix Potter. It was their

[56] Thompson, *Here I Lie*, 114. *Dangle's Mixture* was also the title of one of Thompson's publications, along with *Dangle's Rough Cut*. On Thompson (1861–1948), *Who Was Who, 1941–1950*, 1144.

[57] *M.A.P.*, 13 Aug. 1904, 170, 29 Oct. 1904, 2, for these. Other advertisements for Marsuma cigars featured the actor–author Weedon Grossmith, and Field Marshal Lord Kitchener; *M.A.P.*, 26 Nov. 1904, 578, 10 Dec. 1904, 642.

[58] Cutting sent to the author by the Corporate Librarian of Imperial Tobacco, 14 Dec. 1998.

[59] *The Tribune*, 1 Aug. 1906, 3.

[60] *T.P.'s Weekly*, 29 Jan. 1904, 161. When Holmes makes his appearance in *A Study in Scarlet* (1887–8), he is introduced as a pipe-smoker of shag tobacco and includes among his accomplishments the authorship of a monograph on cigar and tobacco ashes. He famously classifies the case of 'the Red-Headed League' a 'three-pipe problem'.   [61] See Masefield's Introduction to *Novels of George Du Maurier* (1947), p. x.

[62] Ormond, *Du Maurier*, 462.   [63] Edith Sichel, *The Life and Letters of Alfred Ainger* (n.d.), 302–3.

[64] Pearson, *Tree*, ch. 9. Tree first staged *Trilby* in Manchester in September 1895, then transferred it to the Haymarket on 30 October.

illustrations that in large part were responsible for this. These costumed the entire animal kingdom as well as provided models for the tiny tots themselves. Tenniel gave Lewis Carroll's White Rabbit a check jacket, high stiff collar, and brolly in addition to the waistcoat required for the tyrannical timepiece; later this would seem sparse compared with the range of wardrobe and household fittings that Beatrix Potter gave her creatures. Sumptuous too was Kate Greenaway's kit: *Under the Window: Pictures and Rhymes for Children* (1879) sold 70,000 copies and generated a minor industry of Christmas cards and valentines, bookplates and birthday books, almanacs and calendars, board games, wallpapers, and tiles, and of Greenaway-style 'aesthetic' clothes. Edith Nesbit attired her daughters in this fashion, to their 'embarrassment and discomfort' at school.[65] The Greenaway look was, in Andrew Lang's words, 'the Mirror of modish Childhood';[66] but it was not worn by young girls alone. At their Bradmore Road home in North Oxford, where Walter Pater ornamented himself in silk stockings and apple-green tie, his sisters designed to match him by their own 'fantastic apple-green Kate Greenaway dresses'.[67] Greenaway herself had been inspired by visits to rural Nottinghamshire during her Hoxton childhood, but in her prime she moved to a house in Hampstead built by the architect Norman Shaw. Looking to make money also, Robert Louis Stevenson was encouraged by the Greenaway boom, as his wife recorded in her diary: 'I had Kate Greenaway's children's birthday book. Lou took it up one day and said, "These are rather nice rhymes, and I don't think they would be difficult to do".'[68] The result was Stevenson's *A Child's Garden of Verse* (1885).

Greenaway's dainty dolls in dirt-free villages amid apple and cherry blossoms excited Ruskin's nympholeptic tendencies; but Beatrix Potter appraised her work with a cool eye and judged that she could not draw.[69] Having been given a Greenaway birthday book as a child, she got rid of it as soon as possible and thereafter developed what she admitted was 'an unreasoning aversion' to such work.[70] Potter herself had no sentimentality about the modern child, 'pampered & spoilt' by too many toys and by books that did nothing to stimulate an imaginative reach to nature.[71] She disparaged the quality of mass consumerism in a manner reminiscent of George Gissing, whose *In the Year of Jubilee* (1894) opens with a sardonic survey of a house in suburban Camberwell, within which, on a chair, symbolically lies 'a broken toy, one of those elaborate and costly playthings which serve no purpose but to stunt a child's imagination'.[72] Potter became an ardent Tariff Reformer in protest against the ruin of the native toy industry

---

[65] Moore, *Nesbit*, 86, 119–20.   [66] Andrew Lang, *The Library*, enlarged edn. (1892), 180.

[67] Vernon Lee's description, quoted in Billie Andrew Inman, 'Mr Pater of Bradmore Road', *Oxford Magazine*, Second Week, Michaelmas Term, 2004, 9.

[68] Margaret Mackay, *The Violent Friend: The Story of Mrs. Robert Louis Stevenson 1840–1914* (1970), 104.

[69] Margaret Lane, *The Magic Years of Beatrix Potter* (1980), 65.

[70] Beatrix Potter to Harold Warne, 20 Nov. 1911, in Judy Taylor (ed.), *Beatrix Potter's Letters* (1989), 189.

[71] Beatrix Potter to Fruing Warne, 29 May 1919, ibid. 257.   [72] Gissing, *Year of Jubilee*, 2.

through the dumping of German imports, though she was no friend of a free-trade Liberal Government on other grounds, being dismayed by its propensity to pass what she termed 'grandmotherly legislation'.[73] This declaration was made during the 1910 general elections, and followed a decade in which Potter had taken an active part in merchandising products associated with her stories. The patent of her Peter Rabbit doll was registered on 28 December 1903; in the next year she conceived a Peter Rabbit board game. She set exacting standards for firms wanting to manufacture and market under licence stuffed toys and painting books, china tea sets and figurines, wallpaper and stationery, birthday and Christmas cards, from which she received royalty payments.[74] It was no small triumph for her to announce as she did in 1917, 'all rabbits *are* called Peter now', although as a modest afterthought (or perhaps in deference to American opinion) she added the qualification, 'either Peter or Brer Rabbit'.[75]

Boys had particular cause to resent Mrs Hodgson Burnett. Her *Little Lord Fauntleroy* (1886) did not initiate the fashion of dressing precious lads in sapphire and pink knickerbockers and velvet tunics, with Van Dyck lace collars and cuffs; but the idealized innocent of that story, Cedric Errol, Lord Fauntleroy, as illustrated by Reginald Birch, now made these adornments obligatory for the dapper young man's wardrobe, eliciting cooing and derision in equal measure. Four-year-old A. A. Milne and his brothers tamely submitted to be photographed like this, a drastic fate avoided by 6-year-old Compton Mackenzie, who wrecked 'that infernal get-up' by throwing himself in the gutter.[76] Yet, Mackenzie's reaction was as nothing compared to an 8-year-old in Davenport, Iowa, who carried his objection to the point of torching the family barn. Saddest of all was the plight of Burnett's son Vivian, cursed for ever with a sissy image. Yet, according to her biographer, 'It was not only Fauntleroy clothes which sold; there were Fauntleroy playing-cards, Fauntleroy writing-paper and toys and models of every sort, wooden, plaster, clockwork and chocolate. There was even a perfume named after him.' The building trade did not ignore him either. In 1889 the developers of a Surrey estate put up some bungalows. Though falling short of the castle ideal, one was named Dorincourt after the stately pile in *Fauntleroy* and, as a publicity stunt, presented to the author.[77]

The uncertainties of authorship also attracted business. Insurance companies cited bankable names in their promotions: 'Sir A. Conan Doyle and Mr Kipling

---

[73] Taylor (ed.), *Potter*, 173–9, 190–1. The dominance of the toy market by Germany before 1914 was generally deplored. About £1.18m was said to be the annual worth of the trade. Home-manufactured toys revived during the war: for example, W. H. Smith established a large factory at Stoke, turning out toys of all kinds including dolls which, it was reported, were 'made amid clean surroundings, and not stuffed, as German dolls often were, with unsanitary straw and other rubbish' (*The Graphic*, 8 July 1916, 58).

[74] A sizeable portion of the correspondence in Taylor (ed.), *Potter*, concerns these matters.

[75] Letter to Fruing Warne, 13 Nov. 1917, ibid. 240. Brer Rabbit was popularized by Joel Chandler Harris (1848–1908), who produced his best-selling Uncle Remus Negro folklore stories from the early 1880s. *Uncle Remus and Brer Rabbit* was first published in 1906.

[76] Thwaite, *Milne*, 2–3 and illus. opp. p. 204; Mackenzie, *Life and Times*, i. 160, 178.

[77] Thwaite, *Burnett*, 82, 90–2, 117–18, 126.

could obtain a policy insuring that any book they wrote would have a sale
running into hundreds of thousands of copies'; and 'Mr Pinero, as a playwright,
would be similarly insured,' so that 'his drama will not be taken off the stage
through failure before a stipulated number of performances'.[78] Perhaps what
authors really needed insuring against was unwise investments. The range of
limited liability companies was much narrower then than now. Overseas
investments, particularly in railway and government stock, accordingly drew
punters. When George Meredith died in 1909 he owed the Army & Navy Stores
£20 10s. 11d. but was owed £7,090 for his share of the Chilean national debt.[79]
Domestic flotations of foreign ventures could involve no more than hot air, as
Trollope classically portrayed in Augustus Melmotte's career in *The Way We Live
Now*. Heedless of this lesson, the peerage again provided a lead. Thus the Marquess of Dufferin and Ava, after a distinguished career as Governor-General of
Canada, Viceroy of India, and HM Ambassador to Russia, Turkey, Italy, and
France, contrived to disgrace himself by succeeding Lord Loch as chairman of the
London and Globe Finance Corporation, one of Whitaker Wright's fraudulent
enterprises which spectacularly collapsed at the turn of the century.[80] *Punch*
caustically cartooned coroneted sandwich-men parading the street with boards
advertising Rainbow Gold Mining Corporation, the Will o' the Wisp Syndicate,
and the Bust Tyre Company, above the caption 'Noblesse Oblige'.[81] Conan Doyle
held a bluff attitude about this, holding that a man will have 'missed a very
essential side [of life] if he has not played his part in commerce'. Such was his
accumulating wealth from authorship, he happily ventured a flutter in a goldmine
which yielded nothing, a coal mine which produced unburnable stuff, and a
treasure-hunting syndicate which failed to locate a sunken wreck. But Doyle was
not generally frivolous. He invested in Newnes's *Strand* magazine and *Tit-Bits*,
and in a motorbike firm; for thirty years he was a director of a postcard and
Christmas card company, and he was also chairman of a brass musical instrument
maker.[82] George Sims, by contrast, was an undisciplined gambler, at the roulette
tables, on horses, on anything; and his marketing of the hair-restorer Tatcho was
fated to end in depilation, if not disaster. A master melodramatist, Sims cut a fine
figure at the Devonshire Club during his prosperity. Gradually, his appearances
there dwindled in proportion to the hairs on his head; eventually he withdrew
because, so mockers said, the club committee refused to sanction him keeping
his hat on.[83]

---

[78] *T.P.'s Weekly*, 8 Nov. 1907, 603.   [79] A. D. Harvey, 'Old Objectionables', *TLS*, 2 Jan. 2004.
[80] On Dufferin (1826–1902), see the biography by his nephew Harold Nicolson, *Helen's Tower* (1937),
265–76; *DNB Supplement 1901–1911*, i. 171–6; Rendel, *Personal Papers*, 160–1; Blunt, *Diaries*, ii. 18; and on
Whitaker Wright (1845–1904), *DNB Supplement 1901–1911*, iii. 711–13.
[81] *Punch*, 13 Aug. 1898, 62. See also *Punch*, 9 Jan. 1897, 18, for a cartoon of aristocrats and sportsmen together in a drawing room in full evening dress with adverts emblazoned across their white
shirt fronts.
[82] Booth, *Conan Doyle*, 142, 167, 253–4. Conan Doyle was also a founder shareholder in the Portsmouth
and South Hampshire Electricity Supply Co. in 1889; ibid. 132–3.   [83] Sladen, *Long Life*, 159.

ALWAYS YOUNG

YOU CAN BE.

Since arrangements of a business nature were completed by Mr. Geo. R. Sims, Author and Playwright, by which the world might benefit by his discovery for the growth of the hair, the registered title of which is "Tatcho," hundreds of thousands have paid tribute to him for this remarkable specific. Many say that they attribute the fact that they are able to keep their berths to their being able to retain their hair in a youthful and wholesome condition. Unconsciously thousands of men and women for the want of this simple precaution have found the first nail driven into the coffin of their business careers. Every year the cry

"TOO OLD AT 40"

becomes more acute. When Professor Osler, who recently took the chair as Professor of Medicine at Oxford, said that people should be chloroformed at sixty, he was not taken seriously. An Oxford Bard wrote :—

Almost bald and forty-one,
So my work on earth is done.
Calm should follow after storm,
Nothing left but chloroform.

How true it would have been if Professor Osler had said that so far from being able to earn a living the bald-headed and grey haired might as well be chloroformed at forty. Now, there is a remedy for all this if people will but apply for it. That remedy is Mr. Geo. R. Sims' "Tatcho." "Tatcho" alone will do it. The aptest simile that can be applied to hair growing is that, just as your harvest is reckoned by the seed you sow in the ground, so will your hair be reckoned by the remarkable grower "Tatcho" rubbed into the roots. Autograph letters have recently appeared in the public press from Officers high in authority in the Army and Navy, well-known Doctors and Society Leaders, all testifying in the most unmistakable terms to the efficacy of "Tatcho" in bringing on the hair and nourishing it, by natural process, to its natural rich colour. A test however in your own hands is the convincing power.

OUR SPECIAL OFFER.

Now, to answer all argument, to let "Tatcho" show for itself what it can do, and to familiarise the public with it on terms within the reach of all, the Company have empowered their Chief Chemist to supply all applicants with

A FULL-SIZE 4/6 TRIAL BOTTLE OF "TATCHO," CARRIAGE PAID, FOR 1/10.

This is tantamount to giving money away; but what is its bearing on the object the Company have in view —the placing of the genuine article on the toilet table of even the poorest in the land? Just this, that each user becomes a living testimonial to the powers of "Tatcho." A hundred thousand such users are of infinitely greater service than a hundred thousand pounds spent in press publicity. It is to the saving in publicity that the public owe the benefit of having "Tatcho" on this mutually beneficial arrangement. Such is the Company's faith in the possibilities of Mr. Sims' discovery. The present offer is made solely to convince you. The rest is in your hands.

"TATCHO": Its Uses.

"TATCHO" FOR BALDNESS.

"TATCHO" FOR PREMATURELY GREY HAIR.

"TATCHO" FOR WEAK, THIN AND FALLING HAIR.

CUT OUT THIS COUPON.

Fill in your Name and Address in the space provided, and send with P.O. for 1/10, in return for which you will receive, carriage paid, a full size 4/6 trial bottle of "Tatcho."

NAME.....................................

ADDRESS..................................

....

"M.A.P." 22 4 05.

Tatcho Laboratories, 5 Great Queen St., Kingsway, London.

FIG. 8.3. Hair apparent or hair presumptive? Tatcho, as advertised by George Sims. *Source: M.A.P.*, 22 April 1905, 396. © Bodleian Library

II

Pecuniary losses troubled still more authors. Several of the worst instances of this were past, it is true. Sir Walter Scott was famously saddled with enormous debts after the collapse of Ballantyne, his publisher–bookseller, in 1826, which he worked for the rest of his life to pay off; and Thackeray found most of his inheritance, £18,000 (over £1 million in modern money), disappear in the Indian bank failures of the early 1830s. He dissipated part of what was left at the gambling tables, in other expensive pleasures, and in newspaper investment, and lost heavily again during the 'railway mania' speculation in 1845–7. None of this experience prevented him from burning his fingers during the banking crisis of 1857 or from investing in American railway stock, which he sold for a loss in the early 1860s.[84] 'Manliness and simplicity of manner go a great way with me,' Thackeray wrote about Tennyson in 1841, at a time when Tennyson was investing the family inheritance, about £8,000, in Dr Matthew Allen's 'wood-carving by machinery' business. When that crashed, Tennyson was hit hard, though not pitched into the penury he claimed. Edward FitzGerald sprang to his rescue with £300 per year; he still had £100 per year from his aunt, and he was earning £500–600 per year from his poetry.[85] This placed him comfortably across the gentlemanly middle-class threshold. And when Dr Allen died in 1845, Tennyson holding an insurance policy on his life, he came into another £2,000. This did not restrain influential friends from trying to wring out of Peel's government a grant to relieve his supposed destitution. Tennyson was twice offered a sum from public funds and twice refused it. He had not been struck by pangs of conscience but was playing for higher stakes. He was rewarded in September 1845 with an annual pension of £200: previous offers of the same amount had been non-recurrent. Tennyson trousered it for the next forty-seven years, thereby accumulating £9,400 (ignoring compound interest or investment income) even when his writing proceeds rose to £10,000 per year.[86] From the start, Tennyson's graspingness deprived a needier author: Sheridan Knowles, then aged 61 and a dramatist whose tragedies had been staged by Kemble and Macready. Tennyson and Knowles had constituted the final shortlist of candidates for State bounty. Tennyson's son later wrote, 'Peel knew nothing of either of them'—a palpable nonsense respecting Tennyson, since Peel had been importuned over several years, Tennyson's cronies even lobbying to bag him the laureateship when Southey died in 1843. Tennyson *fils*'s legend included a family joke that, as a tie-breaker, Tennyson's ally Monckton Milnes invited Peel to read Knowles's *Ulysses*, 'whereupon the pension was granted to Tennyson'.[87] In fact, Milnes, then a Peelite Conservative MP, told Peel that if charity alone governed the decision, the choice

---

[84] Harden (ed.), *Thackeray Letters*, 28, 89, 125, 128, 138, 318, 353; and D. J. Taylor, *Thackeray* (2000), 36, 64, 108–9, 375.   [85] Martin, *Tennyson*, 272.
[86] Ibid. 282–3, 292–3.   [87] Tennyson, *Tennyson*, 188.

was Knowles; but if Peel wanted to endow literature it must be Tennyson.[88] This was indisputably the case; yet it is right also to observe that Knowles lacked well-placed supporters. Following a religious conversion in 1843, he became a Baptist preacher, though this did not stop him penning two novels subsequently. Knowles was not the sole author done out of sustenance. Tennyson's persistent banking of his pension depleted the Civil List allocation for literature. Bulwer Lytton upbraided Tennyson for this, in 1846. Though Tennyson was not worsted in their literary duel, sensitivity to criticism remained one of his characteristics.

There was little sign later that authors, in the round, learned lessons from these episodes, although Thomas Hardy, close with his money as with most else, would not imitate Thackeray or Tennyson and fall for a speculative venture. When his sister-in-law was dying in 1900, he recommended his wife to

get good advice—e.g. from a respectable *banker*, or *lawyer*, on the re-arrangement of your sister's affairs; Corporation stock, of a large & thriving town, like that of Plymouth, for instance, is as good as anything. It pays about 3 per cent; & if you are offered more anywhere you may be sure there is some risk. A Government Annuity, which ceases at death, is a good thing for a person alone, & of course it brings more annually than an investment in which the principal is retained.[89]

Risk avoidance was no guarantee of contentment. Hardy, who liked to monitor the operations of unpredictable fate in his novels, felt himself on the receiving end of a stock-market injustice in 1902. His spirits not improved by flu, he complained to his banker friend Edward Clodd about 'a general slump in my few poor "securities"—as you bankers facetiously call the most insecure kickshaws on earth'.[90] Mixing conservative and adventurous strategies hardly seemed the answer either, if Kipling's example was followed in selecting the worst of both. He was duped into buying 20 acres of Canadian wilderness, and into paying taxes on it, while all the time the property legally belonged to someone else; and in 1892, during a Cook's world cruise on his honeymoon, he lost practically his entire savings, around £2,000 in fixed deposits, when the New Oriental Banking Co. crashed.[91] Kipling's Canadian investments improved after he befriended Max Aitken, Lord Beaverbrook; nor was it a bad move for his bank balance to be pally with Cecil Rhodes. Grand imperial prospects were apt to dematerialize without a guiding hand. Canada, specifically the Canada Tanning Extract Company, was one of Samuel Butler's many unwise investments. He wasted time there in the

---

[88] Martin, *Tennyson*, 292. Gladstone also importuned Peel on Tennyson's behalf.

[89] Hardy to Emma Hardy, 23 Oct. 1900, in Purdy and Millgate (eds.), *Hardy Letters*, ii. 270–1.

[90] Hardy to Edward Clodd, 17 May 1902, ibid iii. 20. Hardy employed stockbrokers. His conservative preferences were revealed in reaction to his first wife's niece: 'what seems to annoy him more than anything is that she has sold the good gilt-edged securities he bought for her and invested in such things as Bovril, Associated Newspapers, etc. without telling him' (Florence Hardy to Sydney Cockerell, 19 Aug. 1919, in Millgate (eds.), *Emma and Florence Hardy*, 161). Hardy's income was then over £2,000 p.a. He was financially generous to his relations, though miserly in domestic economy; thus, his house Max Gate remained largely bereft of sanitation and other services.

[91] Lord Birkenhead, *Rudyard Kipling* (1978), 135–7.

mid-1870s trying to salvage his capital. His independent means were reduced, not extinguished, however: 'Even when things were at their worst, I never missed my two months' summer Italian trip since 1876,' he wrote in 1890, 'except one year and then I went to Mont St. Michel and enjoyed it very much.' That no doubt helped to maintain his equanimity; but there were shocks still to come, notably in 1897, when Charles Paine Pauli died and Butler discovered his deceits. Pauli, an apparently impecunious lawyer, he had first encountered in New Zealand in the 1860s and supported to the tune of some £200 a year. Butler had fallen out with his father about this; in 1897 it was disclosed that Pauli's estate was worth £9,000. He had tricked others as well as Butler; yet, the odd thing was that Butler knew that Pauli never even liked him.[92] Butler's uselessness with money puzzled him, therefore. He mused about the difference between him and his grandfather, a headmaster of Shrewsbury, who made money all his life—'until he became a bishop'. 'Money is always on the brain,' Butler reflected; concluding, 'Money losses are the worst, loss of health is next worst and loss of reputation comes in a bad third.'[93] Happily, British authors had no monopoly in financial incompetence. Mark Twain made a gallant bid for victor ludorum by disastrous investments in a typesetting and publishing firm and in a milk-food company. This earned him 'a world-wide reputation for financial inadequacy'.[94] It then became a duty for patriotic business moguls to rescue the popular king of American letters. Henry Rogers, of Standard Oil, subsequently directed Twain's portfolio; and the Twain name was affixed to a brand of five-cent cigars as well as to a cure for indigestion.[95]

III

It was a revealing comment in 1900 in *The Times*'s obituary of R. D. Blackmore, author of *Lorna Doone* (1869), that 'To the world he was known only by his books. Personally he was of a retiring disposition, and he detested with all his heart the publicity in which the writer of today is expected to live.'[96] Blackmore mostly lived quietly as a fruit-grower and market gardener; but, as a business proposition, his 16-acre smallholding was a mistake, and it consumed much of the revenue earned by his books.[97] Blackmore had apparently shunned the limelight at a time when writers were enjoying an increasing amount of exposure. The qualifying adverb 'apparently' should be explained. R. C. Lehmann, in his parodies of bestsellers for *Punch* in 1890–1, insinuated that Blackmore's modesty was sham; in effect, just another marketing device.[98] Blackmore had been a strong believer in

---

[92] Jones, *Butler: A Memoir*, ii. 286–7.   [93] Jones (ed.), *Notebooks of Samuel Butler*, 3, 36–7, 172–3, 371.

[94] *T.P.'s Weekly*, 24 Jan. 1908, 100.

[95] *M.A.P.*, 25 Feb. 1905, 184. See also Fred Kaplan, *The Singular Mark Twain: A Biography* (New York, 2004); Karen Lystra, *Dangerous Intimacy: The Untold Story of Mark Twain's Final Years* (Berkeley, 2004).

[96] *The Times*, 22 Jan. 1900.   [97] Sutherland, *Companion*, 67–8.

[98] 'Marian Muffet' by 'R. D. Exmoor', *Punch*, 23 May 1891, 244.

the potency of press advertising for his novels, thinking (like most authors) that his publishers did too little of it.[99] He also became a client of the premier literary agent A. P. Watt. When Hall Caine was pondering how to improve his own stock in 1890, he understood that Blackmore was close to the top division: 'The present value of [Rider] Haggard, taking serial rights only, is about £1500, that of Blackmore £1000, and [Walter] Besant less. Curiously enough [Thomas] Hardy, whom I together with many others look upon as our greatest living English novelist, does not appear to command so high a figure.'[100] Caine's first novels, *The Shadow of a Crime* (1885) and *A Son of Hagar* (1886), copied the Blackmore model of rural romance, set in a wild and backward region, dense with dialect customs, family feuds, and dark secrets that allow the author to moralize. *A Son of Hagar* was dedicated to Blackmore, whom Caine had sought out. Blackmore followed Caine's career with interest: 'Take your time,' he advised, 'take hold of rapid emotion or drift of the public's rotten tastes; but work to your best mark.'[101]

Blackmore, then, was not green about the new market conditions for authorship, though shy about personal publicity. This was coming to be counted unavoidable, even indispensable. One facet was the progress of photography. Julia Cameron led by snapping Tennyson after they became neighbours on the Isle of Wight in the 1860s.[102] Tennyson also agreed to sit for that other pioneer photographer the Revd C. L. Dodgson (Lewis Carroll), whose study of Alice Liddell, aged 7 and posing in rags as 'The Beggar Child', he much admired.[103] Dodgson made a habit of photographing nymphettes: 'I am fond of children (except boys).' He trained his lens too on assorted royalty, prelates, and politicians, and included in his bag of authors George MacDonald, Ruskin, the Rossettis, Tom Taylor, Aubrey de Vere, and Charlotte Yonge. Mrs Humphry Ward was even persuaded to don her wedding dress, complete with bridesmaids, a fortnight *after* the ceremony, for him to photograph.[104]

Dickens had demonstrated what use might be made of an author's image to publicize his work. Posters of his face appeared not just on fixed sites but on vehicles; and when photography arrived, he submitted to over eighty studio sittings, including 'an exclusive sitting for the photographer Gurney in New York

---

[99] See his correspondence with Macmillan's, publishers of his first novel, *Clara Vaughan* (1864), calling for 'the drenching horn of advertisement' to counter hostile reviews, and offering £50 towards the cost; Blackmore to Alexander Macmillan, 23 May 1864, in Nowell-Smith (ed.), *Letters to Macmillan*, 63–4.

[100] Allen, *Caine*, 208.   [101] Ibid. 181, 271.

[102] Tennyson, *Tennyson*, 487, 886. Mrs Cameron also photographed Browning, Carlyle, Sir Henry Taylor, and Aubrey de Vere. In 1875 she left for Ceylon, where she died in 1879.

[103] Morton N. Cohen, *Lewis Carroll* (New York, 1996), reproduces Carroll's photographs of Liddell and Tennyson on pp. 63, 159.

[104] Ibid. 162–4, 240. Regarding the photographs of children, naked and otherwise, Cohen emphasizes that Carroll always had parental consent and chaperonage. The charge of latent paedophilia is now commonly laid against Carroll; but there is no evidence to substantiate this and no child ever seemed scarred by Carroll's attentions. Victorian attitudes to childhood were not the same as ours; on the other hand, not every Victorian cultivated the friendship of young girls as Carroll did. For further commentary on this, see Morton N. Cohen, 'When Love was Young: Failed Apologists for the Sexuality of Lewis Carroll', *TLS*, 10 Sept. 2004, 12–13.

to promote his American reading tour' in 1867.[105] Dickens died in 1870; thereafter improvements in photographic publishing stimulated a greater exploitation of and by popular authors. Naturally, Americans were (or felt themselves to be) ahead of the game. The lecture agent Major Pond wrote, 'It is quite singular to note how little personal and popular knowledge there is in Great Britain of the men who really mould intellectual thought. If we Americans do not personally know a man who has written books and sung poems for us, we do at least strive to know his face, by wide possession of a "counterfeit presentment".' Mass-produced portraits and photogravures of Browning and Tennyson hung on the walls of thousands in the United States and made them better known than in Britain, Pond maintained; and when he eventually induced the poet Sir Edwin Arnold to tour North America in 1891–2, it was a 'constant surprise' to Arnold to find himself so readily recognized.[106] But if Britain had ever been behind, it caught up fast. In May 1890 W. T. Stead's *Review of Reviews* remarked, 'authors are more read about than read'.[107] Now they could be seen too. Stead included in the August issue, along with regular summaries of articles and books, a listing of the more important new photographs; and he reproduced the supposedly most interesting.

Authors were hardly unique in wanting to disseminate their official likeness to the world. Celebrities of every sort, athletes, actors, artists, academics, lawyers, politicians, ecclesiastics, soldiers, travellers, society beauties, and royalty, all passed through photographers' studios. Neville Cardus remembered as a boy doting on these, from the studios of Elliott & Fry and the like. He was then alert to recognize his heroes, on one memorable day spotting on Manchester's streets the actor Sir Henry Irving, the conductor Hans Richter, and the Lancashire and England cricketer A. C. Maclaren.[108] Literary men and women joined them as pin-ups, striking the cerebral or glamorous pose as mood and market prescribed. The official photograph of Sir Edwin Arnold emerged thus: 'Powerful, expressive head; shoulders covered with heavy fur coat'.[109] As for Stephen Crane, famed author of *The Red Badge of Courage* (1895), who settled in England in 1897 after reporting the Graeco-Turkish war, his publicity photograph displayed him in tunic, riding breeches, and spurs, with a revolver holstered at the hip. He sat on crags, though the rocks were of the stage sort, thoughtfully supplied by the studio.[110] Soon there would be no protection against recognition. Cecil Roberts was travelling by train from Kidderminster to Paddington in 1918 when 'a small, neat man got into my carriage at Oxford. He was about forty, quietly dressed. I started when I saw him sit down opposite me. There could be no doubt that this was John Masefield, whose portrait as England's foremost living poet was to be seen everywhere.'

---

[105] Curtis, 'Dickens in the Visual Market', in Jordan and Patten (eds.), *Literature in the Marketplace*, 236.
[106] Major J. B. Pond, *Eccentricities of Genius* (New York, 1901), 377.
[107] *Review of Reviews* (May 1890), 448.   [108] Cardus, *Autobiography*, 9.
[109] *Review of Reviews* (Aug. 1890), 192.
[110] The photograph is reproduced in Christopher Benfey, *The Double Life of Stephen Crane* (1994), 214.

It took Roberts until Reading to approach Masefield, saying how he admired his work and that he too wrote poetry. They agreed to lunch together and Roberts 'was so excited by this encounter that later, on the Underground, I was carried two stations beyond my destination'.[111] Arnold Bennett also failed to pass incognito. He was 'astonished that anybody can recognise me from my photographs. But people do. Often I see them leaning towards each other and I hear them say in a whisper audible a hundred yards off: "There's Arnold Bennett".' In 1929 he declined to make himself more interesting, rebuffing a professional photographer who wanted to encapsulate him gazing at a Modigliani.[112]

Illustrated papers existed from the mid-nineteenth century. The likenesses of a handful of outstanding writers, such as Dickens, Tennyson, and Carlyle, were thereby fixed in the public mind. Thackeray's daughter Anne noted: 'only a few days before his death [24 December 1863], my father came home one afternoon saying that he could not get accustomed to the number of people whom he did not know, who seemed to know him in the street, and took off their hats as he went along'.[113] Edmund Gosse owed his first meeting with Swinburne in 1868 to his recognizing him 'instantly from his photographs which now filled the shop windows'. They did not exchange words on that occasion because Swinburne was being carried past Gosse and out of the British Museum, borne aloft on a chair by stalwart, silent attendants after the poet had banged his head on a desk.[114] The best-known papers to reproduce portraits were the sixpenny weeklies, the *Illustrated London News* and *The Graphic*, established in 1842 and 1869 respectively. These used woodcut drawings to provide the public with pictorial presentations of people in the news. Only their pretensions to seriousness distinguished them from *Punch* (established in 1841) or illustrated fiction magazines such as the *London Journal* (established in 1845). Artists whom publishers used to illustrate novels found employment on these papers. What changed with the 1880s was the intensity of the rivalry, signified when the *Illustrated London News* began to serialize fiction.[115] A host of light-entertainment papers also sprang up. Clement Shorter was at the heart of these developments, as editor of the *Illustrated London News* (1891–1900) and first editor of the *Sketch* (1893–1900). Appropriately, Shorter's marriage to the Irish poet Dora Sigerson in 1896 had its origin in his being captivated by her photograph in a paper.[116] In 1900 John Latey— editor of the *Penny Illustrated Paper*, where Shorter (briefly, in 1890) was his assistant—succeeded Shorter as editor of the *Sketch*.[117] Latey's own new assistant and eventual successor, Keble Howard, left an insider's account of life on such a

---

[111] Roberts, *Years of Promise*, 173.

[112] Bennett, *Journal 1929*, 106–7, 120. Bennett, at a private view of Modiglianis in a West End gallery, was pleased that he had bought a portrait of a woman by Modigliani ('certainly one of the greatest painters of this century') eight years earlier for £50: 'There were no £50 items in this show.'

[113] Fuller and Hammersley (eds.), *Thackeray's Daughter*, 93. [114] Gosse, *Life of Swinburne*, 178.

[115] Sutherland, *Companion*, 317. [116] Ibid. 574–5.

[117] On John Latey (1842–1902), *Who Was Who, 1897–1916*, 412. His father (also John Latey) had been editor of the *Illustrated London News*, on which Latey began. Latey then became joint editor, with Mayne

paper, which generated a 'handsome revenue', in the late 1890s and early 1900s. Finding his office walls decorated with photographs of actresses, Howard completed their embrace by covering the ceiling as well. An important part of his job, aside from feature-writing, proof-reading, and correspondence, was to select photographs from the thousands submitted—'When I say thousands, I mean thousands. I am sure that fully two thousand photographs would come to the office each week...'. Black-and-white artists were not displaced; if anything, their market expanded with the number of illustrated papers, because drawings were easier to reproduce than photographs. The *Sketch* employed many, including Phil May and Max Beerbohm. Naturally, too, the *Sketch* contained a regular literary feature: the 'Literary Lounger' column, written by the ubiquitous Robertson Nicoll, using the cipher 'O.O.'.[118]

The quality broadsheets were generally more sparing, but on landmark occasions they employed the same device. The first Mrs Hardy cut out the portrait of Ruskin from the *Daily Chronicle* that saluted his eightieth birthday in 1899, and hung it in her day room.[119] Meanwhile, the periodicals competed in the inventiveness with which they presented the 'human interest' angle. In January 1891 George Newnes launched the sixpenny monthly *Strand Magazine* as a middle-class stablemate for his popular miscellany *Tit-Bits*. By 1896 it enjoyed a monthly circulation of half a million copies.[120] Now best known for its Sherlock Holmes serializations, illustrated by Sidney Paget,[121] the *Strand* from the start pushed star-name features. The October issue, for example, carried an illustrated article on Tennyson's early days and a profile of W. S. Gilbert. Gilbert also appeared in the *Strand*'s photographic section, which that month displayed the ex-Empress (of France) Eugénie, the novelist and MP Justin McCarthy, the apostle of self-help Samuel Smiles, and the physician Sir Morrell Mackenzie, who unavailingly treated the throat cancer of the German Emperor, Frederick III. No incongruity was too great for these ensembles. February's edition combined Gladstone, Ruskin, Cardinal Manning, Mrs Langtry, and T. H. Huxley; and November's joined Thomas Hardy and Charlotte M. Yonge. Hardy was further invited to participate in the *Strand*'s series of 'Portraits of Celebrities at Different Times of their Lives'. He cooperated by sending four photographs of himself at various ages.[122]

Reid, of the *Boys Illustrated News*, and author of romantic novelettes. He described himself as a 'steadfast advocate of all manly exercises calculated to promote a sound mind in a sound body'.

[118] Howard, *Motley Life*, 138–9, 142–3, 168–71.

[119] Emma Hardy to Rebekah Owen, 14 Feb. 1899, in Millgate (eds.), *Emma and Florence Hardy*, 14.

[120] Sutherland, *Companion*, 609.

[121] A Holmes story would add 100,000 copies to the *Strand*'s circulation; Booth, *Conan Doyle*, 178.

[122] Hardy to George Newnes, 29 Aug. 1891, in Purdy and Millgate (eds.), *Hardy Letters*, i. 242. Conan Doyle featured in December; Booth, *Conan Doyle*, 145. On the copyright of photographs and reproduction fees paid by the press, see Joseph, *Commercial Side of Literature*, 222–3. Usually, the studio retained copyright. In 1925 reproduction fees ranged from a half to 4 guineas in the London press, with the provincial press paying less. Photographs of actresses and Society women, not authors, were then the ones that commanded higher sums: 'Editors are well aware that by publishing an author's photograph they are giving him useful publicity—ergo, why pay for it?'

The artificiality of such studies was satirized by Hubert Henry Davies in *Lady Epping's Lawsuit*, which was staged at the Criterion in 1908. To accompany an interview, which is equally fabricated, the playwright Paul Hughes, who has just scored a hit, is instructed to strike poses for the photographer. First comes 'standing up in a natural attitude...This is "Good morning. Glad to see you." Look pleasant, please'; the second, as Paul is placed in a chair, 'in a posture of despair with his head on his hand', expresses 'Oh, dear, I can't work to-day somehow'; third, with one hand caressing the books in the library, is dubbed 'My silent friends'. Paul, having invited the publicity, is now beginning to think better of it. He refuses to submit to a garden shot; unperturbed, he is pointed to the sofa, to assume 'a sprawling summer-like attitude': the photographer 'will fill in the shrubs and a sun-dial afterwards'. The final requests are for photos with wife and child; but Paul, and particularly his wife, Evelyn, call halt at this point. Interviewer and photographer leave, nonetheless content that they have enough to satisfy the readers of their journal the *Gentleman's Friend*; whereupon the inquest ensues:

EVELYN. ....[In] the old days you said that advertising one's self with interviewers and snapshots was so contemptible.
PAUL. No one wanted to interview me or snap me then.
EVELYN. Don't change, Paul.
PAUL. Of course not, dear—but it's not my fault if the press wants to make an idol of me.
EVELYN [*indignantly*]. An idol! You mean an Aunt Sally!
PAUL. Really, Evelyn, I don't think you should speak so to a public man. With new dignities come new duties. They have a right to know exactly what I'm like.
EVELYN. Who?
PAUL. The people!
EVELYN. Oh, Paul—how can you talk like that? The other day a monkey was interviewed—think of it—a monkey.
PAUL. They say it has genius.[123]

Such attention startled some authors. Following his publishers' promotion of *In the Year of Jubilee* (1894), and to accompany the serialization of *Eve's Ransom* in the *Illustrated London News* in 1895, George Gissing was asked by the editor Clement Shorter to attend the studio of a photographer who was portraying the 'sixteen leading novelists' of the day. Soon afterwards a snippet appeared in the *Literary World* referring to a Gissing 'boom', at which the doleful drudge noted in his diary: 'Didn't know of the "boom".'[124]

There was also cause to snigger at how some authors sought to beguile their public—Hall Caine, particularly, with his supposed facial resemblance to Shakespeare. Caine's effrontery was boundless, and he had his own laugh at editors who lapped up whatever he offered. Like Hardy, he was invited by the *Strand* to send four photographs, taken at different times, to accompany a

---

[123] 'Lady Epping's Lawsuit' (1908), in Davies, *Plays*, i. 153–5.   [124] Halperin, *Gissing*, 214.

sycophantic article on the Great Author. Thus he appeared at ages 6, 25, 33, and 38: all very well, except that two were not photographs of Caine. The 6-year-old was his son Ralph, and the 25-year-old was Caine's brother Willie.[125] Authors needed smartly to balance commercial calculation and vanity. 'Fluffy', or 'Fluffina' to her friends, Mrs Hodgson Burnett was actually short and stout, with a moon face of poor complexion topped with hair that, the spiteful suggested, was dyed or a wig. She did her best to avoid photographers and artists, but magazines could not do without a vision of the creator of *Little Lord Fauntleroy*. Her son Vivian appalled her in 1906 by collaborating with *Munsey's Magazine*, which he allowed to make a drawing from a photograph he had, to illustrate an article about her:

Never have I seen anything as monstrous as the thing Munsey drew from your picture of me—and I have seen monstrous things in my time . . . Your photograph was not flattering but the 'drawing' is that of an elderly, battered and drunken Irish cook with a bottle nose and deep cuts in her cheeks. It is a thing so coarse and revolting that it is bad business. I have not a doubt that it has absolutely injured me, and lowered my market value by thousands a year . . . [126]

It was the studio image, posed and touched up, that authors most favoured. The only photograph Mrs Hodgson Burnett pronounced 'really excellent' was by Barrauds of Oxford Street.[127]

The gossip magazine *M.A.P.* noted waspishly how others, too, contrived to mislead admirers: 'In a photograph, Mr Kipling looks sturdily and strongly built, whereas in reality he just escapes being puny; and a recent photograph of Mr W. W. Jacobs represents him with a straight Grecian nose, instead of the prominent arched organ which is his dominant feature.'[128] Although like the rest of the world he passed through Messrs Elliott & Fry's studios, the duodecimo J. M. Barrie was anxious to avoid situations which exposed his (lack of) stature. An automobilist since 1900, he nevertheless shunned an invitation from the editor of *Motoring* to be featured in the magazine, declaring 'I do not care to be photo-graphed.'[129] Shaw later took the perverse view that Barrie's shortness made him all the more grand. At Hardy's funeral in 1928, when the pall-bearers included Kipling, Galsworthy, and Housman, and the prime ministers Baldwin and MacDonald, Shaw stood out by his tallness but, he added about his little friend, 'Barrie, blast him! Looked far the most effective. He made himself look specially small.'[130]

Photographs could dispel the mystique surrounding an author. In 1912 Gosse recalled the moment in 1871 when, together with other juniors toiling in the bowels of the British Museum, he was summoned upstairs to be presented to Tennyson, who was being shown around on one of the days on which the public was excluded.

[125] Allen, *Caine*, 216.   [126] Thwaite, *Burnett*, 214.   [127] Ibid. 112.
[128] *M.A.P.*, 27 Aug. 1904, 249.   [129] Letter, 8 May 1903, in Meynell (ed.), *Barrie Letters*, 42.
[130] Asquith, *Barrie*, 2.

The feeling of excitement was almost overwhelming ... Tennyson was scarcely a human being to us, he was the God of the Golden Bow; I approached him now like a blank idiot about to be slain, 'or was I a worm, too low-crawling for death, O Delphic Apollo?' It is not merely that no person living now calls forth that kind of devotion, but the sentiment of mystery has disappeared. Not genius itself could survive the kodak snapshots and the halfpenny newspapers.[131]

Easy recognition did have its compensations. Barrie's favourite eating places were the Savoy (nearby the Adelphi, where he lived), the Ritz, Berkeley, and Claridge's. Part of his pleasure derived from memory of hungry days during his writer's apprenticeship in London, whereas now he could not enter one of these exclusive restaurants without being 'greeted by his name by a smiling, bowing commissionaire or head waiter'. Barrie found the same in Brighton when putting up at the Royal Albion, where the hotelier Harry Preston hailed him as 'My Lord and Master' and loaded him with champagne and cigars.[132]

Authors exercised what control they could over the medium. Zack (Gwendoline Keats, who never published under her real name) would not send her photograph to *The Bookman*, this being her remonstrance against the 'whole modern spirit of self advertisement'. So she told the nervously shy May Sinclair in 1898, who in that year posed for her own publicity photograph to launch her second novel *Mr. and Mrs. Nevill Tyson*. Sinclair's was a romantically dreamy pose which made her appear taller than her 5-foot nothing.[133] Anthony Trollope had been characteristically down-to-earth: 'I do not like photographs, and dislike my own worse than all others.' Still, he realized that he needed a stock of them to send out to admirers, to keep them from further pestering him. The one he chose in the 1870s, a mere inch square, had him look disapproving and 'very much like a conspirator'.[134] In the 1890s Hardy likewise found it useful to send correspondents copies of Elliott & Fry's formal photograph, and to authorize its reproduction in newspapers for articles about him. This studio image was updated at intervals, by his friend the photographer Hermann Lea, by Russell & Sons of 17 Baker Street, and by the Stereoscopic Co. The publicity shot was one thing, but now authors had to avoid cameras being pointed by unlicensed hands. Hardy complained of 'an unpleasant experience' in 1904 when he walked from his home, Max Gate, to the cottage at Higher Bockhampton where he was born and where his brother and two sisters were still living: 'I was unknown to myself, Kodaked by some young men who were on the watch.'[135]

Marie Corelli was especially notorious for gaining height and shedding weight and years in her publicity photographs. The last she would authorize dated from

---

[131] Edmund Gosse, 'A First Sight of Tennyson', in Gosse, *Portraits and Sketches*, 131–2. The quotation is from Keats's *Hymn to Apollo* (1815).   [132] Asquith, *Barrie*, 59, 63; Preston, *Memories*, 207.

[133] Suzanne Raitt, *May Sinclair: A Modern Victorian* (Oxford, 2000), 79, and pl. 5 for Sinclair's publicity photograph. For Zack (Gwendoline Keats, d. 1910), Kemp *et al.* (eds.), *Edwardian Fiction*, 430.

[134] Booth (ed.), *Trollope's Letters*, 345, 368, 400.

[135] Hardy to Hermann Lea, 12 Nov. 1904, in Purdy and Millgate (eds.), *Hardy Letters*, iii. 146.

1906, which made her look ten years younger; and she was still autographing this in 1919, when 'she was sixty-four and looked like eighty'.[136] Gabell's studio was responsible for the 1906 confection, and for another favourite, Corelli as Pansy at a Shakespeare Festival ball in 1903. That was the permanent image she held of herself when she paraded about her home town of Stratford, as a beauty, wearing 'pale, conspicuous colours: lilac, and faint pinks, and creams—like the Royal family, with whom she identified herself'. So Marguerite Steen wrote: she was a student at Ruby Ginner's School of Revived Greek Dance in Stratford in 1918 when she came across Corelli in the doorway of W. H. Smith's bookshop. Steen was amazed by Corelli's china figurine appearance: 'I am five feet six on my flat feet; her head reached a little above my elbow. Her enormous torso, which was that of a normal adult, only looked enormous because of her dwarfed arms and legs, which would have fitted a child of ten. Her face was a ball of pink putty into which were pushed the dark beads of her eyes, and trimmed with yellowish curls.' The opportunity was irresistible. Having a camera with her, Steen snapped the shutter, only to be pounced upon and berated by Corelli's live-in companion, Bertha Vyver—'Fat Bertha, mountainous in rusty black'—who threatened to report her to Ruby Ginner.[137] When gliding along the Avon in her gondola, Corelli and Vyver would pull blankets over their heads to defeat photographers.[138]

Forerunners of the paparazzi were already massing. Authors at ease were not, therefore, off limits. Barrie was upset in 1899 when reporters and photographers converged on the Cotswold village of Broadway, where he and his celebrity team of cricketers, the Allahakbarries, were playing against rivals wearing the colours of the former actress Mary Anderson (now Madame de Navarro), in an annual fixture which they began unpublicized in 1897.[139] Abroad was no sanctuary either for the writer craving privacy, as Jerome K. Jerome and Rudyard Kipling found in 1909 during a winter sports holiday in Switzerland: 'the Kodak fiends followed . . . in their hundreds', richly enjoying Kipling's maladroitness on skis and skates.[140] In 1902 Kipling had moved to the seclusion of Bateman's, a manor house on the Sussex Weald, in part because day trippers from Brighton were pressing their faces at the windows of his previous home, The Elms, at Rottingdean.[141] But authors also aimed the invasive camera. 'I must some day write about how I hunted the late Bishop of Carlisle with my camera, hoping to shoot him when he was sea-sick crossing from Calais to Dover,' wrote Samuel Butler with malicious glee in 1892.[142]

---

[136] Scott, *Corelli*, 73.   [137] Marguerite Steen, *Looking Glass: An Autobiography* (1966), 54–5.
[138] See the photograph opp. p. 185 in Scott, *Corelli*.   [139] Dunbar, *Barrie*, 112, 123.
[140] Jerome, *Life and Times*, 175. Critics of Kipling also deployed photography as a hostile metaphor. The Liberal editor of the *Daily News*, A. G. Gardiner, while acknowledging the 'astonishing intensity of his vision', argued that 'the essential fact' was that 'Kipling is a precocious boy with a camera. He has the gift of vision, but not the gift of thought' (Gardiner, *Prophets, Priests and Kings*, 324–30).
[141] Martin Seymour-Smith, *Rudyard Kipling* (1989), 305–7. Rottingdean was also where the painters Sir Edward Burne-Jones (Kipling's uncle) and William Nicholson had homes; Rothenstein, *Men and Memories, 1900–1922*, 141–2.   [142] Jones (ed.), *Notebooks of Samuel Butler*, 254.

IV

Authors did not neglect the conventional means by which their renown might be registered for posterity: portraiture and sculpture. Generally, the exercise bene-fited artist and author. Thomas Hardy was portrayed several times both by William Strang and by William Rothenstein. In 1906 Jacques-Émile Blanche asked to paint his portrait. This was exhibited in the Salon de la Société nationale in Paris, before passing to the Tate Gallery. In 1908 Hardy also sat for Sir Hubert von Herkomer, who had illustrated the serial version of *Tess of the D'Urbervilles*. It was the right contacts that had led to the portrait of Hardy by Winifred Thomson in 1897, this resulting from Lady Jeune's introduction.[143] Similarly, it was rich American admirers, Mr and Mrs Charles Fairchild of Boston, who commissioned John Singer Sargent to portray Robert Louis Stevenson in 1884, a study that was repeated in 1885 picturing Stevenson in velveteen jacket, twisting his moustache, and with Fanny, his American wife, robed as a Red Indian. In 1886 the American artist J. W. Alexander attended on Stevenson at Bournemouth, making a drawing of his head which Stevenson thought 'a mixture of an aztec idol, a lion, an Indian Rajah, and a woman'.[144] Later that year Sidney Colvin escorted Stevenson to Hammersmith to sit for Sir William Richmond;[145] and, when he retired to Samoa, a bust was done by John Hutchison, who was famed for his studies of the Queen and Prince Consort and of imaginary subjects such as Hamlet and Don Quixote.[146] The fans' favourite Stevenson icon was the medallion sculpted in New York in 1887 by Augustus St Gaudens, depicting the romantic invalid sitting up in bed wearing a South American poncho and holding his manuscripts. The original had him holding a cigarette in his right hand, but a pen was substituted for the bas-relief reproduction in St Giles's, Edinburgh.[147]

How an author posed, and was posed, was an essay in character idealization. Tennyson's 'official' portrait, that liked best by his family and presented to the National Portrait Gallery, was a repainted version of Samuel Laurence's from 1838. After Tennyson's death his widow approached G. F. Watts to retouch Laurence's work; on his refusing, Burne-Jones undertook the required alterations,

---

[143] The Purdy and Millgate collections of Hardy's letters contain details about these commissions. See also Florence Hardy to Sydney Cockerell, 31 Jan. 1921, in Millgate (ed.), *Emma and Florence Hardy*, 173, for her initial dislike of the Blanche portrait. Blanche (1861–1942) was nicknamed the French Sargent for the way in which he sought out celebrities and Society people.

[144] Letter to Mr and Mrs Thomas Stevenson, 7 July 1886, in Colvin (ed.), *Letters to Family and Friends*, ii. 39. For the Sargent portraits, see the letters to W. H. Low, 3 Jan. and 22 Oct. 1885, ibid. i. 333, 362–3.

[145] Sir Arthur Richmond, *Twenty-Six Years, 1879–1905* (1961), 23. Richmond's Stevenson is in the National Portrait Gallery.

[146] Stevenson's account in Colvin (ed.), *Vailima Letters*, 307—'I am being busted here by party named Hutchinson. Seems good'—misspells the sculptor's name. On Hutchison (d. 1910), *Who Was Who, 1897–1916*, 363–4.

[147] Mackay, *Violent Friend*, 134, 143–4, 161–2; and letter to Colvin, end Sept. 1887, in Colvin (ed.), *Letters to Family and Friends*, ii. 65–6. Stevenson's poncho was a gift from Sir Henry Taylor (1800–86), a neighbour during the Stevensons' Bournemouth years, on whom, see *DNB* lv. 410–12.

to background and costume and, it is thought, to facial expression, 'in order to present a more suitable romanticized likeness of the poet to the world'.[148] It was generally assumed that the peculiar source of an author's genius would best be divined if the artist felt close to the subject. Gerald Kelly knew Somerset Maugham from 1902 and painted him thirty times; yet it was not until he saw Graham Sutherland's portrait (1949) that Kelly realized that, all the while, 'disguised as an old Chinese madame', Maugham looked as if he had been keeping 'a brothel in Shanghai'.[149] Even when the artist admired the author there was no guarantee that the author would be satisfied. In 1907, Charles Shannon being unavailable, Augustus John was lured to Coole Park, Lady Gregory's estate in Ireland, by the prospect of drawing W. B. Yeats and by the £18 fee coughed up in advance. John believed that he triumphantly caught the image of the hieratic poet; yet Yeats complained that John's 'savage imagination' transformed him into a 'tinker, drunken, unpleasant and disreputable', or as 'an unshaven, drunken bartender'. The plan was abandoned of using one of John's etchings as a frontispiece for the Yeats collected edition then being prepared for publication. A Sargent charcoal (paid for by Lady Gregory) was substituted instead;[150] and a quarter of a century would elapse before John was invited to try his hand again. The arrangements were made by Oliver St John Gogarty, but the prelude was an awful dinner party at which Yeats reeled off a series of practised anecdotes about George Moore for Lord and Lady Longford, which produced 'stentorian laughter' from the lordship and a 'more discreet whinny' from the ladyship. John's 'difficulties while painting Yeats were not lightened by the obligation of producing an appreciative guffaw at the right moment, and I fear my timing was not always correct'.[151] John persevered; nor did Yeats's death and his own failing powers dim the ambition. In the 1950s he planned a vast statue of Yeats to awe Dublin, but could not decide between 'trousers or a more classic nudity'.[152]

'It was the sight of your maimed strength and masterfulness that begot John Silver in *Treasure Island*,' wrote Stevenson to the crippled poet–editor W. E. Henley, who was more regularly cast in a bust by Rodin and in a drawing by Will Rothenstein.[153] In the 1890s Rothenstein went the rounds of author celebrities, as, slyly, did Max Beerbohm with his caricatures. Rothenstein was barely 21 in 1893 when the publisher John Lane gave him his first commission: to

---

[148] Martin, *Tennyson*, 553.

[149] Quoted in Morgan, *Somerset Maugham*, 525. Maugham nevertheless bought the Sutherland portrait, which eventually found its way into the Tate Gallery in 1951.

[150] R. F. Foster, *W. B. Yeats* (1997), i. 371, 373; Michael Holroyd, *Augustus John* (1974–5), i. 259–62, where it is noted that in subsequent editions of Yeats's collected works one or another of John's portraits of Yeats is invariably used.   [151] Holroyd, *John*, ii. 138.

[152] Letter to Joe Hone, 9 Feb. 1956, in Holroyd, *John*, ii. 201.

[153] Letter to Henley, May 1883, in Colvin (ed.), *Letters to Family and Friends*, i. 270; Rothenstein, *Men and Memories, 1872–1900*, 297. The bust by Rodin, of whom Henley was one of the first advocates in England (they had met in Paris in 1881), was done in 1886. Rodin made a replica of it for the memorial to Henley, unveiled in St Paul's Cathedral in 1907. The Rothenstein drawing was done in 1897; there was also an oil by William Nicholson in 1901; *DNB Supplement 1901–1911*, ii. 246.

draw twenty-four Oxford notables at £5 per head. Rothenstein had yet to learn that what the artist saw and what the sitter and his supporters wanted may not correspond. The aesthete Walter Pater summoned his sisters to denounce Rothenstein's presentation of him as (in Grant Richards's words) 'a gambling major, and whisky-sodden at that'.[154] There was a consciousness about serving History by these records. Hence it did not matter (except to the artist) when book reproductions of these figures did not sell strongly, as was the fate of Rothenstein's *English Portraits* (1898), which contained another lithograph set of twenty-four worthies including Hardy, Henley, Robert Bridges, Arthur Pinero, and Grant Allen, as representatives of Literature.[155] Even worse befell Rothenstein's portraits of rising writers who, at the point of production, had no sizeable fan club. This was the *Liber Juniorum* (1899), and it sold not a copy. It contained prints of Aubrey Beardsley, Laurence Binyon, Laurence Housman, Max Beerbohm, W. B. Yeats, and Stephen Phillips. Revealing was the planning that went into it. Rothenstein consulted Arthur Symons, who had been

discussing it with Yeats, and we both strongly feel that [William] Watson and [John] Davidson should *certainly* form part of it. Why not then a dozen somewhat thus:

1. Watson	5. [Herbert] Horne	9. Housman
2. Davidson	6. [Reginald] Savage	10. Stephen Phillips
3. F.[rancis] Thompson	7. Lionel Johnson	11. Binyon
4. Yeats	8. [Ernest] Dowson	12. A.[rthur] S.[ymons]

This at once gives more weight, and allows more chance for the one or two names which *we* think interesting but editors may not. I find I have forgotten Max. I fear Dowson or Binyon might have to go if you want the dozen.[156]

In due course, Rothenstein would depict—frequently several times—practically every literary celebrity of the period. In addition to those named, he drew George Gissing, Henry Newbolt, W. H. Hudson, Joseph Conrad, Maurice Hewlett, Edmund Gosse, Stopford Brooke, Æ (George Russell), Arnold Bennett, Walter de la Mare, Ralph Hodgson, Siegfried Sassoon, and A. E. Housman. The last never failed to tell Rothenstein 'how repellent he appeared to himself in my drawings'.[157]

Some writers were so entranced by having their likenesses drawn as to appear almost professional sitters. Swinburne got to know the Pre-Raphaelite fraternity at Oxford and was perfectly endowed by nature as a grotesquerie to figure in their designs, having an undersized body and huge head, pallid face and green eyes, and copious red hair like an aureole made from blood oranges. And figure he did, in paintings, engravings, bookplates, and stained glass, so many times that Philip

---

[154] Lambert and Ratcliffe, *Bodley Head*, 76.

[155] The inclusion of Grant Allen, surprising in this company, was engineered by the publisher Grant Richards, who was his cousin. On this and other squabbles over the selection of subjects, Mary Lago (ed.), *Men and Memories: Recollections 1872–1938 of William Rothenstein* (1978), 107–14, 211–12.

[156] Rothenstein, *Men and Memories, 1872–1900*, 330.

[157] Rothenstein, *Men and Memories, 1900–1922*, 39.

Webb reported workmen at the Scarborough glass factory exclaiming, as yet another Morris image of Swinburne was exposed, 'Blest if they haven't put in little Carroty-locks.'[158] Swinburne's successor as leading male model among writers was George Moore. It was a great moment when they met. This was in the 1870s, when all were 'carried away on the hurricane winds of Swinburne's verses', and it was every poet's dream to glimpse him. Encouraged by W. M. Rossetti, Moore ascended the stairs in Great James Street, where Swinburne had rooms, opened a door, and, instead of finding the poet in an armchair poised to offer a cigarette and chatter about Shelley, Moore espied a naked man on a bed. Worse, the nude Swinburne resembled a 'dreadful caricature' of Moore himself: red hair, thin frame, high forehead, long nose, and pointed chin. Moore's nerve failed: 'I just managed to babble out, "Does Mr Jones live here?" The red head shook on a long thin neck like a tulip, and I heard, "Will you ask downstairs?" I fled and jumped into a hansom . . .'.[159] Moore never saw Swinburne again. This excursion apart, Moore dwelt among artists in Paris during his struggling years in the 1870s. He was portrayed then by Edouard Manet, later by Jacques-Émile Blanche, Walter Sickert, Henry Tonks, J. B. Yeats, and William Orpen.[160] These are only the most famous representations. Moore was so frequently painted by the New English Art Club that, to commemorate his return to live in Chelsea after 1909, Max Beerbohm sketched a revolt of artists' models, one confronting Moore thus: 'Ought to be ashamed o' yerself—coming an' taking the bread out o' us poor girls' mouths.'[161] In spite of having 'a muddy skin and a battered long nose',[162] and resembling 'an extremely decayed lemon',[163] Moore was egregiously vain. Manet's recollection circulated: 'Ce pauvre George Moore! Il était si embetânt!'[164]—but Moore could not be dissuaded from posing.

Moore's own successor as artists' model was Bernard Shaw. No writer was more enthusiastic about having his physiognomy and frame captured for posterity. 'Roger Fry likened him to Christ,' wrote Rothenstein. 'I could not see the resemblance; but I admired Shaw for one thing especially—he did not wait until he was famous to behave like a great man.'[165] Shaw was one of Rothenstein's

[158] Gosse, *Life of Swinburne*, 71, 201. Gosse likened Swinburne, because of his movements, to 'some orange-crested bird—a hoopoe, perhaps'.

[159] Moore to Gosse, 2 Dec. 1912, in Gosse, *Life of Swinburne*, 330.

[160] Bruce Arnold, *Orpen: Mirror to an Age* (1981), ch. 8 for Moore's association with Orpen.

[161] J. G. Riewald (ed.), *Beerbohm's Literary Caricatures* (1977), 253. Oscar Wilde applauded an earlier caricature of Moore by Max as a 'masterpiece', being 'a most brilliant and bitter rendering of that vague formless obscene face' (letter to Reginald Turner, 3 Feb. 1899, in Hart-Davis (ed.), *Wilde Letters*, 348).

[162] Nash, *Life*, 17.

[163] Mrs Hodgson Burnett's description, on seeing a picture of Moore in the *Yellow Book* in 1895; Thwaite, *Burnett*, 161.

[164] Agate, *Shorter Ego*, 36 (14 Apr. 1933). Manet's remark might translate as 'Poor George Moore! He was so irritatingly boring!'

[165] Rothenstein, *Men and Memories, 1872–1900*, 208; id., *Men and Memories, 1900–1922*, 108–9, 183–4. Shaw himself wrote in 1901 that G.B.S. was 'one of the most successful of my fictions, but getting a bit tiresome' (G. B. Shaw, *Sixteen Self Sketches* (1949), 54). Mrs Patrick Campbell, wooed by Shaw to star in his plays, evidently felt the same when she wrote on 24 July 1912: 'I do wish you wouldn't send me your

earliest sitters; and he pedalled miles across London in 1894 to importune Max Beerbohm, then still an Oxford undergraduate but whose reputation as a cartoonist was already spreading. Eventually, Max would do over forty caricatures of Shaw, more than of anyone, himself and Edward VII apart. Shaw was largely impervious to their barbs, although Mrs Shaw shredded one and committed it to the flames.[166] In sum, there was no artist, sculptor, or photographer who could not have Shaw at any time and in any attitude: wearing a broad-rimmed hat for Rothenstein and papal robes for Neville Lytton, or clothed in nothing but his thoughts for Alvin Langdon Coburn. The more risqué the reputation of chiseller, dauber, or snapper, the keener was Shaw to pose. Naturally, he sought out Rodin, whose power to shock earned him the sobriquet 'the Zola of sculpture'; but he also sat for sculptures by Troubetskoy, Davidson, Kathleen Bruce; paintings by Augustus John, Sir John Lavery, John Collier, Bertha Newcombe, Nellie Heath, William Strang; and photographs by anyone able to point a camera. H. G. Wells declared, 'It is impossible to move without coming up against Shaw in effigy'; and Beerbohm, repelled by the self-satisfaction radiating from Shaw's smug 'temperance beverage face', remained troubled by the thought of 'that tremulous beard in marble—rigidly fluttering its way down the ages'.[167] In 1914 occurred Shaw's proudest moment. He appeared in Mme Tussaud's waxworks.[168]

Shaw was excessive, yet authors such as Joseph Conrad and Henry James, who despised the commercialization of their profession, did not uphold this objection to the extent of avoiding canvas and camera. Well-known portraits of each exist by, respectively, Walter Tittle and John Singer Sargent. Coburn also photographed both. The justification for sitting for Coburn—a handsome Bostonian with an independent income—was that he was as supreme an artist as Bellini, Holbein, Hals, or Gainsborough. This was Shaw's puffery for Coburn's one-man show at the Royal Photographic Society in 1906.[169] It also helped that Coburn was a confessed Hero-Worshipper.[170] Progressively, Coburn photographed practically every celebrated British author, from Barrie and Belloc to Yeats and Zangwill, between 1904 and 1917, not to mention artists, composers, and prime ministers; and the finest examples were published as *Men of Mark* (1913) and *More Men of Mark* (1922). Coburn was also commissioned to peregrinate Europe photographing scenes for the definitive New York edition of Henry James's works in

photographs—I dislike photographs, I have given all yours away at the theatre—My dresser particularly liked the one of you as Jesus Christ playing the piano' (Alan Dent (ed.), *Bernard Shaw and Mrs. Patrick Campbell: Their Correspondence* (1952), 29).

[166] Behrman, *Max*, 20, 74; Riewald (ed.), *Beerbohm's Literary Caricatures*, 76–89.

[167] St John (ed.), *Terry and Shaw Correspondence*, 393; and Cecil, *Max*, 262. Also Blunt, *Diaries*, ii. 136 (10 Apr. 1906). For Shaw's own account, *Sixteen Self Sketches*, 121–6; Holroyd, *Shaw*, ii. 180–5.

[168] *Punch*, 7 Jan. 1914, 8.

[169] Catalogue quoted in Alvin Langdon Coburn, *An Autobiography* [with over seventy reproductions of his work], ed. Helmut and Alison Gernsheim (1978), 36.

[170] Alvin Langdon Coburn, *More Men of Mark* (1922), 18.

1906;[171] and he illustrated the American edition of Maeterlinck's *The Intelligence of Flowers* (1907) and Chesterton's *London* (1914).

By his frequent poses—Coburn photographed him over fifty times[172]—Shaw was incrementally making an investment in future reputation. The issue was more urgent for those who were dying or had just departed life. The convention of mortuary artistry still held. Works in this mode, such as Sir John Millais's *Dickens after Death*, elicited awed approval. In August 1907 Wilfrid Blunt summoned Neville Lytton down to Sussex for the purpose of sketching the moribund poet Francis Thompson, who was being nursed in one of Blunt's estate cottages. Blunt was delighted by the resultant 'profile in coloured chalks. It is an exact presentment of what he is, and will be very valuable as a record in the days to come. He, Thompson, is pleased with it himself.'[173] Swinburne, with a lifetime's posing behind him, met a different fate when an unseemly dispute broke out as he lay on his bier in 1909. Rothenstein's wife, the actress Alice Kingsley, proposed that a death-mask be made. She offered to persuade Epstein to do the job at once. Swinburne's guardian, Watts-Dunton, discountenanced the idea: not of having a death-mask made but of having it done by Epstein, who was insufficiently famous. He called in Alfred Drury, who made a mould. The result was black comedy. Drury never delivered, claiming to have lost the mould.[174] And Epstein's reputation grew, though first as a notoriety with his nude figures on the British Medical Association building in London and tomb for Oscar Wilde in the French national cemetery, Père Lachaise, Paris. Finished in 1912, Wilde's monument was arrested in transit by French customs officials. When released and sited, it was draped in tarpaulin by authorities disturbed by the angels' genitalia. Further mutilated by persons unknown, it was refused an opening ceremony for two years.[175]

For the greatest men of letters only the greatest artist would do. In Victorian estimation, valuing his allegorical power above all, this meant G. F. Watts. He portrayed Tennyson six times;[176] and in 1898, when Watts was aged 81, he began to sculpt the great statue of Tennyson which was completed in 1903. Chesterton wrote in 1904: 'He scarcely ever paints a man without making him about five times as magnificent as he really looks. The real men appear, if they present themselves afterwards, like mean and unsympathetic sketches from the Watts original.'[177] As well as his Tennyson of 1865, Watts portraited Browning (1866),

---

[171] Edel, *James*, ii. 635–7.

[172] Coburn, *Autobiography*, 26. Shaw was himself a keen and knowledgeable photographer, including this as one of his recreations for the first time in *Who's Who* (1901), 1016.

[173] Blunt, *Diaries*, ii. 181 (30 Aug. 1907).

[174] Rothenstein, *Men and Memories, 1900–1922*, 236. On Drury (1856–1944), *DNB 1941–1950*, 221–2.

[175] Borland, *Robert Ross*, 136, 170–1, 200, 207.

[176] Geoffrey H. White (ed.), *The Complete Peerage* (1953), xii. 668, also notes portraits by Herkomer (1878) and Millais (1881), a chalk drawing by Arnault now in the National Portrait Gallery, and two busts by Woolner (1857, 1873).

[177] Quoted in Wilfrid Blunt, *'England's Michelangelo': A Biography of George Frederic Watts* (1975), 59. There was a retrospective exhibition of Watts in 1905. The daughters of Leslie Stephen, the later Virginia Woolf and Vanessa Bell, were grievously disappointed. Virginia thought it *'atrocious: my last illusion is*

Swinburne (1867), Carlyle (1868–9), William Morris (1870), Matthew Arnold (1880), and Leslie Stephen (1880), as representatives of Literature for inclusion in the National Portrait Gallery, which was founded in 1856.[178] In 1892 Watts turned to Tennyson's successor as the King of Letters, George Meredith, offering to portray his head as a gift to the nation. Meredith showed some resistance. He could have no happy memories of posing. In 1856, the year his first novel was issued, he starred as model for that masterpiece of tragedy *The Death of Chatterton*, by the artist Henry Wallis, who then rewarded him by running off with his wife. Meredith's philosophy now, confided in J. M. Barrie, was that 'No one should be painted except beautiful women and great men, and I am neither the one nor the other.'[179] He also told Mrs Leslie Stephen, 'I have no ambition to provoke an English posterity's question, Who is he? and my grizzled mug may be left to vanish.'[180] This turned out a coquettish demur, though Meredith maintained this pretence to the last, protesting to Alvin Langdon Coburn in 1904 before he posed in profile, his determination 'not . . . to be photographed at the age of seventy-six and made to look like an old monkey, as Tennyson did!'[181]. Watts completed his portrait of Meredith in 1893; and in 1896 John Singer Sargent, who in turn followed Watts as the doyen of portraiture—indeed, was 'the Van Dyck of our times', according to Rodin—did a further two drawings of Meredith.[182] Two years before, Edmund Gosse had made the arrangements for Coventry Patmore to sit for Sargent. Having come up to London specially, Patmore left nothing to chance: 'in order to be in good looks for Sargent, I have spent the greater part of every day, since I came, in bed'. And how thrilled he was when Sargent smoothly said 'I ought to have two portraits painted of me as it is impossible to give the whole character in one'.[183]

---

gone. Nessa and I walked through the rooms, almost in tears. Some of his work indeed most of it—is quite childlike.' Shortly afterwards she was at a dinner party given by her doctor, Sir George Savage, when 'every person I talked to spoke almost with tears of the greatness and beauty of Watts—and wouldn't admit the possibility of criticism, and this, I suppose, is the sample British Public' (letters to Madge Vaughan, early Jan. 1905, and to Violet Dickinson, mid–Feb. 1905, in Nicolson and Banks (eds.), *Flight of the Mind*, 174, 179).

[178] Only his Leslie Stephen found its way into a private collection rather than the National Portrait Gallery.   [179] Letter to Lady Cynthia Asquith, 13 Apr. 1931, in Meynell (ed.), *Barrie Letters*, 222–3.

[180] Quoted in *G. F. Watts: The Hall of Fame* (1975), 17.

[181] Coburn, *Autobiography*, 30. The photograph, in which 'he resembled a Greek bust, a head of Zeus, calm in its tranquillity, regal in its dignity', was used as the frontispiece for the first of the twenty-seven-volume memorial edition of his works in 1910.

[182] Sassoon, *Meredith*, 216–17; James Lomax and Richard Ormond, *John Singer Sargent and the Edwardian Age* (1979), 72–3. William Strang also did a painting and drawing of Meredith, 1906–8, and T. Spencer-Simson a bronze medallion.

[183] Patmore's letters to his wife, in Patmore, *Coventry Patmore*, 208–9.

9

The Star Turn

I

Hero-worship could be a trial, but many author–heroes were equal to it. It was standard form for poets to be asked to declaim their verses, when a guest at some function or when receiving company themselves. The copious would even include a running commentary on their marvels, much like Humpty Dumpty. '*I* can repeat poetry as well as other folk,' Humpty boasts to Alice; further, he could 'explain all the poems that ever were invented—and a good many that haven't been invented just yet'.[1] Certain authors were all too eager to hog the limelight. The Society hostess Mary Jeune considered that Browning 'spoke louder, and with greater persistency than anyone I have ever come across in my life'. Only once did she know him out-talked. This was by Carlyle, who silenced him at a tea party specially arranged by Lady Augusta Stanley so that Queen Victoria could meet informally both these literary giants.[2] In the early 1870s Browning frequently dined at the Chelsea home of the newly married Sir Charles Dilke. In 1872 he read there *Red Cotton Nightcap Country* (1873)—'at his own request'.[3]

Certain performances were judged immortal. At a Literary Society dinner in 1891 Lord de Tabley, a poet himself, remarked that the most inspiring he ever came across was the Dorset poet William Barnes, then dead some five years; but Swinburne could claim the prize for peculiarity. In the 1870s, when Edmund Gosse knew him best, Swinburne

would arrive at a friend's house with a breast-pocket obviously bulging with manuscript, but buttoned across his chest. After floating about the room and greeting his host and hostess with many little becks of the head, and affectionate smiles, and light wavings of the fingers, he would settle at last upright on a chair, or, by preference, on a sofa, and sit there in a state of rigid immobility, the toe of one foot pressed against the heel of the other. Then he would say, in an airy, detached way, as though speaking of some absent person, 'I have brought with me my "Thalassius" or my "Wasted Garden" (or whatever it might happen to be), which I have just finished.' Then he would be folded again in

---

[1] Lewis Carroll, Alice's *Adventures in Wonderland and Through the Looking-Glass* (Oxford, 1982), 191, 193.
[2] Lady St Helier [Mary Jeune], *Memories of Fifty Years* (1909), 159–60. On Carlyle's conversational capacity—'a monarch of talk'—see Balfour Browne, *Recollections*, ch. viii.
[3] Gwynn and Tuckwell, *Dilke*, 1, 160.

silence, looking at nothing. We then were to say, 'Oh, do please read it to us! Will you?' Swinburne would promptly reply, 'I had no intention in the world of boring you with it, but since you ask me—' and out would come the MS. I do not remember that there was ever any variation in this little ceremony, which sometimes preluded many hours of recitation and reading.

Swinburne's 'pure Ashburnham voice'—his cousin's description—was generally equal to the task; but 'sometimes, in reading, he lost control of his emotions, the sound became a scream, and he would dance about the room, the paper fluttering from his finger-tips like a pennon in a gale of wind'. *The Triumph of Time* regularly did for him, as 'his voice took on strange and fife-like tones, extremely moving and disconcerting, since he was visibly moved himself...It was a case of poetic "possession", pure and simple.'[4]

These performances continued after 1879 at The Pines, Putney, where Swinburne passed his long twilight years. His keeper Watts-Dunton's sanitized recollections were that his 'reading aloud was...a greatly favoured form of entertainment. Swinburne was a sympathetic reader, possessed of a voice of remarkable quality and power of expression, and he would read for the hour together from Dickens, Lamb, Charles Reade, and Thackeray.'[5] R. D. Blumenfeld put things differently in 1901: 'they hold a sort of Poet's Court down at "The Pines" in Putney, with Swinburne on a dais usually surrounded by a lot of admiring dames of the Swinburne cult, draped in Liberty clothes and all in rapture-like attention while the great man pours forth words of Putney wisdom'.[6] This was a far cry from days when Swinburne liked to shock those of delicate sensibility. Tennyson was not delicate but he would stand no nonsense from an upstart. In 1857, after Tennyson read *Maud*, he told Swinburne that he would be grateful if 'he did not press upon me any verses of his own'.[7] Soon Swinburne would not be checked. In 1862, as a 25-year-old rebel (albeit of Eton and Balliol extraction) and with little published reputation, he took it on himself to scandalize a dinner party at Fryston. His target was not his host, Richard Monckton Milnes, who was practically unshockable. An assiduous collector of pornography, he was the person who initiated Swinburne into the work of the marquis de Sade. Nor was Swinburne particularly showing off for Thackeray, a fellow guest and known to Milnes since Cambridge. His aim was directed more at the rest of the table: Thackeray's two daughters and the new Archbishop of York, William Thomson, who had made a parade of his orthodoxy in *Aids to Faith* (1861) to counter the liberal theology of *Essays and Reviews* (1860). Swinburne read 'Les Noyades'. The Archbishop was disgusted, the young ladies giggled, and the occasion was saved by the butler announcing, 'Prayers! my Lord!'[8]

---

[4] Gosse, 'Swinburne', in Gosse, *Portraits and Sketches*, 48–51.
[5] Watts-Dunton, *Old Familiar Faces*, 19.   [6] Blumenfeld, *Diary*, 187–8 (29 Dec. 1901).
[7] Gosse, *Life of Swinburne*, 52.
[8] Ibid. 95–6; Gérin, *Anne Thackeray Ritchie*, 134–5; Fuller and Hammersley (eds.), *Thackeray's Daughter*, 91–2. 'Les Noyades' was included in *Poems and Ballads* (1866). Thackeray's daughters were Anne, afterwards Lady Ritchie and a novelist herself, and Harriet Marion (Minnie), who married Leslie Stephen and

> Birds in the high Hall-garden
> When twilight was falling,
> Maud, Maud, Maud, Maud,
> They were crying and calling,

I asked her what bird she thought I meant. She said, "A nightingale".

This made me so angry that I nearly flung her to the ground: "No, fool! . . . Rook!", said I.'[18]

Mary Gladstone also had her experiences of Tennyson reading *Maud* in 1878, in 1879, and again in 1882. On the first occasions she was transfixed: 'It was wondrous the fire and fervour and despair he alternately put into it. More like a passionate youth than a worn-out old man.' The third time was different, Mary meanwhile having rejected the suit of Tennyson's son Hallam: 'He glared at me and explained everything as if I had never heard of it. He also read "Sir Galahad" and "St. Agnes' Eve", saying "any fool cd. read them".'[19] Previously, in November 1876, when a guest of Gladstone at Hawarden, Tennyson read the whole of his new play, *Harold* (1877), 'with great vigour and power and evident enjoyment to himself; now and then he paused to praise the passage or to ask an opinion'. Unfortunately, not all his audience was up for it. The marathon session began at 11.30 and continued for two and a half hours, during which Gladstone nodded off and other minds turned to 'such earthly things as luncheon'.[20]

There soon came a time when luncheon did not have to wait. It was the poet who was put on hold. Such was the miracle of technology that even the dead were made to speak when commanded; at least, Edison's phonograph permitted their messages to be reproduced. In 1892 the *Review of Reviews* hailed that 'notable moment in the history of science and literature' when, to a select and solemn gathering of six persons, the voice of the recently deceased Robert Browning was transmitted, 'perfectly distinct and of life-like fidelity'.[21] Asked to recite a poem, Browning had embarked on *They Brought the Good News from Ghent to Aix*, always a favourite; he started then stopped, having 'forgotten me own verses!' The replay was on the first anniversary of the poet's death. Dr Furnivall represented the Browning Society there, to the disgust of Browning's sister, who called the affair an 'indecent séance'.[22] The moment of actual recording could resemble a devotional service. The Dean of Westminster was at Farringford in May 1890,

---

[18] Margot Asquith, *Autobiography* (1920), i. 196–8.

[19] Masterman (ed.), *Mary Gladstone*, 137, 151, 243 (12 Apr. 1878, 22 Mar. 1879, 16 Mar. 1882).

[20] Masterman (ed.), *Mary Gladstone*, 111 (1 Nov. 1876).

[21] The occasion was illustrated in *Review of Reviews* (May 1892), 468. See also St Helier, *Memories*, for a photograph (opp. p. 332) and description (p. 334) of a similar occasion when the voice of the recently deceased Cardinal Manning was transmitted.

[22] Benzie, *Furnivall*, 263, where it is noted that Furnivall further alienated Browning's family by releasing for publication a photograph of the poet taken shortly before he died and, worse, by pursuing genealogy to 'prove' that Browning was descended from a footman and that his father was 'half-Creole'.

when Tennyson 'at the Dean's suggestion spoke some of his own well-known lines into the machine, after which we sat side by side on the little sofa with the conductors in our ears, and heard the grand voice come back from the cylinder: an experience never to be forgotten'.[23] Others were also excited by Edison's contraption. Sir Richard Burton offered to yell the muezzin's prayer into one.[24] Unhappily, his invitation was declined.

The ability to reproduce sound was not yet a mass medium. Possession, therefore, largely maintained a traditional appearance. In 1905 the De La More press issued *The Robert Browning Calendar and Birthday Book* (selected by M. E. Gibbings, price 2s. 6d.).[25] Such confections, with a daily quotation from a favourite author, were quite the rage. One publisher, F. Palmer, with enterprising ecumenicalism, issued for 1912, *The H. G. Wells Calendar* and *The Arnold Bennett Calendar*; for 1913, calendars for J. M. Barrie, Anatole France, and George Moore; and for 1914, calendars for Hilaire Belloc, Marie Corelli, Henrik Ibsen, and Walter Pater.[26] Palmer's also had a calendar series of statesmen. It would be interesting to know who, having bought the firm's *Bismarck Calendar* for 1914, still displayed it in the British Isles after 4 August.

II

The tramp of literary tourists constituted another profitable sideline for publishers. Messrs A. & C. Black produced a popular 'Pilgrimage' series: *The Scott Country, The Burns Country, The Blackmore Country*, and so forth.[27] In March 1905 Virginia Stephen reviewed *The Thackeray Country* by Lewis Melville and *The Dickens Country* by F. G. Kitton for the *Times Literary Supplement*. She disdainfully styled them 'two trashy books' in private; but among her own first published articles was an account of the Brontë parsonage at Haworth.[28] Probably, there was no single inventor of this fashion for literary pilgrimages. Positivists were undoubtedly keen on the idea, Frederic Harrison declaring in his memoirs in 1911 that 'One of the most popular forms of commemoration which we instituted was that of a pilgrimage to the home, or tomb, and associations of great men, and visits to scenes of historical interest.'[29] Literary tourism pre-dated the late nineteenth century; yet it was then that the crusading journalist W. T. Stead sought to give it more organization so as to generate a vital national culture. Thomas

---

[23] Rawnsley, *Memories*, 143. According to Martin, *Tennyson*, 573–4, the poet recorded over several days extracts and shorter poems, including 'Blow, Bugle, Blow', 'The Charge of the Light Brigade', and 'Come into the garden, Maud'; latterly, the recording has been transferred to disc, though the quality is poor and the voice high-pitched (Tennyson said it 'sounded like the squeak of a dying mouse').

[24] Byron Farwell, *Burton: A Biography of Sir Richard Francis Burton* (1963), 392.

[25] Listed in *TLS*, 3 Feb. 1905, 40. [26] *TLS*, 2 Nov. 1911, 434, 10 Oct. 1912, 427, 20 Nov. 1913, 558.

[27] New volumes in the series were welcomed in *T.P.'s Weekly*, 12 May 1911, 590.

[28] Nicolson and Banks (eds.), *Flight of the Mind*, 158, 178. [29] Quoted in Benzie, *Furnivall*, 210.

Hardy welcomed Stead's suggestion, albeit with characteristic Victorian caution about class sensitivities:

The idea of a Pilgrimage—at any rate to the haunts of the men now dead, if not to spots brought into notice by the living—is an interesting one, and in these days when all classes seem to be waiting for a lead in respect of emotions, dreams, views, and religion, might be carried out I should think rationally and systematically. The only real difficulty would be probably in the mixing together of persons of different classes previously strangers.[30]

Hardy, for all his lamentations about living in the public eye, was actually an assiduous agent of the Wessex industry, with his elaborate maps combining real and fictional place-names. The first was published in *The Bookman* in October 1891. Hardy was annoyed by freelancers muscling in on his territory, such as Wilkinson Sherren's *The Wessex of Romance* (1902) and Charles G. Harper's *The Hardy Country: Literary Landmarks of the Wessex Novels* (1904). As early as 1893 Hardy told his publisher, Macmillan, 'I fancy I shall be compelled, in self defence as it were, to publish an annotated edn. giving a really trustworthy account of real places, scenery, *etc.* (somewhat as Scott did): since it does not seem to be quite fair that capital shd. be made out of my materials to such an extent as promises to be done.'[31] When a new edition of the novels was being planned in 1902, Hardy stressed to Macmillan the importance of keeping the generic title Wessex Novels, 'the novels being now unexpectedly used more & more as a species of guide books to this part of England there seems no reason to suppose the sales will diminish':

For commercial reasons, not to speak of literary ones, I fancy the words should be retained. Many people have heard of the Wessex novels who do not know their individual titles. This inclusive title is, moreover, copyright, & as several writers have used 'Wessex' in their productions since I began it they may annex 'Wessex Novels' if we let the name drop.[32]

Accordingly, Hardy cooperated in the making of Bertram Windle's *The Wessex of Thomas Hardy* (1902) and Hermann Lea's *Handbook to the Wessex Country of Thomas Hardy's Novels and Poems* (1905); and he supplied a preface for F. R. and Sidney Heath's *Dorchester (Dorset) and its Surroundings* (1905).[33] Talking to Henry Nevinson in 1906, he 'thought the books appearing on Wessex might help to advertise his own books a little!'[34] The message was also spread by formal associations. Hardy accepted the nominal presidency of the Wessex Society of Manchester, and a vice-presidency of the Society of Dorset Men in London,

---

[30] Hardy to W. T. Stead, 31 May 1893, in Purdy and Millgate (eds.), *Hardy Letters*, ii. 10.
[31] Hardy to Frederick Macmillan, 31 Mar. 1902, in Purdy and Millgate (eds.), *Hardy Letters*, iii. 16.
[32] Hardy to Frederick Macmillan, 22 Mar. and 11 Oct. 1902, ibid. 13, 36.
[33] Hardy to Bertram Windle, 7 Nov. 1901, to Hermann Lea, 6 Oct. 1904 et seq., and to Frank Heath, 23 Sept. 1905, in Purdy and Millgate (eds.), *Hardy Letters*, ii. 302, iii. 137–8, 182.
[34] Diary, 26 Apr. 1906, in Nevinson, *More Changes*, 165.

established in 1897 and 1905 respectively.[35] Hardy even named his dog Wessex. This terrier, which Hardy kissed every night before going to bed,[36] had a personality much like its owner. The ultimate test was John Galsworthy, a campaigner for all good causes, including the humane treatment of animals. When Galsworthy visited, Wessex bit him.[37] The dog was eventually buried under a stone inscribed: 'Wessex—Faithful and Unflinching'.

Where the subject of the literary pilgrims' devotion was dead, there were sites to inspect and a mood to be evoked. Most railway companies advertised day trips to places of interest along their lines. In the Edwardian period Thomas Burke took advantage of the Great Western Railway's cheap fares to make excursions out of London: 'to Stoke Poges (Gray), to Beaconsfield (Waller), to Horton and Chalfont (Milton), to Laleham (Matthew Arnold), to Marlow (Shelley), to Chertsey (Cowley), to Halliford (Peacock)'.[38] In East Anglia in 1897 Arnold Bennett was curious to stay at the Great White Horse Inn, famed as Pickwick's inn. He was allotted an immense bedroom, labelled 'Pickwick' outside. On its walls was 'an extremely bad oil painting of a Pickwick banquet'; and a notice recorded that a 'facsimile of this hotel was erected at the World's Fair, Chicago, as one of the celebrated old inns of this country'.[39] The fate of Hawes Inn at Queensferry also caused vexation. This 'sacred haunt' for lovers of Sir Walter Scott and Robert Louis Stevenson—the setting for scenes in *The Antiquary* (1816) and *Kidnapped* (1886)—was after 1890 'overstridden and overridden by that monster of utility the Forth Bridge, which has added so immensely to the convenience and detracted so materially from the romance of that locality', declared a disappointed Lord Rosebery.[40]

As well as shrines to visit, literary tourists required, ideally, sextons and vergers to consult. It was a happy chance for Arthur Benson, touring in 1911 about Ecclefechan, round which Carlyle used to perambulate in a rage, that he should meet a woman some 50 years of age, suitably 'hard-featured [and] grim . . . who introduced herself as Carlyle's niece, daughter of his sister. She had little information to give; but she was very anxious we should realise who she was, and repeated it several times.'[41] Shakespeare was beyond reach of oral memory but W. S. Blunt gained a frisson by discovering that Anne Hathaway's cottage was

---

[35] Hardy to E. H. Coombs, 10 Nov. 1897, and to William Watkins, 25 Feb. 1905, in Purdy and Millgate (eds.), *Hardy Letters*, ii. 181, iii. 158. The original president of the Society of Dorset Men in London was Sir Frederick Treves, the surgeon now best known for his association with the 'Elephant Man', Joseph Merrick; Hardy succeeded him as president, 1907–9, 'much against my wish', he noted gloomily to Florence Henniker, 31 Dec. 1907, ibid. iii. 288.

[36] Florence Hardy to Rebekah Owen, 18 Jan. 1916, and to Sydney Cockerell, 27 Dec. 1919, in Millgate (ed.), *Emma and Florence Hardy*, 114, 164–5, where it was reported that Wessex was inadvisedly fed with goose and plum pudding at Christmas, which he then threw up.

[37] Flower, *Just as it Happened*, 93. This was Wessex's standard behaviour. Florence Hardy, therefore, thought worthy of record his remarkable 'adoration' of Edmund Blunden when he stayed at Max Gate. Letter to Siegfried Sassoon, 21 July 1922, in Millgate (ed.), *Emma and Florence Hardy*, 186.

[38] Burke, *Son of London*, 203.   [39] Flower (ed.), *Bennett Journals*, i. 39–40 (20 June 1897).

[40] Geake (ed.), *Appreciations*, 91.   [41] Lubbock, *Benson*, 219–20 (31 Aug. 1911).

'quite untouched and unrestored . . . [and] inhabited still by a descendant of the Hathaways'.[42] At Haworth there were people alive who had known the Brontës, so Will Rothenstein, born in nearby Bradford, recollected; and a house at Guiseley was pointed out as where Jane Eyre first taught as a governess.[43] It was the Lake District, however, that ran second only to Stratford as the principal destination for literary tourists. After 1900 Ruskin's home, Brantwood, by Lake Coniston, was added as a bonus on top of the established venues of the Lakeland poets. When Arthur Benson visited in 1907, he was gratified to be taken over the house, still with Ruskin's things intact, by Ruskin's niece Mrs Severn, who 'told me how he died, sitting up in bed; two days before he had been perfectly well. She cried a little as she told the tale . . .'.[44] He met with no disenchantment either at Wordsworth's former home—though 'they are terribly harried by trippers'— because Mrs Fisher-Wordsworth, 'rather a pretty woman, showed us everything, the chests, the little old parlour, etc., with great zest'.[45] Visiting Dove Cottage in 1908, the deputy editor of the *Quarterly Review* and keen Wordsworthian John Bailey also discovered it 'very well kept by an old woman who had shaken hands with the poet, which gave me pleasure in shaking hands with her'.[46] That same summer a 16-year-old Nottingham boy, Cecil Roberts, sat in the garden hut facing the lake and recited Wordsworth's poem describing the scene in 1802 for Mary Hutchinson. Having observed the custodian's routine, next day Roberts hid in the hut in anticipation of Dove Cottage being closed at lunchtime; then, with the garden gate locked, he sneaked inside, parted the cords which protected Wordsworth's bed, and lay there for a couple of hours, 'hoping the divine afflatus might descend on me'.[47] Properly inspired, he earned 3 guineas by evoking the Lakeland Poets for the weekly magazine *Great Thoughts*.

Others also had their thrills. A curiosity of the 500th meeting of the Johnson Society—specially held at the Doctor's Oxford college, Pembroke, in 1896—was the presence as guest of one Alexander Boswell, a descendant of the unique biographer; and Johnson's teapot was passed round for inspection.[48] As for devotees of Shelley, there was the opportunity, provided one had the right contacts, to converse with the offspring. Thus, for the newly wed Alice and Wilfrid Meynell, the poet Aubrey de Vere effected an introduction to Sir Percy and Lady Shelley at Boscombe Manor near Bournemouth, 'in order that

---

[42] Blunt, *Diaries*, i. 228 (17 May 1896). Anne Hathaway's cottage was bought in 1892 by the trustees of Shakespeare's house in Stratford, for the sizeable sum of £3,000; *Review of Reviews* (May 1892), 519–20. A reproduction of Ann Hathaway's cottage was erected in Jackson Park, Chicago, for the World's Fair in 1893.   [43] Rothenstein, *Men and Memories, 1872–1900*, 13.

[44] Lubbock, *Benson*, 177 (3 Oct. 1907). Benson published *Ruskin: A Study in Personality* (1911).

[45] Lubbock, *Benson*, 122–3 (20 July 1905).   [46] Bailey (ed.), *Letters and Diaries*, 112–13 (12 Aug. 1908).

[47] Roberts, *Years of Promise*, 18–20. Another oddity of this Lake District holiday was Roberts's encounter on the road with the first American he ever met. This turned out to be the future President, Woodrow Wilson, who was staying with Canon Rawnsley.

[48] Grant Duff, *Diary, 1896 to 1901*, i. 81–2 (23 June 1896). The occasion was attended by the literary critics and scholars Austin Dobson, George Saintsbury, and Canon Ainger, and by the Regius Professor of Modern History, York Powell, who deigned to cross the road from Christ Church.

they might see Shelley relics, and . . . [have] the strange experience of hearing a portly middle-aged man refer to the immortal youth as "my poor father" '.[49]

An outstanding promoter of literary tourism was Hall Caine, who put the Isle of Man on the map with himself at its centre. The Isle had not been altogether ignored by writers. Wordsworth wrote a sonnet on Tynwald Hill and Crabb Robinson composed several, to which Matthew Arnold, who holidayed there, added 'To a Gypsy Child by the Sea-Shore' (1843). Walter Scott's *Peveril of the Peak* (1823) also contained Manx scenes, though drawn from imagination because he never set foot there. Some would have known that F. W. Farrar based *Eric; or, Little by Little* (1858) partly on his own schooldays on the Isle at King William's College; others too acknowledged his schoolmate T. E. Brown, the Manx dialect poet and classical scholar. But none had anything like the impact of Hall Caine in shaping popular perceptions of the Isle. The Manx themselves had mixed feelings about the living legend of Hall Caine. He was not born on Man; he had Manx paternity but his mother was from Cumberland, which region provided the setting for his first two novels, *The Shadow of a Crime* (1885) and *A Son of Hagar* (1886). Neither book initially captured a large readership or brought Caine financial reward; and he turned instead to use the Isle of Man for the making of *The Deemster* (1887).[50] This was written in six weeks at a lodging house in Douglas, although it was not yet (or ever entirely) the case that Caine settled on Manx lore and locations for his work, because he had literary ambitions of Tolstoyan magnitude. Thus Caine's next novel, *The Bondman* (1890), shifted scene between Iceland and the Isle of Man, and *The Scapegoat* (1891) was set in Morocco. The great change in Caine's relationship with the island came with *The Manxman* (1894), whose action, unlike *The Deemster*, took place in the Man of his own day. It was 'one of the most remarkable books of the century', proclaimed the review in *Queen*.[51] Again, Caine had written this story in lodgings on the Isle, this time at Peel; but its vast success was the means of his now taking up residence there. When Robert Sherard interviewed him in 1895, Caine was torn between building himself a house on the Creg Malin headland overlooking the bay at Peel, or buying the early nineteenth-century Greeba Castle.[52] He settled on the latter, for £1,025—a knock-down price, reckoned jealous critics, who bridled at what was seen as typical of Caine's sharp practice. The sum had been determined in the Manx Chancery Court. The vendor, with delicious irony for Caine, was the widow of a partner in Chatto & Windus, who he believed had exploited his naivety and penury as an inexperienced novelist and whom he had by now deserted for Heinemann's. The judge in the case commented that £1,025 seemed a

---

[49] Meynell, *Francis Thompson and Wilfrid Meynell*, 60. Later, in 1912, at the sale of Browning's effects, Wilfrid Meynell bought for £13 Mrs Leigh Hunt's posthumous bust of Shelley; ibid. 200–1. See also Meynell, *Alice Meynell*, 63.   [50] C. Fred Kenyon, *Hall Caine: The Man and the Novelist* (1901), 111–18.
[51] Quoted, with other reviews, in Samuel Norris, *Two Men of Manxland: Hall Caine, Novelist, T. E. Brown, Poet* (Douglas, 1947), 12, 227–43.
[52] Robert Harborough Sherard, 'Hall Caine: A Biographical Study', *Windsor Magazine* (Dec. 1895), 572.

miserable sum for a castle; but it was the best offer received, albeit less than previously paid for it. The widow, who had a mortgage outstanding of £1,000, was in deficit after paying legal fees.[53] It was the final straw when Caine's next best-seller emerged, entitled *The Christian* (1897). The *Saturday Review* responded with mock appreciation under the headline 'Glory at Greeba Castle, A Vision'. Its second sentence ran: 'On to the battlements of a Castle that he had purchased, for a fourth of its value, from the widow of a publisher . . . there stepped forth a figure concealed, for commercial purposes, in the garb of a Christian.'[54]

Greeba Castle, when Caine was in residence—though he often wintered abroad and also acquired a house in Hampstead, became for the next thirty-five years of his life a magnet to draw tourists to the Isle of Man. Compton Mackenzie reckoned it all 'a little ridiculous'. Invited there in 1910, he expected 'Gothic grandeur' but found the equivalent of 'a medium-sized red brick villa'.[55] In August 1897 Caine had held his first open day. *The World* described the charabanc loads of excursionists who flocked to meet the celebrity author, who appeared suitably 'picturesque with grey sombrero and pointed beard and flowing locks'.[56] In 1903 *T.P.'s Weekly*, recommending holiday destinations for its readers, nominated the Isle of Man as 'Hall Caine's Island'.[57]

Caine's part in marketing the resort was direct and close. He wrote a guide-book for the Isle of Man Steam Packet Co., which plied between Douglas and Liverpool. This revived memories of Thackeray or, rather, of what Carlyle supposed Thackeray guilty of when he wrote *Notes of a Journey from Cornhill to Grand Cairo* (1846), that is, to puff P & O in exchange for a free passage. This Carlyle compared 'to the practice of a blind fiddler going to and fro on a penny ferry-boat in Scotland, and playing tunes to the passengers for halfpence'.[58] Thackeray protested innocence, but others were quite shameless about the practice. Douglas Sladen penned *On the Cars and Off* (1895) for Sir William Van Horne, president of the newly completed Canadian Pacific Railway, 'in return for his giving me free passes for myself and my family from Montreal to Vancouver and back'.[59] Most of Sladen's books were planned with commercial spin-offs in mind. Among his novels was *The Admiral* (1898), timed to catch the commemoration wave on the centenary of Nelson's victory over the French at Aboukir Bay (the battle of the Nile). More obvious were his country guides, such as *In Sicily* (1901) and *Sicily, the New Winter Resort* (1904), the result of Sladen wintering there from 1896; and *How to See Italy* (1911), which was 'written for the Government of Italy'. Sladen added, 'When the White Star Steamship Company

---

[53] Norris, *Two Men of Manxland*, 18.

[54] *Saturday Review*, 14 Aug. 1897, in Purdy and Millgate (eds.), *Hardy Letters*, ii. 180.

[55] Mackenzie, *Life and Times*, iv. 95.

[56] The World (Aug. 1897), in Norris, *Two Men of Manxland*, 15–16.

[57] *T.P.'s Weekly*, 3 July 1903, 108.

[58] Sir Charles Gavan Duffy, *Conversations with Carlyle* (1892), in James Sutherland (ed.), *The Oxford Book of Literary Anecdotes* (Oxford, 1975), 235–6.   [59] Sladen, *Long Life*, 349.

established their excursions from America to Italy, they bought an edition of 3,000 copies to present to the passengers . . . '.[60] As for Hall Caine, a consortium was organized of 'bankers, land speculators and amusement caterers', to promote tourism to the Isle; and Caine's brother was placed in charge of their London office.[61] Caine himself became a member of the island parliament. Though his activity both as writer and as elected representative roused hostilities locally, that he was exploiting the Manx connection, many citizens also knew on which side their bread was buttered. It was Caine who performed as host when Edward VII visited the Isle. It was not good for business when Caine took himself off, say, to Rome to research *The Eternal City* (1901) or to Egypt for *The White Prophet* (1909). Thus the editor of the *Isle of Man Times* hailed *The Master of Man* (1921) in gratitude that once again he had set a story entirely on the Isle. For Caine had rescued Man from obscurity, and worldwide it was 'identified with your name. The name of Hall Caine is the most valuable asset the Isle of Man has ever had or ever will have.'[62] This link in the public mind was not just secure, it became imperishable, according to the address given at the memorial service for Caine in St Martin-in-the-Fields in 1931, by R. J. Campbell:

The soul of Scotland sang to the poetry of Robert Burns; that of Wordsworth revealed itself anew to every dweller in the Lake District who is conscious of its mystic charm; in the pages of Thomas Hardy historic Wessex, the matrix of England, arose from its long slumber; in Arnold Bennett the mingled pathos and shrewdness of the Five Towns became vocal; and for all time to come the genius of that little self-contained kingdom, the Isle of Man, would be associated with the name of Hall Caine.[63]

In 1928 Caine had been made a freeman of Douglas, where a bronze statue of him now stands. His body was buried in the churchyard at Maughold, where briefly he had been a schoolmaster; and a Celtic cross over the grave is inscribed with characters from his novels.

There was no Corelli Country—many scenes in that best-seller's books took place in some unlocatable psychic realm—but Marie Corelli's devotees were ready to take to the road whenever she favoured them with a sign. *The Mighty Atom* (1896), her novel denouncing the 'infamous' action of 'self-styled "Progressivists"' in promoting secular education, brought fame to Combe Martin in north Devon, where 'the villagers point out with pride to tourists the old pulpit where Lionel and Jessamine are supposed to have fallen asleep'. This was a rare instance of Corelli actually visiting a place she wrote about—she never travelled to Naples, where *Vendetta* (1886) was set, or to Norway, which provided a backdrop for *Thelma* (1887). As a consequence, she made old Mr Norman, the sexton—Reuben Dale in the novel—quite a personage. Corelli gave him an

---

[60] Ibid. 352.   [61] Norris, *Two Men of Manxland*, 8, 52–6.

[62] John A. Brown to Hall Caine, 1 June 1921, in Hall Caine (ed.), *Letters to the Author from the Friends to Whom Copies of the Privately-Printed Edition of 'The Master of Man' were Sent* (1921).

[63] *The Times*, 9 Sept. 1931. For Caine's association with Campbell, see below, Ch. 21.

autographed copy of *The Mighty Atom*, which he displayed in the church, secured in a wall casing to prevent her less scrupulous fans from making off with it. Thanking Corelli for her gift, Norman signed himself 'Reuben'; and a postcard of him sold to the 'hundreds and hundreds' of visitors. Norman's nice little earner ended with his death from consumption in 1898, whereupon an unpleasant wrangle broke out about a memorial to him, the *Daily Mail* charging Corelli with interfering for the purpose of self-advertisement; but the association of her novel with the church was still being noted in guidebooks a generation later, when Corelli herself was no longer alive.[64] Combe Martin was an out-of-the-way place, but loyal readers were never deterred by hardships; and for those disposed to undergo a transatlantic voyage, then traverse half a continent, there was always Corelli City to head for in Colorado, so named by her fans on the frontier. Occasionally, the humanity of these ambulant literary disciples shone through, as George Moore discovered when he met a zealot of George Borrow. This individual was so inspired by *Wild Wales* (1862) that he determined to follow Borrow's trail from village to village: 'I shall not be accused by anyone', he declared, 'of lacking sympathy for any place visited by Borrow, but all I remember of my walk from Caernarvon to Ethelgebert is that the beer at Ethelgebert was the best I ever drank.'[65]

There were substantial drawbacks to this literary tourism for an author in residence. Tennyson's moodiness did not put off the pilgrims, and right up to the end he was besieged. 'It's horrible the way they stare,' Tennyson exclaimed miserably to Canon Rawnsley in 1884 when a charabanc of tourists debouched onto a lane near his home, Farringford, on the Isle of Wight. 'And their impudence is beyond words,' he added as he 'turned his face to the bank and began prodding violently with his stick'. He recounted with grim satisfaction how once he deceived an American woman who strode across his lawn, asking him if he had seen Tennyson. He had sent her scuttling off in the wrong direction 'like a thing possessed'; but his walk with Rawnsley was not made more pleasant by their discovering graffiti chalked on his gate, which informed them 'Old Tennyson is a fool.'[66] In 1890, when Staff Officer at the Freshwater gunnery school, Arthur Lee prevailed on Tennyson's niece to arrange an entrée: 'I already knew most of *In Memoriam* by heart. To me he was Merlin, an almost

---

[64] Kent Carr, *Miss Marie Corelli* (1901), 54–5; Thomas F. G. Coates and R. S. Warren Bell, *Marie Corelli: The Writer and the Woman* (1903), 314–15; Ransom, *Corelli*, 92–5. The sexton is variously called James or Edward Norman. For the guidebooks, see the Ward, Lock & Co. *Pictorial and Descriptive Guide to Barnstaple, Ilfracombe, Bideford, Clovelly and North-West Devon*, 11th edn., rev. (n.d.), 29. The booming sales of *The Mighty Atom* during the tourist season in North Devon in 1912, when the novel was reissued in a shilling edition, are noted below, Ch. 18. When Corelli wrote to the press in 1906 to explain that her new story (*The Treasure of Heaven*) was set in Somerset, not Devon it was remarked in (*Punch*, 8 Aug. 1906 98), that 'the news has thrown a pall of gloom over one of England's fairest counties, but does not specify which county'.

[65] George Moore, *Salve* (1912), 56; Michael Collie, *George Borrow: Eccentric* (Cambridge, 1982), 234–40, for Borrow's huge pedestrian achievements and the uselessness of trying to follow in his footsteps.

[66] Rawnsley, *Memories*, 100, 102–3.

legendary seer, and the thought that I might really meet him in the flesh excited my imagination as few things ever before.' Lee found the Laureate an 'obdurate recluse', vigilantly protected by his family and by an 'old and wary butler'. Eventually, the poet unburdened himself, how he had selected Farringford

because it was so retired from the world, but the tourists persisted in intruding upon his peace. Looking round at the high walls of the garden, he said: 'They even come in here and saunter up to me, asking "Is this private?" This spring they rooted up nearly all the daffodils in the drive'; and then he added with withering scorn: 'Yes, they like to keep them as *souvenirs of Tennyson*.'

Having shared one Laureate's horror at being mistaken for another, Lee did not return until 1892, when Tennyson ventilated his fury against interviewers who made up lies, and against acquaintances who pretended intimate friendship. 'Mosquitos' he called them disdainfully. Tennyson now preferred London to the Isle of Wight: 'I am far less mobbed in Regent Street than in a country lane here.'[67]

Fans underwent immense exertions out of devotion to their idols. A Balliol undergraduate in the 1890s, Mark Tellar cycled about Dorset to visit sites mentioned in Hardy's novels. Twice he maintained a vigil outside Max Gate, in the hope of catching sight of Hardy. He did not, though 'I speculated whether if he suddenly appeared I would dare to address him.'[68] Such shyness was not generally imitated. Newman Flower, a Dorset man himself who became head of Cassell's, told how tourists were unloaded at Max Gate from charabancs, whereupon they marched up the drive, 'rang the bell noisily . . . peered into his windows . . . tore pieces from his bushes and trees as souvenirs [and] broke off large branches so that they might share bits with their friends'. Hardy's wife was fully stretched on these occasions, warding off the unbidden visitors so that the poet–novelist could enjoy his creative solitude; still, it was breached by one brazen caller who presented a visiting card inscribed as 'Herbert Spencer', only to emerge as an entirely fictitious philosopher.[69] It was clear that Hardy's fans would not brook disappointment. 'The usual rank & file of summer tourists have called here,' Hardy reported wearily in 1903, '& I have given mortal offence to some by not seeing them in the morning at any hour. I send down a message that they must come after 4 o'clock, & they seem to go off in dudgeon.' Others milled around, with cameras peering over hedges.[70] Not just Max Gate, but also the

---

[67] Clark (ed.), *Lee*, 43–6: for the 'mosquitoes', Watts-Dunton, *Old Familiar Faces*, 136. Watts-Dunton recounted Tennyson coming across two men, dressed as gentlemen, perched up trees surrounding his garden, having been refused admission at the gate; and Constance Flower's journal (4 June 1881) noted that Tennyson 'spoke much of the prying spirit of the tourists, and gave anecdotes of men he had waylaid in his own grounds' (Cohen, *Lady de Rothschild and her Daughters*, 193).

[68] Tellar, *Young Man's Passage*, 82–3.   [69] Flower, *Just as it Happened*, 101.

[70] Hardy to Florence Henniker, 13 Sept. 1904, and to Hermann Lea, 9 Nov. 1904, in Purdy and Millgate (eds.), *Hardy Letters*, iii. 74, 145.

cottage at Higher Bockhampton in which he was born, fell victim to his admirers' vandalism, according to an adulatory press profile about 'The Wizard of Wessex'. The natal home was missing part of its thatch because 'the straws . . . have gone to America, for Americans, who appreciate Hardy even better than we do, flock to the spot to carry away relics'.[71] Hardy's mother, still living in the cottage, made a handsome profit from this ritual, because the Americans would 'give her a sovereign for a straw'.[72] The topography of Hardy's Wessex tales also spelled trouble for other residents. Entertaining the founder of the Society of Dorset Men in London, William Watkins, Hardy took him to a house near Shaftesbury which was where his imagined Tess had lodged:

He knocked at the door. For quite a while they waited on the step. Then the door was opened. Hardy revealed his identity, and asked if he and his friend could see over the house, only to be met with this answer:

'So you're the man who's caused this plague of people trying to visit this house, are you?' And the door was slammed in his face.[73]

Authors in their own younger days knew what it was to revere a writer. Theodore Watts-Dunton, author of the best-selling Gypsy romance *Aylwin* (1898), recalled how as a boy he encountered George Borrow braving the sea at Yarmouth in a biting March wind:

I had plunged into the surf and got very close to the swimmer, whom I perceived to be a man of almost gigantic proportions, when suddenly an instinct told me that it was Lavengro himself . . . and the feeling that it was he so entirely stopped the action of my heart that I sank for a moment like a stone, soon to rise again, however, in glow of pleasure and excitement: so august a presence was Lavengro's then! . . .

Although I would have given worlds to go up and speak to him as he was tossing his clothes upon his back, I could not do it. Morning after morning did I see him undress, wallow in the sea, come out again, give me a somewhat sour look, dress, and then stride away inland at a tremendous pace, but never could I speak to him.

Not until years later did Watts-Dunton gain an introduction to Borrow, through a mutual friend, the poet Dr Gordon Hake, whereupon Watts-Dunton tried to

---

[71] *M.A.P.*, 12 May 1906, 442. The thesis that Hardy was less appreciated at home was sustained by arguing that in Dorchester Hardy was better known as a magistrate than as a writer; but the whole piece reads as a gross exercise in legend: 'He cares nothing for Society; in conversation he seems unconscious of his own cleverness . . . Moorland and meadow are his delight, and storm and the stress of tempests hold no terrors for him, for he rejoices in the wonderful freedom of God's air.'

[72] Flower, *Just as it Happened*, 85. Hardy's mother died in 1904, aged 90. Flower also broadly affirmed the ignorance about Hardy locally. Though Flower as boy read and idolized Hardy, his family could tell him only '(1) that Hardy was a person of considerable celebrity: (2) that he was a person of mystery who hid in a house nearby—a house surrounded by a brick wall and a belt of trees: (3) that he wrote very important books which only one of my aunts ever read'. When he endeavoured to pursue the matter by tackling a local shepherd, asking if he knew Hardy, he was met with an expression which suggested that 'I might have asked him what was the *menu* when he dined with the Prince of Wales last Wednesday.' He eventually drew the decisive information that Hardy had nothing to do with sheep, so far as the shepherd knew.   [73] Flower, *Just as it Happened*, 93.

impress Borrow with erudition about Romany lore and recondite literature.[74]
It was ineffectual. A self-absorbed curmudgeon, Borrow was reluctant to concede
precedence on subjects he knew nothing about, and utterly resistant on those
he did.

The first author to whom Barrie penned a letter was Ascott R. Hope,[75]
misspelling many words in it because the boys in his school stories couldn't spell.
Barrie 'used to think that Hope (or else Ballantyne or Marryat) ought to be made
King of England'.[76] Wondrous though such boyhood heroes were, they were
then eclipsed in Barrie's imagination by Carlyle. There was a local connection
here because, when at school in Dumfries, Barrie would encounter the tortured
sage moping along the country roads. He doffed his cap fifty times or more, and
devised stratagems to extract a word from the great man; to no avail. Crowds
of Carlyle devotees were a familiar sight to Barrie. They came to inspect the
birthplace in Ecclefechan, including 'an American clergyman who reverently
sipped of the polluted water of the burn and carried off a stone from it as a relic
in his pocket-handkerchief'. When in later years Barrie's father paid his inaugural
visit to London to see his son, now embarked as a writer, 'the first place we
sought out together was neither Westminster Abbey nor the Tower, but Carlyle's
house in Cheyne Row'.[77] The cycle was repeated in the Edwardian period, this
time with Barrie in the role of idol to the young Neville Cardus: 'I nearly went to
London to call on Barrie. My plan was to invade his rooms, exactly as Sentimental
Tommy invades Pym's rooms, and not leave until he had given me a job as his
secretary. But my courage failed; I did not even begin the journey.'[78]

Hardy also knew what it was to be a fan. He had idolized Dickens and, when
Hardy was an apprentice architect, he lunched at the same coffee house. Once,
having eaten, he got up and moved beside Dickens, ready to devour another meal
if it would cause Dickens to 'look up, glance at this strange young man beside
him and make a remark—if it was only about the weather. But he did nothing of
the kind. He was fussing about his bill. So I never spoke to him.'[79] Replies, when
they came, were not always the anticipated agreeable ones. E. M. Forster was a

[74] Watts-Dunton, *Old Familiar Faces*, 43–5. Borrow's *Lavengro* was first published in 1851. On his
swimming feats and show-off tendencies, Michael Collie, *George Borrow: Eccentric* (Cambridge, 1982), 232–3.

[75] 'Ascott R. Hope' was one of several aliases adopted by Robert Hope Moncrieff (1846–1927), prolific
author and member of several London clubs, including the Athenaeum and Savile. On 20 November 1893
Barrie wrote to Maarten Maartens (J. M. W. Schwartz, 1858–1915): 'It interested me to see that Ascott R.
Hope's *My Schoolboy Friends* was one of your boyish favourites. That is another bond of union between
you and me. Do you know him? He goes to the Savile. Great talker who writes on his knee and thinks this
his worst book. A good fellow, yet it is a mistake to meet those giants of our boyhood, we loved them so
much' (Meynell, *Barrie Letters*, 28). When Cosmo Hamilton first got into print in the late 1890s with
Through a Keyhole, Hope invited him to dine at the Authors' Club 'for the purpose of choking me off, of
proving to me how foolish it was to imagine that I could write' (Hamilton, *People Worth Talking
About*, 82). [76] Barrie, *Two of Them*, 197.

[77] Barrie, *Greenwood Hat*, 37–40, 87. Carlyle's home, 24 Cheyne Row, Chelsea, was bought by public
subscription in 1895 and became the first London property owned by the National Trust when it was
transferred to its management in 1936. [78] Cardus, *Autobiography*, 50.

[79] Flower, *Just as it Happened*, 88–9.

generous writer of fan letters to fellow authors and formed several friendships in this way—but not with A. E. Housman, whose savage riposte was 'so fearful that Forster hurriedly threw it on the fire.'[80]

III

Autograph-hunters were another plague. Andrew Lang wryly remarked about Oliver Wendell Holmes's perpetual good nature: 'the worst thing I have heard of him is that he could never say "no" to an autograph hunter'.[81] Autographer-hunters were determined and devious. The wife of the Dorset magistrates' clerk Mrs Ffooks spent hours contriving 'a hundred ways of getting into touch with well-known people, and merely to extract autographs'. She was ecstatic when she duped Joseph Conrad into sending her 'a long and very nice letter . . . It is a mania with her.'[82] Some zealous collectors were people of considerable station such as Lady Dorothy Nevill or Lady Gregory. The latter, a writer herself, prevailed on other authors as well as public figures such as Gladstone and Rosebery to inscribe their signatures on a fan.[83] The Duchess of Sutherland's attitude to her book of autographs was like a general's surveying his forces and strengthening its command. In 1902 she evidently realized that she lacked the signature of George Meredith, who was now widely acclaimed as the King of Letters. He was also elderly and immobile with infirmity; hence she motored to Surrey, and 'I was haled out of my obscurity to meet her. We had 40 minutes talk. For this I was made to pay subsequently by the arrival of a precious book from Dunrobin, containing Czar and Kaiser, signature and verse— and with the request for what I could not refuse and always hate to do.'[84] Otherwise, a supreme champion of the breed was the civil servant-turned-poet Frederick Locker, who eventually upgraded himself to Locker-Lampson. He demonstrated exceptional cunning by compiling, ostensibly for his daughter, a bound collection of favourite verses and getting their authors to append their signatures. Robert Browning, whose father had been friendly with Locker, fell for this in 1879, even transcribing three stanzas on request.[85]

Society people the more easily concealed their collecting vice behind the convention of the visitors' book. It was similar for the wife of the Dean of Christ Church, Lorina Liddell, a terrible snob and chaser after royalty and titles. She was hungry too to ensnare famous writers and so prized a brief letter from Thackeray that she itemized it in her will.[86] Even George Gissing, who cheerlessly described

[80] Lago and Furbank (eds.), *Forster Letters*, vol, i. p. xii.   [81] Lang, *Adventures among Books*, 96.

[82] Florence Hardy to Sydney Cockerell, 13 May 1923, in Millgate (ed.), *Emma and Florence Hardy*, 198–9.

[83] Elizabeth Coxhead, *Lady Gregory: A Literary Portrait*, rev. edn. (1966), 31.

[84] Meredith to Lady Ulrica Duncombe, 30 Aug. 1902, in Cline (ed.), *Meredith's Letters*, iii. 1462–3. For Meredith's letter to the Duchess of Sutherland, returning her autograph book, 28 Aug. 1902, ibid. 1461.

[85] DeVane and Knickerbocker (eds.), *New Letters of Robert Browning*, 253–4.

[86] Cohen, *Carroll*, 513.

literary failure in *New Grub Street* (1891), started getting requests for his autograph.[87] Tennyson's reluctance to part with his signature stretched back decades, as the Rawnsley family, old Lincolnshire connections, well understood. Willingham Rawnsley struggled to obtain one for his prize copy of *Idylls of the King*, won for recitation at Uppingham School in 1861. To Rawnsley *père*, who officiated at Tennyson's marriage in 1850, made himself a student of the works, and thereafter irritated the poet with requests for favours, Tennyson once sent 'a half sheet of notepaper with several of his autographs, adding only one line— "There, will that do for you?" ' When Willingham married, Tennyson sent his works as a wedding present; but the volume was uninscribed and the couple had to press him when he visited them, Tennyson grumbling, 'People would say you had decoyed me here on purpose.'[88] Lewis Carroll also resisted giving his autograph, although he was an avid collector himself and pestered other celebrities on his own account and on behalf of child friends.[89] Mischievously, he persuaded chums to masquerade as Lewis Carroll and answer his correspondence. He chuckled 'to picture the astonishment of the recipients of these letters, if by any chance they ever came to compare his "autographs" '.[90] There was a certain justice in this because no sense of propriety curbed the collector.[91] Max Beerbohm was intercepted on leaving the memorial service for George Meredith in Westminster Abbey in 1909 by an autograph-hunter who mistook him for J. M. Barrie. Max rose to the occasion and scribbled in the girl's book, 'Aye lassie, it's a sad day the noo, J.M.B.'[92] Hardy was more furtive in his evasions. Yeats once asked him what he did about the many books sent to him for signature, whereupon Hardy navigated him to the top of his house to disclose volumes piled floor to ceiling.[93] Hardy stopped autographing books because people were reselling them at inflated prices. This was a grudge he developed against Clement Shorter, whom, he was appalled to remember when he came to revise his will in 1922, he had nominated as a possible literary executor.[94]

IV

Relatively innocuous ways existed by which fans could express discipleship. The theatre critic James Agate once worshipped Kipling. When 21 and working in the Manchester cotton trade, he was devastated by newspaper reports that Kipling was dangerously ill in New York, whereupon he vowed that 'if he died I would

---

[87] Halperin, *Gissing*, 229. [88] Rawnsley, *Memories of the Tennysons*, 133–4.
[89] Cohen, *Carroll*, 295–6. [90] Collingwood, *Carroll*, 225.
[91] As Norman Douglas found when *South Wind* (1917) brought him fame after years of indifference. He reproduced samples of the letters he received in his autobiography, *Looking Back*, 501–4.
[92] Cecil, *Max*, 260. [93] Sutherland (ed.), *Literary Anecdotes*, 281.
[94] Florence Hardy to Rebekah Owen, 3 Nov. 1916 and 13 Dec. 1917, and to Sydney Cockerell, 3 Aug. 1922, in Millgate (ed.), *Emma and Florence Hardy*, 124–5, 136, 187.

wear a black tie for the rest of my life!'[95] Kipling's recovery spared Agate this necessity until 1936. Births provided happier opportunities. Naming an offspring after a favourite fictional character was a fashion marked from the eighteenth century, when epidemics of Clarissa and Pamela (Samuel Richardson) and Amelia (Henry Fielding) were succeeded by outbreaks of Nicol (Sir Walter Scott), Leila (Byron and Bulwer Lytton), Christabel (Coleridge), Shirley (Charlotte Brontë), Pippa (Robert Browning), Lorna (R. D. Blackmore), and Maud and Vivien (Tennyson).[96] Jude remained a distinct minority taste, tainted by the association with Christ's betrayer and not improved by the dismal hand dealt by Thomas Hardy in 1895, until the best-sellers' own successors, the Beatles pop stars, refurbished its image for a post-Christian age with their song 'Hey Jude' in 1968. Wanda, a bogus Teutonic or Slavonic-sounding name, was launched by the eponymous heroine of Ouida's 1883 novel, and Thelma, supposedly Norwegian, by Marie Corelli's 1887 best-seller. Corelli then achieved a double in 1895, her heroine in *The Sorrows of Satan* creating a fad for Mavis. A similar one–two was scored by B. C. Stephenson, librettist of the comic opera *Dorothy*, which ran for almost three years from 1886, followed by *Doris* in 1889.[97] Worse was to come with a wave of Wendys after Barrie's *Peter Pan* (1904) and *Peter and Wendy* (1911). These baptisms were a reverent action which injured only the infant recipient. Barrie himself was childless, yet still played the game. He renamed his St Bernard dog (originally called Glen) Porthos after the same in George Du Maurier's *Peter Ibbetson* (1891), which in turn was a salute to Dumas's musketeer. Du Maurier's own daughters were called Sylvia and Beatrix after his best-loved Mrs Gaskell and Thackeray heroines;[98] but the dignity of livestock remained uppermost in Leicestershire, from where a farmer in 1877 asked Tennyson 'if Isolt in your beautiful Idyll of Guinevere is a female character. I am founding a family of highly bred short horns descended from a . . . cow called Guinivere [*sic*] & I propose to call her female produce Isolt 1st, 2nd, 3rd, etc. but I cannot quite satisfy myself from the context as to the sex of Isolt.'[99] The pedigree of the police dog in one of the last stories by Maarten Maartens, the Dutch novelist popular in England, was altogether clearer: it was Sherlock, 'the detective incarnate'.[100] Max Beerbohm too was quite explicit about the naming of his own pets: James, for a fox-terrier he acquired in 1913, to celebrate Henry James's seventieth birthday and 'his books [which] had given me more pleasure than those of any other living man'; and Strachey, for a kitten in 1920, to remind him of the feline amusement he found in Lytton Strachey's *Eminent Victorians* (1918).[101] Homage to Robert Louis Stevenson

---

[95] Agate, *Shorter Ego*, 118.

[96] Patrick Hanks and Flavia Hodges, *A Dictionary of First Names* (Oxford, 1990), p. xx.

[97] Mackenzie, *Life and Times*, i. 138–9. Stephenson died in 1906; the musical score for both plays was by Alfred Collier (1844–91).

[98] Meynell (ed.), *Barrie Letters*, 7; and Ormond, *Du Maurier*, 153. Sylvia is from Mrs Gaskell's *Sylvia's Lovers* (1863), Beatrix from Thackeray's *Henry Esmond* (1852). Du Maurier also took the name of his hero in *Trilby* (1894), Little Billee, from a Thackeray ballad.   [99] Martin, *Tennyson*, 520.

[100] *Punch*, 5 June 1912, 439.   [101] Beerbohm to Strachey, 7 July 1920, repr. in *The Times*, 7 July 2003.

was more in John Buchan's mind when it came to horseflesh. Alan Breck was the name he chose for a pony he rode in South Africa when on Milner's staff during the Boer War; and he called an aged hunter the same which he rode about Elsfield following the Great War.[102]

Back in the world of *Homo sapiens* there was a piquancy about Lady Diana Manners's forename. She was so christened after Meredith's *Diana of the Crossways* (1885). For those in the Souls and others in the know, this choice by her mother was almost reckless: the child had resulted from an affair with Harry Cust, though the proprieties were otherwise observed and she was brought up as the third daughter of the future eighth Duke of Rutland.[103] The eventual Lady Glendevon was also stamped by her parents' choice of name, signalling their irregular relationship. Baptized Elizabeth but always known as Liza after the tragic heroine *Liza of Lambeth* (1897), she was the daughter of Somerset Maugham, born while her mother, Syrie, was married to the chemist Henry Wellcome.[104] Sentiment, perhaps mixed with pride, caused other authors to lumber their children with names drawn from their creations. The peculiarly named Chudleigh Garvice, who won the DSO in the Boer War and became commandant of police at Alexandria, was born in 1875, the year his father published his first novel, *Maurice Durant*, whose hero was Chudleigh Chichester.[105] Others took matters into their own hands. Far away in Ontario, Canada, in 1878 Florence Nightingale Graham was born. She duly went on to become a nurse before opening a beauty salon on New York's Fifth Avenue in 1910 and founding a cosmetics empire as Elizabeth Arden, the surname derived from her favourite lovelorn hero, Tennyson's *Enoch Arden* (1864).[106] Hector Munro also renamed himself. He took the pseudonym Saki from *The Rubáiyát of Omar Khayyám*, translated by Edward FitzGerald in 1859.[107]

Rather than a character's, an author's own name was commonly adopted. The Revd W. Stuart Scott, a devotee of Marie Corelli's novels since childhood, named his first-born, happily a daughter, Marie, at which the effusive spinster authoress expressed herself 'delighted to be fairy godmother'.[108] Authors themselves were not averse to playing the mutual admiration game. One of Dickens's sons was baptized Henry Fielding after the author of *Tom Jones*, and another Edward Bulwer Lytton after the author of *The Last Days of Pompeii*. There was also a Walter Landor Dickens, a Sydney Smith Dickens, a Francis Jeffrey Dickens, and

---

[102] Smith, *Buchan*, 222.

[103] See *DNB* for Harry Cust (1861–1917) and Lady Diana Cooper, *née* Manners (1892–1986); also Lady Diana Cooper, *The Rainbow Comes and Goes* (1961), 65–6, 72. Cust's serial seductions caused him to be deselected as MP in 1893–4; Jane Ridley and Clayre Percy (eds.), *Letters of Arthur Balfour and Lady Elcho* (1992), 87, 103–5. His principal redeeming feature was the invention of a game called 'Boring the Bore', as Walter Raleigh described it to Mrs Walter Crum, 30 June 1911: 'He does it by flat long interminable reminiscences of his childhood, till even the Bore screams' (Raleigh (ed.), *Raleigh Letters*, ii. 366–7).

[104] For an obituary of Lady Glendevon (1915–98), see *The Times*, 31 Dec. 1998.

[105] Chudleigh is a place in Devon, of which county Garvice was fond.

[106] *Sunday Times*, 29 June 2003.   [107] Langguth, *Saki*, 61–2.

[108] Scott, *Corelli*, 69. The self-centred Corelli never gave little Marie a thing; ibid. 173.

an Alfred D'Orsay Tennyson Dickens. Squeezed between the poet's names for this last child was homage to Count D'Orsay: both he and Tennyson stood as godfathers.[109] That was not possible in 1896, when George Gissing named one of his sons Alfred out of respect for the late Laureate; but, previously, Coventry Patmore too had embarked on a Dickensian-style comprehensiveness. Patmore named his first son Milnes, after his patron, the poet–politician Richard Monckton Milnes, and his second son Tennyson, after his then friend and idol. These inspirations were suitably rewarded. Milnes grew to hate his father, and Tennyson served as a painful reminder of a breach between the paternal poets which persisted from the early 1860s until death thirty years later.[110] No better fortune followed Hall Caine's naming of his second son, Derwent, in 1891, the same as that chosen by Coleridge for his younger son.[111] Caine's _Life of Samuel Taylor Coleridge_ had appeared in 1887, that _annus mirabilis_ for him, when his novel _The Deemster_ launched his best-selling career. Son Derwent proved an exceptionally horrid and selfish individual with a foul temper who, though always adored by his father, would land Caine with an illegitimate granddaughter, whom Caine and his wife raised as their own. Finally, spare a thought for the future editor of the _New Statesman_, Kingsley Martin. He was christened thus in 1897 because his father, a Congregationalist minister, so admired Charles Kingsley's writings. There were, however, additional reasons why young Kingsley was bullied at school.[112]

V

An author's postbag was another index of fame. This was _the_ great age of letter-writers. Hall Caine wrote 'hundreds of letters every month' and, as a best-seller conscious of public image, declared that this duty meant more to him than his books.[113] A register kept by the Revd C. L. Dodgson (Lewis Carroll) records 98,721 letters sent and received between 1861 and his death in 1898; but, wanting to shelter his life as a mathematics don at Oxford, Dodgson regularly returned unopened letters that addressed him as Lewis Carroll.[114] What Dodgson sought to avoid was pathetically exhibited by Robert Browning. Calling at his London home in De Vere Gardens in 1888, Anne Thackeray Ritchie found the elderly poet at bay, cornered between American celebrity-seekers in one room and members of the Browning Society in another. He lamented that she had 'no conception what it was like', especially the daily deluge of fan mail, which, by the time he answered it, left him exhausted to begin his work.[115]

---

[109] Edgar Johnson, _Charles Dickens_ (1953), for this and the naming of other children.
[110] Patmore, _Coventry Patmore_, ch. 11; Martin, _Tennyson_, 324–5, 534–5.   [111] Allen, _Caine_, 216.
[112] C. H. Rolph, _Kingsley: The Life, Letters and Diaries of Kingsley Martin_ (1973), 32.
[113] Allen, _Caine_, 8.   [114] Collingwood, _Carroll_, 218; Cohen, _Carroll_, 191, 262.
[115] Gérin, _Ritchie_, 226.

Belatedly, George Gissing too experienced this consequence of popularity. His quasi-autobiographical *Private Papers of Henry Ryecroft* (1903) generated a crop of correspondents, including a clergyman who wished to employ the late Mr Ryecroft's housekeeper.[116] True to form, Gissing himself failed to savour this for long: he was dead by the year's end.

Readers were also inclined to burden authors with intimacies. Their preferred targets were authors who defied the conventions in their treatment of personal relationships, as George Moore did in *Esther Waters* (1894) and *Evelyn Innes* (1898) or as H. G. Wells did in *Ann Veronica* (1909) and *The New Machiavelli* (1911). These attracted confidences from readers with problems that paralleled those in the fiction. Moore received 'long letters asking for sympathy and advice, and love-letters too. He was getting them daily from some Viennese woman—long love-letters full of psychology and passion.' Wells also told of 'letters received from women who believed he would understand their difficulties—difficulties of the heart.'[117] It was a measure of Henry James's standing that he was never besieged by popular attentions. Visitors to Lamb House at Rye, where James settled in the late 1890s, came by invitation. The only time anything like a crowd gathered was in June 1900, when Lord Wolseley called on James. Led by town officials, people assembled to salute the former Commander-in-Chief.[118] The refined novelist, however, had no power to restrain the fantasist. This came in the shape of Miss Emilie Busbey Grigsby, a 23-year-old from Kentucky. Having met James at a tea party in London in 1903, she declared herself the 'original' of Milly Theale, heroine of *The Wings of the Dove* (1902). That she would claim also that George Meredith, on meeting her, recognized the heroine of *The Ordeal of Richard Feverel* (1859) is some token of her delusion; still, gossip columnists so embroidered her relationship with James that the celibate and sexagenarian author was said to have proposed marriage. This, James told his brother, 'would be worthy of the world-laughter of the Homeric Gods, if it didn't rather much depress me with the sense of the mere inane silliness of this so vulgarly chattering and so cheaply-fabricating age'.[119] But it was impossible to stop the fan from living the dream. A bold declaration was made by a female fan of W. J. Locke, author of the bohemian romances *The Morals of Marcus Ordeyne* (1905) and *The Beloved Vagabond* (1906). His wife, Aimée, related in 1912 how 'a complete stranger rushed up to her and folding her in her arms, exclaimed: "You are the only woman I have ever envied!" "She was quite an old lady", she added dryly.'[120] Perhaps she was aware of the Lockes' romantic complications. Aimée had been married when she and Locke met. Having fallen in love, they lived together until

---

[116] Halperin, *Gissing*, 338.

[117] Rothenstein, *Men and Memories, 1900–1922*, 171. See also Allen, *Caine*, 351, for the letters Hall Caine received from women following *The Woman Thou Gavest Me* (1913), his best-selling novel about divorce and illegitimacy.　　　　　　　　　　　　　　　　　　　　　　　　[118] Edel, *James*, ii. 373.

[119] Henry James to William James, 6 May 1904, ibid. 506.

[120] Lowndes (ed.), *Lowndes Diaries and Letters*, 39 (28 July 1912).

her divorce allowed them to marry in 1911. That they had been cut from some social circles made Locke's attachment the stronger—'his idolatry of her was so extravagant that when she slightly burned a finger in lighting a gas jet he flew into a passion with the Gas, Light and Coke, had the entire lighting system ripped out and electricity installed within twenty-four hours'.[121]

A writer could easily make waves without evident design. The son of an archbishop of Canterbury, and himself an Eton master and Cambridge don, Arthur Benson reached a vast public with his urbane essays and fiction *The House of Quiet* (1904), *The Upton Letters* (1905), *The Thread of Gold* (1905), and *From a College Window* (1906). These were first published anonymously

because all that one says in public, above one's own signature, is commented on from the standpoint of one's own profession and reputation; and in England, where the standard of artistic values is not very high, and where people are frankly more interested in personality and position than in ideas, it is tiresome not to be able to say frankly what one thinks, without having it all accounted for by one's birth and nurture and circumstances and occupations.

Once Benson's authorship was identified, he 'suffered . . . from being supposed to be an extremely secluded and leisurely person, turning from ancient folios to contemplate the sunset, and back again to my folio, without anything particular to do except to rejoice in gentle sentiments'. In fact, he was a much-occupied man, with innumerable engagements and a large correspondence: and 'on the whole I enjoy such a life more than the contemplative life'.[122] His reading public would not be shaken out of its illusion. Given a glimpse of a magical world of apparent civilized ease, permeated by the 'high-minded and sincere and beautiful', they lapped up

the donnish and the aristocratic flavour . . . in episcopal palaces and county society and Eton and Cambridge—and believe they have really found the charm of culture. It is humiliating in a sense, because I don't think it is a critical or an intellectual audience; but it is there, and its real and urgent goodwill is there.

Who these people were he didn't actually know—'clerks, tradesmen, doctors, teachers, their wives and daughters', he was informed after one public lecture.[123] Arnold Bennett, who loathed Benson's faux philosophy—'All of it has the astounding calm assurance of mediocrity'[124]—thought he knew. He dubbed him minister to Mudie's. But Benson did not go in for self-deception. 'My desire is to

---

[121] Steen, *Looking Glass*, 44. Steen's relationship with Locke cooled after her own remark about Aimée's fading beauty got back to him: she described Aimée as resembling 'an alcoholic magnolia'.

[122] A. C. Benson, Preface to the Second Edition, Oct. 1916, of *Father Payne* (1917), 6–7.

[123] Lubbock, *Benson*, 204–5 (17 Jan. 1911). See also Nicoll, *Bookman's Letters*, ch. xiii, on the popularity of Benson's essays.

[124] *New Age*, 1 Sept. 1910, in Bennett, *Books and Persons*, 239–41. *Punch* also repeatedly treated Benson as a laughing-stock, the author of smoothly worded banalities. Benson complained of such critics accusing him of penning platitudes, in *At Large* (1908); for a review of this 'latest (but surely not his last) book of distilled-water essays', see *Punch*, 4 Nov. 1908, 342. Previously, it had invented spoof titles by

write a great and beautiful book,' he mused in 1906; 'instead I have become the beloved author of a feminine tea-party kind of audience, the mild and low-spirited people, who would like to think the world a finer place than they have any reason for doing.'[125] Their enthusiasm for his work was unmistakable. Benson's fan mail kicked off with an epistle 'from a virgin of 30, written to me as the unknown author of the *College Window*—in a beautiful, simple style, a most interesting personal document'.[126] By 1911 he had received numerous requests for assignations and several offers of marriage from female admirers, singularly inappropriate proposals to a confirmed bachelor with homosexual proclivities; and 1915 brought a gift of £40,000 from an American lady, whom he never met.[127] With this enormous sum—some £2 million today—Benson was able to indulge his friends and college, a consideration which perhaps influenced Fellows, who elected him to the mastership of Magdalene. Though he vented his irritations— 'A disgusting morning of letters—I wrote about 30...'—Benson courteously replied to all sorts, even 'the ingenuous spiritualistic ladies who write to me, who tell me the absurdest stories, and wish me to be instantly converted to spiritualism'.[128] Cecil Roberts was grateful for Benson's conscientiousness. In 1911 Roberts was 19, ambitious to be a writer, yet stuck in a clerkship in a corporation office in Nottingham. He sent Benson a 300-page typescript over which he had laboured at nights. Its style 'was too obviously inspired by [Oliver Wendell Holmes's] *The Autocrat of the Breakfast Table* [1857]' but Roberts was 'hoping of course for recognition of genius' from Benson:

He sent my book back with a four-page letter of criticism and encouragement, and paid the postage! When I think of my audacity in burdening such a busy man with my scribbling, I marvel at his kindness to an unknown youth. It had a lasting effect on me. When, in due time, I, too, was pestered by the unsolicited manuscripts of budding authors, I repressed my impatience and responded as A. C. Benson had responded. I wrote kindly, and paid the postage, if not enclosed.[129]

With the death of his brother Hugh—Catholic priest and writer of best-selling historical romances and mystical works—in 1914, Arthur Benson found himself saddled with additional correspondence, the core comprising 'about 12 spinsters

---

Benson: *Parlour Pathos; Warblings from a Scholar's Sanctuary; Mezzanine Musings; Great Thoughts from a Best Bedroom; The Slop-over Letters; or, The Ordeal of Tony Toshpot*, etc. (*Punch*, 23 Oct. 1907, 302). See also Beerbohm, *Christmas Garland*, 21–30, for 'Out of Harm's Way', Max's parody of Benson. Unhappily, a companion caricature—with the caption 'Mr Arthur Christopher Benson vowing eternal fidelity to the obvious'—has been lost.

[125] Lubbock, *Benson*, 153 (31 Dec. 1906).   [126] Newsome, *Edge of Paradise*, 191.

[127] The American lady is identified as Madame de Nottbeck, originally an Astor, in Newsome, *Edge of Paradise*, ch. 11. See also Lubbock, *Benson*, 157–8, 223, 278–9.

[128] Lubbock, *Benson*, 135, 162 (9 Feb. 1906, 2 Mar. 1907).

[129] Roberts, *Years of Promise*, 41. Benson's Preface to the second edition of *Father Payne* starts: 'It always interests me to find how many of the literary aspirants who asked me to read and comment on their work say that they have no desire to get money or fame, but only wish to do good.' Later in that book Benson gave advice about how to write.

who write once a week, several of them Hugh's pets, yet I can't bring myself not to answer—and so it goes on day by day'.[130]

Kipling would have thought these trifling difficulties. He was dogged by a lunatic from England to South Africa and back over several years. This climaxed with the stalker firing a revolver as Kipling was leaving the Athenaeum.[131] Conan Doyle also drew worldwide attention. He himself was an eager writer of letters to newspapers; nor was he shy of personal publicity. 'A Day with Dr. Conan Doyle', a profile by Harry How, complete with photographs of author, wife, tandem tricycle, and house, in August 1892, adorned the *Strand Magazine*, in which Doyle serialized his stories. Interviews with him were also published in *The Idler* in Britain and in *McClure's Magazine* in America.[132] Amid the multitude of letters Doyle received, many were addressed to his fictional detective Sherlock Holmes and ally Dr Watson with pleas, including financial inducements, to solve distressing cases. Nuisance though he found this, Doyle cannot be exculpated because he sometimes answered letters as Holmes or Watson. People wanted to believe in them, having little confidence in the police to counter crime or deliver justice. Threatening letters followed after Doyle killed off Holmes at the Reichenbach Falls in December 1893, an event which the press reported as real news. Obituaries of Holmes appeared. The *Strand* slumped in circulation. Over 20,000 subscribers cancelled, to the consternation of the proprietor, Newnes, the editor, Greenhough Smith, and shareholders, among whom was Doyle himself.[133] Angry readers badgered the Prince of Wales and MPs, demanding Holmes's resurrection. Doyle submitted in 1901 when Holmes returned to pursue *The Hound of the Baskervilles*; and new adventures periodically appeared for another quarter-century, the author being compelled to accept that he would be forever 'identified with what I regarded as a lower stratum of literary achievement'.[134]

G. K. Chesterton's postbag was also among the largest and most varied, as the inventor of Father Brown, and as poet, literary critic, purveyor of paradoxes, popular theologian, and controversialist. He took to employing secretaries: 'no letter was left unanswered [but] autograph hunters were a pest, and we kept a very large sheet of signatures, and I cut off one as needed'.[135] A spouse, secretary, or both were the usual factotums employed by a writer to parry unwanted correspondence or gifts designed to elicit a reply. During his American tour in 1882 Oscar Wilde claimed to employ three secretaries: one to receive the flowers that arrived at ten-minute intervals, a second to spend all day scribbling his autograph, and a third to surrender locks of hair for dispatch to 'myriad maidens'. The last two became invalids, the one with writer's cramp, the other with

---

[130] Newsome, *Edge of Paradise*, 329–30.   [131] Birkenhead, *Kipling*, 233.

[132] Booth, *Conan Doyle*, 171–2.

[133] Ibid. 142, 190. Holmes was the first fictional character to be the subject of a biography (by Vincent Starrett).

[134] Pearson, *Conan Doyle*, ch. vi. Circulation of the *Strand Magazine* rose by 30,000 in August 1901, when the first episode of *The Hound of the Baskervilles* appeared.

[135] One of Chesterton's secretaries, Winifred Pierpoint, in Ward, *Return to Chesterton*, 151.

premature baldness.[136] As the country's most successful playwright in the early 1900s Barrie, too, saw the wisdom of taking on a secretary after his correspondence and accounts piled up chaotically. Not all was in response to his own work, because such was his fame that the public identified the Barrie whimsy everywhere and was unwilling to believe his disclaimers of authorship. This was the case with Daisy Ashford's comic best-seller *The Young Visiters* (1919), for which Barrie wrote a preface after establishing that the author, then aged 38, had genuinely written it when 9 years old. Barrie emphasized this to his American publisher, Charles Scribner:

It is printed word for word as originally shown me. I think I say this in the preface, and I rather resent people's not accepting my word. The whole affair has been something of a trial for me, as hordes of parents here keep sending me their children's work, and now they are doing it from America. I have to employ a secretary.[137]

Barrie minus Ashford was still big business. A principal part of his secretary's job was dealing with the 'hundreds of letters from silly women asking *what it is that "every woman knows"*'. The occupation proved predictable in other ways—'a *schwärm*-ing appeal for signed photographs from two schoolgirls', counterbalanced by 'heartrending ones from actresses, clamouring for engagements, sending photographs, etc.'. Aside from umpteen social invitations and begging letters, pleas for autographs or advice about manuscripts, appeals to act as godfather to a child who was to be christened Peter or Wendy, and commercial requests for product endorsement, translation rights, or a preface for this and that book, the routine was broken only by crackpots whose letters were either binned or replied to on St James's Theatre notepaper rather than from Barrie's Adelphi Terrace address.[138]

In respect of volume and variety of correspondence, the extraordinary Silas K. Hocking is worth exhuming, extraordinary because it is likely that his books outsold most best-sellers. True, there were a lot of books by Hocking: *Punch*, parodying the *Tit-Bits* style of imparting useless 'Facts You Ought To Know', informed everyone in 1905 that 'Mr Silas Hocking has not written more than 1123 novels.'[139] When Arnold Bennett was investigating popular authors for *The Academy* in the late 1890s, Hocking's publisher Frederick Warne & Co. confided his sales: 1,093,185 altogether, or about a thousand a week.[140] In part, this was explained by format and price: Hocking never went in for the triple-decker, and the majority of his stories sold at 3s. 6d., after serialization in Nonconformist periodicals. In 1894 Hocking, then a Methodist minister, became editor of the

---

[136] Richard Ellmann, *Oscar Wilde* (1987), 159. [137] Meynell (ed.), *Barrie Letters*, 66.
[138] Asquith, *Diaries*, 455, 461, 469, 471 (26 June, 24 July, 29 Aug., 3 Sept. 1918); id., *Barrie*, 8, 11, 19, 29.
[139] *Punch*, 6 Dec. 1905, 397.
[140] E. A. Bennett, *Fame and Fiction: An Enquiry into Certain Popularities* (1901), 145. Bennett's own fame was so small at this time that the publisher of this collection of articles, Grant Richards, misspelled his surname on the book's cover as 'Bennet'.

Family Circle; and in 1896 he co-founded the *Temple Magazine* (subtitled *Silas K. Hocking's Illustrated Monthly*). In Society London, Hocking's stories were disregarded; in the provincial centres of Dissent—Hocking was the son of a Cornish tin-mine owner—his work was in huge demand.[141] *M.A.P.*, in a profile of Hocking in 1904, noted that his audience was chiefly 'the country folk and lower middle classes' and, if 'not great readers, they generally buy what they read'. His success derived from 'the tonic qualities' of his simple fables, conveying plain moral lessons.[142] *Punch* gently mocked this virtuousness, including in its 'Masterpieces Modernised' series *Tom Jones* updated by Hocking, and suggesting as a title for one of the greatest unwritten books Hocking's *Rabelais as a World Force*.[143] Yet,

daily he has letters from all over the world saying what help and cheer they have found in his books. All the letters in the postbag, however, are not so pleasant. Many, verging on the abusive, are from persons who denounce Mr. Hocking because he is not sufficiently doctrinal—by which they probably mean dogmatic. And, of course, like every public man, Mr. Hocking suffers from the autograph hunter and the begging-letter writer. A large and curious part of his correspondence consists of uninvited autobiographies from people who are certain Mr. Hocking could utilise them in his novels.[144]

Fans could get very indignant when their favourite failed to respond to cue. Samuel Butler did not have many fans and he disliked most of those. In 1931 Ford Madox Ford acknowledged that Butler's posthumously published *Way of All Flesh* (1903) was one of the 'greatest milestones on the road of purely English letters between *Gulliver's Travels* and Joyce's *Ulysses*'; but he evidently still smarted at maltreatment by him: 'I disliked Samuel Butler more than anyone I knew. He was intolerant and extraordinarily rude in conversation—particularly to old ladies and young persons.'[145] Butler was especially sardonic about admirers who, having read *Erewhon* (1872), 'wanted me at once to set to work and write another book like it'. He did eventually issue the sequel, *Erewhon Revisited* (1901); but, when a woman had accosted him in the British Museum, making this proposal just after he had published *Life and Habit* (1877), he felt like replying that had she known Shakespeare she would doubtless have ticked him off for writing *Henry IV*

---

[141] Ibid. 146. Having read Hocking's latest, Bennett found his popularity almost inexplicable but suspected it might lie in his 'tact', so as not to offend the Dissenting readership for whom sensationalism was the devil. Thus excitement was kept down, the intelligence not challenged, and everything was simplified while bowing to the spiritual ideal. When Bennett met Hocking in 1915 he 'found him decidedly agreeable, rather devil-may-care with his fine beard. He said he hadn't been doing much lately; getting older [Hocking was then 65]; only worked in mornings; and had been living on dividends. However, he had recently had demands for five serials, and had contracted to do three. He evidently had the right trade attitude towards his work'. (Flower (ed.), *Bennett Journals*, ii. 131 (15 May 1915)).

[142] *M.A.P.*, 24 Dec. 1904, 732.

[143] *Punch*, 14 Feb. 1900, 117, 24 Aug. 1912, 307. In the greatest unwritten books series it also proposed Hilaire Belloc's 'Life and Teachings of Sir Wilfrid Lawson'—Lawson being the leading parliamentary advocate of temperance reform, and Belloc a confirmed boozer.   [144] *M.A.P.*, 24 Dec., 732.

[145] Ford, *Return to Yesterday*, 133–4.

instead of another *Titus Andronicus*—'Now that was a sweet play, that was.' In his club Butler encountered a member who needed repeated assurances from a third party that Butler was who he was: 'It was plain he thought a great deal of *Life and Habit* and had idealised its author, whom he was disappointed to find so very commonplace . . .'. When people wrote to him, or used an intermediary, asking to be introduced, he usually assented but

it always ends in turning some one who was more or less inclined to run me into one who considers he has a grievance against me for not being a very different kind of person from what I am. These people however (and this happens on average once or twice a year) do not come solely to see me, they generally tell me all about themselves and the impression is left upon me that they have really come in order to be praised. I am as civil to them as I know how to be but enthusiastic I never am, for they have never any of them been nice people, and it is my want of enthusiasm for themselves as much as anything else which disappoints them. They seldom come again.[146]

As the twentieth century dawned and developed, a new sort of correspondent, ultimately more dreadful than any, and completely unstoppable, entered authors' lives: the Ph.D. student and academic. Bernard Shaw was one of the first to attract this class of person: the American Archibald Henderson, who cross-examined him from 1904 and published the first of several studies in 1911.[147] H. G. Wells also achieved the status of guru. His Essex home was placed firmly on the academic map:

Every 'professor of English Literature' in an American college (and there must be a couple of million, or more) regards it as a sort of Mecca pilgrimage to sit at least once in his lifetime on the mat of Mr Wells's door. The old Great Eastern Railway used to make a handsome addition to its revenue out of these Wellsian pilgrimages.[148]

Wells was bored by these visits. Other authors, whether from vanity or presumption that scholarly interest must be distinguished from ordinary intrusions by its intellectual and moral seriousness, apparently welcomed this attention. In 1922 the poet Alice Meynell, aged 75 and in the last months of life, wrote to her son from her home in Sussex: 'Miss Tuell, a Wellesley (New England) professor who has actually come to England on purpose to study my various works for the thesis for her degree, we have asked to stay with us here.'[149] Later in the decade Richard Little Purdy, then a doctoral student at Yale, began his lifelong association with Thomas Hardy, although his first visit to Max Gate did not occur until 1929, the year following Hardy's death.[150]

Until the academic lit. crit. industry was cranked up, among the worst of the many sorts of correspondent was the aspiring author who presented some

---

[146] Jones, *Notebooks of Samuel Butler*, 156–8.   [147] Laurence (ed.), *Shaw: Letters 1898–1910*, 471 ff.

[148] Blumenfeld, *All in a Lifetime*, 177.

[149] Meynell, *Alice Meynell*, 335. Anne Kimball Tuell published *Mrs Meynell and her Literary Generation* (New York, 1925).   [150] Millgate (ed.), *Emma and Florence Hardy*, 281–2, 310.

effusion for endorsement. Even the saintly Alice Meynell flagged: 'It is a good thing to be nice to the poor dear Miss B–'s of this world, but the result is that they bring you their poems to read on the spot, in front of them.'[151] This stratagem was generally unsuccessful and should have been abandoned ever since Dr Johnson gave his verdict on *Dido* and its author: 'Sir, I never did the man an injury. Yet he would read his tragedy to me.'[152] No doubt, different authors attracted a different volume and type of literary incompetence. Thomas Hardy was naturally a magnet for the regional saga enthusiast. To one, George Morley, who sent his story about rural Warwickshire, *A Bunch of Blue Ribbons* (1907), Hardy patiently explained the commercial risks: 'Literature is a precarious profession at the best of times, & in average cases requires a greater expenditure of labour than any other to produce a steady income from—certainly than any trade. The sale of a book is largely a matter of chance. A book may be good, but not sell: it may be bad, & sell well.' Consult a knowledgeable publisher, he counselled, before adding aridly, '& even they are often wrong'.[153]

Few could rival the Laureate's correspondence for quantity; certainly, he was the loudest to complain. In 1885 his publisher Macmillan had to intervene and not for the first time, placing this letter in the press:

We are requested by Lord Tennyson to inform his correspondents through *The Times*, that he is wholly unable to answer the innumerable letters which he daily receives, nor can he undertake to return or criticise the manuscripts sent to him. A similar statement was published two years ago, but its repetition now seems necessary in consequence of the mass of correspondence which has reached Lord Tennyson since the publication of his new volume of poems [*Tiresias and Other Poems*].

Tennyson moaned that he would need to be 'a hundred-armed Briareus with all his hands writing at once' in order to answer requests for autographs. As for the unsolicited poetical rubbish, he calculated in 1890 that 'I get a verse for every three minutes of my life.'[154] No wonder he was inclined to 'vomit morally' from the flattery which enveloped him when a fellow sufferer from celebrity, Marie Corelli, drew from him the admission that 'Modern Fame is too often a crown of thorns and brings all the vulgarity of the world upon you. I sometimes wish I had never written a line'—whereupon she published, and rebuked him for, his sentiments.[155] Nor was Corelli content with that. She contrived a witticism from

---

[151] Meynell, *Alice Meynell*, 256–7.

[152] Birrell, 'The Johnsonian Legend' (1897), in Birrell, *Self-Selected Essays*, 95.

[153] Hardy to George Morley, 5 July 1907, in Purdy and Millgate (eds.), *Hardy Letters*, iii. 259–60.

[154] Lang and Shannon (eds.), *Tennyson Letters*, iii. 300, 307, 331–2, 390, 399. Tennyson usually left the answering of such correspondence to his wife and son; Tennyson, *Tennyson*, 635. *Tiresias, and Other Poems* was dedicated to Robert Browning and contained poems new and old, including 'The Charge of the Light Brigade'.

[155] Lang and Shannon (eds.), *Tennyson Letters*, iii. 416–17. Corelli prompted the reply from Tennyson by sending him *Ardath* (1889). Corelli also suffered from requests for autographs and from 'the begging letters which beset me and my work' (Brian Masters, *Now Barabbas was a Rotter: The Extraordinary Life of Marie Corelli*, (1978) 160; Bertha Vyver, *Memoirs of Marie Corelli* (1930), 81).

this meagre connection with the Laureate, although it failed to impress the aunt of Mrs H. H. Penrose:

M[arie]. C[orelli]. Do you like tennis?
  The aunt makes a perfunctory answer.
  M.C. The only tennis I like is Tennyson.
  Pause.
  M.C. The dear old man sent me a beautiful letter once.
  'I tried to look', said the excellent aunt afterwards, 'as if Tennyson had been in the habit of sending me a letter every day.'[156]

Well-meaning strangers who wrote to recommend cures for rheumatism (a burnt cork under the bed or a diet of snails) provided Tennyson with small consolation. Perhaps a change of subject was called for, to summon a more useful stream of generosity. A. A. Milne was the recipient of such bounty:

At a crisis in the war I wrote some pathetic verses called 'The Last Pot,' and never lacked for marmalade again. When I had exhausted the benevolence or the larders of English women, the nearer colonies and the more distant Dominions took up the torch, so that the Empire became for me a place in which marmalade is always setting.[157]

For sheer pleasure, the response to Walter de la Mare's *Memoirs of a Midget* (1921) was difficult to surpass. Readers presented him with a multitude of miniatures for his heroine, Miss M.—tiny books, shells and 'a small gold frog dug up from the mud of the Nile'.[158]

VI

Not all attentions were unwanted. The effusive illuminated address was standard form in Victorian England, as constituents saluted retiring MPs or parishioners their vicars. It was not surprising, when authors got in on the act, that Edmund Gosse was found orchestrating so many performances. He organized this congratulatory address on parchment scroll for George Meredith's seventieth birthday on 12 February 1898:

You have attained the first rank in literature after many years of inadequate recognition. From first to last you have been true to yourself and have always aimed at the highest mark. We are rejoiced to know that merits once perceived by only a few are now appreciated by a wide and steadily growing circle. We wish you many years of life, during which you may continue to do good work, cheered by the consciousness of good work already achieved, and encouraged by the certainty of a hearty welcome from many sympathetic readers.

---

[156] Flower (ed.), *Bennett Journals*, i. 42–3 (16 July 1897). On Mrs H. H. Penrose, Kemp *et al.* (eds.), *Edwardian Fiction*, 312–3. [157] Milne, *Autobiography*, 236.
[158] Russell Brain, *Tea with Walter de la Mare* (1957), 36.

[Signed:]

J. M. Barrie	F. W. Maitland
Walter Besant	Alice Meynell
Augustine Birrell	John Morley
Austin Dobson	F. W. H. Myers
Conan Doyle	J. Payn
Edmund Gosse	Frederick Pollock
R. B. Haldane	Anne Thackeray Ritchie
Thomas Hardy	Harry Sidgwick
Frederic Harrison	Leslie Stephen
John Oliver Hobbes	Algernon Charles Swinburne
Henry James	Mary A. Ward
R. C. Jebb	G. F. Watts
Andrew Lang	Theodore Watts-Dunton
W. E. H. Lecky	Wolseley[159]
M. London (Mandell Creighton)	

The organization of this obeisance was no straightforward matter. Six weeks before, Gosse consulted Hardy, who advised floating the idea among two or three others, 'beginning with Leslie Stephen, who had experience in a similar kind of tribute to Carlyle on his reaching his 80th year. I think one or two insidious objections were raised in that case, though I cannot remember what they were, & they would probably have no weight in this.' Hardy was right to counsel caution, although too pessimistic to expect a repetition of the farce which attended one tribute to Carlyle in 1875. Prior to the birthday, Carlyle's Chelsea home had been broken into, the burglars making off with his dining room clock; hence a dozen female admirers, including Lady Stanley of Alderley, Lady Ashburton, the Countess of Airlie, Mrs Oliphant, Mrs Tennyson, Mrs Froude, and Anne Thackeray, thoughtfully subscribed a pound each for a replacement. On 4 December the birthday arrived, but it was

a dismal winter's day, the streets were shrouded in greenish vapours, and the houses looked no less dreary within, than the streets through which we had come. Somewhat chilled and depressed, we all assembled in Lady Stanley's great drawing-room in Dover Street, where the fog had also penetrated, and presently from the further end of the room, advancing through shifting darkness, came Carlyle. There was a moment's pause. No one moved; he stood in the middle of the room without speaking. No doubt the philosopher, as well as his disciples, felt the influence of the atmosphere. Lady Stanley went to meet him. 'Here is a little birthday present we want you to accept from us all, Mr. Carlyle', said she, quickly pushing up before him a small table upon which stood the clock ticking all ready for his acceptance. There followed silence, broken by a sadly sounding knell.

---

[159] Sassoon, *Meredith*, 241. Not all these names were foremost literary people, of course: Creighton was a bishop and historian, and Lord Wolseley was Field Marshal and Commander-in-Chief of the Army. The latter's inclusion is explained by Meredith's support of the idea of national military service, a cause championed by Wolseley.

'Eh, what have I got to do with Time any more?' he asked. It was a melancholy moment, nobody could speak. The unfortunate promoter of the scheme felt her heart sinking into her shoes.[160]

Gosse evidently hoped for a better reception from Meredith for his memorial; but there were hurdles to overcome. About the signatories Hardy had counselled, 'Swinburne ought to be in it, or perhaps Meredith would not value it.' Here was a tricky assignment, because it was pretty common knowledge amid the inner circle of letters that Meredith and Swinburne could not stand each other and had rarely met since the early 1860s; but Meredith's seventieth did indeed prove opportune to effect a temporary reconciliation. Following a correspondence, Swinburne accepted Meredith's invitation to Box Hill.[161] In his next letter to Gosse, Hardy recommended the inclusion of Morley and Harrison, wondered about Doyle—'I doubt if G.M. knows Conan Doyle, but he may'—and queried Herbert Spencer; but his main point was, '*Most* of the names should I think be those of personal friends.' Two days later, having approved the wording of the tribute, drafted by Leslie Stephen, Hardy deliberated again about the signatories:

When you first mentioned the matter my impression was from 25 to 30—so that the list may not have an indiscriminate appearance, or of being other than nearly all personal friends. I don't quite see how A.J.B. [Balfour, Conservative Leader of the House of Commons] could sign to 'comrades in letters' . . . The women seem the most ticklish business—3 or 4, including J. O. Hobbes, would do, I suppose. I question if he would care for many.

Hardy further suggested cabling Kipling, who had left for Cape Town, for his consent to be included.[162] This was wise. Kipling had once met Meredith:

Imagine an old withered man very deaf in one ear who, as did Dragonet in the *Morte d'Arthur*,

'skips like a withered leaf upon the floor'.

He is full to a painful overflowing of elaborated epigrammatic speech which on the first fizz strikes one as deuced good. Five minutes later one cannot remember what on earth it was all about. And neither time, tide, Heaven nor Hell, nor the sanctities of five o'clock tea seem to be able to stop that flow of talk. The raucous voice continues; the little old man balances himself on his toes like a Shanghai rooster to command attention, and that attention *must* be given or he sulks like a child.

Having met Meredith, Kipling concluded, 'I don't want to see him any more.'[163]

It is clear from the correspondence about the Meredith tribute that there was often a clandestine motive in these events. Signatories celebrated themselves as well as the honorand; they also snubbed those excluded from the list. The

---

[160] Anne Thackeray's account, in Fuller and Hammersley (eds.), *Thackeray's Daughter*, 129–30.
[161] Gosse, *Life of Swinburne*, 92–4, 105–6.
[162] Hardy to Edmund Gosse, 4, 7, 9, 16 Jan. 1898, in Purdy and Millgate (eds.), *Hardy Letters*, ii. 184–5. J. O. Hobbes was John Oliver Hobbes (Pearl Craigie). [163] Birkenhead, *Kipling*, 111–12.

omission of W. E. Henley—he was a studious Meredithian, who reviewed *The Egoist* (1879) three times—was conspicuous, and a consequence of Gosse's and Henley's mutual loathing. Meredith was alert to this possibility of hidden agendas, writing to Edward Clodd: 'I know what they mean, kindly enough. Poor old devil, he *will* go on writing; let us cheer him up. The old fire isn't quite out; a stir of the poker may bring out a shoot of gas.'[164] Meredith's ruminations were well aimed. The impresario Gosse confessed to Henry James and Thomas Hardy that Meredith was unreadable. Though he liked him well enough personally, he found Meredith's unquenchable optimism intolerable in more than short doses. Accordingly, Gosse had declined an invitation from Clement Shorter to write on Meredith, not trusting his ability to mask his distaste for the work.[165]

The fuss made on Meredith's seventieth birthday was unobtrusive compared with the 'orgy of homage and adulation' that occurred on his eightieth in 1908. Anthony Hope, Herbert Trench, and Israel Zangwill descended on Flint Cottage with an address from the Society of Authors; and Clement Shorter and Edward Clodd followed with a vellum signed by 250 names representing literature, art, science, and public life. The cantorial peal of congratulatory telegrams and letters from around the world was headed by a message from the King; and leading articles in most newspapers sounded the fanfare of his certain immortality in literature.[166] Naturally, this publicity ensured that Meredith was also deluged by a cataract of unwanted correspondence from desperate authors seeking permission to adapt plays from his stories, and 'begging letters, letters of great gush, idiotic letters; one from a piteously-voiced bankrupt clergyman!'[167] As for some of the accredited authors, again polite form had overriden private doubt. Hardy's and Meredith's philosophies were antipoles. After the two talked in June 1905, Meredith had felt 'afflicted' by Hardy's 'twilight view of life'.[168] Hardy commented sardonically: 'It is curious (& very good of him) that he was concerned for my pessimism, for I was afraid after leaving that I had shaken his optimism, & G.M. converted to pessimism by me is too terrible a catastrophe to think of. It would lead to my speedy "removal" by the young Meredithians.' Plainly stung, Hardy mounted a resolute defence of his position: 'Why people make the mistake of supposing pessimists, or what are called such, incurably melancholy, I do not know. The very fact of their having touched bottom gives them substantial cheerfulness in the consciousness that they have nothing to lose.'[169] Nevertheless, Hardy subscribed to the birthday tribute in 1908, while also sending Meredith a copy of the recently published Third Part of *The Dynasts*.[170] And, as fate would have it, Hardy's studious refusal of the *Daily News*'s invitation to write about

---

[164] Sassoon, *Meredith*, 151–2, 241–2. For the Henley–Gosse rift, Thwaite, *Gosse*, 217, 539.
[165] Thwaite, *Gosse*, 401–2.   [166] Sassoon, *Meredith*, 257–8.
[167] Meredith to John Morley, 25 Feb. 1908, in Cline (ed.), *Meredith's Letters*, iii. 1634.
[168] Meredith to Edmund Gosse, 2 July 1905, ibid. 1529.
[169] Hardy to Edmund Gosse, 7 Nov. 1905, in Purdy and Millgate (eds.), *Hardy Letters*, iii. 187.
[170] Hardy to Clement Shorter, 16 Feb. 1908, ibid. 296.

Meredith—'I have known Mr Meredith for so long a time—forty years within a few months—& his personality is such a living one to me, that I cannot reach a sufficiently detached point of view to write, as you request, a critical estimate of his great place in the world of letters'—was simply ignored. The *Daily News* published this, having carefully omitted the phrase 'as you request'.[171]

The self-congratulatory element in these tributes was judged too pronounced in 1913 by Alice Meynell (who had contributed to the Meredith) when a proposal was made to present Thomas Hardy with a Festschrift of poems inscribed in the versifiers' own handwriting. Gosse, again, was behind it, reinforced with a committee comprising the Laureate and other poets. This was no birthday decennial—Hardy's seventieth passed in 1910—and he had already been decorated by the Royal Society of Literature in 1912, its gold medal being presented to him by Henry Newbolt and W. B. Yeats. For that occasion Hardy prepared press releases of his acceptance speech in which he inveighed against the deterioration of the English language.[172] The year 1913 had brought the Litt.D. from Cambridge, and also saw Macmillan's completion of the twenty-volume Wessex Edition of Hardy. The notion of a Festschrift now provided a rare occasion when Alice Meynell was overruled by her husband. To one of their children, she explained: 'I, being asked to contribute, thought I never would agree to join such a self-advertising and intrusive assault upon Hardy. I had written a courteous refusal. And lo! your father quashed the answer, not yet posted, and now I am to say Yes. I should have thought it a moral impossibility.'[173] The Great War then supervened; but its end, and Hardy's longevity, released the authors' pent-up emotions in a new surge of sycophancy. In 1919, for his seventy-ninth birthday, came the 'Poets' Tribute', a collection of autograph poems by forty-three writers, including Bridges the Laureate and Kipling, which Siegfried Sassoon transported to Max Gate. On Hardy's eightieth, a delegation of Augustine Birrell, John Galsworthy, and Anthony Hope presented the Society of Authors' address; but such harmony was as ever illusory. In 1921, when his eighty-first generated the gift of a first edition of Keats's *Lamia, Isabella, The Eve of St. Agnes, and Other Poems* (1820), together with an address signed by over 100 'younger comrades in the craft of letters', the Hardy household 'received several indignant letters from authors demanding of us *why* they had not been asked to join in the address' including one 'very grieved letter' from ancient Mrs W. K. Clifford, to whom they had not the heart to point out that it was designed to represent 'younger authors'.[174]

---

[171] Hardy to H. W. Smith, 9 Feb. 1908, ibid. 295.

[172] Millgate, *Hardy*, 477. Hardy approved of the English Association (est. 1906), being 'appalled at the ruin that threatens our fine old English tongue by the growth of American phraseology of the worst sort in our newspapers, which influence the speech of the people more than is realised. For instance to-day I heard a farm woman say to her child, "Hurry up!" Ten years ago she would have said "Come hither!" ' (Hardy to Sidney Lee, 22 Nov. 1906, in Purdy and Millgate (eds.), *Hardy Letters*, iii. 237).

[173] Meynell, *Alice Meynell*, 283.

[174] Florence Hardy to Louise Yearsley, 10 Aug. 1919, to Macleod Yearsley, 16 May 1920, to E. M. Forster, 17 June 1921, in Millgate (ed.), *Emma and Florence Hardy*, 160, 166, 177.

10

Playing the Press: Entry and Exposure

> As to what you gather from newspapers, they are not to be trusted. They
> deal in gossip and gossip gets its fee in these days. I forbear to contradict
> them in the press, thinking it useless when once a tale has been started. And
> besides an author should not value himself so highly as to join in any tem-
> porary buzz concerning him.
>
> (George Meredith to Mrs W. J. Trimble, 9 April 1909)

I

'The Penalties of a Well-Known Name' was the title chosen by Ouida in 1892 for
an article in which she pronounced maledictions against the intrusions and
misrepresentations of reporters. Their fell stratagems in pursuit of interviews
were facilitated by new technology:

Whoever else may deem that the phonograph, the telephone, and the photographic
apparatus are beneficial to the world, every man and woman who has a name of celebrity
in that world must curse them with the deadliest hatred . . . . He who bends beneath the
decrees of the sovereign spy is popular at the price of dignity and peace. Those who
refuse to so stoop are marked out for abuse and calumny from all those who live by or are
diverted by the results of the espionage.

This was bad enough; worse, it encouraged the public to act similarly and to take
more interest in celebrities' personal habits than in their work. People clamoured

to know what any famous person eats, drinks, and wears, in what way he sins and in what
manner he sorrows, than it does to rightly measure and value his picture, his position, his
romance, or his poem. Journalistic inquisitiveness has begotten an unwholesome appetite, an impudent curiosity, in the world which leaves those conspicuous in it neither
peace nor privacy.[1]

It was hard in these circumstances to withhold sympathy from the victims—
except that Ouida, then a declining force in the literary marketplace and living far
away in Italy, might have dropped out of sight were it not for these articles in

---

[1] Ouida, 'The Penalties of a Well-Known Name', *North American Review* (June 1892), *Review of Reviews*
(July 1892), 43. cf. Israel Zangwill, 'The Penalties of Fame', in Zangwill, *Without Prejudice* (1896), 236–48.

which she broadcast strident opinions about everything from canine spirituality to the cut of men's trousers.

Authors not only regularly cooperated with journalists, they frequently were journalists. To become a journalist the writer first needed to acquire the trade tools. J. M. Barrie came to London knowing nobody; moreover, as a Scotsman he liked to recall with a twinkle, 'I did not even quite know the language.'[2] But he did have Roget's *Thesaurus* with him. He paid incidental tribute to that reliable companion in *Peter Pan* (1904), which begins in Bloomsbury because Roget lived there. Better still, his legend of Captain Hook was that 'The man is not wholly evil; he has a *Thesaurus* in his cabin . . .'.[3] In 1887 David Anderson, a quondam leader-writer for the *Daily Telegraph*, offered the aspirant rather more when he founded the London School of Journalism. This lured pupils for a fee of 100 guineas with the bait that they could soon be earning 'from £300 to £1,000 a year'. For a fee of that magnitude it was plain that Anderson had in mind, not the awakening of raw talent from humble circumstances, so much as the fleecing of the ingenuous rich. His school was two upstairs rooms off Fleet Street, and his classes consisted largely of talk, mostly desultory, sometimes libellous. Anderson's principal limitation as a professor of journalism was his contempt for journalism—apart from the *Daily Telegraph*. Still, he could dilate upon the proper construction of a leaderette; moreover, he had a 'fixed idea that wealth beyond the dreams of avarice awaited any man who could discover a trade which had no trade organ and supply it with one'. Anderson's alumni afterwards took revenge in their reminiscences or novels which, as Francis Gribble (Anderson's third pupil) observed, 'rarely strike a note of gratitude'. Among them was Robert Hichens, the son of a wealthy clergyman and educated at Clifton College. His *Felix* (1902) was 'almost photographically exact' in its description of Anderson and his School of Journalism.[4]

Whether Gribble, Hichens, or other pupils gained more than copy from their experience is unclear. The only job that Anderson found for Gribble was an assistantship on a newspaper in Yokohama, for which he was pronounced medically unfit. As for Hichens, he wrote his first novel *The Coastguard's Secret* when he was 17; that is, before he attended Anderson's school. But he had been endeavouring also to prove himself as a lyricist at the Royal College of Music— one of his songs was sung by Patti—and it may be that, almost inadvertently, the year at Anderson's was important in confirming his decision to become a writer. Hichens actually collaborated with Anderson in testing the latter's conviction that there was a fortune to be seized by filling a gap in the trade market. This they

---

[2] Barrie, *Courage*, 24.

[3] Barrie, *Plays*, 17, 71. Peter Mark Roget (1779–1869) studied at Edinburgh University (like Barrie later), where he read medicine; he became a professor of physiology and secretary to the Royal Society and was a leading spirit in the foundation of the University of London. He published the *Thesaurus of English Words and Phrases* in 1852. See Werner Hüllen, *A History of Roget's Thesaurus: Origins, Development and Design* (Oxford, 2004).   [4] Gribble, *Seen in Passing*, 88–99.

aimed to do for domestic service with a new paper called *Mistress and Maid*, Hichens supplying the money and Anderson the flair; but the venture flopped, and Anderson closed his academy and returned to the *Daily Telegraph*. Hichens, however, took to journalism, succeeded Bernard Shaw as music critic on *The World*, and then enjoyed a *succès de scandale* with *The Green Carnation* (1894), a skit on the aestheticism and depravity of the Wilde circle.[5] He followed it with *Flames: A London Phantasy* (1897), whereupon he was offered (and turned down) £2,000 a year by Lord Burnham to join the *Daily Telegraph*.[6] Hichens finally triumphed with an international best-seller, the desert romance, *The Garden of Allah* (1904).[7] Nor was he alone among Anderson's scholars to establish a reputation in journalism, authorship, or the theatre: the names of Guy Beringer, Stuart Erskine, C. L. Freeston, Cranstoun Metcalfe, H. Greville Montgomery, Bazil Tozer, and Herbert Vivian convey little now, but all struck some figure in Edwardian newspaper and literary circles.[8]

George Gissing was suitably horror-struck. In *The Private Papers of Henry Ryecroft* (1903), he wrote: 'There has come into existence a school of journalism which would seem to have deliberately set itself the task of degrading authorship and everything connected with it; and these pernicious scribblers (or typists, to be more accurate) have found the authors of a fretful age only too receptive of their mercantile suggestions.' He went on to express how much 'do I loathe and sicken at the manifold baseness, the vulgarity unutterable, which, as a result of the new order, is blighting our literary life. It is not easy to see how, in such an atmosphere, great and noble books can ever again come into being.'[9] This wretched

[5] Sutherland, *Companion*, 294–5, and *DNB 1941–1950*, 385–6. Heinemann, publisher of *The Green Carnation*, insisted on the book being anonymous: 'That will make people talk about it.' Authorship was variously attributed to Alfred Austin, Marie Corelli, and Andrew Hichens (the author's cousin); the *Pall Mall Gazette* even suggested that Wilde was the author. Also under suspicion was Ada Leverson, who was a friend of Wilde and a contributor to *Punch*. When the true authorship was publicized, Wilde (who had guessed it) wrote to her: 'Of course, you have been deeply wronged. But there are many bits not unworthy of your brilliant pen: and treachery is inseparable from faith. I often betray myself with a kiss. Hichens I did not think capable of anything so clever. It is such a bore about journalists, they are so very clever' (Hart-Davis (ed.), *Wilde's Letters*, 124). See also Sherard, *Wilde*, 117, for his distaste for the manner in which Hichens 'had won his way into their intimacy, and had collected his material'.

As well as satirizing the Wilde circle, *The Green Carnation* guyed practically every other celebrity author, actor, artist, or figure of the day: Mrs Lynn Linton, Lewis Morris, George Meredith, Ouida, Edna Lyall, Olive Schreiner, George R. Sims, George Moore, Mrs Humphry Ward, Sarah Grand, Rhoda Broughton, Max Beerbohm, G. A. Sala, Lady Jeune, Wilson Barrett, George Alexander, and Hubert Herkomer. Its model was E. F. Benson's *Dodo* (1893); Robert Hichens, *Yesterday* (1947), 65–75. *The Green Carnation* was reprinted, with the addition of Hichens's name, in 1894, but withdrawn during Wilde's trials in 1895, both author and publisher agreeing that it would 'be in very doubtful taste to continue selling such a "skit" on a famous man who had got into trouble'. See Hichens's Introduction to the 1949 reissue of the novel (p. xiii).

[6] Hichens, *Yesterday*, 40, 104–6; and pp. 44–54, for his account of Anderson's School of Journalism. The Hichens family was well connected. A cousin married Mary Prinsep (who, when widowed, married the second Lord Tennyson, the poet's son); another cousin became chairman of the Stock Exchange.

[7] *The Garden of Allah* was the third best-selling book in the United States in 1905; Alice Payne Hackett, *Fifty Years of Best Sellers 1895–1945* (1945), 21.   [8] *T.P.'s Weekly*, 9 Oct. 1903, 584.

[9] Gissing, *Henry Ryecroft*, 214–15.

state of affairs was too close to the mark, as Gissing grimly recounted in *New Grub Street* (1891), where the painstaking novelist Reardon is overtaken by the facile journalist Milvain. In 1893, in *The Author*, the magazine of the Society of Authors, its founder, Walter Besant, proposed that the Society itself should undertake the examination of journalists. This was consistent with Besant's animus against ignorant drama critics and reviewers of novels who were devoid of literary taste; but his suggestion was predictably derided by *Punch*, which asked, 'who'll examine you?'[10]

Anderson's academy was not the only racket in town. Also masquerading as a seminary for authors was the School of Fiction located in St John's Wood and run by Florence Marryat. She was the youngest of several novel-writing daughters of the famed Captain Marryat, author of *Mr Midshipman Easy* (1836) and *The Children of the New Forest* (1847). Florence's stories did not have the same staying power, but she was a prolific and, in staid circles, notorious 'purveyor of dangerously inflammatory fiction, unsuitable for reading by young ladies, but much to their taste'.[11] She was also a playwright and toured with her own theatrical company; but her School of Fiction contained little by way of instruction:

She is said to have addressed her first pupil—a very shy and timorous youth—as follows:

'Are you in love? No? Have you ever been in love? No? Then go away and fall in love at once, and when you have done so, come back and tell me all about it. No one can possibly write fiction until he has fallen in love'.

And the blushing youth is said to have run away from the school, sacrificing his fees, and never to have dared to return to it.[12]

Perhaps, Gissing was referring to Mrs Marryat's School of Fiction when he reported in *Henry Ryecroft* 'an astonishing fact': 'I heard not long ago, of an eminent lawyer, who had paid a couple of hundred per annum for his son's instruction in the art of fiction—yea, the art of fiction—by a not very brilliant professor of that art'.[13]

The models for these academies for teaching people how to write were the music and art schools. Samuel Butler attributed his own failure as a painter to attendance at art school; he was therefore thankful that he never submitted to the same in respect of his literary and musical ambitions.[14] None of these schools of journalism or of fiction was a means of popular access to the profession of letters, but the literary aspirant from the lower-middle classes and below was not otherwise ignored. In 1890 George Bainton edited a symposium called *The Art of Authorship*. It contained 356 pages for 5s. and, according to the *Review of Reviews*, 'Mr. Bainton seems to have applied to every English writer of standing . . . Among those who have sent interesting literary reminiscences and advice to beginners

---

[10] *Punch*, 1 Apr. 1893, 150.

[11] Michael Sadleir quoted in Sutherland, *Companion*, which summarizes the career of Florence Marryat (1838–99) and her father (1792–1848) on pp. 411–14.   [12] Gribble, *Seen in Passing*, 122.

[13] Gissing, *Ryecroft*, 211.   [14] Jones (ed.), *Notebooks of Samuel Butler*, 103–5.

are William Black, Robert Browning, J. A. Froude, Andrew Lang, and George Meredith'.[15] How far such advice was honestly obtained is debatable. Bainton was reproved by the Authors' Society for not having made it clear that he intended to publish his correspondents' replies. Peter Keating notes that both a romanticization and demystification of the craft of authorship characterized the plethora of literary handbooks being published.[16] It was a recurrent feature of the late Victorian press to include some advice to the budding writer. The *Pall Mall Gazette* in the late 1880s ran a series, 'How Plays are Written', to which various dramatists contributed; and in July 1892 the *Monthly Packet*, edited by Charlotte M. Yonge and Christabel Coleridge, featured 'How the Stories Come: Fifteen Statements of Fact by Writers of Fiction', being a summary of replies to questionnaires sent out to (as the conventional puff had it) 'well-known authors'.[17] The girls' magazine *Atalanta*, having absorbed the *Victorian Magazine* in 1892, celebrated by serializing Robert Louis Stevenson's *Catriona* (1893)—then known as *David Balfour*—and by inaugurating a series of articles on novel-writing. This kicked off with 'Style in Fiction' by the romantic novelist W. E. Norris; but the overall plan was to establish a school of fiction run on the lines of a Reading Union, 'to help to form style, and to correct that want of method and unity in the construction of plot, which characterises the work of most beginners'. A scholarship of £20 a year, tenable for two years, was the main reward, together with other prizes, for readers who sent in the best essays on 'the mystery and art of writing novels'.[18] *T.P.'s Weekly* was, therefore, following a well-trodden path by the Edwardian period when it set up a Literary Advice Department. This, for a modest tariff, provided individual reports on manuscripts, whether short stories or novels, general literature, poetry, plays, lyrics, and illustrations.[19] T.P. O'Connor was also involved in Max Pemberton's Quill Club, which sought to encourage literary beginners; and his *Weekly* regularly advertised the Literary Correspondence College, which promised a ' "Success" Course of Literary Training' from lessons by Barry Pain, 'whose name and work are world-famous'.[20]

That a vast amount of aspiration was waiting to be satisfied there can be no doubt. The first mass literate society was excited by newly acquired powers, and reading inspired creative imagination and emulation. In 1883, responding to a working man who harboured hopes of becoming a professional poet and

---

[15] *Review of Reviews* (May 1890), 448.   [16] Keating, *Haunted Study*, 71–3.

[17] *Review of Reviews* (July 1892), 37.

[18] *Review of Reviews* (Oct. 1892), 388. On *Atalanta*, its editor, L. T. Meade (1854–1915), and W. E. Norris (1847–1925), see Sutherland, *Companion*, 32, 427, 468, and Kemp *et al.* (eds.), *Edwardian Fiction*, 261, 276–7, 297–8.

[19] See also Wilfred Whitten's articles 'How to Write an Essay', 'The Better Word', 'What is Style?', etc. in O'London, *Unposted Letters*, 40–7, 52–8, 140–4.

[20] See the advertisements reproduced opposite. *Punch* regularly mocked such literary advisers: see the parody of an article by the novelist Ellen Thornycroft Fowler, 'To Would-Be Women Writers', 12 June 1905, 23, and 'Hints on Literature as a Career', 9 Aug. 1905, 104–5.

TO AUTHORS

AND

JOURNALISTS.

The writer, whether he aspires to write novels, short stories, or articles, often spends years in uncongenial work; rebuffs and drudgery being the only return for time and labour spent.

The "Success" Course of Literary Training, promoted by the Literary Correspondence College, teaches the aspirant to serve his apprenticeship to Literature in the briefest time possible. The lessons are written by a well-known novelist whose name and work are world-famous.

For full particulars write at once for pamphlet A.L. to

The Literary Correspondence College,

9, ARUNDEL ST., STRAND, W.C.

First Lessons in Story Writing.

By BARRY PAIN.

2s. 6d. net.

Sent post free by the Publishers, The Literary Correspondence College, for 2s. 8d.

Of this work the *Westminster Gazette* writes: "The beginner who takes these lessons to heart may be quite assured of an advantage over his competitors."

Learning the Profession of Literature.

A careful study of the principles that underlie literary success, and a judicious training not only in literary form, but in that business knowledge the literary man or woman must acquire, will help you to success as an author.

Our Success Course

is written by a novelist whose name is a household word. It will save you years of fruitless striving, because it will teach you the principles essential to success. It consists of twelve practical lessons (with exercises corrected by experts), and forms a complete apprenticeship to literature. We criticise students' MSS. free, and have excellent channels for placing every description of literary work from paragraph to novel.

For full particulars write for Pamphlet H I to—

THE LITERARY CORRESPONDENCE COLLEGE,

9, Arundel Street, Strand, W.C.

THE QUILL CLUB.

President: MAX PEMBERTON.

Vice-Presidents: T. P. O'Connor, M.P., W. W. Jacobs, H. B. Marriott Watson, A. St. John Adcock, A. E. W. Mason, M.P., Hilaire Belloc, M.P., G. K. Chesterton.

LITERARY ASPIRANTS and those interested in the study of Literature are invited to join the Quill Club. Conducted by honorary officers. Affords London and provincial literary beginners assistance, publishing advice, criticism of manuscripts, protection against fraud, etc. Monthly Social Gatherings at Bedford Hotel, Southampton Row, W.C., and at Liverpool. Subscription, Ten Shillings per annum; no entrance fee.—For full particulars write the Chairman,

JUAN W. P. CHAMBERLIN,
177, Great College Street, London, N.W.

FIG. 10.1. Businessmen of letters: selling savvy to aspirant authors.
Source: T.P.'s weekly, 8 February 1907, 183, 20 December 1907, 817, and 14 February 1908, 208

enclosed a specimen, Tennyson wrote:

As to your poem it is so much the habit of the age to try and express thought and feeling in verse, each one for himself, that there are not I suspect many listeners (for such work as yours), and therefore poetry is not generally profitable in a money point of view. By all means write, if you find solace in verse, but do not be in a hurry to publish.[21]

An astonishing number of poets actually found their way into print, mostly in newspapers and magazines rather than in book form; but, confining the count only to the book, Catherine Reilly has identified 2,964 persons in the United Kingdom who published poetry in the 1880s and 1890s. They came from all walks, the great majority pursuing livings apart from writing. Their occupations included

accountant; actor; archaeologist; architect; artist; auctioneer; banker; barrister; blacksmith; botanist; carpenter; civil servant; clergyman (of all denominations, and ranking from curate to archbishop); clerk; company director; composer; cowherd; diplomat; draper; engraver; estate agent; farmer; flax dresser; glazier; governess; house painter; ironmonger; journalist; lace maker; landowner; librarian; local government officer; maidservant; manufacturer (of cotton, jewellery, metal, silk, wool, etc.); merchant seaman; mineralogist; musician; newspaper proprietor; pattern maker; physician; policeman; postman; railway worker; school inspector; shepherd; shipowner; soldier (of all ranks from private to general); solicitor; spinner; stockbroker; stonedyker; storekeeper; surgeon; teacher (parish school to university level); warp dresser; watchmaker; weaver.

The circumstances that caused expression of their poetic strivings were also various. Although love clearly led, and outstripped memorial or funereal occasions, meditation on the mysteries of religion and nature was widespread. Inspiration too was found in history and mythology, in contemporary politics and social situation, in local neighbourhood and holiday travel, and in national events such as royal jubilees, and imperial triumphs and disasters. Evident was real pride in the possibility of achievement, that the ordinary individual might, if not take wing and join the immortals, then at least leave an impression on the hearts and minds of some few others. In this regard, Reilly singles out a factory operative from Ossett in Yorkshire, George Henry Wilson, who prefaced his *Miscellaneous Poems* (1896):

I am perfectly aware that the country is almost flooded with books of poems, and that the general reader has not much taste for this class of literature. Yet I hope, notwithstanding the adverse criticism which I know this small volume will receive, that nevertheless it may do some little good to those who peruse its contents.[22]

It was a motivation well understood by the acting editor of *T.P.'s Weekly*, Wilfred Whitten, to whom the question was frequently put: What is the use of poetry?, to

---

[21] Tennyson, *Tennyson*, 650. From the context, it would appear that the working man's poem was inspired by a bereavement. Tennyson more often complained about the quantity of bad verse he received than responded sympathetically: see above, pp. 392–3.

[22] Catherine Reilly, *Late Victorian Poetry 1880–1899: An Annotated Bibliography* (1994), pp. ix–xiii.

which he always answered: 'the use of poetry is to raise us above merely useful things'.[23]

This was the bright side. Then there was the dark, on which George Gissing was a specialist:

With a lifetime of dread experience behind me, I say that he who encourages any young man or woman to look for his living to 'literature', commits no less than a crime . . . . Hateful as is the struggle for life in every form, this rough-and-tumble of the literary arena seems to me sordid and degrading beyond all others. Oh, your prices per thousand words! Oh, your paragraphings and your interviewings! And oh, the black despair that awaits those down-trodden in the fray.

Last midsummer I received a circular from a typewriting person, soliciting my custom; some one who had somehow got hold of my name, and fancied me to be still in purgatory. This person wrote: 'If you should be in need of any extra assistance in the pressure of your Christmas work, I hope', etc.

How otherwise could one write if addressing a shopkeeper? 'The pressure of your Christmas work'! Nay, I am too sick to laugh.[24]

The original businessman of letters Anthony Trollope had dispatched downright advice in 1874: 'Though the profession of Literature is very pleasant to those who are successful, it is very precarious and as full of peril as of allurements. Out of ten who make the attempt nine fail to earn their bread at it'.[25] Trollope did not relinquish his Civil Service salary until nineteen years after he published his first novel; later, in his prosperity and fame, he served as treasurer of the Literary Fund, vetting proposals to relieve indigent authors.

The founder of the Society of Authors, Walter Besant, also knew how few made a good living by their pens. On occasions he allowed facetiousness to get the better of him: thus, in the *New Review* in February 1892, expatiating 'On Literary Collaboration'—he had written novels with James Rice—he advised the budding author (male) to seek out an 'intelligent, quick and sympathetic' collaborator (female). Proposing marriage was optional; the important thing was that she should be 'a girl of quick imagination, who does not, or cannot write—there are still, happily, many such girls'. This collaboration, then, would not involve joint penmanship, so much as the development of a rough story outline which the female partner might chatter into life.[26] However, writing in *Forum* in August 1892 on 'Literature as a Career', Besant spelled out the precariousness of the business. London alone contained 15,000 persons trying to make a living from literature. At the top, about fifty novelists each made around £1,000 a year; perhaps a hundred novelists, plus half-a-dozen dramatists and a handful of writers

---

[23] O'London, *Unposted Letters*, 18–21.

[24] Gissing, *Ryecroft*, 54–5. In 1902 Gissing unexpectedly benefited from a legacy, worth £300 p.a., which at last gave him a basis of independence. With predictable misfortune, Gissing did not live long to enjoy it, dying in 1903 at the age of 46.

[25] To W. Donald, 27 Feb. [1874], in Booth (ed.), *Trollope's Letters*, 315–6.

[26] *Review of Reviews* (Feb. 1892), 181.

of successful educational books, lived by literary work. That was to exclude journalism from the reckoning. Besant conceded that the proliferation of papers and periodicals acted as an incentive; yet, the established sort operated like a closed shop and it was difficult for the outsider, without personal connection, to break into these. *Punch* was particularly off-putting. Regularly its issues bore this 'NOTICE. Rejected Communications or Contributions, whether MS, Printed Matter, Drawings, or Pictures of any description, will in no case be returned, not even when accompanied by a Stamped and Addressed Envelope, Cover, or Wrapper. To this rule there will be no exception.'[27] Awash with unsolicited pieces, *Punch*, even when it did accept any, paid low rates.[28] As for the new magazines, most did not last and, during their fugitive existence, maintained only the editors. For their contributors, the pay was little better than a crutch. The plain truth was that the great majority of writers were poor.[29]

Soon after Besant made this evaluation, the book world was revolutionized by the demise of the three-decker novel; nevertheless, the hard facts remained. When Besant recapitulated his own career, he again emphasized the risk of relying on literature as a sole means of livelihood: 'The great thing in literary work is always the same—to be independent . . . and not to be compelled to do pot-boiling. I could afford to be anxious about the work and not to be anxious about the money.' He also stressed that he 'began by producing a book on a subject [French literature] on which I desired to be a specialist. The work had a *succès d'estime*, and in a sense made my literary fortune,' because it opened doors for him on magazines and newspapers, which employed him as a reviewer; and he followed it by another such book before he turned to novel-writing.[30]

The best-seller Hall Caine further highlighted the problem in his memoirs in 1908: 'Open to everybody, having no tests, no diplomas, issuing no credentials and being practically without organisation, the literary profession is perhaps the easiest of all for the rank and file to enter, and the most difficult for them to rise in.'[31] Still, no amount of warnings about the odds stacked against them deterred newcomers, because Caine himself, the son of a Merseyside shipwright, stood as an example of the riches which the fortunate could win. Moreover, it was not just the money or the prospect that their names might last beyond their lives that drew literary aspirants. In 1904, when aged 18, Thomas Burke quit his junior clerk's job in the City. He was determined to live by his pen. He had long been practising writing and at 16 had his first short story published, in *Spare Moments*, which offered a weekly guinea prize for such efforts. *Spare Moments* was one of the new miscellany papers, modelled on the success of George Newnes's *Tit-Bits*; but Burke held no illusions that his path as a writer would be smooth. Already he had enough rejection slips to prove this. He had also spoken or written to a range of people for advice: to Wilfred Whitten at *T.P.'s Weekly*, to a literary agent, and to Jack London, Morley Roberts, and Robert Sherard.

[27] See *Punch*, 7 June 1890, 276.   [28] Thwaite, *Milne*, 106, 111–12.
[29] *Review of Reviews* (Sept. 1892), 258.   [30] *T.P.'s Weekly*, 9 Jan. 1903, 270.
[31] Hall Caine, *My Story* (1908), 379.

Unanimously, they warned against literary work if he had no other source of income. They used such language as 'precarious', 'edge of a precipice', 'bitter struggle', and 'nerve-racking'. Yet Burke went ahead. In after years he explained why: 'When they spoke of the stress and anxiety of the literary life, and its dolours, and advised me to read Gissing's *New Grub Street* (which I did), I could only surmise that they had had no opportunity of comparing the literary life with life in a commercial office in Fenchurch Street.' To be a writer was to have the opportunity to be more 'fully alive than any of the well-to-do and secure whom I had encountered'.[32]

The same feelings animated Cecil Roberts, who at 15 left school in Nottingham to start as an office boy. This was in 1908, the year his father died, leaving Roberts and his mother with precious little and needing to take in lodgers. At 19, he was earning a pound a week in the local weights and measures inspectorate, supplemented by occasional sums paid for articles and poems he had written. This extra was invested in a dinner suit with tails, in which uniform he presented a lecture on the tragic life of Francis Thompson, first in Nottingham, then in Leicester. The year 1912 saw him win the Kirke White Prize Poem, annually offered by the University of Nottingham, for his poem 'The Trent'. He was also published in the *Contemporary Review* and the *Poetry Review*; but, like Thomas Burke, he suffered piled-up rejection slips, notably from the *English Review*, whose editor, Austin Harrison, he bombarded with poems and even browbeat in his office. In 1913, through the generosity of the owner of a local brush-making business, he was able to pay for his first book to be published, *Phyllistrata and Other Poems*, copies of which were dispatched to A. C. Benson, Kipling, Alice Meynell, and more. When 350 copies had been sold, costs were covered; and in 1914 his patron both subsidized a second book of poems and stumped up money to hire the Mechanics Hall in Nottingham and the Bechstein Hall in London for a recital of the poems, with tickets on sale at between 2s. and half a guinea. By such means, part talent, part persistence, part luck, it was possible to build up a name as a writer and to dream of becoming a professional author. In 1915 Roberts handed in his notice, feeling that 'I must get out of that office with its drab life-long security, its pension at sixty.'[33] It was a momentous step, foolhardy according to his employer who was then paying him 22s. a week and expecting him to sit the qualifying examination for promotion to inspector. Roberts did not, of course, achieve financial self-sufficiency as an author straight away; but wartime brought him an opening, to replace Dixon Scott as literary and drama critic of the *Liverpool Daily Post* at £3 a week. He was appointed after being asked to write 1,200 words on Henry James, who was reportedly dying; a severe test, because Roberts had read no James. He bagged ten volumes from the library and gave himself twenty-four hours. It was a rush, it was a fraud, but it was writing and it was living.

This lure to live by the pen, especially by imaginative work, was not confined to poor boys such as Thomas Burke and Cecil Roberts. J. H. Balfour Browne

---

[32] Burke, *Son of London*, 180–2.   [33] Roberts, *Years of Promise*, 60.

echoed their sentiment. He came from a comfortable professional background and in due course married a judge's daughter and rose to be a KC. But, while reading for the bar, he and his fellow students all 'wished to be literary'. In part, this was a reaction against the 'withered sticks of lawyers' who delivered dull lectures to them. They also reckoned that success in such 'plodding professions', even if success was attained, must come slowly, unlike in 'literature, where, in the imagination at least of the aspirant, the returns are as quick as in a ready-money business'. While Browne stuck to the law, he led a double life, publishing poems, novels, and literary essays. For a long time he did so anonymously, lest solicitors assume that a literary barrister was not a serious barrister; but, though his literary work did not much touch the public's taste, it gave him greater satisfaction than all the legal books he wrote.[34]

Such a compromise was rejected by Thomas Burke and, later, when he in turn was approached by literary aspirants, he gave opposite advice to that which he had received: 'I told them to throw up everything, to plunge in and take their chance. I told them not to embrace a dull certainty and lose a shining risk, not to become a piece of office furniture in what is called a job for life but is most often a job for death.'[35] The same point was made differently by D. H. Lawrence's father, to whom a life devoted to writing seemed sissy and its rewards, however meagre, akin to money for old rope. When *The White Peacock* (1911) was published,

my father struggled through half a page, and it might as well have been Hottentot.
'And what dun they gi'e thee for that, lad?'
'Fifty pounds, father.'
'Fifty pounds!' He was dumbfounded, and looked at me with shrewd eyes, as if I were a swindler. 'Fifty pounds! An' tha's niver done a day's hard work in thy life.'[36]

Just like Lawrence, Burke did not regret his decision, though he did struggle to support himself, by casual journalism and by writing articles, short stories, sketches, verses, even ghosted features on behalf of the famous. Only one in four of the pieces he submitted found acceptance in the early years; nonetheless, he was struck by the kindliness of editors to an unknown, and the pains they took to point out how his work might be improved. He particularly celebrated Wilfred Whitten of *T.P.'s Weekly*, who, once Burke had ignored his initial advice not to attempt to become a writer, now encouraged him. He found equal helpfulness in J. P. Collins, literary editor of the *Pall Mall Gazette* and assistant editor of the *Pall Mall Magazine*; A. W. Evans, assistant editor of *The Nation*; Alfred Orage, editor of the *New Age*; Percy Everett, editor of *Pearson's Magazine*; James Milne, literary editor of the *Daily Chronicle*; J. M. Bullock of *The Graphic*; and D. M. Sutherland of the *Evening Standard*.[37] Cecil Roberts paid a similar tribute to Holbrook Jackson,

---

[34] Balfour Browne, *Recollections*, 8–26.   [35] Burke, *Son of London*, 182.
[36] Worthen, *Lawrence: The Early Years*, 144.
[37] Most of these individuals were associated with more than one paper. Thus D. M. Sutherland was successively London editor of the *Manchester Daily Despatch*, editor of the *Sheffield Daily Telegraph*, editor of the *Evening Standard* (1914–15), and editor of the *Pall Mall Gazette* (1915–23), before becoming director of

who as editor of *To-day* published his anti-war poem 'Futility' in February 1918 and gave practical advice, introductions, and hospitality.[38] Thus, the literary life was not so unstructured and unsupportive, so bleak and miserable, as its detractors both inside and outside alleged.

II

One literary tipster was Arnold Bennett, who published *How to Become an Author* (Pearson, 1903, price 5s.), at a time when he had scarcely cast off his own novelist's nappies. He was unabashed about disclosing tricks of the journalist's trade, and cheerfully cynical in telling the aspirant freelance to pursue popularity before trying to educate the public, because the cardinal objective was to get into print. To appeal to a large audience, begin with the paragraph, he advised—popular papers would pay from 2s. 6d. to 3s. 6d. for a brisk paragraph—and it was necessary to get known to an editor before launching into an article. The second maxim was to think of all human life, however mundane, as potentially exciting copy. Thus, when the scribbler caught an omnibus, ideas for articles should swim in his brain: 'How an Omnibus is Built' for *Pearson's Magazine*; 'The Ailments of Omnibus Horses: A Chat with a Vet. of the London General' for the *Westminster Gazette*; 'An Omnibus Horse's Views about Policemen' for a comic paper; 'Ways of the Omnibus Thief' for *Tit-Bits*; 'London Stables: An Inquiry' for the *Daily News*; 'Stopping and Starting', a sketch for *Queen* or for the Saturday women's page of the *Daily Chronicle*. Family misfortune should not be private either: when an uncle perishes in a railway accident, an illustrated article must be dispatched to the *Strand Magazine*. Perhaps Bennett had J. M. Barrie in mind. By publishing *Margaret Ogilvy* (1896), which milked his mother's memory (and the death of his older brother David, when aged 13, in a skating mishap), Barrie was fulfilling a prediction in *When a Man's Single* (1888), where his fictional journalist Noble Simms declares, 'My God! I would write an article, I think, upon my mother's grave!' H. G. Wells also saluted Barrie for having signposted the 'true path to journalism' through this creation: 'For years I'd been straining after lofty and original topics. The more articles I had rejected, the higher I aimed. All the time I was shooting miles over the target. Noble Simms, bless him, taught one that all I had to do was to lower my aim—and hit.'[39] But Bennett suspected that hits might not be scored regularly enough. So, when the penman was starving, having foolishly abandoned a secure, if modest, clerk's position in the hope of striding along Fleet Street, he should compose a bright piece about 'How to Live on a Shilling a Day'.[40]

political propaganda for the Anti-Socialist and Anti-Communist Union in the inter-war period. On him, see *Who Was Who, 1951–1960*, 1060. On Whitten's views, see 'Is Literature a Career?', in O'London, *Unposted Letters*, 104–7.

[38] Roberts, *Years of Promise*, 208–10.   [39] Asquith, *Barrie*, 182, 221.

[40] This also occurred to Roy Flecker, in one of his allegorical, semi-autobiographical stories, 'N' Jawk'. It features the poet Slimber, 'author of an exquisite volume of verse in the Doreskin Library of modern

The moral of all this amoral advice was that authorship was a vampiric business. This characteristic was preyed upon by the New Journalism, which revelled in writers who wrote about writing or, better still, about writers. Authors and authorship constituted prime human-interest material. 'All the leading papers nowadays are to some extent magazines,' J. M. Barrie wrote in 1893, noting that each contained 'short leaders or essays on social, literary, or artistic subjects'. And, with deliberate absence of chivalry, he considered women better suited than men to the New Journalism's trivial pursuits. Women were more sharp-eyed than men in picking out personal details at 'private views' and 'first nights', noticing who was there and what they wore.[41] Especially, women made the better interviewers. In 1895 *Punch* versified 'To a Lady-Journalist', complete with cartoon showing her cross-dressed in long skirt and male top hat and tailcoat, with lorgnette and severe expression, standing at a door with the knocker firmly grasped. The caption read: 'Coming for an Interview'.[42] In 1897 the Society for Women Journalists was treated to a lecture on the Art of Interviewing;[43] and, on cue, *The New Barmaid*, a two-act vaudeville performed at Charles Hawtrey's Avenue Theatre in 1897, included a 'Lady Journalist', Dora, who sings:

> With my pencil and my pocket book
> I'm ready for the fray,
> And I make a note of everything
> That comes along my way.
> What's that? Down it goes,
> It never must be missed,
> It's naughty, but it's copy for
> The Lady Journalist.[44]

In 1891 the *Girl's Own Paper* had carried an article on 'Young Women as Journalists'; and, though its author, Holden Pike, warned about the overcrowded and precarious state of journalism and about the dangers for young women working late at night, he stated: 'A great deal of the most effective work on our newspapers has been done by women; and, could it be told, the public to-day would be surprised to learn how much of the total is still done by them.'[45] It was the miseries that Florence Dugdale most remembered, thus providing her with a suitable dowry to marry Thomas Hardy in 1914. In her spinster days she had been a schoolteacher, secretary, and journalist; the last she considered 'the most degrading work anybody could take up—typewriting is a lady's occupation by contrast'.[46] Hilaire Belloc's sister Marie

---

Masterpieces', whose 'articles to "Tit Bits" and "Pearson's Weekly", though the real source of his modest revenue, were even less well known than his poems. Yet his unsigned essay on "How to make money by writing" was not only deservedly popular among that wide public to which "Tit Bits" appeals, but had also saved him from death by starvation' (Flecker, *Collected Prose*, 35).

[41] Barrie, *Two of Them*, 187–91.   [42] *Punch*, 15 June 1895, 281.   [43] Ibid., 6 Feb. 1897, 65.
[44] Frederic Bowyer and W. E. Sprange (music by John Crook), *The New Barmaid* (n.d. [1897]), 15.
[45] *Review of Reviews* (Apr. 1891), 364.
[46] Told to Rebekah Owen, *c*.1916, in Millgate (ed.), *Emma and Florence Hardy*, p. xiii n. 6.

also recalled discouragements. In her twenties, before her marriage in 1896 (to a *Times* journalist), she was used by the *Pall Mall Gazette*, the *Strand Magazine*, and more, to interview the leading French authors Dumas *fils*, Anatole France, Sardou, Jules Verne, and Zola:

In London it was still regarded as unfitting in some quarters, and amusing and absurd in others that a young woman should be doing the kind of journalism on which I was then engaged. I was never confronted with that attitude in Paris; there the men and the women I went to see, seemed to think it quite natural I should be gathering material for English papers. No one appeared to feel my sex had anything to do with the way of life I chose to lead. But the French have always respected the profession of letters.[47]

Perhaps; yet, Belloc's Francophilia generally caused her to see that side of the Channel bathed in sunshine, and she was not so bowed down that journalism served to launch her career as a woman of letters. When la Belloc started out on the *Pall Mall Gazette*, the editor was W. T. Stead, a supporter of female suffrage; and the position of 'Chief Interviewer' on the paper was occupied by a woman, Hulda Friederichs.[48] Stead employed more women—Marie Belloc among them—when he began the *Review of Reviews* in 1890; remarkably, he paid women the same as men.[49] Though now sure to be denounced as a sexist presumption, it was then reckoned that women wrote the best gossip columns—as Eliza Aria did for *Truth* ('Mrs. A's Diary') and *Black and White* ('Diary of a Daughter of Eve')[50]—because women were their most avid readers. The unhappily married Ada Leverson told George Moore, with whom she was 'madly in love' in the early 1890s: 'I am not afraid of death but I am of scandal. The idea of being "talked about" is one of which I have a weak terror—then, think of those evening papers!'[51] Yet in 1893–4, Leverson, while writing sketches and parodies for *Punch*, was also employed as an interviewer for *Black and White*, her subjects including W. S. Penley (of *Charley's Aunt* fame), the actor–manager George Alexander, Lillie Langtry, and Weedon Grossmith (*Diary of a Nobody*), and ranging in diversity from the exiled Russian nihilist Sergius Stepniak to a Cornish coastguard.[52] Hubert Henry Davies, perhaps having been on the receiving end, began his satirical drawing room drama *Lady Epping's Lawsuit* (1908) with a newly successful playwright, Paul Hughes, being interviewed for *The Gentleman's Friend* by Miss Ferris, whom the stage directions depict as 'a hustling blonde about thirty-five. She is rather overdressed in a cheap way . . . . Her manner is extremely genial and effusive.'[53] The interview is farcically dishonest: Miss Ferris makes things up

[47] Lowndes, *Love and Friendship*, 192.
[48] Lucy Brown, *Victorian News and Newspapers* (Oxford, 1985), 162. On Friederichs (d. 1927), *Who Was Who, 1916–1928*, 382–3. She left the *Pall Mall Gazette* in 1893, when the paper changed ownership and politics, and joined the *Westminster Gazette*, editing the *Westminster Budget* from 1896.
[49] Joseph O. Baylen, 'The Review of Reviews', in Sullivan (ed.), *Literary Magazines 1837–1914*, 354.
[50] See her memoirs: Mrs. Aria, *My Sentimental Self* (1922).
[51] Julia Speedie, *Wonderful Sphinx: The Biography of Ada Leverson* (1993), 30.   [52] Ibid. 61.
[53] 'Lady Epping's Lawsuit' (1908), in Davies, *Plays*, i. 149.

and twists words to suit herself and her readership, and is as much the star of the interview as Hughes himself. This might seem a coarse caricature; but it was also J. M. Barrie's impression that women made

the best interviewers, because they can go where men are not admitted and ask questions at which even the male interviewer would blush. The celebrity into whose study the lady interviewer pushes her way is in an awkward position. It is quite within his right to tell his servants to remove the male interviewer with their feet; but the lady is here, and the question is how to get her out. How did she get in? Probably by pretending to be somebody else, if indeed she has not tripped in behind some visitor. She may have been despatched to the work after the other sex has failed to gain an entrance, and she is determined to succeed. She may wait calmly for hours until she sees the door ajar. If her victim is a lawyer she will take the name of one of his clients; if a doctor she will call herself a patient; if a politician she pretends to be the wife of his agent. In short, there is no lie to which she will not resort, and her conscience is so dead that she boasts of her methods when they have succeeded. Now she has borne down on her victim, and he tells her politely that he must decline to be interviewed. She then takes a chair and insists on interviewing him. His wisest course is not to answer any question; but it is a course not easy to pursue, for she is an adept at exasperating. Even if he is dumb to her she examines the room. She 'takes in' the furniture, and her 'host's' dress, and pounces on the papers that litter his writing-table. On her way out she may have the good fortune to see her victim's little boy, and him she at once cross-examines. The servants are also pressed. It is the lady interviewers who ask their victim whether it be true that he is applying for a divorce, and what his proof is, and which is the stool his wife flung at him. This would read like exaggeration were it not notorious that the New Journalism is ever on the scent of scandals, and that the ladies are its best servants.[54]

Given these requirements, not all 'ladies' measured up. Janet Hogarth was a vicar's daughter who read philosophy at Lady Margaret Hall, Oxford, then taught at Cheltenham Ladies College. Aged 26 in 1891, she had done some reviewing for *Murray's Magazine* before she applied for another position:

The Editor asked me to call, but as soon as he saw me, and almost before he had looked at my somewhat academic testimonials, he said unhopefully, 'Well, you know, this isn't your job. What I want is an interviewer, and interviewing needs bounce. When I read your letter, I said to myself, "A lady and a scholar. No, no, no" ', and with that he politely showed me down the office stairs.[55]

That 'lady' interviewers might still descend on an unwary author, bearing unimpeachable credentials, Thomas Hardy learned to his cost. This was the case with Constance Smedley, who founded the Lyceum Club for literary and intellectual women. In 1907 she motored down to Max Gate, the home that Hardy designed for himself near Dorchester in 1885. Hardy was asked to receive her by Kenneth Grahame's wife, Elspeth, the sister of Winifred Thomson, who had painted his portrait. Though Smedley did not arrive on the day expected,

---

[54] Barrie, *Two of Them*, 187–91.   [55] Courtney, *Recollected in Tranquillity*, 169.

Hardy enjoyed her visit. 'She is most bright & interesting, & we had a long talk,' he told Mrs Grahame. Later he was dismayed to discover Smedley using their conversation for an article in *T.P.'s Weekly*.[56] Suitably, the last letter that 81-year-old George Meredith penned, five days before his death in 1909, was an animadversion on this score to Ella Hepworth Dixon. She was a New Woman novelist who had fictionalized some of her own struggles in *The Story of a Modern Woman* (1894); she also edited the *Englishwoman's Review*. Meredith wrote that he would be happy to see her, but with this proviso:

For you are that fearful thing, a Journalist, and one commanding an audience, and therefore eager for matter, however small. It is, that you hold your hand from an 'interview'. Let me be spared that infliction. I have received visitors, and have seen myself exhibited to the public some days later, hatefully to my feelings. That is why I dare to petition a running pen to spare me for my privacy—and there may be no need.[57]

Not that the male of the species was to be trusted more. 'Everyone has heard of Lewis Carroll's hatred of interviewers,' wrote his nephew and biographer Stuart Dodgson Collingwood. Carroll, who was also a clergyman don, rejected all interviews. Only once were his defences breached when, having corresponded on some question of faith, he invited the troubled individual to his rooms at Christ Church. The troubled individual turned out to be a reporter with notebook, primed to ask the 'usual questions', until briskly shown the door.[58] The best of bona fides could prove worthless. That was Thomas Hardy's experience of Clive Holland, a fellow novelist. They corresponded for a decade from 1897, Holland seeking Hardy's cooperation in various ventures; and he published several articles and books about Hardy and Wessex. It was through Holland that Hardy agreed to a visit by 200 members of the Institute of Journalists in 1905. Hardy was chagrined to read a production from Holland's pen shortly afterwards: 'Nearly the whole article is fictitious,' he railed, 'except the two or three passages that are plagiarised from other writers. The editor appears to have been hoaxed. I will keep it as a curiosity.'[59] He was more philosophical a few weeks later: 'There was no harm in it, I suppose,' he told a friend, 'except that it seemed as if I had assented to its publication, which I had not done.'[60] Hence, the decision Hardy reached, of which he informed Bram Stoker in 1907 when Stoker sought to interview him for the *New York World*: 'for a long time I have been compelled to refuse interviewing by any paper'.[61]

---

[56] Hardy to Elspeth Grahame, 31 Aug. 1907, in Purdy and Millgate (eds.), *Hardy Letters*, iii. 270. Smedley's article appeared in *T.P.'s Weekly*, 7 Jan. 1910.

[57] Meredith to Ella Hepworth Dixon, 13 May 1909, in Cline (ed.), *Meredith's Letters*, iii. 1697.

[58] Collingwood, *Carroll*, 333–4.

[59] Hardy to Clive Holland, 7 Dec. 1905, in Purdy and Millgate (eds.), *Hardy Letters*, iii. 188. Holland was the pen-name of Charles James Hankinson (1866–1959), on whom, see Kemp *et al.* (eds.), *Edwardian Fiction*, 190.

[60] Hardy to Florence Henniker, 21 Dec. 1905, in Purdy and Millgate (eds.), *Hardy Letters*, iii. 190.

[61] Hardy to Bram Stoker, 1 July 1907, ibid. 258–9.

interviewers at arm's length and was not to be coaxed by fellow authors. As his
fame soared in the early 1890s, he was approached by Gilbert Parker, whom he
had met only once, to interview him for *McClure's Magazine*; and by Harold
Frederic, who 'wanted to do a joint-author talk with me, a thing in which author
(a) says "When did you first feel genius springing up within you?" and author (b)
(the owl) gravely tells him, and then (a) tells (b) which he considers his masterpiece, etc. etc.' Barrie declined these invitations, and others that followed, such
as from Bram Stoker in 1907.[69] So, though it might have surprised his detractors,
did H. G. Wells, when his friend Arnold Bennett offered to supply the *New Age* in
1908 with an article on Wells or an interview. Bennett went to stay with Wells
and Wells talked absorbingly; but he discountenanced an interview—'Said
interviews must "occur", with which I agreed'.[70] The more mysterious and
elusive the writer the more pressing, and grotesque, were the petitions. After
Francis Thompson became a published poet, he was pursued by an American
woman poet, visiting London, who proposed 'a quiet talk *à deux*' by a journalist
who desired to interview him as a 'Celebrity at Home'; and by the photographers
Elliott & Fry, who wished to portray him 'in his study'.[71] They were not to know
that Thompson was quartered in a dingy bedsit off the Harrow Road, where he
flopped in drug-induced stupor.

The Harold Frederic request to interview Barrie merits, in retrospect, high
points on the brass scale. Frederic was London correspondent of the *New York
Times* and a novelist, whose *Illumination* (1896; the American title was *The
Damnation of Theron Ware*) encouraged Arnold Bennett to emulate this portrayal
of Methodism's hold on small-town America by depicting the same about
his native Potteries. More piquantly, Frederic's private life involved two
Mrs Frederics. Each had a household of children, one in Hammersmith, the other
outside Croydon. Frederic more than most authors, therefore, was alert to the
danger of interviews, which might uncover his irregularities; and he went to
lengths to avoid being subject or else situated it on neutral turf. The short-story
writer and novelist Robert Barr, a friend of Frederic and aware of his double life,
evidently neglected to brief George Burgin,[72] who applied to interview Frederic at
home for *The Idler* magazine. 'Barr knows very well that, for family reasons, I can't
be interviewed for your "Lions in their Dens" series,' Frederic growled. 'The
reasons don't matter,' he added; 'but if you want this interview, I'll see one of
you at the National Liberal [Club].'[73] That paradigmatic New Woman George

---

[69] Meynell (ed.), *Barrie Letters*, 5–6, 55.   [70] Flower (ed.), *Bennett Journals*, i. 279 (5 Mar. 1908).
[71] Meynell, *Thompson and Meynell*, 85. The American was probably Agnes Tobin, the journalist R. S.
Warren Bell, whose series 'The Houses of Celebrated People' ran in *The Windsor Magazine* in 1895.
[72] For G. B. Burgin (1856–1944), see Sutherland, *Companion*, 93–4, where he is described as the author of
'torrents of fiction'; and Sladen, *Twenty Years*, 164–5, where it was noted that his *Shutters of Silence* (1903) had
been through thirty editions. Burgin became literary editor of the *Daily Express*, was secretary of the Authors'
Club (1905–8), and vice-president of the Dickens Fellowship: Kemp *et al.* (eds.), *Edwardian Fiction*, 49.
[73] Stanley Weintraub, *The London Yankees: Portraits of American Writers and Artists in England 1894–1914*
(New York, 1979), 114.

Egerton, author of *Keynotes* (1893) and *Discords* (1894), refused all her publisher John Lane's attempts to publicize her, again probably from a concern to shield her unconventional private life, though she made a principle out of prohibition: 'Interviews I bar—also portraits in ladies' papers. I would burn every exclusively woman's paper in England . . . I suppose in my way I am an irritable little person, but I can't stand cant of any kind, and not too much flattery.'[74] Authors were naturally most comfortable when the publicity was organized on their own terms. Bernard Shaw devised the most perfect by interviewing himself.[75] Others were less free; accordingly, inducements were offered. The most tasteless example concerned Oscar Wilde, who, about to be discharged from Reading Gaol, was told by the governor that two journalists, Americans, were waiting to interview him about prison life, for which they were prepared to pay handsomely, even £1,000.[76] Wilde refused with contempt (in spite of his impecunious condition), maintaining that journalists were never gentlemen (in spite of his having been a journalist).

III

Softer options were preferred by many authors, the cosiest being to supply a selective reminiscence which featured them winning fame against the odds. *The Idler*'s instant popularity—Jerome K. Jerome and Robert Barr were founding co-editors in 1892—was in part due to the series 'My First Book', in which well-known writers described their initial experiences.[77] Published by Chatto & Windus, *The Idler* was actually edited in a flat at Arundel Street, off the Strand, where every Wednesday afternoon contributors talked literary 'shop' over tea. The sub-editor, George Burgin, was also organizing secretary of the Vagabonds Club, a monthly dining society for literary sorts; and most 1890s' star or emerging names would appear at one or another—W. L. Alden, Hall Caine, John Davidson, Conan Doyle, George Manville Fenn, Francis Gribble, Bret Harte, G. A. Henty, Anthony Hope, E. W. Hornung, W. W. Jacobs, Coulson Kernahan, Rudyard Kipling, William Le Queux, Phil May, Frankfort Moore, Arthur Morrison, Barry Pain, Gilbert Parker, Eden Phillpotts, Pett Ridge, William Watson, H. G. Wells, Stanley Weyman, and Israel Zangwill. 'The great advantage of those Idler teas', Douglas Sladen recollected, 'was that women as well as men could be present.' Most dining clubs, the annual function of the Authors' Society excepted, then excluded women. Sladen recalled meeting at *Idler* teas Marie Corelli, Mona Caird, Mrs Campbell Praed, Mrs Humphry Ward, Eliza Lynn Linton, Alice Meynell, Lucas Malet, Ellen Thorneycroft Fowler, and other women authors.[78]

---

[74] Lambert and Ratcliffe, *Bodley Head*, 98–9.   [75] Jerome, *Life and Times*, 2–3.
[76] Sherard, *Wilde*, 222.
[77] Stevenson, for example, told the story behind the making of *Treasure Island* (1883) in August 1894. On *The Idler*, see Sullivan (ed.), *Literary Magazines, 1837–1914*, 177–82, and Jerome, *Life and Times*, 126–7.
[78] Sladen, *Twenty Years*, 164.

In this way, 'a charmingly pretty young American', Alice Livingston, was introduced into London's literary set, and met her future husband, C. N. Williamson, with whom she wrote best-selling travel fiction.

From such conviviality there emerged not just literary relationships but literary gossip, and with it an expanding branch of journalism. A pioneer practitioner was the novelist Edmund Yates. He was 'The Lounger at the Clubs' columnist for the *Illustrated Times* and 'Atlas' for *The World: A Journal for Men and Women*, the sixpenny weekly which he founded in 1874.[79] In 1881 he started sending Robert Browning a copy of it each week, much to the poet's surprise, though he was gratified by the occasional puff Yates would slip in.[80] *The World* had plenty going for it, with sparkling contributions from a variety of talents, such as Henry Lucy, whose parliamentary sketches he afterwards transferred to *Punch*; and the opening issue included a typically spiky piece from Mrs Lynn Linton entitled 'Jezebel *à la Mode*'. Novels were also serialized, Yates's own, naturally, and others by Wilkie Collins, Miss M. E. Braddon, Hawley Smart, and Walter Besant; but *The World*'s success largely rested on its personality focus with features such as its 'Celebrities at Home' series, which was later imitated by the *Windsor Magazine*. Yates was rebuffed— by Trollope for one—but by 1884, when Yates penned his memoirs, nearly 400 'celebrities' had consented to display their domestic harmony, headed by the Prince of Wales at Sandringham.[81] Gossip journalism was not a risk-free occupation, however. Yates had been ejected from the Garrick in 1858 for writing about a fellow member, Thackeray, his source being a private conversation at the club. In 1885 Yates even suffered a spell in prison following a criminal libel action by the Earl of Lonsdale, the source for that story being Carlton Club gossip. Risks were much reduced when the gossip columnist both specialized in one subspecies, authors, and was flattering, even unctuous, in his remarks.[82] *Punch* in 1890 jocularly demanded a Society for the Protection of 'Celebrities' and suggested that they should start charging for interviews, autographs, and photographs. It credited *The World* with having begun this tittle-tattle trend, whereupon there followed the modern 'deluge, of biographies, autobiographies, interviewings, photographic realities, portraits plain and coloured— many of them uncommonly plain, and some of them wonderfully coloured— until a Celebrity who has *not* been done and served up, with or without a plate, is a Celebrity indeed'.[83]

What Yates and *The World* initiated was extended by Douglas Sladen, who made a substantial career out of it. Born in 1856, he was educated at Cheltenham

[79] Edmund Yates, *His Recollections and Experiences* (1884), i. 277–9, for his work on the *Illustrated Times* (est. 1855), under Henry Vizetelly as editor: 'This was the commencement of that style of "personal" journalism which is so very much to be deprecated and so enormously popular.' He had earlier attempted something similar—'a column of "literary and artistic gossip" '—for the *Weekly Chronicle*; ibid. 266.

[80] DeVane and Knickerbocker (eds.), *New Letters of Robert Browning*, 289.

[81] Yates, *Recollections*, ii. 232–3, 330–3.

[82] Ransom, *Corelli*, 75–6, tells of Yates (1831–94) being converted to Marie Corelli's charms in the last months of his life.   [83] *Punch*, 25 Oct. 1890, 201.

and Oxford. There he won a First in Modern History; he also took legal action against a fellow undergraduate for writing a barbed personal sketch.[84] Sladen afterwards spent significant periods abroad—some five years in Australia as professor and apprentice author and where he married; three years as a peregrinating resident in Europe and Egypt, establishing himself as a travel and fiction-writer, as a poet and anthologist; then three years in North America, capped by a protracted stay in Japan. When he published *The Japs at Home* in 1892, Sladen reminisced, 'I shed my label of the "Australian Poet", and became known as the author who has been to Japan. I even enriched the English language with a word—*Japs*. It had long been in use in America, but no one had ventured to put it into a book in England. Some thought it was undignified; some thought that it would incense the Japanese'; but Sladen relished the common touch, and his book sold 150,000 copies before 1914, such was the popular fascination with that little-understood country.[85] The instant authority on Japan was also a harbinger of the Americanization of the London literary scene, when he settled there from 1891. This had two aspects, the first being a replication of the style of New York and Boston literary receptions in the Sladen home, 32 Addison Mansions, 'at which so many people, now famous, used to meet every Friday night, regaled only with cigarettes, whiskeys-and-sodas, claret cup, bottled ale and sandwiches'.[86] The second was the development of

the habit of personal journalising. Certain popular newspapers devoted columns and columns every week to giving every species of good-natured gossip about the biographies and home-lives of well-known people. It was this movement which culminated in the production of *Who's Who*. Interviewing was a feature of the day. From living like hermit-crabs, English authors suddenly began to realise the value of publicity in the sale of their wares.[87]

---

[84] This was E. B. J. Iwan-Müller (1853–1910), afterwards with the *Pall Mall Gazette* and *Daily Telegraph*; see *Oxford DNB*.

[85] Sladen, *Twenty Years*, 35–6, 204–5; and *Who Was Who, 1941–1950*, 1062, for Sladen (1856–1947). Philip Gibbs recalled that when he was working for the newspaper syndicate Tillotson's, 'one series of articles we published in the evening paper of a Lancashire cotton town was entitled "Queer things about Japan", by Douglas Sladen. The mill girls, who in those days wore clogs and shawls, used to line up in queues to get the next instalment, which brought the colour, romance and glamour of the East into the dank fog and drabness of their own lives.' See Gibbs's Introduction to Sladen, *Long Life*, 16.

[86] Sladen, *Twenty Years*, 58. Cf. Jerome, *Life and Times*, 78: 'Douglas Sladen was the most successful At Home giver that I ever knew. Half *Who's Who* must have come to his receptions at Addison Mansions from ten-thirty to the dawn. He had a wonderful way when he introduced you of summarising your career, opinions, and general character in half-a-dozen sentences, giving you like information concerning the other fellow—or fellowess. You knew what crimes and follies to avoid discussing, what talents and virtues it would be kind to drag into the conversation.' Sladen himself did not drink after dinner, and was a non-smoker. Sladen's wife, Maggie Muirhead, was Australian, the daughter of a 'big Western District squatter', as Sladen put it. They married in 1880 but, though she lived until 1919, she was invalided after a difficult childbirth and they took to employing a secretary–companion Norma (Norrie) Lorimer (1864–1948), who also made a name as a novelist. She lived and travelled with them and acted as joint hostess at their functions. See Sladen, *Long Life*, ch. 8 and p. 71; and Kemp *et al.* (eds.), *Edwardian Fiction*, 247, 365.

[87] Sladen, *Twenty Years*, 146, 203.

Sladen's family was well connected among the upper-middle and public-service classes, his relations including Sir Charles Sladen, Prime Minister of Victoria, Sir Edward Sladen, British Resident in Rangoon, and General John Sladen, brother-in-law of Field Marshal Lord Roberts. To family connections, Sladen added networks of Oxford contemporaries, such as S. H. Jeyes, editor of the *Standard*, and Sidney Low, editor of the *St James's Gazette*. Throughout his life Sladen displayed a genius for friendship or, putting it functionally, was an adept at collecting people. With Jerome K. Jerome's encouragement, he quickly made his mark in London literary journalism and joined forces with George Burgin to reconstitute the Vagabonds dining club, bringing in more writers—'The idea of letting in women members was mine'—and persuading Lord Roberts to act as president.[88] Sladen in turn helped Jerome to formulate the new illustrated weekly *To-Day* in 1893. Sladen acted as literary editor, and proposed 'that we should have a book of the week, in which we told as much about the author as we knew, and that biographical gossip about authors and artists and actors should be one of our chief features'.[89] *To-Day* was not Sladen's sole vehicle for personal journalism. His 'Table-Talk Notes' appeared in the *Literary World*; and his 'Diner-Out' *causerie*— which he started under Lewis Hind's editorship for the *Pall Mall Budget*—he transferred to *Queen* when he succeeded Clement Shorter as literary editor. 'I kept the "Diner-Out" for biographical gossip about authors chiefly', he recalled, 'and for announcements of forthcoming books, which could be made interesting by personal gossip. Actual reviewing I kept as far as possible out of that column.'[90] The crowning moment came in 1896, when Sladen signed a three-year contract to edit a remodelled *Who's Who* for Messrs A. & C. Black, who had just bought the copyright.

The late nineteenth century witnessed a proliferation of biographical directories of professional bodies and assorted worthies in town and country. It made a comfortable living for publishers. The market was reasonably predictable and remunerative: reference libraries and, above all, the individuals and families listed therein, who relished seeing their credits in print. *Punch* thought it a racket, preying on people's conceit and competitiveness. Thus the compiler of *Notable Nonentities of Norwood and its Neighbourhood* persuades Mr Mark Lane to subscribe to its 'two handsome quarto volumes', by emphasizing that a guide to this superior suburb would be 'incomplete indeed, were it to include no reference

---

[88] The original Vagabonds had held 'eighteen-penny weekly dinners at the Cock Tavern, that Tudor restaurant at the gates of the Temple, where they talked over their affairs, and put up with a great deal of Socialism from a man, who was so tiresome that, as soon as I had anything to do with it, I got them through their Secretary, George Burgin ... to refound the club as the "New Vagabonds", leaving the Socialist out, and taking in all the other young authors and artists who frequented the "Idler" teas' (Sladen, *Long Life*, 140–1).

[89] Sladen, *Twenty Years*, 188. On *To-Day*, see Sullivan, *Literary Magazines, 1837–1913*, 416–17.

[90] Sladen, *Twenty Years*, 189–90. Sladen was gratified to learn that the actual Queen, Victoria, had his column 'read to her every week, and was most amused by it'.

to so distinguished a resident as yourself'. So the notebook is produced, solemnly to record what the world is eager to know:

Any remarkable traits recorded of you as an infant, Mr Lane? A strong aversion to porridge, and an antipathy to black-beetles—both of which you still retain? Thank you, *very* much. And you were educated? At Dulborough Grammar School? Just *so!* Never took to Latin, or learned Greek? Commercial aptitudes declaring themselves thus early— curious, *indeed!* Entered your father's office as clerk. Became a partner? Married your present lady—when? In 1860? Exactly!—and have offspring? Your subsequent life comparatively uneventful? That will do admirably . . . and we will send down a competent artist, in a day or two, to take the photographs.

Another subscriber is now ensnared—for two copies: one 'for your children after you have gone, Mr Lane!', and another for a married sister in Australia, to 'amuse her'.[91]

Sladen had bigger trophies in his sights than Norwood's Notable Nonentities. It was he who devised the formula by which *Who's Who* attained its lasting popularity and usefulness. To persuade individuals to supply biographies, he drafted forms on special stationery and enclosed them in long blue envelopes, following Lord Rosebery's intelligence that these were employed for Cabinet communications and liable to cause 'a strange flutter of expectation'. Specimen biographies were included as models, Sladen having induced the Duke of Rutland and A. J. Balfour to allow theirs to be used for, respectively, peers and commoners. His greatest stroke was the idea of adding 'recreations' to the standard data. Newspapers thereafter never tired of quoting these, 'thus giving the book a succession of advertisements of its readability, and shop-keepers who catered for their various sports bought the book to get the addresses of the eminent people, who were, many of them, very indignant at the Niagara of circulars which resulted'.[92]

The old *Who's Who* originated in 1848: it was 'a handbook of the titled and official classes only', and 'as futile as an 1840 Beauty Book'. Sladen's aim now was to produce a reference work 'of an entirely new kind, avowedly modern, light, and autobiographical'. To achieve this he would need to incorporate the celebrated in every walk of life, 'whether their prominence is inherited, or depending upon office, or the result of ability which singles them out from their fellows in occupations open to every educated man and woman'. The last was important, to acknowledge the contribution made by women in an age that took its name from one. Sladen was also clear that 'what the Victorian era . . . has witnessed more than anything else, is the growth of a new empire'; not so much territorial as 'the empire of the mind, meaning the power of literature—of the Press and of the Pen'. He was unabashed, therefore, that in his first editorial production, the 1897 *Who's Who*, 'literature is over-represented'. Perhaps, he conceded, 'the tendency of the age . . . pays what may be thought an exaggerated homage to writers'; but

[91] *Punch*, 14 Mar. 1891, 121.   [92] Sladen, *Twenty Years*, 236.

it was necessary at last to redress the deficiency, 'that we have had in England no adequate guide to tell us *Who's Who* in literature'.[93] The 1897 edition contained altogether some 6,000 biographies; the 1898 added another 1,000 (including Lucas Cleeve and W. W. Jacobs among the new literary stars); the 1899 a further 1,500. And the attraction (or drawback) of the formula was that it lacked all proportion. Length of entry was not tailored according to estimated importance, as was done for the dead in the *Dictionary of National Biography*.

Perhaps for this reason not all complied with the invitation to appear in the revamped *Who's Who*. Among politicians, the Prime Minister, Lord Salisbury, and Colonial Secretary, Joseph Chamberlain, declined. Sladen also noted the curiosity that naval officers were inept, army officers obliging, about form-filling.

Architects and literary men filled up their forms best, artists and actresses worst, though actors were almost as bad. You would have thought that the actual formation of the letters in framing a reply was a torture to artists, actors and naval officers.

Rude responses were plenty, the rudest coming from W. S. Gilbert:

He said he was always being pestered by unimportant people for information about himself. So I put him down in the book as 'Writer of Verses and [of] the libretti to Sir Arthur Sullivan's comic operas'. He then wrote me a letter of about a thousand words, in which he asked me if that was the way to treat a man who had written seventy original dramas. Next year he filled up his form as readily as a peer's widow who has married a commoner.[94]

This was how Sladen behaved: if celebrities did not deliver, he invented a CV for them. It usually brought them into line. Most jumped at the opportunity, if not all so splendidly as Bernard Shaw, who included among his recreations 'showing off',[95] or Marie Corelli, who disclosed that 'she is at present unmarried'.[96] Consequently, the new *Who's Who* was a roaring success: 'newspapers gave it column reviews, chiefly consisting of the unsuitable recreations of prominent people'.[97] The publishers, however, did not renew Sladen's contract. In 1914 Sladen bitterly regretted that he had not insisted on 'the clause which has gone into all my other agreements', namely, that if a book was not as profitable as the publisher hoped, it should become his property. Sladen implied that Messrs A. & C. Black cynically ditched him after taking his 'ideas, whose originality and value has abundantly been proved since'.[98] He was right, certainly, about the success of

[93] *Who's Who* (1897), preface.
[94] Sladen did not always allow accuracy to get in the way of a good story. Gilbert's entry in *Who's Who* (1897), 334, and *Who's Who* (1898), 390, were the same, as was that for *Who's Who* (1899), 432, except that the legend 'writer of verses, and of the libretti to Sir Arthur Sullivan's comic operas' was dropped.
[95] *Who's Who* (1897), 595. 'Cycling and showing off were Shaw's then recreations; next year—*Who's Who* (1898), 704—he amended the declaration thus: '*Exercise*: cycling. *Recreations*: change of work, Nature, Art, human intercourse, anything except sport'. This edition was also the first in which he put: '*Trade Union*: Authors' Society'.
[96] *Who's Who* (1897), 254; *Who's Who* (1898), 290. The 'at present' was dropped from the 1899 edition.
[97] Sladen, *Twenty Years*, 65, 237–8; *Punch*, 10 Apr. 1897, 169, and 5 Mar. 1898, 105.
[98] Sladen, *Twenty Years*, 233–4; and *Punch*, 3 Jan. 1900, 17, for Henry Lucy's tribute to Sladen's innovativeness, on the publication of the first *Who's Who* to appear without his editorship.

Who's Who. Its market matched a good-selling novel: 10,000 sales in 1901, at price 5s., and 12,000 in 1910, notwithstanding the price having doubled.[99]

Sladen thereafter pursued his own literary interests, principally of the formulaic kind; yet, although out of England for several months annually, he and his wife kept up their literary receptions at Addison Mansions, until 1911, when they moved to Richmond. Sladen also directed the Vagabonds and Authors' clubs' dining and entertainments programmes, and edited other personal directories: *Sladen's London and its Leaders* and *The Green Book of London Society*. But his dismissal from *Who's Who* rankled:

There was no one in London with the same knowledge as I had as to who should be included in the book, because my three years' work in New York papers had made me take up biographical journalism—a profession which did not exist in London till I brought it over from America, and which never took permanent root in England. In fact, it very soon withered out of existence.[100]

Sladen's verdict about the evanescence of personal journalism must be read in the context of his disenchantment, although it found some support from Ford Madox Ford, who in 1911 sought to summon the style of the 1890s for his daughters:

In those days writers were interviewed; their houses, their writing desks, their very blotting pads, were photographed for the weekly papers. Their cats even, were immortalized by the weekly press.[101]

'Think of that, now!' he exclaimed, as if these habits were no more. What happened meanwhile was not the passing of personal journalism as such; rather, that writers gradually lost the limelight to other celebrities film stars, sports stars, and social butterflies. It may be that personal journalism never spread so pervasively as in America, but to argue that it quickly perished in Britain was excessive. Certainly, authors had been accorded extraordinary attention in the 1890s. Some misreporting was easily borne and in good humour. Barrie wrote to Quiller-Couch from his home town, Kirriemuir in Scotland, on Christmas Day 1893: 'I see from the papers that I am in Switzerland with Maarten Maartens. Hope I'm enjoying myself.'[102] But legitimate boundaries were crossed. When Tennyson was ill in February 1890, the press presumed that the 80-year-old Laureate was dying. Reporters gathered at Aldworth and, finding the family unco-operative, paid a local beggar to convey kitchen gossip from his daily call for food scraps.[103] Soon, children were not sacrosanct either. H. G. Wells's wife came home one day in 1911 to find her two small sons being interviewed about Wells's latest book—though, admittedly, a book involving children's games.[104]

---

[99] Derek Hudson, citing figures provided by A. & C. Black, in Nowell-Smith (ed.), *Edwardian England*, 316.   [100] Sladen, *Twenty Years*, 234.
[101] Ford Madox Hueffer [Ford], *Ancient Lights and Certain New Reflections, Being the Memories of a Young Man* (1911), 153–4. Cf. *Punch*, 30 Oct. 1901, 321, for a spoof 'Diary of an Author'.
[102] Meynell (ed.), *Barrie Letters*, 5.   [103] Martin, *Tennyson*, 573.
[104] Lowndes (ed.), *Lowndes Diaries and Letters*, 26 (3 Dec. 1911).

Sladen was still in business in 1914; and many an author was an accomplice in his publicity drive. Others required cajolery; if so, Sladen was the man to apply it. His memoir *Twenty Years of my Life* (1914) involved a fund of anecdotes. Sladen's surviving papers show that this was the outcome of an extensive correspondence with authors who, through soft soap and virtual blackmail, were persuaded to contribute. Thus to W. W. Jacobs:

In going through my memoirs, which have to be with the printer next week, I seem to have treated you very inadequately in my chapter upon the principal authors of my time. I expect that what I have written is also inaccurate, which is a pity, for you have such a tremendous public, who would be immortally interested to know how you came by the knowledge which has made your books unique. I should be so grateful if you would substitute a few hundred words about the way in which you came to write the books which we all love. That I know it in a vague way, is shown by the paragraph that I have written. Of course, I shall print what you send me as emanating from myself, though I could say that you had told me the anecdotes. It does not matter how many words you write: I know that verbosity is not one of your pleasures, but I should like one whom I have known so long, and whose work I admire so immensely, to be a leading figure in my memoirs.[105]

The same approach, with minor variations, was made to most others. Several, such as Charles Garvice and H. A. Vachell, rewarded Sladen with several pages of autobiography which he simply stitched into his text. When some demurred, he responded by pretending that they had been singled out for prominence or by redoubling the threat that, if they did not send something, they would be treated perfunctorily. Sladen's standard lines included: 'You are such a great writer that I want you to be an outstanding figure' (to Richard Whiteing); 'You ought to have a page, not a paragraph' (to Compton Mackenzie); 'You, above all people, should be properly represented in my memoirs' (to Mrs W. K. Clifford). At his best, Sladen achieved classic proportions of effrontery and puffery:

My dear old chap,
    In going through my memoirs, which have to be with the printer next week, I find that I left it to you to write it, and then forgot to send the blank form to you. Will you write several hundred words about yourself, saying everything that you want to have said in the most anecdotic and human way possible? You needn't blush about saying it, because I shall have said it, not you, and I wish to say the best and most effective things possible about my dear old friend, so that the critics may quote what *I* have said about him . . .
    With best regards,
        I am,
        Yours affectionately,
P.S. Will you let me have it back by the end of the week, because it will have to be marked into its place?[106]

---

[105] Sladen to W. W. Jacobs, 17 Dec. 1913; copy in Richmond Reference Library, Local Studies Collection, Sladen papers, box 66, fo. 10.
[106] Sladen to unidentified correspondent, 17 Dec. 1913, Sladen papers, box 66, fo. 12.

Clement Shorter, a hustling editor who played the field of authorship with as little scruple as Sladen, was evidently wise to his strategy; but he cooperated all the same, as Sladen's follow-up letter indicated:

You made a legitimate point in chaffing me about getting other people to write my memoirs, but, in fact, I have only asked a mere handful of the greatest authors to do so. I felt that if I wrote to anybody, I must write to you, because you have been such a consistent friend in keeping my books in notice . . . [107]

The recycling or promotion of other people's memoirs was another course adopted by Sladen, encouraged by such as Walter Crane, who replied:

It is very good of you to wish to expand about me a bit more—but haven't I said enough about myself in my 'Reminiscences' (Methuen 1907) which no doubt you have seen?

However, I will see if I can send you a few special notes for *your* book which is sure to be full of interesting things about yourself and other celebrities. [108]

Yet others exuded the vanity, wreathed in mock modesty, which Sladen's approach was designed to arouse; as in Edgar Jepson's reply:

Many thanks for all those nice things you say about me. But I am not a fencer at all as it happens. If you like to say that the experts are agreed that on any day I am the second-best, if not the best, auction bridge-player in England that would be accurate enough.

I can't think of anything in the way of literary anecdotes. Unless you like to say that I am a walking warning against writing fiction since from my first book I made 0, from my 2nd £6-19-9, and from my 3rd £9-10-3. [109]

IV

Arthur Pinero was aged 60 when he cried enough of this self-advertisement. It is true that Pinero by then was out of, or above, the rat race, being rich and a knight of the realm; but neither had he been conspicuous in courting personal publicity during the period of his greatest fame, the 1890s. Pinero ventilated his disgust in *The Big Drum*, staged at the St James's in 1915. The protagonist is an author, Philip Mackworth, who writes a novel, *The Big Drum*, in which he denounces 'the hustlers of the pen'. This disappoints a friend, who thinks that Mackworth is too prissy about pushing himself:

What I want to see are paragraphs concerning you mixed up with the news of the day, information about you and your habits, interviews with you, letters from you on every conceivable topic . . . I entreat you, feed the papers. It isn't as if you hadn't talent; you *have*. Advertising *minus* talent goes a long way; advertising *plus* talent is irresistible. Feed the papers. The more you do for them the more they'll do for you. *Quid pro quo.* [110]

[107] Sladen to Clement Shorter, 23 Dec. 1913, copy, Sladen papers.
[108] Walter Crane to Douglas Sladen, 21 Dec. 1913, Sladen papers, box 66, fo. 54.
[109] Edgar Jepson to Douglas Sladen, 19 Dec. 1913, Sladen papers, box 66, fo. 22.
[110] Quoted in Fyfe, *Pinero*, 298.

It is not difficult to identify whom Pinero had in mind. Bernard Shaw peppered the press 'on every conceivable topic'; but, according to Pinero, 'vulgar ostentation or almost superhuman egoism' was now so general and shameless that authors would attend the funerals of famous people whom they had not known simply to get their names in the papers. Yet, Pinero also understood that writers were not alone in having abandoned all modesty, to force themselves upon public notice. Mackworth's novel

shows the bishop and the judge playing to the gallery, the politician adopting the methods of the cheap-jack, the duchess vying with the puffing draper; it shows how even true genius submits itself to conditions that are accepted and excused as 'modern' and is found elbowing and pushing in the hurly-burly. It shows how the ordinary decencies of life are sacrificed to the paragraphist, the interviewer and the ghoul with the camera; how the home is stripped of its sanctity, blessed charity made a parade-ground for display; the very grave-yard transformed into a parade-ground; while the outsider looks on with a sinking of the vitals because the drumstick is beyond his reach and the bom-bom-bom is not for *him*.[111]

Naturally, Mackworth's *Big Drum* becomes a best-seller—but only because his nouveau riche fiancée, fearing the book will fail, contracts with the publisher to buy up 25,000 copies. It is another instance of literary market manipulation.

The Cassandras were not without consolations, especially when Hugh Walpole was at hand to illustrate the pratfalls of penmanship. In 1909 the literary agent Hughes Massie commissioned him to compile *Careers for Young Men*. The celebrities earmarked for interview included the best-seller, Hall Caine, together with the Bishop of London, A. F. Winnington-Ingram, the manager of Drury Lane Theatre, Arthur Collins, and a writer on cricket. Twenty years later Walpole still shuddered at the recollection. The cricket writer was interviewed first. At Walpole's question, what preparation was required for this career, he exploded: 'My God! I don't know. It isn't a Career. It's a bloody bore.'[112] No more interviews were conducted, and the assignment was abandoned in farce.

[111] Quoted ibid. 301–2.   [112] Hart-Davis, *Walpole*, 66–7.

11

Securing the Future

When a popular writer dies, the question it has become the fashion with a nervous generation to ask is the question, 'Will he live?'

(Walter Raleigh, *Robert Louis Stevenson* (1895))

No one so obscure nowadays but that he can have a book about him.

(J.M. Barrie, *Courage* (1922))

The idea to me is intolerable that when I am dead and gone my naked thoughts and unguarded expressions may be raked up and made to serve some dirty purpose or other. I have already had enough of notoriety.

(George Borrow to John Hasfield, 23 June 1843)

Many authors saw no reason to rely on the interview to keep their names before the public or to address posterity. The habit of keeping correspondence and journals, with a view to publication, was endemic and ancient; indeed, traceable back to Rome, which was 'the seat of coteries of literary log-rollers'.[1] 'I think it is impossible for literary men to write natural letters any more,' Thackeray told a friend to whom he was confiding his financial troubles in 1848; adding, 'I was just going to say something, but thinks I in future ages when this letter comes to be etc.—they will say "he was in embarrassed circumstances he was reckless and laughed at his prodigality he was etc." '[2] Most authors seemed well aware of the rules of the game or else devised their own. It hugely disappointed admirers of his genius that Robert Louis Stevenson should choose to remove himself from civilization in order to voyage around the Pacific from one 'undecipherable cannibal-island' (Henry James's complaint) to another;[3] but in 1890 he concluded his odyssey by settling in Samoa and, wrote the syrupy Sidney Colvin, 'to my infinite gratification, [he] took to writing me long and regular monthly budgets as full and particular as heart could wish; and this practice he maintained until within a few weeks of his death'. The result was the *Vailima Letters* (1895). How far it was a planned exercise by both men from the start may be questioned; but by 1892 the character of the correspondence was established, Stevenson writing, 'It came over me the other day suddenly that this diary of mine to you would

---

[1] Sir Edward Cook, 'A Ramble in Pliny's Letters', in Cook, *More Literary Recreations*, 111.
[2] Thackeray to Mrs Bryan Waller Procter, 13 Sept. 1848, in Harden (ed.), *Thackeray Letters*, 157.
[3] To William James, 29 Oct. 1888, in Edel (ed.), *James Letters*, iii. 242.

make good pickings after I am dead, and a man could make some kind of book out of it without much trouble.' Colvin even instructed Stevenson about the sort of 'revelations' he required, namely, 'that his letters should not be so entirely taken up as some of the past winter [1893–4] had been with native affairs, of relatively little meaning or interest to his correspondent'.[4] Keeper of the department of prints and drawings at the British Museum, Colvin preened himself on being an arbiter of taste both artistic and literary. Tall, thin, and (beneath what Chesterton called his 'frigid refinement')[5] a neurotic, Colvin was irritable towards underlings and ingratiating towards the famous. Kipling met him in the early 1890s and pulled no punches in his description: 'an all-fired prig of immense water . . . [who] suffers from all the nervo-hysterical diseases of the 19th Century. Went home with him as far as Charing Cross in a 3rd smoking which made him sick. He recounted all his symptoms, and made me sick. A queer beast with matchstick fingers and a dry unwholesome skin'.[6] When another emerging authorial talent, Compton Mackenzie, newly elected to the Savile in 1912, saw Colvin for the first time, he too was put off from approaching him by 'the chill' he cast, not to mention 'his deafness and the cold drop at the end of his nose'.[7]

Theodore Watts-Dunton was another self-appointed keeper of the flame, in his case primarily for Swinburne, though he also prided himself on intimacies with William Morris and the Rossettis. 'He is a hero of friendship,' Gabriel Rossetti declared, the recollection of which baffled Arthur Benson when he called on Watts-Dunton in 1903 in preparation for the book he was planning about Rossetti for Macmillan's English Men of Letters series: 'I can't understand this enigma— how this egotistical, ill-bred little man can have established such relations with Rossetti and Swinburne. There must be something fine about him—and his extraordinary kindness is perhaps the reason; but his talk, his personal habits, and his egotism would grate on me at every hour of the day.'[8] When a crop of Rossetti memoirs and letters was published in the 1880s and 1890s, by Gabriel's brother William and by Hall Caine, George Birkbeck Hill, and more, Watts-Dunton had hurried to stake out the moral high ground. He emphasized the fiduciary position of the dead writer's family, friends, and literary executors, as 'a sanction of the deepest religious kind'. Some disclosure of biographical information, for

---

[4] Colvin (ed.), *Vailima Letters*, pp. xv–xvi, 200, 328. 'Vailima' was the name of Stevenson's estate, meaning 'five rivers'. See also Mackay, *Violent Friend*, 197–8, 228–9, for Colvin's disapproval of Stevenson's involvement in South Seas politics; and, for a recent selection, Robert Louis Stevenson, *His Best Pacific Writings*, ed. Roger Robinson (Brisbane, 2004). Oscar Wilde, finding the *Vailima Letters* tedious, parodied them in letters to Robbie Ross; Hart-Davis (ed.), *Wilde Letters*, 280, 285.

[5] Chesterton, *Autobiography*, 93. Chesterton added that, apart from a mutual love of Stevenson, he and Colvin 'differed upon every subject in earth and heaven; he was both Imperialist in politics and a Rationalist in religion . . . He hated Radicals and Christian mystics and romantic sympathisers with small nationalities, and in fact everything that I had any tendency to be.'   [6] Birkenhead, *Kipling*, 111.

[7] Mackenzie, *Life and Times*, iv. 136.

[8] Lubbock, *Benson*, 68 (4 Apr. 1903). Henry James, on the other hand, couldn't understand Benson writing on Rossetti: 'No, no, no, it won't do. *Dear* Arthur, we know just what he can, so beautifully do, but no, oh no, this is to have the story of a purple man written by a white, or at the most, a pale green man' (told by Percy Lubbock to George Lyttelton, in Hart-Davis (ed.), *Lyttelton Hart-Davis Letters*, 264 (28 Feb. 1957)).

example, business letters that evidenced conditions under which a piece of work was produced, was valuable and legitimate; but there was no excuse for exhuming slashing remarks such as Rossetti made about Tennyson's reception of his poems in 1870 because this belied the admiration that Rossetti always felt for Tennyson. None would imagine from Rossetti's letters what a perceptive critic he was; their publication betrayed his reputation. In sum, argued Watts-Dunton, 'the greatest injustice that can be done to a writer is to print his letters indiscriminately'. Late in life Rossetti had become conscious of their potential treachery and started to weed his correspondence, but death overtook him before he progressed further than the early 1860s. This practice, Watts-Dunton thought, deserved systematic imitation: Rossetti 'realised what all eminent men would do well to realise, that owing to the degradation of public taste, which cries out for more personal gossip and still more every day, the time has fully come when . . . it behoves every man who has had the misfortune to pass into fame to burn all letters'.[9] Only following a holocaust of private papers would authors attain that happy position occupied by Shakespeare, about whose personal life an almost complete dearth of information existed. Shakespeare therefore was known by his work alone. A great many authors would try to follow this plan during this period, from the Poet Laureate Robert Bridges downwards. Bridges made an exception in the case of Gerard Manley Hopkins, whose letters he preserved because these represented a vital statement of his philosophy and poetic intent at a time when Hopkins's inhibitions bottled up his production and prevented the publication of his poetry. Still, Bridges destroyed his own correspondence with Hopkins, as also his own juvenile verses, and requested that no biography of him be written.[10]

Henry James also let his feelings be known. When the acclaimed editor, critic, and poet James Russell Lowell, who had served as American Minister in London, died in 1891, James observed the pieties in writing to Lowell's fellow Boston Brahmin, Charles Eliot Norton, who was poised to edit Lowell's letters for publication: 'It's a blessing . . . to feel that such an office is in such hands as yours.' This was a deft allusion to Norton's part in the controversy when, following the alarmingly frank treatment of Carlyle by his executor J. A. Froude, Norton had been commissioned by Carlyle's niece to expose Froude's carelessness and to restore the sage's reputation by editing his correspondence with R. W. Emerson (1883) and his *Letters and Reminiscences* (1887). James had been dismayed by newspaper notices of Lowell's death. They were not hostile, indeed 'extremely worshipful about him—but all with that colourless perfunctory note, that absence of the personal tone and of individual talent, which makes English journalism almost unreadable to me nowadays'. It was these 'posthumous vulgarities of our day', James told Norton, which 'add another grimness to death'.[11]

---

[9] Watts-Dunton, *Old Familiar Faces*, 83.   [10] Thompson, *Robert Bridges*, 1, 10, 87–8.
[11] James to Norton, 28 Aug. 1891, in Edel (ed.), *James Letters*, iii. 353–4. Norton (1827–1908), Professor of the History of Art at Harvard, was also appointed Ruskin's executor.

A scholar like Norton was obviously superior to a hack journalist, yet James was uneasy about the whole business. This disquiet did not prevent him from enjoying and reviewing literary biography and correspondence; but he continued to brood about this 'idea of the *responsibility* of destruction—the destruction of papers, letters, records, etc. connected with private and personal history'.[12] Three of his stories, *Sir Dominick Ferrand, The Aspern Papers*, and *John Delavoy*, reflect his anxiety that a man's work should not be subordinated to whatever discreditable details about his personal life may be ferreted out by unscrupulous biographers and gossip-fixated journalists hired by some 'publishing scoundrel'. The ideal was presented in *John Delavoy*, in which the artist was 'the most unadvertised, unreported, uninterviewed, unphotographed, uncriticized of all originals. Was he not the man of the time about whose private life we delightfully knew least?' James so acted upon this as to destroy his manuscripts and the myriad letters he received; but he had no power to compel the destruction of letters that he had written to others or the copies that they had made of theirs to him. Perhaps 12,000–15,000 survive, out of the *c.*40,000 letters that James wrote; a four-volume selection was published by Leon Edel in 1974–84, and now a thirty-volume complete edition is planned.[13] All this is in plain defiance of James's testamentary wishes, as expressed to his nephew in 1914:

My sole wish is to frustrate as utterly as possible the post mortem exploiter—which, I know, is but so imperfectly possible. Still one can do something, and I have long thought of launching, by a provision in my will, a curse no less explicit than Shakespeare's own on any such as try to move my bones. Your question determines me definitely to advert to the matter in my will—that is to declare my utter and absolute abhorrence of any attempted biography or the giving to the world by 'the family', or by any person for whom my disapproval has any sanctity, of any part or parts of my private correspondence. One can discredit and dishonour such enterprises even if one can't prevent them, and as you are my sole and exclusive literary heir and executor you will doubtless be able to serve in some degree as a check and a frustrator.[14]

The first interview with a journalist to which James assented was not until 1904, when he was aged 61. This took place in America, conducted by a young woman, a 'pathetic bore', for whom James apparently felt pity. He used the opportunity to emphasize his philosophy, namely, 'One's craft, one's art, is his expression, not one's person, as that of some great actress or singer is hers.' He declined to identify a 'moral purpose' or to resolve unanswered questions in his stories, because 'is that not the trick that life plays? Life itself leaves you with a question—it asks you questions.' But he did enjoy castigating the American reading public as 'dissolute'; in the words of Leon Edel, 'he said it was omnivorous, gulping, either ignorant or weary, reading to soothe or indulge. He felt that people in America did not like to think,'[15] unlike some older civilizations.

---

[12] Edel, *James*, ii. 82.   [13] See Philip Horne (ed.), *Henry James: A Life in Letters* (1999).
[14] Edel, *James*, ii. 472–3. See also Hamilton, *Keepers of the Flame*, 207–21.
[15] Edel, *James*, ii., 558–9.

James did not test this comparison by relaxing his guard before the British reading public. Still, no reticence on his part could prevent his being written and talked about.

Watts-Dunton was a doughty champion of the James position. He reserved his strongest condemnation for this new type of public, whose influence he believed pestilential for the art of literary biography and for the formation of a literary canon. He counted it as such an unalloyed disaster for an author 'to pass from the sweet paradise of obscurity into the vulgar purgatory of Fame, that it almost behoves a man of genius to avoid, if he can, passing into that purgatory at all'. Watts-Dunton was so pleased by this formula that he repeated this phrase, 'the purgatory of fame', in obituary panegyrics for both Rossetti and Tennyson.[16] In another memoir, concerning his friend Dr Gordon Hake, who had been close to George Borrow, Watts-Dunton identified a virus of 'new criticism', defined as 'that vulgar greed for notoriety that in these days, when literature to be listened to must be puffed like quack medicine and patent soap, has made the atmosphere of the literary arena somewhat stifling in the nostrils of those who turn from "modernity" to poetic art'.[17] Authors' executors, their biographers, and editors of literary memorials were sometimes guilty of serious crimes, such as allowing raw manuscripts and private letters to be sold at auction and permitting publication of unfinished or inferior work which an author had wished suppressed. Still more frequently were they guilty of lapses in taste by publicizing the petty transactions of an author's life. Naturally, therefore, Watts-Dunton set strict limits to a study which James Douglas published about him in 1904. When the bookman Robertson Nicoll reviewed it, he acknowledged Watts-Dunton as novelist and poet, while chiefly saluting his literary criticism, for the *Examiner* in 1874, then for the *Athenaeum* from 1876. Notable was his treatise on poetry for the ninth edition of *Encyclopaedia Britannica* in 1885. Nicoll hailed Watts-Dunton as a truly great critic, with a 'masterly grasp of principles', 'singularly beautiful and poetical' style, and 'nobly catholic temper', which allowed him to deliver judgements 'entirely devoid of envy, spite, and malice'. Yet, all this could be divined from Watts-Dunton's published work. Douglas's study contained few biographical particulars, Watts-Dunton 'guarding his privacy for many years with something very like ferocity'. This frustrated Nicoll: there was 'too little of Mr. Watts-Dunton' in Douglas's book. Strangely, there was also 'too little of Mr. Douglas', whom Nicoll described as 'best known to the public as a master of what may be termed personal criticism—the only criticism which seems likely to be read in the immediate future'.[18]

In 1890 *Punch* had thought it timely to advise a strategy which, if authors followed it, would ensure that their correspondence was unlikely to be auctioned

---

[16] Watts-Dunton, *Old Familiar Faces*, 78, 126.   [17] Ibid. 209.

[18] Nicoll, *Bookman's Letters*, ch. xv. James Douglas, an Ulsterman, was at this time literary critic and assistant editor of the *Star*; later, editor of the *Sunday Express*, 1920–31. A recreational poet, he boasted of having had published a coronation ode for Edward VII in 1902: he also wrote a novel, *The Unpardonable Sin* (1907).

or even preserved. It was not enough to decorate the simplest missive, such as a formal reply to an invitation, with standard forbidding phrases, 'Not negotiable', 'This letter is the property of the Writer', 'Not for publication', 'All rights reserved', and to attach your solicitor's address. Far better to introduce into each letter some 'antidotal abuse' about your executors—that 'x' is an ass, 'y' wears a toupee, and 'z' is a twaddling old bore, shunned by society. Yet even this might not deter those who combined greed with thick skin. Hence, 'perhaps the best plan will be, not to write at all. The telegraph, at the end of the century, costs but a halfpenny a word, and we seem to be within measurable distance of the universal adoption of the telephone.'[19] *Punch* did not anticipate the advent of telephone bugging and other recording devices. As things stood, most executors dutifully endeavoured to fulfil commissions to polish the images of the departed for posterity. Lewis Carroll's death in 1898 generated particular curiosity: the inventor of Wonderland was not only a clergyman and mathematics don but a photographer and frolicsome friend of young girls. His nephew and godson Stuart Dodgson Collingwood was quickly off the mark with a discreet *Life and Letters* published in the year of Carroll's death. This was the 'St Lewis' version, and Collingwood completed his mission by destroying a portion of Carroll's diaries and correspondence; but it did not take long for some of his former circle to exploit their experiences. Isa Bowman, whom Carroll got to know when she was a child actress and who played a small part in the West End production of *Alice*, published *The Story of Lewis Carroll* in 1899 and auctioned letters he had written to her about kissing.[20] Watts-Dunton did not so much pillory these agents as

blame the public, whose coarse and vulgar mouth is always agape for such pabulum . . . Although the 'public' acknowledges no duties towards the man of literary or artistic genius, but would shrug up its shoulders or look with dismay at being asked to give five pounds in order to keep a poet from the work-house, the moment a man of genius becomes famous the public becomes aware of certain rights in relation to him.[21]

Watts-Dunton denied that the public had any property in the matter, being disqualified by its propensity for asinine idolatry and appetite for trivia:

Without the smallest real reverence for genius—without the smallest capacity of distinguishing the poetaster it always adores from the true poet it always ignores—the public can still fall down before the pedestal upon which genius has been placed by the select few—fall down with its long ears open for gossip about genius, or anything else that is talked about.[22]

A fatal flaw in Watts-Dunton's argument was the widespread failure of authors to destroy their private papers. Pruning was no doubt undertaken, but the preferred action was for authors to commit their papers and with them their posthumous reputation to a trusted guardian or disciple rather than to consign

---

[19] *Punch*, 13 Dec. 1890, 282.   [20] Cohen, *Carroll*, 186, 532.
[21] Watts–Dunton, *Old Familiar Faces*, 104–5.   [22] Ibid. 194–5.

wholesale their letters and diaries to the flames. It was particularly rich of Watts-Dunton to have criticized William Rossetti's judgement in publishing some of Gabriel Rossetti's letters when 'it was only after waiting in vain for thirteen years for the promised biography of his brother by Theodore Watts-Dunton that Rossetti set about the *Memoir, with Family Letters* (2 vols., 1895)'.[23] William Rossetti might have been a bore and humbug, but he was a perceptive and radical art critic and he was an experienced literary editor, having produced editions or appraisals of Blake, Keats, Shelley, and Whitman, as well as of his brother's work. Gabriel's reputation could hardly have been in safer hands; and the same was true for Christina Rossetti, although as an unbeliever William was notably far from sharing her religious position. It was simply naive to suppose that William Rossetti would publish everything that survived his brother's cull of papers or give others licence to hold forth about his sister. He excised significant passages from the correspondence and had many a dispute with Christina's first biographer, Mackenzie Bell, who issued *Christina Rossetti* in 1898.[24]

Watts-Dunton's halo slipped further when it came to the test. In the month following Swinburne's death, the sub-editor on the *English Review*, Douglas Goldring, called on him to negotiate for one of Swinburne's manuscripts, about the Jacobean playwright Francis Beaumont. He found Watts-Dunton a sharp bargainer. They wrestled over a fee for contingent American rights and, altogether, 'his lowest offer was exactly ten pounds more than the highest price which I was authorised to bid'. Watts-Dunton was sure that Swinburne was a still rising stock, not only the last of the old generation of poets but the first of the new: 'He added, as I got up to go, that Swinburne's death would immensely increase his "sales", and thus the market value of his copyrights!'[25] Goldring turned out to be the least of Watts-Dunton's problems. More insistent were the attentions of the bibliographer, manuscript-dealer, and forger Thomas Wise, who was now exploiting an alliance with Watts-Dunton's jealous rival for control of Swinburne's literary remains and legend, Edmund Gosse. There was also a sister and cousin of Swinburne to reckon with. The whole business developed into an ugly and unedifying wrangle, full of duplicity and greed.[26] Watts-Dunton tactfully died in 1914, leaving his widow, Clara, to issue her risible *The Home Life of Swinburne* (1922).[27] Gosse's largely veiled *Life of Swinburne* had appeared in 1917. 'The fatuity of the Swinburne family, something venal and odious in the partly virtuous character of Watts-Dunton, Swinburne's own strange habits—these

---

[23] Frederick Page's notice of W. M. Rossetti (1829–1919), in *DNB 1912–1921*, 480. Wilde, still incarcerated in Reading gaol, regarded the published Rossetti letters as 'dreadful', adding: 'Obviously forgeries by his brother' (to Robert Ross, 6 Apr. 1897, in Hart-Davis (ed.), *Wilde Letters*, 246).

[24] Anthony H. Harrison (ed.), *The Letters of Christina Rossetti*, i: *1843–1873* (Charlottesville, Va., 1997); Hamilton, *Keepers of the Flame*, 136–7. [25] Goldring, *Reputations*, 219–23; id., *Life Interests*, 194–6.

[26] Hamilton, *Keepers of the Flame*, 184–96.

[27] A mockingly ironical review of it in the *Observer* by J. C. Squire, who hoped that other great poets would be so fortunate in their biographers, initially took in Thomas Hardy: see Florence Hardy to Sydney Cockerell, 2 Apr. 1922, in Millgate (ed.), *Emma and Florence Hardy*, 182.

combined to make the biography of the poet like the path that Christian had to traverse in the *Pilgrim's Progress,*' was Gosse's own retrospect of his endeavours, tailored to conform to the partialities of his correspondent, the religious-minded critic John Bailey in 1918.[28] To the differently constituted Harold Nicolson, Gosse by contrast gossiped about 'Swinburne's love of being beaten (if possible by muscular ladies)', as Nicolson in turn enjoyed telling Rupert Hart-Davis.[29]

Dwelling in a glasshouse did not inhibit Gosse from throwing stones. He objected to the two-volume *Letters and Literary Remains*, which the widow of J. H. Shorthouse published in 1905 about the author of *John Inglesant* (1880), as having presented 'not an imperfect so much as a false impression of a very singular person'. Expanding in 1912, he opined 'The great danger of twentieth-century biography is its unwillingness to accept any man's character save at the valuation of his most cautious relatives, and in consequence to reduce all figures to the same smooth forms and the same mediocre proportions.'[30] More candour was evidently Gosse's call; but he had no compunction about employing the pruning shears to excise the manuscript of the biography (1895) of John Addington Symonds by his literary executor H. F. Browne, and then later burning papers that Symonds had left to the London Library which candidly examined the nature of homosexuality.[31]

It was lapses in taste by official biographers and executors that also disturbed those who professed the sternest standards. They were not satisfied that an author's surviving family or friends could be trusted to protect reputations, still less advance them. No damage was more catastrophic than that dealt inadvertently by Edward FitzGerald's literary executor William Aldis Wright, who in 1889 published in three volumes the *Letters and Literary Remains*.[32] Included in the correspondence was one of 15 July 1861, in which FitzGerald observed lightly:

Mrs. Browning's death is rather a relief to me, I must say: no more Aurora Leighs, thank God! A woman of real genius, I know; but what is the upshot of it all? She and her sex had better mind the kitchen and their children; and perhaps the poor: except in such things as little novels, they only devote themselves to what men do much better, leaving that which men do worse or not at all.

Offensive to women everywhere and especially hurtful to the widower, this misogynistic humour caused bitter ructions when, with FitzGerald dead for half a dozen years, Browning apostrophized him in the *Athenaeum*:

To Edward FitzGerald

I chanced upon a new book yesterday:
I opened it, and where my finger lay
  'Twixt page and uncut page, these words I read

---

[28] Letter, 30 Jan. 1918, in Bailey (ed.), *Letters and Diaries*, 181.

[29] Hart-Davis (ed.), *Lyttelton Hart-Davis Letters*, 239 (13 Jan. 1957).

[30] Gosse, *Portraits and Sketches*, 10.

[31] See *Oxford DNB's* notice of Symonds (1840–93) by Rictor Norton.

[32] On Wright (1831–1914), a Fellow of Trinity College, Cambridge, and noted Shakespearean and biblical scholar, see *DNB 1912–1921*, 595–7. The *DNB* notice ignores the FitzGerald–Browning clanger.

> —Some six or seven at most—and learned thereby
> That you, FitzGerald, whom by ear and eye
> She never knew, 'thanked God my wife was dead.'
> Ay, dead! And were yourself alive, good Fitz,
> How to return you thanks would task my wits:
>   Kicking you seems the common lot of curs—
>   While more appropriate greeting lends you grace:
> Surely to spit these glorifies your face—
> Spitting from lips once sanctified by Hers.

For once, there was no uncertainty about Browning's meaning. Admirers of both writers were upset by their failure to persuade Browning to withdraw his commination in the few months remaining before his own death.[33]

Dr Wright's blunder was a startling reminder of the pitfalls awaiting literary trustees. A blithe defiance of all evidence to the contrary was the course adopted by Dickens's eldest daughter Mary (Mamey) and sister-in-law Georgina Hogarth, who had published an edition of his letters in 1880 as a supplement to what they called that 'perfect and exhaustive' biography (1874) by John Forster. The preface established their intent:

In publishing the more private letters, we do so with the view of showing him in his homely, domestic life of showing how in the midst of his own constant and arduous work, no household matter was considered too trivial to claim his care and attention. He would take as much pains about the hanging of a picture, the choosing of furniture, the superintending of any little improvement in the house, as he would about the more serious business of his life; thus carrying out to the very letter his favourite motto of 'What is worth doing at all is worth doing well'.[34]

This was designed to enforce the conspiracy of silence about Dickens's brutal separation from his wife in 1858 and keeping of a mistress, Nelly Ternan, for the last dozen years of his life, tucked away in houses first in Slough and then in Peckham. Georgina Hogarth, indeed, had been a key member of the plot, acting as chatelaine at Gad's Hill, Dickens's official residence, superintending his children and receiving visitors there. In the 1890s hints about the deceits practised by Dickens began to leak out, but the domestic halo largely remained in place for the public.[35]

In general, the problem for family and trustees was how to draw the line between too much concealment and too much disclosure. Erring from the ideal at one end of the scale was John Walter Cross, whom George Eliot married shortly before her death. His biography (1885) of her was less a Life than 'a Reticence in three volumes'.[36] At the opposite pole was J. A. Froude's behaviour as Carlyle's literary executor: his publication—a month after Carlyle's death—of

---

[33] Fuller and Hammersley (eds.), *Thackeray's Daughter*, 163–8, for letters from Browning and Emily Tennyson, 16 and 20 July 1889, about this.

[34] *The Letters of Charles Dickens, Edited by his Sister-in-Law and his Eldest Daughter*, i: *1833 to 1856* (1880), preface.   [35] Claire Tomalin, *The Invisible Woman*, 170, 235–7.

[36] Quoted in Nash, *Life*, 60, who attributed the remark to Gladstone.

the *Reminiscences* (1881), followed by *Letters and Memorials of Jane Welsh Carlyle* (1883) and the four-volume biography of Carlyle (1882-4). In his preface to the last, Froude calmly observed:

When a man has exercised a large influence on the minds of his contemporaries, the world requires to know whether his own actions have corresponded with his teaching, and whether his moral and personal character entitles him to confidence. This is not idle curiosity; it is a legitimate demand. In proportion to a man's greatness is the scrutiny to which his conduct is submitted . . . The publicity of their private lives has been, is, and will be, either the reward or the penalty of their intellectual distinction.

Froude acknowledged that in his will and in his journal Carlyle had expressed the wish that no biography be written; but, he added, 'Carlyle knew that he could not escape. Since a "Life" of him there would certainly be, he wished it to be as authentic as possible.' Carlyle's ideal was plain truth-telling and portrayal of man in the round, as he thought had been achieved by Lockhart in his *Life of Sir Walter Scott* (1838). Reviewing it, Carlyle had defended Lockhart from the charge that he was 'too communicative, indiscreet, and has recorded much that ought to have lain suppressed . . . How delicate, decent, is English biography, bless its mealy mouth. A Damocles' sword of *Respectability* hangs for ever over the poor English life-writer (as it does over poor English life in general), and reduces him to the verge of paralysis.'[37] Carlyle was not to know the liberties that Lockhart had taken with the evidence; it was enough that he sanctioned more candid and realistic biographical assessment. Froude too engaged in suppression, though he left for his own trustees to use if they saw fit, to defend him, evidence suggestive of Carlyle's sexual inactivity, if not impotence. Nevertheless, he disclosed sufficient of what Frederic Harrison termed the 'Brobdingnagian' scale of the Carlyles' marital misery to outrage those who held the Positivists' belief that biography of great men should be a means of inspiring future generations. Perhaps a lesson was indeed learned, if Jerome K. Jerome is followed: 'Froude ventured to mention the fact that the married life of Mr. and Mrs. Carlyle had not been one long-drawn-out celestial harmony. The entire middle-class of England and America could hardly believe its ears. It went down on its knees and thanked God that such goings-on happened only in literary and artistic circles.'[38] By contrast, Frederic Harrison's quarrel with Cross's *Life of George Eliot* was not about his gliding over the romantic side of her relationships with John Chapman, Herbert Spencer, and George Henry Lewes, but about his intellectual and literary assessments.[39]

 The protracted agonies about Froude's Carlyle highlighted anew the purpose and consequence of biography, whether its detail informed or injured the subject's work. The Carlyle controversy resembled previous scandals concerning Byron and Shelley; it was also a forerunner of umpteen future conflicts involving the surviving family and friends of departed literary figures who vied for control

---

[37] Quoted in James Anthony Froude, *Thomas Carlyle (1891)*, vol. i, pp. v–xiii.
[38] Jerome, *Life and Times*, 4.   [39] Vogeler, *Harrison*, 292–3, 315–16.

of copyrights and reputation.[40] Literary biography was and remains a much disputed genre. There still exist authors and critics who contend that no knowledge of a writer's life can properly explain the imaginative process and product, and that therefore literary biography is not merely futile but untrustworthy. This philosophically defensible position was strengthened during the twentieth century by the increasing dominance of a type of literary biography whose primary accent was a voyeuristic obsession with the subject's sex life in pursuit of a psychoanalytical retrospect; invariably this was underpinned by a zeal for household detail akin to an auctioneer's arrangement of lots. Social historians, while not exempt from charges of keyhole-peeping, generally hold a different set of interests from the intellectual historian or literary scholar. They are less concerned to 'read' an author's work via his life, than to set the author in context.

The English language is richer than any other in biographical literature. So Asquith declared with patriotic pride in an address at the Edinburgh Philosophical Institution on 15 November 1901. It was exemplified for him by '*Colonel Hutchinson's Life* by his wife, Roger North's *Lives of the Norths*, Boswell's *Johnson*, Lockhart's *Scott*, Carlyle's *Sterling*, Stanley's *Arnold*, Lewes' *Goethe*, Mrs Gaskell's *Charlotte Brontë*, Trevelyan's *Macaulay*—these are only the titles which first suggest themselves in a brilliant and inexhaustible catalogue.'[41] Bookmen had long vied in issuing such exhortatory lists. George Saintsbury having presented his own evaluation in 'Some Great Biographies'—the quintet of Boswell's *Johnson*, Moore's *Byron*, Lockhart's *Scott*, Carlyle's *Sterling*, and Trevelyan's *Macaulay*[42]—it was inevitably answered by others, especially Robertson Nicoll, who declared, 'Biography is my favourite form of reading, and I have beside me in the room where I am writing at least four thousand biographical works.'[43] There were various critical tests. Asquith pondered the occupational hazards of the biographer. One was to avoid 'the production of that which is trivial and ephemeral'. Just as necessary was to avoid the homiletic: 'It is not the function of a biography to be a magnified epitaph or an expanded tract.' Biographers should serve the truth, he averred, donning his legal silk; yet he thought that, if the biographer had done his job properly, and made vivid the personality of individuals who had done great work, biography 'brings comfort, it enlarges sympathy, it expels selfishness, it quickens aspiration'. So, Asquith believed, biography had an edifying role to play after all. He attributed the 'enormous increase, not only in the number but in the popularity of this class of books' to this desire of readers to

---

[40] Hamilton, *Keepers of the Flame*, for a broad study of this phenomenon from John Donne to Philip Larkin.

[41] 'Biography', in Rt. Hon. H. H. Asquith, *Occasional Addresses, 1893–1916*, (1918) 42–53.

[42] George Saintsbury, 'Some Great Biographies', *Fortnightly Review*, (June 1892), in Saintsbury *Collected Essays and Papers 1875–1920*, i: *Essays in English Literature*, ch. xvi.

[43] Nicoll, *Bookman's Letters*, 17. Nicoll's top six were: (1) Boswell's *Johnson*, (2) Lockhart's *Scott*, (3) Gaskell's *Charlotte Brontë*, (4) Trevelyan's *Macaulay*, (5) Froude's *Carlyle*, (6) Morley's *Gladstone*.

enhance their understanding of the purpose and meaning of life through acquaintance with the trials and tribulations of great figures.[44]

It was natural for a biographer who admired his subject to want readers to share that sentiment, but a too frequent vice was to make a subject conform to the biographer's ideal. Before 1914, and especially before 1900, an outstanding model was the exemplary Christian life. As agent for the Bible Society, which service took him throughout Europe, George Borrow had appeared perfect for the part; and that was how an American clergyman and Professor of Spanish, W. I. Knapp, presented him in the first major account of the writer, *Life, Writings and Correspondence of George Borrow* (2 vols., 1899). His task was not eased by the dispersal of Borrow's papers following his death in 1881; but Knapp engaged in deliberate suppression. Though vehemently anti-Catholic, Borrow had not been a convinced Christian; moreover, as a perennial egoist, he pursued his own agenda during his Bible Society employment. Knapp disclosed this dilemma to a correspondent in 1894: 'If I tell the truth will Borrow ever be read again? If I embellish him, make him a hero, I must burn his papers and letters afterwards—that no quizzing fool 50 years later may make his fortune by bringing out a new life—and prove it by the tell-tale archives'.[45] Knapp's whitewash coloured every other significant assessment of Borrow before the Great War and for many years after. It was not, for example, seriously disturbed by Clement Shorter's *George Borrow and his Circle* (1913), even though Shorter had acquired some of Borrow's papers; still less by Herbert Jenkins's *The Life of George Borrow* (1914), which intoned that 'there was something magnificent in his Christianity' and that he was unequalled as a missionary.[46]

Asquith had had nothing to say about the biographer who deliberately sought to deflate a reputation—whether, for example, Froude intentionally 'set himself to the discrowning of the old king', as Robertson Nicoll thought.[47] The debunking biography is more of a twentieth-century phenomenon, following Lytton Strachey's *Eminent Victorians* (1918) in particular; yet it should not be imagined that friendliness towards a subject always spared the biographer trouble in the past. The hornets' nest stirred up by Mrs Gaskell's *Life of Charlotte Brontë* (1857) served as a warning. Gaskell embarked on it from the best of motives, to 'make the world (if I am but strong enough in expression) honour the woman as much as they have admired the writer'. She also had the historical urge to set down accurate details of the life while they were still fresh, to prevent these from being lost to memory or supplanted by misinformed accounts which were already in circulation in newspapers and magazines. She won the consent of the family, notably Charlotte's husband and father. Yet there was no plain sailing because Charlotte's and her sisters' fiction had excited moral censure from some contemporaries for its unladylike passionateness and scenes of violence and dissolute behaviour; and this needed explaining, if not justifying. Mrs Gaskell's

---

[44] Asquith, *Occasional Addresses*, 42–55.   [45] Collie, *Borrow*, 4.   [46] Ibid. 55, 260.
[47] Nicoll, *Bookman's Letters*, 24.

commitment to truth-telling stopped short of disclosing Charlotte's love for a married man, the Brussels schoolteacher M. Heger; instead, she decided that the problem lay with Bramwell Brontë, Charlotte's brother. By describing his 'wreck and ruin', in particular his affair with his employer's wife, Mrs Gaskell courted disaster because, though Bramwell was dead, the woman concerned was not; indeed, having remarried and been widowed a second time, the erstwhile Mrs Robinson was now a Society hostess, Lady Scott. She threatened a libel suit, which was headed off by a retraction published in *The Times*; but Lady Scott's action encouraged others too to call for the removal of offending passages or for corrections of fact, including Charlotte Brontë's father, who otherwise approved of the work. Thus, in spite of reviews that extolled a classic biography, the author and publisher were beset with misfortune. Unsold copies of the first edition were called in, and a second edition, ready for issue, was withdrawn.[48] Perhaps for this reason, Mrs Gaskell rejected all approaches made to her to impart biographical information to students of her own novels. She persisted in 'an entire refusal to sanction what is to me so objectionable and indelicate a practice, by furnishing a single fact with regard to myself. I do not see why the public has any more to do with me than to buy or reject the wares I supply to them.'[49] Her daughters maintained this vigil after her death, and it was owing to the control exercised by one of them, Meta Gaskell, that Clement Shorter's typescript for a volume on Mrs Gaskell in the English Men of Letters series in 1909 was aborted. When Meta Gaskell died in 1913, her instructions were carried out to burn all papers in her possession relating to her mother.[50] Shorter, notwithstanding, had already established himself in the vacant post as interpreter of the Brontës to the world. Having supplied an introduction to a reissue of *Jane Eyre* in 1889, he published *Charlotte Brontë and her Circle* in 1896. The previous year he had bagged a cache of Brontë manuscripts, of which he boasted over dinner at the Savile Club to Edward Clodd and George Gissing: 'Last summer he went to the village in the middle of Ireland where, for many years, Nicholls, Charlotte's husband has lived. Got round the aged man, and bought all MSS for some £500 (I suspect for less). Nicholls has hitherto refused all approaches.'[51] Now on a roll, Shorter produced a new version of Mrs Gaskell's *Life of Charlotte Brontë* in 1899, *Charlotte Brontë and her Sisters* (1905), and *The Brontës: Life and Letters* (2 vols., 1908), all of which used material acquired from Nicholls.

The proper balance between privacy and publicity was debated again around the turn of the century because of two publications. The first, in 1897, was Frederic G. Kenyon's two-volume edition of *The Letters of Elizabeth Barrett Browning*. In the preface Kenyon admitted that the Brownings had 'more than

---

[48] Winifred Gérin, *Elizabeth Gaskell* (Oxford, 1980), chs. xv–xvii.
[49] Letter, 4 June? 1865, quoted ibid., p. vii. [50] Ibid., p. viii.
[51] Coustillas (ed.), *Gissing's Diary*, 400 (11 Jan. 1896). Nicholls was the Revd Arthur Bell Nicolls, former curate to the Revd Patrick Brontë, Charlotte's father. Nicolls married Charlotte in 1854, shortly before she died.

once expressed their strong dislike of any such publicity in regard to matters of a personal and private character'; yet, he continued,

They could not but be aware that the details of their lives would be of interest to the public which read and admired their works, and there is evidence that they recognised that the public has some claims with regard to writers who have appealed to, and partly lived by, its favour. They only claimed that during their own lifetime their feelings should be consulted first; when they should have passed away, the rights of the public would begin.

The letters that Kenyon published had been reclaimed from correspondents by Robert Browning after his wife's death (in 1861); and he had not destroyed them—as he had many of his own letters, Kenyon deliberately remarked. Thus preserved, they passed after Browning's death (in 1889) to their only son; and it was with his consent that they were now released.[52] The finger thus pointed to the son, R. W. (Pen) Browning, who had sizeable schemes of his own, publishing in 1899 his parents' love letters running to two volumes and over 1,100 pages. Pen justified himself thus:

In considering the question of publishing these letters, it seemed to me that my only alternatives were to allow them to be published or to destroy them. I might indeed have left the matter to the decision of others after my death, but that would be evading a responsibility which I feel that I ought to accept.[53]

The public endorsed his decision. Kenyon's volumes had already sold so keenly that a third reprinting was achieved in the sixteen months before the Browning love letters appeared. These now became a general favourite. They inspired Florence Barclay to conceive her own best-selling romances;[54] nor was she alone dewy-eyed. Thomas Hardy told Florence Henniker, with whom he was not a little in love, that 'the Browning Loveletters . . . made such an excellent novel, & a true one'.[55] They even caused Arthur Benson to wish that he too could enjoy such a marriage—until he remembered that he didn't actually like women.[56] George Meredith also recognized their force. 'I can see why B[rowning] sanctioned publication,' he wrote, feeling it amounted to 'a miracle surpassing all previous tales and all fiction of the power of love', although he added, still no doubt burning from his own first wife's betrayal and desertion, 'I could not have done it.'[57] Those who doubted the wisdom of publication felt vindicated when, following the death of Pen Browning, control over the letters passed out of the

---

[52] Frederic G. Kenyon (ed.), *The Letters of Elizabeth Barrett Browning* (1897), vol. i, pp. v–vi. Letters to her sister Henrietta were held back, until published in an edition by Leonard Huxley in 1929.

[53] *The Times*, 15 Feb. 1899. For a critical assessment, see Daniel Karlin, *The Courtship of Robert Browning and Elizabeth Barrett* (Oxford, 1985).					[54] See below, Ch. 20.

[55] Hardy to Florence Henniker, 24 Dec. 1900, in Purdy and Millgate (eds.), *Hardy Letters*, ii. 277.

[56] Lubbock, *Benson*, 151, 157 (16 Dec. 1906, 31 Jan. 1907).

[57] Meredith to Louisa Lawrence, Mar.? 1899, and to Alice Meynell, 13 Mar. 1899, in Cline (ed.), *Meredith's Letters*, iii. 1323–4.

family's hands. Lord Tennyson, the former Laureate's son and biographer, wrote fiercely to *The Times* in 1913:

Cannot Robert Browning's nearest relatives stop this infamy of the sale of the Browning love-letters? Browning, walking one day with me in Eaton-place, said to me:—'Tell your father that I have destroyed 1,500 letters of mine to my father. He will rejoice, for he loathes as much as I do the casting of one's heart into the streets as garbage for fools.'[58]

Tennyson himself had expressed feelings on the subject in stronger fashion, as was his wont. To the photographer Julia Cameron in 1860, he declared 'that every crime and every vice in the world were connected with the passion for autographs and anecdotes and records,—that the desiring anecdotes and acquaintance with the lives of great men was treating them like pigs to be ripped open for the public . . .'.[59]

A different stir arose in 1901 from Graham Balfour's *Life of Robert Louis Stevenson*. It was not the writing that caused the sensation so much as the review in the *Pall Mall Magazine* by Stevenson's embittered one-time intimate W. E. Henley. Henley, according to Bernard Shaw, was 'a tragic example of the combination of imposing powers of expression with nothing important to express';[60] but on this occasion Shaw was wrong, for Henley had plenty to unburden. He had been Stevenson's originally designated biographer, but that became impossible after 1887–8, when Henley alienated Stevenson by accusing his wife of plagiarizing another's work. The problem over the biography had not ended there, because doubts existed about Stevenson's next choice, Sidney Colvin. Colvin lacked the widow's blessing; nevertheless, so Edmund Gosse gossiped to Arthur Benson in 1895, 'Colvin comes posting to Gosse, to beg *him* not to take the position, because it ought to belong to him by rights. A piece of the grossest ill-taste. I had always thought Colvin refined, if stiff and feeble. But now I know that he is vulgar.'[61] Having finally secured the 'sacred command', Colvin made too slow progress. Part of his hesitation lay in deciding how much to disclose about Louis and Fanny Stevenson's premarital relationship when Fanny was not yet divorced from her first husband, and about Stevenson's relationship with Colvin's own future wife. Colvin's embarrassment was compounded when, while he procrastinated, Eve Blantyre Simpson, the sister of a student friend of Stevenson, published *Robert Louis Stevenson's Edinburgh Days*, which recounted his youthful excesses and which Fanny Stevenson denounced as 'most malicious'. Colvin, whose financial dependency on Stevenson deepened the murkiness, was induced to step down in 1899, not, however, without presenting a bill for time spent, to the tune of £483 6s. 8d., and publishing in that year a two-volume *Letters of Robert Louis Stevenson to his Family and Friends*;[62] whereupon the biography

---

[58] *The Times*, 4 Mar. 1913.   [59] Martin, *Tennyson*, 552.
[60] Quoted in Goldring, *South Lodge*, 223.   [61] Newsome, *Edge of Paradise*, 89.
[62] The *Letters* were reprinted twice in 1899, twice again in 1900, and entered a tenth edition in December 1911. Thomas Hardy found Stevenson's correspondence attractively lightweight: 'The very fact of his not being quite "Thorough", as a man & as an author (i.e. critic of life), makes the letters, perhaps,

was offered to Stevenson's cousin Graham Balfour. He, after an initial refusal, completed the task in 1901.[63] From the family's vantage point and that of many Stevenson fans, it was more than competently executed, Balfour (a lawyer) showing tact in all the right areas, indeed omitting all mention of the Stevensons' quarrel with Henley. Henley, however, was set on releasing the pent-up passion of thirteen years. The result was what Mrs Meynell dubbed his 'assassin article'. Entitled 'The Two Stevensons', it dwelt on the difference between 'the Stevenson who went to America in 87; and the Stevenson who never came back. The first I knew, and loved; the other I lost touch with, and, though I admired him, did not greatly esteem.' The targets of Henley's scorn were threefold: foremost, Fanny Stevenson, who had deprived him of his deepest friendship; secondly, Stevenson himself, who Henley believed had become disfigured by vanity and self-absorption; lastly, the doe-eyed public, who had been duped by the assiduously cultivated image of Stevenson as the 'Catechist of Vailima', 'this Seraph in Chocolate, this barley-sugar effigy of a real man'.[64] What Henley wrote publicly and vituperatively, Henry James expressed privately and politely to Graham Balfour. It was an impeccable Pontius Pilate performance by James, who had earlier wriggled out of an invitation from Fanny Stevenson to act as literary executor.[65] The biography, he felt, made Stevenson too '*personally* celebrated'; thus, from Stevenson's books 'a certain supremacy and mystery (above all) has, as it were, gone from them'. James acknowledged that Stevenson was in part responsible for manufacturing the exotic image which now preoccupied the public; but being a showman could not explain 'literary vision, the vision for which the rarest works pop out of the dusk of the inscrutable, the untracked'.[66] Subsequently, Walter Raleigh, who had known both Stevenson and Henley, endeavoured to umpire the feud when Henley was also dead:

Henley was a much richer, greater, more generous nature than R.L.S. And Henley violated all the proprieties, and spoke ill of his friend, and R.L.S. wrote nothing that was not seemly and edifying. So the public has its opinion and is wrong. You couldn't quarrel with Henley—not to last—because the minute you showed a touch of magnanimity or affection, he ran at you, and gave you everything and abased himself, like a child. But R.L.S. kept aloof for ten years and chose his ground with all a Pharisee's skill in selecting sites. He had not a good heart. He said many beautiful and true things, but he was not humble. There is nothing falser than the shop-window work called literature. R.L.S.'s sermons and prayers stick in my throat. It is no good calling them insincere, the worst of it is they are as sincere as possible, and quite unreal. His history, even as you can read it in his published letters, is another chapter in Shelley's 'Triumph of Life'. He was offered a

all the more pleasant reading' (Hardy to Florence Henniker, 17 Mar. 1903, in Purdy and Millgate (eds.), *Hardy Letters*, iii. 55).

[63] Mackay, *Violent Friend*, 169–76, 312–38; Hamilton, *Keepers of the Flame*, 197–209. The reviewer in *Punch*, 23 Oct. 1901, 296, gave a respectful notice, apparently swallowing the official line that Colvin abandoned the commission owing to 'ill health'.

[64] The review is extensively quoted in Connell, *Henley*, 365–8. For a rejoinder, see *Punch*, 4 Dec. 1901, 402.

[65] 26 Dec. 1894, in Edel (ed.), *James Letters*, iii. 497–501.   [66] Quoted in Edel, *James*, ii. 474.

little godship by a doting public, and he took it, and cut away all ties that might hamper him in his new profession. Henley didn't understand it, he thought it was a bad joke, or the tongue of slanderers or something, and he was puzzled and (ultimately) angry.[67]

This was a far cooler assessment of Stevenson than that which Raleigh had given in a memorial lecture to the Royal Institution in 1895, when in presenting the case for Stevenson's achievements as a writer he had included such statements as 'Stevenson himself was singularly free from the vanity of fame.'[68] The effect of Henley's spectacular performance was mostly to explode his own rather than Stevenson's reputation.[69] The Stevenson image was repolished regardless, with J. A. Hammerton's *Stevensoniana* (1910) and a special issue of *The Bookman* devoted to him in 1913.[70] It was, therefore, impossible to legislate for the loose cannon. Henley's action could not be blamed on the type of biography commissioned by Stevenson's family and literary executors: whether by Colvin, Balfour, or whom-ever, Henley was always lying in wait to take his revenge on his former friend. There remained for the likes of Watts-Dunton, who desired appropriate literary memorials for great authors, to recommend an exemplary model. This was the two-volume memoir of Tennyson, written by his son Hallam under the watchful eye of widow Tennyson, and dedicated to the Queen, in 1897. Reviewing it for the *Athenaeum*, Watts-Dunton pronounced Tennyson unusually fortunate, both in the years since his death as well as in his life's achievements:

Fortunate, indeed, is the famous man who escapes the catchpenny biographer. No man so illustrious as Tennyson ever before passed away without his death giving rise to a flood of books professing to tell the story of his life. Yet it chanced that for a long time before his death a monograph on Tennyson by Mr Arthur Waugh—which, though of course it is sometimes at fault, was carefully prepared and well considered—had been in preparation, as had also a second edition of another sketch of the poet's life by Mr Henry Jennings, written with equal reticence and judgement. These two books, coming out, as far as we remember, in the very week of Tennyson's funeral, did the good service of filling up the gap of five years until the appearance of this authorised biography by his son. Otherwise there is no knowing what pseudo-biographies stuffed with what errors and nonsense might have flooded the market and vexed the souls of Tennysonian students. For the future such pseudo-biographies will be impossible.[71]

---

[67] Quoted in Connell, *Henley*, 370.   [68] Raleigh, *Stevenson*, 10.

[69] Mostly, but not for everyone. Kipling wrote: 'Henley's demerits were, of course, explained to the world by his loving friends after his death. I had the fortune to know him only as kind, generous, and a jewel of an editor'—a reference to Henley's publication of Kipling's 'Cleared', his bitter indictment of the Gladstone Government's supposed whitewashing of the Parnellites' complicity in atrocities in Ireland, in the *Scots Observer*, on 8 March 1890, when other editors shied away. Henley's and Kipling's mutual admiration was based on 'an organic loathing of Mr. Gladstone and all Liberalism' (Kipling, *Something of Myself*, 50). In March 1903 a well-wisher gave a motor car to Henley, who was a cripple. Henley had little time to enjoy it: he died in June. See Hardy to Florence Henniker, 29 Mar. 1903; also to J. Nicol Dunn, 16 Feb. 1904, explaining why it would be inappropriate for him to contribute to a proposed memorial to Henley. Purdy and Millgate (eds.), *Hardy Letters*, iii. 57, 106–7.   [70] Terry, *Stevenson*, p. xxii.

[71] Watts-Dunton, *Old Familiar Faces*, 152–3. Also Hamilton, *Keepers of the Flame*, 177–83. Hallam, as Lord Tennyson, served as Governor-General of Australia, 1902–4; in 1908 he published the Eversley Edition of his father's work. He also served as President of the Royal Literary Fund, which allocated pensions

Hallam Tennyson's was indeed the classic Life, according to the Watts-Dunton prescription: it involved systematic 'scrubbing' of Tennyson's past 'to remove all traces of the rough Lincolnshire poet with his black blood, his inability to keep his friendships cultivated, his reluctance to marry, his occasional obscenity and bad language, his terrible fits of depression, his obsessive fear of poverty, and his slowness to assume the responsibilities of maturity'.[72] The call had been sent out for Tennyson's letters to be returned and, when Hallam had selected what he thought useful to tint the image of hieratic poet, some 30,000 of the 40,000 letters were destroyed.[73]

Not always having a dependable filial hagiographer, several authors seized the initiative by writing autobiographies or keeping journals for publication. Certainly the public liked to devour these, but on occasion its appetite was whetted for nothing. 'I see in the papers that I am writing an autobiography,' 74-year-old George Meredith remarked in 1901; 'I would as soon think of composing a treatise on the origin of Humpty-Dumpty.'[74] On the other hand, George Moore was quick to demonstrate that mature years and realized achievement were not prerequisites for autobiography. Moore issued his first, *Confessions of a Young Man* (1888), while in his thirties. 'Interesting but disgusting', was George Gissing's mirthless reaction.[75] *Memoirs of my Dead Life*[76] followed in 1906 as an hors d'oeuvre to Moore's scandalous *Hail and Farewell* trilogy of 1911–14; and he resumed his intellectual striptease after the war with *Conversations in Ebury Street* (1924), in which he belittled the reputations of rival performers in literary art, Joseph Conrad, Henry James, and Thomas Hardy.[77] Moore's title as original callow autobiographer was snatched in 1926 by Beverley Nichols, who opened his with the proclamation, 'Twenty-five seems to me the latest age at which anybody should write an autobiography.' When he reached 'the decrepitude of thirty', he planned to write another, to be called 'Making the Most of Twenty-Eight'.[78] Perhaps he had in mind Bruce Cummings, who, under the pen-name W. N. P. Barbellion and at the age of 30 in 1919, issued his *Journal of a Disappointed Man* based on diaries he had kept since he was 13.[79]

and aid to impecunious authors and their families. On Hallam Tennyson (1852–1928): *Who Was Who, 1916–1928*, 1030.

[72] Martin, *Tennyson*, 553.   [73] Ibid. 583.

[74] Meredith to Lady Ulrica Duncombe, 23 Dec. 1901, in Cline (ed.), *Meredith's Letters*, iii. 1411.

[75] Coustillas (ed.), *Gissing's Diary*, 27 (25 Apr. 1888).

[76] Parodied in *Punch*, 5 Sept. 1906, as *Prattle of my Dead Past*. Max Beerbohm also parodied Moore in 1906, in the *Saturday Review*, reissuing it in 1912 in *Christmas Garland*, 177–85.

[77] Hardy was the only one of this trio then still living. For his hurt, see Florence Hardy to John Middleton Murry, 30 Mar. 1924, in Millgate (ed.), *Emma and Florence Hardy*, 207.

[78] Beverley Nichols, *Twenty-Five: Being a Young Man's Candid Recollections of his Elders and Betters* (1930), 9–10.

[79] Cummings was an assistant at the British Museum. More extracts from his journal, as well as reprinted articles, were published in W. N. P. Barbellion, *Enjoying Life and Other Literary Remains* (1919). One of these pieces examined 'The Passion for Perpetuation'. There (p. 104), *inter alia*, he poked fun at Moore: 'When his youth died, wrote George Moore about his "Confessions of a Young Man", the soul of

Where narcissism did not come naturally, publishers could always be found to encourage it. When the author–illustrator W. Graham Robertson was 29 or 30—this would be in 1896—he sought to interest a publisher in a picture book. The publisher rebuffed him by singing from the standard 'No demand for that sort of thing' hymn sheet. But, he added brightly, 'if you would write your Reminiscences for me—'. Robertson protested. He was so young and had earned no distinction, though in due course he would find celebrity as an authority both on William Blake and on bob-tailed Old English sheepdogs and as a designer for the Edwardian stage hit *Pinkie and the Fairies* (1908). Still, it was not Robertson's actual or potential achievement that attracted the publisher: 'No,' said he, 'but you have known a great many Distinguished People,' Robertson enjoying friendship or acquaintance with Rossetti and Burne-Jones, Henry Irving and Ellen Terry, and many others.[80] It was the same for Virginia Stephen. She was aged 25 when, dining out in Chelsea in 1907, she was advised to launch her memoirs. A fellow guest understood that she was the daughter of the late Sir Leslie Stephen, who had been close to Thackeray, George Eliot, George Meredith, and a host of other eminences. Their conversation ran:

'In the course of your life Miss Stephen, you must have known many distinguished people. [Robert Louis] Stevenson, I suppose?' Yes and George Eliot, and Tennyson before he grew a beard I said. But the astonishing thing is that these great people always talked much as you and I talk; Tennyson, for instance, would say to me, 'Pass the salt' or 'Thank you for the butter'. 'Ah indeed; you should write your memoirs; one gets paid for that kind of thing', he said; being a dealer in pictures.[81]

Virginia Stephen was pulling his leg—George Eliot, for instance, had been dead thirteen months before she was born—but, in time, she would act differently. As the author Virginia Woolf, she and the Bloomsbury Group, to which she belonged, would hold the twentieth-century record for incestuous memoir-writing and letter- and diary-keeping. Such publications always appealed to some writers as a kind of insurance or second chance, in case their own creative output was insufficiently strong to secure lasting recognition. It had even been remarked about Robert Louis Stevenson that 'he may live by his letters when nearly all the rest of his work is forgotten'.[82]

As for the journal method, that had been raised to a high level of indiscretion by the Goncourt brothers in France, a practice that Arnold Bennett then

---

the ancient Egyptians awoke in him. He had the idea of conserving his dead past in a work of art, embalming it with pious care in a memorial, he hoped, as durable as the pyramids of Rameses II! Poor George Moore!' When *Journal of a Disappointed Man* was first published, with an introduction by H. G. Wells, some supposed it was a work of fiction by Wells himself.

[80] W. Graham Robertson, *Time Was* (1955), p. vii.

[81] Letter to Violet Dickinson, 20 July 1907, in Nicolson and Banks (eds.), *Flight of the Mind*, 300.

[82] Nicoll, *Bookman's Letters*, 97. This view was attributed to a 'Dr. Dawson'—perhaps W. J. Dawson (1854–1928), a Methodist minister who was well known as a writer and lecturer on literature as well as on theological subjects.

comprehensively followed.[83] Bennett's journal stretched to over a million words. His publisher Newman Flower cut it to 400,000 words, in three volumes: 'if the diaries had been published as they stood Cassells would have sold a quarter of a million copies, and then gone into bankruptcy as the result of the libel actions. Careful as I was, Cassells had one action over them, and lost it.'[84] Inevitably, the biter was sometimes bit. Will Rothenstein was amused to hear Edmond de Goncourt complain that when George Moore dined with the brothers he took notes on his shirt-cuff.[85] Inevitably, too, there was disingenuousness. Thomas Hardy declared piously, in recollecting his encounter with George Meredith in 1869 when Meredith was publisher's reader for Chapman & Hall: 'Unfortunately I made no notes of our conversation: in those days people did not usually write down everything as they do now for the concoction of reminiscences'.[86] Instead, Hardy hid behind his wife's petticoats in issuing his autobiography, which was published posthumously as if it were her biography of him. Notebooks and correspondence, on which it was based, were destroyed along the way.[87]

Hardy had approved when his friend Edmund Gosse published, anonymously (though his authorship was widely known), an autobiography of his unusual childhood, *Father and Son* (1907). Hardy allowed that the intrinsic interest of those experiences was reason enough for Gosse to write; but he speculated whether even

such a clear statement would prevent misrepresentation when you would be no longer able to correct it. It has become a serious question what people ought to do now-a-days in respect of the flood of fictitious gossip that gets into the snippety press about them. I myself, who lead such an obscure private life, have been compelled often to put into handbooks *etc.*, personal details that I detest printing, solely to give this gossip the lie.[88]

Such pre-emptive action was squarely in the tradition of Tennyson, who, a quarter-century before his son produced the definitive official biography, invited Thackeray's daughter, who had known and idolized him for twenty years, to write about him for *Harper's Magazine* in 1882. In their conversations he divulged all sorts of supposed 'confidences' about his past—his struggles against poverty,

---

[83] A two-volume selection from the journal and correspondence of the Goncourt brothers was translated and edited by Marie Belloc and Marie Shedlock and published by Heinemann in 1894. The edition was not large, recalled Marie Belloc, and it soon disappeared. She was paid a paltry £40: on this, and her recollection of Edmond de Goncourt, who spoke of his fellow writers 'sometimes... with contempt, and always with malice [and]... was the only snobbish Frenchman I have ever known', see Lowndes, *Love and Friendship*, 150–3.   [84] Flower, *Just as it Happened*, 167.

[85] Rothenstein, *Men and Memories, 1872–1900*, 162.

[86] Sassoon, *Meredith*, 70; and, for the making of the two-volume Life of Hardy, see Millgate *Hardy*, 516–19, and Hamilton, *Keepers of the Flame*, 241–50. It was not financially rewarding for Hardy's widow; see Millgate (ed.), *Emma and Florence Hardy*, 305, 321.

[87] Florence Hardy to Sydney Cockerell, 7 Feb. 1918 and 30 Jan. 1919, in Millgate (ed.), *Emma and Florence Hardy*, 139, 155.

[88] Hardy to Edmund Gosse, 3 Nov. 1907, in Purdy and Millgate (eds.), *Hardy Letters*, iii. 282.

loneliness, self-doubt, and critical rejection, and the inspiration he gained from landscape and from the belief in his poetic gift held by his friends, who included Thackeray. The manuscript of the article was submitted to Tennyson for alteration before forwarding to *Harper's*; but he was thoroughly satisfied and did not amend it.[89]

[89] The article was reprinted in book form, together with Anne Thackeray Ritchie's memoirs of Ruskin and the Brownings, following Tennyson's death in 1892; Gérin, *Ritchie*, 222-4. Tennyson's son Lionel had been best man at Anne Thackeray's marriage to her cousin Richmond Ritchie in 1877. See also Martin, *Tennyson*, 446–8.

12

Titles and Laurels

KING [OF UTOPIA]. Our Peerage we've remodelled on an intellectual basis,
    Which certainly is rough on our hereditary races—
CHORUS. We are going to remodel it in England
KING. The Brewers and the Cotton Lords no longer seek admission,
    And Literary Merit meets with proper recognition—
CHORUS. As Literary Merit does in England!
KING. Who knows but we may count among our intellectual chickens,
    Like you, an Earl of Thackeray and p'r'aps a Duke of Dickens—

      (W. S. Gilbert, *Utopia Limited; or, The Flowers of Progress* (1893))

I

Though he grumbled about press attention ('Most of the things said of me in the papers are lies, lies, lies'), Tennyson was gratified on 6 August 1889 by eightieth-birthday tributes from fellow authors, led by Browning, Swinburne, Alfred Austin, Lewis Morris, and Theodore Watts-Dunton. Tennyson's son recollected: 'By his side in the study he kept a big box full of congratulatory letters and telegrams, into which he dived at intervals while he was smoking; and on his table was a splendid bouquet of eighty roses from Princess Frederica.'[1] Here was Lord Tennyson—the first author ennobled solely for services to literature. Macaulay and Lytton, the two previous authors made peers, had been active politicians. Tennyson was offered a baronetcy four times: in 1865 by Palmerston, in 1873 by Gladstone, in 1874 by Disraeli, and in 1880 by Gladstone again. As each was refused, it appeared plain that Tennyson was angling for a peerage and plainer still when he and Gladstone went cruising to Scandinavia in September 1883 aboard the brand new *Pembroke Castle*, both guests of the shipping magnate, philanthropist, and Liberal MP Sir Donald Currie.[2] Gladstone held a lofty view of the status of poet compared with politician, and a particularly lofty view of Tennyson:

Tennyson's life and labour correspond in point of time as nearly as possible to my own; but he has worked in a higher field, and his work will be more durable. We public men

---

[1] Tennyson, *Tennyson*, 720.
[2] Martin, *Tennyson*, 463, 501, 528–9, 541–2; Masterman (ed.), *Mary Gladstone*, 294.

play a part which places us much in view of our countrymen, but the words which we speak have wings and fly away and disappear ... [whereas] the Poet Laureate has written his own song on the hearts of his countrymen that can never die.[3]

Tennyson, for his part, had even hoped that their two families would be joined. This was dashed in 1879 when Mary, Gladstone's daughter, rejected the courtship of Hallam, Tennyson's son.[4] Matters had not been helped by Tennyson himself making clumsy advances on Mary, 'harping on my eyes' (which he compared to Carlyle's), brushing her cheek, stroking her 'petit nez retroussé' and, after a reading from *The Princess* (1847), '*He kissed me.*' She took refuge at the piano, 'and played and played with my heart in my mouth'.[5]

Promotion to the peerage had raised two practical questions: about Tennyson's financial sufficiency, and about his politics. There was no cause to worry on the first score, except that Tennyson's obsessiveness about money (and receipt of a state pension of £200 annually since 1845) made it seem that he might be short of it. Gladstone's secretary's enquiry put Tennyson's income at £5,000 (£3,000 from investments) in 1883.[6] Almost as this assessment was made, it needed upward revision, because Tennyson was signing a lucrative contract with Macmillan's.[7] According to his grandson, Tennyson several times made over £10,000 a year from royalties.[8] Publishers were apt to make fools of themselves in their eagerness to secure him for their lists. Having fallen out with Moxon & Co., his publisher since 1832, Tennyson was tempted to Strahan's in 1868 by a five-year contract so lavish that it proved disastrous for the firm: £4,000 per year for the right to publish old works and, with respect to new, Tennyson would pay all expenses in return for all profits, minus a mere 5 per cent commission for Strahan. The contract also allowed Tennyson to veto 'distasteful' advertisements. Tennyson himself was staggered by its liberality.[9] At his death he would leave an estate of over £57,000—about £3 million in today's money—but he was determined not to spend a farthing when he could get others to pick up the bill. He accepted the peerage on condition that the State waive the fees involved, as if he were a military veteran on half-pay.[10]

There was more concern about the second matter, Tennyson's politics. Though personally fond of Gladstone, Tennyson was increasingly critical of his policies, regarding foreign affairs, empire, the armed services, parliamentary reform, and Ireland.[11] When the Duke of Argyll—also disenchanted by

---

[3] Morley, *Gladstone*, ii. 358.   [4] Ann Thwaite, *Emily Tennyson: The Poet's Wife* (1996), 540–2.
[5] Masterman (ed.), *Mary Gladstone*, 158–61 (5–9 June 1879).
[6] Sir Edward Hamilton's diary, 26 Sept. 1883, in Lang and Shannon (eds.), *Tennyson's Letters*, iii. 264.
[7] Martin, *Tennyson*, 549, says that this ten-year contract, which Tennyson signed on 15 January 1884, 'gave him a third of the advertised price of all books sold, with a minimum guarantee of £1,500 annually'. Morgan, *Macmillan*, 173–4, states that £4,000 p.a. was 'always comfortably exceeded'.
[8] Sir Charles Tennyson, *Stars and Markets* (1957), 12.
[9] Patricia Thomas Srebrnik, *Alexander Strahan, Victorian Publisher* (Ann Arbor, 1986), 100–7.
[10] Martin, *Tennyson*, 542–3, 578.
[11] Morley, *Gladstone*, ii. 148, 372, 787–8; Rawnsley, *Memories of the Tennysons*, 103–4.

Gladstone's Irish policies—visited Farringford, Tennyson read his *Ode on the Death of the Duke of Wellington* (1852), and at the lines

> Who never sold the truth to serve the hour,
> Nor paltered with eternal God of power,

Tennyson muttered, 'As I am afraid Gladstone is doing now'.[12] Tennyson revelled in a reputation for downrightness. The views which he ventilated in private were the opposite of statesmanlike. He growled to Arthur Lee in 1890: 'If there are any people I hate in this world they are the French and the Russians . . . I hate all humbug as heartily as the Duke of Wellington did and he hated the French too.' Though he admired the House of Lords as an institution and believed in the hereditary principle (for good and ill), he told Lee, 'They made me a Peer too late; if I had been one 30 years ago I might have done something in the House, but now I am too old.'[13]

It was true that Tennyson showed some failing power. Gladstone late one night converted him to Home Rule. By breakfast, he had recovered his senses: 'I never said anything half bad enough of that damned old rascal.'[14] He took his seat in the Lords on the cross benches, an assertion of his independence of party and particularly of Gladstone, so that he was 'free to vote for that which to himself seemed best for the Empire'.[15] But Tennyson never spoke in the House, seldom attended, and embarrassingly acted as agent for the Queen in 1885 by putting her (improper) suggestion to Gladstone that he might wish to retire. For all that, Tennyson delighted in the elevation. He was prepared to shoulder the burdens involved: 'My sisters say I shall have to pay more for my wine.' His ambition was to be dubbed Lord d'Eyncourt, as one in the eye for the family of his crazy and snobbish uncle who changed their name to Tennyson d'Eyncourt. In the end he was persuaded to opt for Baron Tennyson of Aldworth and Freshwater (the location of his two homes), and to declare that he accepted the promotion only as an honour for Literature: 'By Gladstone's advice I have consented to take the peerage, but for my own part I shall regret my simple name all my life.'[16] No mention here of the desire to secure public promotion for his son Hallam, which all along was a leading element in Tennyson's calculations.[17]

The world did not greet Tennyson's peerage as he supposed. *The Spectator* remarked: 'The news has been received with universal and, we think, legitimate depression.'[18] But *The Spectator*'s affected despondency was just another way of extolling Literature, as something supernal that could only be degraded by secular recognition. Honours had garlanded literary men before; Walter Scott accepting

---

[12] Grant Duff, *Diary, 1896 to 1901*, i. 20 (18 Feb. 1896).   [13] Clark (ed.), *Lee*, 44, 47.
[14] Martin, *Tennyson*, 575.   [15] Tennyson's wife's journal, in Martin, *Tennyson*, 546.
[16] Martin, *Tennyson*, 542–4.
[17] Thwaite, *Emily Tennyson*, 547. Hallam, as second Baron Tennyson, became Governor of South Australia, 1899–1902, then Governor-General of Australia, 1902–4.
[18] *The Spectator*, 15 Dec. 1883. Also Lang and Shannon (eds.), *Tennyson's Letters*, iii. 472, for press opinion.

a baronetcy, for example. They were also rejected. Robert Southey declined a baronetcy. So, more recently, had Carlyle. This was in 1874, when Disraeli offered him the choice of a baronetcy or, because he was poor and childless and therefore might not appreciate hereditary honours, the GCB and a pension. Carlyle refused both, though moved by Disraeli's magnanimity, Disraeli being 'the only man I almost never spoke of except with contempt'. It was Lord (more likely, Lady) Derby who conceived the idea, which was then pressed on Disraeli with the recommendation that Carlyle was 'for whatever reason, most vehement against Gladstone . . . Anything that could be done for him would be a really good political investment.'[19] That politicians were now calculating the premium to be won for themselves by patronizing authors marked a change from past form. The Duke of Somerset told the Earl of Kimberley that he once asked Lord Melbourne (Prime Minister, 1835–41) 'to give some assistance to Carlyle who was then in very poor circumstances. Who is he? Said Lord M. A very original writer was the answer. "D–mn your original writers," replied Lord M. "I hate them." '[20] Carlyle was not seduced by Disraeli's offer; he did, however, accept the Prussian Order of Merit, ostensibly because it was solely for merit and not embroiled with social class hierarchy, though he told his brother that 'Had they sent me ¼lb of good tobacco, the addition to my happiness had probably been suitabler and greater!'[21]

Following Tennyson's elevation, no more peerages went to literary men, though this level of recognition was advocated by Walter Besant on behalf of the Society of Authors.[22] Gladstone briefly weighed Ruskin's qualifications for a peerage in 1893, but Ruskin's mental instability made it impossible to think of him taking a seat in the Lords. Moreover, now unproductive, Ruskin was 'not like Tennyson known to a wide public', commented a dismissive Gladstone, who was not prepared to go beyond considering a Civil List pension. Ruskin himself remained clear enough in mind to feel slighted. Sir Henry Acland reported in 1897 how Ruskin was 'much disappointed that he had had *no* public recognition at the Jubilee';[23] and Acland sought to revive the question of a peerage. Walter Besant meanwhile persisted in pressing authors' claims to honours. At the very least, he thought, they merited knighthoods, such as were all too readily bestowed on provincial mayors; and 'he was impatient to see how little progress this idea made' before his death in 1901.[24] The threshold was increasingly crossed, however. Starting with Besant himself and Lewis Morris (1895), knighthoods or baronetcies were bestowed on Gilbert Parker and Conan Doyle (1902), W. S. Gilbert (1907), Arthur Pinero (1909), Arthur Quiller-Couch (1910), Rider Haggard (1912),

[19] Froude, *Carlyle, 1834–1881*, ii. 458–64; W. F. Monypenny and G. E. Buckle, *The Life of Benjamin Disraeli, Earl of Beaconsfield* (1910–20), v. 355–68.

[20] Hawkins and Powell (eds.), *Kimberley Journal*, 279 (28 June 1873).

[21] Letter to John Carlyle, 14 Feb. 1874, quoted in James Walton (ed.), *The Faber Book of Smoking* (2000), 191. [22] *Review of Reviews*, (Jan. 1892), 79; (Sept. 1892), 258.

[23] Gladstone to Sir Henry Acland, 15 Aug. 1893, and Acland to Gladstone, 13 Aug. 1897, in Matthew (ed.), *Gladstone Diaries*, xiii. 279. [24] Nicoll, *Bookman's Letters*, 149.

J. M. Barrie (1913), Henry Newbolt (1915), William Watson (1917), and Anthony Hope (Hawkins) and Hall Caine (1918). The first two editors of the *Dictionary of National Biography*, Leslie Stephen and Sidney Lee, were knighted too, in 1902 and 1911 respectively, counterbalanced by knighthoods for successive editors of *Punch*, Francis Burnand and Owen Seaman, in 1902 and 1914. The definition of Literature was stretched further by Walter Raleigh's knighthood in 1911. This affirmed the rising status of academic lit. crit., which the recipient himself was disposed to call 'parasitic'. According to Desmond MacCarthy, 'the "cultivation" of taste, indeed the whole business of making a cult of literature, seemed silly to him'.[25]

There was no gong for Tennyson's successor as Poet Laureate, Alfred Austin. He confided in Wilfrid Meynell, who in turn told Wilfrid Blunt, in 1908 that 'he has been sounded as to his willingness to be given a title (we suppose a knighthood), but that he has answered that the only title he aspires to is "one that would give him the right to address his peers in parliament". He may whistle for that,' commented Blunt.[26] Austin's own successor, Robert Bridges, accepted the laureateship only on condition that 'there must be no damned nonsense of knighthoods or anything of that kind'.[27] Thomas Hardy also refused a knighthood, to Emma's dismay in 1908; but, like Bridges, he accepted the Order of Merit.[28] Hardy was listed as a possible peer, sympathetic to the Liberal interest,[29] during the Parliament crisis in 1911, along with J. M. Barrie, Anthony Hope, R. C. Lehmann, and Robertson Nicoll.[30] Barrie had turned down a knighthood, almost

[25] MacCarthy, *Portraits*, i. 209, 217.   [26] Blunt, *Diaries*, ii. 214 (27 Sept. 1908).

[27] Thompson, *Bridges*, 83.

[28] Hardy to H. H. Asquith, 5 Nov. 1908, in Purdy and Millgate (eds.), *Hardy Letters*, iii. 353. Hardy was nominated for the Order of Merit by the Prime Minister, Asquith, who prevailed against the opposition of that *éminence grise*, Viscount Esher. The vacancy occurred in 1909 on the death of Meredith who had been awarded the OM in March 1905. Esher's thoughts first focused on the question in 1908 when Meredith was in a coma and not expected to survive. Writing to the Duchess of Sutherland, Esher lamented the contemporary 'eclipse of all high literary ideal, and the poverty of writers both in verse and prose', compared with the richness of the 19th century. Believing that 'high literature and high endeavour went hand in hand', he feared for Britain's ability to face off competition from Germany when, 'except for John Morley, the last of the Titans, there is hardly a writer alive . . . who is above mediocrity'. In 1909 Esher wrote a memorandum for the King opposing the OM for Hardy. His journal summarized the case: 'Hardy's best work is the *Dynasts*, which nobody reads. His realistic novels are not of the highest calibre. Kipling's service to the Empire entitles him to a preference. But I suggested James Bryce as a writer much more in the "grand style", if the Order is to be given at all' (Brett, *Esher*, ii. 331, 388–9). The OM was a highly coveted order, invented by Edward VII to mark his coronation in 1902 and restricted originally to twelve members who had given distinguished military and naval service or who were eminent in arts, letters and science. In 1907 a further category, of high public service, was added, leading to the appointments of Lord Cromer, the retired Consul-General in Egypt, and Florence Nightingale, the heroine of the Crimea, then aged 87 and the first woman member of the Order. See *The Times*, 30 Nov. 1907.

[29] Hardy was generally Liberal in sympathy, though he had reservations about major articles of Liberal policy such as Home Rule: interview with Hardy in 1906, in Nevinson, *More Changes*, 180.

[30] Millgate, *Hardy*, 470–1; list of potential peers in J. A. Spender and Cyril Asquith, *Life of Herbert Henry Asquith, Lord Oxford and Asquith* (1932), i. 329–31. Lehmann was well known as a comic writer for *Punch*; but it was his politics that mattered more in this connection. He was, briefly, editor of the *Daily News* and a Liberal MP, 1906–10. Robertson Nicoll's inclusion also should be attributed to his Liberal politics, influencing the Nonconformist vote, more than to his literary quality. He had been knighted for political services in 1909. By contrast, Hilaire Belloc, who was a Liberal MP, was not listed. His maverick views

proudly so, in 1909; and in *The Twelve-Pound Look* (1910) he mocked the vanity that made people crave these things. In the play, fat Harry Sims, worth £¼ million and greedy of doubling it, is at home with his wife, trying on the robes to be worn when he will receive his knighthood. They practise the motions. Harry waddles up to his wife, who, 'going on one knee, raises her hand superbly to his lips. She taps him on the shoulder with a paper-knife and says huskily, "Rise, Sir Harry". He rises, bows, and glides about the room, going on his knees to various articles of furniture, and rising from each knight.' An agency typist is summoned, to prepare 'hundreds' of replies to the congratulations they expect—along the lines of: Harry is 'an exceptional case. He did not try to get this honour in any way. It was a complete surprise to him...is not a man who cares for honours...would have asked to be allowed to decline had it not been that I want to please my wife', etc., etc.[31] In 1913, presumably having thought things through, Barrie accepted a baronetcy.[32] Since he was not only divorced but impotent, the chances of his gratifying a wife by fathering an heir were slim. However, A. E. W. Mason refused a knighthood for one such reason: 'honours mean nothing to a childless man'.[33]

Knighthoods were further refused by W. B. Yeats and John Galsworthy, in 1915 and 1918 respectively, and by Arnold Bennett and H. G. Wells, both in 1919.[34] Their abstemiousness appears all the more remarkable given Asquith's recollection of the general clamour for gongs he encountered as Prime Minister—a 'voracity for honours, so widespread and so shameless as to be incredible for anyone who has not been at the fonthead'.[35] There was piquancy about the invitation to Bennett. Only a year before, in *The Title*, he too had poked fun at the system. 'Examine the Honours List', says Culver, 'and you can instantly tell how the Government feels in its inside. When the Honours List is full of rascals, millionaires, and—er—chumps, you may be quite sure that the Government is dangerously ill.' And Tranto adds, 'Literature's always a good card to play for Honours. It makes people think that Cabinet Ministers are educated.'[36] Bennett's view was that 'there are only two decorations free from some kind of stain of undeservingness. One is the O.M. and the other is the V.C. And I have doubts about even the O.M.'[37] George Moore did not. He told his secretary that he had been 'approached unofficially on several occasions regarding a knighthood... [but] that the only decoration he would accept was the O.M.'[38] Moore liked to

and hostility to the Servile State probably account for this omission, though when he and his wife dined with Wilfrid Blunt during the constitutional crisis, 'he expects a great creation of peers, hoping he himself may be one' (Blunt, *Diaries*, 284 (5 Dec. 1909)).

[31] Barrie, *Plays*, 719–23.   [32] Dunbar, *Barrie*, 174, 201. The OM followed in 1922.
[33] *DNB 1941–1950*, 580.
[34] W. B. Yeats to Lily Yeats, 10 Dec. 1915, in Wade (ed.), *Yeats Letters*, 604; Galsworthy to Lloyd George, 1 Jan. 1918, in H. V. Marrot, *The Life and Letters of John Galsworthy* (1935), 437; Margaret Drabble, *Arnold Bennett* (1975), 238.   [35] Quoted in J. W. Robertson Scott, *'We' and Me* (1956), 46.
[36] Arnold Bennett, *The Title* (1918), 41, 131. The play opened at the Royalty Theatre, 20 July 1918, and ran for 285 performances: Flower (ed.), *Bennett Journals*, ii. 248 (27 Mar. 1919).
[37] Bennett, *Journal 1929*, 153 (13 Nov. 1929).   [38] Scott, *'We' and Me*, 28 n. 1.

impress the ladies; but whatever the truth about the knighthoods, he was never offered the OM.

Literary merit was not the only or overriding consideration in the awards that were made. In Besant's case, it was not his initiative in establishing the Society of Authors (1884), to promote copyright reform and writers' interests, that was being recognized, or his general prowess as novelist and historian of London. Rather, according to Lord Rosebery, who as Prime Minister was the source, the knighthood saluted Besant's part in founding the People's Palace in East London.[39] Besant acquiesced but would have preferred a citation that recognized his services to Literature. The irony was still more marked for Richard Burton, whose knighthood arrived in 1886. This was compensation for a lifetime's failure to secure the kind of posting he wanted in the consular service, and it came just when he was emerging into his own as an erudite pornographer with the serial issue (for private subscribers) of the *Thousand Nights and a Night*.[40] And Conan Doyle's knighthood in 1902 did not reward the creator of Sherlock Holmes and Brigadier Gerard so much as the apologist of British action in South Africa.[41] *The Great Boer War* was first issued in 1900, then regularly updated by Doyle in the sixteen editions that followed before the war's end.[42] The Colonial Secretary, Joseph Chamberlain, was the prime mover both of the war and of Doyle's knighthood.[43] Likewise, Lewis Morris and Quiller-Couch, those tireless workers for the Liberal Party and educational progress in, respectively, Wales and Cornwall, were honoured in preference to Morris the poet and Quiller-Couch the anthologist and author of historical romances.[44] It was the same for Rider Haggard, whose knighthood came as reward for public work; Newbolt also was a public servant as well as poet, and Parker was a Conservative MP as well as novelist. Both Anthony Hope and Hall Caine were knighted in 1918 for propaganda services in the war;[45] it was the CH that followed for Caine in 1922 that marked his contribution to literature. Altogether, then, fewer authors *qua* authors gained titles than did, for example, publishers or newspaper editors

---

[39] Lord Rosebery, 'London', 7 Dec. 1896, in Geake (ed.), *Appreciations*, 123–4.

[40] Burton's wife—an Arundell, tracing an ancestry back to Elizabethan recusants—was a persistent lobbyist for the knighthood; Farwell, *Burton*, 318, 384.

[41] Foreign monarchs were less shy about recognizing Conan Doyle's contribution to literature: an honorary Italian knighthood in 1898, and an award from the Sultan of Turkey in 1907; Booth, *Conan Doyle*, 217, 285.

[42] The war, he argued, was 'not only just but essential'. The Empire emerged stronger, sealed in 'blood brotherhood' as colonial volunteers fought side by side with British Army regulars; and for South Africa itself, the 'British flag under our best administrators will mean clean government, honest laws, liberty and equality to all men' (Arthur Conan Doyle, *The Great Boer War* (1902), 741–3). See *Punch*, 15 Jan. 1902, 44–5, for praise of the 13th edition.

[43] Booth, *Conan Doyle*, 256. Conan Doyle hesitated about accepting; ibid. 241.

[44] Quiller-Couch became Professor of English Literature at Cambridge in 1912 but seemed more gratified by his position at Fowey, Cornwall—Troy in his novels—where he lived from 1892. There he was 'quite a little potentate', observed Arthur Benson: landowner, Chairman of the Harbour Commission, and Commodore of the Yacht Club. 'One felt that Q is slightly ashamed of literature, and proud of local influence and county prominence' (Newsome, *Edge of Paradise*, 358).

[45] Mallet, *Hope*, 233–5; Allen, *Caine*, 367, 395.

and proprietors,[46] although some individuals occupied more than one category. Thus Francis Burnand, knighted in 1902, was both a long-standing editor of *Punch* (1880–1906) and a comic playwright with over 100 titles to his name. This elevation did not deter *Punch* in 1904, from concocting a spoof debate on the subject 'Should Novelists Accept Decorations?' in which celebrity authors' vanities were mocked and the proposal was made that new orders be established: the 'C.F.P. (Commander of the Fountain Pen); E.T.T. (Employer of a Thousand Typists); I.F.A. (Inspirer of the Fulsome Ad.)'.[47]

Actors and play producers as well as authors were now being accorded recognition too. Theatre stardom was as old as the stage itself, but a new phenomenon was apparent: that transition in status of actors from the 'brass-bowelled barnstormers' (Bernard Shaw's phrase) of the Georgian and early Victorian period to the Establishment knights and dames of the modern entertainments industry. Following Henry Irving's elevation in 1895, knighthoods regularly lapped over the stage: Squire Bancroft (1897), Charles Wyndham (1902), John Hare (1907), Beerbohm Tree (1909), George Alexander (1911), Johnston Forbes-Robertson (1913), Frank Benson (1916). Shaw again coined the right phrase to describe it—'the tofffication period'. He was upset that more actors and managers than dramatists were honoured.[48] Beerbohm Tree's gong came after energetic lobbying from the Duchess of Rutland and Viscount Esher, and from W. T. Stead and Mrs Tree. Having a German parentage and education, Tree received an order from the Kaiser prior to his knighthood. Tree was part of what Sidney Lee called Edward VII's 'histrionic circle'; like Bancroft, he made for Homburg or Marienbad when Edward happened to be visiting these spas.[49] Tree also mixed socially with the Asquiths, no disadvantage at the final count. Previously, when introduced to Gladstone in 1889, Tree was asked about actors' politics. Solidly Conservative, said Tree. Deplorable, said Gladstone; whereupon,

---

[46] Among the press honorands were: Algernon Borthwick, proprietor of the *Morning Post* (knighted 1880, baronetcy 1887, peerage as Lord Glenesk 1895); George Armstrong, proprietor of the *Globe* and *The People* (baronet 1892); H. H. Gibbs, founder of the *St James's Gazette* (peerage as Lord Aldenham, 1896); Edward Levy Lawson, proprietor of *Daily Telegraph* (baronetcy 1892, peerage as Lord Burnham 1903); John Robinson, manager of the *Daily News* (knighted 1893); Thomas Wemyss Reid, editor of *Leeds Mercury* and *Speaker* and manager of Cassell's (knighted 1894); W. H. Russell, the *Times*'s war correspondent (knighted 1895); George Newnes, founder of *Tit-Bits*, *Strand Magazine*, and *Westminster Gazette* (baronet 1895); E. T. Cook, editor of *Pall Mall Gazette, Westminster Gazette*, and *Daily News* and of Ruskin's *Works* (knighted 1912); Alfred Harmsworth, proprietor of the *Daily Mail* and *The Times* (knighted 1903, baronetcy 1904, and peerage as Lord Northcliffe 1905); Arthur Pearson, founder of *Daily Express* (baronet 1916).

[47] *Punch*, 3 Feb. 1904, 78. The authors parodied were: Anthony Hope, Conan Doyle, Gilbert Parker, William Le Queux, A. E. W. Mason, Guy Boothby, Henry Harland, Kipling, Henry James, Hall Caine, and Marie Corelli.

[48] Shaw to William Archer, 7 Sept. 1903. Hence, Shaw lobbied Lord Esher and Margot Asquith for Pinero's knighthood, which came in 1909; Laurence (ed.), *Shaw's Letters*, 365, 801, 843, and James Lees-Milne, *The Enigmatic Edwardian: The Life of Reginald, 2nd Viscount Esher* (1988), 174–5.

[49] Sir Sidney Lee, *King Edward VII* (1925), i. 570–2. When Edward, as Prince of Wales, celebrated his fiftieth birthday in 1891, 'a body of actors and theatre managers' presented him with 'an eighteen-carat gold cigar box, weighing a hundred ounces, on which his plumes and feathers were picked out in diamonds of the first water' (Magnus, *Edward VII*, 293). Edward's primary interest in the stage was in bedding actresses.

Tree added, 'But the scene-shifters are radical to a man.'[50] Painters were on the rise too: it was during Gladstone's first premiership that artists began to be invited to State banquets.[51] They were also being dubbed with increasing regularity. John Millais (baronet, 1885) was the first to receive a hereditary title, and Frederic Leighton (knighted, 1878) became the first (and only) artist raised to the peerage. This was for the briefest duration, on the day before his death in 1896. Earlier in the nineteenth century knighthoods generally went to court favourites or presidents of the Royal Academy:[52] David Wilkie (1836), Edwin Landseer (1850), and so forth. The book and periodical illustrator John Gilbert was knighted in 1872, but it was from the 1890s that a broader tide of titles flowed: Edward Burne-Jones (baronet, 1894), Edward Poynter (knight, 1896; baronet, 1902), William Richmond (knight, 1897), Lawrence Alma-Tadema (knight, 1899), Luke Fildes (knight, 1906), and Hubert Herkomer (knight, 1907).[53]

II

Authors, therefore, were hardly being accorded special favour. Such honours as came their way were all very agreeable; still, something was felt to be missing. Some writers might now have public recognition, but they had no authority; especially, they had none over the profession of letters itself. There was no point in looking to the British Academy for this. Established in 1901 and granted a royal charter in 1902, it was inaugurated with forty-nine, and an intended maximum of 100 members. It was designed both as a hall of fame for those distinguished in the arts and as a vehicle to promote further study in the humanities, including history, philosophy, law, politics, economics, archaeology, anthropology, philology, and literature. The supervision and promotion of fiction, poetry, and other imaginative writing were excluded from the Academy's purview,[54] which was rather, in the words of one founder member, the ancient historian Thomas Hodgkin, 'that of a body advising, co-ordinating and reporting on the work of other learned bodies', in particular, university scholarship and research. From the start, there were signs of those invidious distinctions being made that would so plague authors who sought to organize an august assembly of their own. With becoming modesty, Hodgkin considered that other historians should have been preferred to him in the original nomination: 'I am troubled at the thought that

---

[50] Pearson, *Tree*, 60, 146–7, 166–8, 222. For an explanation of the Trees' connection with the Duchess of Rutland, Lady Angela Forbes, *Memories and Base Details* (n.d. [1922]), 12.

[51] [Escott] *Society in London*, 150–1.

[52] Ibid. 152, considered these terms interchangeable: 'It is necessary for the President of the Royal Academy to be not only an artist but a courtier . . .'.

[53] G. F. Watts twice refused a baronetcy, in 1885 and 1894, though he accepted inclusion in the first batch of the Order of Merit in 1902; and John Singer Sargent refused a knighthood in 1907, pleading his American citizenship.

[54] See *Punch*, 3 Sept. 1902, 155, for 'The Uninvited Graces', which cartooned a haughty Academician sweeping past the distressed and outcast figures of Poetry, Drama, and Romance.

some, like [George] Prothero and Percy Gardner, who have certainly better claim than I, yet are not included in the mystic 49.' Having attended the Academy's inaugural meeting, he wrote: 'We are an elderly lot and I must say that we seem rather dull dogs.'[55]

Patronage was also at the disposal of the Royal Society of Literature, established in 1823. From a foundation fund of 1,100 guineas, pensions and prizes were awarded to supposedly meritorious writers; but its fellowships and professorships were distributed almost as bonbons. Consider the Revd Anthony Deane, author of sundry volumes of light verse (*Frivolous Verses*, 1892; *Holiday Rhymes*, 1894; etc.), a selection of George Crabbe's poetry, and various theological works. When he was made a Fellow, it was through the string-pulling of his friend Henry Newbolt; still, as Deane had grace to admit, 'the Royal Society of Literature ... is so modest and does so little that most people are unaware of its existence'.[56] England had nothing comparable to the Académie française, which was incorporated in 1634–5 with a commission to exercise authority over the country's language and literary style. Or, rather, it did; the Royal Society of Literature itself—one of its defining objects was 'to preserve the purity of the English language'—but the Royal Society either did not exert itself or was not heeded. The idea of establishing an equally authoritative English Academy had been debated, off and on, for over 200 years ever since Dryden, the first official Poet Laureate, lent his advocacy to the cause. Among the Victorians, Matthew Arnold was well known as a champion; but it was no coincidence that the most serious consideration of this question occurred in the 1890s and early 1900s. Then, leading men of letters were vexed about the supposed degradation of literary standards, epitomized in their eyes by the popular press and best-seller phenomenon. They bridled that there was no tribunal other than the market.

In July 1890, in the third issue of *The Author*, the Society of Authors' journal, Oswald Crawfurd questioned whether 'the *ex cathedra* pronouncements of an official Board of Letters would ever carry much weight'; yet he considered that the Society itself might 'in a humble way [do] some useful work ... to resolve the doubts and uncertainties that exist on many points in syntax, spelling, prosody and phraseology'. He instanced 'the admission of useful provincial words into general usage' as one such service.[57] This was a moderate enough proposal, yet pregnant with consequences; accordingly, the Society's leader, its founder, Walter Besant, felt obliged to comment. He was sceptical about attempts to direct the language, believing in its natural evolution; yet in 1892 he expressed the

---

[55] Louise Creighton, *Life and Letters of Thomas Hodgkin*, 2nd edn. (1918), 255–6. Both Prothero, then President of the Royal Historical Society, and Gardner, Professor of Classical Archaeology at Oxford, were shortly afterwards incorporated members of the British Academy.

[56] Anthony C. Deane, *Time Remembered* (1945), 195.

[57] Bonham-Carter, *Authors by Profession*, 206. On Crawfurd (1834–1909), former Consul in Portugal, poet, novelist, magazine editor, and director of the publishers Chapman & Hall, see *DNB Supplement 1901–1911*, i. 439–40.

hope that the Society of Authors might develop into a centre for the management of the literary profession's common interests, much like the Inns of Court did for lawyers or the College of Physicians for doctors; and he called specifically for the establishment of an equivalent to the Académie française.[58] The press, and literary periodicals especially, were provided with a field day for speculation. In 1897 *The Academy*[59] was still playing this game when it drew up a list of forty (the same number as members of the Académie française) names for a British Academy of Letters, including the former Prime Minister (and Homeric scholar) Gladstone, Edmund Gosse, W. E. Henley, Henry James, Kipling, Meredith, Alice Meynell, Ruskin, Swinburne, and W. B. Yeats. The Poet Laureate, Alfred Austin, was conspicuously excluded; so was the disgraced Oscar Wilde. Bernard Shaw wrote to complain about this treatment of Wilde, as did H. G. Wells, who advanced the names of Shaw himself, George Gissing, and George Moore. Generally, Wells condemned the exercise as a 'parlour game', although he was less forceful than Swinburne, who in a missive to *The Times* called it 'too seriously stupid for farce and too essentially vulgar for comedy'.[60]

It was nonetheless too good an opportunity for satirists to pass up. *Punch* declared open season on the Roaring Forties or the New Menagerie of Letters. It led with a supposed letter from Hall Caine, hailing this incentive for 'even the Greatest Writers to become, if possible, Greater Still'. Other authors' vanities and partialities, mutual admiration and loathing, were etched in fabricated epistles, from the feminist novelist Sarah Grand ('Man is a bestial, if necessary, blot upon creation. Could I and similar matrons have our way, he should be soundly smacked. Sexual jealousy, I take it, has kept my name from this arbitrary list'); from the historian W. E. H Lecky ('I am glad to observe my name among The Forty. I do not, however, altogether subscribe to the other thirty-nine articles. Yours, sceptically . . . '); from Marie Corelli, author of the *Sorrows of Satan* (1895), who, while principally saddened by Satan's exclusion from the Elect, pursued her vendetta against Swinburne and demanded his replacement by her half-brother the poetaster Eric Mackay; from Richard Le Gallienne and John Davidson, who each nominated the other, and Clement Scott, who recommended Max Beerbohm (their dislike was well known); from Bernard Shaw, who eliminated everyone but himself; and from Gladstone, who, in prolix style, announced himself as 'the actual author of the so-called Homeric cycle of poems' and with 'an impregnably-rooted sense of the justice of this arrangement' was gratified at 'how relatively low a position the merits of humour, as exemplified in the persons of Messrs. W. S. Gilbert and "Lewis Carroll", have been relegated'. The ludicrous pitch was sustained by William Watson counting it an honour to be excluded

---

[58] *Review of Reviews* (Sept. 1892), 258.

[59] *The Academy* was bought in 1896 by the American businessman John Morgan Richards. His daughter, the author John Oliver Hobbes, sought to influence *The Academy*'s editor, Charles Lewis Hind, in the selection of the names for this Academy; see her letter, 3 Nov. 1897, in Richards, *John Oliver Hobbes*, 121.   [60] Karl Beckson, *London in the 1890s* (1992), 227; *Punch*, 4 Dec. 1897, for a parody.

from a list which also ignored Alfred Austin; and it was capped by a salutation in pidgin English to 'Sir Punch, Mister', from Émile Zola.[61]

In 1902–3 *The Author* again debated the question, soliciting its members' views. The Ibsenite William Archer thought that an Academy might do some good. As a rationalist, Archer favoured simplified spelling reforms, a movement then making progress in America.[62] Others were pessimistic that an Academy could raise standards, Israel Zangwill remarking forlornly about the 'vulgarity of the epoch' and Violet Hunt judging their age as resolutely 'non-critical'. The poet Herbert Trench, then senior examiner for the Board of Education, was emphatic about the need:

The lower forces of literary productiveness are amply organised. The higher are without representation. There is no council at the head of literature to control or keep order, or by example to discountenance the indecencies of advertisement . . . Our Society of Authors—admirable body that it is—exists only to protect literature as an article of commerce, not with literature as an art, and as more than art.

Again, there was the sense of inferiority compared with other professions, which

all have their societies, to influence, to keep order, to recognize rank and confer honour. Pure literature . . . has no society whose aim is to sustain the name, and publicly to represent to foreigners and to the community the power of English intelligence and imagination.[63]

Even in America, where the market appeared most to rule literature, action had been taken, first with the establishment of the National Institute of Arts and Letters in 1898, then with the Academy of Arts and Letters in 1905. The latter was limited to fifty names, initially elected from members of the Institute and afterwards autonomous. The model again was the Académie française; similarly, its composition and role, far from settling argument, ruffled feathers. Thus the pragmatic philosopher William James declined membership, ironically pretending insult that 'my younger and shallower and vainer brother', alias the novelist Henry James, was elected prior to him.[64]

Respondents to *The Author* sustained the debate about an English Academy. Max Beerbohm thought Trench resembled a beachcomber 'looking for forty fossils'; Morley Roberts too reckoned that, because 'an academy is nothing if not academic', it was bound to end 'in imposing senility'. Rider Haggard, however, advocated something more specific, an Academy of Imaginative Literature.

---

[61] *Punch*, 20 Nov. 1897, 238, and 27 Nov. 1897, 244–5.

[62] Archer became secretary of the Simplified Spelling Society, established in 1908. On this question generally, see P. J. Waller, 'Democracy and Dialect, Speech and Class', in P. J. Waller (ed.), *Politics and Social Change in Modern Britain* (Brighton, 1987).

[63] *The Author*, Oct. 1902, in Bonham-Carter, *Authors by Profession*, 207. See also Trench's remarks in *T.P.'s Weekly*, 23 Jan. 1903, 334. On F. H. Trench (1865–1923), *DNB 1922–1930*, 852–3. He was artistic director at the Haymarket Theatre subsequently. [64] Edel, *James*, ii. 605.

Instead, the Society of Authors proposed a committee—James Bryce, James Frazer, Thomas Hardy, William Lecky, George Meredith, and Swinburne—to explore the question. Because several of these individuals were uninterested in or opposed to the idea of supervising contemporary literature, the matter lapsed until 1910, when the Royal Society of Literature invited the Society of Authors to collaborate in establishing an Academic Committee, each body to propose fourteen names, whereupon the twenty-eight would elect a further dozen to complete the fabulous forty. A list was compiled by a subcommittee of the Society of Authors' management committee, then passed to the Society's council, at which point Mrs Humphry Ward objected to the absence of any woman's name and Bernard Shaw moved that the Society should abstain from the enterprise.[65] Shaw was torn between reforming and wrecking instincts. A reformed Academy would contain more novelists, poets, and playwrights than critics and scholars; it would also ensure vitality by a compulsory retirement clause and another that insisted that 'at least ten Academicians shall always be under 50 years of age'.[66] A wrecking strategy involved different tactics:' 'I think you could do a great deal by threatening to nominate Frank Harris,' Shaw impishly told Gilbert Murray.[67]

The Royal Society of Literature proceeded alone, therefore. Its guiding hand was Edmund Gosse. Not discouraged by such evidence of an imperfect world as emanated from the Society of Authors, he now outlined a constitution for 'An Academic Committee of English Letters'. Its main purposes were to incorporate a literary elite, representing literary criticism, the novel, poetry, and drama, and to uphold standards of language and style. This it would do by public lectures and prizes; it might take a role too in censorship. Functioning under the aegis of the Royal Society of Literature, the Academic Committee would start with some thirty members, who would progressively co-opt others, to a maximum of forty. As well as Gosse himself, the nominated praetorians of excellence were: Alfred Austin, Laurence Binyon, A. C. Bradley, Robert Bridges, S. H. Butcher, Joseph Conrad, W. J. Courthope, Austin Dobson, Edward Dowden, J. G. Frazer, R. B. Haldane, Thomas Hardy, Maurice Hewlett, Henry James, W. P. Ker, Andrew Lang, Sir Alfred Lyall, J. W. Mackail, John Morley, Gilbert Murray, Henry Newbolt, E. H. Pember, Sir Arthur Pinero, George W. Prothero, Walter Raleigh, G. M. Trevelyan, A. W. Verrall, George Wyndham, and W. B. Yeats. The last named replied to Gosse's invitation:

Of course I accept and am flattered at being asked to do so. An English Academy would save us, perhaps, from the journalists, who wish to be men of letters, and the men of letters who have become journalists . . . This is the first generation in which the spirit of literature has been conquered by the spirit of the press, of hurry, of immediate

---

[65] Bonham-Carter, *Authors by Profession*, 207–8.
[66] To Mrs Humphry Ward, 10 Sept. 1910, in Laurence (ed.), *Shaw Letters*, 939.
[67] To Gilbert Murray, 24 July 1910, ibid. 936.

interests, and Bernard Shaw is the Joseph whose prosperity has brought his brethren into captivity.[68]

There was the welfare of literature to promote; there was also the welfare of Willie himself. The ground for a Civil List pension for Yeats, whose annual income hovered around £180, was already being tilled by Gosse, who had been enlisting the support of the right people: Asquith, the Prime Minister; Birrell, Chief Secretary for Ireland; Crewe, former Lord Lieutenant of Ireland, now Liberal leader in the Lords; Justin McCarthy, Irish Nationalist veteran; and so forth. Inclusion in the Academic Committee would, as Gosse wrote prettily to Yeats's patroness Lady Gregory, give him 'a claim which cannot be put by'. Lady Gregory, however, was bent on her own arrangements. She and Gosse spat and scratched about the best technique of pulling the strings that would bag for Yeats the coveted double of Irish revolutionary and King's client. In August 1910 Yeats got his pension of £150 per year, this sum largely being found courtesy of the dour Scots poet John Davidson, whose suicide by drowning in March 1909 left a void in the Civil List.[69]

Yeats had been disposed to view the Academic Committee as a means of rescuing literature from Shavian smartness. Nonetheless, he had proposed Shaw for membership, in part because he was a useful tool in another cause, the campaign against the theatre censorship. Yeats wanted Gosse to mobilize the Academic Committee on this question; he himself had arranged the Abbey Theatre's production of Shaw's *The Shewing-up of Blanco Posnet* in Dublin in 1909, after it was banned in England. Shaw, however, was rejected by the original Committee; and G. K. Chesterton was not even considered. Rejected too were Hilaire Belloc and H. G. Wells. Wells, as a Fabian Socialist, had been drawn to the idea of an Authors' Guild that might stamp a 'hall-mark' on literature; but his notion of a stamping authority was remote from an Academic Committee composed of 'Uninspired Respectability'. Rather, it should involve 'that Intrusive Bounder, who is the living soul of literature'—an author much like Wells.[70] Otherwise, he declared himself 'bitterly, incurably, destructively against Literary Academies'.[71] As for Kipling, though he appeared to want 'a judicial body that can maintain and impose standards', he refused to join the Academic Committee; so did J. M. Barrie, both men apparently following the advice of Anthony Hope.[72]

These doubts about a literary establishment matched experiences from the art world. This was riven with cliques; and rival clubs or rebel schools naturally emerged in repudiation of the prestige and patronage of the Royal Academy. 'Herein lies the real evil of Academies,' wrote William Rothenstein; 'they

---

[68] Yeats to Edmund Gosse, 12 Apr. 1910, in Wade (ed.), *Yeats Letters*, 549.

[69] Foster, *Yeats*, i. 424–8. Davidson's pension, £100 p.a., was awarded in 1906.

[70] Bonham-Carter, *Authors by Profession*, 207.

[71] Quoted in Thwaite, *Gosse*, 453. See also Parrinder and Philmus (eds.), *H. G. Wells's Literary Criticism*, 13.   [72] Newsome, *Edge of Paradise*, 276; Kipling quoted in Thwaite, *Gosse*, 453.

encourage intrigues and suspicion . . . '.[73] This was always an argument against an Academy of Letters. J. Stanley Little, executive secretary (1887–8) of the Society of Authors, was a particularly fierce exponent. In 1890, when *The Author* carried an article advocating an Academy as 'an antiseptic power in literary art' to counter the philological contagion spreading from an unlettered democracy and from transatlantic neologisms, Little warned of a worse danger: a literary equivalent of the Royal Academy 'which has done nothing for English art in the concrete sense, and in regard to individual artists of the highest distinction, has done all it could to crush them out of existence'. The RA was an abuse; its members were 'the carriage folk of art'. Little was 'convinced that there is not an evil of over-production, nor of gold, or notoriety-hunting, which the institution of an Academy of Letters would not increase tenfold'.[74] George Moore was equally direct: 'That nearly all artists dislike and despise the Royal Academy is a matter of common knowledge . . . From Glasgow to Cornwall, wherever a group of artists collects, there hangs a gathering and a darkening sky of hate.'[75]

Gosse's Academic Committee nonetheless came into being, with John Morley (Lord Morley) as president. There was a farcical air to its first meeting in November 1910, when the chair was taken by A. C. Benson. Benson had not been included in Gosse's core thirty: in the original ballot his name was ranked no. 32, and he was elected only because of others refusing. The membership of G. M. Trevelyan now occasioned a row. It was Sir George Trevelyan whose inclusion was wanted, but Sir George declined while engineering the election of his son instead. J. W. Mackail became 'purple with emotion'; and Gosse and the secretary, Pember, displayed pettishness to one another.[76] Benson was disposed to take the whole business lightly but not so as to refuse any gong that was going: he accepted a so-called professorship of English Fiction from the Royal Society of Literature in 1911, as did Henry Newbolt. Progressively, the Academic Committee sought to make amends by courting those excluded from its first intake. Bernard Shaw had been incorporated in June 1911, whereupon he championed the membership of Chesterton against the protests of Gosse and Maurice Hewlett. Hilaire Belloc, Arnold Bennett, John Galsworthy, John Masefield, and H. G. Wells were invited to join at the same time. Bennett was not impressed at the thought of taking his place in such a 'grotesque institution'. He communicated this to Wells, who similarly resisted appeals made to him by Gosse and Henry James:

I have an insurmountable objection to Literary or Artistic Academies as such, to any hierarchies, any suggestion of controls or fixed standards in these things . . . This world of

---

[73] Rothenstein, *Men and Memories, 1900–1922*, 193.

[74] H. G. Keene and J. Stanley Little, 'English Academy', *The Author*, 15 Dec. 1890, *Review of Reviews* (Jan. 1891), 64. On Little (1856–1940), minor novelist with experience in South Africa and a friend of Rider Haggard; Sutherland, *Companion*, 378.   [75] *Review of Reviews* (June 1892), 600.

[76] Newsome, *Edge of Paradise*, 244, 276–7, where E. H. Pember is wrongly indexed as 'N. Pember'. He served as first secretary of the Academic Committee but died shortly afterwards in 1911. A lawyer, Pember found admission to the *Dictionary of National Biography* both for his forensic skills and as man of letters.

ours, I mean the world of creative and representative work we do, is I am convinced best anarchic. Better the wild rush of Boomster and the Quack than the cold politeness of the established thing . . . [77]

The first woman elected was Thackeray's daughter Lady Ritchie. If there was disagreement about other names, there was agreement about this, that Mrs Humphry Ward should not be the first female member.

A decade after the Academic Committee emerged, as 'a modest and partial experiment . . . for the protection and encouragement of pure English style in prose and verse', Gosse presented a sanguine assessment of its prospects: 'It was assailed, as was natural and right, by satire and by caricature, but it has survived the attacks . . . and there can be little doubt that, with good luck, it may become a prominent feature of our intellectual and social system.'[78] This optimism proved misplaced. The Committee maintained a life of sorts until 1939; but it never attained the authority of the Académie française. Thus, literary men were compelled to cope as best they may with the existing system of random honour and informal influence.

III

The laureateship, £100 per annum but 'no sack' (Tennyson), was the classic instance of a literary honour where literary excellence was incidental. Opponents of the office maintained that it was no coincidence that poet laureates came in as court jesters went out: proof of England's genius only for continuity in institutions. Ostensibly a member of the royal household, the laureate generated odes to occasion, whereupon even the best faltered with false feeling. Tennyson found his trough with a threnody on the death of the Duke of Clarence some months before his own.[79] There was a certain symmetry that the nineteenth-century laureateship should close with Austin as it began with Pye. Even when the right appointment was made, the wrong one had sometimes been pursued in vain. Before Tennyson succeeded Wordsworth in 1850, the post was offered to Samuel Rogers and Sheridan Knowles.[80] The laureateship was left vacant between Tennyson's death in 1892 and Austin's appointment in 1896. *Punch* in 1893, mindful of the mood of the age, reckoned that the most suitable appointee would be a music-hall lyricist, vivid and versatile, and accustomed to produce patriotic patter by return of post.[81] Gladstone, who had the first opportunity, let the

He was a classicist, poet, and playwright whose work, while unpublished, circulated among the select of The Club and Dilettanti Society. Pember was joint secretary of the latter from 1893 to 1911; he is frequently cited in the published journal of Sir Mountstuart Grant Duff who was a stalwart of both clubs.

[77] Norman and Jeanne MacKenzie, *H. G. Wells* (1973), 277–8.
[78] 'The Foundation of the French Academy', in Gosse, *Aspects and Impressions*, 145.
[79] For Tennyson's struggles to compose this, Rawnsley, *Memories*, 145.
[80] Tennyson's friends had lobbied for him to succeed Southey in 1843; correspondence ibid. 88–9.
[81] 'The Lay of the (Music-Hall) Laureate', *Punch*, 21 Jan. 1893, 33.

laureateship lapse, partly because he felt Tennyson's stature incomparable and partly because the two (in his view) next greatest poets held unacceptable opinions. One was William Morris, who 'was supposed to have socialistic or Nihilist proclivities'.[82] A relieved Gladstone was told that Morris would refuse it if offered;[83] but, if Wilfrid Blunt's diary can be relied upon, Morris felt that he had been misused. On 4 November 1892 Blunt found Morris at work in Hammersmith:

'It is all a lie', he said, 'about their having offered to make me Laureate. Bryce came to see me and talked of it, but it was only on his own private account. I was fool enough to tell Ellis, and he told his son, who must needs repeat it at the National Liberal Club, and so it got into the papers. I fancy from what I have heard if they don't offer it to me they will offer it to Swinburne, but perhaps he won't take it.' *I.* 'It is five to one he will take it.' *He.* 'That's about the betting, but Theodore Watts declares he will refuse. That's perhaps all the more reason.'[84]

Morris was right to think that Swinburne was in the frame; but he too was suspect, from personal notoriety as well as on political grounds. One of Gladstone's private secretaries, Sir George Murray, told a former colleague, Sir Algernon West, that

he had visited the British Museum and discovered that Swinburne had never withdrawn a word of his poems and ballads [*Poems and Ballads*, 1866], but on the contrary had published a pamphlet in defence of them, and had circulated a poem against the execution of the Manchester Fenians; so I am afraid that his chances of the Laureateship are over.[85]

The political objections, however, gradually changed. In a state of ecstasy Swinburne had composed his *Ode on the Proclamation of the French Republic* in 1870 and, in a way that caused disgust, gloatingly dashed off 'The Saviour of Society' in 1873 to celebrate the death in exile of the deposed Napoleon III;[86] but he had no sympathy with the 'verminous and murderous muckworm of the Parisian

---

[82] Horace G. Hutchinson (ed.), *Private Diaries of the Rt. Hon. Sir Algernon West, G.C.B.* (1922), 65.

[83] Hon. Lionel A. Tollemache, *Talks with Mr. Gladstone* (1898), 124–5. Morris was 'sounded' by one of Gladstone's Cabinet, 'with Mr Gladstone's knowledge and approval' (Mackail, *Morris*, ii. 302–3). This was the Chancellor of the Duchy of Lancaster, James Bryce, who, while assuring Gladstone that Morris's *Songs for Socialists* did not involve 'any incitement to violence' and contained 'nothing to cause scandal', told him that Morris had said that as 'a sincere republican' he would not accept the post if offered. Bryce to Gladstone, 18, 26, 28 Oct. 1892, in Matthew (ed.), *Gladstone Diaries*, xiii. 117. Morris previously refused to stand for the professorship of Poetry at Oxford, when the chair was vacant in 1877: on that occasion, when Morris was not yet a Socialist, the reason was his confessed inability to lecture about the scholarly theory of poetry. By 1892 Morris was no longer a productive poet; and his opinion of Tennyson, once admiring, was that he had ceased to appeal to him after *Maud* (1855).

[84] Blunt, *Diaries*, i. 82–3. 'Theodore Watts', later Watts-Dunton, was Swinburne's guardian. 'Ellis' is more problematical. Perhaps, this was T. E. Ellis (1859–99), the Liberal deputy whip. At Oxford in the early 1880s Ellis admired Morris's artistic sensibility and anti-industrialism, and even declared himself a Whitmanite; see Neville Masterman, *The Forerunner: The Dilemmas of Tom Ellis, 1859–1899* (Swansea, 1972), 46, 48.

[85] Hutchinson (ed.), *West*, 63–4. See also Gladstone's correspondence with Lord Acton, 7, 8, 10, 17, 18 Oct. 1892, in Matthew (ed.), *Gladstone Diaries*, xiii. 104, 107, 114.

[86] Gosse, *Life of Swinburne*, 186, 209.

Commune', and he denied the compatibility of 'the republican principle with the disintegrating instinct of Parisian anarchists or Irish reactionaries'.[87] This last reference disclosed another development: Swinburne was appalled by Gladstone's Home Rule scheme. In spite of his poem appealing for clemency for the Manchester Fenians, who had been executed in 1867, Swinburne never advocated a republic for Ireland as he had for Italy and France.[88] His opinion of Gladstone was the reverse of friendly, holding him in contempt after General Gordon was abandoned in Khartoum in 1885:

> Forsaken, silent, Gordon dies and gives
> Example: loud and shameless Gladstone lives,
> No faction unembraced or unbetrayed,
> No chance unwelcomed and no vote unweighed . . .[89]

This vituperation in verse went unpublished; but an anonymous essayist in the *Fortnightly Review* in 1890, endeavouring to stake out Swinburne's claims two years before Tennyson's demise, advertised that Swinburne 'in his hot youth was a fiery Republican, but he is now a vigorous Unionist—whose recent poems show that his riper judgement accepts the English Monarchy'.[90] Certainly his Jubilee ode, published in the *Nineteenth Century*, June 1887, impressed the Queen's eldest daughter, the future Empress Frederick of Germany, who recommended it to her mother as 'fine and striking' and hoped that it had been read to her.[91] Whether this would have sufficed for Lord Salisbury, the Unionist premier, had the vacancy occurred at that time, is questionable; still, it was said that both Arthur Balfour, leader of the Unionist Party in the Commons, and the Prince of Wales wanted Swinburne to follow Tennyson.[92] The Queen herself remained adamant because of the immorality of his early poetry and advocacy of regicide (tyrannicide in Swinburne's terminology) in the case of the French Emperor and Russian Tsar. The Queen would have been further horrified if she had received a whiff of Swinburne's performances in his cups, when he revisited Balliol in the early 1870s. For the edification of undergraduates, Swinburne sketched a play he was minded to write, a fanciful picture of early Victorian England. The country is on the brink of revolution caused by libertinism at 'Buckingham's Palace', where the Queen disports herself with her paramour Lord John Russell. The latter's jealous rival is 'Sir Peel' who passionately addresses the Queen: 'I know why you love Lord John Russell. He is young, he is beautiful, he is profligate. I cannot be young, I cannot be beautiful, but I will be profligate'; whereupon he follows

---

[87] Quotations from 'Whitmania' (1887) and 'Social Verse' (1891), repr. in Algernon Charles Swinburne, *Studies in Prose and Poetry* (1915), 102, 140.　　[88] Gosse, *Life of Swinburne*, 174.

[89] Quoted in Beckson, *London in the 1890s*, 101.

[90] 'Tennyson and After', *Fortnightly Review* (May 1890), *Review of Reviews* (May 1890), 398. The article advocated the abolition of the office of Laureate, were Swinburne not to be appointed, rather than allow it to sink to an unacceptably low level.

[91] Ramm (ed.), *Beloved and Darling Child*, 52–3 (9 June 1887).

[92] Hutchinson (ed.), *West*, 64, 68–9.

the stage direction 'Exit for ze Haymarket', that well-known resort for harlots. Later in the drama it transpires that Victoria has an illegitimate daughter, sired by Lord John, who plies her trade on the streets as 'Miss Kitty' and does 'everything which might have made a Messalina blush'. Swinburne was in full flow now, but another glass of port caused him to switch direction, explaining the *Poems and Ballads* in his own clandestine experiences, until yet another glass, consumed in one swig, rendered him comatose.[93]

'The general sense of the Government is in favour of Swinburne, and it has been ascertained that Swinburne would like to be appointed,' recorded Blunt in 1893, when the office had been kept vacant for a year. This followed a conversation with Spencer Lyttelton, Gladstone's principal private secretary.[94] Whether 'the Government' included Gladstone himself may be doubted because, committed as Gladstone was to a second Home Rule Bill, Swinburne's Unionist conviction was no recommendation. The partisan Liberal press aligned against Swinburne at this time, Lady Battersea—wife of a former Liberal whip—writing in her journal in 1893 'how ungenerous and rude the *Daily News* is to the poet. The *Pall Mall* of course is, being rancorous and vindictive always, but I was ashamed to read that paragraph in the *Daily News*.'[95] If he was not to have it, then Swinburne's own preference was for Canon Dixon, once of the Pre-Raphaelite set at Oxford and a poet of some originality, who was admired also by Robert Bridges and Gerard Manley Hopkins; but though Dixon's *Mano* (1883) was known, his was not a name high in the public reckoning. The same applied to Swinburne's second choice, Lord de Tabley, who published verse under various pseudonyms before issuing two series of *Poems, Dramatic and Lyrical* (1893–5).[96] In desperation, Gladstone had even considered Ruskin, who was 'seventy-three, nearly out of his mind, and never wrote a poem anyone ever read'.[97] Not that Ruskin ever belittled the business: 'He says Poetry is *the* living art of modern days.'[98] The problem was, as one critic remarked, adapting Tacitus, 'all would have agreed Mr. Ruskin was capable of writing poetry, if he had not written it'.[99]

One stage beyond the desperate was the pathological, personified by Marie Corelli. She harboured ambitions of the laureateship, not for herself but for her (putative) half-brother Eric Mackay. 'I wonder if Miss Marie Corelli remembers

<hr />

[93] W. H. Mallock, *Memoirs of Life and Literature* (1920), quoted in Sutherland (ed.), *Literary Anecdotes*, 274–5. Swinburne varied the performance, on another occasion having the Queen confessing (in French) to the Duchess of Kent her lapse in virtue with Wordsworth: see Bailey (ed.), *Bailey Letters and Diaries*, 175.

[94] Blunt, *Diaries*, i. 114 (10 Oct. 1893). Lyttelton was Gladstone's principal private secretary, 1892–4.

[95] Cohen, *Rothschild and her Daughters*, 244.

[96] Gosse, *Swinburne*, 277. On Dixon (1833–1900) and de Tabley (1835–95), see Drabble, *Companion*, 278, 1045; Reilly, *Late Victorian Poetry*, 138–9, 498–9.

[97] Hutchinson (ed.), *West*, 69. This suggestion actually came from Gladstone's friend the historian Lord Acton, who, as a Catholic, was very hostile to Swinburne's candidacy; but Ruskin was eliminated after Gladstone consulted the Regius Professor of Medicine at Oxford, Sir Henry Acland. See also Beckson, *London in the 1890s*, 101–2.   [98] Masterman (ed.), *Mary Gladstone*, 129–30 (14 Jan. 1878).

[99] *The Academy*, 14 Jan. 1899, quoted in R. G. Cox (ed.), *Thomas Hardy: The Critical Heritage* (1970), 322.

a meeting on the Terrace of the House of Commons,' wrote Robert Farquharson coyly in 1911, describing how she had made herself 'specially charming' to MPs in order to press Mackay's claims.[100] Eric, it is fair to remark, passed one basic test: he did pen verses. Moreover, these sold in quantity. *Love Letters of a Violinist* (1886) sold 35,000 copies; and he was considered sufficiently significant to warrant inclusion in H. D. Traill's list of sixty-six living writers who had authentic claim to the title of poet, which was published in the *Nineteenth Century* in January 1892.[101] Eric was astute enough to publish several loyal odes, to the Queen herself, and on the marriage of the Duke of York to Princess Mary of Teck (1893) and the birth of their son the future Edward VIII (1894).[102] Otherwise, he was a wastrel who sponged off Corelli, even claiming that he authored her books.[103]

Press tipsters provided no shortage of runners, but the pedigree in every case was wanting by personal, poetic, or political deficiency. The other Morris, Lewis, was considered a public favourite and a disciple of Tennyson. He was very productive. His *Poetical Works* were published in four volumes in 1882 and 1890, including an ode for the Queen's Jubilee in 1887; and *A Vision of Saints* (1890) he planned as a Christian complement to the *Epic of Hades* (1876–7). The latter— *Punch* liked to report that most of it was composed on the London Underground steam railway[104]—was his most famous work; it eventually sold over 50,000 copies in his lifetime.[105] Morris's actual contact with Tennyson was not close. When meeting, Tennyson preferred to talk about insects, not poetry. On Tennyson's elevation to the Lords, Morris was suitably servile: 'in the opinion of a subaltern in the army of which you are Commander in Chief, the Queen has done the most graceful thing in offering you a Peerage'.[106] Morris's impatient cunning got the better of him in 1887, when he put about the idea that Tennyson, then approaching 80, ought or was about to retire. These rumours Tennyson's son Hallam quashed by affirming the Laureate's continued inspiration. He further turned the knife by suggesting that the laureateship would probably be abolished after his father's demise. It must have been a crestfallen Morris, therefore, who saw a new Tennyson, *Demeter and Other Poems*, appear in the bookshops in December 1889, receive encomiums from the critics, and sell 20,000 copies in a week.[107] His self-confidence was not easily shredded, however. *Murray's Magazine*

---

[100] Farquharson, *In and Out of Parliament*, 122.

[101] Traill followed this up with another eight (who included Kipling, Richard Le Gallienne, and Canon Dixon), left out of the original list, in March, making a total (because the Revd E. C. Lefroy had died meanwhile) of seventy-three, of whom fifty-seven were deemed minor and sixteen major. Eric Mackay was in the minor category. *Review of Reviews* (Jan. 1892), 49, (Mar. 1892), 292.

[102] Reilly, *Late Victorian Poetry*, 304–5.

[103] Corelli had a breakdown following Eric Mackay's death. She was not secretive about it: see *Who's Who* (1905), 347. She removed this reference from later entries (see *Who Was Who, 1916–1928*, 228) and wrote a pamphlet, which has not survived, denouncing Eric's treachery. On this unsavoury episode, see Masters, *Corelli*, 154–60. For a better opinion of Eric, see Sladen, *Twenty Years*, 126: Sladen was obliged to the father, Charles Mackay, for an early commission.   [104] *Punch*, 22 Mar. 1905, 207.

[105] *DNB Supplement 1901–1911*, ii. 649–52, for Morris (1833–1907).   [106] Martin, *Tennyson*, 545.

[107] Ibid. 561, 571.

in July 1891 contained 'Some Thoughts on Modern Poetry', in which Morris gave generously of what was in his mind. He demanded that the modern poet rid himself of 'the devastating pests' of obscurity and pedantry, 'rely more upon metrical harmonies than upon the mere jingling of sound', and cease looking backwards:

the great gains of science should not be ignored by him, nor the insoluble but ever recurring problems of the relations of the Human to the Divine. Great as is the wealth of English poetry, I confess that to me the great bulk of it—and indeed, of the poetry of the world—even when it is not mere caterwauling, seems trivial, insincere, and ineffectual to the last degree.[108]

Morris's appeal did not carry to the right places. Gladstone grimly informed Lord Acton on 17 October 1892 how 'L. Morris circuitously puts himself forward—here I can find no one to speak for him.'[109] A year later, reporting the Government's views to Wilfrid Blunt, Spencer Lyttelton declared, 'The one thing we are afraid of is having Lewis Morris thrust on us.'[110] The high critics shared this repugnance, counting his very popularity as an unmistakable disqualification. As Roy Flecker put it, 'If you cannot see that the *Epic of Hades* (it sells by the hundred thousand) is beneath contempt, you are not fit to read *Paradise Lost*. If you don't know how bad the bad is you can never tell how good the good is.'[111] In 1890 the *Fortnightly Review* had drawn a correlation between Morris's bombastic inanity and his readership—'His view of things in general is precisely that which is dear to the half-educated middle classes, a facile optimism garnished with cheap philosophical phrases, and using the most awful names and ideas of religion as the counters of sentimental platitude. His principles consist in repudiating the whole history of English poetry since Byron...'.[112] George Saintsbury ranked Morris with the recently deceased Martin Tupper, whose name was a byword for banality.[113] Those who met Morris, as Balfour Browne did at a dinner given by the poet Mrs Emily Pfeiffer at Putney, described 'a biggish, fleshy man...whose conversation was costive, and when it did come was not remarkable'.[114] 'Knows right from wrong like the palm of 'is 'and, and ain't afraid to say where one begins and t'other ends' was Max Beerbohm's satirical summary of Morris's virtue as expressed by John Bull.[115] Morris did have allies, yet even these were slightly unnerved by his inflated idea of himself. Robert Farquharson, an 'intimate friend', considered that 'his political services, combined with his poetical merits, should deserve official recognition'; but Farquharson admitted to being 'Philistine enough to prefer his *Epic of Hades* to Dante'.[116] When Morris

---

[108] *Review of Reviews* (July 1891), 40.   [109] Matthew (ed.), *Gladstone Diaries*, xiii. 114.
[110] Blunt, *Diaries*, 114 (10 Oct. 1893).   [111] 'The Public as Art Critic', in Flecker, *Collected Prose*, 249.
[112] *Fortnightly Review* (May 1890).   [113] Saintsbury, *Scrap Book*, 24.
[114] Balfour Browne, *Recollections*, 157.
[115] 'De Arte Poetica' (1901), in Riewald (ed.), *Beerbohm's Literary Caricatures*, 196–8.
[116] Farquharson, *In and Out of Parliament*, 122.

asked what he ought to do about the 'conspiracy of silence' ranged against him for the laureateship, Oscar Wilde advised: 'Join it'.[117]

Young poets made no concealment of contempt. 'L. Morriss', snorted Ernest Dowson, the casual misspelling signifying dismissal. The very idea that the laureate should be at all popular horrified Dowson; on the contrary, an urge to flay the public was a vital prerequisite. For this reason, Dowson also eliminated William Morris. Dowson was 'sorry that Tennyson has crossed the bar', because he was 'un grand poète . . . Above all, I love him because he did sacredly hate the mob—which whether it be the well dressed mob whom Browning pandered to, or the evil smelling mob to which William Morris does now, to the detriment of his art and of his own dignity still pander, I hold alike to be damnable, unwholesome and obscene.'[118] This marked a substantial difference from W. B. Yeats, whose advice was sought by *The Bookman*. They had one common ground: Yeats refused even to discuss 'the claims of all kinds of perfectly absurd people' such as Lewis Morris, who, he noted, styled himself '"of Penbryn" to be distinguished from his namesake of Parnassus'. Yeats's main purpose, in hope of inducing William Morris to accept, was to argue for 'nationalising the Laureateship'; that is, abolishing the courtly character and making it a genuine public office with a responsibility to celebrate 'matters of national importance, great battles if he held them to be waged in a just cause, the deaths of famous men of thought and action, and the ever-coming never-come light of that ideal peace and freedom whereto all nations are stumbling in the darkness'. As an illustration of the superannuated state of the currently constituted office, he averred that Tennyson's

Idylls of the King are marred a little by the dedications to the Prince Consort and to the Queen . . . because . . . [this] lessened the significance of the great imaginative types of Arthur and Guinevere, and cast round the greatest romantic poem of the century a ring of absurdity. We can only just tolerate Spenser's comparison of the Queen of the Fairies to Queen Elizabeth, for even then all such comparisons were growing obsolete, whereas we can hardly forgive at all this injury which the Court poet of our day has done to the laurelled poet of the people.[119]

With no prospect of reforming the office, the press continued its perambulation of the poetic field. Another popular favourite was Sir Edwin Arnold, though as chief editor of the *Daily Telegraph* in the years when it moved from support of the Liberal Party to the Conservatives and championed Lord Lytton's forward

[117] H. M. Hyndman, *The Record of an Adventurous Life* (1911), 381. Wilde favoured Swinburne, writing in *The Idler* (Apr. 1895): 'Mr Swinburne is already the Poet Laureate of England. The fact that his appointment to this high post has not been degraded by official confirmation renders his position all the more unassailable. He whom all poets love is the Poet Laureate always' (Hart-Davis (ed.), *Wilde's Letters*, 191 n. 1). The contempt of Wilde's circle for Morris was captured by Robert Hichens in *The Green Carnation* (1894) in which Esmé Araminth laments his own hyperactive intelligence: 'I so long for the lethargy, the sweet peace of stupidity. If only I were Lewis Morris!' (p. 88).
[118] To Victor Plarr, *c*.8 Oct. 1892, in Flower and Maas (eds.), *Dowson's Letters*, 243.
[119] *The Bookman* (Nov. 1892), in Wade (ed.), *Yeats's Letters*, 218–20.

policy in India and Turkey's side in the Balkans conflicts, he stood little chance with Gladstone. Arnold's poetic reputation rested on his epic portrayal of the life of the Buddha, *The Light of Asia* (1879), which achieved sixty editions in England, eighty in America, and numerous translations. Now almost unread, *The Light of Asia* found its way into countless Victorian homes and still exercised an influence on burgeoning poets in the new century. Herbert Read, in politics and circumstance far removed from Arnold, nevertheless acknowledged its significance during the incubation of his own first poems, *Songs of Chaos* (1915). His brother's employer, a Leeds tailor who adopted the orphaned Read, had awakened his love of literature by lending him '*The Light of Asia* telling me that all his life it had been his favourite poem'.[120] Arnold's ambitious sequel, *The Light of the World* (1891), was written while he was living in Japan; and his third wife was Japanese. Douglas Sladen recollected how Arnold, when not tutoring the daughters of wealthy Japanese, would consult Buddhist monks and sages. Sladen added: 'he could put his mind on an Eastern plane of thought. He looked quite Oriental when he was in Japanese dress; his dark skin, his Oriental type, the deep reserve which lay behind his affability, all suggested the child of the East.'[121] Japanese porcelain and decoration owed their late nineteenth-century vogue to Whistler and others, but Arnold was important in stimulating interest in Japanese drama, his *Japonica* appearing in 1892 and his adaptation of a Noh play, *Adzuma* (or *The Japanese Wife*), in 1891. There were other poems, *Lotus and Jewel* (1887) and *Poems: National and Non-Oriental*, collected in 1888; and, notwithstanding a tepid reception given to *The Light of the World*, he 'confidently expected the reversion of the laureateship after Lord Tennyson's death'.[122] Had Tennyson been able to decide the question, Arnold was almost the last person he would have chosen. In March 1892 Arthur Lee made notes of Tennyson's table-talk:

He was particularly incensed . . . by an alleged interview with him which had been published by Sir Edwin Arnold and which he denounced as entirely fictitious. 'He talks of me as an intimate friend, whereas I have only seen him once. He accuses me of "soft arrogance"; what does that mean I should like to know? He describes my hair as "sable-silvered", whereas I have never had one grey hair in my head. He alleges I stood with him on the top of Blackdown and said 'It was here that I parted with General Gordon before he left England for the last time.' Could anything be more absurd! I only saw Gordon once and that was in Eaton Square in London. He said that I spoke of his (Arnold's) poems, whereas I have never read a line of any of them in my life.[123]

---

[120] Diary, 22 May 1917, in Read, *Contrary Experience*, 96.   [121] Sladen, *Twenty Years*, 117.
[122] *DNB Supplement 1901–1911*, i. 60. Arnold's confidence was shared by William Rossetti, who, dining with the Garnett family on 23 October 1892, declared that 'Swinburne and Wm. Morris should have the refusal of it, after them perhaps Coventry Patmore. He thinks Sir Edwin Arnold will probably get it, and would keep out Lewis Morris at any price' (Marsh, *Rossetti*, 559).
[123] Clark (ed.), *Lee*, 44. The offending article, 'A Day with Lord Tennyson' by Sir Edwin Arnold, appeared in the American journal *Forum* (Nov. 1891), and was substantially reproduced, with a photograph of Tennyson in cloak and sombrero, in *Review of Reviews* (Jan. 1892), 38–9, where it was noted that Arnold 'has been hailed already by some as the Poet Laureate in succession to Lord Tennyson'.

Not content with traducing Tennyson, Arnold laid claim to the royal seal. When in the company of admirers of his verses, he waxed expansively, and casually mentioned that 'the Queen favoured his candidature for the Laureateship'.[124]

By contrast with Arnold, whose ambitions were all too patent, George Meredith, though Liberal in sympathies, was ruled out by not being popular enough. 'Mr Meredith the poet troubles himself even less than Mr Meredith the novelist to conciliate the indolent reader' by making himself comprehensible, it was remarked in 1890.[125] An indication of this want of popularity was the anthology *Victorian Poets*, published in 1891 in a new University Extension Series by Amy Sharp, local secretary for the Rugby centre: it contained chapters on Tennyson, the Brownings, Clough, Matthew Arnold, Rossetti, William Morris, and various minor poets—but not Meredith.[126] In 1892 he was elected president of the Society of Authors in succession to Tennyson. This raised his public standing; and that year saw a reprint of *Modern Love* (1862), following the activity of the *Poems and Lyrics of the Joy of Earth* (1883) and *Ballads and Poems of Tragic Life* (1887). His poetry was lauded in the *Fortnightly Review* in March 1892, by the Shakespeare and Shelley scholar Edward Dowden, from his perch as Professor of English Literature at Trinity College, Dublin. Notwithstanding philosophical differences, especially concerning personal immortality, Meredith had admired Tennyson as poet;[127] and he now sought to scotch the prospects of those whom he deemed unworthy successors. ' "Stilted prose" was the rapid and unhesitating reply' to whether he reckoned *The Light of Asia* a very fine poem, to the dismay of his questioner, who had 'read and re-read it with the greatest possible pleasure' and thought it 'beautiful'.[128]

In the event, Gladstone, with the Queen's agreement, left the office vacant. '[Alfred] Austin, [Robert] Buchanan, and other shadows flit in the distance,'[129] he wrote wearily on 17 October 1892; but, essentially, once Swinburne, William Morris, and Ruskin were eliminated, he had abandoned the search. He retired from the premiership in 1894 and his Liberal successor, Rosebery, did nothing further. Rosebery had sufficient political distractions, of course; but, though bookish, he was little inclined towards poetry. 'To appreciate poetry one must be in the heights rather than in the depths,' he told Lord Crewe. With his insomniacal melancholia, there was little doubt into which category Rosebery fell;[130] and no amount of poetic importunity could stir him. Lewis Morris was

---

[124] Farquharson, *In and Out of Parliament*, 122. See also Douglas, *Looking Back*, 388–9, for Arnold's mixture of affability and vanity.   [125] *Fortnightly Review* (May 1890).
[126] *Review of Reviews* (Sept. 1891), 307.   [127] Nicoll, *Bookman's Letters*, 12–14.
[128] Farquharson, *In and Out of Parliament*, 121–2.
[129] Letter to Acton, 17 Oct. 1892, in Matthew (ed.), *Gladstone Diaries*, xiii. 114.
[130] Robert Rhodes James, *Rosebery* (1963), 211. The death of his wife, the Rothschild heiress, in 1890 was an obvious factor, but it has also been suspected that he feared the exposure of a homosexual affair with Viscount Drumlanrig, who died (probably committed suicide) during a shooting party in October 1894. Drumlanrig was the heir of the Marquess of Queensberry; the youngest son was Lord Alfred Douglas, key figures in the trials of Oscar Wilde in 1895. See Ellmann, *Wilde*, 402; and articles in the *Oxford DNB* on both Rosebery and Queensberry by John Davis.

particularly pressing. Active in the Reform Club, he had twice bid to enter Parliament as a Liberal, in 1886 and 1892; and, though his zeal for Irish Home Rule and Welsh Disestablishment was not shared by Rosebery, Morris's services to the Welsh university movement were marked. He was also performing as de facto laureate, issuing odes on the marriage of the Duke of York in 1893[131] and the opening of the Imperial Institute in 1895. Rosebery tossed him a knighthood, not the laureateship, and in June 1895 his Government fell from office.

By omission, therefore, the nomination passed to the Conservative premier, Lord Salisbury. Even at the start of that year, the farcical aspect of one ministry after another shuffling off the responsibility was all too apparent, as also the naked ambition of certain poets and the wild inconsistency of certain pundits. *Punch* invented the Amalgamated British Society for the Supply of Laureates and reported its annual general meeting, attended by authors, reviewers, and publishers. Grant Allen, voted into the chair, sorrowfully announces the Society's repeated failure to fill the vacancy, despite his own exertions—'He had discovered a new sun in the firmament of poetry at least once a month, and had never hesitated to publish the name of his selection in one of the reviews. He was still willing to take seven to four about Mr. John Davidson and Mr. Francis Thompson, Mr. William Watson barred.' The Society's assets are looking thinner—only so many sonnets and odes, and strictly limited editions (a dig at the Bodley Head's stable of poets)—and it is 'becoming more and more costly and difficult to feed the public on geniuses'. At this, Richard Le Gallienne, notorious for his booming reviews of Bodley Head poets, of whom he is one, protests and is removed by the police, whereupon the meeting is turned over to other subscribers:

MR. ALFRED AUSTIN asked where he came in. He had never allowed a birth, a wedding, or a death in the upper circles of Royalty to pass unsung...Besides, he had discovered Ireland last year. MR. LEWIS MORRIS and MR. ERIC MACKAY made similar complaints. The latter offered to write patriotic poems with plenty of rhymes in them against any other living man. Would the meeting allow him to recite—?[132]

But no recitals are allowed, to 'loud murmurs of dissatisfaction' from the poets present. *Punch* thus seasoned the search with a silliness but, as Lord Salisbury assumed the premiership once more, much the same parade of long shots remained, though death had removed one, Frederick Locker,[133] and a new Ministry meant a revival in prospects for those with known Conservative and Unionist opinions, such as W. E. Henley, Coventry Patmore, William Watson, Sir Edwin Arnold, and Alfred Austin.

---

[131] Satirized in *Punch*, 27 May 1893, 241.   [132] *Punch*, 26 Jan. 1895, 47.

[133] Locker (1821–95) had become the double-barrelled Locker-Lampson in 1885, adding the maiden name of his second wife. His first wife was a daughter of the Earl of Elgin. As a poet, his reputation rests on his only volume, *London Lyrics* (1857), which ran into twelve editions by the time of his death, though he also published an anthology, *Lyra Elegantiarum of vers de société*, in 1867. The Locker and Tennyson families were joined when their children married; see Tennyson, *Stars and Markets*, ch. 4.

The first of these, Henley, editor of the *National Review*, had plumped for Swinburne when the laureateship was vacated in 1892, adding as a half-joking afterthought the names of Andrew Lang and Sir Edwin Arnold, and still more ludicrous, George R. Sims and Alfred Austin.[134] Arnold stepped up the pace in 1895 by dedicating his *Tenth Muse and Other Poems* to the Duchess of York; and *Punch* in October still counted him first favourite in the betting stakes, adding that 'Sir Lewis Morris is very much fancied—by himself. A somewhat sensational wager of £3,000 to £10 was booked against Sir Lewis and Mr. Henley "coupled".'[135] Events now moved beyond a joke, although Owen Seaman's parodies of the poetic contenders in *Punch* (published as *The Battle of the Bays*, 1896) sustained that side. Patmore, who (it was maliciously observed) 'survived all attempts to laugh him down', had issued a timely publication (*Religio Poetae*) following Tennyson's death, as had Austin (*Fortunatus the Pessimist*) and Watson (*Lachrymae Musarum*). The last contained a widely praised elegy for Tennyson. Watson appeared rather too conspicuously angling for the succession—his previous publication was *Wordsworth's Grave and Other Poems* (1890);[136] and this had brought a ringing declaration in the *Fortnightly Review* from Grant Allen, who cited W. D. Howells, Walter Besant, and Edward Clodd as endorsing his verdict that Watson was no minor poet. Since *In Memoriam*, Allen averred, he had 'not heard from any new tongue so large and whole an utterance'.[137] Watson's evolutionary theology naturally found favour from this agnostic and atheist party, but his lyricism—'April, April, Laugh thy girlish laughter'—also attuned to popular sentiment about what a poet should be. Big of build, Watson was decidedly manly, which meant anti-decadent, anti-aesthete, and anti-French— 'such rubbish and such filth'—in his poetic credo. Off duty, this disposition led him to smash up furniture when the mood seized him, and to treat his publisher John Lane to descriptions of his 'fiddling around with Mrs Watson's twat' during his progress to the Isle of Man armed with a cache of condoms.[138] In public, Watson's manly attitude caused him to strike a position as a political poet. Unfortunately for the Watson party, a mental breakdown had prostrated their favourite for well over a year after its onset in 1895. When Gladstone had read Watson's *Poems* (1892), sent to him by R. H. Hutton, it was with a view to obtaining for him a Civil List pension, not the laureateship.[139]

Other names had also been canvassed, often without much conviction, though there was genuine poetry in each: Robert Bridges, Aubrey de Vere, Austin

---

[134] Connell, *Henley*, 258.　　[135] *Punch*, 26 Oct. 1895, 198.

[136] He sent a copy to Hardy, who replied appreciatively that he had already read it while staying with Edward Clodd: 'I was immediately struck with the power of the poetry, & the absence of that affection which seems to be the rule with so many modern writers of verse, or at least rhyme' (Hardy to William Watson, 9 Aug. 1891, in Purdy and Millgate (eds.), *Hardy Letters*, i. 241).

[137] *Review of Reviews* (Aug. 1891), 174.　　[138] Lambert and Ratcliffe, *Bodley Head*, 82.

[139] Gladstone did not support Hutton's request: Matthew (ed.), *Gladstone Diaries*, xiii. 122 (28 Oct. 1892). A petition for a grant to relieve Watson was circulated in 1894; see Hardy to John Lane, 8 and 13 Feb. 1894, in Purdy and Millgate (eds.), *Hardy Letters*, ii. 49–50.

FIG. 12.1. Pin-up poets bidding to succeed Tennyson as Poet Laureate.
Source: *Review of Reviews*, November 1892

Dobson, Andrew Lang, and Sir Alfred Lyall. The outsiders also included a trio of women poets. No woman had—has even now—held the post, although the Victorian age gave prominence to many. Douglas Sladen, conduit for so much literary gossip in the 1890s, reported a movement in favour of Margaret Woods. A poet himself, Sladen reckoned her 'the best of all poetesses in the English language', having 'the gifts of both Brownings'. She was, besides, he thought, 'one of the best novelists of the day', starting with *A Village Tragedy* (1887).[140] All this was hyperbolic and distinctly partial: Sladen had been an undergraduate at Trinity College, Oxford, where Mrs Woods was wife of the President. She was altogether excessively well connected in the academic and ecclesiastical establishment: her father, having been Master of University College, Oxford, became Dean of Westminster, and her uncles included the philosopher F. H. Bradley and the literary scholar and Professor of Poetry at Oxford A. C. Bradley. She was renowned as a conversationalist.[141] Henry James also held a good opinion of her. Nonetheless, her claims paled when set against those of Christina Rossetti. In the *New Review*, November 1892, having nominated Swinburne foremost, Edmund Gosse then mentioned Christina Rossetti together with William Morris, Coventry Patmore, Austin Dobson, and Robert Bridges as other genuine poets who were possible successors to Tennyson—the first article to propose a female poet for the office.[142] Rossetti even composed an elegy, 'A Death of a First-Born', to commemorate the demise of Prince Albert, Duke of Clarence, in 1892, which was published in *Literary Opinion*. She further won the plaudits of Putney, appreciated both by Swinburne himself and by Swinburne's guardian Theodore Watts-Dunton, who had been a friend of her brother D. Gabriel Rossetti. Watts-Dunton was also the *Athenaeum*'s leading critic and author of the influential essay on 'Poetry' written for the ninth edition of *Encyclopaedia Britannica* in 1887. Other critics too acknowledged Rossetti's quality, George Saintsbury for one.[143] Still more emphatic was Walter Raleigh, then Professor of Literature at Liverpool. Writing to his sister on 11 January 1892, he declared:

I have been reading Christina Rossetti—three or four of her poems, like those of her brother, make a cheap fool of [Robert] Browning—and leave E.[lizabeth] B.[arrett] B.[rowning] barely human. I think she is the best poet alive. You read *Wife to Husband* and then try to read *Any Wife to Any Husband*—it is like going out of Heaven on a visit to a monkey-house.[144]

But Rossetti was already in her seventies, and death removed her at the very end of 1895. Swinburne's poetic tribute followed, 'A New Year's Eve', published in the *Nineteenth Century*, February 1895. Not that her succession to the laureateship had

---

[140] Sladen, *Twenty Years*, 129. On Margaret Woods (1856–1945), see Kemp *et al.* (eds.), *Edwardian Fiction*, 423–4.
[141] M. G. Brock and M. C. Curthoys (eds.), *The History of the University of Oxford*, vii: *Nineteenth Century Oxford* (Oxford, 2002) 243.   [142] Beckson, *London in the 1890s*, 100.
[143] Grant Duff, *Diary 1896 to 1901*, i. 82–3.   [144] Raleigh (ed.), *Raleigh Letters*, i. 164–6.

been at all likely, if only because of her own retiring disposition. Ford Madox Ford later reported that, when told of the movement favouring her, she had 'shuddered' at the thought of unwanted eminence.[145]

Rossetti was intensely religious, both in her personal duties and in her poetry. So too was the third woman talked about for the laureateship: Alice Meynell, a Catholic convert, otherwise Rosetti's 'effective literary heir'.[146] When Tennyson died in 1892, Mrs Meynell had published little poetry except *Preludes* (1875). In the *Fortnightly Review*, December 1892, assessing 'Mrs Meynell: Poet and Essayist', Coventry Patmore lauded her prose more than her poetry. Subsequently, in the *Saturday Review*, December 1895, he passionately promoted her claims for the laureateship. What had happened meanwhile? Meynell published a second volume of verses, *Poems*, in 1893; yet, this was mostly a reissue of *Preludes*, long out of print, with some of the weaker poems excised and a few new ones added. More decisive in forming Patmore's position was the publication of her essays *The Rhythm of Life* (1893). This contained a eulogy of Patmore's own poetry; *The Unknown Eros* (1877), Meynell argued, raised Patmore to the rank of the immortals. It was the start of an intense relationship which dominated the last years of Patmore's life. Equally besotted by Mrs Meynell was Francis Thompson, whom she and her husband nursed through his opium and drink addiction and whose poetry they first published and promoted. Thompson's 'Love in Dian's Lap' (*Poems*, 1893) was inspired by her; and, though without public influence, Thompson joined Patmore in ardently pressing Meynell's claims for the laureateship, while fearing the appointment of Sir Edwin Arnold.[147]

Both Thompson and Patmore were Catholic co-religionists of Meynell, Patmore being like her a convert. In the competition for the laureateship, the weight placed on the scale of things by a poet's religious affiliation is difficult to estimate. Coventry Patmore's descendant Derek Patmore reckoned that his 'conversion to Catholicism . . . made his appointment an impossibility'; but it was not the fact of his turning Catholic that counted so much as what Patmore subsequently made of it in his devotional verses and prose meditations. Ever anxious, Lewis Morris suspected Patmore of bidding for the laureateship when he abandoned retirement in Lymington after 1892 to reappear in Society. At one 'immensely swell affair' at Lady Jeune's, he rewarded Patmore with 'a very sour look'. Age (he was 70 in 1893) was not on Patmore's side, but more fatal to his suit initially was his pronounced hostility to Gladstone, exclaiming in a notorious ode, 'His leprosy's so perfect that men call him clean!' Accordingly, when Patmore's name cropped up in discussions about the laureateship—'not a great poet, still he

<hr />

[145] Hueffer, *Ancient Lights*, 57–8. See also Marsh, *Rossetti*, 559–60, for the talk about Rossetti and the laureateship; and Hudson, *Munby*, 415, for another poet's advocacy of Rossetti.

[146] Marsh, *Rossetti*, 537, though Rossetti and Meynell never met.

[147] Patmore, *Patmore*, 215, and Meynell, *Thompson and Meynell*, 110. *The Rhythm of Life* 'quite quickly achieved two ordinary editions of 500 copies each' (Lambert and Ratcliffe, *Bodley Head*, 39).

is a poet, which some of the other aspirants are not', wrote James Bryce—Gladstone coldly remarked that Patmore 'had died many years before'.[148]

Roman Catholicism proved no bar to Alfred Austin's eventual appointment by Lord Salisbury in 1896. Yet it appeared scarcely relevant in his case because, though he never publicly renounced, he married an Irish Protestant, denounced Cardinal Manning and the ultramontane party, attended Anglican services out of good form, and actually believed in no religion.[149] It was his political journalism, as leader-writer for the *Standard* and editor of the *National Review*, that recommended him to Salisbury; and his wife was active in the Primrose League. Austin's lyric poetry did draw admirers and these included Thomas Hardy;[150] but his narrative poems, blank-verse drama, and subsequent official confections, excited ridicule. Following the 'Pax Britannica' ode of 1898, *Punch* carried 'An Austiniad', which mocked both content and manner and advised him to give up.[151] This was actually politer than George Meredith, who, notwithstanding Austin's dedication of *Fortunatus the Pessimist* (1892) to him, thought from the start that he 'ought to be locked up ... and his pen impounded'.[152] 'In poetry', he added grimly, 'our Alfred is on the level of our Ministers in the art of Government.'[153] The most widely circulated witticism was that Alfred the Little had succeeded Alfred the Great,[154] an unkind reference to Austin's height as well as his poetry: he stood about 5 foot nothing. He was big on the idea of manliness, however, telling Vernon Lee when she stayed at his home, Swinford Old Manor, near Ashford in Kent, in 1885, that 'a poet should be a man in the first instance, a gentleman in the second, and then only a poet'. Imbued with this code, he would bang on about the 'necessity of horse exercise, warrior aristocracy, etc.', and address the local peasantry in booming voice.[155] Frank Harris thought Austin

---

[148] Patmore, *Patmore* 212–13, 227–8. See Bryce to Gladstone, 28 Oct. 1892, in Matthew (ed.), *Gladstone Diaries*, xiii. 117; and Hutchinson, *West*, 69, for Bryce's recommendation.

[149] Grant Duff, with whom Austin stayed in the summer of 1900, 'thought he talked best when the subject was the Catholic Church, to which he belonged originally but left in his early manhood, finding it impossible to hold her dogmas though retaining the strongest regard for her' (Grant Duff, *Diary, 1896 to 1901*, ii. 241 (27 Aug. 1900)). In 1908 Austin confessed to Wilfrid Blunt that 'he has leanings once more towards it [Catholicism] now he is getting old'. Austin was then aged 73. Blunt, who was also born a Catholic, enjoyed with Austin 'long talks and discussions on theology, philosophy, and the Catholic church. He is an acute and ready reasoner, and is well read in theology and science. It is strange that his poetry should be such poor stuff, and stranger still that he should imagine it immortal.' Blunt's conclusion was that, ridiculous though Austin's appointment was, he 'is better anyhow than Lewis Morris, the Liberal candidate, or than Watson, Dobson, Davidson, and the rest of the sons of their own penny trumpets' (Blunt, *Diaries*, i. 212, 369 (5 Jan. 1896, 15 July 1900), and ii. 213 (11 Sept. 1908). See also Nevill, *Reminiscences*, 324, for Lady Dorothy Nevill's similar eulogy: 'Mr. Alfred Austin is one of the best conversationalists I know.'

[150] Hardy to Alfred Austin, 14 June 1891, fulsomely reporting his enjoyment of *Lyrical Poems* (1891). Austin repaid the compliment the following year, sending Hardy a copy of the *National Review* which contained a 'generous' review of *Tess*; Hardy to Austin, 6 Feb. 1892, in Purdy and Millgate (eds.), *Hardy Letters*, i. 238, 258. Hardy inscribed a presentation copy of *Tess* for Austin. This was offered for sale in 1998 for £45,000; see *Art and Antiques* supplement of *The Times*, 2 June 1998.

[151] *Punch*, 3 Dec. 1898, 257. See also the mock interview, with cartoons, *Punch*, 18 June 1902, 438–9.

[152] Meredith to Edward Clodd, 15 Jan. 1896, in Cline (ed.), *Meredith's Letters*, iii. 1219.

[153] Meredith to Louisa Lawrence, 22 Sept. 1901, ibid. 1402.   [154] *Punch*, 11 Jan. 1896, 15.

[155] Gunn, *Vernon Lee*, 124.

possessed as much poetic spirit as a house fly. When Austin announced with sham modesty that he must write a certain amount of verse to keep the wolf from the door, this invited the riposte: 'I see . . . you read your poetry to the wolf, eh?'[156]

Following his appointment, Austin revelled in the position of premier poet. The publisher Eveleigh Nash was told by Austin's sister-in-law that, when receiving visitors, Austin would enter his drawing room with a servant, who announced, 'The Poet Laureate'.[157] Max Beerbohm was delighted to discover this formality. He wrote to Austin under an assumed name, claiming to want to interview him for the *English Illustrated*: 'This morning comes an exquisite letter saying that "The Poet Laureate greatly regretted that owing to his rules" etc. Isn't it rather marvellous of him to call himself these names—to a stranger?'[158] As for the Prime Minister who appointed him, Lady Frances Balfour reported, following Austin's effusion about the relief of Mafeking: 'I asked Salisbury if he thought "wrestle" and "Cecil" a good rhyme. He said he had thought it best not to read the poem of his Poet Laureate.'[159]

On 11 January 1896, George Gissing, unusually for him, was living the high life. First, he lunched at the Grosvenor with the poet John Davidson, who spoke 'with disgust' about Austin's appointment. In the evening he dined at the Savile Club with Edward Clodd, where they were joined by Clement Shorter and more. All registered a predictable verdict on the day's topic: 'Universal contempt thrown on Alfred Austin, of course'.[160] The cognoscenti's disdain did not preclude a public popularity. 'Jameson's Ride', which critics then and now rank against stiff competition as the worst of Austin, met with calls for reprints, even that it be set to music, after *The Times* first published it.[161] In 1900 Austin was awarded a Civil List annual pension of £200.[162] Outwardly the decencies were upheld about his station; in practice he was displaced by the Eton schoolmaster, afterwards Cambridge don, A. C. Benson, who acted as unofficial court laureate. His first involvement was as the author of a wedding hymn, chosen to be sung at the marriage of Princess Maud of Wales to Prince Charles of Denmark in July 1896. Queen Victoria commissioned other odes, hymns, and canticles from Benson: for her Diamond Jubilee, for her visit to Ireland, for the Boer War, and for family rites of passage. This duty continued under Edward VII, resulting in 'Land of Hope and Glory', verses which accompanied Elgar's *Pomp and Circumstance March* at the Coronation. It was Benson too who in 1903 was chosen for the sensitive

---

[156] Harris, *Life and Loves*, 435–6. Nash, *Life*, 122, attributed the quip to the Scottish judge Lord Young; on Young (1819–1907), see *DNB*.   [157] Nash, *Life*, 122.

[158] Rothenstein, *Men and Memories, 1872–1900*, 290. Also Blunt, *Diaries*, i. 279–80 (27 June 1900) for Austin's naive self-importance; and Nowell-Smith (ed.), *Letters to Macmillan*, 188–9, for Austin's draft press release in 1898 about the duties of his office.

[159] Letter to George Saintsbury, May 1900, in Lady Frances Balfour, *Ne Obliviscaris* (1930), ii. 326–7.

[160] Coustillas (ed.), *Gissing's Diary*, 400.

[161] *The Times*, 11 Jan. 1896. *The Times* paid Austin £25 for it. Cf. 'The Laureate's First Ride', *Punch*, 18 Jan. 1896, 33.   [162] *Annual Register for 1900* (1901), pt. ii, 19.

(and lucrative) job of publishing a filleted version of Queen Victoria's letters for the period 1837–61, which appeared in three volumes in 1907. Rather pointedly, the press described Benson as having been 'a great personal favourite' of the Queen; and his eminence was such that *Punch* now ascribed to him the authorship of the Apocrypha and Shakespeare's plays.[163]

For all his unmistakable Toryism, Austin had deemed that 'to take a polemical part in Party Politics would ill consort with the office I have the honour to hold'. So he wrote to F. Carruthers Gould, an unabashed Radical and searing critic of the Boer War, whose immorality and incompetence he cartooned in the *Westminster Gazette*. What had drawn Austin into this unexpected communication with an opposite was Joseph Chamberlain's tariff reform campaign. This split the Conservative and Unionist Party from 1903, and alienated Austin, who was a dedicated free trader like Carruthers Gould, the Liberal Party, and majority opinion in the country. Hence his surreptitious approach to Gould, suggesting that he devise a cartoon depicting a spectral Disraeli demanding of Chamberlain, 'What have you done with my Legions?'[164]

The appointment of a successor to Austin in 1913 appeared altogether less political. Many again expressed the opinion that the office had outlived its purpose. The Prime Minister, Asquith, was once among them, having wanted the post suspended on Tennyson's death; now, the new King, George V, also thought it should lapse.[165] In a spirit of compromise, Beerbohm Tree jocularly proposed that the laureateship be preserved but conferred, mandarin-style, on a deceased poet—'to benefit his family and to point out the beauties of his works to an otherwise indifferent posterity'.[166] The post survived unreformed in this or other ways. Asquith's own literary preferences were conventional—the classics and Shakespeare foremost—but his embrace was wide. Marie Belloc Lowndes wrote, 'I have known many men with an extensive knowledge of English literature, but I never knew a man whose knowledge was so extensive...'.[167] For relaxation during the Great War, he translated Kipling's ballads into Greek verse and, having been deposed by Lloyd George, he would spend 'a happy morning with a Rhoda Broughton'.[168] As a debater, his phraseology was meticulous. When seeing Asquith in the Commons pause for perfect expression, Max Beerbohm always wanted to help by shouting out, 'Don't worry, sir; the word you are looking for is "the".'[169] Of poets, Asquith judged Milton the finest but was fond of quoting

---

[163] Lubbock, *Benson*, 33–4, 42–3, 69, 147–8; Newsome, *Edge of Paradise*, 99–110, 115–8, 136, 226, 233.
[164] Scott, *'We' and Me*, 82.
[165] Hutchinson (ed.), *West*, 19, and Kenneth Rose, *King George V* (1983), 313.
[166] *The Times*, 17 July 1913.
[167] Lowndes, *Merry Wives*, 203. Alexander Mackintosh, the parliamentary reporter who assisted Asquith in compiling his several books of speeches and memoirs in the 1920s, also noted his fastidious choice of quotations and minute knowledge of literature; Mackintosh, *Echoes of Big Ben*, 112, 166. Cook, *More Literary Recreations*, 61–7, paid a similar tribute.
[168] Flower, *Just as it Happened*, 141; Asquith, *Diaries*, 324 (6 Aug. 1917).
[169] Kennet, *Self-Portrait*, 265 (14 Feb. 1929).

from Dryden, Pope, Wordsworth, Tennyson, and Coventry Patmore. Yeats, who sat next to Asquith at a dinner given by Edmund Gosse, 'found him an exceedingly well read man, especially, curiously enough, in poetry'.[170] *In Memoriam* he knew by heart, according to J. A. Spender, who once had cause to test him.[171]

Asquith's preferences for the laureateship excluded Edward Marsh's Georgian poets, whom he called a 'spavined team'. The press advanced various names: Laurence Binyon, Robert Bridges, Austin Dobson, Thomas Hardy, John Masefield, Alice Meynell, Henry Newbolt, Alfred Noyes, Stephen Phillips, Quiller-Couch, and Owen Seaman. Noyes had been encouraged in poetry by George Meredith and, following *The Loom of Years* (1902), *The Flower of Old Japan* (1903), and his collected *Poems* (1904), he had stirred the nation with a two-volume epic, *Drake* (1906–8), a copy of which Admiral Beatty kept by him during the Great War.[172] In 1913 Noyes presented the Lowell Lectures at Boston on 'The Sea in English Poetry'. This won for him a professorship in Modern English Literature at Princeton, not the laureateship. The talk of Masefield—who would obtain the laureateship in 1930—was also considered something of a joke, not least by the candidate himself, who reported to his brother: 'I haven't got a ghost of a chance, and never had . . . I am at once too young, too rebellious, and too coarse, to be in the running.' He was nonetheless invited to 10 Downing Street on 16 April 1913, the occasion being a birthday dinner party for the Prime Minister's daughter Violet, which included J. M. Barrie, Augustine Birrell, Rupert Brooke, Edmund Gosse, Edward Marsh, and Bernard Shaw.[173]

William Watson had again been in the frame. Indeed, in the *Observer*'s poll of writers, scholars, and publishers, he came second (after Kipling).[174] Douglas Sladen wrote that Watson 'is accustomed to think and write upon large national and international movements, and he has a splendid gift of sonorous and epigrammatic diction . . . In my mind, there was no question that the laureateship lay between him and Kipling.'[175] Watson's stock was high in 1913 with the publication of *The Muse in Exile*. In it he both lamented the public neglect of poetry and expressed fears for the security of Empire. This last sentiment was not calculated to commend him to Asquith; but Watson, now aged 55, had turned out loyal sentiment to order—a coronation ode for Edward VII in 1902—and had previously stood well with the Liberal conscience. The failure to succour Armenian Christians, massacred by the Turks in 1895–6, profoundly upset Watson, who

---

[170] W. B. to J. B. Yeats, 20 Nov. 1909, in Wade (ed.), *Yeats Letters*, 540.

[171] Spender, *Life, Journalism and Politics*, i. 153–5. The occasion was at Mells in 1900, when Asquith accused Spender of misquoting two lines. It transpired that both men were correct. The offending lines were included in a later edition than that which Asquith possessed. See Wilson Harris, *J. A. Spender* (1946), 88.

[172] *DNB* 1951–1960, 776–8, for Noyes (1880–1958). Otherwise, Beatty's preferred reading was the 'Morning Post and Pink 'Un [the *Sporting Times*]'; Stephen Roskill, *Admiral of the Fleet Earl Beatty, the Last Naval Hero: An Intimate Biography* (1980), 255.

[173] Constance Babington Smith, *John Masefield: A Life* (1978), 109, 114.

[174] *Observer*, 8 June 1913, cited by Derek Hudson, 'Reading', in Nowell-Smith (ed.), *Edwardian England*, 308.   [175] Sladen, *Twenty Years*, 106.

poured out anti-Turkish verses in *The Spectator*. 'Poet and Sultanicide', *Punch* dubbed him;[176] yet Watson's stance was not singular. The contest was not between pro- and anti-Turkish versifiers but about excelling in anti-Turkish declamation. Swinburne then proved a match for anyone—'I enter myself . . . for the anti-Turkish cursing-and-swearing stakes!';[177] still, Watson's coinages for the Sultan ('Abdul the Damned') and his ministry ('The Vice-Regency of Hell') were impressive. *The Year of Shame* (1896) was Watson's 'patriotic appeal, intended to provoke men to serious thought about national honour and duty'. Watson complained about the steep price that his publisher John Lane charged for this work—'I have not reached the mass of the people'; but, when he lambasted those who 'look upon international duty as something that is to be measured chiefly, if not entirely, by financial and material interests', then dismissed Kipling's 'Recessional' (1897) as 'merely barbarous and primitive', and championed the Boers' 'noble' cause in the South African war, Watson's stock stood high with radical Liberals.[178] For the sterner critics, this very topicality devalued Watson's muse. Further, his sense of continuing in a great poetic tradition seemed too self-promoting. So thought Roy Flecker, whose own best work, *The Golden Journey to Samarkand*, appeared in 1913. Flecker scorned Watson as worse than Stephen Phillips, and inveighed against his attempt 'in a most brazen manner to re-write Keats, Tennyson, and even Stevenson—(he begins a poem: "Under the dark and piny steep"). The temporary reputation acquired by Mr Watson is particularly pernicious to the well-being of Poetry; and it is ridiculous as well as aggravating that any notice should be taken of his pompous outcries.'[179]

The press, now that there were many more popular newspapers, took a greater interest in the laureateship in 1913 than in 1892. Critics were canvassed and their opinions reported. Alice Meynell, a volume of whose *Collected Poems* appeared in 1913, gained the endorsement of the editor of the *Observer*, J. L. Garvin, and of the *British Weekly*, Robertson Nicoll; and in a plebiscite in *T.P.'s Weekly*, she 'beat everyone by an enormous number—except Kipling'. Commenting on this, her daughter admitted: 'I had asked two people to vote for you—just so that you should not be entirely out of it! But I needn't have troubled.'[180] A year later

---

[176] *Punch*, 15 June 1904, 416.

[177] Swinburne to Watts-Dunton, 11 Sept. 1896, in Metcalf, *Knowles*, 347; and Gosse, *Swinburne*, 233, for Swinburne's contributions during the Balkans crisis in 1876. Even the Laureate Austin joined the anti-Turkish fray in 1896, thus to excite the ridicule of *Punch*, 10 Oct. 1896, 173, which cartooned him bestride a turkey.

[178] Lambert and Ratcliffe, *Bodley Head*, 112–13. Watson collected his pro-Boer verses in *For England: Poems Written during Estrangement* (1903); for a slashing review, see *Punch*, 28 Oct. 1903, 296–7.

[179] Flecker, *Collected Prose*, 218. To his future biographer Geraldine Hodgson, 15 Dec. 1913, Flecker wrote, 'I am so sorry you admire William Watson.' Flecker, now fatally stricken with consumption, for which he was being treated in Switzerland, found his own muse being extolled at this time, writing to his father, 'Do you realise your son is thought by Gosse, Yeats, Gilbert Murray, and also, thank God, some editors, to be far the greatest poet of his day, barring Yeats?' (Hodgson, *Flecker*, 202, 225, 249).

[180] Meynell, *Alice Meynell*, 282. W. S. Blunt, a long-standing friend, also favoured Mrs Meynell: see his letter to Wilfrid Meynell, 27 June 1913, in Meynell, *Meynell and Thompson*, 81. Eighteen months earlier, however, before the vacancy arose, Blunt was dining with Hilaire Belloc, who 'asked me who I thought

sort of thing. But as for me—*I say*—it's all damned nonsense!' Like Coventry
Patmore, Bridges always wrote with a quill and he was a vehement anti-socialist,
a doctrine he associated with 'downleveling', 'the Lower Ethick', and 'the class-
hate that kindleth in disorder'd times'. Thompson accused Bridges of economic
ignorance and political complacency. He supposed that 'if Bridges had possessed
more intellectual curiosity and had acknowledged a wider range of ideas, even
heretical and subversive ideas, as being at least of interest, he would have been a
still greater poet'. Some of Bridges' Boer War verses, *Matres Dolorosae* (on soldiers
from his old school, Eton, killed in South Africa) and his *Peace Ode* (to celebrate
the victory in 1902) were poor things; still, he could never perform as wretchedly
as Austin and, concluded Thompson, when all was added up, 'it amounts to
about the smallest amount of bad writing that any first-rate English author has
produced'. Later Bridges would so revise his judgement about the Boers,
following the contribution that a self-governing South Africa had made to the
Empire in the Great War, that he dedicated *October and Other Poems* (1920) to
General Smuts. Moreover, there was no gainsaying that the principal path taken
by Bridges in his poetry lay in a direction other than politics; as he proclaimed, he
was 'born to beauty'.[194]

   This was why Bridges' appointment as Laureate was generally deemed to
have been made on poetical, not political grounds. Such a verdict could never
have been given about Kipling, although that did not obscure his poetical gifts or
automatically disqualify him from this office. He was admitted the best choice
even by those who held contrary views about poetry and politics. Roy Flecker's
biographer Geraldine Hodgson emphasized how much 'Flecker loathed the
whole business of message-mongering'[195] in poetry; but he was both realist and
tolerant enough to allow an exception for the laureateship, an institution he
believed worth preserving. He wrote to the *Daily Chronicle*, 11 June 1913: 'It is not a
post which is meant to be given to the best living poet—or we should have
to give it to Mr Yeats without hesitation. It is a post for a good poet who is willing
to be a Court Poet.' Flecker discountenanced the notion of Thomas Hardy
becoming Laureate—he appeared blind to Hardy's muse when he wrote that
'The greatest of our novelists is an odd person to propose as Poet Laureate'—and
instead he recommended Kipling:

I am an honest Liberal and I know Kipling is a Conservative, and has written sad doggerel
against the Budget. But for all that what a fine thing it would be for the Government to
drop the party question and advise the King to appoint to the post of Laureate the poet
who seems to have been inevitably born for the position.[196]

---

[194] Thompson, *Bridges*, 58–65, 80, 83, 110–11. See also Walter Raleigh to Lady Elcho, 30 Oct. 1912: 'He
[Bridges] is delightfully grumpy. He mentions thing after thing which is commonly believed and says that
of course it's not so. He's always right. His intellect has been so completely self-indulged that it now can't
understand rubbish. He has never obeyed anyone or adapted himself to anyone, so he's as clear as crystal,
and can't do with fogs' (Raleigh (ed.), *Raleigh Letters*, ii. 390–1).   [195] Hodgson, *Flecker*, 272.
   [196] Ibid. 188.

Kipling was obviously the most popular poet of the day. He had long been tagged the People's Laureate. The fastidious, led by Max Beerbohm, loathed him for having cheapened and betrayed an immense gift.[197] But it was not just the hoi polloi that favoured him. In 1898 the Warden of Merton College, Oxford, reckoned that 'an undergraduate *plébiscite*' would cast for Kipling;[198] and, in the *Times Literary Supplement* in 1912, Bridges himself extolled Kipling's vitality, especially his ingenious use of 'the idioms and actual converse of common folk', although 'Mr. Kipling's method seems to shut him out from such heights' as Wordsworth reached.[199] Kipling enjoyed unusually large sales, and all commercially successful poets were judged in relation to him. Thus Robert Service, who shot to fame with his Yukon ballads *Songs of a Sourdough* (1907), and other rough rhymes about rough characters such as Dan McGrew and Sam McGhee, Pious Pete and Blasphemous Bill, was naturally dubbed the 'Canadian Kipling'.[200] As a convinced imperialist and anti-Liberal, Kipling had been in Salisbury's thoughts when scouring for a successor to Tennyson; he was sounded but refused. This answer he maintained consistently whenever honours were offered: he rejected the KCB in 1899, 'feeling he can do better without it', the KCMG in 1903, the OM in 1916, the CH in 1917, and more in the 1920s, despite the general opinion that, with his pen, he had (in Lord Esher's words) 'accomplished for the Empire quite as much as Cromer or Kitchener'. When he learned that his name was going forward for the Companion of Honour, he blazed at Bonar Law: 'How would you like it if you woke up and found they had made you Archbishop of Canterbury?'[201] Kipling did, however, accept an honorary D.Litt. from Oxford and the Nobel Prize for Literature (in 1907).

IV

Thomas Hardy's wry comment 'It is odd to associate him with "peace" ' notwithstanding,[202] Kipling was celebrated as the first British writer to win the Nobel. He remained the only one until the inter-war years, unless Rabindranath Tagore, who won it in 1913, counts, as being from British India. A Brahman, born

---

[197] Beerbohm waged a vendetta against Kipling: at least twenty-six caricatures and numerous biting parodies, reviews, and essays; Riewald (ed.), *Beerbohm's Literary Caricatures*, 194–207; Behrman, *Max*, 49–58.

[198] George C. Brodrick, 'The University of Oxford in 1898', *Nineteenth Century* (Aug. 1898), 217.

[199] Thompson, *Bridges*, 80–2. Bridges was a friend of Bruce Richmond, editor of the *TLS*, and frequently contributed articles.

[200] Robert Service (1874–1958) was actually born in Preston and grew up in Glasgow. He emigrated to North America in 1895. *Songs of a Sourdough* was followed by *Ballads of a Cheechako* (1909) and *Rhymes of a Rolling Stone* (1912). See James Mackay, *Vagabond of Verse: Robert Service, a Biography* (1995). Stanley Unwin was responsible for securing *Songs of a Sourdough* for his uncle's publishing firm, T. Fisher Unwin: Rose and Anderson (eds.), *British Literary Publishing Houses, 1881–1965*, 4.

[201] Birkenhead, *Kipling*, 275 and app. B.

[202] Hardy to Florence Henniker, 31 Dec. 1907, in Purdy and Millgate (eds.), *Hardy Letters*, iii. 288. Interviewed in 1906, Hardy said that 'he liked Kipling very much as a companion, and thought he would have been a very great writer if the Imperialists had not got hold of him' (Nevinson, *More Changes*, 180–1).

in Calcutta, Tagore first came to England in 1878 and was already a published poet when he was at University College London. He wrote mostly in Bengali; his work became known in Britain chiefly through translation, a cultish following growing up with his *Gitanjali: Song Offerings* (1913), prefaced by W. B. Yeats. The translation was the poet's own, adapted by Yeats and Sturge Moore. Yeats was infatuated by Tagore, not just by his lyricism, but his religion, philosophy, and politics, which for Yeats marked a parallel between the Indian and Irish spiritual revivals that would loosen the British yoke more surely and healthily than would physical-force nationalism. He was thus delighted when Tagore won the Nobel Prize, doubly so because Gosse out of 'malice' had blocked Tagore's election to the Academic Committee of English Letters.[203] Tagore was not the only Indian poet to visit England—T. Ramakrishna did so in 1911[204]—but he it was who most stirred the literati and intelligentsia. Among those to whom he was introduced in 1912 and 1913—between times he sailed for America, where the cult lapped in his wake—were the octogenarian man of letters and ex-Anglican clergyman Stopford Brooke, and Robert Bridges, Edward Carpenter, John Galsworthy, W. H. Hudson, John Masefield, Ezra Pound, Bertrand Russell, Bernard Shaw, and H. G. Wells.[205] In 1914, reviewing *Chitra* ('Beauty'), 'a fairy play in seven scenes', which Tagore originally published in 1895, E. M. Forster noted:

London is the City of booms, of transient fanaticisms that raise the spirit to fever heat and pass leaving it a little weaker. There is no connection between one boom and the next. The rams are driven hurriedly from altar to altar, and their blood has scarcely cooled to Emil Reich before it is poured in unexampled profusion to Mr Tagore. The reviewer, while affecting to be above such hysteria, is really involved in it, and it is difficult to listen through the noise and nonsense of the last two years and catch the authentic voice of Tagore beyond.[206]

Forster had already made his first visit to India and caught the siren spell of the East, but his verdict on Tagore was almost deflating. The poetry had charm but was not 'strong stuff'; nor was Tagore 'a seer or a thinker', to be classed with Whitman or Nietzsche. Yet, in 1901 Tagore had founded his own school at Bolpur in Bengal, the Santiniketan (Abode of Peace), and he was now projecting it as an international institute for a new universal religion, inspired by the perception of perfect unity between Man and Nature. Once consciousness of this was realized,

---

[203] Foster, *Yeats*, i. 469–73, 616.

[204] On Ramakrishna (b. 1854), who was educated at Madras Christian College and became Professor in Dravidian Languages at Madras University, see *Who Was Who, 1916–1928*, 867.

[205] Krishna Kripalani, *Tagore: A Life* (Oxford, 1971), 126. See also *DNB* for Tagore (1861–1941); and Krishna Dutta and Andrew Robinson (eds.), *Selected Letters of Rabindranath Tagore* (Cambridge, 1997).

[206] E. M. Forster, 'Chitra' (1914), in Forster, *Abinger Harvest*, 314–16. Emil Reich (1854–1910), from Hungary, was hailed as historian, theologian, philosopher, and all-purpose polymath. Having moved to England, he gave lectures at London, Oxford, and Cambridge universities. He was also consulted by HM Government in preparing the British case in the Venezuelan boundary dispute, it was remarked amid the multiple vanities of his entry in *Who Was Who, 1897–1916*, 591.

not only would love permeate the world but man would feel truly free.[207] Hence, not just respect but reverence was accorded him;[208] and a knighthood followed in 1915. P. G. Wodehouse, dispensing advice in *Vanity Fair* to Christmas-present shoppers in 1915, gave his salute by recommending a shiny-backed edition of Tagore as ideal to attract flies which would then shoot off at amazing speed and stun themselves against the wall.[209] Tagore was to renounce the knighthood in 1919; and when Forster reviewed *The Home and the World* in that same year, the Tagore phenomenon seemed much ado about nothing.[210]

The Nobel Prize for Literature, first awarded in 1901, was the most prestigious of an abundance of prizes which, by 1914, gave prominence to authorship. Another was the Polignac, an annual award of £100. In 1912 it went to John Masefield for his poem *The Everlasting Mercy*, in a ceremony orchestrated by the Royal Society of Literature in the Caxton Hall.[211] Poets in the pupal stage were spurred on by this. In 1913 Siegfried Sassoon produced a pastiche of Masefield's prize-winning performance as *The Daffodil Murderer*, which in turn alerted Edmund Gosse to his promise.[212] Unsung authors valued such patronage. The Polignac's winner in 1913 was James Stephens, scion of Dublin's slums. A diminutive figure, 4 feet 6 inches small, with scarcely any schooling, Stephens was 'discovered' by Æ (George Russell), who encouraged him to publish his first book of poems, *Insurrections*, in 1909; he was then taken up by W. B. Yeats, through whose influence with the Royal Society of Literature the Polignac was awarded for his prose fantasy *The Crock of Gold* (1912). Yeats lavished praise on Stephens's work in the presentation address.[213] This sort of service, dishing out other people's money to friends and clients, and distributing pats on the backs of the *proxime accesserunt*, was greatly appreciated. Flecker, though disappointed not to win the Polignac in 1914, was cheered that 'Gosse, Yeats, Gilbert Murray all did

[207] See C. F. Andrews (ed.), *Rabindranath Tagore: Letters to a Friend* (1928). Andrews was a missionary with the Cambridge Brotherhood and present at Rothenstein's Hampstead home on 30 June 1912, when, before a select audience, including H. W. Nevinson, Tagore was introduced and Yeats gave readings from the *Gitanjali*. Andrews thereafter became an associate of Tagore and a worker at the Santiniketan. Andrews had been in South Africa to observe and then lend support to Gandhi's passive resistance struggle against the system of indentured Indian labour there and, like Tagore himself, worked to extend the movement into Fiji and other colonies and eventually to the Indian subcontinent. In the interlocking passages between the letters of the 1928 book, Andrews usually refers to Tagore not by name but, awesomely, as 'the Poet'. On Andrews's association with Tagore, see Benarsidas Chaturvedi and Marjorie Sykes, *Charles Freer Andrews*, foreword by M. K. Gandhi, (1949), esp. chs. 6 and 7.

[208] For a critical account of the cult: Lago (ed.), *Rothenstein*, 168–71, 191–2. Rothenstein produced *Six Portraits of Sir Rabindranath Tagore* (1915). See also Nowell-Smith (ed.), *Letters to Macmillan*, 290–2, 295, 309; Jacks, *Stopford Brooke*, ii. 586, 624, 671; Raitt, *May Sinclair*, 194; *Punch*, 10 Dec. 1913, 494, and 18 Feb. 1914, 129.

[209] The article—written by Wodehouse under the pen-name P. Brooke-Haven—was reprinted in *The Times*, 17 Dec. 2001.

[210] Forster, 'The Home and the World' (1919), in Forster, *Abinger Harvest*, 316–17.

[211] *The Times*, 29 Nov. 1912; Smith, *Masefield*, 105–9. Prince Edmond de Polignac died in 1901; the prize was established by his American wife, Winnie, an heiress to the Singer sewing machine fortune.

[212] Wilson, *Sassoon*, 156–60.

[213] Foster, *Yeats*, i. 486, 493. On Stephens (1882–1950) see Kemp *et al.* (eds.), *Edwardian Fiction*, 82, 373.

their best for me'.[214] Unlike the Polignac, the Nobel Prize was not restricted to imaginative or fictional writing: the stipulation was literature of 'an idealistic tendency'. This explains the otherwise mysterious choice of an ad hoc Nobel Prize Committee, established by the Authors' Society, in 1902. It nominated as Britain's candidate the octogenarian philosopher Herbert Spencer.[215]

Billiards apart, Spencer had little time for frivolity and used earplugs to exclude conversation he felt might excite him. He had not been a favourite of Carlyle. When Monkton Milnes as a boy was taken to visit Carlyle in Cheyne Row, he told the sage that he was the second famous man his father had introduced him to that day, the other being Spencer. Whereupon Carlyle advised, 'then you can boast to your young companions that you've met the most unending ass in Christendom'.[216] Gosse wrote: 'On the solitary occasion when I sat in company with Herbert Spencer on the committee of the London Library he expressed a strong objection to the purchase of fiction, and wished that for the London Library no novels should be bought, "except, of course, those of George Eliot".'[217] Spencer's friendship and philosophy were important for Eliot (to whom he once proposed marriage); but many other novelists and poets carried his imprint on their work. Grant Allen was perhaps an extreme case, both in his fiction and in his pronouncements on education and public policy generally;[218] but Olive Schreiner's *Story of an African Farm* (1883) was also strongly influenced by her reading Spencer; and Spencer it was who suggested the theme for Wilfrid Blunt's 'individual protest against the abominations of the Victorian Age', the poem *Satan Absolved* (1899).[219] Naturally, Spencer had decided views on the function of poetry. 'Poetry', he declared, 'shd. diminish the friction between the minds of the writer and reader'; and for this reason he had disliked Robert Browning's, which increased it.[220] Spencer himself was no light read; as the radical politician Joseph Chamberlain put it in 1883, 'Happily, for the majority of the world, his writing is not intelligible, otherwise his life would have been spent in doing harm.'[221] Yet Spencer could coin a phrase, and his 'survival of the fittest' became lethal after it was taken up by Aryan fascist ideologues. Sales of his works,

[214] Hodgson, *Flecker*, 218; Goldring, *Reputations*, 22–3. The Polignac was last awarded in 1914—to the poet Ralph Hodgson.

[215] Lord Avebury was chairman of the nominating committee, whose membership included A. C. Benson, Austin Dobson, Richard Garnett, Edmund Gosse, Mrs J. R. Green, and Thomas Hardy; see Newsome, *Edge of Paradise*, 94; Hutchinson, *Lubbock*, ii. 164–6; Millgate, *Hardy*, 438. In 1897 a public fund had been established to pay for a portrait of Spencer by Hubert Herkomer, in celebration of Spencer's conclusion of his Synthetic Philosophy. To this, Hardy donated 1 guinea: see Purdy and Millgate (eds.), *Hardy Letters*, ii. 142–3. Hardy preferred Swinburne to Spencer for the Nobel nomination in 1902; Mrs Humphry Ward also protested about it, writing to the secretary of the Society of Authors to argue that George Meredith had stronger claims than Spencer. See her letter, 19 Jan. 1902, in Trevelyan, *Mrs. Ward*, 180–1. The actual winner in that year was the historian Theodor Mommsen. For a satire, *Punch*, 22 Jan. 1902, 63.

[216] Related to Compton Mackenzie by Edmund Gosse; Mackenzie, *Life and Times*, iv. 152.

[217] Gosse, *Aspects and Impressions*, 2.   [218] Allen, *Post-Prandial Philosophy*, 23–4.

[219] Blunt, *Diaries*, 410–11.   [220] Masterman (ed.), *Mary Gladstone*, 121 (14 Apr. 1877).

[221] Norman and Jeanne MacKenzie (eds.), *The Diary of Beatrice Webb*, i. (1982) 91.

at first received with 'stolid indifference', grew such that at the end of his life he was receiving £800 per year from British royalties and £500 per year from America, sums that made comfortable an otherwise miserable old age.[222] Already there was reason to think that Spencer's synthetic philosophy, evolutionary logic, scientific materialism, and constipated individualism were an unhealthy influence on literature. R. C. Lehmann, providing *Punch*'s parody of Olive Schreiner, mocked her allegorical manner and phoney philosophical allusions to Life and The Ideal, Wealth and Vastness, Health and Infinity, Wisdom and Love, Reflection and Joy. Like the Lord Mayor's Show, 'The Real was not there . . . And it was all a striving and a striving and an ending in Nothing.'[223]

Max Beerbohm, with his instinct for the ludicrous, enjoyed inventing spoof titles for improbable books: *The Love Poems of Herbert Spencer* was a favourite.[224] Arnold Bennett too, when reading Spencer's posthumously published *Auto-biography* (1904), found the account 'disappointingly deficient in emotion'. But Bennett was emphatic about his own debt to Spencer: 'When I think how *First Principles* [1862], by filling me up with the sense of causation everywhere, has altered my whole view of life, and undoubtedly immensely improved it, I am confirmed in my opinion of that book. You can see *First Principles* in nearly every line I write.'[225] The Society of Authors' Nobel Prize Committee continued annually to nominate British contenders, in 1903, for instance, forwarding Swinburne's name.[226] In 1914 it nominated Thomas Hardy.[227] News of this was broadcast. Far away in America, while on tour, the actor Jack Barnes came over all misty-eyed. He was then penning his memoirs *Forty Years on the Stage*, recollecting his part as Sergeant Troy in J. Comyns Carr's adaptation of Hardy's *Far from the Madding Crowd* (1874) in 1882; and he recorded it as fact, having read in the newspapers that Hardy 'has been justly awarded the "Nobel" prize for literature'.[228] Barnes's memoirs went to press still bearing that legend; but this would be the year in which, because of the Great War, no award was made. It was the kind of conjunction that Hardy the grim fatalist might happily have planned.

---

[222] Ibid. ii. 159.

[223] *Punch*, 16 May 1891, 229. The parody was entitled 'Gasps' by 'Olph Schreion, Author of "Screams", "The Allegory of an Asian Ranche" '. Schreiner originally published *The Story of an African Farm* under the pseudonym Ralph Iron. [224] Cecil, *Max*, 371.

[225] Flower (ed.), *Bennett Journals*, i. 383 (15 Sept. 1910).

[226] The Committee preferred Swinburne over John Morley, George Meredith, and Kipling; Newsome, *Edge of Paradise*, 94. [227] Sladen, *Twenty Years*, 253.

[228] J. H. Barnes, *Forty Years on the Stage: Others (Principally) and Myself* (1914), 134–5. When Bernard Shaw was awarded the Nobel in 1925, Hardy registered it as 'rather a blow . . . He had not counted on it exactly, but had always had the feeling that he had been passed over for some unjust reason' (Florence Hardy to Sydney Cockerell, 17 Nov. 1926, in Millgate (ed.), *Emma and Florence Hardy*, 245).

the son of a Kirriemuir weaver, but they were humble enough, Buchan being born the son of a Fifeshire manse. In his pomp Buchan was 'consistently kind about everyone except Barrie. He laughs at him. "Ma caneerie and I were heving a talk," et cetera', Buchan would say, mocking the kailyard style which brought Barrie his first flush of fame. Lady Kennet, who recorded this, rightly supposed that Buchan and Barrie had 'just enough in common . . . to make a slight rivalry.'[9] Unlike Barrie, Buchan went to Oxford, albeit the socially and intellectually unfashionable Brasenose College. At Oxford he cultivated the Balliol set of Raymond Asquith, eldest son of the future Prime Minister, and Auberon Herbert, later Lord Lucas; and he became President of the Union in 1899. Barrie, a graduate of Edinburgh, was irritated by the affected superiority and streamlined progress of these pampered and privileged alumni from the deep south. Thus, Mr Purdie in *Dear Brutus* (1917): 'He is the most brilliant of our company, recently notable in debate at Oxford, where he was president of the Union, as indeed nearly everybody one meets seems to have been. Since then he has gone to the bar on Monday, married on Tuesday, and had a brief on Wednesday.' Purdie delights in his own cleverness: he made such 'charming company for himself.'[10] This was not the first time Barrie allowed himself a dig at the Oxford type. *The Will* (1913) begins with Robert Devizes at work. He is aged 23, lately down from Oxford, and now junior partner in his father's firm of solicitors. And what is he doing?—'we catch him skilfully balancing an office ruler on his nose'. This is not all that Oxford has taught him. The first scene opens with a discussion between Robert, his father, and the put-upon chief clerk, Surtees, about how a client's letter has gone missing:

ROBERT. You were out, father, and Surtees brought me in some letters. His mouth was wide open. [*Thoughtfully*] I suppose that was why I did it.
MR DEVIZES. What did you do?
ROBERT. I must have suddenly recalled a game we used to play at Oxford. You try to fling cards one by one into a hat. It requires great skill. So I cast one of the letters at Surtees's open mouth, and it missed him and went into the fire.

During the play decades pass; later Robert is pictured in charge of the firm, 'a middle-aged man who has long forgotten how to fling cards into a hat'. To a new chief clerk, Sennet, we now have Robert issuing orders:

ROBERT [*Frowning*]. And, Sennet, less row in the office, if you please.
SENNET [*glibly*]. It was those young clerks sir—
ROBERT. They mustn't be young here, or they go. Tell them that.
SENNET [*glad to be gone*]. Yes, sir.[11]

This is an unattractive picture; but Buchan was not so easily written off. Indisputably, he was an achiever at Oxford, where he won a First in Greats, and the

---

[9] Kennet, *Self-Portrait*, 288 (8 May 1932). Lady Kennet was the sculptress Kathleen Bruce.
[10] Barrie, *Plays*, 473–4.
[11] Ibid. 693–4, 704. Barrie was awarded an honorary degree by Oxford in 1926 (and by Cambridge in 1930).

Stanhope Historical Essay and Newdigate Poetry prizes. Moreover, he was already supporting himself by his writings. He listed five publications in the 1898 edition of *Who's Who*, in which he was possibly the only person whose occupation was defined as 'undergraduate'.[12] His contacts in the world of publishing grew as he became a reader for the Bodley Head, and later a partner in Nelson's (he was at Oxford with Tommy Nelson); but it was his articles in *The Spectator* while training for the bar that brought him to the notice of Leo Amery, who recommended him to the High Commissioner for South Africa, Sir Alfred Milner, as assistant private secretary. Both before and after his South African service, 1901–3, Buchan assiduously participated in the weekending round of country-house parties. He was conscious too of connections to be made through London clubs. These were then 'in their hey-day, their waiting lists were lengthy, and membership of the right ones was a stage in a career'. The most celebrated were out of reach; he contented himself initially with young men's clubs such as the Bachelors' in Hamilton Place and the Cocoa Tree in St James's Street, until John Lane, the publisher at the Bodley Head, sponsored his membership of the Devonshire.[13] His rise became irresistible with his marriage to Susan (Susie) Grosvenor in 1907. She was 'pretty and flaxen and brainless . . . [and] must have a man to hold her handkerchief', wrote Virginia Stephen, reporting one view of the match by the MP Jack Hills, who predicted tragedy from her marrying a very clever man.[14] Yet her heart was 'excellent' and Buchan had what he wanted. He entered the 'enchanted land' and became a patrician by adoption with 'a vast new relationship—Grosvenors, Wellesleys, Stuart-Wortleys, Lytteltons, Talbots'.[15] Though he had written many books and would write more, he had now so far risen socially as to be deemed an upper-class businessman who dabbled in literature. His wife recalled: 'At this stage of his life no one thought of him primarily as a writer. "Why do you go on writing?" one of my relations naively asked him. "Why do you play the piano and do embroidery?" he retorted. "One must have some touch with art".'[16]

None was so successful as Buchan in exploiting a social system in which Celtic charm could flourish without the disadvantages attending the English working-class provincial. The philosopher–historian Sir Ernest Barker, who was born

---

[12] Smith, *Buchan*, 61.

[13] Lambert and Ratcliffe, *Bodley Head*, 118; Buchan, *Memory Hold-the-Door*, 93. Smith, *Buchan*, 83, cites the Piccadilly, the Devonshire, and Cocoa Tree as his clubs in 1900–1. In *Who's Who* (1905), 215, Buchan gave only the Bachelors' and the Union.

[14] Letter to Violet Dickinson, 20 Nov. 1906, written when the Grosvenor–Buchan engagement was known; Nicolson and Banks (eds.), *Flight of the Mind*, 248. Hills (1867–1939) was educated at Eton and Balliol. His first wife, who died in 1897, was Stella Duckworth, a half-sister of Virginia Stephen.

[15] Buchan, *Memory*, 137. Susan Grosvenor's father was first cousin to the Duke of Westminster. She and Buchan married at the Society church St George's, Hanover Square, the bride being conveyed in the Grosvenor family coach. They started their honeymoon at Tylney Hall in Hampshire, home of Sir Lionel and Lady Phillips, before travelling to Austria and Italy. Their three sons subsequently went to Eton, 'and we were lucky as Cyril Alington, the Headmaster, married to a cousin of mine, welcomed us yearly for a week-end'. See Lady Tweedsmuir (ed.), *John Buchan by his Wife and Friends* (1947), 39, 95.

[16] Tweedsmuir (ed.), *Buchan*, 43–4.

Athenaeum. Given its name, the Garrick was intended as a theatrical rather than literary club, founded to give 'actors the opportunity of meeting gentlemen and patrons of the drama on equal terms'.[27] But the generally low status of the theatre and its performers meant that, by mid-Victorian times, 'members of no profession, of the literary profession, of the learned professions, and of the army had rather elbowed out the actors'. So Frank Burnand recollected: he was elected in 1865, being a burlesque-writer and on the staff of *Punch*. But not for these credentials alone. His uncle, already a Garrick member, was his sponsor; and Burnand was an Etonian. Moreover, at Cambridge he had founded the University's Amateur Dramatic Club. The Garrick then seemed 'old-fogy-ridden'; and when Burnand and other new members, still in their twenties or thirties—the musicians Arthur Sullivan and Frederick Clay, and that budding novelist of the sporting and army life Captain Hawley Smart—re-created an atmosphere of jollification there, they were met with steely reprimands from such as Sir Charles Taylor.[28] The passing of years and introduction of a different theatrical order then registered themselves at the Garrick. Squire Bancroft, John Hare, Henry Irving, Cyril Maude, and J. L. Toole were among its best-known actor members in the late nineteenth century; and in the Edwardian period, when Gerald Du Maurier was elected, he would lunch there most days.[29] Theatrical behaviour was apparently felt obligatory by members who were not connected to the stage. Scribner's London agent Lemuel Bangs swigged champagne by the pint at the Garrick and dressed up to the nines, in a selection from one of his 188 ties and twenty-six gaudy waistcoats.[30]

Among the dramatist members around 1900 were Barrie, Comyns Carr, Arthur Pinero, and Louis Parker. Anthony Hope, a sizeable part of whose sizeable literary income came from playwriting, was elected in 1903—'a luxury for idle evenings', he noted rather grandly in his diary.[31] Aspiring playwrights looked upon the place with awe. Alfred Sutro repaired there as a guest of Joseph Hatton after they attended the first night of Henry Arthur Jones's *The Case of the Rebellious Susan* (1894), starring Charles Wyndham. Thus it was, wrote Sutro, that 'for the first time I entered that club of clubs'.[32] Garrick members included several authors not primarily known as playwrights such as Kenneth Grahame, who was further distinguished as secretary to the Bank of England; but actors tended to rule the roost, at least in Irving's time, and it was wise not to cross them. *Obiter Dicta* (1884), which made Augustine Birrell's reputation as a belletrist, contained an essay on actors that 'prevented a friend from putting me up for election at the Garrick for, so my friend told me, "the essay had irritated Henry Irving"'.[33]

---

[27] Quoted in Irving, *Irving*, 230. Its founders included the Duke of Sussex (sixth son of George III).
[28] Burnand, *Records*, ii 18–19.   [29] Daphne Du Maurier, *Gerald: A Portrait* (1935), 112, 118.
[30] Thwaite, *Burnett*, 127.   [31] Mallet, *Hope*, 169.
[32] Alfred Sutro, *Celebrities and Simple Souls* (1933), 60. On Hatton (1841–1907), Sutherland, *Companion*, 284, and Kemp *et al.* (eds.), *Edwardian Fiction*, 177.
[33] Birrell, *Things Past Redress*, 100. Ironically, Irving was blackballed when first put up for membership in 1873, though his supporters rallied to elect him in 1874. In 1882 he was elected a member of the

This revived memories of previous spats. Thackeray was once an active member, elected at the age of 22 in 1833; as was Dickens, elected at the age of 24 in 1837, largely at the instigation of his publisher Bentley. Famously, the Garrick was the scene of their estrangement when Dickens refused to back the expulsion of Edmund Yates for writing a scurrilous sketch of Thackeray, based on club gossip, in 1858. Dickens then resigned from the committee and eventually the club in 1865, when a candidate whom he proposed for election, W. H. Wills, editor of *All the Year Round*, was blackballed.[34] Thackeray had died in 1863; and his committee place was filled by Anthony Trollope, who had joined the Garrick two years before. He dined there seldom but thought it 'a festival' when he did. His popularity in the club compensated for his misery at school and solitariness in his working life.[35] Charles Reade also occupied a place in Garrick lore. Barrie was told by a long-time member how 'he used to watch Reade writing his invectives there, and that the fiercer they were the sweeter his smile'.[36] The club moved premises from Probatt's Family Hotel, King Street, to the current building in *palazzo* style, designed by Frederick Marrable, in Rose Street in 1864, the year in which George Meredith was elected. Meredith remained a member until 1899, when he resigned as no longer able to make use of it in his seventy-first year.

The Garrick therefore acquired authors almost as a by-product of its principal business, the stage. The Arts Club, founded in 1863, and later amalgamated with the Hogarth, did the same, though its first chairman was the author of *Tom Brown's Schooldays*, Thomas Hughes. The founder's object was the commingling of 'those connected either professionally or as amateurs with art, literature and science';[37] still, it was naturally the painters, illustrators, and cartoonists, Frederic Leighton, John Tenniel, John Leech, Charles Keene, and George Du Maurier, who were most evident, although towards the end of his life Du Maurier would become a best-seller too. The eventually most famous author member was Swinburne, elected in 1864. Alas, his tantrums did not do much for the reputation of writers in general. Mislaying his hat one summer evening in 1870, he gathered up the headgear of other members and stamped on them. Compelled by the committee to resign, he long brooded about his victimized condition and would not ever seek election to a club again.[38] New clubs such as the Authors' afterwards emerged as a haven for fugitive penmen. The Authors' Club was founded by Walter Besant in 1891. Its secretary was also the Society of Authors' secretary,

---

Athenaeum; but, though eventually Irving was a member of six clubs, including the Marlborough and the Savage, it was at the Garrick where he appeared most and where as 'Sir Enery' he lorded it; as his grandson put it, where 'he seemed to preside over rather than to be part of their fellowship' (Irving, *Irving*, 230–3, 239, 392–3, 407, 412, 521–2, 654). As for Birrell, he did not pine for eternity: he was afterwards elected to the Athenaeum. His other clubs were the National Liberal and the Johnson.

[34] *The Times*, 21 Jan. 1937; Harden (ed.), *Thackeray's Letters*, 330–1, 355–6; *DNB* notice of Thackeray by Leslie Stephen.   [35] Trollope, *Autobiography*, 147–9.

[36] To Maarten Maartens, 20 Nov. 1893, in Meynell (ed.), *Barrie Letters*, 27.

[37] Quoted in Charles Graves, *Leather Armchairs: The Chivas Regal Book of London Clubs* (1963), 93.

[38] Gosse, *Swinburne*, 198–9, tactfully spares readers details of the episode.

is time the ladies learnt these things—though the knowledge may mean the final over-throw of our masculine supremacy, already tottering to its fall. It is time they knew that one member never accosts another to whom he has not been introduced. It is no wonder that—like the illustrious 'Bertie'—we 'look sad'. We are thinking of our absent wives and absent womankind generally, and gloomily recognising that the separation of the sexes is a mistake. I once took a frivolous French friend to the Junior. He looked round with an affrighted gaze on the miscellaneous collection of seedy coats and trousers there assembled, and, exclaiming, 'Ça manque de femmes', incontinently fled. There is the whole matter in a nutshell. Ça manque de femmes.[47]

As Walkley suspected, the heyday of the West End club as an all-enveloping male institution was already passing. In 1881 for the first time lunchers exceed diners at the Athenaeum, numbering 15,584 to 15,530; in 1911 these totalled 18,520 and 7,678 respectively, and in 1913, 14,459 and 4,844. The waiting list of men seeking election likewise fell, from 1,673 in 1884 to 1,011 in 1914.[48] That new clubs had been founded meanwhile provided no sufficient explanation, because the same trends were observable in them also. Moreover, the country's population, especially that of Greater London, was adding millions at the same time. It was changing social custom among the middle and upper classes that cumulatively mattered more and decided the different pattern of club life: the newer habits of country-house weekending and restaurant dining, both of which included the attraction of female company, not to mention the draw of suburban family life.

Several women's clubs, or clubs that accepted women, did exist: the Albemarle, Alexandra, Bath, Empress, New Victoria, Pioneer, and Sesame.[49] As befits its name, the Pioneer came first. A tongue-in-cheek Jerome K. Jerome recalled, 'All the most desperate women in London enrolled...'. They then invited Bernard Shaw, 'assumed to be a feminist', to address them; but, since he chose as his text Ephesians 5: 22 ('Wives submit yourselves unto your own husbands, as unto the Lord'), reports had it that he was 'torn limb from limb'.[50] Thomas Hardy's first wife, Emma, was a member of the Alexandra Club at 12 Grosvenor Street. The Alexandra was particularly severe about excluding men. Whereas the Albemarle allowed male guests and visitors, the Alexandra barred the entire trousered sex, even husbands and brothers; and, if Baroness Orczy's memory of the Alexandra in the 1890s served her accurately, 'it was easier to enter the Kingdom of Heaven

---

[47] Walkley, *Frames of Mind*, 273–4. The Junior is an invention here, though there were several clubs with that word in their title. Walkley's own club at this time was the Devonshire; he was also a member of the Johnson and Omar Khayyám dining clubs. Later he was a member of the Garrick; and he finally made it into the Athenaeum in 1923, when aged 68 and with three years to live. Cf. Goldwin Smith, *Reminiscences* (1910), 158: 'Instead of being denounced as hostile to marriage, the Clubs ought to be credited with keeping young men fit for it' by secluding them from the temptations of promiscuity. 'Blessed are Clubs, and above all Clubs in my memory the Athenaeum, with its splendid library and its social opportunities,' he wrote about his time in London in the 1850s; and when he emigrated to Canada he endeavoured to reproduce it by assisting 'in the foundation of a good Club for young men in Toronto'.

[48] [Cowell], *Athenaeum*, 98, 140–4.

[49] Elinor Glyn was a member of the Bath, and Mona Caird of both the Pioneer and the Sesame.

[50] Jerome, *Life and Times*, 75.

than the membership of the club'.[51] This, no doubt, delighted Emma Hardy. Her husband's aristocratic friend and collaborator Florence Henniker, on the other hand, was a member of the Empress Club, founded for 'Ladies of social position' in 1897 at 35 Dover Street. Hardy joshed her about the club's name: 'what lofty titles we see! To go one better than that, the next Ladies' Club will have to be called the—well—Virgin Mary's I suppose?'[52] Arnold Bennett's French wife, whom he married in 1907, also joined the Empress when they returned to live in England, though naturally Bennett hated the idea and fact of women's clubs.[53]

Female authors of various description enjoyed quasi-collegiate association in professional bodies such as the Women Writers' Club and the Society for Women Journalists, which met for luncheon and other occasions; but these were vagrant, without the fixed premises needed to inspire a vital sense of corporation. This advance was achieved by the Lyceum, which formally opened in 1904. It was the first women's club to penetrate the centre of clubland, Piccadilly, and it was 'a distinct pioneer in the recognition of women and their introduction into public life on a normal footing of friendly equality'.[54] Such was the account of its founder, Constance Smedley, author of *An April Princess* (1903), whose one-act play *Mrs Jordan* (1900)—about the actress and mistress of William IV—had been staged by Mrs Patrick Campbell. Her father, a chartered accountant and director of several companies, having two daughters as well as one son, had been determined to encourage their intellectual interests so as to equip them to make a mark and to live civilized and rounded lives. This was especially important for Constance, crippled since childhood, probably by polio: thereafter she needed crutches and later a wheelchair.[55] Her younger sister Ida studied chemistry at Newnham College, Cambridge, while Constance herself proceeded to London, there to develop her passion for the theatre both as set designer and as play-wright. Smedley *père* did not now drop out of the picture; on the contrary, it was his support, to the tune of £30,000, that enabled Constance to establish the Lyceum in premises vacated by the Imperial Service Club when it went into liquidation. The Lyceum took over the building, lock, stock, and billiard table. The last was preserved after a vote deemed billiards 'just the right form of exercise for intellectual women'.[56] Smedley's financial guarantee defrayed both refurbishment and running costs. When the Lyceum opened with 1,000 members, half paying 2 guineas subscription and half at 1 guinea, the annual expenditure in rents and rates alone was £5,000.[57] By comparison, the Cavalry Club next door had a rent and rates bill of £4,500 with a subscription list yielding over £14,000

---

[51] Orczy, *Chain of Life*, 67.

[52] Hardy to Florence Henniker, 26 Feb. 1905, in Purdy and Millgate (eds.), *Hardy Letters*, iii. 15.

[53] Bennett, *Bennett*, 143, 151.   [54] Constance Smedley, *Crusaders* (1929), 96.

[55] See Grace Brockington's notice of Constance Smedley (1876–1941), *Oxford DNB*

[56] Smedley, *Crusaders*, 100, where Lady Strachey, a club vice-president, is nominated as particularly adroit at billiards.

[57] W. T. Smedley's speech at the Lyceum, 10 Feb. 1909, in Smedley, *Crusaders*, 66–7. Another financial backer was Trevor Williams, Chairman of the Gramophone Company.

annually. The Lyceum's difficulty was that so many professional women or, to be more precise, the kind of women with the intellectual and other attainments that the Lyceum wanted to include, possessed limited incomes. Thus the subscription was deliberately set low. The club could have been self-supporting from the start if it had had ambitions to be a ladies' social club only and not rejected over 1,200 applicants. The membership rose to 2,000 during the first year, yet could 'have been much larger but for the holocausts that ensued at each committee meeting . . . Qualifications were almost too rigorously analysed and many desirable members were refused, until even thoroughly qualified women became quite nervous about applying.'[58]

Constance Smedley's first thought had been to establish a club for writers and artist-illustrators, her own twin interests. Using the Literary Year Book and consulting her friends, she fired off letters to sixty women authors and journalists. Already a line was being drawn: 'How carefully we considered their pretensions to good standing intellectually! What heated serious discussions as to their exact position in the world of literature! Popularity as usual was not smiled upon. There must be a sound foundation of achievement for the names we wanted.'[59] From those sixty, two replies carried especial weight, from Mrs W. K. Clifford and Pearl Craigie (John Oliver Hobbes), both well-known novelists and socially influential. Further discussions now sharpened the criteria for membership. Ida Smedley suggested taking in women with university degrees or who were active in educational work; more significant still, it was decided to allow 'the wives and daughters of distinguished men'. Constance Smedley later defended this: 'The wives and daughters of men of letters and artists and eminent professors would belong to interesting circles, and would keep the Club in contact with men in the professions.' 'It would not be so exclusively a feminine affair,' she added;[60] but an important distinction was being breached here. Women were being judged by women not solely for their accomplishments but on the basis of their husbands' and fathers' accomplishments too. Perhaps this strategy was justified by results in cases such as Mrs Oscar Beringer, who was promoted to the executive. How otherwise to get close to her husband, the director of the Philharmonic, who, in *Who's Who*, stated with off-putting Germanic rigour: '*Recreations*: no time to indulge in hobbies'.[61]

The Lyceum really got under way when Lady Frances Balfour was persuaded to preside over the first Provisional Committee. The fifth daughter of the eighth Duke of Argyll, she was sister-in-law to the Prime Minister. Her husband, Eustace, the youngest Balfour brother, was actually not much of a catch. Nominally an architect, trained by Basil Champneys, he was whisky-sodden and perished of drink in 1911. Lady Frances was made of sterner stuff, a forthright churchwoman, outspoken opponent of gambling, and trusty lieutenant of

---

[58] Smedley, *Crusaders*, 70.   [59] Ibid. 59.   [60] Ibid. 61.
[61] *Who Was Who, 1916–1928*, 84, for Oscar Beringer (1844–1928), who was born in Baden and trained at Leipzig and Berlin and whose first appearance was in Saturday Concerts at the Crystal Palace in 1860.

Mrs Millicent Fawcett in the suffrage movement. She served as president of the Lyceum and chaired its executive for fifteen years. The support of the Countess of Aberdeen was also valued. Some, such as Sir Horace Plunkett, who had dealings with her over schemes for agrarian reform in Ireland, where her husband was Lord Lieutenant (1906–14), held substantial reservations. 'Much as I admire her philanthropic work and aims', he told the novelist Shan Bullock, 'there are two things about her which repel me: a morbid craving for notoriety and an addiction to political intrigue.'[62] The public face was what mattered, however. Lady Aberdeen's promotion of smallholdings, village crafts, and servants' education, and her involvement in women's and children's health and welfare work, the town and country planning movement, the international Red Cross and later the League of Nations, appeared exemplary of the Christian mission she held dear.[63] She was an author of sorts: *Through Canada with a Kodak* resulted from her period as consort to the Governor of Canada, 1893–8. More to the point, she was president of the Women's Liberal Federation and, in 1898–9, had been president of the International Council of Women. Of more day-to-day practical assistance was Mrs Moberly Bell, a clergyman's daughter and wife of the general manager of *The Times*. Appointed the first vice-chair, she was 'one of the most devoted and loyal promoters of the Lyceum, who proved a tower of strength in future trials'.[64]

Three provisional committees conducted the planning during the year before the Lyceum's formal opening and, most importantly, vetted applications. The largest committee represented literature, journalism, and music: sixty-nine names, including two duchesses, of Leeds and Sutherland, and several peers', baronets', or knights' wives. Some of these qualified simply as patronesses of arts and letters, but Lady Burghclere, daughter of the fourth Earl of Carnarvon, had written a biography of George Villiers, the second Duke of Buckingham; Lady Gilbert was the Irish novelist Rosa Mulholland; Lady Lindsay was both poet and painter; and Lady Lugard was *The Times*'s specialist on colonial affairs, Flora Shaw. This committee also included a galaxy of well-known women writers: Miss M. E. Braddon, Rhoda Broughton, Sarah Grand, Beatrice Harraden, Alice Meynell, Edith Nesbit, Mrs Campbell Praed, Violet Martin and Edith Somerville (Somerville and Ross), Flora Annie Steel, Katharine Tynan, and Mrs Humphry Ward. Several qualified under a double ticket, being well known themselves and with a well-known or influential husband, such as the Irish poet Dora Sigerson, who was married to the editor Clement Shorter; Agnes Castle, who wrote historical romances with her husband, Egerton Castle; or the journalist–playwright Mrs T. P. O'Connor. It is not denying the individual talents of others to suggest that their incorporation might be owed principally to their husband's name or

---

[62] Plunkett to Bullock, 18 Jan. 1910, copy in the Plunkett Foundation for Co-operative Studies archive, Long Hanborough, Oxfordshire.

[63] On Lady Aberdeen (*née* Majoribanks; 1857–1939), see *DNB 1931–1940*, 348–9.

[64] Smedley, *Crusaders*, 62–3. Both Lady Frances Balfour and Lady Aberdeen produced two volumes of memoirs—respectively, *Ne Obliviscaris* (1930) and (written with Lord Aberdeen) *We Twa* (1925)—but none mentioned her part in the Lyceum.

position. This was the case, perhaps, with the publisher's wife Mrs John Lane, a rich Swiss American, who was a light essayist and author of a promotion for grapefruit.[65] Mrs G. K. Chesterton, both Mrs Thomas Hardy, Mrs George Bernard Shaw, and Mrs Paget Toynbee, all were less notable than their husbands; so was Mrs H. G. Wells, who later became a member. Another remarkable feature was the inclusion of overseas names, such as the novelist Ada Cambridge, who, though born in Norfolk, lived largely in Australia upon marriage to her clergyman husband in 1870. The founders had desired to establish an international chain of sister Lyceums, and the *Lyceum Annual* was published with that objective from 1905.[66]

The Lyceum's purpose, wrote Constance Smedley, 'was never merely to provide entertainment for its members: it was conceived, organised and worked for as a Club whose chief *raison d'être* was the advancement of the status of women in the world of arts and letters'.[67] This it did by putting on numerous functions—debates, recitals, exhibitions, and formal dinners to which supposedly sparkling non-members were invited. These were not always appreciated. Somerville and Ross attended an Irish Evening at the Lyceum in 1906, at which Standish O'Grady was chief guest. They thought it a pity, after suffering his 'very long and wandering and dreary' speech, that he had 'left a rest cure in order to make it'. Worse followed: 'a horrid youth who spoke as if his mouth was full of fish bones', a Miss Hull who sermonized on her part in the Gaelic revival 'in a thin mouselike squeak', and 'a mad person from Australia', before 'Miss Coleman Smith chanted Yeats's poetry'. Thoroughly browned off, they declined to be guests of honour at a St Patrick's Day dinner held at the Lyceum in 1907.[68]

Still, by encouraging its component sections to advance their members' special interests and professional association, the Lyceum developed momentum. Advisory boards had been created in 1906: an Authors' Board, a Dramatists' Board, Journalists' Board, Arts and Crafts Board, and so forth, each of which elected two representatives to serve on the club's executive. The first Authors' Board had Flora Annie Steel as its chair; the vice-chair was G. E. Mitton (later Lady Scott), who was a multifaceted author: a contributor to Walter Besant's London survey, and writer of novels such as *A Bachelor Girl in London* (1898), of biographies such as *Jane Austen and her Times* (1905), and of various guidebooks. Other members included the scarcely less prolific Mary Sweetman, who generally issued novels under the pseudonym M. E. Francis and was the sister of Agnes Castle; and Ella Hepworth Dixon, daughter of an editor of the *Athenaeum*. Dixon herself edited the *Englishwoman's Review* and wrote painful novels, among them *The Story of a Modern Woman* (1894).

New Woman ardours and dilemmas were the particular forte of another colleague on the Authors' Board, Beatrice Harraden. Initially influenced by

[65] Lambert and Ratcliffe, *Bodley Head*, 133–5, 149.
[66] Smedley, *Crusaders*, 87–9. Notable foundations of Lyceums in Europe were Amsterdam (1904), Berlin (1905), Paris (1906), and Florence (1908).   [67] Ibid. 257.
[68] Collis, *Somerville and Ross*, 141–3, 147.

Eliza Lynn Linton, Harraden shot to fame with *Ships that Pass in the Night* (1893). The impact on women of their forging professional careers which upset their personal lives was a recurrent theme of her fiction. Michael Sadleir attributed this to 'the one tragic experience of her life, for she fell deeply in love with a man who falsified his clients' accounts and whose body was found not long after in a crevasse on a Swiss glacier'.[69] Harraden stayed unmarried and pitched in with the militant wing of the suffrage movement, unlike another colleague on the Authors' Board, Mrs Burnett Smith. A doctor's wife and protégée of Robertson Nicoll, she was a virtual manufactory of romantic fiction, publishing over 250 titles under her maiden name, Annie S. Swan, or as David Lyall; in addition, she reached a large audience through *The Woman at Home* (of which she was editor, 1893-1917) and *Annie S. Swan's Penny Stories* and *Annual*, in which she dispensed advice in response to readers' letters about personal, domestic, and work-related problems, as well as penned short stories. Completing the first Authors' Board were two other noted writers, the poet–essayist Alice Meynell, and the poet–novelist Katharine Tynan. Both were Catholics, a creed that conspicuously influenced their philosophy and work; but the historian can make too much of formal contrasts. Beatrice Harraden, for example, was among the friends Mrs Burnett Smith made when she and her husband established their first London home, at Camden Square, in 1892; later, they became neighbours in Hampstead.[70] More important in the context of the Lyceum was their position as working women, whose income from authorship sustained their independence or their families. It was this understanding of the predicament of the woman writer that united all members of the Authors' Board, and committed them to widening their opportunities through the Lyceum. That was the thrust too of male well-wishers such as George Meredith, whose message was read out at one dinner by his daughter-in-law, a member of the Music Board: 'Hasty expectation causes fits of disappointment. This is a slow movement, but sure. Women must learn that it is by strengthening the mind that superior muscle will be subdued to acknowledge the state of equality.'[71]

The Lyceum was thus launched. The press generally avoided ridiculing the women's efforts; indeed, 'referred to the Club as a rose garden in the stern domain of Club-land and invariably presented a charming and attractive picture of its activities'.[72] But the contradiction inherent in it, that the country's leading women's club was bankrolled by a man, eventually had to be faced. A membership of 2,000 was testimony to the Lyceum's success, yet male clubs charged between ten and forty times more in subscriptions. In 1909 reconstruction

---

[69] *DNB 1931–1940*, 402; also Sutherland, *Companion*, 280, and Kemp *et al.* (eds.), *Edwardian Fiction*, 174–5.

[70] Mildred Robertson Nicoll (ed.), *The Letters of Annie S. Swan* (1945), 19, 42, where Harraden is described as 'small, dark, vivacious, with one of the first "bobbed" heads to be seen in London, and charmingly dressed by Liberty'. [71] Smedley, *Crusaders*, 113.

[72] Ibid. 69–70. Constance Smedley had particular cause to appreciate this. In the interviews she gave, reporters 'never alluded to my physical handicap; it gave me a fair chance and allowed me to take my part in the normal working world without arousing sentimentality or curiosity'.

became unavoidable when Constance Smedley resigned as secretary upon marriage to Maxwell Armfield, the symbolist painter and designer; and the Lyceum was compelled to change from a proprietary to a members' club.

IV

The Lyceum enabled women authors to establish a presence in London's clubland; nevertheless, that culture remained preponderantly masculine in character. It was epitomized by the political clubs, the Carlton (Tory–Conservative) and the Reform (Whig–Liberal), although these, established for party purposes in the wake of the 1832 franchise extension, generally appeared more welcoming and congenial than others of this stripe. Thus the atmosphere at Brooks's, which had started as a gaming club in 1764, then became a Whig club after it moved to St James's in 1778, was alarming, likened in the 1850s to 'a country house with the Duke lying dead upstairs';[73] and its frigidity and hauteur did not diminish as the century progressed.[74] Alongside of such formally constituted clubs existed various dining associations which included literary conversation as part of the menu. The most exclusive were The Club, Grillion's, and the Literary Society. The Club began in 1764 when its original eight members, Dr Johnson, Sir Joshua Reynolds, Edmund Burke, and Oliver Goldsmith among them, convened at the Turk's Head in Gerrard Street; and the names of James Boswell, the actor David Garrick, the historian Edward Gibbon, and the politician Charles James Fox were soon added. There were thirty-eight members (and three honorary members) when the retired Governor of Madras Sir Mountstuart Grant Duff was elected in 1889. By this date, The Club used Willis's Rooms, and the dominating presence was the State leadership, represented by the politicians Salisbury, Gladstone, Derby, Selborne, Carnarvon, Rosebery, Goschen, and Sir George Trevelyan. The Duke of Argyll also fell into this category; there were two other dukes besides, plus senior figures from the armed services, the diplomatic, and judiciary—Viscount Wolseley, the Marquess of Dufferin and Ava, and Lord Coleridge. History was represented by Lord Acton, W. H. Lecky, and J. A. Froude, and science by professors Huxley and Tyndall. Many members were authors of various description, such as the Anglo-Indian official Sir Alfred Lyall, who wrote poetry, history, and studies of religion and folklore; but the only one who merited the description by earning his bread in this way was the Poet Laureate Tennyson. He was invited to join The Club in 1865, rather to his surprise because (he maintained) he had never heard of it. 'I suppose one has not to pay some 25 guineas entrance and some 7 ditto a year, because then, I would not say that the game is not worth the candle, but that the candle is too dear for me. Does one only pay

---

[73] St Algernon West, *Recollections, 1832 to 1886* (1899), 98.
[74] Farquharson, *In and Out of Parliament*, 90.

for one's dinner when eaten, or how is it?', Tennyson responded gruffly; but the Duke of Argyll allayed his anxieties, and he was admitted to the exclusive circle.[75]

For the majority of ordinary and even extraordinary writers—Thackeray was proposed and rejected in 1861[76]—The Club was simply out of bounds by the late nineteenth century. The same obtained for Grillion's, founded in 1812 by a couple of Old Etonian diplomats as neutral territory where Westminster and Society leaders might set aside their controversies by dining together and discussing intellectual interests.[77] Lord Houghton's preface to the annals of Grillion's in 1880 declared it 'indisputable that all that connects the men of thought with the men of action is at once a rare and appreciated pleasure and a stimulus to the loftier studies'.[78] That ideal was not always realized. Gladstone's journal, 13 April 1885, recorded, 'Dined at Grillion's: alone!'; and he ordered a bottle of champagne to soothe his solitude.[79]

By 1889, when Grillion's convened in the Grand Hotel, its membership was double that of The Club: seventy-seven ordinary and a dozen honorary members, of whom twenty-three also belonged to The Club. Again, Tennyson was admitted to this rare elect. There was yet further overlap with the Literary Society, of which thirteen of its thirty-five ordinary and five honorary members belonged to The Club, although these did not include Tennyson. The Literary Society was another monthly dining club of early nineteenth-century foundation and, with elections occuring at irregular intervals rather than annually, its entire membership during its first ninety years was a mere 200. Practising literary men were not much more conspicuous at the Literary Society than at Grillion's, even though Wordsworth had been a founder and Sir Walter Scott was elected in 1815, George Crabbe following in 1819, Washington Irving and Sir Francis Palgrave in 1822, Lockhart in 1826, and Southey in 1832. By 1891, when it met in the Bristol Hotel, Henry James and Andrew Lang were the only professional authors on the roll; still, others—such as Lord de Tabley and George Du Maurier—were well known as writers.[80] When Arthur Benson was admitted in March 1907, the meal resembled the high-table fare he was used to in Cambridge; but the charge was a steep 12s., the venue was Prince's in Jermyn Street, and the company, which included Austin Dobson, Basil Champneys, Spencer Walpole, and the Archbishop

---

[75] Tennyson, *Tennyson*, 432–3. Martin, *Tennyson*, 461, includes Lord Houghton with Argyll as Tennyson's sponsors, and adds that Tennyson attended The Club once in the year of his election and only twice thenceforward. He did not join the Athenaeum until 1887.

[76] Thackeray to the Revd Whitwell Elwin, 2–31 May 1861, in Harden (ed.), *Thackeray's Letters*, 355. His proposer was Spencer Walpole (1806–98), the historian who was three times Home Secretary.

[77] Grillion's took its name from a French chef, in whose restaurant the club first dined. Dinners were usually held on Wednesdays during parliamentary sessions.

[78] Quoted in H. Hensley Henson to Dr Elston Grey Turner, 18 Feb. 1947, in Evelyn Foley Braley (ed.), *Letters of Herbert Hensley Henson* (1950), 201.

[79] Matthew (ed.), *Gladstone Diaries*, xi. 322. Gladstone was a member of Grillion's from 1840, and of The Club from 1857.

[80] On these clubs' membership and character, see Grant Duff, *Diary, 1889–1891*, i. 75–9, 105–6, 153–5. In the inter-war period, when his cousin Stanley Baldwin was leader of the Conservative Party and Prime Minister, Kipling was a member of both The Club and Grillion's.

of Canterbury, Randall Davidson, was altogether 'rather more interesting than the ordinary don'. At his next dinner, in April, Benson was regaled by the former Prime Minister, Balfour, who spoke freely about his predecessors.[81] The year 1911, when the constitutional crisis over the House of Lords and Irish Home Rule was at boiling point, saw the foundation of another inner-circle dining club. This was The Other Club. The lead was taken by F. E. Smith and Winston Churchill, supplemented by Lloyd George, each a leading partisan in the crisis; and it was stipulated that 'nothing in the Rules or intercourse of the Club shall interfere with the rancour or asperity of party politics'. Hence the admission of select and sociable literary men was regarded as beneficial, a prophylactic against party-political acrimony, although one of the original author members Anthony Hope (Hawkins) was listed by Asquith as a potential peer in the Liberal interest. The actor–manager Sir Herbert Beerbohm Tree was likewise included as a comic turn; still, to the end of his life, Hope relished their spirited dinners and the opportunity to talk intimately to men at the centre of things. Arnold Bennett too was incorporated after the war; and at one of their dinners in 1925, they debated birth control, Bennett and Hope pro, 'F.E. [Smith, then Lord Birkenhead] violently *con*'.[82]

Because of the inaccessibility of these elite dining clubs to most authors, the late nineteenth century had seen the burgeoning of new shoots with a more pronounced literary flavour. Among these were the Johnson Club, founded in 1884 for enthusiasts of the eighteenth-century sage, who had as their bursar the publisher T. Fisher Unwin; the Sette of Odde Volumes, founded in 1878 and comprising twenty-one bookmen of supposed special talents who included the prolific Max Pemberton, adventure-writer, playwright, and periodical-editor;[83] and the Whitefriars, which met on Fridays at Anderton's Hotel, Fleet Street, for debate over walnuts and wine. The Whitefriars involved authors and journalists with literary interests, such as Robertson Nicoll of the *British Weekly* and *The Bookman*, Clement Shorter of the *Illustrated London News*, the *Sphere*, and more, J. A. Spender of the *Westminster Gazette*, Heath Joyce of *The Graphic*, William Senior of *The Field*, T. P. O'Connor of *T. P.'s Weekly*, and Arthur Spurgeon of the National Press Agency. In 1901 Whitefriars' members and guests made a pilgrimage to Max Gate, Thomas Hardy's Dorset home: 'There were 100 in all, & of course we did not know a quarter of them,' Hardy reported irritably. 'We put up a marquee, opening from the drawing room, & they had tea in it.'[84]

More intellectually distinguished was the Rabelais Club, founded in 1879 by Walter Besant, who, among his many talents, was the author of studies about the great French satirist. Initially it operated almost as a cell of the Savile Club, being

---

[81] Lubbock, *Benson*, 163–4; and Newsome, *Edge of Paradise*, 276, which notes Sidney Colvin, Lord Crewe, Bernard Holland, and John Murray as members of the Literary Society at that time.

[82] Mallet, *Hope*, 208, 232, 257, 272–3.

[83] The publisher John Lane became club secretary in 1890, and its Master of Ceremonies in 1891. The membership was so limited because 'this was the number of volumes in the 1821 Variorum Edition of Shakespeare' (Lambert and Ratcliffe, *Bodley Head*, 35–6).

[84] Hardy to Florence Henniker, 25 July 1901, in Purdy and Millgate (eds.), *Hardy Letters*, ii. 293.

made up mostly of Savileans who met to discuss and publish their appreciations of Rabelais. When it expanded to include prominent actors, artists, musicians, and miscellaneous literary men as well as scholars and critics, it evolved into a dining club, lost coherence, and petered out after 1889.[85] Its successor as idiosyncratic association was the Omar Khayyám, founded in 1892 by Edward Clodd, Clement Shorter, and George Whale.[86] In 1893 its members planted a rosebush—raised from a hip taken from beside Omar's grave in Iran—over Edward FitzGerald's grave at Boulge in Suffolk.[87] Paganism (rationalism was the preferred designation) was the common philosophy of the club, following FitzGerald's own freethinking. There appeared no obligation also to subscribe to FitzGerald's dietary regime: vegetarianism. In a 'mild orgy of red wine and red roses' the club met three times a year, twice in London (usually at Frascati's restaurant) and once in the country (usually at Great Marlow), when one of the company would produce a poem in FitzGerald's metre.[88] George Gissing was brought in from the

[85] The members, seventy in all, for 1885 are given in Saintsbury, *Last Scrap Book*, 203–5. Among well-known author members were Henry James, Thomas Hardy, and George Meredith. The actors included Henry Irving and J. L. Toole; the artists, Lawrence Alma-'Tadema and E. A. Abbey; the musicians, Charles Hallé; the critics, Andrew Lang and Joseph Knight; and the scholars, F. W. Maitland and A. J. Duffield. Foreign members included Victor Hugo (who never dined), Bret Harte, and Oliver Wendell Holmes. Henry Longfellow was also proposed, but died soon after (in 1882). The Rabelais disintegrated because of what Saintsbury termed 'some looseness of rules', in particular that once a person had been a guest he might henceforth consider himself a member. This appeared to Saintsbury 'to partake of insanity', and he never dined thereafter. It was at the Rabelais that a farewell dinner was given for Irving, about to embark on his first American tour, in 1883; for a boring account of this by the obnoxious Charles Brookfield, see his *Random Reminiscences* (1911), 51–3.

[86] Clement Shorter, 'The Story of the Omar Khayyám Cult', *T. P.'s Weekly*, 26 Feb. 1904, 275, adds that the inaugural dinner of twelve on 13 October 1892 included Richard Le Gallienne, Justin Huntly McCarthy, William Watson, and the painters William Simpson and Arthur Hacker. Edmund Gosse, Augustine Birrell, and the publisher William Heinemann participated in the second, in January 1893. On Edward Clodd (1840–930), see *DNB 1922–1930*, 190–2. Clodd, banker and freethinker, had been a co-founder of the Johnson Club; he was prominent too in the Folk-Lore Society. For George Whale (1849–1925), see *Who Was Who, 1916 1928*, 1113–14. Whale was active in local government in London, being Mayor of Woolwich 1908–9, and an unsuccessful Liberal parliamentary candidate for Marylebone. By profession he was a solicitor. He amassed considerable wealth, living at York Terrace, Regent's Park; Arnold Bennett in his diary described his 'great ugly sitting-room'. Whale was another freethinker, and Bennett made use of notes which Whale compiled about superstitious beliefs rife during the Great War. Whale was also active in the Folk-Lore Society, a Fellow of the Royal Historical Society, a member of the Johnson Club, and a founder of the Pepys Club. On his part in London government reform, see John Davis, *Reforming London: The London Government Problem, 1855–1900* (Oxford, 1988), 209–11.

[87] Members and guests of the club, including Clodd, Shorter, Thomas Hardy, Anthony Hope, Dr James Frazer (of *The Golden Bough*), and the Anglo-Indian official Sir George Robertson, renewed the pilgrimage to FitzGerald's grave in 1901; see Hardy to Florence Henniker, 2 June 1901, and to Sir George Douglas, 5 June 1901, in Purdy and Millgate (eds.), *Hardy Letters*, ii. 288–9.

[88] Gosse, *Aspects and Impressions*, 281; and *T.P.'s Weekly*, 22 May 1903, 888. See also the invitation to Coventry Patmore to be the club's guest of honour in 1896, when Edmund Gosse was President. Gosse mentioned that among the other diners would be Conan Doyle, Pinero, John Davidson, Sidney Colvin, and the sculptor Hamo Thornycroft; Patmore, *Patmore*, 229–30. Another occasion when the club met under Gosse's presidency is described in Grant Duff, *Diary, 1896 to 1901*, i. 190–2 (25 Mar. 1897); the annual poem was then composed by Austin Dobson. Grant Duff, together with Field Marshall Lord Wolseley, went as Gosse's guests; and among the diners were J. M. Barrie, Augustine Birrell, and Conan Doyle. Henry Newbolt was President in 1904. It continued after the war: Anthony Hope was President in 1933, the last year of his life. Mallet, *Hope*, 280.

him, and he was seconded by Professor Sir Walter Raleigh, who had known him from Oxford.[99]

A crucial test of strength for this cadre occurred in March 1877, when G. O. Trevelyan's name was in the ballot for membership. The family was no upstart, owning some 20,000 acres, though the father was only recently a baronet. His mother was sister to the historian and politician Thomas Babington (later Lord) Macaulay, whose classic *Life and Letters* he published in 1876. Educated at Harrow and Trinity College, Cambridge, where he won a First and was made an Honorary Fellow, Trevelyan became a Liberal MP and eventually entered the Cabinet. At the time his name was before the Athenaeum, it was as the champion of a meritocracy that Trevelyan was principally known, having been to the fore in the administrative reform movement, which opened senior positions in the Civil Service to candidates chosen by competitive examination and which abolished the purchase of commissions in the armed services. It was for this last action that some military members determined to blackball him in 1877 but, as his son G. M. Trevelyan wrote in 1932, this incited a stronger movement in his favour in the club which 'was then, even more than now, the focus of the intellectual life of the nation. His nomination card was signed by an unexampled galaxy of names famous in letters, science and public life.' One was Carlyle, then aged 82, and he 'not only signed but came down to vote and urged others to vote for him'.[100] Trevelyan was elected by 389 votes to twenty: the new intellectual aristocracy, which now included the foremost men of letters, had proved capable of protecting their own.

It was thus demonstrable that the Athenaeum, by whatever method, did incorporate individuals of uncommon ability. 'It is an English idea of literary distinction—one of the prominent instances of their Humour', wrote George Meredith in 1894, regretfully withdrawing his name from consideration for membership, as he had done previously, because his crippled condition made travel to London virtually impossible.[101] Among the earliest members were Sir Walter Scott, Bulwer Lytton, Thomas Campbell, Thomas Moore, Samuel Rogers, and Henry Crabb Robinson. The originator of its name, and for long the Athenaeum's moving force, had not, however, been an irenic figure: J. W. Croker was a partisan Tory. He was notorious for his slashing criticism of Keats's *Endymion* and for mutual enmity with Macaulay, who had been elected in 1830. The club's heavy debts thereafter had caused it to seek increased income by enlarging the membership. Famously in 1838 forty newcomers were elected in one batch; still, these included Charles Darwin, Charles Dickens, George Grote, Richard Monckton Milnes, Arthur Stanley, and the architects Philip Hardwick and Sydney Smirke.[102] The ideal remained that of incorporating a cultural elite,

---

[99] Sybille Bedford, *Aldous Huxley* (New York, 1974), 121, 124.

[100] G. M. Trevelyan, *Sir George Otto Trevelyan* (1932), 100. G. M. Trevelyan was himself a member from 1910.

[101] Meredith to Frederick A. Maxse, 19 Feb. 1894, in Cline (ed.), *Meredith's Letters*, iii. 1155.

[102] [Cowell], *Athenaeum*, 25.

what Theodore Hook archly termed a 'mental' club, unlike the United Service Club (established in 1815), which was 'regimental'.[103] When the Order of Merit was founded in 1902, eleven of its original twelve recipients were members of the Athenaeum;[104] and by 1907 sixty-nine of its company had been buried in Westminster Abbey and thirty-two in St Paul's Cathedral.[105] The 1,200 members in 1900 paid an entrance fee of 30 guineas and an annual subscription of 8 guineas. For all this, there was a sizeable waiting list; but Rule II empowered the club committee to circumvent it by electing annually not more than nine persons eminent in science, literature, the arts, or for public service. Ruskin was elected by this device in 1849, Carlyle in 1853. Thackeray, proposed in the ordinary way, had been blackballed in 1850 but made it under Rule II in 1851; and the club now preserves his billiards cue.[106] Trollope's moment came—better as he put it, 'received the honour of being elected by the Committee at the Athenaeum'—in 1864. His sponsor was Lord Stanhope, the founding chairman of the National Portrait Gallery. Trollope confessed, 'I never was more surprised' when told of his election.[107] In 1882 he was further elated when his son Harry was elected as an ordinary member, by 204 votes to four.[108] This comfortably exceeded the desiderata: one blackball in ten excluded.

Matthew Arnold (elected in 1856) always experienced 'something resembling beatitude'[109] whenever he entered the Athenaeum, yet some held reservations about the club. 'A compliment, but an expensive one, as I didn't really want another Club', fretted Anthony Hope, who was elected under Rule II in 1899.[110] He was then aged 36; even younger was Kipling, aged 31, when he was admitted under the same rule two years earlier. It was a 'great, but frightening, honour', he recalled. As the youngest member by some distance, he thought the atmosphere resembled 'a cathedral between services'. Kipling preferred the company at the Beefsteak when need drove him to London; yet he allowed that 'if one wanted to know anything from forging an anchor to forging antiquities one would find the world's ultimate expert in the matter at lunch' at the Athenaeum.[111] So also Walter Raleigh discovered: 'You can't talk politics, for instance, because the idiot who did it is probably at the next table.'[112] One of his first meals there was with

---

[103] Ibid. 44.   [104] Ibid. 155.

[105] Arthur Griffiths, 'London Clubs: Past and Present', *Fortnightly Review* (Apr. 1907), 657.

[106] Thackeray's sponsor in 1850 was the barrister Abraham Hayward, who translated *Faust* and was also esteemed as an essayist: on Hayward (1801–84), see *DNB*. The historian Henry Hallam (1777–1859) and the Dean of St Paul's, Henry Milman (1791–1868), also spoke out for Thackeray; see his letter to Hayward, 1 Feb. 1850, in Harden (ed.), *Thackeray's Letters*, 186–7, when he attributed the rebuff to offences he had caused as a satirist, on which, see also Cowell, *Athenaeum*, 49, and Hugh Tait and Richard Walker, *The Athenaeum Collection* (2000), 199–201.   [107] Trollope, *Autobiography*, 149.

[108] Booth (ed.), *Trollope's Letters*, 464, 468, 471–4, for Trollope's nervousness and lobbying. Harry—Henry Merivale Trollope (1846–1926)—was in publishing.

[109] Quoted in Tait and Walker, *Athenaeum Collection*, 3.   [110] Mallet, *Hope*, 134.

[111] Kipling, *Something of Myself*, 84–5. Henry James was one of his sponsors. Tait and Walker, *Athenaeum Collection*, 61, 121, for the club's portraits of Kipling. Kipling was also a member of the Conservative Party's club, the Carlton.

[112] Letter to his wife, 19 Nov. 1905, in Raleigh (ed.), *Raleigh Letters*, ii. 285.

actors, academics, physicians, and servicemen.[126] Henry de Mosenthal, a Fellow of the Institute of Chemistry, contributed a dull history of dynamite. This rather epitomized the whole: the world of Literature was not going to be detonated by Savages.

It was thus not difficult for literary newcomers to find acceptance there. E. Phillips Oppenheim was elected at the age of 22 after the dramatization of his first novel, *Expiation* (1887);[127] and Keble Howard was nominated by the boys' story-writer Manville Fenn at an equally tender age in 1900, when he had achieved nothing more than assistant to the editor of the *Sketch*. Howard later became a prolific author and also joined the Society of Authors; but he never attended their meetings—'I should be terrified of so many great people all gathered together'—and it was the very unliterary atmosphere of the Savage which attracted him. That was frankly boisterous, some might say undignified; Saturday night dinners commonly featured sing-songs, musical chairs, and practical jokes.[128] Jerome K. Jerome was a Savage and, Bateman-like, remembered the man who ordered tea there: 'It was the talk of the club for a fortnight. Most of the members judged it to be a sign of the coming decline and fall of English literature.'[129] Conspicuous among the Savages then were professional entertainers such as Brandon Thomas and W. S. Penley, the stars of *Charley's Aunt* (1892); Lionel Brough, character actor and clown; Harry Fragson, who was usually working two or three music halls at £200 per week; and Phil May, cartoonist and drunk.[130] The Savage had been the first club to elect Barrie, the Reform next; but he soon awoke to the self-discovery that their club life held few attractions and he rarely entered the half a dozen, including the Garrick and Authors', to which he belonged. In the 1905 edition of *Who's Who*, Barrie (like Raleigh) listed one only: the Athenaeum.[131]

The Athenaeum's restrictiveness had given opportunity to the Savile, which evolved out of the Eclectic, established in 1868. The original title reflected an intention to incorporate the distinguished in most walks of life—diplomats and

---

[126] Cf. the review in *Punch*, 3 July 1907, 18, of the half-centenary history, Aaron Watson's *The Savage Club* (1907). Like most clubs, the Savage had by then formal categories of membership: Science, Music, Literature, Art, Drama.   [127] Oppenheim, *Pool of Memory*, 8.

[128] Howard, *Motley Life*, 144–57, 252–3. Also Sutro, *Celebrities*, 48–9, for the hearty Saturday nights.

[129] Jerome, *Life and Times*, 56.

[130] For candid, albeit friendly, pen portraits of May, see Gribble, *Seen in Passing*, 137–54, and Jerome, *Life and Times*, 140–1. Gribble was editor of *Phil May's Annual. Review of Reviews* (Nov. 1891) 451, contains a profile of May, together with a photograph of him at work in his studio on Holland Park Road. May died in 1903, aged less than 40.

[131] On 8 January 1922 Barrie wrote to Quiller-Couch, 'A few years ago I was elected to another club and went into it for the first time with a member who said he knew I didn't go much to my other clubs but hoped I would come oftener here, to which my reply, "Dear Sir, I *have* now been oftener here than to my other clubs".' Earlier, on 26 March 1895, he told Q, 'as for clubs, after one look inside I conceived a desire to resign my membership' (Meynell (ed.), *Barrie Letters*, 8, 23; Barrie, *Greenwood Hat*, 252–6; *Who's Who* (1905), 90). Barrie was put up for the Garrick by Frederick Greenwood, the editor who first 'discovered' him; Scott, *Pall Mall Gazette*, 306. The Garrick celebrated Barrie's baronetcy, together with Johnston Forbes-Robertson's knighthood, at a special dinner on 29 June 1913; see Sichel, *Sands of Time*, 237, where the menu card designed by Harry Furniss is reproduced. Barrie later became a member of Grillion's, through his connection with the Asquiths.

dons, judges and lawyers, medical men and scientists, ecclesiastics, politicians, architects, painters, editors, and omnibus 'gentlemen'. It was renamed the Savile in 1871 on moving premises to Savile Row. This address in retrospect suggests more style than was evident then. Charles Brookfield reported the 'superstition prevalent among the non-scientific members that the smoking-room at the back of the house, with its top light, had in its time served as a dissecting-room'.[132] The Savile name stuck in spite of its re-establishment at 107 Piccadilly after 1882. If it too had an exclusiveness, this was designed to be intellectual rather than social. The Savile aimed at the interesting more than the rich, by an entrance fee of 10 guineas and subscription of 4.[133] A table d'hôte dinner, provided every week-day for 3s., was central to the club's life; and the maximum membership, set at 500 in 1871, was raised to 550 in 1876 and 600 in 1882. The Savile gained a reputation for advanced thinking. 'They won't elect you unless you're an atheist or have written a book' was the outsider's view.[134] The first of these assumptions was probably a stab at Edward Clodd and John Cotter Morison, freethinkers both, who served as committee members in the 1880s; but this hardly described the Savile in its entirety because it was also commonly said that the *Saturday Review*—conservative in politics and theology—was edited there, the editor, W. H. Pollock, and assistant editor, George Saintsbury, both being active members.[135] Surprisingly, perhaps, Pollock was one of thirty-two members who supported Oscar Wilde for membership in 1888;[136] but Wilde's name did not progress, and he had to content himself with membership of the Albemarle, to which club the Marquess of Queensberry famously directed the letter in 1895 addressed 'To Oscar Wilde posing Somdomite'.[137] While patrons or practitioners of literature

---

[132] Brookfield, *Reminiscences*, 44.

[133] The subscription was raised to 5 guineas in 1882; but a proposal by the committee to raise the entrance fee to 15 guineas in 1884 was defeated—'the only time, so far as is known, that a change of the rules directly recommended by the Committee has failed to obtain acceptance' ([Stephen], *Savile Club*, 43). By the mid-Edwardian period the entrance fee for most London clubs was between 20 and 40 guineas, and the subscription between 7 and 12 guineas p.a. In part, these charges reflected increased costs from the installation of lifts, electric lights, and telephones; there was also a lavish staff, including well-paid managers and secretaries. Head chefs were paid £200–300 p.a. Griffiths, 'London Clubs', *Fortnightly Review* (Apr. 1907), 662. When Compton Mackenzie was elected to the Savile in 1912, both entrance fee and annual subscription were 6 guineas; *Life and Times*, iv. 150.

[134] Quoted in [Stephen] *Savile Club*, 35; see also *T.P.'s Weekly*, 15 May 1903, 867.

[135] Pollock was editor of the *Saturday Review* from 1883 to 1894, whereupon Frank Harris took it over as proprietor–editor and briefly revived its circulation until he sold it on in 1898. See Kerry Powell, 'The Saturday Review', in Sullivan (ed.), *Literary Magazines, 1837–1913*, 379–83; and Saintsbury, *Second Scrap Book*, 326–39, for his fond reminiscences of the Savile, where he used to lunch and do pieces of work at least three times a week for nearly twenty years.

[136] Others who backed Wilde's candidature included W. E. Henley, Henry James, Edmund Gosse, Rider Haggard, Walter Besant, George Macmillan, and J. W. Mackail; Hart-Davis (ed.), *Wilde's Letters*, 73 n. 3. Henley's support at this date is worth noting; it is improbable that he would have done so later, having through his newspaper the *Scots Observer* taken a leading part in attacking Wilde's *Picture of Dorian Gray* in 1890. Wilde sent a note of condolence to Henley on the death of his only child in 1894; but by 1898, when Henley dispraised *The Ballad of Reading Gaol*, the distance was unbridgeable, Wilde writing of Henley's review that it was 'very coarse and vulgar, and entirely lacking in literary or gentlemanly instinct' (ibid. 115, 304, 330). [137] Ellmann, *Wilde*, 412.

invitations; and from 1904 to 1910 he resorted to 'Fletcherism',[5] the prolonged
mastication of food, which later he blamed for his 'digestive crisis', 'food
loathing', nervous debility, and depression. Yet, in and out of season, James
specialized in ruminative talk. The style did not appeal to everyone. Dorothy
Richardson vulgarly compared it to the 'non-stop waggling of the backside as he
hands out, on a salver, sentence after sentence'.[6] This compulsion to disgorge in
conversation what he had chewed over in mind meant that James could not
stay secluded for long. He had come out again after 1909 in order to shepherd
Edith Wharton about Society, accompanying her to the Elchos at Stanway, the
Astors at Cliveden, the Marchioness of Ripon at Coombe Court, Lady St Helier
at Arlington Manor, Newbury, and her town house in Portland Place, the
Charles Hunters at Hill Hall, the Ranee of Sarawak at Ascot, Lady Charles
Beresford, *et omnes*.[7]

This commitment to club and social life James could justify as artistic
dedication. Close inspection of upper-crust 'manners, customs, usages, habits,
forms, upon all these things matured and established', furnished him with
materials essential to his work, as a novelist of a great society in slow decline. It
was not a distinction that won universal applause—Somerset Maugham in *Cakes
and Ale* (1930) would write that 'Henry James had turned his back on one of the
great events of the world's history, the rise of the United States, in order to report
tittle-tattle at tea parties in English country houses'[8]—and in 1911 the combined
efforts of Gosse in England and W. D. Howells in America, and the orchestration
of Edith Wharton throughout the northern hemisphere, to obtain for James the
Nobel Prize for Literature, proved a failure. Compensation then came on 15 April
1913, James's seventieth birthday, when 269 admirers paid homage by subscribing
a 'golden bowl' (actually a silver-gilt Charles II porringer and dish), plus a
commission for John Singer Sargent to paint that 'large and luscious rotundity'.[9]

---

[5] Named after the American Horace Fletcher. The start of this fad was described by his friend R. D.
Blumenfeld: 'Horace Fletcher, the man who is mostly responsible for the infliction of Japanese fans and
other cheap Oriental gewgaws on Europe and America, has developed a new one . . . he has found youth
by chewing every morsel of food until it is no longer chewable, and this has reduced Fletcher from fifteen
stone to ten stone in weight, and given him the strength and endurance of a young giant. A year ago he
was just a fat, flabby, helpless invalid, and we had to assist him into a four-wheeler. Now he rides a bicycle
before breakfast for twenty miles and never tires' (Blumenfeld, *Diary*, 122 (31 Oct. 1900)). While less alert
to the commercial possibilities of mastication manuals, the Liberal premier Gladstone's rule that all food
be chewed thirty-two times before swallowing made a deeper impression on schoolboys than all his wise
statesmanship; see J. C. Masterman, 'My Mr Gladstone', in Masterman, *Bits and Pieces* (1961), 93–7.

[6] Rosenberg, *Richardson*, 50.

[7] See Powers (ed.), *Letters*. All these Society names are well-known to historians, with the possible
exception of the Charles Hunters. His wealth derived from coalmines, and they entertained literary and
other celebrities at their estate in the north of England as well as at Hill Hall, Epping Forest. Mary Hunter
was the daughter of a major-general. George Moore was a favourite of hers. He dedicated *The Brook Kerith*
(1916), his musing about the character of Christ, to her, as a belated return for the Bible she had given him
in 1898.   [8] Maugham, *Cakes and Ale*, 72.

[9] See the five-volume biography by Leon Edel (1953–72), esp. v: *The Master 1901–1916*, 438–9, 484–9. Also,
Edel's editions of James's letters, esp. ii: *1875–1883* (1980) and iii: *1883–1895* (1981); Simon Nowell-Smith, *The
Legend of the Master* (1947; Oxford, 1985), 54–6; Lomax and Ormond, *Sargent*, 69–70.

The finished portrait hung in the Royal Academy until it attracted the attentions of an elderly suffragette with a meat cleaver in 1914. After repair and James's demise, it was willed to the National Portrait Gallery. James had thus become an eminence.

II

There was a suitableness about authors and aristocracy coming together. Figures alike, if Wilde's aphorism is followed, that the peerage 'is the best thing in fiction the English have ever done'.[10] Hugh Walpole was avid in pursuit of both. Charles Marriott, author of *The Column* (1901) and recipient of one of Walpole's frequently posted fan letters, recalled that 'not long after we were settled in London [in 1909] Hugh had engaged to dine with us but threw us over for an invitation from old Lady Lovelace, explaining quite frankly that she would be of more use to him in that stage of his career as a writer'.[11] Drawing-room life in aristocratic town houses or weekending in their country piles was a favourite subject for dramatists and novelists, even for those of severe intellectual disposition such as Mrs Humphry Ward, who struggled to maintain the eighteenth-century mansion Stocks in Hertfordshire which she occupied from 1892. She also settled into the Tudor mansion Levens Hall in Cumbria in 1896–7 while writing *Helbeck of Bannisdale* (1898). After her first great success, *Robert Elsmere* (1888), she was invited to spend a week with Lady Wemyss, whom, she declared,

I love more than ever, but the party in the house was large and very smart, and with the best will in the world on both sides it is difficult for plain literary folk who don't belong to it to get much entertainment out of a circle where everybody is cousin of everybody else, and on Christian name terms, and where the women at any rate, though pleasant enough, are taken up with 'places', jewels and Society with a big S.[12]

The entertainment may have been limited—what Arthur Pinero, in *The Times* (1891), called 'the gaiety of climbing a flight of stairs to clutch at a haggard hostess on a landing'[13]—but it was the publicizing of these occasions that mattered foremost. Max Beerbohm affirmed that for an author admission to 'Society is a sort of substitute for an Academy of Letters'. Such parties might involve tiresome, even humiliating, horseplay; a junket that included Asquith, Cromer, and Haldane, ended with 'eggs being fried in Max Beerbohm's hat'. Still, Max could be consoled, as when Lady Desborough invited him to dine with 'the de Greys,

---

[10] Oscar Wilde, *A Woman of No Importance* (1893), Third Act, in Wilde, *Plays*, 117.

[11] Hart-Davis, *Walpole*, 74. On Charles Marriott (1869–1957), Sutherland, *Companion*, 411, and Kemp *et al.* (eds.), *Edwardian Fiction*, 267–8. He struggled as a novelist after the success of *The Column* and ended his days as art critic for *The Times*. Compton Mackenzie knew him when he was living in St Ives, where Walpole originally sought him out; Mackenzie, *Life and Times*, iv. 53–5.

[12] Mrs Ward to Mrs A. H. Johnson, 21 Oct. 1888, in Trevelyan, *Mrs. Ward*, 72.

[13] Fyfe, *Pinero's Plays*, 72.

literary society like the plague all the rest of my life as Wellington avoided military society'. Why was this? Shaw's father had been second cousin to a baronet but otherwise, the son wrote with disgust, 'a hypocrite and a dipsomaniac'.[25] Shaw smarted about his family's dive down the social scale before he assumed his unembarrassable pose and embraced socialism. He joined several literary societies in the 1880s—the New Shakspere, Browning, and Shelley—as well as political societies, most famously the Fabians. He also joined the Authors' Society, but this he characteristically termed his 'trade union'. In 1909, for the first time, he recorded in *Who's Who* membership of a club, Royal Automobile, clarifying his position in 1910 by adding 'motor driving' to his established exercises of 'cycling, swimming, public speaking'.[26] In a conventional sense, therefore, Shaw never was a clubman or regular at salons.

Arnold Bennett, who did relish club life but also considered himself a socialist, would not be ensnared in salons either. He mocked the notion of 'a literary bachelor living with a cause and holding receptions of serious people in chambers furnished by Roger Fry'.[27] That description indicated a shift in the trappings of the bohemian lifestyle during this period. Irregular it may have remained in several respects, it was also chic and needed a fair income to support it. Ambrose Byars, in Guy Thorne's *When it was Dark* (1903), declares: 'The days when you couldn't be a genius without being dirty are gone . . . I was staying at St. Ives last summer, where there is quite an artistic settlement. All the painters carried golf-clubs and looked like professional athletes. They drink Bohea in Bohemia now.'[28] Guy Thorne (C. A. E. Ranger-Gull), a fervent High Churchman and snob, was cutting; but, since he had been a hard-drinking journalist in London and then moved to Cornwall, where he continued to imbibe copious quantities, he cannot be dismissed as a witness. This assessment of a changing bohemian style, from the sordid to the pseudo, was not in conflict with that of the more sympathetic Arthur Ransome, whose *Bohemia in London* (1907) shocked only by the absence of shocking behaviour to report. 'Bohemia is an abominable word,' he decided, 'with an air of tinsel and sham, and of suburban daughters who criticise musical comedies seriously, and remind you twice in an afternoon that they are quite unconventional'.[29] Bohemian in the sense of hanging about Soho coffee-houses and taverns was a developmental phase for many a writer, like the pupal period for a bug. Eventually, they would evolve into Hampstead, where 'long and matted hair is quite intelligibly worn by the young men who are mad to "return to the primitive emotions of healthy barbaric life" (I quote from a Hampstead conversation).' Hampstead was where a 'dozen charming middle-aged women struggle, with the aid of Messrs Liberty and a painful expenditure of taste, to turn

---

[25] Holroyd, *Shaw*, i. 8, 15, 99.   [26] *Who's Who* (1909), 1717; (1910), 1758.
[27] Bennett, *The Title*, 26.   [28] Guy Thorne, *When it was Dark* (1904), 15.
[29] Ransome, *Bohemia in London*, 7.

their drawing-rooms into salons' and to catch 'the meanings and messages of "the newer movements" '. Ransome elaborated:

The room has half a dozen nooks and corners, and in each corner, seated on cushions, are a young man with long hair and flowing tie, and a maiden out of a Burne-Jones picture, reading poetry, listening to the talk or to the music made by a youthful Paderewski at the piano. The hostess will be draped in green or brown, to tone with the wall-papers, and she will talk anxiously with one or another young man, thinking all the time about the intellectual level of the conversation and the balance of her sentences . . . Some cause, some movement, some great and vital matter will stir the whole salon . . . A man will address the hostess and shake his fist, and talk of Ireland, and the brutality of English rule; of the deplorable condition of the Russian peasants; of the open shame of the Ipecacuanha Indians, who prefer tattoo to decent clothing . . . Several committees will be formed at once.[30]

Bennett did not pass through a bohemian phase, only because he had his own idea about the proper decoration of a literary bachelor's apartment. This betrayed a different weakness, to imitate a luxurious imperial lifestyle. When furnishing his small flat, 4 rue de Calais, after his move to Paris, he visited the Fontainebleau Palace:

He fell in love with the furniture of Napoleon's period—he had to have that style for his home. He hunted round for bargains, with tips given to him by his devoted friend, Henry Davray. Napoleonic furniture inspired him; I do not mean Napoleon did, but certainly Napoleon's love of pageantry, his tenacity, perseverance, his success, did encourage the worker in him; the man afraid of splendour, sumptuousness and power, yet striving to get them all.[31]

The successful author was thus acquiring status trappings; still, being indulged at home or in Hampstead was different from being on parade in Mayfair. The marquess inherited rather than bought his furniture, while the millionaire simply scooped it up, quality and quantity alike. Hence the self-assurance of authors was often tested by the aristocratic and plutocratic embrace. Many were both flattered and flustered. The deference demanded of them rankled with the status-sensitive or class-confused writer, who suspected his own sycophancy. George Du Maurier made merry with the torment in 1879 in his *Punch* cartoon 'The Reward of Merit'. This depicted the Duchess of Stilton 'being introduced to a famous writer for the ninth time of the season, complacently conscious of giving pleasure, but quite unconcerned with her failure to recognise him'.[32] Among his other cartoon characters was Mrs Lyon Hunter. The super-rich Americans Waldorf and Nancy Astor were not yet transmogrified into super-rich British aristocrats, but the first stage was begun when for their marriage dowry in 1906 William Waldorf Astor gave them several millions and a palace, Cliveden, which he had bought from the Duke of Westminster in 1893. There, Nancy Astor became one of the most lavish Society hostesses. She would handpick a famous author or two to mix with native

---

[30] Ibid. 229–31.   [31] Bennett, *Bennett*, 22.   [32] Ormond, *Du Maurier*, 341, 343.

and foreign royalty and aristocracy. Barrie, Belloc, and Kipling, all feature in her visitors' book and none appears to have been at ease.[33] As an author's experience and confidence grew, a disclosure of real feeling might occur, as in Barrie's *Twelve-Pound Look* (1910), where Kate tells her gross and conceited ex-husband, who is about to be knighted and already calling himself Sir Harry, why his attitude revolted her:

KATE. How you beamed at me when I sat at the head of your fat dinners in my fat jewellery, surrounded by our fat friends . . .
SIR HARRY. [*shouting*]. . . . We had all the most interesting society of the day. It wasn't only business men. There were politicians, painters, writers—
KATE. Only the glorious, dazzling successes. Oh, the fat talk while we ate too much— about who had made a hit and who was slipping back, and what the noo house cost and the noo motor and the gold soup-plates, and who was to be the noo knight.[34]

In *Dear Brutus* (1917) Barrie introduces 'Lady Caroline Latey of the disdainful poise, lately from the enormously select school where they are taught to pronounce their *r*'s as *w*'s; nothing else seems to be taught, but for matrimonial success nothing else is necessary. Every woman who pronounces *r* as *w* will find a mate; it appeals to all that is chivalrous in man.'[35] In the Midsummer Night's mayhem that follows, Barrie marries her off to the rough butler Matey, who has a past of shady dealings. In *Mary Rose* (1920) Barrie was in more lenient mood; but the confessional of the peculiarly pedantic Cameron, who rows the Blakes—from Sussex gentry and officer stock—to the Scottish isle, rings true. Cameron is aware that he is better read and all-round more intelligent; indeed, he has tested this assumption, yet still feels the need to copy something in Mr Blake:

It iss not Mr Blake's learning; he has not much learning, but I haf always understood that the English manage without it. What I admire in you iss your ferry nice manners and your general deportment, in all which I haf a great deal to learn yet, and I watch these things in Mr Blake and take memoranda of them in a little note-book.[36]

Authors might smoulder, but they went on accepting the invitations, alike from dim Lady Lisping of old feudality and from brassy Lord Muck of new manufacture. Douglas Goldring, who left Oxford to join the staff of *Country Life* and the *English Review*, wrote:

I shall never forget an occasion when, at a dance given by a millionaire armaments manufacturer in a palatial house in Knightsbridge, I heard my hostess say to an unobtrusive man in steel-rimmed spectacles: 'Oh Mr. Kipling, will you take Mrs. Humphry Ward down to supper?' I was struck dumb with astonishment. 'Good heavens', I thought, 'what are *they* doing here?' It amazed me to see two genuinely distinguished people among so many rich nobodies.[37]

---

[33] Maurice Collis, *Nancy Astor* (1960), ch. 3; Jerome, *Life and Times*, 98, for Barrie's touchiness about this or a similar experience.   [34] Barrie, *Plays*, 730–1.
[35] Ibid. 465.   [36] Ibid. 563.   [37] Goldring, *South Lodge*, 45.

Arthur Benson thought much the same about his brother Fred, who moved in the fashionable swim after the success of *Dodo* (1893): 'he goes to stay with absurd countesses like Lady Radnor whose vagaries I cannot think that he would tolerate if she was Mrs Tompkinson'.[38]

Perhaps the best course was to be utterly cynical about the whole thing. In 1890 *Punch* entertained readers with a communication purportedly from a retired author. His original ambition had been modest enough, to make enough money to spend six weeks by the seaside at Herne Bay; but he succeeded beyond expectation when 'an elderly lady of unstable views' was so taken by a story of his that she bequeathed to him 'a very handsome legacy'. How was this feat accomplished? 'My plan briefly was to write a quasi-religious Novel with a Purpose. I knew nothing about religion, and had no literary experience'; but, having invested in a dozen penny novelettes, he constructed his plot and dialogue by scissors-and-paste method. The finishing touch required 'a reading ticket for the British Museum Library, and from the writings of Herbert Spencer, Huxley, Emerson, Matthew Arnold, Ruskin, Dr Momerie, and Mr Walter Pater, and largely from the more pretentious Reviews and Magazines, I made copious and tolerably bewildering extracts, which I apportioned among the vacant spaces in my story'. The product had no difficulty finding a reputable publisher and was immediately taken up by salon types:

I became for one dazzling season a second-rate lion of the first magnitude. I was pointed out by literary celebrities whom nobody knew, to social recruits who knew nobody. I figured prominently in the Saloons of the Mutual-exploitation Societies, and when my name appeared in the minor Society papers among those present at Mrs Ophir Crowdy's reception, I felt what it was to be famous—and to remain unspoiled.[39]

The spoof scribbler was satisfied by his one season; but several real authors were set on becoming social somebodies in their own right. Mrs Humphry Ward, it has been noticed, was chatelaine of a Hertfordshire mansion. Kipling embarked on the same in 1902 when he bought Bateman's in East Sussex for £9,300, initially with 33 acres, which he progressively extended to 300 acres. As a landlord with tenant farmers, Kipling 'enjoyed the cachet of owning a small estate, which allowed him to discuss hunting and poaching with the aristocratic friends of his later years'.[40]

III

In her *Memories of Fifty Years* (1909) Lady St Helier[41] ascribed the increasing cosmopolitanism of Society to the initiative of Lady Waldegrave, the principal

[38] Arthur Benson's diary, July 1906, in Newsome, *Edge of Paradise*, 191.
[39] *Punch*, 7 June 1890, 276.
[40] Andrew Lycett, 'Everything a Man Could Want', *National Trust Magazine* (summer 1999), 54–7.
[41] Born Susan Stewart Mackenzie, of a Scottish landed family—her aunt was a lady-in-waiting to the Queen—she married the judge Sir Francis Jeune, who was created Baron St Helier in 1905, the year of his

Whig–Liberal party hostess following the death of Lady Palmerston in 1869. Lady Dorothy Nevill, on the other hand, awarded the palm to Lady Waldegrave's rival Lady Molesworth as being the better at 'drawing out clever people and making them talk—a social quality of the highest possible value'. This disagreement between Lady St Helier and Lady Dorothy Nevill—themselves the best-known salon hostesses in the late Victorian and Edwardian period—reflected their own political loyalties. Lady Waldegrave had been the first to capture Dickens, though apparently he was too tongue-tied to be launched at a large Society gathering and it was Lady Molesworth who first succeeded in getting him to shine at a dinner party of six.[42] Literary salons given under the patronage of a titled hostess had been seen before, the best known in the 1830s and 1840s being associated with the widowed Countess of Blessington. She supplemented her jointure by the proceeds of her pen, turning out 'silver-fork' novels and editing annuals such as *The Book of Beauty* and *The Keepsake*. Disraeli, Bulwer-Lytton, and Dickens had attended her functions; so had the then best-seller Harrison Ainsworth, who was famously handsome. This was a distinct social step up for Ainsworth, a Manchester solicitor's son, though he had distant aristocratic connections through his mother; still, it makes sensible, if not altogether accurate, Somerset Maugham's observation that 'Ainsworth was the first English man of letters to move in English society on terms of equality,' until with the collapse in the popularity of his work from the 1850s, he retreated to the shadows.[43]

Each of these hostesses was in her own origins on the margins of Society or even from beyond: Lady Molesworth, for instance, had been a singer, and Lady Dorothy Nevill's immediate family invited disrepute by their misbehaviour. Lady Dorothy's own youngest son, Ralph, who co-authored her memoirs, was the rumoured offspring of her affair with Disraeli. Breeding remained a paramount consideration for Society proper. Lord Frederic Hamilton, who was born in 1856 and enjoyed Society functions in the late 1870s, emphasized that 'London society was so much smaller then, that it was a sort of enlarged family party'—an apt observation, since Hamilton was one of fourteen children of a duke.[44] Before the 1880s the old order was intimate and generally exclusive, the barriers being social as well as party-political. Activities such as drama and professions such as medicine were mostly beneath notice. Lady St Helier instanced only Mr and Mrs Alfred Wigan and Miss Helena Faucit (Lady Martin)[45] from the first, and the

death. He was a member of Grillion's, the most exclusive of dining clubs. Jeune was her second husband, her first being Colonel Stanley, son of Lord Stanley of Alderley. Her entry in *Who's Who* (1905), 857, recorded that 'Lady Jeune is indefatigable in service of the poor, and in Society is famed for her brilliant art of entertaining.' The St Heliers' only son died of fever in India, also in 1905.

[42] Nevill, *Reminiscences*, 171–5; and [Escott], *Society*, 37–8. For Lady Waldegrave (1821–79), Lady Molesworth (c.1809–88), and Lady Dorothy Nevill (1826–1913), see *Oxford DNB*.

[43] Maugham, *Cakes and Ale*, 86; and *Oxford DNB*, for Ainsworth (1805–82) and Blessington (1789–1849).

[44] Hamilton, *Days before Yesterday*, 195.

[45] For Alfred Wigan (1814–78) and his wife, Leonora Pincott, and for Helena Faucit (1817–98), who married Theodore Martin (knighted in 1880), see *DNB*. Martin was the official biographer of the Prince

surgeon Sir Henry Thompson[46] from the second, who were admitted. Lady Molesworth's liberality was afterwards imitated by Lady Dorothy Nevill, whose Sunday luncheons brought together 'all the best representatives of every kind of society', her circle including the actors Squire Bancroft and Henry Irving as well as Cabinet ministers. It was, however, her cultivation of authors that was most signal and systematic. 'Literary people have always attracted me,' she wrote.[47] In her reminiscences—a plodding account which makes almost incomprehensible Edmund Gosse's opinion that Lady Dorothy was 'the finest female wit of her age'[48]—she noted her mother's friendship with the poet Samuel Rogers and wanted particularly to recall her own with Matthew Arnold, Walter Pater, J. A. Froude, Hepworth Dixon (editor of the *Athenaeum*), Ouida, and Oscar Wilde. The last named acquired Zola's autograph for her: she was a ruthless collector and unblushingly solicited them. Thus it was that Lady Dorothy united strange company such as Cardinal Newman and Zola, if only as signatures in her book. Her seizing on certain authors was inspired by family interest: the poet Austin Dobson, known for his eighteenth-century literary studies, in 1893 wrote an appreciation of one of her forebears, Horace Walpole. Otherwise, the remarkable thing about Lady Dorothy was the way in which she spanned the generations and genres in her literary network: Thackeray (whose sardonicism rather unnerved her), Tennyson, Frederick Locker, Thomas Hardy, Alfred Austin, Kate Greenaway, Miss M. E. Braddon, and Edmund Gosse, who dedicated his only novel, *The Secret of Narcisse* (1892), to her.

Consort (1875–80), and his wife was also favoured by the Queen. The actor Charles Brookfield (*Reminiscences*, 219) cattily remarked about the Wigans: 'Alfred and his wife were frequently honoured by a command from Her Majesty to bring their company to perform at Windsor. It is not to be wondered at that her social success rather turned the head of the gifted Leonora—that is to say, that she became a little apt to give herself airs among her brother and sister artists who had been less favoured.'

[46] Thompson (1820–1904), from a trade and Nonconformist background, was very unusual. A surgeon at University College London, whose speciality was urinary disorders, he operated (successfully) on King Leopold I of Belgium in 1863 and (unsuccessfully) on the exiled Napoleon III of France in 1872–3. He was founder of the Cremation Society of Great Britain in 1874, a cause supported by Anthony Trollope and Sir John Tenniel; the practice was legalized in 1884, and the first cremation took place at Woking in 1885. Thompson was also an astronomer, artist, and novelist (under the pseudonym Pen Oliver) and a collector of Chinese porcelain (which Whistler celebrated in his canvases). This versatility made Thompson an attractive catch for Society; and his own entertaining at Wimpole Street was much praised, particularly his 'octaves', dinner parties of eight courses for eight people served at eight o'clock. He started these in 1872: they involved 'the most famous persons in the worlds of art, letters, science, politics, diplomacy, and fashion'. The Prince of Wales (the future George V) attended the 300th; the last, the 301st, took place just before Thompson's death. See *DNB Supplement 1901–1911*, iii. 503–5; Nevill, *Reminiscences*, 298–9. Perhaps this sufficiently explains why he was the first of medical men to be singled out for social promotion; but he also treated the aristocracy and the famous for venereal complaints. Thackeray was one of his patients (Harden (ed.), *Thackeray's Letters*, pp. xvi, xxii, 72, 323, 327, 369); so was Lord Colin Campbell (G. H. Fleming, *Victorian 'Sex Goddess'* (Oxford, 1990), 10, 41) and, quite possibly, the Marquess of Queensberry (*Oxford DNB*, article by John Davis), whose body was cremated at death. Thompson was thus a privileged keeper of secrets.   [47] Nevill, *Reminiscences*, 319.

[48] Thwaite, *Gosse*, 327. Thwaite states that it was at the home of the general Sir Redvers Buller that Gosse first met Lady Dorothy Nevill, who became thereafter one of his closest friends; ibid. 310. See also [Escott], *Society*, 119–20, for Nevill's salon.

The inclusion of authors, as also actors and actresses and (to adopt T. H. S. Escott's designation) 'impostors and impostresses', had one obvious justification. Escott, editor (1882–6) of the *Fortnightly Review*, explained it as Society's 'anxiety to secure prophylactics against boredom'.[49] Some authors, once admitted, were rather too keen to make up for lost time, such that they 'are quite as much courtiers, even parasites, by profession, as they are poets or men of letters by achievement'. This was particularly true of the older generation, so long excluded. Primed by his election to the Athenaeum in February 1862, Robert Browning was now seen to live 'for society, and in society'. He had become 'a professional diner-out', a fixture of all drawing rooms, aristocratic and plutocratic, great and small, where he appeared 'full of anecdote accommodated to his audience, profound or superficial, light or serious, literary, scientific, poetic, historical, or what you will'. A widower since 1861, he also congratulated himself on being considered 'irresistible by ladies of all ages and all degrees'—reasonably enough in the case of the equally widowed Lady Ashburton, who twice proposed marriage to him, 1869–71. Matthew Arnold was another such 'orb of literary light in the social empyrean', though 'less conspicuously or aggressively the man of the world, pure and simple, than Mr Browning'.[50] Browning's 'engagement book [was] filled a month ahead each year from December until August';[51] and Hallam Tennyson suspected that when Browning expired it would be 'in a white choker at a dinner party'.[52] Browning's correspondence shows him staying at various country piles, among them Alton Towers (the Earl of Shrewsbury), Highclere (the Earl of Carnarvon), and Hatfield (the Marquess of Salisbury). Shortly before his death in 1889 he dined with Lord Rosebery to meet the Shah of Persia; but his Liberal leanings otherwise caused him to turn down an invitation to sup with General Boulanger, the enemy of the Third French Republic.[53] Mary Gladstone, the GOM's daughter, had not liked Browning at first: 'He talks everybody down with his dreadful voice, and always places his person in such disagreeable proximity with yours and puffs and blows and spits in yr. face.' But she began to think better of him during the Eastern Crisis, when he turned his rhyming talent against the music-hall jingoes, coming up with this coarse gem at a breakfast party:

> We don't want to fight,
> By Jingo, if we do,
> The head I'd like to punch
> Is Beaconsfield the Jew.[54]

---

[49] [Escott], *Society*, 52.   [50] Ibid. 130–1.

[51] DeVane and Knickerbocker (eds.), *New Letters of Robert Browning*, 2. The London Season proper ran from Easter/April to the end of July, whereupon the shooting season and/or autumnal visits to Continental spas and resorts took over.   [52] Miller, *Browning*, 272.

[53] DeVane and Knickerbocker (eds.), *New Letters of Robert Browning*, 379–81.

[54] Masterman (ed.), *Mary Gladstone*, 116–17, 135, 240, 411, 454 (9 Mar. 1877, 4 Apr. 1878, 11 Feb. 1882, 18 Dec. 1889, 14 Mar. 1901).

Politics generally now counted for less in these gatherings. Many of the literary figures whom Lady Dorothy invited to her table were Liberal in inclination, whereas their hostess was a decided Tory, proud to proclaim that Lord Randolph Churchill originated the idea of the Primrose League at her house; she herself was on its Ladies' Grand Council.[55] But authors would always forgive, if not every lady, then at least the titled ones. In this they behaved no differently from others on the rise: Joseph Chamberlain was friendly with Lady Dorothy in his anti-aristocratic period when they talked about orchids and French literature and avoided contentious politics.[56] An exception to this accommodation of political differences was briefly made for followers of Parnell's more aggressive brand of Irish nationalism, if Justin McCarthy's experience is a guide. In the 1870s he enjoyed a double success as leader-writer for the Liberal *Daily News* and romantic novelist, author of *Dear Lady Disdain* (1875) and *Miss Misanthrope* (1878). He was then earning, according to T. P. O'Connor, 'the gigantic income of two or three thousand a year' and, with his 'fascinatingly agreeable manners, gentle, modest, as brilliant in talk as in writing, he was the darling of London society'. In 1879 McCarthy was returned as Parnellite MP for Longford, whereupon, as both Liberal and Conservative parties denounced the terrorism of the Irish land campaign and the obstructive tactics of the parliamentary party, he found Society doors closed. He was then ostracized by 'all his old social friends, with the honourable exception of Lady St. Helier, then Mrs. Jeune'.[57] This did not last. Society hostesses generally renewed their competitive pursuit of talent; and McCarthy instead found himself pilloried as an 'Anglicized Irishman' by the more extreme Irish Nationalists, following the split in Parnellite ranks caused by the leader's disgrace and demise.[58]

In only one respect did Lady Dorothy Nevill regret Edwardian Society's failure to uphold the exclusivity that had prevailed in early and mid-Victorian society. This was in the admission of the nouveaux riches or plutocrats who had no social virtues. Indeed, she 'questioned whether Society, as the word used to be understood, now exists at all ... The question is not now asked, "Is So-and-so clever?" but instead, "Is So-and-so rich?" ... Now all is changed; in fact Society (a word obsolete in its old sense) is, to use a vulgar expression, "on the make".'[59] This was because the old landed and leisured aristocracy, to offset falling agricultural rents, angled for City directorships. Mayfair needed to pick the pockets of the Stock Exchange; alternatively, to play the marriage market by embracing a transatlantic bride who came blessed with dollars. It was W. T. Stead who coined the phrase 'gilded prostitution' in *The Americanization of the World* (1902). Equally indelicate was Marie Corelli: 'there is always a British title going

---

[55] Nevill, *Reminiscences*, 327–35.   [56] Ibid. 224–7.

[57] O'Connor, *Memoirs*, ii. 66–7, 70–1; and [Escott], *Society*, 136, where McCarthy is described as doing himself harm by transforming 'from an English *litterateur* into an Irish politician'.

[58] Sheehy, 'Irish Journalists', 254. Parnell himself disdainfully styled McCarthy 'a nice old gentleman for a quiet tea-party'.   [59] Nevill, *Reminiscences*, 121–2.

a-begging,—always some decayed or degenerate or semi-drunken peer, whose fortunes are on the verge of black ruin, ready and willing to devour, monster-like, the holocaust of an American virgin, provided bags of bullion are flung, with her, into his capacious maw'.[60] The racket was well organized: in Corelli's story *Thelma* (1887) Mrs Rush-Marvelle is paid 500 guineas commission to broker the marriage of Marcia Van Clupp to Lord Masherville.[61]

Corelli further claimed to be able

to name at least a dozen well-known society women...who make a very good thing...by accepting huge payments in exchange for their recommendation or intro-duction to Royal personages, and who add considerably to their incomes by such means, bringing the names of the King and Queen down to their own sordid level of bargain and sale, with a reckless disregard of the damaging results of such contemptible conduct.[62]

A persistent theme of Corelli's novels was that in modern Society everything could be had for a price. In *The Sorrows of Satan* (1895) the author Geoffrey Tempest, who has become a multi-millionaire by selling his soul, is presented at a court levée. The introduction has been purchased for him by Prince Lucio Rimânez—the Devil incarnate. Corelli scornfully depicted the 'flunkeydom... sham and humbug' that went with these events; yet she exculpated the Prince of Wales himself, who presided on this occasion:

the heir-apparent to the greatest empire in the world expressed in his very attitude and looks an unaffected and courteous welcome to all, surrounded as he was, and as such in his position must ever be, by toadies, parasites, sycophants, hypocritical self-seekers, who would never run the least risk to their own lives to serve him, unless they could get something personally satisfactory out of it, his presence impressed itself upon me as full of the suggestion of dormant but none the less resolute power.[63]

What accounts for this exception? Later in the story the reader is privileged to peep inside Lily Cottage, the Warwickshire home of Mavis Clare, the best-selling novelist whom venal critics decry and the public adores for her fearless honesty and romantic passion: 'There were flowers everywhere, books, rare bits of china—elegant trifles that only a woman of perfect taste would have the sense to select and appreciate—on one or two of the side tables and on the grand piano were autograph-portraits of many of the greatest celebrities in Europe.' Among these were the Tsar of Russia, the Queen of Italy, and the Prince of Wales. 'You know the Prince?', Tempest asks, 'in a little surprise'. 'Well, it would be more correct to say that he knows me,' the authoress replies with becoming modesty. 'He has been very amiable in taking some little interest in my books. He knows a great deal about literature too—much more than people give him credit for.

---

[60] Corelli, 'American Women in England', in Corelli, *Free Opinions*, 119. See also Maureen E. Montgomery, *'Gilded Prostitution': Status, Money and Transatlantic Marriages, 1870–1914* (1989).

[61] Marie Corelli, *Thelma: A Norwegian Princess* (1896), 290, 413–14.

[62] Corelli, 'The Vulgarity of Wealth', in Corelli, *Free Opinions*, 100.

[63] Corelli, *Sorrows of Satan*, 151–4.

He has been here more than once . . .'.[64] Mavis Clare was an idealized self-portrait of Marie Corelli, who made sure the world knew of the favour her novels found among native and foreign royalty. To her publisher Bentley she had written ecstatically when the Prince of Wales requested her first two novels, *A Romance of Two Worlds* (1886) and *Vendetta* (1886): '*If you can manage it* will you put a paragraph on this in some of the leading evening papers[?]' And Corelli just happened to be in Homburg in 1892 when the Prince was there, which brought her an invitation to dinner. Her triumph was complete when her attendance was commanded at his coronation.[65]

For authors and aristocrats possessed of aesthetic sensibility, neither financiers nor royalty came up to scratch. Esmé Amarinth, the cartoon Oscar Wilde figure in *The Green Carnation*, remarks:

I wonder what a stockbroker is like. I don't think I have ever seen one. I go out in Society too much, I suppose. Society has its drawbacks. You meet so few people in it nowadays, and Royalties are of course strictly tabooed. I was dining with Lady Murray last week, and mentioned the Prince by mistake. She got quite red all down her neck, and snorted . . . — 'One must draw the line somewhere.' The old aristocracy draws it at Princes now, and who can blame them.[66]

Nor was the new aristocracy always willing to lower its standards to a princely level. E. F. Benson's Society novel *Dodo* (1893) was taken to be a skit on Margot Tennant and, when she dined at the Russian Ambassador's shortly after its publication, the Prince of Wales came up to her and enquired: 'How do you do, Miss Dodo?' An appalled Lady Emily Lytton, to whom Margot reported this, commented: 'He is the only man who would have had the bad taste enough to do such a thing.'[67]

It was nothing new for Society to flirt with Sensation, but it entirely recoiled from Scandal. The real Oscar Wilde would soon know the difference, although his doppelgänger Amarinth might still joke in 1894: 'One has to choose between being dangerous and dull. Society loves to feel itself upon the edge of a precipice, I assure you. To be harmless is the most deadly enemy to social salvation.' But it was important not to tip over the edge:

'Society only loves one thing more than sinning,' said Madam Valtesi, examining the moon magisterially through her tortoiseshell eyeglass.
  'And what is that?' said Lady Locke.
  'Administering injustice.'[68]

The upper-crust attitude to sexual adventure and eccentricity was not naturally censorious. Not a few aristocratic males might well have experienced homoerotic sensations, even seduction, at public school and, reclining in leather armchairs at

---

[64] Ibid. 180–1, 191.   [65] Ransom, *Corelli*, 38–9, 64–6, 116.
[66] Hichens, *Green Carnation*, 118–19.
[67] Letter to the Revd Whitwell Elwin, 4 July 1893, in Lutyens, *Blessed Girl*, 207.
[68] Hichens, *Green Carnation*, 69; and [Escott], *Society*, 134–5, for Wilde's success with Society women.

their St James's clubs in old age, with testosterone diminished or altogether dead, stare vacantly into the middle distance fondly recollecting such adolescent dalliances. But to make a career of homosexuality and to flaunt it as Wilde did was incorrigible and utterly infra dig. Homosexual transgressions whose sordid details ended up in court and a blaze of publicity were far more horrifying than homicide, which might involve glamour and romance. The well-bred appreciated stylish slaughter in the drawing room as in the field, or so J. M. Barrie suggested with a twinkle. In *Seven Women* (1917) Tovey itemizes for an old friend the guests invited to a dinner party in his honour, who include a murderess. Tovey explains: 'Fact is . . . the order of the day for dinners has become a celebrity at any cost'; and he swells with pride that the murderess 'had a much more exalted engagement', which she broke to join their party.[69]

Generally, the literary man had preceded the millionaire (or murderess) in gaining access to Society. In the late Victorian period, as conventions were beginning to be relaxed, and new habits of town-house at-homes and supper parties and country-house weekending were taking root, 'the world began to realise the enormous crowd of brilliant men and women who had hitherto lived unrecognised and unappreciated at their very gates; and those into whose houses they were welcomed found their rooms filled with distinguished guests, and the *beau monde* flocking in numbers to make their acquaintance'. This was Lady St Helier's description; and it was her receptions and dinners, in the 1880s and afterwards, that were marked by this social mixing, such that those who attended

were always convinced that every person they did not know was distinguished, either for some political, intellectual, or literary reason, or even from some less elevated point of view. I think . . . it amused them to see those of whom they had heard, but whom they had never known, and, above all, to feel that every person who trod on their gown or knocked up against them was remarkable in some way or other.[70]

All this impressed members of the foreign aristocracy such as Constantine Benckendorff, who thought there was 'no other country where the ruling few mixed so easily with the literary and artistic world'.[71] Of course, this progressive liberality did not obtain universally. When Elinor Glyn married into county Society in 1892—her husband's estate was Sheering Hall in Essex—one dowager instructed her in correct form: 'Remember, my dear, it is only to garden parties that you must ask the lawyers and doctors—never to luncheons or dinners!' Glyn added: 'Brains did not count; the Army, the Navy, the Diplomatic Service, the Church or the Bar were the only undisputed professions of "Gentlemen". Those who earned money in other ways, whether by professional, literary or artistic

[69] Barrie, *Plays*, 636.
[70] St Helier, *Memories*, 186–7; and Nevill, *Reminiscences*, 340, for Lady Dorothy's eulogy. Burnand, *Records*, ii. 285 choruses this: 'At "the Jeunes" you met everybody who was anybody and rarely anybody who only thought himself somebody. Not to have the *entrée* to "the Jeunes" was to argue yourself unknown.'   [71] Quoted in Ridley and Percy (eds.), *Balfour–Elcho Letters*, 12.

ability, or by business interests, were ruled out, and were only seen at Hunt balls and charity entertainments.' When making the rounds of aristocratic establishments, Glyn was more likely to meet, rather than some author, a 'handsome young man in a velvet smoking-suit . . . sprawling on a rug before the fire playing with his rough-haired terrier . . . a typical product of Eton and Oxford, endowed with a splendid physique, personal charm and innate good qualities of the highest order, but intellectually and emotionally sound asleep'.[72]

On visits to London from Dorset, Thomas Hardy would stay occasionally at Lady St Helier's. 'He was a delightful companion,' she recalled, 'always glad to talk about his books, and the reasons and events which had influenced him in his different novels.' This, it was implied, was a confidence Hardy reserved for her, because 'society had no attractions for him. He was shy and retiring, and the adulation and interest which he awakened was a cause of annoyance instead of being any pleasure to him.'[73] There was misjudgement here. Hardy's limit of agreeableness (or of fawning) was rarely reached where titled ladies were concerned. Although he did once chance a criticism of Lady Grove's description of her brush with an unhelpful shop assistant when he read the proofs of *The Social Fetich* (1907), her study of contemporary manners, it paled beside his wife's review of its failings.[74] Fundamentally repressed and calculating, Hardy stoically maintained a dutiful deference in aristocratic company, and harboured his resentments for a posthumous and covert autobiography (published under his second wife's name), in which, for example, he declared apropos the banal conversation at the Carnarvons': 'A row of shopkeepers in Oxford Street taken just as they came would conduct the affairs of the nation as ably as these.'[75] This was different from his accounts at the time. Describing to his first wife (who did not accompany him) a reception at Lady Carnarvon's in May 1885, which Robert Browning and Mrs Oliphant also attended, Hardy swelled with wide-eyed pride at

---

[72] Glyn, *Romantic Adventure*, 63, 133.

[73] St Helier, *Memories*, 240. Cf. Maugham, *Cakes and Ale*, preface, for the only time he met Hardy, which was at a dinner party at Lady St Helier's, when 'there was in him a curious mixture of shyness and self-assurance'.

[74] Millgate, *Hardy*, 454–6; Emma Hardy to Lady Grove, 9 Dec. 1907, in Millgate (ed.), *Emma and Florence Hardy*, 36–7. Lady Grove not only roused Emma's jealousy but alienated her by criticism of her religious views. The daughter of General Pitt-Rivers, the anthropologist and archaeologist Lady Grove was both extremely beautiful and proud of her looks. She was also known for her directness; Lowndes, *Merry Wives*, 40. Lady Grove was also author of *Social Solecisms* (1903), and of that esoteric classic *Seventy-One Days Camping in Morocco* (1902), a suffragist and anti-vaccinationist, see *Who Was Who, 1916–1928*, 441–2. *The Social Fetich* was dedicated to Hardy. It was scornfully appraised by G. K. Chesterton as a form of aristocratic mystification, upsetting what she called 'middle-classdom' by pronouncing whether it is more correct to say 'port wine' instead of 'port', 'napkin' rather than 'serviette', and causing further social anxieties about pillowcases, bedspreads, and so forth. Lady Grove referred alarmingly to 'gateless barriers', which blocked the social acceptability of people who perpetrated these vulgarisms. Her book was a precursor of the U and non-U speech and behaviour debate of the 1950s. See Chesterton, *All Things Considered*, 237–43; Nancy Mitford (ed.), *Noblesse Oblige* (1956); and K. C. Phillipps, *Language and Class in Victorian England* (Oxford, 1984), 1, 57–8, 129, 135.

[75] Florence Emily Hardy, *The Life of Thomas Hardy 1840–1928* (1972), 172. An expanded version edited by Michael Millgate (1985) restores more of Hardy's pleased recollections of titled ladies.

his mixing with 'the Portsmouth sisters', that is, the daughters of the Earl and Countess of Portsmouth, who included Lady Carnarvon herself, Lady Dorothea and Lady Margaret Wallop, and Lady Winifred Herbert, although regrettably Lady Camilla Gurdon was missing:

Nearly all the ladies were wearing the same dresses as before. Lady Winifred's divine blue looking decidedly crumpled about the neck—the stick-up ruff I mean—not so well as when we saw it in all its new glory. Lady Margaret was in black lace, with gloves between salmon & buff, & a dull red fan—& necklace of brilliants & black ornaments between—dress low— Both the sisters tell me in confidence that they feel shy of meeting so many people having been shut up in the country so long. Lady W. slaved away at the tea-pouring—complaining bitterly of the heaviness of the teapot—which was an enormous one.[76]

In March Hardy had stayed at Eggesford House in Devon, home of the Portsmouths, having been met at the station by

Ld. P's brougham waiting to take me up to the house, so there was no trouble at all . . . I have had tea with Lady P. & the ladies—the only members of the family at home—Lord P. not having returned from hunting yet (6 p.m.) The young ladies are very attentive & interested in what I tell them. Lady P. charges them to take care of me—& goes away to her parish people etc.—altogether a delightful household . . . I shd say that a married daughter, Lady Rosamond Christie, I think she is, who is here, strikes me as a particularly sensible woman. If Lady P's orders are to be carried out my room will be like a furnace— she is particularly anxious that I shd not take cold etc.[77]

By 1893–4, Hardy was in his prime, attending regularly at aristocratic tables. He passed what might be called the Frank Harris test, that of being invited back (Harris, according to Wilde, could boast of having been to all the great houses of England—once). Hardy was particularly smitten by Florence Henniker, who had writing ambitions about which she consulted him.[78] Fifteen years younger than Hardy, she was the sister of Lord Houghton, Viceroy of Ireland and later Marquess of Crewe and Leader of the House of Lords. Hardy's correspondence with her betrays the author at his most grand, as when penning the imperishable lines: 'Our friend the Duchess of Manchester wanted me to dine with her last Sunday; but I did not stay in town. She sd she had a lot of interesting people coming'; or, 'I have accepted also an invitation to Lady Shrewsbury's dinner on the 29th but I can throw her over if necessary.'[79] As things turned out, Hardy did grace Theresa, Dowager Countess of Shrewsbury's dinner with his presence; and he was rewarded when his 'partner at the table was Lady Gwendolen Little, Lady S's daughter—by far the brightest woman present, as I found afterwards, on

[76] Hardy to Emma Hardy, 16 May 1885, in Purdy and Millgate (eds.), *Hardy Letters*, i. 132–3.

[77] Hardy to Emma Hardy, 13 Mar. 1885, ibid. 131.

[78] Florence Henniker's *In Scarlet and Grey* (1896) included 'The Spectre of the Real', written jointly with Hardy.

[79] Hardy to Florence Henniker, 20 June and 1 Dec. 1893, in Purdy and Millgate (eds.), *Hardy Letters*, ii. 16, 43.

sounding them all round. The lady on the other side of me was Lady Julia (?) Wombwell—to whom I did not say 3 words the whole dinner-time—although I meant to.'[80] Among the round of dinners, luncheons, picnics, and other functions that Hardy attended at this time were ones given by Lady Londonderry, Lady Pembroke, and the Hon. George Curzon.

Hardy was living proof that by authorship men of modest origins could transmogrify into 'gentlemen'. Some ruthlessness and deviousness were required to fashion this magic, but Hardy could summon the necessary. In the genealogy he composed in old age and in his autobiography, some family members were raised in status while others, including whole branches, were lopped off. Puddletown relations who were servants or labourers were not only not received at Max Gate, they were ignored by Hardy and his wife as they passed through the streets.[81] In *Who's Who* Hardy was unspecific about his birth, giving only the county Dorset of which he became a magistrate; but he made a point of styling his wife, Emma, the 'niece of Archdeacon Gifford'.[82] This distance which Hardy placed between himself and his origins was integral to the making of him as a writer. He continued to live in the district but, mentally, he moved on and needed to do in order to write about the changes that were affecting country people and landscape, and the conflict of rural custom and urban culture, with the imaginative force that he did. In his autobiography, revealing in spite of its evasions, Hardy wrote uncomfortably of his 'triple existence . . . a life twisted of three strands—the professional life, the scholar's life, and the rustic life combined'.[83] Born in the hamlet of Higher Bockhampton, the son of a master mason who was ingrained in the Dorset vernacular, Hardy had been taught Latin and French in the county town of Dorchester,[84] then London-trained as an architect and church restorer before turning to live as an author, by preference a poet, by necessity a story-writer.

The emotional strangulation entailed in this evolution was not always understood by others. No sympathy could be expected from George Gissing, who was as socially detached and deracinated as Hardy became, but in a generally downward rather than upwardly mobile trajectory. When Gissing visited Hardy in 1895, he 'grieve[d] to find he is drawn into merely fashionable society, talks of lords and ladies more than ordinary people'; yet, Gissing, belatedly in receipt of critical acclaim, was also beginning to get invitations to country weekends and club dinners. Gissing bought a dress suit so that he might attend, taking care always to leave behind his working-class wife.[85] A rule of ignoring wives in invitations issued to male celebrities was firmly implemented by most Society

---

[80] Hardy to Florence Henniker, 30 June 1893, ibid. 19.
[81] Robert Gittings, *Young Thomas Hardy* (1975) is particularly good on this.
[82] *Who's Who* (1905), 708.   [83] Hardy, *Life*, 32.
[84] Hardy's choice of phrase in *Who's Who* (1905) was 'Latin and French private tuition'.
[85] Halperin (ed.), *Gissing*, 190, 210, 220, 228, 234. For H. G. Wells's meeting Gissing at the Omar Khayyám Club, Wells, *Autobiography*, ii. 563, 567.

hostesses—and upheld by most male celebrities from Dickens onwards. George Du Maurier was outstanding for refusing to attend without his wife. He cartooned the hypocrisy in 1886 when he depicted Lady Snobbington (*née* Shoddy) 'At her Old Tricks Again', telling Mr Löwe (the Eminent Banjoist), 'I've a nice little Bohemian dinner-party on Sunday—nice clever people you will like. Come and dine, and bring your banjo, if Mrs. Löwe will spare you, just for once!'[86]

IV

Authors practised their own patrician–clientship system. The one-legged 'super-tramp' W. H. Davies became an instant celebrity with the publication of *The Soul's Destroyer* (1905), hailed by Arthur Symons as being 'full of uncouth power, queer individuality, and a kind of bitter personal reality'.[87] There followed his *Autobiography* (1908), boosted by a preface from Bernard Shaw. Davies received a Civil List pension, largely through the intercession of Edward Garnett and his circle. Son of Richard Garnett, who had been keeper of printed books at the British Museum, a poet, and man of letters, Edward Garnett was a writer and, above all, an influential publisher's reader, and adviser to umpteen authors: Conrad, Galsworthy, W. H. Hudson, D. H. Lawrence, and more. His wife, Constance, was the respected translator of Russian classics, which she pursued for little financial reward and at the cost of failing eyesight. A strong air of being the tsar of a literary dynasty hung about Edward Garnett, thought Douglas Goldring, who stated that 'almost the only experiences I can recall of sheer unprovoked rudeness—apart from contacts with British officials and diplomatic attachés, who specialise in "high-hatting"—have been at the hands of this distinguished family'. In 1908–9, when Goldring was not known as an author, Garnett seemed to judge his position as sub-editor on the *English Review* as akin to office boy, to whom offensiveness was the right attitude to adopt. Goldring also noticed:

His manner to all the 'rising' authors present was so heavily patronising as to suggest that they had no business to 'rise' without his consent and approval . . . Of his personal qualities, apart from his boorish manners and quite remarkable ugliness, I know nothing . . . It was merely as a Literary Pontiff that he seemed to me then, and seems to me still, largely a fake. It is claimed that he 'discovered' Conrad, D. H. Lawrence, and other geniuses, but actually he got Lawrence from Ford and Conrad from Galsworthy. His personal judgment may have been fairly sound, but it is doubtful if he would have achieved his reputation as a publisher's reader had he not been in a position to pick the brains of his betters.[88]

---

[86] Ormond, *Du Maurier*, 343. Cf. Maugham, *Cakes and Ale*, 24, 41, for the aristocratic condescension shown towards celebrity authors' wives and for their social exclusion.

[87] *Outlook*, 19 July 1905, quoted in Beckson, *Symons*, 302, where Davies's opinion is given that it was Symons's review that launched his success.

[88] Goldring, *South Lodge*, 171. Garnett was responsible for expurgating Lawrence's *Sons and Lovers* for publication by Duckworth in 1913. Among the decisions taken by Garnett which dismayed a later

At this time Garnett, who was a big man, unkempt, and a smoker of herbal cigarettes, presided over informal weekly literary lunches at the Mont Blanc restaurant in Soho. These W. H. Davies occasionally attended, meeting there Conrad, Hudson, Belloc, Masefield, Ford Madox Ford, Norman Douglas, and other now lesser-known figures such as Stephen Reynolds, Thomas Seccombe, and H. M. Tomlinson. With Edward Thomas, who was enduring the life of a literary hack and had not yet emerged as a poet, Davies struck a chord and, following the Mont Blanc meal, they would repair to the St George's vegetarian restaurant in St Martin's Lane for another literary gathering over tea, at which Thomas presided.[89] Davies preferred this to the Mont Blanc session. Not being used to literary company, he was uneasy in Garnett's circle and 'bored with their long, lifeless talk on books and art'. Davies was at a disadvantage: the authors at the Mont Blanc knew his work and he did not know theirs, because he was not a book-reviewer and could not otherwise afford to buy books by living authors.[90] Davies, 'Celtic, sardonic, animal, curiously simple, primitive', according to Arthur Symons,[91] relished therefore the St George's group, which included poets in a similar mould, struggling and strange, such as John Freeman and Gordon Bottomley. He hit it off especially with Ralph Hodgson, who was accompanied everywhere by a bull terrier. Hodgson and Davies shared a fiercely strong pipe tobacco and 'talk of dogs and prizefighters instead of poets and poetry'.[92] Davies then resumed his tramping, until the onset of the Great War, when he returned to London, to a flat in Holborn, ready to answer the call to duty. For a 43-year-old cripple without a trade, the options appeared strictly limited; but he was wooed by Society women to perform on behalf of their war charities. These involved poets reading their works, and actors reciting the poems of others, in some vast drawing room, for which tickets were sold at high prices and large sums raised as a result.

Gatherings such as these had many a late Victorian precedent and advertised the hostesses's reputation for intellectualism as well as good works. In 1893 Lady Emily Lytton described one of a course of lectures on the 'Uses of Poetry' given by Churton Collins at Lady Cowper's London home in St James's Square. Lady

---

generation, his rejection of James Joyce's *A Portrait of the Artist as a Young Man* (1916) is frequently cited. Ezra Pound led the denunciation of Garnett's judgement about this at the time. For an appraisal, see George Jefferson, *Edward Garnett: A Life in Literature* (1982).

[89] Thomas had reviewed *The Soul's Destroyer* (1905) in the *Daily Chronicle*. Afterwards, Davies lived with the Thomases for a while, dedicated his *New Poems* (1907) to them, and was encouraged by Thomas to compose his autobiography. Cooke, *Thomas*, 45–51.

[90] W. H. Davies, *Later Days* (1925), 39. The account by Davies is shot through with resentments against the literary men he met. He seems to have formed a particular dislike of W. H. Hudson, until he got hold of a copy of *Green Mansions* (1904), which drew his admiration. Also Garnett (ed.), *Galsworthy Letters*, 9–10; Douglas, *Looking Back*, 405–6, for the Mont Blanc lunches.   [91] Beckson, *Symons*, 302.

[92] Davies, *Later Days*, 73; also Rothenstein, *Men and Memories, 1900–1922*, 351–2. For another pleasing description of Hodgson, see Roberts, *Years of Promise*, 208–9; and for his life (1871–1962) and work, Drabble, *Companion*, 466. His first book of poems, *The Last Blackbird*, was published in 1907; he was the last recipient of the Polignac Prize, awarded for his poems 'The Bull' and 'The Song of Honour', in 1914.

Cowper was the daughter of the fourth Marquess of Northampton; her husband, the seventh Earl, had been Lord Lieutenant of Ireland; but Lady Emily was not easily impressed. 'There were many fine ladies listening to the lecture and the solemnity of everyone was quite painful,' she wrote. The high spot for her was not anything Collins said about poetry being 'the embodiment of ideal truth'; it was

the entrance of Margot Tennant. She arrived in the middle of the lecture and the butler opened the door very gently so that she might quietly slip in, but Margot was determined to be noticed. She banged the door and marched up the room with a great noise, patted me on the back and seated herself beside me, and afterwards made remarks in a loud whisper.[93]

The Professor of Literature at Oxford, Walter Raleigh, also did 'a Society Cakewalk'. At one dinner, seated next to the actress Mrs Patrick Campbell, he was asked to recommend passages from Wordsworth for her to recite. Raleigh was shocked: Wordsworth was not for reciting and on no account was she to do so in his presence. Fiddlesticks, Mrs Pat countered—until Raleigh prevailed and 'shunted her on to Jean Ingelow, which she did very well. Jean Ingelow is *best* recited.' But the significant intelligence was Mrs Pat telling him that she had once received £60, 'the most she ever got for 12 lines, all for reciting [Wordsworth's] "She dwelt among the untrodden ways" '.[94]

Poetry readings at London town houses during the Great War starred soldier–poets foremost. Siegfried Sassoon performed at Lady Colefax's on 15 November 1917, together with Robert Nichols, who returned for an encore on 12 December. Wykehamist and Oxonian, and of solid county family, Nichols flaunted his war wounds in front of the shirkers when he reappeared on a bill that included the three Sitwells, T. S. Eliot, and Aldous Huxley. The last left a famous account:

Gosse in the chair—the bloodiest little old man I have ever seen—dear Robbie Ross stage-managing, Bob Nichols thrusting himself to the fore as the leader of us young bards (*bards* was the sort of thing Gosse called us) and myself, Viola Tree, a girl called McLeod and troops of Shufflebottoms, alias Sitwells bringing up the rear: last and best, Eliot. But oh—what a performance: Eliot and I were the only people who had any dignity: Bob Nichols raved and screamed and hooted and moaned his filthy war poems like a Lyceum villain who hasn't learned how to act...the Shufflebottoms were respectable, but terribly nervous.[95]

The first such function at which W. H. Davies read was at Baroness 'Baba' D'Erlanger's, in Byron's former house in Piccadilly. The Cabinet minister and belletrist Augustine Birrell was in the chair, and Lady Cynthia Asquith selling

---

[93] Lady Emily Lytton to the Revd Whitwell Elwin, 3 May 1893, in Lutyens, *Blessed Girl*, 188.
[94] Letter to Mrs C. A. Ker, 16 July 1909, in Raleigh (ed.), *Raleigh Letters*, ii. 344–5. On Jean Ingelow (1820–97), Drabble, *Companion*, 494.
[95] John Pearson, *Façades: Osbert and Sacheverell Sitwell* (1980), 117. On Nichols (1893–1944), *DNB 1941–1950*, 626–7.

programmes. 'It was', she wrote, 'a most amusing idea, ten live poets reading their own poems.' The decimal bards were Hilaire Belloc, Laurence Binyon, Emile Cammaerts (the Belgian poet, now a war refugee), Davies, Walter de la Mare, Maurice Hewlett, Henry Newbolt, Owen Seaman, Margaret Woods, and W. B. Yeats. The last 'recited four poems preciously, but really rather beautifully'; by contrast, Belloc 'complained of being the "sport of the rich at forty-six"', though he gave a 'very funny' recital of *Doris*.[96] So successful was the affair that a sequel was arranged. Lady Cynthia was in the front row this time but, perhaps because of aristocratic caprice, the event was not so well attended. Gilbert Murray presided, too flippantly for Lady Cynthia's taste, and the poets now included a khaki-clad and nervous W. J. Turner and clerically intoning John Drinkwater. Walter de la Mare performed attractively, Hewlett tediously, and Yeats rose to the occasion like 'the stage poet—a pale hand checking a lock trained into rebellion—a cathedral voice and a few editing remarks before delivering a poem'. For Lady Cynthia, '*far* the most lovable was little Davies who read delicious poems very sweetly. I felt him to be a real poet and when one sees him one loses any lingering impression of artificial, strained simplicity. He is so obviously nature-inspired and not a retailer.'[97] Lovable little Davies revelled in these events. Socks crumpled over his ankles and collar without stud, the antithesis of gentility, 'I was treated so well at these houses that I never once had cause to complain.' So might a family pet write. Davies added that his readings for charity 'led me into another kind of life, where I met some interesting people. One of the most brilliant hostesses was Lady Cunard, whose luncheons were often attended by the Prime Minister and his family, by Balfour and others. Lady Cunard was so straightforward that I took to her at once . . .'. But, he maintained, 'I knew what I was doing; and stood ready at any moment to call a halt.'[98]

Davies had travelled from street to salon. Eventually he returned to the road in search of a wife.[99] There were other writers who, though the distance between them and the rich and titled was not so vast as for Davies, also came from socially impossible backgrounds. One of these, H. G. Wells, whose mother knew life below stairs, much enjoyed being upstairs with the Souls at Lady Desborough's at Taplow Court and Lady Elcho's at Stanway. It confirmed 'my natural disposition to behave as though I was just as good as anybody'[100]—apt because, if marital infidelity was the test, Wells was equal to this aristocratic set. Wells's amorous exploits made him a pariah for some but not for the Souls and, after his

---

[96] Asquith, *Diaries*, 152 (11 Apr. 1916).   [97] Ibid. 314 (21 June 1917).

[98] Davies, *Later Days*, 130–2, 142, 146. The straightforwardness of Lady Cunard, the American-born Maud Burke, nicknamed Emerald, was not always apparent to authors: 'Filson Young, the shilling-shocker novelist once came to lunch with her and found his books lying thick on her tables. He remarked that one was missing and she said she hadn't been able to get it from the book shop. He hurried round and indignantly asked why they hadn't provided it to Lady Cunard. They said, "Lady Cunard—why she had all your books up yesterday and returned them in the afternoon"' (Asquith, *Diaries*, 449 (7 June 1918)).

[99] W. H. Davies, *Young Emma*, Foreword C. V. Wedgwood (1980).

[100] Wells, *Autobiography*, ii. 636.

Though less dramatic, the case of Lord Ernest Hamilton was scarcely less interesting. A nephew of the former Prime Minister Lord John Russell and a son of the first Duke of Abercorn, Hamilton enjoyed 'a fatal facility for doing everything easily'. Having played cricket for Harrow and taken up steeplechasing, he had a spell in the 11th Hussars before sitting as Conservative MP for North Tyrone, 1885–92, when he declared himself 'ready to support further measures for the establishment of an independent farming proprietary'.[128] Now married, Hamilton abandoned politics for golf, music, and photography, then produced a clutch of historical novels and society romances between 1897 and 1905, 'and very successful some of them were, until it finally dawned on him that his real vocation in life was that of a historian'. One of his brothers, Lord Frederic Hamilton, whose account this was, fondly recalled a Gilbertian verse Lord Ernest wrote, entitled 'The Curse of Versatility';[129] but this was something of a family trait because Lord Frederic edited the *Pall Mall Magazine* and wrote novels after retiring from the diplomatic service and Parliament. Less talent and more pose were evident in 1917, when Virginia Woolf met the Hon. Evan Morgan, the heir of Viscount Tredegar, at Garsington Manor: he was 'most carefully prepared to be a poet & an eccentricity, both by his conversation, which aimed at irresponsible brilliance, & lack of reticence, & by his clothes, which must have been copied from the usual Shelley picture'.[130] Scarcely less absurd was Lady Florence Bourke, who wrote *Faithfulness in High Places* (1912). This was a 'fatuous novel', thought Lady Cynthia Asquith, who was delighted to be privy to a telephone conversation between Lord Basil Blackwood and the insistent authoress: 'He rashly embarked on saying he was reading her book (he hasn't opened it). She immediately asked him how far he had got. He appealed to me, "For God's sake, where have I got to?" holding his hand over the receiver. I prompted him to say, "Where the mother has an accident". There is no mother and no accident!'[131] Later Lady Florence told Lady Cynthia 'the story of the play she had just finished and given to Mrs Pat[rick Campbell]—she said, patronisingly, she "wouldn't mind her doing the part of the Duchess" '.[132]

The aristocracy contained more gifted authors than these, though the most gifted tended to be qualified as aristocrats only by distant (or deviant) line. Swinburne's mother was daughter of the third Earl of Ashburnham—a title deriving from William III's reign—and his father, an admiral, descended from

---

[128] Michael Stenton and Stephen Lees (eds.), *Who's Who of British Members of Parliament*, ii: *1886–1918* (Hassocks, 1978), 153–4.

[129] Hamilton, *Days before Yesterday*, 116–18. On Lord Ernest Hamilton (1858–1939), see Sutherland, *Companion*, 272; Kemp *et al.* (eds.), *Edwardian Fiction*, 171; on Lord Frederic Hamilton (1856–1928), see Stenton and Lees (eds.), *Who's Who of M.P.s*, ii. 154.

[130] Bell, *Woolf Diary*, i. 78–9 (19 Nov. 1917). Morgan—'The inimitable Evan Morgan, poet, painter, musician, aristocrat and millionaire . . . the unique fairy prince of modern life'—became a friend of Aldous Huxley, who featured him in *Crome Yellow* (1921). They, too, first met at Garsington during the war. See Bedford, *Huxley*, 85, 123.   [131] Asquith, *Diaries*, 63–5 (5, 7 Aug. 1915).

[132] Ibid. 177 (17 June 1916).

a Border family who had acquired a baronetcy from Edward II. Swinburne's romanticism was charged up by this:

The poet never forgot the ancestral castle of Swinburne, which had passed from his forebears two centuries ago, never the fierce feuds and rattling skirmishes under the hard Northumbrian sky. He talked with freedom and manifest pleasure of these vague mediaeval forefathers, of their bargaining and fighting with the Umfrevilles and the Fenwicks; of the unspeakable charm of their fastness at Capheaton, where so much of his own childhood was passed.[133]

Aubrey de Vere was in the same mould. His family could trace descent to the Norman Conquest, though their days of power as Earls of Oxford were long extinct, much like their ruined seat, Hedingham Castle in Essex. Aubrey de Vere sported the same Christian name as umpteen forebears, including his father, who was also a poet; but their home was now in Ireland and, though de Vere was famed for his friendships with Wordsworth (whom he idolized), the Brownings, and Tennyson, his own standing as a poet suffered from his conversion to Rome in 1851.[134] This was the year of the Ecclesiastical Titles Act, passed by Russell's Government to counter the restoration of the Catholic hierarchy in Britain. De Vere's reputation was judged accordingly; for example, dismissively by the Lord Lieutenant of Ireland, later Colonial and India Secretary, the Earl of Kimberley, as being 'of the sentimental, aesthetical turn of mind which is closely allied to superstition—clever, amiable but priestridden'.[135] It was thus against the grain in 1898 when W. Macneile Dixon, Professor of English Literature at Mason College, Birmingham, lauded de Vere's *Alexander the Great* (1874) as the finest poetic drama of the century; but then it was precisely for his independence of fashion, peculiar psychology, and unusual diction that he was being singled out.[136] The *Athenaeum*'s reviewer of de Vere's *Recollections* (1897) scored the point by styling him 'a man of letters in a sense peculiar to a day now disappearing, a man of responsible leisure, of serious thought, of grave duties, of high mind'.[137] The succeeding sort of man of letters, professional not gentlemanly, and prone to think religion cant, was epitomized by Edmund Gosse when he contrived to meet de Vere in 1896. De Vere was then in his eighty-third year, and it was rather as a relic, who had known Wordsworth and Newman, for which he was valued. And value he gave: Gosse 'never knew a more persistent speaker... Mr. de Vere talked, with no other interruption than brief pauses for reflection, for three hours . . . without the smallest sign of fatigue.' Slyly, Gosse noted the unmarried

---

[133] Gosse, 'Swinburne', in Gosse, *Portraits and Sketches*, 45. When his father died in 1877, he inherited £5,000 and his books, valued at another £2,000; Gosse, *Life of Swinburne*, 234–5. Swinburne's cousin was the first Lord Redesdale (1837–1916), father of the Mitford sisters.

[134] See Aubrey de Vere, *Recollections* (1897).

[135] Hawkins and Powell (eds.), *Kimberley Journal*, 166 (27 June 1865).

[136] W. Macneile Dixon, *In the Republic of Letters* (1898), 64–118, praising both Aubrey de Vere's and his father's poetic achievements. Dixon became professor at Glasgow in 1904.

[137] Quoted in the publisher Edward Arnold's catalogue, Oct. 1898, 13.

salon hosts at their London home, 47 Palace Court, Bayswater. They were not well off: they had sunk most of their money into the house and had a large family to support from writing. Their drawing room was notably less crowded with furniture than was common then, and Alice dressed without the richness usual to women of her social position, though this simplicity made her beauty stand out the more.[148] Sunday was the day for the Meynells' open house, which often meant, as the editor of *The Academy*, Charles Lewis Hind, put it, 'arriving at about half-past three, staying till midnight, and meeting in the course of the year most of the literary folk worth knowing'. In the 1890s this included Aubrey Beardsley, Oscar Wilde and brother Willie, Richard Le Gallienne, Lionel Johnson, H. W. Nevinson, Coventry Patmore, Stephen Phillips, Herbert Trench, Richard Whiteing, William Watson, Katharine Tynan, and W. B. Yeats.[149] Affectedly grand and snide, Wilde was wont to speak of Bayswater with horror— 'A Bayswater view of life meant, from his lips, a severe condemnation for mediocrity'[150]—but Sheila Kaye-Smith counted herself fortunate to be invited to one of the Meynells' at-homes, following the publication of her second novel, *Starbrace* (1909). She was aged 22 and under instruction from her literary agent to spend time in London, in order to broaden her horizons. A Sussex doctor's daughter, Kaye-Smith was raised in that evangelical style that ensured that she possessed 'working knowledge' of the Bible before she was competent even to read it. Introduced for the first time to other literary people at the Meynells, she was 'profoundly shaken by the experience. The atmosphere—artistic, cultured, casual—was entirely different from that of my own home, where Sunday supper meant the family sitting down in state to eat cold beef and prunes and talk about the evening's sermon.'[151] In 1929, together with her Anglican parson husband, Kaye-Smith would convert to Rome; but there was a republic of letters here that reached beyond the Catholic literary circles of which the Meynells were the recognized leaders. Arthur Symons acknowledged this in 1900, telling his future wife how he was 'forcing' himself to attend Alice Meynell's at-home because her invitation bore 'some significance in one who for so long professed a pious horror of me and my works. One reason for going is that she has great influence journalistically.'[152] Symons first met Mrs Meynell in 1889. His opinion of her *Preludes* (1875) was that it contained 'some of the most truly poetical poetry any woman has ever written'. He also noted, 'There is something pathetically weary and harassed about her, but she talks really like a poet.'[153]

Alice Meynell was either serene or prone to migraines at her own at-homes. The 'most exciting parties' she still judged to be those at Stafford House, the great town house in St James's, where Millicent, wife of the fourth Duke of Sutherland,

[148] Lowndes, *Merry Wives*, 10–11.   [149] Meynell, *Alice Meynell*, 142–5.
[150] Sherard, *Wilde*, 73.
[151] Brook, *Writers' Gallery*, 78. Kaye-Smith (1887–1956) was best known for her rural novels which, like Mary Webb's and D. H. Lawrence's, were parodied in Stella Gibbons's *Cold Comfort Farm* (1932).
[152] Beckson, *Symons*, 207–8.   [153] Ibid. 48.

reigned. Robert Hichens concurred, writing soapily that the Duchess was 'perhaps the most absolutely charming woman in the London world of that time, and very beautiful into the bargain'.[154] William Rothenstein remembered her with equal fervour, while candid about the comical way in which writers and artists (himself included) tumbled over themselves to meet 'this gracious and beautiful lady'.[155] J. M. Barrie was another author whom the Duchess culti- vated;[156] but she became closest to Anthony Hope. They first met in 1896 and thereafter conducted an extensive correspondence, this literary friendship supplemented by Liberal Party politics. When Hope eventually married, he named his first child Millicent; previously, however, he refused her request that he dedicate a book to her, lest he be thought snobbish. The Duchess, an omnivorous reader—'she could begin the day with reports on technical education in Prussia, continue it with Huxley's Life and Shakespeare, and . . . polish off seven love-stories at the same time'[157]—could hold up in literary cross-examination. In 1904, over tea at Eton with Arthur Benson, she 'talked of poetry—Yeats etc.— with a good deal of discrimination';[158] and Mrs Belloc Lowndes recorded that the Duchess 'published at least one novel anonymously' and had 'a lively, eager mind'.[159] Some notes of dissent were registered, notably by Arnold Bennett in *The Card* (1911). This lampooned the Duchess's record of good works in the Potteries, where, operating from the family seat at Trentham Hall, she gained the title Meddlesome Millie.[160] Let, however, Alice Meynell describe one of the Duchess's 'little parties' at Stafford House, as reported to her children:

She is giving 'intellectual' Friday evenings. The Duke of Argyll (who has literary ambitions) was there, the Duchess of Rutland, Winston Churchill, Lord Ribblesdale, Mrs Hunter, Andrew Lang, Herbert Trench, the Beerbohm Trees, Laurence Binyon, Oliver Lodge, who said he has read all I have written, Mr [Augustine] Birrell—I cannot remember any more; the gathering was small. Percy Grainger played.[161]

---

[154] Hichens, *Yesterday*, 97, 187.   [155] Rothenstein, *Men and Memories, 1900–1922*, 70–1, 206–8.

[156] Dunbar, *Barrie*, 168–72.

[157] Mallet, *Hope*, 160. Cf. the Duchess telling Regy Brett, 'I have dinner on a tray [and], in between mouthfuls of fried sole and partridge, read [Ruskin's] *Sesame and Lilies* [1865] and [Marie Corelli's] *Barabbas* [1893] by turn.' It was Brett who had recommended Corelli's novel as a must-read, together with George Eliot's *Daniel Deronda* (1876) and Charlotte Brontë—an extraordinary menu. See Lees-Milne, *Enigmatic Edwardian*, 85.   [158] Lubbock, *Benson*, 92 (3 Nov. 1904).

[159] Lowndes, *Merry Wives*, 102–3. Anthony Hope acted as her agent in dealing with the publisher: Mallet, *Hope*, 134–8. According to Kemp et al. (eds.), *Edwardian Fiction*, 134, the novel, published in 1899, dealt with 'socialist agitators during a strike'. There were also books of short stories published in 1902 and 1925; in addition, her sister Lady Angela Forbes turned to novel-writing for money after her marriage collapsed, *The Broken Commandment* (1910) being 'banned by the libraries' and dubbed by *The Times* as 'a compound fracture of the seventh commandment'.

[160] The Duchess appears in *The Card* as the Countess of Chell, nicknamed Interfering Iris. Bennett first met the Duchess, in some embarrassment at a dinner party, following its publication. He afterwards wrote to her claiming that he was 'admiring, apologetic, and unrepentant' (Drabble, *Bennett*, 159, 184). On the Duchess (1869–1955), see *Who Was Who, 1951–1960*, 1059; the Duke died in 1913, and the Dowager Duchess twice remarried and eventually settled in France.

[161] This was probably in June 1908. Grainger played previously for the Duchess of Sutherland at Dunrobin Castle in Scotland in August 1905; see Kay Dreyfus (ed.), *The Farthest North of Humanness: Letters*

And on another occasion:

The Stafford House party last night was very good. Your father came on with Wilfrid Blunt from dinner, and with Lord Osborne Beauclere. There were a good many people we know, and in any case Violet Meeking stuck to me all evening, so I was not lonely. Your father and Wilfrid Blunt enjoyed themselves 'listening to each other', as Violet well said.[162]

The Meynells had an additional attraction for Blunt beyond their own merits. They were intriguing because of their rescue and promotion of the mysterious Francis Thompson, who, when not sleeping rough, in derelicts' hostels or in drab lodgings, harboured with them. Thompson's first published poem appeared in the Meynells' magazine *Merry England* in 1888.[163] The discerning then recognized the quality of Thompson's *Poems* (1893), which contained 'The Hound of Heaven'. *Sister Songs* (1895) and *New Poems* (1897) followed and, in 1898, Blunt wrote to remind Wilfrid Meynell, 'you have often promised me that I shd. make Thompson's acquaintance'. The day was chosen, 12 October; but only the day because, though Blunt invited them to stay overnight, Meynell tactfully explained that this was unwise, 'the poet having an inconvenient habit of setting his bed on fire'. Under the influence of De Quincey and his own torments—a Manchester doctor's son, Thompson had studied medicine and been intended for the Catholic priesthood—he had become a laudanum addict. This, together with an enfeeblement caused by consumption and a further weakness for alcohol, rendered him unconscious of surroundings. Meynell's anxiousness about Thompson's combustible propensity was, therefore, well founded. In 1897 Thompson had burned himself out of his Harrow Road lodgings; and, after a succession of these accidents, landladies considered him 'a mental case'. Whereupon Thompson moved in with the Meynells and promptly started another fire in a cupboard by leaving a lit pipe in his coat pocket. Eighteen ninety-seven was not a good year for Thompson's well-being: he was hospitalized after being run over by a hansom at High Holborn. Since he generally walked the streets in a trance, it was a marvel that he was not struck more often; but a railway journey seemed scarcely safer. Meynell's son Everard, who wrote the *Life of Francis Thompson*, was witness in a railway carriage when an umbrella fell on Thompson from the rack: 'I am the target of all disasters!', the poet cried tremblingly.[164] When Blunt finally met

---

of Percy Grainger 1901–14 (1985), pp. x, 48, 214. The gimmick of getting Grainger to play at parties was taken up by rival hostesses such as Mrs Charles Hunter, whose sister was the composer Dame Ethel Smyth (1858–1944). Grainger was paid £25 for an evening's work at Mrs Hunter's at homes, rising to £50 when the guests were unusually grand, as when she entertained the Duke and Duchess of Connaught, General French, and Rodin; see John Bird, *Percy Grainger* (1982), 139. Grainger, for all his peculiar sexual make-up and practices, was a general favourite with women. He had shown himself a strong supporter of the Lyceum Club; Smedley, *Crusaders*, ch. viii.

[162] Meynell, *Alice Meynell*, 246; cf. Blunt, *Diaries*, ii. 353 (14 July 1911).
[163] Blunt, *Diaries*, i. 147–8 (6 Aug. 1894), ii. 181–4 (30 Aug. 1907).
[164] Meynell, *Alice Meynell*, 247; Meynell, *Thompson and Meynell*, 79, 115–6.

Thompson, he rather liked his ingenuousness but found it 'difficult to think of him as capable of any kind of strength in rhyme or prose'. As 'the poet of nature', Thompson was a huge disappointment. Meynell told Blunt that, as their train passed through the countryside, Thompson ignored the scenery and was 'wholly absorbed in the *Globe* newspaper'. On escorting Thompson into the woods after luncheon, Blunt confirmed this. Thompson was 'quite ignorant of the names of the commonest trees, even the elm, which he must have seen every day in London. I pointed one out to him, and he said, "I think, a maple".' Physically, too, Thompson was unprepossessing. While acknowledging that Thompson was a Lancastrian, indeed preserved his accent and a passion for Lancashire County Cricket, Blunt considered him 'a true Cockney', by which he meant 'a little weak-eyed, red-nosed young man of the degenerate London type, with a complete absence of virility . . .'. There was not much going for Thompson in Blunt's estimation, therefore, except for his 'look of raptured dependency on Mrs Meynell which is most touching'.[165] Still, Blunt fulfilled the role expected of him as aristocratic patron. In 1907, when Thompson was dying, Blunt provided nursing for him in a cottage on his estate.[166]

---

[165] Blunt, *Diaries*, i. 297–8 (12 Oct. 1898).   [166] Ibid. ii. 179 (24 Aug. 1907).

15

Looking and Acting the Part

[LADY LOCKE]. London is not the same London it was ten years ago . . . Men
did not wear green carnations . . .

[MRS WINDSOR]. You don't understand. They like to draw attention to
themselves.

[LADY L.]. By their dress? I thought that was the prerogative of women.

[MRS W.]. Really, Emily, you *are* colonial. Men may have women's minds, just
as women may have the minds of men.

[LADY L.]. I hope not.

[MRS W.]. Dear, yes. It is quite common nowadays.

(Robert Hichens, *The Green Carnation* (1894))

Though not affected myself, I like other people to be.

(Ada Leverson)

It is expected, generally, of a poet that he should be of somewhat eccentric
appearance. He should be above the prevailing fashion in dress, and wear a
costume entirely of his own creation and the tailor's make.

(Sir Francis Burnand, *Records and Reminiscences* (1904))

So few people look like themselves.

(Max Beerbohm)

Dress mattered for the self-advertising author as for the modish aristocrat. It
was easy to make a statement in this way because dress codes were then so rigid,
both at business and at play. The American R. D. Blumenfeld was struck, when
he first came to London in the mid-1880s, by the sight of 'horse omnibuses on
which were perched one by one a dozen men adorned with top hats. The Strand
from a roof looked astonishingly like a field that is covered with glossy crows.'[1]
Particular occupations had their defining uniform—the peasant's smock, the
butcher's apron, the barrister's wig, the don's gown—but headgear especially
marked out the classes. The change wrought by the Great Reform Act in 1832 was
famously measured by the Duke of Wellington, surveying the new Commons:
'I have never seen so many bad hats in my life!'[2] Wearing the right clothes in the

---

[1] Blumenfeld, *All in a Lifetime*, 37, and pp. 105–6 for the relaxation of dress codes during the Great War.

[2] Elizabeth Longford, *Wellington: Pillar of State* (1975), 350.

right place at the right time was a matter of supreme importance; hence the enormity of the rebellion entailed by departure from custom.

An author's choice of unconventional apparel was a sure means of being talked about. It was 'an age of easy publicity', wrote Holbrook Jackson about the *fin de siècle*.[3] Jerome K. Jerome attracted it by wearing an old tweed cap, Keir Hardie-style, to offset an immaculate frock coat. This was scarcely big-league stuff. Nor was Bret Harte's trick of commanding a daily buttonhole from a Piccadilly florist, sent in a little box to him wherever he occasioned to stay.[4] For a really booming statement, it was necessary to behold Mark Twain in his gleaming white suits. Equally magnificent, Wilde invented himself as an exquisite—or harlequin, Theodore Watts-Dunton preferred to call him. Wilde even lectured on 'Dress' during his provincial tour in 1884–5;[5] but, corporeally, he was never up to it. A 'great fat oily beast', thought Edith Somerville, who met him in 1888.[6] This was only marginally more flattering than 'the great white slug', proposed in the same year by Lady Colin Campbell, whom Edmund Gosse then maliciously planned to seat next to Wilde at a dinner held by the Authors' Society to advance Anglo-American copyright.[7] In Paris in 1894 Wilde admitted to 'an ever-growing difficulty in expressing my originality through my choice of waistcoats and cravats'.[8] This signified that even the highest forms of life must ultimately accept limits to the evolutionary process. The beautification business had attracted Wilde initially 'to impress the Philistines with due respect for letters, ragged and pitiable no longer, but curled and scented, and in costly raiment'. It was important not to remain in one mode for too long. Accordingly, the accoutrements of his American tour were discarded in Paris, where he 'delighted in the elegancies of a Lucien de Rubempré, and modelled the arrangement of his hair after a bust of Nero in the gallery of the Louvre'. Wilde's 'originality' actually involved imitation: from Victor Hugo he copied his writing paper, and from Balzac his dressing gown with monkish cowl, as also the ivory cane with the turquoises' head. Some of his selections did not travel. In London 'gorgeous fur coats' conveyed glamour; but 'in Paris, . . . they are the distinctive garb of dentists and opera-singers, people with whom men of the world in France do not care to associate'.[9] No author suffered more terribly the price of fame when the mask was torn from his face:

From two o'clock till half-past two on that day I had to stand on the centre platform of Clapham Junction in convict dress and handcuffed, for the world to look at . . . Of all possible objects I was the most grotesque. When people saw me they laughed. Each train as it came up swelled the audience. Nothing could exceed their amusement. That was of

[3] Holbrook Jackson, *The Eighteen Nineties* (1939), 82.
[4] Fyfe, *O'Connor*, 135. Mrs T. P. O'Connor thought Harte's habit sweet, O'Connor thought it silly.
[5] Ellmann, *Wilde*, 245–6.   [6] Collis, *Somerville and Ross*, 48.
[7] Bonham-Carter, *Authors by Profession*, 142–3.
[8] Recalled by Robert de Billy and quoted in George D. Painter, *Marcel Proust* (1977), i. 160.
[9] Sherard, *Wilde*, 21, 26, 33, 47, 115.

course before they knew who I was. As soon as they had been informed, they laughed still more. For half an hour I stood there in the grey November rain surrounded by a jeering mob. For a year after that was done to me I wept every day at the same hour and for the same space of time.[10]

Wilde was not the first to use costume as a calling card, and decidedly he was not the last. In 1894 an Oxford undergraduate Max Beerbohm composed 'A Defence of Cosmetics' for the *Yellow Book*, whereupon the humorist Barry Pain lost his humour. He recommended 'a whiff of grapeshot' to be discharged against the author and every such decadent. Max, however, had been undertaking 'an exercise in euphuism'; neither then nor later did he approve of the application of rouge by women, still less by men.[11] A dandy tradition nonetheless asserted the liberation of the individual from the tyranny of social convention. Beerbohm recognized that this entailed hard work: he once cartooned the young Disraeli, with the legend 'A Well Known Dandy, Who Afterwards Followed a Less Arduous Calling'.[12] Fundamentally, dandyism represented a state of mind more than the contents of a wardrobe. Hence the appropriateness of Arthur Symons's remark, that Wilde aspired to be 'an artist in attitudes'.[13]

The swelled-head syndrome cannot be discounted altogether, for dandies also made a philosophy of narcissism. Their object, as defined by Baudelaire, was to live and die in front of the mirror. An amount of real accomplishment obtained in many authors, however curiously attired; still, an element of vanity was unmistakable, and this was captured by the child's innocent retort to Tennyson after he complained of being stared at—'Then why do you wear a purple cloak?'[14] Tennyson was, declared Watts-Dunton, 'the most poetical-looking poet I have ever seen';[15] but Watts-Dunton, who resembled a pug according to Edmund Gosse (or a toad according to Lady Ritchie),[16] was himself a model of social manufacture. For sixty-four years this solicitor's son, who initially followed his father's profession, appeared content to be Theodore Watts. In 1896 the man of letters decided to incorporate his mother's maiden name. Alas, the hyphenation did not draw the hoped-for deference, rather the telegraphed query: 'Theodore— What's Dunton?'[17] Watts-Dunton made the most of what little nature endowed him. In 1909, when Watts-Dunton was aged 77, Douglas Goldring called at his home in Putney. He was awestruck when the door opened: Watts-Dunton 'seemed to be about four feet high. He was dressed in a long, shiny, black frock-coat, and wore white woollen socks. He had on black spectacles, and his white hair was long and unkempt . . . Watts-Dunton had undoubtedly the manner and

---

[10] Wilde to Lord Alfred Douglas, Jan.-Mar. 1897 (*De Profundis*), in Hart-Davis (ed.), *Wilde's Letters*, 219.
[11] Behrman, *Max*, 40–1.   [12] Ibid. 74.   [13] 'Dandies', in Jackson, *Southward Ho!*, 135–41.
[14] Tennyson's cloak-wearing was not a pose, argued George Saintsbury, merely a failure to abandon a habit adopted in the 1820s when fashion-conscious Londoners and Oxbridge undergraduates copied the garb of Spanish political refugees in exile in England; Saintsbury, *Scrap Book*, 199–202.
[15] Watts-Dunton, *Old Familiar Faces*, 210.
[16] Fuller and Hammersley (eds.), *Thackeray's Daughter*, 126.
[17] Lambert and Ratcliffe, *Bodley Head*, 40.

bearing of a "personage".' Goldring reflected how keenly his own generation attempted to achieve this kind of presence, but without comparable success; and he saluted the Victorians, who had such style about them.[18]

George Meredith, of much the same age as Watts-Dunton, also knew the importance of making an impression. Before increasing paralysis seized him—and before he fell out with them over salary—he used to spend one day a week as publisher's reader in Chapman & Hall's offices, where 'his punctilious attire attracted the attention of many visitors, especially women: one remembered his lavender gloves, another his crisp hair'.[19] Furthermore, throughout his writing life, and especially when he ascended to the throne of English letters after Tennyson's death, he covered up his origins as a (bankrupt) tradesman's son and implied that he had patrician beginnings.[20] Speculation of another kind was excited by George Eliot's public appearances. 'Have you seen a horse, sir? Then you have seen George Eliot,' ran a cruel joke of the time.[21] Her unfortunate physiognomy was not improved by partnership with George Henry Lewes. Where her features were equine, his were simian. Robert Hichens's father once sat next to them at a concert in St James's Hall. Mesmerized by their ugliness, on returning home he could not stop talking about the most repulsive couple he had ever seen, adding that Lewes's complexion was 'painfully scorbutic'.[22] When he was a Board of Trade translator in the 1870s, Edmund Gosse used to walk to work in Whitehall and several times encountered them, travelling together in a victoria. This gave Gosse plenty of opportunity to study this 'strange pair', the one 'hirsute, rugged, satyr-like, gazing vivaciously to left and right', the other

a large, thickset sybil, dreamy and immobile, whose massive features, somewhat grim when seen in profile, were incongruously bordered by a hat, always in the height of the Paris fashion, which in those days commonly included an immense ostrich feather . . . The contrast between the solemnity of the face and the frivolity of the headgear had something pathetic and provincial about it.[23]

Here was an outward symbol of Eliot's intellectual evolution, the hat serving as a relic of her early enthusiasm for French culture before her mind became thoroughly 'Teutonized'; but a different construction was imagined by the religiously inspired novelist Elizabeth Charles when, to the shock of her many admirers, Eliot, following Lewes's death, married J. W. Cross in 1880:

Remember that she is an English woman of the middle classes, imbued with English prejudice, and perhaps to her the name of *wife* may have seemed a refuge from all the agony of years. She told me she used to *tremble* when she met anyone. She felt it

---

[18] Goldring, *Reputations*, 220; id., *Life Interests*, 194.

[19] Arthur Waugh, *A Century of Publishing* (1930), quoted in Sassoon, *Meredith*, 69.

[20] Sassoon, *Meredith*, 37, 110. Meredith confided in Alice Meynell about this; Blunt, *Diaries*, ii. 247 (21 May 1909).　　　　　　　　　　　　　　　[21] Colvin, *Memories*, 91.

[22] Hichens, *Yesterday*, 16.　　　[23] Gosse, *Aspects and Impressions*, 1.

all so bitterly. She had given up everything, good position and respectability for Mr. Lewes.[24]

Robert Louis Stevenson also reinvented himself by dropping his third Christian name (Balfour) and Frenchifying his second (originally, Lewis). He further equipped himself with velvet jackets and long hair. All this went with a roving disposition which, to the Edinburgh burgesses who were reluctant to contribute to the Stevenson memorial there in 1896, seemed redolent of loose morals and theology.[25] His stepson and sometime collaborator Lloyd Osbourne loyally attempted a defence at the unveiling of yet another Stevenson memorial in 1915, this at the Baker Cottage, Saranac Lake, New York. Stevenson was not a poseur, Osbourne argued, there being no affectation in the long hair, which the consumptive grew to avoid catching cold, or in the shawls and cloaks which he wrapped about him to spare the exertion of dressing and to keep him warm while recumbent.[26] But invalidity could not explain the striped cricket jackets, the blue sea-cloth suits, the collarless shirts, the outlandish neckties, worn with a range of hats: straw, sailor's, Tyrolese, and more. Charles Brookfield recollected his first sight of

Stevenson at the Savile; his 'get-up' was perfectly astounding. His hair was smooth and parted in the middle and fell beyond the collar of his coat; he wore a black flannel shirt, with a curious knitted tie twisted in a knot; he had Wellington boots, rather tight, dark trousers, a pea-jacket and a white sombrero hat (in imitation, perhaps, of his eminent literary friend, Mr W. E. Henley). But the most astounding item of all in his costume was a lady's sealskin cape, which he wore about his shoulders, fastened at the neck by a fancy brooch, which also held together a bunch of half a dozen daffodils.[27]

Yet, another considered justification of Stevenson's garb came from Sidney Colvin, who, like Osbourne, baulked at the charge of affectation ('affectation is affectation indeed only when a person does or says that which is false to his or her nature'): 'His shabby clothes came partly from lack of cash, partly from lack of care, partly . . . from hankering after social experiment and adventure, and a dislike of being identified with any special class or caste.'[28] The charm was not felt alike by everyone. Andrew Lang recalled a moment in an Edinburgh drawing room when Stevenson removed his jacket and sat in his shirt sleeves until his hostess declared: 'You might as well put your coat on again, no one is taking any notice of you.'[29]

Poet, critic, and scholar, Lang too was not without vanity or velvet jacket. W. B. Richmond caught his languorous pose—what Stevenson called 'too good-looking, delicate . . . a la-de-dady Oxford kind of Scot'[30]—in the portrait of

---

[24] Quoted by Anne Thackeray Ritchie, in a letter to Emily Ritchie, 1880, in Fuller and Hammersley (eds.), *Thackeray's Daughter*, 154. On Elizabeth Charles (1828–96), author of *The Chronicles of the Schönberg Cotta Family* (1863), Sutherland, *Companion*, 116–17, 126, and Elizabeth Jay's notice *in Oxford DNB*.
[25] Mackail, *Barrie*, 256. Barrie gave the address at the unveiling: Meynell (ed.), *Barrie Letters*, 11–12.
[26] Terry, *Stevenson*, 133.   [27] Brookfield, *Reminiscences*, 48–9.
[28] Colvin, *Memories*, 108. Colvin argued the same in his Introduction to *Stevenson's Letters*, vol. i, p. xi.
[29] Green, *Lang*, 178.   [30] Terry, *Stevenson*, 57.

1885, exhibited at the Grosvenor Gallery and now in the National Gallery of Scotland.[31] Violet Martin—the Ross of Somerville and Ross—had dinner with Lang when they met in St Andrews in 1895. She enjoyed the encounter because he admired their *The Real Charlotte* (1894); but she felt that she had been granted an audience, when he spoke 'with a kind of off hand fling' and 'talked of R. L. Stevenson, Mrs Humphry Ward and others, as personal friends, and exhibited at intervals a curious silent laugh up under his nose'.[32] Mrs Belloc Lowndes was also keen to meet Lang in the late 1890s because 'Dear Andrew with the brindled hair' had known Stevenson but, when she encountered him at Scottish country houses, 'always he behaved like a spoilt child, either making himself agreeable by talking in a brilliant and amusing way, or remaining silent and sulky. What aroused my anger and contempt was that he always showed he was bored when local worthies, such as the minister and his wife, were asked to meet him.' Lang's spouse, Leonora (Nora), a niece of Lord Aberdare, was a notable picturesque addition. At their marriage in 1875, she was referred to as 'Lang's Dresden china shepherdess'.[33]

Not all authors were favoured with Lang's handsome exterior. Indeed, very few were, if Phil May's cartoon for *Punch* in 1897 is followed, featuring a literary and artistic banquet at which the assembled diners are all ugly mugs, variously balding or hirsute and with misshapen faces. Behind them stand two waiters, one saying to the other: 'Well, they 'ave the intellec', Fred, but we certainly 'as the good looks!'[34] Still, there was a popular expectation that an author's appearance would, if not extend to the beau idéal or even to flamboyance, nevertheless suggest something of the part. Most people thought Henry James physically resembled Napoleon but, while James was masterful enough, the late French Emperor was no literary model. James's faithful typist Miss Theodora Bosanquet, whom he took on in 1907, preferred to think of him as Coleridge—'in figure'. She considered that he would look best 'wearing a flowered waistcoat—very expensive—"unrestrained" in the lower part'. When he had interviewed her for the job, however, James 'wore green trousers and a blue waistcoat with a yellow sort of check on it and a black coat—that was rather a shock. I'd imagined him as always very correctly dressed in London.'[35] By contrast, Violet Asquith was pleased when she met Æ, the Irish poet G. W. Russell, who looked '*exactly* as he ought—hairy visionary'.[36]

None could compete for audacity with Hall Caine, who cultivated a likeness to the iconic image of Shakespeare. In his younger days, before his ego fully inflated, he contrived to pick up compliments regarding his resemblance to a lesser order

---

[31] It is reproduced in the frontispiece of Green, *Lang*.

[32] Quoted in Collis, *Somerville and Ross*, 104.

[33] Lowndes, *Merry Wives*, 20. Lord Aberdare (1815–95) was the former Henry Bruce, Home Secretary in Gladstone's first ministry. [34] *Punch*, 8 May 1897, 217.

[35] Edel, *James*, ii. 655.

[36] Violet Asquith diary, 24 Apr. 1910, in Bonham Carter and Pottle (eds.), *Lantern Slides*, 205.

of genius, Richard Monckton Milnes being reminded of Keats, Ruskin remarking on his closeness to Burne-Jones, and the journalist Robert Sherard reckoning him a Zola lookalike.[37] Others ignored the Van Dyck beard, black, wide-brimmed hat, and cloak, and focused on the small stature, red hair, and beady eyes which incorporated Caine into the squirrel family.[38] Characteristically, Caine preferred to settle for Shakespeare. To his legion of fans, this was confirmation of their idol's greatness; but the notion of such a reincarnation was ridiculed by fellow authors, whose objectivity was not without an admixture of envy at his success. Watts-Dunton's friendship with Caine did not restrain him from writing tartly: 'The only man who ever really looked like that [Stratford] bust was the late Dion Boucicault, who did so without trying.'[39] Others joked that Caine's appearance now resolved all controversy about the authorship of the Shakespearean œuvre because, when he landed at New York to display himself to his transatlantic disciples, total strangers embraced him as Francis Bacon. For the titillation of Caine's native critics in 1901, Harold Begbie and F. Carruthers Gould combined to produce a poem and a cartoon to commemorate the resemblance. Following after Ben Jonson's designation of Shakespeare as the Swan of Avon, the poem was entitled 'The Goose of Sulby' (Sulby in the Isle of Man, where Caine resided in great style); and, as a pleasing gratuitous insult, it was dedicated to Marie Corelli, a jealous rival best-seller.[40] Corelli, moreover, had settled in Stratford, and malicious wits reported that she found inspiration for her own work by contemplating the portrait of Shakespeare above her desk—which was actually of Hall Caine.[41]

If Caine and Corelli went in for aggrandizement, another tendency was evinced by Robert Browning, at least in his last years when his youthful Byronic dandyism was long past. The actor–manager Squire Bancroft thought that he looked 'more like a highly respectable man of affairs than a great man of letters'. This was a higher elevation than Quiller-Couch's, that 'Browning was a bit of a grocer in real life'; but that remark, coming from one who (in Arthur Benson's eyes) resembled 'a racing tout', may be discounted.[42] Benson's disparagement would have shocked Q himself, who apparently took care over selecting his 'picturesque clothing'; still, Compton Mackenzie perhaps corroborated it by describing Q at his Fowey home 'wearing a brown tweed suit with a *café au lait* shirt and a tie the colour of a *clarissimo* cigar'.[43] Browning, in any case, did have his eccentricities. When he returned to live in London after his wife's death, he kept a pet owl; and

---

[37] Robert Harborough Sherard, 'Hall Caine: A Biographical Study', *Windsor Magazine* (Dec. 1895), 568–9.

[38] Roberts, *Years of Promise*, 39.

[39] Watts-Dunton, *Old Familiar Faces*, 208. On Boucicault (1820?–1890), the playwright and actor–manager, see *DNB*.

[40] Harold Begbie and F. Carruthers Gould, *Great Men* (1901), 46–7. See Fig. 15.1. On the Shakespearean likeness, see Kenyon, *Caine*, 16; Stephen and Lee, *Lives of the 'Lustrious*, 20; Norris, *Two Men of Manxland*, 13–14, 61.

[41] Fred Benson related this to his brother Arthur in 1906; Newsome, *Edge of Paradise*, 191.

[42] Ibid. 288.   [43] *DNB 1941–1950*, 703 (notice by F. Britain); Mackenzie, *Life and Times*, iv. 35.

SHAKESPEARE
MR. HALL CAINE.

FIG. 15.1. Best-seller as Bard. *Source*: Harold Begbie, *Great Men*, illus. F. Carruthers Gould (London: Grant Richards, 1901)

the hostess Mrs Skirrow, keen to win his friendship, gave him for a Christmas present a brass inkstand with a glass-eyed owl figurine on top.[44] Browning also had a fondness for drinking only port at dinner. When he was Squire Bancroft's guest, a bottle was placed by him 'that he might help himself as he pleased and not be offered other wines'.[45] Mrs Skirrow, having neglected to arrange this, was mortified to see Browning in a sulk at her table.[46]

Wine selection and wardrobe were immaterial to the opiated and mendicant Francis Thompson. Even on the hottest days he wore a brown ulster cape, what *The Academy*'s assistant editor Wilfrid Whitten called 'his disastrous hat', a cast-off suit, and a crucifix round his neck. When calling at *The Academy*'s offices, he used a shoulder bag, like a fish basket, to pick up books for review or to drop off his copy, though he was reliable in neither enterprise: his copy was usually late and

[44] DeVane and Knickerbocker (eds.), *New Browning Letters*, 194, 204–5. Mrs Skirrow was the wife of the Master in Chancery, Charles Skirrow.   [45] Bancroft, *Recollections*, 394.
[46] DeVane and Knickerbocker (eds.), *New Browning Letters*, 190–1.

he was apt to sell a book before he reviewed it.[47] Struggling writers who were determined to rise adopted different strategies. J. M. Barrie and H. G. Wells made their initial appearances in editorial offices in spectacularly ill-fitting top hats.[48] Both men found fame in the 1890s. Barrie, spotted by Arthur Benson at a party at Edmund Gosse's in 1900, still appeared woebegone: 'a little pale, ill-dressed, weary man, very taciturn, and with no look of the gentleman. I should have taken him for an over-worked clerk.'[49] By 1914 Wells was in the happy position of witnessing the next generation of struggling writer make fools of themselves in attempts to impress him. For a party at Wells's Hampstead home, D. H. Lawrence donned a newly purchased dress suit and insisted John Middleton Murry do the same, with the result that he appeared as 'a callow acolyte of the Reverend Mr Stiggins'.[50] Disguise was chosen by the fierce atheistical Scot and former dominie John Davidson: he wore a toupee. This was so effective that it passed unnoticed by Will Rothenstein while drawing the poet, but not by Max Beerbohm. When challenged, Davidson excused the hairpiece by claiming that he adopted it not to look younger but because a bald head would damage his prospects as a journalist.[51] It is just possible; yet, as a member of the Omar Khayyám club, Davidson must have known from his FitzGerald how 'A hair perhaps divides the False and True.' Whatever the case, the accessory was not multifunctional. Edith Nesbit enjoyed telling 'how, playing cricket on the Downs, Davidson would take off his wig and carefully hang it on the stumps'.[52] A full head of hair, by contrast, did not console Barrie. In later life his thatch remained resolutely black and he was 'afraid people might suppose he used dye!'[53]

A. E. Housman smothered his poetic soul beneath the stuffy silences of a professor of classics. The part was so overplayed that he resembled 'an absconding cashier', thought Max Beerbohm, after Housman had ventured nothing in conversation apart from the speculation, 'there is a bit of a nip in the air, don't you think?'[54] This anti-climactic gem deserved being ranked with Dickens's sole reflection on Wordsworth, after elaborate arrangements were made for the two literary stars to meet: 'Rum old cock'.[55] Disappointment also befell those who encountered Thomas Hardy. The commonest reaction was that here was a grey provincial architect; but Hardy told Rothenstein that he was often mistaken for a detective because of the cocked expression of his eyes.[56] His first wife, Emma, reversed the criminal pursuit by saying that he looked like Dr Crippen and wouldn't be surprised if she ended up in the cellar.[57] Hardy did,

[47] Meynell, *Alice Meynell*, 221–3; Meynell, *Thompson and Meynell*, 121–2.

[48] Barrie, *Greenwood Hat*, 18–19; Wells, *Autobiography*, i. 356–8.

[49] Newsome, *Edge of Paradise*, 89.

[50] John Middleton Murry, *Between Two Worlds* (1935), in Sutherland (ed.), *Literary Anecdotes*, 340–2. Stiggins is the character in Dickens's *Pickwick Papers* (1837) who arrives drunk at a temperance meeting.

[51] Rothenstein, *Men and Memories, 1872–1900*, 181.　　　[52] Moore, *Nesbit*, 101.

[53] Asquith, *Barrie*, 2.　　　[54] Cecil, *Max*, 262.　　　[55] Asquith, *Diaries*, 426.

[56] Rothenstein, *Men and Memories, 1872–1900*, 303.

[57] Reported by the future second Mrs Hardy in a letter to Edward Clodd, 19 Nov. 1910, in Millgate (ed.), *Emma and Florence Hardy*, 68.

however, excite the gossip columnists by one sartorial eccentricity, his wearing two waistcoats even in broiling weather.[58]

Hardy was a genuine poet and tragic novelist, whereas Richard Le Gallienne, a poetaster and picaresque novelist, compensated for deficient talent by 'looking more like a poet than any man has ever looked, before or since', according to Grant Richards.[59] John Gallienne, his father, the manager of a Birkenhead brewery, had Channel Islands origins, and Richard further Frenchified his sur-name by the prefix 'Le' when he published his first book of poems. 'Why does the man's very name sound ungrammatical?', complained Max Beerbohm.[60] He acquired matching spouse as well, if the description by two female visitors to George Meredith's, where they met the Le Galliennes in 1892, is not too con-taminated for truth: 'a boneless heap of green Liberty smocking—over her happy aestheticism she pokes her chin, while Richard Le G. is charming, handsome, with a look of being delicately set apart'.[61] Mrs Le Gallienne's costume was regulation for the distressed female, a part played to perfection by Pearl Craigie (John Oliver Hobbes), who for the last six years of her short life wore loose Liberty-style satin gowns.[62] Le Gallienne himself appeared as 'a great beauty'; indeed, seated at the theatre, he was mistaken for a woman.[63] The naturalist W. H. Hudson was entirely disgusted by the preening. Le Gallienne, he wrote, 'comes to you, as it were, fresh from the dressing-table, with all the cosmetics, powders and perfumes on him. One would like to kick him.'[64] Yeats later admitted to having been duped by Le Gallienne, 'who had what seemed like genius'; but instead of his showy element falling away, as Yeats imagined it would as Le Gallienne matured, it grew to consume the rest.[65]

Not even Le Gallienne outdid Aubrey Beardsley, of whom it was said that even his lungs were affected. With chestnut hair, parted at the middle and falling over his forehead, beneath which lay what Wilde called that 'silver hatchet' face, Beardsley enjoyed natural advantages. These he developed by a preference for padded-shoulder suits and butterfly ties. The walls of his rooms in Pimlico he

---

[58] *M.A.P.*, 13 Aug. 1904, 173.

[59] Lambert and Ratcliffe, *Bodley Head*, 47. Also Sladen, *Twenty Years*, 108, 259, and Jerome, *Life and Times*, 130, for his dress. Rothenstein, *Men and Memories, 1872–1900*, 132, said that he looked like Botticelli's head of Lorenzo, and he itched to draw him. Naturally, the 'Henley Regatta'—the *National Observer* school of manly poets, led by the editor W. E. Henley—felt a strong aversion for Le Gallienne.

[60] Riewald, *Beerbohm's Literary Caricatures*, 168–9.

[61] Michael Field [Katharine Bradley and Edith Cooper], *Works and Day* (1933), quoted in Sassoon, *Meredith*, 220. Michael Field's—Edith (1862–1913) was the niece of Katharine (1846–1914)—own sartorial statement was conveyed via their hats, which they selected once a year from Kate Riley, a Dover Street milliner; Rothenstein, *Men and Memories, 1900–1922*, 115. The Mrs Le Gallienne whom they described, Mildred, a former waitress, died in 1894. Le Gallienne remarried in 1897: this wife was Danish and, when Arnold Bennett met her in 1904, 'she had had enough of the artistic temperament' and separated from him. Flower (ed.), *Bennett Journals*, i. 184 (30 June 1904). [62] Richards, *John Oliver Hobbes*, 47.

[63] Jerome, *Life and Times*, 144.

[64] Ruth Tomalin, *W.H. Hudson: A Biography* (1984), 213. For a friendlier picture of Le Gallienne in 1895, when he was 'the chief of our Amorists' (Wells, *Autobiography*, ii. 552–3).

[65] Yeats to Florence Farr, July 1905, in Wade (ed.), *Yeats Letters*, 455.

painted orange, the doors and skirtings black. This décor imitated the interior of the chateau inhabited by the aristocratic aesthete Des Esseintes, whose philosophy of revolt against Nature was defined in Huysmans's *A Rebours* (1884). And in his bedroom and studio Beardsley hung Utamaro's pornographic prints which his friend Rothenstein had picked up in Paris.[66]

Little touches mattered. As if living together 'in sin' in London in 1911–12 was not enough, J. Middleton Murry and Katherine Mansfield liked to startle by their odd appearance. The result was not as they imagined. At the Duke of York pub in Theobald's Road, where they ate occasionally, 'he in his old fisherman's jersey, she in her exotic coiffures, [they] were taken for a music-hall turn'.[67] Dressing down had drawbacks. Robert Louis Stevenson, 'in search of local colour', once strolled the streets costumed as a working man and 'came upon one definite and mortifying side of life. He found that women completely ignored him. As if he had been invisible!'[68] Pseudo-plebeians proliferated. W. Pett Ridge, famed for his East End stories, always smoked a pipe at public dinners, to demonstrate that he was 'one of the people'.[69] His peculiarity otherwise lay in the immutability of his attire—'cut-away coat with fancy vest, grey striped trousers, kid boots buttoned at the side (as then worn by the best people), spotless white shirt and collar, speckled blue tie, soft felt hat, and fawn gloves'—the same at home or abroad, in his club or in the Alps.[70] By contrast, the democrat in William Morris was asserted by a dark-blue serge suit worn with a linen shirt dyed indigo in his vats. This apparel signified, according to J. W. Mackail, 'something of the look of a working engineer and something of that of a sailor'. Walter Raleigh harboured suspicions: 'He [Morris] was a hale old party, with a skipper's beard and a loud voice, but I cannot get rid of the impression that there was a strain of the school-girl in his soul. A little, just a little, silly, I think. Everyone who writes about him is just a little silly, too.'[71] Alternatively, Morris wore a French workman's blouse. His solidarity with the manual labouring class was also exhibited by feats of strength for his friends, lifting a chair under each arm, then bending to pick up a coal scuttle with his teeth. He had long since ceased to wear a necktie; gone too were the purple trousers of his Pre-Raphaelite period, and the capitalist's tall hat, in which he attended the board meetings of the mining company which supplied him, his mother, and sisters with a large slice of income. Still, it was dismaying for Morris the reborn communist when he took over Kelmscott Manor. There he

---

[66] Rothenstein, *Men and Memories, 1872–1900*, 134, 187. There was a large traffic in Utamaro prints in France at this time—166,000 were sold there in the 1890s—and the leading dealer, Hayashi Tadamasa, collaborated with Edmond de Goncourt in writing the first biography of Utamaro. See the review of the exhibition of Utamaro's art at the British Museum, *The Times*, 5 Sept. 1995.   [67] Lea, *Murry*, 33.

[68] Ford Madox Ford, *It was the Nightingale* (1934), 71.

[69] Howard, *Motley Life*, 265. On W. Pett Ridge (1860–1930); Sutherland, *Companion*, 536–7, and *Oxford DNB*.

[70] Jerome, *Life and Times*, 86–7. Pett Ridge married a sister of Carl Hentschel—Harris in Jerome's *Three Men in a Boat* (1889).

[71] Raleigh to Percy Simpson, 4 Sept. 1913, in Raleigh (ed.), *Raleigh Letters*, ii. 396.

found the housekeepers, Philip Comely and his wife, insistent on preserving the class proprieties: ' "as though it were a trick of machinery" . . . Philip's hand rose to the brim of his hat, or lacking that to his forelock, with every word he uttered'.[72]

Morris's fellow socialist, the children's book illustrator and poet Walter Crane, held a different vision, an egalitarian utopia in which the proletariat was decorously dressed; and he showed the way with his 'velvet coat and flowing yellow silk tie'.[73] R. B. Cunninghame Graham's sartorial socialism led him down both tracks, though he remained the poseur in whatever costume. He so loved dressing up for photographers and artists that Beatrice Webb called him 'a barber's block'.[74] In Latin America he wore gaucho's gear, while at home he was the impeccable dandy aristocrat. Sir John Lavery painted him in that style in 1893, but the parliamentary sketch-writer for *Vanity Fair* was more caustic when he described his appearance in the Commons in 1887: 'Something between Grosvenor Gallery aesthete and waiter in Swiss café. Person of "cultchaw", evidently, from the tips of taper fingers to loftiest curl of billowy hair, and with sad, soulful voice to match. Drawls out some deuced smart things. Effect of speech heightened by air of chastened melancholy.'[75] Bernard Shaw took off in yet another direction in 1885, ordering the first of his red–brown, hygenic woollen suits from Dr Jaeger's prescription. The effect, thought Frank Harris, was to make him look like a radish. Shaw's Jaeger outfit, along with his vegetarianism, henceforth became the badge of a progressive writer, rivalled only by Edward Carpenter's sandal-wearing fellowship, yoga, and buggery.[76] The more confusing the ideology, the more mixed-up the sartorial statement. At a Poets' Club dinner for the Futurist Marinetti in 1912, Maurice Hewlett, presiding, rebelliously sported 'sandals over bare feet below tails and white tie'.[77]

Edwardian authors did not comprehensively fall short of their Victorian forebears in display. In 1911 Compton Mackenzie was the only man in London to wear a white suit. This was not from discipleship to Mark Twain but because that summer saw a prolonged heatwave. Even so, Mackenzie's tailor was shocked by his audacity and asked when he would be leaving England.[78] The oriental not the tropical caught Roy Flecker's fancy. Douglas Goldring recalled the poet at a flat in Torrington Square in south London, sitting at the piano, 'dressed up in a Japanese kimono, smiling his pleasant, rather sardonic smile and thumping out

---

[72] Mackail, *Morris*, i. 222–4, 242.   [73] Rothenstein, *Men and Memories, 1872–1900*, 293.

[74] Beatrice Webb, *Our Partnership*, ed. Barbara Drake and Margaret Cole (1948), 23 (Sept. 1889).

[75] Watts and Davies, *Cunninghame Graham*, 57.

[76] Holroyd, *Shaw*, i. 123, 159–61; Chuschichi Tsuzuki, *Edward Carpenter 1844–1929: Prophet of Human Fellowship* (Cambridge, 1980). A census conducted by *The Vegetarian Messenger* in 1890 enumerated thirty-three vegetarian restaurants in London, seven in Manchester, two each in Liverpool and Portsmouth, and one each in Belfast, Birmingham, Bristol, Leeds, Newcastle, Nottingham, and Ventnor. See *Review of Reviews* (June 1890), 527. J. C. Squire, the *New Statesman*'s literary editor, also attired himself in Jaeger; Flower (ed.), *Bennett, Journals*, ii. 75 (8 Dec. 1913).   [77] Mackenzie, *Life and Times*, iv. 148.

[78] Ibid. 129.

the tune of "La branche de Lilas" or "Navaho" while the rest of us shouted the choruses'.[79]

Belligerence was more the hallmark of the editor of *The Academy*, T. W. H. Crosland, which he signalled by always keeping on his hat, indoors as well as out.[80] He relished the part of the proverbially blunt Yorkshireman. North-country men were not generally disposed to be flashy. Arnold Bennett was described by Gerald Cumberland as 'the least picturesque and literary of figures'. Jokes about Bennett's provincial appearance were legion. Chesterton said that he looked like a man who had gone up to London for the Cup Final and forgotten to go back.[81] Yet, Bennett was more cosmopolitan than most gave him credit. Following marriage in 1907, he liked to stride about Avon-Fontainebleau, the village outside Paris where he and his wife had settled, looking 'terribly English in his well-cut suit'. Alternatively, he turned out 'as a country squire...in his baggy knickerbockers, his leggings, his cap and his stick in hand'. Unfortunately, the locals passed remarks, and dogs barked and attacked him.

Grotesque though it was for the urbanized English provincial to play the country gent abroad, it was complemented when the foreigner adopted the same in rural England. This was Joseph Conrad, who, with his beard, monocle, mannerisms, and check suit, seemed to imagine that this was the correct attitude for a squire. Especially 'startling and unforgettable' was the sight of 'Conrad standing on Ashford station, with a bowler hat surmounting the rest of the outfit'.[82] It was not easy to recall that here was a former sailor: Conrad bore 'the air of a diplomat, more familiar with the Faubourg St. Germain than the bridge of a ship'.[83] Not daunted by his Fontainebleau experiences, Arnold Bennett went on to have a peacock period in London too. Perhaps cockatoo is more apt, considering his quiff. Bennett did not like women to use cosmetics; but himself he liked to present as 'the man-about-town, dressed somewhat ostentatiously, wearing the very best make of clothes, shoes, hats, shirts, gloves, handkerchiefs, ties;...his button-hole decorated, his hat somewhat on one side, his stick and his heels clapping the pavement of Bond Street, Piccadilly, etc'.[84] Unimpressed, H. G. Wells called Bennett's fob 'gastric jewellery'.[85]

If Bennett still seemed the solicitor's clerk pretending the playboy, one could set against him G. K. Chesterton with his swordstick, flowing cloak, flopping hat, Porthos figure, and ringlets. This ensemble became as essential to his

---

[79] Goldring, *Reputations*, 8–9; id., *Life Interests*, 38. Geraldine Hodgson, the family-approved biographer of Flecker, took issue with Goldring's account of Flecker's bohemianism as untypical; Hodgson, *Flecker*, 115.

[80] Wilson, *Sassoon*, 146.   [81] Lowndes, *Merry Wives*, 128.   [82] Goldring, *South Lodge*, 30.

[83] Roberts, *Years of Promise*, 165.

[84] Bennett, *My Arnold Bennett*, 31–2, 35, 138. The Bennett buttonhole was a carnation, grown by his own gardener at his Essex mansion, and sent up daily whenever he was in town. Cf. the sartorial style of Albert Grapp, ladies' man of the Fire Towns, in 'Scruts', Max Beerbohm's parody of Bennett: *Christmas Garland*, 92.   [85] Flower (ed.) *Bennett Journals*, ii. 179 (7 Dec. 1916).

personality as paradox and unreliability. It made him 'the most conspicuous figure in the landscape of literary London'.[86] Henry James deplored it and, one morning in 1908, insisted his typist 'peep through the curtain to see "the unspeakable Chesterton" pass by—a sort of elephant with a crimson face and oily curls. He [James] thinks it very tragic that his mind should be imprisoned in such a body.'[87] Yet Chesterton's display was tame stuff compared with the gypsy exhibitionism of Augustus John and modesty itself compared with the studied unconventionality of Lytton Strachey. Both favoured vast overcoats or Quaker capes, long hair, and, on occasion, earrings; but, where John exuded unwashed virility, Strachey exaggerated his style as an elongated epicene. The effect of either could be devastating. When John, 'very magnificent-looking, huge and bearded', arrived for lunch at Lady Howard de Walden's, his appearance reduced her 2-year-old daughter to 'terrified tears'.[88] Strachey did not specialize in making little girls cry; still, when for outdoor wear he sported a mouse-coloured corduroy suit with orange waistcoat and yellow coat, he created consternation among the peasantry. The Irish Catholic countryside equally took fright at W. B. Yeats. On excursions from Lady Gregory's Coole, brooding all in black, he was confused for a proselytizing Protestant missionary.[89] More deliberately, Strachey made a philosophy, if not quite a religion, out of attire. He asserted that the conventional middle- and upper-class Englishman's uninterest in clothing apart from the quality of its material reflected the national character: 'One sees it everywhere—in their substantial food with its abominable cooking, in their magnificent literature with its neglect of form, in their successful government with its disregard of principle.'[90]

It needed an American to underline the point. Step forward Ezra Pound, who burst on London in 1908 with auburn hair, pointed moustache and beard, and David Copperfield curls. He wore, variously, a rimless pince-nez on a black ribbon, a single turquoise earring with sky-blue shirt, apricot or Japanese hand-painted tie secured by a gold finger-ring, pink coat with blue-glass buttons, and billiard-table green trousers, or open-necked shirt, no tie, brown velvet coat, and pearl-grey trousers.[91] The effect was highlighted by his complete lack of humour. Grace Lovat Fraser remembered his appearance only too well.[92] She

---

[86] Gardiner, *Prophets, Priests and Kings*, 331–41. Chesterton attributed the cloak, hat, swordstick—and his moustache—to his wife's design and insistence; Ward, *Return to Chesterton*, 61, 70, 80.

[87] Edel, *James*, ii. 660.

[88] Asquith, *Diaries*, 298 (27 Apr. 1917). On Augustus John's appearance, see W. B. Yeats to John Quinn, 4 Oct. 1907, in Wade (ed.), *Yeats Letters*, 496–7. John was painting a portrait of Yeats at the time. When staying at the Rothensteins', John preferred to climb in through the window rather than take a front-door key; Rothenstein, *Men and Memories, 1872–1900*, 352.

[89] Coxhead, *Lady Gregory*, 46. Violet Martin—the Ross of the writing duo Somerville and Ross, who was also Lady Gregory's cousin—found Yeats at Coole in 1901 in much the same condition: 'a cross between a Dominie Sampson [the schoolmaster in Sir Walter Scott's *Guy Mannering* (1815)] and a starved R. C. curate—in seedy black clothes—with a large black bow at the root of his long naked throat' (Collis, *Somerville and Ross*, 129). [90] Holroyd, *Lytton Strachey*, ii. 82.

[91] Goldring, *South Lodge*, 40, 48. [92] Grace Lovat Fraser, *In the Days of my Youth* (1970), 124–44.

was the daughter of American parents who had settled in London in 1896 when her father was financial manager for Buffalo Bill's Wild West Show. Grace befriended Ezra on his arrival; but the earring served as a trigger for Papa Fraser. Forearmed by familiarity with circus characters, he advised her to end the relationship.

16

Lecture Tours

A great author visiting America is received with more attention than a Prince or a Chief Justice.

(Douglas Sladen, Preface, *Who's Who* (1897))

I

Ezra Pound came to London the victim of mid-Western Grundyism, which brought about his expulsion from a tutorship at Wabash College, Indiana. Having arrived, he was certain that 'London, deah old Lundon, is the place for poesy.'[1] The reverse held for many a British writer; at least, if they did not exactly follow inspiration there, they sought a more appreciative audience in youthful and keen republican America than in old and tired aristocratic England. Whenever George Meredith was depressed by the defective understanding of domestic reviewers (which was often), he would remark how 'Americans appear to have received my work very generously.' He told his friend Jessopp in 1889, 'To the Americans I am indebted for their having bent a serious examination to my works, instead of the jeer and round shoulder of the Lout. Consequently I feel that I am an American writer; and it is for the money simply that I publish here.' Meredith prided himself on being a democrat and, after the resolution of the American civil war, he 'looked on the American people as leaders of our civilisation'.[2] Towards the end of his life, in an interview for the *Daily Chronicle* in 1904, his enthusiasm was moderated only a little. America, he said, 'has given us Emerson, that very great writer. The Americans have dowered the world with priceless inventions, promise of the great things to be expected of them, and they are a human, a

---

[1] To William Carlos Williams, 3 Feb. 1909, in D. D. Paige (ed.), *The Selected Letters of Ezra Pound 1907– 1941* (New York, 1971), 7.

[2] Quotations from Meredith's letters to W. Morton Fullerton, 15 Nov. 1886, Augustus Jessopp, 1 July 1889, Edmund Gosse, 17 Nov. 1889, in Cline (ed.), *Meredith Letters*, ii. 838, 983, iii. 1222, 1709. Meredith had his embarrassing moments in his relations with the Americans. Between 1860 and 1868, when pressed for money, he had written for the *Ipswich Journal* and, conforming to the policies of that paper, criticized Bright, Lincoln, and the Union side in the civil war, though his personal sympathies were with them. See Sassoon, *Meredith*, 66, 191-2. On Meredith's eightieth birthday in 1908, American admirers presented him with an address; see *Annual Register for 1908*, ii. 4.

large-hearted people, but very young, and hitherto perhaps the country has been too big for them.'[3]

Meredith did not go so far as to test his belief by travelling to America. Probably increasing invalidism prevented it. Such abstention was unusual, for America was regarded as *the* place where authors could exploit celebrity. 'Sooner or later', wrote Jerome K. Jerome, 'it occurs to the English literary man that there is money to be made out of lecturing in America.' He did so in 1908, then returned for a second helping in 1912—abstemiousness personified compared with Hall Caine, who made four American visits before Jerome made his first.[4] The transatlantic tour was already a proven money-spinner by 1879, when the American publisher James T. Fields told Tennyson that he could make £20,000: 'By lecturing? By reading?' 'No,' said Fields, 'by standing in a room and shaking hands with 20,000 people.'[5]

This—£19,000–20,000—was the sum which Dickens reputedly made on his last American tour in 1867–8. Such a mountainous profit was never scaled again, although Gladstone told the Warden of Merton in the 1880s, 'with a full sense of its comical aspect, that he had received an invitation from an eminent American to visit the United States upon a guarantee of £250 a night'.[6] Edward VII knew likewise. Asked what he would do if the monarchy were abolished, he replied, 'I could support my family by lecturing on the Constitution in America.'[7] The Prime Minister and King defaulting, it was left to authors to occupy the bill. One was George MacDonald, a former Congregationalist minister who toured for eight months in 1872–3. His reputation was based on a talent for fantasy stories. Elinor Glyn recalled *The Princess and the Goblin* (1872) being read to her as a child: this proved 'a turning-point in my life, and influenced me more profoundly than any other which I have ever read. It aroused a sleeping interest in mystic things, and turned my religious ideas into these channels, and away from orthodox beliefs.'[8] MacDonald, whose speech was stuttering, was relatively cheap at £30 per lecture. On the other hand, a 'copyright testimonial' was raised for him by American friends ashamed by their publishers' piracy, which deprived him of thousands of pounds over the years; and he was offered the pastorate of a church

---

[3] Nevinson, *More Changes*, 36.

[4] Jerome, *Life and Times*, ch. xi; Connolly, *Jerome*, 142–3, 162–3; Caine, *My Story*, ch. ix.

[5] Lang and Shannon (eds.), *Tennyson's Letters*, iii. 300. In 1861 Tennyson was offered £3,000 plus expenses to give readings in America, according to James Bryce, who was told this by Tennyson himself. See Bryce's letter to his mother, 10 Apr. 1861, in H. A. L. Fisher, *James Bryce* (1927), i. 53. Martin, *Tennyson*, 551, says that the lecture agent Major Pond tried to draw him for a fifty-lecture tour in the 1880s, guaranteeing $1,000 per lecture. This would have resulted in a fee total of about £10,300. The publisher James T. Fields (1817–81), who first became friendly with Dickens after meeting him in England in 1859, was involved in the arrangements for Dickens's 1867–8 American tour.

[6] Brodrick, *Memories and Impressions*, 237. Sums were liable to inflation in the retelling. If the 'eminent American' was the lecture agent Major Pond, then his final offer was £4,000 for twenty lectures, or £200 per session: for this, and Gladstone's polite refusal—pleading age, though he had another three premierships ahead of him—dated 7 February 1880, see Pond, *Eccentricities*, 348–9.

[7] McMillan, *Way we Were*, 31, citing the *Daily Express's* special issue commemorating the King's death in May 1910.　　　　　　　　　　　　　　　　[8] Glyn, *Romantic Adventure*, 14.

on New York's Fifth Avenue at $20,000 (*c.*£4,100) per annum. MacDonald returned with lecture receipts of about £1,000, enough to pay off some debts and to sustain his family of eleven children, but 'a sum he could have easily earned at home'.[9]

MacDonald's relations with his tour organizer, James (Jim) Redpath of the Boston Lyceum Bureau, had been strained. MacDonald demurred at plans to maximize the exploitation of his fame; nor was he really in the premier division. Anthony Trollope, having once sat next to MacDonald at dinner, thought he had everything—'He is a clever, honest, industrious, imaginative man, with a large intellect'—except 'the art of expression to make him so successful a writer as he might have been'.[10] Still, those who occupied the top flight served only to emphasize the gap between that level and the one-man super-league, Dickens. Thackeray, for instance, cleared £2,500 after expenses during his first tour in 1852–3, and £3,000 from his second visit in 1855–6.[11] Similarly, Wilkie Collins made £2,500 from a five-month tour of America and Canada in 1873–4. Collins was a popular author. He was thrilled when a trotting stallion was named after him: 'A printed pamphlet . . . records his virtues, and says "Wilkie Collins covers mares at $75 each"!!!' But Dickens had been an actor as well as a supremely popular author. He presented dramatic readings in ways that few could rival. Collins had not the voice, temperament, or stamina to undertake so many engagements as Dickens; moreover, halfway through the tour he broke with his agent, who, he believed, cheated him.[12] To add insult to injury, the Dickens show rolled on after the great man's death in 1870. His eldest son and namesake made an American tour, reading from his father's works, in 1887.[13]

For thirty years until his death in 1903, the most enterprising agent was the redoubtable Major James Burton Pond, civil war veteran and retired Indian-fighter. In 1901 it could be plausibly remarked that Kipling was 'the only young literary man of eminence who has never lectured for Major Pond'.[14] Kipling's reasons for rebuffing Pond provide a salutary check to facile assumptions that lecturing was a pain-free exercise, a licence to print money combined with holidaying. For one thing, when Pond made his overtures in 1895, Kipling was domiciled in Vermont and had already travelled about the States. He recoiled at having 'to face again some of the hotels and some of the railway systems' that he had experienced. There were other matters to calculate:

the bother, the fuss, the being at everybody's beck and call, the night journeys and so on, make it very dear. I've seen a few men who've lived through the fight, but they did not look happy. I might do it as soon as I had two mortgages on my house, a lien on the horses, and a bill of sale on the furniture, and writer's cramp in both hands; but at present I'm busy and contented to go on with the regular writing business.

[9] William Raeper, *George MacDonald* (1987), ch. 27.
[10] To Cecilia Meetkerke, 29 Mar. 1877, in Booth (ed.), *Trollope's Letters*, 368.
[11] Gérin, *Anne Thackeray Ritchie*, 69, 105.   [12] Peters, *Collins*, 345–7, 355–66, 424.
[13] Sutherland, *Companion*, 186, for Charles Dickens junior (1837–96).
[14] Stephen and Lee, *Lives of the 'Lustrious*, 49.

shot him?'[46] Altogether, Wilde accounted his tour a failure;[47] but he was now a
recognized name in the New World as well as at home, and he had contracts for
the staging of two of his plays in America. He returned in August 1883 to oversee
the production of *Vera; or, The Nihilists*, made topical by the assassination of Tsar
Alexander II; but no sooner was it launched than it sank.[48]

For authors of established reputation, money—'the filthy greenbacks' (Charles
Kingsley)—was much the strongest motive to visit America. Kingsley had been
promoted to a canonry of Westminster in 1873, but his wife's keenness to
redecorate their homes sent him (accompanied by elder daughter) off to America
to pay the bills. The exhausting tour, back and forth for seven months through
America's east coast cities and into Canada, then to the South and Rocky
Mountain states for California, practically killed him. He had once harboured
dreams, when in torment following graduation, of going out to the frontier 'and
throw myself into the wild life, to sink or swim, escaping from a civilization
which only tempted me and maddened me with the envy of a poor man!'[49] His
son Maurice had recently done just that, helping to complete the Denver–
Colorado Springs railway in 1870, and marrying an American. Kingsley hoped of
himself that he would return home 'a wider-hearted and wider-headed man' from
'the vast experience of new people and new facts'.[50] He certainly had some
prejudices to combat, for he had disliked post-bellum America before he set foot
there. Having 'exterminated their southern aristocracy', Americans had, in
Kingsley's view, then forced the 'northern hereditary aristocracy, the Puritan
gentlemen of the old families, to retire in disgust from public life'.[51] American
hospitality now disarmed him. He dined with President Grant; he patched up an
epistolary quarrel he had had with Senator Charles Sumner (who an hour later
collapsed and died); and the Speaker of Congress invited him to open its session
with prayers. The demonstration of a new Gatling gun in his honour was less well
received, Kingsley deploring the waste of ammunition. He also appeared diffident
about his literary reputation and took more seriously his clerical duties, preaching
to large congregations, though he snubbed an offer from 'the tyrant' Brigham
Young to address the Mormons of Salt Lake City in his tabernacle, instead taking
the pulpit at St Mark's, the newly consecrated Episcopal church there.[52] The
principal lecture in his quiver, on Westminster Abbey, was of this order too; he
had another on Culture, a different thing entirely from learning, so he emphasized to students at Berkeley.[53] Other venues were arranged by Redpath and
Pond; and in Washington he found himself styled 'Sir Canon Kingsley'. Wilde,
too, would discover America's keenness to confer titles. He was addressed as

---

[46] Ellmann, *Wilde*, 194.   [47] Sherard, *Wilde*, 83, recorded that he preferred not to talk about it.
[48] Ellmann, *Wilde*, 227–9.
[49] Written from Omaha, 11 May 1874, in *Charles Kingsley: His Letters and Memories of his Life*, ed. his wife
(1877), ii. 433.   [50] Written from St Louis, 4 May 1874, ibid. ii. 432.
[51] Susan Chitty, *The Beast and the Monk: A Life of Charles Kingsley* (1974), 285.
[52] Written from Salt Lake City, 17 May, in *Kingsley: Letters and Memories*, ii. 433.
[53] See the report in the students' paper the *Berkeleyan*, ibid. ii. 438–40.

Captain on crossing into Texas, raised to Colonel by the time he reached the centre of the state, and promoted to General the closer he got to Mexico.[54] Utterly unforgivable was Wilde being called Professor, at which one's heart indeed bleeds for him still. Kingsley himself had found audiences more sizeable— he lectured to nearly 4,000 people in the Opera House at Philadelphia[55]—and reporters less respectful, in the east than in the west; but ultimately all that mattered was his profit, over £600, largely because his hosts' generosity (railway directors provided free passes) spared much personal expenditure.[56]

III

It was true that authors visited the New World not entirely for mercenary reasons. One motive for J. M. Barrie accompanying Robertson Nicoll in 1896 was to meet the Louisiana novelist George Washington Cable, with whom he had corresponded and whose stories of Creole life were comparable to Barrie's Scottish tales. As a schoolboy, Barrie had been entranced too by Fenimore Cooper: a play that Barrie wrote for the Dumfries Amateur Dramatic Club, *Bandelero the Bandit*, was based on one of his stories.[57] Walter Besant's visit in 1893 had been still more purposeful, designed to seal new copyright arrangements (an issue repeatedly raised by Dickens during his first visit in 1842) and to promote the federation of English-speaking peoples. As a boy Besant had read American authors avidly, in such quantity that he felt he knew America almost as well as his own country. To the young Besant, America was 'my Land of Romance' and he could not bear to read about the War of Independence which separated it from Britain. When at last he set foot in America, he feared that his image of it might be dispelled; but he was heartened by the welcome: 'Among the better class of Americans one seldom finds any trace of hatred to Great Britain. I think that, with the exception of Mr W. D. Howells,[58] I have never found any American gentleman who could manifest such a passion.' The romance of America remained real, and not just in the superior technology of its cities, endowment of colleges and schools, and embrace of immigrants: 'it is in the atmosphere of buoyancy, elation, self-reliance, and energy, which one drinks in everywhere'.[59]

Besant's ecstasy was shared. Constance Smedley's favourite childhood reading was that transcendentalist and proto-feminist classic Louisa May Alcott's *Little Women* (1868–9). When she came to write children's books herself, she drew on

---

[54] Ellmann, *Wilde*, 226.   [55] *Kingsley: Letters and Memories*, ii. 425.

[56] Chitty, *Kingsley*, 288–9.   [57] Dunbar, *Barrie*, 31, 35, 107–9; and Meynell (ed.), *Barrie Letters*, 10–11.

[58] Howells (1837–1920) served as American Consul at Venice, 1861–5; editor of *Atlantic Monthly* from 1871, and associate editor of *Harper's Magazine*, 1886–91; critic and novelist, best known for *The Rise of Silas Lapham* (1885). A favourite theme of Howell's was to inveigh against the decadence of modern literature in England compared with America; see *Review of Reviews* (Mar. 1890), 219–20.

[59] 'The Land of Romance' and 'The Land of Reality' (1893), in Walter Besant, *As we Are and As we May Be* (1903), 203–45.

Evening Play Centres' Fund, the Children's Recreation School, the Passmore Edwards Settlement, and the Quebec Battlefield Fund.[71]

Mendicancy on behalf of a good cause had previously propelled the Revd S. Reynolds Hole across the Atlantic, in 1894. Hole was Dean of Rochester, a diocese whose income was halved by agricultural depression;[72] and all profits from his lecturing went towards the cathedral restoration fund. Hole was a practised raconteur, proud of his friendship with Thackeray (they stood the same height, 6 feet 3 inches[73]), and primed to spout on sundry topics: authors and artists, ecclesiastics and preachers, aristocracy and working classes, education and marriage, bores and impostors, drama and poetry, sports and games—in sum, the condition of England. Nor did he neglect to slip in an appreciation of American authors, Washington Irving, Fenimore Cooper, Hawthorne, Longfellow, and more. Hole was famed too as a rose-grower; and his progress was reckoned by Pond as the most successful made by an Anglican clergyman since F. W. Farrar, Dean of Canterbury, undertook a four-month North American tour in 1885.[74]

Originally invited by the Bishop of Pennsylvania to present a theological course, Farrar had then combined preaching with lecturing. It reflected his double life as author of two different types of best-seller: the moralistic school story, *Eric; or, Little by Little* (1858), and the epitome of liberal theology, *The Life of Christ* (1874). These books accumulated, respectively, thirty-six and thirty editions in his lifetime. His lectures on Browning now proved an especial hit, and he was credited with rescuing the poet from oblivion and launching his popularity in the United States. Demand to hear Farrar grew, such that Pond paid him the magic $1,000 (*c.*£200) fee for each of his last three lectures;[75] and he was received by President Cleveland and other notables. In 'Farewell Thoughts on America', delivered in Boston, Philadelphia, and New York, Farrar intoned his wonderment about 'the irresistible advance, the Niagara rush of sweeping energy, the magnificent apparent destiny of the nation'; and he expressed himself gratified that it was founded on sound Christian faith. Yet Farrar also felt the need to berate the 'intrusiveness of the baser portion of your Press', after a journalist somehow gained entry to his bedroom and the morning afterwards treated readers to a 'detailed, but not very accurate, description of his dressing-gown and slippers'.[76]

IV

The sensitive sort of author commonly complained about American brashness. Max Beerbohm suffered in 1895, acting as secretary to his half-brother Beerbohm

---

[71] Sutherland, *Mrs Ward*, 288–92.

[72] Dean Hole, *More Memories* (1894), 10. Ironically, the depression was a result of the influx of cheap North American cereals. Both *More Memories* and its predecessor, *Memories* (1892), reflected Hole's lecture topics.   [73] Hole, *Memories*, 78.

[74] Pond, *Eccentricities*, 122–9.   [75] Ibid. 118.

[76] Reginald Farrar, *The Life of Frederic William Farrar* (1905), ch. xii.

Tree, whose theatre company was on tour. Vulgarity affronted him with his first sight of the Statue of Liberty: 'It must come down,' he told a reporter.[77] While in America, Max was approached with an invitation to undertake a lecture tour, a proposal he considered grotesque, because not only had he then achieved little, but Tree had just then relieved him of his post as press officer on account of his incompetence and aversion to publicity.[78] The newspaper interview was a scourge in itself, usually intrusive and frequently untruthful. Henry James cautioned Thackeray's daughter Lady Ritchie against visiting America for this reason, 'that that terrific country is in every pulse of its being and on every inch of its surface a roaring repudiation and negation of anything like Privacy, and of the blinding and deafening Publicity you might come near to perish'.[79] During her visit in 1905–6 May Sinclair was reduced to tears when she saw one article, based on a conversation over tea, which she felt included too intimate personal details: her father, in the Liverpool shipping trade, had died a bankrupt alcoholic in 1881. Fortunately, she had been presented with a draft and was allowed to veto; but she had to 'struggle against incessant temptations to take the next steamer home'.[80]

The booming of Mrs Humphry Ward in 1908 was grievous more for its inaccuracies. A New York publisher circulated the American press with biographical details which included the intelligence that she was the granddaughter of 'the famous Dr Arnold, who wrote the *Tom Brown* stories'.[81] Mrs Ward herself likened to 'Pekinese spaniels' the journalists and photographers who boarded her liner as it docked in New York; and she was dismayed when in Philadelphia a female journalist filled a column on the strength of exchanging 'six words' on the train with her daughter.[82] Even the academic sort such as Sidney Lee, the Shakespearean scholar and editor of the *Dictionary of National Biography*, found himself besieged by the press. He went to America to give the Lowell Lectures and to present learned papers on Elizabethan and Jacobean authors at various colleges; yet journalists quizzed him about Anglo-American friction over Venezuela, about Kipling, Stephen Phillips, and much else, hoping to lure him into dropping some incautious remark.[83] Still, Jerome K. Jerome reminded fellow authors, 'without the American interviewer to boom us in advance, and work up the local excitement for us when we arrive, we would return with empty pockets'.[84] Jerome also saw the funny side:

I have been described, within the same period of seven months, as a bald-headed elderly gentleman, with a wistful smile; a curly-haired athletic Englishman, remarkable for his youthful appearance; a rickety cigarette-smoking neurotic; and a typical John Bull. Some of them objected to my Oxford drawl; while others catalogued me as a cockney, and invariably quoted me as dropping my aitches.[85]

---

[77] Cecil, *Max*, 114.   [78] Behrman, *Max*, 48.   [79] Letter, 25 Mar. 1913, in Gérin, *Ritchie*, 290.
[80] Raitt, *Sinclair*, 3–5, 98.
[81] *Westminster Gazette*, 20 July 1908, cited in *Punch*, 29 July 1908, 78. During his 1883–4 tour, Matthew Arnold had been styled 'Son of Tom Brown of Rugby' (Murray, *Arnold*, 322).
[82] Sutherland, *Mrs Ward*, 288–9.   [83] July 1903, in Archer, *Real Conversations*, 244–5.
[84] Jerome, *Life and Times*, 187.   [85] Ibid. 185–6.

'for some reason I have never had to endure such biting, personal, newspaper attacks in the States as I have in England, although I was certainly presented in the rôle of an absolutely fantastic "houri"!'

The rougher, egalitarian side of urban democracy appealed to Glyn less. In New York 'shop assistants and waiters were nearly all rude, even insolent'. Nor did American Society, the fabled Four Hundred, emerge much better in *Elizabeth Visits America* (1909), written along the lines of her first novel, *The Visits of Elizabeth* (1900). Their boasting made an easy target. It was bad enough that nearly everyone stated that 'their great-great-grandfather came over in the *Mayflower*', such that it must have been twice the size of a Cunarder to have held them all; some even claimed the Virgin Queen, Elizabeth I, as an ancestor. As the apostle of romantic love, Glyn was affronted too by the mercenary standard which seemed to rule, and she was unsparing of the quantity of 'fluffy little gold-diggers' in American Society. She herself was propositioned by a multi-millionaire: 'If I would come away with him and have a son, he would "square" the husband—settle a fabulous amount upon my little daughters— with a million for myself—and the rest of his entire personal fortune upon the son-to-be!'[93]

Little of this came within the general experience of British authors visiting America; but others too were pulled up by strong impressions. Jerome K. Jerome was disappointed that so much material progress was at the cost of spiritual life: there was standardization of thought, like commodities. Above all, he was distressed by what he saw, heard, and read about the maltreatment of American blacks;[94] and at Chattanooga, where he departed from his text in order to denounce the lynchings, he was received in stony silence. Galsworthy, who paid a three-month visit in 1912, was tortured by scruples of his own. Ostensibly he went to promote his play *The Pigeon* in New York. A stronger incentive was to renounce his love for the dancer Margaret Morris, which was endangering his marriage. In America he tried to escape reporters—he was always loath to release biographical details—but he became unpleasantly aware of the pace and rootlessness of metropolitan American life. He summarized his impressions, like a headmaster who thinks the pupil could do better:

Found a curious state in America of aspiration towards good literature and art, but practically no present production of it. Success still the standard, not the thing for thing's sake, but success meaning less perhaps monetary success than it did. Terrible disposition to short cuts in everything, especially among dramatists. Drama in the hands of commercial Jews mainly, and no one making resolute front against this. No central radiating

---

[93] Quotations from Glyn, *Romantic Adventure*, chs.xiii–xv, and Glyn, *Elinor Glyn*, 130–59.

[94] Jerome, *Life and Times*, 182–3. Note, by contrast, W. H. Davies, who returned from America with a prejudice against coloured people. Davies visited America as a 'super-tramp', crossing the Atlantic in the holds of a cattle-boat, and thence plying the railroads. He was not then a published poet, and seems to have formed a jealousy against English poets of (in his view) modest powers who returned from lecture tours of the United States with swollen pockets and heads. 'Why do the Americans think so much of our worst writers?', he asked. Davies, *Later Days*, 18–20, 28–9, 75–6.

point for Art of any kind. New York trying but not yet succeeding. Therefore no standard. At the same time much apparent wish for change, to judge by talk.[95]

V

How financially profitable most American tours were is difficult to judge. Jerome K. Jerome admitted that his own first tour in 1908 yielded less than it might. For this he blamed himself. His name was certainly a draw, *Three Men in a Boat* (1889) having been hugely pirated, to which he had added a reputation as popular playwright. Accordingly, he had been booked by the Pond Agency, then run by widow Pond, for a 'stupendous tour', comprising 'every state in the Union, together with Canada and British Columbia', at an average of five readings a week, each to last an hour and twenty minutes. It was more than he could bear, and after a fortnight he cabled his wife to bail him out in order to avoid a funeral. His contract was renegotiated, to share platforms with a local favourite and seasoned campaigner, the monologuist Charles Battell Loomis (1861–1911). He was physically 'the ugliest man I have ever met', thought Jerome, but in all else beautiful; and Jerome envied his ability to perform whatever the venue.[96]

Conan Doyle, who had gone out in 1894, had not needed carrying like Jerome; still, he also recognized that an American tour needed careful calibration if it was to be worth it. He packed in over forty engagements, mostly public readings, in the autumn and early winter. His lecture repertoire included addresses about George Meredith, Stevenson, and Barrie; also about Kipling, whom he visited in Vermont and tried to convert to golf. Doyle had long been captivated by American literature, by Poe, Hawthorne, Fenimore Cooper, and Bret Harte, and by tales with American settings such as *The Scalp Hunters* (1851) by Mayne Reid, the Ulster-born adventurer who settled (and fought) in the United States in the 1840s. Doyle was an enthusiast for Anglo-American reunion, to which cause he dedicated *The White Company* (1891); and his greatest creation, Sherlock Holmes, was in all likelihood named in salute to Oliver Wendell Holmes. Doyle netted £1,000 profit from his tour, which sum (and more) he invested in the American publisher McClure's;[97] but, back home in 1895, he argued that the bonanzas reaped by Dickens and Thackeray from their American tours were exceptional, and that agents' fees or hotel and travel bills would leave a writer with scarcely more than he could earn by his pen in the same time. Accordingly, Doyle recommended the experience chiefly to see the places and people.[98] Pond was put out by this, whereupon Doyle wrote to *The Critic*, New York, to correct any impression that

[95] Marrot, *Galsworthy*, 341. On the relationship with Margaret Morris, Catherine Dupré, *John Galsworthy* (1976), chs. 22–3.   [96] Jerome, *Life and Times*, 190–2.

[97] Booth, *Conan Doyle*, 29, 37–8, 198–203. His second North American visit was in 1914, just before the outbreak of war; ibid. 293–5. He presided at an Authors' Club centenary commemoration of Poe's birth, in 1909; ibid. 105.

[98] Conan Doyle's letters, July and Sept. 1895, in Gibson and Green (ed.), *Unknown Conan Doyle*, 45–7.

his tour had been unrewarding; on the contrary, it was 'successful beyond all possible expectation'. Doyle's visit was short, but only because of a promise to his invalid wife that he would be home at Christmas. Pond had had to turn down more requests for engagements than Doyle could accept; and he declared in 1900, 'I would give him more money to-day than any Englishman I know of if he would return for a hundred nights'—a tribute tarnished only by the misclassification of Doyle as an Englishman. The explanation of Doyle's appeal lay not just in the popularity of his work but in his preaching and practising good Anglo-American relations.[99] Almost the only discomfort Doyle experienced was from the American habit of overheating buildings; but as an outdoors man he revelled in its spaces and sports.

Doyle nevertheless had raised the issue of the relative rewards gained by lecturing or by the pen. The variable in this equation was what a particular author's usual earning power was over several months. Thackeray, who did not reap the Dickensian profits that Doyle supposed, had sailed for Boston clutching an advance copy of *The History of Henry Esmond* (1852), in which his principal hopes were invested of making the money he needed to support his two daughters and mentally ill wife. On departure, he told one of these daughters that 'if I have the luck I may secure nearly a third of the sum that I think I ought to have behind me by a six month's tour in the States'.[100] Boston, New York, Philadelphia, Baltimore, Washington, and Richmond, Charleston, Savannah, and the South were visited on this first tour; 'but o how sick I am of the business!', he declared in March 1853, upon which he aborted his 'circuiteering', giving up St Louis and the West and Montreal and Canada. He showed greater pertinacity in 1855–6, taking in more places and altogether racked up £3,000 profit. The purses paid for lecturing were not the only money made: in 1852 Harper's offered him $1,000 (just over £200) to publish his lectures (on 'The English Humorists of the Eighteenth Century'), and he struck another deal with Appleton's to reprint five other works for £100 or £200, less than they were worth though more than he could expect in a pirates' market if he had not been on the spot.[101] Further spin-offs he discountenanced. He would not, like Dickens (*American Notes*, 1842), issue a stock-taking: 'No man should write about the country under 5 years of experience, and as many of previous reading.'[102] Altogether, then, Thackeray did not exploit America to the full, but he was content with his proceeds: 'an hour's reading was often as profitable as a fortnight's work'.[103]

Fifty years later the visit of Alice Meynell was also revealing about the relativities. She went as the guest of Agnes Tobin, the daughter of a San Francisco banker. Tobin spent several years in England as a budding poet and literary

[99] Pond, *Eccentricities*, 502–9, where Doyle's speeches are reproduced.
[100] Letter to Anne Thackeray, Oct. 1852, in Harden (ed.), *Thackeray's Letters*, 225. Generally, on Thackeray's two American tours, see Taylor, *Thackeray*, chs. xvi and xviii.
[101] Letter to George Smith, 26 Nov. 1852, in Harden (ed.), *Thackeray's Letters*, 231.
[102] Letter to Albany Fonblanque, 4 Mar. 1853, ibid. 239.   [103] *The Times*, 30 Oct. 1952.

tuft-hunter. Mrs Meynell 'discovered' her in 1895, and contributed an introduction to Tobin's Petrarch translations, *Love's Crucifix* (1902). They were united by Roman Catholic devotion as well as by literary interests. Tobin also cosied up to George Meredith (who in turn was smitten by Mrs Meynell), Arthur Symons, W. B. Yeats, and Joseph Conrad, who dedicated *Under Western Eyes* (1911) 'To Agnes Tobin who brought to our door her genius for friendship from the uttermost shore of the west'.[104] Mrs Meynell travelled to America in September 1901, with Tobin's brother and sister, and looked forward to this 'part of the romance of my romantic life'. The arrival in New York dashed the romance as it coincided with news of President McKinley's assassination; nor did her plans proceed without hitch. Though she had a commission from the *Pall Mall Gazette* for a series of articles, she intended staying little more than a month, travelling around with Agnes Tobin, before they returned to England. The idea of lecturing was entirely casual, such as Tobin could arrange—'Agnes strongly recommends a Dickens causerie, as well as lecture, at San Francisco, before a woman's club called The Century.'[105]

Everything changed in October when Tobin developed a cough, decided she could not face the Atlantic in winter, and prevailed on Meynell to stay to nurse her. Meynell greeted the suggestion with tears and remained until April. There followed the need to enlarge her lecturing revenue, not for subsistence in America—Tobin the valetudinarian covered most costs—but to compensate husband Wilfrid and their seven 'chicks' for mother's lost income. To 'darling Cuckoo', alias son Everard, Meynell described the arrangements for San Francisco:

Agnes is herself the Impresario. She is too sweet and dear, she is simply devoted. She has hired the hall, got the tickets printed, advertised, published portraits, got an article into a paper, and raised H——generally. Nothing could be better. Yet I cannot persuade myself that anyone will go. How I wish I could turn a better honest penny! Would I had put myself into Major Pond's hands![106]

This last registered a note of doubt about the amateur Agnes; and, to her husband, Meynell betrayed worries that although 'Agnes has done all that mortal could do for me, Celia [Agnes's sister] helping her nobly . . . the hall is very small, so it cannot hold a big sum.' Still, she was thrilled to meet Robert Louis Stevenson's widow, who told her that when her *Poems* (1893) and *The Rhythm of Life* (1893) had reached Samoa, Stevenson kept them under his pillow to prevent them from being pinched before he could read them; and her appearance before the dames of the Century Club was a gushing success: 'What is remarkable is the wish of everybody to exaggerate in one's favour. It is the old lionising

---

[104] Frederick R. Karl, *Joseph Conrad: The Three Lives* (New York, 1976), 701. Tobin acted as intermediary for John Quinn's purchase of Conrad's drafts and manuscripts, and was the agent of André Gide meeting Conrad. She also devoted herself to nursing Arthur Symons when he collapsed into insanity in 1908; Beckson, *Symons*, 238 ff.

[105] Alice to Wilfrid Meynell, 1 Oct. 1901, in Meynell, *Alice Meynell*, 172–3.

[106] Alice to Everard Meynell, 18 Oct. 1901, ibid. 176.

passion still surviving. They *want* to believe you are the most remarkable woman in the world.'[107]

Meynell's inaugural lecture ensued, 'The Great Transition in English Poetry from the Seventeenth to the Eighteenth Century'. Though to herself she seemed to have been 'roaring' at the audience, a newspaper criticized her weak voice. During November 1901 she worked up another three lectures for giving in San Francisco and for recycling anywhere that would have them. These were 'The Children', drawn from her published essays (of 1897) with that title; 'The Treble Note', about Charlotte Brontë; and 'Dickens as a Man of Letters'. The last two were adapted from periodical articles she had written, and they turned out a long-run investment. Together with 'The Great Transition in English Poetry', Meynell published these in modified form in *Hearts of Controversy* (1917). 'Dickens' was delivered in San Francisco before the end of November, and 'Brontë' in early December; but the organization for the latter was bungled: 'We had intended to advertise, and then we thought we would not, and we tried the experiment of an evening instead of an afternoon lecture, as a man told me that more men would go. I also lowered my admission. The consequence was comparative failure—£12, out of which I have to pay for the hall and the tickets.'[108] By this time she had received invitations to lecture in New York for £15 and in Chicago for £20: 'modest sums, but Agnes thinks I can repeat them indefinitely'. The plan now was to take her four lectures on tour after Christmas, 'for Monterey, then for Los Angeles, and if Agnes can bear the roughish travelling, for [New] Mexico. After that our course ought to be eastward to New Orleans, then by degrees up to Washington, Philadelphia, Chicago, Boston, and New York.' All this was through Meynell's and Tobin's own arranging; but it was not from choice. Meynell had corresponded with Major Pond before leaving San Francisco, hoping that he would undertake the management; and a friend went to see him. The Major's position was that he could not make 'any serious "bookings"' without six months' notice; whereupon, Meynell raised the question with her husband, 'Shall I come out again in the summer and have a real innings?'[109] She determined to make the best of a bad job. Los Angeles brightened her spirits. 'The Great Transition in English Poetry' lecture, to an audience of 300 or 400, moved some to weeping; but she was able to send only £15 home, having spent £6 on opals. 'Dickens', delivered in the same place a month later, made £15 8s.; then, after a farewell banquet, she took to the railroad. Her itinerary was revised. Despite 'a charming note' from the new First Lady, Mrs Roosevelt, she could not fit Washington into the schedule. In the mid-West, in Indianapolis, she enjoyed a success, notwithstanding a delay in recovering her baggage from the train, 'so that I had to lecture in my travelling dress (with the grey blouse I got at Ponting's!) to a great gathering of people in evening dress. It was rather painful, but

---

[107] Alice to Wilfrid Meynell, 24 Oct. 1901, ibid. 177.
[108] Alice to Wilfrid Meynell, 13 Dec. 1901, ibid. 181.
[109] Alice to Wilfrid Meynell, 13, 29 Nov., and 13 Dec. 1901, ibid. 178–82.

they congratulated me on the fact that my skirt was not really short'. The dinner that followed, 'to which the most literary Indianapolites were invited', was dazzling: 'The knowledge of literature struck me as ever—the interest in Coventry Patmore, for instance. They know my work by heart.'[110]

The climax of Meynell's tour came in Chicago, where the 'Brontë' lecture was so applauded she spontaneously recited one of her poems 'The Shepherdess', and was cheered again; and in Boston, where she spoke in the city and at nearby Harvard University and Wellesley College. It was a personal rather than pecuniary triumph: 'I have made only £17 this week.'[111] Afterwards, she was for home. So, what was the balance after all? Bearing in mind the improvised organization, there was credit. Probably, Meynell was paid less than any author who made an American lecture tour in this period; yet, the remittances she sent back, between £12 and £20, were about the same as her husband's fluctuating weekly earnings.[112] It also must be remarked that Alice Meynell was a coterie not a public figure; above all, she was not a novelist, and was unable to market herself commercially. Within these limits, she tried. It has been noted already that she continued to write for the *Pall Mall Gazette* while in America, and that afterwards she published her American lectures. Moreover, following her return, she gave her 'Brontë' lecture at Newcastle, her first public lecture in England. However, though she then presented the 'Dickens' at the Pioneer Club in 1905, this was the end of her lecturing enterprise.

Here we may need reminding how relatively rare it was for English women authors to speak in public. Female professional performers existed, such as singers and actresses; otherwise, Constance Smedley emphasized, 'at that time women who spoke in public were of the propaganda-platform type'[113]—that is, women active in philanthropic work or in the emerging suffrage movement. Among the few women authors who were reckoned accomplished platform performers was Mrs Burnett Smith (Annie S. Swan) and this was largely because of experience gained from temperance and missionary work. She was in demand at formal literary dinners, and she fulfilled such responsibilities as presiding at the Women Writers' Dinner in 1905 or over the Society for Women Journalists in 1906, with distinction.[114] A Scotswoman, she was considered an even better after-dinner speaker than Mrs T. P. O'Connor—who, as an American, was without the traditional diffidence supposedly afflicting the English.

Pearl Craigie (John Oliver Hobbes) too was proud of her American origins. Though resident in England from infancy, she more than once accompanied her businessman father, who crossed the Atlantic some forty times. The family was well connected. A cousin was senior judge of the Supreme Court and, during a four-month visit in 1895–6, she combined the promotion of her playwriting with

---

[110] Alice to Wilfrid Meynell, 7, 16 Feb., 11, 16 Mar. 1902, ibid. 187–91.
[111] Alice to Wilfrid Meynell, 21 and 28 Mar. 1902, ibid. 191–2.
[112] Meynell, *Thompson and Meynell*, 135–6.   [113] Smedley, *Crusaders*, 94.
[114] Nicoll (ed.), *Letters of Annie S. Swan*, 46–8.

the social whirl of Washington and New York, as a guest at presidential and ministerial functions. But it was not until 1905–6, the last year of her life, that she undertook a lecture tour in America with the J. B. Pond Lyceum Bureau, permutating three addresses: on Dante and Botticelli, on 'The Artist's Life' (Balzac, Brahms, and Turner), and on 'The Science of Life', the last illustrated by reference to Ignatius Loyola (Craigie was a Catholic convert), Wesley, and Tolstoy. A fierce winter and extensive railway travel took their toll, and she foreshortened her tour; she had, however, written articles for the American press and, on returning to England in February, she presented her impressions of America in speeches at a dinner of the Imperial Industries Club and at the National Liberal Club. Her 'Science of Life' lecture was recycled for a Manchester University audience in May, a busy month in which she also addressed meetings of the National Vigilance Association and Invalid Children's Aid Association. In this last respect, she conformed to type. It was in support of that charity that she had given her first public speech; her last was at a presentation banquet for the actress Ellen Terry in June 1906.[115] Whether Mrs Craigie had actually anything to say in her lectures was questionable. Inside his own copy of *The Artist's Life* (1904), which reproduced her essays and speeches, Max Beerbohm parodied her platitudinous style ('the level of any high school girl who has dipped into a popular encyclopaedia') and her self-satisfaction ('My hat, at which so many of you are looking, cost 17 guineas').[116] Still, it was for some women achievement enough to spout in public.

Mrs Hodgson Burnett was another hybrid: English-born in 1849, an emigrant to America in 1865, then a regular visitor to England from the late 1880s. Her fight in the courts for copyright protection against unauthorized dramatizations of *Little Lord Fauntleroy* in 1888 caused her to be fêted by fellow authors. This, while obviously gratifying, was an ordeal. At a Society of Authors dinner she was able to escape with few words, no more than she gave when opening a Boys' Club Reading Room dedicated to her teenage son, who died from consumption in 1890. On 30 November 1895, however, she was compelled to deliver her first speech as such, at a New Vagabonds Club dinner in her honour, before an assembly of 400. Only five months before, at a previous New Vagabonds Club dinner, it had been Anthony Hope who had replied on behalf of 'the Ladies', to the sniggering of those who thereby deduced that the advent of the 'New Woman' had failed to produce even one speaker. The *Literary World*, which reported this deficit, observed tartly, 'The only sign of novelty we detected about the ladies present was that a few condescended to puff cigarettes, to the evident scandal of some less advanced ladies'; and *Punch* produced some comic verses to mark the occasion.[117] At the November dinner Mrs Burnett's nerve was strengthened by friendly support from Israel Zangwill, who was by nature uninhibited; but there was no disguising her new departure. There were three

[115] Richards, *Hobbes*, 31–5, 93–7, 317–21.
[116] Lawrence Danson, *Max Beerbohm and the Act of Writing* (Oxford, 1991), 164–5.
[117] *Punch*, 22 June 1895, 299.

things she had always wished to avoid: being hanged, drowning, and having to make a speech. She added: 'I am torn between two emotions—one is the hope that I shall be able to make you hear me; the other the fear that it might be better for me and you, if I could not.' She then talked about her writing and, when she resumed her seat, it was to 'prolonged cheering'. Next year, in July 1896, she attended an Authors' Club dinner in her honour, 'the first public dinner which we have ever given to a lady writer'.[118] Such occasions remained a rarity after 1900. Constance Smedley was particularly conscious of this failing in most English women authors, and it was through her in 1905 that the Lyceum Club formed a debating society, meeting in private, to allow women to practise public speaking, especially 'the art of after-dinner speaking'. Her Lyceum colleagues had been embarrassed at their first international function when four American women, including the Dean of Barnard College and the presidents of Mount Holyoke and Wellesley, each spoke confidently and wittily, whereas the home team was petrified into silence. Alice Meynell's predicament in 1901, in giving her first public speeches and lectures in the United States, is better understood in this context. On returning to England, she would be a founder member of the Lyceum. Another was the novelist May Sinclair; and it was through the Lyceum that she battled against shyness and eventually made her own maiden speech, though that would be in monotone, like a ventriloquist's dummy. In 1905–6, during a visit to America, Sinclair had been the despair of her publishers and friends, for it proved impossible to coax her into a publicity campaign.[119] Placed next to Mark Twain during a banquet to hail his seventieth birthday, she was thanked at its end by the honorand for maintaining a 'remarkably interesting silence'.[120]

VI

Picking the moment to visit America, when an author was on a crest, plainly made a difference. Few left it as late as Edith Somerville, who was 71 when she toured in 1929, fourteen years after the death of Violet Martin, her co-author of the popular *Irish R.M.* stories. The debt-ridden condition of her estate caused the visit, and it yielded material for another book, *The States through Irish Eyes*.[121] Still, there were some whom no inducement would move. Andrew Lang resisted the offer of a lecture tour in 1898, citing a poor voice as excuse, only to be told: 'It is not necessary to talk . . . Come and let us look at you—we will do the talking!' Whereupon *The Academy* remarked: 'America's talking powers are just what he dreads!'[122] Nor, though he made himself available at home to Americans who enthused about his work, would Thomas Hardy abandon his inhibitions to parade on lecture platforms. Such invitations as came his way were refused.

[118] Thwaite, *Burnett*, 164–5, 170. [119] Smedley, *Crusaders*, 94–9. [120] Raitt, *Sinclair*, 97.
[121] As well as lecturing, she sold some of her paintings for £1,500; Collis, *Somerville and Ross*, ch. 21.
[122] Green, *Lang*, 202.

The most grotesque was an all-expenses-paid trip 'with wife or daughter' to attend the dedication of the Pittsburgh Institute's new building in 1906, when Hardy was 66 years old, childless, and with a failing marriage.[123] By contrast, there was the Revd John Watson (Ian Maclaren). When he made his first tour, 1 October–16 December 1896, he was at the peak of popularity. He twice achieved the feat of having two books in the top ten American best-seller charts in the same year: in 1895 *Beside the Bonnie Brier Bush* (1894) was number 1, and *Days of Auld Lang Syne* (1895) at number 6; in 1896 *Kate Carnegie* (1896) was number 7, while *Beside the Bonnie Brier Bush* held on at number 10.[124] So oversubscribed were his engagements—to give sermons as well as ninety-six readings and lectures— that Pond offered him a further $24,000 (c.£5,000) to stay on for twelve more weeks. Watson declined, having his congregation in Liverpool to minister to; yet, during the previous ten weeks, receipts amounted to $35,796 (c.£7,365), unmatched in Pond's experience except by Henry Morton Stanley. In his memoirs Pond lavished more pages to describe Watson's reception than he did for any other performer, recording how 'multitudes with bated breath and outstretched necks, sat and listened to him with intermingled laughter and tears, like sunshine making the rain radiant'.[125] Again, Watson was notable for his handling of the press; and he would return for a second successful tour, under Pond's direction, 19 February–10 May 1899. Watson's third, following his retirement from the ministry, began on 30 January 1907; but the strains of the lecture circuit took their toll of his weakening health, and he died in the Brazelton Hotel, Mount Pleasant, Iowa, on 6 May, aged 57.[126]

This matter of timing one's American visit, picking the right moment to exploit celebrity, is pointed up by Winston Churchill's tour in December 1900–January 1901, although there were many unusual aspects to it. The most bizarre was the coincidental rise to fame of an American Winston Churchill (1871–1947), whose first novel, suitably titled *The Celebrity,* appeared in 1898. He followed that with *Richard Carvel,* which was the third best-selling book in America in 1899 and the effective launch of a remarkable career as a writer of chiefly historical fiction. The sardonic remarked that it was surely 'impossible that the world can contain two Winston Churchills at the same time';[127] but the American was probably the best-selling author of the entire period from the turn of the century up to the Great War, in his own country, heading the charts in 1901, 1904, 1906, 1908, and

---

[123] Hardy to the Trustees of the Pittsburgh Institute, late July 1906, in Purdy and Millgate (ed.), *Hardy Letters,* iii. 220. Hardy sustained a particularly warm correspondence with one American fan, Rebekah Owen (1858–1939), the daughter of a New York businessman, from 1897. Following his death, his second wife was invited to undertake an American lecture tour on Hardy; see Barrie's letter to her, 21 May 1930, in Meynell (ed.), *Barrie Letters,* 159.

[124] Hackett, *Best Sellers,* 11–12. Before starting his circuit with Pond, Watson had given the Lyman Beecher Lectures on Preaching, at Yale University, which awarded him the DD; Nicoll, *Maclaren,* 189.

[125] Pond, *Eccentricities,* 405–51.

[126] Watson died an exceptionally wealthy man, leaving almost £60,000: see *Oxford DNB.*

[127] Stephen and Lee, *Lives of the 'Lustrious,* 28.

1913.[128] The English Winston Churchill may not have liked the idea of masquerading as his namesake, any more than Matthew Arnold liked being mistaken for Edwin Arnold; but it could not be ruled out that he might benefit financially from the confusion. Just turned 26, the English Winston was three years younger than the American; yet he had cause to believe he was famous in his own right. Son of the late Lord Randolph Churchill and of an American heiress, Jennie Jerome, who had now largely dissipated her fortune, Winston had established a name as soldier, war correspondent, and author. In 1898 he published *The Story of the Malakand Field Force,* and in 1899 *The River War;* but 1900 was the *annus mirabilis,* with three new books by him, a Ruritania-style novel, *Savrola,* and two accounts of his Boer War experiences, *London to Ladysmith via Pretoria,* and *Ian Hamilton's March.* Especially thrilling was the publicity he attracted by his escape from captivity at the hands of the Boers. Moreover, in the general election in October, he was elected MP for Oldham. This raised his market value, not least in his own estimation. Enquiries were made of Major Pond, initially by Lady Randolph in the spring when Winston's star was beginning to soar. Winston wanted a guarantee of at least £1,000 a month for a three-month North American tour, and hoped to clear £5,000 altogether.

Churchill's bargaining counter was the sum he could expect from a lecture tour of British cities. In July 1900 Churchill grandly informed Major Pond that he had offers totalling over £2,000 for a month's tour at home, lecturing about Boer War strategy. He peremptorily ordered Pond to 'show me something very much better than that', adding,

and I don't want to wear myself out by talking to two-penny-half-penny meetings in out of the way places. In all my social arrangements I shall exercise my entire discretion. When I come to Canada I shall stay with the Governor General [Lord Minto] whom I have known for some years and I have a certain number of friends in America of whose hospitality I shall avail myself. I don't want to be dragged about to any social functions of any kind nor shall I think of talking about my experiences to anybody except when I am paid for so doing.[129]

The domestic lecture tour in November was even more profitable than Churchill predicted: he made £3,782 15s. 5d.[130] By comparison, his subsequent American–Canadian tour lasted twice as long for less than half the money: £1,600. What explains the discrepancy? Everywhere Winston could count on powerful family friends and on the cachet of the Churchill name to draw distinguished men to preside at his meetings: lords Wolseley and Rosebery, and Joseph Chamberlain,

---

[128] Hackett, *Best Sellers.* Churchill was also eighth on the best-sellers list for 1900, and second in 1910 and 1915. Both Winston Churchills were included in *Who's Who* for the first time in 1899.

[129] W. S. Churchill to James B. Pond, 31 July 1900, in Randolph S. Churchill, *Winston S. Churchill, Companion vol. ii/1: 1901–1907* (1969), p. xxix.

[130] This is the sum given in Churchill, *Churchill,* 542. Winston himself claimed, 'Altogether in the month of November I banked safely over £4,500, having toured little more than half of Great Britain' (*My Early Life* (1959), 367).

in London, Edinburgh, and Birmingham, respectively; Mark Twain in Boston, and so forth. Moreover, interest concerning Winston's mother, always considerable, was particularly keen. She now flourished unsuspected intellectual credentials by launching the *Anglo-Saxon Review,* a transatlantic literary quarterly, garlanded with celebrity contributors: Swinburne, Henry James, and assorted aristocrats, politicians, and sages from both countries.[131] Priced 1 guinea in Britain and $5 in America, the *Anglo-Saxon Review* had an appeal that was decidedly snobbish. More piquantly, Lady Randolph had married again, this time to a man as young as Winston. All this excited Major Pond, who wrote to her:

Have you any idea how green your memory is here in New York City? I would suggest that you accompany your son on the voyage and witness his reception here. It seems to me it would be a very proud day for you, and your friends here would appreciate it, and I need not add it would doubly enhance the value of the lecture.[132]

Lady Randolph did not desert her new husband and Winston made the trip alone. His market stock also slumped because of adverse attitudes to the Boer War in America. Winston noted a 'strong pro-Boer feeling, which has been fomented against me by the leaders of the Dutch, particularly in New York'. He further complained bitterly about Pond's organization, for selling him too cheaply and for taking too large a commission. Mostly, Pond passed him on to local agents in various towns, sometimes not even arranging public lectures but merely appearances at private parties; and Pond's press management backfired: 'He is a vulgar Yankee impresario and poured a lot of very mendacious statements into the ears of the reporters and the whole business has been discussed in whole columns of all the papers'.[133]

Churchill's more successful domestic tour had been arranged by the Lecture Agency, run by Gerald Christy from offices in The Strand, London. He 'handled all the big lectures . . . in this country', according to Keble Howard, who signed up with Christy after the Great War.[134] Curiously, evidence about these domestic agents who arranged writers' lecture tours in Britain is generally more elusive than about their corresponding factors in the United States. The exception is Dickens, whose public readings are well documented. Dickens's last manager (from 1866), George Dolby, had genially exploited his association in *Charles Dickens as I Knew Him* (1885); so had John Camden Hotten, who cobbled together reports of fifty-six of Dickens's speeches and sped these into print in the year of Dickens's death, 1870.[135] Dickens's stardom was unmistakable. Following a

---

[131] Thomas Hardy, however, declined to write for the *Anglo-Saxon Review;* see his letter to Earl Hodgson, 31 Oct. 1900, in Purdy and Millgate (eds.), *Hardy Letters,* ii. 271.

[132] Pond to Lady Randolph Churchill, 2 Nov. 1900, in Ralph G. Martin, *Lady Randolph Churchill,* ii: *1895–1921* (1972), 200–1.

[133] Winston to Lady Randolph Churchill, 21 Dec. 1900 and 1 Jan. 1901, in Churchill, *Churchill,* i. 543–4.

[134] Howard, *Motley Life,* 337–8.

[135] Hotten's unreliable record was supplemented by Richard Herne Shepherd in 1884, until both were displaced by K. J. Fielding's edition in 1960. While disclaiming any title to be definitive—the problem is

banquet in his honour at St George's Hall, Liverpool, in 1869, when Dickens was making his way to the station, he was repeatedly stopped 'by persons of the working classes wanting to shake hands with him; and all of them eager to thank him for the pleasure his books had afforded them'.[136]

Thackeray too regarded the domestic circuit as a sound 'investment', before and after his two American visits. His first lectures, on 'The English Humourists of the Eighteenth Century', were given (nervously) in 1851, in Willis's Assembly Rooms in King Street, St James's, before an audience of titled ladies and Society figures. A second set on 'The Four Georges' took him to Scotland and about England in 1857–8, to the disgust of the Queen, who did not approve his lampooning her Hanoverian ancestors.[137] The logistics of these lecture tours and other appearances are less easily discovered than reports of audience reactions.[138] It is not obvious from Thackeray's correspondence how the arrangements for his lectures were made. Not all venues were settled at the start but were added to in ad hoc fashion. In February 1857, however, he was boasting of having 'found a Barnum who pays me an awful sum for April & May and let us hope June—shall make £10,000 by my beloved Monarchs one way or the other—and then & then—well I don't know what is going to happen'.[139] This 'Barnum' was Thackeray's tour manager, Thomas Willert Beale; a lawyer, he was principally an impresario of music festivals at Crystal Palace and in the provinces.[140] His agency, Cramer & Beale, assigned George Hodder to chaperone Thackeray at subsequent fixtures.[141] Thackeray had the Dickens barometer always in mind—even while sightseeing in Rome in 1854 ('When I read of Dickens's triumphs before the Hoperatives at Manchester my soul is full of envy . . .')[142]—but he himself had not done badly, reporting between engagements at Bradford and Manchester in 1856 that his lectures

are a much greater success here than in America—as great even pecuniarily. People knowing the subject better more familiar with the allusions etc. like the stuff—I am glad for my part that this should be the opinion—for I know in America it was thought that I had brought them an inferior article—glass beads as it were for the natives—But no newspaper in this country will say like Bennett [editor of the *New York Herald*] that any young man could sit down in their office and write such lectures in an evening.[143]

---

insurmountable that 'Dickens never wrote out his speeches before they were given, and only rarely did so afterwards'—Fielding collated reports of 115 speeches that Dickens delivered at special occasions, in both Britain and America, the first on 3 May 1837, at the anniversary dinner of the Literary Fund, and the last on 30 April 1870, at the annual banquet of the Royal Academy.

[136] George Dolby, in Fielding, *Dickens's Speeches*, 393.

[137] Gérin, *Ritchie*, 55–9, 69; Fuller and Hammersley (eds.), *Thackeray's Daughter*, 87, 170; Farquharson, *In and Out of Parliament*, 68–9, comparing Thackeray and Dickens as speakers.

[138] Taylor, *Thackeray*, 315–8, 322–6, 386–91, for audience reactions.

[139] Letter to Frederick Swartout Cozzens, 8 Feb.–5 Apr. 1857, in Harden (ed.), *Thackeray's Letters*, 314.

[140] On Beale (1828–94), *Oxford DNB*.   [141] Taylor, *Thackeray*, 389–90.

[142] Letter to Mrs Bryan Waller Procter, Jan.–4 Feb. 1854, in Harden (ed.), *Thackeray's Letters*, 264.

[143] Letter to Mrs Frank Hampton, 10–12 Dec. 1856, ibid. 308.

Fees varied, of course. Four London engagements early in 1857 bagged him over £1,000; the university towns of Oxford and Cambridge scored between £100 and £150; and a good-sized provincial city audience, as at Newcastle, also yielded about £100. At Liverpool he drew 1,200 folk for one lecture and, after several presentations in Edinburgh, he reckoned that 3 per cent of that city's people had listened to him—some 6,000 altogether, if he calculated aright.[144] Cumulatively, he criss-crossed the land: Scotland, and England's north-west and north-east, parts of the midlands and East Anglia, the West Country, and the capital and its environs. On occasion Thackeray performed for (to him) as little as £25, as at a London suburb on 26 January 1858, after which he handed the money over to his doctor, Henry Thompson, 'who attended me all last year without a fee'. 'It was easily earned money, wasn't it?' Thackeray chirruped, though soon he was declaring, 'I am sick of letting myself out for hire.'[145]

Thackeray thus amassed a considerable fortune and, while Dickens remained out in front, he opened up a sizeable gap between himself and the rest of the field. Following in their wake—Thackeray died in 1863, Dickens in 1870—lesser sorts needed to scale down expectations. Anthony Trollope, as always, was a realist about these things. He made several public appearances, speaking on current affairs such as 'The Zulus and Zululand' at Nottingham on 23 October 1879, here drawing on the experience of his visit to South Africa two years earlier; and on literary matters, such as 'The Art of Reading', at the annual prize-giving of the Quebec Institute, London, on 2 March 1876.[146] Like Thackeray a former parliamentary candidate, Trollope was not shy on the platform. Thomas Hardy heard him in December 1876, at a rally on the Eastern Question chaired by the Duke of Westminster, when he shared the limelight with Gladstone, Lord Shaftesbury, and others. Trollope ignored his allotted span; the Duke rang the bell, gesticulated, and, still failing to halt Trollope, pulled at his coat-tails, whereupon Trollope eyeballed him, menacingly said 'Please leave my coat alone,' and carried on.[147] But Trollope was not enamoured of lecturing, if only because 'I am better paid for writing.' So he told his American friend, the author–journalist, actress–singer Kate Field, who was a noted lyceum lecturer and keen to try out England:

I do not doubt you would have very large audiences; —but they do not pay well. £10 a lecture is about the mark if you can fill a large room—600 or 700—for our rooms are not as large as yours,—and our lectures are chiefly given to audiences who do not pay for tickets, but pay by the year. So that the managing committees cannot afford to pay much. I had a word to say the other day about fiction, and I lectured in four places, receiving £15 in two and £10 in two.[148]

[144] Taylor, *Thackeray*, 389.
[145] Letter to William Duer Robinson, 23 Jan.–25 Feb. 1858, in Harden (ed.), *Thackeray's Letters*, 323–4.
[146] Booth (ed.), *Trollope's Letters*, 352–3, 429.   [147] Hardy, *Life*, 112–13.
[148] To Kate Field (1838–96), 15 Apr. 1870, in Booth (ed.), *Trollope's Letters*, 261.

This was in 1870. Higher fees were obtainable on special occasions and for well-managed tours, featuring glamorous names. Dickens's rate was £80 for a night's readings by 1870, increased from the £50 per night he was paid in 1866;[149] but Trollope's observations were otherwise sobering about the different structures of the American and British local club and provincial institute circuits.

It is well known that many writers took to the circuit subsequently, some with bewildering frequency such as G. K. Chesterton, prompting in his case the famous telegram to his wife: 'Am in Market Harborough. Where ought I to be?'[150] What the mechanisms, above all what the profits were, is an altogether different issue, and deserving research. A couple of examples can be given. Oscar Wilde made so few (or so soon spent) profits from his American tour that he 'was obliged, much against his will' to tour Britain too. So wrote Robert Sherard, who added: 'It was a real penance to him, and I could understand this after I had seen how his lectures were advertised in the provincial papers. But his money needs were pressing, and perforce he had to lend himself to this exploitation of the notoriety gained in the period which he had renounced.'[151] Wilde in fact made two tours, during July 1883 and from autumn into spring 1884–5, the cycles being interrupted by a return visit to the United States and by his courtship and marriage. His agent was Colonel Morse, who had arranged the American tour in 1882; and his repertoire was the same, now reinforced by 'Impressions of America', 'The Value of Art in Modern Life', and 'Dress'. It was a gruelling schedule, appearing in some fifty places in England, twenty-one in Ireland, and several in Scotland and Wales, the Colonel remorselessly counting over 150 bookings, the majority from mechanics institutes. Fees were much lower than Wilde received in America, generally between 10 and 25 guineas per lecture;[152] but they assuaged some of the pain. At intervals Wilde would return to London to dine at the Café Royal, 'and on more than one occasion pulled out of the pocket of his fur coat a handful of notes and gold which he had earned so distastefully in the provinces'. Apart from the loot, Wilde used the provincial tour to educate himself in German: he 'beguiled the tedium of the journeys . . . by studying that language with a copy of the Reise-Bilder and a little pocket dictionary'.[153] Matthew Arnold appeared only resentful. He disliked the experience of lecturing in America in 1883 and 1886; when induced to lecture in Britain, he liked this no better. He wrote to the Warden of Merton on 26 January 1888, 'I am just off for the North to make a horrid discourse about America at Hull and at Bradford; I have then to prepare a horrid discourse about Milton . . . all before the middle of February.'[154] Still, once the intellectual investment had been made, it was vital that it should pay maximum dividends. J. A. Spender's first editorship was of the *Eastern Morning News*, based in Hull, where one day he was astonished to find Matthew Arnold striding

[149] See Michael Slater's notice of Dickens, *Oxford DNB*.

[150] Chesterton, *Autobiography*, 334–5; and Ward, *Gilbert Keith Chesterton*, 161, 313–14, for his topics and his shortcomings as lecturer. [151] Sherard, *Wilde*, 87–9.

[152] Ellmann, *Wilde*, 224–9, 245–7. [153] Sherard, *Wilde*, 156. [154] Brodrick, *Memories*, 263.

night'. Blunt further recorded how a war correspondent covering the Italian invasion of Tripoli 'arranged to give a course of lectures in the principal towns in England on the Italian barbarities. I offered to help him financially, but he said his lectures were to be well paid by a business firm, which had undertaken it at £10 a night.'[165] F. Carruthers Gould, assistant editor of the *Westminster Gazette*, had also lectured about the country 'on parliamentary subjects' which were illustrated by lantern reproductions of his cartoons. He endured the circuit for four years before retiring, not, however, from disappointment at the fees; rather, he averred, 'the hospitality he received was too much for him'.[166]

These examples are more properly classified as current affairs rather than literary lectures, and in this domain Bernard Shaw led for productivity. A Fabian Socialist, he gave sixty-six lectures in 1887 and had notched up almost 1,000 ten years later. Sunday was his favourite day for spouting. He had no set venue: indoors or outdoors, town hall or lamp-post. In 1908 he added 'public speaking' to his recreations in *Who's Who*.[167] This jocularity aside, Shaw suffered some self-disgust about booming himself; yet he cannot be convicted outright of mercenariness. It is indisputable that here was an author driven by serious political commitment. Shaw was pinched for money until the late 1890s brought him significant royalties from his plays and marriage to an heiress, but 'I have never spoken a word in public for money, though I have been offered absurdly large sums to break that rule.'[168]

Having a topical or sensational case counted on the organized lecture circuit. H. G. Wells, basking in the notoriety of *Ann Veronica* (1909) and *The New Machiavelli* (1911), enjoyed a one-off appearance at the *Times* Book Club in 1911, presenting a lecture on 'The Scope of the Novel'. Arnold Bennett attended and relished Wells's defiance; but he was more curious to study his audience, 'the "library" public in the mass!'—who turned out to be 'a thousand women and Mr. Bernard Shaw'.[169] Unmatched was the thriller-writer and 'professional alarmist' William Le Queux, whose *Invasion of 1910* was serialized by the *Daily Mail* prior to publication in 1906. Le Queux's campaign against German spies and call for their internment flourished during the Great War, when he delivered 228 lectures; but it is uncertain whether or what he was paid.[170] Better documentation exists for Arthur Benson. The Lecture Agency offered him £20 a night in January 1914 after receiving a report of how he enthralled an audience of 1,400 at Whitfield's Tabernacle with a lecture on Lewis Carroll, which Benson himself thought fell flat. By this time Benson was an established favourite with a suburban middle-class and aspiring working-class public, earning large sums by his writing: £20,000 in four years, he reckoned in 1910. He had produced poetry and novels, co-edited Queen Victoria's Letters, and furnished three studies for Macmillan's English Men of Letters series on Rossetti (1904), Edward FitzGerald

---

[165] Blunt, *Diaries*, ii. 341, 372 (26 Feb., 5 Dec. 1911).
[166] Robertson Scott, *'We' and Me*, 88; *Who's Who* (1905), 645.   [167] *Who's Who* (1908), 1658–9.
[168] Holroyd, *Shaw*, i. 192–6.   [169] *New Age*, 25 May 1911, in Bennett, *Books and Persons*, 315–16.
[170] Stearn, 'Mysterious Mr. Le Queux', 22.

(1905), and Walter Pater (1906); but it was his desultory homiletic essays that won him the largest following—'you are a kind of chaplain, you know, to many of us!', said Silvester Horne, the Liberal MP and Congregationalist minister.[171] Given his sales in Britain and America, Benson could reasonably calculate that 'about half-a-million people are interested in what I say'. The attacks he received—dubbed complacent and superficial by critics in the *British Review, The Academy*, and *New Age*[172]—while they added to his omnipresent sense of unworthiness, were evidence of his prominence. Hence the numbers willing to turn out to hear him: a capacity audience of 800 at the City Temple in 1911 apparently swelled to 1,000 when he returned there in 1912, and he needed bodyguards to shield him from admirers who followed him through the streets to King's Cross. At Kingsway Hall 1,200 people heard him lecture on 'Leaders of Men', and 1,500 packed into the Birmingham Institute. The occasional miscue notwithstanding—at the Lyceum in 1915 an audience assembled for a lecture on George Gissing when he came prepared to talk about Charlotte Brontë—Benson proved an outstanding success.[173]

VII

Several of the locations where Benson was invited to speak were citadels of religious Nonconformity. They had been equally thronged during the previous decade by audiences drawn to hear these sects' champion novelist, Silas K. Hocking.[174] The lecture, like the sermon, was a favoured medium of Victorian missionaries, combining uplifting accounts of the thousands converted from heathenism in obscure parts of the world with vivid descriptions of their own hardships and adventures. Janet Courtney, born in 1865, the daughter of an Anglican vicar in Lincolnshire, always associated them with ill-sung blasts of the hymn 'From Greenland's icy mountains', and amused herself by anticipating whether they would compare the size of their mission district to 'Yorkshire, or Ireland, or even the United Kingdom. There seemed to be a regular competition amongst them as to who had the biggest field of effort.'[175] Companion to the missionary lecture was the lecture designed to abet public improvement. So widespread was it that J. H. Balfour Browne even wrote of 'lecture mania' being 'an epidemic of the nineteenth century—a century which was under the impression that education and diffusion of knowledge by spoken words was the assurance for the progress of the race'.[176] As a loyal Scotsman, he attributed this

---

[171] Silvester Horne (1865–1914) is misspelled Sylvester Horne in Benson's diary, 11 Jan. 1914; Lubbock, *Benson*, 266. He was the author of histories of Free Church activities, of a biography of David Livingstone, and of volumes of sermons. In *Who's Who* (1905), 796, he described himself as an 'impenitent Radical, and advocate of modern Puritanism', listing 'agitating' among his recreations.

[172] The *New Age*'s critic was Arnold Bennett, as Jacob Tonson; see *New Age*, 1 Sept. 1910, in Bennett, *Books and Persons*, 239–41.

[173] Lubbock, *Benson*, 204, 230–1, 263, 267 (23 Jan. 1912, 21 Dec. 1913, 21 Jan. 1914); Newsome, *Edge of Paradise*, 243, 271–5.   [174] *M.A.P.*, 31 Dec. 1904, 766.

[175] Courtney, *Recollected in Tranquillity*, 73.   [176] Balfour Browne, *Recollections*, 124.

are incalculable.'[185] Still, he did not think these rivals dealt the death blow to the circuit. Good lecturers and big names remained in demand, 'as may be seen from the fact that I am regularly corresponding with some three thousand different persons associated with the management of lectures and platform entertainments, and at least sixty per cent of them are women'.[186]

Pond was dead when W. B. Yeats made his first North American visit, in November 1903–March 1904; but there was no question of him using Pond's agency (which continued under his widow). Yeats's arrangements were made by the rich Irish American lawyer John Quinn, who was a collector and patron of art and literature.[187] He had met Yeats in 1902, supported his and Lady Gregory's plans for an Irish theatre, produced small editions of their plays to secure their American copyright, and commissioned a portrait of Yeats by Charles Shannon. Yeats, who had begun writing for the *Boston Pilot* in 1889, gave over forty lectures on his 1903–4 tour in both America and Canada, on Irish history and Fenian heroes as well as on literature. According to Walter de la Mare, Yeats boasted an ability 'to lecture for an hour on any subject without preparation'. De la Mare doubted the worth that resulted: 'When Yeats talked, you could always see where he was getting to, but it was difficult to see what he was getting at. Perhaps that is true of a good many Irishmen.'[188] This question did not matter now because Yeats's North American audiences were chiefly Irish clubs and societies, and Catholic colleges ('who say they don't mind my heretical theology').[189] Yeats 'for the first time in his life earned a substantial sum of money', substantial, that is, relative to his penury: Yeats reached 50 years of age before he earned over £200 in a year from his books.[190] In fact, his American purses were exactly what Churchill had deemed disappointing: mostly £40, though sometimes £70, per lecture, totalling £1,600. The price—boredom, hoarseness, exhaustion, homesickness— was worth paying; and Yeats returned for another two-month lecture series in February 1914. In between he visited briefly with the Abbey theatre company, in 1911. He was drawn too to see his father, the painter J. B. Yeats, who was also on Quinn's payroll. Yeats *père* was supported in New York from 1908 by Quinn (in exchange for manuscripts from Yeats *fils*) and liked it so much that he resisted all family pressure to return to Dublin.

---

[185] Pond, *Eccentricities*, 548.   [186] Ibid. 550.

[187] Subsequently, in 1909, Quinn and Yeats quarrelled and ceased to communicate for five years when Quinn accused Yeats of trying to seduce his mistress. In 1911 Quinn began to invest in Joseph Conrad manuscripts, which sold for a large sum when Quinn auctioned them in 1923, much to their author's disgust. Quinn also bought and sold the manuscript of Joyce's *Ulysses*. Karl, *Conrad*, 701–2, 840; John Kelly and Schuchard (eds.), *Yeats Letters*, iii. 728–31, for a biographical sketch of Quinn.

[188] Brain, *Walter de la Mare*, 27, 59.

[189] Yeats to Lady Gregory, 16 Nov. 1903, in Wade (ed.), *Yeats Letters*, 413. Yeats also appeared in demand at genteel ladies' colleges on the east coast; Bryn Mawr, Smith, Vassar, Wellesley, and so forth. See John. S. Kelly, *A W. B. Yeats Chronology* (Basingstoke, 2005), 89–93, for a summary itinerary.

[190] Wade (ed.), *Yeats Letters*, 275. See also Yeats's correspondence with A. H. Bullen and Charles Elkin Matthews, 30 Oct. 1904, after Yeats received a demand for income tax on an estimated £500 a year. Inland Revenue inspectors had been misled by Yeats's reputation into thinking that he was earning a comfortable middle-class income. Yeats was compelled to appear at an inquiry and to submit detailed

W. B. Yeats made more than dollars by his tour. There was reputation too. In May 1904 Wilfrid Blunt noticed the difference at a dinner party involving Yeats, who was 'just back from America, where they have made a great fuss with him, and he takes himself very seriously in consequence'.[191] Some preening was forgivable in the circumstances. Yeats delightedly told Lady Gregory that a letter from some American schoolgirls at once found him in an envelope addressed simply 'Mr Yeats, Ireland'.[192] This confidence enabled him to go his own way lecturing in Britain. He informed the actress and co-explorer of the occult Florence Farr in 1906 that, though he had been refused by the lecture agencies because his reputation and his subjects were 'too esoteric for the general public outside certain university towns', he had nonetheless 'made hundreds of pounds' as one lecture engagement led to another. He had recently lectured in Dublin, and was planning other appearances in Leeds, Edinburgh, Oxford, and Cambridge.[193]

In spite of Conan Doyle's cautionary note, and a grumbling Winston Churchill, the consensus among authors therefore suggests that there was both money and renown to be gained from a North American tour. Confirmation of such profits, direct and indirect, is exemplified by J. M. Barrie and Arnold Bennett. Barrie's first visit—to New York, Boston, Washington, and New Orleans—was in 1896 and under the wing of his then patron, Robertson Nicoll; but it was the connection he made there with the theatre impresario Charles Frohman that was the key to Barrie's conversion from chiefly novelist to chiefly playwright, beginning with the adaptation of *The Little Minister* (novel 1891; play 1897) which inaugurated his prodigious moneymaking.[194] An American promoter was also indispensable for Arnold Bennett's progress. His American reputation flowered only from 1909, owing to the publisher George Doran, whose wife admired *The Old Wives' Tale* (1908).[195] As Bennett recorded in his journal on 27 October 1909, 'A year ago no American publisher would publish my work'; and, though Bennett was disgusted by the garishness of the American edition of *The Old Wives' Tale*—'an awful vermilion and gilt binding'—Doran's enthusiasm was vital in building up Bennett's name. In 1910 Doran's sold 12,000 copies and acquired Bennett's permission to republish a dozen earlier works; in addition, Bennett signed with Dutton's of New York a contract for £1,000, with generous royalty, for his next three novels.[196] The crowning moment came in March 1911, when Bennett was saluted from 'the Editor's Easy Chair' of *Harper's Monthly*: its author was the veteran

accounts before the inspectors accepted the truth of his modest income. Letters in Kelly and Schuchard (eds.), *Yeats's Letters*, iii. 664–5.

[191] Blunt, *Diaries*, ii. 100 (10 May 1904).

[192] Yeats to Lady Gregory, 10 Dec. 1909, in Wade (ed.), *Yeats Letters*, 543.

[193] Yeats to Florence Farr, 6 Feb. 1906, in Kelly and Schuchard (eds.), *Yeats's Letters*, iv. 334.

[194] Dunbar, *Barrie*, 107–10; Meynell (ed.), *Barrie Letters*, 10–11, 32.

[195] Bennett, *My Arnold Bennett*, 54–66, for a comical account of Bennett's preparations to impress Doran when he visited him at Fontainebleau.

[196] Flower (ed.) *Bennett Journals*, i. 329–30, 335, 361, 384, 390 (6, 27 Oct. 1909, 25 Feb., 21 Sept., 11 Nov. 1910).

commissioners. Writing to Hollingshead, he had endorsed the principle that a novelist should have property in his plot; then added,

I cannot imagine myself to feel much injured by the adaptation to the stage of any novel of mine. Indeed, I do not think I should refuse the use of a plot to any respectable dramatist who might pay me the compliment of asking for it. But I do feel very bitter against those who endeavour to palm off as their own the work of others.[5]

Trollope had been stung in 1872 when Charles Reade lifted the plot of *Ralph the Heir* (1871) for his play *Shilly Shally*, this being the same Reade who vigorously protected his own novel *It is Never Too Late to Mend* (1856) against unauthorized stage adaptations and mordantly complained about authors' inadequate security in *The Eighth Commandment* (1860)—'Thou shalt not steal. Except from authors'.[6] Francis Burnand, a prolific writer of burlesques and *Punch*'s editor from 1880, remained notably unsympathetic to the protectionists. Responding to a lecture on dramatic property, given by Hollingshead to the Society of Authors in 1887, he commented:

What law can prevent 'coincidences?' and what just remedy can there be for a sufferer by a coincidence? Old materials must be used over and over again, and the greater the genius the more utter is his disregard of what ordinarily talented men would consider from a narrow-minded and selfish point of view, their private and personal property. Why should the Dramatic Author who has hit upon what is to all intents and purposes the same plot as the Novelist be debarred from producing his play because the Novel comes out first?[7]

The novelists' cause, however, would shortly be won when Mrs Hodgson Burnett took to the courts, arguing for copyright infringement against an unauthorized adaptation of *Little Lord Fauntleroy*, in 1887–8.[8]

Stage adaptations thus constituted a thorny aspect of the copyright debate; but the most vexatious question concerned the republication of published work from country to country. Foreign authors enjoyed protection in British law so long as their countries extended similar safeguards to British subjects; and this generally European network became more widely international (while still excluding America and Russia) after the Berne Convention, 1885.[9] The prospects that beckoned for a commercially successful author were intoxicating. In 1886 Thomas Hardy and Aubrey de Vere 'made a calculation that if an international Copyright

---

[5] To John Hollingshead, 21 Apr. 1873, in Booth (ed.), *Trollope's Letters*, 308.
[6] Sutherland, *Companion*, 522–3.   [7] *Punch*, 26 Mar. 1887, 154.
[8] *Punch*, 10 Mar. 1888, 117; Thwaite, *Burnett*, 108–11.
[9] A notable pioneer, before copyright became binding throughout Europe, was the German publisher Tauchnitz (est. 1837), who published cheap, one-volume reprints of English novels for English readers and travellers on the Continent. Tauchnitz could have proceeded by piracy, but preferred to enter into contracts (for a £50 fee) with authors and to purchase rights. It was noted, at the half-century of Tauchnitz's business in 1887, that he had 276 British and 165 American writers on his list; and that the largest honorarium he had paid for the Continental edition of an author's works was to Macaulay, the largest for any single romance to Bulwer Lytton. See *T.P.'s Weekly*, 1 Apr. 1904, 448.

Bill were passed, in 50 years hence a writer of Scott's popularity (£10,000 a year to him) wd. be making £100,000 yearly—allowing for increase in the world's population'. Reporting their arithmetic to Edmund Gosse, Hardy queried: 'Can it be possible [?]'[10] Hardy subsequently learned, from tortuous negotiations with European translators and publishers, that it was no straightforward matter to execute profitable and reliable contracts abroad;[11] still, he found that 'a translation helps a book in England by a curious reflex action on the public. As you know, they are like sheep, & when they discover that foreigners think it worth while to translate a book, & are discussing it in their press, they feel that they, too, ought to read it.'[12] Hardy also knew, as a member of the Society of Authors, which persistently agitated about copyright, that authors would be deprived of the largest portion of this potential bonanza if America was not a party to agreement. As he put it in 1889, 'we shall be almost written out before anything is done with incorrigible America'.[13]

America was the largest market for English literature to stand outside this civilized intercourse. Though individuals received occasional ex gratia payments from American publishers—among the earliest was Dickens in 1838—British authors were substantially cheated of royalties by American pirates. F. J. Furnivall remembered Wordsworth furiously waving an American newspaper advertisement at his publisher: 'All my poems, Mr. Macmillan—for threepence!'[14] Henry James was thoroughly ashamed of his compatriots as yet another international copyright bill, the twelfth since 1843, went crashing in Congress in 1890: 'It seems as if this time we had said, loudly, that whereas we had freely admitted before that we in fact steal, we now seize the opportunity to decide that we *like* to steal.'[15] Malpractice had not been confined to one side of the Atlantic. Seventeen British publishers rushed to produce unauthorized versions of Mrs Beecher Stowe's *Uncle Tom's Cabin* (1852) when that book was the seasonal sensation;[16] and other popular American authors, such as Fenimore Cooper and Nathaniel Hawthorne, had cause for complaint. Nevertheless, the Americans' abuse appeared the more extensive. Anthony Trollope scaldingly wrote an Open Letter in the *Athenaeum*,

[10] Hardy to Gosse, 8 Sept. 1886, in Purdy and Millgate (eds.), *Hardy Letters*, i. 151.

[11] See numerous letters in the Purdy and Millgate collections, especially those from Hardy to Madeleine Rolland, 11 June, 7 and 25 July, and 21 Sept. 1897, to Henry Davray, 14 Nov. 1900, to Frederick Macmillan, 23 Mar. 1903.

[12] Hardy to Frederick Macmillan, 19 Mar. 1908, in Purdy and Millgate (eds.), *Hardy Letters*, iii. 309.

[13] Hardy to W. Moy Thomas, 7 Aug. 1889, ibid. 197. See also Hardy's letter to the editor of *The Graphic*, Arthur Locker, 18 Nov. 1889, negotiating serialization rights for *Tess*. Hardy said that he averaged £550 for serial rights in the UK (though he had received £600 for the last) and reckoned an average £250 from the United States for 'advance sheets exclusive of book rights', these sheets usually being used in Canada too. He added, 'What the book right is worth in the United States I cannot tell, the figures fluctuating greatly—about £50 it seems, the pirates keeping it down so low' (ibid. 202).   [14] Benzie, *Furnivall*, 259.

[15] To William Dean Howells, 17 May 1890, in Edel (ed.), *James Letters*, iii. 284.

[16] Over $20,000—more than £4,000—was raised, largely through a 'Penny Offerings' scheme, to compensate Mrs Stowe for this deprivation of royalties, during her British tour in 1853. She returned to England in 1856 specifically to secure copyright for the publication of *Dred*. Hedrick, *Harriet Beecher Stowe*, 240, 262.

6 September 1862, protesting against the American publisher Fletcher Harper's piracy of his travelogue *North America* (1862). American publishers had British authors over a barrel. Some simply published their own version of a British work without compunction; the more reputable houses would approach their British counterparts with a price, invariably a mean one, for the rights to publish in America, yet always with the implicit threat that they would copy the work anyway if their price was refused. Trollope and his publisher Chapman & Hall had succumbed to this kind of 'negotiation' by Fletcher Harper in regard to previous works; now, when for *North America* Trollope contracted with Lippincott's to publish in the United States, Harper brought out a pirated edition four days before Lippincott's and marketed it cheaply as a spoiling strategy. Trollope appealed for justice and honest dealings for British authors; sagaciously, he further observed that international copyright served the interests of American publishers too by affording them security against the piracy of their colleagues whenever they undertook British works.[17] In 1866 Trollope contributed a paper on the matter for the National Association for the Promotion of Social Science;[18] but a generation would pass before such arguments proved persuasive. Meanwhile, the Americans' piracy (or 'transfer' as Fletcher Harper euphemistically termed it) became more flagrant in the 1870s and 1880s, as publishers competed to feed a growing appetite for fiction with dime series of popular classics and current novels.[19] New sensations were eagerly snapped up. Mrs Humphry Ward's best-seller *Robert Elsmere*, published in Britain in February 1888, sold 100,000 copies in America by November, three times its British sales. In this case, the American pirates overestimated demand: stores were reportedly advertising it at the knock-down price of 4 cents or offloading it free with a bar of Balsam Fir Soap, which perhaps explains why an American publisher sent a mere £100 conscience money, to which Macmillan's, which exported its colonial edition to the United States added £250.[20]

In 1890 the young Kipling again exposed Harper's sharp practice by returning with contempt an ex gratia payment of £10 after it published without permission a collection of his short stories; and he savaged Walter Besant, William Black, and Thomas Hardy in his 'Rhyme of the Three Captains' for pleading that Harper's treatment of them had been 'just and liberal'. This appeasement, especially that by Besant, the founder of the Society of Authors, requires a little explanation. Kipling's outburst was unfortunate in its timing, Besant fearing that it would jeopardize the Society's discreet lobbying and endanger the Copyright Bill then being debated in Congress. In any case, he thought,

It was absurd to keep calling the Americans thieves and pirates while our people did exactly the same thing on a smaller scale. It exasperated Americans and weakened the

[17] Booth (ed.), *Trollope's Letters*, 119–26, for the *Athenaeum* letters, 6 Sept. and 25 Oct. 1862, the second being Trollope's rejoinder after Fletcher Harper had replied to the first.   [18] Ibid. 190.
[19] Reynolds, *Fiction Factory*, 29–30, 75–6.
[20] Trevelyan, *Mrs. Ward*, 75; Sutherland, *Mrs Ward*, 129–31.

efforts of those who were manfully fighting in the cause of international honesty. Such influence as we possessed we brought to bear in this direction, with, one hopes and believes, a certain allaying of irritation.[21]

Cultivating the sympathy of American authors was the Society's preferred method, as, for example, by its dinner to honour James Russell Lowell and others, on 25 July 1888. Only with strong domestic support was the American Copyright Act in 1891 made possible; and the *Review of Reviews*, in welcoming its passage, credited Robert Underwood Johnson, of the *Century Magazine*, and the publisher George Putnam, with having been to the fore in the movement.[22]

Until this point was reached, authors considered various stratagems to avoid American theft. The most drastic was an arranged marriage, that is, to accept an American co-author. Wolcott Balestier, arriving in London in 1888 as agent for the New York publisher John W. Lovell, sought to promote himself in this style, with overtures to Mrs Humphry Ward and all. His ambition, he liked to say, was to have his finger on the pulse of literature. According to Edmund Gosse, he achieved this and more:

There was not one English novelist from George Meredith and Mr. Thomas Hardy down to the most obscure and 'subterranean' writer of popular tales, with whom he did not come into relations of one sort or another . . . Balestier knew them all, knew their current value, appraised them for future quotation . . . Within twelve months he knew the English book-market as, probably, no Englishman knew it.

Gosse first met Balestier at Mrs Humphry Ward's, and thereafter saw him 'almost daily for nearly three years'. It was he who alerted Balestier about Kipling as the rising literary star.[23] True to form, Balestier then made it his business to get close to Kipling. He so far succeeded as to collaborate with him over *The Naulahka*. This was published in 1892, too late for Balestier to enjoy his triumph: he died a week short of his thirtieth birthday, of typhoid in December 1891, though Kipling afterwards married his sister Caroline and moved to Vermont, where their house was named Naulakha.[24]

The orthodox way of circumventing American piracy was to publish first with an American publisher. In the early 1870s Tennyson accepted an annual fee of £500 from James T. Fields, for advance copies of his poems prior to their publication in Britain.[25] This sum was considerably less than Tennyson's fees at home; nor, as Trollope had pointed out, did such agreements guarantee protection. Wilkie Collins, who published with Harper's, profited little when another American publisher cashed in by selling 120,000 copies of *The Woman in White* (1860): 'He

---

[21] Besant, *Autobiography*, 222–3. For a defence of Hardy's position, see Millgate, *Hardy*, 308; and Purdy and Millgate (eds.), *Hardy Letters*, i. 218–20, 223. [22] *Review of Reviews* (Apr. 1891), 319–20.

[23] Gosse, 'Wolcott Balestier, 1861–1891', in Gosse, *Portraits and Sketches*, 215-25. Conan Doyle was also on Balestier's payroll; Booth, *Conan Doyle*, 167.

[24] Birkenhead. *Kipling*, 115-17, 132–3. The difference in spelling—*Naulahka* and 'Naulakha'—is explained by Birkenhead: the first was perhaps a mistake by Balestier. It referred to a fabulous jewel.

[25] Martin, *Tennyson*, 502.

never sent me sixpence,' Collins fumed.[26] Jerome K. Jerome also suffered. His original best-seller *The Idle Thoughts of an Idle Fellow* (1886) was taken up by the hundred thousand in America, from which he derived nothing; and he fared little better from his principal best-seller *Three Men in a Boat* (1889), which sold over a million there. He had published it in America through Henry Holt, whose integrity Jerome later acknowledged for sending him annually a small cheque; but other American publishers issued pirated editions aplenty and, Jerome ruefully reflected, 'I reckon my first and worst misfortune in life was being born six years too soon; or, to put it the other way round, that America's conscience, on the subject of literary copyright, awoke in her bosom six years too late for me.'[27]

American publishers and editors would make periodic visits to London, touting for business. In August 1889 Joseph Marshall Stoddart, the Philadelphia publisher of *Lippincott's Magazine*, entertained Conan Doyle and Oscar Wilde at the Langham Hotel, Portland Place, and snapped up *The Sign of Four* and *The Picture of Dorian Gray* as a result.[28] A stipulation of publishing first (or simultaneously) with an American publisher was built into legislation in 1891 and 1909, when American copyright was at last extended to foreign authors provided they deposited in the Library of Congress two copies of their book, which must be printed and bound within the United States. This was not ideal for British authors; still, it was a distinct improvement upon piratical anarchy and, appropriately, one of the first beneficiaries of the 1891 Act was Mrs Humphry Ward, who sold the American rights of *David Grieve*, sight-unseen, to Macmillan's for the record sum of £7,000.[29] Other opportunities followed. In 1896 the publisher Charles Scribner, who was issuing *Sentimental Tommy* serially in magazines before bringing out the book, suggested to J. M. Barrie that they utilize the 1891 Act to launch a uniform edition of his works, with some minor textual revisions and prefaces so as to cloak the recycling as a 'new' product.[30]

Several British authors now made substantial sums from America, and their titles featured regularly in that country's best-seller charts before 1914. But it was not a tenable prospect for the majority. In the *Fortnightly Review*, July 1890, Gosse anticipated that, were American copyright to be gained, certain British authors— 'perhaps at the extreme limit, fifteen'—would profit hugely and a considerable number, mostly novelists, would be able to make better terms. Otherwise,

the bulk of the writing tribe, and among them some of the most celebrated of living names, will find that American copyright improves their financial condition not an iota. The people who will benefit from the adoption of copyright, and that instantly and largely, are the authors of America. The present condition of the law is positively annihilating American literature. The first direct action of the Copyright Law, when it

---

[26] Peters, *Collins*, 357.   [27] Jerome, *Life and Times*, 61,

[28] James Payn, the *Cornhill*'s editor, had acted as intermediary; Booth, *Conan Doyle*, 132.

[29] Sutherland, *Mrs Ward*, 137–8. The American Macmillan's became an independent company in 1896; Morgan, *Macmillan*, 163–4.   [30] Dunbar, *Barrie*, 102.

passes, will be to destroy an immense crop of base English fiction, and to give the young American novelist, of the better class, a chance of being heard.[31]

Gosse was not the first to see this. It was a point made by Dickens when he waged his one-man campaign for international copyright during his first American tour, though his hosts were so upset that they were blinded to the case. In Boston, on 1 February 1842, Dickens had implored America to enter into an international arrangement: 'It becomes the character of a great country,' he declared; '*firstly*, because it is justice; *secondly*, because without it you never can have, and keep, a literature of your own.'[32] That prediction was confirmed by Hall Caine, after he represented the Society of Authors to the government of Canada on the copyright question.[33] As he put it in 1908, American copyright did

more than secure justice for the English author—it had created the American author as a professional man of letters. Literature as a profession was for the first time beginning to live; and it is no matter of surprise to me that in the few years that have intervened, America's books have ousted English books in the favour of the American people.[34]

II

The need to manage American outlets encouraged more writers both to seek advice from the Society of Authors and to turn to literary agents.[35] These developments received stimulus in any case from authors' anxieties to secure better terms from indigenous publishers. Some agents, it emerged, were no better than the worst publishers. Conan Doyle and J. M. Barrie were defrauded of £8,000 and £16,000 respectively by the theatrical agent Arthur Addison Bright.[36] Wilkie Collins was also the victim of an unscrupulous agent, Stefan Poles, on whom he

---

[31] *Review of Reviews* (July 1890), 54.   [32] Fielding (ed.), *Dickens's Speeches*, 21.

[33] Canada caused problems for British authors, again because of its government's desire to include a 'manufacturing clause' in legislation, by which the copyright of foreign authors was conditional upon their works being actually printed in Canada. On Caine's visit in 1895, see his entry in *Who's Who* (1905), 244; and *DNB 1931–1940*, 137. The Authors' Society felt that further representations were needed in 1898, when it sent out to Canada the secretary, G. H. Thring; see Thring's entry in *Who Was Who, 1941–1950*, 1151. Wilkie Collins was apparently the first to check a piracy in Canada by arranging for the separate publication there of *Man and Wife*, in 1870. The problem of the American market was complicated by this, as Canadian copies crossed the border; Peters, *Collins*, 316.   [34] Caine, *My Story*, 370.

[35] Arnold Bennett found literary agents especially good at placing his journalism in America: Hepburn (ed.), *Bennett Letters*, i. 237. See also Thomas Hardy's letter to G. Herbert Thring, secretary of the Society of Authors, 4 March 1902, when Hardy was uncertain of his position in America following the publishing takeover of Osgood McIlvaine & Co. by Harper's; Purdy and Millgate (eds.), *Hardy Letters*, iii. 7–8.

[36] Booth, *Conan Doyle*, 284; Mackail, *J.M.B.*, 389–90; Dunbar, *Barrie*, 148–9. The frauds came to light when Bright committed suicide, having fled to Switzerland, in 1906. He had acted for Barrie since 1894 and was instrumental in establishing Barrie's American editions and connections with the impresario Charles Frohman, who owned theatres on both sides of the Atlantic. Remarkably, Barrie thereafter entrusted his theatrical business to R. Golding Bright, who was able to sort out his elder brother's affairs because Addison, equally remarkably, had banked rather than spent the misappropriated money. Conan Doyle, on the other hand, first turned to another theatrical agent, Arthur Hardy, then took charge of negotiations himself; and for his other literary work used A. P. Watt.

rate[50]—because 'I have for many years been able to get good prices for my books from the magazines & from the publishers for the early and costly editions.'[51]

Having a genius for misery, Gissing was admittedly no easy man to market. Still, once he started using literary agents his income rose. From 1886 to 1891 he averaged £120 p.a. and from 1892 to 1899, £345 p.a., though cause and effect are not straightforward. The equation ignores the changing nature of his work and public taste. Even in the better period he experienced another dire year, 1897, when he earned £102; and during the last years of his short life his income was erratic, £297 in 1900, £723 in 1901 (his best ever), and £442 in 1902–3. When Gissing first employed an agent, A. P. Watt, he hardly strengthened his hand by insisting that the manuscript of *Born in Exile* be sold quickly because he needed cash. After doing the rounds of reluctant publishers, Watt sold it outright to A. & C. Black for £150, half down and half on publication, which, after Watt's commission, left Gissing with £135. Gissing on his own negotiated better terms for *Denzil Quarrier* in the same year, when Lawrence & Bullen offered £100 down and a royalty of one-sixth of sales. Gissing had not entrusted Watt to take over his entire affairs. In 1893 he ditched him for William Morris Colles when he resumed short-story writing and required an agent who was versed in this expanding sector. 'I am entered upon the commercial path,' Gissing declared. 'But I shall try not to write rubbish.' Colles did well for Gissing in screwing higher rates out of that 'scoundrel' Shorter—Clement Shorter, who was then editor of three journals, the *Illustrated London News*, the *English Illustrated Magazine*, and *Sketch*.[52] Colles also persuaded Gissing to join the Society of Authors, with which in its formative years Colles was closely involved.[53] Again, however, Gissing's relations with his agent began to cloud. He bypassed Colles in sending *Eve's Ransom* (1895) to Lawrence & Bullen, and he would not maintain the output of short stories, preferring to concentrate on longer fiction. In 1898 Gissing changed agents a second time, moving to J. B. Pinker, whose fresh approach, he believed, would help him both to realize his literary ambitions and to produce the money he needed to support three establishments, this being the cumulative wreckage from his disastrous private life. And it seemed to work: he reported with satisfaction to H. G. Wells that, whereas Colles had obtained £250 advance from Methuen for *The Town Traveller* (1898), Pinker raised £300 for *The Crown of Life* (1899).[54]

Gissing's mobility between agents was hardly unique. Somerset Maugham shuffled the same pack in different sequence, moving from Colles to Pinker to

---

[50] To George Bentley, 10 Feb. 1875, ibid. 333.   [51] To Thomas Hardy, 27 Mar. 1877, ibid. 367.
[52] Shorter (1857–1926) was a former civil servant. *DNB 1922–1930*, 771–2 suggests that he turned to journalism as 'a joyous adventure, out of which he made much less profit than he might have done if money had been his main object'. By 1897 he was simultaneously editor of five journals; he further founded *Sphere* (1900) and the *Tatler* (1903). Marshall, *Out and About*, 126, recalled that Shorter was known as Dirty Clem on account of his 'being dark in appearance and not too well brushed'.
[53] Bonham-Carter, *Authors by Profession*, ch. 8. Colles himself was once a journalist.
[54] Duffy, *Methuen*, 46. Other information on Gissing's income and dealings contained in this paragraph is from Halperin, *Gissing*.

Watt;[55] and H. G. Wells, originally with Pinker, quarrelled with most agents.[56] May Sinclair demonstrated both jitters and an amount of independence. Unhappy about the half-profits system under which she published her first novel, *Audrey Craven* (1897), with Blackwood's, she joined Watt; but she became concerned that this move had alienated Blackwood's when her second novel, *Mr. and Mrs. Nevill Tyson*, sold poorly. She broke with Watt in 1904—'the best day's work I ever did'—after she found for herself an American publisher, Henry Holt, for her third novel, *The Divine Fire*. When that became a hit in the United States and accordingly generated interest at home, Sinclair held an auction between Pinker and Curtis Brown for her account, eventually settling on Brown. There was a double irony about this: not only was Henry Holt hostile to literary agents, but *The Divine Fire* also attacked the commercialization of literature.[57]

Henry James too dipped a toe before plunging. He first considered joining Watt in 1888 after the shock of having a short story ('The Pupil') refused by the *Atlantic*;[58] but he did not stable himself permanently with an agent, Pinker, until 1898, when he was wanting to put all his literary affairs on a sounder footing and find money to purchase Lamb House in Rye.[59] By 1906 he was describing Pinker as 'a blessing unspeakable—I simply couldn't live without him'.[60] In 1915 Pinker's name was among the signatories supporting James's application for British nationality. The introduction of agents into the literary marketplace was bound to cause friction, however, and not simply with publishers who sought to preserve former relations and vested interests and, as may be, inefficient or dishonest practices. The poet John Davidson, not in the greatest demand and not an easy man to deal with, confided to George Gissing over lunch in 1896 that he was 'having trouble with editors etc. because of his employing Watt as his agent. Asks £25 for any poem but the very shortest.'[61]

Even without prickly personalities, authors' assumptions required delicate handling. When an author received modest terms, he rarely reckoned that an accurate measure of his work but rather blamed the agent's poor performance and begrudged his 10 per cent. When he was well rewarded he presumed the agent had a simple task because the work was self-evidently excellent. Agents were little use to new authors, indeed to anyone without some market reputation. Not even Pinker could make money for Frederick Rolfe, Baron Corvo;[62] or from the first book written by A. A. Milne, *Lovers in London* (1905), which he placed for

[55] In 1909 Maugham was successfully sued by Colles for withholding his commission, to the dismay of the Society of Authors; Morgan, *Maugham*, 64–6, 110–11, 116–17, 142, 171–2, 268, 513.

[56] Bonham-Carter, *Authors by Profession*, 183–4.   [57] Raitt, *Sinclair*, 79-96.

[58] Edel (ed.), *James Letters*, iii. 194. See his letter to Edmund Gosse, 3 Jan. 1888, ibid. 210–11.

[59] Edel, *James*, ii. 13–14, 350–2, 790.

[60] Henry James to Edith Wharton, 2 July 1906, in Powers (ed.), *Letters*, 65. James introduced Wharton to Pinker after Pinker told him that 'he yearned to have you for a client'.

[61] Coustillas (ed.), *Gissing's Diary*, 399–400 (11 Jan. 1896).

[62] A. J. A. Symons, *The Quest for Corvo* (1940), 123, 128. Rolfe severed relations with his first agent, Stanhope Sprigge, on discovering that he was a Catholic. Rolfe had also converted to Catholicism, but he had a paranoia about a Jesuit conspiracy to ensnare him.

£15 with an unheard-of publisher, Alston Rivers, dubbed 'the Alston Rivers Mining and Exploration Company' by the embarrassed author.[63] Curtis Brown, whose agency started in 1899, was quite candid about the market conditions:

Much that has been written about the literary agent has been futile, because the writers have not understood that authors can be divided into two classes: first, those whose work the publisher doesn't particularly want; and second, those whose work the publisher does want, or would want if he knew of it; and that it is only with the second class that a sound literary agent has, or should have, to do. Unless an author's work gives decided promise, he is of little interest to the publisher, or to the first-class agent. No agent, except one who takes 'retainers', can afford to spend much time over him. He can generally find a market for his work as well as a good agent, and better than a bad agent; and he can afford a more thorough canvass than either . . . The only agent who really counts, either for the author, or with the publisher, or with his own banker, is the one who sells the kind of work for which publishers are in competition, and who takes advantage of that competition to get the best market price for the author.[64]

Both Curtis Brown and his partner, Hughes Massie, were Americans; and this made them attractive to British authors wanting to exploit opportunities in that country. A friend of Curtis Brown and his wife, who lived in St John's Wood, was Constance Smedley, founding secretary of the Lyceum; and she for a time acted as European commissioning agent for two American magazines, *Everybody's* and *Delineator*. It was through her that Kenneth Grahame placed *The Wind in the Willows* (1908) with Curtis Brown; she also introduced May Sinclair, W. J. Locke, and others.[65] It was Curtis Brown too who sought to relaunch Mrs Humphry Ward's best-selling appeal in 1908 by auctioning her stories to American mass-circulation magazines, despite her demurral about this downmarket character.[66] Naturally, Curtis Brown was a conduit for authors wanting to move in the opposite direction, promoting American authors in Britain. He was agent for Edgar Rice Burroughs, author of the aristocratic ape-man Tarzan, whose inaugural tale Methuen published in Britain in 1917.[67] Other agents also processed this two-way traffic: Jack London asked A. P. Watt to negotiate the British serialization of *The Call of the Wild* in 1903.[68]

---

[63] Thwaite, *Milne*, 113–15, where it is noted that 'Milne eventually bought back his copyright for £5 to prevent a reprint.' Milne left Pinker for Curtis Brown during the Great War.

[64] Curtis Brown, 'The Commercialisation of Literature', *Fortnightly Review* (Aug. 1906), quoted in Bonham-Carter, *Authors by Profession*, 170. Cf. *Punch*, 14 June 1905, 421, for its satirical account of 'The Shelley Literary Agency', with its object of assisting 'young, inexperienced, or (more rarely) bashful' authors.   [65] Smedley, *Crusaders*, 153–5.

[66] Sutherland, *Mrs Ward*, 286–7. Dorothy Richardson was also on Curtis Brown's books, and Julia Frankau (Frank Danby) and Arthur Ransome had Hughes Massie as their agent; see Rosenberg, *Richardson*, 95; Gilbert Frankau, *Self-Portrait: A Novel of his Own Life* (1939), 186; and the prefatory note in Ransome, *Bohemia in London*.

[67] Duffy, *Methuen*, 75, 77. *Tarzan of the Apes* appeared in America in 1914, followed by *The Return of Tarzan* (1915) and *The Son of Tarzan* (1917). Burroughs (1875–1950) had never been to Africa. Methuen also published in 1919 the first of his Martian series, *A Princess of Mars* (1917), but this was not so successful.

[68] Jack London, *The Call of the Wild, White Fang, and Other Stories*, introd. and ed. Earle Labor and Robert C. Leitz III, World's Classics (Oxford, 1990), p. xxiii.

In 1912 the Society of Authors advised its members to make agreements with agents only for a year at a time, to allow them to negotiate all rights but not to complete any contract without specific permission or for a commission exceeding 10 per cent. This was inspired by the knowledge that there existed 'not so much authors' agents as agents' agents and publishers' agents';[69] but it was not just the Authors' Society that had qualms. Publishers were peeved when authors who, they felt, owed their success to them, turned to literary agents in order to exploit that success. Thus John Lane fumed when M. P. Willcocks went to Curtis Brown after *Wingless Victory* (1907): 'd—n literary agents', he wrote, 'especially Curtis Brown'. Lane had only himself to blame. He was notoriously tight-fisted; as the centenary history of the Bodley Head explained, 'Lane was never one to economize, except on his authors.'[70] The publisher William Heinemann had been so vexed by A. P. Watt's activities that he endeavoured to snuff out agents at their birth, as a species of parasite, by appealing in the *Athenaeum* in 1893 for publishers to unite against them;[71] yet in time Heinemann and the rest of the publishing world would accommodate not just the agents' 10 per cent but royalty rates for best-selling authors of 25 per cent and more—33 ⅓ per cent if Robertson Nicoll's report about Hall Caine, the champion best-seller on Heinemann's list, is credited.[72]

Publishers' avidity to acquire popular idols made them silly, like gamblers. They offered 'grotesquely inflated' terms and, when these were not recovered, they complained of having been swindled. Arnold Bennett had no sympathy: 'though I have often met publishers who have got the better of literary agents, I have never met a literary agent who has come out on top of a publisher'. Publishers pelting big-name authors with fantastic sums, on the assumption that everything they wrote would be a hit, was a disaster entirely of their own making, rather than a tribute to the hypnotizing power of their agents. The majority of authors did not enjoy such market leverage; thus, publishers suffered little in the round, although, Bennett added sardonically, 'I have heard that one publisher, hitherto accustomed to the services of twenty gardeners at his country house, has

[69] Quoted in Bonham-Carter, *Authors by Profession*, 171.

[70] Lambert and Ratcliffe, *Bodley Head*, 119, 159. On M. P. Willcocks (1869–1952): Kemp *et al.* (eds.), *Edwardian Fiction*, 418–19.

[71] Watt defended himself by issuing *Letters to A. P. Watt*, a collection of testimonials from authors who enjoyed his services. A notable coup was the inclusion of a letter from Andrew Chatto, founder of the publishing firm of Chatto & Windus in 1873, who published Wilkie Collins, Walter Besant, and other popular authors in Watt's stable. Chatto testified that, in arranging for the magazine serialization of books, literary agents could be especially helpful. See Peters, *Collins*, 369–70; *The Academy*, 3 Apr. 1897, 380.

[72] James Hepburn, *The Author's Empty Purse and the Rise of the Literary Agent* (Oxford, 1968), 89. Note the spoof in Stephen and Lee (eds.), *Lives of the 'Lustrious*, 40: 'HEINEMANN, WILLIAM, Publisher, was born at Greeba, in the Isle of Man, and educated at Mill Hill, where among his schoolfellows was Mr. A. P. Watt. The two boys soon became inseparable; more than once they saved each other's lives; and the friendship then began grows stronger with every year. Mr. Heinemann's enterprise as a publisher stops only at his own dramas, which have been issued from the Bodley Head. Authorities: Information supplied Messrs. Hall Caine, John Lane, and the Queen of Greeba.' Greeba Castle, Isle of Man, was Hall Caine's residence, purchased from the profits of his novels.

been obliged to reduce the horticultural staff to eighteen.'[73] Still, a publisher's prejudice against agents and desire to wean authors off them could improve their lot. When the young Irish poet and novelist James Stephens intimated to Frederick Macmillan in 1913 that he was planning to abandon Pinker, Macmillan instructed: 'We must see that we treat him liberally so that he may realise that he is losing nothing by dealing with us direct.' The offer was made to raise his royalty from 10 to 25 per cent; and the firm was later prepared to do the same for Æ (George Russell) and W. B. Yeats, assuming that Stephens would confide his rate to these friends.[74] Going it alone was not impossible. Characteristically seeking to be independent of everybody was Bernard Shaw. By organizing the entire publication of *Man and Superman* (1903), subcontracting the printing to Clark's of Edinburgh and inducing Constable's to take a commission on the distribution, Shaw tried to do without *both* agents *and* publishers in a formal sense. In this, however, he was only following the example of John Ruskin and Herbert Spencer.[75]

Generally, literary agents professionalized and systemized the role of middle-man between author and publisher which had many antecedents, in the form of solicitors, publishers' readers, and well-connected authors' friends and relations, such as John Forster's negotiations on behalf of Leigh Hunt, Dickens, and others, or Theodore Watts's on behalf of Swinburne.[76] Walter Besant had signed up with A. P. Watt in 1883 only after the death in the previous year of his regular co-author James Rice, who had been editor of *Once a Week*, had legal training, and freely served as Besant's agent.[77] Personal connections likewise were exploited by Robert Louis Stevenson. One was Charles Baxter, a friend from student days, who endeavoured to bring order to the sometimes conflicting agreements which Stevenson had made with different publishers. Stevenson also used another friend, the poet and editor W. E. Henley, to whom he paid what he euphemis-tically termed 'loans' for the agent services he rendered, such as arranging £100 advance for *Treasure Island*.[78] These informal ministrations were not now dis-placed so much as supplemented by literary agents. Thus, Winston Churchill's first book was handled by A. P. Watt after Watt was recommended by Lady Randolph Churchill, herself advised by Arthur Balfour, the Conservative leader, who was a client of Watt.[79] However, when it came to finding a publisher for the

---

[73] *New Age*, 20 June 1908, in Bennett, *Books and Persons*, 22–5.

[74] Nowell-Smith (ed.), *Letters to Macmillan*, 302–7.

[75] Bernard Shaw to Daniel Macmillan, 11 Sept. 1943, ibid. 190–4.

[76] James A. Davies, *John Forster: A Literary Life* (Leicester, 1983); Gosse, *Life of Swinburne*, 214–5.

[77] See Simon Eliot's notice of Besant in *Oxford DNB*.

[78] See letters to Henley, Apr. 1882, to Edmund Gosse, 20 May 1883, to Charles Scribner, 20 or 21 Nov. 1887, in Colvin (ed.), *Stevenson's Letters*, i. 238, 268, ii. 74; Mackay, *Violent Friend*, 126, 165, 173. Stevenson collaborated with Henley in playwriting, *Beau Austin* (1890) and others.

[79] Balfour published works on the philosophy of religion. Robertson Nicoll, acting as literary adviser to Hodder & Stoughton, conducted an unusual negotiation with him in 1913: 'A. J. Balfour has given me his new book to publish. He actually refused the terms I offered, on the ground that they were too high! This has happened to me only once before in a long experience' (Nicoll to Sir George Riddell, 21 Feb. 1913, in

potentially best-selling biography of his father, Winston in 1905 turned to Frank Harris, the retired editor and still restless roué. Harris had known Lord Randolph; more to the point, Harris boasted of knowing the literary market. Winston was thrilled by what he regarded as Harris's coup: Macmillan's gave £8,000 for the copyright. Harris also seemed satisfied with a commission of 5 per cent, for which in addition he undertook proof revision duty; but Morris Coles, whose agency held a letter from Churchill asking him to submit offers, was thoroughly put out and demanded to be paid too.[80] Coles had also been chagrined in 1894 when George Meredith broke with him in order to place his literary affairs—and stock-market investments—in the hands of his own son Will, who would shortly become a partner in the publishers Constable & Co.[81]

A. P. Watt was probably the first of the modern agents, beginning irregularly around 1875 and formally styling himself as such in 1881. It was Watt who first charged the 10 per cent commission still generally used. Watt was previously involved in the Scottish publishing firm of Alexander Strahan, having married Strahan's sister. His move into literary agency seems to have been a natural progression of two activities: selling advertising space in Strahan's magazines, and redirecting to other publishers fiction that Strahan could no longer afford to buy.[82] Walter Besant introduced Rider Haggard to Watt in 1885 on the strength of the service he had given both him and Wilkie Collins.[83] The boldest move was made by John Buchan, who, in his first year as an Oxford undergraduate, in 1895–6, started to use Watt to handle the serial rights of his stories; and, while for the moment retaining control of his book negotiations, Buchan declared his intention 'never for a moment [to] go below ten per cent royalty, which is as much as I could get through Watt'.[84] For others, Watt appeared a miracle-worker, a veritable Jeeves, or, as Ford Madox Ford dubbed him, a cross between 'a bishop and a butler'.[85] A particular pleasure in 1897 was to capture Robert Hichens, who published with Heinemann. Watt told Hichens that he could more than double his earnings if he joined him. Hichens did so, and remained with the firm for the rest of his life, testifying in 1947: 'Almost as soon as Mr Watt took charge of my business affairs my finances became much more prosperous.'[86]

Darlow, *Nicoll*, 228). The intended book was based on Balfour's Gifford Lectures, 'Theism and Humanism', which he gave at the University of Glasgow in 1914, and which Hodder & Stoughton published in 1915.

[80] Frank Harris to Winston Churchill, 14 Oct. 1905, in Churchill. *Churchill*, Companion vol. ii/1. pp. 469. The saga can be followed on 467–94.

[81] Meredith to William M. Coles, 15 Jan. 1894, and to W. M. Meredith, 12 Nov. 1894, in Cline (ed.), *Meredith's Letters*, iii. 1151–2, 1177. Coles had been employed by Meredith only since 1892, on a reduced commission of 5 per cent.   [82] Srebrnik, *Strahan*, 182, 242.

[83] Higgins, *Haggard*, 85.

[84] Smith, *Buchan*, 50, 104, 293, who notes that for several of his early books Buchan enjoyed a 15 per cent royalty, and subsequently obtained 25 per cent rising to 30 and 33⅓ per cent.

[85] Ford, *Return to Yesterday*, 50.

[86] Hichens, *Yesterday*, 106. Most of Hichens's subsequent best-sellers, *The Garden of Allah* and *The Call of the Blood*, were placed with Methuen, though *Bella Donna* was again with Heinemann.

Grant Allen, G. K. Chesterton, S. R. Crockett, Conan Doyle, Anthony Hope, William Le Queux, Baroness Orczy, Sir Gilbert Parker, M. P. Shiel, and Stanley Weyman, all used Watt. So did W. B. Yeats, who placed most arrangements with him from 1901, though this generated little revenue. Royalties on *Samhain*, which Yeats edited in 1901, amounted to £5 14s. 3d., from which Watt deducted his 10s. and sundry pence;[87] and in 1902 Yeats was telling Lady Gregory how 'desperately hard up' he was.[88] Watt's greatest prize had come ten years before, in 1890–1. This was Kipling, who recalled no serious difference with the firm in a profitable association lasting four decades.[89] In earning power in the Edwardian period, however, even Kipling was probably outstripped by Marie Corelli, who placed all her literary affairs with Watt from 1904.[90] She was an important catch, not just in terms of revenue: Corelli was on record as boasting of not employing literary agents and of managing her own business.[91]

At the Authors' Club in 1910 Robertson Nicoll pronounced that on the whole literary agents had well served the interests of both authors and publishers over the past quarter-century.[92] Though a known friend of Watt, Nicoll was assuming the part of peacemaker, and he had sufficiently diverse experience as author, critic, editor, and publishers' adviser to give credibility to his verdict. As a prolific author, Arnold Bennett had no doubts. Altogether there were some thirty literary agencies offering services by 1913, when he argued in the Society of Authors' magazine, *The Author*, that 'every author of large and varied output ought to put the whole of his affairs into the hands of a good agent'.[93] George Egerton (Mary Chavelita Dunne), famed author of *Keynotes* (1893), did so comprehensively: her third marriage, in 1901, was to the literary and dramatic agent R. Golding Bright, whereupon she also began to supply agency services to such as Bernard Shaw and Somerset Maugham.[94] However, a great many authors, particularly novices, continued to operate on their own account. To a wily operator such as the publisher Grant Richards, they were lambs to the slaughter. Philip Gibbs, knighted in 1920 for his work as war correspondent, told Cecil Roberts how

[87] The proceeds were given to the Gaelic League; see Yeats to Lady Gregory, 20 Jan. 1902, in Wade (ed.), *Yeats Letters*, 364. The royalties on *Poems, 1899–1905* and *Ideas of Good and Evil* were also tiny; see F. Sidgwick to A. P. Watt, 3 and 30 Oct. 1907, in Bodleian Library, Oxford, Sidgwick & Jackson MSS, Letter-book 1, fos. 283, 312.

[88] Yeats to Lady Gregory, 13 June 1902, in Kelly and Schuchard (eds.), *Yeats Letters*, iii. 202. In 1910 Yeats told W. S. Blunt that he was making 'only about £30 a year by the sale of his poetry' (Blunt, *Diaries*, ii. 310 (5 June 1910)).

[89] Kipling, *Something of Myself*, 50–1; Birkenhead, *Kipling*, 129. Watt was recommended to Kipling by Walter Besant. A. P. Watt died in 1914 but his firm continued to flourish under his son A. S. Watt. See also Robertson Nicoll's tribute to Watt, appearing under his Claudius Clear byline in *British Weekly*, 12 Nov. 1914.

[90] Vyver, *Memoirs of Corelli*, 193. A. S. Watt was named as an executor of Corelli's estate in 1924, together with her companion Bertha Vyver; *The Times*, 9 May 1924.

[91] Carr, *Corelli*, 76; Coates and Bell, *Corelli*, 121–2. In fact, until his death in 1898 Corelli's half-brother, Eric Mackay, handled some of her literary affairs, in a thoroughly disreputable way; Masters, *Corelli*, 155–6.

[92] Darlow, *Nicoll*, 334–5.   [93] Quoted in Bonham-Carter, *Authors by Profession*, 184.

[94] On George Egerton (1859–1945), see Sutherland, *Companion*, 209–10.

Richards had paid him a mere £25 for all rights to his first novel, *The Street of Adventure* (1909). The sequel was worse: 'Thirty years later, when Gibbs was famous, Richards demanded £500 to buy back all rights, otherwise he would republish the novel. "This was sheer blackmail," said Gibbs . . . "I refused, so Richards republished the old novel as a new one by me, which seriously jeopardised the sales of my new novel." ' Gibbs's experience especially interested Roberts because Richards published his own first novel too. This was *The Chelsea Cherub* (1917). Roberts was not proud of it—he later tried to buy up every copy he came across—but he was most embarrassed by the contract he was foolish enough to sign. Roberts was working in the Overseas Transport section of the Ministry of Munitions when his departmental chief suggested that he show it to Arnold Bennett, whom he knew through the Royal Thames Yacht Club. Bennett returned it with two pages of appraisal, acknowledging that 'Richards is very clever in his advertising and he has a reputation for publishing clever things'; on the other hand, 'This agreement is in my opinion very vicious. The first clause is the worst as it gives the publisher absolute control of the book anywhere.' Bennett's advice was unavailing. Roberts confessed, 'His comments on the Agreement were so scathing that I never dared to show the letter to my debonnaire publisher; moreover, at this point in my career, I was not prepared to jeopardise publication.'[95]

In the same year that Bennett perused Roberts's contract he published *Books and Persons*. In it he reprinted his obituary of George Meredith from 1909, when, reflecting on Meredith's publishing arrangements in the Victorian period, he had exclaimed: 'My only wonder is that human ingenuity did not invent literary agents forty years ago.'[96] Bennett's enthusiasm was understandable. In 1913 he was receiving a shilling per word for his journalism; in the previous year he had earned £16,000, the sum of his entire previous income. He now bought a Queen Anne house in Essex, and a yacht—'just to show these rich chaps that a writer can make money too'.[97]

---

[95] Roberts, *Years of Promise*, 174.

[96] *New Age*, 27 May 1909, in Bennett, *Books and Persons*, 138. Sassoon, *Meredith*, 189–90, for Chapman & Hall's poor treatment of Meredith.

[97] Swinnerton (ed.) *Bennett Journals*, 251 (31 Dec. 1912). Bennett joined Pinker in 1901. In 1913 Bennett earned even more, £17,166 10s. 1d. (reduced to £15,449 17s. 1d. after Pinker's 10 per cent), plus £405 11s. 3d. from investments. It is worth noting that Bennett's plays accounted for over half of his earnings.

III
BEST-SELLERS

A best-seller is the gilded Tomb of a mediocre talent.

(Logan Pearsall Smith, *All Trivia* (1933))

Every author, be he grave or gay, should try to make his book as ingratiating as possible. Reading is not a duty, and has consequently no business to be made disagreeable.

(Augustine Birrell, 'The Office of Literature' (1886))

I strongly hold the view that a work written solely with that object [of becoming a best-seller] can, with the rarest exceptions, never achieve it. It is time that the legend of the completely cynical best-selling author were exploded, even though many of them fondly pretend to answer to that description. 'Writing down to the public' is, in point of fact, no better for the pocket than it is for the soul.

(B. Levy, of the publisher Jarrold's, in Michael Joseph,
The Commercial Side of Literature ([1925]))

In trying to understand the appeal of best-sellers, it is well to remember that whistles can be made sounding certain notes which are clearly audible to dogs and other of the lower animals, though man is incapable of hearing them.

(Rebecca West, *The Strange Necessity* (1928))

He wrote a shilling shocker, just to show he *couldn't* write.

(E. J. Goodman, in J. E. Muddock (ed.), *The Savage Club Papers* (1897))

M-Money is n-no use, my boy, except in l-l-l (then, with a high explosion)—
LARGE quantities.

(Arnold Bennett, advising Neville Cardus, 15 Sept. 1919)

18

Market Conditions

It is not because a story is bad or an author a fool that either should not be popular nowadays, as you and I know, who see so many donkeys crowned with laurels, while certain clever fellows of our acquaintance fight vainly for a maintenance or a reputation.

(W. M. Thackeray to Richard Bedingfield, 1 June 1845)

. . . .novels may be expected to continue as a large business product—feeding new appetites, being turned out as the day's loaves are: & consumed & forgotten as the day's loaves are, without demand for anything in them that need be remembered after consumption.

(Frederick Greenwood, c.1897)

I

We learn about the past as much from its ordinary or inferior articles as from its treasures; as Robert Louis Stevenson put it in 1874, 'the most imbecile production of any literary age gives us sometimes the very clue to comprehension we have sought long and vainly in contemporary masterpieces'.[1] In the late nineteenth century there were certain genres that the mass reading public favoured. Among them, adventure, romance, horror, crime, and sport clearly led. Stevenson himself, by supplying a range of products that critics valued on the quality side of the adventure and horror market, came to be a beneficiary of this. Having abandoned the law for authorship, his first earnings by his pen were disappointing, yielding but £109 in 1879. In 1883, when *Treasure Island* was published in book form, his proceeds were £465; by 1887, following *Dr Jekyll and Mr Hyde* and *Kidnapped*, he was clocking up £4,000 to £5,000 a year,[2] equivalent to an annual income of some £¼ million today. Amid this new-found wealth Stevenson remained anxious that his frail health would not permit him to go on performing at this rate; indeed, he died in 1894, at the very time when the book market was entering upon a new wave of expansion that brought the best-seller boom.

---

[1] 'Victor Hugo's Romances', *Cornhill Magazine*, Aug. 1874, in Stevenson, *Familiar Studies of Men and Books*, 3.   [2] Financial information from Colvin (ed.), *Stevenson's Letters*, i. 164, 304, ii. 284.

It is important to emphasize that the size of this market was of a different magnitude from the readership of, say, Henry James or Joseph Conrad, whose biggest-selling works in their lifetimes were in the region of 10,000 copies; different too from that achieved by the younger generation of now 'classic' authors such as E. M. Forster, whose *A Room with a View* (1908) and *Howards End* (1910) sold 2,312 and 9,959 copies respectively in the quinquennium 1908–13.[3] By contrast, popular authors such as Arnold Bennett were capable of selling 13,350 copies of a novel (*These Twain*, 1916) in a week, following 'some rotten reviews';[4] and outstanding best-sellers sold hundreds of thousands and reached an audience of millions.[5] The public response to James and Conrad conformed to Martial's maxim *Laudant illa sed ista legunt* ('Those they praise but the others they read'). They had their devotees, of course. So smitten by Conrad's power was Bertrand Russell that he named *both* his sons Conrad. However, the relative position of James and his like in the literary market place was generally understood. It was made plain in a publication of 1901, entitled *Lives of the 'Lustrious*, whose entry for James ran:

Six-shilling Sensationalist, was born at Hangman's Gulch, Arizona, in 1843. This favourite author, whose works are famous for their blunt, almost brutal directness of style and naked realism, passed his early years before the mast, and is believed at one period of his career to have sailed under the skull and crossbones. Mr Henry James, on settling on shore, turned to the pen for a livelihood, and under a variety of pseudonyms produced in rapid succession a large number of exciting stories, the most popular of which are probably *The Master-Christian*, *The Red Rat's Daughter*, *The Mystery of a Hansom Cab*, *The Eternal City*, and *The Visits of Elizabeth*. Authorities: Jacobite Papers; Daisy and Maisie or The Two Mad Chicks.[6]

We do not need telling that this was a spoof, but it is worth dwelling on its targets. One was the *Dictionary of National Biography*, edited by Leslie Stephen and Sidney Lee. By 1900 the *DNB* stretched to some sixty volumes, having appeared with awesome regularity at every quarter from its inception in 1885. *Lives of the 'Lustrious* was subtitled 'A Dictionary of Irrational Biography'. The editors were an enigmatic pair, 'Sidney Stephen' and 'Leslie Lee'. They were satirizing that exercise which is now dubbed 'literary canon formation': the assembly of a roll-call of classic authors who each contributes to a great tradition of English Literature. A second target, equally obviously, was Henry James himself. James was already being worshipped by a coterie of literary disciples who spoke of him as the Master.[7] So awestruck was E. M. Forster when introduced to James that his

---

[3] Information provided by Forster's publisher, Edward Arnold, and cited in Derek Hudson, 'Reading', in Nowell-Smith (ed.), *Edwardian England*, 315.   [4] Flower (ed.), *Bennett Journals*, ii. 152 (22 Jan. 1916).

[5] Joseph, *Commercial Side of Literature*, 11: 'For every reader of Henry James and D. H. Lawrence there are a hundred readers of Nat Gould and Ethel M. Dell.'

[6] Stephen and Lee, *Lives of the 'Lustrious*, 47.

[7] Edel, *James*, ii. 39–41; Nowell-Smith, *Legend of the Master*, 22. Edmund Gosse and John Bailey agreed, following James's death, that 'H. J. is being treated too solemnly, too hieratically', although Gosse

mind seized up and he started talking gibberish.[8] It must, therefore, have seemed a particularly good joke to lampoon James by way of a best-seller's curriculum vitae, because the paucity of his book sales was as well known as his pronouncements about the novel as a high order of art. The publisher Methuen made a virtue out of this necessity in 1905 with his advertisement of *The Golden Bowl*:

The publication of a new book by Mr Henry James is a great literary event, and Mr James is one of the very few men of whom this statement can be made. It cannot be said that he is the darling of the multitude but he is what he prefers to be—the giver of untold pleasure to the lover of style and of a profound psychological analysis.[9]

A third target of *Lives of the 'Lustrious* is less obvious: this was the pretensions of the best-selling authors themselves. The entry for James was not all invention: the books may not have been written by him but they did represent real titles. *The Master-Christian* (1900) was by Marie Corelli, *The Red Rat's Daughter* (1899) by Guy Boothby, *The Eternal City* (1901) by Hall Caine, and *The Visits of Elizabeth* (1900) by Elinor Glyn. These authors are not so widely known today and their works largely forgotten or ignored. That things were different then may be illustrated by another of the misattributed titles, *The Mystery of a Hansom Cab*. A detective story, subtitled 'A Startling and Realistic Story of Melbourne Social Life', it was originally published in Australia in 1886. Hume dedicated it to James Payn, who was editor of the *Cornhill Magazine* (1883–96) and a reader for the publisher Smith, Elder. Payn was also a sensation novelist and unabashed about his prolific output: 'I should not get so much for one first-rate book as I do for three second-rate ones.'[10] The first London edition of the *Hansom Cab* appeared in 1887, and the 100,000 mark was soon passed, to the chagrin of the hapless author, who had sold the copyright for £50.[11] Hume gained some compensation from a

---

acknowledged that Percy Lubbock's introduction to the two-volume selection of James's letters, which were published in 1920, was, 'from a sacerdotal point of view, about as good a thing as could be produced'. Gosse to Bailey, 14 Apr. 1920, in Bailey (ed.), *Bailey Letters and Diaries*, 204.

[8] To Edward Joseph Dent, 10 Feb. 1908, in Lago and Furbank (eds.), *Forster's Letters*, i. 92. Later, in Egypt during the Great War, Forster applied himself to read James. Struggling with *What Maisie Knew* (1897), he rather thought that 'she is my very limit—beyond her lies *The Golden Bowl, The Ambassadors* and similar impossibles'. (ibid. 240).   [9] Duffy, *Methuen*, 36.

[10] Scott, *Pall Mall Gazette*, 97, which states that Smith & Elder (who published the *Cornhill*) paid Payn £3,000 a year. On Payn (1830–98), see Sutherland, *Companion*, 493–4. He was a friend of Robert Louis Stevenson, who in 1882 wrote to the *New York Tribune* and *Athenaeum* to acquit Payn of having plagiarized from his work; see Colvin (ed.), *Stevenson's Letters*, i. 251–3. One of Payn's daughters married the editor of *The Times*, G. E. Buckle. Robertson Nicoll was a particular fan, saying that he had read all of Payn's hundred stories and many several times; Darlow, *Nicoll*, 419. Payn was also a favourite of *Punch's* reviewers: see *Punch*, 10 May 1890, 221, and 15 Nov. 1890, 233.

[11] Accounts of the speed and scale of the success of *The Mystery of a Hansom Cab* vary. Sutherland, *Companion*, 313, 454–5, reports that Hume had the book privately printed and that it 'made little stir in Australia', only taking off in the English edition; but there is some internal contradiction in Sutherland's record because on p. 182 it is stated that 'in 1886, *The Mystery of a Hansom Cab* . . . sold a quarter of a million copies in a year'. Desmond Flower, *A Century of Best-Sellers* (1934), 16, put things differently again: 'The first Melbourne edition was 5,000 and was sold in a week; the first London edition was 25,000 and went in three days . . . All traces of the first edition have vanished, and the earliest known copy is marked 100,000.' The earliest edition possessed by the Bodleian Library, Oxford—it was acquired by the Johnson

dramatization of his story. This opened at the Princess's Theatre in February 1888 in an adaptation made by Hume himself in collaboration with Arthur Law;[12] meanwhile, the book remained a monster best-seller. *Punch* could include a sketch in 1898 entitled 'The Mystery of a Handsome Cad', confident that its readers would identify the punning allusion;[13] and in 1901 when Arnold Bennett's *Grand Babylon Hotel* (1902) was about to be serialized in the *Golden Penny* magazine, the publishers delighted him by their promotion, which 'in a whirl of adjectives describes the thing as "the most original, amusing and thrilling" serial written this decade—the best thing of the sort since *The Mystery of a Hansom Cab*'. Bennett mused: 'Fancy writing a story as good as *The Mystery of a Hansom Cab!*'[14]

II

What qualified a book as a 'best-seller'? In 1934, in a pamphlet on the phenomenon, Desmond Flower surveyed the century from 1830 to 1930. He chose as the first criterion for admission to this peculiar pantheon that a book should have achieved at least 100,000 sales. Some measure of this achievement is evident from data given by Michael Joseph in *The Commercial Side of Literature* (1925).[15] The sales of most novels, according to Joseph, did not reach 1,000 copies, and what he called 'the averagely successful' sold between 2,000 and 3,000. Thus: 'Anything from 5,000 to 10,000 copies may be regarded as a substantial success; and over 10,000 as an outstanding success. From thirty thousand onwards we are in the region of the "best-seller" '.[16] By Joseph's reckoning, therefore, Flower was pitching a very high threshold at 100,000 for his best-sellers; and, when account is also taken of the trade supposition that each copy sold was read by at least two people, it is clear that the books on Flower's list reached an exceptionally large audience. Indeed, they might even be termed super best-sellers; but an immediate

Collection in 1968—is styled the 175th thousand but not dated. This was published by 'The Hansom Cab Publishing Co., 60 Ludgate Hill, E.C.', which was described as holding the rights, although it acknowledged that the author reserved the dramatic rights. Other copies in the Bodleian are: the 250th thousand (1888), the 377th thousand (Jarrold's 3s. 6d. popular novels, 1896), and the 550th thousand (Jarrold's tenpenny popular novels, 1916). On the author Fergus Hume (1859–1932), see Sutherland, *Companion*, 313, Kemp et al. (eds.) *Edwardian Fiction*, 199, and *Who Was Who, 1929–1940*, 677. He was born in England but his parents emigrated to New Zealand. Educated at the University of Otago, he then qualified as a barrister before spending three years in Australia. He moved to England in 1888, and continued as a prolific fiction-writer. His last address was Rosemary, Grove Road, Thundersley, near Southend-on-Sea, Essex. His will was probated at £201 6s. This is perhaps the smallest amount left by any best-selling author in this period. There is now a notice of Hume, by Robin Woolven, in the *Oxford DNB*.

[12] *Annual Register for 1888*, pt. ii, 88; J. B. Booth, *Life, Laughter, and Brass Hats* (1939), 77.
[13] *Punch*, 3 Dec. 1898, 256.   [14] Flower (ed.), *Bennett Journals*, i. 109 (18 Jan. 1901).
[15] Joseph had insider's knowledge of the trade. He was a sub-editor on various weekly magazines, then advertising manager for Hutchinson's before joining the Curtis Brown literary agency; and he was the author of advice manuals, *Short Story Writing for Profit* (1923) and *Journalism for Profit* (1924). *The Commercial Side of Literature* itself sold well, ranking among the top eight titles in the summer of 1925; later, in 1935, Joseph founded the publishing firm that bears his name. See Richard Joseph, 'Michael Joseph Limited', in Rose and Anderson, *Literary Publishing Houses*, 175–7.   [16] Joseph, *Commercial Side of Literature*, 179.

question arises about the length of time allowed for the figure of 100,000 sales to be passed. Stevenson's *Treasure Island*, for instance, began inauspiciously as a serial in the children's magazine *Young Folks* in 1881–2 and, though acclaimed when published in book form in 1883, sold no more than 5,600 copies in Britain in the first year.[17] Sales of *Dr Jekyll and Mr Hyde* (1886) again began slowly until, following a lengthy review in *The Times* and a sermon in St Paul's Cathedral in January 1887, it sold nearly 40,000 copies in the next six months.[18] Flower also noted that some best-sellers such as Edgar Wallace's *Four Just Men* (1905) 'did not sell at all originally, but caught like wildfire in cheap editions; others, for instance *The Mystery of a Hansom Cab*, started at a breath-taking pace and fell away with time'. Sensibly, Flower included both kinds, because his chief criterion was that best-sellers were books that, 'during the long or the short life that fate allowed them, took the country by storm and, in many instances, affected the reading tastes of the British public'.[19]

There remain unresolved problems about Flower's selection. The principal difficulties stemmed from his decisions to identify one title for each best-selling author and, if possible, to nominate the first of these authors' books that achieved 'really great success'. This practice was not always followed;[20] anyway, several authors produced a string of best-sellers and their first success was not always their biggest. Furthermore, Flower simplified the data by compiling a calendar, attempting to itemize one best-seller per annum, 1830–1930. He did not consistently adhere to this rule, and on occasions there were gap years or years in which more than one title was listed. (It is strange, for instance, that Flower overlooked Hugh Conway's *Called Back* and William Le Queux's *The Invasion of 1910*, best-sellers in, respectively, 1884 and 1906.) It was particularly the case from the late nineteenth century that more than two or three best-sellers might be published in the same year. Flower's catalogue, therefore, contains an amount of arbitrariness and even error; nevertheless, it is worth reproducing his nominations for the period *c*.1870–1918 as a starting point to a discussion:

1875 Helen Mathers, *Comin' Thro' the Rye*[21]
        Mrs Walton, *Christie's Old Organ*[22]

---

[17] It sold faster in America, though mostly in pirated editions; Mackay, *Violent Friend*, 105–7, 124–5.

[18] Ibid. 145, where it is noted that it also was widely pirated in America, selling there some quarter of a million copies before the author's death in 1894. In addition, sales were boosted by the popular stage adaptation in 1887.   [19] Flower, *Best Sellers*, 3.

[20] For example, for Nat Gould, Flower cited *The Boy in Green* (1905), but this was a long way behind Gould's first best-seller, *The Double Event* (1891).

[21] Flower gave no best-seller between the years 1867—for which he cited two, Rhoda Broughton's *Cometh Up as Flower* and Ouida's *Under Two Flags*—and 1875. On Helen Mathers (pseud. Ellen Buckingham Mathews, 1853–1920) and *Comin' Thro' the Rye*, see Sutherland, *Companion* 144, 421–2. Sutherland considers it clearly influenced by Broughton's best-seller; he also notes that it sold 35,000 copies for her publisher Bentley over the next twenty years, which if that was its total sales should not earn it entry into Flower's list.

[22] Desmond Flower, *Best Sellers*, 15, notes that it was published by the Religious Tract Society.

1876 Walter Besant and James Rice, *The Golden Butterfly*[23]
       Mark Twain, *The Adventures of Tom Sawyer*[24]

1877 Anna Sewell, *Black Beauty*

1882 Edna Lyall, *Donovan*

1883 Robert Louis Stevenson, *Treasure Island*[25]

1885 H. Rider Haggard, *King Solomon's Mines*

1886 Frances Hodgson Burnett, *Little Lord Fauntleroy*

1887 Fergus Hume, *The Mystery of a Hansom Cab*[26]

1888 Mrs Humphry Ward, *Robert Elsmere*

1889 Jerome K. Jerome, *Three Men in a Boat*

1891 J. M. Barrie, *The Little Minister*

1892 Arthur Conan Doyle, *The Adventures of Sherlock Holmes*

1893 Sarah Grand, *The Heavenly Twins*
       Stanley J. Weyman, *A Gentleman of France*

1894 George Du Maurier, *Trilby*
       Rudyard Kipling, *The Jungle Book*
       H. S. Merriman, *With Edged Tools*[27]

1895 Marie Corelli, *The Sorrows of Satan*

1896 Guy Boothby, *Dr Nikola*
       W. W. Jacobs, *Many Cargoes*

1897 Hall Caine, *The Christian*

1898 Anon., *Elizabeth and her German Garden*[28]
       Charles Garvice, *Just a Girl*

1899 E.W. Hornung, *The Amateur Cracksman*

1901 Victoria Cross, *Anna Lombard*[29]
       Lucas Malet, *The History of Sir Richard Calmedy*[30]

1902 A. E. W. Mason, *The Four Feathers*

1903 Jack London, *The Call of the Wild*

---

[23] Its protagonist, Gilead P. Beck, is 'probably the first American millionaire to be portrayed in English fiction', suggests Sutherland, *Companion*, 252.

[24] Desmond Flower, *Best Sellers*, 15, notes that Chatto & Windus's British edition 'preceded the American by six months'.   [25] Flower wrongly dated this to 1885; *Best Sellers*, 16.

[26] Flower gives no date for this but includes it notionally at 1890. I have placed it at the date of its success in England, in 1887. See above, n. 11.

[27] Merriman was the pseudonym of Hugh Stowell Scott (1862–1903), on whom, see *DNB Supplement 1901–1911*, iii. 278–9; Sutherland, *Companion*, 560–1; Kemp *et al.* (eds.), *Edwardian Fiction*, 279; Flower, *Just as it Happened*, 41–3.

[28] The author was the Countess von Arnim, later Countess Russell (1866–1941), born Mary Annette Beauchamp in Australia. See *DNB 1941–1950*, 748–9; Sutherland, *Companion*, 547.

[29] For her first well-known book, *The Woman Who Didn't* (1895), the author's surname was spelled 'Crosse'. Victoria Cross was the pseudonym of Anne Sophie Cory (1868–1952); see Kemp *et al.* (eds.), *Edwardian Fiction*, 7, 84–5, and Charlotte Mitchell's notice in the *Oxford DNB*, which reports Cory's claim that *Anna Lombard* sold 6 million copies by 1928.

[30] Lucas Malet was the pseudonym of Mary St Leger Harrison (1852–1931), who was Charles Kingsley's daughter. See *DNB 1931–1940*, 405–6; Sutherland, *Companion*, 282; Kemp *et al.* (eds.), *Edwardian Fiction*, 124, 186–7, 262.

Guy Thorne, *When it was Dark*[31]

1904 Frank Danby, *Baccarat*[32]

O. Henry, *Cabbages and Kings*[33]

Robert Hichens, *The Garden of Allah*

1905 Nat Gould, *The Boy in Green*

W. J. Locke, *The Morals of Marcus Ordeyne*

Baroness Orczy, *The Scarlet Pimpernel*

Edgar Wallace, *The Four Just Men*[34]

1907 Elinor Glyn, *Three Weeks*

1908 Maurice Leblanc, *The Seven of Hearts*

Henry de Vere Stacpoole, *The Blue Lagoon*

1909 Florence Barclay, *The Rosary*

1910 Richard Dehan, *The Dope Doctor*[35]

Jeffery Farnol, *The Broad Highway*

1912 Ethel M. Dell, *The Way of an Eagle*[36]

Zane Grey, *Riders of the Purple Sage*

1914 Edgar Rice Burroughs, *Tarzan of the Apes*

1915 Ian Hay, *The First Hundred Thousand*[37]

1916 H. G. Wells, *Mr Britling Sees it Through*[38]

1918 P. G. Wodehouse, *Piccadilly Jim*

The list can be fleshed out from other sources. One is the record of the top ten books in the United States, compiled annually by *The Bookman* from 1895 to 1912, from sales registered at twenty to thirty 'representative' bookshops throughout the country, and after 1912 by the *Publishers' Weekly*, from sales at seventy to 100 such bookshops. This sampling system excluded direct mail-order sales and book club purchases, although these methods of book-buying did not grow significantly until the 1920s.[39] Still, important from our point of view was the establishment of a rural free delivery service in the United States in 1895, which

[31] Guy Thorne was the pseudonym of Cyril Arthur Edward Ranger Gull (1876–1923). He published fiction using both names. *When it was Dark* sold half a million copies by the time of his death: *Who Was Who, 1916–1928*, 443–4; and Kemp *et al.* (eds.), *Edwardian Fiction*, 165, 413–4.

[32] Frank Danby was the pseudonym of Mrs Julia Frankau (1864–1916), on whom, see Sutherland, *Companion*, 233; Kemp *et al.* (eds.), *Edwardian Fiction*, 88–9, 316.

[33] O. Henry was the pseudonym that William Sydney Porter (1862–1910) adopted after serving a prison sentence in Texas. See Browning and Cousin, *Literary Biography*, 533–4.

[34] Flower, *Best Sellers*, misdates this as 1907.

[35] Richard Dehan was the pseudonym of Clotilde Inez Mary Graves (1863–1932), who wrote plays, pantomimes, and many other novels under her own name. See *Who Was Who, 1929–1940*, 545, and Kemp *et al.* (eds.), *Edwardian Fiction*, 94, 103.

[36] Ethel M. Dell was the maiden name, retained as the pen-name, of Ethel Savage (1881–1939); see *DNB 1931–1940*, 785–6.

[37] Ian Hay was the pseudonym of John Hay Beith (1876–1952), on whom, see *DNB 1951–1960*, 79-80, and Kemp *et al.* (eds.), *Edwardian Fiction*, 178, 316.   [38] Flower, *Best Sellers*, 20, misdates this 1917.

[39] The most important exception was Mark Twain, whose books 'never appeared on bookstore best-seller lists, for most of them were issued by subscription companies whose house-to-house sales were not recorded in best-seller reports from bookstores' (Hackett, *Best Sellers*, 14).

boosted retailing of all kinds, including books; further, the price for new fiction was little different in America from that in Britain during this period. A newly published novel at the turn of the century typically sold for $1.50, and by 1910, $1.35 or $1.30, with reprints for the big sellers in 50-cent editions. Below this was a vast market for 'dime novels', pulp fiction at 10 cents apiece.[40] Naturally, there were fashions peculiar to the American book-buying public, and some indigenous authors had large reputations that were not matched by an equivalent success in Britain. Thus, while the same appetite was shown for historical romances—one of the best-selling genres in both countries from the 1890s to the 1920s[41]—the American best-seller list was dominated by such home-grown exponents as Winston Churchill, Paul Leicester Ford, and Charles Major. It was a question Arnold Bennett endeavoured to explain, why particular works of historical fiction by American authors, which sold over 200,000 copies in the United States, did not take off in Britain.[42] *Punch*'s book critic also pondered the same in 1912, when faced with Major's *The Touchstone of Fortune*. This seemed destined to be 'devoured by thousands from the Everglades of Florida to Melonsquashville, Tenn.', if Major's first best-seller, *When Knighthood was in Flower; or, The Love Story of Charles Brandon and Mary Tudor* (1899), which sold half a million copies, was any guide. *Punch*'s reviewer was mystified. The stories were long and lumbering; and, in his dialogue Major appeared to make few concessions to verisimilitude: 'the most interesting thing about *The Touchstone of Fortune* is the breezy American way in which the characters speak. "Do you suppose we could have made a mistake?", asks Wentworth on page 203. "You surely did," says King Charles (champing irritably, I have no doubt, at his chewing-gum, as he spoke).'

Despairingly, *Punch* protested that the 'American "best-seller" is a sort of uncouth growth on literature. It is like nothing else in the world of print.'[43] There appeared, therefore, an instinctive resistance on the part of British readers to this incongruous Americanization of their history; they remained more comfortable with their own practitioners' Victorianizations of the past. A similar failure to transfer a success from one side of the Atlantic to the other also occurred in additional cases. Thus, while the popularity of children's books was marked in both countries, America had its own favourites such as Helen Bannerman, *Little Black Sambo* (1899), Kate Douglas Wiggin, *Rebecca of Sunnybrook Farm* (1903), Gene Stratton Porter, *Freckles* (1904), and Eleanor H. Porter, *Pollyanna* (1913). Nevertheless, this was a period in which British authors featured strongly in

---

[40] When the normal pre-First World War rate of exchange was $4.86 to the pound sterling, the equivalent sums were 6s. ($1.50), about 4s. 6d. or 5s. ($1.30–1.35), 2s. (50 cents) and 5d. (10 cents).

[41] Stanley Weyman and Baroness Orczy are names that still are well known but, as Kemp *et al.* (eds.), *Edwardian Fiction*, 185–6, emphasize, 'A list of Edwardian writers who dabbled in it [historical romance] would include a considerable proportion of all the writers included in this *Companion*.'

[42] He instanced Churchill's *Richard Carvel*, Paul Leicester Ford's *Janice Meredith*, and James Lane Allen's *The Choir Invisible*; Bennett, *Fame and Fiction*, chs. iii–xv.   [43] *Punch*, 10 July 1912, 39.

American best-seller charts: 1906 was the only year in which no book by a British author appeared in the top ten titles.

It is a possible objection to the historian using American evidence to draw conclusions about British best-sellers, that particular books by British authors might have captivated American readers more than their home public. Over lunch at the Pall Mall Restaurant in 1912, Aimée Locke, wife of W. J. Locke, declared that 'he made all his money in America'.[44] Locke was certainly very big there, while resisting all invitations to lecture. Yet his novels also topped the British best-selling lists; and it was said about the Bodley Head, which published Locke in Britain, that profits from his books paid all the firm's running costs. Locke was 'a living gold mine'.[45] There are other examples that might be considered. Robert Hichens recorded in his memoirs that, 'as a rule, I have had more success in America than in my own country'. *The Garden of Allah* (1904) sold in America more than double the quantity in Britain. It was soon being cited as one of those cases that give heart to authors everywhere, being an instance of a publisher's miscalculation. Mary Bisland, representing an American publisher in London, for years had been recommending Hichens, to which the stock response was that his work would not sell. According to Marie Belloc Lowndes, who had it from Bisland herself, this publisher took *The Garden of Allah* only after her persistent pleading, and offered 10 per cent royalty instead of a lump sum.[46] Its phenomenal success made Hichens's fortune; and the spin-off play, adapted by Hichens in collaboration with Mary de Navarro,[47] broke records throughout the country after its premier at the New Century Theatre, New York, on 21 October 1911. It was not staged in Britain until 1920, when Arthur Collins overcame his own reservations about the Hichens–Navarro adaptation and gave it the full Drury Lane treatment, sandstorms and all.[48] Nevertheless, though American

---

[44] Lowndes (ed.), *Lowndes Diaries and Letters*, 39 (28 July 1912).

[45] Lambert and Ratcliffe, *Bodley Head*, 143, 188. On the nature of Locke's novels—essentially adult fairy stories, based on reversals of fortune and an agreeable bohemianism—see Kemp *et al.* (eds.), *Edwardian Fiction*, 26–7, 244, 284–5, where the plots of *The Morals of Marcus Ordeyne* (1905) and *The Beloved Vagabond* (1906) are summarized. *The Joyous Adventures of Aristotle Pujol* (1912) was another best-seller for Locke, who also made profitable dramatizations of his stories.

[46] Lowndes (ed.), *Lowndes Diaries*, 29 (5 Mar. 1912). The American publisher was not named in this account, and *The Garden of Allah* had two different publishers in the United States in 1904: Grosset & Dunlap and F. A. Stokes, both of New York.

[47] (1859–1940); born Mary Anderson, she was an American actress who became a leading player in Stratford and London in the 1880s, best known for Rosalind in *As You Like It* and Perdita and Hermione in *The Winter's Tale*. W. S. Gilbert wrote *Comedy and Tragedy* (1884) for her, and Wilde *The Duchess of Padua* in 1883. She retired from the stage in 1889, marrying Antonio de Navarro and living at Broadway in Worcestershire. The common verdict on her acting was that it was limited, and she was principally appreciated for her beauty. See the diary entries in Masterman (ed.), *Mary Gladstone*, 297, 304–6, 333, 403.

[48] Collins, in New York in 1911, reported that he was 'bored to tears' and even fell asleep during the performance; he therefore opposed its transfer to London. But, as well as making 'an immense amount of money' in the United States, the play also turned out to be one of Drury Lane's greatest money-makers and ran for 359 performances; see Hichens, *Yesterday*, 168–79, 233, 279–85, 293–7; Collins, *Best Riches*, 84–5.

interest in *The Garden of Allah* was massive, the book was also a huge best-seller in Britain. Methuen first published it on 14 October 1904, and issued the second, third, and fourth editions in November and a fifth in December. Another seven editions followed in 1905, and when the first illustrated edition appeared in 1914, that was the twenty-fourth altogether. And these were all at standard price: a cheaper edition (the thirtieth) was held back until 1920, to ride the stage-play wave. In addition, two silent movies were based on it, in 1916 and 1927, and a third in Technicolor in 1936 by David O. Selznick, starring Marlene Dietrich and Charles Boyer.[49] The book was in its forty-fourth edition in Britain at the time that Hichens wrote his autobiography in 1947. Nor was it the case that he was a one-book best-seller. *The Call of the Blood* (1906) also sold well and was made into a film; *Barbary Sheep* (1909) was twice sold as a film; and *Bella Donna* (1909), both as a novel and in its dramatized form (adapted by J. B. Fagan), was 'one of the greatest selling successes I ever had'. The real point about *The Garden of Allah* is not that it sold more in the United States than in Britain but that it was an *international* best-seller. Furthermore, not all Hichens's best-sellers prospered in America rather than in Britain: *The Fruitful Vine* (1911) sold strongly in Britain and weakly in the United States, and Hichens stated that he 'gave back to my American publisher a thousand pounds of the four thousand pounds on account of royalties which he had paid to me for it on the day of publication, partly to compensate him for his loss on it'.[50]

For the most part, the Hichens formula, of an Englishwoman infatuated with a foreign lover, proved a winner on both sides of the Atlantic. It was to reach its apogee after the Great War with the publication of Mrs E. M. Hull's *The Sheikh* (1919), which sold over a million and was brought to the screen in 1921 with Rudolph Valentino in the title role. Mrs Hull lived with her pig-farming husband in Derbyshire, but her book, according to her publisher, made 'a strong appeal to the great number of unmated and unsatisfied women who, though virtuous in the eyes of the world, have a mental double life in which they find themselves carried away by the type of man who arouses in them the desire for the supreme experience. It means much to those who lead small, smothered lives.'[51] Mrs Hull's heroine, Lady Diana Mayo, put it rather more explicitly after being repeatedly violated by the Sheikh:

He was a brute, but she loved him, loved him for his very brutality, and superb animal strength. And he was an Arab! A man of different race and colour, a native; Aubrey [her brother] would indiscriminately class him as 'a damned nigger'. She did not care. A year ago, a few weeks even, she would have shuddered with repulsion at the bare idea, the thought that a native could even touch her had been revolting, but all that was swept away and was as nothing in the face of the love that filled her heart so completely . . . She was deliriously, insanely happy!

---

[49] Hichens preferred the second version, directed by Rex Ingram; Hichens, *Yesterday*, 242–5. The original was directed by Herbert Brenon; see Robinson, *World Cinema*, 407.
[50] Hichens, *Yesterday*, 184, 234.   [51] Nash, *Life*, 131–2.

There was no need to fret. The Sheikh is eventually disclosed not to be Arab at all but (as Claud Cockburn put it) the son of 'a tip-top British peer'; and his mother came from 'one of the oldest noble families in Spain—so old and so noble that it is quite all right to hint that they may have had Moorish blood from way back'. Thus, 'everything is race-wise and class-wise O.K.'.[52] Probably, this was necessary given the majority's sensibilities, but many Victorians—perhaps Mrs Hull herself—might have been aware of the life of Jane Digby el Mezrab. An admiral's daughter, she was briefly the second wife of the Earl of Ellenborough, who afterwards became Governor-General of India. They divorced in 1830, he citing her adultery with Prince Schwartzenberg; but, following another marriage and a series of lovers, she saved her best until last. As prim Isabel Burton—wife of the morally suspect Sir Richard Burton—described it, having established a friendship with Jane in the late 1860s, 'She was a woman of great beauty and linguistic and artistic talents. After an adventurous but dubious career in Europe she married at Damascus the Sheikh Mijual of the tribe Mezrah, a branch of the Anazeh Bedouins. She subsequently resided for many years in camp in the desert near Damascus.'[53] Isabel Burton was herself put out and put off by the Sheikh's pigmentation: Jane's 'contact with that black skin I could not understand. His skin was dark—darker than a Persian—much darker than an Arab generally is. All the same, he was a very intelligent charming man in any light but that of a husband. That made me shudder.'[54]

Hichens had been the first best-seller really to exploit 'the exotic fallacy' of the Middle East, having taken that 'trip in a dahabiyeh as far as Biskra' which Max Beerbohm subsequently recommended to all female novelists.[55] Hichens was advertised by the *Tatler* as 'The Man . . . Who Possesses an Unrivalled Knowledge of "The Eternal Feminine" ';[56] but there was a good deal of ambiguity about the gender roles of the two protagonists of *The Garden of Allah*, Dominic Enfilden, a peer's daughter, of wavering Roman Catholic faith, and Boris Androvsky, the Trappist monk with whom she has a charged relationship in the desert—an ambiguity shared by the author himself, who had once been part of Wilde's circle and who never married. Domini is a 32-year-old spinster and stands 5 feet 10 inches. The desert serves throughout as a metaphor for and as a means towards religious truth and personal fulfilment. The key ingredients in the story are not mere physical passions, rather spiritual union and the element of tragic

[52] Claud Cockburn, *Bestseller: The Books that Everyone Read, 1900–1939* (1972) 131–4.

[53] Quoted in J. A. Hamilton's notice of the Earl of Ellenborough (1790–1870), *DNB* xxxii (1892), 227.

[54] Farwell, *Burton*, 276.

[55] Quoted in E. M. Forster, 'Salute to the Orient!' (1923), in Forster, *Abinger Harvest*, 249. Forster instead recommended Marmaduke Pickthall (1875–1936) as 'the only contemporary English novelist who understands the nearer East . . . He has written novels about England also, and their badness is instructive: he appears to be one of those rare writers who only feel at home when they are abroad.' Biskra was a health resort in Algeria, which Hichens visited several times and, he claimed in the Preface to the 1914 edition of *The Garden of Allah* (1904), thus became 'familiar with the wonderful desert region in the midst of which it lies'.   [56] Margot Peters, *Mrs Pat: The life of Mrs Patrict Cambell* (1984) 305.

impossibility. It was this sacramental character that attracted Mary de Navarro, a devout Catholic, to collaborate with Hichens, the son of an Anglican clergyman, in adapting *The Garden of Allah* for the stage; and she injected much of her own spirituality into it, as he acknowledged. The novel struck a chord with romantic women everywhere, from the royal family downwards. Queen Alexandra was known to have read it and, Hichens wrote triumphantly, the Duchess of Connaught told him how upset she was by the book's ending:

She said I had been too cruel in parting the two lovers, Domini and the Monk. It was a heart-rending end and must have distressed many readers. (It did, for I received hundreds of letters protesting against it.) I stuck to my guns, however, and told Her Royal Highness that from the first moment I conceived the book I made up my mind that Religion must triumph over human love, and that the Monk, after having known the joys of passion in the world, must resign them for the sake of his monkish soul.[57]

The example of Hichens, some of whose books sold more in the United States than in Britain, should not therefore inhibit the historian from using American evidence to throw light on the character of the British best-selling list, because Hichens was also a best-seller at home. 'Garden of Allah' parties, at which guests attired themselves in what they took to be Arabian costume, were all the rage.[58] Indeed, it is most unlikely that there existed British authors whose books sold hugely in the United States and were a complete flop at home; it is more likely that their success in Britain was a cause of the interest taken in them by Americans. Historians of the best-seller in Britain may, then, derive useful data from the American best-seller charts, not to assign an exact rank order of popularity but rather as a general indication of best-selling status. Below is a list of the titles by British-based authors which appeared in the top ten of annual best-sellers in America:

1895 Ian Maclaren, *Beside the Bonnie Brier Bush* and *Days of Auld Lang Syne*
       George Du Maurier, *Trilby*
       Hall Caine, *The Manxman*
       Israel Zangwill, *The Master*
       Anthony Hope, *The Prisoner of Zenda*
1896 Gilbert Parker, *The Seats of the Mighty*
       Ian Maclaren, *Beside the Bonnie Brier Bush* and *Kate Carnegie*
       J. M. Barrie, *Sentimental Tommy*
1897 Hall Caine, *The Christian*
       J. M. Barrie, *Sentimental Tommy* and *Margaret Ogilvy*

---

[57] Hichens, *Yesterday*, 148. Hichens conceived of the book when staying in the Trappist monastery of Stovëli in Algeria, and wrote it during his frequent sojourns in Italy and Sicily. The matinée idol Lewis Waller played the part of the monk Androvsky in the stage play in America, Henry Ainley having turned it down.   [58] Duffy, *Methuen*, 34.

1898 Mrs Humphry Ward, *Helbeck of Bannisdale*
Rudyard Kipling, *The Day's Work*
Stanley Weyman, *Shrewsbury*
Anthony Hope, *Simon Dale*
Gilbert Parker, *The Battle of the Strong*

1899 Rudyard Kipling, *The Day's Work*
Theodore Watts-Dunton, *Aylwin*
Richard Whiteing, *No. 5 John Street*

1900 Mary Cholmondeley, *Red Pottage*

1901 Gilbert Parker, *The Right of Way*
Elinor Glyn, *The Visits of Elizabeth*
Maurice Hewlett, *Richard Yea-and-Nay*

1902 Gilbert Parker, *The Right of Way*
A. Conan Doyle, *The Hound of the Baskervilles*
Lucas Malet, *Sir Richard Calmedy*

1903 Mrs Humphry Ward, *Lady Rose's Daughter*

1904 [Katherine Cecil Thurston], *The Masquerader*

1905 Mrs Humphry Ward, *The Marriage of William Ashe*
Robert Hichens, *The Garden of Allah*
[Katherine Cecil Thurston], *The Masquerader* and *The Gambler*
C. N. and A. M. Williamson, *The Princess Passes*

1907 Gilbert Parker, *The Weavers*

1908 Gilbert Parker, *The Weavers*

1909 W. J. Locke, *Septimus*

1910 Florence Barclay, *The Rosary*
Katherine Cecil Thurston, *Max*
W. J. Locke, *Simon the Jester*
C. N. and A. M. Williamson, *Lord Loveland Discovers America*

1911 Jeffery Farnol, *The Broad Highway*
Florence Barclay, *The Rosary*

1912 Anne Douglas Sedgwick, *Tante*

1913 Sir Gilbert Parker, *The Judgment House*
Jeffery Farnol, *The Amateur Gentleman*
Hall Caine, *The Woman Thou Gavest Me*

1914 W. J. Locke, *The Fortunate Youth*
W. B. Maxwell, *The Devil's Garden*

1915 W. J. Locke, *Jaffery*

1916 H. G. Wells, *Mr Britling Sees it Through*
Ethel M. Dell, *Bars of Iron*

1917 H. G. Wells, *Mr Britling Sees it Through*
W. J. Locke, *The Red Planet*
Robert Hichens, *In the Wilderness*

Jeffery Farnol, *The Definite Object*
Ethel M. Dell, *The Hundredth Chance*
Ian Hay, *The First Hundred Thousand* and *Getting Together*
Donald Hankey, *A Student in Arms*
1918 May Sinclair, *The Tree of Heaven*
Ethel M. Dell, *Greatheart*
E. Phillips Oppenheim, *The Pawns Court*
Stephen McKenna, *Sonia*

III

One foundation for one sort of best-seller lay in the 'penny dreadfuls',[59] sometimes also called 'bloods' for their offering of 'blood and thunder' yarns; but the classification was a loose one, derogatively applied not only to much adult and juvenile cheap fiction but also to newspapers and magazines which primarily purveyed sensation. Three-quarters of all the vast quantity of periodical literature published in the late nineteenth century consisted of fiction, either serialized novels or short stories.[60] Now, however, there was evident a new kind of competition from papers whose chief attraction was neither reportage nor the sustained story but miscellaneous entertainment. In 1892 the largest distributor, W. H. Smith's, which had 600 bookstalls, disclosed that the circulation of daily papers was showing little increase, but the weekly medley of the *Tit-Bits* type popularized by George Newnes was multiplying fast and appeared

likely to choke all other literature . . . . The days on which the greatest pressure is felt are Friday and Saturday, when they [Smith's] have respectively fifty-eight and a hundred weeklies to despatch, besides the dailies . . . The back number department has a gross income of £12,000 a year, from which it would seem that Mr Smith's customers call for a million and a half back numbers in the twelve months.[61]

In 1893 Alfred Harmsworth's response to *Tit-Bits*, his penny weekly suitably titled *Answers* (established in 1888), was enjoying sales close to 400,000. Village as well as town was seized by the fad. Flora Thompson recalled of rural Oxfordshire and Buckinghamshire that *Tit-Bits*

was taken by almost every family, and the snippets of information culled from its pages were taken very seriously indeed. Apparently it gave deep satisfaction . . . to know how many years of an average life were spent in bed and how many months of his life a

---

[59] The phrase is dated to 1884 by the *Oxford English Dictionary*.
[60] *Review of Reviews* (Jan. 1890), 14.
[61] W. M. Acworth, 'W. H. Smith and Son', *English Illustrated Magazine* (July 1892), *Review of Reviews* (Aug. 1892), 162.

man spent shaving and a woman doing her hair... The title of *Tit-Bits* furnished a catchword which could always be used with effect when an unfamiliar taste was discovered or an unfamiliar opinion expressed. Then 'Don't try to be funny. We've read about you in *Tit-Bits!*' said scathingly was, in the slang of the day, 'absolutely the last word'.[62]

There was another side to *Tit-Bits* (established in 1881). It also published slices of the eighteenth-century essayists Addison, Steele, and Goldsmith, of the early and mid-nineteenth-century classic novelists and thinkers Lamb, Scott, Carlyle, Macaulay, Kingsley, George Eliot, and Thackeray, of Victor Hugo and Jules Verne, and of American authors from Washington Irving, Poe, Hawthorne, and Emerson, to Longfellow and Oliver Wendell Holmes. It encouraged readers to become writers, as Arnold Bennett, the winner of 20 guineas in a *Tit-Bits* competition, was afterwards proud to acknowledge. Intelligibility and readability were its criteria; these probably account for the rejection of pieces submitted by Joseph Conrad and Virginia Woolf.[63] The sensible author was alive to it as a force for public good and made it an ally. Conan Doyle, who earned about £1,500 from his writings in 1891, the year he abandoned medicine for authorship, bought 250 shares in Newnes Ltd in July, invested £260 in 200 shares in *Tit-Bits* in November, and acquired still more in December.[64] He put behind him the indignation he felt in 1884 when he had failed to win a *Tit-Bits* competition and had wagered £25 for an independent umpire to arbitrate between his entry and the winner.[65] In 1893 *Tit-Bits* serialized both *A Study in Scarlet* (1888) and *The Sign of Four* (1890).[66] The serialization of Doyle's stories yielded him four times the income that they produced in book form.[67]

Critics were inclined to include in the fiction category the *Illustrated Police News*, which luridly reported more-or-less true crimes and sold 300,000 copies a week in 1888. More properly, it referred to such as *Princess's Novelette* with its romantic tales and weekly sales of 168,000. Outselling both together was the *Boy's Own Paper* with over half a million sales each week; but, if the common assumption is allowed, that each copy passed to another two or three people, every issue reached perhaps 1.5 million readers.[68] Following G. A. Henty and Rider Haggard, the 'strong, silent Englishman' type commonly featured in these stories, advancing the imperial service as fearless and benevolent warriors, explorers, or administrators, and all with unconquerable boyish high spirits, especially as the toll of corpses mounted. 'More even than with the contemptible inexpressiveness

---

[62] Thompson, *Lark Rise*, 516.

[63] John Carey, *The Intellectuals and the Masses: Pride and Prejudice among the Literary Intelligentsia, 1880–1939*, (1992), 109–10.   [64] Pearson, *Conan Doyle*, 106; Booth, *Conan Doyle*, 167.

[65] Booth, *Conan Doyle*, 103. His offer was not taken up.

[66] *A Study in Scarlet* first appeared in *Beeton's Christmas Annual*, 1887, and *The Sign of Four* in *Lippincott's Magazine*; see Sutherland, *Companion*, 576, 613.   [67] Booth, *Conan Doyle*, 255.

[68] See J. J. McAleer, Jr., 'Patterns of Popular Reading in Britain 1900–1950' D.Phil. (Oxford, 1990). *BOP* became a monthly in 1914.

of the whole thing', Henry James wrote after reading *She* by 'the unspeakable Haggard',

I am struck with the beastly *bloodiness* of it—or it comes back to the same thing—the cheapness of the hecatombs with which the genial narrative is bestrewn. Such perpetual killing and such perpetual ugliness!...In *She* the Narrator himself shoots through the back (I think) his faithful servant Mahommed, to prevent his being boiled alive, and describes how he 'leaped into the air like a buck', on receiving the shot. He himself is addressed constantly by one of the personages of the tale as 'my Baboon'! *Quel genre!* They seem to me works in which our race and our age make a very vile figure...

Perhaps the vilest figure of all for James was 'the fortieth thousand' he read on the title page of his copy of *She*. This moved him to 'a holy indignation. It isn't nice that anything so vulgarly brutal should be the thing that succeeds most with the English of today.'[69]

Haggard appeared more a man for his times than did James. Although, according to Douglas Goldring, 'in real life Empire-builders are usually strong, silent bores, with tropical livers, whose occasional eruptions of speech will empty a smoking-room in the dullest club in London inside fifteen minutes',[70] it becomes difficult, if newspaper reports of the period are consulted, to decide where reality ended and fiction began. The *Daily Mail*'s correspondent G. W. Steevens described the actions of the young officer of a navy gunboat during Kitchener's Sudan campaign:

Steaming up and down the river in command of a ship of his own, bombarding here, reconnoitring there, landing elsewhere for a brush with the dervishes, and then again a little way farther to pick up loot,—the work had all the charm of war and blockade-running and poaching combined. If a dervish shell did happen to smash the wheel where would the boat be; perhaps seventy miles from any help? It was said the Sirdar was a little nervous about them, and to my inexperience it was a perpetual wonder that the boats came back from every trip. But somehow, thanks to just a dash of caution in their audacity, they always did come back. Impudently daring in attack, with a happy eye

---

[69] Henry James to Robert Louis Stevenson, 2 Aug. [1886], in Edel (ed.), *James Letters*, iii. 128. Edel dates this letter 1886, but *She* was not published in book form until 1 January 1887. Tolstoy was also appalled by *She*, pronouncing it and other books by Haggard as the lowest form of literature. He expressed himself astonished that so many English readers lapped them up, although this sat well with his view that along with the Zulus, 'the English are the most brutal nation on earth'. See the interview conducted by Isabel Hapgood, *Atlantic Monthly*, (Nov. 1891), *Review of Reviews* (Nov. 1891), 498. H. G. Wells was of the same opinion, lambasting Haggard's bloodthirstiness during his period as reviewer for the *Saturday Review* in 1895; Parrinder and Philmus, *Wells's Literary Criticism*, 55–7. This disgust was best captured by *Punch's* parody of Rider Haggard in a story narrated by 'Smallun Halfboy' (Allan Quatermain), who declares: 'no one ever killed more Africans, men and elephants, than I have in my time. But I do love blood. I love it in regular rivers all over the place, with gashes and slashes and lopped heads and arms and legs rolling about everywhere. Black blood is the best variety; I mean the blood of black men, because nobody really cares twopence about them, and you can massacre several thousands of them in half-a-dozen lines and offend no single soul. And, after all, I am not certain that black men have any souls, so that makes things safe all round' (*Punch*, 17 Jan. 1891, 28). [70] Goldring, *Reputations*, 94.

to catch the latest moment for retreat, they were just the cutting-out heroes of one's youth come to life. They might have walked straight out of the 'Boy's Own Paper'.[71]

The *Boy's Own Paper* and its companion *Girl's Own Paper* were established by the Religious Tract Society in 1879, actually as *counter*-attractions to the supposed unwholesome concentration of penny dreadfuls upon gory crimes, tawdry romances, and shoddy sensationalism. *BOP* was not only read by boys, it was also partly written by them; at least, it encouraged young writing talent such as Keble Howard, who at the age of 17 had the first product from his pen accepted by *BOP* and received a cheque for half a guinea—a largesse that meant that 'for a few weeks I walked on air'.[72] Conan Doyle was another, writing on *BOP* 's twenty-fifth anniversary how it had been 'one of the first papers which grew tired of returning my MSS., and began to print them instead.'[73] The salience of *BOP* and *GOP* can be measured by the fact that *The Times* even reviewed their Christmas annuals, when it was made clear that, amid the miscellaneous hobby and informative features, and the frequent homily, the main course was fiction of a spirited sort; and *The Times* thundered applause more than criticism.[74]

This should be emphasized. Though the penny magazines ('dreadful' or otherwise) never lacked critics, neither did they want apologists.[75] Robert Louis Stevenson wrote an essay in praise of 'A Penny Plain and Twopence Coloured';[76] and Wilkie Collins was long interested in making contact with this 'unknown public'. In 1858 he had studied the serialized stories in the 'penny journals' and reported for Dickens's *Household Words* that they were all much the same, 'a combination of fierce melodrama and meek domestic sentiment . . . incidents and characters taken from the old exhausted mines of the circulating library'. In the last decade of his life, the 1880s, Collins encouraged his agent, A. P. Watt, to place his work in this market; but it was not straightforward, in spite of his reputation as the author of sensation novels. Collins was, several journal proprietors thought, too superior an artist for mass consumption. When eventually the newspaper syndication rights of his divorce novel *The Evil Genius* were sold in 1885 to Tillotson's for £1,000, the highest price he had received for a story, he fumed at Tillotson's complaints about the suitability of his product.[77] Collins's difficulties were of manufacture, not morality. The founder of the firm,

[71] G. W. Steevens, *With Kitchener to Khartum* (1898), 83. Steevens died of fever at the age of 31, during the siege of Ladysmith in 1900. [72] Howard, *Motley Life*, 81.

[73] Letter, 31 Oct. 1903, in Gibson and Green (eds.), *Unknown Conan Doyle*, 99.

[74] *The Times*, 20 Dec. 1892.

[75] *Punch*, 15 Mar. 1899, 130, for a skit, 'The Penitent Pirate', in response to the press reporting that 'Abuse of the "penny dreadful" has become a magisterial commonplace.'

[76] Stevenson, *Memories and Portraits*, 213–27.

[77] Peters, *Collins*, 394–5, 416–7. When bragging to readers of the American magazine *Lippincott's* about the operations of his small empire of syndicated newspaper fiction, Tillotson declared: 'I buy the author; I don't buy the story, and I would rather give four thousand dollars for a "Braddon" or a "Wilkie Collins" than forty dollars for an intrinsically better story by an author without a name'. *Review of Reviews*, Jan. 1890, 68. Both Collins and W. F. Tillotson—who had founded Tillotson's Newspaper Fiction Bureau in 1873—died in 1889.

W. F. Tillotson enjoyed striking a cynical pose when defining for a journalist what sort of story stood the best chance of success: 'Stories of English domestic life, with a good deal of incident and a little immorality'.[78] But this last was, for the most part, unimpeachable, and Tillotson's shied away from serializing Thomas Hardy's *Tess*, in which it had originally expressed interest and offered 1,000 guineas for the rights.[79] In 1890 an article on 'Penny Fiction' in the *Quarterly Review* had made standard noises about the shortcomings of popular fiction as literature, yet also noted that it was 'singularly pure in tone, and that any violation of decency would inevitably lead to such a falling off of circulation as would practically amount to ruin of the paper guilty of it'.[80] Especially at the adolescents' end of the market, it was the sheer excitement and escapist fantasy of the stories that were captivating. J. M. Barrie and the schoolfriend he made on his first day at Dumfries Academy agreed to call themselves Sixteen-String Jack and Dare Devil Dick in tribute to the heroes of penny stories they both consumed.[81]

G. K. Chesterton, who loved to shock, maintained that it was easier to write 'ten *Times* articles than one *Tit-Bits* joke'.[82] Solemnity was straightforward; brightening a reader's day was a tough proposition. He also wrote 'In Defence of Penny Dreadfuls' (1914). His axiom was that 'Literature is a luxury; fiction is a necessity'. But, as the champion of Dickens's pre-eminence, Chesterton was concerned to distinguish types of popularity, the universal and everlasting from the particular and passing. 'Men read a Dickens story six times', Chesterton asserted, 'because they knew it so well. If a man can read a Le Queux story six times it is only because he can forget it six times.' Dickens, he added, 'filled the literary world in a way hard to imagine . . . The man in the street has more memories of Dickens, whom he has not read, than of Marie Corelli, whom he has.' With the exception of Sherlock Holmes,[83] no character in the literature of their own day was readily recognized by ordinary people: even Kipling had failed to invent personalities who had become 'common property like the Dickens characters'. Yet, notwithstanding this inferiority of all recent popular

---

[78] *Review of Reviews* (Jan. 1890), 68. A recent shift away from a focus on domestic life was noted: 'The rage nowadays is all for strong sensation, rapid movement, and complicated plots.' Arnold Bennett sold one of his first stories to Tillotson's for £75 in 1899: this was *For Love and Life*, which Bennett wrote under the pseudonym 'Samson King' and which was later republished under his own name as *The Ghost* (1907). Bennett continued to send stories to Tillotson's, although as his reputation and value grew, Bennett issued an ultimatum in 1910 'refusing to work any more at the old price' (Flower (ed.), *Bennett Journals*, i. 356 (31 Jan. 1910)).

[79] Hardy to Tillotson & Son, 12 Mar. 1887, in Purdy and Millgate (eds.), *Hardy Letters*, i. 162–3.

[80] *Review of Reviews* (Aug. 1890), 165.   [81] Dunbar, *Barrie*, 31.

[82] Chesterton, *All Things Considered*, 2.

[83] Chesterton was undoubtedly correct about Holmes having passed into the common lore: Holmes was even cited as the archetypal detective in stories by fellow novelists, for example, in Sir Walter Besant, *The City of Refuge*, new edn. (1897), 77. However, sales of the Holmes stories in *book form* were relatively poor in the years before the Great War. *The Return of Sherlock Holmes* (1905) averaged only 750 copies p.a, in 1908–14, at 3s. 6d.; and the collected edition of Conan Doyle's works, in twelve volumes, averaged only forty sets p.a. 1903–14. Information provided by Doyle's publisher, John Murray, and cited in Derek Hudson, 'Reading', in Nowell-Smith (ed.), *Edwardian England*, 314. The popularity of the Holmes stories was through their serialization in the *Strand* magazine.

writers when compared with Dickens, Chesterton objected to the assertion that 'the people likes bad literature, and even likes literature because it is bad'.[84]

IV

What kind of literature the people liked can be glimpsed in the social survey of Middlesbrough iron-workers and their families published in 1907 by Florence, Lady Bell. She drew on her knowledge of the district over almost thirty years. The habits of some 200 couples were detailed:

17 women who cannot read.

8 men who cannot read.

28 houses where no one cares to read.

8 men who actually dislike reading.

3 women who actually dislike reading.

7 women who say they 'have no time for it'.

50 houses where they only read novels.

58 houses where they read the newspapers only.

37 houses where they are 'fond of reading' or 'great readers'.

25 houses where they read books that are absolutely worth reading (this includes the men who read books about their work).

The popularity of fiction among these readers was marked. Dispassionately, Lady Bell observed that after a strenuous day's labour most working men and their wives were unlikely 'to wish anything that involves an effort of attention'. Their aim was 'purely recreative', and for the most part there was little selection about their reading, rather picking up what was available. Many of the women readers, Lady Bell was told, 'prefer something about love, with a dash of religion in it' or 'something with a little love and a little murder'; above all, 'something that will take one away from oneself':

This is the character of most of the penny stories which form the bulk of the literature accessible to them. They like some relief to the greyness of their lives, some suggestion of other possibilities; but for many of them anything that excites laughter goes too far in the other direction, although they are usually ready to laugh at something humorous if read to them more than if they read it themselves. But they generally prefer something emotional and not laughable . . . I have looked through a number of the penny stories that the women mostly read. They are irreproachable, and they have the most curious resemblance of plot. In four that I read, one after another, the poor and virtuous young man turned out to be a long-lost son, and became rich and powerful.[85]

What was true of industrial Middlesbrough in the early 1900s held also for rural Oxfordshire and Buckinghamshire in the 1880s, according to Flora Thompson,

---

[84] Chesterton, *Dickens*, 100–4.

[85] Lady Bell, *At the Works: A Study of a Manufacturing Town* (Newton Abbot 1969), 167–8.

whose grandmother enjoyed the *Princess Novelette* and similar penny series, 'and she had a large assortment of these which she kept tied up in flat parcels, ready to exchange with other novelette readers'. This was a pretty general phenomenon among the village women who 'were fond of what they called "a bit of a read"', and these novelettes

were handed round until the pages were thin and frayed with use. Copies of others found their way there from neighbouring villages, or from daughters in service, and there was always quite a library of them in circulation.

The novelette of the 'eighties was a romantic love story, in which the poor governess always married the duke, or the lady of title the gamekeeper, who always turned out to be a duke or an earl in disguise. Midway through the story there had to be a description of a ball, at which the heroine in her simple white gown attracted all the men in the room; or the gamekeeper, commandeered to help serve, made love to the daughter of the house in the conservatory. The stories were often prettily written and as innocent as sugared milk and water; but, although they devoured them, the women looked upon novelette reading as a vice, to be hidden from their menfolk and only discussed with fellow devotees.

The novelettes were as carefully kept out the children's way as the advanced modern novel is, or should be, to-day; but children who wanted to read them knew where to find them, on the top shelf of the cupboard or under the bed, and managed to read them in secret. An ordinarily intelligent child of eight or nine found them cloying; but they did the women good, for, as they said, they took them out of themselves.[86]

This reading of novelettes was so widespread that an author like W. W. Jacobs who aimed to capture the flavour of 'real life' could introduce it into a story, as in this piece of backchat from 'In Limehouse Reach', in *Many Cargoes* (1896):

'Nancy's so discontented,' said the mother, looking at the girl who was reading quietly by her side. '. . . She gets her head turned reading those penny novelettes.'

'You look after your own head,' said Nancy elegantly, without looking up.

'Girls in those novels don't talk to *their* mothers like that', said the elder woman severely.

'They have different sorts of mothers,' said Nancy, serenely turning over a page.[87]

There were no shocking impurities of language and behaviour in these novelettes, and no subversive philosophy, simply the twin sentiments of getting on in the world and marrying happily. The only thing that Lady Bell deplored about these publications was their small print, which damaged eyesight and brought on headaches; still, it was unreasonable to 'expect for a penny to get a complete novel in pica'.[88] Such sympathy and experience were rare. A minor novelist and playwright, who wrote in French and English, Lady Bell spanned the divided worlds of London drawing rooms and Middlesbrough manufacture.[89] Her

---

[86] Thompson, *Lark Rise*, 47, 84, 99–100.

[87] W. W. Jacobs, 'In Limehouse Reach', in Jacobs, *Many Cargoes*, 33rd edn. (1912), 140–51.

[88] Bell, *At the Works*, 168.

[89] Lady Bell (1851–1930) was the daughter of Sir Joseph Olliffe, former physician to the British Embassy in Paris. Her husband, Sir Hugh Bell, was a Middlesbrough ironmaster and Lord Lieutenant of Yorkshire,

sociology of reading habits highlighted similarities more than differences:

The *Illustrated Police Budget* is a sensational and much-read paper. In a number which has lately come into my hand there is a special double-page illustration headed 'Father Murders Six Children.' Outside the page, on one cover, is a picture of a man cutting his wife's throat, on the other of an actress being thrashed by an irate wife—the counterpart, in a cruder form, of the detective stories revelled in by readers of more education and a wider field of choice, such stories as 'Monsieur Lecoq'[90] and 'Sherlock Holmes.'

Lady Bell's drawing-room friends were just as predictable and imitative as the working classes in their reading:

The first fifty who were asked had all during the previous six months been reading the same books... five or six large biographies, a book of essays, some letters that had attracted attention, one or two novels by personal friends, one or two novels by writers of position: that is, all these educated people had been reading, exactly like the uneducated, the books that came under their hand or that other people had talked to them about... In the face of this very hand-to-mouth course of reading of the well-to-do, we can hardly wonder that the average working-man and his wife, who do not hear much talk of books or of writers, should not eagerly seek for the masterpieces of literature... It seems undeniable that for the great majority of people reading means recreation, not study: it is a pity we have only the one word to designate the two pursuits.[91]

Lady Bell did come across working-class readers with unusual interests—self-taught students of Greek, German, and French—and those who named Shakespeare, Dickens, and Thackeray, or biography, military history and science, and religious belief and unbelief, as their preferred reading. Flora Thompson's recollection was much the same, for she herself was of this type;[92] but what united all classes was the appetite for fictional sensation, adventure, and romance. Proof of this later came as a revelation to Sean O'Casey in his encounters with those leading men of letters and poets of Ireland, Oliver St John Gogarty and W. B. Yeats. Their godlike intellectual image was dented when he saw an Edgar Wallace novel fly out of Gogarty's burst-open suitcase, and a pile of westerns and detective stories crowding Yeats's mantelpiece.[93] People liked to be thrilled and preferred not to be made miserable by what they read. This was indicated by the literary agent W. M. Colles when he badgered Thomas Hardy in 1892 for 'a strong story suitable for working-class reading, melodramatic rather than

---

where he owned two substantial properties, Mount Grace and Rownton. Arthur Benson, who visited the Bells in 1911, recorded in his diary that their income was about £60,000 p.a., a massive sum; Newsome, *Edge of Paradise*, 287. For other family connections, see G. M. Trevelyan, *An Autobiography and Other Essays* (1949), 225. Lady Bell was a friend of Henry James in the 1890s; see Edel, *James*, ii. 121; and Kemp *et al.* (eds.), *Edwardian Fiction*, 9, 25.

[90] Book (1869; pub. in English, 1888) by Émile Gaboriau (1832–73), French pioneer of crime fiction. Fergus Hume's *The Mystery of a Hansom Cab* (1886) was inspired by Gaboriau's success; Sutherland, *Companion*, 313. Arnold Bennett also thought extremely highly of Gaboriau, who 'filled me with big, epic ideas for fundamental plot' (Flower (ed.) *Bennett Journals*, i. 110, 163–4 (26 Feb. 1901, 25 Mar. 1904)).

[91] Bell, *At the Works*, 146, 169–70.   [92] Thompson, *Lark Rise*, 100, 337, 359, 426–8.

[93] Sean O'Casey, *Inishfallen, Fare Thee Well* (1949), in O'Casey, *Autobiographies* (1963), 166.

tragic'.[94] Much the same phrase that had struck Lady Bell about popular reading habits was picked up by Holbrook Jackson in the years before the Great War: people avoided what they called 'heavy stuff' and rather wanted something 'that will take them "out of themselves"'. Jackson regarded this as symptomatic of the modern world, evident too in the popularity of musical comedy and of picture papers, postcards, and cinemas. Transient sensation was the thing, that which 'just passes the time and prevents its devotees thinking or realising or doing anything beyond the immediate more or less mechanical moods of the hour'. Hence, the trivial and ephemeral was 'the most important product of our day, because it is produced deliberately to satisfy the needs of a weary population': 'We just do our work without interest because we have to, and we are therefore forced to use all sorts of artistic narcotics to prevent our being bored with ourselves when we are not working . . . Our inner lives are bankrupt because we have bartered away the riches of thoughtful silence. Civilisation is in the shadows.'[95]

This was portentous stuff. Implicit in Jackson's polemic was the assumption that a structure of life once existed that trained previous generations to be more contemplative and to appreciate the profound. Historians, however, should guard against drawing large inferences from the habitual division of literature into 'serious' and 'light' categories; nor can they easily know how books were read, what sensations passed through readers' minds, what things held or lost their attention, and what experiences remained with them. But there is sufficient concrete and impressionistic evidence to cast doubt on the notion that the classics always roused in readers different emotions from so-called inferior works. The popular writer Annie S. Swan was quite aware of the close interest that her many readers took in the fate of her fictional characters:

Some years back I had a story running in the *People's Friend* in which there were two minor characters, a woman who had been for years a faithful and devoted servant in the family whose fortunes I was writing about. She married a man called George, who had faithfully 'followed' her for years. They had no children—a cross in Jess's life, for she had helped to bring up some children in the house she had left—so I thought she had better have one, just to satisfy a long-felt want. How wonderful to be able to wave the wizard's wand like this and fill up all the empty spaces! One day a friend of mine who lived in Kirkcaldy, happened to be in the news shop in the afternoon, when the women were crowding in to buy their *Friends*. On the pavement one woman, eager to get the next instalment, opened out the page, and suddenly, just as my friend passed by, gave a leap into the air, crying excitedly:

'Hurrah! Jess's gaun tae hae yin!'

Once, when she was addressing a political meeting of 2,000 women at Paisley, a note was passed from the audience to the chairman: 'Will Mrs. Burnett Smith [Annie S. Swan] tell us whether Captain Hannay is going to marry Jean Adair?'[96]

[94] Colles to Hardy, 24 Mar. 1892, in Purdy and Millgate (eds.), *Hardy Letters*, i. 261. Hardy was continually courted by Colles for stories, and mostly fended him off.

[95] Jackson, *Southward Ho!*, 191–6.   [96] Annie s. Swan, *My Life: An Authobiography* (1934) 294–5.

Compare this with Sidney Colvin's account of a reception half-a-century earlier at The Priory, the London home of the country's leading intellectual couple George Eliot and George Henry Lewes:

During the serial publication of *Middlemarch* [1871–2] I particularly remember his [Lewes's] taking me apart one day as I came in, and holding me by the button as he announced to me in confidence concerning one of its chief characters, 'Celia is going to have a baby!' This with an air at once gratified and mysterious, like that of some female gossip of a young bride in real life.[97]

No one will equate George Eliot and Annie S. Swan as authors of similar philosophical weight and permanent literary value; yet historians need to allow that a good story gripped alike the cerebral select of a literary salon and the humble housewife at her local newsagent's. Readers of George Eliot may not have been drawn to her for cogitation about evolutionary science and other such profound matters, and may well have skipped such passages as there were. Many a so-called classic had this in common with a best-seller, a story well told, containing a cast of individuals whose deeds and relationships made readers care and whose rites of passage they followed as closely as if they were members of their own families. 'Desperately in love with the hero', 26-year-old Mary Gladstone confided to her journal in 1874 after finishing Julia Kavanagh's *Nathalie* (1850). It was a mock confession, of course; and she did not kid herself that here was a great novel. But that was not the point: it was 'an enthralling book, and there is a scene towards the end wh. wd. melt the stoniest heart'.[98] By convention and popular preference, tears of sorrow should at the last give way to tears of joy. A precondition of a certain sort of story-reading was this willingness to embark on a roller-coaster ride of the emotions; and for the Victorians, that usually involved moral tests and struggles before virtue was rewarded and vice confounded. Such reading provided a kind of therapeutic or enhancement, strengthening the fibre so as to turn refreshed to tackle the serious cares of life. Mary Gladstone, in the next few days, also devoured Julia Kavanagh's *Adèle* (1858), but that did not work the spell. Indeed, it was 'rotten rather'. Even *Nathalie* she did not think measured up to the same author's *Daisy Burns* (1853), although her recommendation had now led her father, lately ejected from the premiership, to read it too. Then normal service was resumed in the Gladstone household: 'Long conv. with Papa evening—Homer, spiritualism, Jevons, ivories, and works of art. Homer before Moses. The redemption hinted at in his pages . . .'.[99] Still, Mary Gladstone would find one of her father's successors later confessing to the same weakness: in 1916 Lloyd George told her, after they chatted about the American Winston Churchill's historical romances, 'He can't read novels that end badly.'[100]

---

[97] Colvin, *Memories*, 92.
[98] Masterman (ed.), *Mary Gladstone*, 91 (17 Apr. 1874). On Kavanagh (1824–77), Sutherland, *Companion*, 343–4. [99] Ibid. 91 (24 May 1874). Jevons was W. S. Jevons (1835–82), the political economist.
[100] Ibid. 483 (22 Feb. 1916).

V

In the Middlesbrough readers' survey in 1907 Mrs Henry Wood had been nominated as a favourite author more times than Shakespeare and Dickens together. Lady Bell was a little puzzled by this. Mrs Wood, after all, had died in 1887 and her best-seller *East Lynne* was published over half a century ago, in 1861. Evidently passé now in higher social circles, she

doubtless delighted many of the educated when they were younger, that is, before their experience had shown what we will call the unlikelihood of some of her combinations. What makes her so popular among the working classes is probably, first of all, the admirable compound of the goody and the sensational: the skill in handling which enables her to present her material in the most telling form, and a certain directness and obvious sentiment that they can understand, while at the same time it is just enough above their usual standard of possibilities to give an agreeable sense of stimulus. 'East Lynne' is perhaps the book whose name one most often hears from men and women both. A poor woman, the widow of a workman, who had gone away to a distant part of the country, and was being supported by the parish, wrote to some one in her former town to say that she thought that if she had 'that beautiful book "East Lynne" it would be a comfort to her.' And on another occasion a workman, wishing to add to the library of a club he frequented, brought a copy of 'East Lynne', saying it was the book he liked best.[101]

The time-lag here was remarkable, proving that best-sellers could endure and not only dazzle for a day. Yet new books rarely enjoyed sustained sales. Nobody really knew the score, but Moberly Bell, planning the *Times* Book Club in 1905, reckoned that many fewer than 15 per cent of all books published would survive five years.[102] Reprints of 'classics' apart, those that did were textbooks more than novels. This was recognized in the vital contributions made to some publishers' fortunes by their education and school book department, such as at Cassell's, which H. O. Arnold-Forster joined in 1885, first as secretary, later as director. A nephew of Matthew Arnold and afterwards Secretary of State for War (1903–5), he was the author of the *Citizen Reader* (1886), which was 'adopted by almost all the School Boards in Great Britain', copied by the Japanese government, and sold 250,000 copies after five years and half a million in twenty years.[103] Few novels of any type could match such a performance. In 1925 Michael Joseph wrote: 'if it were possible to compile a list of the fifty biggest sellers among books in this country . . . the average author would be surprised to discover how many educational works figured in the list'. He instanced J. R. Green's *Short History of the English People* (1874) as one that still accumulated sales 'years after the meteoric novel published on the same day has sold its five or ten, or even twenty thousand

---

[101] Bell, *At the Works*, 166.   [102] Bell, *Moberly Bell*, 252.
[103] Nowell-Smith, *Cassell*, 108; *The Right Honourable Hugh Oakeley Arnold-Forster: A Memoir*, by his wife (1910), 62–5; Grant Duff, *Diary, 1886–1888*, ii. 131 (7 July 1888).

copies and, its little day over, passed into the limbo of forgotten books'.[104] Biography too could easily rival the best-selling novel. The most spectacular instance was John Morley's *Life of Gladstone*, which Macmillan's published on commission for the Gladstone family in three volumes in 1903. Some 25,000 copies were sold in the first year, and the family had pocketed over £30,000 by the time the *Life* was reproduced in fifteen sixpenny parts and two five-shilling volumes in 1906. To these were added a 50,000 print run of a five-shilling Lloyd's Edition in 1908–9, and a renewed three-volume edition in Macmillan's Shilling Library in 1911–12.[105]

It was textbooks that generally proved the longest-distance runners. Arnold Bennett's ruminations in his journal in 1929 underscore this point. He recorded how an elderly author at table with him had been making envious noises about novelists' royalties, remarks obviously directed towards him; and Bennett discovered that this elderly author's most popular book had, in the previous year, sold 'only 7,800 copies'. He asked him when it was published, and was surprised to learn that it was about 1900. The book was a textbook. Bennett did not come clean to this complainant, but he could have

informed him that the number of modern novelists whose novels reach an annual sale of 7,800 copies after being extant for thirty years is as near zero as makes no matter. We might have informed him that the sale of the ordinary fairly successful novel comes to an end within six months of publication, if not sooner; though of course a small percentage of novels do achieve the cheap-edition stage—a stage, however, which brings but relatively trifling sums to the author.

Bennett pondered his own case, doubting whether any of his novels had matched in a 3*s.* 6*d.* edition its sales in original form; moreover, books priced more cheaply would not 'stand' much advertising by publishers fearful of losing money. As clinching proof, he stated that 'the most popular of all my seventy-four or -five books, published some twenty years ago, has an annual sale of about 3,000 copies, with which I am well content'. That too had been a textbook of sorts: *How to Live on Twenty-Four Hours a Day* (1912).[106] Bennett's friend H. G. Wells was acute enough both to perceive this and to act upon it. In 1917 he moaned, 'I've had my boom. I'm yesterday'; then in 1920 he published *The Outline of History*. This amassed sales of 3 million and earned Wells more than all his other works combined. His complaint to Bennett now was different: 'He said "The Outline of History" was ruining him—in income tax.'[107]

---

[104] Joseph, *Commercial Side of Literature*, 52–3; Morgan, *Macmillan*, 107, for the fee (£30 outright) paid to Green. Joseph also cited technical books on 'wireless, tennis, cricket, dancing, football, motoring, gardening, engineering, photography, spiritualism', as commonly achieving sales of 50,000 and even 100,000 in cheap editions, though these usually required a well-known 'name' on the title page to take off. Looking to the future, he reckoned the economics textbook a profitable market to pursue.

[105] Morgan, *Macmillan*, 191–2.   [106] Bennett, *Journal 1929*, 133–5.

[107] Flower (ed.), *Bennett Journals*, ii. 206, 265 (10 Oct. 1917, 14 Apr. 1920); and Mackenzie, *Wells*, 413.

East Lynne, therefore, was a marathon seller, exceptional in its stamina. Moreover, it was not the case that the intellectual or upper classes had all forgotten Mrs Wood since the 1860s. Francis Hirst noted in his journal in 1899 a dinner conversation between John Morley and Mary Drew ('the cleverest of Mr. Gladstone's daughters') who both 'praised Mrs. Henry Wood';[108] and Lady Cynthia Asquith's diary recorded about one January Sunday in 1917, 'Stayed in bed until dinner. I read *East Lynne* until my eyes ached.'[109] According to the *Daily Express* in May 1910, *East Lynne* had been Edward VII's favourite novel.[110] Edward, of course, was not to be reckoned either upper- or intellectual class, being above the one and below the other; but in this choice of fiction he was closest to his ordinary subjects. It is a reasonable assumption for the historian to make that, if a late Victorian or Edwardian household contained any book apart from the Bible, Bunyan, and Shakespeare, that book would be *East Lynne*. Annie Swan, born in 1859, was raised on a Berwickshire farm and then at Leith, where the family reading matter was limited by her father's religious zeal—he joined the Evangelical Union, influenced by the Morisonian revival—but she vividly recalled the occasion when her mother 'surprised us all by retiring to her room for a whole day, abandoning everything. The mystery was explained by a copy of *East Lynne*, which had been brought surreptitiously into the house, and in which she became so engrossed that she ceased to "care a hang", as we expressed it, for anything or anybody.'[111] The sales of *East Lynne* actually climbed as the late nineteenth century progressed. It was first serialized in the *New Monthly Magazine* in 1861 and, famously, when Mrs Wood was seeking to publish it as a book, Chapman & Hall were advised to reject it by their reader, George Meredith.[112] Bentley's accepted it, and a review in *The Times*, 25 January 1862, launched it. The book went into its fifth imprint in that same year. The 65th thousand copy was issued in 1876, the 141st thousand in 1887.[113] Bentley's 1897 edition was described as the 460th thousand; a year later the firm was bought out by Macmillan's, whose 1899 edition boasted the half-million, the 1902 edition that of the 560th thousand. The popularity of *East Lynne* carried Mrs Wood's other titles with it. When Thomas Seccombe wrote his notice for the *DNB* in 1900, he observed that, of her many other books, *The Channings* (1862) was also still selling strongly, the 140th thousand in 1895 and the 200th thousand in 1898; *The Shadow of Ashlydyat* (1863) had reached its 150th thousand and *Within the Maze* (1872) its 112th thousand, in 1899; and that the sale of *Mrs Halliburton's Troubles* (1862), *Lord Oakburn's Daughters* (1864), *Roland Yorke* (1869), and *Edina* (1876), 'shows at present no sign of diminution'.[114] Altogether, some forty of Mrs Wood's titles featured in Macmillan's list, and a newspaper advertisement by the firm in 1904 boomed that

---

[108] Hirst, *Golden Days*, 182 (13 Sept. 1899).   [109] Asquith, *Diaries*, 256 (14 Jan. 1917).
[110] McMillan, *Way we Were*, 31.   [111] Swan, *Life*, 22.
[112] Meredith wrote: 'Opinion emphatically against it. In the worst style of the present taste.' He was not unsupported, however: the senior partner Edward Chapman also 'considered that the tone of the book was not good for the general public' (Sassoon, *Meredith*, 67).   [113] *The Times*, 11 Feb. 1887.
[114] *DNB*, lxii (1900), 356–7.

these had sold over 3 million copies. Less than three years later Macmillan's advertisements claimed sales of over 4.7 million copies, price 2s. in green cloth, 2s. 6d. in red.[115]

Book-borrowers behaved in the same way as book-buyers. In the late 1890s the librarian of Bootle asked his colleagues in other free libraries about the most popular authors among their readers. The largest libraries were unable to give details, but twelve medium-sized towns and fifteen smaller ones did so, and heading the list in sixteen libraries was Mrs Henry Wood.[116] As for the numerous stage adaptations of *East Lynne*, the most famous was that by T. A. Palmer, which opened at Nottingham in 1874. It was in this, not in the novel itself, that the tragic heroine Lady Isabel Vane shrieks at the death of her son, 'Dead! Dead! and . . . never called me mother'. The *Times* obituarist of Mrs Wood in 1887 noted that stage adaptations of *East Lynne* were being 'almost nightly performed in different parts of England and France, as well as in the United States', and the *DNB* in 1900 stated that these remained 'one of the staple productions of touring companies both in England and abroad'.

All this was well known to people in the theatre. Henry Irving once took a drive through Norfolk with his son Laurence and the fashion-writer Mrs Aria, whose sister was the novelist Frank Danby (Mrs Julia Frankau). Having enjoyed tea at a farmhouse, Irving proposed to reward the farmer's wife with a signed photograph and perhaps some books, for there was none in the living room. Mrs Aria was sent into the parlour to communicate this:

'Would you like some books?'
  She replied decisively, 'No, thank you, I have one.'
  My thoughts flowed reverentially.
  'We take to it at Christmas-time.' I was the more impressed by the certainty that the book was the Bible; I could see it in its black binding, gold-lettered, all tenderly lifted from its shelf . . .
  'It is *East Lynne*: have you heard of it? We read it aloud in the winters when it is too dark to work.'
  In the landau later I recounted my miscarried mission. '*East Lynne, East Lynne*', repeated Irving, 'strange', and he fell at once to telling me that provincial theatres presented the play continually.[117]

Over a long career most actors at one time or another would have played in *East Lynne* at some provincial or suburban theatre. Irving himself had done so in Birmingham and Liverpool in 1865, taking the part of Archibald Carlyle; and it was in the same role at the Surrey Theatre in 1867 that Wilson Barrett first achieved recognition in London.[118] Wilde paid his respects in his first play, *Lady*

---

[115] *Pall Mall Gazette*, 8 July 1904, 4; *T.P.'s Weekly*, 8 Feb. 1907, 181.
[116] J. J. Ogle, *The Free Library* (1897), cited in Kelly, *Public Libraries*, 193.
[117] Aria, *Sentimental Self*, 95.
[118] R. J. Broadbent, *Annals of the Liverpool Stage* (Liverpool, 1908), 278; Irving, *Irving*, 702–3; *DNB Supplement. 1901–1911*, i. 101, for Barrett. Q recalled, of his childhood in Cornwall in the 1860s and 1870s, that

Windermere's Fan (1892), in which Lady Windermere's mother is disclosed as Mrs Erlynne, the woman with a past.[119] In the social survey of Norwich, published in 1910, it was remarked that the only theatre still surviving in the city, which had not become a music hall or cinema, 'restricts itself to third-rate companies in such plays as "East Lynne" and "The Bad Girl of the Family"'.[120] The cinema itself caught up with *East Lynne* in 1902: there were nine such films before 1918. So well known was the book (or play or film) it elicited a film parody, *East Lynne with Variations*, by Mack Sennett in 1919.

Sustained popularity, more than critical reputation, marked Wilkie Collins's works also. Swinburne complained about this disparagement when Collins died in 1889. Though Collins 'was no more a Dickens than Dickens was a Shakespeare', Swinburne nonetheless argued that *The Woman in White* (1860) and *The Moonstone* (1868) displayed 'incomparable ability', and *Armadale* (1866) would have been considered a notable achievement if anyone but an Englishman had written it.[121] In fact, the *Times* obituary of Collins had been respectful about *The Woman in White*: pronounced 'the first of English novels of plot and situation', it was, while avowedly a sensational story, 'a novel of character as well, and Count Fosco is a creation almost of the first order'.[122] It was, moreover, true that numerous best-selling novelists copied Collins's characteristic craft of construction, the chessboard technique of telling a story through the correspondence or voices of several characters. The epistolary formula survived to serve Elinor Glyn well enough in *The Visits of Elizabeth* (1900) and C. N. and A. M. Williamson in *The Lightning Conductor* (1902), just as it had Bram Stoker in *Dracula* (1897). Also essaying to revive Collins's standing in 1904, *T.P.'s Weekly* argued by analogy with the epicure who went into raptures when he discovered the mutton chop. The 'mere cleverness' of modern writers was becoming 'a little shrill, and the alleged epigram is proving too incessantly the paste of platitude'; hence it hoped that contemporary literary gourmets might turn away from such decorative but thin and unsatisfying dishes and rediscover with relish the nourishing sturdiness of Collins. A pessimism shadowed the panegyric, however: 'Nobody has quite taken his place; nobody gives us the fireside thrill of mystery that this novelist gave to his generation. Perhaps it is our own fault; perhaps we have become too sceptical, too ironical on the score of prepared conclusions, to accept the old-fashioned hypnotism.'[123] These critical debates were rather lost on the public. 'There is no necessity to dwell upon the characteristics of "The Woman in White",' *The Times* had observed in 1889, 'for everybody has read it, and many people have read it

---

East Lynne was among the fare staged by the touring Theatre Royal company from Plymouth when it played in Bodmin during the Whitsun holiday; Quiller-Couch, *Memories*, 16. Nicoll, *Late Nineteenth Century Drama*, ii. 671, lists nine adaptations by anonymous hands.

[119] Powell, *Wilde*, ch. 2 for the sources and interplay of this comedy.

[120] Hawkins, *Norwich*, 310. Frederick Melville's *The Bad Girl of the Family* was premiered at the Elephant and Castle Theatre, 4 Oct. 1909, before moving to the Aldwych after Christmas.

[121] Swinburne, *Studies*, 110–28.   [122] *The Times*, 24 Sept. 1889.

[123] Article by L.L.L. in *T.P.'s Weekly*, 27 May 1904, 701.

several times over'.[124] And they continued to do so: *The Woman in White* sold a further 300,000 copies when a sixpenny paper edition was brought out in the 1890s.

Nor did ordinary readers need reminding of the merits of Miss M. E. Braddon's *Lady Audley's Secret* (1862). Lady Bell's survey of the Middlesbrough working class in 1907 naturally noted her name.[125] At that date Braddon was still an active producer of fiction; indeed, her productivity was always astonishing. When Bernard Shaw was reviewing for the *Pall Mall Gazette* in the late 1880s, he termed her 'a princess among novel manufacturers', then added: 'There ought to be legislation against this sort of thing—on the lines of the Factory Acts.'[126] Her popularity was not just with the groundlings. Among her early admirers were Bulwer Lytton, Charles Reade, and Thackeray; Robert Louis Stevenson enjoyed her too; and Mr Gladstone left behind the cares of state by reading her.[127] Miss Braddon was 'a top favourite with the circulating library subscriber [and] with the railway reader (by 1899, fifty-seven of her novels had appeared in yellow backs)'.[128] Indeed, there appeared to be no sanctuary where she was not encountered. Readers beginning lessons on the Pitman language course, issued in penny weekly parts with English in one column and a German translation opposite, started off with a passage from the *Windsor Magazine* which described Braddon at work on her novel-writing.[129] 'It is a fact', wrote Arnold Bennett at the turn of the century, 'that there are thousands of tolerably educated English people who have never heard of Meredith, Hardy, Ibsen, Maeterlinck, Kipling, Barrie, Crockett; but you would travel far before you reached the zone where the name of Braddon failed of its recognition.'[130] Again it was the case, as with Mrs Henry Wood, that performances of the many plays she had written and of the umpteen stage adaptations (many of them piratical) of her novels spread her popularity. The young Henry Irving impersonated Talbot Bulstrode at the Theatre Royal, Manchester, in 1864 in the stage version of *Aurora Floyd* (1863), and played Harry Thorncote at the Prince of Wales's Theatre, Liverpool, in 1866 in the splendidly titled *Only a Clod*;[131] and *Lady Audley's Secret* was first filmed in 1912, and again in 1915 and 1920. In an admittedly 'somewhat unscientific' survey of twenty-one public libraries in 1907, Woolwich's librarian had concluded that Miss Braddon was the most popular author.[132]

---

[124] *The Times*, 24 Sept. 1889.

[125] Bell, *At the Works*, 147, 165. Ogle's survey of the most popular authors among borrowers from free libraries in 1897 placed Miss Braddon the equal of Dickens: out of twenty-seven libraries making returns, each headed the list in four libraries. See Kelly, *Public Libraries*, 193.

[126] Holroyd, *Shaw*, i. 214.

[127] See e.g. his reading *Gerard* (1891) and *The Venetians* (1892); Matthew (ed.), *Gladstone Diaries*, xii. 414, xiii. 32, 63.

[128] Sutherland, *Companion*, 80–1; also Michael Sadleir's notice in *DNB 1912–1921*, 377–8. Kemp *et al.* (eds.), *Edwardian Fiction*, 42–3, like Sutherland, gives the year of birth as 1835 instead of 1837.

[129] *Pitman's German Weekly*, 2 Oct. 1897, 3.   [130] Bennett, *Fame and Fiction*, 24–5.

[131] Irving, *Irving*, 114, 697, 703.

[132] Ernest A. Baker, 'The Standard of Fiction in Public Libraries', *Library Association Record*, 9 (1907), cited in Stearn, 'Mysterious Mr. Le Queux', 9, 25.

It was her most famous title that carried the rest: her novels were commonly advertised as having been written, not by Miss Braddon as such, but by the 'author of *Lady Audley's Secret*'.[133] The immense success of that particular story, with sales reckoned nearly a million copies in her lifetime, was also something of a curse. Not only was she 'foolishly and savagely attacked during the seventies and eighties . . . as the most dangerous of the "sensation novelists", whose work was liable to corrupt the minds of young people by its violence and by its power to make wickedness alluring', but her other work was apt to be 'dismissed as without proportion, thought, or character-analysis, by critics who based their judgement solely on this one preposterously successful melodrama.'[134] *Punch's* reviewer of *One Life, One Love* in 1891 had nonetheless remained enraptured: 'Marvellous, Miss Braddon! Very few have approached you in sensation-writing, and none in keeping up sensationalism as fresh as ever it was when first I sat up at night nervously to read *Aurora Floyd*, and *Lady Audley's Secret*.'[135] Moreover, Miss Braddon did develop as a writer, thought Arnold Bennett, who sought to explain her popularity in 1901. He was impressed—'astonished', he put it—by 'the sound vigour' of her style, by 'the slow and various ingenuity' by which she unravelled her plots, and by her 'vast embracing sympathy'. 'Good sense and broad charity' characterized her work and 'the tone is often frankly religious', by which Bennett meant that

Sin must be punished; the future must pay for the past: but, this being granted, let us have riches and bright tempers, and eat well and dress well and live in glorious old mansions . . . she represents the best aspect of average humanity—that 'ultimate decency' which resides somewhere in everyone. It is this quality which is the deepest root of her success.[136]

Her portrait was painted by W. P. Frith, the scenic artist of *Ramsgate Sands* (1853), *Derby Day* (1858), and *The Railway Station* (1862), who had also produced a famous study of his friend Charles Dickens (1859).

By the Edwardian period Miss Braddon was being treated by popular literary journals much like a national treasure. Yet there was also a hint of mystery and impropriety. As *M.A.P.* put it, her entertaining at Lichfield House, Richmond, made her a familiar figure in literary, theatre, and art circles; and this handsome Georgian 'home, her method of work, her horses and her dogs have often been described in the Press, but she herself has never yet been interviewed; indeed, the interviewer is the only literary person who is not a welcome guest'.[137] The reasons for this reticence are not hard to fathom. The product of a broken marriage, Braddon compounded adversity and social unacceptability when, having begun to write stories to support her mother and herself, and having had a spell on stage as an actress, she embarked on a liaison with the magazine

---

[133] *Review of Reviews* (June 1892), 82.   [134] Michael Sadleir, *DNB 1912–1921*, 377–8.
[135] *Punch*, 7 Feb. 1891, 65.   [136] Bennett, *Fame and Fiction*, 32–3.
[137] *M.A.P.*, 9 July 1904, 35.

publisher John Maxwell. She then had five children—a sixth died—by him at a time when Maxwell had five other children and his wife was consigned to an insane asylum. That was in the 1860s, when Maxwell's business was precarious. He was bailed out largely by the prodigious earnings of his paramour, who, for a while, acted more or less as her own publisher. Maxwell and Braddon married in 1874 when the first Mrs Maxwell was dead and, after she herself had become a widow in 1895, the earlier scandal of her marital life had run its course. Lady Dorothy Nevill, for example, counted her a 'great friend of mine' in the Edwardian period.[138] In her own memoirs in 1910 Mrs T. P. O'Connor recorded how she was thrilled to meet 'the authoress of *Lady Audley's Secret*, which I thought and still think the best novel of the kind ever written. Mrs Maxwell was a tall, dignified woman, dressed in black and white, her face wore a very kind expression, and she was as modest and as feminine as a woman who had done nothing'.[139]

This modesty struck Ford Madox Ford who also visited her at Richmond; but it was a personal, not professional, characteristic. She 'took her work more seriously than herself'; and Ford like Bennet admired her style. She composed 'sound English—like Cobbett's'. Braddon was then in her eighties, yet her intellectual energy was unabated, and she had set herself to learn Greek in order to read Homer in the original.[140] 'Gracious and indomitable' was the description of her by Walter Sichel, who also made her acquaintance in this later period.[141] When she died in 1915, the funeral took place in Richmond parish church, where, a few months later, a memorial tablet was unveiled that proclaimed 'Miss Braddon (Mrs. Mary Elizabeth Maxwell)' to have been a 'writer of rare and refined scholarship, who gave profitable and pleasurable literature to countless readers in her library of three score and ten works of fiction'. Present was a large attendance of worthies including the local MP and soon-to-be Home Secretary George Cave, a posse of clergymen, several titled personages, and a miscellaneous band of authors, from Mrs Humphry Ward to Bram Stoker and Charles Garvice.[142] Braddon's three sons now constituted a minor literary dynasty—the eldest, Gerald Maxwell, was drama critic of the *Court Journal* and author of several plays and stories; Edward, a barrister, was a writer on legal and social questions; and William, initially a journalist on *The World*, had embarked on his own path as a popular novelist, and ended his career as chairman of the Society of Authors and of the National Book Council.[143]

Miss Braddon had appeared still uneclipsed at the turn of the century. As Edmund Downey put it in 1903, 'It is no mean record for a book published nearly forty years ago to sustain as "Lady Audley" does, as strong a hold upon novel-readers to-day as it promptly established when it appeared in its three-volume

[138] Nevill, *Reminiscences*, 322.   [139] O'Connor, *I Myself*, 161.
[140] Ford, *Nightingale*, 73.   [141] Sichel, *Sands of Time*, 219.
[142] See the newspaper cutting in Richmond Library, Local Studies, ref. L920.089.BLE 35.
[143] Kemp *et al.*(eds.), *Edwardian Fiction*, 273–4.

dress.'[144] The income it generated was remarkable: having bought the copyright for £250, the original publisher, William Tinsley—who was a gamekeeper's son, 'quite witless and quite *h*-less', according to George Moore—built himself a villa near Barnes, which he called Audley Lodge.[145] Moore pinpointed his own awakening interest in fiction to overhearing his parents discussing whether Lady Audley murdered her husband. Then aged 11, Moore 'took the first opportunity of stealing the novel in question. I read it eagerly, passionately, vehemently,' afterwards progressing to the rest of Braddon's fiction, including *The Doctor's Wife*, about 'a lady who loved Shelley and Byron', which in turn led him to take up those poets and to fall under Shelley's spell in particular. He was thus grateful to her on both accounts.[146]

It was this trio—Wilkie Collins, Mrs Henry Wood, and Miss Braddon—who had given rise to the phenomenon of the sensation novel.[147] James Joyce saluted them in *Ulysses* (1922) via Molly Bloom's soliloquy in which she recounts how her friend Hester 'gave me the Moonstone to read that was the first I read of Wilkie Collins East Lynne I read an the shadow of Ashlydyat Mrs Henry Wood Henry Dunbar by that other woman . . .'.[148] The ingredients of the sensation novel were: passion aplenty (including much fainting), adulterous secrets (ideally, bigamy), multiple murders and myriad disguises, solemn oaths and family curses (insanity preferred), apparitions and deathbed scenes, missing letters and con-tested wills, cryptograms and forgeries, chases and accidents (railway crashes a speciality, although colliery explosions, storms, and cataclysms allowed), and aristocratic, professional, and humble folk who are all intriguingly inter-connected and who often bear significant facial resemblances. Importantly, some central female character must be not only beautiful but wicked or, at least, devious and guilty. The homicidal heroine was Miss Braddon's particular hall-mark, which is why latter-day feminist critics enthusiastically decode her work as that of a prototypical revolutionary, surreptitiously casting off the corsets of Victorian restraints on women.[149] Marriage law and its hardships were also

---

[144] Edmund Downey, 'Miss Braddon and her Work', *T.P.'s Weekly*, 24 July 1903, 203.

[145] On Tinsley's, see Sutherland, *Companion*, 630–1; and Sutherland's essay 'Tinsley Brothers', in Anderson and Rose (eds.), *British Literary Publishing Houses*, 299–303. The firm was bankrupt in 1878, owing over £30,000. Eveleigh Nash, who saw Tinsley in his old age in the 1890s, was told that at one period Tinsley was spending £1,000 a year in entertainment at the Gaiety Restaurant: Nash, *Life*, 30–1. Hardy's first three novels were published by Tinsley, *Desperate Remedies* (1871), *Under the Greenwood Tree* (1872), and *A Pair of Blue Eyes* (1873). He retained bitter memories of Tinsley's mean treatment; Flower, *Just as it Happened*, 89–90.   [146] Moore, *Confessions*, 2–3, 167, 211.

[147] The *Edinburgh Review* commented in 1864: 'two years ago nobody would have known what was meant by a Sensation Novel; yet now the term has already passed through the stage of jocular use . . . and has been adopted as the regular commercial name for a particular product of industry for which there is just now a brisk demand' (quoted in Winifred Hughes, *The Maniac in the Cellar: Sensation Novels of the 1860s* (Princeton, 1981). Sutherland, *Companion*, 562–3, includes Dickens and Reade as pioneers of the genre.

[148] Joyce, *Ulysses*, 677, the obscurer references being to Wood's *The Shadow of Ashlydyat* (1863) and Braddon's *Henry Dunbar* (1864).

[149] Elaine Showalter, *A Literature of their Own: From Charlotte Brontë to Doris Lessing*, rev. edn. (1982), ch. vi, esp. 157–68.

crucial to Mrs Wood's *East Lynne*, but she was otherwise politically Conservative, conventionally anti-Catholic, and a churchgoer with a passionate concern for temperance reform. Markedly, therefore, it was towards Braddon, not Wood, that Mrs Oliphant[150] pointed an accusing finger, for being 'the inventor of the fair-haired demon of modern fiction'.[151] More judiciously, Henry James, while also writing on the subject of Braddon, decided that to Wilkie Collins 'belongs the credit of having introduced into fiction those most mysterious of mysteries, the mysteries that are at our own doors'. The sensation novel had domesticated the gothic romance, and its terror was all the more terrible for having been removed from some improbable, faraway castle and placed in an English country house, a suburban villa, or 'in the heart of civilised London'.[152]

The shift was dramatically contrasted by the *Westminster Review* a decade before: 'It was the fashion then to construct a story out of strange and unnatural *circumstances*, it is the fashion now to elaborate it out of morbid *feelings* and overwrought *sensibilities*.'[153] By playing on psychic disturbances, the sensation novel was perceived as a threat to family stability by fostering morbid neuroses among middle-class women who, it was thought, showed a narcotic craving for this class of literature. Here Mrs Oliphant indicted the method of distribution, noting that 'the violent stimulus of serial publication—of *weekly* publication—with its necessity for frequent and rapid recurrence of piquant incident and startling situation—is the thing above all others most likely to develop the germ, and bring it to fuller and darker bearing'.[154] Yet the originality and impact of these novels may both be questioned. They had much in common with the melodramas that dominated the Victorian stage; and critics then and since have debated how to measure their influence, whether their chaotic improbabilities and teeming immoralities represented an anarchic challenge to Victorian religious and social orderliness, or whether anything so grotesquely unrealistic and transparently escapist can be dignified with philosophical content and carry serious implications. The sensation novels in any case were congeries, and they soon burst apart into subspecies: adventure, thriller, detective, romantic, horror, and fantasy fictions. It was in these styles that the late nineteenth and early twentieth centuries' successors to Wilkie Collins, Mrs Wood, and Miss Braddon as best-sellers were principally to be found.

---

[150] Mrs Oliphant (1828–97) was also a best-seller in the 1860s with a seven-volume series known as *The Chronicles of Carlingford*, but in a more domestic vein; and her need as a young widow to support her family by her pen won a wide circle of admirers, among them Queen Victoria, who was represented at her funeral; *The Times*, 28 June 1897. A memorial was unveiled at St Giles', Edinburgh, by J. M. Barrie in 1908; Mackail, *Barrie*, 403.

[151] 'Novels', *Blackwood's Magazine*, Sept. 1867, in Elizabeth Jay (ed.), *The Autobiography of Margaret Oliphant* (Oxford, 1990), 178.

[152] Henry James, 'Miss Braddon', *The Nation*, 9 Nov. 1865, 594, in Taylor, *Secret Theatre*, 1.

[153] 'The Progress of Fiction as Art', *Westminster Review* (Oct. 1853), 358, in Taylor, *Secret Theatre*, 6.

[154] Margaret Oliphant, 'Sensation Novels', *Blackwood's Magazine* (May 1862), 568, in Taylor, *Secret Theatre*, 5.

VI

The term 'best-seller' post-dated the appearance of the sensation novel: it was of American coinage in 1889, although the adjectival 'best-selling' remained commoner in England, where *The Bookman* from the 1890s published lists of books most in demand.[155] The 'best-seller' concept arrived, therefore, with the maturing of the first generation to be educated under the 1870 Act and at the point where the three-decker novel of restricted sales and commercial library circulation began to be eclipsed by single-volume fiction of popular sales and public-library borrowing. The previous position was well defined in the statement with which the *Review of Reviews* habitually headed its column listing new works of fiction: 'Two and three-volume novels are rarely purchased; readers can always obtain them in abundance at the circulating libraries.'[156] Signs were plentiful that artists of all kinds could not presume for ever upon the public's patience as an age of increasing hurry generated competing demands upon people's attention. The vogue for short stories was already pointing the way, and when the triple-decker novel was finally challenged, it tumbled to the ground with startling suddenness. Between 1894 and 1895 the publication of three-volume novels fell from 184 to fifty-two; in 1896 it halved again, to twenty-five; and in 1897 only four were published. The *coup de grâce* had been administered by the runaway success of one best-seller, Hall Caine's *The Manxman*, issued in one volume in 1894, priced 6*s*., although other authors who had had titles published in this format—George Moore, *A Mummer's Wife* (1885), and Rider Haggard, *She* (1886)—subsequently would claim a supporting or starring role in this victory.[157]

The supremacy of the six-shilling novel had a seismic effect on the world of publishing. At the Authors' Club in 1910, reviewing progress over the past quarter-century, Robertson Nicoll declared: 'The great difference between publishing in 1886 and publishing in 1910 is that in the former year the author was still seeking the publisher, whereas in the latter the publisher is seeking the author.'[158] In 1912 Edmund H. Peer, of W. H. Smith's, noted: 'Publishers are keener than ever for best sellers and pray ardently' for them.[159] They did more than pray, being not averse to priming both author and market. Throughout the Victorian period and after, publishers endeavoured to persuade, even dictate, what an author should write. In the case of authors who had written one best-seller, this generally meant that they should write their next book along the same lines, while authors who had not so far written a best-seller should model theirs on

---

[155] *Oxford English Dictionary, New Supplement*; Keating, *Haunted Study*, 439–40.

[156] *Review of Reviews* (Jan. 1890), 78. Barrie expressed the same more humorously; publishing a novel in three volumes, he wrote, was a form whose 'drawback . . . is that the author cannot see his book bought' (Barrie, quoting his own article written in the late 1880s for the *St James's Gazette*, in *Greenwood Hat*, 41).

[157] Keating, *Haunted Study*, 26, 423; Guinevere L. Griest, *Mudie's Circulating Library and the Victorian Novel* (Newton Abbot, 1970), 208–9.   [158] Darlow, *Nicoll*, 334.

[159] *Newsbasket* (Aug. 1912), 186. Dr J. J. McAleer kindly supplied me with this reference.

someone who had.[160] The crime writer Dick Donovan was in this second category, plodding along in Conan Doyle's footsteps. In 1906 he lamented:

There are very few professional writers, as far as my experience goes, who are able to write exactly what they would like to write; to descend to trade phraseology, they must follow the market, and it cannot be doubted, painful as it is to have to acknowledge it, that the public demand at the present day is for sensationalism. Sensationalism is the key-note of success, whether it be in connection with the stage, writing books, or running newspapers. Notwithstanding this irrefutable fact, the very papers that depend upon sensationalism for their existence, and often descend to very low depths in order to pander to the morbid tastes of the public, are the first to lecture an author severely on what they are pleased to term his 'sensational and melodramatic style'.[161]

Best-selling authors for their part could play hard to get, whereupon publishers might have to spend more than they wanted not only in fees or royalties but also in advertising. This had been evident already in the case of Dickens. Thus Chapman & Hall, having had Dickens and lost him, were desperate to keep him when he returned to them after 1859. This climaxed with the £7,500 advance he was offered for *The Mystery of Edwin Drood* (1870), the firm having previously issued a million handbills to publicize his last completed novel, *Our Mutual Friend* (1865). Advertising might even turn a book by a little-known author into a best-seller. The effectiveness of a spicy slogan or gimmick was never better demonstrated than in Cassell's launch of Rider Haggard's *King Solomon's Mines* (1885). Having made neither name nor money with his first effort, the triple-decker *Dawn* (1884), and dejectedly taken up legal practice, Haggard had knocked off *King Solomon's Mines* in six weeks, some of it scribbled on a pad on his knees during weekend train journeys between Norwich and London, and all because of a five-shilling bet with his brother that he could write a story as good as *Treasure Island* (1883). Cassell's being Stevenson's publisher, it was natural for Haggard to turn to them; he was also conscious of the entrancement which the map in *Treasure Island* had worked on the reader. He urged that his map in *King Solomon's Mines* be 'drawn with real blood to get the desired effect'. Cassell's demurred and instead

became very busy—secretly. They prepared long narrow posters—each as long as a hoarding—on which was printed in huge type:

> *King Solomon's Mines—The Most Amazing Book Ever Written.*

Some nights after the publication of Haggard's book they put these posters up *after dark* on hoardings all over London. People went to their work on the horse-buses in the morning to find this message at every turning. '*King Solomon's Mines—The Most Amazing Book Ever Written*'.

They could not get away from it. They went out to their lunch—rich men and poor—and found the same statement staring them in the face. They began to believe it. What was this book? They must know.

---

[160] J. A. Sutherland, *Victorian Novelists and Publishers* (1976) is very good on this.

[161] On Dick Donovan (J. E. Muddock, 1843–1934) and his financial plight, see Kemp *et al.* (eds.), *Edwardian Fiction*, 102–3.

education,[180] Wallace had disenjoyed a succession of dead-end jobs before enlisting in the Army in 1894. It was in South Africa, to which he was sent as a medical orderly in 1896, that the writing bug stirred in him, by first imitating Kipling's verses. He even got to meet his hero, although Kipling sought to dampen his ambition of becoming a professional author with the dictum 'Literature is a splendid mistress, but a bad wife!'[181] Literature was no worse than the Army, from which Wallace shrewdly purchased his discharge just after the outbreak of the Boer War. He stayed on as a war correspondent, became editor of the *Rand Daily Mail*, then returned to London to join Alfred Harmsworth's *Daily Mail*, which assigned him a series on the unemployed. He accepted only for reasons of self-advertisement, social concern being fashionable: 'I hate the British working man; I have no sympathy with him; whether he lives or dies, feeds or starves, is not the slightest interest to me.'[182] What was of interest was making money as an author. He reckoned that a melodrama, *An African Millionaire*, based on Cecil Rhodes, would mint it for him; but it flopped, even in South Africa. A switch to another genre was called for. Love was not Wallace's strong suit, so romance was out. It would have to be what every reporter should have instincts for: detection and sensation.

The result was *The Four Just Men*, involving a plot by anarchists to dispose of a troublesome foreign secretary. The story had some topicality—the conspirators wanted to stop an Aliens Extradition Bill—but, the *Times Literary Supplement* noted, it marked an advance of 'murder as a fine art'. 'Modern science', the reviewer explained, 'lets the novelist revel in dark and deadly methods of sudden death.' Wallace revelled more than most: he 'undertakes with immense gusto to make the flesh of his reader creep'.[183] The book was also no ordinary production since Wallace had failed to persuade a publisher to take it on. He therefore decided to publish it himself and bribe the public into buying it by splashing out £1,000 on newspaper and bookshop advertisements and on a poster campaign all over London, offering a further £1,000 in prizes to readers who best solved the mystery of how the murder was committed in a locked room in Downing Street. This was not an original ploy; for instance, E. J. Goodman's *The Only Witness* (1891), a shilling paperback published by Trischler, was a 'sensational novel which breaks off in mid-career, a prize of £30 being offered to the reader first successful in solving the mystery of the plot'.[184] But the sums held out by Wallace were mesmerizing and some 38,000 copies of his novel were snapped up.[185] This was recklessness on a grand scale, and quite in character for one who was an undisciplined gambler on cards and horses. It was also close to fraud because

---

[180] Until he was more certain of himself, Wallace lied about his place of education. His entry in *Who's Who* (1905), 1670, reads: '*Educ.*: London, privately'. In later entries he told the truth: '*Educ.*: London Board School'; see *Who Was Who, 1929–40*, 1405. In 1905 Wallace was back in London, but he had compiled the entry when thousands of miles away in Johannesburg.

[181] Lane, *Wallace*, 100. Lane was Wallace's daughter-in-law.

[182] Ibid. 173.   [183] *TLS*, 10 Oct. 1905, 387.   [184] *Review of Reviews* (July 1891), 96.

[185] Frank Swinnerton, *The Georgian Literary Scene*, rev. edn. (1938), 444.

Wallace had no means of paying for either advertisements or prizes until bailed out by Harmsworth, who fretted that his paper's reputation would suffer through association.[186] Ruin remained only round the corner, however, because Wallace's reporting shortly involved the paper in two expensive libel actions; and he was dismissed. The transition from careless reporter to racy novelist was thus started, and a writing career of almost unrelieved cynicism embarked upon. After the Great War, following a period as racehorse tipster, all the plant was then in place to set in motion the Wallace fiction factory that boomed for the next decade—quantity over quality, the author as mass producer, generating over 150 books at breathtaking pace, almost faster it seemed than the newspaper presses that first printed him.[187] The 'Weekly Wallace' sped into the 'midday Wallace'.[188] It was a modern parable, fitting to a tee the indictment made by the Guild Socialist A. R. Orage in 1915, concerning 'the standard of the mob in literature . . . the mere capacity to tickle the ears of the groundlings. The popular author of to-day (there are at least a hundred making several thousand pounds a year) is very often the counterpart of the profiteer and, like him, exploits ignorance and other disabilities.'[189]

From 1921 Wallace found his way into Hodder & Stoughton's stable, which trademarked all his books with a bloody crimson circle and his signature on their covers. By 1928 it was reckoned that, excepting the Bible, a quarter of all books published and bought in England was a Wallace.[190] Initially spurned by publishers, he had begun with do-it-yourself bravado; but, meanwhile, publishers were endeavouring to spot and sign up future stars. T. Fisher Unwin ran a prize competition for the best novel by a new author, and turned up the prolific Ethel M. Dell through this.[191] The book was *The Way of an Eagle* (1912); its author, the 30-year-old daughter of an employee at the Equitable Life Assurance. Her manuscript was apparently much revised by Unwin's before publication but, when publicized with an intriguing advertisement as 'the novel with an ugly hero', it shot through twenty-seven impressions before 1915. Some quarter of a million copies were printed in cheap editions during the Great War. Having

---

[186] Wallace never forgot the debt although he did forget to repay it. Only a half was deducted from his salary, to Harmsworth's subsequent fury; see Lane, *Wallace*, 198, 297, and the fulsome letter from Wallace to Harmsworth (now Lord Northcliffe), 5 May 1922, in Pound and Harmsworth, *Northcliffe*, 850–1. In it Wallace described himself as 'semi–illiterate' when he first joined the *Daily Mail*; a revealing designation, because convention favours 'semi-literate'.

[187] One indication of Wallace's breakthrough into the league of best–sellers was his being recruited to write for the New York publishers Street & Smith, who commanded the largest slice of the American market for popular books and magazines. Wallace signed for his first story for Street & Smith in 1918, whereas Charles Garvice, Hall Caine, Marie Corelli, Rider Haggard, Conan Doyle, Anthony Hope, Stanley Weyman, and Kipling, had appeared in Street & Smith publications for many years previously. See Reynolds, *Fiction Factory*, 176–7. [188] Lane, *Wallace*, 287.

[189] *New Age*, 17 (1915), 13, in Martin (ed.), *Orage*, 58. By comparison, in 1892 Walter Besant had reckoned there were about fifty novelists earning £1,000 a year.

[190] David Glover's notice of Wallace (1875–1932), *Oxford DNB*. Wallace was represented by A. S. Watt's literary agency from 1920 to 1921.

[191] Gerber (ed.), *Moore*, 32. G. K. Chesterton was a reader for Fisher Unwin.

cannily indentured Dell's services with a four-novel contract at the outset, Unwin's then discovered that their fortunes were more or less tied to her. She accounted for half the firm's sales and, though more generous terms were conceded to her for her fifth novel, *Greatheart* (1918), she broke with them subsequently after disagreement over the quantity of free copies allowed her. Thus weakened, the firm could not survive the strike seasons of 1925–6, and was merged into Ernest Benn Ltd.[192]

Dell's outstanding popularity during the Great War and inter-war periods evidenced a distinction clearly understood by booksellers and ignored at peril by publishers: she was not a first-class novelist in the sense of winning highbrow appreciation, but she was a first-class storyteller in the appeal she held to thousands whose principal requirement was 'a good read'. This difference was impressed on Gilbert Frankau during his own writer's apprenticeship by F. S. Bradley, who managed a W. H. Smith's bookshop in Reading: 'Bradley told me how the girls at Huntley & Palmers' biscuit factory clubbed together to buy the novels of Ethel M. Dell,' and he likened Dell in this respect with Charles Garvice.[193] Michael Sadleir too recognized that as a popular novelist she belonged to the class of Garvice and Florence Barclay:

that is to say, her public was an ingenuous and uncritical one, which asked only for a well-sustained, romantic narrative, with dangers averted, innocence unsmirched, and characters recognisable from the first for what they proved to be. All of these she provided . . . Her heroes (often short of stature and rather plain) are whipcord or tempered steel. Her heroines are proud, unhappy, and inclined to be fierce before marriage, although when at last they yield to their faithful lovers' pleas they become utterly submissive. Her villains are unmistakable 'Sir Jaspers' . . . [but she] rises above the *Peg's Paper* formula of duke and dairymaid, and also above the pure and lovely woman whose radiant influence transforms an unconvincing sinner into an intolerable saint . . . Passion is under ultimate control, and, however black things may look, deviation from the path of propriety is checked in time.[194]

What particularly interested people in the publishing trade was that Dell—after her prizewinning debut—sustained her best-selling status largely without publicity. When Michael Joseph pondered the phenomenon in 1925, no photograph of her, to his knowledge, had been issued, yet she was 'perhaps the most widely read writer of our time'. He considered whether her shyness was itself a publicity ploy, lending an air of mystery which worked an equivalent effect; but he doubted whether this really mattered, and reckoned Dell did not need personal publicity to sustain her sort of readership. Nor did she require reviews: she was 'independent of press criticism'.[195]

[192] Anderson and Rose (eds.), *British Literary Publishing Houses*, 306, 310.

[193] Frankau, *Self-Portrait*, 221

[194] *DNB, 1931–1940*, 785–6. See also Kemp *et al.* (eds.), *Edwardian Fiction*, 96. For Garvice and Barclay, see below, Chs. 19–20. [195] Joseph, *Commercial Side of Literature*, 212–19.

Unwin's was far from being the pioneer in mounting the type of competition which brought on young authors such as Miss Dell; half a century earlier the Scottish Temperance League had offered a prize of £100 to the author of a story that best exemplified its cause, and it was this that had tempted Mrs Henry Wood to expand her magazine short-story writing into her first full novel, *Danesbury House* (1860), thus launching her best-seller career.[196] As in many aspects of the popular-literature market, the real originators of these competitions were the mid- and late Victorian newspaper and periodical proprietors and editors. Annie S. Swan's long association with the publisher John Leng of Dundee began when she won second prize in a Christmas story competition in the *People's Journal*, the popular weekly magazine that Leng's firm published.[197] The quality weeklies were generally more sedate, but John Morgan Richards, the American advertising man who bought *The Academy* in 1896, sponsored prizes of 100 and 50 guineas to the authors of the two best new books voted by its readers, in order to increase the magazine's circulation. Lists of best-selling books, from figures supplied by booksellers in various towns and cities, were also published. The first year of *The Academy's* competition, 1897, saw Stephen Phillips carry off the 100 guineas for his poems; the runner-up, W. E. Henley, was consoled with 50 guineas for his essay on Burns. Such was the interest generated that, next year, 150 guineas were split equally between Maurice Hewlett's *Forest Lovers*, Joseph Conrad's *Tales of Unrest*, and Sidney Lee's *Shakespeare*; and in 1899 six prizes of 25 guineas were awarded to W. B. Yeats, *The Wind among the Reeds*, Gwendoline Keats, *On Trial*, Hilaire Belloc, *Danton*, G. M. Trevelyan, *England in the Age of Wycliffe*, H. G. Graham, *The Social Life of Scotland in the Eighteenth Century*, and Constance Garnett for her translation of Turgenev. Formal competition was abandoned in 1900 'for a system of wider interest, in which amateur authors were encouraged by liberal awards to contribute essays, on general and miscellaneous subjects to the journal'.[198]

Competition gimmickry had by this date reached around the newspaper world, from *Tit-Bits* to *The Times*.[199] Even the *Daily News*, the Cadbury-owned Liberal newspaper which eschewed racing news in order to discourage gambling, ran a Reading Contest over four months in 1908, offering prizes from £1 to £1,000.[200] In 1891 Grant Allen had carried off the jackpot £1,000 prize offered by *Tit-Bits*, for his story *What's Bred in the Bone*.[201] Such a sum cast into the shade periodicals such as *Cassell's Family Magazine*, which offered prizes of £30–50 for the best short stories of between 7,500 and 9,000 words, with a 'domestic interest, bright in style, original in plot, and adapted for family reading' in 1892.[202] It was this sort of

---

[196] *D.N.B.* LXII (1900), 355.   [197] Swan, *Life*, 30–1.

[198] Richards, *John Bull and Jonathan*, 100–1.

[199] See advertisements in *T.P.'s Weekly*, 27 Feb. 1903, 510, and 10 April 1903, 685.

[200] Advertisement in *T.P.'s Weekly*, 10 Jan. 1908, 48.

[201] *Review of Reviews*, July 1891, 199. This was in marked contrast to the wages of philosophy. So Allen learned from the experience of his first publication, *Philosophical Aesthetics* (1877). Allen paid £120 to have it published; it sold 300 copies and Allen made a net loss of £40 or £50: *Review of Reviews*, Sept. 1892, 266.

[202] *Review of Reviews*, July 1892, 69.

timidity that had nearly finished Cassell's by the early 1900s, a sorry contrast with the buoyant years when they energetically marketed Rider Haggard. When Newman Flower joined Cassell's in 1905, he felt as if he had 'walked into an open grave'. Having worked as a sub-editor for Harmsworth's, he was qualified to diagnose the sickness. Cassell's periodicals reeked of staleness, largely recycling copy from past numbers or books. Under the management of Sir Wemyss Reid, Cassell's suffered from chronic under-investment in new authors, in fresh stories and layout, and in advertising. Harmsworth's, Flower knew, 'were spending £20,000 at that time for publicity alone, on every new publication they put out'. When Flower launched the *Story-Teller* in 1907, which was to restore Cassell's fortunes, 'all we could afford to spend on the first number—literary, publicity, everything—was £1,600, for we had nothing more in the till'. Flower brought to the *Story-Teller* the short-story talents of E. Phillips Oppenheim, Somerset Maugham and W. J. Locke, and Maurice Leblanc and G. K. Chesterton—all the Arsène Lupin and Father Brown detective stories were published there—as well as re-energizing former favourites such as Max Pemberton. Later, from a chance meeting in a railway carriage with Kipling, Flower discovered that he had read the magazine almost from the first.[203]

VII

The hectic pattern of the best-seller world was thus emerging. The statistical reliability of best-seller listings was frequently suspect;[204] moreover, it made many authors uncomfortable. Chagrined that Mudie's had ordered far fewer of his *Thyrza* than of Rider Haggard's *She* in 1887, George Gissing predicted that he would still be read when Haggard and the other 'petty scribblers of the day' were 'waste paper'. By 1900, when more stuffing had been knocked out of him, Gissing was bewailing how 'humiliating' it was to be so outsold by the likes of Hall Caine and Marie Corelli.[205] Thomas Hardy also had his doubts, although he possessed more of a public name than Gissing and he was also more successful in the

---

[203] Kipling apparently admired Oppenheim's short stories the most: see Oppenheim, *Pool of Memory*, 194–5; and Flower, *Just As It Happened*, 25–32. Flower assumed the general management of Cassell's in 1913. Warwick Deeping (1877–1950) was one of the best-sellers Flower promoted. He also brought Robert Hichens and Horace Vachell to Cassell's; but his biggest coup was in securing Arnold Bennett and H. G. Wells from 1916.

[204] Not much has changed a century later. The credentials of weekly best-seller lists published by Bookwatch are questionable, not least because of the possibility of manipulation by the trade. In 1992 (admittedly during a recession when book-buying was in the doldrums) a sale of only 300 copies was sufficient to pitch a book into the number 10 slot. Such a figure might be obtained by concerted purchases at targeted booksellers, on top of actual sales to libraries and genuine customers, whereupon the *éclat* received from an appearance in the best-seller lists would generate its own advertising momentum. See Derwent May, 'Publish and Be Remaindered', *Times*, 20 July 1992, for this and complaints about the Net Book Agreement and discounting; and *Sunday Times*, 12 May 1996, for the first best-seller list to include estimated weekly sales, extrapolated from data obtained from 628 bookshops.

[205] Halperin, *Gissing*, 100, 305, 345.

marketplace. The experimental publication by Harper's London branch of *Tess of the D'Urbervilles* (1891) in a sixpenny edition saw all 100,000 copies sold within the twelve-month period June 1900–June 1901, with another 45,016 copies sold of the sixpenny edition of *Far from the Madding Crowd* (1874). He received a penny per copy on each (just under 17 per cent royalty) and as much as 25 per cent on the ordinary six-shilling editions of them and the rest of his works; but altogether the sales of these were 'rather steady than brilliant'—a total for the year of about 3,000.[206] For all his renown, hustle, and occasionally impressive sales figures, Hardy was not regarded (and did not regard himself) as a best-seller. Indeed he deplored the commercialization of literature with its tendency to 'exalt numbers above quality', disliking especially 'that pernicious custom in some so-called literary papers of publishing lists of "best-selling" books—which in the interests of all literary art should be kept a dead secret.'[207]

The empirical basis of the best-seller lists became better established with the inauguration of *Newsbasket* in 1908. This house magazine of the biggest retailers, W. H. Smith, surveyed the monthly trade of its principal railway bookstalls and urban bookshops. Taking a sample of its 'best-selling books' feature for a six-month period in 1912, the following authors stood out in the popular fiction and new editions categories: Florence Barclay, Harold Begbie, Hilaire Belloc, Arnold Bennett, R. H. Benson, George A. Birmingham, Rhoda Broughton, Marie Corelli, Frank Danby, Richard Dehan, Ethel M. Dell, Maud Diver, Conan Doyle, Jeffery Farnol, Charles Garvice, Elinor Glyn, Rider Haggard, Thomas Hardy, Beatrice Harraden, Ian Hay, Maurice Hewlett, Robert Hichens, Anthony Hope, Baroness von Hutton, W. W. Jacobs, Mrs Belloc Lowndes, Rudyard Kipling, Compton Mackenzie, A. E. W. Mason, W. B. Maxwell, Horace Newte, Baroness Orzcy, E. Phillips Oppenheim, Barry Pain, Max Pemberton, Eden Phillpotts, H. de Vere Stacpoole, R. L. Stevenson, Bram Stoker, Guy Thorne, Katherine Thurston, H. Ainsley Vachell, E. Charles Vivian, Lew Wallace, and H.G. Wells.[208] A good many of these writers continue to carry literary importance; missing were some names who had still to establish a popular reputation in 1912. The prolific John Buchan, for example, had not yet published a book which sold more than 2,000 copies in Britain, with the possible exception of *Prester John* (1910); his breakthrough into the best-seller league came with *The Thirty-Nine Steps* (1915) and *Greenmantle* (1916).[209] The *Newsbasket* snapshot is interesting also for the mixture of genres represented: historical and contemporary romance and adventure; fantasy, horror, and detection; and realist or 'problem' novels with regional or sociological emphasis. The *Newsbasket* listing contained no figures of actual copies sold, but it included several authors who consistently outstripped the rest.

---

[206] Hardy to Frederick Macmillan, 22 March 1902, in Purdy and Millgate, *Hardy Letters*, iii. 13–14, 77–8, 80.

[207] Hardy to Henry Newbolt, 4 Nov. 1906, ibid. 233–4.

[208] *Newsbasket*, 'Best-selling Books' feature, March–September 1912; copy kindly made for me by Dr J. J. McAleer Jr. [209] Smith, *Buchan*, 293–8.

conversations he had with Garvice and on an autobiographical statement which Garvice compiled for him.[3] Sladen declared: 'Garvice, undoubtedly, has the largest sales of any one in the world. I have seen the figures. Last year's sales [1912–13] alone amounted to 1,750,000 copies—books of all prices.' Garvice's career was, he added, 'one of the most remarkable literary successes on record—more than six millions of his books have been sold'.[4]

Piecing together fragmentary information about him, it would appear that Garvice was born in 1850.[5] When living at The Retreat, Cookham, Berkshire, he published a collection of songs and poetry, *Eve: And Other Verses* (1873), and a three-decker novel, *Maurice Durant* (1875).[6] *Eve* Garvice dedicated to his wife. The preface suggests the struggling young author: most of 'these poor verses' were conceived 'at midnight when the hand was too weary to write and the brain to forge stronger work; some few were born under the cloud of a heavy sorrow, others scribbled on foreign steam-boats and in railway carriages; but all were thrown off to fill the gaping corners of a magazine or provide some composer with pegs whereon to hang his music'. Their sentiment and themes are conventional—about Nature and the Seasons, about Love, or to 'Italia'— although one perhaps was inspired by personal experience. 'Preaching and Practising' rebuked a parson who sermonized about humility and charity yet sent pompous letters to a neighbour whose dog had strayed on the rectory grounds.[7]

Maurice Durant was dedicated to the actor Henry Irving, 'with the warmest admiration and esteem'. Whether Garvice actually knew Irving or was merely hopeful of interesting him in a stage adaptation, it is impossible to say. Originally serialized in a weekly fiction periodical, the story obtained 'a fair share of success', according to the preface, 'notwithstanding its too palpable inconsistencies and crudity'. It was written 'some years ago when the Author's acquaintance with the world, the flesh, and His Satanic Majesty was small in degree and imaginative in quality'. Immaturity was everywhere evident, and the reader's incredulity needs to be suspended as the fortunes and misfortunes of stock characters are

---

[3] This survives in Richmond Reference Library, Local Studies collection, Sladen papers, box 66, fo. 16. Garvice wrote it in December 1913.

[4] Sladen, *Twenty Years*, 281. Sladen's figures were endorsed (or perhaps repeated) by the *Times Literary Supplement*, 6 May 1915. The *Times* obituary, 2 Mar. 1920, also stated that he had 'a larger circulation than any other purveyor of fiction'; and the *Richmond Herald*'s obituary, 6 Mar. 1920, spoke of sales in Britain and the United States 'at the rate of over a million a year'. Garvice, obviously proud of his sales, made a habit of showing people his tally. Horace Collins, who was the press and publicity officer at the Drury Lane Theatre, recalled: 'Charles Garvice was a friend of mine and his books were the best-sellers of his day. He once showed me the returns from his literary agent and they were fabulous. When at his zenith the number of his novels sold all over the world each year reached nearly a million' (Collins, *My Best Riches*, 174).

[5] In *Who's Who* Garvice did not disclose his year of birth; he died on 1 March 1920. The death certificate gives his full name as Charles Andrew Garvice and his age as 69. No birth certificate has survived, but Garvice was baptized on 18 September 1850, at St Dunstan's Church in Stepney, the son of Andrew John Garvice and his wife, Mira.

[6] Garvice told Sladen that he was 19 when he wrote his first book, but he did not specify it.

[7] Charles Garvice, *Eve: And Other Verses* (1873), 18–19.

sensationally recounted. The eponymous hero, we are told, had vanished twelve years before the story opens, to the continent where he has contracted a disastrous liaison, news of which kills his father, the Rector of Grassmere. The village squire is a virtuous baronet of the old school, Sir Fielding Chichester, now unhappily debt-ridden and fearful that his magnificent library may be forfeited. His daughter Maud—named, perhaps, in homage to Tennyson—is instantly smitten when Maurice dramatically enters the novel on page 75; and little wonder—dark and brooding, Maurice has not entirely misspent his time abroad, especially in Italy, where he has won fame as 'Lucian', the greatest painter and musician of the age. This supreme artist turns out to be a man of action too, a fearless rider, deadly shot, and, as most other Garvice heroes subsequently, useful with his fists. Maud and Maurice are betrothed, yet there is many a twist before they are allowed to enjoy marital bliss. Maurice's Mediterranean period yields sufficient gold to clear off Sir Fielding's mortgage but also casts a shadow in the form of a wife: Felise Faustine, a wild Corsican woman with a weakness for drink, who is in cahoots with a gang of thieves based in London's Italian colony around Hatton Gardens. The unprincipled Latins are responsible for a string of robberies in Chelsea and in the countryside, which ultimately requires Maurice to face up to his past when his former wife's body is found in the local pond. Maurice goes missing and is sought by the police for her murder. Two years pass—during which the versatile Maurice follows the life of a trapper on the American plains— but Maurice's love for Maud burns undiminished and he decides to return. Maud meanwhile is pining away, made distraught by Maurice's abandonment and apparent uxoricide. On his journey home Maurice happens on a cottage wherein lies dying the thieves' ringleader, Lorenzo Spazzola. Assuming the guise of a priest, Maurice administers the last rites and hears Lorenzo confess that he was already husband to Felise when they conspired to marry her to a rich Englishman who later returned to his own country. They had tracked down this rich Englishman (Maurice's masquerade is obviously sufficiently intricate for him not to be identified as the same) and quarrelled about blackmailing him, whereupon Lorenzo drowned Felise in the Black Pool. With characteristic presence of mind, Maurice now gets the fast-fading felon to write out and sign a confession in order to rush to another deathbed, this one adorned by the beloved Maud; and she, upon learning that Maurice had never been legally married and is innocent of murder, speedily recovers in time for wedding bells.

The modern reader may suppose that enough is told here to occupy all three volumes and more; yet *Maurice Durant* also contains an extensive sub-plot, another story of suffering true love, this involving Maud's brother, the handsome and noble-hearted heir to the baronetcy, 23-year-old Chudleigh (nicknamed Chud) Chichester. Like Maurice, he experiences trials enough. In matters of the heart he is initially worsted by the Hon. Clarence Hartfield, a villainous, lisping, and intriguing sort who holds Sir Fielding Chichester's debts and steals Chudleigh's love, Carlotta Lawley. Hartfield having succeeded to the title of Lord

Crownbrilliants and bagged Carlotta for his bride, game, set, and match appear to
have been declared on Chud; but he comes back strongly as the degenerate side to
Crownbrilliants is on ample display in his Park Lane mansion, where he embraces
alcohol in preference to Carlotta, who plans to abscond with Chud. This proves
unnecessary because a collision with a horse and cart kills Crownbrilliants; and the
delights of Florence now beckon for a honeymoon, as Carlotta and Chud's nuptials take place only a month after the demise of the unlamented Crownbrilliants.
Chud has not otherwise let time idle. He has become MP for the semi-industrial
district in which his family's lands lie. The account of the election is revealing for
what it discloses about Garvice's own politics. The opposition is provided by a
bluff, self-made millionaire, Gregson, now retired from business and the builder
and occupant of the folly bordering on the park of ancient Chichester Hall.
Gregson stands as a Liberal, advancing all sorts of anti-aristocratic declarations
and abstract proposals designed to promote working-class improvement and
freedom; but there is also another alleged labourers' friend standing, a working-
class republican called Gideon Giles. He is the very caricature of subversive
agitator, with big red hands, greasy hair, and a torrent of revolutionary rhetoric;
moreover, he organizes roughs to disturb Chud's meetings and to set about Chud
himself, who is thankful for Maurice Durant's pugilistic prowess in his defence.
This assault swings the election Chud's way as the majority of voters perceive
the darkness lurking behind liberal claptrap. Thus the people recognize that their
real interests are best served by Tory Democracy:

Mr Gregson's rampant Liberalism and Mr Gideon Giles's florid invective have fallen to
dust and ashes beneath Chudleigh's outspoken determination to uphold the British
throne and constitution, and when as a climax he declared that he meant to be the
working-man's friend by voting for the reduction of taxes and the labour time, he was
answered from the dense throng by a roaring cheer . . . [8]

These politics remained fixed for the author throughout his life. Garvice believed
that a noble class—noble not just by pedigree but by character too—was the best
guarantor of the country's liberties, prosperity, and progress.

When published as a book, *Maurice Durant* was not a success, being prolix and
pricey for the popular market. This conclusion—characteristically expressed in
commercial, not artistic, terms—Garvice came to later when he rewrote and
reissued it in a cheap edition; and for two decades he concentrated on serials for
fiction magazines on both sides of the Atlantic. He edited as well as provided
most of the copy for one which sold for 7*d.* in England and was owned by the
American publisher George Munro. These serials 'had an enormous—to me a
fabulous—sale, and are still selling', Garvice wrote in 1913:

I worked nearly night and day, and was so fully occupied and contented that, absurd as it
may sound, I never gave a thought to publishing the serials in book form here in England;

---

[8] Charles Garvice, *Maurice Durant* (1875), ii. 182.

notwithstanding that the books were so popular in America that one of George Munro's rivals hit upon the extremely ingenious idea of waiting until half a novel of mine was published in serial form, getting someone else to finish it and issuing it in volume form before I had finished the story. Of course this was before the International Copyright Act. Blessings on its name![9]

By his own admission, Garvice was well remunerated. He had been living at Boathyde in North Devon and, with increasing wealth, he bought a farm, Moorlands, in the same county.[10] He even became president of the Farmers and Landowners Association. His public life expanded when he was elected a Conservative county councillor for the Northam district and he served as Conservator of Rivers. Again, beginning at the Bideford Debating Society by presenting 'recitals linked together by biographical notes', he discovered a talent for lecturing—also that it was lucrative. In 1913 he was elected president of the Institute of Lecturers.

II

It was not until 1898 that Garvice had his first success in England, with *Just a Girl*. This had been published previously in America;[11] and it was a copy of an American edition that 'my friend, that brilliant journalist, Robert Harborough Sherard, while sitting at my writing-desk, took up . . . [and] asked my permission to take it away and try to place it. He took it to Mr. Coulson Kernahan who recommended it to the publisher for whom he was reading.'[12] The publisher was James Bowden, who managed Ward, Lock & Co. (then Ward, Lock & Bowden) in the 1890s;[13] and *Just a Girl* was published under James Bowden's own imprint. This was certificate of its impeccable moral tone: Bowden's list included Methodist sermons and novels by Joseph Hocking, well-known for their 'tendency towards preachiness'.[14] *Just a Girl* had sold 100,000 copies in the United States. It was boomed in England on the strength of that and two highly favourable reviews, one by Douglas Sladen (in *Queen*) and the other by the editor of *The British Weekly*, Robertson Nicoll. Nicoll's seal of approval was decisive for the Nonconformist novel-reading public, which wanted romance and adventure without affront; as Rebecca West described it, 'This public wanted to read fiction,

---

[9] Garvice's statement [Dec. 1913], Sladen papers, box 66, fo. 16.

[10] He wrote about his experiences in *A Farm in Creamland: A Book of the Devonshire Countryside* (1911). He began to farm directly in 1903, but owned the property earlier.

[11] *Just a Girl; or, One Strange Duchess* was published in New York in 1895 by A. L. Burt and in 1896 by George Munro.

[12] Garvice's statement [Dec. 1913], Sladen papers, box 66, fo. 16. On Sherard (1861–1943) and Kernahan (1858–1943), see Sutherland, *Companion*, 350, 572.

[13] R. M. Healey, 'Ward, Lock and Company', in Anderson and Rose (eds.), *British Literary Publishing Houses*, 321–7.

[14] Sutherland, *Companion*, 300–1, for Joseph Hocking (1860–1937), brother of Silas K. Hocking (1850–1935), probably the Methodist reading public's favourite novelist.

but felt uneasy in doing so unless it had an appearance of religious and moral propaganda.'[15]

It took a literary agent to give Garvice that final propulsion to sustained best-seller circulation. This was Eveleigh Nash, who was aged 25 when he set up his own agency in 1898 in Norfolk Street, The Strand, London, in offices vacated by the Transvaal Delegation. Nash came from a well-connected Edinburgh family; he had arrived in London in 1892 and made his start in publishing in the newly formed partnership of Bliss, Sands & Foster, each of whom had served with Kegan Paul, Trench & Co. Their new firm was small, with mean-looking premises at 15 Craven Street, The Strand, and with a subscribed capital of only £4,500; and the partnership was dissolved after five years when Bliss and Foster left to work for John Murray. But in their brief activity they made a stir in the trade by launching a reprint series, led by *The Arabian Nights* and *Robinson Crusoe*, entitled The Cheapest Books in the World—a misnomer because they were priced 2s., yet they were 'made to look in appearance like a guinea volume . . . and they sold like wildfire'.[16] When the firm broke up, Nash started his literary agency and, having been proposed for membership of the Authors' Club by Douglas Sladen, used that base to make connections. Garvice was among these first clients, having approached Nash to read four serial stories he had written for the *Family Reader*, a wide-circulation weekly magazine. Garvice was wondering about publishing these as books. Nash reckoned that

there was a big public that would read the stories if they knew of their existence and could obtain them at a cheap price. The Garvice style of book is perhaps best described when it is stated that in one of his novels the young peer with wavy hair, blue eyes, silky moustache and pink cheeks, marries the dark-eyed maid who brings in his morning tea at the lodgings where he has been compelled to put up owing to financial stringency. But let no one think hastily it was a *mésalliance*, for it turns out that she was the grand-daughter of a 'heartless Earl' who disowned his son because he had married beneath him. However, when the old man was on his death-bed he repented that he had 'shut the gates of mercy' on the girl, who was taken into the family fold, and all was well. As for the young peer, his rascally solicitor who had misappropriated for years some of his client's rents, was found out, and his honest partner paid in full all the money that had been filched. She was dark, and he was fair, and these being eternal fountains of romance, Charles made them play through many of his tales of love; and the simple public that likes this kind of fare (some people are rude enough to call it tripe) devoured it eagerly, and felt happier for doing so.

I took the serials to Willie Sands; and, after explaining their character to him, I read out, at his invitation, some of the 'best' sentimental scenes, while he laughed till he cried and there and then accepted my suggestion that he should bring out the four stories simultaneously and advertise their titles under the heading Charles Garvice's Novels, together with a paragraph which we thought would make an emotional appeal to the unsophisticated reader. The books took their public by storm; and when, later, they

---

[15] Rebecca West, *The Strange Necessity: Essays and Reviews* (1987), 321.   [16] Nash, *Life*, 23.

appeared in paper covers at sixpence, they were as numerous in the shops and on the railway bookstalls as the leaves of Vallombrosa. Charles Garvice was now on the road to Fortune . . .[17]

The four books were: *Nance, A Coronet of Shame, Her Heart's Desire*, and *The Outcast of the Family*. Published together in 1900, these had sold some 300,000 copies by 1905.[18]

Garvice was launched, but he did not remain with Nash, who closed his agency in 1900 in order to re-enter publishing, first for Archibald Constable & Co. and then on his own account in 1902. Nash recommended Garvice and his other clients to place their business with A. P. Watt, who acted for Garvice until his death in 1920.[19] The format in which Garvice was first marketed in 1900 was kept, and was one key to his success. This was the one-volume standard, initially priced 6s. with illustrations, but moving quickly into the 3s. 6d. edition and down to sixpenny editions. The sixpenny edition was the best-seller and goldmine. Arnold Bennett's agent J. B. Pinker told him in 1909 that 'of all the *"Daily Mail* Sixpenny Novels", Charles Garvice's sold the best'; Garvice was also a star of T.P.'s Sixpenny Library, published by Hodder & Stoughton.[20] These were paperbacks, generally unillustrated yet with a brightly coloured cover featuring the heroine. Thus Nora Ryall, 18-year-old daughter of the Grange, is pictured on the cover of *In Wolf's Clothing* (1908): as a study in pink, with flowing dress and matching bonnet, which highlight her auburn tresses. She is seated, with one hand holding a closed fan, the other pertly poised on the hip; and her blue china eyes, set in an oval face with rosebud lips and lightly blushed cheeks, stare directly at the potential purchaser of the novelette. It was all irresistible, though the reader who hurried through the first 124 of its 128 pages would find the denouement interrupted by two pages of advertisements for 'Whelpton's Purifying Pills' to combat indigestion, 'Southall's Sanitary Towels' for women's comfort, 'Every Man's Book of the Dog', and 'Keating's Powder Kills Bugs, Fleas, Moths, Beetles, Mosquitos'. The author who mass-marketed his wares saw no point in standing on dignity.

Garvice's output was sizeable, publishing some forty or more novels between 1903 and 1919.[21] These tales were not all written in the last twenty years of Garvice's life. Many were rehashed from his long apprenticeship of writing

[17] Ibid. 33–4. Nash's simile about the leaves of Vallombrosa was, of course, a scholarly jest; it was Milton's originally, in *Paradise Lost*, depicting the quantity of fallen angels.

[18] See advertisement, citing a notice in *Queen*, at the front of Charles Garvice, *Linked by Fate* (1905).

[19] Nash, *Life*, 46.

[20] Swinnerton (ed.), *Bennett Journals*, 347 (entry for 30 Dec. 1909); advertisement in *T.P.'s Weekly*, 27 Dec. 1907, 859.

[21] *In Cupid's Chains* (1903); *The Rugged Path* (1903); *Love Decides* (1904); *A Jest of Fate* (1904); *Linked by Fate* (1905); *Love, the Tyrant* (1905); *Diana and Destiny* (1906); *A Girl of Spirit* (1906); *The Gold in the Gutter* (1907); *Where Love Leads* (1907); *In Wolf's Clothing* (1908); *The Fatal Ruby* (1909); *The Mistress of Court Regina* (1909); *Queen Kate* (1909); *Lorrie* (1910); *Staunch as a Woman* (1910); *Once in a Life* (1910); *The Heart of a Maid* (1910); *Barriers Between* (1910); *A Girl from the South* (1910); *For Her Only* (1911); *The Woman in It* (1911); *The Other Girl* (1911); *Iris* (1912); *Sweet Cymbeline* (1912); *Two Maids and a Man* (1912); *Doris* (1912); *His Guardian Angel* (1912); *Love in a Snare* (1912); *A Relenting Fate* (1912); *The Verdict of the Heart* (1912); *Elaine* (1913); *All is not Fair in Love*

Chronicle' that Mr Garvice's novels have already found more than six million readers. The writer of the 'Chronicle' article endeavours to account for this amazing vogue . . . 'Being a born story writer, Mr Garvice's first, last, and only aim is to tell a story just as well as he can, and to make it as interesting and real to others as it is to himself. His extraordinary breadth of sympathy prevents his harbouring prejudices and tendencies for or against any class of people. He delineates human nature without bias or advocacy. He engages in no fictional dispute on vexed social questions, takes no hand in debating sex problems, does no human sums in eugenics, grinds no philanthropic axe, voices no grievance, pleads no cause, shuns the didactic, and eschews propagandism. Life for Mr Garvice is not to be disputed, it is to be lived; not a matter for cross questions and crooked answers, but a fine romantic adventure, 'neath sunlight and shadow, a very holiday to be enjoyed with faith and hope, and no questions asked.'[29]

That Garvice was no social scientist or political reformer masquerading as a novelist was plainly the case; but that did not make his fiction impartial in its social observation. Garvice had decided views about his duty as a novelist. He liked to declare that he had 'never written a line to which the most typical British matron, resident in Brixton, Bloomsbury, or Birmingham, could take the slightest possible exception or offence'. Thus, 'sexual problems are out of my line, and, indeed my readers wouldn't stand them'. He condemned 'the tendency of the modern novel to the abnormal or the unhealthy. That is destructive of the whole art of the story.' Garvice was proud of the vast circulation of his fiction, but more proud of the way he had achieved it:

I shouldn't like to boast of an enormous circulation out of betting and racing stories, or some of the disgracefully immoral novels of the day . . . The writers of such books ought to be whipped at the cart's tail. I know they say that they write from experience and that they are mere photographers. Bosh! I know one must write from experience, but why choose only nasty experience? . . . I, too, have drawn from life. Only I have tried to see the sweeter side of life; it's just as real and a great deal more pleasant.

He advocated a labelling system for novels, which would give

some indication of the character of its contents. I once found my daughter reading a book. I asked her what it was. 'Oh,' she replied, 'It's "Maggie," or some such name, and it's by ——,' mentioning a well-known writer. Well, it sounded innocent enough, and I took it up, expecting to find it a simple record of a young girl's life, as masterly a study of a girl's life as that study he had once given us of war. I picked the book up, and to my horror I discovered it was the story of a New York courtesan, the scene of the story being pitched in the very vilest places you could imagine . . . Such a book is soul-damning, and it is an outrage upon the modesty of our young daughters . . . A girl's mind can be polluted almost before she knows what she is reading.

It does not take a Sherlock Holmes to identify this author who roused Garvice's parental concern: Stephen Crane, whose *Maggie: A Girl of the Streets* was published in 1892, the year before his classic civil war novel *The Red Badge of Courage*. Crane

---

[29] *T.P.'s Weekly*, 5 May 1911, 556.

was safely dead when Garvice gave this interview, but he also 'mentioned two or three famous books by name with a disgust and loathing which left no doubt . . . as to the sincerity of his opinions'. Garvice continued:

All this is new in our time. Who ever had to label Dickens, Thackeray, Kingsley or Trollope? Why pick out only immoral people to write about? . . . Tell the English people the story of their lives as simply and purely as you can and you will never want for readers. That is my only secret of work, and possibly it is also the secret of any success I may have had.

Garvice generally adhered to his formula; on occasion, however, strong feelings caused him to deviate. 'I don't as a rule believe that a novel should be a pamphleteer or written with a purpose,' he said, adding,

Sometimes I write with a purpose. For instance, in my present novel I am vigorously attacking the sweating system, which I have recently been studying on the spot in the East-End. Ah! How the East-End has changed! Once it was all law-abiding English, and now it is filled with these nasty, cheap-living aliens with frightfully insanitary habits.[30]

This anti-alienism was all of a piece with Garvice's political partisanship. For fourteen years he was chairman of the Conservative and Unionist constituency association in North Devon.[31] Yet it must be remarked that anti-alienism was a common enough prejudice, evident in sections of the Liberal Party and Labour movement also. Such an ideology probably strengthened Garvice's bond with his readers. It did not strike contemporaries as something that sat ill with his reputation for good nature.

III

The standard Garvice story involves members of the landed classes, the traditional squire or noble family, and is set on their country estates with interludes at London town houses and excursions abroad, in the Empire and North America and on the Continent. These overseas forays lend an amount of exotic adventure to the stories but are principally deployed as part of some complicated plot, in which the aristocratic heir is masquerading as a commoner before claiming his rightful inheritance from those who would cheat him. A recurrent theme is the

---

[30] Raymond Blathwayt, 'The Widest Read Author: A Talk with Mr. Charles Garvice', in *Great Thoughts*, 8–10; cutting in Richmond Reference Library, Local Studies collection, catalogue ref. L920. The cutting is undated, but internal evidence would suggest 1911.

[31] Exactly when is difficult to determine. The obituary in the *Evening Standard*, 2 Mar. 1920, stated that this was when 'Sir Stafford Northcote was contesting the Barnstaple division'. Northcote, Chancellor of the Exchequer (1874–80) and afterwards Conservative leader in the House of Commons, represented the old Northern constituency of Devon between 1866 and 1885. It is possible that Garvice was chairman in the last years of Northcote's representation, though he would have been in his early thirties. The constituency was split in 1885, principally divided between North-West (or Barnstaple) and North (or South Moulton), in which Liberals generally won majorities.

debt encumbrance of those old landed families. Garvice has little complimentary to say about the moneylenders who hold them in thrall and the nouveaux riches, characteristically either northern factory-owners or City speculators, who become their neighbours and seek to dispossess them. In *Olivia and Others* the villainous Bartley Bradstone, a stock-market millionaire, schemes to marry—bigamously, as it turns out—the daughter of the Squire of Hawkwood Grange, whose mortgages he holds. Garvice writes with snobbish distaste for this type—'Your *parvenu*, while he would give half his newly gotten wealth to be a gentleman, invariably hates every gentleman he meets.'[32] Bradstone has bought an estate in North Devon—where Garvice himself farmed—and has demolished a ramshackle, fine old house and built 'a huge mansion which, by its highly florid architecture, was far more suitable to South Kensington': it is 'all gables and turrets' and made 'terribly conspicuous' by its 'red brick with white stone facings'. Bradstone's dinners likewise are over-elaborate, with 'too many covers, too many wines, with too much plate, and too many servants'; and, horror of horrors, his mahogany is new too. Bradstone's vulgarity is painful. By contrast, Squire Vanley is unworldly: 'Twice a baronetage and once a peerage had been offered to the Vanleys; but to a Vanley the old English and old Devonshire title of "Squire" was too dear to be exchanged for any other, though it might be higher; and so Squire Vanley, the master of the Grange, refused, and certainly was not the less respected for his refusal of, a peerage.'[33] And it is not just social standing, manners, and ethics that distinguish Bradstone from the Vanleys and their circle; it is manifested too in physical appearance. Bradstone has 'plebeian' looks. These are contrasted with Harry Faradeane's 'tall, patrician figure and handsome face', over which Olivia Vanley 'would sigh heavily—and ah! So wistfully'.[34] Faradeane, another new neighbour, is the mystery figure in the story; needless to say, he wins Olivia's hand, rescues her family from Bradstone's machinations, and conveniently turns out to be the Earl of Clydesfold in disguise.

Heroic characters in Garvice's stories conform to this mould, conspicuous for their pedigree, uprightness, and sterling English virtues. Garvice's initial best-seller, *Just a Girl*, had set the pattern. The story opens with the discovery of a 3-year-old girl lying by a woman's corpse near a gold-digging camp in Australia. The foundling is won at poker by a professional gambler, Varley Howard, who christens her Esmeralda. Esmeralda, who has reached 17 by chapter 2, is regarded by the entire camp 'as a kind of queen. Besides, it was well known that her guardian, Varley Howard, would not permit of any love-making, and that the man who should venture to propose marriage to Esmeralda would far more probably be the chief figure in a funeral than in a wedding. So that Esmeralda had grown up as innocent of love and love-making—indeed, far more innocent—as nineteen out of twenty English girls.'[35] At this point Esmeralda has a dramatic

---

[32] Charles Garvice, *Olivia and Others: A Novel of Incident* (n.d.), published by Hutchinson. Smith had published it as *Olivia; or, It was All for her Sake*, in New York in 1897.   [33] Ibid. 10.
[34] Ibid. 91.   [35] Charles Garvice, *Just a Girl* (1898), 45.

meeting with an Englishman, young Lord Norman Druce, who is in Australia to recover his family's fortunes. Lord Norman is shot at and the bullet passes through Esmeralda's hat. Her pluckiness under fire as well as her beauty impress the young aristocrat. However, it is not Lord Norman who ultimately wins her. He, having cornered five of the best claims in the goldfields, instead marries Lilias, the ward of Lord Selvaine; but it is through Norman, as the story switches scene to England's stately homes and town houses, that Esmeralda falls in love with and marries his cousin, the Marquis of Trafford, eldest son of the Duke of Belfayre. Esmeralda meanwhile has been revealed to be a multi-millionairess, actually a Miss Chetwynde, once mislaid by her guardian Lady Wyndover. Lord Norman first interests Esmeralda in Trafford by describing him thus:

'He's a first-rate shot—you should see him stalking deer! There's no tiring him. And then he rides—it's a treat to see him going across country as straight as a line, taking everything as it comes, just like a bird. And then, he's the best-looking fellow in London'.

'What is he like?' she asked, with a woman's curiosity on this most important point.

'Oh,' replied Norman vaguely, 'he's tall—not too tall—and what you women call graceful; all muscle, and not an ounce of fat. He can knock a man down with a straight one from the shoulder.'

'There's heaps of men who can do that,' she said, half jealously.

The heroic high-born of Garvice's fiction also honour virtue in whatever guise it comes. Within an ordained hierarchy of rank, they yet act as natural egalitarians. Varley Howard experiences this when he accompanies Esmeralda to their grand houses: 'It was wonderful how unanimous was the verdict in Varley's favour, how everybody conspired to make a lion of him, much to his surprise, and how eager everyone was to show him the best side of this old but not altogether worn-out England.'[36]

There was usually some humorous spin to Garvice's descriptions, coupled with generally illiberal sentiments about below-par types, in the manner of armchair attitudinizing. Vane Mannering, the hero of *Linked by Fate* (1905)—previously serialized in the penny weekly the *London Reader*, beginning 10 October 1903—is introduced as 'athletic and strong', 'one of those good-looking young men the public schools and the 'Varsities turn out with machine-like regularity'. By page 100 he has transmuted into the Earl of Lesborough, but the story opens with a small party shipwrecked on 'one of the islands which lie off the eastern shore of Australia': in addition to Mannering the party includes Arthur Fleming, a consumptive clergyman, Vernon, a delirious doctor, and his daughter Nina. The potential love interest is established early, when Mannering knocks 'at the rough door of the hut'. (Apparently desert islands off the eastern shore of Australia come provided with purpose-built huts: there are a convenient three on this island—one for Mannering and Fleming, one for the doctor and his

---

[36] Ibid. 397.

daughter, and one for the crew.) Nina opens the door of hers in response to Mannering's knock:

'Oh, good evening, Mr Mannering!' she said, with quiet cheerfulness, and her voice rang like a low note of music in the pine-perfumed air. 'Will you come in? My father is out, he went out for a stroll. Is anything the matter?' . . .

Mannering knew enough of women to know that with this one, young as she was, the proper course was the direct one. His eyes rested reflectively for a moment on her lovely face, on the small, shapely head with its soft, black hair resting on the forehead, and wound into a knot at the back, then he said:

'I am afraid there is, Miss Nina.' He had grown to call her by her Christian name: ship-wrecked people are apt to be slack on extreme points of etiquette. 'The men are getting impatient. They entertain the absurd idea that we have smuggled the specie and valuables from the ship in your father's medicine chest.'

The men referred to are the half a dozen motley crew and, the reader presumes, it is their incompetent navigation and inept seamanship that have brought about the wreck because 'the party owed their lives to Vane Mannering, whose energy, alertness, coolness and presence of mind had brought them from the doomed ship'. Mannering is quite blasé about the whole operation, being now concerned that 'this beastly island is one of the numerous group which is quite out of the line of shipping', though exactly where they were he is unable to say— 'If they had taught me geography at Eton or Oxford, instead of Latin and Greek, and several other still more useless things, I might give a guess . . .'. The crew, however, serves one useful purpose, that of supplying some villainous opposition. Mannering reflects on the problem in conversation with the clergyman:

'No, they are not all bad: but there are one or two black sheep amongst them. I mistrust that Lascar and the other stoker, Munson. He is always haranguing the rest . . . If they were Englishmen one would not have any misgiving: but—!' He shrugged his shoulders.

'We man our ships with the scum of the earth, Fleming, just as we fill the East-end of London with aliens to take the bread out of the mouths of our own poor.'

Naturally, this crew—the calculating rascally leaders and the impressionable weak-willed followers—have been at the keg of rum that has been washed ashore. When thoroughly inflamed with liquor, they confront Mannering about the gold they think is in the doctor's medicine chest. It is the Lascar who is their spokesman, 'in his thick, sibilant voice, his black eyes rolling evilly on the faces of the listeners. "Ve are bein' played vith! It ish thish Mishter Mann'rin' that ish trickin' us: 'im and the Padre, ah, and the Medico, too! They hab the money. I who speak know it . . .".' Mannering and Fleming are armed with revolvers, which appear to resolve the argument until the Lascar produces his master stroke, a sneer about the English love of fair play:

'You speak bravely, Misther Mann'rin'! Ah, you 'ave ze gun! . . . If you had only ze little knife like zis, we would settle the matter, ah, so ker-vickly! You are ze one coward!'

Then Mannering did a foolish thing—the foolish thing which Englishmen, individually and collectively, so often do; he gave away his advantage. It was inexcusable; but, ah, well, let the man who has meekly borne the taunt of a Lascar and been called a coward pitch the first stone; I will not; and I have an idea that the reader will not.

So Mannering gives up his gun in order to have a man-to-man knife fight with the Lascar. The parson, now under instructions to shoot the first man to interfere, is doubtful about the wisdom of the enterprise, but 'I learnt a trick or two when I was in Malacca,' says Mannering reassuringly as he rolls up his sleeves and straps a bowie knife to his wrist. The strap is a handkerchief supplied and tied by Nina, whose 'face was white as death, her eyes were like "the violets steeped in dew", her lips, white as her face, were set tightly'. The knife fight has its dicey moments—the Lascar is 'as agile as a snake'—and Mannering is slashed down his shoulder and side before he disarms his adversary. Flinging aside his own knife, he declares: 'Now, we'll fight it out English fashion.' This means boxing Queensberry Rules: 'Suffice it that the Lascar was as a child in the hands of the man who had carried all before him with the gloves at Christ Church.' Apparently Oxford had not been so useless after all. The horizontal Lascar is carried away and Nina greets the victor: 'You are bleeding! Oh, Mannering, how—how nobly you fought! It was wicked, very wicked, but, oh, how—how—I admire you for it! God forgive me!' So, Nina also has her part to play, dressing the dreadful wound of the slashed warrior, who demurs: '"It is too slight to be called a wound", said Mannering casually.'[37]

It would be superfluous to quote more or to pass further commentary—except to remark that all of the above takes place in chapter 1! There was nothing leisurely about a Garvice romance. Nor, though the intricate plots defied belief, did Garvice put any obstruction in the way of reader understanding of his characters: for example, chapter 1 of *In Wolf's Clothing* (1908) is entitled 'Enter the Heroine', chapter 2 'The Hero', and chapter 3 'The Bounder'. Garvice was quite happy to talk about his method. R. D. Blumenfeld recorded in his diary:

I have from Charles Garvice his secret of success in the making of a popular novel designed to cause every cook and housemaid in Europe and America to weep copiously. He says: 'First take a wicked Earl; then an innocent village maiden; next some irate parents, a background of soldiers and sailors, a family solicitor and an elopement scene; a church door; snow falling, detectives, and finally Villainy defeated and Virtue triumphant. There's a firm in New York who would take one of these novels a week if I could furnish it. But, alas! I can only do about six a year!'[38]

IV

Garvice was talented enough to understand the limits of his talent or, rather, what the mass market wanted. Douglas Sladen applauded: 'His romantic love-stories

[37] All quotations are from the book version *Linked by Fate* (1905), 1–16. The serialization in the *London Reader*, 10 Oct. 1903, contains minor differences, mostly of punctuation, though here and there a word is changed.   [38] Blumenfeld, *Diary*, 215 (8 Feb. 1908).

are conspicuous not only for their thrilling plots—Garvice is a born story-writer—but for their freedom from all deleterious influence. There is nothing goody-goody about them; they are just wholesome, straightforward romances—an almost lost art.'[39] Garvice dubbed his stories 'the currant bun of literature', his role being to supply the masses with a nourishing fare, flavoured with the spice of romance and adventure. On his death it was said that he 'understood that the great public is really a child, that its imagination is illimitable, and, above all, that the only respite in its life of dust and work lies in the magic of that fairy wand which can turn a pumpkin into a gilded coach'.[40] Others questioned whether his audience was confined to the Cinderella class. Garvice, was bought and read practically universally, thought Francis Gribble, who was both an experienced journalist and a novelist himself. There was a demand for Garvice's books 'in the drawing-room as well as in the servants' hall—in the suburbs, and even in Mayfair, as well as in the provincial towns'; and after 1914 this demand, if anything, increased because Garvice's books 'satisfied a sentimental need which the war, somehow or other, intensified. Men devoured them in the trenches when not engaged in killing Germans, and also in the hospitals. During those strenuous years they plastered the windows of nearly all the booksellers' shops in the country, and their author was called upon to pay super-tax....'.[41]

Kipling's knowingness about this was shown in 'Mary Postgate' (1915), in the scene, heart-rending in its pathetic detail, in which the personal effects of the dead nephew—Second Lieutenant W. Fowler, killed during a trial flight—are wheelbarrowed down the garden to be burned: the inventory begins with his 'thumbed and used Hentys, Marryats, Levers, Stevensons, Baroness Orczys, Garvices, schoolbooks, and atlases', and continues load upon load until it ends with the 'undistinguishable wreckage of tool-boxes, rabbit-hutches, electric batteries, tin soldiers, fret-saw outfits, and jig-saw puzzles'.[42] Garvice was thus in good company, a dearly loved possession. Francis Gribble understood this too. Though no fan of the books, he cited a friend, a professor at a military college who ventured a comparison, absurd in principle, between George Meredith

---

[39] Sladen, *Twenty Years*, 281.   [40] *Richmond Herald*, 6 Mar. 1920.

[41] Gribble, *Seen in Passing*, 241–2. The popularity of Garvice among hospitalized soldiers was also noted by the novelist Beatrice Harraden in an article in *The Bookseller* in 1917. Joseph McAleer, *Popular Reading and Publishing in Britain 1914–1950* (Oxford, 1992), 77, in citing this, rightly remarks that availability also influenced reading habits, because people read virtually anything they could get hold of; yet there is little reason to doubt Garvice's wartime popularity. An undated newspaper cutting in the Richmond Reference Library, Local Studies collection (ref. L920.089 BLE) reports Garvice's view that his work satisfied genuine needs in wartime. He made three points. First, 'no possible good can be derived from brooding over the horrors of this war . . . [and] serious books would only make us more serious than we are now'. Secondly, his stories provided 'the paper-maker, the printer, the binder' with employment, though he added that he had not found it easy to continue writing in the prevailing atmosphere and 'I . . . have not written a line of fiction for over twelve months.' Thirdly, he argued, 'if the people do not read novels, and decline to read the serious books, what are they going to do with their time during this coming winter? They can't all go to the front. Susie has sewn quite enough shirts for soldiers, the hospitals are well supplied with nurses—and Satan still finds mischief for idle hands to do.'

[42] Kipling, 'Mary Postgate', in Kipling, *Mrs Bathurst and Other Stories*, 110–11.

and Charles Garvice: 'I could see that Meredith's stuff was awfully clever, but it bored me stiff. A critic, no doubt, would say that Garvice's stuff was rubbish; but I'm bound to say that I found it interesting in every line.' Garvice, thought Gribble, was the supreme master of the story both sentimental and gripping, yet 'he used to speak of himself as having been "lucky" . . . the lucky novelist being one who, by the accident of his temperament, supplies a want which is keenly felt, but not articulately expressed. But business ability is also needed to make the most of that sort of luck, and Garvice possessed it.'[43]

Garvice suffered but one setback in his best-selling years, a failure to sustain his break into the West End theatre. His debut there occurred with a comedy, *The Fisherman's Daughter*, which opened at the Royalty Theatre on Boxing Day 1881, a good many years before his popularity as a novelist was established. Having emerged as a playwright, he then retreated, although he told Douglas Sladen in 1913 that some of his books had been dramatized 'and others are on their way to the stage'.[44] At one point he had approached Horace Collins, who was press agent at the Drury Lane, where his brother Arthur was general manager. An occasional short-story writer, Horace Collins had some experience at adapting work for the popular stage. According to him, Garvice

was very anxious to have one of his stories turned into a play and wanted me to undertake it. I would have gladly done it, because his name would have been a draw, but after plodding through a number of his books, I reluctantly came to the conclusion that the material was unsuitable for play purposes . . . he seemed to me to ring the changes on the old plot of children being changed at birth by a wicked foster-mother, and that had been used on the stage from time immemorial . . . readers of novels, I suppose, are more unsophisticated and more easily pleased than play-goers. Anyway, I felt it would do neither of our reputations much good to concoct a play. I expect I offended Garvice, as he seldom spoke to me afterwards.[45]

Collins's memoirs, written several decades after the event and filled with self-conceit, cannot be taken as entirely trustworthy; but in essentials he was right. Garvice was not included in John Parker's first edition of *Who's Who in the Theatre* (1912), extensive though its coverage was. The most complete hand-list of plays performed in British theatres between 1850 and 1930 also notes only one other Garvice play, a comedy, *Marigold*, adapted for the stage in collaboration with Allan Abbott and given its first showing at the Royalty Theatre, Glasgow, on 30 March 1914.[46] On the other hand, Garvice was describing himself in *Who's Who* in 1905 as 'novelist, *dramatist* and journalist', and he retained this designation thereafter.[47]

---

[43] Gribble, *Seen in Passing*, 240.

[44] Garvice's statement [Dec. 1913], Sladen papers, box 16, fo. 16.

[45] Collins, *Best Riches*, 174–5.

[46] Nicoll, *Late Nineteenth Century Drama*, ii. 376; id., *English Drama*, 663.

[47] *Who's Who* (1905), 601 (my italics); and *Who Was Who, 1916–1928*, 394, which include *A Life's Mistake* and (as part author) *A Heritage of Hate* among the few play titles. *Punch*, 15 July 1914, 61, facetiously reported, 'A movement is on foot to induce Mr Charles Garvice to change the name of his play, *A Heritage*

It was not the case, though, that Garvice was ignorant or incapable of writing in a different vein. His first novel, *Maurice Durant*, in the text and chapter epigraphs, showed that Garvice had had some brush with the classics (or else possessed an anthology), citing Æschylus, Marcus Aurelius, Ovid, Pliny, Sophocles, and a range of English poetry, from Shakespeare to Swinburne. Edgar Jepson recounted how Garvice 'did not strain himself to write Literature; he just lured away Ford Madox Ford's lady secretary, for he felt sure that, working so much with Ford, she must have caught it from him'.[48] This was a good joke, but Garvice was able to take it. He could and did write for a discriminating audience, placing with the *Westminster Gazette* a series of witty short stories about the literary and journalistic marketplace in which he poked fun at himself and others in the trade: 'The Prodigal at the Scribblers', about a short-story writer 'of the impressionist and staccato school', who is simultaneously 'grinding away at "Why Did She Kill Herself?" for the *Green Book*' and at ' "Janet's First Sweetheart" for the *Young Lady's Only Companion*'; 'The Transformation of a Great Novelist', about an author who eventually murders his illustrator, fed up with misrepresentations of his heroines; 'The Ideal Editor', about a publisher who protests to an author that his manuscript of 300,000 words is too short, and insists on paying both straight away and more than the author asks for—and is therefore certified insane; and 'The Interview', about the fabrications of journalists who profile celebrity authors and invent details to fit the romantic preconceptions of their readership, in this case the author Norbut:

Norbut is the man who wrote 'Polly Put the Kettle On: a Study in Black'. It came out quietly enough and no one expected it to do anything wonderful; but a certain great statesman . . . read it during a fit of insomnia and found rest—and said so in enthusiastic terms in one of the Reviews. The book ran to seven editions and Norbut found himself famous.[49]

But, generally, Garvice stuck to his romantic potboilers. He conformed to the prescription of Miss Prism, who was 'not in favour of this modern mania for turning bad people into good people at a moment's notice . . . The good end happily, and the bad unhappily. That is what Fiction means.'[50] Unlike that redoubtable creature, who mislaid the all-important handbag containing her treasured work of fiction, Garvice was thoroughly professional. Every morning he went up to his London office in Milton House Chambers, off the Strand, where he spent a business day in dictating his novels at up to 100 words a minute, pipe-smoking hard all the time.[51] This was in the years before the Great War

of Hate, as so many patrons of melodrama have experienced difficulty in pronouncing the title as it stands at present'—reference, no doubt, to their struggles with aspirates.

[48] Jepson, *Memories of an Edwardian and Neo-Georgian*, 53.

[49] Charles Garvice, *The Scribblers' Club* (1909), 115. Few readers of the *Westminster Gazette* would fail to pick up and enjoy this reference to the former Prime Minister, Rosebery.

[50] Oscar Wilde, 'The Importance of Being Earnest' (1895), in Wilde, *Plays, Prose Writings, and Poems*, 367.

[51] Sladen, *Twenty Years*, 281. Garvice had this at least in common with Henry James, who dictated most of his later works, calling it 'this blest mechanism'; see Henry James to Archibald Marshall, 18 Jan. 1914,

when Garvice lived at 4 Maids of Honour Row, abutting the palace at Richmond; he also had a thatched cottage at Hambledon, near Henley-on-Thames. These were the rewards of best-selling fiction-writing, by which Garvice was progressively transformed into a City gent; but he had most enjoyed playing the farmer in Devon, and his obituary in the *Richmond Herald* said that 'he certainly looked more like a farmer than a literary man'. The publicity photograph in his prime, copyrighted by George Newnes & Son, showed a handsome erect figure with Kitchener moustache, wearing a flat cap, Norfolk jacket, striped waistcoat, and jodhpurs, and holding a crop in his leather-gloved hands. Garvice told Raymond Blathwayt, 'I have been a farmer, and I can plough a field with any man'; and the *Evening Standard* recollected that, in his period as constituency party chairman in North Devon, 'at one of the meetings Mr. Garvice got down from the platform to quieten a noisy opponent, who gripped him by the collar and tore the front of his shirt out. But Mr. Garvice knocked him down.'[52] Such an incident, if true—it bore some resemblance to the election scene in *Maurice Durant*—suggested that the author might easily have taken the part of one of his own romantic heroes.

In town Garvice exercised by cycling, although this conveyance eventually lapsed, with wealth and age, in favour of motoring and sailing. He was clubbable, a popular member of the Garrick and Whitefriars; he was also involved in the Primrose League and Freemasons. Nor did success isolate him from other writers. On the contrary, he earned their respect in 1908 by taking the lead in the reconstitution of the Authors' Club when most were resigned to seeing it fold.[53] Gratitude for his part in this (or as a tongue-in-cheek action) led to his being made a Fellow of the Royal Society of Literature. He was now much in the swim of literary life. Shortly before his death Garvice was co-founder, with Douglas Sladen and Mrs Baillie Reynolds, of the After-Dinner Club, 'a sort of *salon* which met six times a year for introductions'. The club committee involved well-known names from the worlds of theatre, art, and literature—Dame Madge Kendal, Solomon J. Solomon, Margaret Woods, Lady Partridge, Lucas Malet— and, wrote Sladen, 'We drew up a list of the people who should be invited to join, and about four hundred accepted.'[54]

Garvice was personally liked because fundamentally unpretentious.[55] The same could not be said for Anthony Deane, the socially and intellectually self-confident

---

in Marshall, *Out and About*, 272. E. Phillips Oppenheim and Edgar Wallace also used the dictation method. Arnold Bennett tried and failed (apart from dictating correspondence); as for that great seer of the scientific future H. G. Wells, he wrote in untidy longhand (Flower, *Just as it Happened*, 174–5).

[52] See Blathwayt, *Great Thoughts*, 8–10; *Evening Standard*, 2 Mar. 1920, which included a more recent photograph of the elderly author, holding a fair-sized black dog. The George Newnes photograph of Garvice is in Richmond Reference Library, Local Studies collection, ref. L920.

[53] See above, Ch. 13.

[54] Sladen, *Long Life*, 170–1, 244–5. The Richmond Reference Library, Local Studies collections, Sladen papers, box 27, contains the correspondence. Refusals to join the After-Dinner Club came from Conan Doyle, Rider Haggard, Thomas Hardy, and Bernard Shaw. On Mrs Baillie Reynolds, see Kemp et al. (eds.), *Edwardian Fiction*, 339.

[55] The obituary in *The Times*, 2 Mar. 1920, is particularly good on this.

chairman of the Society of Authors committee of management, 1918–21. Deane was singular in being the first clergyman to hold that position. Wellington- and Cambridge-educated, he was a descendant of his namesake Sir Anthony Deane, a member of the Navy Board in Charles II's time; and the curacies and incumbencies he held in Bath, Malvern, and Hampstead, and his eventual canonry of Windsor and chaplaincy to the King, were symptomatic of the rich patronage enjoyed by a member of the Establishment.[56] Naturally, he became a member of the Athenaeum but, when a curate at Midhurst around the turn of the century, he joined the Authors' Club in order to use its overnight facilities during visits to London. There, he got to know Garvice; and, while patronizing about Garvice's writing, he highlighted qualities of sincerity and warmth:

> I ought not to forget Charles Garvice, that genial, astute, amazingly successful manu-facturer of pure rubbish. The adjective is doubly justified; his novels were unadulterated drivel and they were wholly innocuous . . . Yet if anyone supposed that it must be easy to make a fortune by writing down to the level of a huge semi-illiterate public, he is mistaken. He will not succeed, as Garvice could not have succeeded, unless he is honestly convinced that his rubbish is not rubbish, but work of real literary value. And to be, as certainly Charles Garvice was, among the kindest and most generous of men may be better worth while than to produce the most artistic works of fiction.[57]

A telling moment came in December 1918 when Deane organized at All Saints, Ennismore Gardens, a memorial service for authors killed in the war, at which Edmund Gosse read the lesson. Afterwards Deane invited a miscellany of authors attending the service, Garvice among them, to take tea at his home in Rutland Gate. Deane was uncertain what might ensue, given Gosse's reputation for being sharp-tongued to inferiors, but when Gosse left the party, 'he chanted a kind of triumphal song . . . "I have lived to-day!" he declared; "I have lived! I have met Charles Garvice!" '[58]

Garvice's amiability was widely remarked upon. A previous chairman of the Society of Authors management committee, Anthony Hope, noted in his diary on Garvice's death: 'a thorough good pleasant fellow. One would do anything for him, except read his books! And one told him so, and his good-nature laughed.'[59] Baroness Orczy also served with Garvice on a Society of Authors committee, this in 1914–15, which sought to assist writers whose livelihood was hit by the war.

---

[56] The novelist May Sinclair, seven years his senior, had fallen for him when she was undergoing a spiritual crisis. Deane had no shortage of certainty about the truth of Christianity, or about the unat-tractiveness of New Women—'insipid', 'deadly', and 'distasteful' he called them in his ill-titled *Holiday Verses* (1894), where he also belittled their aspiration to take university degrees. See Raitt, *Sinclair*, 69 n. 88. On the other hand, Deane was quite a talented parodist. Two of his series of nursery rhymes in the style of a famous author—'Mary, Mary', as by Edward FitzGerald, and 'Jack and Jill', as by Kipling—are reprinted in Simon Brett (ed.), *The Faber Book of Parodies* (1984).

[57] Deane, *Time Remembered*, 109. On Deane (1870–1946), see *Who Was Who, 1941–1950*, 300.

[58] Deane, *Time Remembered*, 192.

[59] Mallet, *Hope*, 241. Garvice is unnamed in the quotation, but its date and context make the identity unmistakable. See also *Punch*, 15 Oct. 1913, 324, for a gentle dig at Garvice's gentleness.

She described him as the 'kindest, most self-effacing' of men.[60] This was possibly the secret of his success as a novelist, thought Rebecca West, to whom that phenomenon was otherwise quite inexplicable:

It was impossible to meet Charles Garvice without realising that here was a dynamic good man; and his abundant eupeptic benevolence forced itself through to the printed word and gave a real warmth to the scenes where the kindly earl, anxious to make his son's mill-girl bride feel at home, took the entrée dish from the butler and helped her with his own hand.[61]

The final evaluation was made by Francis Gribble, who was moved to resuscitate his Virgil, finding appropriate to Garvice's reputation two lines from *The Aeneid*:

Parva metu primo, mox sese attollit in auras,
Aggrediturque solo, et caput inter nubila condit.[62]

At his death on 1 March 1920 Garvice left an estate probated at £71,049 6s. 9d.— perhaps £1.5 million in modern money. His will indicated that he had already made provision for his family, which comprised five daughters and two sons. Very little weight can be placed on comparisons made between the values of authors' estates, because of all-too-significant variables involving inheritance, investment, expenditure, and tax avoidance; but, as a rough indication of Garvice's fortune from writing, it can be noted that, with another ten years' earning power available to him, Arnold Bennett would leave substantially less.[63] There is much, therefore, that is creditable to the tradesman of letters in Garvice's case. Garvice researched his market over the years, progressively adapted his product, and turned out quantity to satisfy: was not that also romantic?

---

[60] Orczy, *Life*, 135.   [61] West, *Strange Necessity*, 322.

[62] Gribble, *Seen in Passing*, 241. From Virgil, *The Aeneid*, book 4, lines 176–7. In David West's translation (Harmondsworth, 1990, 86): 'From small and timorous beginnings, she soon lifts herself up into the air, her feet still on the ground and her head hidden in the clouds.' I owe this reference to my colleague Dr N. J. Richardson.

[63] Bennett left £36,600, plus securities estimated at £7,900, copyrights at £4,225, and manuscripts at £7,500: altogether some £15,000 less than Garvice. For an interpretation of the Bennett estate, see Drabble, *Bennett*, 352–3, and Swinnerton, *Bennett: A Last Word*, 1, 6, who emphasizes how much Bennett had given away in his lifetime, in support of his brothers and their families, and in charitable gifts. Bennett was also divorced.

20

Hymns and Heroines:
Florence Barclay

I

By contrast with the gradual rise, patient and planned, of Charles Garvice, Mrs Barclay's spectacular success was almost adventitious. She was a month short of her forty-seventh birthday when she issued her best-seller *The Rosary*, in 1909. It was not her first novel. That was *Guy Mervyn* (1891), a triple-decker written under a pseudonym, Brandon Roy, and published by Spencer Blackett.[1] *Jane Annie; or, The Good Conduct Prize* followed in 1893; meanwhile, Mrs Barclay became seriously ill with 'a form of peritonitis . . . [which] all but cost her life'.[2] Literature was largely set aside until she published a short devotional story, *The Wheels of Time* (1908), in which the heroine of *The Rosary*, Jane Champion, was introduced. She had written most of it in 1905 while again convalescing, this time from strain brought on by too much bicycling. *The Rosary* sold 150,000 copies within nine months; at its peak, two impressions per month were appearing. On her death in 1921 it was available in nine languages: English, French, German, Spanish, Norwegian, Swedish, Finnish, Dutch, and Polish. Mrs Barclay was relatively prolific in her final ten years, publishing more or less annually, all with the same house, the American G. P. Putnam's Sons, simultaneously in New York and London.[3] Sales were immense, but none eclipsed *The Rosary*, which was a monster best-seller on both sides of the Atlantic. When the first complete[4]

---

[1] Spencer Blackett, based at 35 St Bride Street, Ludgate Circus, London, had a generally undistinguished list of novice authors, such as Rider Haggard's triple-decker *Dawn* (1884), though it also issued cheap reprints of already successful titles, Conan Doyle's *The Sign of Four* (1890), and stories by G. A. Henty and Ouida.

[2] *The Life of Florence L. Barclay: A Study in Personality*, by 'one of her daughters' (1921), 105.

[3] Other titles: *The Mistress of Shenstone* (1910), *The Following of the Star* (1911), *Through the Postern Gate* (1912), *The Upas Tree* (1912), *The Broken Halo* (1913), *My Heart's Right There* (1914), *The Wall of Partition* (1914), *The White Ladies of Worcester* (1917), *Returned Empty* (1920). The choice of Putnam's was at the instigation of Mrs Barclay's sister, living in New York. On this firm, whose later best-sellers were Marie Stopes, *Married Love* (1919) and Erich Maria Remarque, *All Quiet on the Western Front* (1929), see James J. and Patience P. Barnes, 'G. P. Putnam's Sons', in Anderson and Rose (eds.), *British Literary Publishing Houses*, 250-7.

[4] 'Complete' because this edition restored some 10,000 words which Putnam's had required her to cut. 'Later on', Mrs Barclay's husband wrote, 'they were only too eager to accept any manuscript she wrote and followed every suggestion she liked to give.'

popular edition, with a brief introduction by her husband, was published in Britain in May 1925, over 1 million copies of the original had been sold. This popular edition went through twenty-six impressions before 1945. *The Rosary* had topped the best-sellers chart in America in 1910, and still held ninth place there in 1911. America's 'song of the year' in 1911 was Irving Berlin's 'Alexander's Ragtime Band', but the hit of 1910 was 'The Rosary', first composed by Ethelbert Nevin in 1898, with words by Robert Cameron Rogers, because it featured in the plot of Mrs Barclay's book. 'Everyone was humming it,' wrote Alice Payne Hackett; and, 'so popular and profitable was the book that its publisher's new building on West 45th Street, in New York, was dubbed "The Rosary"'.[5]

The Rosary was dedicated to Angela, Mrs Barclay's last daughter, who had been born in 1900. There were five other daughters and two sons. If her intermittent illnesses and the raising of eight children are thought insufficient explanation of her late-flowering authorship, then reference must be made to her duties as the daughter and wife of clergymen. Indeed, it is essential to note her religious life. She published a booklet in 1905, *A Notable Prisoner*, recounting the Passion of Christ as if told by Barabbas; and her fiction was conceived in this spirit:

My aim is never to write a line which could introduce the taint of sin, or the shadow of shame, into any home. Never to draw a character which would tend to lower the ideals of those who, by means of my pen, make intimate acquaintance with a man or a woman of my own creating . . . Too many bad, mean, morbid characters already, alas! walk this earth. Why should writers add to their numbers, and risk introducing them into beautiful homes, where such people in actual life would never for one moment be tolerated.

There was, her filial biographer added, 'a good deal of allusion to religion in her books. But it was never dragged in. It was a natural expression of her own point of view.'[6] The same point was made, more cruelly, by Rebecca West:

Heaven knows how in the tepid pages of *The Rosary* its million readers detected the power that lived in Mrs Florence Barclay, that made her physically as radiant as a young girl when she was a woman of sixty and permitted her to enjoy complete confidence that she was directly inspired by the Holy Ghost; but it must have leaked through by some channel.[7]

II

Mrs Barclay was born Florence Louisa Charlesworth in 1862. The middle of three sisters, she was nicknamed Benny by her mother, perhaps because (her

---

[5] Alice Payne Hackett, *Fifty Years of Best Sellers 1895–1945* (1945), 26, 106. On the composer Nevin, see Peter Gammond, *The Oxford Companion to Popular Music* (Oxford, 1991), 418. According to Mrs Barclay's daughter, the song sold 40,000 copies in England in the year after the publication of the story; Barclay, *Life*, 264.   [6] Barclay, *Life*, 177, 240, 244.
[7] West, 'The Tosh Horse', in West, *Strange Necessity*, 322.

own daughter speculated) 'she was more like a very active small boy than a mid-Victorian small girl; or because Mrs Charlesworth had longed so greatly for a son'.[8] This tomboy trait would permeate her later fiction. Education was conducted at home by a governess until, at 17, she was sent briefly to Belstead, her mother's former school. Her father, Samuel, ministered at Limpsfield, Surrey, and Florrie (as she was afterwards generally called) throughout her life regarded the Limpsfield vicarage as home.[9] In 1870 the Revd Charlesworth, who was prone to 'fits of intense depression', moved from this rural idyll to an East London problem parish, St Anne's, Limehouse. He was supported by a young curate from a wealthy family—Charles Barclay, born at the mansion Bury Hill, near Dorking—whom Florrie married when she was 18. The Barclays translated to Holy Trinity, Little Amwell, Hertfordshire (near Haileybury College), where Charles ministered until retirement in 1921. Florrie shared her father's and husband's evangelical devotion. Her honeymoon was spent in the Holy Land, where she was credited with identifying the mouth of Jacob's well. For her the Bible was the word of God; Christ's presence she knew to be real, as also that of Satan, 'who made people wicked, [and] it was most desirable that Satan should be reformed without delay'.[10] Mrs Barclay started and led a men's Bible class and mothers' meetings in her parish, where she also organized counter-attractions to its pubs through concerts and recitals. Discovering that she possessed healing powers in her hands, she became much interested in telepathic and psychic communication, yet she remained anxious to guard her parishioners against 'the tremendous increase and popularity of spiritualism', about which 'she had an intense horror . . . she believed that to have anything whatever to do with it would be a grave sin, and a violation of God's laws'.[11]

Mrs Barclay was otherwise an extraordinary all-rounder in which for long periods the writer lay submerged. A lifelong passion was for music. This provides the means by which love is revealed in *The Rosary*. Her father intended sending her to the College of Music before her early marriage put a stop to that. She sang a rich contralto and played the violin and piano; and in her parishes she trained the choirs and played the organ. Mrs Barclay was no simpering vicar's wife. A fellow best-selling authoress, the equally determined Annie S. Swan—who lived at neighbouring Hertford—appreciated her as 'an understanding creature' but emphasized that 'there was not a suggestion of mushy sentimentality about the sturdy little figure in homespun, crowned by a queer sort of velvet hat, a cross between a beret and a Scotch cap, without which she was never seen'.[12] Mrs Barclay did not so much overcome illness as beat it off. She was an apostle of fitness, following Sandow's exercises towards harmony of the spiritual and

---

[8] Barclay, *Life*, 14.
[9] The Barclays returned to Limpsfield in the last year of Mrs Barclay's life and she is buried in its churchyard. Limpsfield is better known to literary scholars as the place where the poet W. H. Davies settled and where Edward and Constance Garnett had their home.   [10] Barclay, *Life*, 22–3, 30–4.
[11] Ibid. 107–18.   [12] Swan, *My Life*, 133–5.

physical life.[13] She also swam, rode, walked, climbed, cycled, rowed, skated, skied, and played golf, tennis, and women's cricket.

In the late nineteenth and early twentieth centuries sport had a social significance greater than the aggregation of pleasures and enhanced health of body and mind that its individual practitioners enjoyed. For women especially it marked an enlargement of the area of acceptable activity for their sex. Implications were thus carried away from the playing fields, into the workplace and home and for gender relations broadly. Together with the amateur versus professional schism, the propriety of women's sports was hotly debated.[14] Lines were drawn differently according to social class culture. A tradition of female participation in country sports, riding to the hounds especially, was well established; and its formidable characters were already stock figures in literature and on the stage, such as the splendid Lady Gay Spanker in Dion Boucicault's *London Assurance* (1841). For the rest, the attitudes of the more conservative-minded middle and upper classes were nicely caught by *Punch*, which habitually found women golfers, cricketers, or tennis players *ipso facto* funny; yet *Punch* also appreciated the importance to women of their receiving respect on the games field.[15] Mrs Barclay's part in this is difficult to caption. Upholding as she did the traditional cardinal virtues of Christian marriage and motherhood, she appears scarcely to merit even a heavily qualified designation of unwitting revolutionary; still, we should not rule out the possibility of her personal example and her fiction inspiring other women to push harder against the social constraints that confined them. The contrast with Marie Corelli is marked. Both best-sellers' stories were permeated by religious themes and language; otherwise, the outlooks of these authors and their heroines were different. Corelli was vehemently anti-sport and, together

[13] Eugen Sandow (1867–1925), the moustached German muscleman, moved from weightlifting feats to develop a string of training schools and a worldwide mountebank medical trade: his thirty-page tract on home treatment, as 'recommended by the highest medical authorities', promised relief in cases of 'Indigestion, Insomnia, Constipation, Nervous Disorders, Weak Lungs, Sluggish Liver, Obesity, and generally the disorders resulting from a sedentary life'. The Sandow System involved a nineteen-part series of exercises, generally using light five-pound dumb-bells. Sandow's mail-order business operated from premises at 17–18 Basinghall Street, London, in the City close to the Guildhall. See the advertisement in *T.P.'s Weekly*, 17 Apr. 1903, 752. Mrs Barclay, who went through a professional course and then conducted her own class in the Sandow regime in her parish, should not be thought especially credulous. The 'Sandow system of physical culture' could also boast a testimonial from (and picture of) Lord Lansdowne, writing from the War Office on 21 March 1900, although Lansdowne's organization of the Boer War effort hardly merited maximum points on a scale of efficiency: advertisement in *T.P.'s Weekly*, 4 Sept. 1903, 445. Not one to miss a trick, James Joyce has Bloom recount his intermittent subjection to Sandow's regime, in *Ulysses*, 602. Conan Doyle, friend and follower of Sandow, contributed a foreword to Sandow's *The Construction and Reconstruction of the Human Body* (1907) (Booth, *Conan Doyle*, 252); and P. G. Wodehouse, while still working at the Hong Kong and Shanghai Bank in the early 1900s, contributed to *Sandow's Physical Culture Magazine* (Donaldson, *Wodehouse*, 57).

[14] There are many articles in the *International Journal of the History of Sport* that examine these issues. For example, Althea Milling, ' "Ray of the Rovers": The Working-Class Heroine in Popular Fiction, 1915–25', *International Journal of the History of Sport* (Apr. 1998), 97–122.

[15] Marilyn Constanzo, ' "One Can't Shake Off the Women": Images of Sport and Gender in *Punch*, 1901–10', *International Journal of the History of Sport* (Mar. 2002), 31–56.

with intermittent strictures in her novels, expressed this animus in *Pearson's Magazine* in 1905, under the captivating title 'Balls on the Brain'. Here she observed as a consequence of the spread of sports 'an alarming tendency to woodenize and leatherize the brain itself'.[16] While bad enough for men to become sports-obsessed, it was far worse for women and represented for Corelli a horrible antithesis to her ideal of Womanhood, as repellent as the morals of the New Woman or the politics of the suffragists and suffragettes; but, then, Corelli was anti-suffrage as Mrs Barclay was not.

Physically fearless and blessed with fine coordination, Mrs Barclay achieved unusual feats of athletic skill and endurance. In 1890, when she was staying at St Moritz during a winter sports festival, she was so taken by the toboggan run, 5 miles downhill, that she volunteered to take the place of a competitor who had withdrawn. 'If I ride, I ride to win', was her philosophy and, on an old-fashioned Swiss toboggan up against racers on the speedier new American models, she beat the field. A powerful swimmer, it was nothing for her, on family holidays on the Isle of Wight, to swim out to the *Warner* lightship $2\frac{1}{2}$ miles across the strong currents of the Solent, then row back. Other family holidays were taken at Overstrand, near Cromer, to which she once cycled the 120 miles from Hertford Heath in a day.[17] Physical exertion also played a decisive part in Mrs Barclay's authorship. First, strenuous bicycling brought on *The Rosary*; then, in 1912, her writing ground to a halt following a blow to the head while motoring, until another smack to the head from an oar while boating on Derwentwater reactivated her mental machinery. This was a highly unorthodox form of brain surgery, although Augustus John was said to have undergone the same when he smashed his skull on a rock while diving into shallow sea and resurfaced an artistic genius.[18] Mrs Barclay, however, ascribed her own recovery to special providence.[19]

Mrs Barclay equipped the heroines of her novels with similar athletic accomplishments. Jane Champion in *The Rosary* is decidedly hearty and much admired by young men for this. One, worsted by her at golf, reports, 'She drives like a rifle shot, and when she lofts, you'd think the ball was a swallow.' Invited by her lover for a tête-à-tête on the river, Jane declares: 'I am not the sort of person to be told off to sit in the stern of a tiny skiff and steer. If I am in a boat, I like to row; and if I row, I prefer rowing stroke.' Jane is a courageous rider, too, 'prepared for any fence or any wall'; and, 'wearing collars and stocks, top boots and short skirts', she impresses the chaps no end by 'whacking her leg with a riding-whip, and stirring the fire with her toe'. Trial by fire provides no test for Jane. At a critical moment of *The Rosary*, she sits close but unbeknown to her now blinded lover, who, having lit a cigarette, 'flung the flaming match straight on to Jane's clasped hands'. When Jane 'smilingly flicked it off', a witness to this episode is rightly

[16] Scott, *Corelli*, 228.   [17] Barclay, *Life*, 128–31.   [18] Holroyd, *John*, i. 51–3.
[19] Barclay, *Life*, 265–6.

awestruck: 'What nerve! Ninety-nine women out of a hundred would have said "Ah!" and given away the show. Really, she deserves to win.' Not surprisingly, Jane is described as walking 'with the freedom of movement and swing of limb which indicate great strength and a body well under control'. The same recurs in other stories. Christobel Charteris, heroine of *Through the Postern Gate* (1912), has 'a tall, athletic figure, fully developed, gracious in its ample lines, yet graceful in the perfect swing of the well-poised walk'. At tennis, which she plays on her own court, Christobel possesses a 'magnificent serve' and 'glowing with the exercise, and the consciousness of being in great form', dispatches the opposition.

Mrs Barclay felt no embarrassment about a confusion of genders resulting from women displaying their physical prowess. In *The Rosary* Jane strides up the Great Pyramid in intense heat in record time,

hardly realising how large a part of her finely developed athletic powers and elastic limbs had played in the speed of the ascent. And Jane stood there, sound in wind and limb, and with the exhilarating sense, always helpful to the mind, of a bodily feat accomplished. She was looking her best in her Norfolk coat and skirt of brown tweed with hints of green and orange in it, plenty of useful pockets piped with leather, leather buttons, and a broad band of leather round the bottom of the skirt.

Jane is, in Mrs Barclay's eyes, functionally yet still femininely attired. Her costume is topped with a 'soft green Tyrolian hat—for Jane scorned pith helmets—which matched it so admirably'. And she is

deeply tanned by the Eastern sun. Burning a splendid brown, and enjoying the process, she had no need of veils or parasols; and her strong eyes faced the golden light of the desert without the aid of smoked glasses . . . 'Nice gentleman-lady', murmured Schehati [Jane's Arab guide] again; and had Jane overheard the remark it would not have offended her; for, though she held a masculine woman only one degree less in abhorrence than an effeminate man, she would have taken Schehati's compound noun as a tribute to the fact that she was well-groomed and independent, knowing her own mind, and, when she started out to go to a place, reaching it in the shortest possible time, without fidget, fuss, or flurry. These three feminine attributes were held in scorn by Jane, who knew herself so deeply womanly that she could afford in minor ways to be frankly unfeminine.[20]

For Mrs Barclay, the conventional idea of a lady so corseted she was incapable of doing anything except faint was no model to imitate. Characteristically, she has Jane go to South Africa

in the very thick of the Boer War . . . nursing; but the real thing, mind you. None of your dabbling in eau-de-cologne with lace handkerchiefs, and washing handsome faces when the orderlies had washed them; making charming conversation to men who were getting well, but fleeing in dread from the dead or the dying. None of that, you may be sure, and none of that allowed in her hospital; for Miss Champion was in command there, and I can

---

[20] Barclay, *The Rosary*, 128–30.

tell you she made them scoot. She did the work of ten, and expected others to do it too. Doctors and orderlies adored her.

This is recounted by one doctor who witnesses Jane, intrepid when a Boer shell crashed through the hospital roof, imperative and businesslike in organization, yet compassionate and tender to the sick and dying, whose heads she 'rested against her womanly breast', bringing 'a sense of mother and home quite near'. 'Just once she broke down. It was over a boy whom she had tried hard to save— quite a youngster,' the doctor adds before describing that particularly distressing case. One lachrymose incident is invariably allowed for the most manly of Victorian fictional men: this enhances rather than diminishes their fine quality.[21] The same is granted for Jane, in whom 'that big, loving heart must often have been racked; but she was always brave and bright'.[22] The Great War would find Mrs Barclay and her children likewise rising to its challenges. Her elder son, who was ministering in Australia, returned as a chaplain with the forces until laid low by typhoid; her other son served at Jutland; four of her daughters became nurses and another, too young for nursing, cooked at a VAD hospital. Mrs Barclay threw herself into charity work, hospital-visiting and comforting the bereaved; she was also undaunted when, on 3 September 1916, a Zeppelin bomb blew out the vicarage windows.[23] 'You always were a *thorough* old thing!' the admiring Sir Deryck Brand says to Jane in *The Rosary*: 'No half-measures would do.'[24]

The heroes of Mrs Barclay's novels have their work cut out to keep up with her heroines; but Guy Chelsea, the daring, record-competing motorist and aviator hero of *Through the Postern Gate*, having ambled outside the said gate, 'threw up his cap, and caught it; then started off and sprinted a hundred yards; then, turning aside, leapt a five-barred gate, and made off across the fields'. Gate-vaulting is sine qua non for a Barclay hero. It began with Sir Guy Mervyn, in her first novel of 1891. Accomplished violinist as well as sportsman, he projects himself with commendable frequency, into the saddle and over inanimate objects. A stile is happily positioned cross-country between Mervyn Hall and The Towers, where the 'dazzlingly lovely' Lady Elaine resides, all the better for Guy to show what he is made of. Once, when Lady Elaine stumbles on a broken step of the stile, bangs her head, and twists her ankle, 'with a wild cry, Guy sprang down the bank and vaulted over the stile' in order to sweep her up. Later in the story, elated after declaring his love, Guy 'bounded joyously over the stile'—this time by moonlight.[25] In *The Rosary* Garth Dalmain, though a painter with a penchant

---

[21] The late Victorian period witnessed the beginnings of a reaction against the weepy writer and weepy scene. Wilde's remark about Dickens—'One must have a heart of stone to read the death of Little Nell without laughing'—is well known. See also *Punch*, 21 Apr. 1888, 189, and 28 Apr. 1888, 202, for hoots of derision in response to Walter Besant's declaration that 'no moving situation was ever yet depicted, the writing of which did not cost the Author anguish and tears'. Yet, only a few weeks before, *Punch's* reviewer freely admitted to having snivelled over *Little Lord Fauntleroy*; ibid., 10 Mar. 1888, 117.

[22] Barclay, *The Rosary*, 222–3.   [23] Barclay, *Life*, ch. xii.   [24] Barclay, *The Rosary*, 240.

[25] Brandon Roy [Mrs Barclay], *Guy Mervyn* (1891), i. 140, ii. 185, iii. 85, 194.

for arty clothes, can not only belt a tennis ball but also hurdle a gate. He performs this action on his Aberdeenshire estate when he 'happened to pass within sight of some fellows rabbit-shooting, and saw what he considered cruelty to a wounded rabbit. He vaulted over a gate to expostulate and to save the little creature from further suffering.' This is an important incident for, not only is Garth fatefully blinded by ricocheting pellets, it also allows Mrs Barclay to pronounce an exception to her otherwise panathletic credo. Garth has given up shooting a couple of years earlier: 'He never really enjoyed it, because he so loved the beauty of life and hated death in every form.' Garth is a late convert compared with Jane. She had never been seen in the hunting field: 'her love of life and of fair play would have kept her out of that.' Indeed, all field sports were detestable:

Passionate love of animal life, intense regard for all life, even of the tiniest insect, was as much a religion with her as the worship of beauty was with Garth. She never could pretend sorrow over these accounts of shooting accidents, or falls in the hunting-field. When those who went out to inflict cruel pain were hurt themselves; when those who went forth to take eager, palpitating life, lost their own; it seemed to Jane a just retribution. She felt no regret, and pretended none.[26]

Thus Mrs Barclay was not an unphilosophical athletic authoress. She was fit but fastidious. Her affinity with wildlife was remarkable, as she demonstrated by taming birds, bats, dormice, and even fish. Her domestic menagerie included Bacco, a monkey, Tammy, a chow, Peter, a poodle, a jackdaw, a toucan, and three pairs of jerboas.[27] Just as with her sporting skills, so Mrs Barclay transferred these abilities to characters in her novels. In *The Broken Halo* (1913) one helpfully describes her method of taming birds. In *The Rosary* the Duchess of Meldrum is known for 'surrounding herself with all sorts of queer birds and beasts' and 'shedding a kindly and exciting influence wherever she goes'. The animals even included 'six Egyptian jerboas', which the Duchess allowed 'in the drawing-room every evening after dinner, awfully jolly little beggars, like miniature kangaroos. They used to go skipping about on their hind legs, frightening some of the women into fits by hiding under their gowns, and making young footmen drop trays of coffee cups.' There was an aviary, too, although Tommy, the talking macaw, and a toucan known as the Magistrate ('Because of the beak') have perches in the house. Mrs Barclay's attitude to animals was loving but firm. Her daughter remarked,

she never allowed herself any foolish weaknesses in the matter, such as a refusal to sanction the *necessary* taking of life, or in adopting fads like vegetarianism, or subscribing

---

[26] Barclay, *The Rosary*, 135. Other unattributed quotations in the previous paragraphs are from this, pp. 11, 17, 19, 37, 136, 250, 254, 262; and from Florence Barclay, *Through the Postern Gate*, 156th thousand, popular edn. (n.d.), 20, 23, 74.

[27] Barclay, *Life*, 40–1, 128, 135–56. There is a photograph of Mrs Barclay with a song-thrush on her lap, opposite p. 160.

III

None could doubt also, from the passionate intensity of Mrs Barclay's romances, that she had read and been influenced by so-called sensation novels. Her own first story, the triple-decker *Guy Mervyn* (1891), while in purpose the 'religious novel' as her daughter defined it, owed many of its devices and preposterous plotting to the sensation genre. Lady Elaine, with whom Guy Mervyn falls in love, is a Woman with a Past. An earl's only daughter, she enjoyed a happy childhood until her mother died, whereupon her father went to ruin, gambling on horses and mortgaging his estates to one particularly ruthless creditor called Monk. Ignoring her adolescent infatuation with another nobleman, Lord Montague Errol, her father sells her in marriage to Monk on her seventeenth birthday. A baby follows when Lady Elaine is herself still 'a child—not fit to be a mother'; she at first rejects the infant boy, then adores him, but her husband, now an MP, insists she accompany him to London without the boy, who falls ill and dies at the age of 6 months.[38] The husband, Monk, is a stage villain:

a short thick-set man, well over fifty; broad-shouldered, dark and sallow; his black bushy beard and moustache did not hide his full sensual lips; and, when he smiled, Guy noticed the white pointed teeth, which gave an almost wolfish expression of cruelty to his face . . . [and] which to a pure true soul rendered his face unutterably revolting.[39]

Monk beats Lady Elaine, cowardly assaults Guy, relishes dirty talk at the dinner table, and dies in a seizure from intoxication; but not before he has hurled into a lake Lady Elaine's locket containing a curl of her dead baby's hair. Hearing of her despair, Guy 'dives like a duck' into the lake, time and again until, in a state of near-exhaustion, he recovers it 'with its contents uninjured by the water'.[40] Lord Montague meanwhile has reappeared on the scene, sadistically invited by Monk to jeopardize Lady Elaine's growing relationship with Guy. Lord Montague turns out to be self-indulgently vicious rather than irredeemably wicked. He torments Guy by pretending that an old letter was recently written, in which Lady Elaine, when only 16, had declared her feelings for him; he also plans to kidnap her, secluding a pair of horses in a darkened wood. Fortunately, his plot is overheard by Guy's sister, concealed in the trees. After a struggle Lord Montague is disarmed of his revolver, whereupon Lady Elaine, instead of berating him, offers up a prayer and Lord Montague kneels and begs forgiveness.[41]

 Incredible coincidences, a dark paternal history, and intercepted letters also characterize the relationship between Guy's private tutor the Revd Cyril Branscome and Lady Elaine's friend Muriel Bruce, whose love affair runs parallel in the story. They had fallen for each other before Cyril went up to Cambridge, intending, when he achieved sufficient security, to marry; however, Muriel's

---

[38] [Barclay], *Guy Mervyn*, ii. 157–72, iii. 73–80.   [39] Ibid. i. 84–5.   [40] Ibid. iii. 102–10.
[41] Ibid. iii, chs. xxxiv, xxxviii.

father, a clergyman but 'a clever, ambitious man', made sure that her letters to Cyril never reached him, or his her, and under pressure from her father she married a rich suitor. Ignorant of this scheming, Muriel felt rejected, and Cyril betrayed; now, years later and in widow's weeds, Muriel is glimpsed at a hotel beside Lake Geneva where Guy and Cyril are staying. Guy recognizes her from a photograph he remembers on Lady Elaine's drawing-room table. Cyril and Muriel, having remained in love, finally marry; and Guy installs Cyril as vicar of his vacant village living. The disclosure of Muriel's father's deviousness, which almost ruined their happiness, provokes an artless intervention from Mrs Barclay, who ends that chapter on an exclamatory note:

Oh fathers, with hard dry hearts, clear heads and cool judgments; think what you have to answer for, when you let your own worldly-mindedness and mercenary ambition interpose between your daughters and those to whom they have given the pure first love of their young hearts! Better were it for you that a millstone were hanged about your necks, and that you were drowned in the depth of the sea![42]

Mrs Barclay then recovers herself. Cyril and Muriel, after all, have been reunited. They forgive her now dead father and give thanks for their present bliss and for their being 'at one *in Him*', Muriel musing that 'perhaps we should neither of us have been drawn to Him, if all had gone right three years ago'. Cyril agrees, for otherwise he would not have met Guy, who was 'the means of leading me to Christ'; at which Muriel chimes, 'And I sought Him in my trouble and loneliness, when I lost you.'[43]

In *Guy Mervyn* Mrs Barclay thus used the conventions of sensation fiction as vehicles to recount a tale of religious experience. At the start, Guy, aged 19, succeeds a crusty old baronet bachelor relation to take possession of Mervyn Hall, living there with his mother and two sisters. He is 'remarkably handsome, tall and broad-shouldered, with a frank, boyish face and the clearest, truest pair of blue eyes you ever saw';[44] and, 'notwithstanding his boyish roughness and lack of polished manners'—he had been apt to roam free at their previous Highland home—he 'had in his veins the blood of generations of true English gentlemen'.[45] A gentleman's creed Guy himself defines: 'Never to do a mean action, and never to tell a lie'.[46] Yet, 'religion did not come naturally to Guy; not even that very easily digested form of religion to be obtained at most country churches', interposes Mrs Barclay. He attends services irregularly, preferring Sunday morning walks in the woods with his dog, at which Mrs Barclay asks: 'And is it rank heresy, or the simple truth, to say that, in thus learning to know and love the beauties of God's glorious universe, his mind and heart were all unconsciously drawn nearer to the great Mind of Omniscient Wisdom, and the great Heart of Eternal Love?'[47]

---

[42] [Barclay], *Guy Mervyn*, iii. 14–15.   [43] Ibid. iii. 31–2.   [44] Ibid. i. 29.   [45] Ibid. i. 11.
[46] Ibid. i. 19.   [47] Ibid. i. 35–7.

sense of religion and hatred of sin. The result was shrewdly and sympathetically analysed by *The Times*:

Mrs. Barclay was essentially a home novelist. She had the home point of view and made the very most of it. This is not to say that she was dull. It was one of the secrets of her success that she managed to be entirely sincere and yet to infuse into an atmosphere which many people regard as narrow a kind of repressed excitement. When reading her books, indeed, one realised the sensational possibilities of repression. For she succeeded in keeping the surface of the lake unruffled, while beneath the surface strong, rather ill-defined currents were whirling about in all directions . . .

The use she made of religious feeling was always attractive, even if it was always sentimental. Her characters . . . [it] is probably fair to describe . . . as what most people, when they are in love for the first time, would like to be like, and what many people are like at Christmas . . . [She] was an apostle of the beauty and holiness of love—for love's sake . . . Zealot-like, and in unchastened phrase, she told the middle classes of this country that men and women mattered much more than goods and chattels. Above all, they mattered more to one another—and God . . . It says much for her capacity as an evangelist that the middle classes agreed with her.[60]

Clever clogs were not so lenient, and a comparison with Mrs Barclay was a handy term of abuse. So Ernest Raymond found when his first novel, the best-selling *Tell England* (1922), was savagely reviewed by Rose Macaulay in the *Daily News*. It was, she wrote, 'sloppy, sentimental, and illiterate'. Still, she did not doubt that there were some schoolboys who 'may like *Tell England* and the novels of Mrs Barclay (you could, by the way, transfer whole sentences and paragraphs from one to the other of these last contributions to literature without detection)'.[61] Macaulay's laugh, smartly formed at Somerville, rings particularly hollow in retrospect, remembering her own religious mother and that now, having turned 40 in 1921, she was involved with a married man, who was a former priest. She withdrew from the Anglican fold because of this relationship, returning to it only after her lover's death.[62] In any case, two of her successors as undergraduates at Somerville were among the many writers of fan letters to Mrs Barclay in 1913.[63]

The Times's obituary placed most of Mrs Barclay's readership in the middle classes, but it comprised a wide social spectrum. At the top was royalty. It was Putnam's London manager, Constant Huntington, who had the bright idea of sending *The Rosary* to Queen Alexandra on publication. Boston-born, Harvard-educated, and related to the Putnams, Huntington married an heiress and moved easily in British aristocratic circles. When the Queen responded by telling Huntington that *The Rosary* was her favourite book of the year, the word spread

---

[60] *The Times*, 11 Mar. 1921.   [61] Quoted in Raymond, *Story of my Days*, 182–3.

[62] See Sarah LeFanu, *Rose Macaulay* (2003). The lover was the novelist Gerald O'Donovan (1871–1942), on whom, see *Oxford DNB*.

[63] Mrs Barclay's reply, 24 Feb. 1913, in Barclay, *Life*, 261–2. It is conceivable, though unlikely, that the original fan letter was jape.

among Society.[64] In 1912 Mrs Barclay made it into *Who's Who* for the first time.[65] Known admirers of *The Rosary* included Field Marshal Sir Evelyn Wood, who won the Victoria Cross during the Indian Mutiny. Lest the modern reader be tempted to dismiss Wood's literary habits as those of an ignorant military buffer, there is the opinion of the publisher Newman Flower that Wood was 'one of the best read men I ever met'. But there are clues in Wood's life that account for his being drawn to Mrs Barclay's stories. One was Wood's always immaculate appearance, wearing a frock coat with, whatever the season, a buttonhole. The other was his religion, like that of his friends Charles Kingsley and General Gordon: 'In his bedroom was a little altar where he said his prayers when he reached the room at evening to change for dinner. Sundays found him in his pew at the village church, straight, upstanding, his hair whitening now, this man with the strong unfaltering faith.'[66] One of Wood's sisters, Katherine, was better known as Kitty O'Shea, Parnell's mistress and belated wife. Wood never spoke or wrote to her after the Parnell affair. Other proclaimed admirers of Mrs Barclay included the cricketer–cleric and public-school headmaster Edward Lyttelton, who was a resolute opponent of 'indecent' novels such as Compton Mackenzie's *Sinister Street* (1913); and the actor–manager George Alexander, who tried to interest Mrs Barclay in a dramatization.[67] There was no class antagonism in her books. She was courteous to all, in her novels as in life, stated her daughter: ' "How nice to be written about by someone who *knows* us, at *last*", remarked a certain dowager duchess to another, as she finished *The Rosary*; and the working people loved her books because whenever they appeared in them it was always as real, simple, likeable characters, never burlesqued, never ridiculed.'[68]

Not that there were many or many sorts of working people in these books. The industrial working classes and urban poor are unmentioned. This is almost certainly from choice. She had met with rough treatment, even been pelted with rubbish, when as a girl she supported her mother's religious revivalist endeavours in Limehouse, visiting workplaces to sing hymns and play her violin. Her own daughter's legend is that little Florrie won over their hearts by her pluckiness.[69] That may be so; and afterwards, as a minister's wife herself, Mrs Barclay took the

---

[64] Anderson and Rose (eds.), *British Literary Publishing Houses*, 254. Huntington later encouraged L. P. Hartley as novelist.

[65] Styled conventionally 'Barclay, Mrs. Charles W.'; *Who's Who* (1912), 99.

[66] Flower, *Just as it Happened*, 181–6. On Wood (1838–1919), see *DNB 1912–1921*, 591–3. In his capacity as a governor of Gresham's School, Holt, Arthur Benson encountered Wood (in full dress uniform) delivering the Speech Day address in 1907: 'the usual rot about ability being the gift of God, but character being in our power to acquire' (quoted in Newsome, *On the Edge of Paradise*, 221).

[67] Mackenzie, *Life and Times*, iv. 197–8; Barclay, *Life*, 219–20. The most comprehensive listing of plays performed in British theatres, 1900–30, that by Allardyce Nicoll (*English Drama*), contains no dramatization of a Barclay story, but Desmond Flower, *Best Sellers*, 20, writing about *The Rosary* in 1934, stated: 'Its fame to-day is a little eclipsed by that of the song and the incredible posters which inferior repertory companies still use in small provincial towns to advertise the play.' *The Mistress of Shenstone* was made into a Hollywood film in 1921; there were French and Mexican film versions of *The Rosary*, in 1934 and 1944 respectively. [68] Barclay, *Life*, 48–9.

[69] Ibid. 55–7.

Bible into suburban Essex, Leytonstone and Walthamstow, where there were also working-class strongholds. But her preferred literary environment is the country estate with its village servant class. Its characters are allowed supporting roles in her fiction, costumed in clichés: the loving and loyal former nanny, the crusty but kindly cook, and so forth. In *The Following of the Star* the aged rector's housekeeper, Sarah Dolman, is 'stout, comfortable, and motherly'; and, when at Christmas she sends a card to the rector's locum, missionary David Rivers, inscribed 'To the Reverant David rivers from Yours rispectfully Sarah', he stands it in place of honour on the mantelpiece. The verger Jabez Bones, in the same story, is always ready with an exclamation, 'Sakes alive, sir!'[70] In *Through the Postern Gate* the heroine Christobel's faithful elderly housekeeper, Martha, has a soft spot for the hero, Guy, with whom she exchanges banter in her immaculate kitchen, though often his clever remarks are beyond her simple understanding. Still, when she permits herself a peep through the storeroom window on the day Guy has proposed to (and been rejected by) Christobel, as his 'erect figure' disappears beyond the postern gate she finds 'an unwonted tear running down the furrows of her hard old face. "Lord love 'im!", she said. "He'll get what he wants in time. There's not a woman walks this earth as couldn't never refuse 'im nothing" ... Then she wiped her eyes with her apron, and chid her nose harshly for an unexpected display of sentiment.'[71] These servant types are all good-natured, humorous souls, with authority and decorum in their own sphere, with anarchic aspirates when flustered, with salt-of-the-earth sagacity when moved to reflect, and with proper sense of place and plain religious faith. They are dependable and dignified, respectful but not obsequious. About old Margery in *The Rosary*, Garth's former nurse and now his housekeeper, Mrs Barclay emphasizes that when the Duchess visits, 'Margery received her Grace as simply as she received the minister's wife, and with the same old-fashioned courtesy— deference without servility, and friendliness without familiarity.'[72]

Needless to say, Mrs Barclay's heroes and heroines were good to their servants, good also to other members of the service class whom they happen to encounter. When in *The Rosary* Jane returns to England after long absence abroad, at Dover railway station she finds a capable porter to manage her baggage. For his efficiency a half-crown, rather than the expected penny, is placed in his palm:

He had a sick young wife at home, who had been ordered extra nourishment, and just as the rush on board began, he had put up a simple prayer to the Heavenly Father 'Who knoweth that ye have need of these things', asking that he might catch the eye of a generous traveller. He felt he had indeed been 'led' to this plain, brown-faced, broad-shouldered lady ...

---

[70] Barclay, *Following of the Star*, 26, 28, 59.   [71] Barclay, *Postern Gate*, 54–5.
[72] Barclay, *Rosary*, 319, 365.

Jane, having now established herself in the waiting train, receives a telegram that causes her such distress that she calls for someone to fetch a coffee. The same porter dashes to get it and is again rewarded:

The train moved on, and the porter stood looking after it with tears in his eyes. Over the first half-crown he had said to himself: 'Milk and new-laid eggs'. Now, as he pocketed the second, he added the other two things mentioned by the parish doctor: 'Soup and jelly'; and his heart glowed. 'Your heavenly Father knoweth that ye have need of these things.'[73]

The central characters of Mrs Barclay's novels are untroubled by money worries and belong to the nobility, intermarried with the upper-middle and professional classes. In *The Rosary* Jane Champion is the Honourable Jane, niece and former ward of the Duchess of Meldrum, while Garth Dalmain has a castle and estate on Deeside. In *Through the Postern Gate* Guy Chelsea is the heir to a peerage, owns a great hall complete with village, and has an annual income of £50,000, while Christobel Charteris, his aunt, is the daughter of a Cambridge professor and sister of a bishop. Naturally, she is also a high achiever in the brains department, a Girton girl who won 'the highest honours in classics as yet taken by a woman'. By contrast, Guy rather misspent his time at Trinity instead of pitching to be Senior Wrangler, and he is apt to flee when Christobel, with 'full, clear, measured, melodious' voice, declaims Greek tragedy; nonetheless, he is intellectually sound enough to dine with the Master of his college.[74] Likewise, in *The Rosary* the hero and heroine have accomplishments other than that of having chosen parents of pedigree: artist Garth is a Royal Academician and passable pianist, and Jane, having 'had the immense privilege of studying with Madame Marchesi in Paris' (as Mrs Barclay herself had done[75]) is well able to warble 'The Rosary' at the Duchess's concert, as a substitute prima donna. The sundry professional classes are top-drawer too. Important support is given to Jane by Sir Deryck Brand, 'the well-known nerve specialist', in Wimpole Street, whose unfailing helpfulness is described by an 'enthusiastic lady patient... with more accuracy of definition than of grammar: "You know, he is always so very *just there*" '.[76]

Mrs Barclay's novels are overcrowded with paragons. The aristocracy is especially unreal, drawn from outside by an idealized imagination. Aristocrats in these stories are and act as the aspiring middle classes would like them to be and to behave: virtuous, courtly, handsome, kind, and loving God. Where they have eccentricities, these are of the delightful dotty sort. This was consistent with

---

[73] Ibid. 140–1.   [74] Barclay, *Postern Gate*, 66, 75, 78.   [75] Barclay, *Life*, 287.

[76] *The Rosary*, 28, 139, 142. Sir Deryck Brand was in all likelihood based on Sir Andrew Clark (1826–93), who treated Mrs Barclay when she was seriously ill in 1892. Clark was physician to the London Hospital, and had private consulting rooms at 16 Cavendish Square, where he was said to be making £12,000 per annum in the 1880s. Clark was Gladstone's doctor and 'a deeply religious man whose patients were reminded of it by the inscription on a wall of his consulting-room ... "Glory Be To God" '. On Clark, see *DNB*, and Reginald Pound, *Harley Street* (1967), 22–3. Mrs Barclay gave another puff of Sir Deryck in *The Following of the Star*, 139.

Mrs Barclay's intent not to use fiction to put people down; as Christobel says in *Through the Postern Gate*, 'non-appreciations do not appeal to me. If a person has meant to be effective and proved inadequate, or tried to do good and done harm, I would rather not know it, unless I can help to put matters right.'[77]

The actual smart set was apt to sneer at this. We do not know whether Lady Cynthia Asquith ever read *Through the Postern Gate*, in which the heroine's surname, Charteris, happened to be her own; but at Stanway in 1916 for her sister's twenty-first birthday, Lady Cynthia entertained family and guests after dinner by reading from *The Rosary*: 'Aloud it is a roaring farce. We all declared we must adopt "soft, white lace".'[78] It is true that Mrs Barclay was prone to overdo the lace at Jane's bosom for evening gown and best day wear.[79] But the hoots of the Asquith circle do not lead us nearer to answering the fundamental question: why did *The Rosary* enjoy such spectacular success? Robertson Nicoll, editor of the *British Weekly*, provided a straightforward answer: 'Duchesses and hymns! Of course the books will sell!'[80] Puzzled fellow novelists and literary critics also debated the question. Archibald Marshall consulted his friend Arthur Hutchinson, editor of the *Windsor Magazine* and *Daily Graphic*, whose own fourth novel, *If Winter Comes* (1921), sold three-quarters of a million copies in Britain and America.[81] Hutchinson

had an extraordinary knowledge of current fiction. His personal preference was for the best, but he could always tell you to what any writer who was not of the best but had a vogue owed his or her popularity . . . The usual explanation of the unrivalled success of *The Rosary* was that its sentimentality struck an answering chord in unsophisticated minds. It was generally agreed that you couldn't strike the chord unless you had an unsophisticated mind yourself, and thoroughly meant it, but that wasn't enough for Hutch. He didn't say that *The Rosary* was a good novel, but he said it contained one of the good story themes . . .[82]

V

The best-selling formula, as developed by Mrs Barclay, in fact contained three chief ingredients: a plot that gripped, romance, and religion. The first requirement, as Hutchinson recognized, was a strong storyline, with unusual incident. The genius of *The Rosary*—and it was a stratagem that Mrs Barclay repeated—was an unexpected twist to the standard tale of love conquering all. Though the hero is strikingly handsome, 'like a young sun-god'—'adored by all the girls for his good looks and delightful manners; pursued for his extreme eligibility by mothers and chaperons; famous already in the world of art; flattered, courted, sought after

[77] Barclay, *Postern Gate*, 112.   [78] Asquith, *Diaries*, 230 (24 Oct. 1916).

[79] For various descriptions of the lace, Barclay, *Rosary*, 50, 92–3, 97, 291, 350, 357.

[80] Darlow, *Nicoll*, 416.

[81] On Hutchinson (1879–1971), see Kemp *et al.* (eds.), *Edwardian Fiction*, 200; West, *Strange Necessity*, 323; Dark, *Other People*, 170, 219.   [82] Marshall, *Out and About*, 236.

in society'[83]—the heroine is no beauty. In most romantic novels the female lead is traditionally alluring of face and figure, generally also of that conventional age for courtship, the late teens or early to mid-twenties. Jane Champion is 30 and thinks, in doubting moments, 'I look thirty-five, and feel forty.' Mrs Barclay corrects this self-denigration and tells the reader,

She looked a calm, pleasant thirty; ready to go happily, year by year, towards an equally agreeable and delightful forty; and not afraid of fifty, when that time should come. Her clear eyes looked frankly out upon the world, and her sane mind formed sound opinions and pronounced fair judgements, tempered by the kindliness of an unusually large and generous heart.[84]

As an 'heiress, independent of parents and guardians, of good blood and lineage', Jane had received 'nearly a dozen proposals of marriage', having seen through a dozen seasons; but these suitors were all firmly refused, being of the predictable type—a bandy-legged and unctuous rector, with an eye to raising parochial income and his own social status; several nice young men of good families whom she helped out of scrapes and who blurted out proposals in maudlin gratitude; and a drove of 'middle-aged men—becoming bald and grey; tired of racketing about town'—who businesslike looked on Jane as a good investment, having the wherewithal to maintain a fine old country pile.[85] Not only is Jane now 30 and, we are repeatedly told, plain of face, indeed 'the plainest woman of his acquaintance' thinks Garth, and a 'real *plain* sort' according to her aunt, she is also tall for a woman (5 foot 11 inches) and solidly built. 'The almost massive proportions of her figure' weigh in at 'twelve stone odd', although as the plot develops over two years, she is scaled down to 11 stone 10 pounds while mooning for her lost love under the North African sun. She sheds more flesh (of unspecified volume) while masquerading as Nurse Rosemary Gray and tending her blinded beau. Nonetheless, she cannot do anything about her broad shoulders, or about her big hands; still, these are better to grasp burning matches as well as to drive golf and tennis balls. There are other compensating qualities, including 'a glorious voice', 'the deep, tender voice' which can sing 'The Rosary'; and, though she is occasionally addressed by young men friends as 'My dear old chap', she 'was in no sense masculine—or, to use a more appropriate word, mannish'.[86] Indeed, in the chapter that introduces Jane, Mrs Barclay emphasizes that she 'had once been described, by one who saw below the surface, as a perfectly beautiful woman in an absolutely plain shell'. It was simply that 'no man had as yet looked beneath the shell . . . and apprehended the wonder of her as a woman, experiencing the wealth of tenderness of which she was capable, the blessed comfort of the shelter of her love, the perfect comprehension of her sympathy, the marvellous joy of winning and wedding her'.[87] Garth Dalmain

---

[83] Barclay, *Rosary*, 46, 154. [84] Ibid. 114, 130. [85] Ibid. 67–8.
[86] Ibid. 17, 36, 40, 62, 100, 118, 171, 210, 297. [87] Ibid. 6–7.

emerges as this man. Significantly, he states: 'Plainness is not ugliness.'[88] He understands how the beauty of a soul can shine through and transfigure a body.

The genius of Mrs Barclay's creation of plain Jane Champion was its appeal to plain Janes everywhere. Most of her readers were not fabulously rich or nobly born pentathletes with operatic voices. They were probably not belles either; and it is manna for the unpretty people of the world to be told that what really counts is spiritual rather than physical beauty. How they could identify with the 'heavy coils of her brown hair [which] never blew about into fascinating little curls and wisps, but remained where, with a few well-directed hairpins, she each morning solidly placed them'.[89] There had, of course, been previous plain Janes in fiction, the most famous being the eponymous heroine of Charlotte Brontë's *Jane Eyre* (1847); and there are obvious echoes of that story in *The Rosary* when the hero, Garth, like Mr Rochester, is blinded. But Jane Eyre's prize, won by her intelligence, fortitude, and devotion, is a much older man. By contrast, look at Jane Champion's catch. On top of the breeding, brains, and integrity which Garth has aplenty, he is aged 27 yet looks, according to one admirer, 17 or, according to a more deliberate Jane, 19.[90] The same trick is repeated in *Through the Postern Gate*, in which Christobel is aged 36 and Guy 26, though this discrepancy was as nothing compared to that in *The Broken Halo* (1913). Recommended to Norman Douglas as 'the worst novel ever written', it concerned 'a penniless agnostic youth who marries a bewitching and pious creature on the wrong side of sixty'.[91] Mrs Barclay's lesson to her readership was clear: the race is still not lost or the shelf-life expired for all the novel-reading old maids of Britain, Europe, America, and beyond.

The love described in Mrs Barclay's novels was no ordinary thing. As the age gaps between her male and female principals might suggest, the element of mother love was pronounced. Both Jane and Garth in *The Rosary* are orphans, but it is the loss of the mother not the father that is dwelt on; indeed, fathers scarcely merit a mention. When love is awakened in Jane, she 'realised how much of the maternal flows into the love of a true woman when she understands how largely the child-nature predominates in the man in love'.[92] Garth's blindness increases his childlike dependency on Jane, who first masquerades as his nurse and afterwards, when married to him, occupies 'the Oriel chamber' at Gleneesh—once his mother's room, adjoining his, and kept locked since her death. Apart from choosing a new carpet to replace 'the rather worn Brussels, in a pattern of faded squares, [which] was certainly a century behind the times',[93] Jane vetoes the Duchess's attempts to persuade her to redecorate and refurnish the room. The novel climaxes with this exchange on their wedding night:

Garth turned the wedding ring; then spoke with his lips against it . . . 'Is it [his mother's, now Jane's room] open to-night?' he asked. Jane clasped both hands behind his

[88] Barclay, *Rosary*, 41.   [89] Ibid. 129.   [90] Ibid. 33, 114.
[91] Quoted in Stanley J. Kunitz (ed.), *Twentieth Century Authors: First Supplement* (New York, 1955), 70.
[92] Barclay, *Rosary*, 106.   [93] Ibid. 368.

head—strong, capable hands, though now they trembled a little—and pressed his face against her . . .

  'Yes, my own boy,' she said, 'it is.'[94]

Again the pattern was established from the first. In *Guy Mervyn* Lady Elaine, 27 to Guy's 19, repeatedly styles him 'my own boy-lover'.[95] Or consider *The Following of the Star*, a romance which Mrs Barclay dedicated to her own elder son. Here the lovers are, rarely for a Mrs Barclay story, much the same age; but we are told that Diana *seems* older than David.[96] Moreover, both have been alone from childhood; he the only child of a couple who married late in life, she fatherless from the age of 3 with a mother ten years older than her father.[97] Towards the end of the tale, David not having long to live,

Her arms tightened around him.

  'Good-night—good-night, my Boy, my own!'

  . . . Then he turned in her arms, moving his head restlessly to and fro against her breast, like a very tired little child seeking the softest place on its pillow; then settled down, with a sigh of complete content.[98]

The image is equally explicit in *Through the Postern Gate*, where Guy is invariably called 'Boy' or 'Little Boy Blue' by Christobel. She had cuddled him as a child when his mother died. 'Does not the love of the sort of wife a fellow really wants have a lot of the mother in it too?', asks Guy.[99] This question is answered by repeated affirmatives as the story progresses.

  These affairs between older women and younger men are no coarse toyboy sagas, because—and this was the second ingredient of Mrs Barclay's best-selling formula—their romance was chaste and ethereal. This again amused Norman Douglas. Whatever irregular thoughts might arise in the mind of the prurient reader were firmly slapped down by Mrs Barclay, who, he wrote, was ever ready to 'damp the glowing embers of the flesh with an aptly-chosen quotation from Nehemiah or Habakkuk'. There was a splendid zealotry about Mrs Barclay's use of biblical reference and metaphor in the service of romantic passion. The courtship in *The Following of the Star* is set at Christmas, and the story divided into three parts entitled Gold, Frankincense, and Myrrh. In *Through the Postern Gate* the romance takes shape over seven days: like the fall of Jericho, whose walls tumbled to the blasts of rams' horns, whereafter 'up the conquerors went, right to the heart of the citadel'. Guy plans the same strategy towards Christobel, who is not slow to get the message—'*I* being Jericho', she remarks, inviting him to 'come blow me your horn!' This excites him to kneel before her:

'I shall walk right up into the heart of the citadel', he said, 'when the gates fly open, and the walls fall down; and there I shall find you, my Queen; and together we shall "inherit

---

[94] Ibid. 392–3.   [95] [Barclay], *Guy Mervyn*, iii. 194–5, 214, 254–5, 258.
[96] Barclay, *Following of the Star*, 34, 80.   [97] Ibid. 100, 107, 112.   [98] Ibid. 418–19.
[99] Barclay, *Postern Gate*, 51.

the kingdom". O dear unconquered Citadel! O beautiful, golden kingdom! Don't you wish it was the seventh day *now*, Christobel?'

This declaration makes Christobel feel 'momentarily dizzy' but she recovers to command, albeit in a whisper, Guy to return to his seat. He obeys and 'neither spoke a word, for some minutes . . . [but] the triumphant happiness in his face was a rather breathless thing to see. It made you want to hear a great orchestra burst into the Hallelujah Chorus.'[100]

All this was a gift to the parodist. *Punch* delivered on cue with 'The Rose Garden', in which 'Jane glanced at the Boy as he lounged in the satin-covered deck chair. The harmony of his pink socks and his purple silk blazer did not blind her to the ardent glow of his eyes.' Jane is 49 and the 'little pink-faced boy' 21. Grandly, he declares: 'Jane, share my poverty with me. I have but fifty thousand a year. It may be a generation before I succeed to the peerage. I hide nothing from you.' When he falls out of his aeroplane and is picked up senseless, Jane declares, 'I too must be deaf and dumb to be *en rapport* with him,' to the relief of the butler, who, 'with the licence permitted to an old retainer', murmurs, 'It'll stop her from singing, anyhow.' Love prevails; there follows 'a simple wedding in the little village church', conducted by the Archbishop, who is almost 'overcome by the scent of the roses, in which the church was ankle-deep'. The church throngs with dukes and duchesses: 'baronets and knights . . . to prevent inconvenient crowding, had been kept in the churchyard'. Having 'chosen poverty, affliction and the pink-faced boy', a 'radiantly happy' Jane 'with calm confidence signed "I will" with her fingers'.[101]

The love interest in Mrs Barclay's stories is invariably located in an idealized home life. The *Manchester Guardian* noted of *Through the Postern Gate*: 'It is a book to turn over in a sunny garden, under shady trees, when one might look up from the clear print and see a happy prince coming in through the green gate to lead one's own self to fairyland.'[102] More than that, love is a sacrament. As Jane declares in *The Rosary*, 'It is "spirit, soul, and body" in the Word, not "body, soul and spirit", as is so often misquoted; and I believe the inspired sequence to be the right one.'[103] 'Holy' is the term regularly used by Mrs Barclay to define the love between her leading characters. When Garth drops to his knees outside Jane's window at night, his thought as well as his action is prayerful:

In moments of deep feeling, words from his mother's Bible came to his lips more readily than expressions of his own thought. Now, looking upward, he repeated softly and

[100] Barclay, *Postern Gate*, 40–1.

[101] *Punch*, 12 June 1912, 446. According to her daughter, this skit delighted Mrs Barclay, 'for she had a keen sense of humour, and appreciated genuine, good-natured fun, even at her own expense' (Barclay, *Life*, 253). She may have been less content by 'The Halo they Give Themselves', A. A. Milne's conception of a story jointly authored by Mrs Barclay and Hall Caine, in *Punch's Almanack for 1914*. The Barclay part features the Virile Benedict (Dr Dick), who specializes in marrying rich old women: 'his fifth or sixth wife had perished of old age only a few months ago', when conveniently he collides in a cycling accident with the Little Grey Woman of the Night-Light (Mrs Beauchamp), who is 82 and has £12,000 a year.

[102] Barclay, *Life*, 308.   [103] Barclay, *Rosary*, 157.

reverently: ' "Every good gift and every perfect gift is from above, and cometh down from the Father of light, with whom is no variableness, neither shadow of turning." And oh, Father,' he added, 'keep us in the light—she and I. May there be in us, as there is in Thee, no variableness, neither shadow which is cast by turning.'[104]

Religious and romantic ecstasy was, therefore, the hallmark of Mrs Barclay's fiction. As the *Sunday Times* obituary put it,

There was a purpose behind all she wrote that lifted her books above the common, and enabled her to reach readers who would turn away from the 'typical best-seller' in disgust.[105]

It is essential to emphasize this aspect of Mrs Barclay's popularity, because most of those who are now judged the significant authors of the period, and who are still read where she is forgotten, conspicuously disregarded or even decried Christian inspiration. Mrs Barclay's work can be placed in that broad class of 'healthy fiction' previously exemplified by Silas K. Hocking's *Her Benny* (1879), a simple fable-cum-sermon, which pressed a lesson about the interdependence of religious conversion, moral improvement, and self-help leading to material wealth and social elevation.[106] Mrs Barclay, though, was uninterested in these last considerations: her characters were not socially petty and they were immune from prosaic want and material ambition. Her message concerned only salvation, insisting that the love between a man and a woman came through the spirit and reflected the love of God. Her work was religious-centred in an unintellectual way. Her heroes and heroines embodied Christian goodness.

VI

Mrs Barclay hardly set out with the design of becoming a best-seller but, once she was one, how did she react? As a Queen of Romance, she behaved regally. On the publication day of her latest novel, she

visited her publisher's office (where she took a personal interest in every member of the staff), and there would be quite a little ceremony. First she would be presented with a beautiful bouquet of flowers—as a rule flowers of a kind mentioned in the new book. Then each member of the staff would come in, and she would have a friendly handshake, a few words for each, and an autographed copy of the book to give.

Then, taking the bouquet with her in the car, she would pay a round of visits to her bookseller friends, receive their smiling congratulations, and see the piles of her new book, which they would assure her were fast beginning to diminish.[107]

---

[104] Ibid. 109. The quotation is from James 1: 17.   [105] Barclay, *Life*, 310.

[106] A United Methodist Free Church Minister, born in Cornwall, who held notable pastorates in Liverpool (where *Her Benny* is set) and Southport, Hocking (1850–1935) wrote some fifty books but made no fortune from *Her Benny* since he sold the copyright for £20. He left the ministry in 1896, aspiring to a career in Liberal politics as well as in authorship. For a sympathetic study, Ian Sellers, *Nineteenth Century Liverpool and the Novelists* (Warrington, 1979), 35–8; also *Oxford DNB*; Sutherland, *Companion*, 301; and Kemp *et al.* (eds.), *Edwardian Fiction*, 188–9.   [107] Barclay, *Life*, 251–2.

An attractive-looking woman, Mrs Barclay was vain enough to enjoy having her picture on the wrappers of her books, and to welcome newspaper interviews and photographs. She also made the obligatory American tour in 1910, heralded as the author of *The Rosary*, in order to publicize her sequel, *The Mistress of Shenstone*. (Naturally Mrs Barclay put the journey to good use: 'She wrote the whole of *Through the Postern Gate* in seven days, half of it on the voyage to America, half on the voyage back.')[108] When she docked in New York, the harbour was crowded with people waving bunches of violets, and the quay was hung with purple banners: *The Rosary* had been bound in purple covers.[109] This was not Mrs Barclay's first visit; her enthusiastic descriptions of America and Americans in *The Rosary* were based on her own letters home from the United States in 1909,[110] when she had toured the country to assist her younger sister Maud (married to a son of the Salvation Army founder 'General' Booth) in preaching the gospel. The lecture agent Major Pond once nominated Maud Ballington Booth 'the ablest woman orator in America'; and he wrote of the extraordinary demand to hear her.[111] In 1909 Mrs Barclay had joined her sister in holding Bible readings and lecturing on 'Palestine and the Bible' to audiences of thousands who gathered at the Chautauqua evangelical congresses. They spoke in twelve states, covering 7,000 miles in three weeks.[112] Mrs Barclay then plugged her sister's work in *The Rosary*, where Sir Deryck instructs Jane:

Seek out Mrs Ballington Booth, the great 'Little Mother' of all American prisoners. I know her well, I am proud to say, and can give you a letter of introduction. Ask her to take you with her to Sing-Sing, or to Columbus State Prison, and to let you hear her address an audience of two thousand convicts, holding out to them the gospel of hope and love,—her own inspired and inspiring belief in fresh possibilities even for the most despairing.[113]

Mrs Barclay's religious dedication, in fact, proved far stronger than any desire to revel in her best-seller stardom. She never wrote stories or articles for ordinary commercial or literary magazines, though begged by their importunate editors, who would relay the spiritual messages and essays that she sent to the religious papers. She also refused all invitations to speak except from religious organizations and she never lectured except on a religious theme. She had been a sought-after speaker *before* she was well known as a novelist, generally to ladies' Bible

---

[108] Barclay, *Life*, 263.   [109] Ibid. 221.   [110] Ibid. 179–82.   [111] Pond, *Eccentricities*, 177.
[112] Barclay, *Life*, 179–206. The original Chautauqua congress was in New York State in 1874, devised to provide educational courses for Sunday-school teachers and adults. The summer-school model was widely imitated by religious and ethnic groups.
[113] Barclay, *Rosary*, 126. Florence Barclay's brother-in-law Ballington Booth was William Booth's second child, born in 1857. In 1885 Ballington was sent to command the Salvation Army in Australasia, with the title of Marshal, in a manner characteristic of his father's dynastic policy. He returned to London in 1886, before moving to America. Ballington bridled at William's dictatorial style—'I am *General* first and Father afterwards'—and effectively made the American branch independent. With his wife, Maud, he established the Volunteers of America, and she became noted for her prison work. Begbie, *General Booth*, ii. 158.

reading groups around Hertfordshire and Essex; also, when in the south of France in 1903, 'she delivered addresses on the Bible, in French, which she spoke like a native'.[114] This was her favourite subject, 'The Inspiration of the Bible'. Manchester's Free Trade Hall was filled with 3,500 people to hear it in 1913; she also packed Spurgeon's Tabernacle, and religious meetings in cities throughout the British Isles. Her daughter commented: 'She could easily have obtained a welcome in any of these big towns under very different circumstances, and been duly "lionized". But she preferred to come to the simple and unliterary and in the name of Christ.'[115]

This more or less described Mrs Barclay's public life. Her popularity was such that she was included in *King Albert's Book*, which Hall Caine compiled in aid of Belgian refugees early in the Great War. *In Hoc Vince: The Story of a Red Cross Flag* was her contribution, also published separately as a shilling booklet. Its handsome English hero was the sort who pre-war 'made the winning stroke, and carried his bat for top score in the match'.[116] In France, following the retreat from Mons, he saves a temporary hospital from German shelling by draping over the roof a Red Cross flag which he has improvised from a white sheet symbolically dipped in the blood of the wounded. A full-length story followed, set in the twelfth century and dedicated 'To Faithful Hearts All The World Over'. *The White Ladies of Worcester* (1917) with its sham archaic dialogue ('Thou good-for-nothing imp!') was no masterpiece; but its fervour was unmistakable, as was the mother substitute theme in this romance between a crusading knight and a prioress.[117] In 1918 Mrs Barclay accepted the presidency of the East Hertfordshire Women's Voters Association, but she refused to advance as a parliamentary candidate. At her death in 1921 she left £33,749 (£21,121 net personalty), all of which went to her husband.[118] The family had been comfortably off before her literary success; and how much of her estate was inherited or derived from literary earnings and how much she had given away is impossible to decide. Her daughter stated that she regarded her royalties as a trust to use for others. She did buy a car, and employed a chauffeur, principally to allow her to fit more religious lecture engagements and pastoral calls into her schedule. Still, it is not difficult to imagine her behaving like Diana Rivers in *The Following of the Star*. The owner of a 'noiseless Napier', Diana relishes speed and instructs her chauffeur, Knox, to cover in twenty minutes the 12 miles between her stately home, Riverscourt, and the rectory where her lover, David, resides; indeed, when bearing him off for Christmas dinner, they do it in eighteen minutes.[119] Sunday travel was frowned upon, however; if Mrs Barclay had to do it, she used a taxi and 'would always give an extra generous tip, *because it was Sunday*'.[120] She contributed to numerous charities, paid for the private

---

[114] Barclay, *Life*, 160.   [115] Ibid. 176.   [116] Florence Barclay, *In Hoc Vince* (1915), 15.
[117] See esp. ch. lix of Florence Barclay, *The White Ladies of Worcester* (1917). This rare excursion into historical romance was inspired by her sitting in the Druid Circle near Keswick, once visiting it by moonlight which 'felt deliciously creepy!'; Barclay, *Life*, 263.   [118] *The Times*, 6 June 1921.
[119] Barclay, *Following of the Star*, 53–4, 65–6, 71.   [120] Barclay, *Life*, 121.

education of sons of friends, and raised the wages of her domestic servants.[121] Of course, it may be too credulous to accept the panegyric of Mrs Barclay by a daughter who presented her like one of the heroines of her novels. Nevertheless, the best-selling status of Mrs Barclay was won by cultivating this image. 'No sadness of farewell, when I embark!', she instructed during her final illness, reciting from Tennyson's *Crossing the Bar* as she had so often. Mendelssohn's *Elijah* oratorio was also a predictable favourite, heard and sung by her many times.[122] There was no fear of the 'fiery chariot' when it came to bear her off; and for her funeral at Limpsfield, a special train was arranged for the many mourners travelling from Victoria station.[123]

[121] Barclay, *Life*, 223–5.   [122] Ibid. 305–6.   [123] *The Times*, 14 Mar. 1921.

21

The Epic Ego: Hall Caine

I

Mrs Barclay possessed an amount of self-confidence but, compared with Hall Caine and Marie Corelli, she was a shrinking violet. They took themselves seriously on a grand scale. In 1898 an envious and contemptuous Joseph Conrad bracketed Caine and Corelli together as twin best-sellers, neither of whom 'belongs to literature', being 'commonplace' in thought and 'without any distinction' of style; but he singled out Caine for special denigration as 'simply mad with vanity', 'a megalomaniac, who thinks himself the greatest man of the century' and believed that 'the lower part of his face is like Shakespeare and the upper like Jesus Christ'.[1] Shakespeare and the Saviour were the sort of company Caine liked to keep; but historians do well to remember that he had cause to think highly of himself when a chapter of *My Contemporaries in Fiction* (1897) by the novelist and critic D. Christie Murray was titled 'Living Masters: [George] Meredith and Hall Caine'.[2] Likewise Edmund Gosse had hailed *The Manxman* (1894) in the *St James's Gazette* as a genuine contribution to literature, stating that 'the most fastidious critic would give in exchange for it a wilderness of that deciduous trash which our publishers call fiction'. Rose Macaulay enjoyed quoting this review in 1923, when Caine, though not yet Gosse, had been knighted. She further amused herself by remarking how another author, 'having in an unguarded hour committed to print an appreciation of Sir Hall Caine, and then having learned his mistake, has changed his name and started life again, unable otherwise to support his disgrace'.[3]

[1] To Aniela Zagórska, Christmas 1898, in Frederick R. Karl and Laurence Davies (eds.), *The Collected Letters of Joseph Conrad, 1898–1902* (Cambridge, 1986), 137–8.

[2] See Meredith to David Christie Murray, 12 Mar. 1897, in Cline (ed.), *Meredith's Letters*, iii. 1261.

[3] Rose Macaulay, *Told by an Idiot* (1923), 115. I owe this reference to Dr A. J. Olechnowicz. Gosse was a reader for Heinemann's, which published Caine; this in some measure might explain his puffery. They lunched together occasionally at the National Liberal Club; Newsome, *Edge of Paradise*, 88. Caine's first book, *Sonnets of Three Centuries: An Anthology* (1882), included five sonnets by Gosse, whose consent was conditional on there being none of Oscar Wilde's: 'I look upon his so-called Poems as the appendage of a social reputation with which literature has nothing to do and as the illustration of vagaries that are hateful to every studious and unaffected mind.' Gosse also welcomed Caine's *Recollections of Dante Gabriel Rossetti*, published later that year, as 'notably honest and courageous'. See Allen, *Hall Caine*, 111–12, 156, for this; and p. 245 for Gosse inviting Caine to dinner at his home in 1896, at which Lord Wolseley and 'the witty old Bishop of Gloucester and Bristol', C. J. Ellicott, would be guests. Gosse was notably inconstant,

Caine could count on selling *second* serial rights; that is, newspaper or magazine serialization of a story that was already published as a book and had already been serialized. In 1925 Michael Joseph cited Caine's work as having 'such universal appeal that it can make successive appearances in different serial markets and thus reach as many different publics'.[15] Norris, indeed, stated that Caine's book royalties generated 'only the smallest part of his income. The serial publication of some of his best stories brought him many thousands of pounds, but his dramatised and film versions yielded greater profits to the author than all his book royalties combined.'[16]

Caine learned this lesson early on, to seize every opportunity of recycling one story in different packages. After unwisely selling the book of *The Deemster* (1887) outright to Chatto & Windus for £150, Caine had his eyes opened by obtaining £400 for the serial rights and £1,000 from the stage adaptation, *Ben-my-Chree* ('Girl of my Heart' in Manx), which Wilson Barrett first produced at the Princess's Theatre in May 1888.[17] According to Caine himself, Barrett pipped Henry Irving in the race to win the adaptation, Irving seeing a splendid role for himself as the Bishop. Irving was an early hero of Caine. In his autobiography Caine wrote admiringly about the obscure Cornishman John Henry Brodribb, who turned himself into the eminence known as Sir Henry Irving, that he 'created a character and assumed it for himself'.[18] Many would remark the same about Caine. Over time, there were not one but many roles: professional Manxman, Pundit and Prophet, and surrogate Shakespeare and Tolstoy.

Caine never succeeded in having a play performed by Irving although, as a friend of Irving's business manager Bram Stoker, he tried to interest Irving in variations on such themes as the Wandering Jew, the Flying Dutchman, and the Demon Lover.[19] In 1890 Caine applied himself to reworking a script sent to Irving about the life of Muhammad, thought it 'by much the best of my dramatic efforts', and was furious when it was aborted, the Lord Chamberlain having intimated that he would refuse it a licence for fear of protests by Muslims in British India and Egypt. Caine afterwards used this case to argue for the abolition of theatre censorship.[20] Notwithstanding setbacks, Caine persisted in writing dramatic versions of his novels. Beerbohm Tree rejected *The Manxman*. It was

[15] Joseph, *Commercial Side of Literature*, 206.   [16] Norris, *Two Men of Manxland*, 58.

[17] £1,000 is the sum commonly cited for Caine's profit from the dramatized version of *The Deemster*; see Sutherland, *Companion*, 98; Robert Harborough Sherard, 'Hall Caine: A Biographical Study', *Windsor Magazine* (Dec. 1895), 572; Norris, *Two Men of Manxland*, 7–8. According to Caine's own account—*My Story*, 345—his contract with Barrett was 2 guineas per performance until his royalties reached £800, when his interest was to end. Barrett's production at the Princess's ran for 100 performances; it was then taken to the provinces, where it was a great success, and to America, altogether holding the stage on and off for seven years, before being again produced in London. Caine's second collaboration with Barrett was *The Good Old Times*, which opened at the Princess on 12 February 1889.   [18] Caine, *My Story*, 350.

[19] Harry Ludlam, *A Biography of Bram Stoker, Creator of Dracula* (1977), 109–10.

[20] *Parliamentary Papers PP* (1909), vol. viii, no. 451, Qs. 5569, 5634–7; and below, Ch. 27. Also Caine, *My Story*, 351–2. Caine told Sherard in 1895 that Irving offered to compensate him for his labour. This he grandly refused, and contented himself by 'sitting on my antagonists in an angry article in *The Speaker*'; Sherard, 'Hall Caine', 572–3.

'unlikely to appeal to the sympathies of the fashionable audiences of the Haymarket Theatre'. Again, it was taken up by Wilson Barrett, who rewrote the script to change the central figure. First staged at Leeds on 20 August 1894, it 'met with a good reception everywhere, except in Manchester and New York. The critics in the latter city wrote that it was a disgrace to the book.'[21] Tree did eventually take a Caine play, the dramatization of his novel *The Eternal City* at His Majesty's Theatre in 1902; it also opened simultaneously in New York. *The Eternal City* was a work on a big scale, set in Rome and spanning seventy years, ending in the mid-twentieth-century future, when Caine envisioned a republic resting on the Lord's Prayer. One of its more damning reviewers remarked that 'to enter Mr Caine's city is rather like plunging into a vast cauldron of primitive hotch-potch'.[22] The story naturally included an imaginary Pope, styled Pius the Tenth. This was a risky move by Caine, because there had already been nine such; indeed, an actual Pius X would soon succeed, on the death of Leo XIII in 1903. It was also unprecedentedly daring to put a Pope on stage, particularly for impersonation by Brandon Thomas of *Charley's Aunt* fame; and the partnership of Tree the actor–manager and Caine the author was more like a collision. Caine attended rehearsals in order to convey his genius directly. At one point Tree as Baron Bonelli was required to fling to the floor Constance Collier as Roma Volonna:

'Stop!' called the author, raising his hand. Everything, including the music, stopped; and Hall Caine, running his hand through his hair, spoke as in a dream:

'I see in my mind an actor, seizing a woman fiercely, and with tense muscles and bated breath hurling her right over his head.'

'I remember,' interposed Tree as in a reverie, 'seeing a famous actor seize a famous actress, lift her up by her feet, and dash her head against the ground, not once, not twice, but three times.'

'In what play was that?' demanded Hall Caine.

'I understand that it was called *Punch and Judy*,' said Tree.[23]

Tree used to dine out on elaborately prepared witticisms at Caine's expense. He proposed that, as a crueller alternative than forced-feeding in gaol, suffragettes should be transported to the Isle of Man and be read to by Caine. Robert Hichens recalled a party given by Mrs Charles Hunter in Marienbad, at which Tree entertained the table by a representation of Caine as cicerone conducting the King around the Isle of Man.[24] Caine certainly enjoyed showing off his castle,

---

[21] Sherard 'Hall Caine', 574. Caine wrote another stage version of *The Manxman*, called *Pete*, which opened at the Lyceum Theatre on 29 August 1908.

[22] Sutherland, *Companion*, 98–9, 216, where it is also noted that 'C. Arthur Pearson commissioned *The Eternal City* for his *Ladies' Magazine* and later sued Caine on the grounds that the work was too immoral to publish.'

[23] Pearson, *Tree*, 140. *Punch*, 8 Oct. 1902, 236, for verses by Owen Seaman mocking Caine's publicity of the play; and 15 Oct. 1902, 258, for a review critical of Caine's script but laudatory of both the acting and production.

[24] Hichens, *Yesterday*, 71, 297–8, where the Duke of Beaufort, Sir Charles Wyndham, and Mary Moore are mentioned as other guests.

lecture agent, the play's success in America alone brought him $500 (over £100) *a day* in royalties.[34]

Caine's stage adaptations provided some employment for his family: his sister Lily, who appeared in several of them,[35] and his son Derwent, who made his acting debut in *The Bondsman*. Caine nevertheless suffered disappointments, for the theatre was a notoriously volatile business. Compton Mackenzie relished describing the preparations for his father's production of *The Bishop's Son* at the Garrick in September 1910. Caine was at his egotistical best, insisting on an inappropriate actor for the lead and altogether dismissive of advice as he interfered in rehearsals. Mackenzie himself was lined up for his debut in the part of a young priest, at £10 a week. Ten pounds was all he got, because the play and his stage career terminated after a week. Both his father and Caine suffered heavy losses.[36] Arnold Bennett was also told on good authority that Caine had been the guarantor for a season of his plays at the Adelphi in 1907, when 'the profits on "The Bondman" averaged £75 a week, and the losses on "The Prodigal Son" £75 a night'.[37] Against this must be set the takings from his new version of *The Christian*. This opened at the Lyceum on 31 August 1907, ran for 182 nights, and, according to Samuel Norris, generated £400 a week for Caine.[38] On the whole, the balance appeared comfortably in the black. There was also popular fame—but no recognition from fellow playwrights. Caine was rejected by the Dramatists' Club in 1909 when put up for membership by Bernard Shaw, who remonstrated with the club's founder, Arthur Pinero:

At the last lunch I attended I raised the question as to whether Hall Caine would be invited to be a member. There was a shriek of 'Good God! No!' which astounded the head waiter into betraying by his face that he had hitherto regarded Hall Caine as being an author so much more eminent than any of us that it would be the height of presumption on our part to hope for his presence.[39]

Shaw discovered some reasons for the members' hostility: that

Hall Caine was a self-advertiser; Conan Doyle had written a pamphlet against him fifteen years ago and would not come to lunches if he came; he was unclubbable; he would go about declaring that he belonged to the Dramatists' Club and speaking in its name &c, &c.[40]

Shaw was indignant about the pettiness of such charges and insinuations. Shaw had his defects but hypocrisy was not one. He knew that, if Caine had

---

[34] Pond, *Eccentricities*, 454.

[35] Lily had parts in *The Christian*, old and new versions, and in *The Prodigal Son*; John Parker (ed.), *Who's Who in the Theatre* (1912), 77.   [36] Mackenzie, *Life and Times*, iv. 94–101, 103, 111–12.

[37] Flower (ed.), *Bennett Journals*, i. 261 (14 Oct. 1907).

[38] Norris, *Two Men of Manxland*, 58; Parker (ed.), *Theatre*, 77.

[39] Shaw to Pinero, 29 Nov. 1909, in Laurence (ed.), *Shaw's Letters*, 884. The Dramatists' Club (est. 17 Mar. 1909) was an outgrowth of the playwrights' campaign against the censorship of plays.

[40] Shaw to Pinero, 17 Mar. 1910, in Laurence (ed.), *Shaw's Letters*, 910. For the Conan Doyle incident, his writing a letter to the *Daily Chronicle* in 1897 denouncing Caine's habit of whipping up pre-publication interest in his novels, see above, Ch. 4.

a challenger for the title of supreme self-advertiser, this challenger was Shaw himself and most judges would vote Shaw the winner. No one promoted himself quite so comprehensively as Shaw, who wrote to the press on every conceivable subject, spoke to audiences on every possible occasion, pushed his views about the theatre in correspondence with leading actresses, badgered critics and editors, occupied acres of newspaper columns, and freely made himself available to every photographer, artist, and sculptor. He reviewed reviews of his work and, when there was no interviewer to hand, he inter-viewed himself.[41] Caine was no innocent but he was not the only criminal self-publicist among authors. Shaw, therefore, accused members of setting personal feelings above the best interests of the Dramatists' Club; and he warned that the club would atrophy into 'a mere clique of cronies', from which he and Pinero 'should have to secede and form a Superdramatists' Club with strenuous rites of initiation'. Actually, Caine was in good company as a recipient of the blackball. Gilbert Murray, whose adaptations from Greek plays scored notable successes, had been rejected as not being an original dramatist; St John Hankin was shunned for what were considered ill-mannered criticisms of fellow playwrights, including Pinero; and Gilbert Cannan became a non-starter when he ran off with Barrie's wife. According to Shaw, several members of the club saw nothing wrong in discriminating against individuals on personal grounds; but Shaw countered this strongly in Caine's case:

Hall Caine takes himself and his work, and consequently takes us and our work, very seriously; but that is why I rather want to have him . . . As to his clubbability, all I can say is that years ago I wrote a shocking attack on him, beginning 'Who is Hall Caine?' which is quoted, to my great shame and grief, to this day. He wrote me a quite nice and human remonstrance; and I replied with infernal brutality. But when we met afterwards, he never betrayed the slightest feeling about it: he treated me with the frankest friendliness . . . How many of our colleagues in the Club would be so clubbable as that?[42]

Shaw certainly tilted at Caine in times past. As the *Pall Mall Gazette*'s reviewer, he upheld *A Son of Hagar* (1886) as the epitome of what was ridiculous and wrong about current fiction.[43] Now, a quarter-century later, Shaw and Caine were ranged on the same side when Shaw sprang to the defence of *The White Prophet* (1909). This story raised such questions about Britain's occupation of Egypt, and about the nationalist culture and spiritual life of the two countries, that it roused a storm of criticism from the imperial administration, orchestrated by the former Consul-General Lord Cromer (Lord Nuneham in Caine's novel), and Cromer's supporters in the press and public life. Shaw championed Caine's case through the

[41] Holroyd, *Shaw*, i. 281, 297–8. Note *Punch's Almanack for 1914*, which cartoons Shaw and Caine together: they 'execute each a modest solo on his favourite instrument', Shaw blowing a brass, and Caine banging a drum.

[42] Shaw to Pinero, 21 Mar. 1910, in Laurence (ed.), *Shaw's Letters*, 913. Shaw's 'shocking attack' on Caine was his review of Wilson Barrett's adaptation of *The Manxman*, in the *Saturday Review*, 23 Nov. 1895.

[43] Holroyd, *Shaw*, i. 209, where 'Hagar' is misspelled 'Hager'.

columns of the *Daily Telegraph*. This polemic Shaw hoped would be adopted as the preface to a second edition of the novel; but, exceptionally for a Caine epic, a second edition did not follow straight away. Indeed, *The White Prophet* was long out of print and unavailable by 1920, when Heinemann was preparing a Collected Edition of Caine's novels. Heinemann did publish Shaw's defence separately as a pamphlet in 1909;[44] yet Heinemann was otherwise aghast at criticisms of *The White Prophet* as a subversive work, and he refused to sanction a second edition. How poorly *The White Prophet* sold is difficult to divine. If Samuel Norris is believed, it fell so flat that Caine bought in copies to avoid the mortification of seeing these offered as 'remainders'.[45] Heinemann, having developed cold feet, could not have helped domestic sales. Abroad it was translated into seven languages, including Arabic, in which form it was serialized in the native Middle Eastern press. Equally in a funk like Heinemann was Beerbohm Tree, who, having been lined up to produce a play version, now dropped it from 'fear of the shadow of the Censor'.[46] Caine organized a copyright performance at the Garrick on 27 November 1909, although no public presentation was ever staged.[47] Further, he made an impressive appearance before a parliamentary Joint Select Committee which considered the question of stage censorship.[48] This testimony was such as to do credit to any member of the Dramatists' Club, whose *raison d'être*, after all, was to relax the Lord Chamberlain's bridle.

III

To resolve why it was that Caine became such a controversial figure and especially such a problem for fellow authors, the historian needs to delineate the circumstances of his career. Thomas (Tom) Henry Hall Caine was born on 14 May 1853 at Runcorn, Cheshire. His father, John Caine, was Manx by origin, the son of a crofter who worked some 60 acres at Ballaugh and who, according to Hall Caine's own account, preferred dissipation in Douglas and thereby alienated his holding. That compelled John Caine to earn his living by other means, which he did first as a blacksmith's apprentice in Ramsey, then as a shipwright on Merseyside. This was a skilled trade, well paid by working-class standards in mid-century. Caine recalled his father earning a basic 36s. a week, with extra piece-work besides, sufficient to keep a wife and family.[49] The mother, Sarah, whose maiden name was Hall, came from Whitehaven in Cumbria. Two other sons were born to the couple: John James, who died aged 21 from tuberculosis in 1877, and William Ralph, whose own path to prosperity in journalism, authorship,

---

[44] Dan H. Laurence and Daniel J. Leary (eds.), *Bernard Shaw: The Complete Prefaces*, i: *1889–1913* (1993), 312–22.   [45] Norris, *Two Men of Manxland*, 66.
[46] Caine's evidence (23 Sept. 1909) before the Joint Select Committee on the Stage Plays (Censorship), *PP* (1909), vol. viii, no. 451, Q. 5506.   [47] Allen, *Caine*, 332–41; Nicoll, *English Drama*, 542.
[48] See Ch. 27 on this.   [49] Sherard, 'Hall Caine', 562–4.

and publishing, and in the development of Isle of Man tourism, intersected with that of his more famous elder brother.[50] Caine recalled little about his early years in Liverpool, this being a less romantic location than the Isle of Man, with which his name became associated by his writing. His grandmother's Ballavolley cottage, where he stayed as a boy, was reverently described (and photographed) in Robert Sherard's profile of Caine for the *Windsor Magazine* in 1895. Seated in the inglenook, Caine would watch his aunts cook oaten cake over the peat fire, and listen to stories about Manx legend and local characters. Precociously bookish, Caine declared that the first he remembered reading was a tome on the German Reformation. This he spent weeks over; 'staggering under its weight, [he] would carry it out into the hayfield where, truant to the harvest, he would lie behind the stacks and read and read'. The book also earned him a beating, for burning candles long past bedtime. He was indignant about the injustice, 'for he felt that candles were nothing compared to knowledge'. Here was a boy who

never played games, but spent his time in reading—not boyish books, indeed, but books in which never boy before took interest—histories, theological works, and, in preference, parliamentary speeches of the great orators, which he would afterwards re-write from memory. At a very early age he showed a great passion for poetry and was a great reader of Shakespeare.[51]

This was the start of another persona which Caine cultivated—the matchless genius—and, like the Manxman image, it would bring him pain as well as profit over the years. A. G. Gardiner, editor of the *Daily News*, remarked that the Edwardian public 'delights in the man who will advertise himself in twelve-foot letters. It worships success, however it is achieved. You may be exposed as often as you like: all will be forgiven if only you will be smart.' Caine was a representative figure for this public, 'moral teacher' for the million.[52] According to his critics, Caine was 'smart' enough to perceive that the public had an unsatisfied thirst for moral certitude and direction. Too many writers were questioning and undermining traditional beliefs; they recoiled from reproducing the simple dramas of the past, about the honest and upright pitted against the legions of evil: the biblical story, in other words, uncluttered by recent criticisms relating to its historical truth, scientific basis, and complex theologies. Caine's *The Prodigal Son* being an obvious pointer to the parable, *Punch* sneered that his ambition was not only 'gradually to rewrite the whole of the Bible' but also to

---

[50] William Ralph Hall Caine (1865–1939), after working on the *Liverpool Mercury*, became editor of the *Court Circular* and *Family Churchman*; also a director of Sir Isaac Pitman & Sons, the shorthand and educational publishers, and in London he represented 'a department of the Isle of Man legislature' and consortium to promote tourism there. He edited *Humorous Poems of the Century* (1890) and *Love Poems of England* (1893), wrote history and geography school books, and contributed 'many of the leading biographies in Cassell's Dictionary'. Afterwards he wrote several books about Lancashire and the Isle of Man. *Who Was Who, 1929–1940*, 208.　　　　[51] Sherard, 'Hall Caine', 565–6.

[52] Gardiner, *Prophets, Priests, and Kings*, 96.

improve on it.[53] For Caine himself, the Bible was a good book in every sense of the term:

I think that I know my Bible as few literary men know it...The Bible has for me very much the same appeal that it had for Bunyan. There is no book in the world like it, and the finest novels ever written fall far short in interest of any one of the stories it tells.

He was unembarrassed about the use he made of it:

Whatever strong situations I have in my books are not of my creation, but are taken from the Bible. *The Deemster* is the story of the prodigal son. *The Bondman* is the story of Esau and Jacob, though in my version sympathy attaches to Esau. *The Scapegoat* is the story of Eli and his sons, but with Samuel as a little girl. *The Manxman* is the story of David and Uriah.

Caine added that *The Christian* again came from the Bible, although 'from a perfectly startling source,' and that '*The Eternal City* is the modern version of Samson and Delilah.' His principal motive in writing was not romance, or to display his dramatic vigour as a storyteller and his mastery of human passions and character-drawing—all of which he naturally had in abundance—but to reveal

the ever-present sense of the controlling power which the Greeks called Fate, but which the profoundly religious spirit of the Modern identified with the will of God. That no man is lost until his soul is lost, and that however low a man may fall, there is salvation for him so long as his soul can be kept alive.[54]

Caine was a novelist who deliberately developed a didactic mission. In his early work this was not so conspicuous. When *A Son of Hagar* (1886) was republished in the Nelson Sevenpenny Library in the Edwardian period, the publisher's advertisement, while puffing its author as having 'the largest popularity of our day', described the novel as 'an excellent example of his earlier and best stories, when he was less inclined to point a moral than to write an engrossing tale'.[55] Caine told Robert Sherard in 1895 that when he wrote his first novel, *The Shadow of a Crime* (1885), 'I only wanted to write a thrilling tale. Now what I want in my novels is a spiritual interest, a problem of life.' In these subsequent novels the central motive was the same: 'It is the idea of justice, the idea of a divine justice, the idea that righteousness always works itself out, that out of hatred and malice come love. My theory is that a novel...must end with a sense of justice, must leave the impression that justice is inevitable.'[56]

This proved an effective formula, made the more so by Caine's arrangement of his work in order to highlight the simplicity and universality of his stories.[57] The six parts of *The Manxman*, for example, were titled: 'Boys Together', 'Boy and

---

[53] *Punch*, 14 Sept. 1904, 181, and 28 Dec. 1904, 451. When Caine's prodigal returns after a scapegrace career, it is as a millionaire and following his father's death.

[54] Interviews with Caine: see Sherard, 'Hall Caine', 575, and Norris, *Two Men of Manxland*, 28–9. Similar statements can be found in Kenyon, *Caine*, 12, and Caine, *My Story*, 283.

[55] See the advertisement in the end pages of Nevill (ed.), *Reminiscences*.

[56] Sherard, 'Hall Caine', 570, 576.   [57] *The Times*, 2 Sept. 1931, for letter from Canon H. T. Knight.

Girl', 'Man and Woman', 'Man and Wife', 'Man and Man', 'Man and God'. But
how genuine was the religious spirit in Caine? His familiarity with the Bible was
obvious. He told Norris that he had read the Bible through seven times, and
Norris conceded that he could quote it in remarkable fashion. Ruskin too
reportedly acknowledged that Caine 'knows it better than any living writer of
fiction'. Yet Caine did not attend any church regularly. In later life he declared
that he belonged to none, only 'the church outside the church—the world at
large'.[58] This non-sectarianism may have derived from his Manx background.
Religion on the island was a simple Bible-based affair, and both Nonconformity
and the Anglican Church generally dispensed with ceremony and appeared
almost interchangeable.[59] In the Edwardian period Caine was drawn to the
interdenominational 'Christian Commonwealth' ideal associated with the mod-
ernist 'New Theology' of the charismatic R. J. Campbell. A Congregationalist,
and pastor of the City Temple in London, 1903–15, Campbell was one of several
high-profile clergymen who lent support to the Labour movement. He pleaded
for 'the reconstruction of society on a basis of mutual helpfulness instead of strife
and competition', and proclaimed: 'I now regard Socialism as the practical
expression of Christian ethics and the evangel of Jesus.'[60] Caine too prided himself
on his progressive politics at the time; and the central doctrine of the New
Theology, the immanence of God, especially appealed to Caine, who liked to
asseverate about the Holy Spirit in sweeping terms without troubling himself
about fine distinctions. Characteristically, in his memoirs in 1908 Caine declared
himself to have been a Christian Socialist and New Theologian before either of
these terms achieved currency.[61] Critics were scathing, however, about the
mishmash in Campbell's creed, and judged it liable to degenerate into pantheism.[62] Campbell himself would renounce the New Theology and withdraw his
works from circulation on joining the Church of England in 1916; but he would
also officiate at the memorial service for Caine in 1931.

Historians should not neglect another unorthodox side to Caine, that which
responded to his Manx grandmother's tales of fairies, the evil eye, and 'belief in
every kind of supernatural influence'. 'The earth and the air were full of spiritual
things for her,' he wrote.[63] Phantasmagorical fascination in part explains Caine's
being drawn to Coleridge and D. G. Rossetti. In 1901 Fred Kenyon's biography,
whose text Caine vetted, noted that both poets had been 'strangely and strongly
attracted towards the supernatural'; also that 'Hall Caine is a firm believer in
many of the phenomena which, by ignorant people, are placed in the category of

---

[58] Norris, *Two Men of Manxland*, 19.

[59] A. W. Moore, *A History of the Isle of Man* (1900), ii. 679. Exemplifying this, Caine's father, an Anglican,
took to attending Myrtle Street Baptist Chapel in Liverpool. See Vivien Allen's notice of Hall Caine in the
Oxford DNB, where she adds that Caine himself 'returned to the Church of England as an adult'.

[60] R. J. Campbell, *Christianity and the Social Order* (1907), pp. vii–ix. On Campbell (1867–1956), see *Who
Was Who, 1951–1960*, 178; G. I. T. Machin, *Politics and the Churches in Great Britain 1869–1921* (Oxford, 1987), 280;
and G. Stephens Spinks, *Religion in Britain since 1900* (1952), 60–1.   [61] Caine, *My Story*, 39.

[62] Robertson Nicoll was a fierce critic of the New Theology in his *British Weekly* columns; Darlow,
Nicoll, 194–5.   [63] Caine, *My Story*, 10, 25.

At Caine's instigation, Heinemann dispatched *The Bondman* to Gladstone, whose verdict ('I recognize the freshness, vigour and sustained interest no less than its integrity of aim') was given wide publicity. The same procedure was adopted for other novels. *The Christian* yielded Gladstone's plaudits for Caine's treatment of 'the things which are unseen as against those which are seen'. Trumpeting such views from a fast-fading octogenarian did not strike everyone as fair game—*Punch* decried the sight of 'an ancient statesman void of guile inveigled drawn and exploited to the full'—but Caine was rewarded by an invitation to Gladstone's funeral at Westminster Abbey in 1898. The statesman's son presented Gladstone's fob watch to Caine, who thereafter displayed it on his study mantelpiece.[74]

Caine thus ended by employing Gladstone, when at the beginning it might have been the other way round, because the stewardship of the Seaforth estate was apparently offered to him at £120 per annum. Instead, Caine became a draughtsman for the Liverpool architect Richard Owens, contributing articles to *The Builder*, the influential architectural journal. Already prone to nervous attacks, however, Caine interrupted his apprenticeship in 1870, when, for reasons of health, he spent a period on the Isle of Man assisting his uncle, the schoolmaster at Maughold, who was also a temperance advocate. Caine himself became a member of the Band of Hope. This temperance connection is a little-noticed aspect of Caine's public life as an author; but it should not be underestimated in assessing his moral appeal to a particular readership.[75] It resulted in *Drink: A Love Story on a Great Question* (1906), a short story that was reissued as a pocket-sized book in 1908, with a forty-page appendix debating questions raised by his story: whether hypnotism might cure alcoholism; whether drink addiction was a sin, a disease, or, as Caine thought, both; and whether legislation might engender improvement. Wider social problems were aired; for example, what should be done to curb London's illicit clubs and other underground haunts which put on indecent entertainments and lured intoxicated customers deeper into vice. Caine argued that, instead of mere condemnation and calls for suppression, the churches would be more effective if they provided counter-attractions and healthy amusements, especially on Sundays. There was nothing in what Caine was proposing that had not been already advanced—and implemented—by others. Still, it was clear from the reactions of church ministers and temperance worthies that they believed that a powerful voice was added to their movement, and Caine stated that he received more letters about *Drink* than about all his then ten published novels.[76]

Caine's brief schoolmaster period also saw him set in motion another important role, the political progressive. He had letters and articles published in the

---

[74] Allen, *Caine*, 81, 202, 256–7, 263. Curiously, Gladstone, who was meticulous in keeping a record of his reading, noted only one Caine novel, *The Scapegoat*, which he read on publication in 1891; Matthew (ed.), *Gladstone Diaries*, xii. 414 (22 Oct. 1891). On the exploitation of Gladstone's name, see Ch. 28.

[75] Kenyon, *Caine*, 221–2.

[76] T. H. Hall Caine, *Drink: A Love Story on a Great Question* (n.d. [1908]), 8. Allen, *Caine*, 313, notes the provenance of *Drink* in a magazine story written by Caine seventeen years earlier; also that *Drink* was refused by Caine's regular publisher, Heinemann, and instead issued by George Newnes.

Manx newspaper *Mona's Herald*, arguing the case for political independence. It is unreasonable to expect of individuals, let alone a teenager, that they devise a coherent political creed and hold to it consistently lifelong; but quite what Caine's politics were was never easy to pin down. Their chameleon quality would be epitomized in the 1924 general election, when Caine wrote the election addresses for both his sons, Ralph, the Conservative candidate in East Dorset, and Derwent, the Labour candidate in Clitheroe.[77] In 1903 it was reported that three constituencies were pressing Caine to stand as their Liberal parliamentary candidate. There was great concern at the time about the incidence of taxation, particularly rising local rates, burdening the poor and others on modest incomes; and *Punch* naturally had it that Caine's radical solution would be the supply of free gas.[78]

In 1931 the *Times* obituary remarked that at an earlier period Caine's 'social and political views, always strongly democratic, were little short of revolutionary. During a short sojourn in the Isle of Man he wrote a series of fervid articles, in defence of the Communards of Paris; and he remained ostensibly a champion of the people's rights, the people's sense, and the people's taste.'[79] The source for this was most likely Sherard's interview in 1895. Sherard actually went further, describing the Caine of the early 1870s as 'a rabid Communist . . . [who] read communistic and socialistic literature with avidity'. Yet, Sherard also stated that in *Mona's Herald* Caine 'preached the virtues of Conservatism and attracted the attention of John Ruskin by his eulogies of Ruskin's work with his recently founded Guild of St George'.[80] This, rather than the communism, was what Caine preferred to emphasize in his 1908 memoirs, where he registered the influence on him of Ruskin's monthly letters 'to the workmen and labourers of Great Britain' published as *Fors Clavigera* (1871–84).[81]

In 1908 Caine was coming to the end of his most politically active period. He had been elected as one of twenty-four members of the Manx House of Keys, representing Ramsey, by a majority of 267 over a Conservative opponent, in 1901. Here was an apparent fulfilment of a call Caine made in a lecture in Liverpool in 1880—five years *before* he published his first novel—that all writers should involve themselves in public affairs.[82] Caine now had cause to rue this. The best surviving account of Caine's part in Manx politics, that published by Samuel Norris in 1947, is not impartial: Norris was secretary of the Manx National Reform League from its formation in 1903 to its disbandment in 1919. Caine's relations with Manx people were ambivalent. The Isle was his adopted *patria*; he prided himself on mixing with ordinary Manx folk, and on having learned their language and lore. In 1901 Man contained 55,000 people; it was a closed community, in which

---

[77] Allen, *Caine*, 401.   [78] *Punch*, 4 Feb. 1903, 79, and 11 Nov. 1903, 339.
[79] *The Times*, 1 Sept. 1931.
[80] Sherard, 'Hall Caine', 568. One of the industrial ventures inspired by Ruskin was the St George's Woollen Mills at Laxey on the Isle of Man. It produced 'Ruskin Manx Homespuns', advertised as 'An honest cloth made of honest thread'; Allen, *Caine*, 26.   [81] Caine, *My Story*, 39.
[82] T. H. Hall Caine, *Politics and Art: A Lecture Delivered at the Royal Institution, Liverpool* (Liverpool, 1880).

literary friends and actors and actresses; that he gave donations to the Wesleyan minister Hugh Price Hughes, at his West London mission; and that he contributed £1,825, or £1 a day for five years, towards a rescue hostel off Piccadilly.[94] *The Christian* had set out some of these concerns. For Kenyon to write of it as if it contained some blueprint for practical social reform was an assessment that erred on the side of generosity; nonetheless, Kenyon was right in recognizing the importance of this novel. Through it Caine launched a millenarian crusade to combat the vices of Babylonian London. It contained resemblances to Mrs Humphry Ward's *Robert Elsmere* (1888)—without the difficult theology. The treatment was melodramatic, but real life does have its garish moments too. When Robert Sherard interviewed Caine for the *Windsor Magazine* in 1895, Sherard was deeply upset by Oscar Wilde's torments during his trials. He evidently related these to Caine and, Sherard afterwards surmised, Caine 'found the story so horrible that I think one finds an echo of it in his account of the martyrdom of John Storm' in *The Christian*.[95] The novel excited praise and scorn in equal measures. This was because, as Kenyon put it, Caine 'dared to criticise the hypocrisies of modern society';[96] and it achieved vast sales.

Caine also undertook public service for the Society of Authors in respect of international copyright law, though this might be construed as in part self-interested and vainglorious.[97] In 1892 he contributed the fifth in a series of articles in *The Idler*, written by now famous authors about their initial experience of publishing. He was paid £40 for it, but in it he proposed that the Society of Authors should establish a fund of £1,000 to provide advance payments on account of royalties, in order to spare novice authors from the need to sell their copyrights.[98] Nothing came of this but, according to Sherard's flattering assessment, Caine 'possesses in a marked degree that sense of solidarity amongst men of letters, in which most successful authors are so singularly lacking, and the great power with which his world-wide popularity has vested him is used by him rather in the general interest of the craft than to his own advantage'.[99]

Caine's most extraordinary public role concerned the plight of east European Jewry, vast numbers of whom were fleeing persecution in tsarist Russia and making painful migrations to Britain and America. Downcast in 1890 when his play based on Muhammad was blocked, and frustrated too by his lack of progress on a planned Life of Christ, Caine had taken himself to Morocco in spring 1891 in pursuit of a big theme, having it in mind to set the scene for a story about the conflicts of Muslims and Jews. This Moroccan sojourn turned out to be no idyll, and he returned disgusted by the country, calling it 'a disgrace to the century';[100]

---

[94] Norris, *Two Men of Manxland*, 71.   [95] Sherard, *Wilde*, 153.
[96] Kenyon, *Caine*, ch. x, esp. 188; also Sutherland, *Companion*, 125, for a summary.
[97] Kenyon, *Caine*, 181–2; Caine, *My Story*, 369–70; see also above, Ch. 17.
[98] Hall Caine, 'My First Book: *The Shadow of a Crime*', *The Idler* (Oct. 1892), *Review of Reviews* (Oct. 1892), 377. The article is also quoted in Kenyon, *Caine*, ch. iv. Allen, *Caine*, 219, for the fee.
[99] Sherard, 'Hall Caine', 574.
[100] Quoted in Sutherland, *Companion*, 556, which also summarizes the plot of *The Scapegoat*.

but it resulted in *The Scapegoat*, which was first serialized in the *Illustrated London News*, then published in two-volume format by Heinemann in 1891. (In 1947 Norris noted grudgingly that most critics had judged it Caine's best work as a storyteller.[101]) The melodramatic plot now matters little; the significance lay in the book's title, symbolic of anti-Semitism everywhere. It was this that arrested Hermann Adler, the Chief Rabbi of the British Empire. He apparently exhorted Caine to visit Russia, to report on conditions there and, perhaps, to gather material for a book about the pogroms. Caine did set out for Russia in June 1892, 'entirely at his own expense, declining all the offers of subsidies made to him by the Jewish Committee'.[102] This was what Caine told Sherard in his usual grand manner and, just as usual, it concealed much. The Russo-Jewish Committee, chaired by Dr Adler, had not wanted publicity given to the mission, still less to suggest that it was sponsoring Caine's fiction; and it is likely that Caine leaked the purpose to the press with a view not only to working up interest in his imagined masterpiece (his normal practice) but also to arranging deals with newspapers, for whom he would send 'Letters from Russia'. The direction of Caine's thinking, and fledgling megalomania, were captured in an allusion in the *Illustrated London News* to *Uncle Tom's Cabin*: Caine could foresee himself rousing the world by bringing succour for the Russian Jews as Mrs Beecher Stowe had done for the American negroes. A livid Dr Adler told Caine that the Committee would repudiate him if such reports continued.[103] All this, plus the birth of his second son and another 'nervous collapse', delayed Caine's departure; but eventually he acquired the necessary accreditation. As protection against the tsarist authorities, he carried a warrant from the Prime Minister and Foreign Secretary, Lord Salisbury, to HM Ambassador at St Petersburg; and, to deflect the suspicion of the Jewish communities, a letter in Hebrew for presentation to their rabbis. Travelling overland, he spent time in Germany discussing problems with the Jews there, before making for the Russian border. The sequel was described by Caine to Sherard:

I went through the pale of settlement, and saw as much of frontier-life amongst the Jews as possible, and found them like hunted dogs. I, however, got no farther than the frontier towns, for cholera had broken out, numerous deaths took place every day, my own health was getting queer, and, to speak plainly, I was frightened. So we turned our faces back and returned home. On my return to London I delivered a lecture before the Jewish Workmen's Club in the East End, in a hall crammed to suffocation. I shall never forget the enthusiasm of the audience, the tears, the laughter, the applause, the wild embraces to which I was subjected.[104]

Caine also contributed articles to *The Times* on the subject, but his projected novel *The Jew* never resulted. As with *The Life of Christ*, Caine had overreached himself. He told the loyal Kenyon in 1901 that he realized that such a subject was

---

[101] Norris, *Two Men of Manxland*, 7.   [102] Sherard, 'Hall Caine', 573.
[103] Allen, *Caine*, 214–15.   [104] Sherard, 'Hall Caine', 573–4.

'altogether too vast for his experience: it would require years of study which he could not give'.[105] Sherard was treated to a little more candour: 'I worked very hard at it, I turned it over in every direction in my mind, but I felt I could not do it. I wanted the experience of a life; I could not enter into competition in their own field with the great Russian novelists.' He showed Sherard a pocket diary for 1893: the whole of January and part of February had '*The Jew*' entered in, evidence of his struggle with the conception. He snapped out of his paralysis in dramatic fashion, taking off to the Isle of Man to write *The Manxman* (1894):

I turned my Jewish story into a Manx story, and *The Jew* became *The Manxman*. In my original scheme, Philip was to be a Christian, Governor of his province in Russia, Pete, Cregeen and Kate were to be Jews. I thought that the racial difference between the two rivals would afford greater dramatic contrast than the class difference, and it was only reluctantly that I altered the scheme of my story.[106]

The Jewish question was dropped, therefore.

This was not the end of Caine's involvement in the cause of the oppressed. Early in the Great War he edited *King Albert's Book* (1914), price 3s., for relief of Belgian refugees: it was an anthology of prose and poetry and messages of goodwill, with facsimile signatures, written by famous authors and public figures. He had done something of the same before, in 1905 and 1908 putting together 'gift books' in aid of Queen Alexandra's charities.[107] Having by 1914 mocked Caine's self-promotion for the best part of two decades, *Punch* now lauded his *King Albert's Book* as this 'Golden Book'[108]—doubtless because *Punch's* editor, Sir Owen Seaman, was a contributor—and a grateful King dubbed Caine with the Order of Leopold, to which the Belgian parliament after the war added a commissioned portrait by Alfred Jonniaux. Caine's service was not unequivocally appreciated at home. The business of producing such an expensive volume, in cooperation with the *Daily Telegraph* and Hodder & Stoughton, meant that Caine upset other publishers at a time of paper-rationing, especially as the source of his paper was his son Ralph, who was a director of paper firms in Canada and South Africa before joining the Ministry of Munitions and avoiding active service. Moreover, having solicited a contribution from Bernard Shaw, Caine met a boycott from printers at the *Telegraph* who refused to set up anything by a writer whom they judged traitorously pacifist and anti-war; and the book could go ahead only with Shaw omitted.[109] Others excluded themselves, Professor Sir Walter Raleigh in no uncertain terms. 'Can't someone bottle the authors?' he asked:

I have just had a loathsome letter from Hall Caine, about a literary album, all gush and rant, to be given to the King of the Belgians. So I said—'Dear Sir, the best present to give to the King of the Belgians is Belgium. Two of the men of this household are at the front

---

[105] Kenyon, *Caine*, 168.   [106] Sherard, 'Hall Caine', 574.
[107] Vivien Allen's notice of Caine in *Oxford DNB*, which adds that he 'did not allow his name to appear other than as a contributor'.   [108] *Punch*, 23 Dec. 1914, 527.
[109] Allen, *Caine*, 356–8, where the Jonniaux portrait of Caine is reproduced.

and a third is drilling, Yours truly.' But nothing will prevent authors and fussers butting in. They feel they don't matter, and they can't bear it. They're like the men of the Basque nation, who take to their beds and receive congratulations when their wives have a child.[110]

Unperturbed, Caine went on to extol the women too, in a commissioned book for the Ministry of Munitions: *Our Girls: Their Work for the War Effort* (1916). This contained the priceless declaration 'Constant intercourse at work has given the men a high opinion of women',[111] a sentiment with which it is impossible to argue. A lecture series in America, designed to draw that country into the war, in 1915 was not well received, either by American opinion or by HM Ambassador in Washington, and was broken off prematurely;[112] but Caine was held in regard by the rising man in politics Lloyd George, who looked to individuals possessing 'push and go'. Caine became involved in propaganda film-making.[113] More significant still was Caine's part in devising what became the Covenant of the League of Nations:

the first document in the earliest development of the League of Nations sent out by the British Foreign Office to the heads of governments of foreign countries was drawn up by me, and a large part of the first document issued by the League of Nations after its establishment was the joint work of Lord [Robert] Cecil and myself.[114]

Besides all this, Caine contributed propaganda articles to British, American, and Italian newspapers. Like many an author who put his pen to patriotic use, he convinced himself that he personally had brought Italy and America into the war on the Allies' side; he also let it be known that he had sacrificed literary contracts in the United States worth $150,000 (over £31,000) in order to write for his country.[115] Caine accepted a knighthood in 1918; and he continued to boast about his influence in high places thereafter. In 1921 a dinner was given by the publisher Heinemann's to introduce their new American partners. This was the firm of Frank N. Doubleday, who had taken a controlling interest when the founder, William Heinemann, died in 1920. Doubleday's were represented by a son of the late American Ambassador Walter Hines Page, at which Arnold Bennett noted: 'Hall Caine made a prodigiously idiotic speech, in which incidentally he proved that he was responsible for the choice of Page's father as U.S. Ambassador'.[116]

V

The summary question remains: why had Caine become an author? 'Money has never at any time been an aim in my life,' Caine wrote in his autobiography in

---

[110] Raleigh to Mrs Walter Crum, 23 Oct. 1914, in Raleigh (ed.), *Raleigh Letters*, ii. 406–7.
[111] Allen, *Caine*, 365.   [112] On this, see below, Ch. 26.   [113] On this, see above, Ch. 1.
[114] Caine to the American Judge Buffington (n.d.), quoted in Allen, *Caine*, 363.
[115] Norris, *Two Men of Manxland*, 62.   [116] Flower (ed.), *Bennett Journal*, ii. 286 (8 Mar. 1921).

1908; 'I have never allowed myself to think of it first in regard to any single thing I have ever done.' He recounted his early struggles, how 'I had been writing for ten years, and had published at least five novels, every one of them considered a success, before I had made a penny beyond what was necessary to meet the most modest of daily needs.'[117] Given this doggedness and what he saw as Caine's entrepreneurial flair, Norris concluded that if Caine had not become a novelist, he would have made an effective businessman. In fact, Caine the novelist did practise business, promoting Isle of Man tourism, marketing his own brand of cigarettes, and appearing in advertisements for Beecham's Pills.[118] Still, Caine knew that, in conventional humane evaluation, the most successful businessman counted for less than the most successful author. Not just the prospect of fame and riches but the possibility of immortality was what drew Caine to authorship: 'of all professions the profession of letters has the largest and most lasting influence'.[119] And, Caine reckoned, such influence was expanding: once discrete national literatures were merging to create a single world constituency, and authors were being hallowed as spiritual guides and forces for international understanding. As an instance, he cited the impact of Tolstoy's writing; he also contrasted the quiet burial of Wordsworth at Grasmere in 1850 with the rapt attention given to Tennyson's passing in 1892, as proof of the growing public respect for authors:

For ten days before Tennyson died the newspapers were filled with the name of the poet, and the eye of England was on him alone. While he still lived we watched by his bed, marking every change in his condition; and when he died we stood in his death-chamber, seeing the moonlight resting on his grand old head and on the hand that held open the page of *Cymbeline*. When his body was put into the coffin we were told of it; and we were told, too, when it was brought on its last night ride from his home in the country to Westminster Abbey. We were told who made his pall, and the nature and design of it; and, when the final page of his history had to be filled up, we read the names of some two hundred out of more than twice two thousand who followed him to the grave.[120]

Needless to say, Caine had been present among this company of mourners.

How, then, did Caine himself rise from obscurity to a commanding position in the league table of best-sellers? Three factors stood out, over and above his intrinsic talent: his cultivation of influential people, choice of material, and manipulation of the media. The first of these meant that his name very early in his writing career gained from notable associations. This involved a series of contrivances and coincidences; it is also some index of the social mobility possible in the nineteenth-century world of letters. When we last retraced Caine's biography, we left him on the Isle of Man in the early 1870s as a £40 per year temporary schoolteacher who had had articles on architecture published in *The Builder*. These attracted the notice of Ruskin, Caine having subscribed to the

---

[117] Caine, *My Story*, 374, 377–8.   [118] Norris, *Two Men of Manxland*, 19, 22; and above, Ch. 8.
[119] Caine, *My Story*, 386.   [120] Ibid. 395–6.

Ruskinian indictment of the vandalism (known as restoration) of ancient buildings.[121] He returned to Liverpool to work as a draughtsman but determined also to pursue his writing. His first efforts were directed towards the stage—he attempted an adaptation of Charles Kingsley's Chartist novel *Alton Locke* (1850)—and into poetry. A long poem of his was published in Liverpool in 1874, anonymously but, as was the fashion, Caine liberally distributed complimentary copies, one of which, sent to D. G. Rossetti, elicited generous praise about it containing 'passages of genius'. While still working in an architect's office, Caine set about multiplying his contacts in the outside world: by co-founding a Liverpool branch of the 'Notes and Queries' Society, by becoming secretary to a Liverpool branch of the Society for the Protection of Ancient Buildings (newly founded by William Morris in 1877), and by embarking on a career as lecturer. That this last action, addressing parochial audiences, should have led Caine anywhere might now amaze us; but in the nineteenth century the press gave wide coverage to such lectures and local publishers readily printed them, the equivalent of an informative general arts programme on Radio 4. It was a series of lectures on Shakespeare—Caine having founded a Liverpool Shakespeare Society and made himself president—that brought him an introduction to Lord Houghton, the former Richard Monckton Milnes who was Keats's biographer and Swinburne's patron. 'You have the head of Keats,' he supposedly exclaimed on seeing Caine.[122] Another lecture series, 'The Supernatural in Poetry', brought a commendation from Matthew Arnold; one in particular, on Rossetti, led to a correspondence with the subject in 1879 and an invitation to London. In his lecture Caine had taken Rossetti's part against Robert Buchanan, whose onslaught against Rossetti in 1871 and libel action against Swinburne in 1875 still reverberated. Rossetti, now aged 50, was living a reclusive existence; Caine, half his age, was treated to a reading of 'The King's Tragedy', which Rossetti would include in *Ballads and Sonnets* (1881). This encounter engendered two further developments; one, Caine's editing of an anthology of English sonnets; the other, quite extraordinary, his being invited to move into Rossetti's house in Cheyne Walk. The anthology was completed as *Sonnets of Three Centuries* (1882). It is now chiefly remembered for Caine's rejection, under Rossetti's advice, of five sonnets sent for inclusion by Gerard Manley Hopkins.[123]

When Caine moved in with Rossetti in 1881, his annual income (he later told Sherard) was '£260, and of this £200 was earned as a draughtsman'. From this he had saved about £50, to which Rossetti in the autumn added £100 commission for Caine's assistance in the sale to Liverpool Corporation of Rossetti's painting *Dante's Dream on the Anniversary of the Death of Beatrice*.[124] Otherwise, Caine ever insisted, he received no money from Rossetti, and their mode of living was monastic. The regime was also a demanding one. On learning that Caine was to

---

[121] Ibid. 262–70.   [122] Sherard, 'Hall Caine', 568–9; Allen, *Caine*, 58.
[123] Marsh, *Christina Rossetti*, 485, reckons that if Christina rather than Gabriel had been advising Caine, a different verdict would have been given.   [124] John Willett, *Art in a City* (1967), 43.

present twenty-four lectures in Liverpool on 'Prose Fiction', for which he would need to survey the line of English novelists, Rossetti insisted that he read the works aloud to him; hence 'I read Fielding and Smollett, Richardson, Radcliffe, "Monk" Lewis, Thackeray and Dickens, under a running fire of comment and criticism from Rossetti. It was terrible labour this reading for hours night after night, till dawn came and I could drag myself wearily upstairs to bed.'[125] It was nonetheless a useful education, though not so useful as Rossetti's death on Easter Day 1882, with Caine in attendance. No doubt, he was the source of the widely reported description that Rossetti died 'in Hall Caine's arms'. To the dismay of Rossetti's brother William, who thought it tastelessly sensational, Caine rushed into print with *Recollections of Dante Gabriel Rossetti*, published in the autumn.[126] It was a necessary move, to deflect insinuations that he had been no more than Rossetti's valet; instead Caine was able to advance, if not as Rossetti's spiritual heir to the world, then at least as his interpreter to the provinces. Later he would exploit the connection again in an episode in *The Prodigal Son* (1904), when the protagonist, Oscar Magnussen, is depicted as raising money to feed his gambling by exhuming musical scores which had been buried with his wife Thora's corpse. George Meredith wrote to Theodore Watts-Dunton in a state of shock:

The Reviews of Hall Caine's latest—I cannot read the book—tell of a part of it concerning all who loved Rossetti and held the incident too sacred for allusion. The man has posed as Rossetti's friend. You will be feeling the same disgust as I . . . on this base and cowardly trick to conceal an incapacity to invent.[127]

Meredith was not mollified by Caine's defence of himself in the press—'the miserable attempt at an exculpation. The fact is that it is the friend who has offered up his dead friend on the pyre for his own purposes is eluded. Certainly he is a master puffer.'[128] But Watts-Dunton may well have blushed at all this: he had stayed with Caine while he was writing *The Prodigal Son*, had talked to him about it, and received an advance copy.[129]

---

[125] Sherard, 'Hall Caine', 570.

[126] About half of Caine's memoirs, *My Story* (1908), were taken up by an account of his relations with Rossetti, being largely recycled from the *Recollections*. Caine revised and reissued *Recollections* in 1928, to catch the market on the centenary of Rossetti's birth. It was appreciatively assessed by Desmond Mac-Carthy, who judged that it 'contains two chapters no literary man, however fastidious, could fail to respect'; that is, Caine's account of his first night and morning spent in Rossetti's house. But, MacCarthy added knowingly: 'Sir Hall Caine has never shown dislike of publicity' (MacCarthy, *Portraits*, i. 226–33).

[127] Meredith to Watts-Dunton, 6 Nov. 1904, in Cline (ed.), *Meredith's Letters*, iii. 1508.

[128] Meredith to Watts-Dunton, 17 Nov. 1904, ibid. 1509. Meredith nonetheless in December 1905 contributed a foreword to *The Queen's Christmas Carol*, an anthology of work freely given by various well-known authors, artists, and musicians, in aid of the Queen's Fund for the Unemployed. It was sponsored by the *Daily Mail* and compiled by Caine, whose name, however, appeared only as a contributor and not as editor, which perhaps accounts for Meredith's action. In the late 1880s and early 1890s Caine and Meredith had been closer, Meredith lending Caine books (which he was remiss about returning); they also attended Browning's funeral together in 1890, and Meredith even appeared to consider accompanying Caine to Tunisia in 1891.

[129] Allen, *Caine*, 300. Caine and Watts-Dunton had what Caine's biographer calls 'a firm friendship which lasted until Theo Watts's death in 1914'. They saw much of each other in the 1880s, were both

Caine's *Rossetti* had brought him little money, earning only £40, but given him openings into journalism. An article on Rossetti's friend the mystical poet–painter William Bell Scott, sent to the *Liverpool Mercury*, led to an offer by the editor, John Lovell, to retain Caine as a regular contributor at £100 per annum. After six months this was raised to £150, enabling Caine to remain in London. A base in the capital was sensible for career purposes, but the move was prudent also because Caine's private life was in a mess. He had started an affair with a girl who worked at a café, Mary Chandler, daughter of a Walthamstow poulterer. She was young—how young, 13, he may not have known until her stepfather pressured him to take responsibility. Technically Caine was not in breach of the law, but this was a time when purity campaigners (who included Christina Rossetti) were petitioning Parliament to raise the age of consent and to protect girls from sexual predators. As the relationship with Mary persisted, Caine needed to deploy concealment and deceit. When a son, Ralph, was born in 1884, the mother was barely 15 and assumed to be Caine's wife. Caine committed perjury by so defining Mary on registering the birth; in fact, they did not marry until 3 September 1886, in a civil ceremony at Edinburgh. He compounded the falsification by then giving her age as 23, not 17; and in *Who's Who* dated their marriage as 1882. The cycle was repeated in the next generation, when Caine's second son, Derwent, fathered an illegitimate daughter, Elin, in 1912. Caine demanded that his wife, then aged 43, pretend that Elin was her own, a lie that racked her health and ruined their marriage. Caine's agonizing about accepting a baronetcy—a hereditary title— from Lloyd George in 1918 is thus explicable from fear of exposing his own elder son's illegitimacy. The recurrence of themes of bastardy and the marriage laws in Caine's stories is also understandable. Dark family secrets obtain in real life as well as in melodramatic fiction.[130]

While sending copy to the *Liverpool Mercury*—book and play reviews, police court and low life reports, and obituaries—Caine produced another book, *Cobwebs of Criticism* (1883), based on lectures given in Liverpool about critical misjudgements of the Romantic poets by their contemporaries.[131] Caine was not yet done with potboiler literary work and, in 1887, he turned out a *Life of Samuel Taylor Coleridge*. Inside his own copy Caine showed Sherard in 1895 that he had inscribed: 'This book was begun Oct. 8th, 1886. It was not touched after that date until Oct. 15th or 16th, and was finished down to the last two chaps. by Nov. 1st. Completed Dec. 4th to 8th—about 3 weeks in all.' In response to Sherard's unctuous verdict that this was 'an excellent piece of work', Caine

present at Rossetti's deathbed, and Caine confided in Watts-Dunton his irregular relationship with his eventual wife, Mary. Watts-Dunton also reviewed Caine's first novel, *The Shadow of a Crime* (1885), enthusiastically. There were, however, testy moments in the friendship, such as when Watts-Dunton refused Caine's request to dedicate his *Coleridge* to him in 1886. Caine's view of Watts-Dunton, expressed in 1890, was: 'what a poseur he is! . . . However, it doesn't matter. He is a good fellow below it all' (ibid., 116, 159, 162, 175, 185–6, 310).

[130] Allen, *Caine*, chs. 11–12 ff., is the best-documented account of Caine's personal life and its impact on his work.　　　　　　　　　　　　　　[131] On this, see above, Ch. 4.

masterfully contradicted him: 'I could have written *the* life of Coleridge.'[132] It earned him £30.[133]

Caine's ambition to become a novelist was already accomplished before *Coleridge* was issued. *The Shadow of a Crime* (1885) was serialized in the *Liverpool Mercury* and published by Chatto & Windus: he received £100 from the former, £75 for the rights from the latter, and 'a burst of eulogy from the Press, but at the time it produced no popular success, and made no difference in my market value'.[134] By his *Liverpool Mercury* work and from freelancing contributions to the *Athenaeum* and *The Academy*, Caine was making about £300 per annum; he was also given the occasional manuscript to vet as a publisher's reader. One was *The Romance of Two Worlds* (1886), the first novel that Marie Corelli sent to George Bentley. Caine advised Bentley against it; though when he afterwards met the author, in 1889, he congratulated her on its success and left her with the impression that it was his recommendation that had swayed the publisher. Bentley, when told about it, tore a strip off Caine.[135] This discomfort, on top of the distress caused by his private life, probably caused him to invent another legend for Robert Sherard in 1895, who reported that 1885–6 was 'a time of need . . . during which Hall Caine beat the streets of London in search of work. He offered himself as a publisher's reader in various houses and was roughly turned away. He suffered slights and humiliations, but these only strengthened his resolve.'[136] Later Joseph Conrad would consider Caine 'a kind of male Marie Corelli. He is a great master of the art of self-advertising'[137]—but the Bentley episode is some indication of the desperate networking that Caine pursued at this time, spanielling towards novice authors as well as towards the established. Regarding the latter category, Caine added to his list of acquaintances Swinburne and Watts-Dunton, Matthew Arnold, and Robert Browning; he even struck up a friendship with Robert Buchanan, who, having recanted his attack on Rossetti, was also now scratching out an existence from novel-writing and melodrama. A second novel followed from Caine's pen in 1886, *A Son of Hagar*. Like his first, this had a Cumberland setting, Caine drawing on his mother's family background. It brought him £300 and, more importantly, into contact with R. D. Blackmore.[138] It was with the intention of imitating Blackmore's success with the regional novel that Caine now decided to represent himself as the storyteller of Manxland; as *Punch* proposed for his motto, 'The proper study of mankind is (the Isle of)

---

[132] Sherard, 'Hall Caine', 571.
[133] Kenyon, *Caine*, 92. Caine's *Coleridge* was published by Walter Scott as no. 2 in its Great Writers series.
[134] Sherard, 'Hall Caine', 570. The later reissue of the novel enabled Caine to dedicate it: 'To my able fellow-journalist JOHN LOVELL, who in a darker hour of labour and misgiving cheered me with an estimate of this novel that the public has since ratified.' It was Lovell who had suggested the title: Caine intended calling it *The City of Wythburn*. On Lovell (1835–90), see Waller, *Democracy and Sectarianism*, 499.
[135] Masters, *Corelli*, 85.   [136] Sherard, 'Hall Caine', 571.
[137] Karl and Davies (eds.), *Conrad Letters*, ii. 137–8.
[138] Kenyon, *Caine*, 90–7, 118–19; Caine, *My Story*, 294–307.

Man!'[139] Caine afterwards liked to attribute this to Rossetti's urging—' "There is a career there", he used to say, "for nothing is known about the island".'[140] He was also aided by T. E. Brown, the Anglo-Manx poet who placed his command of Manx dialect, history, and folklore at Caine's disposal: 'I did nothing without consulting him, and took no serious step without his sanction.' When Brown died in 1897, 'something of myself died too, the better part of myself', Caine wrote movingly.[141] Norris, however, regarded these as so many crocodile tears shed over one who had served his purpose. When there was a move to build some memorial to Brown on the Isle of Man, Caine was a nominal leader but inactive in practice.[142]

Caine continued to acquire contacts with famous writers, of his connection with whom (when they were safely dead) he would freely boast. *The Deemster* yielded a laudatory letter and advice from Wilkie Collins, which Caine made available to Fred Kenyon in 1901 and reproduced in his memoirs in 1908.[143] He did not disclose—possibly did not know—that Collins, when dying in 1889, contemplated inviting Caine to complete *Blind Love* (1890), which he had begun to serialize and for which he had outlined the remainder. But, in Collins's final judgement, Caine was insufficiently qualified and, through his agent A. P. Watt, Collins asked Walter Besant to do it instead.[144] By equipping himself with a new regional base in Manxland, Caine had nonetheless broken through into widespread recognition. Even George Gissing, never easily pleased, thought *The Deemster* contained 'some really strong romantic writing', although 'the characterization is feeble, when one thinks of Scott'.[145] Caine, however, was canny: he did not forget Blackmore's lament that the huge success of *Lorna Doone* caused the public subsequently to treat him as a one-book man. To avoid being typecast, Caine diversified the settings for his stories: he introduced Iceland as a backcloth to *The Bondman* and returned to it for *The Prodigal Son*; he used Morocco for *The Scapegoat* and intended to use Russian Poland for the aborted novel *The Jew* in 1893; for *The Christian*, he exploited his reporter's knowledge of London; and *The Eternal City* he set in Rome. Scenic mobility gave his stories the appearance of freshness, albeit ultimately only so much colouring to themes that were invariably drawn from a common source, the Bible.

Atonement and redemption was the message he iterated; but it was not only in this way that Caine was a formulaic writer. George Saintsbury noted in the *Fortnightly Review* in January 1895 that Caine also recycled storylines: five out of the six novels he had then published involved the same plot, two brothers (or half-brothers or cousins) in love with one girl. Illicit passion was a recurrent feature, and most of Caine's characters were conventional types: unsophisticated country girls who are seduced and betrayed and who come to repent their sins,

[139] *Punch*, 8 Sept. 1894, 120. [140] Sherard, 'Hall Caine', 570.
[141] Kenyon, *Caine*, 111–18. Caine, *My Story*, 325. [142] Norris, *Two Men of Manxland*, 74–6, 307–24.
[143] Kenyon, *Caine*, 108–10; Caine, *My Story*, 327–43. [144] Peters, *Collins*, 429–30.
[145] Coustillas (ed.), *Gissing's Diary*, 22 (29 Feb. 1888).

heroes who are steadfast and spotless, villains who get their come-uppance. It was
all rather childish sentiment, thought Saintsbury, who in addition had a poor view
of Caine as a stylist.[146]

Saintsbury was not the first to get at Caine. Ahead in the queue was R. C.
Lehmann, whose parody of *The Bondman* enlivened Mr Punch's Prize Novels series
in 1891. Retitled 'The Fondman' by 'Called Able, Author of "The Teamster" ', it was
introduced by a note from 'the eminent Author' to the editor, which instructed:
'don't call this a novel. It's a right-down regular Saga'. He then mused:

Do you know what a Saga is? Nor do I, but this is one in spite of what anybody may say.
History be blowed! Who cares about history? Mix up your dates and your incidents ... put in some Northern legends, and a tale about MAHOMET (by the way, I've
written a play about him) ... [and] thunder-storms, and passions, and powers and
emotions, and sulphur-mines, and heartless Governors, and wicked brothers ... [147]

The story, switching erratically between Iceland and the Isle of Man ('And thus
are Sagas constructed') contained many incidental delights: the Governor of
Iceland is called Gorgon Gorgonsen, and the six brothers of Greeba, whose names
are Asher, Jacob, John, Thurstan, Stean, and Ross, 'preferred addressing one
another as Jobbernowl, Wastrel, Gomerstang, Blubberhead, Numskull, and
Blatherskite. It saved time, and made things pleasant all round.'

Still, Mr Punch sticking out his tongue ranked almost as a compliment: the
standard tribute paid to fame. It is probably right, therefore, to pinpoint Saintsbury's
article as registering the official end of Caine's honeymoon with the press and the
reviewing fraternity. Until then his prestige stood high. In November he gave the
opening lecture ('Moral Aim in the Novel and the Drama') of the winter session of
the Edinburgh Literary and Philosophical Institution, an honour measured by
reckoning that his predecessors were the distinguished man-of-letters, now Cabinet
Minister, John Morley and the former Chancellor of the Exchequer G. J. Goschen.[148]
Caine also cut a figure at Society functions such as Lord Edward Cecil's marriage to
Violet Maxse, which the *Illustrated London News* recorded in 1894:

The signatories to the register included Lord Salisbury, Mr Chamberlain, Mr Balfour,
Mr John Morley, and Mr Asquith ... Mr George Meredith, who is seldom present at such
society functions, came with his daughter, and had as neighbours in the church other
representatives of literature, including Mrs Humphry Ward, Mr Oscar Wilde, and
Mr Hall Caine.[149]

Following Saintsbury's onslaught, though, it became de rigueur for reviewers
with some intellectual credibility to despise Caine's pretentious melodramas.
Iconoclasts such as H. G. Wells positively relished the task. In March 1895, just

---

[146] Norris, *Two Men of Manxland*, 23–4. Saintsbury had previously lauded Caine's anthology *Sonnets of
Three Centuries* (1882); see Allen, *Caine*, 138.   [147] *Punch*, 10 Jan. 1891, 13.
   [148] Sherard, 'Hall Caine', 574; Allen, *Caine*, 237.
   [149] Sassoon, *Meredith*, 225. Meredith's presence was explained by his being an old friend of the Maxse
family.

before his own first novel, *The Time Machine*, was published, Wells set about Caine in the *Saturday Review*; thereafter he regarded him as the reference point for all that was contemptible in best-selling literature. On 22 January 1898 Wells sent Gissing a letter with cartoon drawings: 'have you seen something like this about[?]. If so—shoot it! It's not human. It's Hall Caine . . . His damned infernal . . . book [*The Christian*] has sold 100,000 (one hundred thousand) copies.'[150] The same curiosity about Caine's sales in defiance of blighting reviews was shown by George Moore, who wrote to the publisher T. Fisher Unwin in 1901: 'The notices of Hall Ca[i]ne[']s book [*The Eternal City*] have been very bad. The book seemed even more absurd than usual. Is it a great commercial success[?]'[151]

Max Beerbohm also exercised his cleverness at Caine's expense. In 1897, on the publication of *The Christian*, he boasted of a 'great "succès"', this being his demolition of Caine in the *Daily Mail*.[152] Andrew Lang too published an 'infinitely droll parody of Hall Caine' in *Punch*. So thought Canon Ainger, who recommended it to Edmund Gosse, in all probability knowing that Gosse had rapturously reviewed *The Manxman* three years previously: 'We do indeed need a few teachers abroad to remind us of the difference between good literature and what is bad and foolish,' the Canon remarked sweetly.[153] The actual review of *The Christian* in *Punch*, a month before Lang's parody, was unremittingly vicious:

If you have absolutely nothing at all to do; if you have no newspapers, no library, no books of any sort (including *Bradshaw's Guide*); if there be no pack of cards handy, or even a solitaire board; if, on a pouring wet day, you are dying for want of something to irritate you into healthy action, then, should you discover a copy of *The Christian* anywhere about, take it up and try it. Impossible to answer for the consequences, but if you are of an iron will and able to control your passions up to a certain point, you will, despite the wretched weather, pull on your thickest boots, struggle into your driest water-proof, and rush out of the house as if you were Abel running away from Caine. Everyone to his taste, and it is reported that the book has had a wonderful sale. Certainly, if this be so, the sale is indeed wonderful, and the fact shows how bad the weather must have been in various parts of the country.[154]

Come the 1920s, and Caine's reputation was so deflated among sharp-witted literary critics that pity was now mixed with scorn, Rebecca West writing

Nothing in the history of literature is more pathetic than the career of this man who, thrown in his youth into the society of the Pre-Raphaelites, realised that they had brought

---

[150] Parrinder and Philmus (eds.), *Wells's Literary Criticism*, 44, 47, 58.

[151] Letter, 26 Aug. 1901, in Gerber, *Moore*, 217; and Goodwin, *Moore*, 53, 238–9, for other jokes about Caine.

[152] Rothenstein, *Men and Memories, 1870–1900*, 300; and Cecil, *Max*, 175. Caine was so upset by this and other attacks that he contemplated composing a rejoinder and even suing one newspaper for defamation. His publisher, Heinemann, restrained him by telling him: 'I've had my fling at that little squirt Beerbohm . . . The book is going magnificently and it's good—very good. So don't you bother and just let' em howl' (Allen, *Caine*, 256).

[153] Ainger to Gosse, 8 Nov. 1897, in Sichel, *Ainger*, 312. For Lang's parody, 'The Heathen', see *Punch*, 6 Nov. 1897, 216.   [154] *Punch*, 9 Oct. 1897, 157.

into being a lovely and exciting world of the imagination, and for the rest of his life tried to bring such a world into being himself by writing immense novels about illegitimate half-brothers called by the same Christian name, who, owing to an exact resemblance, serve each other's sentences in Portland, while all the female characters become nuns.[155]

Caine was always ready to expose the hurt he felt from these attacks. He admitted to 'feeling greatly depressed under the wilful as well as, in some cases, unconscious misrepresentation to which I am being exposed on all sides'. Thus he complained to Annie S. Swan in 1901, reeling from 'the misjudging my book [*The Eternal City*] has gone through, not on the literary side only. That was to be expected, but on the side of the intellectual intention, its political, its religious, and above all, its purely human motive.' They had met by chance at Douglas Sladen's, when Swan found herself

jammed in the passage beside a melancholy-looking individual whom I had no difficulty in recognising as Hall Caine. We stood there for about twenty minutes talking. At least, he talked and I listened ... I was prodigiously entertained, for he was an interesting personality, who took himself and his work very seriously. To my surprise, a week or so later, I received a copy of *The Eternal City* and a letter from Greeba Castle, in which he thanked me warmly for the delightful conversation we had had at Sladen's party. There was no conversation, only an oration to an audience of one ...[156]

In 1902 Caine fought back: 'The persons who sneer at a public success are wallowing in the backwater of their own incompetence,' he declared, only to excite still louder hoots of derision from *Punch*.[157] He also took on the critics with the reissue of *Cobwebs of Criticism* (1883) in 1907.[158] Moreover, while he never succeeded in recovering their good opinion or the favour of English Literature schools at the universities, the verdict must be that Caine emerged overall victorious in his day. It was not every author's family that received messages of condolence on his death from the King and Queen, and from the Prime Minister, Ramsay MacDonald, who was both 'very grieved' and moved by the 'pride and distinction of his great career'.[159] That the same King George had once confided to Augustine Birrell that personally he detested Caine only strengthens the case.[160] The royal advisers knew that it was impossible for him to disregard such sales receipts. Caine was unmistakably a public favourite.

Caine's ability to manipulate the media probably also accounts for the interview by Sherard in the *Windsor Magazine* that appeared in 1895, the year of Saintsbury's attempt to burst Caine's bubble. It concludes with an elaborate description of the author's habits of composition (as well as a trailer for his next novel, which would not in fact appear until 1897):

My work is as follows: I first get my idea, my central motive, and this usually takes me a very long time. The incidents come very quickly, the invention of incidents is a very

---

[155] West, *Strange Necessity*, 322.   [156] Swan, *My Life*, 90–1.   [157] *Punch*, 31 Dec. 1902, 454.
[158] See above, Ch. 4.   [159] *The Times*, 2 Sept. 1931.
[160] Birrell to Violet Asquith, 7 Sept. 1911, in Bonham Carter and Pottle (eds.), *Lantern Slides*, 283.

easy matter to me. Then labour like mad in getting knowledge. I visit the places I propose to describe. I read every book I can get bearing on my subject. It is elaborate, laborious, but very delightful. Then make voluminous notes. Then begins the agony. Each day it besets me, winter or summer, from five in the morning till breakfast time. I awake at five and lie in bed, thinking out the chapter that is to be written that day, composing it word for word. That usually takes me up till seven. From seven till eight I am engaged in mental revision of the chapter. I then get up and write it down from memory, as fast as ever the pen will flow. The rest of the morning I spend in lounging about, thinking, thinking, thinking of my book. For when I am working on a new book I think of nothing else; everything else comes to a standstill. In the afternoon I walk or ride, thinking, thinking. In the evenings, when it is dark, I walk up and down my room constructing my story. It is then that I am happiest. I do not write every day . . . and when I do write, I never exceed fifteen hundred words a day.

I do not greatly revise the manuscript for serial publication, but I labour greatly over the proofs of the book, making important changes, taking out, putting in, recasting. Thus, after 'The Scapegoat' had passed through four editions and everybody was praising the book, I felt uneasy, because I felt I had not done justice to my subject; so I spent two months in re-writing it, and had the book reset and brought out again. The public feeling was that the book had not been improved, but I felt that I had lifted it up by fifty per cent.

IMPORTANT: MR HALL CAINE'S NEW WORK

Arrangements have just been concluded under which the next great work Mr Hall Caine does in succession to the 'The Manxman,' will be written for the WINDSOR MAGAZINE, *and will appear in serial form in England in the* WINDSOR MAGAZINE *alone. Mr Hall Caine has already begun to write this story, the opening chapters of which, we hope, will be published in the* WINDSOR MAGAZINE *some time next year.*[161]

By behaving as he (and the public) believed a great author should behave, agonizing over his creations, Caine became a great author *ipso facto*.

Caine thrived on publicity. Not for nothing did *Punch* nickname him 'The Boomster': he was everywhere, a perpetual din or, worse, a disease. In order to get rid of him, *Punch* in 1908 canvassed his claims for the throne of Serbia, together with those of Christabel Pankhurst and Winston Churchill; but, modestly, Caine declines the honour, just as he has also determined not to become Pope, preferring to remain 'the uncrowned king of his little island'.[162] *Punch* also maintained that it was privy to the contract Caine had signed for a new novel in 1902: this stipulated 'that it shall be another work of genius'.[163] As explanation of all this fanfaronade, Norris emphasized Caine's background as a journalist: he had 'a close knowledge of the ways of the Press, not excelled by any other living novelist, and he exploited the free publicity which could be had for the asking by any accepted writer, provided only that he would be audacious, unconventional and impervious to public criticism'.[164] There was nothing more

---

[161] Sherard, 'Hall Caine', 577.
[162] *Punch*, 19 Mar. 1902, 215, 15 Jan. 1908, 50, and 21 Oct. 1908, 297. *Punch* awards the throne of Serbia to another unabashed self-publicist, William Le Queux.   [163] *Punch*, 6 Aug. 1902, 77.
[164] Norris, *Two Men of Manxland*, 16.

audacious and unconventional than a novelist who lived in a castle among 'his own people'. Fred Kenyon—author of the biography published in 1901 when Caine was still in mid-career—had been a guest at Greeba Castle during its writing; and he submitted the text to Caine for approval. Accordingly, Kenyon's study included such judgements as (about *The Bondman*) 'one of the most powerful novels ever written', and (about *The Eternal City*), 'This last great novel of Hall Caine's is not a picture of life; it *is* Life.'[165] Understandably, Edmund Gosse was now desperate to recover face after his original over-assessment of Caine, and he relished relating how, on a visit to Rome, 'he heard a deep sepulchral voice exclaim slowly behind him: "The Vatican will hide no secrets from me!" He turned round and recognised the wide-brimmed hat of Hall Caine.'[166] The advent of *The Eternal City* had been smoothed by a sycophantic account of its making, in *The Bookman*, August 1901:

When Mr Hall Caine first decided upon the central idea, he had thought of setting his story in London, or Paris, or New York. He tried all cities and found them impossible . . . Rome alone seems to Mr Hall Caine the city worthy, in the dawn of an immense social revolution, to be the heart and soul of humanity, renewing itself in hopes and aspirations now, and promising in the future pacific civil and moral glory.[167]

But not everything in such obsequious notices was bunkum. Caine *did* take pains to research the background for his novels—what *Punch* scorned as 'cheap guide-book erudition'.[168] He also laboured over their writing, and he revised new editions.[169] In this respect he resembled George Moore, who repeatedly recast his work, and was unlike Arnold Bennett, who told his agent Pinker in 1910: 'I never rewrote any portion of any book. My first draft is always also the final writing. I would much sooner write a complete fresh novel than rewrite two chapters of an old one.'[170] In this way, Caine created a reputation for being a perfectionist. This did not make him an author of masterpieces, but there was cause to acknowledge an artisan. Critics might decry the 'audacious garrulity', 'factitious pomp of melodrama', 'ignorance of human probabilities', and 'meretricious merit that attracts and stimulates the commonplace mind that likes to think it is thinking';[171] but in Caine's case, the best-seller did not equal slick and shoddy. Even Joseph Conrad, for whom the very thought of Caine invariably released ducts of bile, seemed to glimpse something of this when he wrote sarcastically to his agent to say that, if Caine could take two years to write a book, he too should be allowed time to compose his work properly and not be badgered about deadlines.[172]

---

[165] Kenyon, *Caine*, 144, 200.   [166] Flower, *Just as it Happened*, 124.
[167] Quoted in Kenyon, *Caine*, 217–18.   [168] *Punch*, 25 Sept. 1901, reviewing *The Eternal City*.
[169] See *Review of Reviews* (June 1892), 614, welcoming the one-volume 3s. 6d. edition of *The Scapegoat*, 'entirely re-written' since the original two-volume publication; and, by contrast, *Punch*, 11 Feb. 1914, 109, for a parody of Caine's painful process of revision.
[170] Arnold Bennett to J. B. Pinker, 9 Feb. 1910, in Hepburn (ed.), *Bennett Letters*, i. 133.
[171] *Punch*, 25 Sept. 1901, 234, 9 Oct. 1901, 258.
[172] To J. B. Pinker, 16? July 1908, in Karl and Davies (eds.), *Conrad Letters*, iv. 92.

Caine's globe-trotting was faithfully recorded by the press and, lest it was not, Caine publicized the whereabouts himself: the introduction to his memoirs, *My Story*, was signed off as from 'Khartoum, 1908', where he was undertaking research for *The White Prophet*.[173] Caine liked to exhibit himself in the best places. Alice Meynell, not normally catty, reported home from the Hotel Excelsior, Rome, in 1913: 'Casting my eye over that sea of vanity, it lighted on Hall Caine, who looked pleased to be spotted.'[174] Caine's travel was not entirely for research. There was the delicate health to protect. This had been offered to the Manx as reason for his absenteeism from the House of Keys, although if they had turned to *Who's Who, 1905*, they would have read that his recreations were the unlikely invalid pursuits of 'horse-riding and mountaineering'. Still, when Jerome K. Jerome came across Caine at the Palace Hotel in St Moritz, he indeed discovered him hard at work in his room, writing a novel. This was *The Christian*; nevertheless, Jerome found Caine not at all grumpy to be disturbed—'He received us gladly and when, after lunch, I proposed a walk, answered with gentleness that he would be pleased.'[175] Their walk ended in fiasco, Caine conducting the party into a snowdrift; yet Jerome's testimonial to Caine's affability should not be ignored. This was remembered also by Robert Hichens and Eveleigh Nash.[176] The vanity seemed almost venial; and Caine was quite capable of telling a story against himself, as in the thrill he had felt to find opposite him in a railway carriage a young lady reading one of his novels, into which he had poured his heart—until she set it aside to read the station names instead.[177]

The vanity did have its monstrous side. The habit was pretty general among authors of sending complimentary copies to fellow authors and people of influence, both as a token of friendship and in the hope of receiving a puff.[178] A step further involved one author getting another to compose a flattering preface to the work; but what Caine did in his last novel, *The Woman of Knockaloe* (1923), was quite extraordinary. This was published by Cassell's, whose head, Newman Flower, had negotiated the deal. Flower was then forced by illness to give up work for several months, and on his return to the office was greeted by the first bound copy of *The Woman of Knockaloe*. Turning the leaves, he was astonished to find 'an introduction of eight or ten pages signed by me. I began to read it. They were pages of adulation of the author and his beliefs. And I had not written nor seen a word of it! I was informed that Hall Caine had told the firm . . . that he could not say these things about himself, but that I should not mind saying them!' Flower was cross, not least to be pilloried in the press; but Caine's brass-necked effrontery won the day because it was far too expensive to contemplate pulping the large first edition.[179]

---

[173] *Punch*, 29 Apr. 1908, 311, on the publicity Caine generated about his three months in Egypt.

[174] Meynell, *Alice Meynell*, 279.   [175] Jerome, *Life and Times*, 167–8.

[176] Hichens, *Yesterday*, 71, 297; Nash, *Life*, 117–21.

[177] Barbellion [B. F. Cummings], *Journal of a Disappointed Man* (Harmondsworth, 1948), 18.

[178] On this practice, see Ch. 4.   [179] Flower, *Just as it Happened*, 231–2.

Two years previously Caine had bound in book form *Letters to the Author from the Friends To Whom Copies of the Privately-Printed Edition of 'The Master of Man' Were Sent*. Among the concerted fanfare two names stood out. One was the co-founder of the Society for Pure English and editor of the *Oxford English Dictionary*, Henry Bradley LL D (Oxon.), who wrote: 'The amazing figures (surely unprecedented) of the circulation of your works imply a great influence, and it has been wholly directed to inspire love of man, reverence for the right, and compassion and hope for the fallen'. Then there was Sir Arthur Pinero, recipient of Shaw's vehement letters in 1910 after Caine had been rejected by the Dramatists' Club. In 1915 Pinero had denounced authors' publicity-seeking practices in his play *The Big Drum*, but now he wrote about *The Master of Man*:

What strikes me, in the first place, is the largeness of its architecture, remarkable at a time when the English novel tends to be rather finicking, to lose itself either in intricate form or loose construction and weak artifice. There is no smallness in your work; all is brought to order and purpose with boldness and breadth... I admire beyond measure the undeviating directness with which you drive home its terrible moral, allowing no super-subtlety, no temptation to display mere ingenuity, to turn you aside for a single moment. Indeed, your relentlessness is so harrowing as almost to be cruel to the reader. 'The Master of Man', in its combined power and simplicity, ranks, in my opinion, with your greatest successes, and, therefore, with the best we have in fiction.[180]

This reference to the 'largeness of architecture' of Caine's work did, however, hit the mark as an explanation for his best-seller stature. Portentousness was a characteristic his novels shared with the old-fashioned epic and the modern blockbuster. When, following a strong scene in *The Prodigal Son*, he thumpingly interjects, 'None of us can see the future. We must all bow before the Unknown,' *Punch*'s reviewer was inclined to remark like Mrs Gamp, 'There ain't no denigin' of it, Betsy'; yet that same superior reviewer acknowledged that altogether it was 'a decidedly powerful novel' which held the reader from beginning to end.[181] Caine's melodramatic storylines and grandiose style naturally came to interest film-makers, eager to project such work onto a still larger canvas. Unauthorized versions of *The Deemster* and *The Bondman* were made by Fox, and of *The Christian* by Vitagraph, before the Great War.[182] *The Christian* and *The Manxman* were then produced as British-made films in 1916 and 1917, followed by *Darby and Joan* (an original film script by Caine) and *The Prodigal Son* in 1922; and there were American-made films of *The Eternal City* in 1915 and 1923, *The Deemster* in 1917, *The Woman Thou Givest Me* in 1919, *The Christian* in 1923 and *The Master of Man* in 1924. Alfred Hitchcock's version of *The Manxman* in 1929, a silent movie made at Elstree

---

[180] Henry Bradley to Caine, 17 May 1921, and Sir Arthur Pinero to Caine, 7 June 1921, in Hall Caine (ed.), *Letters to the Author from the Friends to whom Copies of the Privately-Printed Edition of 'The Master of Man' were Sent* (1921), 17, 24. On Pinero's play *The Big Drum*, see above, Ch. 10; and for the background of *The Master of Man*, see Allen, *Caine*, 373, 380–4.   [181] *Punch*, 23 Nov. 1904, 378.
[182] Allen, *Caine*, 364, for the copyright problem.

studios with the leads taken by foreign stars, has good claims to be considered that famous director's worst film.[183]

Caine's influence was most continuously deployed in the world of publishing itself. It was Heinemann's publication in 1894 of *The Manxman* in one volume, price 6s., and its sale directly to bookshops, that had largely broken the stranglehold of the circulating libraries and triple-decker format.[184] Caine first published with Heinemann's in 1890: *The Bondman* was also its first publication and was the making of the firm, as it accumulated sales of 450,000. Rejected by Caine's previous publisher, Chatto & Windus, and by Cassell's, Heinemann secured Caine for £300 in advance of royalties.[185] Heinemann not only profited from Caine, he believed in him. When he first read the manuscript of *The Scapegoat* (1891), he regarded it as 'the finest novel that had ever been written'.[186] For a long while Caine remained a pillar of the firm and acted as one of its literary advisers. Such services did not prevent Sydney Pawling, who became a partner in Heinemann's in 1893, from being snide about Caine, telling how he 'would sneak into Heinemann's office by the trade entrance to spend many a clandestine hour drafting their advertisements for his bestsellers'.[187] Gilbert Frankau recorded this remark: Frankau would become a best-seller in the inter-war years and (if such were possible) an even more swollen-headed one than Caine. Additionally, Frankau related that Caine once told him, 'You are lucky young man, to be writing novels at a time when a novelist is no longer expected to be a gentleman.' An old Etonian and monumental snob, Frankau thought this betrayed 'a touch of envy'; yet it also conveys something of Caine's feelings about the decades of condescension, even contempt, he had encountered because of his self-promotional enterprise. His clubs remained second-class: the Authors, National, Whitefriars, and Macabeans, never the Savile or Athenaeum.

In the final analysis, when the excessive applause and abuse that Caine received are levelled out, what is the historian left with that might explain his success? Undoubtedly, it was his capacity as a storyteller on a big scale. Sidney Low, who

---

[183] Robinson, *World Cinema*, 150.

[184] Griest, *Mudie's*, 182, 210. A later experiment by Heinemann with a Caine novel was not so successful, when the publisher endeavoured to break the 6s. standard by varying price according to length. He therefore inaugurated the Heinemann Library of Modern Fiction, whose first title was Caine's *The White Prophet* (1909), published in two volumes at 4s. each. No other publisher was prepared to imitate him, and the circulating libraries also objected to paying what amounted to a price rise; but it may have been the political furore roused by *The White Prophet* that made this an ill-fated choice to venture a new publishing practice. See Allen, *Caine*, 336–7.   [185] Nowell-Smith, *Cassell*, 189.

[186] Hueffer, *Ancient Lights*, 181, where he also cites his grandfather, the artist Ford Madox Brown, calling it 'a work of genius'.

[187] Frankau, *Self-Portrait*, 279. On Pawling, a nephew of the proprietor of the subscription library Charles Edward Mudie, see Linda Marie Fritschner, 'William Heinemann Limited', in Rose and Anderson (eds.), *British Literacy Publishing Houses, 1881–1965*, 152. Pawling was a family friend of the Frankaus, a director of the Frankau cigar-importing business; also captain of Hampstead Cricket Club. It was Pawling's inconsiderate treatment of Jack London in 1910–11 that lost him for Heinemann's, London thereafter publishing with Mills & Boon; see Joseph McAleer, *Passion's Fortune: The Story of Mills & Boon* (Oxford, 1999), 32–3.

had met Caine in Egypt, captured this quality in conversation with Arnold
Bennett in 1910: 'Low insisted on Hall Caine's powers as a *raconteur*, as proved at
Cairo, when he kept a dinner-party of casual strangers interested for $1\frac{1}{2}$ hours
by a full account of the secret history of the Druce case, which secret history he
admitted afterwards was a sheer novelist's invention.[188] This was classic Caine.
The Druce case was a series of sensational applications and lawsuits beginning in
1896 and relating to the estate of the eccentric and reclusive fifth Duke of Portland
(1800–79), who, it was contended, had lived a double life as Thomas Charles
Druce, a Baker Street shopkeeper. The concluding trial involved a fine cast of
perjurors, including members of the Druce clan who had come over
from Australia to claim their inheritance.[189] Caine had attended court during the
trial, which finished in January 1908, then advertised to the press his intention of
romancing the story in novel or play.[190] He never did—but he did have time in
which to prepare the 'spontaneous' version which so impressed Sidney Low.

[188] Flower (ed.), *Bennett Journal*, i. 351 (4 Jan. 1910).
[189] See Theodore Besterman. *The Druce-Portland Case* (1935).
[190] *Punch*, 8 Jan. 1908, 26, and 15 Jan. 1908, 50.

22

The Demonic Dreamer: Marie Corelli

TIPS FOR CRITICS

If you want a great *casus belli*,
If you would be thumped to a jelly,
  Just *dare* to suggest
  That *the* greatest and best
In the world is *not* Marie Corelli!

(*Punch*, 9 May 1896)

I am generally judged of a frivolous disposition because I am small in stature, slight in build, and have curly hair—all proofs positive, according to the majority, of latent foolishness. Colossal women, however, are always astonishingly stupid, and fat women lethargic—but a mountain of good flesh is always more attractive to man than any amount of intellectual perception.

(Irene Vassilius in Marie Corelli, *The Soul of Lilith* (1892))

A man has been arrested for firing shots in Miss Marie Corelli's garden. From a statement he made he is apparently a reader of Miss Corelli's books. The state of his mind is to be enquired into.

(*Punch*, 23 December 1908)

I

Hall Caine had one obvious rival, and that was Marie Corelli. 'They were both self-centred and supersensitive, imagining slights where none were intended,' wrote Annie S. Swan.[1] They shared other characteristics—both 'rode the Tosh-horse at full gallop', sneered Rebecca West[2]—but, for all the sensational nature of Caine's own rise and career, it was almost pedestrian compared with Corelli's. Born Mary (Minnie) Mackay in 1855, the illegitimate (though, possibly, adopted) daughter or even granddaughter of Charles Mackay, then editor of the *Illustrated London News*, Marie Corelli spent part of her childhood as a neighbour of George

---

[1] Swan, *Life*, 91.   [2] West, *Strange Necessity*, 322.

Meredith at Box Hill, Surrey.[3] She liked to recall this brief association with great-ness; that is, Meredith's association with her greatness. He supposedly informed Mackay that 13-year-old Minnie had 'divine fire', having heard her play the piano. In 1892, in *The Silver Domino*, her retaliation against hostile reviewers and against contemporary authors more highly esteemed than herself, she patronized Meredith as 'an Eccentricity—a bit of genius gone mad—an Intellectual Faculty broken loose from the moorings of Common Sense and therefore a hopelessly obstinate fixture in the "groove" of literary delirium', finding him 'distinctly amusing—and never more so than when he thinks he is impressive'.[4] Later, on being told that Meredith closed her *Treasure of Heaven* (1906) with tears in his eyes, Corelli took this as a high mark of approbation.[5] The possibility that the old man was grief-stricken from her massacre of the English language, she had ruled out.

Corelli's relationship with her family was the more intense for the obscurity of her birth. In *Who's Who* entries she described herself as being 'of mingled Italian and Scotch (Highland) parentage and connections, adopted in infancy' by Mackay. To W. Stuart Scott in 1919, Corelli made this dramatic declaration about her paternity: 'I never knew my own father—he died *before* I was born!'[6] If Mackay was her father, then the likely natural mother was a Mrs Mills—a domestic servant-cum-laundress, formerly married to a scenic artist—who became the second Mrs Mackay in 1861, after Mackay's estranged first wife died in 1859. Corelli worshipped Mackay, who published several novels, including *Luck and What Came of It* (1881); but not much befell Mackay thereafter. He was seized with a stroke in 1883 and nursed until death in 1889 by Corelli.[7] During his last illness *Punch*, which later would mercilessly guy Corelli herself, saluted Mackay as 'the People's Poet', who had gladdened hearts everywhere with his verses *There's a Land, a dear Land, A Good Time Coming*, and *Cheer, Boys, Cheer!*:

> Poet and patriot, champion still
> Of simple manhood and honest skill,
> Of pure Home-love, and of frank good-will.
>
> Friend of JERROLD, and foe of wrong;
> Very Voice of the toiling throng,
> Its needs and yearnings, in touching song:
>
> *Punch's* greetings! The world should see
> That needless sorrow come not to thee,
> Broken yet cheery at Seventy-three.
> Let all who have heard, under many a sky,
> The manly music he lifted high,
> Thank-offering render to CHARLES MACKAY!

[3] Ransom, *Corelli*, 22, 206, 225–31, for the inconclusive evidence about Corelli's parentage. This, generally, adds little to the pioneering work by Brian Masters, *Now Barabbas was a Rotter: The Extra-ordinary Life of Marie Corelli* (1978). [4] Stevenson, *Meredith*, 169, 302.
[5] Vyver, *Corelli*, 195. [6] Scott, *Corelli*, 83.
[7] Corelli later told Scott that *A Romance of Two Worlds* (1886) and *Vendetta* (1886) 'were written at his [Mackay's] bedside' (ibid. 112).

This was in February 1888, when a fund was being raised to relieve Mackay's hard-pressed circumstances. *Punch* implored its readers to subscribe generously and, in November, to buy a selection of his poems and songs which Whittaker & Co. had newly published.[8]

The second Mrs Mackay had predeceased the People's Poet in 1876; but she was practically banished from Corelli's memory and scarcely ever referred to. She was supplanted in Corelli's affections by Bertha van der Vyver, 'Mamasita' and 'dearest Ber', who joined the household in 1878. She was the daughter of a putative Belgian countess and Belgian–Spanish merchant; her mother, then separated from the father, lived with an American in Cleveland Terrace, Bayswater. Vyver and Corelli played together as children, having first met in Brighton. They also attended convent school together, in Paris in the late 1860s. Neither married. Sniggers greeted the first issue of the newly formatted *Who's Who*, edited by Douglas Sladen in 1897, when Corelli's entry read: 'she is at present unmarried'. The 'at present' survived into the 1898 edition and was dropped from the 1899.[9] In her early fifties she was smitten by the painter Arthur Severn; but nothing came of it, other than the anguished *Open Confession: To a Man from a Woman*, published posthumously in 1925.[10] Corelli and Vyver lived together until Corelli's death in 1924. Vyver, an executor and principal devisee for life of her estate,[11] published a memoir of Corelli in 1930. Her role was always, as Robert Hichens remarked, that of 'praiser-in-chief' to Corelli.[12]

The Mackay connection had not ended for Corelli with Charles Mackay's death. Eric, one of four children by the first marriage, then acted as her self-appointed guardian—though Corelli was now in her thirties. A tempestuous relationship ensued. Jerome K. Jerome, who knew her when she was sharing a home with Eric at 47 Longridge Road, in south-west London, described her as

an erratic worker and contracts would often get behind time . . . and occasionally when her agent would come to the house tearing his hair because of an instalment that an editor was waiting for, and that Marie did not feel like writing, they [the agent and Eric] would take her up and lock her in her study; and when she had finished kicking the door, she would settle down, and do a good morning's work.[13]

[8] *Punch*, 4 Feb. 1888, 59, and 3 Nov. 1888, 209. The reference to Jerrold is to Douglas Jerrold, the hugely popular mid-Victorian writer who had nicknamed Mackay 'the British Béranger'—itself a reference to Pierre Jean de Béranger (1780–1857), then considered the greatest of French songwriters. The popularity of Mackay's songs was in large measure owed to Henry Russell, who set them to music and performed them. On these individuals, Michael Slater, *Douglas Jerrold, 1803–1857* (2003), and *DNB Supplement*, iii (1901), 332–3, for Russell (1812–1900). Mackay himself was also recognised in *DNB* xxxv (1893), 120–1, and more appreciatively by Angus Calder in the *Oxford DNB*.

[9] *Who's Who* (1897), 254; (1898), 290.

[10] Severn was married to a cousin of John Ruskin, thereby inheriting Ruskin's home Brantwood, by Lake Coniston. Corelli owned several of Severn's paintings, and six of his pictures illustrated Corelli's *The Devil's Motor* (1910).

[11] *The Times*, 9 May 1924, 20–1. Corelli's will is reproduced in Scott, *Corelli*, 269–73. Her wish was 'to be buried with and beside my dearest life long friend Bertha Vyver'. Vyver, one year older than Corelli, died in 1941.   [12] Hichens, *Yesterday*, 90–1.

[13] Jerome, *Life and Times*, 91. One reason for his friendship with Corelli was 'We discovered we were precisely the same age.' But Corelli had a habit of dropping years. Jerome was born in 1859; Corelli in fact

There is doubtless fancy in this anecdote, yet it encapsulates one truth at least: Eric Mackay was an exploitative bully. Having sponged off his father, this put him in the frame of mind to sponge off Corelli. A musical training in Italy had been planned for him, for which Charles Mackay coughed up £120 per annum, but the several years that Eric spent there were idled. Charles excluded Eric from his will, and Corelli inherited the entirety, £2,718 6s. 9d.[14] Eric meanwhile turned to versifying. Corelli paid for his poetry to be published, invented the captivating title *Love Letters of a Violinist*, and reviewed it under a pseudonym.[15] She also included some of his poems in her novels, in *Thelma* (1887), for example. Most bizarre of all, Corelli campaigned for the poet laureateship for him.[16] This included importunate letters to newspaper editors. Surviving among the papers of Ernest Parke, who presided over the *Star* and *Morning Leader*, is an epistle from Corelli describing Eric as 'my only relative, one of the kindest, truest-hearted gentlemen that ever lived, and loved by all who have come into contact with him'. She was aggrieved about 'the bitter animosity of the Press against him and myself'; to which Eric added his own note of complaint about people who 'have been particularly insolent to me'. He asked if Parke would 'honour me by publishing the enclosed in tomorrow's issue—all editions, on front page, somewhat prominently at the top of column? I don't want anything for it but a prominent place.'[17] Corelli's mood changed following Eric's death in June 1898, when the extent of his duplicity and parasitism—he had put it about that he wrote Corelli's books—became clear.[18]

This revelation came at a time when Corelli herself was ill, requiring surgery, possibly for a hysterectomy. This breakdown put a halt to her writing; as she put it melodramatically, but also with startling candour, in *Who's Who* in 1901,

At the end of 1897, a dangerous illness, nearly ending in her death, interrupted her work, and while slowly recovering from this during the spring of 1898, George Eric Mackay (second son of Charles Mackay), who had been nominated at his father's death as her legal guardian, being many years her senior, died suddenly of pneumonia, leaving her entirely alone in the world. The shock of this bereavement prostrated her again with serious illness, and it was not until the end of April 1899 that she recommenced her literary labours . . .[19]

Corelli made up for lost time with two publications in 1900. One was the monster best-seller *The Master-Christian*. The other, *Boy*, was an amplification of a short

---

was four years older. By 1924 the discrepancy between her alleged and actual age had stretched to ten years. *The Times* reported her death, between 7 and 8 a.m. on 21 April, thus: 'she was 59 on May 1 last year. She wished it stated that the time she died was to be called "God's time", because she would not adopt summer time' (*The Times*, 22 Apr. 1924). Summertime, introduced in 1916, cannot explain the missing decade, which Corelli made disappear for reasons of vanity and to disguise her illegitimacy.

[14] Ransom, *Corelli*, 57.   [15] Ibid. 27.   [16] On this, see above, Ch. 12.
[17] Scott, *'We' and Me*, 178.
[18] See Corelli's bitter allusion to this in 'Accursëd Eve', in Corelli, *Free Opinions*, 158–9; also Masters, *Corelli*, 154–60; Ransom, *Corelli*, 97.
[19] *Who's Who* (1901), 294–5. This confessional remained in *Who's Who* until the 1909 edition.

story 'contracted for previously to her illness in 1897'. *Punch*, which habitually lampooned Corelli and decried her work (*The Master-Christian* was dismissed as 'meretricious'[20]), had rapturously received *Boy* as 'a work of genius'. Its reviewer predicted for it classic status, certain 'to establish her reputation among the very few of our novelists whose works English readers would not willingly let die'.[21] Such extraordinary acclaim is testimony to how susceptible readers in that day were to sentimentalism about children, previously manifested in the response to *Little Lord Fauntleroy*, to which *Boy* was now deemed superior. *Punch*'s reviewer may also have been moved to declare an armistice at such a low point in Corelli's fortunes. *Boy* had been dedicated thus: 'To my dearest friend in the world Bertha Vyver who has known all my life from childhood and has been the witness of all my literary work from its very beginning this simple story is gratefully and lovingly dedicated'.[22] The publisher Hutchinson also included a Note, highlighted in red: 'This NEW LONG STORY is the *most important* volume by MARIE CORELLI published for some years, and the first issued since the Author's serious illness.' Dated 31 May 1900, it continued to be inserted in impressions of the book issued in 1901, which were styled the 'Fifty-third Thousand'. These also included an advertisement for Corelli's *The Mighty Atom* (1896), which was then entering a new edition 'completing 97,000 copies'.

Writing had not always been Corelli's ambition. Following after Charles Mackay's minstrelsy, she had received what she termed 'a first-class musical training', becoming 'proficient on the piano and mandolin'. To this statement in *Who's Who* she added: 'She commenced to write an elaborate opera entitled Ginerva Da Siena, when barely 14'. She also wrote two songs, 'My Sweet Sweeting', and 'Romeo's Good Night'.[23] It appeared that she had been planning a professional concert career because it was then, like many a British musician imbued with a sense of native inferiority, she adopted a foreign name, Marie di Corelli, when giving recitals.[24] A propensity for self-glamorization—in plain English, lying—had taken hold. To the editor of *Blackwood's Magazine* in 1883 she introduced herself as 'a Venetian, and the direct descendant (through a long

<hr />

[20] *Punch*, 9 Oct. 1901, 258.   [21] *Punch*, 25 July 1900, 60–1.

[22] *Thelma* (1887) was also dedicated 'To my dearest friend, Bertha Vyver, in recognition of her sweet companionship, tender sympathy, and most faithful love'.   [23] *Who's Who* (1905), 347.

[24] On this habit of British musicians adopting foreign names, see Cyril Ehrlich, *The Music Profession in Britain since the Eighteenth Century: A Social History* (Oxford, 1985), 104, 186–8. The quality of Corelli's concerts is praised by her lifelong companion; Vyver, *Corelli*, 48–52. Music remained as a recreation. When Francis Gribble, editing *Phil May's Annual* in the early 1890s, approached Corelli for an article, she replied that she was 'far *too* busy as it is, and can take no more work this year unless in the form of a "correspondence" from Bayreuth for the Festival, for which I have just got the best places in the theatre. I could do something there for somebody, as I am a musician as well as scribbler, and I carry letters to Frau Wagner' (Gribble, *Seen in Passing*, 150–1). In 1901 Corelli nominated Wagner, Schubert, Chopin, and Bizet as the composers she most liked; Masini, Tamango, and Plançon as her favourite male singers; and, as for female singers, 'none!' Kent Carr, *Corelli*, 73. Bernard Shaw, as a dedicated Wagnerite, was qualified to spot the borrowings Corelli made from Wagner's operatic dramas in both *Thelma* and *The Sorrows of Satan*; see his review of the stage adaptation of the latter, 16 Jan. 1897, in Shaw, *Plays and Players: Essays on the Theatre* (Oxford, 1950), 164.

line of ancestry) of the great Michael Angelo Corelli, the famous composer and also on another side of the family from one of the Doges of Venice'. Corelli joined incompetence to fantasy—the forename of the composer and violin virtuoso Corelli (1653–1713) was actually Arcangelo—and she compounded improbability by declaring that Lord Neaves had encouraged her to approach Blackwood's, 'but travelling and residence abroad banished the idea for some time'.[25] Neaves, a former solicitor-general, was not in a position to contradict: he died in 1876.

The career changed but the name—minus the 'di'—stuck. Corelli published her first novel, *A Romance of Two Worlds*, in 1886. She had been reading Hugh Conway's best-seller *Called Back* (1884), and thought of calling her own story 'Lifted Up', until her father, impressed by Lewis Morris's *Songs of Two Worlds* (1871), suggested the final title.[26] Another thirty stories would follow, all, as A. G. Macdonell described them, 'full-blooded, "Turkey-carpet" slabs of nonsense' or, as E. F. Benson put it, like a 'series of geysers continuously exploding'.[27] Their popularity brought her first fame; the wealth would come later. Her original publisher, George Bentley, while apparently besotted by her, ran true to form and exploited her. She complained to the Revd W. Stuart Scott in 1919 that 'I only got £40 for *A Romance of Two Worlds*' and that

Bentley made a fortune out of *Thelma* [1887] and gave me £150. I did not get another penny for it until I got it out of his hands. I have a letter blocked out which I sent to him, saying that I really could not accept £250 for *Ardath* [1889], as I could not live on what I was getting out of my books.[28]

Corelli's bank balance subsequently improved. In *The Sorrows of Satan* (1895), she referred scornfully to critics, who earned a pound a week, regarding 'as their natural enemies the authors who make thirty to fifty pounds a week', a sum (of between £1,560 and £2,600 per annum) which may have reflected her own income at the time.[29] Later she was reckoned to make £10,000 from each book; and in the new century her annual income was in the region of £18,000, as she commanded advances from publishers of £7,000 or more.[30] She boasted to Robert Hichens that on one occasion 'the head of a firm of big publishers asked her to lunch at the Carlton and offered her thirty thousand pounds down if she would sell to him the world rights of her next long novel'—which she refused to do.[31]

[25] Ransom, *Corelli*, 24–5. Writing to the publisher George Bentley in 1889, she alluded to 'my dear, sweet, beautiful Venetian mother' (Scott, *Corelli*, 84).

[26] Scott, *Corelli*, 22–3; and Sutherland, *Companion*, 100–1, 222–3, for *Called Back*.

[27] Scott, *Corelli*, 33; Masters, *Corelli*, 12–13.   [28] Scott, *Corelli*, 86, 97.

[29] Corelli, *Sorrows of Satan*, 259–60.

[30] See Robertson Nicoll's report of Hodder & Stoughton's offer in 1909, according to Riddell, *Diary, 1908–1914*, 16; and Ransom, *Corelli*, 160, for Methuen's advance of £7,000 for *Holy Orders* (1908): 'Their confidence was justified—in the first month the book sold 112,450 copies and earned £7,505 10s.' *Thelma* (1887) and *The Sorrows of Satan* (1895) alone were yielding £5,000 a year in 1906; Scott, *Corelli*, 232. See also *Punch*, 7 Nov. 1906, 331, for comic speculation about the amount of income tax Corelli was paying.

[31] Hichens, *Yesterday*, 71.

Corelli used many publishers: Bentley, Lamleys, Methuen, Skeffington, Hutchinson, Arrowsmith, Constable, Hodder & Stoughton, and Collins. Methuen became her main publisher. Its catalogue in August 1910 included an impressive fifteen titles, all at 6s.: *The Sorrows of Satan* led, in its fifty-fifth edition (or impression); *Barabbas* (1893) was in its forty-fourth; *Thelma* (1887) its fortieth, *Vendetta* (1886) its thirty-seventh, and so on. There is, generally, no reliable correlation between numbers of impressions and volume of sales. Alfred Sutro's play *The Cave of Illusion* (1900) features a publisher who brazenly boasts of manipulations. When he grumbles about one of his titles being a dead failure, his interlocutor is shocked: 'But you advertise the seventh edition?', to which the publisher rejoinders, 'That means nothing—I haven't sold out the second! I must boom it, to help off the *edition de luxe*, which, between you and me, drags terribly.'[32] Methuen's took a high line about such fiddles: 'To print say 750 copies of a novel and to divide this into five "editions" of 150 each, announcing the exhaustion of each puny infant with a prodigious flourish is ridiculous, and perhaps immoral. At all events it is meant to bamboozle the public.'[33] Four of Corelli's Methuen titles advertised in 1910 disclosed both data: *Holy Orders: The Tragedy of a Quiet Life* (1908) was in its second edition (120th thousand); *Temporal Power: A Study in Supremacy* (1902), second edition (150th thousand); *God's Good Man: A Simple Love Story* (1904), thirteenth edition (152nd thousand); and *The Master-Christian* (1900), twelfth edition (177th thousand). *Temporal Power* had established a record for the largest first print run for a six-shilling novel on 28 August 1902, when 120,000 copies were issued.[34] It was a measure of the Corelli phenomenon that, only six years before, Hutchinson's, ecstatic at having Corelli on its list for the first time, considered it was breaking records with a first printing of 20,000 for *The Mighty Atom* (1896).[35]

Methuen served Corelli well. It made a splash of pre-publication publicity, much as Heinemann's did for Hall Caine. In 1904 it ran this advertisement for several weeks:

Messrs Methuen have much pleasure in announcing that they will publish shortly a new romance by Miss Marie Corelli. They do not think it advisable at present to give the title or any description of the contents of the book, but they may say on their own part that it is a work of extraordinary vivacity and charm, with an intense human interest which will appeal to an enormous circle of readers. It is a story of pure love and faith, and is more on the lines of 'Thelma' than any book which the author has written since that favourite romance. The demand for this novel is already very great, and orders should be sent to the booksellers' without delay.[36]

---

[32] Alfred Sutro, *The Cave of Illusion* (1900), 31–3.

[33] *Methuen Gazette*, the publisher's house magazine, quoted in Duffy, *Methuen*, 8.

[34] Coates and Bell, *Corelli*, 247.   [35] Scott, *Corelli*, 44.

[36] Advertisement in *Pall Mall Gazette*, 4 July 1904, 3. Repeated in *Pall Mall Gazette*, 18 July 1904, 4. Methuen observed with some satisfaction at the year's end: 'Depression may reign in the book trade and the purse of the burdened taxpayer be very light but everyone has enough money to buy Miss Corelli's new romance. And so edition after edition has been exhausted, and even the critics, not always generous

Eventually, the title was unveiled—*God's Good Man: A Simple Love Story*—and another barrage of advertising accompanied it: 'The excitement about this book increases every day, and the demand bids fair to exceed the wonderful one for Miss Corelli's last romance [*Temporal Power*], a demand which passed all records made either by this author or by any other author. You should order a copy of this delightful book without delay.'[37] All this, it should be noted, was exactly what Corelli had denounced as malpractice in *The Sorrows of Satan*, where the instruction is given to 'let your publisher advertise to the effect that the "First and Second Large Editions" of the new novel by Geoffrey Tempest, are exhausted, one hundred thousand copies having been sold in a week! If that does not waken up the world in general, I shall be much surprised!'[38]

According to Corelli's own account, 'her first attempts in literature were three sonnets on Shakespearean themes, and were published by Clement Scott, then editor of *The Theatre*'. Her first novel, *A Romance of Two Worlds* (1886), which dealt with 'spirit power and universal love', was published in the then standard format of three volumes by Bentley. It owed its origin, she claimed, to 'a curious psychical experience occurring to herself personally'.[39] Bentley's readers had taken violently against it. One was Hall Caine, and this kick-started a lasting enmity between the best-sellers.[40] Both fancied themselves a modern Shakespeare; each held an idiosyncratically divine mission; each was invited by publishers to write a Life of Christ; and their megalomania was fuelled by a detestation of critics and rival authors. When it was alleged in 1903 that her *Temporal Power* (1902) was inspired by Caine's *The Eternal City* (1901), Corelli announced that:

There are absolutely no points of resemblance. Miss Corelli has never read *The Eternal City* or any of Mr Hall Caine's books except *The Christian* [1897]. She declares, however, that she searched in vain for a real follower of Christ in that work. It is interesting to note, by the way, that although the two novelists met years ago at a social function, they are practically strangers to one another, and are probably content to remain so.[41]

Corelli had as little liking for publishers' readers as for book-reviewers. She lost no opportunity to denigrate them in the course of her stories:

These 'readers', I learned, were most of them novelists themselves, who read other people's productions in their spare moments and passed judgment on them. I have

---

to the distinguished author, have been forced to lay down their stilettos and admire' (quoted in Duffy, *Methuen*, 34).

[37] *Pall Mall Gazette*, 21 July 1904, 3.

[38] Corelli, *Sorrows of Satan*, 65. 'The loud hawking of literary wares' is compared to 'the rival shouting of costermongers in a low neighbourhood'.   [39] *Who's Who* (1901), 294–5.

[40] Carr, *Corelli*, 29–32, 84–5; Gribble, *Seen in Passing*, 150. The spoof *Lives of the 'Lustrious*, ed. Stephen and Lee, 20, suggested for Corelli's motto: 'Cave Cainem'. *Punch* repeatedly played on Corelli and Caine's mutual loathing; e.g. 31 Oct. 1900, 310, or 18 Jan. 1905, 38. When they both attended the Warwick Pageant, it reported that 'Each . . . was the observed of all observers, except one' (ibid. 11 June 1906, 26).

[41] Coates and Bell, *Corelli*, 257.

always failed to see the justice of this arrangement; to me it seems merely the way to foster mediocrities and suppress originality.[42]

II

George Bentley made an astute judgement about *A Romance of Two Worlds*. He reasoned that a work that sparked such a violent reaction from his publisher's readers was bound to create a stir.[43] He advanced Corelli payment for one year's rights. Around the turn of the century, when two authorized biographies of Corelli appeared, it was already legend that *A Romance of Two Worlds* received only four summary and unfavourable reviews; in 1909, when *The Bookman* devoted a special issue to the Corelli phenomenon, the legend was so improved that it appeared the novel elicited only two reviews and both 'condemnatory', as Corelli herself liked to report.[44] Four seems the generally agreed total. The loyal Bertha Vyver in 1930 quoted selectively from these, making them appreciative— that the *Pall Mall Gazette* had heralded 'An Audacious Novel'; that the *Athenaeum*, 13 March 1886, also took it seriously; that *The Globe*, 16 March 1886, reckoned it 'wild and fantastic; but it is also clever and ingenious'; and that the *Whitehall Review*, 4 March 1886, noted, so completely did the author believe her own story that the reader 'is carried away from the world into the land of dreams'.[45] Vyver's tweaking apart, the consensus was that the press had done nothing to assist its promotion. Instead, 'the public discovered the book for themselves, and letters concerning its theories began to pour in from strangers in all parts of the United Kingdom. At the end of its first twelve months' run, Mr Bentley brought it out in one volume in his "Favourite" series. Then it started off round the world at full gallop.'[46] 'Edition followed edition,' enthused her first biographer, Kent Carr, in 1901; 'it was translated into many tongues; learned Brahmins studied its teachings; while a clergyman of the Church of England wrote to say that its revelations had

---

[42] Corelli, *Sorrows of Satan*, 6. And later, on p. 43: 'I know the kind of people who "read" for you—the gaunt, unlovable spinster of 50—the dyspeptic bookworm who is a "literary failure" and can find nothing else to do but scrawl growling comments on the manuscript of promising work—why in heaven's name should you rely on such incompetent opinion?'

[43] In correspondence with Corelli, 27 May 1889, Bentley noted that Rhoda Broughton also was regularly abused by reviewers and it never did her any harm with the public. After the success of *Thelma* (1887), Bentley took to beginning his letters to Corelli with 'Dear Thelma'. Letters quoted in Coates and Bell, *Corelli*, 125–7. The last book Corelli published with Bentley was *The Soul of Lilith* (1892). The firm was taken over by Macmillan's. Corelli would not entertain the idea of placing any new title with Macmillan's so long as they persisted in sending out her manuscripts to a publisher's reader: 'I have long ceased to be the slave of the publisher's "reader" . . . that often narrow and prejudiced "oracle".' She enclosed with her letter a press cutting which read, 'The Queen, it is said, is reading Marie Corelli's book, *A Romance of Two Worlds*, with the deepest interest' (Corelli to Macmillan, 22 Mar. 1892, in Nowell-Smith (ed.), *Letters to Macmillan*, 244–5). [44] Scott, *Corelli*, 97.

[45] Vyver, *Corelli*, 56–8.

[46] Coates and Bell, *Corelli*, 43. The second edition (1887) of *A Romance of Two Worlds* included a new Introduction by Corelli, affirming her Electric Creed, and an Appendix, quoting from readers' letters.

saved him from suicide.'[47] Others were frankly mystified. George Gissing had read it in 1888. He commented: 'a queer piece of juvenile fanaticism', adding: 'Don't know whether she is in earnest, though.'[48]

It is a challenge to summarize this extraordinary tale's crackpot complexity.[49] Written in the first person, its heroine, having suffered a breakdown, consults a Chaldaean named Heliobas, who, via psychical electricity, ultimately affirms for her the essential truths of Christianity. The action takes place variously between the south of France and the outer reaches of the solar system. Still, as Corelli's first biographer, the awestruck Kent Carr commented, Corelli's 'implicit belief in what she related robbed it of every trace of charlatanism'. He further observed, with a nice mixture of canniness and bathos:

The book, too, came at a time when the world was primed to welcome any addition to its occult knowledge. The new creed was neither spiritualism nor hypnotism, but then neither was it science...It promised them so much too; not only the sure hope of immortality, but certain material advantages which no man may despise—eternal youth among other things, and absolute immunity from doctors' bills.[50]

Corelli herself appeared anxious to avoid a potentially damaging charge of heterodoxy. Interviewed for Jerome K. Jerome's *The Idler* magazine, she stated: 'I distinctly wish it to be understood that I am neither a "Spiritualist" nor a "Theosophist" . . . and I have no other supernatural belief than that which is taught by the Founder of our Faith.'[51] Later she waxed scornful about W. T. Stead's *Letters from Julia* (1897), in which the popular editor acted as automatic amanuensis for a ghost spirit; about the inventor of Sherlock Holmes, Conan Doyle, being duped by 'the trickery of mediums' and spiritualist 'clap-trap'; and about Sir Oliver Lodge's *Raymond; or, Life and Death* (1916), in which the respected scientist recorded how his son, killed in the Great War, still communicated. 'Poor man,' Corelli wrote of Lodge, 'the death of his son has struck the soft spot in his brain!... he has studied science *without* humility—and that is why he can be so easily "fooled".' Yet it was chiefly these individuals' so-alled 'proofs' that she objected to, especially their use of mediums: 'Spirits—(who *do* exist) never descend to such common and personal parlance.' Corelli herself was superstitious in trivial matters—page 13 of her scrapbook, otherwise chock-full of press items about herself, was not used.[52]

In spite of her professed hostility to spiritualism, Corelli's Electric Creed contained many elements in common. Certainly, Corelli played up to the current mood of speculation, that maybe the world was full of spirits seeking to make contact with the living. Her short story 'The Lady with the Carnations', published first in a magazine and reprinted in *Cameos* (1896), combined this with a dig at her critics. It concerned the spirit presence of an artist's model, murdered by her lover, the artist himself, who mistakenly believed her unfaithful. The theme of 'a faithful

---

[47] Kent Carr, *Corelli*, 32.   [48] Coustillas (ed.), *Gissing's Diary*, 22 (29 Feb. 1888).
[49] There is a splendid digest in Sutherland, *Companion*, 543.   [50] Carr, *Corelli*, 40–1.
[51] Quoted in Coates and Bell, *Corelli*, 47.   [52] Scott, *Corelli*, 168–70.

woman deeply wronged' was a favourite of Corelli, who saw herself in this part. This particular story was also narrated in the first person, by the only person to whom the spirit would manifest itself. Scepticism is expressed by her friends, among them a Mrs Fairleigh: she 'was one of those eminently sensible persons who had seriously lectured me on a book known as "A Romance of Two Worlds", as inculcating spiritualistic theories, and therefore deserving condemnation'.[53]

The scenarios of Corelli's stories frequently involve pseudo-scientific jargon, purloined from chemistry and physics, about radiation, atomic energy, and the like. 'Religion and science, viewed broadly, do not clash so much as they combine,' she wrote. 'To the devout and deeply studious mind, the marvels of science are the truths of religion made manifest.'[54] She abhorred the unethical implications inherent in the random aspects of the Darwinian theory of natural selection; on the contrary, God was in charge, and the Law of Nature was God's Law. 'You should study science, it is such a fascinating and romantic thing,' she advised an admirer, before recounting how she once visited Professor Sir William Crookes: 'He showed me a row of crystals hanging from a line; by directing a beam of powerful electric light upon these glasses he played the musical scale. It was to demonstrate how light evolves sound.'[55] No doubt, the gallant scientist enjoyed putting on this party trick for a diminutive authoress who liked to dress as 'Pansy'; yet the great experimentalist further made 'excursions into psychical research'. These brought him much criticism, but 'he thought all phenomena worthy of investigation and refused to be bound by tradition and convention'.[56] In her own scatterbrained way, Corelli took all this on board, then simplified it. There was only 'one Light, containing in itself both the divine and human essence of absolute power, wisdom, and purity. The power . . . is obtainable, but only through absolute faith in Christ.'[57] This conviction remained with her, even strengthening through age, until in 1919 she wrote: 'there is a much Higher Hand moving behind the scenes of this wild scrimmage of misrule, disorder, and immorality, and what the world dreams of, is *imminent*! I cannot tell or know *what* it is, but I *feel* it!—and "Blessed is he who when his Lord cometh is found *watching*".'[58] Corelli's Electric Christianity gave Bernard Shaw much amusement; but it was entirely genuine, he had concluded in 1897. Corelli was 'the apostle of romantic religion', glorifying the miraculous with almost medieval superstition and, fired by an uncontrollable imagination, painting its marvels in luminous colour.[59] Previously, in the late 1880s, when he reviewed novels for the *Pall Mall Gazette*, Shaw had recommended to Corelli, as also to Ouida, that they take a course in political economy. Now, he realized that, in Corelli's case at least, he was dealing with a metaphysical condition of an incurable kind.[60]

[53] Marie Corelli, 'The Lady with the Carnations', *Cameos* (1919), 119.
[54] Corelli, 'Society and Sunday', *Free Opinions*, 236.   [55] Scott, *Corelli*, 166.
[56] *DNB 1912–1921*, 136–7, and *Who Was Who, 1916–1928*, 247–8, for Crookes (1832–1919).
[57] Scott, *Corelli*, 56.   [58] Letter, 11 Mar. 1919, in Scott, *Corelli*, 95.
[59] Review of the stage adaptation of *The Sorrows of Satan*, 16 Jan. 1897, in Shaw, *Plays and Players*, 161–9.
[60] Holroyd, *Shaw*, i. 210, 342.

Corelli's Christian faith was both strong and strange. As a child, she believed passionately in angels, was privileged to have visitations from them, heard voices, and had visions. She said of her convent period: 'I became for a time so absorbed in the mysteries of the religious life, that I had some vague idea of founding a "New Order" and of being the leader of an entirely original community of Christian workers, who should indeed follow Christ in spirit and in truth.'[61] Corelli did not establish her own Order but she did consider herself part of one. Without naming it, she outlined her beliefs and practice for the vicar of Stratford upon Avon in 1900:

I am one of a very numerous 'fraternity' (we are, perhaps, between 50,000 and 100,000 altogether)—who are bound to try our best to follow the teachings of Christ as enunciated by Himself—and we are not, by the rules of our Order, allowed to attend public worship, 'That we may be seen of men' . . . We are all at one in our Faith in the Divinity of Jesus Christ and His Message, as being the only way to truth and life; of final salvation, so far as this earth and its inhabitants are concerned, and any doubter of this first grand principle would be requested to resign his or her membership. But we do not accept any of the Church forms. We simply, as far as it is humanly possible to do, obey the *words of Christ* as spoken by Himself—even at all risk of inconvenience to ourselves and misjudgment by our friends.

With regard to the Scriptures, I do not think any *woman* has ever studied them so deeply and devoutly as I have, or, let me say, *more* deeply and devoutly.

I have had the advantage of the teaching of one of the finest Hebrew scholars in Europe, and he has instructed me as to the actual weight and symbolic meaning of every word and line. My religion is *my very life*—I have no thought without it, or beyond it . . . [62]

The ultimate test came in 1911 when Corelli had tea with the octogenarian leader of the Salvation Army, William Booth. The 'General' was enamoured by her combination of gaiety and dedication: 'She was far more free, friendly, and gossipy than I expected to find her; more interested in the Army she could not have seemed to be, and promised to write something when there is an opportunity.'[63] Corelli's track record belied Booth's expectation of acquiring another convert. In spite of their having much common ground—that 'the Soul of the Nation is . . . starving to the point of inanition in all forms of spiritual food', and that the 'Spirit of the Ideal is crushed and kept down by the iron hand of Materialism'—Corelli averred that the 'way out of the labyrinth' would be neither through the established churches nor 'by "revival" meetings or Salvationist assemblies'. 'Why should there by followers of Luther, Wesley, or any other limited human preacher or teacher', she asked, 'when all that is necessary is that we should be followers of Christ?'[64]

The singularity of Corelli's religious position did not disturb her public. Much like Hall Caine, who also emphasized the gospel uncomplicated by ecclesiastical

[61] Quoted in Carr, *Corelli*, 12.
[62] Corelli to the Revd Arbuthnot, 28 Apr. 1900, quoted in Vyver, *Corelli*, 167–8.
[63] Begbie, *Booth*, ii. 411.   [64] Corelli, 'The Soul of the Nation', in Corelli, *Free Opinions*, 340–53.

ceremony and formulary, she appealed to the widest audience—including many ministers of different denominations. Each had their clerical critics, of course. Anthony Deane, newly ordained in the Church of England and ambitious to make his own reputation as an author, wrote what he later acknowledged to have been a 'truculent' attack on the 'religious' novels of both Corelli and Caine for the *National Review* in the late 1890s;[65] yet, when Raymond Blathwayt made a study of 'England's Taste in Literature' in 1911, he was told that Corelli held a peculiar appeal for Anglican clergy.[66] *Punch*'s reviewer of *Barabbas* (1893) had been wide of the mark when he stated that he 'cannot imagine that this novel form of treating Holy Writ will ever be popular with any section of our ordinary reading public'; and he predicted that her publisher would come a cropper with it.[67] Instead, Corelli's rendering of the Resurrection in *Barabbas* was read from the pulpit on Easter Sunday at Westminster Abbey by the Dean.[68] Leading Nonconformist ministers, the Independent Baptist Charles Spurgeon, the Wesleyan Hugh Price Hughes, and the Congregationalist Joseph Parker corresponded with her and used her work as texts for sermons.[69] She was pressed to open a great bazaar in aid of Congregational and Baptist funds, held in the Brighton Dome in November 1902. Corelli pulled out at the last moment, after reading a press report in which a Methodist minister took issue with her latest work, *Temporal Power*. It is difficult to judge the more striking characteristic involved in this episode: Corelli's hypersensitivity to criticism or her ignorance. She appeared to have little idea what Nonconformity represented, let alone what distinguished Baptism or Congregationalism from Methodism.[70] Still, Corelli had enjoyed a wide range of clerical support. Even the Anglo-Catholic priesthood responded, Father Ignatius calling her 'A prophet in our Israel':[71]

Thousands and tens of thousands throughout English-speaking Christendom will bless the author who has dared to pen the pages of *The Sorrows of Satan*; they will bless Marie Corelli's pen, respecting its denunciation of the blasphemous verses of a certain 'popular British poet' [Swinburne]. Where did the courage come from that made her pen so bold that the personality of God, the divinity of Christ, the sanctity of marriage, the necessity of religious education should thus crash upon you from the pen of a woman?[72]

---

[65] Deane, *Time Remembered*, 84–5.

[66] *Fortnightly Review* (Jan. 1912), 160–71. Blathwayt (1855–1935) was well able to judge this point: his father was a clergyman and he too had been ordained.   [67] *Punch*, 28 Oct. 1893, 198.

[68] Vyver, *Corelli*, 166.

[69] Scott, *Corelli*, 28; Coates and Bell, *Corelli*, 309–10. The editor of the *British Weekly*, Robertson Nicoll, wrote to Corelli on 3 November 1920: 'I always think of you in connexion with my old friend Dr. Parker, who liked nothing so much as to lie on his sofa and hear your books read to him' (quoted in Darlow, *Nicoll*, 297). The chairman of the Congregational Union, Parker, who died in 1902, ministered at the City Temple.

[70] Scott, *Corelli*, 121–9. Scott, a Congregationalist minister himself, was particularly qualified to pronounce about Corelli's ignorance of Nonconformity.   [71] Scott, *Corelli*, 23.

[72] Coates and Bell, *Corelli*, 152. The animus against Swinburne—'this satyr-songster . . . [whose] works have been deadlier than the deadliest poison, and far more soul-corrupting than any book of Zola's or the most pernicious of modern French writers'—which Corelli expressed in *The Sorrows of Satan* (see esp. pp. 325–7), marks a contrast with, for example, *Thelma* (1887), where she had deployed his verses as

This was before Corelli's anti-Romanism was made explicit in *The Master-Christian*. However, because that book's main theme was religious hypocrisy, it could be read as a commination against all organized or established churches. Corelli prefaced it with a dedication: 'To All Those Churches Who Quarrel In The Name of Christ'. Her semi-official biographers, Thomas Coates and R. S. Warren Bell,[73] in 1903 denied that the novel was

a bitter attack upon the Roman Catholic faith . . . If the man-made portion of the Roman Catholic dogma has hidden the teachings of Christ on which that Church was founded, that is the fault and the misfortune of the Church of Rome, and not of Marie Corelli, who is bold enough to speak the truth about the matter. That faith in God which is her stand-by is what she would wish to see in the ministry of the Roman Catholic Church, instead of, as she fears, a mere degenerate, priest-built, superstitious reliance upon symbolic shams.[74]

Corelli unbuttoned herself elsewhere too: in 'Pagan London', 'A Question of Faith', and 'Unchristian Clerics', articles that appeared in periodicals both at home and in America and were republished as *Free Opinions, Freely Expressed on Certain Phases of Modern Social Life and Conduct* (1905). She denounced most church-based religion, especially communions involving ornate ritual and ministerial authority.[75] 'Personally', she wrote, 'I have no more objection or dislike to Romanism than I have to any other "ism" ever formulated'—except that, in Corelli's view, Romanism was not so much a form of faith as 'an intolerant system of secret Government'.[76]

Corelli's animosity towards Catholicism had not been previously so exceptional and sharp. Indeed, the eponymous heroine of *Thelma: A Norwegian Princess* is a Catholic, a consequence of her having received a French convent education. 'My mother came from Arles,' she explains, whereupon the hero and her eventual husband—Sir Philip Bruce Errington, Baronet—cross-examines her:

'She was French, then?' he exclaimed with some surprise.

'No', she answered gravely. 'She was Norwegian, because her father and mother both were of this land. She was what they call "born sadly". You must not ask me any more about her, please!'[77]

chapter epigraphs. Previously, in her musician phase, Swinburne had given her two poems to set to music. It is likely that she was ignorant of much of Swinburne's work before the 1890s and until his name was being canvassed as a successor to Tennyson as laureate, when she was pushing the claims of her half-brother Eric Mackay.

[73] Thomas F. G. Coates was the author of a Life of the Prime Minister, Rosebery. R. S. Warren Bell (1871–1921) was the son of a clergyman, whose ministry was at Henley-in-Arden, near Stratford, where Corelli lived. Bell got to know Corelli thereby. A one-time schoolmaster who was also a minor novelist writing mostly for youngsters, Bell became first editor (1899–1910) of *Captain: A Magazine for Boys and Old Boys* (see Sutherland, *Companion*, 56–7). It is perhaps an index of Corelli's decline in reputation that Bell listed the biographical study of Corelli among his publications in his earlier entry in *Who's Who*, e.g. *Who's Who* (1905), 116, but omitted it from later editions (see *Who Was Who, 1916–1928*, 79). For a predictably withering reception of Coates and Bell, *Corelli*, see *Punch*, 1 July 1903, 452.

[74] Coates and Bell, *Corelli*, 211–12.   [75] Corelli, 'Pagan London', in Corelli, *Free Opinions*, 32.
[76] Corelli, 'A Question of Faith', ibid. 51–3.   [77] Corelli, *Thelma*, 141.

Corelli's romance about her own origins was reflected here, and again in Errington's admission that his own 'mother was an Austrian and a Catholic, and I have a notion that as a small child I was brought up in that creed; but I'm afraid I don't know much about it now'.[78] Still, the principal villain in book 1 of *Thelma* is an anti-Romanist preacher. He, a Lutheran clergyman, the Revd Charles Dyceworthy, is exposed as a hypocrite who lusts after Thelma and, when sottish, 'says all religion is nonsense, fable, imposture'.[79] Later in the story he is reported as having been drummed out of his parish in Yorkshire 'for carrying on love-affairs with the women of his congregation', then fetched up as a rabble-rousing street preacher in Glasgow, before being sentenced to a month's hard labour for 'drunken, disorderly, and indecent conduct'. Will that be the end of him, therefore? ' "Don't be too sure of that!" said Sandy cautiously. "There's always America, you know. He can make a holy martyr of himself there! He may gain as big a reputation as Henry Ward Beecher—you can never tell what may happen—'t is a queer world!" '[80] This Sandy Macfarlane, one of Errington's close friends, personifies Corelli's alternative vision of a true ministry. He sacrifices a bequest of £70,000 (a multi-million-pound fortune nowadays) in order to settle in 'one of the lowest streets in the East-end of London . . . where there's misery, starvation, and crime of all sorts'. His aim is first to befriend the heathen poor rather than to preach to them—'there's too much of that and tract-giving already . . . I would remind you that Christ himself gave sympathy to begin with,—He did the preaching afterwards.' Macfarlane has rejected the regular ministry, such as 'the Established Kirk', as 'useless': he doesn't want to be 'one of those douce, cannie, comfortable bodies that drone in the pulpit about predestination and original sin, and so forth,—a sort of palaver that does no good to any reasonable creature'. In fact, Macfarlane declares that the person who set him thinking about these things was Thelma's father, who is a frank pagan— Corelli invents for him a mishmash of Norse mythology, comprising Odin, Thor, and all, for a credo—on the ground that 'he's better worthy respect than many a so-called Christian'.[81] Likewise, Errington confesses,

I suppose I should call myself a Christian, though, judging from the behaviour of Christians in general, I cannot be one of them after all,—for I belong to no sect, I go to no church, and I have never read a tract in my life. I have a profound reverence and admiration for the character and doctrine of Christ, and I believe if I had had the privilege of knowing and conversing with Him, I should not have deserted Him in extremity as His timorous disciples did. I believe in an all-wise Creator . . .[82]

At this stage of Corelli's career, then, Catholicism had not been singled out more than any other institutionalized church for special execration. Her main purpose in *Thelma* was to expose the corrupt soul of Society. That all religion counts for nothing other than for show is the thrust of her indictment; but, since an old English Catholic aristocracy survived and was supplemented during the

---

[78] Corelli, *Thelma*, 80. [79] Ibid. 93. [80] Ibid. 522–3. [81] Ibid. 519–21.
[82] Ibid. 80.

III

Who constituted Corelli's readers? Coates and Bell observed that there was

a very big public which has practically nothing to do except eat meals, sleep, take exercise, and read novels. Such people are necessarily more introspective than busy folk, and many of them are exceedingly anxious as to what will become of them when it shall please Providence to put an end to their aimless existence in this vale of smiles and tears. Marie Corelli supplies them with ample food for thought and argument.[102]

That Corelli's public was vast, even worldwide, none could doubt. Coates and Bell stated in 1903 that *Barabbas* had been 'translated into more foreign tongues than any other novel of either past or present—the translations comprising thirty to forty languages'. They considered her 'perhaps the most extensively read of living novelists in Holland, Russia, Germany and Austria'. Some books, because of their location or theme, had special vogue in different countries. In India it was *Barabbas* and *A Romance of Two Worlds*, both having been translated into Hindustani; in Scandinavia, *Thelma*; in Italy, *Vendetta*; and in France, *Wormwood* (*Absinthe* in the French version). Still,

there is no country where her name is unknown, and no European city, where, if she chances to pass through, she is not besieged with visitors and waylaid with offerings of flowers. Were she to visit Australia or New Zealand she would receive an almost 'royal' welcome, so great is the enthusiasm in the 'New World' for anything that comes from her pen.[103]

A Corelli City was planned in Colorado, in the United States.

Corelli's global audience was amassed almost entirely by means of the printed word. She wrote articles and the occasional short story for newspapers and periodicals; otherwise, she issued books. She resisted having her novels published in serial form. This was unlike Hall Caine; also unlike his novels, Corelli's never really made it to the stage. Her attitude to the theatre and thespians was no more consistent than to most anything else. She told the Revd W. Stuart Scott, 'When Dr. Mackay sent me to the convent in France I was destined for the stage. I should have been there today had it not been that Dr. Mackay fell ill.'[104] This was a different fantasy from her usual claim that she was originally destined for fame as a professional musician. Her first entry in *Who's Who*, in 1897, stated that 'she is extremely fond of the theatre, and takes the keenest interest in the principal dramatic events of the day'; a declaration retained in 1898, then omitted in 1899 and thereafter.[105] 'Faked women' was how she styled actresses, which led to lively exchanges in the *Daily Express* in 1904;[106] yet she invited most stage stars,

---

[102] Coates and Bell, *Corelli*, 113–14.
[103] Ibid. 141, 326–7. See also Carr, *Corelli*, 60–5, for her worldwide sales. Carr mentions Spanish and Persian translations; also that she was popular among combatants on both sides in the Boer War.
[104] Scott, *Corelli*, 112.   [105] *Who's Who* (1897), 254; (1898), 290.
[106] On which, see *Punch*, 10 Aug. 1904, 97.

among them Sarah Bernhardt,[107] to her home, Mason Croft, when they were playing in Stratford; she counted Constance Collier and Lilian Baylis among her friends; she even spoke well of the American beauty Mary Anderson. Mrs Patrick Campbell too got in her good books by reciting at the Alhambra a Christmas Message from Corelli, to benefit a Great War charity. As for Ellen Terry, Corelli idolized her: when inducing her to visit, she composed 'perhaps the only truly humble note she ever wrote to anyone'. She also gave Terry some turquoise earrings, saying that they were 'specially precious' because presented by Mrs Siddons to her mother.[108] The question of the theatre and morality, however, brought out the contradictions in Corelli. In one breath she defended the acting profession against the censures of Grundyism and scorned bowdlerized versions of Shakespeare; in another, she deplored 'the sham, paint and tawdry hypocrisy of the modern stage!!', and denounced it as a 'hot-bed of vice and shame'.[109] The position she had reached by the time her will was declared was that her home should be preserved to provide hospitality to distinguished visitors 'for the promotion of Science Literature and Music among the people of Stratford', but 'absolutely excluding actors actresses and all persons connected with the stage'.[110]

An exception to the otherwise complete absence of the Corelli opera from the stage was a production of *The Sorrows of Satan*. Dramatized by Herbert Woodgate and Paul M. Berton, it opened at the Shaftesbury Theatre on 9 January 1897. Neither Lewis Waller as Prince Lucio Rimanez (the Devil) nor Yorke Stephens as Geoffrey Tempest could rescue it from derision, Bernard Shaw noting that Stephens played his role 'with the air of a man who has resolved to shoot himself the moment the curtain is down'.[111] This failure mortified Corelli: it was her brother Eric who arranged the adaptation.[112] She received £500 'for the use of her name', but the disastrous production made managers thereafter wary of adaptations from her work.[113] Corelli never succeeded in adapting one of her own novels for the West End theatre.[114] There is circumstantial evidence that this was not for want of trying.[115] She once excitedly told Bertha Vyver that Lillie Langtry wished to discuss a staging of *Vendetta*, with Langtry herself keen to play the heroine Nina Romani. Corelli had actually dedicated *Vendetta* to the actor–manager Wilson Barrett, 'whose Genius needs no flattery'—a blatant solicitation.[116] Two copyright performances were arranged: for *The Master-Christian* at the Grand,

---

[107] See Corelli, *Free Opinions*, 215, for a compliment paid to Bernhardt.
[108] Scott, *Corelli*, 21, 84, 112.   [109] Ibid. 113.
[110] Masters, *Corelli*, 285; and Scott, *Corelli*, 270, for the will.
[111] Shaw, *Plays and Players*, 169. Corelli afterwards believed that Shaw plagiarized *The Sorrows of Satan* (1895) for *The Devil's Disciple* (1896); see Masters, *Corelli*, 218.   [112] Masters, *Corelli*, 151–2.
[113] Scott, *Corelli*, 159. Corelli herself had hoped to persuade Beerbohm Tree to stage *The Sorrows of Satan* at the Haymarket, according to Sidney Dark, who as a drama critic was privy to theatre gossip. Dark, *Mainly about Other People*, 88.
[114] Corelli, for instance, merited no entry in the first *Who's Who in the Theatre* (1912), edited by John Parker.   [115] Howard, *Motley Life*, 135.
[116] Scott, *Corelli*, 112, 157. A dramatization by Neville Doone eventually made the stage at Kennington, on 28 March 1904, but got no further; Nicoll, *English Drama*, 611.

Leeds, on 18 August 1900, and for *Temporal Power* at the Royalty, Morecambe, on 23 August 1902.[117] These readings, to secure legal protection, never led to commercial performance.

The authorized version, given by Corelli's companion Bertha Vyver, was that she only once attempted to dramatize one of her books. This was *Barabbas*, for Wilson Barrett; but it allegedly fell foul of the Lord Chamberlain's office, which banned the representation of biblical subjects. Later, Corelli discountenanced a film of it, the request having come from the painter Hubert von Herkomer, who was experimenting in cinematograph production at his Bushey school of art.[118] In 1913 Corelli did, however, provide another film script for Herkomer, which was prized by his son Siegfried. It was, he wrote, 'the simplest of love-tales'. Because the script was 'entirely free from sensationalism'—an almost unnatural achievement for Corelli—he lauded her as 'a dramatic futurist'; by which he meant, not only had she glimpsed how film focused on 'deeds rather than words and idle introspection', but she 'contrived to suggest, in a dozen different visually obvious ways, the mental incentive that actuates each character in the piece'.[119] Apparently, Corelli made a present of this to Herkomer; and, according to Scott, she also 'sold for a song' the film rights to *Vendetta*, *Temporal Power*, and *The Treasure of Heaven*.[120] Unauthorized adaptations of *The Sorrows of Satan* went into production in 1911 and 1916, and the influential Danish director Carl Theodor Dreyer loosely based *Leaves from Satan's Book* on the same story in 1919;[121] but it was not until 1926 that D. W. Griffiths gave it the full Hollywood treatment.[122] Adaptations of *Thelma* had also been made, in 1916, 1918, and 1922; *Holy Orders* in 1917, *God's Good Man* in 1919, and *Innocent* in 1921, the last two by the Stoll picture company, which yielded £1,300 to her estate.[123]

Corelli had, then, acquired her popularity largely through the conventional printed media. In Britain it was commonly supposed that her public was predominantly middle-class and above. In 1906 Hubert Bland, no admirer, qualified this, judging that Corelli's readership was not confined to a particular class so much as to persons of a certain type and tastes in every class. He still reckoned that more working-class than middle-class readers shunned her books. This was speculation, reflecting the Fabians' assumptions about culture, rather than the fruits of any audience survey.[124] Corelli's devotees nonetheless argued likewise. For them, it was a certificate of her merit that the middle classes and people of superior education mainly bought her books. There is indirect evidence to support this view. Corelli's publishers did not issue her in cheap sixpenny form until the end of the Edwardian period, and it was mostly middle- and upper-class

---

[117] Nicoll, *English Drama*, 576. See also Scott, *Corelli*, 156, 160, 237–8, for her involvement in (and brushes with) Edwardian variety theatre and music hall; and Ransom, *Corelli*, 152–3, for her efforts to check unauthorized American adaptations.   [118] Vyver, *Corelli*, 134–7.

[119] Quoted in Scott, *Corelli*, 160.   [120] Ibid. 161.   [121] Robinson, *World Cinema*, 85.

[122] Ransom, *Corelli*, 154–5, for the legal actions taken by Corelli.   [123] Masters, *Corelli*, 286.

[124] Ian Britain, *Fabianism and Culture* (Cambridge, 1982), 255.

purses that controlled the six-shilling novel market. In Switzerland in 1908 Arnold
Bennett met in his hotel an Anglo-Indian army major with the usual 'brick-
coloured face', 'monotonous voice', and 'excellent stupidity which commands
respect'. Bennett thought of engaging his opinions about Indian government
reform until he noticed the book which the major was reading. It was Corelli's
Holy Orders (1908), whereupon, Bennett recorded, 'I then gave up hope.'[125]

In trying to identify who read Corelli there is borrowing as well as buying to
conjure with. There were many different kinds of libraries, including the floating
sort; and the Seamen's Mission appealed for donations of Corelli novels because
they were so popular among men at sea.[126] As for the subscription libraries, the
secretary of Boots' Book-Lovers Library declared in 1911 that Boots never stocked
fewer than 2,000 copies of every new book Corelli published.[127] The pattern in
the free public libraries appeared the same. The son of a Belfast shipyard worker,
W. Stuart Scott as a boy was captivated by Corelli, but his pursuit of her books
through the public library in the early 1900s was invariably frustrated because
they were 'out'.[128] Corelli herself regarded public libraries as a scourge. They
deprived authors of royalties, sapped working-class providence, and spread
germs; and she roundly abused their principal benefactor, Andrew Carnegie.[129]
Yet, it was said of the free libraries in 1903 that 'the Corelli novels are in as
constant demand wherever books are to be obtained for nothing, as at railway
bookstalls, where there is not a halfpenny abatement of the full published
price'.[130] This corroborated a survey made by the librarian of Bootle in 1897,
concerning reading habits in the free libraries of twenty-seven medium-sized and
small towns. It emerged that Corelli was the most popular author in eleven of
these, running second overall only behind Mrs Henry Wood, who was pre-
eminent in sixteen places. Corelli's scrapbook contained a magazine article from
July 1906 which put her way ahead of all other contemporary authors, with
annual book sales of 100,000. A straggling second was Hall Caine, 45,000; third,
Kipling, 40,000; then Mrs Humphry Ward, 35,000; followed by a queer mix, Mary
Cholmondeley, Marion Crawford, John Oliver Hobbes, and W. W. Jacobs, each
above 20,000; and Conan Doyle and H. G. Wells with 'a steady annual 15,000'.[131]
This was an angled snapshot—it ignored the vast novelette and paperback sales of
Charles Garvice or Nat Gould—but it captured Corelli probably at the summit of
her success. Signs of decline were contained in a Birmingham newspaper report,
in February 1914, which also found its way into her scrapbook, indicating that the
city's bookshops had overstocked Corelli and were slashing the prices of her
novels.[132] Still other evidence indicated that a demand was sustained, both in
time and across the length of Britain. In 1915, when Harmsworth's were planning
a new weekly, the *Sunday Pictorial*, they approached the literary agent J. B. Pinker

[125] Flower (ed.), *Bennett Journals*, i. 302 (17 Dec. 1908).   [126] Scott, *Corelli*, 28.
[127] Raymond Blathwayt, 'England's Taste in Literature', *Fortnightly Review* (Jan. 1912), 160–71.
[128] Scott, *Corelli*, 43.   [129] On this, see above, Ch. 2.   [130] Coates and Bell, *Corelli*, 325–6.
[131] Scott, *Corelli*, 233.   [132] Ibid. 238.

with a view to securing some star contributions for the first issue; and the names they had in mind were Marie Corelli and Rider Haggard.[133] Again, in 1917, the Carnegie Trust, which was now promoting free libraries in rural areas, noted that in the north of Scotland Corelli was one of the most popular authors, along with Ethel M. Dell, Rider Haggard, W. W. Jacobs, Jack London, and Baroness Orczy.[134]

This ubiquitousness of popular choice possibly reflected an increasing standardization of taste under the impress of marketing. In the final chapter of *Lark Rise to Candleford* (1939–43), entitled 'Change in the Village', Flora Thompson ended her account of small market town and village life in the late Victorian and Edwardian period by describing the Green family, whom she placed in 'the lower fringe of the lower middle class'. They occupied one of the new houses springing up, were home-proud, and 'had a great dislike of common things and especially of common people'. They were not comfortably off, for Mr Green, who was a Post Office clerk, earned around £2 a week; and, though they were nominally Christian believers, 'in reality, their creed was that of keeping up appearances. The reading they did was mass reading. Before they would open a book, they had to be told it was one that everybody was reading. The works of Marie Corelli and Nat Gould were immensely popular with them.'[135]

Corelli, then, was read by all social classes, with perhaps a preponderance in that expanding group of aspiring upper-working class and lower-middle class; but it was certainly the middle classes and, especially, the literary classes who were most vocal in proclaiming or questioning Corelli's quality. Hesketh Pearson related how Corelli was the cause of his parting company with a former schoolfriend in 1906–7. This friend responded monosyllabically to Pearson's attempts to involve him in discussion about politics, religion, literature, and the theatre. The crunch came during a walk on Hampstead Heath. Pearson made his final effort: 'Do you ever read anything?' 'Yes.' 'What?' 'Marie Corelli.'[136] The school friendship was outgrown. It was with similar scorn that James Elroy Flecker wrote that Marie Corelli was 'the novelist of the people', as 'their poet [was] Ella Wheeler Wilcox, their artist Blair Leighton, their musician Paul Rubens'. He regarded it as a sure mark of the incompetence of ordinary people to judge quality that 'they honestly think Miss Corelli profound, Miss Wilcox passionate, Mr B. Leighton chivalrous, and Mr Rubens lyrical and sparkling...But if the middle classes should exclaim "Our gods are better than these", I should reply that the devotees of Robert Hichens and the thumpers of Rachmaninoff

---

[133] Pinker disabused Harmsworth's of the idea of securing Corelli (whose agent was A. P. Watt) and proposed H.G. Wells and Arnold Bennett from his own stable. In the end Bennett recorded, 'the *Sunday Pictorial*'s star trio was me, Horatio Bottomley and Austin Harrison!' (Flower (ed.), *Bennett Journals*, ii. 125 (13 Mar. 1915)).

[134] Kelly, *Public Libraries*, 193, 215. See also Sichel, *Sands of Time*, 225, for an anecdote about Corelli's popularity among ordinary Scottish folk.

[135] Thompson, *Lark Rise*, 550–4. For Nat Gould, see below, Ch. 23.

[136] *Hesketh Pearson by Himself*, 84–5.

preludes are in a far worse case . . .'.[137] Flecker was endeavouring to be impartial in his contempt for popular taste across the classes; and the same obtained, in typically more belligerent manner, when the Vorticists came to plan the first number of *Blast* for 20 June 1914. The editorial meeting, presided over by Wyndham Lewis and Ezra Pound, drew up a hit-list of persons to be blown up— those 'whose publicity was considered boringly excessive'. This again featured Corelli, albeit this time in incongruous company with the two Beechams (the Pill and Sir Thomas), 'the Bishop of London and all his posterity' (the bishop was a bachelor), the Italian liberal philosopher Benedetto Croce, the entire clans of Meynells, Stracheys, and Thesigers, A. C. Benson, John Galsworthy, Sidney Webb, and 'an unidentified lady named Ella', whom Douglas Goldring, involved in the business production, took to be Wheeler Wilcox.[138] Leaving aside the other well-advertised individuals who excited the blasters' wrath, if Corelli was once more harnessed with Mrs Wilcox, it is some testimony to her worldwide fame because, according to *The Times*'s estimation on her death in 1919, Mrs Wilcox was 'the most popular poet of either sex and of any age, read by thousands who never open Shakespeare'.[139] Mrs Wilcox was American, but her vogue in England was enormous. When she visited in 1913, she was presented at court; yet she also understood her place in the pecking order. Invited to Mason Croft, she paid homage to Corelli by kneeling at her feet.[140]

Academic interest in Corelli was not naturally keen. This only goes to prove, 'funny thing the Life Scholarly, as M. Corelli would call it!'[141] So Walter Raleigh, Professor of English Literature at Oxford, remarked. He met Corelli in 1902. Raleigh liked leading fools on, and he proposed that she should write 'a book in defence of Shakespeare'. He also thought of another

three things to say to her and they all suited very well:

    (1) 'O Miss Corelli, how *do* you think of all those lovely things?'
    (2) 'O Miss Corelli, since I read *Barabbas*, I think that Christianity is just too sweet!'

---

[137] 'The Public as Art Critic', in Flecker, *Collected Prose*, 248–9. For Edmund Blair Leighton (1853–1922), whose sentimental paintings were much reproduced in photogravures and engravings, see *Who Was Who, 1916–1928*, 620; and for Paul Alfred Rubens (1875–1917), composer of songs for a string of popular musical comedies, *Florodora* (1899), *Country Girl* (1902), etc., see *Who Was Who, 1916–1928*, 915, and Peter Gammond, *The Oxford Companion to Popular Music* (Oxford, 1991), 507. Rubens was not just a popular favourite, he was a Society favourite too; see Viscount Esher's account of an evening organized by Alfred Rothschild in 1903, when his party attended the theatre, then supped at the Carlton Club, where they heard Paul Rubens and his brother give a piano recital; Brett, *Esher*, i. 402 (6 May 1903). Rubens was at Oxford, at University College, in the 1890s: see Howard, *Motley Life*, 91–2, for a reminiscence.

[138] Goldring, *South Lodge*, 67–9. On *Blast*, see Alvin Sullivan (ed.), *British Literary Magazines: The Modern Age, 1914–1984* (1986), 61–9.

[139] *The Times*, 31 Oct. 1919, quoted in Harvey, *Companion*, 850. The poetry of Mrs Wheeler Wilcox (1850–1919) was formulaic—: 'Poems of Pleasure', 'Poems of Passion', 'Poems of Hope', 'Poems of Experience', 'Poems of Progress', 'Poems of Love', 'Poems of Cheer', etc. Her most memorable lines (from *Solitude*)—'Laugh and the world laughs with you; Weep, and you weep alone . . .'—share with cosmetic dentistry the primary responsibility for turning Western humanity into a grinning machine.

[140] Scott, *Corelli*, 25, 27, 256.

[141] Raleigh to John Sampson, 9 Dec. 1909, in Raleigh (ed.), *Raleigh Letters*, ii. 346. Cf. Corelli, 'The Happy Life', in Corelli, *Free Opinions*, 326–39, in which she waxed about 'the Life Literary'.

(3) 'O Miss Corelli, isn't it wonderful to know that there are thousands and thousands
of people in the world who have no ideas but what you put into their heads?'[142]

Later, after Raleigh had taken on journalists, editors, and proprietors in his
polemic *The War and the Press* (1918), he came to understand, if not appreciate,
Corelli a little more. Raleigh wrote to his publisher R. W. Chapman

You won't have noticed, nor will anyone, but no paper or journal or weekly that I have
seen has reviewed my last book. It occurred to me the other day that it's a boycott of
The War and the Press. This sort of boycott has happened to only one other writer that I
know of, Miss Marie Corelli, and for exactly similar reasons. *She was very angry.*[143]

The critics' rejection upset Corelli all the more because she considered herself
erudite. This raises questions about the provenance of her work. She was sitting
in a chair when she died in 1924, but at her bedside were 'a Tennyson, a Psalter,
Thackeray's *Vanity Fair* and Dante's *The New Life*'.[144] It is perhaps significant that
the last should have been in translation, because Corelli was apt to boast about
her facility in Italian as in French. Her detractors suspected both were as faulty as
her English; Dante, nonetheless, made an impression, Corelli admiring him for,
among other things, his defiance of critics. Corelli's authorized biographers at the
turn of the century assembled a bran-tub of her alleged favourite reading. As well
as Dante, the Bible, and Shakespeare, this included Balzac, Montaigne's essays,
Plato, and Sir Walter Scott.[145] A contrived air hangs over these compilations.
Corelli's show-off propensity was especially marked when she referred to the
recently dead Tennyson, in a preface to the second edition of *The Silver Domino*
(1892), 'whom I was privileged to call "friend" '—this on the strength of one letter
extracted from the Laureate in response to her sending him a copy of *Ardath*
(1889).[146] While vestiges of great authors' works may be traced in her writings,
their importance to her is demonstrable largely in her eagerness to follow in the
footprints of their fame, even to step into their shoes. She may, for instance, have
been charged by the emotional power of the Brontë sisters' novels, yet perhaps
even more by the story of their lives, their emergence from obscurity to classic
status. Corelli's Shakespearean fixation was of the same order. No doubt she knew
her Shakespeare, whose sonnets she imitated. She was ever ready to sound off
about (mis)interpretations of his work in productions at the Memorial Theatre;
but her decision to live in Stratford involved a design to occupy his limelight. She
bought an oak refectory table supposedly used by Shakespeare and a painting
allegedly of his daughter.[147] Ultimately, all reputations were grist to her own mill.
Thus, when she lectured in Northampton Town Hall on the subject of 'Work',
and proclaimed 'We have today no Scott, Thackeray, or Dickens', it was with the
expectation that her audience would as one cry out, 'But we've got *you*, Miss!'[148]

---

[142] Raleigh to Mrs Dowdall, 9 Mar. 1902, in Raleigh (ed.), *Raleigh Letters*, i. 238–9.
[143] Raleigh to R. W. Chapman, 30 Jan. 1919, ibid. 505.   [144] Scott, *Corelli*, 199.
[145] Carr, *Corelli*, 73; Coates and Bell, *Corelli*, 316.   [146] Scott, *Corelli*, 82; and above, Ch. 10.
[147] Scott, *Corelli*, 200, 246.   [148] Ibid. 226. Scott pinched this joke from *Punch*, 25 Jan. 1905, 68.

Gossip had it that Corelli's merits were once debated in a London club. After an apologist observed that she had plenty of vitality, J. M. Barrie was said to have rejoindered: 'Very much alive—yes . . . But you see that's just what we are complaining about.'[149] It would be wrong to think of Corelli as an isolated figure in the literary world, however. She had been relatively quick to join the Society of Authors, in 1892; and, though slower to acquire a literary agent, she secured the formidable A. P. Watt in 1904.[150] Nor was she without friends and advocates among fellow authors. These included Coulson Kernahan, literary adviser to the publishers Ward, Lock & Tyler. He did not shirk controversy: he advised them to publish Wilde's *The Picture of Dorian Gray* in 1891.[151] This was hardly the sort of advice to commend him to Corelli, who waged war on degenerates; but Kernahan was skilled at keeping incompatible friendships, such as with the ravaged Swinburne during his Putney purdah.[152] Kernahan himself enjoyed large sales with *The Child, the Wise Man and The Devil* (1896);[153] and, like Corelli, he condemned spiritualism. Meeting him one day at Charing Cross station, G. K. Chesterton said, 'do you know I think that we are the only two men in Fleet Street who believe in God'.[154] Another of Corelli's literary friends and supporters was the novelist and biographer W. H. Wilkins, who collaborated with the widow and sister-in-law of the explorer and sensualist Sir Richard Burton in adapting for publication his unfinished work, especially the anti-Semitic treatise *The Jew, the Gypsy and El Islam* (1898).[155] A bachelor and strong Conservative, Wilkins was secretary of two of the earliest organizations to campaign for statutory restrictions on immigration and, as author of *The Alien Invasion* (1892), he warned against the free admission of diseased, lunatic, criminal, and destitute Jews, fleeing the pogroms in tsarist Russia, and against giving asylum to foreign revolutionaries, seeing this as 'a sign of the canker which in time ate away the heart' of the ancient Roman Empire.[156] Corelli too fancied herself in the part of Cassandra, denouncing 'the social blight' of 'atheism, infidelity, callousness and indifference to honourable principle,—the blight of moral cowardice, self-indulgence, vanity and want of heart'.[157] Anti-Semitism formed a very occasional

---

[149] Hichens, *Yesterday*, 92. The novelist Fred Benson also enjoyed reporting gossip about Corelli to his brother Arthur; see Newsome, *On the Edge of Paradise*, 191, 264.

[150] Those joining the Society of Authors at the same time as Corelli in 1892 were Samuel Butler, Anthony Hope, E. Phillips Oppenheim, Eden Phillpotts, Morley Roberts, Brandon Thomas, Arthur Waugh, and Israel Zangwill, an altogether bizarre party. See Bonham-Carter, *Authors by Profession*, 141. In her will Corelli made Watt's agency an executor; she also wished that the use of her home to provide hospitality for distinguished visitors to Stratford would be managed by trustees nominated by the Council of the Society of Authors. Scott, *Corelli*, 269–70.   [151] Hart-Davis (ed.), *Wilde's Letters*, 93.

[152] Watts-Dunton, *Old Familiar Faces*, 15–18.

[153] On Kernahan (1858–1943), see Sutherland, *Companion*, 350, and Kemp *et al.* (eds.), *Edwardian Fiction*, 222–3. Kernahan gave support to Corelli when the extent of Eric Mackay's misrepresentations of her became known; Masters, *Corelli*, 156–9.   [154] Ward, *Return to Chesterton*, 236.

[155] Farwell, *Burton*, 404–5.

[156] Quoted in Bernard Gainer, *The Alien Invasion* (1972), 127. Wilkins also wrote a number of Society novels, marked for their strong moral tone. On Wilkins (1860–1905), Sutherland, *Companion*, 674, and *DNB Supplement*, iii. 666–7.   [157] Corelli, 'The Social Blight', in Corelli, *Free Opinions*, 82.

and subordinate aspect of this theme. The novel *Temporal Power* features an unscrupulous press baron, David Jost—'the fat Jew-spider of several newspaper webs', Corelli terms him. Repeatedly he is styled 'Jost the Jew' as he flits in and out of the story; the physical description is repellent, with 'his little, swine-like eyes retreating under the crinkling fat of his lowering brows', and 'his life was black with villainy and intrigue of the most shameless kind'. These intrigues involve 'a carefully-concocted rumour of war . . . [that] had sent up certain stocks and shares in which he had a considerable interest', Jost acting in league with other 'Jew sharks, lying in wait among the dirty pools of speculation'. Corelli was here tapping into one seam of opposition to the Boer War, that it had been a ramp on behalf of the Randlords, owners of gold- and diamond mines in South Africa, among which Jewish names were prominent.

Characteristically, Corelli threw into the pot her own pet prejudices, for instance, against a national theatre, which in *Temporal Power* is also pictured as a 'project of various cogitating Jews', chorused by 'the Snob-world', all exploiting the gullibility of the masses.[158] As in her novels, so in her essays, Corelli deplored how

the men and women who are faithful, who hold the honour of their King dearer than their own lives, who refuse to truckle to the spirit of money-worship, and who presume to denounce the sickening hypocrisy of modern society and life and its shameless prostitution of high ideals, are 'hounded' by those portions of the Press which are governed by Jew syndicates, and slandered by every dirty cad that makes his cheap living by putting his hand secretly in his neighbour's pocket.[159]

It was these politics, among other qualities, that brought out another declared fan in Walter Sichel, ex-Harrow and Balliol, one-time editor of the monthly *Time* and failed Conservative candidate for the first London County Council in 1889. He met Corelli only once, at a wedding, but he fervently hoped that

at this hour of seditious internationalisms she would bend her talent to the theme of Bolshevism and track the subterranean ramifications of its hideous decadence . . . [Her] appeal would reach to the uttermost ends of the earth and be translated into every language . . . Miss Corelli would convert the thoughtless. By the mere throb and sob of her unreined style she might shatter the octopus tentacles of this neurotic monster.[160]

Corelli had a year to live when Sichel offered up this imprecation in 1923, and the spread of communism thus persisted unarrested by her pen.

Not only the politically conservative sang her praises. Two fellow authors at Methuen, Anthony Hope and Robert Hichens, were also publicized as admirers of Corelli.[161] In Hope's autobiography and in his authorized biography by Sir Charles Mallet, there is no reference to this; and in Hichens's memoirs, written in

---

[158] Marie Corelli, '*Temporal Power': A Study in Supremacy* (1902), 193, 298, 369–70, 373, 420.
[159] Corelli, 'The Vulgarity of Wealth', in Corelli, *Free Opinions*, 101.
[160] Sichel, *Sands of Time*, 225–6.
[161] Carr, *Corelli*, 67. Carr added that Corelli's friends included 'many of the French and Italian writers', without specifying names.

1942–3, by which time Corelli's reputation was risible, he was catty in his few remarks about her. Hichens did not remind the world how he had once swooned over *Boy* and cherished a vision of Corelli: 'People say she is small and fair. So she ought to be—a fairy stirring up the world with a wand dipped in ink.'[162] Hichens first met Corelli when they were both dinner guests of the Laboucheres. Here was another surprising connection: Henry Labouchere was a wit and political intriguer in the Liberal Party. He was also a religious sceptic, although in order to win Nonconformist votes alienated by Charles Bradlaugh, his atheist colleague in the constituency they both represented, he cheerfully called himself the 'Christian member for Northampton'. Labouchere offended the Queen by moving for reductions in Civil List expenditure; he also owned and edited the magazine *Truth*, dedicated to exposing financial malpractice and Society mischief. This made him a not altogether strange bedfellow for Corelli, who persistently ranted against a corrupt Society and business world and against court hangers-on and flunkeydom. She was equally persistently two-faced about such purveyors of gossip, however. In *Thelma* it is given as a sign of the unprincipled character of scheming Lady Winsleigh that *Truth* is displayed in her drawing room, where Mrs Rush-Marvelle, who for a hefty fee of 500 guineas acts as a marriage broker between a vulgar American heiress and a dim-witted aristocrat, 'amused herself by searching the columns of *Truth* for some new titbit of immorality connected with the royalty or nobility of England'.[163] *Truth*, and its prototype, Edmund Yates's *World*, Corelli tells us, are also avidly read in the servants' hall. Her account conveys a salivating censoriousness before, later in the story, she gathers herself up to occupy the moral high ground by inventing a particularly vicious scandalmongering journal, *Snake*, which publishes lies designed to ruin the spotless Thelma. It has been fed these by the roué Sir Francis Lennox, but Corelli tells the reader that its usual sources were

discarded valets or footmen, who came to gain half a crown or five shillings by offering information as to the doings of their late masters and mistresses,—shabby 'supers' from the theatres, who had secured the last bit of scandal concerning some celebrated stage or professional 'beauty'—sporting men and turf gamblers of the lowest class,—unsuccessful dramatists and small verse writers—these, with now and then a few 'ladies'—ladies of the bar-room, ballet, and *demi-monde*, were the sort of persons who daily sought private converse with Grubbs[164]—

that is, Mr Snawley–Grubbs, the weaselly proprietor–editor of *Snake*. With sadistic relish Corelli describes how the author Beau Lovelace horsewhips Grubbs in his office, thus avenging Thelma's honour.

Corelli nonetheless cemented her ties with Labouchere, who was an avid reader of romantic fiction. She would appear at his receptions, and there is a strong suspicion that he, as well as Corelli's putative half-brother Eric Mackay, collaborated in *The Silver Domino*, her anonymously published tirade against

---

[162] Masters, *Corelli*, 164.   [163] Corelli, *Thelma*, 298.   [164] Ibid. 536.

envious reviewers and other novelists' stock.[165] Discovering the principal author
was not difficult, but it added spice to Corelli's reputation, even making her a
suspect in 1894 when *The Green Carnation* was published anonymously too. This
wittily malicious portrait of the Wilde circle and salon London, which became the
talk of the town, addressed targets similar to those Corelli attacked; but its
lightness, smartness, and, above all, humour, were all qualities lacking in Corelli,
and its actual author was Robert Hichens. Still, it makes understandable
Labouchere's part in bringing Corelli and Hichens together. They afterwards
shared the same publisher, Methuen; indeed, Methuen's historian dubs Hichens the
'male Corelli'[166]—referring to his best-selling status as an overwrought romancer,
author of *The Garden of Allah* (1904) and more. Corelli herself professed shock at
Hichens's passionate stories. When a clergyman friend reported that his wife
'loved' them, she wrote incredulously: 'Does she *know* his most *salacious* (excuse
the word!) books?!! I won't believe it . . .'.[167] There was a certain lip-smacking
about Corelli's denunciation of Hichens's 'positively *wicked*' tales—and Hichens
himself became a personal favourite. She invited him to stay at Stratford, where she
drove him round in her carriage, showing him everything Shakespearean, then
over to Warwick Castle, where she appeared to have the run of the place, rooms as
well as grounds.[168] In 1909 Hichens would contribute to the celebration of Corelli
in a special edition of *The Bookman*.[169] This was put together by A. St John Adcock,
one of the magazine's editors, who had written novels about East End slum life and
the Boer War.[170] Corelli's enormous readership lay not just in lowbrow suburbia,
Adcock noted; it was an 'easily discoverable fact that many of her most enthusiastic
admirers are men of the professional classes—doctors, barristers, lawyers, writers,
men of education and intelligence'. All this, he argued, 'brings one to realise that
the ridicule and petty abuse she has had to endure have been but the loud noise of a
small minority, even of the critics'. Plainly considering himself both an intellectual
and a fastidious critic, Adcock was prepared to stick his neck out:

I can speak only for myself and say that highest of all her novels, and with the few living
novels of our time, I rank 'Ardath', 'Barabbas', 'Thelma' and 'The Sorrows of Satan'.
The conception of Satan, in the latter, is as magnificent as it is strikingly original. I know of
nothing to compare with it, for its forcefulness and shadowed majesty, in modern fiction.[171]

IV

In 1899 Corelli had moved to Stratford upon Avon, settling from 1901 at Mason
Croft, in Church Street, a house reputedly lived in by Shakespeare's daughter.

[165] Masters, *Corelli*, 121; Ransom, *Corelli*, 69–73.   [166] Duffy, *Methuen*, 34–5.
[167] Scott, *Corelli*, 113, 119.
[168] Hichens, *Yesterday*, 90–1. Hichens also met Corelli at the Navarros' home in Broadway (p. 226).
[169] *The Bookman* (May 1909), 75–6.
[170] On Adcock (1864–1930), see Sutherland, *Companion*, 9, and Kemp *et al.* (eds.), *Edwardian Fiction*, 2–3.
[171] *The Bookman* (May 1909), 76–8.

At Stratford she was as big a draw as Shakespeare—bigger, thought Sir Horace Plunkett, who once found himself with time to explore Stratford when his motor car broke down. Accordingly, he hired a guide. He was amazed when 'the first and chief object submitted for my devotion was Marie Corelli's house'. No doubt Shakespeare, Plunkett ruefully reflected, had succeeded in his own small way, but on nothing like this scale.[172] When the Shakespeare scholar and editor of the *Dictionary of National Biography*, Sidney Lee, published his monograph *Stratford-on-Avon* (1907), *Punch* expressed mock horror that he disregarded its best-known resident. To make up for this, and to stand alongside the Omar Khayyám Club, Johnson Club, Pepys Club, Boz Club, Vagabonds, and Whitefriars, as venues for the brightest sparks in literary London, why not, therefore, found a Corelli Club, with Sidney Lee as chairman?[173] Her entry in *Who's Who* was, after all, longer than anyone's.[174] Corelli's sense of grandeur was the inverse of her sense of the absurd. A daily ritual was her progress round Stratford in a miniature phaeton, like Cinderella, pulled by two Shetland ponies, called Puck and Ariel, complete with coachman perched on high behind. In 1910 she published *The Devil's Motor*, which denounced automobilism together with her usual omnium gatherum— 'the Press, the Pulpit, Parliament, millionaires, manufacturers, women of society, etc., etc.'—only to buy a 38 h.p. vehicle from the proceeds.[175] Best of all, she was regularly piloted down the Avon in her own gondola, named *The Dream*. This vessel was specially imported from Venice complete with gondolier, until the Latin's quarrelsome inebriation compelled his replacement by her costumed gardener. Yeats, in Stratford for the Shakespeare Festival in May 1905, was offered use of the gondola by Corelli, and tactfully declined.[176]

Corelli maintained a sizeable establishment, a major-domo, two maids, a cook, gardener, houseman-cum-assistant gardener, and latterly a chauffeur, to all of whom she made bequests in her will;[177] but her hospitality had its peculiar aspects. The publisher Eveleigh Nash, invited for a weekend party, travelled up by train with another guest and friend of his, the much married Poppy Radnall, who was then Lady Byron. Why she was invited is a mystery, except that Corelli in common with many swooned over the original Lord Byron and would make a gushing defence of his moral stature in lectures.[178] Corelli having met them with her carriage at the station, Nash was disconcerted when he was deposited at the Shakespeare Hotel, albeit with instructions that he must come for all meals including breakfast. Reaching Mason Croft for dinner, he found installed there

---

[172] Sir Horace Plunkett to Shan Bullock, 9 Aug. 1921 (Bullock MSS 49/1; papers in the Plunkett Foundation, Long Hanborough, Oxfordshire). Cf. 'The Mighty Atom', verses celebrating Corelli's superiority over Shakespeare in Stratford; *Punch*, 10 Sept. 1902, 178.

[173] *Punch*, 18 July 1906, 37, and 10 Oct. 1906, 270.   [174] Ibid., 31 Dec. 1902, 454.

[175] Scott, *Corelli*, 152. For another rant against motoring, see Corelli, 'Society and Sunday', in Corelli, *Free Opinions*, 240–1.   [176] Yeats to Lady Gregory, 30 May 1905, in Wade (ed.), *Yeats Letters*, 449.

[177] Scott, *Corelli*, 271–2.

[178] Scott, *Corelli*, 241–2, cites her address at Harrow County School during the Great War. This was evidently a repeat or reworking of a lecture given previously in Nottingham, on which, see below, p. 806.

Henry Labouchere. The two then speculated why Nash was consigned to the hotel when space existed in the house: was it because Labouchere was the more famous, some forty years senior to Nash, and, although alone on this occasion, married and therefore constituted less menace to a spinster, or was it because the bachelor Nash had been known to be arriving with a glamorous married female guest, of questionable reputation, and Corelli wished to separate them? Also at the dinner were local gentry Sir Henry and Lady Fairfax-Lucy, from Charlecote Park; the final member of the party was the Shakespearean scholar–publisher A. H. Bullen, whom Corelli coquettishly called 'shock-headed Peter' on account of his wild hair.[179] Dinner talk entered a sticky patch when Corelli claimed that publishers had cheated her out of £10,000 from her novels. Instead of murmuring polite acquiescence, Labouchere proceeded to cross-examine her and prove her contention unfounded, whereupon Corelli rose, formally slapped Labouchere's cheek, then resumed her seat and redirected the conversation. After dinner Corelli played the piano beautifully, judged Nash, though he had difficulty preserving a straight face when she burst into song, rendering 'Within a Mile o' Edinburgh Toon'. The next day Bertha Vyver navigated Nash towards a glass cabinet. In it were displayed 'all the original manuscripts of Miss Corelli's novels'. When Corelli, Nash, and Lady Byron met up again shortly afterwards as guests of the millionaire grocer Sir Thomas Lipton aboard his yacht, 'a great coldness arose between the ladies', observed Nash, who attributed it to Lady Byron receiving more attention from the men.[180]

Corelli could not be convicted of lack of effort. In June 1907 she succeeded in drawing Mark Twain to Stratford, engaging a special train to bring him to luncheon with her; alas, she held on to him such that he had no time to see Shakespeare's birthplace, Anne Hathaway's cottage, and the church, and Twain remembered this as 'the most hateful day my seventy-two years have ever known'.[181] Corelli also graciously invited Mrs Barclay to call, following the success of *The Rosary* (1909).[182] On the other hand, she avoided and tried to block unlicensed photographs.[183] Tiny and tubby and conscious of advancing age, she shed many years and more pounds of flesh in her official photograph issued in 1906. This was manna for the satirist: 'In reply to a correspondent who asks his opinion as to whether the photograph of Miss CORELLI in her new book was in any way "touched up", *Mr Punch* begs to say that the answer is in the negative. It may be seen on application at the photographer's.'[184]

Corelli's conviction of her own unique beauty and artistry was protected only by a very thin skin. Her relations with journalists were always volatile. That she courted them and sought to use them there is no doubt. In 1900 she received the

---

[179] *Shock-Headed Peter* was a popular children's play put on at Christmas as an alternative to pantomime; see *Annual Register for 1901* (1902), pt. II, 91. It derived from Hoffmann's *Struwwelpeter* (1844) verses.

[180] Nash, *Life*, 79–80, 82. On Lady Byron, who married for a third time in 1924 to Sir Robert Houston, see J. Wentworth Day, *Lady Houston D.B.E.* (1958).

[181] Scott, *Corelli*, 230–1; Masters, *Corelli*, 214–16.   [182] Masters, *Corelli*, 211.

[183] Scott, *Corelli*, 228–30; and above, Ch. 8.   [184] *Punch*, 15 Aug. 1906, 109.

Whitefriars Club, which included a large body of journalists, at her home; and afterwards she employed Annie Davis, who reported this occasion fulsomely for the *Stratford Herald*, as her secretary.[185] Her other side was registered by the romantic novelist Annie S. Swan. When Swan became president of the Society for Women Journalists, she expressed herself keen to invite every leading female writer to the annual dinner and 'specially anxious to get Marie Corelli, to see whether it would not be possible to pour some balm of Gilead on her difficult relations with the press'.[186] It was not possible: Corelli would not attend. Notoriously, after her sales soared, she refused to allow her books to be sent out for review; nor would she be edited. When, in a move to boost the ailing circulation of the *Daily Tribune*, its literary editor invited Corelli to contribute and assured her that her piece would not be cut, he was gratified to secure her agreement by a postcard bearing the legend 'You are the only gentleman in Fleet Street'. He repented when the article arrived. It was unusable, being 'a violent and libellous attack upon almost every other newspaper'. He informed Corelli that he could not print it. Another postcard followed by return, this time with the bold inscription 'You are an unspeakable cad'. He pinned up both postcards over his desk.[187]

From the start there was an unavoidable ridiculousness about Corelli. In 1908, when Margot Asquith wanted to take the rise out of the anti-socialist polemicist W. H. Mallock, who was also a poet and novelist, she innocently asked him how long it had taken him to write *The Mighty Atom*.[188] Corelli had dedicated her story to 'Those self-styled "Progressivists" who by precept and example, assist the infamous Cause of *Education without Religion* and who by promoting the idea, borrowed from French Atheism, of denying to the children in board-schools and elsewhere, *The Knowledge and Love of God* as the true foundation of noble living, are guilty of a worse crime than murder'. This was Mallock's philosophy too; but Margot's question was closer to the bone than she perhaps realized. In 1889 Mallock had written to Corelli to express his appreciation of *Ardath*, then followed it up with a visit, in company with Ernest Beckett, Conservative MP for Yorkshire North Riding. Corelli celebrated her triumph by a letter to Bertha Vyver:

Mr Mallock . . . is one of the leading writers of the time, and he is a very great admirer of mine. You must not mind when you see any abuse of me in the papers. I have had the courage to attack truthfully the cliques of criticism and the party spirit pervading all art and literature, and of course, those who are stung retaliate. But it does not in the least matter while all the best literary men are rallying around me . . .[189]

Mallock had made a fatal move by paying court to Corelli. She could now patronize him, as in that essay in which she broadcast her joys from living 'the

---

[185] Masters, *Corelli*, 168–9; Ransom, *Corelli*, 106.   [186] Swan, *Life*, 104.

[187] Gibbs, *Pageant*, 63–4. On the *Daily Tribune*, which survived for less than two years (1906–8) and lost the Thomasson family almost £300,000, ibid. 59–68; Camrose, *British Newspapers*, 4–6; Lee, *Popular Press*, 167.

[188] Raymond Asquith to his wife, 1 Oct. 1908, in John Jolliffe, *Raymond Asquith: Life and Letters* (1980), 159.   [189] Letter, n.d. [c.1889], in Vyver, *Corelli*, 90.

Life Literary'; among its many delights were that 'We can reject commoners and receive kings, or *vice versâ*', and that 'it is just as easy to converse in one's own library with Plato on the immortality of the soul as it is good-humouredly to tolerate Mr. Mallock and his little drawing-room philosophies'.[190]

The Babylonian-cum-biblical epic *Ardath*, which Corelli always believed her *chef d'œuvre*, had excited other reactions. G. H. Hardy was astonished by 'the look of hysteria which pervades the thing'. 'The most striking feature of the book', the great mathematician observed, 'is the colossal number of notes of exclamation—I counted 39 in 3 pages. Indeed it mostly consists of !'s ?'s and quotations from the Book of Esdras.'[191] Similarly, Rupert Brooke advised Geoffrey and Maynard Keynes against attempting *The Sorrows of Satan*, Corelli's principal best-seller: 'It is the richest work of humour in the English (?) language: but the effects it produces on the unwary reader...! I am now a positive wreck.'[192] Schoolboy and undergraduate irreverence nonetheless paled beside the superstition of age and authority. Gladstone spent an hour with Corelli on 4 June 1889. Supposedly, he recognized in her 'a great power to move the masses' and '*a thinker* of no ordinary calibre and ability, as well as a perfect mistress of the pen'.[193] Perhaps the great man was temporarily unhinged by his recent engagement with Mrs Humphry Ward's *Robert Elsmere* (1888), which did earnestly wrestle with questions of religious faith and social service. Not all the Gladstone family had been captivated by Corelli: his daughter Mary and her husband, the Revd Harry Drew, read *Vendetta* together in 1887, noting 'goodish plot but rot rather otherwise'.[194] Gladstone's own ardour for Corelli seems quickly to have cooled. He read *The Romance of Two Worlds* before he met her and started on *Ardath* a couple of days afterwards; but when he returned to it after two months, he was doing no more than skimming it. He styled it 'a sag', this being family slang for dull. Nor would Gladstone succumb to Corelli's plea for him to review her work.[195] This disappointment was set aside in 1891 when Queen Victoria commanded that all Corelli's books be sent to her. It was the Duchess of Roxburghe, the Queen's Mistress of the Robes and Lady of the Bedchamber, who had recommended her. The Queen then took to Corelli, although there is some doubt about how far she sustained this enthusiasm after her daughter the Empress Frederick of Germany, opined that 'her writings were trash', and her private secretaries Henry and Sir Frederick Ponsonby added for good measure that they were 'bosh'

---

[190] Corelli, 'The Happy Life', in Corelli, *Free Opinions*, 327.

[191] G. H. Hardy to R. C. K. Ensor, n.d. [c.1895], Bodleian Library, Oxford, Ensor MSS. Hardy and Ensor were Wykehamist contemporaries.

[192] Letter to G. Keynes, Sept. 1906, in Keynes (ed.), *Letters of Rupert Brooke*, 61. Cf. Arnold Bennett to George Sturt, 29 Oct. 1895: 'I have just read Marie Corelli's new book—my first of hers. I can now understand both her popularity and the critics' contempt' (Hepburn (ed.), *Bennett Letters*, ii: *1889–1915*, 24–5).

[193] The Gladstone visit was a favourite of Corelli's admirers, lovingly described in Carr, *Corelli*, 65–7; Coates and Bell, *Corelli*, 13, 125–6, 334; and Vyver, *Corelli*, 105–7. See also Scott, *Corelli*, 83; Masters, *Corelli*, 86–91.   [194] Masterman (ed.), *Mary Gladstone*, 394 (15 Feb. 1887).

[195] Matthew (ed.), *Gladstone Diaries*, xii. 208–9, 222, 224.

and that 'the secret of her popularity was that her writings appealed to the semi-educated'.[196] Nevertheless, in March 1893 the Empress Frederick thanked Corelli at Buckingham Palace for the enjoyment her late husband had taken in her books; meanwhile, Corelli had been busy leaking to the press the royal fascination with her work, although her publisher Bentley restrained her from overt advertisement.[197] Receptions at Downing Street and the Foreign Office, at the behest of Lady Salisbury, wife of the Prime Minister and Foreign Secretary, also gave Corelli the kudos she craved; and this was completed when she was the only novelist invited to King Edward's coronation.[198] She also attended George V's coronation, sitting next to the journalist Philip Gibbs, who suspected her of eating his sandwiches.[199] Corelli sold her impressions of the occasion to the *Daily Mail* in 1911, though she had made great play of refusing similar newspaper requests in 1902.[200]

It was by extraordinary coincidence, remarkable in view of her publicized distaste for 'tuft-hunters and worshippers of Royalty', that almost all Corelli's holidays were taken in 'places where princes, princesses, or prime ministers happened to be staying'.[201] Many of her early novels contain lavish defences of the royal family, combined with contempt for the multitude; this spoken by the hero of *Thelma*:

Look at that victim of the nation, the Prince of Wales! The poor fellow hasn't a moment's peace of his life,—what with laying foundation stones, opening museums, inspecting this and visiting that, he is like a costermonger's donkey, that must gee-up or gee-wo as his master, the people bid. If he smiles at a woman, it is instantly reported that he's in love with her,—if he frankly says he considers her pretty, there's no end to the scandal. Poor royal wretch! I pity him from my heart! The unwashed, beer-drinking, gin-swilling classes who clamour for shortened hours of labour, and want work to be expressly invented for their benefit, don't suffer a bit more than Albert Edward, who is supposed to be rolling idly in the very lap of luxury, and who can hardly call his soul his own. Why, the man can't eat a mutton-chop without there being a paragraph in the papers headed, 'Diet of the Prince of Wales'.[202]

In 1892 Corelli chased after Edward by travelling to Homburg, which he was visiting, in order to gain an introduction.[203] She would also turn up at Marienbad and Braemar; indeed, once upbraided the *Gentlewoman* magazine for not listing her name among the select company in the royal enclosure at Braemar, while in the same breath demanding an apology in another journal for an unauthorized reproduction of a portrait of her.[204] Reward came when Edward invited her to a luncheon which the future King George V also attended, and both told her that they had read *all* her books.[205]

---

[196] Arthur Ponsonby, *Henry Ponsonby* (1942), 84–5; Sir Frederick Ponsonby, *Recollections of Three Reigns* (1957), 51–2. [197] Master, *Corelli*, 103–7; Ransom, *Corelli*, 64.

[198] Coates and Bell, *Corelli*, 306. [199] Gibbs, *Pageant*, 119. [200] Scott, *Corelli*, 155.

[201] Ibid. 163. [202] Corelli, *Thelma*, 217–18. [203] Vyver, *Corelli*, 119–27.

[204] *Punch*, 29 Oct. 1902, 296.

[205] Carr, *Corelli*, 58–9. See also Masterman (ed.), *Mary Gladstone*, 425, for a diary entry (4 June 1894) in which the Duke of York (later George V) is recorded as much recommending *Barabbas*.

At the death of Queen Victoria in 1901, when G. K. Chesterton broke down and wept, Corelli had the presence of mind to issue a poetic lament;[206] still, questions arose in 1902 with the publication of *Temporal Power*. Subtitled 'A Study in Supremacy', it was grandly 'Dedicated with such Devotion and True Service as he alone may Command to A King'. Corelli also included on the title page an epigraph from St Paul: 'For we wrestle not against flesh and blood, but against principalities, against powers, against the rulers of darkness of this world, against spiritual wickedness in high places'.[207] In the September issue of the *Review of Reviews* W. T. Stead criticized Corelli for having based her royal characters and statesmen on British models: King Edward, Queen Alexandra, and Prince George, and the Marquess of Salisbury and Joseph Chamberlain. The last two, respectively Prime Minister and Colonial Secretary, appeared in the story as the Marquis de Lutera and Carl Pérousse and were thoroughly disreputable. In physical appearance and pedigree the likeness was unmistakable. As for their politics, the Marquis 'was "made" to be a stock-jobber, not a statesman. His bent was towards the material gain and good of himself, more than the advantage of his country'; and Pérousse 'possessed a conveniently elastic conscience, which could be stretched at will to suit any party or any set of principles'.[208] Their machinations and warmongering, and lust for power and profit, while burdening the people with food taxes, all bore parallels in charges laid against the Salisbury administration's conduct of the Boer War. Corelli's King also created some difficulty. Though he foils the war party and a Jesuit plot, the story ends with his death in a storm at sea, after he has abdicated in order to sail away aboard a vessel containing the corpse of the socialist republican beauty Lotys. Their illicit passion had been thwarted when she is murdered by a jealous revolutionary rival; yet, the King was 'the best man in the whole story', observed Corelli's own loyal biographers, 'and is represented as winning the love of his people'. Corelli's Queen was more troublesome, being depicted as chilly and unhappy; still, Corelli was able to refer Stead and the world to her 'Christmas Greeting', published at the end of 1901, for her high evaluation of 'The Soul of Queen Alexandra'. There was also the compliment she paid to her dignified bearing, such a contrast to Society women, who had 'this fantastic dread of "looking old"': 'our gracious Queen Alexandra, who supports her years with so much ease and scarcely diminished beauty'.[209] That was probably heartfelt rather than feline; further, Corelli held up the King and Queen as model rulers of the realm because they 'most strictly set the example to all their subjects of attending Divine service at least once on Sunday'—again unlike Society, which 'prefers a pack of cards'.[210] Nonetheless, the Prince Humphry character in *Temporal Power* was altogether doubtful,

---

[206] The lament is partly quoted in Duffy, *Methuen*, 29. Ward, *Return to Chesterton*, 54, for the weeping. This was of high significance because, apparently, 'Gilbert wept rarely and with extreme difficulty.'
[207] The epigraph is from Eph. 5: 12.   [208] Corelli, '*Temporal Power*', 211, 246.
[209] Corelli, 'The Decay of Home Life in England', in Corelli, *Free Opinions*, 214–15.
[210] Corelli, 'Society and Sunday', ibid. 233–4.

carrying dark echoes of the legend about Prince George having contracted a morganatic marriage while serving as a seaman and, therefore, having committed bigamy when he married Princess May of Teck.[211] Apparently, Corelli was not wanting to give credence to these rumours so much as to condemn marriage alliances between royal families. She proclaimed that 'it will soon be necessary for heirs to thrones to enjoy the same honest freedom of purpose in their loves and marriages as the simplest gentleman in the land'—perhaps even to marry famous authoresses? Corelli's scenes of court toadyism also made for uncomfortable moments; but, her biographers emphasized, 'from certain letters and messages Miss Marie Corelli has received from both the King and Queen (if she cared to make them public), it is very evident that she is thoroughly appreciated by the Royal Family, and that they are the last people in the world to believe the numerous adverse statements circulated about her merely on account of her brilliant success'. Were this insufficient, there was a convenient diversion to hand: 'The authoress readily admits that an attack on Jesuitism is contained in the book, nor is she the only one who has waylaid that persuasion. She is strenuously opposed to the political and educational system of Jesuitry, and believes that the whole civilised world is with her.'[212]

Corelli's relations with foreign royalty also merit notice. She numbered several among her admirers. These were not confined to Europe. The Maharajah of Chhatarpur, 'as a tribute of homage and admiration', endowed her with silk woven with gold; he also expressed the mysterious opinion, 'If Christianity were taught in India as *you* teach it, we should understand it better.'[213] This Maharajah was decidedly an oddball; as his former tutor Sir Theodore Martin advised E. M. Forster, who was about to meet him in 1912, 'he *will* talk Herbert Spencer and Marie Corelli till one nearly screams'. This was his preference since he loathed the actual business of ruling; but Forster warmed to him, 'the ugliest little man you can imagine . . . [who] has certainly read bad books as well as good and . . . can't distinguish between them'.[214] Corelli did in fact write a sympathetic portrait of such a figure in her short story 'The Silence of the Maharajah', contrasting his sense of honour, dignity, and gentlemanly conduct towards women with the race arrogance and coarseness of a British so-called 'officer and gentleman'.[215] Generally, it was European royalty who swooned over Corelli's stories. Leader of the field was Queen Marguerite (Margharita) of Italy. Corelli claimed, in a publicity draft for Bentley's in 1886, that 'My godmother is a dame d'honneur to Queen Margharita, to whom I have been presented and who honours me with her interest, because once as a small child I contemporised [*sic*]

[211] On this legend, see Rose, *George V*, 82–6.

[212] Coates and Bell, *Corelli*, 251–6; and Corelli, *Free Opinions*, 7–8, for her denunciation of Stead's charges. [213] Masters, *Corelli*, 7, 133.

[214] To Alice Clara Forster, 21 Nov. and 1 Dec. 1912, in Lago and Furbank (eds.), *Forster's Letters*, i. 158 (for a photograph of the Maharajah), 162, 164.

[215] Marie Corelli, 'The Silence of the Maharajah', in Corelli, *Cameos*, 50–81.

a short poem in her presence.' It was advertised subsequently that this Queen gave Corelli her photograph, asked for her books, and was visited by Corelli in 1889.[216] The Empress of Austria, Princess Louise of Holland, and the last Tsarina of Russia were also Corellians.[217] Corelli's pet terrier was named Czar in homage. But Corelli was not to be seduced from her principles; rather, a demotic note sounded whenever her divine mission was touched. A problem for Corelli was that so many Continental monarchies were Catholic. In March 1906 *The Rapid Review* mounted an advertising campaign: 'THE TOPIC OF CONVERSATION for some time to come will be the striking article by MARIE CORELLI on the marriage of Princess Ena and King Alfonso.' This referred to the pending nuptials between Alfonso XIII of Spain and a granddaughter of Queen Victoria, Princess Ena of Battenberg, who would convert to Catholicism as a condition of the marriage. A second advertisement boomed that Corelli's theme would be 'Faith versus Flunkeyism'. The article duly appeared; then, in April, a further half-page box advertisement in the daily press, containing this message from the authoress:

At the moment of going to press I have received a remarkable communication from an unquestioningly authentic source, giving me detailed information as to how and by whom certain newspapers were 'approached', and persuaded into 'a conspiracy of silence' concerning Princess Ena's 'perversion' to Rome. I beg to thank my distinguished correspondent for his straightforward statement, which, however, cannot be used here. I am also told that 'orders' have been issued to various journalistic centres to 'take no notice' of anything which either I or others may write on this subject in the *Rapid Review*. I place this statement at once in possession of the public, and leave them to judge of its truth by the results.

MARIE CORELLI[218]

V

It was, therefore, a very odd salience which Marie Corelli achieved. When William Archer was in America in 1899, he was impressed by the comprehensive range of courses on offer at its universities, until told, albeit 'with a sneer': 'You can take an honours degree in Marie Corelli.'[219] Corelli's overwrought

---

[216] Masters, *Corelli*, 57, 85–7, 92.

[217] Carr, *Corelli*, 65; Vyver, *Corelli*, 164–5. In *The Sorrows of Satan*, 181, Corelli's alter ego, Mavis Clare, displays in her fragrant drawing room 'autographed likenesses' of her royal admirers: 'the Autocrat of all the Russias, . . . Her Majesty of Italy, and . . . the Prince of Wales'.

[218] Advertisements placed by the *Rapid Review* in *Pall Mall Gazette*, 10 Mar. 1906, 223, 17 Mar. 1906, 264, 14 Apr. 1906, p. ii. To be fair to Corelli, the royal family also showed some concern for Ena's fate as Queen of Spain; but, if what the Princess Henry confided in Arthur Benson was representative, this was because Ena was 'compelled to watch bull-fights . . . nearly fainting at the horrors' (Newsome, *On the Edge of Paradise*, 212). The emphasis would have been better placed on her safety. Following the marriage ceremony on 31 May, a bomb was thrown at the royal carriage and the bride's dress was bespattered with blood, though both she and the King were unhurt. See *The Times*, 1 June 1906.

[219] William Archer, *America To-Day: Observations and Reflections* (1900), 57.

imagination and style was a gift to satirists, but she affected to interpret their arrows as reward. Beau Lovelace, the Corelli-like author in *Thelma*, who is both a Society favourite and yet immune to its deceits, declares: 'I want to be jeered at by *Punch*! I want *Punch* to make mouths at me, and give me the benefit of his inimitable squeak and gibber. No author's fame is quite secure till dear old *Punch* has abused him ... Heaven forbid that I should be praised by *Punch*! That would be frightfully unfortunate!'[220] *Punch* duly delivered; and it is improbable that Corelli was not wounded by the drubbing she received over two decades and more. Thus, her *Wormwood* appeared as *Germfood* by Mary Morally ('Author of "Ginbitters", "Ardart" etc.');[221] still, a full page of parody in Mr Punch's Prize Novels series was a tribute of a kind. In the same way, her *Ziska* was deemed big enough to warrant the parody 'Zut-ski' by Bret Harte in his *Condensed Novels*.[222]

Corelli also enjoyed for over a decade a secondary career as a public lecturer. This began in modest enough circumstances, standing on a box at a church bazaar at Henley-in-Arden, not far from Stratford. The vicar's son Keble Howard, who had writing ambitions, claimed a scoop by reporting the occasion for the *Sketch* on 26 July 1899.[223] Corelli confessed to being 'dreadfully nervous' about making this inaugural speech, and for a while she kept to the neighbourhood. She addressed Stratford working men on 'The Secret of Happiness' on 6 January 1901; emboldened, thenceforward she did not confine her oratory to the local and the unsophisticated.[224] On 19 November 1901 she gave her first public lecture as such, to the Philosophical Society of Edinburgh. She was thus instantly ranked with previous giants of letters, Macaulay, Carlyle, Dickens, Thackeray, Kingsley, and Emerson, and with the prime ministers Gladstone and Rosebery, who had all lectured there in the past. Gladstone, who had died in 1898, may well have done the proverbial spin when the chairman, introducing Corelli, remarked that 'Mr Gladstone's prophecy of a great future for her was one of few modern prophecies that had been fulfilled.' Corelli's subject was 'The Vanishing Gift', by which she meant 'Imagination', 'Inspiration', or 'the Divine Fire'. She developed the theme in two ways. One was to puff herself as standing in a great tradition of imaginative writers, Shakespeare, Burns, Scott, Wordsworth, and Tennyson; the other was to bemoan the disease of the imaginative spirit in their moribund contemporary society. What they now had was a 'constant output of decadent and atheistical literature'; 'the repulsive "problem" play and the comic opera' instead of 'noble and classic forms' of drama; 'the splashy daubing of good canvas called "impressionist" painting'; 'the vilest doggerel verse' considered poetry; and a 'wretched return to the lowest forms of ignorance displayed in the "fashionable" craze for palmistry, clairvoyance, crystal-gazing, and sundry other quite contemptible evidences of foolish credulity concerning the grave issues of life and death,—combined with a most sorrowful, most deplorable indifference to the

---

[220] Corelli, *Thelma*, 527.   [221] *Punch*, 11 Apr. 1891.
[222] Bret Harte, *Condensed Novels: The Two Series Complete* (1903), 231–48.
[223] Howard, *Motley Life*, 132–8.   [224] Coates and Bell, *Corelli*, 263–79; *The Bookman* (May 1909), 67–8.

simple and pure teachings of the Christian Faith'. This 'mental and moral decay' had resulted from 'a morbid craving for incessant excitement, and a disinclination to think'. Accordingly, 'creative work of a high and lasting quality is not possible'. 'For truly', she lamented, 'we live at present under a veritable scourge of mere noise. No king, no statesman, no general, no thinker, no writer, is allowed to follow the course of his duty or work without the shrieking comments of all sorts and conditions of uninstructed and misguided persons...'.[225] The silver rose bowl presented to her on this occasion, and the silver candelabra given to her when she lectured to an audience of over 3,000 for the Scottish Society of Literature and Art in Glasgow, were bequeathed to her literary agent Watt in her will.[226] Corelli also counted among her scalps the Royal Society of Literature: she was the first woman to address it.

Great numbers flocked to hear Corelli's lectures. Cecil Roberts left an account of her appearance in Nottingham when she opened an exhibition about Byron in aid of a building fund for the Mechanics Institute:

She was small and stout, pretty in a fluffy way, somewhat like an ageing chorus girl . . . But what she lacked in stature she compensated in personality and will-power. She held her audience with the subtlest of all platform arts, a diffidence that was coolly accomplished, and she radiated charm. She was clear in her diction and audible. The audience forgot the physical presence in the personality.

This was an especially big day for Roberts himself, then still a teenager. An aspiring writer, he had been asked to write a poetic tribute linking Byron and Corelli. This improbability was printed in the programme and read out by Roberts following Corelli's lecture. Corelli graciously autographed the programme and invited Roberts for a weekend at Stratford.[227] She was not otherwise appreciative of this audience, who had awarded her '*rounds and rounds* of applause': 'I enjoyed *driving* Byron's *poetry* home into the *cotton-wool brains* of people who had never read a line of him.' But she consented to be president of an emergent Nottingham Byron Society, and the publisher John Murray, guardian of Byron's reputation, sent her a snip from the poet's hair, so pleased was he that she had focused on the literature and ignored 'the human frailties of the man'.[228]

Corelli also came out as a noted anti-suffragist. It was contended, although unprovable, that most of Corelli's readers were men, a distinction thought worthy of emphasis because it was believed by publishers, authors, and reviewers alike that women formed the majority of the novel-reading public. Certainly, more men than women wrote to Corelli.[229] These may have been stimulated by carefully posed photographs of the authoress, whose unmarried state conveyed a supplementary sensation. Corelli was 'England's premier virgin', recalled Edgar Jepson sarcastically.[230] While deploring what she called the modern sex novel,

---

[225] Corelli published the lecture in *Free Opinions*, 273–91.   [226] Scott, *Corelli*, 272.
[227] Roberts, *Years of Promise*, 38–40, where part of his Corelli–Byron poem is reproduced.
[228] Masters, *Corelli*, 210.   [229] Coates and Bell, *Corelli*, 113.
[230] Jepson, *Memories of a Victorian*, 232.

Corelli saturated her own with a copious romanticism and emotional intensity which sanctified the erotic. This drew 'hundreds of love-letters' and 'continual offers of marriage', she boasted in the early 1900s.[231] Indeed, what male could resist the poetic appeal to release the repressed, from *The Life Everlasting*?

> Come to me, then, thou angel-love of mine!
> Mate with that half of me which is divine,
> Mix with my soul and its immortal breath,
> And rise with me triumphant over Death![232]

But the historian does not need to invoke pseudo-psychological speculation to establish reasons why Corelli might be popular among male readers, because she propounded in her novels, essays, and pamphlets what was, to many, a compelling vision of Womanhood. Not that she was soft on men, if the dictum is correctly ascribed to her, that a woman had no need of a man when she had three pets—'a dog that growled all morning, a parrot that swore all evening, and a cat that stayed out all night'.[233] Even the adulatory Coates and Bell protested about *The Murder of Delicia*, which Corelli prefaced with the blunt statement that 'a great majority of the men of the present-day want women to keep them'. They termed it the 'least worthy' of her books: 'It is far too full of railing against men; it is far too one-sided and far too bitter.'[234] This was not an aberration: in her essay 'Accursed Eve' she wrote roundly, 'I do not know any man who is not absolutely under the thumb of at least one woman';[235] and in her anti-suffrage statement *Woman or Suffragette?* (1907), 'a man is seldom anything more than a woman's representative'. 'Suppose', she added, 'after many struggles with the police and frantic button-holing of worried Members of Parliament, I did secure my own *one* vote, should I be better off than with the certainty of 50 male voters ready to do precisely as I bid them?' Hence, the suffragette's pursuit of the franchise was 'an open confession of weakness . . . For if she is a real Woman with the mystic power to persuade, enthral and subjugate man, she has no need to come down from her throne and mingle in any of his political frays.' Here was the kernel of the Corelli conception of Womanhood. It was most threatened by unwomanly women, as she deemed suffragettes to be; 'and a masculine woman is nothing more than a libellous caricature of an effeminate man'.[236] Corelli and her companion Bertha Vyver had a story primed about Christabel Pankhurst and Annie Kenny once coming for tea, presumably for the purpose of proselytizing the renowned authoress. The suffragettes' sentiments, or possibly Kenny's 'vulgar laugh', caused an orchid to droop; and the consensus was that they were 'Mad women . . . raving lunatics!'[237]

---

[231] Corelli, 'The Happy Life', in Corelli, *Free Opinions*, 336.

[232] Quoted in J. Cuming Walters, 'A Personal Tribute', in Vyver, *Corelli*, 258. Walters was editor of the *Birmingham Daily Post*; and, after an initial tiff when he questioned Corelli's alleged fluency in Latin, Greek, and Hebrew, he became a devotee. See Masters, *Corelli*, 129.

[233] See letter from Celia Ennis, *The Times*, 5 Feb. 1997.   [234] Coates and Bell, *Corelli*, 192, 194.

[235] Corelli, 'Accursed Eve', in Corelli, *Free Opinions*, 155.

[236] Quoted in Mitchell, *Queen Christabel*, 97–8.   [237] Scott, *Corelli*, 131.

At the other end of Corelli's anathematized scale were Society women, too corrupted and pampered to realize the feminine ideal. Few popular authors had a kind word to say about such creatures; and the Social Season was habitually the subject of scorn. In Guy Boothby's *The Red Rat's Daughter* (1899), debutantes are described as being 'brought up to London, to be tricked out, regardless of expense . . . [and] paraded here, there, and everywhere, like horses in a dealer's yard'.[238] Even more severe was Hubert Henry Davies in *Outcast*, which played at Wyndham's Theatre in 1914. He has his protagonist, Geoffrey, exclaim, after his fiancée jilts him to marry a baronet, 'I don't respect her. How can I? Neither she nor any of the women of her class who do what she's done—sell themselves for a title and three houses. I see no difference between them and those poor wretches . . . walking the pavements of Piccadilly.'[239] Corelli was equally hot on this question but, when declaiming against the 'Modern Marriage Market', she did not lose sight of her overall concern:

Follies, temptations, and hypocrisies surround, in a greater or less degree, all women, whether in society or out of it; and we are none of us angels, though, to their credit be it said, some men still think us so. Some men still make 'angels' out of us, in spite of our cycling mania, our foolish 'clubs'—where we do nothing at all,—our rough games at football and cricket, our general throwing to the winds of all dainty feminine reserve,—delicacy and modesty,—and we alone are to blame if we shatter their ideals and sit down by choice in the mud when they would have placed us on thrones.[240]

In Corelli's mind this throne for women was correctly positioned in the home. Not that she was blind to the necessity of preventing their exploitation—she welcomed the Married Women's Property Act as 'a great and needful boon'—or that she was insensible to the public good accruing from female schools inspectors, doctors, and lawyers. But she stopped short of the admission of women into Parliament: 'I should detest it. I should not like to see the sex, pre-eminent for grace and beauty, degraded by having to witness or to take part in such "scenes" of heated and undignified disputation as have frequently lowered the prestige of the House of Commons.' It was vital that, while 'claiming and securing intellectual equality with Man, she [Woman] should ever bear in mind that such a position is only to be held by always maintaining and preserving as great an Unlikeness to him as possible in her life and surroundings'.[241] In sum, she implored women 'not to part with their chief charm—womanliness'.[242] She must be 'the Goddess and he the Worshipper'.[243] Hence, if women were to 'throw open the once sweet and sacred homes of England to the manoeuvres of the election agents' or, worse, themselves abandon their homes for active politics,

---

[238] Boothby, *Red Rat's Daughter*, 36.   [239] Davies, *Plays*, ii. 218.
[240] Quoted in Coates and Bell, *Corelli*, 153.
[241] Corelli, 'The Advance of Woman', in Corelli *Free Opinions*, 176, 181–2.
[242] Corelli, 'The Power of the Pen', ibid. 299.
[243] Corelli, 'The Advance of Woman', ibid. 183.

then 'the foundation of Empire, their God-appointed centre, the core of the national being', would all come 'tottering to a fall'.[244]

This message ran through many of Corelli's novels, most notably in her depiction of Mavis Clare in *The Sorrows of Satan* (1895). That Clare was a narcissistic self-portrait was guessed by many critics. It was not just the identical initials of the names but the profession that gave it away. Mavis Clare is a best-selling author of healthy Christian fiction, and for that is traduced by venal and envious reviewers. Clare keeps a dog to raven their pernicious notices—as, in reality, Corelli's own dog was trained to do.[245] The physical description of Clare was alluring. She is 'as unlike the accepted ideal of the female novelist as she can well be'; that is, she is not 'an elderly, dowdy, spectacled, frowsy fright'. She is 'a quiet, graceful creature, so slight and dainty, so perfectly unaffected and simple in manner . . . she rather resembled a picture by Greuze in her soft white gown with a pale rose nestled amid the old Flemish lace at her throat—and she turned her head towards us, the sunlight caught her fair hair and turned it to the similitude of a golden halo'.[246] Thus equipped, Clare courageously exposes Society's debaucheries, upholds Christian virtue, and, quite literally, repels the Devil. Corelli issued denials that this was an impersonation; but her first, flattering biographer, Kent Carr, allowed that Mavis Clare might be 'the unconscious working out of a personal ideal'.[247] The moral of the melodrama was clear: 'The book is a grand and successful attempt to show how women who are good and true hold the affection, the esteem, the devotion, the homage of men; it is an incentive to women to be in men's regard the Good Angels that men best love to believe them; it is a lesson to women how to attain the noblest heights of womanhood.'[248]

Corelli, therefore, considered herself a crusader on behalf of her sex. This creates problems for historians' classification of her. There is no one-size-fits-all definition of feminism within which an independent woman such as Corelli snugly settles. On the franchise question, one litmus test, she excluded herself from the reckoning; and, although she eventually withdrew her opposition and accepted it as a token of justice and equality when in 1918 women were partially granted the suffrage, she sustained her abhorrence of the idea of women becoming MPs. On other points of philosophy she differed too; yet she was no self-effacing female of the conventional kind, and in her criticisms of

[244] Quoted in Mitchell, *Queen Christabel*, 97–8.

[245] Vyver, *Corelli*, 125. Corelli's first novel, *A Romance of Two Worlds* (1886), included a psychic dog, a device perhaps owed to Ouida, who was a firm believer in the unconscious cerebral capacity of canines.

[246] Corelli, *Sorrows of Satan*, 182–3, 193–4. It was a standard Victorian joke that authoresses of romances always imagined themselves beauties: see 'The Secrets of Literary Composition', *Punch*, 24 Jan. 1891, in which George Du Maurier cartoons the authoress of *Passionate Pauline* sitting in front of the mirror and writing, 'I see a pair of laughing, *espiègle* forget-me-not blue eyes, saucy and defiant; a *mutine* little rose-bud of a mouth, with its ever-mocking *moue*; a tiny shell-like ear, trying to play hide-and-seek in a tangled maze of rebellious russet gold; while, from underneath the satin folds of a *rose-thé* dressing-gown, a dainty foot peeps coyly forth in its exquisitely-pointed gold morocco slipper etc., etc.' Du Maurier's picture depicts a frump, not a beauty. [247] Carr, *Corelli*, 68–70.

[248] Coates and Bell, *Corelli*, 153.

their sons. And the centre of their influence should be, as Nature intended it to be, the Home. Home is the pivot round which the wheel of a country's highest statesmanship should revolve,—the preservation of Home, its interests, its duties and principles, should be the aim of every good citizen . . . If I were asked my opinion as to the chief talent or gift for making a home happy, I should, without a moment's hesitation, reply, 'Cheerfulness.' A cheerful spirit, always looking on the bright side, and determined to make the best of everything, is the choicest blessing and the brightest charm of home.[255]

If this was Corelli's prescription for the self-realization of her sex, then it was a vision of ideal womanhood that many romantic men were happy to embrace.[256]

VI

In the end Corelli's philosophy, such as it was, hardly mattered. Corelli was famous for being a best-seller, and this fame acted as a spur to other budding best-sellers. After resolute preparatory reading of the range of world literature, seeking inspiration from the terror of Dostoevsky, the exactitude of Henry James, the psychology of William James, the amorality of D'Annunzio, the cold, scientific observation of Flaubert and Maupassant, the spirituality of Tolstoy, the sensibility of Turgenev, the melancholy of Maeterlinck, and a self-conscious correspondence with George Moore about the art of fiction, Anne Douglas Sedgwick was ready to throw all erudition aside, crying out on her twenty-eighth birthday: 'why *can't* I be a Marie Corelli!'[257] A writer could not become a best-seller by research or training, however:

No one can write a best-seller by taking thought. The slightest touch of insincerity blurs its appeal. The writer who keeps his tongue in his cheek, who knows that he is writing for fools and that, therefore, he had better write like a fool, may make a respectable living out of serials and novelettes; but he will never make the vast, the blaring, half a million success. That comes of blended sincerity and vitality.

With self-belief amounting to mania, Corelli possessed this blend in super-abundance. She had 'a mind like any milliner's apprentice', an 'incurably com-monplace mind [that] was incapable of accurately surveying life, but some wild lust for beauty in her made her take a wild inventory of the world's contents and try to do what it could with them'. She had, therefore, 'like the toad, a jewel in

---

[255] Corelli, 'The Decay of Home Life in England', in Corelli, *Free Opinions*, 212, 228. Cf. J. Cuming Walters, 'Personal Tribute', in Vyver, *Corelli*, 257 ff.

[256] G. K. Chesterton's anti-suffrage views were similar; see Ward, *Return to Chesterton*, 49–50.

[257] To Mrs James Pitman, 21 Feb. 1901, in Basil de Selincourt (ed.), *Anne Douglas Sedgwick: A Portrait in Letters* (1936), 25. Sedgwick at this stage had two novels to her name, *The Dull Miss Archinard* (1898) and *The Confounding of Camelia* (1899). She finally made it into the best-seller league with *Tante* (1911). Edwin Montagu, Asquith's former parliamentary secretary and afterwards a minister, was nicknamed Tante as a consequence of 'his resemblance to the moody central character' in the novel; Bonham Carter and Pottle (eds.), *Lantern Slides*, 330 n. 2. On the American-born Sedgwick, see Kemp *et al.*(eds.), *Edwardian Fiction*, 356.

the head: this jewel of demoniac vitality'.[258] 'Well, you are a dreamer,' a character says in *The Life Everlasting*; 'you do not live here in this world with us—you think you do—and yet in your own mind you know you do not. You dream—and your life is that of a vision simply. I'm not sure that I should like to see you awake. For as long as you can dream you will believe in the fairy tale.'[259] Corelli induced thousands to join her in this dreamland. Realism in literature was loathsome to her; imagination was everything, the ruling passion of her books, the refrain of her lectures.

From 1916 Corelli deliberately fell out of step. When British Summer Time (daylight saving) was introduced, Corelli refused to observe it, except of necessity when catching trains. She persisted in this romantic obstinacy for the eight years left to her. It was God's time that she held dear. Inviting Annie Swan to luncheon in 1921, she asked her to come for noon, 'for we do not conform to the senseless "Govt. time" whose 1 o'clock is the blessed sun's mid-day. I never have conformed to it and never *will!*'[260] A low point in her personal reputation came in 1917 when tradesmen and local worthies in Stratford upon Avon, whom she had antagonized by opposing their crude development of the town as a tourist trap, brought about her prosecution for hoarding food.[261] It was a spiteful action, if the innocent explanation of her sugar requirements—for jam-making—was true. Friends rallied, the grocery baron, Sir Thomas Lipton, yelling down the line: 'You'll never want for sugar so long as Tom Lipton's on the 'phone!'[262] Corelli published a vindication, *My Little Bit: A Record of War Work*, in 1919. War provided new outlets for her impulsiveness, both generous and ungenerous, rather than ironed out her inconsistencies. In 1913, in *Nash's Magazine*, she had questioned, 'In what ways is "Patriotism" served by slaying its able-bodied men in thousands?' 'Honour', she argued, was exploited as a face-saving device to cover governments' errors and lust for conquest, at the cost of murdering countless innocent men actuated by 'their fine obedience to duty'. Come the Great War, and Corelli mounted recruiting platforms, denouncing as cowards men who hung back, and urging women to prove their love 'by sending them away to join the Army and putting no difficulties in their path of honour'.[263] She published patriotic articles and, for a year in the London *Evening News*, 'The Journal of the Lonely Soldier'.[264] In Stratford she was president of the Soldiers' Club;[265] and the building she owned next to her home she converted into a rehabilitation centre for injured American officers, a use it still served in 1919. Her relationship with the new transatlantic power was inevitably speckled too. She had taken the lead in the restoration of Harvard House, the sixteenth-century Stratford home of the mother of the founder of the great American university. This was formally

---

[258] West, *Strange Necessity*, 320–2.   [259] Quoted by J. Cuming Walters in Vyver, *Corelli*, 258.
[260] Corelli to Mrs Burnett Smith, 17 Apr. 1921, in Nicoll (ed.), *Letters of Annie S. Swan*, 85.
[261] Vyver, *Corelli*, 231–4.   [262] Scott, *Corelli*, 88.
[263] Ibid. 152–3, citing her address to an audience of 5,000 in the De Montfort Hall, Leicester, in 1915.
[264] Ibid. 241.   [265] Hichens, *Yesterday*, 268–70.

warning to literary historians that they risk missing a great deal if this area of human striving and conflict is ignored. Bernard Darwin composed a rare appreciation in 1948: 'Good writing is good writing whatever the subject and the nineteenth century is rich in good writing on sport, ranging from some of the acknowledged masterpieces of English prose to that which is at least pleasant, racy, and full of vigorous life.'[3]

Winston Churchill attested to the classic status of one at least of this pack of sporting authors when, in a description of his father's intellectual universe, he itemized the three books that Lord Randolph knew best: the Bible, Gibbon, and Jorrocks.[4] The last, Robert Surtees's creation, needs no introduction, yet Surtees's novels, 'now quoted by every enthusiastic fox hunter and which were powerful enough to convert one of Kipling's heroes to the sport, were neither widely read nor much appreciated in the hunting circles of his own day'.[5] That was the early Victorian period; afterwards, Surtees's characters and situations came to occupy pride of place in the sporting literary firmament. Siegfried Sassoon recounted how he and a friend, who were members of a hunt in the Edwardian period, knew almost by heart Surtees's stories, facetiously adopted his language, and dubbed each other after his characters.[6] And if Surtees failed to provide a relevant reference, there was always George Whyte-Melville, whose succession as the premier fox-hunting novelist was suitably terminated in the field, killed when thrown from his hunter in 1878. John Galsworthy, who relished days in the saddle, paid tribute by styling Digby Grand—the eponymous hero of Whyte-Melville's first novel (1853)—the idol of Jolyon in *The Forsyte Saga* (1906); and among Sassoon's hunt colleagues was a well-preserved retired colonel who 'modelled himself on what I may call the Whyte-Melville standard'.[7] Hunting thus had its own distinctive traditions, complete with literary pedigree. This included Anthony Trollope, who crafted many a hunting scene in his novels. Whether living in Ireland or in England, he was

constant to the sport, having learned to live it with an affection which I cannot myself fathom or understand. Surely no man has laboured at it as I have done, or hunted under such drawbacks as to distances, money, and natural disadvantages. I am very heavy, very blind, have been—in reference to hunting—a poor man, and am now an old man. I have often had to travel all night outside a mailcoach, in order that I might hunt the next day. Nor have I ever been in truth a good horseman. And I have passed the greater part of my hunting life under the discipline of the Civil Service. But it has been for more than thirty years a duty to me to ride to hounds; and I have performed that duty with a persistent energy. Nothing has ever been allowed to stand in the way of

---

[3] Bernard Darwin, 'Sporting Writers of the Nineteenth Century', in Cumberlege (ed.), *Essays Mainly on the Nineteenth Century*, 117. On Darwin (1876–1961), see *DNB 1961–1970*, 271–2; he was the evolutionist's grandson, and famed both as a Dickensian and as a golfer.

[4] R. F. Foster, *Lord Randolph Churchill: A Political Life* (Oxford, 1981), 11.

[5] Raymond Carr, *English Fox Hunting: A History*, rev. edn. (1986), 140–2, for explanation of this. On Surtees (1805–64), see Sutherland, *Companion*, 614–15.   [6] Sassoon, *Fox-Hunting Man*, 132–3.

[7] Ibid. 143. On Whyte–Melville (1821–78), Sutherland, *Companion*, 671–2; Carr, *Fox Hunting*, 143, 208–9.

hunting,—neither the writing of books, nor the work of the Post Office, nor other pleasures. As regarded the Post Office, it soon seemed to be understood that I was to hunt; and when my services were re-transferred to England, no word of difficulty ever reached me about it. I have written on very many subjects, and on most of them with pleasure; but on no subject with such delight as that on hunting. I have dragged it into many novels,—into too many no doubt,—but I have always felt myself deprived of a legitimate joy when the nature of the tale has not allowed me a hunting chapter.[8]

Trollope mounted a vigorous defence of hunting in the *Fortnightly Review* after that journal published 'the first serious and intellectually respectable attack' on the sport, by the Oxford historian E. A. Freeman, in 1869.[9] Trollope enjoyed the hunting field as a social leveller as much as for its theatre of courage and skill. In his eyes, it was *the* national sport whose constituents were so peculiarly English that it was 'almost impossible for an Englishman to give to a foreigner an adequate idea of the practice'.[10] In eagerly defending his passion, Trollope allowed his patriotism to distort proportion. Hunting was not so English as to exclude other parts of Britain and Ireland, or so virile as to sideline women. In 1899 the balance was redressed by another classic of hunting literature: *Some Experiences of an Irish R.M.*, written conversationally by Edith Somerville and Violet Martin (Somerville and Ross). From 1903, for five years, Edith was MFH of the West Carbery Hunt, which supplied material for *Further Experiences of an Irish R.M.* (1908), *Dan Russel the Fox* (1911), and *In Mr. Knox's Country* (1915).[11]

By the early twentieth century sport had become a national obsession, a vast entertainments industry with a mass following. League soccer, county cricket, rugby union and rugby league, horse-racing, tennis, boxing, golf, athletics, and the rest absorbed millions as participants and spectators;[12] and an ever expanding sporting press acted as cheerleaders to them. Other nations had their sporting enthusiasms, yet it was generally acknowledged that Britain, especially England, was unrivalled in its inventiveness and leadership of games. The actress Sarah Bernhardt paid unusual homage when, on seeing a football match, she gushed, 'J'adore ce cricket—c'est tellement anglais!'[13] Not that this supremacy emerged or continued unchallenged. A deep ambivalence existed about time taken from work, reflecting a Puritan tradition which distinguished between 'amusement', signifying idleness and dissipation, and 'recreation', involving spiritual renewal. Moreover, certain sports that had a close association with the aristocracy—not just hunting but most other field sports that were buttressed by property rights and long shielded by Game Laws—excited a republican distaste for Privilege. Condemnation of sports on moral grounds, for their cruelty to animals, or attendant rowdyism, drinking, and gambling, persisted; yet the healthy character-building propensities of sports, which required physical training, rule discipline, teamwork, and competitiveness, were correspondingly lauded. Sport

---

[8] Trollope, *Autobiography*, 71–2.   [9] Carr, *Fox Hunting*, 204–12.
[10] Trollope, quoted in Carr, *Fox Hunting*, 132–40.   [11] Collis, *Somerville and Ross*, 135–6, 159.
[12] See Richard Holt, *Sport and the British* (Oxford, 1989).   [13] Roberts, *Years of Promise*, 127.

was becoming a measure by which individuals and groups, towns and nations, were tested.

Of the many individually pursued sports, it was angling that probably led. C. B. Hawkins's social survey of Norwich, published in 1910, noted over 100 fishing clubs attached to public houses there, each with a membership averaging thirty to forty. They drew mostly on the better-paid working class, although some dozen clubs were said to depend largely on labourers earning under £1 a week. These were all subscription clubs, which organized outings and awarded prizes; as for those anglers who were unassociated, it was impossible to count their number. Other towns and villages, in different regional settings, followed different recreational customs. In Norwich the local fancy was canary-breeding, which was part sport and part industry: there were some 2,000–3,000 breeders in the city who exported over 30,000 birds annually. But the Norwich male, in common with the sex everywhere, was most keen on football. It cost 3*d.* to watch the professional league team on a Saturday afternoon, the same sum as would gain admission to the cheapest section of the music hall. Essays on 'How I Amuse Myself', written by elementary schoolboys and made available to Hawkins, mentioned football more times than anything else, and a long way ahead of cricket, although this might in part be explained by the minor-county status of Norfolk.[14] The same obtained elsewhere. Writing in 1911 the book that would become *Life in a Railway Factory* (1915), Alfred Williams declared about the community life around the Great Western Railway works at Swindon:

Sport and play, and especially football, claims the attention of the juveniles. The love of the last-named pastime has come to be almost a disease of late years—old and young, male and female, of every rank and condition, are afflicted with it. Whatever leisure the youngsters have is spent in kicking about something or other amid the dirt and dust; from one week's end to another they are brimful of the fortunes of the local football team. Many a workman boasts that he has denied himself a Sunday dinner in order to find the money necessary for him to attend Saturday's match. Politics, religion, the fates of empires and governments, the interest of life and death itself must all yield to the supreme fascination and excitement of football.[15]

Known as the Hammerman Poet, Williams worked for twenty-five years at the forges in the GWR works and otherwise taught himself French, Latin, and Greek, acquired a wide knowledge of English literature, and published verses and prose studies of Wiltshire village life.[16] The spirit of Richard Jefferies flowed through Williams; but this devotion to Nature and Literature made Williams a singular presence in the workshop, the butt of foremen and workmates alike who worshipped coarser images, among which Sport was now a recognized deity.

The composer Edward Elgar was prepared to travel miles to watch Wolves— Wolverhampton Wanderers Football Club—play; and Frank Benson, the

---

[14] Hawkins, *Norwich*, 312–16.   [15] Alfred Williams, *Life in a Railway Factory* (1969), 287.
[16] See Leonard Clark, *Alfred Williams: His Life and Work* (Bristol, 1945).

Shakespearean actor–manager, was so keen on sport that 'members of his company were always expected to play games as well as to act parts'. He would 'advertise in the theatrical papers for "a good juvenile lead who can field at cover-point", and for "a heavy man able to play half-back" '.[17] Many authors were a part of this sporting culture, which, as we have seen in the case of Florence Barclay, did not exclude women.[18] Even that philosopher of aesthetics the fastidious Walter Pater made a habit of entertaining the sporting hearties of Brasenose College, though whether from ulterior motive it is indelicate to venture. Bernard Shaw was active on several fronts: he was an energetic (and accident-prone) cyclist, he enjoyed swimming, he played cards with his wife, mother, and Sidney Webb, he regularly turned out to watch the Boat Race, he occasionally hit a golf ball, he even took up the boxing gloves. Shaw's fourth novel *Cashel Byron's Profession* (1885) concerned prizefighting. For a reprint he composed a preface in which he debated 'The Morals of Pugilistic Fiction'. Here Shaw strived to counter the suspicion that he had glamorized the business; rather, he outlined his hope that 'It may even help in the Herculean task of eliminating romantic fisticuffs from English novels, and so clear them from the reproach of childishness and crudity which they certainly deserve in this respect. Even in the best nine-teenth century novels the heroes knock the villains down.'[19] It was a vain hope. Best-selling fiction continued in this style: witness Jeffery Farnol's Regency adventures *The Broad Highway* (1910) and *The Amateur Gentleman* (1913). Farnol was no mere romancer: 'his first job with a Birmingham firm of brass founders ended when he knocked down a works foreman for calling him a liar'.[20] In his prosperity as an author, Farnol was chummy with the retired amateur boxer, the hotelier Harry Preston. They travelled together to Atlantic City in 1921 to attend the Dempsey–Carpentier world title fight, where they found that American reporters mixed up their credentials, styling Preston the famous novelist and Farnol the famous pugilist.[21] The world of boxing, with its aristocratic patrons and murky practices, was in principle anathema to Bernard Shaw; yet there is no doubt that he was enthralled by it. It remained a lifelong passion, which the vegetarian Vitalist thinly disguised by contending that the pugilists' ring represented an allegory of capitalism.[22] Shaw did hold a principled objection to one sport, fox-hunting; and he championed the Humanitarian League's case against it as a cruelty that caused suffering to the animal victim and degradation to those who pursued it.[23] But this was an exception, much as with the muscular invalid George Meredith before him. It was generally Shaw's game to maintain that he abhorred games. In *Who's Who* he spelled out the philosophy: '*Exercise*: cycling,

---

[17] Dark, *Mainly about Other People*, 96.   [18] See above, Ch. 20.

[19] G. B. Shaw, *Cashel Byron's Profession* (1914), 17. See also *Punch*, 11 Jan. 1890, 16, for an enthusiastic review of a previous one–shilling reprint.   [20] *DNB 1951–1960*, 348–9, for Farnol (1878–1952).

[21] Preston, *Memories*, 198–200, 256. Preston also took Arnold Bennett to his first boxing match.

[22] Holroyd, *Shaw*, i. 104–5, 267–8; St John Ervine, *Bernard Shaw: His Life, Work and Friends* (1956), 151. Shaw subsequently corresponded with the heavyweight champion Gene Tunney.

[23] Carr, *Fox Hunting*, 206–7.

swimming . . . *Recreations*: anything except sport'.[24] Here was another case of Shaw *contra mundum*: 'I cannot endure the boredom of sport.' Worse, he contended that baseball, though a mad pursuit, was better than cricket, which 'in slowness and stupidity is without parallel or rival'.[25]

Most of this might appear harmless bravado but Shaw was actually taking a great risk. It was all very well to stick out a tongue at Shakespeare, Henry Irving, or the Church, but it was foolhardy for Shaw to criticize sport. Perhaps Shaw was asserting his Irishness in his antipathy to cricket; but he stood little chance of becoming the hero of English or colonial democracy with these views, unlike the whimsical J. M. Barrie, who was a cricket-lover supreme. Unusual for a Scot, Barrie had played cricket since boyhood, in his home village of Kirriemuir and at school in Dumfries. After he moved to London in 1885, Barrie was a regular spectator at Lord's, often in the company of his friend H. B. Marriott Watson, who had arrived in the capital from the antipodes at much the same time and with similar literary ambitions.[26] Games, and cricket above all, occupied a far larger place in Barrie's scheme of things and concept of what made a civilized individual than did music, painting, and poetry.[27] It was through cricket that Neville Cardus got to know Barrie, who had been one of his own boyhood heroes. Barrie, wrote Cardus, 'was crazy about cricket . . . He not only admired Charles Macartney, the most brilliant of all Australian batsmen with the single exception of Victor Trumper; he actually envied him. "He can do all that he wants to do", was his significant tribute.'[28] It was a great day for Barrie and his colleagues when they actually played at Lord's, albeit in a friendly for an authors' team against representatives of the press. But it was not necessary to perform well in order to participate in the cricket culture, any more than it was essential for a romantic to be a great lover. Barrie was no great shakes in either department: like Treherne, pining for Lady Catherine in *The Admirable Crichton* (1902), he was 'a second eleven sort of chap'.[29] Not only was it not necessary to perform well, it was not necessary to perform at all to feel the beauty of the sport, as the weird Francis Thompson proved. Cricket, along with opium, Catholicism, and an unrequited love for Alice Meynell, was what inspired him to compose verse.[30] All the same, there were several authors such as E. W. Hornung and John Galsworthy who, according to Cardus's estimation, reached 'some measure of technique in good club cricket'; and the appreciation which his own writings on cricket drew from men of letters led him to identify the existence of 'a cricket Intelligentsia'.[31]

---

[24] *Who's Who* (1905), 1456.   [25] Quoted in Gardiner, *Certain People of Importance*, 215.

[26] Dunbar, *Barrie*, 22, 30, 65. On Marriott Watson (1863–1921), who became assistant editor of *Black and White* and literary editor of the *Pall Mall Gazette*, a novelist and co-author with Barrie of the play *Richard Savage*, see Sutherland, *Companion*, 661, and Kemp *et al.* (eds.), *Edwardian Fiction*, 409–10.

[27] Peter Llewelyn Davies—one of the five brothers adopted by Barrie—quoted in Dunbar, *Barrie*, 205.

[28] Cardus, *Autobiography*, 148, 187–91.

[29] Barrie, *The Plays*, 206. Treherne does, however, win Catherine in the end.

[30] Meynell, *Thompson and Meynell*, 168–9. See the poem 'At Lord's' in Francis Thompson, *Works* (1913), i. 174.   [31] Cardus, *Autobiography*, 149, 183.

The Allahakbarries, the touring team of amateur cricketers founded by Barrie in 1887 and captained by him, included a cast of authors and artists: at different times, Conan Doyle, A. E. W. Mason, Maurice Hewlett, E. W. Hornung, Jerome K. Jerome, Charles Whibley, E. V. Lucas, Owen Seaman, Charles Turley Smith, Marriott Watson, P. G. Wodehouse, Henry Ford, Bernard Partridge, Augustine Birrell, Alfred Parsons, and E. T. Reed.[32] Conan Doyle was a vigorous all-rounder: cricketer and footballer, swimmer and ice-skater, hockey and rugby player, boxer, and billiards and bowls player.[33] As a cricketer, Doyle played occasionally for the MCC and had the distinction of bowling out W. G. Grace (a compliment Grace soon returned); as a footballer, he had been a founder member of Portsmouth FC. Doyle's enthusiasm for boxing, bare-knuckle or gloved, inspired his Regency melodrama *The House of Temperley*, which was staged at the Adelphi Theatre in 1910. Doyle shouldered the lavish production costs himself, over £2,000, and bore a substantial loss. Female theatregoers were repelled, and the adventitious death of the King in May delivered the knock-out blow to it. Still, as a member of the National Sporting Club, Doyle enjoyed such reputation in boxing circles that he was invited to referee the world heavyweight title fight in Reno, Nevada, in 1910, when Jack Johnson beat Jim Jeffries. He also chaired the committee set up to prepare the British team of sportsmen for the 1916 Olympic Games. The Great War aborted that—the venue had been set for Berlin—but during the 1908 Olympics, staged in London, Doyle was one of the group of onlookers who rushed to help the Italian marathon runner Pietri Dorando stagger exhausted over the winning line, only to be disqualified. Doyle defended Dorando's cause and led a subscription for him; it was an expression of his forthright championship of 'fair play' and of the amateur spirit against encroaching professionalism in sport.[34] Practically the only major sport about which Doyle showed ignorance was horse-racing. No one who knew anything about the subject would site race stables on Dartmoor as Doyle did in the Sherlock Holmes 'Adventure of the Silver Blaze'.[35]

Conan Doyle's virtual all-round sporting activity was not easily matched, but William Hope Hodgson, now chiefly remembered by enthusiasts of his horror stories, had run a School of Physical Culture in Blackburn before he turned to writing, and his sporting competence ranged across athletics, swimming, boxing, and judo.[36] Nor was the pious or intellectual sort entirely anchored to the armchair. One of the highlights of *Hadrian the VII* (1904) occurs when the sterling

---

[32] Barrie, *Greenwood Hat*, 96–105; Meynell, *Barrie Letters*, 35, 39–40, 43. The name Allahakbarries was a comical conflation of Barrie's name with the north African for 'Heaven help us'. Broadway, Worcestershire, where the American actress Mary Anderson (Mrs Antonio de Navarro) lived, was a favourite venue for the Allahakbarries.   [33] Pearson, *Conan Doyle*, 14, 70–1, 104.

[34] See Bill Mallon and Ian Buchanan, *The 1908 Olympic Games: Results for All Competitions in All Events, with Commentary* (Jefferson, NC, 2000), for the controversies over the interpretation of rules.

[35] Booth, *Conan Doyle*, 27, 96–7, 156, 198, 205–6, 274–5, 282–3, 294.

[36] On Hodgson (1877–1918), who was killed in the Great War, see Kemp *et al.* (eds.), *Edwardian Fiction*, 189.

English Pope, the author Frederick Rolfe's alter ego, meets the Kaiser, because His Holiness had clearly been working out in preparation for this audience: 'He took the imperial hand and shook it in the glad-to-see-you-but-keep-off English fashion. Spring-dumb-bells had given the Pope a grip like a vice and an arm like a steel piston-rod. The Emperor blinked once.'[37] Ping-pong was what young J. Middleton Murry excelled in in the 1890s; afterwards, he enjoyed stag-hunting, though he was declared unfit for army service.[38] Among the most popular of the new suburban sports was golf. This was Horace G. Hutchinson's game: he had been swept up in what late Victorians jokingly called the 'Great Golf Stream' which had flowed from Scotland to England and then worldwide. Hutchinson played to a high level and wrote an instruction book, *Hints on the Game of Golf* (1886), before weaving sport into his fiction.[39] There were other notable performers. 'I have always been fond of games', wrote E. Phillips Oppenheim casually, adding, 'I have made my hundred at cricket once or twice, I have won some very tough sets of tennis, and I have a small collection of silver bowls.'[40] These last were golf prizes: Oppenheim was president of his club at Woking, and once progressed to the final of the Italian championship. For P. G. Wodehouse too sport mattered a great deal. It was what brought him happiness at Dulwich College from 1894 to 1900 and, before he left England altogether, he would regularly revisit and report its football matches for the school magazine. He had also been a fast bowler and member of an unbeaten school team one year; he continued to play cricket when he could, though his batting was memorable chiefly for Barrie's 'telling of the first time he saw Plum bat, when he made 1, "but in the second innings wasn't so successful"'.[41] Wodehouse's yearning to visit America, which he did for the first time in 1904, and to establish himself as an author there, was 'due principally, I think, to the fact that I was an enthusiastic boxer in those days and had a boyish reverence for America's pugilists—James J. Corbett, James J. Jeffries, Tom Sharkey, Kid McCoy and the rest of them'. All these games featured in his early school stories and later fiction, including especially golf: 'Wodehouse is said to have immortalized the game of golf as Surtees immortalized fox-hunting.'[42] And in how many other writers their youthful sporting exploits remained exhilarating. H. A. Vachell related that his 'small triumph, which perhaps I overvalue, was the winning of the half mile race for Sandhurst against Woolwich which gave us the victory in the Sports of that year, 1881'.[43] This appeared becomingly modest, yet it had lingered long enough in his mind to bear this retelling in 1913.

[37] Fr. Rolfe, *Hadrian the VII* (Ware, 1993), 224–5.　　[38] Lea, *Murry*, 8, 17, 26.

[39] On Hutchinson (1859–1932), Kemp *et al.* (eds), *Edwardian Fiction*, 200–1.

[40] Oppenheim, *Pool of Memory*, 12.

[41] Hart-Davis (ed.), *Lyttelton Hart-Davis Letters*, 394 (29 Nov. 1957).

[42] Donaldson, *Wodehouse*, 48, 52, 78, 118.

[43] H. A. Vachell to Douglas Sladen, n.d. [Dec. 1913], Richmond Reference Library, Local Studies collection, Sladen papers, box 66, fo. 27. On Vachell (1861–1955), see Kemp *et al.* (eds.), *Edwardian Fiction*, 399.

Alas, for those authors born too soon to exploit the mercenary potential of sport. 'Orion' Horne, author of the 'farthing epic' published in 1843, was preposterously vain about his physical stamina and skill and, according to his own legend, these included fighting as a volunteer in the War of Mexican Independence and mastering a Red Indian in hand-to-hand combat. Nor was he content merely to sit by the hearth in old age. According to Edmund Gosse, Horne 'was nearly eighty when he filled us, one evening, with alarm by bending our drawing-room poker to an angle in striking it upon the strained muscles of his forearm'. Aquatic performance was Horne's principal mode of exhibitionism, and this included swimming beneath Niagara. Such exploits seemed 'strangely incompatible with the appearance of the little man, with his ringleted locks and mincing ways. But he was past seventy before he ceased to challenge powerful young swimmers to feats of natation, and he very often beat them, carrying off from them cups and medals, to their deep disgust.' During his time in Australia, Horne had given lessons in gymnastics as well as in swimming; later, he was dejected that he had opted for the wrong sports, writing to Gosse after Australia's cricketers first toured England in 1878:

I learn that the cricketers have made *each* £1,000 over here! Why, oh! why did I not become an Australian cricketer, instead of an unprofitable swimmer? When years no longer smiled upon my balls and runs, I might have retired upon my laurelled bat, and have published tragedies at my own expense. Is there any redress for these things in another world? I don't think so; I shall be told I had my choice.[44]

Authors who were less accomplished practitioners in the field could not for that be indifferent to the sporting ethic. When Henry James settled in Rye in Sussex, he was invited to be vice-president of the local cricket club. This may have meant little to an American; but as an American James could hardly have been asked to be mayor and, to the citizens of Rye, vice-president of their cricket club was obviously the next best thing. James declined, but he did join the golf club, albeit to take tea not to play golf.[45] H. G. Wells was not handicapped by being American but, to his consternation as the son of a sometime cricket professional, he found that an astigmatism made his own playing of that game poor; and he fared no better at football when, as a student teacher at a Calvinistic Methodist academy at Wrexham, he suffered a damaged kidney and lung from a foul committed on him by pupils. Wells's recuperation from that assault was put to good use, in reading and in beginning to write: he 'ground out some sonnets' and he poured out 35,000 words of a first-effort novel.[46] But Wells was not done with games; on the contrary, 'until the years closed about him Wells exercised himself

---

[44] Gosse, '"Orion" Horne, 1802–1884', in Gosse, *Portraits and Sketches*, 97–115. Swimming (especially sea-bathing) was Swinburne's favoured sport, too, although with his puny frame he was more courageous than competent. Famously, he nearly drowned off the Normandy coast in 1868, an occasion which led to his meeting the youthful Guy de Maupassant; see Gosse, 'Swinburne', ibid. 22–36. *Punch* predictably nicknamed him 'Swimburne'. [45] Edel, *James*, ii. 263.

[46] Wells, *Autobiography*, i. 105, 296–306.

continuously'. The gruelling hockey matches at his home near Dunmow in Essex every Sunday during the Great War gained him a notoriety, because Wells played like a 'fiend', as a bruised, panting, and irritated Arnold Bennett remarked. R. D. Blumenfeld put the case succinctly: 'I have played hockey with H. G. Wells. Anyone who has played hockey with H. G. Wells more than once and can still remain on friendly terms with him may claim reasonably to have the right to write about him intimately.'[47] Nor was it all hockey: Wells 'invented a ball game played in his barn—a game which would reduce one by about a pint of per-spiration in half an hour, and one's figure to shapely proportions in a week or two'. This was a variant of squash; and, when Wells's guests sought refuge in the house, they were not spared there, for Wells had written two books about indoor games, many of them devised by himself.[48]

Wells was excessive, yet sport did make for enthusiasts. Sport was not a topic that Andrew Lang can be imagined to have overlooked because, as *Punch* remarked, no subject escaped his touch. He freely discoursed on 'Theology or Conchology, or Mythology, and all the other ologies, in this instance, Golfology, with equal skill and profundity of wisdom'. That was said in praise of Lang's contribution—together with the Conservative Party leader Arthur Balfour's—to the book on golf edited and principally written by Horace G. Hutchinson, which *Punch* reckoned one of the best volumes in the Badminton Library series on sports and games, published in 1890.[49] Lang was actually useless at the game. Like that other great journalist H. W. Massingham, he 'played golf for its gentle exercise and . . . could occasionally hit the ball, but where it went to he seldom knew and never cared'.[50] Lang's preferred recreation was angling; but cricket, though he played it as incompetently as golf, was the game he loved to watch, declaring, 'My idea of Heaven is a place where I should always find a good wicket and never exceed the age of twenty-four!'[51] It was the opinion of C. B. Fry, the greatest all-rounder in the history of sport, that Lang 'wrote a better essay on cricket than he wrote on any other subject'.[52] Fry himself was once guest of honour at dinner at the Vagabonds Club, where authors were always well represented. 'There were some people in the Club that night', wrote Douglas Sladen, 'who expressed their disapproval to me at the Club's entertaining a mere athlete.'[53] Fry was not that: boasting a First in Classical Moderations at Wadham College, Oxford, he could also past muster in the iambics league. Fry claimed to be 'the first cricketer and footballer to write about sport under my own name', which he had started to do for the *Windsor Magazine* and as a columnist for the Manchester-based paper *Athletic News;*[54] by 1913 he was also a member of the

[47] Blumenfeld, *All in a Lifetime*, 173.   [48] Flower, *Just as it Happened*, 157–8, 172.

[49] *Punch*, 17 May 1890, 231. Hutchinson was afterwards given a weekly column in the *Westminster Gazette*; Spender, *Life, Journalism and Politics*, ii. 152.

[50] Scott, '*We*' *and Me*, 160, citing H. Cozens-Hardy on Massingham.   [51] Green, *Lang*, 207.

[52] C. B. Fry, *Life Worth Living* (1986), 167. On Fry (1872–1956), see *DNB 1951–1960*, 380–1.

[53] Sladen, *Twenty Years*, 172.   [54] Fry, *Life Worth Living*, 152–3.

General Council of the Authors' Club. The Vagabonds was not being original when it toasted Fry. The Johnson Club previously hailed the Australian cricketer George Bonnor at its annual dinner. This rather astonished Bonnor himself, who told the gathering that until their invitation he had never heard of Dr Johnson 'and what is more, I come from a great country where you might ride a horse sixty miles a day for three months, and never meet anybody who had'. But, he added graciously, he was now of the opinion that, were he not a cricketer, he would like to have been Johnson.[55]

Athletes were becoming editors as well as authors. Keble Howard, not long down from Oxford where Fry had been his idol, persuaded his brother R. S. Warren Bell to give Fry a regular feature in the new boys' magazine *Captain*, which he was launching for George Newnes in 1899. It was Howard's belief that the magazine would be more profitable if it was turned altogether into a sports periodical, 'aiming at the undergraduate and the medical student and the young clerk instead of mere schoolboys'.[56] Such a readership would have more money to spend than would boys, and valuable advertising might be won from the makers of sports equipment and sportswear. Warren Bell could not agree to this: his heart was set on editing *A Magazine for Boys and Old Boys* (as the *Captain*'s subtitle had it), and he remained just 'a great, big boy to the very end'.[57] Subsequently, the *Captain* was remembered as one of the magazines that gave P. G. Wodehouse his start by serializing his school stories; but Bell so far endorsed his brother's idea that he appointed Fry as his athletics editor, a position Fry occupied until 1904, when he pioneered his own periodical for Newnes, *C. B. Fry's Magazine*. This flourished until 1913, in its last year independently of Newnes, with whom Fry fell out because of the firm's habit of paying more heed to the advertising department than to the editor. Fry always had larger ambitions than to act as the commercial voice of sport: from 1908 he became director of a training ship for boys wanting to adopt a naval career, and he was a supporter of Field Marshal Lord Roberts's National Service League. For several years, however, *C. B. Fry's Magazine* was a success, Fry having had the sense to consult T. P. O'Connor for editorial advice. Its first issue had startled Newnes when Fry wrote about G. F. Watts's equestrian statue *Physical Energy*; but explicitly sporting features were the magazine's staple. It ran a series on 'Outdoor Men and Women', which included well-known authors among the sportsmen and -women and spotlighted these authors' recreational pursuits more than their prose or

[55] See Augustine Birrell, 'The Transmission of Dr Johnson's Personality' (1898), repr. in Birrell, *Self-Selected Essays*, 73–4. On Bonnor, who stood 6 feet 6 inches tall and was famed both as a slogger and for the distance over which he could throw a cricket ball, see W. G. Grace, *'W.G.': Cricketing Reminiscences and Personal Recollections*, new edn. introd. E. W. Swanton (1980), 328–9.

[56] Howard, *Motley Life*, 100.

[57] Obituary panegyric of Warren Bell (1871–1921) in the *Captain* (Nov. 1921). As editor, which he remained until 1910, he used the sobriquet 'Old Fag'; hence, it was said, 'Few, comparatively, had heard of Warren Bell; but where all over the Empire was "the Old Fag" unknown?' At 6 feet 4 inches in his socks, Warren Bell was a big boy physically, as well as in outlook.

poetry. Among Fry's regular contributors was E. V. Lucas, whose articles were later turned into 'the best book ever written on cricket of olden times—*The Hambledon Men*, a book which is in the library of everyone who likes to read about the game'.[58] Lucas was otherwise a staff writer for *Punch*, where there was also to be found R. C. Lehmann, wicked parodist for the most part yet an ardent rowing coach too and author of *Rowing* (1898) and *The Complete Oarsman* (1908).[59]

Sport did not win the hearts of every author. In 'The Islanders' (1902) Kipling expressed contempt for the 'muddied oafs' and 'flannelled fools' whose 'witless' preoccupation impaired their ability to defend the Empire. Arthur Benson was another notable opponent of the philathletic culture he had observed in the ascendant as a tutor at Eton and Cambridge. 'Schoolboys worship a successful athlete,' wrote Lord Frederic Hamilton, remembering his own days at Harrow.[60] It was this to which Benson objected, because actually he was quite a sportsman himself, 'indeed rather a martyr to exercise and the open air'. Benson rowed, captained his college football team, and scaled mountains with the Alpine Club. 'I do not at all want to see games diminished, or played with less keenness,' he wrote in 1906; 'I only desire to see them duly subordinated.' Principally, he deplored how sport was being promoted above books: 'It is the complacency, the self-satisfaction that results from the worship of games, which is one of its most serious features.' Sport was becoming 'a species of social tyranny'. Benson understood that it required more courage to write this than it did for him to question the Decalogue, 'because the higher criticism is tending to make a belief in the Decalogue a matter of taste, while to the ordinary Englishman a belief in games is a matter of faith and morals'.[61]

The belief in sport was affirmed by the highest. Lord Rosebery, whose horses twice won the Derby during his brief term as Prime Minister, and who was assailed from some quarters as a corrupting influence because of it, was unrepentant. In 1896 he averred that

no one can watch the progress of our nation without seeing the enormous predominance that is given everywhere to-day to outdoor sports. I welcome that tendency. I think it is a healthy and rational tendency, but of course it may be carried too far. What we do see in the tendency to outdoor sport at this time is that it weans the race from occupations that might be objectionable, and it is rearing a noble and muscular set of human beings; and it subserves other objects which are not so immediately apparent.

[58] Fry, *Life Worth Living*, 169. On Lucas (1868–1938), see *DNB 1931–1940*, 549–50.
[59] Both books included chapters by others. See *Punch*, 5 Aug. 1908, 108, for high praise of *The Complete Oarsman*.   [60] Hamilton, *Days before Yesterday*, 109.
[61] A. C. Benson, *From a College Window* (1906), 251–64. See also Lubbock, *Benson*, 35, 141, 162; Newsome, *On the Edge of Paradise*, 69–70; Clive Dewey, ' "Socratic Teachers": The Opposition to the Cult of Athletics at Eton, 1870–1914, Part II: The Counter-Attack', *International Journal of the History of Sport*, 12 (Dec. 1995), 18–47. Benson was no advocate of an unrelenting classical curriculum either: he opposed compulsory Greek at Cambridge.

Among these he instanced the competitive spirit between major towns' football teams:

I am given to understand, though I have never seen one of the great northern or midland football matches, that they are almost Homeric in their character, in their strenuousness, and the excitement they engender . . . I hope very soon to see some such match, because I think we have lived in vain if we have not seen one. I have seen the crowds going to those matches, and I have never seen anything in public life or elsewhere comparable to the eagerness and the enthusiasm of those crowds.

Rosebery also cited the cricket matches between England and Australia as strengthening the connection between the countries; and it was this aspect and application that principally justified sport in Rosebery's mind: 'We have to maintain a great Empire. We have to develop a great Empire, and for imperial purposes you need a race of muscle, of strength, and of nerve. All these are developed by these sports.'[62] Brains were needed too, Rosebery admitted. These should be trained and exercised by reading, diffused through the free public-library system; the two combined, sport and literature, would then prove irresistible in the imperial service.

The Poet Laureate Robert Bridges subscribed to this school of thought: 'I've always b'lieved—in living a man's life!', he declared in 1914. Now aged 70, Bridges was still athletic in body and mind. He had been a batsman 'of the imperious aggressive kind' and had stroked the Corpus boat at Oxford, when it was second on the river, and at a Paris regatta in 1867.[63] 'Manly' was one of Bridge's favourite words, but the pre-eminent spokesman among poets for this philathletic-cum-imperialist and militarist culture was Henry Newbolt. His *Admirals All* (1897) ran through four impressions in the first fortnight of publication; and it remained a popular choice in recitals. When John Bailey read poems to an evening audience of forty or fifty at the Working Men's College on Guy Fawkes Night 1914, the Great War was already 3 months old. He found that Wordsworth was the least well received, whereas '*Admirals All* won the first outburst of applause! and *The Revenge*'.[64] Leslie Stephen so delighted in *Admirals All* and *Drake's Drum* that 'he would declaim [them] to his daughters as they walked to Kensington Gardens.'[65] The sporting ethic was yoked with the spirit of sacrifice in the service of nation and empire, in Newbolt's 'Vitae Lampada':

> There's a breathless hush in the Close to-night—
> Ten to make and the match to win—
> A bumping pitch and a blinding light,
> An hour to play and the last man in.

[62] Address at the opening of the Passmore Edwards Free Public Library, Uxbridge Road, London, 25 June 1896, in Geake (ed.), *Appreciations*, 235–7. [63] Thompson, *Bridges*, 3–5, 78–9.

[64] Bailey (ed.), *Bailey Letters and Diaries*, 153 (5 Nov. 1914). He added, 'The *Ode on Wellington* [by Tennyson]; Kipling's *Return*; and Bridges' *Wake up England*, were all obviously successful.'

[65] Nicolson and Banks (eds.), *Flight of the Mind*, 47. The daughters were the later Virginia Woolf and Vanessa Bell.

And it's not for the sake of a ribboned coat,
  Or the selfish hope of a season's fame,
But his Captain's hand on his shoulder smote—
  'Play up! play up! and play the game!'
The sand of the desert is sodden red,—
  Red with the wreck of a square that broke;—
The Gatling's jammed and the Colonel dead,
  And the regiment blind with dust and smoke.
The river of death has brimmed his banks,
  And England's far, and Honour a name,
But the voice of a schoolboy rallies the ranks:
  'Play up! play up! and play the game!'[66]

Attendances at Test matches did not approach the 70,000 or 100,000 plus at the big football games; yet, cricket seemingly moved the public mind more than did politics or empire. For many, the nickname GOM (Grand Old Man) signified the cricketer W. G. Grace, not the statesman W. E. Gladstone. In reality an avaricious bully and 'shamateur', Grace secured his hero's status by breaking all records in the summer of 1895, at the advanced age of 47.[67] His importance was appreciated even by the scrupulously unathletic Max Beerbohm. When a national subscription was raised for a presentation to Grace, Max contributed his humble shilling along with thousands of other Englishmen—though Max said that he did so 'not because I am a great admirer of cricket, but as an earnest protest against golf'.[68] In 1902, when the news broke that Rhodes was dead, the common response was, 'That's a bad blow for Yorkshire.' The public apparently knew better the spectacular performances on the cricket field of the still lively Wilfrid Rhodes (1877–1973) than the lustrous deeds of the deceased imperialist Cecil Rhodes (1853–1902).[69] But the thousands who followed cricket closely were as nothing compared with the millions who gambled on the horses. Reviewing the first supplemental volumes of the *Dictionary of National Biography* in 1901, Augustine Birrell perused the letter 'A' and noticed that close together came the names of 'Fred Archer, the jockey; Lord Armstrong, the maker of big guns and compiler of huge fortunes; and Matthew Arnold, poet and critic. Of these men', he opined, 'the jockey was probably the widest known at the date of his death. He was a great popular favourite, and could he have had a public funeral, and his admirers

---

[66] Henry Newbolt, *Collected Poems, 1897–1907* (n.d.), 131–2. This collection of poems was dedicated to Thomas Hardy, a connection which perhaps requires a little explanation. Newbolt was an admirer of Hardy's verses; especially, Hardy's poetic drama of the Napoleonic Wars, *The Dynasts* (1903–8), drew them into correspondence at a time when national commemorations of the centenary of the battle of Trafalgar brought into the public eye poets such as Newbolt who celebrated England's naval heroes. On this culture, see J. A. Mangan, *Athleticism in the Victorian and Edwardian Public School* (Cambridge, 1981), and id., 'Duty unto Death: English Masculinity and Militarism in the Age of the New Imperialism', *International Journal of the History of Sport*, 12 (Aug. 1995), 10–38. For Newbolt (1862–1938), see *DNB 1931–1940*, 650–1.   [67] For a recent appreciation, see Simon Rae, *W. G. Grace: A Life* (1999).
[68] Quoted in Davies, *Later Days*, 194.
[69] A Colonial Cricketer, 'The Two Sides of Cricket', *Fortnightly Review* (July 1902), 120.

been free to follow it, no other man's obsequies would have attracted such crowds.'[70]

It was one of the most divisive questions concerning the press in the late nineteenth and early twentieth centuries, whether to publicize the starting prices (with tips and forecasts) for horse-racing, because this would encourage gambling—a largely illegal activity because cash betting off-course was discountenanced by law until 1960.[71] It was an especial dilemma facing newspaper proprietors who held strong religious and ethical objections to betting, as did the Quaker George Cadbury, owner of the leading Liberal paper, the *Daily News*. For a while the *Daily News* pursued what its editor called a 'well-intentioned but mistaken experiment' of eliminating all racing news from its pages. Its eventual surrender brought protests from leading members of the Quaker community such as the Lord Justice of the Court of Appeal and British Plenipotentiary to the Second Hague Conference Sir Edward Fry, who endeavoured to rouse a campaign in the Quaker periodicals *The Friend* and the *British Friend*; but the editors were unwilling to open their columns to its discussion.[72] This abject surrender delighted *The Spectator*, which accused the Quakers of 'cant and hypocrisy'. Sir Edward Fry's daughter wrote, 'betting tips continued to appear in papers owned and managed by Friends and my Father continued to deplore the great evil wrought day by day in the incentive to betting—an evil which he believed was equal to that produced by drink. "When I think of the harm those people are doing every day, I *can't* understand it," he would say, deeply moved between sorrow and indignation.'[73]

This subject was also one of the blind spots in the otherwise keen-sighted populist agenda of W. T. Stead when he set out his 'Ten Commandments' for newspaper editors in 1891. Number 6 was 'Leave out all reports of horse-racing, gambling, prize-fighting and the like.' Stead was a puritan zealot: his final commandment was 'Recoup yourself in the Churches for what you lose on the turf or the Stock Exchange.'[74] This was unwise counsel if the commercial viability of a newspaper was judged the overriding consideration. Stead was not without allies. These included those municipal authorities that adopted a policy of blacking out sporting news in the newspapers on display in their free public libraries.[75]

---

[70] Birrell, *Self-Selected Essays*, 187–8. Archer, who committed suicide at the age of 29 in 1886, rode 2,748 winners in his career. His *annus mirabilis* was 1885, when he won the Two Thousand Guineas, the Oaks, the Derby, the St Leger, and the Grand Prix.

[71] Municipal by-laws operated to curb the activities of street bookmakers in many places, and these were codified in national legislation, the Street Betting Act (1906), which made illegal all off-course betting. See R. I. McKibbin, 'Working-Class Gambling in Britain, 1880–1939', in McKibbin, *The Ideologies of Class: Social Relations in Britain, 1880–1950* (Oxford, 1990).

[72] A. G. Gardiner, *Life of George Cadbury* (1923), 220–1. For the dilemmas of newspaper proprietors and editors concerning this question, see Lee, *Origins of the Popular Press*, 128, 164, 172, 215, 219. Spender, *Life, Journalism and Politics*, ii. 152–3, described the compromise position adopted by the *Westminster Gazette*, which he edited. It recorded the odds and results in horse-racing but never employed a tipster. Sports reporting on the *Westminster* largely meant golf, cricket, and rugby.   [73] Fry, *Sir Edward Fry*, 252.

[74] *Review of Reviews* (Oct. 1891), 415.

[75] Ibid. (Feb. 1892), 165 cited Aston, Leicester, and Paisley. See also Kelly, *Public Libraries*, 172–3: Kelly suggests that the practice began at Aston in 1893 but, as the *Review of Reviews*' reference made plain, it was

Nevertheless, it was obvious where the majority interest and profits lay. The one-time compositor-turned-newspaper magnate Edward Hulton started on his path to riches by printing a single sheet of racing news for circulation in Manchester's pubs. This grew into the immensely successful *Sporting Chronicle*.[76] Likewise with the *Star*: it is a little-emphasized reason for the success of that London evening paper which T. P. O'Connor started in 1888, most historians preferring to attribute it to its politics, the combination of progressivism and Home Rule, or to its galaxy of new writing talent, Bernard Shaw and all. O'Connor himself admitted to another cause. Conscious of his lack of editorial experience, he had sought advice from Edmund Dwyer Grey, of the *Freeman's Journal*; and 'I remember with what surprise I heard . . . that sport would be necessarily one of the most important features of the paper.' Accordingly, he poached from another paper Charles Mitchell, 'who had immense reputation as a sporting tipster', using the nom de plume Captain Coe. O'Connor afterwards reflected how lucky he was to secure him.[77]

The shrewd author recognized this, and allied himself with the sporting cult. Gentlemanly patronage and practice were enshrined in the quantity of sporting clubs established in the capital from the mid-Victorian period, among them the Victoria (1860), Turf (1868), Hurlingham (1869), Flyfishers' (1884), Queen's (1886), Bath (1897), Royal Automobile (1897), Royal Aero (1901), and the Roehampton (1902).[78] Books about sport constituted a conspicuous element of the publishing boom. The number of titles of non-fictional sports literature showed a great leap from ninety-two in the decade 1870–9, 222 in 1880–9, 449 in 1890–9, to 516 in 1900-9.[79] Later it would appear that sport almost displaced literature. In 1937 the BBC ignored the tercentenary of the death of Ben Jonson, whereupon Edward Agate reflected: 'The Englishman does not want to hear a ten minutes' talk on Jonson . . . He prefers to accord a two minutes' silence to a football trainer who died recently in the North.'[80]

II

The amount of fiction in the late nineteenth and early twentieth centuries that included a sporting feature or turned upon a sporting contest is impossible to

---

in existence there a year or two earlier. Kelly adds that the practice 'was for a time widely adopted, especially by library authorities in the Midlands and in and near London'; and he cites a source that noted, 'it was still in use in nearly forty libraries in 1910'. It was continued or reintroduced in some libraries in the inter-war period, and the last known example was at Kirkcaldy in Scotland between 1962 and 1968.

[76] Thompson, *Here I Lie*, 41–2. Thompson wrote the 'Echoes of the Day' feature for the *Sporting Chronicle*.   [77] O'Connor, *Memoirs*, ii. 255–6; Scott, *'We' and Me*, 174–5.

[78] Graves, *Leather Armchairs*.

[79] I owe this information to Matthew Bryant, graduate student of St Catherine's College, Oxford, who in 1995 counted the titles of sports literature in the Bodleian Library catalogue for the period. The sports comprised angling, athletics, boxing, cricket, croquet, cycling, rugby and association football, golf, rowing, swimming, and tennis.

[80] Edward Agate to James Agate, 3 June 1938, in Agate, *Shorter Ego*, 227.

quantify. This was a regular part of the school story for juveniles;[81] but it would be wrong to suppose that its appeal slackened or ceased for adults when their schooldays were left behind. The best-selling status of Nat Gould gives some indication of the size of this market. Here was a literary phenomenon who at his death in 1919 had written about 130 novels, all about horse-racing. Of these, twenty-two were still in the pipeline, ready to be issued at his regular rate of five per annum. Very properly, Gould was accorded notice in the *Dictionary of National Biography*, where Frederick Page reckoned that, at the time of writing (1927), some 24 million copies of his works had been sold.[82] If this estimate is accurate, then it may be that Gould was the best-selling of all best-sellers in the late nineteenth and early twentieth centuries, outstripping Barclay, Caine, Corelli, and even Garvice; but since the *DNB* notice, which ran to one column, Gould's fame has shrunk almost from sight in standard literary reference works.

Gould told something of his own story in a book suitably entitled *The Magic of Sport* (1909), in which autobiography jockeyed for position with reminiscences of famous horse races and riders. At the time of writing his appearance was not very sportsmanlike—plump, bald, and with luxuriant Bismarckian moustache— but his philosophy was downright. In the preface he declared: 'It will be a bad day for England or any other country, when sports decay and maudlin sentimentality obtains the upper hand.'[83] Gould was born in Manchester on 21 December 1857. His father, originally from London, was a tea merchant, with an office in Market Street and home in Cheetham Hill. His mother's family were Derbyshire squires, the Wrights, whose members farmed land both as owner– occupiers and as tenants of the Duke of Devonshire in Dovedale and around Ashbourne. Gould was sent to a private school, Strathmore House, at Southport, where he developed as an all-round games player: captain of cricket, keen footballer and rugby player, and follower of coursing—the premier trophy in that last sport, the Waterloo Cup, was competed for annually near Southport. Indoors, Gould's favourite subjects were 'History, Shakespeare, and Scripture'. The family was Low Church in religion, Gould's father being a churchwarden at St Ann's in the centre of Manchester; and, though Gould never made a big thing of it in his work, he remained steadfast to creed and Church throughout his life. Yet even the religion was combined with sport. In the Middlesex village of Bedfont, where Gould eventually settled (and which London's Heathrow airport later obliterated), his closest friend was the Revd N. G. Pilkington, vicar for thirty-eight years and a clergyman of the traditional sort. In his eighties Pilkington still played cricket and cycled. Gould loved to talk to him about past sporting moments.

Towards the end of his schooldays Gould's circumstances had been transformed by his father's death. Gould was the only remaining child, two brothers

---

[81] See Isabel Quigly, *The Heirs of Tom Brown: The English School Story* (Oxford, 1984).
[82] *DNB 1912–1921*, 221.   [83] Nat Gould, *The Magic of Sport: Mainly Autobiographical* (1909), 5.

having died in infancy; now, he was required to seek work. He first tried his father's business, the tea trade. He did not stick it for long. Gould admitted to taking time off to attend race meetings and cricket matches, and the theatre and music hall, which exhausted the patience of his father's former partner. He left for Derbyshire, to help out on the farms of his various maternal relations. The experience and setting stayed permanently with Gould, who thereafter regarded this part of England both as his real home and as the most gorgeous and inspirational place in the world. Gould generally prided himself on his matter-of-fact style as a writer, but his autobiography burst with emotion at this point:

I have travelled in many lands—in Australia, on the Continent, throughout England, Scotland and Wales—but I have never seen a more beautiful view than can be obtained from the old hill at the back of Hanson Grange. It is small wonder that these memories of country life never left me, no matter where my lot was cast. The love of Nature was bred and born in me; no amount of city life has stamped it out. When I feel dull, or my brain and body require rest, I flee to the solitude of these dear old hills, and my youth comes back to me; a flood of memories pleasantly overwhelms me, and I return to my work invigorated, a new man . . . I have sat on the Nabbs [the hill behind the farm] and watched the shadows creep over hill and dale as the day gently waned. What colourings, what marvellous tints. No artist could catch and hold them. Here are pictures more beautiful than in all the galleries of Rome, Florence, Milan, Paris, Naples, Antwerp, Brussels, Bruges, London and a hundred other places; and I see them alone, with no guide-book in my hand, no description, no one to point out the glorious blending of colours; and I have no need of them.[84]

Gould quit paradise because the prospect of acquiring a farm of his own was remote. To appease his mother he again tried the tea trade until, in 1877, he answered an advertisement for staff on the *Newark Advertiser*. This had been placed by Cornelius Brown, who was part-proprietor of the paper and its editor for thirty-three years. Gould remembered him with great affection: Brown was a notable local historian, the vice-president of the Thornton Society, and a Disraelian Conservative. Gould himself was less interested in the politics, though as a reporter he attended speeches in the town by Disraeli and Gladstone, John Bright, Joseph Chamberlain, and Lord Randolph Churchill, the best of whom he thought was Bright because 'magnificently simple in his language'.[85] Newark also had a racecourse; again, Gould was drawn by the sport. But, much as he enjoyed his time there, ambition dictated that he move on. In 1884, armed with letters of introduction from Brown and from Edward Lloyd (of the *Daily Chronicle*), he embarked for Australia.

Gould intended to stay in Australia for about a year. In fact, he remained for eleven years, married there (in 1886), and began a family, which eventually comprised three sons and two daughters. His first position was chief reporter on

---

[84] Ibid. 74–5. Gould included a photograph of the wondrous spot, opposite p. 66.   [85] Ibid. 111.

the *Brisbane Telegraph*, at £250 per annum: it was a jack-of-all-trades job, covering commercial intelligence, theatre notices, and the turf. He then moved to Sydney, contributing racing news for the *Referee*. The reporter of horse-racing was also a punter. On one unforgettable afternoon he backed all six winners; throughout his life he was quite untroubled by gambling as a moral question. Now freelancing, and suffering spells out of work, Gould was briefly editor of an up-country paper in New South Wales, the *Bathurst Times*. He also began to write stories, the first of which, 'With the Tide', was serialized in the *Referee*:

The plot came naturally; it worked itself without much effort on my part. I wrote about what I had seen, and men I knew; about horses, trainers and jockeys; about that great and wonderful mass of human beings who flock to all racecourses. I had ample material to work upon; there is no better hunting-ground in the world for all sorts of characters than the racecourse.[86]

The story got into book form largely through an introduction to Walter Home, a traveller for the publisher George Routledge & Sons, who was visiting Sydney. He astonished Gould by offering him a three-figure sum for it and by also buying the rights to two other serials he was contemplating. 'With the Tide' was published in 1891 as a cheap 'yellowback'[87] with a new title chosen by Routledge's: *The Double Event*. That referred to the most famous fixtures in the Australian racing calendar, the 'double event' being the Caulfield Cup and the Melbourne Cup, to coincide with which an autumn publication date was chosen; and the book, which intertwined a detective story with the races, became an instant best-seller in Australia and Britain. A dramatized version, by the actor–author George Darrell, played at the Theatre Royal, Melbourne, in 1893. Gould was suitably encouraged and, though he had not yet hit the rhythm that regulated most of his subsequent career, that of producing four full novels and one shorter story annually, he turned out another seven or eight novels before leaving Australia in 1895.

Gould's wife had never been to England. Gould himself was frankly homesick, but he remained fond of Australia and was shocked by the 'colossal' ignorance of colonial subjects he found on his return:

I have seen Melbourne described as the capital of New South Wales in a leading London daily; one can understand anything after that. Things are better now, but even in 1908 Australia is little better than an unknown land to Englishmen. The recent 'White City' Exhibition must have opened the eyes of millions to the possibilities of Australia.[88]

---

[86] Ibid. 170.

[87] The name given originally to the novels reprint series pioneered by Chapman & Hall in the 1850s, for distribution through W. H. Smith's and designed for railway reading, priced 2s. or 2s. 6d. See Sutherland, *Companion*, 685.

[88] Gould, *Magic of Sport*, 181. Gould wrote two books about Australia, immediately on his return to England. Even these contained their sporting episodes: *On and Off the Turf in Australia* (1895) and *Town and Bush* (1896).

Gould was not one to mount a platform about anything, however. Rather, he simply saddled up as an author and headed for the winning post. He became master of the horse-racing story, though he was not its pioneer. Advertisements of his early work proclaimed him as 'the Hawley Smart of Australia', a reference to H. Hawley Smart (1833–93), who had been an officer in the Crimea and Indian Mutiny; after 1869 Smart turned out a couple of novels a year, which mixed horse-racing, hunting, and service life.[89] By about 1904 Gould had out-stripped Smart's total of some fifty novels; and when he paused to compose the autobiography that appeared in 1909, he had completed over seventy novels and numerous short stories, for which his publishers claimed sales of nearly 6 million.[90] At his death in 1919 his reputation was unrivalled: as *The Times* obituary put it, 'Whenever the name of Nat Gould was mentioned, one of the con-versationalists was bound, by some irresistible impulse, to recall some stirring finish' in a race.[91] As a result of this popularity, Gould lived comfortably but, in view of these vast sales, it is somewhat surprising that he left only £7,795[92]—a substantial sum for the times but no more than one-ninth the amount left by Charles Garvice, who died in the following year.

The possibility of Gould having taken steps to shelter some of his fortune from the tax man, as Hall Caine did, or of his having dissipated money through gambling, as the popular playwright G. R. Sims did, cannot be discounted; but part of the explanation might be found in his relations with publishers, of whom he only ever had two, Routledge's followed by John Long. Gould prided himself on that loyalty, which he liked to think was mutual; yet, perhaps he would have done better had he used an independent literary agent to take fuller advantage of the market and especially of the royalty system. On returning to England, he struck up a friendship with Colonel Robert Routledge, who was senior partner, following the death in 1888 of his father, the firm's founder. 'Colonel Routledge', wrote Gould, 'was the sort of man anyone could get on with'; but, he added cryptically, 'the old firm fell on evil times, and there was trouble and many changes in Broadway.'[93] That was Gould's charitable way of referring to what another of Robert Routledge's friends, Eveleigh Nash, explained about the circumstances by which the Colonel 'was obliged to retire, as he had been living beyond his means and had overdrawn his account by nearly £10,000'.[94] Forced out by his younger brother Edmund, the Colonel set up as a literary agent, and Gould placed his books with him, 'more as an act of friendship than anything else. I promised him I would stick to the firm so long as he was in it.'[95] That handsome gesture on Gould's part was not tested more than briefly, because both Routledge brothers died suddenly in 1899. Gould had several books in press

[89] Sutherland, *Companion*, 585.
[90] Gould, *Magic of Sport*, 203. According to an advertisement in *The Bookseller* in 1909, the sales *exceeded* 6 million; quoted in Derek Hudson, 'Reading', in Nowell-Smith (ed.), *Edwardian England*, 316.
[91] *The Times*, 26 July 1919.   [92] Ibid., 15 Sept. 1919; *Oxford DNB*.
[93] Gould, *Magic of Sport*, 195.   [94] Nash, *Life*, 38.   [95] Gould, *Magic of Sport*, 195.

with the firm and others already committed, but in 1902 he was courted by John Long, and after 'a conversation, which lasted about half an hour', Gould offered to 'do him a dozen novels and three annuals in three years, if he cared to take it on'.[96] The arrangement was renewed, and continued for the rest of Gould's life.

Except for the interlude with the discharged Colonel Routledge, who, Gould emphasized, 'merely acted as a friend', he never employed a literary agent:

What is the use of an agent when you can transact the business yourself? An agent requires his commission—probably he is worth it—but I cannot speak from experience. My plan is to go straight to the publisher and ask him what sort of terms he is willing to give me for my work. I never take in a manuscript and bargain for it; I always believe in making an agreement before I begin writing.[97]

About his relations with John Long, whose hospitality at his Surbiton home Gould often enjoyed, he wrote:

He has never met me with a refusal when it came to asking a certain sum for a book. I do not think I have a grasping disposition; I am sure he has not. An author and a publisher ought to row together, pull in the same boat, to their mutual advantage . . . .The author ought to know his public, and what they want; the publisher ought to know how to get at that public. A good deal of advice is given to authors. They are told their work ought to be written with a view to elevating the public taste—write literature, have style, no matter whether it pays or not; money is a matter that should never be considered in connection with writing. All I can say in reply is that I write to please my public, and I write to make a living. A dead man does not get much satisfaction because his work happens to have caught on with posterity, mainly because what he has written is sold in a cheap, attractive form. Some publishers appear to exist on dead men's brains; I prefer a publisher who pays cash down to living authors.[98]

This last remark would suggest that Gould usually sold his work outright. The preferred format remained the 'yellowback'. This made him very distinctive as an author at this date. Memoirs by individuals who remembered reading Gould—such as Gilbert Frankau, who read him when at Eton at the turn of the century—referred to 'Nat Gould's yellow-backed racing novels'.[99] In 1909 Gould thought that his were the only novels still published in that style. 'I was never a believer in high-priced novels,' he explained. 'It is far better to have millions of readers and purchasers at a reasonable rate than a select few at an enhanced price. There is another advantage in issuing a book at a moderate price; it can never be reduced from six shillings to a shilling in six months, a process not flattering to the author.'[100] In addition there were his shilling annuals. These were actually paperbacks: it is quite wrong to think that paperbacks were invented by Allen Lane and Penguin in 1935.[101] *Nat Gould's Annual* seldom contained more

---

[96] Ibid. 198.   [97] Ibid. 195.   [98] Ibid. 199–200.
[99] Frankau, *Self-Portrait*, 53.   [100] Gould, *Magic of Sport*, 203–4.
[101] Desmond Flower, *The Paper-Back: Its Past, Present and Future* (1959).

was as a field for redemption, for characters who had once fallen now to make amends. In *A Hundred To One Chance* Henrietta Berkley, who has deserted her children to return to a former lover, is rediscovered later in the story as a Mrs Gilles:

For some years she had been actively engaged in charitable work in the poorest slums of London, where the name of Mrs. Gilles was almost venerated. The bulk of her income she gave to others, living modestly in quiet retirement, trying to atone for the past. They knew nothing of this, and it was not for her to tell them.[110]

Gould accepted the class system, but he did not defer to it. What mattered was that individuals made the most of their lot by conscientious endeavour and showed regard for others who did likewise. Gould preferred nature's rugged gentlemen to the pampered and privileged kind. The snobs and the servile, and the workshy at all points of the social compass, were anathematized. The first chapter of *A Race for a Wife* introduces an apparently alpha male specimen, Clifton Charlemont, aged 40, 6 feet tall and broad-chested, handsome and rich. The son of an MP, he is a power in the City, a shipping magnate, colliery owner, large landowner, and possessor of a magnificent stud; and, on his estate at Oakhurst, he 'dealt even justice with a firm hand; the workers relied upon him, the shirkers feared him, idle men were of no use and were speedily dismissed'.[111] It seems probable that this masterful figure will win the fair 20-year-old Polly Mossley, particularly as she is badly bitten by his fiery thoroughbred when bravely trying to rein it in after it had thrown a stable hand; whereupon Clifton sweeps her up in his arms and carries her into his mansion, from where a doctor is summoned. Yet Polly is an independent creature, and this independence was bred in Australia. There she was born and raised before coming to England to live with her uncle on an estate which neighbours Clifton's. When not locating his racing stories in Australia itself, Gould repeatedly deploys the Australian experience as a democratic calling card. Polly rides where she wants: 'Australia's a free country, no danger of being caught trespassing there,'[112] she tells Clifton, who has too strong a sense of his private property. She also rides unattended, to the dismay of county society—'stuck-up people [who] think it is not proper'.[113] Among her other suitors is Jim Rowley, a frank and hearty character who is decidedly not top-drawer. He is in the wholesale butchery business, purchasing herds for the meat market; and, having made sufficient money, he indulges his love for horse-racing, competing in a minor way with Clifton and settling on Moat Farm nearby. The same county people who are affronted by Polly's free manner are stand-offish about Jim, which Polly cannot understand: 'In Australia it was different; one man was good as another.'[114] Eventually, Polly refuses Clifton's proposal of marriage and accepts Jim's. Both men are equally astonished. Jim, in his elation, blurts out that he had vowed to 'throw up the beastly trade' if

[110] Gould, *Hundred to One Chance*, 269.   [111] Gould, *Race for a Wife*, 13.
[112] Ibid. 33.   [113] Ibid. 206.   [114] Ibid. 193.

Polly consented to be his wife. 'You must do nothing of the kind; we can have some splendid trips about the country buying cattle,' she says; to which Gould appends the line 'And they do.' Gould also informs the reader that Jim and Polly 'were a success at Moat Farm; contrary to expectations "the people" called on them and were made welcome'.[115] Polly's delight is redoubled thereafter whenever one of Jim's horses finishes ahead of Clifton's; and she smartly scores over Amy Hammersley, a socially ambitious widow who, having married one rich man for his money and position, now becomes Clifton's wife. Amy is

rather jealous of the popularity of Moat Farm and its hospitalities. She was talking to Polly one day, and unfortunately remarked,

'I thought at first Clifton admired you, that he intended asking you to be his wife.'

'He did,' said Polly calmly, 'and I declined his proposal; I much prefer Jim.' Thus Polly 'took her down a peg'.[116]

They are the last words of the story.

These affairs of the heart, as in all Gould's novels, develop in the interstices of thrilling descriptions of races at Brighton, Doncaster, and Newmarket. It is there that the tales really come alive, with talk of owners, trainers, jockeys, punters, touts, and journalists. There is invariably some skullduggery present, but it is exposed and defeated; and nothing in the end detracts from the excitement of the horse race. The reader feels part of the crowd and, like most at a racecourse, so caught up in the action as to be almost riding the steed, striving with bursting lungs to cross the finishing line first. Doubtless, Gould would have agreed with George Borrow, who declared, while struggling to break in a half-Arab mount, 'What a contemptible trade is the author's compared with that of a jockey';[117] but Gould's evocativeness made it easy for his readers to change places.

The sort of person who read Gould naturally drew condescension. Thus 'a big man with a purple face and a signet ring as large as a carriage lamp' was imagined by *Punch*: 'he looked absolutely the type that reads only a half-penny daily and a sporting sheet and puts in the rest of its leisure at gossip or cards . . . I set him down for a Nat Gould man.'[118] By contrast, Andrew Lang, ever one to appreciate action in storytelling, was prepared to give credit. He nominated Gould for the presidency of a Sixpenny Academy because he 'shines by a candid simplicity of style, and a direct and unaffected appeal to the primitive emotions, and our love for that noble animal the horse'.[119] This vividness chiefly accounts for the huge readership amassed by Gould; and his unvarnished egalitarian philosophy underpinned the attraction. Unlike many pre-war bestsellers, Gould ran and ran in the inter-war years too, his popularity little diminished.[120] During the Great War itself, amid the grief and pain, his stock was at its height, providing entry for

[115] Ibid. 319. [116] Ibid. 320.
[117] Collie, *Borrow*, 252. [118] *Punch*, 8 Apr. 1914, 266.
[119] Lang, in *Longman's Magazine*, quoted in the publisher's advertisement in Gould, *Race for a Wife*, 8.
[120] McAleer, *Popular Reading*, 10.

everyman to the winner's enclosure. The novelist Beatrice Harraden, who served as librarian to a military hospital in Endell Street, London, wrote in the *Cornhill Magazine* in November 1916:

We had to invest in any amount of Nat Gould's sporting stories. In fact, a certain type of man would read nothing except Nat Gould. However ill he was, however suffering and broken, the name of Nat Gould would always bring a smile to his face. Often and often I've heard the whispered words: 'A Nat Gould—ready for when I'm better.'[121]

[121] Quoted in publisher's advertisement in Gould, *Race for a Wife*, 8.

IV
WRITERS AND THE PUBLIC: PENMEN AS PUNDITS

. . . I confess that I think public opinion much more likely to be influenced by steady firm action than by much talking and writing.

(Tennyson's refusal to assist in starting a Liberal Unionist journal, 1889)

24

The Campaign Trail

I

Literary people naturally declaimed about literary questions, but it was a sign of the pretensions of authorship that they also pronounced on most other subjects. Publishers positively encouraged topical fiction. When the City of Glasgow Bank, with 133 branches throughout Scotland, crashed in 1878, umpteen small savers and businesses faced ruin. The then Lord Provost (Mayor) of Glasgow was the publisher William Collins, and he set about organizing a relief fund. One feature was a series of Shakespeare readings by the actress Helen Faucit, which raised £470; further, Collins sought to commission Charles Reade to write a novel that would rouse public indignation about such financial malpractices and elicit charity for the victims. Reade, whose first great success, *It is Never Too Late to Mend* (1856), had pressed the cause of penal reform, nevertheless demurred. He felt old and worn-out (he would die in 1880); he also perceived certain problems.

It is most proper that the pen should take up the cause in this case, should expose the iniquity and paint the misery of the sufferers so as to excite universal sympathy if possible. But I do not think fiction is the proper form. The reader of fiction is narrow and self-indulgent. He will read no story the basis of which is not sexual. I feel I could not write a good fiction or command readers on such a subject. Indeed, I have made a trifling experiment in that line already. Guided by the deaths and lunacies that followed the stoppage of the Leeds Bank, I endeavoured in my novel *Hard Cash* [1863] to impress upon the novel-reader that a fraudulent Banker is a murderer as well as a thief. I even wrote a list of victims to prove it. It was wisdom wasted. Neither the novel-reading ass, nor the criticism ass received it. It was never commented on, and I believe everybody skipped it.[1]

It was not thought right, however, that fiction should be frivolous. Even the leading sensational novelist paraded his serious side. In the preface to *Basil: A Story of Modern Life* (1852) Wilkie Collins scorned 'the mob of ladies and gentlemen who play at writing . . . who coolly select as an amusement "to kill time", an occupation which can only be pursued, even creditably, by the patient, uncompromising, reverent devotion of every moral and intellectual faculty, more

[1] Keir, *The House of Collins*, 192–3.

or less, which a human being has to give'.[2] Having established that Literature was a profession, to be conducted as a Science, Collins freely used his novels to ventilate his views on social questions. *Man and Wife* (1870) was a fictionalized treatment of the married women's property law. It also targeted the philathletic cult in public schools and universities. The preface noted 'the recent spread of grossness and brutality among certain classes of the English population'. Whereas other writers tut-tutted about a savage underclass, 'the dirty Rough in fustian', Collins pilloried the toff, 'the washed Rough in broadcloth'. 'Is no protest needed', Collins concluded fiercely, 'in the interest of civilisation, against a revival of barbarism among us, which asserts itself to be a revival of manly virtue . . . ?'[3] Repeatedly, Collins tilted at Grundyism and at marriage and divorce laws. This nicely satisfied Charles Reade's test that, if a topical novel was going to grip the public, sexual intrigue must be central. Collins, whose domestic arrangements were unconventional,[4] decidedly had a special interest in this area; but these questions engaged many other authors, particularly from the 1880s, a period that witnessed radical reappraisals of the position of women in both public and private spheres. Thereafter, it was not just a matter of authors insidiously implanting challenging opinions and behaviour in their stories; authors were boldly stepping outside the shelter of their fiction and onto platforms or else debating these questions in the pages of journals. Arnold Bennett comically scored the point in *The Title* (1918). This play features a pseudonymous author, Sampson Straight, who, it emerges, is female and, 'being a young woman of advanced ideas, [she] has written about everything, *everything*—yes, and several other subjects besides'.[5]

II

Some first made a reputation as controversialists *before* they became widely known as authors. Mona Caird seized the limelight by her contributions to the debate 'Is Marriage a Failure?', initiated in the *Daily Telegraph*. Her articles in the *Westminster Review* in 1888–9, in the *Fortnightly Review* and *North American Review* in 1890, and in the *Nineteenth Century* in 1892, brought her fame, where none of her early novels had done; and this paved the way for the success of her *Daughters of Danaus* (1894).[6] She was born Alica Mona Alison, her father being

---

[2] Peters, *Collins*, 116. For an extended analysis of *Basil*, Taylor, *Secret Theatre*, ch. 2.

[3] Taylor, *Secret Theatre*, 214; Peters, *Collins*, 321.

[4] Collins scandalized Victorian society when his will was published in 1889, bequeathing his estate equally to two mistresses: Caroline Graves, who had lived with him from 1859 and resumed her relationship with him in the 1870s, having married another meanwhile; and Martha Rudd, whom he stationed nearby and by whom he had three illegitimate children. See William M. Clarke, *The Secret Life of Wilkie Collins* (1988).   [5] Arnold Bennett, *The Title* (1918), 24.

[6] On Caird (1854–1932), see Beverly E. Schneller's notice in *Oxford DNB*, and Sutherland, *Companion*, 99–100, 172, although Sutherland gives her birth year as 1858. Thomas Hardy acted as sponsor of one of

John Alison, 'inventor of the vertical boiler', as she proudly recorded in *Who's Who*. Raised partly in Australia, at the age of 23 in 1877 she married a son of Sir James Caird, the authority on agrarian matters.[7] Sir James, a one-time MP and president of the Statistical Society, was a friend of John Bright and T. H. Huxley; and it was this mid-Victorian network of political and intellectual liberals who influenced Mona Caird through their writings, particularly John Stuart Mill on *The Subjection of Women* (1869), though a love of Shelley also left its mark. She contended that for women the conventions governing marriage were akin to slavery because of incessant childbirth, overwork, and subordination. The double standard revolted her. Women were expected to practise self-control, men not; accordingly, many innocent wives had their health and reason destroyed by their husbands incurring venereal diseases.

'The married martyrs' was Caird's sarcastic toast at a Literary Ladies' dinner, held in the Criterion Restaurant in 1889.[8] Her ideal marriage was contracted between a consenting couple. Any infraction provided sufficient cause for separation or divorce. 'A more morally developed people' required this 'greater freedom'. She swept aside one supposed defence of existing marriage, that it protected the interests of children. On the contrary, its abolition should be sought for their sake; in any case, she smartly added, parents who dispatched their offspring to boarding schools just at the age when they most required 'the beneficial influence of home life, have no right to indulge in platitudes concerning the necessity of parental influence'. She dismissed too the criticisms of other women novelists, such as Eliza Lynn Linton, who had finger-wagged about a proper 'woman's sphere' and opposed female suffrage in a succession of scalding articles and essays over thirty years, beginning in the *Saturday Review* in the late 1860s.[9] *Punch*, reviewing her fragmentary memoirs, *My Literary Life*, posthumously published in 1899, remarked that while 'in looks and manner the model of a kindly-hearted lady, [she] was accustomed when she took pen in hand to dip it in gall. She loved few women and suspected all men.'[10] 'The Wild Woman' was how she had termed the New Woman, who 'smokes after dinner with the men; in railway carriages, in public rooms . . .'. 'Marriage, in its old-fashioned aspect as the union of two lives, they repudiate as one-sided tyranny; and maternity, for which, after all, women primarily exist, they regard as degradation,' raged Mrs Linton, who, as if to pile paradox upon paradox, had been a pioneer independent woman author in her younger days, had separated from her husband, and never had children of her own. All this was a trifle disconcerting. 'Mrs Linton's articles are really getting so very noisy,' says Mrs Windsor in

her articles, on evolution in marriage, seeking to interest the editor of the *Contemporary Review*, who rejected it; see Hardy to Percy Bunting, 13 Jan. 1890, in Purdy and Millgate (eds.), *Hardy Letters*, i. 207–8.

[7] On Sir James Caird (1816–92), *DNB Supplement* (1901), i. 365–7.   [8] *Punch*, 15 June 1889, 296.

[9] The best account of her critique and explanation of her extraordinary misogyny, is Nancy Fix Anderson, *Woman against Women in Victorian England: A Life of Eliza Lynn Linton* (Bloomington, Ind., 1987).   [10] *Punch*, 7 Mar. 1900, 164.

The Green Carnation (1894), adding, while drawing on her gloves, 'Don't you think they rather suggest Bedlam?'[11] Driving Mrs Linton mad hardly bothered Mrs Caird: 'If the new movement had no other effect than to rouse women to rebellion against the madness of large families,' she declared, 'it would confer a priceless benefit on humanity.'[12]

Mrs Caird's views generated a great quantity of articles and essays, and the subject remained a hardy perennial. In 1904 Pearl Craigie, the author John Oliver Hobbes, was asked to write on marriage for the *Daily Telegraph*. 'Articles have appeared in all the papers on the subject,' she noted; and 'the *D.T.* has been on the marriage question for years.'[13] Married in 1887 at the age of 19, she left her husband after four years. This experience, together with the publicity given to her divorce in 1895, when unusually she was assigned sole custody of their son and the father allowed no legal access, caused lasting emotional damage, which was not assuaged by her conversion to Catholicism in 1892.[14] As well as articles, the marriage question inspired heated fiction, notably Grant Allen's *The Woman Who Did* (1895) and Victoria Crosse's *The Woman Who Didn't* (1895), which established the publishing firm of John Lane.[15]

It was the position adopted by these authors on issues of social morality that mattered. Branded by James Payn as 'our Neo-Neurotic and "Personal" Novelists',[16] their books, judged as stories or for their characterization and style, were (to put it politely) undistinguished—an inferiority that was also regretted by those who were sympathetic to their aims and thought that a noble mission ought to elicit a better class of literature. H. G. Wells, reviewing *The Woman Who Did*, 'was the more infuriated because I was so nearly in agreement with Grant Allen's ideas, that this hasty, headlong, incompetent book seemed like treason to a great cause'. Its heroine, who defies convention by having an illegitimate child of 'her very own', was absurdly overdrawn with 'spotless' soul, supreme beauty, and 'silvery voice', 'enthroned amid the halo of her own perfect purity', according to Allen's descriptions. Wells likened her to a plaster saint typical of any inferior novelette. He also thought that Allen preached a

---

[11] Hichens, *Green Carnation*, 78. The model for Mrs Windsor was Ada Leverson.

[12] Sutherland, *Companion*, 20–1, 377–8, 677–8; *Review of Reviews* (March 1890), 198 (for Caird), (June 1890), 511 (for Allen), (July 1890), 171, and (May 1892), 500 (for Caird); and Constance Rover, *Love, Morals and the Feminists* (1970), 135–6, for the quotations from Mrs Linton's articles in the *Nineteenth Century* (July and Oct. 1891). Mrs Caird was active too in the anti-vivisectionist movement, and wrote tracts about this.

[13] Letter to Moberly Bell, 22 Sept. 1904, in Richards, *John Oliver Hobbes*, 263–4.

[14] The damage was more than emotional, her husband's infidelities infecting her with syphilis: see Mildred Davis Harding's notice of Craigie (1867–1906) in *Oxford DNB*. Because she was not a Catholic at the time of her marriage, Craigie was forbidden in the divorce order to bring up her son in that faith. See her letter to Arthur Benson about sending the boy to Eton in 1899; Richards, *John Oliver Hobbes*, 167. For a cloying obituary by the editor of *Punch*, Owen Seaman (once romantically involved with her), see *Punch*, 5 Sept. 1906, 167.

[15] For a parody, 'The Woman who wouldn't Do. (She-Note Series)', *Punch*, 30 Mar. 1895, 153; and cartoon, 'The latest Literary Success. "The Woman Who Wanted To"', ibid., 26 Oct. 1895, 202.

[16] 'None of the authors of these works are story-tellers,' he said dismissively; *Punch*, 1 Sept. 1894, 99.

muddle-headed gospel:

He does not propose to emancipate them [women] from the narrowness, the sexual savagery, the want of charity, that are the sole causes of the miseries of the illegitimate and the unfortunate. Instead he wishes to emancipate them from monogamy, which we have hitherto regarded as being more of a fetter upon virile instincts. His proposal is to abolish cohabitation, to abolish the family—that school of all human gentleness—and to provide support for women who may have children at the expense of the State . . . Now Mr. Grant Allen must know perfectly well that amorous desires and the desire to bear children are anything but overpowering impulses in many of the very noblest women. The women, who would inevitably have numerous children under the conditions he hopes for, would be the hysterically erotic, the sexually incontinent. *Why* he should make proposals to cultivate humanity in this discretion is not apparent.[17]

In 1895 Wells also reviewed Allen's *The British Barbarians: A Hill-Top Novel*. Again, Wells protested about Allen's abuse of the novel to launch 'diatribes against the existing laws relating to morality and property'. *The Woman Who Did* was then in its nineteenth edition; but Wells decried the entire 'Woman Who' genre, asserting that this school of fiction was 'without the faintest appeal to any human being . . . except to those who are still in the "curious" stage of sexual development'.[18]

Contempt for Allen also came easily to Joseph Conrad, who, despising public taste, assumed that every best-seller was *ipso facto* artless and a product of 'inferior intelligence'. The 'imbécile' Allen wrote 'popular scientific manuals' as well as novels; still, Conrad disclosed a sneaking admiration for this confidence trick, whereby Allen presented himself as 'a man of letters among scholars and a scholar among men of letters'.[19] Allen indeed was a social Darwinist of an extreme kind, who analysed the relations of the sexes as he did those of classes, races, and nations, alike with (he thought) dispassionate rationalism. Readers of the *Westminster Gazette* had already been treated to his meditative essays, twenty-five of which were republished as *Post-Prandial Philosophy* (1894). 'A Glimpse into Utopia' imagined 'the position of woman in an ideal community'. This was determined by biology, women's reproductive function. He reckoned: 'An average of something like four [children per mother] is necessary, we know, to keep up population, and to allow for infant mortality, inevitable celibates, and so forth.' The question to resolve, therefore, 'if women endure on our behalf the greater public burden of providing future citizens', was how 'to render that burden as honourable and as little onerous as possible'. Allen answered:

in order that she may possess this freedom to perfection, that she may be no husband's slave, no father's obedient and trembling daughter, I can see but one way: the whole body of men in common must support in perfect liberty the whole body of women . . . In

---

[17] *Saturday Review*, 9 Mar. 1895, quoted in Wells, *Autobiography*, ii. 549–51.

[18] *Saturday Review*, 13 May and 14 Dec. 1895, and 21 Sept. 1896, in Parrinder and Philmus (eds.), *Wells's Literary Criticism*, 44–7, 59–61, 82.

[19] To Aniela Zagórska, Christmas 1898, in Karl and Davies (eds.), *Conrad Letters*, ii. 137–8. *Punch* also regularly targeted Allen as an egotistical fraud: for example, 23 Nov. 1895, 241, or 14 Dec. 1895, 285.

the ideal State, I take it, every woman will be absolutely at liberty to dispose of herself as she will, and no man will be able to command or to purchase her, to influence her in any way, save by pure inclination.

Allen did not envisage women working in the economy; rather, they would be supported by State endowment.[20] Such views exasperated not only Conrad and Wells but also the suffrage leader Mrs Millicent Fawcett, who coldly advised supporters

to remember that Mr. Grant Allen has never given help by tongue or pen to any practical effort to improve the legal or social status of women. He is not a friend, but an enemy, and it is as an enemy that he endeavours to link together the claims of women to citizenship and social and industrial independence with attacks upon marriage and the family.[21]

In after years Wells came to appreciate how he and many writers who aspired to dismantle social convention, to promote female independence, and to treat the sexes' relationships in a mature way, owed 'a certain mental indebtedness' to the pioneering efforts of such as Grant Allen; and the irony was not lost on Wells when his *Passionate Friends* (1913) 'was slated furiously and in much the same spirit by the younger generation in the person of Rebecca West'.[22] For all their inadequacies, therefore, 'New Woman' novels and plays constituted one of the most important categories of literature in the late nineteenth century.[23] Moreover, since the majority of fiction-readers was female, several of these productions enjoyed huge sales. Sarah Grand's *The Heavenly Twins* (1893) was one that flourished in spite of rejection slips from Blackwood's and Chapman & Hall, the latter advised by George Meredith. 'She has ability enough and a glimpse of humour here and there and promises well for the future,' he wrote; but she did not understand 'the art of driving a story', which was overwhelmed by the 'ideas'.[24]

Meredith's *congé* appears in retrospect dismally myopic, given the thickets of thought impeding the narrative in his own work; but for a publisher's reader hacking through ten manuscripts a week, it is unreasonable to expect infallibility. Meredith's overall record of service to the women's cause was substantial. It was

---

[20] Allen, *Post-Prandial Philosophy*, ch. xxiii; also ch. xxv, for his rejoinder to those who questioned whether women could be genuinely independent if men (through State taxation) supplied their income. That fewer young men of the middle class—defined as that 'stratum of society, roughly bounded by a silk hat on Sundays'—were now marrying, he attributed to the stresses of urban life. This led to 'an increase in sundry hateful and degrading vices', among them homosexuality (ch. xiv).

[21] *Contemporary Review* (1895), quoted by Elaine Showalter, letter to *TLS*, 27 Aug. 1993.

[22] Wells, *Autobiography*, ii. 548. Rebecca West had previously taken issue with Wells's *Marriage* (1912): her review in *Freewoman*, 19 Sept. 1912, is reprinted in Parrinder (ed.), *Wells: Critical Heritage*, 203–8.

[23] See Showalter, *Literature of their Own*, esp. chs. vii–viii; and, for a summary, see Sutherland, *Companion*, 460–1.

[24] Sassoon, *Meredith*, 68, 223, 250. Grand visited Meredith in 1896, when he was recorded as observing that she 'will improve, for she has said she has begun to care for nothing but literature'; and in July 1904 she was to the fore of a party of some fifty members of the Whitefriars Club who called at Box Hill to pay homage to Meredith.

he who had persuaded Chapman & Hall to take on *The Story of an African Farm* (1883) by Olive Schreiner; and in 1891 she told W. T. Stead that 'Ibsen and George Meredith are the only men of modern times who understand women.'[25] Wilfrid Blunt, whose amatory adventures qualified him as a different kind of expert, composed a similar testimonial in 1912. Though he considered the female characters in Meredith's novels to be fanciful and even weak and wearisome, he acknowledged that 'they have had a considerable influence on our modern ladies—who like to think of themselves as he represents them. He has certainly had a great deal to do with their present sex emancipation.'[26] The painful experience of his desertion by his first wife was refracted in his poetry and fiction; inexorably, he was drawn out to pronounce on the marriage question. In 1904, in the *Daily Mail*, his invitation for people to practise marriage initially in the form of a ten-year probationary period roused 'an outcry from the whole army of Mrs. Grundy'. 'Yet', he observed, 'that powerful person might reflect on the number of Divorces, and consider that when distaste is between couples, it is worse for the offspring. Happily there is a majority of marriages where the two jog along contentedly—with, however, too great an indifference to the minority.'[27] And later, to a married daughter of Alice Meynell—a Roman Catholic—he remarked equably, 'Well, girls are now earning an independence. Few of them see happy marriages around them, and the indissolubility of the tie scares them.'[28]

Meredith was confident that female suffrage would come and he welcomed the prospect, while fearing that suffragette 'intemperateness' would retard the day.[29] But it was always larger questions that concerned him, telling one correspondent in a letter intended to be publicized: 'At present our civilization is ill-balanced, owing to a state of things affecting women, which they may well call subjection.'[30] Hence his concern for education: marriage would remain a rough lottery until boys and girls were schooled together.[31] He denied that there was 'natural hostility between the sexes', yet they must 'have learnt to step forward together'. Fulfilling marriages was only one good to be obtained; even more important was the necessity to transform attitudes and to enlarge capacities. All society suffered when women were 'confined to the domestic circle—consequently a wasted force'.[32] The culmination of his meditations was this, published in the *Manchester Guardian*, 28 March 1905:

Since I began to reflect I have been oppressed by the injustice done to women, the constraint put upon their natural aptitudes and their faculties, generally much to the degradation of the race. I have not studied them more closely than I have men, but with

---

[25] *Review of Reviews* (Feb. 1891), 187; First and Scott, *Schreiner*, 118–19.
[26] Blunt, *Diaries*, ii. 404–5 (22 Nov. 1912); and Max Beerbohm's tribute 'Euphemia Clashthought', in *Christmas Garland*, 187–97.   [27] To Mrs Simons, 17 Nov. 1904, in Cline (ed.), *Meredith's Letters*, iii. 1510.
[28] To Mrs C. W. Saleeby, 17 Oct. 1908, ibid. 1673.
[29] To the editor of *The Times*, c.28 Oct. 1906, ibid. 1576–7; also pp. 1615, 1634, 1686, for similar statements on the unwisdom of militancy and violence.   [30] To Miss Rachel Wheatcroft, 13 Apr. 1907, ibid. 1591.
[31] To Lady Ulrica Duncombe, 19 Apr. 1902, ibid. 1438.
[32] To Mrs A. E. Fletcher, The Dorking Women's Liberal Association, 19? May 1904, ibid. 1497–8.

more affection, a deeper interest in their enfranchisement and development, being assured that women of the independent mind are needed for any sensible degree of progress. They will so educate their daughters, that these will not be instructed at the start to think themselves naturally inferior to men, because less muscular, and need not have recourse to particular arts, feline chiefly, to make their way in the world.[33]

Meredith saw the vote as but one step towards effecting this metamorphosis. It was unhealthy for a society that its womenfolk should be kept in a state of immaturity, like perpetual children, psychologically as well as financially dependent, and chiefly expressing themselves frivolously, deviously, or in tantrums.

Meredith's advice to Chapman & Hall to reject Sarah Grand's *Heavenly Twins* was an artistic judgement, therefore, and not for reasons of morality or male prejudice. He held such doubts about several women writers whom critics saw as his literary disciples, John Oliver Hobbes as well as Sarah Grand.[34] Notwithstanding Meredith's cold douche, Grand had her novel printed privately, whereupon it was picked up by Heinemann and reprinted several times in the year.[35] John Sutherland ascribes its popularity to 'Grand's unusually frank description of syphilis' in the course of indicting the sexual double standard.[36] This was no imagined world to Grand, whose husband, a former army doctor, worked in a lock-hospital for prostitutes suffering from venereal diseases. For Arnold Bennett, who served his journalistic apprenticeship on the magazine *Woman* and who in the late 1890s endeavoured to explain Grand's popularity for readers of *The Academy*, she was a classic instance of a person who became a writer not from natural literary talent but from having a prophetic message:

The titles of her first books—*Singularly Deluded: A Domestic Experiment* and *Ideala*—naively disclose her tendency. Without opening them you can see the passionate reformer running amok through all the cherished humbugs of an established system. *The Heavenly Twins*, equally famous and notorious, was a fierce onslaught which, it is safe to say, made a fearful breach in the walls of the Home—that demure fabric so long and faithfully defended by Charlotte Yonge and Miss Rhoda Broughton . . . The book was eagerly and gratefully accepted by women, who perceived in it not only the bold utterance of their timid aspirations, but also a distant hope of release from the somewhat Ottoman codes of

---

[33] To Hugh W. Strong, Jan. 1905, ibid. 1513.   [34] Stevenson, *Ordeal of Meredith*, 306.

[35] There is some discrepancy from the account given in Sutherland, *Companion*: 'the novel sold 20,000 copies and was reprinted six times in the first year' (p. 258), and 'Heinemann claimed a sale of 40,000 within a few weeks' (p. 288). It was not noticed by *Punch* until 24 Feb. 1894, when its reviewer, while critical of 'the somewhat meandering story', acknowledged 'a remarkable book' which had been greatly taken up by the public.

[36] On Sarah Grand, (Frances Elizabeth Bellenden McFall, *née* Clarke 1854–1943), see Sutherland, *Companion*, 257–8; Kemp *et al.* (eds.), *Edwardian Fiction*, 159; *Who Was Who*, 1941–1950, 458. Thomas Hardy, midway between *Tess* and *Jude*, read *The Heavenly Twins* in 1893; and he affected to be unimpressed. Grand had not 'such a sympathetic & intuitive knowledge of human nature . . . [but she] has yet an immense advantage . . . in the fact of having decided to offend her friends (so she told me)—& now that they are all alienated she can write boldly, & get listened to'. See Hardy to Florence Henniker, 7 and 20 June, 16 Sept. 1893, in Purdy and Millgate (eds.), *Hardy Letters*, ii. 12,18,33.

men. It was a bad novel—artistically vicious in its crudity, violence, unfairness, literary indecorum, improbability, impossibility—but it was a brilliant, though unscrupulous, argument against the 'criminal repression of women' for the selfish ends of men. Its bitter temper is summed up in a single phrase, a phrase not bearing on the main point: 'All that women ask is to be allowed to earn their bread honestly: but there is no doubt that the majority of men would rather see them on the streets'. . . If any recent novel has been saved, instead of damned, by its purpose, *The Heavenly Twins* is that novel. It is the modern equivalent of *Uncle Tom's Cabin*.[37]

Unfortunately, Bennett added, Grand could not leave it there: 'She had fallen into the habit of fiction, and she persisted in it, blind to the fact that she had exhausted the one ingredient which could vitalise her work.' Hence the inferior sequels such as *The Beth Book* (1897), though this was equally potent in generating debate. It provoked the editor of the Conservative *St James's Gazette*, Frederick Greenwood, to consider 'the influence of such writing, & of the "revelations" of women by women upon marriage. That is to say, how strongly they must persuade young men not to marry—young men having many cogent dissuasions from it already wh. did not exist a century ago. And how much would that consequence improve the position of women or conduce to "purity"?'[38] Then there was *Babs the Impossible* (1900): 'does not the title constitute a menace?', Bennett mused. To promote it, the publisher issued 'a pamphlet-interview exegetical of the author's higher aims', in which she 'glibly' pronounced on the plight of women left behind in rural areas as men migrated to towns and on wives trapped at home while their husbands gadded about the wide and wicked world.[39] *Punch*, which likewise bridled at having been sent the interview transcript together with a review copy of *Babs the Impossible*, had the bright idea of including in its 'Masterpieces Modernised' series an adaptation by Grand of Mrs Gaskell's *Cranford* (1853).[40]

Grand did not rest her advocacy of the women's cause on her (dis)abilities as a novelist. She lectured on the need to produce the New Man, by abandoning those attitudes which from nursery age indulged a boy's worst instincts and so made him in adulthood 'a weak-willed, inconsistent creature' and veritable Caliban.[41] Her addresses on this theme and on women's education and marriage law reform were published as *Modern Men and Maid* (1898); she became president of the Tunbridge Wells branch of the National Union of Women's Suffrage Societies and, when in her seventies, she served as Mayor of Bath. Hence, Grand, who had

---

[37] Bennett, *Fame and Fiction*, 72–6.

[38] Scott, *Pall Mall Gazette*, 297. On *The Beth Book* (1897), see Showalter, *Literature of their Own*, 207–9, and Sutherland, *Companion*, 61–2. Again, perhaps surprisingly, it received praise in the review in *Punch*, 4 Dec. 1897, 261.

[39] Bennett, *Fame and Fiction*, 77–9. *Punch*, 24 Apr. 1901, 318, also bridled at the booklet containing the interview with the author, enclosed by the publisher with the review copy.

[40] *Punch*, 11 Apr. 1900, 259, 24 Apr. 1901, 318.

[41] *Pall Mall Gazette*, 16 May 1894, generating a satirical ode, 'A Ballade of the New Manhood', in *Punch*, 26 May 1894, 249.

separated from her husband and supported herself and son by writing, was an exemplary New Woman in fact. Moreover, *pace* Bennett, Grand's work was thought perspicacious by other women. It was a great moment for Marguerite Steen when, attending the dedication of a memorial to the actress Mrs Siddons at Bath in the 1920s, she met Mayor Grand: 'I have learned more about character from Sarah Grand's novels than I had learned from anybody since Thackeray.'[42] What was said as a smartness in *The Green Carnation* (1894), that 'Sarah Grand has inaugurated the Era of women's wrongs,'[43] appears close to truth.

III

The women's suffrage question involved prominent authors on both sides. Where there was a Sarah Grand in favour, there was a Marie Corelli against.[44] Naturally, the Poet Laureate Alfred Austin held a traditional view of the sexes to a grotesque degree: 'Will any one deny that, in great emergencies, men are, as a rule and collectively, calmer and more submissive to sound judgment than women, whose virtues reside rather in another direction? Give women the franchise and it is conceivable that war might be brought about by women against the effort of men to avert it.'[45] Austin found a ready home for his opinions in the *Daily Express*, whose editorials and correspondents devised numerous ingenious remedies for suffragette violence, from birching to wedlock.[46] It was female militancy that unnerved the *Express*, because the suffrage cause had not been proscribed at the outset. It was first promoted in its columns in October 1900, soon after the *Express* was started by Arthur Pearson, whose fortune was in part based on periodicals which targeted women readers.[47] The popular author Mrs George Corbett[48] then told the *Express* how she had 'provided wholesome entertainment for millions of readers and employment for thousands of workers. I am compelled to pay the same rates and taxes as if I were a man, and I am also compelled to do my share towards paying for the free education of children, who are thus enabled to compete with those of the professional and highly-taxed classes.' Women, she stated, had made enormous strides in recent years, 'and the tricky way in which several of our Franchise Bills have been shelved only proves that we are feared as equals in brains and possible influence, not despised as irresponsible inferiors'. She especially decried the injustice of denying the vote to women like herself, and instead endowing hordes of drunken and illiterate layabouts who were prey to malevolent agitators. These fine conservative

---

[42] Steen, *Looking Glass*, 61.   [43] Hichens, *Green Carnation*, 78.
[44] For Corelli's position, see above, Ch. 22.   [45] Quoted in McMillan, *Way we Were*, 96.
[46] Ibid. 94, 101.   [47] Dark, *Pearson*, 67.
[48] On Mrs Corbett (1846–1930), see Kemp *et al.* (eds.), *Edwardian Fiction*, 76–7, where she is identified as the author of crime and nautical fiction and of novels with a distinct feminist slant: *New Amazonia: A Foretaste of the Future* (1890) and *The Marriage Market: A Series of Confessions Compiled from the Diary of a Society Go-Between* (1905).

sentiments were capped by a peroration in which Mrs Corbett declared that it was

quite clear that women of education want to vote very badly; that they have petitioned for it in their thousands; that failure does not daunt them; that they mean to have the vote and that the time will come when Universal Adult Suffrage will be recognised as the only just method of acknowledging the growing usefulness of women's work and influence.[49]

Women's suffrage involved more than placing a cross on a ballot paper. Helena Swanwick wrote: 'Let there be no mistake about it—this movement was not primarily political; it was social, moral, psychological and profoundly religious.'[50] The economic aspect was problematic. The officially counted female proportion of the workforce in 1900 was much the same as in 1850, around 30 per cent. The decline in women's farm work was counterbalanced by an expansion of home workers, outworkers, and those entrapped in sweated trades. Domestic service remained the largest category of female employment, greater than the factory work that involved women, such as in the northern textile districts; and the numbers being recruited into unskilled or semi-skilled jobs in 'new' light industries, such as confectionery or bicycle manufacture, and into secretarial and clerical posts, shopwork and service trades, did not substantially revolutionize female economic expectations and enhance their independence.[51] Underpinning the movement into work were demographic trends, the so-called 'surplus women' problem (there were a million more women than men in 1881). Vaudevilleans found this funny and depicted the consequences at every social level. Ethel Joy, the new barmaid in the 1897 musical of that name, sings:

> Two girls to one boy in the birth-rate alarms
>   Each pessimist born of the age,
> So girls as typewriters now show off their charms,
>   Even Duchesses dance on the stage.[52]

More crucial in the formulation of discontents were changing social philosophies, the questioning of that culture which situated women in the home and confined them to purely domestic chores and child-rearing, intermitted by charitable endeavours, while men worked and politicked in a separate sphere and at a distance. Yet the majority of women did not expect to pursue careers in full-time paid employment. Most gave up jobs on marriage or else (usually more from financial necessity than choice) took on part-time or by-employment. 'Emancipation' for them meant freedom from work into the fulfilment of service

---

[49] Mrs Corbett's article in the *Daily Express* is reproduced in McMillan, *Way we Were*, 87–8.

[50] Swanwick, *I Have Been Young*, 187. Helena Swanwick, married to a mathematics don at Manchester University, was Walter Sickert's sister.

[51] The best summary is Elizabeth Roberts, *Women's Work 1840–1940* (1988).

[52] *The New Barmaid* (n.d. [1897]), words by Frederic Bowyer and W. E. Sprange, music by John Crook, 10.

to home and family, not freedom from home and family through work; as a result, most jobs categorized as 'women's work' were low-status, poorly paid, and unorganized. For many, therefore, the New Woman was not seen as an economically and socially independent individual, well able to stand on her own, but a figure in turmoil who fretted about her prospects and about what her relationships with men might involve now and in future. These anxieties were compounded among women who came from professional or propertied families, by the expanding debate about civil rights for working men whose cultural preferences were deemed vulgar.

Not only were pens wielded with vehemence on the suffrage issue, authors also took to the platforms—or, as Virginia Stephen (later Woolf) did, 'spent an afternoon or two weekly in addressing envelopes for the Adult Suffragists'.[53] This was in 1910, and her activity was soon curtailed by nervous breakdown; but it had signified a departure from her general antipathy to political work. Politicians she previously ranked with journalists as 'the lowest of God's creatures, creeping perpetually in the mud, and biting with one end and stinging with the other'.[54] The women's cause now drew out authors who otherwise might have been content (or compelled by force of circumstances) to devote themselves to literature. Some so far achieved recognition by their public work that it is almost forgotten that they were ever novelists. This is the case with Clementina Black—sister of the famous translator of Russian novels Constance Garnett—whose involvement in the suffrage movement, Fabian Society, and Women's Industrial Council, pressing for a minimum wage and women's trades unions, has entirely eclipsed her novel-writing.[55] The anti-establishment character of such campaigning was unmistakable. Suffragette militancy especially meant outlawry. *The Times* noted wryly that, though *Who's Who* was annually growing in size, there was still no place for Mrs Pankhurst or daughter Christabel in the expanded 1911 edition.[56]

Violence alienated erstwhile sympathizers. John Galsworthy appealed to them through the *Daily News*, now that they commanded public notice for the suffrage, to abandon their attacks: 'it is by reason, and not by force, that the battle will be won . . . The violent tactics give the impression that women have no real faith in their cause—which is the cause of Justice.'[57] The epitome of the gentleman who chivalrously if coolly extended a hand to all creatures in distress, Galsworthy reflected the mood at a time when opinions were both polarizing and hardening, and suffragette outrages were being countered by rough policing and forced

---

[53] Letter to Janet Case, 1 Jan. 1910, in Nicolson and Banks (eds.), *Flight of the Mind*, 421.

[54] Letter to Lady Robert Cecil, May 1908, ibid. 332.

[55] On Black (1853–1923), see Sutherland, *Companion*, 64, and Kemp *et al.* (eds.), *Edwardian Fiction*, 33, for an assessment of her novels; and Ellen F. Mappen's introduction to Clementina Black (ed.), *Married Women's Work* (1915, 1983).   [56] *The Times*, 26 Dec. 1910.

[57] Letter to unnamed correspondent, 22 Oct. 1909, repeating the arguments of his *Daily News* letter of the previous week, in John Galsworthy, *Glimpses and Reflections* (1937), 319–21.

feeding of prisoners.[58] Conan Doyle also earned the militants' wrath. In truth, he was never much of a sympathizer with the suffrage cause, though he accepted the admissibility of women to the franchise where they were taxpayers and he was a doughty champion of divorce law reform. Adhering to a traditional ideology of what constituted manliness and womanliness, he waxed indignant about suffragette assaults against property and person. His reward was an avalanche of abusive mail, seasoned by sulphuric acid tipped through his letter box.[59] 'Stirring times!' indeed, reflected Anthony Hope, a former Liberal candidate and, according to his friend J. M. Barrie, the ideal person 'to represent his craft in Parliament as the member for literature'. Hope, however, kept his distance in 1912 as 'the "Suffragettes" broke the Bond Street and other plate-glass windows, my tailor's among them'.[60]

IV

The New Humorists had enthusiastically embraced the New Woman. Jerome K. Jerome was their spokesman in 1886:

Now-a-days we light a pipe, and let the girls fight it out amongst themselves. They do it very well. They are getting to do all our work. They are doctors, and barristers, and artists. They manage theatres, and promote swindles, and edit newspapers. I am looking forward to the time when we men shall have nothing to do but lie in bed till twelve, read two novels a day, have nice little five o'clock teas all to ourselves, and tax our brains with nothing more trying than discussions upon the latest patterns in trousers, and arguments as to what Mr. Jones's coat was made of and whether it fitted him.[61]

Topsy-turviness remained a comic standby. *Punch* in 1898 gave its 'vision of the future' in the form of a letter to the editor of the 'Daily Telephone', on the theme of 'Should Husbands Work?'[62] Then there was *The Maiden Queen*, a two-act comic opera, storyline by Robert Buchanan and Charles Marlowe, music by Florian Pascal, which delighted audiences in 1908. Again set in the future, c.1970–1980, women ('the stronger sex') hold all offices of Church and State, chorused by the Amazons ('the flower of the Army'); men are subordinate and voteless, kept cloistered until ripe to be married off. Naturally, Lady Rosalind Millstone, 'the democratic Home Secretary', is nicknamed the Grand Young Woman; and when the Revd Annabel Lee, excited at being made Bishop of Putney, exclaims, 'I shall faint!', she is told, 'Courage! Bear it like a woman!' The education of Prince Edgar—in direct succession to the throne, though likely to be passed over on account of being male—provides occasion to satirize political correctness. Newnham is now a single-sex men's college, where the hapless Professor Dingo is

---

[58] Angela V. John and Claire Eustance (eds.), *The Men's Share? Masculinities, Male Support and Women's Suffrage in Britain, 1890–1920* (1997), 101–2.   [59] Booth, *Conan Doyle*, 267–9, 294.
[60] Mallet, *Hope*, 212, 282.   [61] Jerome, *Idle Thoughts*, 50.   [62] *Punch*, 3 Sept. 1898, 108.

cross-examined by Lady Bustleborough, the Lady Chancellor, about the Prince's syllabus:

LADY CHANCELLOR. You have taught him the duties of his sex and position?
DINGO. Quite so.
LADY C. Your course of study has embraced—
DINGO. French and the piano. Calisthenics and the Fashion Plates; the Moral Philosophy of Man as an inferior biped; Modesty and Deportment...
LADY C. Very good. You allow him to read no carnal books?
DINGO. None!
LADY C. No pagan authors, such as Thackeray, the arch-enemy of our sex.
DINGO. Certainly not. Even Kipling is forbidden, on the ground that his works describe the achievements of Man. He is thoroughly grounded, however, in the masterpieces of the female novelists of the last century—more particularly Ouida —
MISTRESS [of Newnham]. Ouida! Good heavens!
DINGO. Pardon me, the study of the works of Ouida has this effect, it shows the wickedness of the male sex in all its ghastly enormity. From this point of view Ouida is strictly moral—and, moreover, Ouida, if tradition is to be trusted, was a female!

The Lady Chancellor then catechizes Lord Eustace, one of the Prince's fellow undergraduates:

LADY C. What is Man's most fitting place?
LORD EUSTACE. [after a look at DINGO, who winks]. The Home!
LADY C. What must he chiefly avoid to fulfil his functions?
LORD E. All public excitement, all enquiry into political questions, which are beyond his intellect—
LADY C. And what, above all, must he reverence?
LORD E. The Perfect Woman, as embodied in those who legislate for his security.[63]

The Maiden Queen ends with Prince Edgar becoming King and true love reigning. The subversion of conventional gender roles was not otherwise cause for light-hearted treatment. G. K. Chesterton noted how, by the Edwardian period, the

popular papers always persisted in representing the New Woman or the Suffragette as an ugly woman, fat, in spectacles, with bulging clothes, and generally falling off a bicycle. As a matter of plain external fact, there was not a word of truth in this. The leaders of the movement of female emancipation are not at all ugly; most of them are extraordinarily good-looking. Nor are they at all indifferent to art or decorative costume; many of them are alarmingly attached to these things. Yet the popular instinct was right. For the popular instinct was that in this movement, rightly or wrongly, there was an element of indifference to female dignity, of a quite new willingness of women to be grotesque.[64]

Just how fractious tempers had become in the succeeding years may be instanced by 'The Political Woman', one of the Modern Types that R. C. Lehmann

---

[63] The Maiden Queen: Comic Opera in Two Acts (n.d. [1908]), 12–13, 16, 27.
[64] Chesterton, All Things Considered, 18.

contributed to *Punch* in 1890–1. A Cambridge-educated lawyer, Lehmann was an enthusiastic clubman, subscriber to the Athenaeum, Brooks, Beefsteak, Bath, Garrick, Reform, and Sports. He enjoyed a career in journalism, as staff member of *Punch* and one-time editor of the *Daily News*; and his study *Charles Dickens as Editor* (1912) still elicits respect. He was also a committed Liberal, once chairman of the party's publication department; and, after contesting general elections in 1885, 1886, and 1892, he was returned as MP for Leicestershire (Harborough), 1906–10. Throughout this time Lehmann published fiction, mostly reprints of comic sketches written for *Punch*; but there was a distinct dearth of humour about 'The Political Woman':

The Political Woman is one upon whom, if she may be believed, the world has never smiled. She avenges herself by recounting her wrongs and those of her sex, to all who can be induced to listen to her. In early youth she will have taught herself by a superficial study of political history that all great movements have depended for their success upon Women, and that men, though they may ride on the whirlwind have had but little hand in directing the storm. The base ingratitude which has hitherto attended feminine effort in general, has aroused in her breast a quite particular and personal resentment against all men who have the misfortune to disagree with her. Hence it comes that the males who bask in the sunshine of her approval are but few. It is noticeable, that although she openly despises men, she makes herself, and wishes to make her fellow women as masculine as is compatible with the wearing of petticoats, and the cultivation of habitual inaccuracy of mind. Moreover, although she has a fine contempt, of which she makes no concealment, for most women, she selects as the associates of her political enterprises and her daily life, only those men whose cast of mind would suit better with the wearing of gowns than of trousers . . .

Few women agree with her, fewer still show any desire for the supposed boons to the attainment of which she is constantly urging them. Yet, the knowledge of these facts only seems to render the Political Woman more determined in the prosecution of her quest, and more bitter in her attacks upon men . . . [She then keeps] company with a Professor, who happens to be unmarried and a Member of Parliament. After making love for some months, by means of an interchange of political tracts, these two will be married in a registrar's office, and will spend their honeymoon in investigating the social requirements of Italian organ-grinders.

From this moment she exists chiefly as a Member or President of innumerable Committees. No sooner does the shadow of a political idea flit through her brain, than she forms a Committee to promote its development. When not engaged in forming or in delivering lectures 'to Women only', or in discussing the Woman's Suffrage question with the Member of Parliament for her district (whom she despises) by means of letters, which she subsequently publishes in the journal of which she is, by this time, the proprietor, editor, and staff combined.

In a regrettable moment of absent-mindedness she bore to the Professor a son, whom she brings up on Spartan principles, and little else. Her home is a centre of slatternly discomfort. She rises early, but, having locked herself into her study, for the better composition of a discourse on 'The Sacred Right of Revolt for Women', she forgets that both the tea and the coffee are locked in with her, and learns subsequently with surprise, but without regret, that her husband drank water to his breakfast. She then proceeds to regenerate the working-man, by proving to him, that his wife is a miserable creature for submitting to his sway, and rouses an audience of spectacled enthusiasts to frenzy by proclaiming, that she is ready to lead them to the tented field for the assertion of rights which the malignity of men has filched from them. Later on, she presides over her various Committees, and she returns home to find that her child has burnt himself by falling on to the dining-room fire, and that her cook has given warning.

She will eventually fail to be elected a member of the School Board, and having written a strong book on a delicate social question, will die of the shock of seeing it adversely reviewed in *The Spectator*.[65]

Most of the gibes and slurs that were flung at feminist politicians over the next century were thus current by the 1890s. Other female admissions to Lehmann's gallery of Modern Types, though more conventional period pieces, reflected little credit on the sex: the Corinthian Lady, the Giddy Society Lady, the Invalid Lady, the Martyr *Incomprise*, the Poor Lady Bountiful, the Lady from Cloudland, the Undomestic Daughter, the Divorcée, the Manly Maiden, the Giver of Parties, and the Lady Shopkeeper.[66] The message affixed to these sketches of distressed and distressing womanhood was that such types were the results of 'the two forces of *ennui* and dissipation acting on a Society that is willing to spend money and desires to kill time'. In Lehmann's opinion, therefore, discontented females were a product of pampering, the diffusion of luxurious living among the middle and upper classes that gave its women too much licence. They frittered away hours at frivolous parties; they imitated the morals of theatre and music hall; they exhibited themselves in smart restaurants and hotels, at Continental gaming tables and on the sports field; they conducted adulterous liaisons, then courted sympathy as victims; and they trifled with serious occupations—social work, business, and politics—for which few had qualifications.

Though it served up gentler versions of these prejudices over the next two decades, *Punch* little deviated from this pattern in its treatment of the Woman Question. In April 1894 it cartooned 'Donna Quixote', a young woman in severe black dress, with primly parted short hair, bespectacled and reading from a book, while holding aloft a key. The caption was from *Don Quixote*, 'A world of disorderly notions *picked out of books*, crowded into his (her) imagination'; and all round is strewn evidence of this—books by Mona Caird, Ibsen, and Tolstoy, the *Yellow Book* and E. F. Benson's *Dodo*, and Blanche Crackanthorpe's essay 'The Revolt of the Daughters' (*Nineteenth Century*, January 1894). By her feet a double-axe-wielding woman is about to slay the dragon Decorum together with a three-headed Mrs Cerberus (representing Chaperon, Mamma, and Mrs Grundy). 'Tyrant Man', decapitated, lies bemused on one side; and looking away from this

---

[65] *Punch*, 29 Mar. 1890, 148.
[66] Respectively in *Punch*, 1 Mar. 1890, 101; 15 Mar. 1890, 124; 29 Mar. 1890, 148; 12 Apr. 1890, 177; 3 May 1890, 208; 24 May 1890, 249; 28 June 1890, 301; 6 Sept. 1890, 109; 11 Oct. 1890, 169; 6 Dec. 1890, 265; 18 Apr. 1891, 185; 4 July 1891, 5. Note also the unpleasant verses about the New Woman, in *Punch*, 10 Jan. 1900, 23.

DONNA QUIXOTE.

[" A world of disorderly notions *picked out of books*, crowded into his (her) imagination."—*Don Quixote.*]

FIG. 24.1. Donna Quixote: women demonstrate that they too can be inspired
to tilt at windmills.   *Source: Punch,* 28 April 1894

scene of havoc is a Volunteer, standing guard with rifle. The cartoon too contained an inset of the reader's mind, in the form of Donna Quixote herself, on horseback and in armour, with lance tilting at a windmill, whose sails bear the legend 'Marriage Laws'. And a companion page of verses ends by warning

> Therefore, dear Donna Quixote, be not stupid,
> Fight not with Hymen, and war not with Cupid,
> Run not amuck 'gainst Mother Nature's plan,
> Nor make a monster of your mate, poor Man,
> Or like La Mancha's cracked, though noble, knight,
> You'll find blank failure in mistaken fight.[67]

Lehmann, it has been noted, was Liberal in his party persuasion. The Woman Question cut across Westminster configurations, and there were adversaries of female suffrage and civil rights legislation as well as advocates among the males of each of the Liberal, Conservative, and Labour parties. The same was true of authors, and it is not obvious what might prove the determining influence. In John Masefield's case the commitment was individual as well as ideological. Masefield enlisted in support of suffragism out of an infatuation for the expatriate American actress Elizabeth Robins, to whom he addressed adoring letters—over 260 in six months—after reading her play *Votes for Women!*[68] This was published in 1909 but was first staged at the Court Theatre in 1907, as part of the Vedrenne–Barker progressivist repertory, and it was Granville Barker who suggested its title. *Votes for Women!*, unabashedly subtitled 'A Tract', complemented Robins's suffrage novel *The Convert*, published in the same year.[69] The play's centrepiece, set in Trafalgar Square, was included in a matinée programme arranged by the Women Writers' Suffrage League in 1912. Reporting that occasion, *The Times* observed:

The scene is, of course, propagandist, but it is particularly true to life, and yesterday its realism and its meaning were underlined by the fact that Mrs Pethick Lawrence and Miss Christabel Pankhurst (the actual personality represented by the Ernestine Blunt of the play) were in the stalls, so that only the footlights separated the drama of the stage from the drama of life.[70]

Robins kept a foot in both camps of the suffrage movement, donating some profits from *Votes for Women!* equally between the constitutionalist National

---

[67] *Punch*, 28 Apr. 1894, 194–5.
[68] Robins was fifteen years older than Masefield (who was married to a Newnham graduate, also older than him). From the evidence of their correspondence one biographer has interpreted Masefield's passion as a mother-fixation; Smith, *Masefield*, 101–4. See also Angela V. John, *Elizabeth Robins: Staging a Life, 1862–1952* (1995), 174–85.
[69] *The Convert* was republished by the Women's Press, London, and by the Feminist Press, New York, in 1980, with an introduction by Jane Marcus. Robins received £1,000 advance for it; John, *Robins*, 4. For the advertisement of it by her first publisher, Methuen, see Duffy, *Methuen*, 44.
[70] *The Times*, 10 Feb. 1912.

Union of Women's Suffrage Societies and the militant Women's Social and Political Union.[71]

Robins had impeccable credentials as a bluestocking. Her husband, a brainless actor, exited from her life, indeed from life itself, by drowning in the Charles River, tied to a suit of armour, before Robins landed in England. Celebrated for her interpretation of Ibsen's *Hedda Gabler* on stage in 1891, she served as nominal editor to a 1s. 6d. reprint of Mary Wollstonecraft's *Vindication of the Rights of Women* (1798), that pioneer classic of the feminist cause which inaugurated the Walter Scott Library series of cheap books in 1892. Robins's novel *George Mandeville's Husband* (1894) then marked the advance of the women's movement from its mid-Victorian position by guying the intellectualism and correctness of George Eliot. This combination of brains and beauty proved irresistible to Masefield; but care had to be taken in approaching Robins. In 1893 Bernard Shaw failed lamentably to court 'Saint Elizabeth' for one of his plays. With his habitual excess of flattery and foolery, Shaw aimed his pitch at her sex appeal, not her professionalism, whereupon she threatened to shoot him.[72] Masefield, however, made a good public speaker, thought Arnold Bennett, who, as a stammerer, was apt to notice these things;[73] and he declared his faith in the suffrage cause at the Queen's Hall on 14 February (Valentine's Day) 1910. He made ritual nods towards Ibsen, cited examples of the abuse of women by men which had been endorsed by the press, and proclaimed that 'the old rule of sex is dead'. But the new rule envisaged by Masefield did not depart from the past, so much as refurbish a chivalric code by which men reverenced and idealized women as mothers and sisters.[74]

The Garden Press, based at the new garden city Letchworth, published Masefield's speech as a pamphlet; and it was reissued by the Woman's Press in 1913. Thus Masefield was twice accorded the progressives' seal of approval. This was in contrast to H. G. Wells, the scheduled speaker at the Queen's Hall until Robins, then president of the Women Writers' Suffrage League, ordered his replacement by Masefield.[75] In *The Convert* (1907)—styled by St John Hankin as 'propagoose', being the feminine version of 'propagander'—Wells had been put in his place, the novel's heroine Vida Levering witheringly observing that 'Even in his most rationalized vision of the New Time, he can't help betraying his old-fashioned prejudice in favour of the "dolly" view of women.'[76] Subsequently Robins's hostility deepened. Wells's *Ann Veronica* (1909) was an unforgivable exploitation of his affair with Amber Reeves, and *The New Machiavelli* (1911) she tried to prevent being published.[77] Wells's advocacy of female suffrage was

---

[71] John, *Robins*, 148.   [72] Holroyd, *Shaw*, i. 312; John, *Robins*, 80–2.

[73] Flower (ed.), *Bennett Journals*, ii. 244 (14 Dec. 1918).

[74] John and Eustance (eds.), *Men's Share?*, 94, 171.

[75] John, *Robins*, 173–4. Masefield was drafted to give the address in place of Wells after Thomas Hardy, Bernard Shaw, and Henry James had all refused.

[76] Elizabeth Robins, *The Convert* (1907; Women's Press edn., intro. Jare Marcus, 1980), 208.

[77] ibid., pp. ix, xii.

unwelcome, therefore, and it came almost as a relief to the suffragettes when he discountenanced militancy as 'ridiculous and irritating'. Patience, however, was preached too by the Ibsenite William Archer. In the 1890s he had achieved what Masefield craved now: Archer and Robins had fallen in love.[78] In 1908 Archer advised a suspension of militancy to allow ministers, whose reputations would not allow them to be seen surrendering to intimidation, breathing space to legis-late. Better still if it was the anti-suffragists who were seen to persist in abusing the suffragists' crusade: 'Hold meetings and let the other side do the breaking up . . . Keep yourselves technically in the right instead of technically in the wrong. Rowdyism and anti-feminist fanaticism will play into your hands fast enough.'[79]

These difficulties of choosing between—or combining—constitutionalist and militant action plagued the suffrage movement; and authors who championed the cause were much exercised in conscience and strategy. One co-founder of the Men's League for Women's Suffrage in 1907 was Henry Nevinson. His career as war correspondent began in the Graeco-Turkish conflict, then proceeded through the Spanish–American War, the Boer War, the Balkans, and sundry other trouble spots, where he came under fire several times. As a pacifist and liberationist, Nevinson believed that women's suffrage would advance the downfall of mil-itarism and imperialism. In after years he liked to retort to critics that, 'almost without exception, all my "lost" causes have won, and are now even popular'. Nevinson also recalled that, just as in the wars he reported, the suffrage struggles he took part in 'were far from pleasing and often deadly serious'.[80] In 1909 he and H. N. Brailsford resigned as *Daily News* leader-writers in solidarity with the suf-fering suffragettes, stating that they could not 'denounce torture in Russia and support it in England'; yet by 1913 Nevinson's continued contact with a Government minister, Lloyd George, was being interpreted as treachery by Christabel Pankhurst, who, worryingly, was expressing 'suspicion and hatred of all men'.[81] It was one thing to put up with blows from a policeman, as Nevinson did as a member of Mrs Pankhurst's deputation to Downing Street in 1910; it was quite another to be victim of a whispering campaign from the paranoid part of the movement. Nevinson advocated stepping up pressure on the Government by electoral exertion and public demonstration, but he was increasingly disconcerted by exhibitionist attacks on property and person, thinking these distasteful, unwise—and likely to cause fatalities.[82]

Nevinson was an author whose professional life made him worry how easily bloodthirsty talk slipped into bloodletting deeds. The same did not cause Israel Zangwill to check his stride when seized by a mission to create a different world order. This included a new nation state for his Jewish co-religionists as well as a new polity for men and women. The London-born son of a Russian refugee,

---

[78] John, *Robins*, 75–80, 85, for this affair.   [79] John and Eustance (eds.), *Men's Share?*, 97.
[80] Henry Nevinson, 'Wars—And Lost Causes that have Won', *Manchester Evening Chronicle*, 30 June 1933, in Sharp (ed.), *Nevinson*, 143–6.   [81] John and Eustance (eds.), *Men's Share?*, 27, 90.
[82] Ibid. 17, 103.

Zangwill first pursued a literary vocation of presenting a faithful picture of Anglo-Jewish life with all its cross-currents, painful or funny, before he was inspired by Herzl's promulgation of territorial Zionism in 1895–6. Thenceforward until his death in 1926 Zangwill was as much politician as author. Disputes over whether the future state should be secular or theocratic, and over its precise location—East Africa, Western Australia, British Honduras, Brazil, Angola, Mesopotamia, or Palestine—pitched Zangwill into internecine controversy. He encountered not just accusations of inconsistency and even perfidy, but also that his political activities were mere publicity stunts for himself as an author. His very panache militated against his acceptance as an interpreter of Judaism and leader of Zionism, in the community he sought to rouse.[83] Zangwill's cause was not evidently assisted by his comic spirit; yet there was no disjunction between the humour and the philosophy. Rather, his witty sketches of Jewish characters were means of posing hard questions. Consider the gem of a short story, 'The Jewish Trinity', in *Ghetto Comedies* (1907). It concerns two young people on the point of engagement: Barstein, a sculptor who holds Zionist ideals, and Mabel, the thoroughly Anglicized daughter of an established Jewish family whose father has been knighted and whose brother is at Oxford. Amid the lavishness of a Jewish charity ball, they ponder whether Mabel's father will discountenance the match. 'At the worst, we can elope to Palestine,' says Barstein; whereupon Mabel shudders, 'Live entirely among Jews!' she cried. She

noted that distinguished Christians were quite sympathetic, but this was the one subject on which Christian opinion failed to impress Mabel. 'Zionism's all very well for Christians—they're in no danger of having to go to Palestine.'

It appears that her objection is that a Jewish state will be nothing more than a giant ghetto, at which Barstein reflects:

'You don't call France a Ghetto or Italy a Ghetto?' There was anti-Semitism, he felt – unconscious anti-Semitism—behind Mabel's instinctive repugnance to an aggregation of Jews. And he knew that her instinct would be shared by every Jew in that festive aggregation around him.[84]

In after years Zangwill confessed that 'he had wasted half his life on Zionism'. Jerome K. Jerome recorded this in his memoirs, published in 1926 when the Balfour Declaration (1917) favouring the establishment of a national home for Jews in Palestine was beginning to take effect. Jerome himself was sceptical,

---

[83] The best account of Zangwill's part in the labyrinthine and factional politics of Zionism is Stuart A. Cohen, *English Zionists and British Jews: The Communal Politics of Anglo-Jewry, 1895–1920* (Princeton, 1982), 85–105. See also his letter, dated 1 February 1914, to Lady Battersea (the former Constance de Rothschild and a lapsed Jew), in Cohen, *Rothschild and her Daughters*, 298–9. He had published in the *Fortnightly Review* (Apr. 1906) his own Zionist proposals, including messages from several authors whom he had invited to comment. Thomas Hardy was one; and Hardy's wife, Emma, wrote to support and subscribe Zangwill's scheme: letter, 30 Apr. 1906, in Millgate (eds.), *Emma and Florence Hardy*, 33.

[84] Israel Zangwill, 'The Jewish Trinity', in Zangwill, *Ghetto Comedies* (1907), 122–5.

believing that the Zionists' Jerusalem, as a Vision Splendid, was always doomed to disappointment when concretized: 'Who in God's name wanted a third-rate provincial town on a branch of the Baghdad railway?' But he shared Zang-will's 'love of Lost Causes, and Under Dogs', and saluted his friend's 'strong personality'—'You either like him immensely or want to hit him with a club.'[85] With equal fervour Zangwill had devoted himself to the cause of women's rights. Sylvia Pankhurst nominated him 'the wit of the Suffrage movement'.[86] His wife and her family, the Ayrtons,[87] had a long history of such commitment. Several of Zangwill's fiery addresses, *One and One is Two* (1907) and *Old Fogeys and Old Bogeys* (1909), became best-selling pamphlets. They berated not just the opponents of women's suffrage but the suffragists' constitutionalist wing, who sought accommodation with Westminster political parties.[88] 'The Parliamentary struggle over Female Suffrage', he wrote contemptuously in 1912, 'is less a struggle against it than a competition for its spoils.'[89] Not only would women's suffrage transform the nation's political institutions, it must also lead to 'a complete re-reading of life, a re-evaluation of all values', Zangwill declared, adding, 'We have done with this man-ridden world.' That was a trifle optimistic; but Zangwill gloried in his sympathies, speaking of himself and his associates in the Men's League for Women's Suffrage as 'suffragettes in trousers'. They fought in a common cause, to banish the customs and prejudices of the past, 'no duel but a duet'. Yet a chivalric code still permeated the minds of many of these male supporters of women's suffrage, and 'at times it was a battle *between* men, *for* the protection of women'.[90]

   An idiosyncratic commitment to suffragism, as to socialism and pacifism, also came from the poet–playwright Laurence Housman. His sister Clemence was a suffragist too; together they compensated for the public reticence (and anti-suffragism) of their brother, the poet A. E. Housman. Dubbed 'Laurence Mad-Housman' for a drawing contributed to the *Yellow Book* in 1896,[91] he achieved further notoriety with *An Englishwoman's Love Letters* (1900);[92] and the Lord

---

[85] Jerome, *Life and Times*, 94.   [86] Sylvia Pankhurst, *The Suffragette Movement* (1977), 375.

[87] On Zangwill's wife, Edith (1875–1945), who also became a novelist, see Kemp *et al.* (eds.), *Edwardian Fiction*, 430. Both her parents received notices in the *DNB*: her mother, Matilda Chaplin Ayrton (1846–83), who as a woman struggled for recognition as a doctor, and her father, William Edward Ayrton (1847–1908), who was an electrical engineer and physicist. Ayrton's second wife, Sarah (Hertha) Marks, whom he married in 1885, was a Girtonian and a distinguished scientist in her own right, winner of a Royal Society medal in 1906. Their daughter was named Barbara Bodichon out of respect for the pioneer feminist who had campaigned for married women's property rights and legal equality for the sexes. She married the writer Gerald Gould, who was also a pro-suffragette militant.

[88] Pankhurst, *Suffragette Movement*, 252; Mitchell, *Queen Christabel*, 138–9.

[89] Israel Zangwill, 'The Awkward Age of the Women's Movement', *Fortnightly Review* (Nov. 1912), 904–12.   [90] John and Eustance (eds.), *The Men's Share?*, esp. 23, 30, 88, 107.

[91] *Punch*, 29 Aug. 1896, 101.

[92] The authorship of *An Englishwoman's Love Letters* (1900), first published anonymously, was variously attributed to Alice Meynell, Marie Corelli, and Oscar Wilde; and Housman made over £2,000 from its first year's sales, in spite of there being sixteen pirated editions produced in America. See Brook, *Writers' Gallery*, 62, 66; and *Punch*, 9 Jan. 1901, 32, 13 Mar. 1901, 198, 200, for review and satire.

Chamberlain laid his ban on several of his plays, *Bethlehem* (1902) and *Pains and Penalties* (1911), as he trespassed on religious and royal sensibilities. He now relished speech-making and political activity. His prime targets were the iniquity of the double standard of sexual morality and the oppressive nature of conventional family life. A homosexual, he was only too aware of the cruelties inflicted by rigid expectations of stereotyped masculinity and femininity; and he was used to being considered a traitor to his sex, a gibe flung generally at male supporters of female suffrage. At Essex Hall in 1912 Housman was cheered to the echo as he exhorted suffragists to end this hypocrisy, which had 'strewn the world with the wreckage of human lives, with death, disease, poverty and the downfall of nations'. 'Thank God,' he rejoiced, 'it is war now . . . war, not to the death, but to the resurrection from the dead, and the new Life to come.'[93] Housman's apocalyptic vision was not a common possession; nor, in truth, was it so freed from conventional preconceptions, because Housman also thought in terms of women naturally expressing 'the communal side of things, [and] man the individual'. The transformation of State and society that was sought—making them less conflictual, more caring and compassionate, to use our own apple-pie comfort language—was imagined as a feminization.[94] Nonconformity was more easily expressed by gesture politics. Indeed, civil disobedience by refusal of taxes, which Housman urged suffragists to adopt, had been initiated by religious Dissenting congregations in protest against the 1902 Education Act. In 1911 Housman enlarged the area of irritation by seeking to sabotage the census enumeration, filling his home on the appointed night with 'a quantity of females, names, numbers, and ages unknown', who bolted his door against him. Thirsting for a share of martyrdom, Housman failed to find the authorities obliging. Arrested at one demonstration, he was detained for a few hours before being discharged unconditionally, whereas women protesters received three months in gaol for similar public-order violations.[95]

Insurgency perhaps came naturally to the wives of authors whose occupational and domestic arrangements got muddled. Literary men were apt to make bad husbands, Andrew Lang remarked after reading Mrs Alexander Ireland's *Life of Jane Welsh Carlyle* (1891): 'The reason is not only that authors are vain, and irritable, and flighty, and absorbed, like artists, in their work; the true, or chief, cause of married misery among writers is probably this: *they do their work at home.*'[96] Most men, from barristers to bricklayers, did their work elsewhere; and, Lang hazarded, the Carlyles' marriage might have been happier if Thomas had decamped daily to scribble in some remote office, thus to avoid having domestic trifles about bakers or butchers launched at him when his head was full of Frederick the Great or Cromwell. It appeared now that the relationship of

---

[93] Mitchell, *Queen Christabel*, 222.   [94] John and Eustance (eds.), *Men's Share?*, 176–7.
[95] Ibid. 117–21. In acknowledgement of his efforts, suffragettes presented Housman with 'a comfortable and dignified library chair, which he still uses daily' (Brook, *Writers' Gallery*, 63).
[96] *Review of Reviews* (Sept. 1891), 294.

W. W. Jacobs and his wife followed the Carlyle model. Jacobs was such a 'tyrannous husband', according to H. G. Wells, that his wife became a suffragette as a 'sublimation of her secret rebellion' against him.[97] Perhaps Wells's judgement was affected by reading one of his own novels; nevertheless, it was true that Jacobs objected to the idea of a socialist redistribution—'there's not enough of the good things of this world to go round evenly, and I want more than my share'. Jerome K. Jerome, who first 'discovered' Jacobs's writing talent and who adopted an egalitarian philosophy contra Jacobs, was otherwise sympathetic to his utopia of a life consisting of 'pipe, two Scotch whiskies a day, and a game of bowls three afternoons a week'.[98] Mrs Jacobs, who was the daughter of a bank accountant, demurred and was imprisoned for smashing a post office window. She told the court that her action was 'prompted by a sense of duty to her children, as she desired that her daughters should grow up to equal duties and responsibilities with her sons. The Magistrate declared her contention so absurd that she must be demented, and announced that he would remand her for a week to have the state of her mind inquired into.'[99]

V

It was not necessary always to throw stones or tantrums in order to gain a hearing and exert influence, as was proved in local government, where women constituted perhaps 17 per cent of borough electorates and secured positions on school and poor law boards, parish vestries, and eventually town and county councils.[100] Campaigning of one kind was no new development. Philanthropic and charitable work—so-called 'good causes'—remained widespread and generally approved. Frances Hodgson Burnett, author of the cloying *Little Lord Fauntleroy* (1886), was active in this tradition. In *Who's Who*, to her death in 1924, she defined as her sole recreation: 'improving the lot of children'. In 1892 she publicized her part in the Drury Lane Boys' Club. This was started, she said, by a boy who persuaded his mother to sell her mangle and to put the 15s. it raised towards fitting out a cellar as a club room. He and other ragged boys devised the club rules, one of which was the prohibition of bad language, whereupon

---

[97] Wells (ed.), *H. G. Wells in Love*, 71. On Jacobs (1863–1943), Sutherland, *Companion*, 324–5.

[98] Jerome, *Life and Times*, 134. Most of Jacobs's stories collected as *Many Cargoes* (1896), his best-selling work, had appeared in *To-day* and *The Idler*. *Many Cargoes*—see *Punch*, 30 Jan. 1897, 54, for a laudatory review—was in its 23rd impression in 1900, and 33rd in 1912. The son of a Thames wharf manager, Jacobs was a civil service clerk before resigning in 1899 to live as a writer. Douglas Sladen (*Twenty Years*, 98–9) recalled: 'He was one of the men to whom the members of the general public, who strayed to literary dinners, were most anxious to be introduced. Their admiration made him shy, and it was a long time before he grew accustomed to do himself justice in his public speeches, for he is one of our most genuine humorists.' See also Michael Sadleir's assessment of Jacobs (1863–1943) in *DNB 1941–1950*, 428–9, rev. Sayoni Basu, in *Oxford DNB*.

[99] Pankhurst, *Suffragette Movement*, 379. The Jacobses had three daughters and two sons.

[100] Patricia Hollis, *Ladies Elect: Women in English Local Government, 1865–1914* (Oxford, 1987), 31–2.

Mrs Burnett took it in hand. She acquired premises at 30 Kemble Street, off Drury Lane, and equipped them with linoleum flooring—Mrs Burnett was impressed by this new material—and a library room, which contained a commemorative window for her son Lionel, who died in his teens in 1890.[101]

There was an equally distinguished tradition of public as well as private good causes. The biggest stir ever made by a novel was by Harriet Beecher Stowe's *Uncle Tom's Cabin* (1852), which generated a wave of emotion for the anti-slavery cause. It sold half a million copies in America within a few months and similarly vast quantities afterwards in Britain,[102] which Mrs Stowe visited three times in the 1850s. She even drew the Queen to meet her at Euston station, a privilege usually reserved for visiting heads of state and not all those.[103] Anthony Trollope had resisted Mrs Stowe's work, with a craftsman's disdain: it was 'falsely sensational and therefore abominable'.[104] More common was Andrew Lang's reaction. In 1905 Lang—born in 1844—recalled: 'The first book that ever made me cry, of which feat I was horribly ashamed, was "Uncle Tom's Cabin", with the death of Eva, Topsy's friend.'[105] The anti-slavery movement had additional significance for the women active in it. Its message of freedom from bondage bore echoes for their own situation, denied equality in marriage, political rights, and standing at law.[106] An article in the *Westminster Review* in 1892, tracing the evolution of the novel, noted that *Uncle Tom's Cabin* was reckoned 'the best-read book in existence, except the Bible and *The Pilgrim's Progress*'.[107]

Nothing quite matched this reception, although Anna Sewell's *Black Beauty: His Grooms and Companions: The Autobiography of a Horse* (1877) was closing fast on the rails and would eventually prove to have the greater staying power. Bought outright for £40 by the East Anglia-based publishers Jarrold & Sons, which specialized in temperance literature and had already enjoyed a million-seller with the poem *Mother's Last Words* (1860), written by Anna Sewell's mother, Mary, *Black Beauty* had reached 100,000 sales by 1890, whereupon it galloped ahead as

---

[101] Mrs Frances Hodgson Burnett, 'The Drury Lane Boys' Club', *Scribner's Magazine* (June 1892), *Review of Reviews* (June 1892), 607. Also Thwaite, *Burnett*, 137–9, 168, for this and her work for Invalid Children's charities, in which she was associated with Mrs Humphry Ward.

[102] The publisher George Routledge was one of the most flagrant and successful pirates of *Uncle Tom's Cabin*; see *Oxford DNB* for Routledge (1812–88).

[103] The Queen also read the sequel, *Dred: A Tale of the Dismal Swamp* (1856), and considered it as good as *Uncle Tom's Cabin*. See Elizabeth Longford, *Victoria R.I.* (1964), 286, where *Dred* is unfortunately misspelled *Dud*. Mrs Stowe's reputation in England dimmed with her *Lady Byron Vindicated* (1870), which sought to document Byron's incestuous relationship with his half-sister; Hamilton, *Keepers of the Flame*, ch. 7.   [104] To Lady Pollock, n.d., in Booth (ed.), *Trollope's Letters*, 500.

[105] Lang, *Adventures among Books*, 18.

[106] See Clare Midgley, *Women against Slavery: The British Campaign, 1780–1970* (1992); also Allen, *Post-Prandial Philosophy*, ch. x ('The Monopolist Instincts'), where men's determination to enjoy exclusive control of women is likened to other forms of possession: slavery, property, capitalism, and patriotism.

[107] Charles James Billson, 'The English Novel', *Westminster Review* (Dec. 1892), 618. The popularity of *Uncle Tom's Cabin* was extended by stage versions: see Raphael Samuel, Ewan MacColl, and Stuart Cosgrove, *Theatres of the Left 1880–1935* (1985), 1–2. The plates off which Thomas Burke's family ate meals at their Brixton lodgings in the 1890s 'were remnants of a set whose centres bore designs based on *Uncle Tom's Cabin*' (Burke, *Son of London*, 25).

societies for the prevention of cruelty to animals at home and abroad, and especially in America, promoted and distributed it. Jarrold's boasted of it being 'the sixth best seller of any books in the world' in 1924; ten years later world sales were reckoned at 20 million.[108] This achievement was exceptional; yet many an author since the 1830s had driven the novel as a vehicle of reform. The pioneer was Bulwer Lytton, if the claim of his grandson (and biographer) is credited: Lytton's *Paul Clifford* (1830)

was the first of that class of fictions, now [1913] common enough in England and elsewhere, which the Germans designate *Tendenzstücke*. The ostensible object of the book was, as stated by its author in a preface to a later edition of it, 'to draw attention to two errors in our penal institutions, viz.:— a vicious Prison Discipline, and a sanguinary Penal Code'.[109]

Still, it was perhaps unwise to be too tendentious. Soon after finishing *Hard Times* (1854), Dickens wrote:

To interest and affect the general mind in behalf of anything that is clearly wrong—to stimulate and rouse the public soul to a compassionate or indignant feeling that it *must not be*—without obtruding any pet theory of cause or cure, and so throwing off allies as they spring up—I believe to be one of Fiction's highest uses.[110]

Dickens's twopenny weekly magazine *Household Words* (1850–9), with a regular circulation of 40,000, reaching 100,000 for Christmas editions, was designed to do this. As well as serializing propagandistic fiction such as *Hard Times* and Mrs Gaskell's *North and South* (1854–5), *Household Words* carried articles that were intended (so Dickens's introductory manifesto put it) 'to help in the discussion of the most important social questions of the time': articles that advocated mass education, safety at work and employers' liability, public health and sanitary reform, and administrative and legal reform, and articles that denounced slum landlordism and cruelty to animals.[111] For ten years, too, Dickens supported the millionaire philanthropist Angela Burdett-Coutts's work for Urania Cottage at Shepherd's Bush, a hostelry for prostitutes and homeless women.[112] Yet, to Dickens's admirers, it all seemed an amount of public work that was incommensurate with his potential. At a banquet in Dickens's honour at St George's Hall, Liverpool, in 1869, when Dickens had barely a year to live, Lord Houghton

---

[108] Adrienne E. Gavin, *Dark Horse: A Life of Anna Sewell* (Stroud, 2004), 182–91; and S. D. Mumm, 'Jarrold and Sons', in Anderson and Rose (eds.), *British Literary Publishing Houses 1820–1880*, 160–1.

[109] The Earl of Lytton, *The Life of Edward Bulwer First Lord Lytton* (1913), i. 360–1.

[110] Letter to Henry Carey, 24 Aug. 1854, in Graham Storey, Kathleen Tillotson, and Angus Easson (eds.), *The Letters of Charles Dickens*, vii: *1853–1855* (Oxford, 1993), 405.

[111] Patricia Marks, 'Household Words', in Sullivan (ed.), *Literary Magazines, 1837–1913*, 170–5.

[112] On Angela Burdett-Coutts (1814–1906), *DNB Supplement 1901–1911*, i. 259–66. Dickens dedicated *Martin Chuzzlewit* (1844) to her. Fielding (ed.), *Dickens's Speeches*, 421, notes that 'Dickens supported the demand for women's legal and social rights but, caring nothing for a vote himself, refused to take the suffrage question seriously,' much to the disgust of John Stuart Mill, who 'was incensed by what he thought the anti-feminism of *Bleak House*' (1852–3).

expressed this regret: 'My friend, Mr. Dickens, has shown little or no interest in the matter of our political life.' Specifically, Houghton was disappointed that Dickens had not stood for election to the Commons and then been raised to the Lords like Macaulay and Lytton. Evidently stung, Dickens now reminded Houghton that he had had to devote himself to a prior purpose, which was to raise the public's esteem of writers of fiction, because when he took it up in the 1830s

it was not so well understood in England as it was in other countries that Literature was a dignified profession [*hear, hear*], by which any man might stand or fall. [*Applause.*] I made a compact with myself that in my person Literature should stand, and by itself, of itself, and for itself [*hear, hear*]; and there is no consideration on earth that would induce me to break that bargain. [*Loud applause.*][113]

More directly active than Dickens in public life were Thomas Hughes and Charles Kingsley, but novel-writing was a secondary, even incidental, occupation for them. Both had been stirred by the Chartist agitation and by F. D. Maurice's Christian Socialist theology. Kingsley was first and last a clergyman. In between he also held professorships in Literature and History, and he used fiction to promote his concerns. His debut work was *Yeast: A Problem*, serialized in *Fraser's Magazine* in 1848. In the preface when it was published in book form in 1851, Kingsley stated his willingness to suffer any obloquy so long as his story might assist in reversing the drift 'towards Rome, towards sheer materialism, or towards an unchristian and unphilosophic spiritualism'. In 1859, in a new preface for the fourth edition, Kingsley reviewed the improvements accruing to the rural labourer from, as he thought, the administration of the Poor Law, free trade, and sanitary and educational reform, and from those landlords and aristocracy whose 'growing moral earnestness . . . is in great part owing (that justice may be done on all sides) to the Anglican movement'.[114] It would be too strong for historians to conclude that Kingsley's novels might as well never have been written, because they dramatized the debate and (Kingsley hoped) persuaded readers to identify with causes he held dear; but his stall was set out in the prefaces almost as a tract, and the story was largely ornament.

Thomas Hughes, similarly, was not foremost a novelist. He was a barrister, later County Court judge, a lay preacher, Liberal MP for half a dozen years, and principal (and co-founder) of the Working Men's College, Great Ormond Street, for over ten years. Industrial cooperation and 'the hope of Christianizing trade in our time' was Hughes's ideal.[115] Having sat on royal commissions that in the 1870s led to legislation which gave trade unions a legal status and protection of

[113] Fielding, *Dickens's Speeches*, 385, 389.
[114] Charles Kingsley, *Yeast: A Problem* (1888), pp. v–xvii.
[115] Letter to the Bishop of Ripon, in H. D. A. Major, *The Life and Letters of William Boyd Carpenter* (1925), 181. Hughes lost much of his money in 1879–80 in the ill-starred co-operative settlement Rugby, in Tennessee. He was assisted thereafter by the generosity of friends such as the publisher George Smith, who had wanted Hughes as first editor of the *Cornhill Magazine* in 1860. See Scott, *Pall Mall Gazette*, 64–5.

funds, Hughes 'believed that their fair and manly policy would rule in the future'. But, he told the Bishop of Ripon in 1893,

I have been grievously disappointed, and have for years now had no connection whatever with the Unions. They seem to me to have drifted into bodies quite as narrowly self-seeking as the old guilds at their worst. Can anything be worse than the attitude (*e.g.*) of the leaders and their dupes in this last great coal strike—utterly regardless of the interests of all the rest of the labourers in other trades, and as cruel as any king or aristocracy have ever shown themselves, to their own poorer brethren whom they call blacklegs?[116]

At Hughes's death in 1896 newspaper obituaries considered that he nonetheless had allowed his sympathy for the poor to override his impartiality as a judge and that no employer in conflict with a working man stood a chance in his court, sentiments that disturbed the Lord Justice of Appeal Sir Edward Fry.[117] As an author, Hughes had written more memoirs of contemporaries, including his elder brother George, the Manchester bishop James Fraser, the missionary David Livingstone, and the publisher Daniel Macmillan, than he had novels. Apart from *Tom Brown's Schooldays* (1857), there was only the inferior sequel, *Tom Brown at Oxford* (1861), and one other, *The Scouring of the White Horse* (1858). Kingsley was the more productive and popular novelist; still, the difference between such as Kingsley and Hughes and the many other writers whose public activities form the theme of this chapter is that the former were activists who became authors whereas the latter were authors who became activists.

Professional authors advanced onto platforms from strong commitment and from self-consciousness about their position; their views were also solicited from an expectation that they would count with the public. Naturally, they met those twin temptations common to persons in public life, to give the public what they judged it clamoured for or to fall in line with those who mattered most. There was more than a hint of the trimmer about the Poet Laureate Tennyson, alleged his eventual successor, Alfred Austin, though when he framed the charge in 1881 he could hardly have envisaged his own promotion. Austin was then a Tory leader-writer and had twice (in 1865 and 1880) stood for Parliament. To his and Tennyson's publisher, Alexander Macmillan, he wrote:

Mr Tennyson has had what some people would call the sagacity to wrap up his political opinions in lavender, and has never yet cared to seem to be on the losing side. I happen to know that he strongly disapproved of the Bulgarian Atrocity agitation, for he loves his country. But he took precious good care not to irritate anybody by saying so publicly.[118]

In fact, Tennyson considered himself above party and equated his prejudices with patriotism. In 1881, while walking with Constance de Rothschild, wife of the Liberal MP Cyril Flower, Tennyson talked about 'Ireland and the terrible state of the country. He mentioned party government with horror and quoted

---

[116] Letter 23 Sept. 1893, in Major, *Carpenter*, 196.   [117] Fry, *Sir Edward Fry*, 279.
[118] Austin to Macmillan, 16 Dec. 1881, in Nowell-Smith (ed.), *Letters to Macmillan*, 187.

Goldsmith's line, "And he gave up to party what was meant for mankind". '[119] After being pitchforked into the peerage by Gladstone in 1884, Tennyson found independence and voice. It was not in the House of Lords that these were expressed. He never made a speech there, and some of his independence seemed mere petulance. His opposition to Home Rule for Ireland was signalled by his refusal to meet Gladstone for almost four years following Gladstone's espousal of that cause.[120] Tennyson was not cut out to match Gladstone on the stump. He was not for that dormant in public affairs, although his forte did not include originality of idea or action. Edmund Gosse put this best, on Tennyson's eightieth birthday in 1889:

He has not headed a single moral reform nor inaugurated a single revolution of opinion; he has never pointed the way to undiscovered regions of thought; he has never stood on tip-toe to describe new worlds that his fellows were not tall enough to discover ahead. In all these directions, he has been prompt to follow, quick to apprehend, but never himself a pioneer.[121]

Yet there was good reason to think of Tennyson as a political poet, certainly by comparison with Browning, thought Stopford Brooke, who made the contrast explicit:

with regard to politics and social questions, Tennyson made us know what his general politics were, and he has always pleased or displeased men by his political position. The British Constitution appears throughout his work seated like Zeus on Olympus, with all the world awaiting its nod. Then, also, social problems raise their storm-awakening heads in his poetry: the Woman's Question; War; Competition; the State of the Poor; Education; a State without Religion; the Marriage Question; where Freedom lies; and others. These are brought by Tennyson, though tentatively, into the palace of poetry and given rooms in it.

At both these points Browning differed from Tennyson. He was not the politician, not the sociologist, only the poet. No trace of the British Constitution is to be found in his poetry; no one could tell from it that he had any social views or politics at all. Sixty years in close contact with this country and its movements, and not a line about them![122]

Browning's avoidance of the contemporary was exaggerated, but it was by articulating widespread anxieties in his poetry, especially about religious faith and political direction, that Tennyson rendered his national service. His jeremiad *Locksley Hall Sixty Years After* (1886) was deemed important enough to warrant a rejoinder from Gladstone in the *Nineteenth Century*.[123] A careful distinction was made. As poetry, the new *Locksley Hall* was reckoned the summit of Tennyson's achievement. 'It certainly has a grand rush and vigour such as he has never surpassed,' wrote Mrs Drew, Gladstone's daughter, who was at Hawarden as Gladstone penned his riposte. Hence Gladstone was 'tender with the Poet', while

[119] Cohen, *Rothschild and her Daughters*, 193.   [120] Metcalf, *Knowles*, 337–8; Martin, *Tennyson*, 575.
[121] Martin, *Tennyson*, 569.   [122] Brooke, *Poetry of Robert Browning*, 37.
[123] Morley, *Gladstone*, ii. 593–4.

bringing 'the heaviest artillery to bear on the Prophet'.[124] Yet Tennyson had been claiming no new privilege in using his verses as the vehicle of an ideology. More of a démarche was his joining in campaigns for a stronger Navy, for a Gordon memorial, and for assisted emigration to the colonies.[125] This was a boundary which George Eliot always refused to cross. She supported Emily Davies and Barbara Bodichon in their promotion of women's higher education, being one of the first subscribers to Girton College, Cambridge; and she donated money to other causes, Octavia Hill's social work, and so forth. But it was done without fanfare, usually confidentially. She would not be drawn to speak on public questions, as she told her friend Clementia Taylor in 1878: 'My function is that of the *aesthetic*, not the doctrinal teacher—the rousing of the nobler emotions, which make mankind desire the social right, not the prescribing of special measures, concerning which the artistic mind, however strongly moved by social sympathy, is often not the best judge.'[126]

VI

The reasons that induced writers to broadcast their views on public subjects or to preserve a reticence are not susceptible to precise taxonomy, because of widely various personal circumstances and philosophical preferences. Generally, women remained more inhibited than men, convention still confining women to certain areas of public life—religious and philanthropic work, educational and social questions; as it were, an extended domestic sphere and ethical rather than political and governmental matters. The rise of a new feminist ideology and female suffrage movement gradually blurred these distinctions, but a generational difference must be allowed weight too. The expansion of the popular press and, especially, the advent of the journalistic interview made more demands on authors, profiling them as public persons and encouraging them to ventilate their concerns on public issues. Consider the first number of the *Windsor Magazine*, published in 1895. That contained an illustrated interview with the author Edna Lyall (Ada Ellen Bayly). Outwardly, she seemed an unexciting subject, a spinster with a heart condition. Descended on her father's side from barristers, and on her mother's from clerics, she lived successively with her two sisters, who were married to clergymen, in Lincoln and London, then, from 1884, at Eastbourne. She published her first romance, *Won by Waiting*, in 1879, the year previous to George Eliot's death. That book made no stir but, before her thirtieth birthday, she had become famous, the result of attention drawn to her next two novels, which dealt with the religious and ethical dilemmas posed by the secularist

---

[124] Masterman (ed.), *Mary Gladstone*, 393 (30 Dec. 1886).
[125] Lang and Shannon (eds.), *Tennyson Letters*, iii. 311–12, 314–16, 350.
[126] Gordon S. Haight (ed.), *The George Eliot Letters* (1954–78), iii. 330, quoted in Hands, *A George Eliot Chronology*, 157.

movement: *Donovan: A Modern Englishman* (3 volumes, 1882) and its sequel *We Two* (3 volumes, 1884), which the Queen herself recommended to her daughter, the future Empress Frederick of Germany, as worthy of George Eliot and Charlotte Brontë.[127] Yet Lyall's *Derrick Vaughan, Novelist* (1889) contained this *cri de cœur*:

Why is it that every other profession can be taken seriously, but that a novelist's work is supposed to be mere play? Good God! don't we suffer enough? Have we not hard brain work and drudgery of desk work and tedious gathering of statistics and troublesome search into details? Have we not an appalling weight of responsibility upon us?—and are we not at the mercy of a thousand capricious chances?[128]

Derrick Vaughan was the first book to appear from the new publisher Methuen, who found that he had a best-seller: 25,000 copies were sold in the first year.

Lyall's apotheosis followed—a parody of her work in *Punch*'s Prize Novels series. This was 'Sonogun' by 'Miss Redna Trial', the author of 'Spun by Prating', etc. The story was preceded by a gloss:

I think you will like this book, writes the fair Author; its tone is elevated and its intention good. The philosophic infidel must be battered into belief by the aid of philosophy mingled with kindness. Take RENAN, HAECKEL, HUXLEY, STRAUSS, and DRAPER—the names, I mean; it is quite useless and might do harm to read their books,—shake them up together and make into a paste, add some poetical excerpts of a moral tendency, and spread thick over a violent lad smarting under a sense of demerit justly scorned. Turn him out into the world, then scrape clean and return him to his true friends. Cards, race-meetings, and billiards may be introduced *ad lib.*, also passion, prejudice, a faithful dog, and an infant prattler. Death-scenes form an effective relief. I have several which only need a touch or two to be complete. That is the way to please the publishers and capture the public.[129]

Punch ridiculed Lyall's formulaic and improbable storylines, banal characterization and style, and tedious moralizing ('Several chapters of theological disquisition omitted.—ED.'); but it could not be gainsaid that Lyall's 'novels with a purpose' stirred the public. This involved brickbats as well as plaudits. The most bizarre was a cameo part in Frederick Rolfe's *Hadrian the VII* (1904), when the

[127] The Queen had then read only *Donovan*, but in sending this to her daughter together with *We Two* she added about the latter that Princess 'Beatrice has and many others and men of intellect who are immensely struck by it' (letter, 17 Feb. 1886, in Ramm (ed.), *Beloved and Darling Child*, 30). The first edition of *Donovan* sold only 320 copies, and Lyall relinquished the copyright of it and of *We Two* for £50; but as her reputation took off from the mid-1880s sales of both books picked up. The popular one-volume version of *Donovan*, for example, was in its 23rd edition in 1896. The diary of Ruth Baily, the young wife of a prep-school proprietor, is evidence for another of Lyall's new admirers. Aged 22, Mrs Baily read both stories in 1887, commenting: '*We Two* . . . The characters beautiful. Some scenes and incidents too exaggerated. *Donovan* . . . Very beautiful. Full of deep thoughts and arguments. Characters—life like and natural' (Baily (ed.), *Ruth Bourne Diaries*, 82).

[128] Duffy, *Methuen*, 3. Lyall's publisher Algernon Methuen was a former schoolmaster and, like Lyall, an active Liberal who was to oppose Britain's part in the Boer War. In January 1910 he stood for parliament, unavailingly in the Conservative stronghold Guildford.

[129] *Punch*, 7 Mar. 1891, 112. R. C. Lehmann was the parodist.

prospective pontiff George Arthur Rose feels inclined to relax with a novel. He picks one at random: 'It was called *Donovan*. He remembered having seen (in an ex-tea-pedlar's magazine) a print of the writer thereof. He also remembered that he had found her self-conscious prose and labial conformation intensely antipathetic.' But he suppresses his repulsion and takes up her novel, for he has had enough intellectual exercise that day, counting the split infinitives in the *Pall Mall Gazette*. Indeed, he now thinks it his duty to read Lyall, because 'she sells her books by tens of thousands while we don't sell ours by tens of hundreds. We'll have a look at her work, and see how she does it.' Thus he reads and, though he 'several times was at the point of closing the book from sheer annoyance', believing that no woman can really understand the mental apparatus of men (and vice versa), he concludes that Lyall is 'a dear, good woman. Her book—well—her book is cheap, awkward, vulgar,—but it's good. It's unfaltering ugly and simple and good. Evidently it's best to be good. It pays . . . '.[130]

Controversy about the Bradlaugh case, and an appreciation of her work by the Prime Minister, Gladstone, accelerated Lyall's rise to prominence. Three times she subscribed to Charles Bradlaugh's expenses in Northampton, where he was compelled to contest by-elections in 1881, 1882, and 1884 after his exclusion from the Commons as an atheist who sought to affirm rather than take the oath. Lyall's support was entirely on grounds of political liberalism. Personally, she held profound religious convictions, and to her brother-in-law's parish of St Saviour's, Eastbourne, she presented three bells, named Donovan, Erica, and Hugo after characters in her novels. It was as a doughty champion of individual liberty and toleration, battling against an over-mighty executive, that Bradlaugh won Lyall's admiration. Following his death in 1891, Lyall penned an appeal to the press for a memorial fund, and led it by donating her last half-year's royalties of some £200. Parallels between Bradlaugh's struggle in the 1880s and parliamentarians' defiance of Charles I's prerogative rule in the 1630s were strong in her mind as she went on to write *In the Golden Days* (1885) and *To Right the Wrong* (1892–3), both set in the seventeenth century and designed as tributes to 'two of the most heroic figures in our history—Algernon Sydney and John Hampden'. The *Windsor Magazine* noted that Lyall's study contained their portraits, next to Cromwell and Milton; and on another wall were Mazzini, the Italian republican patriot, and Grattan, the champion of a separate Irish parliament in the eighteenth century; while on a bookshelf stood 'the latest portrait of Mr Gladstone, for whom the author has the highest respect and admiration, and of whose Irish policy she is a warm supporter'. Lyall's novel *Doreen* (1894), dedicated to Gladstone, made a passionate appeal for Home Rule.[131]

---

[130] Fr. Rolfe [Frederick Baron Corvo], *Hadrian the VII*, 7, 11–13.

[131] Sutherland, *Companion*, 193. Gladstone responded on 25 Nov. 1894 by praising 'the singular courage with which you stake your wide public reputation upon the Irish cause'. See *DNB Supplement 1901–1911*, i. 114–16.

Lyall was secretary of the Women's Liberal Association in Eastbourne. She told the *Windsor Magazine* that 'she is not at all averse to women speaking in public, if they have a real gift for it, but she herself invariably refuses to speak on the platform, pleading her weak voice and want of ready words'. She had done so only once, moving a resolution in eight words in favour of Home Rule; she also held reservations about the propriety of women canvassing, yet 'I fail to see anything unwomanly in voting.' Indeed, it was emphasized that she considered 'woman suffrage as an act of right and justice, and although she admits that it is not likely to be just yet, cannot understand any woman being indifferent to the subject, who takes even the smallest interest in her country'. She rejected the interviewer's provocative suggestion that the Modern Woman question was a got-up cause 'conducive to novel writing, inasmuch that it provides a cheap subject of interest to the general public'. Lyall remained a public fighter for liberal causes. In 1896 she published *The Autobiography of a Truth* and assigned its profits to the Armenian Relief Fund in protest against the Salisbury Government's apparent indifference to Ottoman atrocities; and her last novel, *The Hinderers*, published in 1902, the year before her death, constituted an indictment of the Government's part in the Boer War. Lyall's obituarist in the *Dictionary of National Biography* averred that 'her earnest political purpose, which came of her native horror of oppression and injustice, militated against her mastery of the whole art of fiction'; but this note of regret was not one that Lyall had shared. In a preface to a book of sermons by her mother's cousin, she proclaimed the need for the novelist to speak out: 'No surface teaching can strengthen and prepare the mind for 19th century life ... We need living words, not dead formalities; fresh thoughts, not empty phrases; the straightforward facing of doubts and perplexities, not the weak and lazy shelving of the subject.'[132]

It was a sign of the ubiquitousness of this phenomenon that such a manifesto, exhorting writers to engage in public controversy, should issue not from a noisy metropolitan habituated to exhibitionism but from a fragile spinster in a polite south-coast resort. The shyest of authors were now more easily drawn out, conscious of the dawning of democratic politics and the importance of ordering public affairs along correct lines. Thus Lewis Carroll, who (as the Revd C. L. Dodgson) taught mathematics at Oxford, was a keen communicant to the press, through which he aired opinions on all manner of subjects from the rules of lawn tennis to a method for resolving strikes. He wrote articles in support of the Anti-Vivisection Society and to counter popular prejudice against vaccination.[133] He also expressed a strong interest in electoral systems. His fifty-six-page pamphlet *The Principles of Parliamentary Representation* (1884), proposing a scheme of proportional representation, was made available to both party leaders, Gladstone and Salisbury, when they were locked in argument during the Third

---

[132] *The Windsor Magazine* (Jan. 1895), 18–25.
[133] Collingwood, *Carroll*, 140–5, 241; Cohen, *Carroll*, 377, 391–3.

ideas and social realism evolved its own stock and stilted characters, banging on about 'the wrongness of the whole social system', Beerbohm began to fear that the new wave might have driven playwriting even further away from art than had the school of unthinking melodrama and entertainment.[140] Beerbohm grieved at the betrayal involved when an author decided to sermonize. Galsworthy, he averred, 'sold his literary birthright for a pot of message'.[141] Not only was this not the way of salvation, in all probability there was no salvation any way:

Life—even such part of it as our limited human brains can conceive—is a very weird, august, complex, and elusive affair. To have any positive theory of it, any single dogmatic point of view, any coherent 'message', is an act of impertinence. To be an optimist or a pessimist, a realist or an idealist, a Thingumyite or a Somebodyan, to belong to any 'school of thought' whatsoever, is to write oneself down an ass—for anyone who can read. The true sage, he who penetrates the furthest, and raises the most of the fringe that surrounds the darkness, dares not enunciate any 'truth' without a hundred-and-one reservations and qualifications. He may be heard by a few in his own land. He most assuredly will not have a European reputation. That sort of thing is reserved for inspired asses like Tolstoi or Nietzsche—for men who have gone off at a tangent, men pre-cipitated along one sharp narrow line which they mistake for the whole dim uni-verse . . . let us, by all means, listen to them; they are great fun. Take them seriously?—ah no![142]

Beerbohm sought a divorce of literature from politics; but politics were inherent in manifestos of this period which debated the role of the writer. Oscar Wilde issued his in 1891 in two essays, 'The Critic as Artist' and 'The Soul of Man under Socialism'. His plays also were carriages by which to challenge conventional values.[143] Not that Wilde kept a straight face for long. His showmanship was incorrigible, and earnestness in others roused his mirth, such that he supposedly

had some intention of producing a revised version of the Bible, with all the inartistic passages cut out, and a rhymed dedication to Mr Stead, whose *Review of Reviews* always struck him as only a degree less comic than the books of that arch-humorist Miss Edna Lyall, or the bedroom imaginings of Miss Olive Schreiner.[144]

Novelists and playwrights did not abstain from debating social and other questions in their fiction and plays, as Lang and Beerbohm advised. Moreover, many ventured further into the public domain to advertise their views directly by tract-writing, lecturing, agitation, and associational activity. Their keenness cre-ated the impression of demanding everything at once; as Anthony Hope put it, 'wanting the millennium in a Pickford van'.[145] Come the 1900s, A. G. Gardiner, editor of the *Daily News*, felt justified in treating 'the most conspicuous literary

---

[140] Cecil, *Max*, 248–9.   [141] Ibid. 267.   [142] Ibid. 179–80.
[143] Sos Eltis, *Revising Wilde: Society and Subversion in the Plays of Oscar Wilde* (Oxford, 1996).
[144] Hichens, *Green Carnation*, 138.   [145] Quoted in Paul, *Men and Letters*, 269.

men of to-day' as 'so largely men of action'. It was this that made them so pleased with themselves:

Mr. Chesterton, Mr. Shaw, and Mr. Wells are engaged less in writing books than in fighting battles. They are concerned not with literature but with life. They do not use words like artists, but like warriors, loving them not for their perfume, but because they hit hard. Each has an enemy and it is the same enemy. It is Things as They Are. Mr. Chesterton takes the world in his vast embrace and tries to heave it back into the Middle Ages. Mr. Shaw and Mr. Wells—flinging jolly gibes at each other, by the way— rush at our poor orb and seek to kick it into centuries unborn. They are all perspiring and they are all happy.[146]

VIII

In 1902, in his posthumously published autobiography, Sir Walter Besant, glossing the transition in strong colours, argued that previous generations had regarded the literary life 'with pity and contempt'. Most writers were 'hacks, dependants, Bohemians, and disreputable', and authorship was not considered an occupation 'worthy of a gentleman and a scholar'. With scarce exception, Besant claimed, literary men were not then regarded as opinion-formers. Too many were asso- ciated in the public mind with irresponsibility.[147] This was how Benjamin Disraeli had been regarded originally. The author of silver-fork Society novels before he entered parliament in 1837, he was thus tarnished as a *flâneur*. During the Peelite ascendancy, he kept up novel-writing as an outlet for his political and religious thinking (and personal revenge) in *Coningsby* (1844), *Sybil; or, The Two Nations* (1845), and *Tancred* (1847); then, after a protracted pause of twenty-three years, during which he rose to the Conservative leadership, he issued *Lothair* (1870). Disraeli's resumption of novel-writing struck the *Saturday Review* as as surprising as if 'he would sing at the opera, dance on a tight-rope at the Crystal Palace, or preach a sermon at Mr. Spurgeon's Tabernacle'.[148] Trollope was disgusted by it, thinking it bore the 'flavour of hair-oil' and, had Disraeli shown any judgement, should have been destroyed at birth.[149] *Lothair* turned out to be another *roman-à-clef*, designed to project Disraeli's political philosophy, this time his unease about the fanaticism inherent in ultramontane Catholicism and revolutionary nation- alism. He also needed the income, because he was not rich like most political leaders. Receiving a 50 per cent royalty, he netted £6,000 from *Lothair* by 1876. Another £2,100 followed from Longman's in 1877 for the reissue of his ten novels in a collected edition. Disraeli was then Prime Minister and Earl of Beaconsfield; and it was in this incarnation that Longman's offered him an unprecedented £10,000 for the rights to *Endymion*, which was published shortly after he lost the

---

[146] A. G. Gardiner, *The Pillars of Society* (1916), 286.   [147] Besant, *Autobiography*, 91–3.
[148] *Saturday Review*, 9 Apr. 1870, quoted in Vernon Bogdanor, Introduction to Benjamin Disraeli, *Lothair* (Oxford, 1975), p. vii.   [149] Trollope, *Autobiography*, 231.

general election in 1880, the penultimate year of his life. *Endymion* was a romanticization of the political world Disraeli had known between 1827 and 1855. Once more, it included characters drawn from life, among them Thackeray, thinly veiled as St Barbe, 'the vainest, most envious, most amusing of men'. This was an uncharitable evaluation of Thackeray, dead since 1863, because, though Thackeray had indeed parodied Disraeli's performances in *Punch*, he had also eulogized him for the reflected glory that his political rise earned for other novelists.[150]

Assessment of Disraeli's standing as a novelist was impossible to divorce from the politician. 'I have finished *Endymion* with a painful feeling that the writer considers all political life as mere play and gambling,' wrote the Archbishop of Canterbury, Tait;[151] but this was to think that surface smartness signified an absence of political ideals. Disraeli's official biographer (and editor of *The Times*) George Buckle preferred to endorse Edmund Gosse's prophecy that Disraeli would endure as 'a minor classic of English Literature', Buckle dubbing him 'the creator, and to some minds the sole really successful practitioner, of a new *genre*, the Political Novel'.[152] Dining with The Club in 1899, Grant Duff found himself agreeing with Arthur Balfour, a successor to Disraeli as Conservative leader, that 'after all allowance had been made for their false glitter and blunders of every sort, there was yet a certain literary element in them which would keep them long alive'.[153] That was always the challenge facing writers of political fiction, that its didacticism and topicality should not squeeze out art. Politicians' ideological and ethical problems would provide themes for a quantity of Victorian and Edwardian authors, and politicians appear as walk-on characters in the works of many more. This dismayed George Moore, who considered them a fundamentally uninteresting subspecies of humanity and their antics antipathetic to literature's proper concerns. About Granville Barker's *Waste* (1907)—which drew the Censor's ban—he averred that it was not his best play, 'But oh, dear me! When you get to politicians . . . ! What can anyone do?'[154]

Only one other creative writer had then come within a distance of matching Disraeli in achieving high office, and even he fell far short. This was Bulwer Lytton, who was briefly Secretary of State for the Colonies in Lord Derby's minority government, 1858–9, some twenty years after making that famous declaration in his play *Richelieu* (1839), 'The pen is mightier than the sword.'[155] Ministerial office came during Lytton's second spell in parliament: he had first served as a Radical Whig 1832–41, then returned as a Conservative in 1852. But, according to his grandson and biographer, Lytton had effectively opted for literature over politics in 1835 when he turned down a junior position in

---

[150] Monypenny and Buckle, *Disraeli*, iii. 347, vi. 563–4.   [151] Buckle, *Disraeli*, vi. 568.
[152] Ibid. 573.   [153] Grant Duff, *Diary, 1896 to 1901*, ii. 175 (15 Nov. 1899).
[154] Goodwin, *Moore*, 237.
[155] See Lytton, *Lytton*, vol. ii, book v, ch. v; and, for a modern assessment, Leslie Mitchell, *Bulwer Lytton: The Rise and Fall of a Victorian Man of Letters* (2003).

Melbourne's Government, offered to him on account of the impression made by his pamphlet *Letter to a Late Cabinet Minister on the Present Crisis* (November 1834).[156] If the odds thereafter appeared stacked against sustaining a double career of politics and letters, then the idea of sequential careers, of moving into politics having first carved a name in literature, remained alluring. Still, the failure rate was almost total. Thackeray, his fame as a novelist made, came a cropper at the Oxford by-election in 1857. These were the days of open voting—the secret ballot was not adopted until 1872—when personal influence, not to mention nefarious practices, exercised a persuasion over tiny electorates. His opponent was Edward Cardwell, a Peelite-turned-Liberal who had been president of the Board of Trade in Aberdeen's Coalition Government. As a past MP for Oxford, Cardwell presented a stiff proposition, against which Thackeray measured his public standing as an author. He boasted an independence in the great tradition of 'Satirical-Moralists—and having such a vast multitude of readers whom we not only amuse but teach'.[157] Thackeray had spurned the chance of standing as an official Whig–Liberal candidate (at Edinburgh) in the recent general election because, though on social terms with party grandees, he was disenchanted by aristocratic government, the Aberdeen ministry's maladministration of the Crimean War, and the new Prime Minister Palmerston's apparent determination to perpetuate much the same ministers and policies. Approached by the whip, Thackeray had replied, 'Sir says I with 15000 subscribers to my books (all this is entre nous), and hundreds of thousands of hearers all over England [attending his lectures] I'm not going to be a Whig under strapper.'[158]

As a younger man Thackeray had espoused radical opinions. Though dismissive of physical-force Chartists, thinking no good could come from an uprising, he too rejected the social system: 'I'm not a Chartist, only a republican,' he told his mother in 1840; 'I would like to see all men equal, and this bloated aristocracy blasted to the wings of all the winds.' His ideal then was 'strong government and social equality'.[159] In 1857 he was more circumspect in his formal declarations: 'With no feeling but that of good will towards those leading Aristocratic Families who are administering the chief offices of the State, I believe that it could be benefited by the skills and talents of persons less aristocratic.'[160] The fires in him had not cooled altogether. Speaking in Oxford Town Hall, he insisted that 'popular influence must be brought to bear on the present government of the country', adding, 'if they flinch remind them that the people is outside and wants more and more'.[161] Thackeray cannot be absolved of self-seeking. It was a device of eighteenth-century politics, with which he had made

---

[156] Lytton, *Lytton*, i. 492–5.
[157] Letter to Mark Lemon, 24 Feb. 1847, in Harden (ed.), *Thackeray's Letters*, 136.
[158] Letter to Mrs Henry Carmichael-Smyth, 9–12 Jan. 1857, ibid. 312.
[159] Letters to Mrs Henry Carmichael-Smyth, 18 Jan., 30 July, 4–5 Oct. 1840, ibid. 53, 65, 76.
[160] Taylor, *Thackeray*, 393.
[161] Address, 10 July 1857, quoted in D. J. Taylor, 'The Newcomer', *Oxford Today*, 2/3 (1999), 31.

himself familiar and of which not a little survived into the 1850s, to angle for a government sinecure by causing a nuisance so as to be bought off. Thackeray did not restrain his agents from splashing money about but, though he won over some university progressives such as the historian J. R. Green, he was uncomfortable about personal canvassing. Thackeray also rather admired his opponent, telling his daughter that he was a covert Cardwellite, which evidenced a certain confusion of mind and purpose. What determined the outcome is hard to pinpoint. Corrupt voters might follow the cash, but there were principles to reckon. Cardwell's agents played up the sabbatarian issue as likely to alienate the clerical party from Thackeray, who advocated the opening of museums (though not theatres) on Sundays; but it is difficult to believe that Thackeray stood high with this section of opinion anyhow. In the event, while fewer than seventy votes separated the candidates, Thackeray overestimated his drawing power. According to George Brodrick, Thackeray told the victor when later they met at the Athenaeum:

Well, Cardwell, you know that I have been down among your d——d constituents. Of course, I did not expect that all of them would have read my novels, but I certainly did expect that most of them would have heard of me; instead of which, I found that the question on every one's lips was—'Who the devil is Thackeray?'[162]

Thackeray apparently regretted having stood. The exercise cost him almost £900, and diverted him from starting his next projected novel, *The Virginians*;[163] yet the thought of Thackeray MP remained beguiling: 'I don't know when I shall have another thousand pounds to spare for an election fight—but having tasted of the excitement, have a strong inclination to repeat it. Novel spinning is not enough occupation for a man of six-and-forty . . . . .'[164]

Thackeray's friend Trollope also determined to pitch for parliament, standing as 'an advanced Conservative Liberal' at Beverley in the 1868 general election. To become an MP, he felt, was 'the highest object of ambition to every educated Englishman'.[165] He had already begun to write 'parliamentary' novels, *Can You Forgive Her?* (1865) proving to be the first in the Plantagenet Palliser series.[166] Broadly content with the mid-century political equipoise, Trollope was disturbed by Palmerston's death in 1865 and the virtual doubling of the franchise in 1867.

[162] Brodrick, *Memories and Impressions*, 225.

[163] Gérin, *Ritchie*, 111; Thackeray to William Duer Robinson, 23 Jan.–25 Feb. 1858, in Harden (ed.), *Thackeray's Letters*, 322.

[164] Thackeray to John Webster, dated only as 1858, in Grant Duff, *Diary, 1889–1891*, ii. 63 (15 Dec. 1890). In a letter to an American friend, Mrs George Baxter, 10–23 Apr. 1858, Thackeray qualified this: 'I have seen my name as a candidate for no less than 4 places in event of a dissolution of parliament, but don't want one now for a while. Let us have some more lectures and some more money first. My expenses . . . are awful. I have a one horse chay and spend £2600 a year *at least*' (Harden (ed.), *Thackeray's Letters*, 326).

[165] Trollope, *Autobiography*, 256.

[166] Others were: *Phineas Finn* (1869), *The Eustace Diamonds* (1873), *Phineas Redux* (1874), *The Prime Minister* (1876), *The Duke's Children* (1880). Joseph Conrad recalled that it was one of these that was the first book he read in English; Conrad, *A Personal Memoir* (1912), in *Collected Works*, ix. 71, 73.

He had no programme of public action to propose. He objected to governments assuming the role of moral policeman, as he perceived in the Permissive Bill, which temperance reformers promoted to empower ratepayers to outlaw pubs in their districts, and which was a popular cry among some Beverley Liberals. Others agitated for the secret ballot; but Trollope 'hated....both these measures, thinking it to be unworthy of a great people to free itself from the evil results of vicious conduct by unmanly restraints'.[167] The cost in loss of liberty, by fruitless attempts to compel people to be good, Trollope reckoned too high. He disbelieved in social progress by legislation, as distinct from education or personal advancement by individual exertion. This last path was not straightforward either, for Trollope valued character above cleverness. Hence his anxiety about unprincipled financial speculators, which he expressed in *The Way We Live Now* (1875); and his scepticism, as a civil servant himself, about the new examinations for Civil Service entry that might elevate mechanical crammers and officious experts above dignified and modest gentlemen, which he expressed in *The Three Clerks* (1857). All this counted for nothing in Beverley, which had a forbidding reputation for corruption: 'my political ideas were all leather and prunella to the men whose votes I was soliciting'. Constituents welcomed elections as weapons to plunder politicians. Over two-thirds of those voting in the last four elections were bribed. One of the sitting MPs, Sir Henry Edwards, owned the largest business in the area, the Beverley Iron and Waggon Co.; and, of the 2,672 electors in 1868, some 300 were dubbed 'rolling stock', to be hitched up by any party for a bribe, and another 500 would not support their side unless paid.[168] Trollope owned to grudging admiration for the brass-necked openness of it—'There was something grand in the scorn with which a leading Liberal there turned up his nose at me when I told him that there should be no bribery, no treating, not even a pot of beer....'. The result was mortifying. Attracting 740 voters, Trollope finished a poor fourth of the four candidates contesting this double-member seat. He had paid an election agent £400 for the privilege. Such money was bagatelle to one who earned £70,000 from authorship, but the time spent was 'the most wretched fortnight of my manhood'.[169] Beverley was disfranchised and sunk into the East Riding constituency in 1870, and Trollope fictionalized his experiences in *Ralph the Heir* (1871).[170]

Both Trollope and Thackeray compensated for thwarted parliamentary ambitions by involvement in an alternative forum for debate, the periodical review. Trollope was co-founder (and chairman of the board) of the *Fortnightly Review*, sinking £1,250 into the venture, and securing George Henry Lewes,

[167] Trollope, *Autobiography* 265.

[168] For Beverley in context, see K. Theodore Hoppen, 'Roads to Democracy: Electioneering and Corruption in Nineteenth-Century England and Ireland', *History* (Oct. 1996), 553–71.

[169] Trollope, *Autobiography*, 264–7.

[170] For Trollope's politics, see Asa Briggs, *Victorian People* (1954, 1965), ch. 4; and for Trollope's genius in depicting political and social types, see R. W. Chapman, 'Personal Names in Trollope's Political Novels', in Cumberledge (ed.), *Essays Presented to Sir Humphrey Milford*, ch. vi.

George Eliot's paramour, as first editor in May 1865. Lewes, in ill health, was replaced by John Morley in January 1867 and, for a period at the end of that year when Morley visited America, George Meredith was acting editor. The *Fortnightly* serialized novels, including three of Trollope's own and five of Meredith's; but it was not for this that the magazine was principally conceived, rather as a platform for eclectic opinion, responsibly argued. Trollope advocated signed articles, then an uncommon practice; he was also inclined to exclude political subjects and to insist that 'nothing should appear denying or questioning the divinity of Christ'.[171] Such conditionality, he admitted, militated against the professed ideal of encouraging freedom of expression; in any case, Trollope's cautiousness was ignored by Morley, whose editorship, which lasted until October 1882, was conspicuous for the promotion of rationalism and radicalism.[172] Trollope was equally disappointed financially. Having struggled during its first year, the *Fortnightly* was sold to the publishers Chapman & Hall for, as Trollope put it, 'a trifle'. Bizarrely too, the *Fortnightly*, which originally came out every two weeks, appeared monthly from November 1866 while still retaining its bi-weekly title.

In his association with the *Fortnightly*, Trollope, who regarded *Henry Esmond* (1852) as 'the greatest novel in the English language', was in many respects imitating Thackeray, who was first editor (January 1860–May 1862) of the *Cornhill Magazine*. Thackeray was actually unsuited to the position, but the first issue of this shilling monthly sold an astonishing 110,000 copies, having secured (according to the publisher George M. Smith) 'the most brilliant contributors', who were paid sums 'lavish almost to the point of recklessness'.[173] Among Thackeray's contributors were Elizabeth Barrett Browning,[174] Carlyle, Mrs Gaskell, Thomas Hood, Ruskin, Tennyson, and Trollope. To the last named he declared: 'One of our chief objects in this Magazine is the getting out of novel-spinning, and back into the world.'[175] Thackeray's prospectus for the first number began in self-deprecating style, not wanting to invite derision that the editor, known as a satirical essayist and novelist, should pose as 'a great reformer, philosopher, and

---

[171] Trollope, *Autobiography*, 172–3.

[172] Sullivan (ed.), *Literary Magazines, 1837–1913*, 131–3. For Morley's own statement of his purpose and achievement, see his 'Valedictory' (1882), in Morley, *Studies in Literature*, esp. 339–47. He considered that 'No article that has appeared in any periodical for a generation back excited so profound a sensation as Mr. [T. H.] Huxley's memorable paper On the Physical Basis of Life, published in this Review in February 1869.'

[173] Trollope, *Autobiography*, 170; Sullivan (ed.), *Literary Magazines, 1837–1913*, 82; Sutherland, *Companion*, 150.

[174] Mrs Browning's 'A Musical Instrument' appeared in the July 1860 edition; but in April 1861 Thackeray rejected 'Lord Walter's Wife', fearing a readers' reaction if he published such a poem, containing 'an account of an unlawful passion felt by a man for a woman'. Mrs Browning indignantly responded: 'I am not a "fast woman"—I don't like coarse subjects, or the coarse treatment of any subject. But I am deeply convinced that the corruption of our society requires not shut doors and windows, but light and air: and that it is exactly because pure and prosperous women choose to *ignore* vice, that miserable women suffer wrong by it everywhere.' Robert Browning, offered the editorship before Thackeray himself, would not contribute at all. DeVane and Knickerbocker (eds.), *New Letters of Browning*, 125–6.   [175] Letter to Anthony Trollope, 28 Oct. 1859, in Harden (ed.), *Thackeray's Letters*, 343.

wiseacre, about to expound prodigious doctrines and truths until now unrevealed, to guide and direct the peoples, to pull down the existing order of things, to edify new social or political structures, and, in a word, to set the Thames on Fire'. Thackeray acknowledged that, to attract readers, they must 'amuse and interest them'; therefore, 'fiction of course must form a part' of the *Cornhill*. But it must be only a part:

We want, on the other hand, as much reality as possible—discussion, and narrative of events, interesting to the public, personal adventure and observation, familiar reports of scientific discovery, description of Social Institutions—*quicquid agunt homines* ['all the activities of man']—a Great Eastern, a battle in China, a Race Course, a popular Preacher—there is hardly any subject we *don't* want to hear about, from lettered and instructed men who are competent to speak on it.[176]

What also mattered to Thackeray was his editor's £2,000 a year; he told his mother, 'we mustn't say a word against filthy lucre, for I see the use and comfort of it every day more and more'.[177] His primary concern was to make his two daughters financially independent, while spending huge sums on refurbishing a Queen Anne red-brick mansion at Palace Green, Kensington: 'It's all built out of Corn Hill money and I shall put 2 wheat-sheaves on the doors.'[178]

The *Cornhill*'s circulation was halved by 1863 and dropped to 20,000 by 1871, when the editorship was assumed by Thackeray's son-in-law Leslie Stephen at £500 per annum. The decline in sales was not arrested—12,000 by 1882—but this was in part because of the very success of the formula, which was adopted by competitors such as *Macmillan's Magazine* (in which Thomas Hughes had a financial interest),[179] *Temple Bar*, *The Academy*, *Belgravia*, *St Paul's*, and *St James's*. This formula, in turn, had been modelled on the American *Harper's Monthly Magazine*, which was founded in 1850 and to which Dickens, Thackeray, and Bulwer Lytton contributed. The aim was to combine fiction serialization with high-quality essays: literary, philosophical, historical, travel, and sometimes polemical and political. It was a winning formula, too, until the literary marketplace was shaken up by the advent of a less sophisticated reading public. In 1884 the largest circulation for a monthly review was claimed by the relative newcomer the *Nineteenth Century*, founded in 1877, which had average sales of 20,000 and a readership several times greater;[180] but literary entrepreneurs were now looking beyond the sort of audiences reached by the quality monthly or weekly. In 1886, when planning a new penny weekly to promote 'social and religious progress'—the *British Weekly*—Robertson

---

[176] Letter to 'A Contributor', 1 Nov. 1859, ibid. 345–6.

[177] Letter, 1 Oct. 1859, in Fuller and Hammersley (eds.), *Thackeray's Daughter*, 88.

[178] Letter to Dr John Brown, 23 Sept. 1863, in Harden (ed.), *Thackeray's Letters*, 356, 368.

[179] Hughes was Smith's original choice as editor of the *Cornhill*. *Macmillan's* preceded the *Cornhill* by two months, and started by serializing Hughes's *Tom Brown at Oxford*.

[180] Metcalf, *Knowles*, 285. What multiple to apply to sales figures in order to estimate readership is a nice question. John Morley was perhaps excessively optimistic when he reckoned that the *Fortnightly Review*, with sales of 3,000 in 1873, was read by 30,000. See Sullivan (ed.), *Literary Magazines, 1837–1913*, p. xxiv.

Nicoll was adamant that 'we must provide popular features, so that it will resemble the *Pall Mall Gazette* more than the *Spectator*'.[181]

IX

The heyday of the shilling literary periodical in the two decades after 1860 nevertheless helped to create an image of the imaginative writer as a serious figure; and this prepared the ground for such authors' enhanced status and enlarged public role after 1880. Walter Besant's activity is a token of this. He came slowly to a position of independence through authorship, after six years in a colonial professorship and eighteen as paid secretary to the Society for the Systematic and Scientific Exploration of Palestine, which gave him the security of £200–300 per annum. He published studies of French literature while moving towards fiction-writing. He never became exclusively a writer of fiction because, after 1894, he embarked on a great historical survey of London,[182] designing to rival the Elizabethan John Stow. Moreover, in addition to his work for the Society of Authors, which he founded in 1884, he was drawn into philanthropy. As he explained in his autobiography, 'It all began with a novel.'[183] This was *All Sorts and Conditions of Men: An Impossible Story* (1882), which imagined a 'Palace of Delight' to brighten the lives of the East End poor. What resulted was a public fund—the recast Beaumont Trust—managed by Sir Edmund Currie[184] and Besant himself, which raised £75,000. The People's Palace, as it was called, was sited facing Mile End Road, Stepney, and the first section, the Queen's Hall, was opened by the Queen during her Jubilee on 14 May 1887.[185] The planned complex included a concert hall for 4,000 people, swimming pools and a gymnasium, a library of 15,000 volumes,[186] a newspaper and magazine reading room, a lecture

---

[181] Nicoll to Professor Henry Drummond, 3 Aug. 1886, in Darlow, *Nicoll*, 69.

[182] Besant's survey originally included the idea of investigating current social conditions, such as was then being conducted by Charles Booth. Booth brought his own work to fruition in the monumental *Life and Labour of the People in London*, 17 vols. (1891–1903). One of Booth's assistants, Beatrice Potter, commented tartly in her diary, 19 Oct. 1887: 'Afternoon had interview with Besant, the novelist. Evidently nothing to be got out of him and his 1,300 investigators. Had no idea how they intended to classify their information. One idea, to prevent early marriages. Struck me as a quack, so far as investigation is concerned.' See Norman and Jeanne MacKenzie (eds.), *The Diary of Beatrice Webb*, i: *1873–1892* (1982), 219.

[183] Besant, *Autobiography*, 243.

[184] Currie (1834–1913), heir to a distillery fortune, was chairman of the London Hospital and active on the London School Board and Metropolitan Asylums Board; see *Who Was Who, 1897–1916*. Also, Deborah E. B. Weiner, 'The People's Palace: An Image for East London in the 1880s', in David Feldman and Gareth Stedman Jones (eds.), *Metropolis. London: Histories and Representations since 1800* (1989), 40–55.

[185] *The Times*, 16 May 1887; St Helier, *Memories*, 348–9.

[186] The library was given a fillip following the death of Wilkie Collins in 1889. The attempt of Collins's friends and fellow authors, including Hardy and Meredith, to raise subscriptions for a memorial to Collins in Westminster Abbey or St Paul's failed when the ecclesiastical authorities blocked the proposal 'on grounds of morality as well as literary merit'. Instead, the £400 that was subscribed was converted into a 'Wilkie Collins Memorial Library of Fiction' in the People's Palace, Besant himself being commissioned to complete Collins's last, unfinished work, *Blind Love* (1890). See Peters, *Collins*, 430, 433; Hardy to Harry Quilter, 13 Mar. 1890, in Purdy and Millgate (eds.), *Hardy Letters*, i. 210.

room, club, and social rooms, an art school and winter garden.[187] In 1890 Currie reported on the first two years' progress: at the library, which was open from 3 to 10 p.m., and at musical performances, the People's Palace attracted an average of 2,000 persons per Sunday; and evening classes drew 5,000 students. Their educational work Currie especially approved.[188] But after the Drapers' Company donated £20,000 for a technical school, this, to Besant's dismay, came to dominate the recreational side, which was run down. Clashes occurred over the upkeep of the library; the provision of billiards was withdrawn because this incited betting; and the 'literary club proved a dead failure; not a soul, while I was connected with the Palace, showed the least literary ability or ambition'.[189] Besant forgot, most certainly deliberately, that Arthur Morrison, son of an engine fitter, worked at the Palace between 1887 and 1890, acting as sub-editor (to Besant as editor) of the *Palace Journal*. Morrison left to become a journalist, a writer of detective stories, and, above all, author of stories about slum life in a realist style markedly different from Besant's own: *Tales of Mean Streets* (1894), *A Child of the Jago* (1896), and *The Hole in the Wall* (1902).[190] Grudgingly, in his autobiography, Besant allowed that 'the successes far outweighed the failures', but he could not conceal his asperity about the transformation of the Palace into a polytechnic.[191]

The fault, if such it was, lay in Besant's naivety: his assumption that the poverty of lives in the East End did not stem from structural economic causes so much as from the absence of proper means of society, amusement, and culture. If the feelings of Oscar Wilde's circle about Besant's capacity as a writer were generally experienced, then Besant was not the man to supply this deficiency. In *The Green Carnation* (1894), Esmé Araminth bemoans his own ceaseless sparkle. He yearns for something to slow him down, having 'experimented with absinthe, but gained no result . . . Opium has proved useless, and green tea cigarettes leave me positively brilliant.' In desperation, he reads 'the collected works of Walter Besant. They are said to sap the mental powers.'[192] *Punch* also highlighted Besant's dismalness when it parodied him in its series of Prize Novels. This was 'The Curse of Cognac' by 'Walter Decant', recommended by its author:

as calculated to lower the exaggerated cheerfulness which is apt to prevail at Christmas time . . . Families are advised to read it in detachments of four or five at a time. Married men who owe their wives' mothers a grudge should lock them into a bare room, with a guttering candle and this story. Death will be certain, and not painless.

---

[187] *Review of Reviews* (Feb. 1891), 157.　　[188] Ibid. (Feb. 1890), 137.

[189] Besant, *Autobiography*, 245.

[190] See P. J. Keating's biographical study in the 1969 edition of *A Child of the Jago*, in which Morrison mocked the People's Palace as the East End Elevation Mission and Panosophical Institute. The artist Will Rothenstein also took classes there (Rothenstein, *Men and Memories, 1872–1900*, 29), and Oscar Wilde had applied for the post of Secretary of the Beaumont Trust in 1886 (Hart-Davis (ed.), *More Letters*, 61–2).

[191] In 1902 it became the East London Technical College and in 1907, a constituent of London University, being renamed Queen Mary College in 1934.　　[192] Hichens, *Green Carnation*, 88.

The story climaxes superbly:

They found George Ginsling feet uppermost in six inches of water in the Daffodil Road reservoir. It was a large reservoir, and had been quite full before George began upon it. This was his record drink, and it killed him. His last words were, 'If I had stuck to whiskey, this would never have happened.'[193]

More damaging to Besant's ambitions than such satire, influential subscribers held different agendas for the People's Palace. The fundraising came at a time when attention was being given to two Royal Commissions, on Technical Instruction and on Depression of Trade and Industry; and their exposure of shortcomings in scientific and technical training, leading to a loss of markets to Germany and America especially, meant that this issue took precedence. 'National Efficiency' was emerging as the new watchword. Its enthusiasts championed physical drill for imperial defence as well as technical education for industrial competitiveness. Moreover, the prevailing grain of Victorian cultural provision for the working classes was 'rational recreation', that is, recreation with an educative function, improvement not mere enjoyment. Finally, there was the fear of violence, if not actual revolution: Bernard Shaw observed how donations to the People's Palace rose with the thermometer of alarm, heated by demonstrations of the unemployed and by the depradations of Jack the Ripper. 'Blood money', Shaw called these donations. It was also the case that an alternative model to the People's Palace existed. This was the Toynbee Hall Settlement, founded in 1884 in nearby Whitechapel, whose residents—university graduates and professional men—undertook social work and a cultural mission among the poor, supervising them as squires in an urban manor. Toynbee Hall represented a more systematic organization of Besant's sentiments, that the superior classes would enlighten the poor by sharing experiences and providing moral leadership. Therefore, Besant's original vision for a 'Palace of Delights' was overtaken and harnessed to other needs, judged more coherent by the subscribers.[194]

Besant was not done with practical philanthropy, however. Again, a novel publicized his concerns. *Children of Gibeon* (1886) lamented the plight of Hoxton's sewing girls. Besant had been drawn into the network of girls' clubs and cooperatives that endeavoured to counter the sweating system.[195] He founded the Home Arts and Industries Association (1884), which, over the next twenty years, established 500 evening schools and put on annual exhibitions of wood- and leather-work, embroidery and weaving; and in 1897, in conjunction with the

---

[193] *Punch*, 13 Dec. 1890, 277.

[194] Weiner, 'The People's Palace', in Feldman and Jones (eds.), *Metropolis*; Asa Briggs and Anne Macartney, *Toynbee Hall: The First Hundred Years* (1984); and Alon Kadish, *Apostle Arnold: The Life and Death of Arnold Toynbee, 1852–1883* (Chapel Hill, NC, 1986), esp. 47, for criticism of 'political' solutions to the East End's problems which Besant made in *All Sorts and Conditions of Men*.

[195] Among the many inspired by Besant's novel to volunteer in the Working Girls' Club movement was Emmeline Pethick, later better known as the suffragette and socialist Emmeline Pethick-Lawrence (1867–1954); see Vera Brittain, *Pethick-Lawrence: A Portrait* (1963), ch. 3.

National Union of Women Workers, his prompting produced a women's employment bureau.[196] The epitaph inscribed on his grave at Hampstead— Besant's home, Frognal End, was built there in 1891, and he died in 1901—was 'Write me as one that loves his fellow-men'.[197]

X

In 1903 an appeal was launched for a public memorial to Besant, for erection on the Victoria Embankment, this being a copy of a bronze bust that George Frampton designed for the crypt in St Paul's Cathedral.[198] Besant had been by nature a doer. It might therefore be argued that his public activity was rather an expression of temperament than of authors' greater prominence or sense of responsibility. The case of George Meredith suggests otherwise. It is true that he always held strong political opinions of a Liberal Radical kind; yet, until later life, these views were mostly reserved for private correspondence. His uncertain literary reputation more than his uncertain health caused this reticence. As he told his friend the quixotically conservative Liberal Admiral Maxse, who was fighting the 1880 general election, 'I have the habit of standing aside in politics, from disbelief that I can be of service.'[199] He first made what he called 'a spanking bid for popularity' with *The Adventures of Harry Richmond* (1871), the longest of all his novels, which, through the office of another of his friends, Leslie Stephen, was serialized in the *Cornhill Magazine* with illustrations by Du Maurier.[200] This propelled the book into a second edition within three months; but it was a false dawn and his career stuttered commercially.

Because of his pagan preference for Nature over orthodox Christianity, Meredith had been castigated by the country clergy—with singular exceptions such as the Revd (later Canon) Augustus Jessopp, who first wrote to Meredith with an appreciation of his *Poems* (1851) and then to register shock at parts of *The Ordeal of Richard Feverel* (1859). Jessopp was headmaster of the King Edward VI School, Norwich, to which Meredith entrusted his son Arthur as one of a handful of boarders in 1862. The bond between Jessopp and Meredith was forged not just from mutual love of learning and literature but from shared Radical leanings.[201]

---

[196] *DNB 1901–1911*, i. 155.

[197] Frognal End was a large red-brick villa 'built bungalow-wise', Besant explained, 'to save the servants as much as possible' (R. S. Warren Bell, 'The Houses of Celebrated People', *Windsor Magazine* (July 1895), 3).

[198] George Meredith to the editor of *The Times*, 23 July 1903, in Cline (ed.), *Meredith's Letters*, iii. 1485–6.

[199] Meredith to Frederick A. Maxse, 6 Apr. 1880, ibid. ii. 593. Though Meredith previously abetted Maxse's unsuccessful contest of Southampton in the 1868 general election, this was described by the author of his *DNB* notice, Thomas Seccombe, as 'his single incursion into active politics' (*DNB Supplement 1901–1911*, ii. 611). Maxse was the model for Nevil Beauchamp, the eponymous hero of *Beauchamp's Career* (1875), which Meredith liked, with *Harry Richmond* (1871), most among his novels 'because it was about Maxse' (Sassoon *Meredith*, 129).   [200] Sassoon, *Meredith*, 106; Ormond, *Du Maurier*,. 370–1.

[201] Sassoon, *Meredith*, 58–9, 240.

However, the decisive shift towards popularity for Meredith—and with it, the opportunity to speak out on public questions—occurred in 1884–5 when *Diana of the Crossways* was serialized (though terminated before completion) in the *Fortnightly Review*, whereupon the novel ran through three impressions shortly after publication.[202] This new-found popularity was highlighted by a parody in *Punch*'s Prize Novels series: 'Joanna of the Cross Ways' by 'George Verimyth' ('Author of "Richard's Several Editions", "The Aphorist", "Shampoo's Shaving-Pot"'). *Punch*'s appreciation was not wholly affectionate. It mocked his long-windedness, indicated that his cleverness entertained Meredith more than his readers, and concluded that his pedantry had careered out of control ever since *Richard Feverel*, which remained his best novel.[203] Still, it was an unaccustomed promotion for Meredith to find himself in the company of best-sellers such as Barrie, Hall Caine, Marie Corelli, Rider Haggard, Kipling, and Mrs Humphry Ward, who were all parodied in the same series. By this date several collected editions of Meredith were under way. The first were produced by Chapman & Hall, for whom Meredith acted as publisher's reader. Most of his novels had fallen out of print, and their first editions were sought by collectors; now nine, greatly revised by Meredith, were republished in 1885–6, in runs of 2,000, priced at 6s. each. From 1889 the novels appeared in a 3s. 6d. edition. Meredith joked about all this to the editor of the *Cornhill*, James Payn, in 1895, remarking about his 'submerged head strangely appearing above the waters in England, where it excites less a literary than a kind of scientific interest, as a new description of cork, which begins to swim after thirty years of steady diving'.[204] From 1896, his surviving son, Will—William Maxse Meredith—having joined Constable's, which took over all Meredith's novels, he had the satisfaction of knowing that there were three editions of his works in hand and that four of his novels were in sixpenny paperbacks.[205] In addition, his renown as an author was widely debated by leading names in the quality weeklies, monthlies, and quarterlies.[206] Whereas in 1864, when Meredith stayed for a fortnight with H. M. Hyndman at Trinity College, Cambridge, undergraduates 'did not know what to make of him', by 1900 Meredith had become 'the smartest bit of intellectual finery a Cambridge

---

[202] It was said that Society took up the novel because it was based on the sensational life of Caroline Norton, who had lately died in 1877. Sheridan's granddaughter, Mrs Norton separated from her husband, an MP, in 1836 when he brought a divorce action, citing as co-respondent the Prime Minister, Melbourne. Mrs Norton, a poet and novelist, then campaigned for divorce-law reform. Meredith acknowledged that she was the prototype of Diana—albeit he 'had to endow her with brains'—and the character 'represents one of Meredith's strongest efforts to forward the emancipation of Victorian womanhood from what she is made to describe as their being "taken to be the second thoughts of the Creator; human nature's fringes, mere finishing touches, not a part of the texture"' (Sassoon, *Meredith*, 184–5).

[203] *Punch*, 18 Oct. 1890, 191–2. See also *Punch*, 16 May 1891, 239; 27 June 1891, 30; 31 Oct. 1891, 213.

[204] To James Payn, 20 May 1895, in Cline (ed.), *Meredith's Letters*, iii. 1194.

[205] Eveleigh Nash, literary adviser to Constable's, 1900–2, claimed the credit for publishing Meredith's novels in a 'half-crown pocket edition on thin paper' (Nash, *Life*, 56). On Meredith's break with Chapman & Hall, and move to Constable's, see Anderson and Rose (eds.), *British Literary Publishing Houses 1820–1880*, 105, and Rose and Anderson (eds.), *British Literary Publishing Houses, 1881–1965*, 66.

[206] Sassoon, *Meredith*, 189, 239, 260.

man could sport, and it was utterly *infra dig* not to admire him'.[207] So Siegfried
Sassoon recalled; and E. M. Forster echoed him, that the young, aged between 18
and 30 in 1900, were so much more in tune with Meredith's idiom, they were 'far
better qualified than their elders to expound him'.[208] From talking to himself, as
he had done in *The Egoist* (1879), Meredith was now able to address a wider public.

It is necessary to emphasize that it was public rather than artistic reputation
that mattered here. Meredith was a regular recipient of homage from fellow
authors, although Henry James always made friends with the man, not his books.
Meredith's penultimate novel, *Lord Ormont and his Aminta* (1894), was, James told
Edmund Gosse, 'unspeakable'. It roused in him such 'critical rage, an artistic fury,
utterly blighting in me the indispensable principle of *respect*', that he could proceed only at 'the maximum rate of ten pages—ten insufferable and unprofitable
pages, a day'.[209] At Meredith's death James turned a phrase in tribute—'He did
the best things best'—but, two years later, he was still 'struggling over George
Meredith' and finding '*Harry Richmond* of a badness almost incredible &
unreadable: the *cheap* (for a rich man) let loose as never!'[210] But a good many
authors both extolled Meredith personally and grappled with the products of his
pen. These included diverse sorts, such as Robert Louis Stevenson, Arthur
Symons, and George Gissing.[211] Even George Moore, generally spiteful, found
reason to applaud. True, he thought that Meredith 'puts on his style so thickly
that we can barely see his people'; but this was because on 'the dazzling
page . . . they are dancing to literary rhythms—a thing which . . . cannot be said of
any other novelist'. Above all, 'there is no trace of the crowd about him; he is
one whose love of art is pure and untainted with commercialism, and if I may
praise it for nought else, I can praise it for this'.[212] Well-placed critics such as
W. E. Henley, George Saintsbury, Leslie Stephen, and H. D. Traill also puffed his
superiority. Meredith was beginning to be recognized as, in Sassoon's words, 'one
of the makers of the modern novel of psychology, introspection and ideas'.
Stevenson's promotion of Meredith was substantial. He called *Rhoda Fleming*
(1865) 'the strongest thing in English letters since Shakespeare died'; and *The Egoist*
he nominated, together with a couple of Scott's novels, a Dumas, Shakespeare,
Montaigne, and Molière, as one of that handful of books which 'form the inner
circle of my intimates' and which he read repeatedly—four or five times in the
case of *The Egoist*, he declared in 1887.[213] Commented Gosse: 'Stevenson's
influence in widening the circle of Meredith's admirers and bringing him into his
popular estate was greater than that of any other person.' Like all Meredithians,

[207] Hyndman, *Adventurous Life*, 78; Sassoon, *Meredith*, 64–5.
[208] E. M. Forster, 'T. S. Eliot' (1928), in Forster, *Abinger Harvest*, 89, where he was arguing that Eliot's
Waste Land held a similar status with the young of the 1920s.
[209] James to Gosse, 22 Aug. 1894, in Edel (ed.), *James Letters*, iii. 485.
[210] James to Edith Wharton, 19 July 1911, in Powers (ed.), *Letters*, 182.
[211] Gissing's early work, like Thomas Hardy's, was encouraged by Meredith as reader for Chapman &
Hall.   [212] Goodwin, *Moore*, 39.
[213] Stevenson, *Memories and Portraits*, 228, 230, 292.

Stevenson sometimes complained of surfeit: 'He is not an easy man to be with,' he wrote to please Henry James; 'there is so much of him, and the veracity and high athletic intellectual humbug are so intermixed.' But Stevenson's determination to meet this heroic writer, when his own career was just forming, had been marked. In 1878 he stayed for several weeks in the neighbourhood of Box Hill, simply to gain an introduction to Meredith.[214] This was bolder behaviour than that displayed by J. M. Barrie, who was later invited by Meredith's literary executor, John Morley, to write the Life. Barrie remembered his first sight of Meredith's home, Flint Cottage, as 'a shrine' or 'little royal residence'; but he ran away when Meredith came slowly towards the gate.[215]

Knowing themselves to be special, Meredithians could be quite careless about their accomplishment. The Foreign Secretary Sir Edward Grey, who recommended reading for pleasure above all, was nonetheless fond of Meredith's novels and said airily to one who moaned that he could not read them, 'Why should you?'[216] Lady Cynthia Asquith even believed that 'Meredith is *very* good for reading aloud.' On 10 March 1916 she tested this proposition by reading 'Mamma [Countess Wemyss] two chapters of *The Egoist* after dinner: she fell asleep'. But Lady Cynthia was gratified to learn that, found in his pocket when Billy Grenfell was killed in battle in 1915 was a Meredith poem, copied out for him by his mother, Lady Desborough.[217] The younger Asquith clan was altogether typical in their divided attitudes towards Meredith. At the age of 18 Violet Asquith, inspired by her father's injunction to 'make my soul', tackled *The Egoist*, which 'I thought brilliant. The first 3 pages made me so angry by their obscureness & incomprehensibility that I nearly left off there & then; but I possessed myself with patience & *loved* the rest . . .'.[218] By contrast, her brother Raymond castigated Meredith as an 'unhealthy mixture between a snob and a contortionist thinly veiling adulation of the upper classes by the disingenuous obscurity of his style'.[219]

From 1882 Box Hill had been a mecca for literary pilgrims and base for the Sunday Tramps, the walking fraternity of alpine intellectuals organized by Leslie Stephen and Sir Frederick Pollock.[220] Others were drawn as a kind of personal challenge. When the weird William Sharp arrived there, he was accompanied

---

[214] Sassoon, *Meredith*, 72, 127, 141–3. Stevenson and Meredith met only once more, in 1879, though they continued to correspond; see Terry (ed.), *Stevenson*, 85–8, 110, 113, 142. The character of Gower Woodseer in Meredith's last published novel, *The Amazing Marriage* (1895), was based on Stevenson.

[215] Barrie, *Greenwood Hat*, 168–74, 192–4. Barrie first wrote about Meredith in the *Contemporary Review* (Oct. 1888); but Meredith made the first move in their friendship. Struck by the sparkle of Barrie's articles for the *St James's Gazette*, he asked the editor, Frederick Greenwood, to be introduced; Dunbar, *Barrie*, 64.

[216] 'Recreation', an address at the Harvard Union, 8 Dec. 1919; in Grey, *Falloden Papers*, 65.

[217] Asquith, *Diaries*, 11–12, 74, 141, 199, 226 (26, 27 Apr., 30 Aug. 1915, 10 Mar., 5 Aug., 15 Oct. 1916).

[218] Bonham Carter and Pottle (eds.) *Lantern Slides*, 65 (5 Aug. 1905).

[219] To Katharine Horner, 9 Aug. 1904, in Jolliffe (ed.), *Raymond Asquith Letters*, 116. Raymond was comparing Meredith unfavourably to Sir Walter Scott. As a Balliol undergraduate, he once took a drive with Meredith, who was in anguish over a possible stage version of *The Egoist*: 'the man who is "adapting" it has put it into some language which he says is not English, and the poor old boy feels that it will be a travesty unless he undertakes the labour himself' (letter to H. T. Baker, 21 Sept. 1898, ibid. 46).

[220] *Diana of the Crossways* (1885) was dedicated to Pollock, the distinguished jurist.

by a woman whom he introduced to Meredith as Fiona McLeod—his own pseudonym.[221] Meredith was a big enough name for the younger generation of writers to gain fame through association. Richard Le Gallienne's *George Meredith: Some Characteristics* (1890) entered its second impression in 1891 (and fifth in 1900) and was assessed by the *Review of Reviews* as

one of the best books of critical eulogy and of blind adulation which we have seen. Mr. Le Gallienne knows his subject and worships him, and has consequently written a work which even Philistines will do well to read, and let us hope that it will be but a stepping stone to the novelist himself. Mr. Meredith's novels are getting so popular nowadays that it only remains for a 'Meredith Society' to be started.[222]

Meredith's sixtieth birthday in 1888 even encouraged commercially minded anthologists to compile birthday books from his works. Conversely, Meredith was a big enough target for young authors to rebel against, as William Watson did against his labyrinthine style in 'Fiction—Plethoric and Anaemic' in the *National Review*, October 1889.[223]

Meredith's diffidence about his standing with the general public still held him back from platforms. He told Edmund Gosse:

I decline many invitations to come up to the footlights. I dislike the station. It is good to leave it to the younger champions. I am besides hopeless of our public. The English have hardened me outside, and there has been a consequent process within. I do my work to the best of my ability, expecting the small result for the same, which I get.[224]

Nonetheless, Meredith's seniority among authors—'the King of contemporary letters', as the new editor of the *Fortnightly Review*, Frank Harris, put it   meant that he was increasingly applied to for his views. In 1887 he allowed himself to respond to the *Pall Mall Gazette*'s invitation to comment about a proposed extension of the railway further into the Lake District (the Ambleside Railway Bill), which he opposed in the manner of Wordsworth's poetic resistance to the Kendal & Windermere Railway a generation earlier.[225] That was the year in which Meredith attended a dinner given by the Liberal Party's Eighty Club and was introduced to Gladstone; and in 1888 he sat down with Asquith, Haldane, and Morley at a banquet in support of Parnell. Morley was an important connection. Agnostic like Meredith, and an influential propagandist for free trade Liberalism, Irish Home Rule, and anti-State individualism, Morley had been taken up by Gladstone in 1886 and made Chief Secretary for Ireland with a seat in the Cabinet.

---

[221] Cline (ed.), *Meredith's Letters*, iii. 1163, 1268, 1553–4, on whether Meredith rumbled the disguise and for the supposition that the woman introduced was Sharp's sister.

[222] *Review of Reviews* (Apr. 1891), 408. See also *Punch*, 20 Dec. 1890, 293, where the book is commended as 'a sort of Meredithian *Bradshaw*'.

[223] This did not prevent Meredith from inviting Watson to dine with him and appreciating Watson's poetry; Nicoll, *Bookman's Letters*, 12.

[224] Meredith to Gosse, 17 Nov. 1889, in Cline (ed.), *Meredith's Letters*, ii. 983.

[225] *Pall Mall Gazette*, 25 Feb. 1887, ibid. 852–3.

Previously, Meredith served as acting editor of the *Fortnightly Review* in late 1867 and early 1868, when Morley had been in America. Meredith was not so convinced by Gladstone as was Morley, Morley writing the classic Life while Meredith was torn: 'Half of him [Gladstone] I respect deeply, and the other half seems not worthy of satire.'[226] However, through Morley, Meredith multiplied links with senior Liberals and allies. Asquith, Grey, Haldane (who also sent him cigars), Lloyd George, John Burns, and the Irish Nationalist John Dillon, all visited Meredith at Box Hill.[227]

Chiefly, Meredith's quiet routine was disturbed in 1892 by his election as president of the Society of Authors upon Tennyson's death. He now became 'The Tribune of Letters'.[228] From this point, a different, more public Meredith emerged, even though his ill health, deafness, and immobility worsened. It was not necessary actually to deliver orations. In 1895, when Meredith replied to the salutations of the Omar Khayyám Club at the Burford Bridge Hotel, he announced that this was the first occasion he had made a speech.[229] Meredith was not otherwise reticent. He rattled off letters to the press, or allowed his name to be broadcast, in numerous campaigns: in literary causes, naturally, decrying the Lord Chamberlain's refusal to license Maeterlinck's *Monna Vanna* (even when performed in the French language) in 1902; also on wider public questions, such as women's emancipation, secular education, the conduct of the Boer War, pogroms against the Jews, the Russian Revolution in 1905, tariff reform, and the menace of Joseph Chamberlain, and the need for vigilance about the German navy.[230] All this, in spite of his continued feeling (in 1904) that 'I am not in touch with the English mind.'[231] Meredith's sense of distance did not stem from want of patriotism; on the contrary, wrote Desmond MacCarthy, who was among the hero-worshippers who journeyed to Flint Cottage, 'few men thought more often of their country, or felt more need of pride in her than Meredith'.[232] The pressure upon him to voice his thoughts was persistent. For example, in January 1903 the *Manchester Guardian* solicited his opinions about modern Liberalism; and in

---

[226] Meredith to Leslie Stephen, 30 Dec. 1902, ibid. 1473.

[227] Sassoon, *Meredith*, 193–4, 249; MacCarthy, *Portraits*, i. 173. For Morley's acknowledgement of debt to Meredith, *Review of Reviews* (Nov. 1890), 428.

[228] Professor Oliver Elton, 'The Tribune of Letters', *Tribune*, 17 Jan. 1906, cited in Cline (ed.), *Meredith's Letters*, iii. 1553 n.   [229] Nicoll, *Bookman's Letters*, 7; Stevenson, *Meredith*, 319.

[230] Cline (ed.), *Meredith's Letters*, iii. 1424, 1427–8, 1452–3, 1479, 1510, 1513, 1549–51, 1576–7. The poet, and universal anti-imperialist, W. S. Blunt, was one whom Meredith approached in 1905 'appealing for funds to help the revolution in Russia, and I have subscribed £10, and yesterday came news that the Grand Duke Serge had been blown up with a bomb, so I am subscribing again. Assassination is the only way of fighting a despotism like that of Russia' (Blunt, *Diaries*, ii. 115 (19 Feb. 1905)). Blunt was a great admirer of *Modern Love* and, though he only read it thirty years after its publication when Meredith sent him a copy in 1892, Blunt was accused of plagiarizing it in his own *Songs of Proteus* (1884). This accusation was made in 1899, when Blunt was execrated in the patriotic press for his 'individual protest against the abominations of the Victorian Age', the poem *Satan Absolved* (ibid. i. 340 (15 Dec. 1899)). Meredith's view of Blunt was that he was 'one of the few honest men we have in public life' (ibid. ii. 247 (21 May 1909)).

[231] Meredith to Richard H. P. Curle, 28 Dec. 1904, in Cline (ed.), *Meredith's Letters*, iii. 1511.

[232] MacCarthy, *Portraits*, i. 172.

June 1904 H. W. Nevinson conducted a major interview for the *Daily Chronicle*. The scope was extensive: his philosophy of life and 'fearlessness of death' ('It is essential for manliness'); the difference between his and the common English ideal of Nature; the contributions made to civilization by English, French, German, and American cultures, and, in the light of their recent war, the potential of the Japanese as opposed to the Russian; his insistence that John Morley, John Burns, and James Bryce should be included in a future Liberal Cabinet; and his belief in the benefits to be gained from the admission of women to all areas of public life— as barristers and clergy as well as doctors, and into all government departments, including the War Office. The report ran to several columns; and Meredith not only carefully prepared for the interview, he also made corrections and additions to the proof before it was published.[233]

One conclusion Meredith drew from the defeat of tsarist forces in the Russo-Japanese War confirmed that drawn from the record of British military incompetence in the Boer War: the unfitness in modern conditions of armed services officered on traditional class lines, 'by a singularly unintellectual, ill-educated and unbusinesslike class. The Salvation army might teach them a lesson or . . . our Railway companies.' Meredith also broadcast his belief in conscription: 'Every manly nation submits to universal service. In the present state of the world it counts among the necessities for safety.' Meredith's advocacy of conscription predated the Boer War. It separated him from official Liberalism,[234] although this was a growing opinion. In 1892 Field Marshal Lord Wolseley had pleaded for it in the *Strand Magazine* in order to enhance racial vigour and civic usefulness.[235] Come the Boer War, and a clamorous lobby came into existence: the National Service League, which was founded in 1901 and boasted over 200,000 supporters by 1912.[236] We should not presume that all possessed belligerent intent. It was an

[233] Much of the interview is republished in Nevinson, *More Changes*, 32–7, including a page of proof corrections by Meredith but excluding Meredith's advocacy of conscription. Nevinson too had approved of compulsory military service ever since he was a student in Germany. It equipped the poor, he thought, with healthy bodies and wholesome food; and in the 1890s he 'took command of a Cadet Company in the hopes of ensuring some small amount of benefit to the enfeebled and undersized youths of Whitechapel and Shadwell, until my ideal of the Workers' University under General Service could be ordained' (Nevinson, *Fire of Life*, 31–3, 38, 56, 87). Following the stir that the publication of his views made, and concerned that they might embarrass his friends in the Liberal party, Meredith disingenuously wrote to John Morley, on 5 Aug. 1904, implying that Nevinson had duped him into such full disclosure. Cline (ed.), *Meredith's Letters*, iii. 1499–1500, 1506, for this and his letter to Nevinson, 7 June 1904, agreeing to talk.

[234] 'Generally I am with the Liberals, but I do not always take Party views' (Meredith to Nevinson, 7 June 1904, in Cline (ed.), *Meredith's Letters*, iii. 1500).

[235] Interview with Wolseley by Harry How, *Strand Magazine*, 14 May 1892, *Review of Reviews* (June 1892), 574. Meredith had welcomed Wolseley's appointment as Commander-in-Chief in 1895; Wolseley in turn signed the memorial celebrating Meredith's seventieth birthday in 1898. See Cline (ed.), *Meredith's Letters*, iii. 1210, 1290, 1369, 1383, 1530, 1706–7, 1719, for this and other contacts between the men.

[236] Actual members of the National Service League, whose president from 1906 was the former Commander-in-Chief Lord Roberts, amounted to 98,931; but 'with adherents (a different class of support involving little more than a signature and a penny donation), a total support of 218,513' was claimed. See Anne Summers, 'Edwardian Militarism', in Raphael Samuel (ed.), *Patriotism: The Making and Unmaking of British National Identity* (1989), i. 244. The Navy League, established in 1895 to campaign for a

Aristotelian precept that the primary purpose of military training was not to enslave others but to resist being enslaved. Though it would improve the efficiency with which war was waged, its chief good was to deter war. To this philosophy was added the republican precept of a citizens' army, as evolved through revolutionary America and France, which is why the notion now appealed also to patriotic socialists such as Robert Blatchford and H. M. Hyndman, the latter a long-standing friend of Meredith. 'Doubtless', Meredith wrote wryly to him in 1909, 'there is an apprehension as to the prudence of schooling the toilers in the use of arms'; but he was unabashed and, in the penultimate of his eighty-one years of life, he published a rousing poem, 'The Call', in the *Oxford and Cambridge Review*.[237] Meredith had welcomed the new Liberal Secretary of State for War Haldane's Territorial Army scheme, though he was more impressed by its shortcoming: 'The Territorial 15 days is ludicrous; and the fear of imposing drill for at least a year seems to me a forecast of the national tragedy.'[238] To the chairman of the Navy League's executive, he wrote urging that organization to join him in pressing 'the cause of Compulsory Service. All the present muddle about our Army comes from the cowardly endeavour to shirk this main question.'[239] 'A large and a strictly drilled army is wanted, even a larger navy; a serious people as well' was Meredith's recipe so that a German aggressor would find England 'armed, stationed, and alert'.[240]

Meredith was not the only well-known author to support the idea of conscription and universal drill. One of the National Service League's organizers, W. P. Drury, a former major in the Marines, was a story-writer and playwright of some popularity, particularly in Royal Navy dockyard towns such as Plymouth (his home) and Chatham, where his debut comic opera *H.M.S. Missfire; or, The Honest Tar and the Wicked First Luff* was staged in 1894–5.[241] Kipling too was a natural supporter—though Meredith had deplored his Boer War verses such as 'The Young Queen', published in *The Times*, 4 October 1900: 'Mob-orator puts on the Muse', he styled it.[242] Compulsory service equally strongly appealed to William Le Queux and E. Phillips Oppenheim, being entirely consistent with their production of thrillers warning against 'the menace of German

---

strengthening of the Navy, had about 100,000 members by 1914. A prominent publicist to warn of the German threat was the editor Leo Maxse (1864–1932), son of Meredith's friend Admiral Frederick Maxse, who in 1893 bought the *National Review* as an organ for his son's journalism.

[237] Meredith to Hyndman, 5 Jan. 1909, in Cline (ed.), *Meredith's Letters*, iii. 1683. 'The Call' was published in June 1908.

[238] To Frederick Greenwood, 3 July 1908, ibid. 1654. Haldane and General Sir John French came out to Box Hill to dine with Meredith in December 1907, proposing to bring Field Marshal Earl Roberts with them the next time. Ibid. 1619.   [239] To Seymour Trower, 2 Aug. 1905, ibid. 1538.

[240] To Lady Ulrica Duncombe, 13 Aug. 1900, and to the editor of the *Daily Telegraph*, 16? Feb. 1903, ibid. 1356, 1479.

[241] Kemp *et al.* (eds.), *Edwardian Fiction*, 108, for Drury (1861–1949); Nicoll, *Late-Nineteenth Century Drama*, ii. 351; id., *English Drama*, 617.

[242] Meredith to Lady Ulrica Duncombe, 25? Oct. 1900, in Cline (ed.), *Meredith's Letters*, iii. 1370.

militarism'.[243] Hall Caine too jumped on the bandwagon, which already contained Rider Haggard, who thought conscription

would be the grandest gift that Heaven could give to Britain; that it would lighten the terrible burden of anxiety which haunts many of us by at least one-half; that it would make men of tens of thousands among us who are now but loafers without ambition, without prospects, save such as the relief that State or private charity may afford; that it would inculcate patriotism and the sense of discipline, lacking which every country must in time come to an inglorious end. Indeed my greatest grudge against Mr. Balfour and his colleagues is that they did not take the opportunity given to them during the dark days of the South African War to introduce this reform, which would then, I believe, have been passed without a murmur.[244]

The theatre was also used as a platform to advocate universal military training, through volunteering in the Territorial Army, if not actual conscription. On 27 January 1909 Wyndham's Theatre staged *An Englishman's Home*, written by 'A Patriot'. The author veiled himself because he was a serving officer in the Royal Fusiliers. This was Captain Guy Du Maurier, son of the author of *Trilby*. He had seen action in the Boer War and would die in France in 1915. His authorship was generally known among politicians and journalists, as also that J. M. Barrie was a party to the production, the first to be mounted by the author's brother the actor Gerald Du Maurier in partnership with the impresario Frank Curzon.[245] As a play, *An Englishman's Home* was crude but effective in its message, about the country's unpreparedness to face foreign invasion. The editor of the *Daily Express*, R. D. Blumenfeld, who attended the opening night, called it 'a great patriotic play which is certain to rouse controversy'.[246] The title said it all. 'Home' was an altar, upon which infinite sentiment was lavished: 'Home, Home, sweet, sweet Home. There's no place like Home.' As W. MacQueen-Pope recollected, Home was

so implanted in the British mind that it really overpowered the idea of national patriotism. When the British were up against it and had to set their teeth and fight like fury—in their minds was no picture of the beauties of their land, its glorious history, its mighty monarchs or heroes, but mostly a half-seen mental picture of the place in which they were born, maybe the house, cottage or villa, or even the village or street—which represented Home.[247]

Edward Thomas, who was to be killed at Arras in 1917, also recognized this common chord: 'We feel it in war-time or coming from abroad, though we may be far from home: the whole land is suddenly home.'[248] *An Englishman's Home* anticipated this. It was a simple tragedy in three acts, the story of Mr Brown, a

---

[243] Oppenheim, *Pool of Memory*, 27–8, 37.

[244] Rider Haggard, *Days of my Life*, ii. 107. This passage was written in 1912. For Hall Caine's views, see Allen, *Caine*, 335.　　　　　　　　　　　　　　　　　　[245] Mackail, *J.M.B.*, 408.

[246] Blumenfeld, *Diary*, 228 (27 Jan. 1909). See also McMillan, *Way we Were*, 294–6; McMillan's book is based on the files of the *Daily Express*, which exploited invasion literature to boost the campaign for conscription and increased defence spending.　　　[247] W. MacQueen-Pope, *Give me Yesterday* (1957), 85.

[248] Cooke, *Thomas*, 220.

comfortably off Essex suburbanite, whose only weakness is for diabolo until, faced with a sudden invasion by an unspecified foreign power (which most of the press and audience read as Germany), he takes up a rifle. It is the first and last time he does so because, in defence of his home, he is shot by firing squad for bearing arms without uniform. The actor playing Mr Brown, Charles Rock, 'became world-famous in a week', according to one newspaper account. As for the author, photographs of Guy Du Maurier's 'classic profile' appeared in shop windows and in every paper 'from *The Times* to the *Draper's Record*', his brother jocularly told him; and 'after each of the three acts the audiences applaud and cheer with a unanimity and vehemence without parallel in the history of the British stage'.[249] Field Marshal Roberts and the War Secretary, Haldane, naturally saw the play. It ran for five months and, from the outset, was exploited by the military lobby. Viscount Esher, present at the first night, wrote in his journal:

Involved all this week in a campaign to get recruits for the Terriers in London. It has made a great stir. The origin of the whole affair was an 'interview' with the *Daily Mail*. I made some remarks about Du Maurier's play *An Englishman's Home* and added that we want men not money, and that the *Daily Mail* might find them. Next day I had a cheque for £10,000 from Harold Harmsworth, but we have only got 7000 men so far, and we want 11,000 for London. Still, the ferment will do good.[250]

The play was also seen by Douglas Haig, later Commander-in-Chief in the Great War. At this time he was about to leave for India as Chief of Staff, having previously been Director of Staff Duties and Military Training with a remit that included Home Defence. About *An Englishman's Home* he wrote:

It is very extraordinary how the play draws crowded houses every night, and how impressed the audience seems to be with the gravity of the scenes. I trust good may result and that universal training may become the law of the land, but for myself last night's performance was not an interesting sight—the incapacity of the whole of the people in defending their homes was disgusting.[251]

The politics behind the licensing of the play were equally intriguing. Colonel Sir Douglas Dawson, who had served in the Egyptian campaign in the 1880s and who was now comptroller of the Lord Chamberlain's department dealing with theatre censorship, told a Joint Select Committee in 1909 that *An Englishman's Home* 'gave rise to a great deal of consideration...before it was allowed'. The Lord Chamberlain's department conventionally refused to license plays that contained 'plots or political allusions that are likely to cause International complications or protest'—a sensitivity carried to extraordinary lengths in 1907 when the licence for Gilbert and Sullivan's *The Mikado* (1885) was temporarily revoked and a revival of the operetta was stymied during a Japanese state visit, in

---

[249] Du Maurier, *Gerald*, 122–9.
[250] Brett, *Esher*, ii. 369 (12 Feb. 1909). 'Terriers' was shorthand for the Territorial Army.
[251] Quoted in Duff Cooper, *Haig* (1935), i. 116–17.

order not to upset Britain's Far Eastern ally. In 1909 the Lord Chamberlain's department took steps to ensure that *An Englishman's Home* pointed at no particular power as the invading enemy, and it banned an intended burlesque of the play by Harry Pélissier's Follies because that did. Such was the official position; but the method of communicating the decision about the Follies was irregular, a telegram bearing a comprehensive embargo, 'No skit will be permitted on "An Englishman's Home"', which then found its way into the press. It is clear from the cross-examination of the Examiner of Plays, George Redford, by the Joint Select Committee, that political pressure was brought to bear on him to forbid the Follies' production. 'Perhaps I had better say at once that I obeyed instructions in respect to that piece entirely,' he said; and, when pressed, he admitted that he would have permitted the skit but the Lord Chamberlain ordered him to ban it. The Lord Chamberlain, Lord Althorp, was not called to give evidence, although Dawson on his behalf denied suggestions that the burlesque was prohibited because *An Englishman's Home* was 'a patriotic play encouraging what he regarded as a desirable notional object', or because a skit might have retarded recruitment to the Territorials.[252]

A year later, at the Adelphi, Conan Doyle's play *The House of Temperley*, set in the Peninsular War and climaxing with the storming of Badajoz, was seized on by Viscount Esher to the same end. 'It is a very virile play,' he purred; and on 11 February 1910 he took over the entire theatre for members of the Territorial Army: 'It was a really fine sight. 1500 people all in uniform—no women—*such* an audience.' In Esher's box were Haldane and his Under-Secretary, Lord Lucas; and Conan Doyle and Barrie joined them during the performance.[253] As it happened, Doyle did not support conscription, believing that involved too much 'revulsion of our habits and dislocation of our lives'; but he shared 'Lord Roberts's ideal of a nation of marksmen' and did not shy from advocating compulsion to achieve this, through legislation to establish rifle clubs that would involve 'every adult in the parish'.[254] By insisting on the duty of every man to keep himself physically fit in the absence of conscription, Doyle was also drawn into movements to shorten the hours of work and to give holiday entitlement to groups of employees who were notoriously ill-organized and bowed down, such as shop assistants.[255]

Meredith's *Daily Chronicle* interview in 1904 thus provoked widespread discussion, about his opinions on conscription and other matters, in many newspapers and periodicals.[256] The Prime Minister of Australia, Alfred Deakin, sharing

---

[252] Joint Select Committee on the Stage Plays (Censorship), *PP* (1909), vol. viii, no. 451, Qs. 454–61, 561–3 (Redford), 1577–94 (Dawson).

[253] Brett, *Esher*, ii. 438–9, 449–50 (21 Jan., 11 Feb. 1910). *The House of Temperley* opened at the Adelphi on 27 December 1909.

[254] Letter to *The Times*, 14 June 1905, in Gibson and Green (eds.), *Unknown Conan Doyle*, 105–7. Conan Doyle started a rifle club in his own neighbourhood at Hindhead in Surrey during the Boer War; see his letter to the *Farnham, Haslemere and Hindhead Herald*, 5 Jan. 1901, ibid. 80.

[255] Letters to the *Grocers' Assistant*, Nov. 1900 and Jan. 1901, ibid. 71, 78; and Booth, *Conan Doyle*, 263, for Doyle's continued disapproval of conscription in 1915.   [256] Sassoon, *Meredith*, 246–7.

his views on conscription, made time to visit Meredith when in England.[257] So, on a different mission in February 1908, did Alex Gray, leader of a march of the unemployed from Manchester to London, where he sought to petition the King through the Home Secretary. Embarrassingly, when he turned up at Flint Cottage he was barred by Meredith's servants under general instruction to spare the author visits by strangers without appointment.[258] Through all this, Meredith endeavoured to keep his sanguineness, but the requests were incessant. As he told a friend during the 1906 general election, when approaching his eightieth year, 'Though I can hardly write, I am entreated day by day "to send some words" to or for candidates, journals and holders of meetings, not to speak of manuscript people panting for print.'[259] When he made the 6-mile journey, in his donkey-chair, to Leatherhead to record his Liberal vote, he was met by the cameras of waiting journalists.[260] Nor were the invitations for Meredith to play the oracle confined to England. He gave interviews to foreign journalists, sometimes with unfortunate consequences, as in 1898 when his indiscreet remarks on Alfred Austin's appointment to the laureateship were relayed home. More grandly, in 1907 he acceded to a request from Milan to compose a poem for Garibaldi's centenary; and, as G. M. Trevelyan noted admiringly, the *Last Poems* (1909) were not, as might be expected from an old man, brooding about imminent death but 'almost entirely concerned with—history and politics! There is no "Crossing of the Bar", no "Epilogue" . . . [Instead], he is gravely concerned in these last poems with such workaday questions as Home Rule and Conscription. His last voice is raised to commemorate Nelson and Garibaldi, and to proclaim sympathy with the struggle for Russian freedom.'[261] Such was Meredith's stature that, following his passing, it was supposed that 'no man of letters great enough to command respect was now living. [St Loe] Strachey said he had seen many people uncover before Meredith at a meeting in Sussex.'[262]

---

[257] Meredith to Alfred Deakin, 17 May 1908, in Cline (ed.), *Meredith's Letters*, iii. 1645.

[258] Meredith to Professor Long, 21 Feb. 1908, ibid. 1631.

[259] Meredith to Mrs J. G. Butcher, 1 Jan. 1906, ibid. 1549.   [260] Sassoon, *Meredith*, 256–7.

[261] G. M. Trevelyan, 'George Meredith', originally published in *The Nation* and partially reprinted in *Clio, a Muse* (1913) and *The Recreations of an Historian* (1919), 99–100.

[262] Bailey (ed.), *Bailey Letters and Diaries*, 123 (10 Nov. 1910). John St Loe Strachey (1860–1927) was editor–proprietor of *The Spectator* from 1898 to 1925, and cousin to Lytton Strachey.

25

Public Service and Party Politics

I

The public's perception of authors' habits and circumstances—profound meditation about the world's problems, while seated in a comfortable armchair before the glow of a fire in a book-lined study—did not always accord with fact. On 19 June 1894 George Gissing wrote: 'Letter from Stead of the *Review of Reviews*, asking me, as one of the foremost novelists of Great Britain, for my signature to a Memorial in the International Peace cause. Of course gave it.'[1] He recorded this diary entry after a night tormented by fleas.

It was easy to laugh at authors' political pretensions. Many did, authors included. In *Diminutive Dramas* (1911) Maurice Baring unveiled 'The Member for Literature'. The premiss was that parliamentary reform had created a new constituency to represent Literature in the Commons. After a poll of every literary club in London, four authors emerge with exactly equal votes: Max Beerbohm, Hall Caine, Rudyard Kipling, and Jerome K. Jerome. As a tie-breaker, a public meeting is called, which each author will address, before allowing the throng to ballot. The venue chosen is Battersea. Perhaps it struck Baring, an old Etonian, as sufficiently comical and plebeian for his purposes, but he would almost certainly know that Battersea's actual MP was John Burns, a former trade union firebrand who became the first working-class Cabinet minister, in which position he was conspicuous for vanity and ineffectualness. The public having assembled, Beerbohm presents his case. He begins, 'No politician I'; then dilates on the reasons why he does not want to be elected and why he should not be elected. Baring relished parodying the supreme parodist. His Max delivers by far the longest address, this non-politician droning on for over half the sketch. Kipling follows in allegorical and vatic vein. This confuses the voters, who misconstrue his fable about ants for some unpleasant truths about their aunts. Jerome K. Jerome alone senses what is required. He stands on the wildly popular slogan 'My politics are Home Rule at Home, and down with Mothers-in-Law'. Hall Caine is entirely brushed aside, as befitting the author with the keenest political ambitions, the greatest appetite for publicity, and the largest measure of

---

[1] Coustillas (ed.), *Gissing's Diary*, 340. For Gissing's opposition to militarism and imperialism, see Gissing, *Ryecroft*, 55–8, and Halperin, *Gissing*, 290–5, 300–1.

self-importance. Five times he rises to speak, but the hecklers have him and the furthest he gets is, 'Mr. Chairman, ladies and gentlemen, loath as I have always been to obtrude upon the public gaze—'. The meeting ends in uproar, invaded by suffragettes. Amid scuffles, the result is declared: Jerome 333 votes (elected), Kipling 12, Beerbohm 3, and Caine 2.[2] Baring's sketch is farcical; yet, amid the pleasure from pricking reputations, two lessons stand out. The first is that the writer with the music-hall mind will generally win acclaim; the second that, though it may be a close-run thing, the non-politician among authors ought to succeed over the politician.

II

It was a well-established English literary tradition to include election scenes in novels, generally for purposes of satire.[3] This tradition was sustained in the late nineteenth and early twentieth centuries, although gory scenes of overt violence and bribery retreated with the introduction of the secret ballot in 1872 and legislation against corrupt practices in 1883. A third extension of the franchise, in 1884, had ushered in an age of mass politics, with new causes and, as may be, new forms of vice. A number of popular authors were now seized with parliamentary ambitions. Some failed, such as Anthony Hope, who stood as a Liberal in Buckinghamshire (Wycombe) in the 1892 general election, Rider Haggard, who contested East Norfolk as a Conservative in 1895, and Silas K. Hocking, who twice was rejected as a Liberal, in Buckinghamshire (Aylesbury) in 1906 and in Coventry in January 1910; but others succeeded, such as Gilbert Parker, who represented Gravesend as a Conservative 1900–18, and A. E. W. Mason and Hilaire Belloc, who were swept up in the Liberal landslide of 1906 to represent, respectively, Coventry and Salford South until January and December 1910.[4] The example was contagious. Those who were not representing or nursing a constituency wondered whether they should be. J. M. Barrie subjected himself to introspective cross-examination in 1905–6. 'What with your committees and things', he wrote to Quiller-Couch, who was a Liberal activist in Cornwall, 'I believe you in Fowey are more in the world than I am in London.' Barrie keenly followed A. E. W. Mason's progress at Coventry, admiring the brio with which he threw himself into electioneering: 'He is loved all over the place and gets wound up by big meetings to great effect.'[5]

---

[2] Maurice Baring, 'The Member for Literature', in Baring, *Diminutive Dramas* (1919), 79–87.

[3] See the selection, edited and introduced by H. G. Nicholas, *To The Hustings: Election Scenes from English Fiction* (1956).

[4] Both Belloc and Mason made use of their experiences in their fiction: Belloc in *Mr. Clutterbuck's Election* (1908), and Mason, intermittently, in *The Turnstile* (1912), wherein Captain Rames throws up the opportunity of a Cabinet seat to renew an expedition to the South Pole. *Punch*, 26 Sept. 1900, 222, produced spoof election addresses for Conan Doyle and Anthony Hope in the manner of, respectively, Sherlock Holmes and Ruritania, although in the event Hope failed to stand in that year's general election.

[5] Barrie to Quiller-Couch, 9 Jan. 1906, in Meynell (ed.), *Barrie Letters*, 18–19.

The trouble was that Barrie shied away from exposing himself and his opinions: 'Dislike of papers and all their ways seems to grow on me.' The fiscal debate, which was the overriding issue of the day, he could not sort out in his mind: 'I find I can't argue intelligently on Free Trade, though I'm still a devout upholder of it. I went to hear Mason and Sir Edward Grey at Coventry on it, and I thought they knew a deal about it at the meeting but was not so sure by supper time.'[6] Barrie was no more satisfied that he was competent candidate material a year later:

I am growing into a complete hermit bounded north south east and west by my own petty little notions which I usually abandon in the middle not because they are actually bad but because they work out so dolefully second class. I have been having a bout of this depressing kind lately and little to show for it but a philosophic countenance.

An opportunity did beckon, to stand for the Aberdeen and Glasgow Universities seat. Barrie hesitated, but only for a few hours before fleeing. He would have been up against Sir Henry Craik of the Conservative and Unionist Party. The permanent secretary of the Scottish Education Department in Whitehall for twenty years, he was a native Glaswegian whose father had been Moderator of the Church of Scotland; he was also a credible scholar and literary man—an authority on Jonathan Swift, historian of Scotland, and English prose anthologist.[7] Barrie had not much to pit against this: Craik 'once said I was badly dressed, but on the whole I couldn't decide that this was sufficient reason to contest his seat with him, all which is far from meaning that I'm not keen on the liberals coming in'.[8] Thereafter Barrie remained 'only a looker-on'.[9] He seldom even voted.[10] Yet, self-deprecation aside, he sustained a commitment to maintaining a liberal democracy throughout every subsequent crisis, the Commons versus Lords struggle in 1909–11, the Curragh 'mutiny' in 1914, the Great War, the labour unrest, and government and financial turmoil of the 1920s and 1930s.

Writers, of course, were not professional or full-time politicians, but neither were the hosts of lawyer and landed or business MPs. Even so, it was never easy to reconcile the demands. Until 1911 MPs were unpaid, and during his time in the House Hilaire Belloc wrote his longest biography, *Marie Antoinette* (1909), two novels (*Mr. Clutterbuck's Election*, 1908; *Pongo and the Bull*, 1910), two topographical and travel books (*The Historic Thames*, 1907; *The Pyrenees*, 1909), four pamphlets, and a volume of poems. He also published four volumes of essays. These were mostly reprinted articles from the *Morning Post*, of which he was literary editor, 1906–9. Party-political fidelity was not Belloc's strongest suit: the *Morning Post* represented the Radical Right of the Conservative and Unionist Party and Belloc was an ostensible Radical Liberal. Still, they were not such strange bedfellows

---

[6] Barrie to Quiller-Couch, 3 Jan. 1905, ibid. 18.
[7] For Craik (1846–1927), see *DNB 1922–1930*, 217–18, and *Who Was Who, 1916–1928*, 241.
[8] Barrie to Quiller-Couch, 3 Jan. 1905 and 9 Jan. 1906, in Meynell (ed.), *Barrie Letters*, 18–19.
[9] Barrie to the Countess of Lytton, 19 Nov. 1922, ibid. 257.
[10] Barrie to Mrs F. S. Oliver, 7 Nov. 1922, and to Charles Scribner, 20 Sept. 1925, ibid. 66, 135.

because they both adopted an anti-Semitic tone and spouted strictures against the expansion of State social services, corruption, and jobbery. In any case, Belloc's job with the *Morning Post* provided him with about a quarter of his income. Lecture tours yielded another £50 per week, but these were time-consuming and tiring.[11] In conversation with Violet Asquith, daughter of his future party leader, in 1905, Belloc had 'harped on a good deal on his penury saying repeatedly I'd do anything to get 10 pounds. I advised him to go to Cave [the Asquiths' resourceful butler] who pays all my clothes on delivery and cabs on arrival.'[12] For a literary man like Belloc, therefore, politics had to be squeezed in and were often squeezed out. In 1908 he collaborated with Maurice Baring and Raymond Asquith in producing the first (and only) issue of the *North Street Gazette*. It contained a treatise by Belloc advocating votes for monkeys. It also broadcast his 'Sonnet Written in Dejection in the House of Commons'. Opening with 'Good God, the boredom!', this proceeded to express Belloc's exasperation about an MP's futility, and ended with the uplifting sentiment:

> The while three journalists and twenty Jews
> Do with the country anything they choose.[13]

Parliament, or even the platform, was never a realistic option for certain writers. Edmund Gosse wrote of Swinburne that 'he might be called "Single-speech Swinburne", since positively his only performance on his legs was an after-dinner oration, in May 1866, when he responded to the toast of "The Imaginative Literature of England" at Willis's Rooms'. Shortly afterwards, his friends met together to consider 'what can be done *with* and *for* Algernon';[14] but the Reform League, comprising trade unionists and Radical Liberals who campaigned for the extension of the franchise to working men, took an interest in him when he issued *An Appeal to England*, a verse pamphlet advocating mercy instead of execution for the Manchester Fenians in 1867. The League now invited him to stand for parliament, offering to find a safe seat and pay expenses. They knew little of him except his public reputation as a poetic champion of republics in Italy and France. Swinburne consulted his oracle, Mazzini, who tactfully told him that his service lay other than in parliament; likewise Gosse, who considered that 'he would have been a portent of ineffectuality in a place where even John Stuart Mill was little better than failure'.[15] Swinburne suffered from no shortage of opinions, only a capacity to deliver them coherently when fired by alcohol.[16] In 1873, at a public dinner, when he was invited to propose a toast to 'The Press', the assembly 'was petrified to see Swinburne rise to his feet and shriek out the words: "The Press is a damnable institution, a horrible institution, a beastly institution", and

---

[11] Robert Speaight, *The Life of Hilaire Belloc* (1957), 241, 259; and Blunt, *My Diaries*, ii. 223 (31 Oct. 1908) for Belloc's overwriting.
[12] Violet Asquith's diary, 2 July 1905, in Bonham Carter and Pottle (eds.), *Lantern Slides*, 52.
[13] Baring, *Puppet Show*, 390–3.   [14] Gosse, 'Swinburne', in Gosse, *Portraits and Sketches*, 6, 16–17.
[15] Gosse, *Life of Swinburne*, 174–5.   [16] Ibid. 214.

then sink back into his seat, and close his eyes'. Mercifully, deafness overtook Swinburne after 1880.

Arnold Bennett's inarticulacy derived from a different disability. In spite of repeated searches for a cure, he remained inhibited by a stammer, an affliction he shared with several celebrity authors of the period, from Lewis Carroll, George MacDonald, and J. H. Shorthouse, to Somerset Maugham. When guest of honour at Stoke Town Hall, Bennett's nervous resistance to making a speech was overborne as the audience clapped until he stood up. He removed his fountain pen from a pocket, displayed it, said, 'Ladies and gentlemen, I don't speak, I write,' and sat down.[17] Bennett did not think of himself as a novelist-cum-social reformer in the way that he felt his friend H. G. Wells was;[18] he also lived abroad for long spells in the Edwardian period, when his name as a writer was starting to carry weight with the public. For all that, Bennett was far from being politically dormant. He considered himself a socialist by 1907 and held strong views about personal living and the class and industrial structure. Tory successes, as in the Peckham by-election in 1908, disgusted him, although he liked to think that 'love of justice, more than outraged sensibility at the spectacle of suffering and cruelty, prompts me to support social reforms. I can and do look at suffering with scientific (artistic) coldness. I do not care. I am above it. But I want to hasten justice for its own sake.'[19] When the opportunity beckoned, as in the January 1910 general election, which followed the House of Lords' rejection of the People's Budget, Bennett threw himself into the fray, even astonishing himself by his productivity as he turned out article after article in the anti-Conservative cause, while at the same time making a start on *Clayhanger*. There was an irony about this that did not escape Bennett, for he was then using the Royal York Hotel at Brighton as his headquarters, where he became 'obsessed by the thought that all this comfort, luxury, ostentation, snobbishness and correctness, is founded on a vast injustice to the artisan class'.[20] After three weeks of intense activity, Bennett tried to establish a perspective:

No doubt the elections are genuinely on my nerves. Depressed about them; preoccupied about them . . . . And I suppose that no politics, however idiotic, can make a great difference to the situation of middling, comfortable persons like me. Yet I continue to worry because the fools won't vote right, and I lie awake at night thinking about their foolishness.[21]

In the end, he took himself off on a motor bus to neighbouring Shoreham in order to see for himself how the elections were going between Brighton and there. Bennett was soon abroad again. He made an American tour in 1911; and, around Easter 1912, he was on the Riviera when a six-week-long miners' strike

---

[17] Bennett *My Arnold Bennett*, 40–1.
[18] Bennett to Wells, 30 Sept. 1905, in Hepburn (ed.), *Bennett Letters*, ii. 197–9.
[19] Flower (ed.), *Bennett Journals*, i. 292 (23 May 1908); cf. p. 299 (6 Oct. 1908).
[20] Ibid. i. 350 (2 Jan. 1910).   [21] Ibid. i. 354 (21 Jan. 1910).

was dividing opinion in England. This coincided with the opening of Bennett's play *Milestones*, written with Edward Knoblock; and Bennett worried whether the coal strike might spoil its success. He also took the measure of wealthy expatriate opinion in Monte Carlo about developments during the strike. When news was reported that the miners had rejected the terms of a Minimum Wages Bill, he overheard one woman declare contemptuously, 'But of course they refuse everything!' And Bennett reflected: 'I must have a strike in my continental novel. It is very funny that all the English inhabitants of grand hotels should be furious because miners insist on a minimum of 5s. per day for men, and 2s. per day for boys.'[22] He himself was now entering upon his most prosperous period since he became a writer, and he was acquiring all the plutocratic trappings to match: a grand house of his own when he was not staying in grand hotels, a chauffeur-driven automobile, yacht, and the rest. He could afford to indulge himself, but he also indulged his political partialities as a publicist for progressivism. In 1915 he accepted an invitation to become a director of the *New Statesman*, the socialist weekly started by Sidney and Beatrice Webb and Bernard Shaw in 1913.[23] In typical Bennett fashion, he had 'the notion of some plainer writing about political facts'.[24]

Bennett was constrained by speech handicap to confine his political activity to the role of columnist; but the inclination towards parliament was evident in a number of writers. In 1911 John Buchan was adopted as the Conservative and Unionist candidate for Peebles and Selkirk constituency, a Liberal seat since 1906. He had genuine Scots roots and was a partner in the publishers Nelson's, which had its headquarters in Edinburgh. He was also well connected, having married a Grosvenor in 1907; and he had experience in public administration after leaving Oxford and qualifying for the law, as a member of Milner's 'Kindergarten' with a commission to abet South Africa's reconstruction following the Boer War.[25] All the same, Buchan was an odd sort of Conservative and Unionist candidate. His admiration for Balfour, sharing his doubts about a whole-hog protectionist trade policy and the drift towards unconstitutional action, was distinctly untimely in 1911, when Balfour was deposed as the party leader and replaced by Bonar Law. Altogether, he recollected, his motives in seeking election to parliament were mixed:

I had always felt that it was a citizen's duty to find some form of public service, but I had no strong parliamentary ambitions. Nor was there any special cause at the moment which I felt impelled to plead. While I believed in party government and in party loyalty, I never attained to the happy partisan zeal of many of my friends, being painfully aware of my own and my party's defects, and uneasily conscious of the merits of my opponent . . . . I wanted the community to use its communal strength when the facts justified it, and

---

[22] Flower (ed.), *Bennett Journals*, ii. 45–6 (6, 23 Mar. 1912).   [23] Ibid. ii. 126 (24 Mar. 1915).
[24] Ibid. ii. 151 (15 Jan. 1916).
[25] Smith, *Buchan*, ch. 5. The best summary account of Buchan is H. C. G. Matthew's notice in the *Oxford DNB*.

I believed in the progressive socialisation of the State, provided the freedom of the personality were assured.... I was a Tory in the sense that I disliked change unless the need for it was amply proved, and that I desired to preserve continuity with the past and keep whatever of the old foundations were sound....

So I went into politics with a queer assortment of interests. I hoped to see the Empire developed on the right lines; the Dominions enabled to grow into self-conscious nations.... Then I wanted something done about resettling the land of Scotland.... For the rest I was critical of the details of Mr Asquith's policy, but approved its purpose—old-age pensions, health and unemployment insurance, and most of the famous 1910 Budget. In the quarrel with the House of Lords I was on the Government's side. By 1914 I had come to differ violently from them on the matter of Ulster, for though a federal home-ruler, after the fashion of my friend, F. S. Oliver, their blundering in the treatment of Ulster roused some ancient Covenanting devil in my blood. I came of a Liberal family, most of my friends were Liberals, I agreed with nine-tenths of the party's creed... But when I stood for Parliament it had to be the other side.[26]

There was some dissimulation in this account. That he had no strong parliamentary ambitions is difficult to credit from the persistence with which he looked to Westminster. Eventually he secured election as MP for the Combined Scottish Universities, 1927–35. His maiden speech was credited with destroying proposals that the Prime Minister, Baldwin, tentatively submitted for further reform of the Lords and was glad to see die. Buchan did not prove an assiduous parliamentarian. He made well-informed interventions in debates on subjects that particularly interested him; but 'He was not prepared to spend on its benches the necessary time. Members who did not know him intimately thought him aloof in manner. It is true he had no taste or leisure for Lobby chatter. When he arrived at the House he went straight to the Library.'[27] His ambition did not rest at being an MP. He had hopes of the Cabinet (Education or the Scottish Office) in 1931; and the governor-generalship of Canada, which he took in 1935 with the title of Baron Tweedsmuir of Elsfield, was second-best to the American ambassadorship. It was not the first time his name had been raised in connection with the Canadian governorship. In 1926 a friend of the Canadian premier, Mackenzie King, dropped heavy hints to the Colonial Secretary, Leo Amery, that King would welcome Buchan's appointment. Amery, who had previously pressed for Buchan's promotion to Director of Information during the wartime propaganda drive in 1917, would have none of it. Mackenzie King's ministry was then in trouble, but in any case Amery let it be known, 'as gently as I could, that he [Buchan] really had not quite the experience or qualifications—much as I loved him and Susie—and that these appointments could not be settled by Dominion PM's picking out their personal friends'. Moreover, the actual King, George V, scoffed at the idea as

---

[26] Buchan, *Memory* (1940), 144–6. See also his 'Democracy and Representative Government', *Fortnightly Review* (Nov. 1913), 858–69, being a published version of an address delivered to the Glasgow Democratic Unionist Association. In it Buchan justified the introduction of the referendum into British constitutional practices.   [27] Mackintosh, *Echoes of Big Ben*, 107–8.

'frankly ridiculous'.[28] A decade on, and Buchan would win his way out of parliament; nonetheless, Sir Charles Petrie wrote in 1950, 'that he should have wanted to go into Parliament at all reflects credit upon that establishment, for it proves that the separation between politics and letters, which is so unhappy a characteristic of the modern age', was not then complete.[29]

<h1 style="text-align:center">III</h1>

Westminster was only one of many platforms, and the author who was denied entry was not otherwise silenced or frustrated. Drawing on his own experiences in South Africa, Rider Haggard created a stir in 1890 by an article in the *New Review* urging the Government to declare a protectorate over Swaziland in order to prevent it from being swallowed by the Transvaal Boers. His was a comprehensive indictment of the Colonial Office's policy of 'wantonness and folly' in the region for the past decade, and he advocated this step in the interests of 'the natives, to whom we are under great obligations and whom it is our duty to protect', and because 'it is useless to blink the fact that a great struggle is in progress, of which the issue is shall Dutch or English rule in South Africa?'[30] Haggard also established a reputation as an agrarian expert, a modern Arthur Young: *A Farmer's Year Book* (1899) and the two-volume study *Rural England* (1902), based on articles written for the *Daily Express*, were his credentials.[31] In Haggard's mind this was a great question, the health of the countryside and of the nation being intimately connected; and he feared for the survival of the British race, now the world's most urbanized people.

Haggard was alarmed to think that a new world order was in process of formation, in which the balance of political, economic, and reproductive power was moving from the degenerate West to the burgeoning East, from the anaemic city-bred white races to the more vital rural-based yellow races. In a speech in Canada in 1905 he alluded to the recent Russo-Japanese War: 'Forty years ago the Japanese dressed themselves up in scale armour, like lobsters, and fought with bows and arrows. And look at them to-day, knocking Russia around the ring.' Imagine the future, Haggard advised, when 'not little Japan but ... great China, with her 400,000,000 people has also made some strides towards civilisation' and laid down a navy; 'imagine these 400,000,000 of stolid, strong, patient, untiring land-bred men having nowhere to live, having not earth upon which to stand, and seeking a home'. They will simply 'walk through your paper [anti-immigration] law', he prophesied; they will overwhelm your miserable

---

[28] John Barnes and David Nicholson (eds.), *The Leo Amery Diaries*, i: *1896–1929* (1980), 448, 452 (1 Apr. and 10 May 1926).   [29] Petrie, *Chapters of Life*, 63.

[30] *Review of Reviews* (Jan. 1890), 41–2.

[31] Haggard consulted Thomas Hardy regarding conditions in Dorset, Hardy having written on 'The Dorsetshire Labourer' in *Longman's Magazine* (July 1883). See Hardy to Haggard, 10 Mar. 1902, in Purdy and Millgate (eds.), *Hardy Letters*, iii. 9–10.

populations who were 'heaped together in the things these white people call cities'; and they will settle your vacant countryside.[32] Haggard was not alone among authors in dilating about the Yellow Peril. This was one of many demons to haunt Tennyson's last years: 'the Chinese, who lived on a very little, could imitate everything, and had no fear of death, would, not long hence, under good leadership be a great power in the world'.[33] Haggard and Tennyson were in august company: 'The Chinese will overrun the world,' Field Marshal Lord Wolseley had predicted in 1890, foreseeing them first destroying the Russian Empire, then expelling Britain from India, and dominating Asia, until 'at last, English, Americans, Australians, will have to rally for a last desperate conflict'.[34] Sinister orientals accordingly became stock figures in English fiction, following the lead of M. P. Shiel's *The Yellow Danger* (1898), which the journalist Arthur Henry Ward, taking the pen-name Sax Rohmer, built upon in his best-selling *The Mystery of Dr. Fu-Manchu* (1913).[35]

Haggard was not issuing his warnings in the manner of a thriller-writer; he spoke in Canada from past experience as a commissioner appointed by the Colonial Office, charged to report on the labour colonies established in North America by the Salvation Army. Subsequently, he published an account of the social work undertaken by the Salvation Army in Britain itself, its urban shelters and homes, and its land and industrial colony at Hadleigh and small holdings settlement at Boxted, Essex.[36] He was also made a member of the Royal Commission on Coast Erosion in 1906, missing only one day's sitting during the five years of its work, and that because he had been detained in the course of his investigation of agrarian cooperatives in Denmark. Haggard tried to use the Royal Commission to advance his ideas of rural resettlement through an afforestation programme.[37] There was a synoptic compass about Haggard's thinking on public questions, but he rightly suspected that his practical influence would be negated by the 'great landed interests' ranged against a comprehensive scheme to diffuse ownership.[38] He also felt that a 'bitter prejudice against the Salvation Army' would inhibit the government from entrusting it with administering a more ample scheme of colonial settlements.[39] As for Haggard's own political ambitions, though he originated from the Tory squirearchy and had contested a parliamentary election for the Conservatives in 1895, he became disenchanted with Balfour's palsied leadership of the party after 1903 and he disputed the notion that Chamberlain's protectionist scheme was the panacea to revitalize rural England. He came to understand, therefore, that 'as a party man I am the most miserable failure', because he 'actually dared to think for himself and to possess that hateful

---

[32] Speech to the Canadian Club in Ottawa, Mar. 1905, as an appendix in Haggard, *Days of my Life*, ii. 261–72.   [33] In conversation with Lord Napier in 1886; Tennyson, *Tennyson*, 693.
[34] Interview with Wolseley in *Review of Reviews* (Sept. 1890), 282–4.
[35] P. J. Waller, 'Immigration into Britain: The Chinese', *History Today* (Sept. 1985), 8–15.
[36] H. Rider Haggard, *Regeneration* (1910).   [37] Haggard, *Days of my Life*, ii. 209–13, 220–5.
[38] Blumenfeld, *R.D.B.'s Diary*, 191 (31 Dec. 1901).   [39] Haggard, *Days of my Life*, ii. 194–5.

thing' from a whip's point of view—'a cross-bench mind'.[40] Haggard was brought back to serve on a government inquiry when the issue of colonial resettlement received a fresh impetus during the Great War, to provide ex-servicemen with a better future; otherwise, he was alienated by the progress of, as he saw it, imperial subversion, and he impotently confided to a diary his disgust about Irish and Indian nationalists, Bolsheviks, Jews, and trade union revolutionaries.[41]

Rider Haggard was a case of an author holding and developing strongly considered political and social opinions, which increasingly marginalized him like a Cassandra. Robert Louis Stevenson had been the same, yet more theatrical, seeking to act out his fiction in the role of nineteenth-century knight errant. A lifelong Conservative in politics, still smarting from the abandonment of Gordon in Khartoum and not liking Gladstone or any aspect of his Irish policy, in 1886 Stevenson conceived the crazy notion of going to Kerry to live with the family of a boycotted farmer under threat of death, in order to encourage British and Irish people to behave with more manliness and more justice to one another. The possibility of losing his own life was reckoned an opportunity to make a martyr's stand: 'a writer being murdered would...throw a bull's-eye light upon this cowardly business'. The alternative for Stevenson, afflicted by lung disease, was to suffer 'a quite inglorious death', wasting away under the bedclothes.[42] The Irish adventure was dropped, but later Stevenson fulfilled himself by interventions in the politics of the Pacific and South Seas: first, a defence of Hawaiian independence on behalf of King Kalakava, who was an avid reader of Stevenson's romances, against the missionary and plantation lobby which was promoting the American annexation that finally took place in 1898; then, a counterblast to critics of the administration of the leper colony on Molokai island run by the Belgian priest Father Damien, who died in 1889; and lastly, his championship of Mata'afa, a chieftain of Upolu, one of the Samoan islands torn by native rivalries which were being exploited by Germany, America, and Britain in their own interests. A resident of Upolu since 1890, Stevenson threw himself into the unfolding crisis with little caution but with his sense of drama and chivalrous instincts primed. He fired off letters to *The Times* hot with indignation, which impeached the motives of the foreign trading, missionary, and consular interests in the islands, and he set aside his fiction to compose a history of the Samoan conflict. He gave material help, even, it was rumoured, smuggled arms as well as enlisted his pen on behalf of Mata'afa. By the end of 1892, he reported with a flourish to a correspondent in Bournemouth, 'I am at daggers drawn with the government'; and to Sidney Colvin he declared, 'I live always on the brink of deportation.'[43]

---

[40] Haggard, *Days of my Life*, ii. 106; and *Punch*, 30 Mar. 1895, 145, for a spoof election address by Haggard.

[41] Morton N. Cohen's notice of Haggard (1856–1925), *Oxford DNB*.

[42] Mackay, *Violent Friend*, 156–7; see also letters to Mrs Fleeming Jenkin, Apr. 1886, in Colvin (ed.), *Stevenson's Letters*, ii. 26–31. In 1887, though then in the United States and destined never to return to England, he joined a Unionist club: see letter to Charles Baxter, 12 Dec. 1887, ibid. 82. On Stevenson's Tory politics, in this following his father, see Terry, *Stevenson*, 30, 49.

[43] Colvin, *Stevenson's Letters*, ii. 268–9.

Eventually, Mata'afa and his followers surrendered, and the cause was lost; but Stevenson's involvement in the islands' politics was to have a lasting mark. Out of gratitude, the native chiefs mobilized their men as a workforce to clear the forest and build a road, named the Road of the Loving Heart, to Stevenson's estate at Vailima. Stevenson did not long outlive this. He was buried on the mountain top of his island, memorialized by his own verses,

> Under the wide and starry sky . . .
> Here he lies where he longed to be;
> Home is the sailor, home from the sea,
> And the hunter home from the hill.

His widow, with a want of reality comparable to Stevenson himself, now campaigned for Samoa's annexation by Britain, so that Stevenson's remains might rest in British soil. This was negated in 1899–1900 when most of the islands were annexed by Germany, the rest being allocated to American administration; and Vailima became the German Governor's residence. During the Great War, however, the British flag was run up over the mansion by occupying New Zealand forces; thereafter, as the islands passed through American and New Zealand mandates to independence in 1962 as the republic of Western Samoa and to membership of the Commonwealth in 1970, Vailima served as the residence for the head of state.

Stevenson's stormy-petrel antics took place in an exotic location; but the home front was the chief setting for Conan Doyle's public life. This was, by any measure, a full one. He was buoyed up by his status as a doctor and by the kudos of having created the world's most famous fictional detective, although his historical novels, such as *The White Company* (1891), which went through fifty editions before 1914, actually outsold the Sherlock Holmes books. Doyle peppered the press with his concerns, having an enthusiasm about national defence, a mania about spiritualism, and a strong nose for miscarriages of justice both individual (the Edalji and Slater cases) and collective (Belgian atrocities; and divorce law reform).[44] He also rushed to defend the heroism of the captain of the *Titanic*, against questions raised by Bernard Shaw. Doyle was twice a Liberal Unionist parliamentary candidate—for Edinburgh Central in 1900, and for the Hawick Burghs in 1906—but, by 1911 he was a declared Home Ruler. He justified this to Ulstermen by letter to the *Belfast Evening Telegraph*. It involved no inconsistency, he maintained. Previously he had asserted that Home Rule for Ireland 'would only be safe with an altered economic condition and a gentler temper among the people, and, above all, after the local representative institutions already given had been adequately tested'. These conditions he believed had now been met: land reform had improved material prospects and, the fanatics apart, both representative Nationalists and Unionists, Catholics and Protestants,

---

[44] Gibson and Green (eds.), *Unknown Conan Doyle, passim*. Atrocities in the Belgian Congo stirred many authors to protest, by formal memorial or by fictional representation, among the latter being Henry de Vere Stacpoole's *Pools of Silence* (1910), which ran through five imprints in its first year.

had shown a willingness to work local government. As he wrote this, England itself had been racked by violent industrial disputes: 'So far as being law-abiding citizens goes, England, which is just recovering from a period of absolute anarchy, is not in a position to criticise Ireland, which remained perfectly quiet during the same time.' Finally, Doyle argued, the success of Home Rule in South Africa, where passions had been even more inflamed than in Ireland and had led to war only a decade ago, convinced him that the experiment was worth repeating in Ireland. It was this big picture, the Empire, which most concerned Doyle and which he now entreated Ulsterman to share:

a solid loyal Ireland is the one thing which the Empire needs to make it impregnable, and I believe that the men of the North will have a patriotism so broad and enlightened that they will understand this and will sacrifice for the moment their racial and religious feelings in the conviction that by so doing they are truly serving the Empire, and that under any form of rule their character and energy will give them a large share in the government of the nation.[45]

Doyle's statement merited reproduction in full in *The Times*,[46] and a leading article in the *Morning Post*.[47] It generated a predictable response from extremists: death threats, though these may also have come from militant suffragettes, whom Doyle unwisely chose simultaneously to sermonize; and a police guard was accorded him for a while.[48]

IV

In certain quarters Doyle's directness and disinterestedness were much admired. Douglas Sladen wrote appreciatively: 'He is not naturally a party man . . . . There have been moments when he has been openly opposed to some measure of the Unionist Party. He really belongs to the Public Service party.'[49] On the other hand, Doyle's bluff conviction about what was the right course struck those who were animated by a different creed as bullying and wrong-headed. Jerome K. Jerome, having Radical and Socialist sympathies, was afterwards perturbed to find himself put down in Doyle's memoirs as ' "hot-headed and intolerant in political matters". When I read that passage I was most astonished. It is precisely what I should have said myself concerning Doyle.'[50]

Yet in his eulogy of Doyle, Sladen inadvertently located one source of many authors' ineffectualness in politics. There was no Public Service Party. Moreover, directness and disinterestedness were often twin to *naïveté* in public affairs. Not that Doyle should be particularly faulted for failing to understand or solve the

---

[45] Letter to the *Belfast Evening Telegraph*, 22 Sept. 1911, in Gibson and Green (eds.), *Unknown Conan Doyle*, 157–8. [46] *The Times*, 22 Sept. 1911. I owe this reference to Chris Collins. [47] To which Conan Doyle replied; see his letter to the *Morning Post*, 28 Sept. 1911, in Gibson and Green (eds.), *Unknown Conan Doyle*, 158–9. [48] Booth, *Conan, Doyle*, 281. [49] Sladen, *Twenty Years*, 74. [50] Jerome, *Life and Times*, 176.

Irish problem; nor was he alone in having taken encouragement from the South African example, though this involved imperfect assumptions, which Sir Gilbert Parker exposed in three articles for the *Morning Post* in 1912. He scotched the analogy drawn between Ireland and the dominions. South Africa, Canada, and Australia were themselves unions, much as Great Britain and Ireland were; and the secession of the Transvaal, Quebec, or Queensland would be no more tolerated by these dominion governments than would be the secession of California from the United States. The Irish Home Rule Bill, in Parker's opinion, constituted an unworkable 'hotch-potch of Dominion and Local Government, a stupid and perilous arrangement of overlapping powers' which would build more, not less, friction into the system and impair, not strengthen, the stability of Union and Empire.[51] Parker, like Doyle, traded on his reputation as a popular novelist, and his name automatically drew public attention to his pronouncements; but unlike Doyle, Parker was a practising party politician, a Conservative and Unionist MP since 1900. Knighted in 1902, he was active in the cause of imperial unity and, in domestic policy, promoted small ownership, though *Punch* was inclined to ridicule his self-importance. 'Politics is an exacting mistress,' it spoofed him as saying in 1904. 'Since I joined the Kitchen Committee of the House of Commons my literary output has dwindled by 250 words daily.'[52] Parker's status was enhanced by the 1906 general election debacle, when so many senior colleagues lost their seats. That he did not gain the sought-for front-bench promotion was due as much to the propensity of his party to pursue intrigue as to his personal shortcomings, though these were unsparingly analysed by a candid friend, the editor of the *Morning Post*, H. A. Gwynne, in 1911. Gwynne was involved in the plot to depose Balfour from the party leadership, amid which Parker was inclined to falter and trim:

for this work in front of us (the deposition of A.J.B[alfour]) he will be no more use than a sick headache. He lacks, for this purpose, the one essential quality—pluck.... [and] I think he might fail us at the critical moment. In the Die-Hard business he was very down on us until I lunched with him & hinted (*Machiavelli*-like!) that with a change of leader his chances would be greater. After that he was lamb-like.... I have written at this length about Parker because, although he is a most excellent fellow au fond, you will find that when there is real work to be done, he isn't there, as the Americans say. But he can always be a very useful help.[53]

Parker's experiences as a practising politician stand as a salutary contrast with Conan Doyle's. The path of public virtue was pitted with conspiratorial infighting. Maybe it was wiser to try to influence events from outside, standing on the rock of impartial goodwill, than from inside, perched on the shifting sands of party factionalism. Better still, perhaps, to do as Kipling did and articulate

---

[51] *Morning Post*, 6, 8, and 9 May 1912.   [52] *Punch*, 3 Feb. 1904, 78.
[53] H. A. Gwynne to Lady Bathurst, 22 Oct. 1911, Brotherton Library, Leeds, Glenesk–Bathurst archive, MS Dept. 1990/1/2174. Chris Collins kindly copied this for me.

unbridled partisanship while pretending not to be a politician at all. Kipling did
not content himself with composing periodic poems of hate for Liberals and their
causes, though he produced many malignant classics of this kind, from 'Cleared:
In Memory of the Parnell Commission' (1890) through to 'Ulster' (1912) and
'Gehazi' (about the Marconi scandal, 1913). He also took to the platform, particularly in the years before the Great War when domestic politics were inflamed
by the Liberals' programme of constitutional and social reform. In October 1912,
for example, Kipling addressed the Junior Imperial and Constitutional League at
Ashton under Lyne, having been invited by the local Conservative and Unionist
MP, Sir Max Aitken, the proprietor of the *Daily Express* (later Lord Beaverbrook).
'In one part of his speech,' the *Morning Post*'s reporter noted, 'he declared "I am
not a politician"—a statement that was received with some hilarity, as well it
might be, for Mr. Kipling made an uncommonly good political speech, which
kept the close attention of a densely-packed audience from start to finish.'
Kipling's theme was that Britain was in the midst of a revolution engineered by
crooked ministers. Their purpose was to feather their own nests; to achieve
this, they had to render ordinary people helpless and to suborn other political
factions even if this meant, as in the case of Welsh Nonconformists lobbying for
Disestablishment or Irish Nationalists demanding Home Rule, imperilling Church,
Union, and Empire. Most Cabinet ministers' livelihoods, Kipling argued, derived
from the perquisites of office. It was, therefore, in their interest both to prolong
their tenure and to remove checks in the way of their exploitation of office. Thus
the House of Lords was emasculated by the Parliament Act and the House of
Commons made compliant by paying MPs; as Kipling put it, the Commons agreed
'to appropriate to itself £400 per annum per head—(laughter)—£100 free from
income tax, out of the public revenue'. The general public required a subtler and
more sinister measure of discipline, the introduction of National Insurance:

This weekly ticketing and being inspected by paid overseers must involve us in slavery
and kill self-respect. The National Insurance Act creates a servile class whose time and
mind and energies are converted from the control of their own and their country's affairs
to a series of degrading exercises calculated to break them into the idea of shameful
dependence on an all-providing Government.

About the Liberals' compact with the Irish Nationalists Kipling was mordant.
Having lost their governing majority in 1910, the Liberals

found themselves compelled to grant Home Rule to Ireland or run the risk of losing their
salaries. (Laughter.) The Irish hunted and hounded them towards Home Rule through
every dirty political by-lane and every black political bog, like cattle in a Connemara
drive. (Cheers.) . . . .Even the hardest-mouthed Radical paper does not pretend that Home
Rule was laid before the electors at the last election or that it has been discussed in the
House of Commons . . . . The Home Rule Bill proposes to sell a million or so of inhabitants of these islands out of the Union against their will to the open and avowed enemies
of the Union.

The *Morning Post* fully reported Kipling's speech, giving him a column and a half, while a short paragraph, comprising three sentences, two of which eulogized Kipling, was allotted to the speech of the actual politician, Sir Max Aitken.[54] This was obviously the most effective strategy for an author to command political attention: repudiate the idea of being a politician, then mount the political platform and deliver a strident political address. Kipling maintained this line into 1914, if anything deepening his support for Ulster's resistance to Home Rule and continuing to lambast the Liberal Government as a corrupt conspiracy. He was a signatory to the Ulster Covenant, which declared the Home Rule Bill unconstitutional and justified 'the taking or supporting any action that may be effective to prevent the armed forces of the Crown being used to deprive the people of Ulster of their rights as citizens of the United Kingdom'. And, at public meetings—for example, in May 1914, at the great demonstration on Tunbridge Wells Common, where he shared a platform with Viscount Hardinge, Viscount Midleton, Lord Ampthill, the local MP Captain Spender-Clay, and other leaders of the Unionist Association and British League for the Support of Ulster—it was 'Mr. Rudyard Kipling's Scathing Indictment' that captured the headlines and enjoyed the most extensive reportage.[55]

Occasions arose, however, when the public-service ethic as espoused by Conan Doyle appeared more fitting and welcome than Kipling's partisanship. During the Boer War, Doyle suspended his normal literary activity, first to work unpaid at a field hospital in Bloemfontein,[56] then to pen an instant history, *The Great Boer War* (1900). The impression it made can be gauged from *Punch*, whose reviewer suspended the house humour and assumed due seriousness: 'The terribleness of the tale is added to by the dispassionate manner in which Mr. Doyle handles his facts, and the judicial style of his summing up of the evidence.' Doyle drew two principal lessons, both silver linings to otherwise dark clouds. The first was his declaration, 'The slogging valour of the private, the careless dash of the regimental officer, these were our military assets; seldom the care and foresight of our commanders.' The second concerned the assistance given by colonial troops to British forces: 'If we have something to deplore in this war, we have much, also, to be thankful for.' As *Punch*'s reviewer summarized, 'it is a melancholy story of dauntless courage and demented direction', and mainly owing to these ordinary soldiers that the Empire was 'delivered.... from the pit dug for it by fatuous administration at home'.[57] Doyle revised and extended his account several times, culminating in a complete edition in September 1902; during the conflict he also issued a 60,000-word booklet, *The War in South Africa: Its Causes and Conduct*, designed to counter misrepresentations of Britain's case in Europe,

---

[54] *Morning Post*, 19 Oct. 1912.

[55] Ibid., 18 May 1914. I am grateful to Chris Collins for a photocopy of this and other references to the *Morning Post*.

[56] Letters to the *British Medical Journal*, 7 July 1900, and *The Scotsman*, 3 Oct. 1900, in Gibson and Green (eds.), *Unknown Conan Doyle*, 60–6; also Booth, *Conan Doyle*, 227–32. [57] *Punch*, 14 Nov. 1900, 357.

particularly by German politicians and press. Its distribution was a feat of
ingenuity and perseverance, which Doyle initiated by an approach through *The
Times* and other newspapers for subscriptions. This awoke a huge response and,
Doyle told Sladen, 'five months later I had the book on my table in twenty
languages'. The King reputedly sent £500, and the former Prime Minister, Lord
Rosebery, £50; but Doyle was moved more by the way 'poor people scraped
together their half-crowns to do their widow's-mites' worth for England.
I sent that pamphlet to every man in Europe whose opinion counted... In
Germany the whole twenty thousand copies were distributed; twelve thousand
of them gratis, and eight sold.' Altogether, some half a million copies travelled
about the world.[58] A hundred thousand were issued free;[59] but this may have
been counter-productive since it acquired the taint of being thought government propaganda.[60] Doyle, however, reckoned that, after expenses were
covered, £1,400 surplus might remain and, not wanting to derive a profit,
he proposed

to set apart £1,000, the interest of which shall form a scholarship for enabling some poor
South African, Boer or British, to pursue his studies at Edinburgh University [of which
Doyle was an alumnus]. From the sum which remains we hope to send a small souvenir
to a few friends of Great Britain abroad who have stood loyally by her at a time when
many of her own children played her false. The balance, if any, I should like to retain in
my hands and to use at my own discretion for the encouragement of the movement for
civilian riflemen.[61]

Doyle's crusading was rivalled in extent by John Galsworthy's, though only
partly in kind. The Boer War, which Doyle supported so wholeheartedly, aroused
misgivings in Galsworthy, which he expressed in his play *The Mob*, though this
was not staged until March 1914. It features a young Cabinet minister who, after
'England declares war upon a weak, semi-civilised nation... sacrifices his career,
his friends, the affection of his family, and ultimately his life, in protesting against
a policy which he feels to be barbarous, greedy, and unjust'. The play was
wooden but high-principled, setting in antithesis two types of patriotism: the 'my
country right or wrong' jingoism of the mob, versus that superior regard for a
country's honour and finer nature, that patriotism which, while knowing it
cannot stop the war, is decided that 'history shall not say when England did
this thing not a voice was raised in protest'.[62] Yet, when the Great War erupted
shortly after his play had been staged, Galsworthy weighed the proprieties

---

[58] Sladen, *Twenty Years*, 156–7. For Conan Doyle's correspondence with the press concerning the
distribution of his pamphlet, see Gibson and Green (eds.), *Unknown Conan Doyle*, 83–94.
[59] Conan Doyle in *Who's Who* (1905), 458.   [60] Booth, *Conan Doyle*, 240.
[61] Letter to *The Times*, 5 June 1902, in Gibson and Green (eds.), *Unknown Conan Doyle*, 92–4. The
Edinburgh scholarship was apparently never introduced; and the balance of the fund was disbursed
among various causes, the combined services Union Jack Club, Indian famine relief, a fund for nursing in
Japan, and a charity to relieve Boer hardship. Booth, *Conan Doyle*, 240–1.
[62] Desmond MacCarthy, review of *The Mob*, 2 May 1914, in *Drama* (1940), 200–5.

differently, and he refused permission for *The Mob* to be performed anywhere during that conflict.[63]

V

Joseph Conrad dubbed Galsworthy a 'humanitarian moralist'. Another friend, J. M. Barrie, while regarding Galsworthy as 'a queer fish', noted how he was 'so sincerely weighed down by the out-of-jointness of things socially'.[64] There survives among Galsworthy's papers a list of causes which, at one time or another, involved his advocacy and money:

ABOLITION OF THE CENSORSHIP OF PLAYS.

SWEATED INDUSTRIES. MINIMUM WAGE.

LABOUR UNREST. LABOUR EXCHANGES.

WOMEN'S SUFFRAGE.

PONIES IN MINES.

DIVORCE LAW REFORM.

PRISON REFORM: (CLOSED CELL CONFINEMENT).

AEROPLANES IN WAR.

DOCKING OF HORSES' TAILS.

FOR LOVE OF BEASTS.

SLAUGHTERHOUSE REFORM.

PLUMAGE BILL.

CAGING OF WILD BIRDS.

WORN-OUT HORSE TRAFFIC.

PERFORMING ANIMALS.

VIVISECTION OF DOGS.

DENTAL EXPERIMENTS ON DOGS.

PIGEON SHOOTING.

SLUM CLEARANCE.

ZOOS.

CECIL HOUSES.

CHILDREN ON THE STAGE.

THE THREE YEAR AVERAGE INCOME TAX.[65]

This did not exhaust his concerns: Galsworthy's *Glimpses & Reflections* (1937), posthumously published, contains a complete alphabet of causes which he supported by public and private correspondence. Nor was he ineffective: his part in bringing about a reduction in the terms of solitary confinement in prisons is well established, from a combination of the stir made by his play *Justice* (1910), and of his persistent letter-writing to newspapers and lobbying of officials and

---

[63] Letter, 9 Sept. 1916, in Galsworthy, *Glimpses and Reflections*, 224.

[64] Dunbar, *Barrie*, 172. See also Beerbohm, *Christmas Garland*, 103–14, for 'Endeavour', Max's perfect parody of Galsworthy's philosophy.   [65] Marrot, *Galsworthy*, 215–16.

ministers.[66] It was with strong conviction that Galsworthy refused a knighthood in 1917–18: 'men who strive to be artists in Letters, especially those who attempt criticism of life and philosophy, should not accept titles'.[67]

Galsworthy had an unusually developed conscience, but it was far from automatic that authors would assemble in the progressive camp on social questions, or that attitudes then considered advanced would be acceptable later. The intellectuals' embrace of eugenics and assumptions about white racial superiority produced a class of writing that now astonishes by its inadmissibility. Ibsen's translator, the drama critic William Archer, was widely admired on intellectual and personal grounds. He was a staunch rationalist, an advocate of simplified spelling; and he was a doughty champion of social and political freedoms at home and abroad, for instance, going to Spain in 1910 to investigate and expose injustice in the case of Francisco Ferrer, the anticlerical leader executed in October 1909.[68] In the previous year he had travelled about America, drawn by reports about the race war. The result was *Through Afro-America* (1910), which he dedicated to fellow progressive H. G. Wells, 'with whom I so rarely disagree that, when I do, I must needs write a book about it'. Archer captioned Wells as naive for supposing that the race enmity in America existed only because of 'the almost insane arrogance and inhumanity of the Southern white man'. Archer himself distributed blame more broadly, including 'the vanity, the resentfulness, and the savagery of the negro himself'; and he considered that, though most pressing for the United States and Britain (because of its Empire), 'The problem of the twentieth century is the problem of the colour line.' He was notably hostile towards racial inter-marriage, being convinced of 'the essential and innate inferiority of the negro race'; and advised the setting up of separate black states within the United States. Though he acknowledged that 'Negroes may have been lynched or shot down, not only for crimes they themselves did not commit, but for crimes that were never committed at all,' he concluded that 'there are quite enough authentic cases of crime—denied by nobody—to justify the horror of the South.'[69]

Such sentiments rather go to prove, as Arnold Bennett recognized, 'every Briton is at heart a Tory—especially every British Liberal'.[70] There was no dissemblance from Joseph Conrad. His cynicism and pessimism about politics were given rein in *Nostromo* (1904), which (out of genuine affection and not a

---

[66] See ibid., chs. vii–viii; Galsworthy, *Glimpses and Reflections*, 159–62, 209–21, 243, 270–7; correspondence between Galsworthy and Churchill (then Home Secretary) in 1910, in Churchill, *Churchill*, Companion vol. ii/2: *1907–1911*, 1148–53, 1187–91; Mackenzie, *Beatrice Webb Diary*, iii. 138 (15 Mar. 1910). Galsworthy even spent two days at Lewes Prison, interviewing convicts undergoing solitary confinement, in order to confirm his view that 'it is a barbarous thing'. See his letter to Edward Garnett, 7 Sept. 1909, in Garnett (ed.), *Galsworthy Letters*, 172.

[67] Letter to Lloyd George, 1 Jan. 1918, in Marrot, *Galsworthy*, 437; letter to Garnett, 6 Jan. 1918, in Garnett (ed.), *Galsworthy Letters*, 232.

[68] William Archer, *The Life, Trial and Death of Francisco Ferrer* (1911).

[69] William Archer, *Through Afro-America: An English Reading of the Race Problem* (1910), pp. ix, 8, 26, 197, 217–44; McMillan, *Way we Were*, 186, where Archer is mistakenly referred to as 'an anthropologist'.

[70] Bennett, *Journal 1929*, 165.

little irony too) he dedicated to John Galsworthy. 'Of course,' says Martin Decoud—'the adopted child of Western Europe'—in that novel, 'government in general, any government anywhere, is a thing of exquisite comicality to a discerning mind.' Latin American politics were merely an exaggeration of the type, like '*opéra bouffe* in which all the comic business of stage statesmen, brigands etc., etc., all their farcical stealing, intriguing and stabbing is done in dead earnest. It is screamingly funny, the blood flows all the time, and the actors believe themselves to be influencing the fate of the universe.'[71] Conrad was not at all enamoured of the humanitarian tendency in modern legislation, writing huffily in the *Daily Mail* in 1910: 'We are too busy at present reforming the silent burglar and planning concerts to soothe the savage breast of the yelling hooligan.'[72] The disagreement with Galsworthy was undisguised: he also wrote to the *Daily Mail* in 1910, stating, 'The broad and quite undeniable fact is that criminality has decreased in proportion as penal methods have become more careful, discriminating, reformative, and less merely severe.'[73]

Penology interested several writers apart from Galsworthy. Not surprisingly after his incarceration in Reading Gaol, Oscar Wilde had campaigned for prison reform, writing lengthy appeals, which were carried by the *Daily Chronicle* in 1897–8, and publishing the pamphlet *Children in Prison and Other Cruelties of Prison Life* (1898).[74] The poet Wilfrid Scawen Blunt also had personal acquaintance of prisons, having served two months in 1888 in Galway and Kilmainham gaols, in solitary confinement with hard labour, for offences under the Crimes Act in Ireland. When Winston Churchill became Home Secretary in 1910, Blunt wrote to remind him of his promise to reform prison discipline: Churchill had previously consulted Blunt when he was compiling the biography of his father, Lord Randolph. Blunt now forwarded to Churchill an extensive memorandum detailing his ideas: these included an end to the silence and separation regime, a distinction between political and common prisoners, abolition of the prisoners' uniform, and enlarged provision for both exercise and education. All this may now strike us as unexceptional, but Blunt reported Churchill as replying that 'he would have liked to adopt the whole of my programme only public opinion was not ready for it yet'. In several respects, though, Blunt was himself against change; indeed, argued for a deterrent penology. He remained convinced of the justice of 'corporal punishment of the severest kind inflicted in cases of rape, wife-beating, cruelty to children, and the like, with capital punishment still for murder'; and he had a crotchet about wanting to restore public executions, not to appeal to the mob so much as to allow the victim 'one last half hour in the light of day outside those [prison] walls'.[75]

---

[71] Conrad, *Nostromo*, 134–5, 138.

[72] Joseph Conrad, 'The Ascending Effort', *Daily Mail*, 1910, in Conrad, *Notes on Life and Letters* (1921), 95.

[73] Letter to the *Daily Mail*, 25 July 1910, in Galsworthy, *Glimpses and Reflections*, 213.

[74] Hart-Davis (ed.), *Wilde's Letters*, 269–75, 334–9.

[75] See Churchill, *Churchill*, Companion vol. ii/2. 1137, 1144–8; Blunt, *Diaries*, ii. 154, 289, 292, 295–7, 315, 321–2, 445–51.

The debate about penal strategies in late Victorian and Edwardian England was actually very extensive and involved imbricating ideologies. Especially, penal policy was related to arguments concerning the reformation of Poor Law institutions and other welfare agencies.[76] Common to all was the enlistment of the expertise of the new 'sciences'—sociology, biology, psychology, criminology—in order to ascertain what influences most counted in determining an individual's actions, nature (heredity) or nurture (environment). Depending on how this equation was resolved, there followed consequences for public policy across the whole range of social work, according to the assessment of whether character and behaviour were reformable and would respond to education and regulation or else were unreformable and required restraint and repression. Behind these concerns of social theorists and professional administrators lay wider questions about the rights and duties of citizenship and the proper role of the State, in the light of an apparently inexorable trend towards universal adult suffrage. Chivvying the government of the day to do more to redress perceived inequities was, therefore, a popular commission eagerly undertaken by a writer such as George R. Sims who, with good reason, prided himself on his common touch. *Dagonet Ballads* (1879), which included heart-rending verse, 'It is Christmas Day in the workhouse', sold 100,000 copies in a year; and his melodramas and burlesques held both West End and provincial stages with record runs. In the 1880s and 1890s he campaigned against slum housing and unfeeling Poor Law administration, publicized the plight of the unemployed and aged, and lent support to a variety of other causes including campaigns to protect vulnerable girls from being drawn into prostitution. Some concrete achievements followed from this activity. Sims's part in the Children's Free Breakfast and Dinner Fund, established by the weekly *Referee*, for which he was a columnist, anticipated the legislative provision of free school meals for needy children which was introduced by the Liberal Government after 1906; and his campaign on behalf of a Norwegian, Adolf Beck, who was twice gaoled as a result of unreliable identification, contributed to the setting-up of the Court of Criminal Appeal, as well as incidentally winning for Sims himself an honorary knighthood from the King of Sweden and Norway. In 1906 Sims took up his pen in service of another downtrodden section of society as he now saw it, the lower-middle classes, whose hard-won security was being imperilled by a crushing burden of rates and taxes and public spending which feather-bedded the improvident. His polemics on their 'bitter cry', published in the newly founded daily *The Tribune*, roused widespread attention and added to those pressures that persuaded the Government to award relief to this class in subsequent budgets.[77]

Certain authors excelled at whipping up righteous indignation. These outbursts were not always received as they wished. When Silas Hocking, author of many

[76] See David Garland, *Punishment and Welfare* (Aldershot, 1985).
[77] See Waller, 'Altercation over Civil Society: The Bitter Cry of the Edwardian Middle Classes', in Jose Harris (ed.), *Civil Society in British History*.

a moral tale, ranted against the House of Lords in 1907, styling its members a collection of 'antediluvian fossils, who breathe in an atmosphere in which free-dom cannot live', and who had been 'replenished by the plutocrats of the drink ring and the gutter press', *Punch* thought this funnier than any of his novels and hoped he would make lots more speeches.[78] Other authors were better qualified to prick at human folly and unreasonable enthusiasms. Edmund Gosse was in this latter category; moreover, as a civil servant he was long habituated to preserve a reticence in public about politically sensitive issues. Retirement for Gosse, therefore, meant not gentle subsidence but mild eruption when he wrote to *The Times* in 1919 as 'an elderly man who is not a politician nor a public character, but merely an individual among millions of honest, sober persons whose liberty is attacked by a moral tyranny'; in this case, to protest against faddists who pressed for alcohol prohibitionism such as was being advanced in the United States.[79]

For those writers who did crave public influence, one problem which persis-tently plagued them was that they did not normally make loyal or even very understanding party men. A. E. W. Mason, for instance, as Liberal MP for Coventry (*Punch* enjoyed cartooning him as a latter-day Lady Godiva),[80] had alienated support by opposing his own party's temperance-inclined Licensing Bill in 1908.[81] 'I am politically a freelance, and must remain so,' wrote Galsworthy, with an amount of satisfaction. He further attested to an impatience which made him unacceptable to party managers: 'If I were (which God will take care I am not) in Parliament, I should have to espouse those measures which seemed the shortest cuts to proportion and justice...'[82] This did not prevent partisan members of the public, upset by his pronouncements and interventions, from attaching party labels to him. In January 1910 he felt obliged to reply to one correspondent: 'By what process of reasoning or right you call me a Socialist I do not know. As a matter of fact I am not one'—before going on to spell out where he stood in the constitutional crisis at that time.[83] When Galsworthy found himself in the rare position of chairing one such meeting, he recorded in his diary: 'How odious are political meetings, with their perpetual sneering scoring-off tones of voice.'[84] This was in September 1910, during the deadlock caused by the Lords' rejection of Lloyd George's 'People's Budget'; and Galsworthy adopted the position of wishing a plague on both Houses. The Radical Liberals' proposals to end the Lords' veto and even abolish the second chamber altogether, and the Radical Conservatives' proposal to make regular use of referendums, he disliked equally:

What's wanted is a Second Chamber of 150, not hereditary, appointed in Conference by both Parties, kept by some automatic machinery (the Prime Minister of the day) as nearly as may be level between the parties. Against a third rejection by this Chamber there

---

[78] *Punch*, 13 Mar. 1907, 181.   [79] *The Times*, 15 July 1919.   [80] *Punch*, 13 Mar. 1907, 194.
[81] Ibid., 10 June 1908, 415.   [82] Galsworthy, *Glimpses and Reflections*, 172, 244.   [83] Ibid. 261.
[84] Marrot, *Galsworthy*, 306.

should be appeal by referendum, which in practice would never be resorted to, for such a body would voice the country with great exactitude. What's wanted is something that will seriously diminish the friction and acrimony of party, not accentuate it . . . [85]

In February 1914 Galsworthy sent what he called 'a rather fiery letter to *The Times* about the cold-heartedness and delays of Parliament, which created some rumpus'.[86] This began by itemizing his (now familiar) list of causes requiring legislative attention: the sweating of women workers; undernourishment of children; blind-alley employment of adolescents; the ease with which paupers were consigned to lunatic asylums; and 'foul housing of those who have as much right as you and I to the first decencies of life'. Again, he waxed indignant about the 'shameful barbarities done to helpless creatures'—the export of worn-out horses, the mutilation of horses by docking, the inhumane methods of slaughtering animals, the caging of wild birds, and the importation of exotic plumes to decorate female attire. But the chief point that Galsworthy was making on this occasion was that the Government, both executive and legislature, had the wrong order of priorities and that 'party measures absorb far too much of the time that our common humanity demands for the redress of crying shames'. Every one of the issues he had listed was

admitted to be anathema; in favour of their abolition there would be found at any moment a round majority of unfettered Parliamentary and general opinion. One and all they are removable, and many of them by small expenditure of Parliamentary time, public money, and expert care. Almost any one of them is productive of more suffering to innocent and helpless creatures, human or not, and probably of more secret harm to our spiritual life, more damage to human nature, than, for example, the admission or rejection of Tariff Reform, the Disestablishment or preservation of the Welsh church, I would almost say than the granting or non-granting of Home Rule—questions that sop up *ad infinitum* the energies, the interest, the time of those we elect and pay to manage our business. And I say it is rotten that, for mere want of Parliamentary interest and time, we cannot have manifest and stinking sores such as these treated and banished once for all from the nation's body . . . [87]

Galsworthy's reading of the public mind as to what it thought lesser questions was almost certainly wrong about the tariff reform controversy, which brought out more people to vote than ever before—and animated more of the disfranchised, such as working-class women, than even the issue of female suffrage—because it was a matter that directly affected them in respect of the state of employment and cost of living. But he was not otherwise foolish or alone in his expression of frustration and anger. Petitions calling for the complete exemption

---

[85] Galsworthy to Edward Garnett , 27 Nov. 1910, in Garnett (ed.), *Galsworthy Letters*, 201. See also Galsworthy to Garnett, 6 June 1918, ibid. 233–4, for his hope that the wartime cooperation between the political parties would persist when the Great War ended.

[86] Garnett (ed.), *Galsworthy Letters*, 390.

[87] Letter to *The Times*, 28 Feb. 1914. It is reproduced, together with a follow-up letter of 9 March, in Galsworthy, *Glimpses and Reflections*, 238–42.

of dogs from vivisection, just one of Galsworthy's causes, had recently attracted 870,000 signatures.[88] In all likelihood he was right to believe that he spoke for a substantial body of opinion that wanted redress of these grievances. Outside the party system their chances of success were much reduced; yet, by articulating and championing the causes of this unrepresented multitude, writers such as Galsworthy fulfilled an important public role.

Galsworthy liked to proclaim himself 'the least politically educated person in the world'; but that was a title to which the majority of his fellow countrymen and women could also lay claim. Not being politicians, they were able to state without equivocation and free from 'cheap-jack nostrums' what kind of life they aspired to. Generally it was one that elevated welfare above wealth. Galsworthy and authors like him sometimes drew up agendas for people to heed, just as politicians did. In an address in America in 1919 Galsworthy highlighted three of the many changes he sought:

(1) The reduction of working hours to a point that would enable men and women to live lives of wider interest.
(2) The abolition of smoke—which surely should not be beyond attainment in this scientific age.
(3) The rescue of educational forces from the grip of vested interests.[89]

Important as these issues were in Galsworthy's mind, he could have chosen other and equally vital topics, and given thirty rather than three. What mattered most, however, was the fact of an author speaking out to advance the quality of life, as a humane and considerate individual, a public figure uncontaminated by any ambition to seek political office.

---

[88] See his letters to *The Times* on this subject in July 1913; in Galsworthy, *Glimpses and Reflections*, 299–303. [89] John Galsworthy, *Address in America, 1919* (1919), 67–72.

do in the first place), and we are to have a 'bureau' with information supplied, a sort of clearing house, as I hope, for articles and interviews and so on.[6]

This miracle of authorial harmony was more apparent than real, if Arthur Benson's diary account of the conference is consulted. Mostly, this consisted of disparaging remarks about the appearance and mannerisms of his fellow authors: 'Arnold Bennett very pert and looking every inch a cad, Newbolt cool and anxious . . . Hewlett, like a little rat, very curt in talk'. About the proceedings, he wrote that 'Trevelyan produced a manifesto, very unwillingly and rudely, and read it. It was moderate in tone and was applauded . . . Zangwill made an interminable speech about the Jews and their importance as journalists,' wanting a petition to be sent to the Tsar about their emancipation. Wells argued for authors to act individually, while Chesterton, whom Benson thought came out of the meeting best, 'spoke humorously—he was ready to write pamphlets, he said, which would appeal even to Americans'. Doyle, ever practical, 'suggested an agency for placing articles'.[7] Arnold Bennett also wrote a diary account; according to this, Masterman directed the proceedings well, but 'Zangwill talked a great deal too much. The sense was talked by Wells and Chesterton. Rather disappointed in Gilbert Murray . . .'.[8]

D. H. Lawrence had not been included. His was not the sort of pen the authorities wished to enlist. He also had a German wife. She was apt to declare how much smarter than the British the German regiments were, and to appear satisfied that 'her countrymen had no sense of what the English mean by "fair play"'. Whenever the war was spoken of, Lawrence collapsed: 'he just sits and gibbers with fury. He sees no hope in the country, nothing but war, and the war he sees as the pure *suicide* of humanity—a war without *any* constructive ideal in it, just pure senseless destruction'. Oscillating violently in mood between acute misery and hysterical resentment, Lawrence actually propounded a simple line: he wanted the war stopped. This ideal was obscured by his accusing any serving British soldier whom he met of 'subconscious "blood-lust"', by his reproaching even volunteer hospital workers of 'subscribing to the war', and by his maintaining that 'the German theory of war—though filthy—was perfectly "logical"'. Lawrence's conviction that men were dying for fighting's sake, as an orgy rather than sacrifice, was not a message people particularly wanted to hear; and by 1917 he and spouse were receiving the attentions of the police, who searched their lodgings in Cornwall, seized letters, and ordered them to leave the area. Lawrence was already minded to quit England for America, sending out feelers to rich and influential friends to assist his passage.[9]

---

[6] Mallet, *Hope*, 218–19. The Writers' Manifesto was published in *The Times*, 18 Sept. 1914.

[7] Newsome, *On the Edge of Paradise*, 312.

[8] Flower (ed.), *Bennett Journals*, ii. 103–4 (3 Sept. 1914). Masterman summoned newspaper editors to a separate conference, which the literary agent A. P. Watt also attended.

[9] Asquith, *Diaries*, 46, 89, 234, 257, 294, 356 (21 June, 17 Oct. 1915, 13 Nov. 1916, 18 Jan., 20 Apr., 16 Oct. 1917).

II

Lawrence's war service was entirely self-centred. He was hardly alone among authors in having doubts and sorrows about the war's causes and course, but others managed to discipline their egotism and essay something for the patriotic good. These contributions varied. J. M. Barrie's war play *Der Tag* was produced at the Coliseum on 21 December 1914 and, as W. A. Darlington described it, while 'it had some of the faults inherent in all art that is made to serve a political purpose . . . it put into dignified language the cause for which the Allies were fighting'.[10] Literature served to relieve suffering materially as well as spiritually. In February 1918 Barrie acted as chairman of the great Red Cross Sale at Christie's, of which E. V. Lucas was secretary of the Books and Manuscripts Committee. Among the choicest lots put up for auction was the copy of *Vanity Fair* (1848) which Thackeray had presented to Charlotte Brontë, though it was a second edition and uninscribed. This had been bought by Clement Shorter from Brontë's widower, then bought from Shorter for £100 by Robertson Nicoll, who now donated it to the Red Cross Sale, where it realized £325 10s.[11] Barrie was one of a number of leading authors who were active in providing aid for Belgian refugees and convalescent soldiers: these included Anthony Hope, W. J. Locke, Laurence Housman, Hall Caine, John Galsworthy, Arnold Bennett, and, until his death in 1916, Henry James. Barrie was a substantial benefactor of the conversions of the Herbert family home, West Park in Bedfordshire, into a hospital and convalescent home for wounded soldiers, and of a chateau at Bettancourt in northern France into a reception centre for refugee mothers and children.[12] Thereafter he put his main effort into writing a series of one-act plays for charity performances which provided relief for servicemen on leave and comfort for those left at home or suffering bereavement.

Though divorced and childless, Barrie was not immune from personal grief. He was devastated by the deaths in 1915 of three individuals for whom he had great affection: the American impresario of his stage successes, Charles Frohman, drowned in the torpedoing of the *Lusitania*; and both Guy Du Maurier and Guy's nephew George Llewelyn Davies, who were killed in France a few days apart. George had been the most loved by Barrie of the five brothers for whom *Peter Pan* had been written and for whom he had acted as trustee after they were orphaned. 'I have lost all sense I ever had of war being glorious, it is just unspeakably monstrous to me now,' Barrie had written to George on learning of his uncle's death, in a letter which George would never receive.[13] The wartime plays—*Dear*

---

[10] Dunbar, *Barrie*, 206–7.

[11] Darlow, *Nicoll*, 270; Barrie to Nicoll, 12 Feb. 1918, in Meynell (ed.), *Barrie Letters*, 31. Professor Sir Walter Raleigh contributed a manuscript page from one of Scott's novels; see his letter to E. V. Lucas, 7 Jan. 1917, in Raleigh (ed.), *Letters*, ii. 461.

[12] Meynell (ed.), *Barrie Letters*, 111–13; Dunbar, *Barrie*, 213–16. Barrie put some of his experience of this into *A Kiss for Cinderella*, first staged at Wyndham's Theatre on 16 March 1916.

[13] Letter, 11 Mar. 1915, in Dunbar, *Barrie*, 210.

Brutus (1917) excepted—were not the best of Barrie but they evidence his acuteness in capturing the sentiments of the time and his insistence that the war should not deflect the British people from their true instinct to play fair. The witch-hunt for German spies was gently deflated in the opening scene of *A Kiss for Cinderella*, in which the artist Bodie has summoned to his studio a constable to investigate the mysterious doings of the poor servant girl who sweeps the building:

BODIE. . . . She knows a number of German words.
POLICEMAN. That's ugly.
BODIE. She asked me lately how one could send a letter to Germany without Lord Haig knowing. By the way, do you, by any chance, know anything against a firm of dressmakers called *Celeste et Cie*?
POLICEMAN. Celest A.C.? No, but it has a German sound.
BODIE. It's French.
POLICEMAN. Might be a blind.[14]

Jane, the Cinderella of the title, turns out to be helping refugee and orphan children; her Fairy Godmother works for the Red Cross; and the policeman eventually wins Jane's heart, the honest, plodding soul recognizing his romantic passion only after he goes completely off his feed. The play also reiterates Barrie's suffragism—a consistent theme of his, most notably in *What Every Woman Knows* (1908), 'back in the strange days when it was considered "unwomanly" for women to have minds'.[15] In *A Kiss for Cinderella* the doctor in charge of the servicemen's convalescent home is a woman, Bodie's sister, who is depicted in ideal manner: expert in her profession and 'born to command', but 'not in the least mannish or bullying'. This the policeman, as the quintessential stolid British male, now ponders, because previously

he had been more than a passive observer of the suffragette in action, had even been bitten by them in the way of business; had not then gone into the question of their suitability for the vote, but liked the pluck of them; had no objection to his feelings on the woman movement being summed up in this way, that he had vaguely disapproved of their object, but had admired their methods. After knowing Dr Bodie he must admit that his views about their object had undergone a change; was now a whole-hearted supporter . . .[16]

The wartime emergency, Barrie implies, must not be made excuse to defer justice for women; indeed, the women's claim was growing. In *The New Word* Barrie further expresses pride in the country's liberal traditions: 'Till the other day we were so little of a military nation that most of us didn't know there were 2nd Lieutenants.'[17] Unhappily, everyone is now familiar with such terminology, and homes have empty spaces once filled with boys' play. Still, the sadness of *Barbara's Wedding* is lifted at the end as the grieving grandparents turn to Dickens's *Pickwick*, 'the best book for war-time'; and soon 'they are both chuckling'.[18]

---

[14] Barrie, *Plays*, 399–400.   [15] Ibid. 349.   [16] Ibid. 442.
[17] *The New Word*, in J. M. Barrie, *Echoes of the War* (1918), 88.   [18] *Barbara's Wedding*, ibid. 125–6.

Barrie also recognized that everyone wanted to do their bit in the war and all had a personal stake in the outcome, even the charwoman who invents a soldier son in *The Old Lady Shows her Medals*.[19] De facto, the headship in families and leadership of the nation were passing or would pass to those who had seen military service and, Barrie intimated in *The New Word*, it would benefit their country if less stiffness existed between the generations. Hence this marvellous pantomime of English reserve, in which father addresses son on the need to set aside past formality and awkwardness about expressing feeling:

'We have, as it were, signed a compact, Roger, never to let on that we care for each other. As gentlemen we must stick to it.'
  'Yes. What are you getting at, father?'
  'There is a war on, Roger.'
  'That needn't make any difference.'
  'Yes, it does. Roger, be ready; I hate to hit you without warning. I'm going to cast a grenade into the middle of you. It's this, I'm fond of you, my boy.'
  Roger squirms. 'Father, if any one were to hear you!'
  'They won't. The door is shut, Amy is gone to bed, and all is quiet in our street . . .'[20]

After the war, in his Rectorial Address at St Andrews in 1922, given in the presence of the Chancellor, Field Marshal Earl Haig, Barrie developed this theme more explicitly, that the older generation had failed the younger, who must now demand a partnership in affairs; and, if they did not, he warned, 'we shall probably fail you again. Do not be too sure that we have learned our lesson, and are not at this very moment doddering down some brimstone path.'[21] Barrie's theme then was Courage; but, during the war, his ability to sound the right notes, of pathos and brightness, had not deserted him. He never pandered to Hun-hatred. *Barbara's Wedding* concerns *inter alia* the tragedy of two boyhood friends, English Billy and German Karl, who die in the same battle; and *A Well-Remembered Voice* features a soldier's ghost who tells his father that he has met the shades of the Germans they had been fighting, 'and they were rather decent; so we chummed up in the end.'[22] Outside of his playwriting, too, Barrie did his best to keep up the nation's spirits with spry humour. Responding to complaints about the introduction of Summer Time (daylight saving) in 1916, he observed that 'everyone ought to be pleased, as it would surely shorten the war by one hour!'[23]

Barrie already had a baronetcy, but William Watson, according to Douglas Goldring's uncharitable assessment, was rewarded with his knighthood during the war for penning 'a sonnet to Lord Northcliffe and one or two other pieces inspired by current events'.[24] Ford Madox Ford remained unrecognized; recognition, indeed, was problematic because as Ford Hermann Hueffer, whose father

---

[19] The character was based on Barrie's landlady from his student days in Edinburgh, and the play proved one of his most popular. Dunbar, *Barrie*, 48, 217–18.
[20] *The New Word*, in Barrie, *Echoes of the War*, 82–3.   [21] Barrie, *Courage*, 8–10.
[22] *A Well-Remembered Voice*, in Barrie, *Echoes of the War*, 152.
[23] Lowndes, *Merry Wives of Westminster*, 156.   [24] Goldring, *Reputations*, 111–12.

was German, he was suspected of espionage by his landlord.[25] Ford, however, was a friend of Masterman—they toured the Rhineland together in 1913, and the Government's National Insurance plans had been adumbrated in the first two numbers of his *English Review* in 1908. Ford now produced for Masterman's ministry two commissioned propaganda books, *When Blood is their Argument: An Analysis of Prussian Culture* and a companion about the value of French culture, *Between St Dennis and St George: A Sketch of Three Civilisations*, both in 1915. This was a year of extraordinary activity for Ford, who also published his masterpiece *The Good Soldier* and, at the age of 42, obtained an army commission with the Welsh Regiment.[26] There was no conscription in Britain before 1916, but Ford in any case was above the age that would be called up.

Active service was never an option for Thomas Hardy. Aged 73 in 1914, he was as morose and agonizing as ever. He had attended the inaugural meeting of the Wellington House author–propagandists, later writing of 'the yellow sun shining in upon our confused deliberations in a melancholy manner that I shall never forget'.[27] Hardy's new bride, just 35 when they married in February, thought he aged another ten years in the month following the outbreak of war.[28] The horrors of war did not entirely explain this mood. *Satires of Circumstances*, published in November, crystallized pain and regrets from his first marriage, which he had been working out in poetry ever since his widowhood in 1912; and from 1917 he turned further in on himself by beginning an autobiography, which he furtively planned to pass off as a biography written by his second wife after his death.[29] He had set out ambivalent feelings about war during the Boer War: 'I constantly deplore the fact that "civilised" nations have not learnt some more excellent & apostolic way of settling disputes than the old & barbarous one, after all these centuries; but when I feel that it must be, few persons are more martial than I, or like better to write of war in prose & rhyme.'[30]Hardy had felt his philosophy confirmed: 'It seems a justification of the extremest pessimism that at the end of the 19th centy we settle an argument by the Sword, just as they wd have done in the 19th Centy B.C.'[31] But, once war was begun, he backed his country to win it. Hardy's letters to his aristocratic friend Florence Henniker were written with particular solicitousness—her husband commanded a battalion of the Coldstreams during the Boer War—but he would have followed its course closely in any case.

---

[25] Ford's landlord in 1914 was Edward Heron-Allen, who thought he looked like 'a typical Prussian bully': see Brian W. Harvey and Carol Fitzgerald (eds.), *Edward Heron-Allen's Journal of the Great War: From Sussex Shore to Flanders Fields* (Chichester, 2002), 15 (23 Aug. 1914). Ford changed his name in 1915 to Ford Madox Hueffer, and in 1919 to Ford Hermann Madox Ford. He previously acquired two forenames, Joseph Leopold, when he converted to Catholicism in 1892.

[26] Goldring, *South Lodge*, 16, 117; Masterman, *Masterman*, 258–60, 290.

[27] Letter to Anthony [Hope] Hawkins, [May] 1920, in Mallet, *Hope*, 243.

[28] Florence Hardy to Rebekah Owen, 5 Sept. 1914, in Millgate, (ed.) *Emma and Florence Hardy*, 100.

[29] Ibid. 131, 137.

[30] Hardy to Florence Henniker, 11 Oct. 1899, in Purdy and Millgate (eds.), *Hardy Letters*, ii. 232.

[31] Hardy to Florence Henniker, 17 Sept. 1899, ibid. 229.

'I take a keen pleasure in war strategy & tactics,' he told her, 'following it as if it were a game of chess; but all the while I am obliged to blind myself to the human side of the matter: directly I think of that, the romance looks somewhat tawdry, & worse.'[32] Hardy even paid a visit to Dorchester barracks, to see the Dorset Yeomanry prepare to embark for South Africa; so, he added in consequence, 'my thoughts are all khaki colour'.[33] These patriotic thoughts, however, were never 'Jingo or Imperial';[34] they turned principally on the suffering men and mangled horses, and found expression in verses such as 'Drummer Hodge', which Quiller-Couch notably undervalued as 'a few drearily memorable lines on the seamy side of war'.[35] In 1902, at the war's end, Hardy dutifully raised a flag at his home, Max Gate;[36] but, in common with much of Hardy's life, it was not a notably cheerful occasion:

The romance of *contemporary* wars has withered for ever, it seems to me: we see too far into them—too many details. Down to Waterloo war was romantic, was believed in: since then even the Jingoes have in their secret hearts an uneasy suspicion that drums & trumpets are not its true insignia—a point I tried to make in some verses called The Sick God.[37]

Hardy set himself to work out this idea in an epic of the Napoleonic Wars, *The Dynasts* (1904–8); and, during the Great War, his dramatization of it was performed by the Hardy Players in Dorchester to raise war funds. He also penned a poetic 'Call to National Service'.[38] Hardy's own form of national service was as a borough magistrate imposing fines for infringement of food-price regulations. This made him unpopular among local tradesmen, including his own grocer. German prisoners of war were detailed to prepare his garden for vegetables and to crop trees; but Hardy felt the war's toll like everyone. The death of a distant cousin at Gallipoli brought the poem 'Before Marching and After', published in the *Fortnightly Review*, October 1915; and *Moments of Vision* (1917) included 'To Shakespeare', written in 1916 to summon inspiration on the tercentenary of the Bard. Florence Hardy, boomed as 'the wife of our greatest novelist', contributed her mite by writing patriotic stories for the *Sunday Pictorial*; yet, she confessed in February 1918, 'from the very beginning of the war, neither of us has ever expected that we should defeat Germany'.[39]

---

[32] Hardy to Florence Henniker, 25 Feb. 1900, ibid. 248.

[33] Hardy to Winifred Thomson, 6 Dec. 1900, ibid. 247.

[34] Hardy to Florence Henniker, 24 Dec. 1900, ibid. 277. Hardy's wife, Emma, was even less 'imperial', writing, 'the Boers fight for homes & liberties—we fight for the Transvaal Funds, diamonds, & gold! . . . Why should not Africa be free, as is America? Peace at any cost of pride, & aggrandisement, is my idea.' Admittedly, this was written to an American, Rebekah Owen, 27 Dec. 1899, when, following Black Week, she was also unconfident of British victory. Millgate (ed.), *Emma and Florence Hardy*, 18–19.

[35] *Daily News*, 9 Feb. 1903, in Purdy and Millgate (eds.), *Hardy Letters*, iii. 51.

[36] Hardy to Edward Clodd, 2 June 1902, in Purdy and Millgate (eds.), *Hardy Letters*, iii. 23.

[37] Hardy to Arthur Quiller-Couch, 9 Feb. 1903, ibid. 51.   [38] Millgate, *Hardy*, 501–2, 511–12.

[39] Florence Hardy to Sydney Cockerell, 24 Feb. 1918, in Millgate (ed.), *Emma and Florence Hardy*, 140.

III

Morale-raising performances appeared more the forte of actors and entertainers such as Frank Benson and Harry Lauder, the latter reckoning that he caused over 12,000 men to join up;[40] but many authors of popular reputation such as Henry de Vere Stacpoole and Kipling also participated in recruiting campaigns.[41] By contrast, the lyric poet Laurence Binyon commemorated those who had already completed their duty in Flanders. An assistant keeper at the British Museum, specializing in oriental art, Binyon composed a poem 'For the Fallen' and sent it to *The Times*, which published it on 21 September 1914. The quatrain

> They shall not grow old, as we that are left grow old:
> Age shall not weary them, nor the years condemn.
> At the going down of the sun and in the morning
> We will remember them

would be recited at innumerable memorials and inscribed on countless grave-stones. Binyon was also confidentially approached by the Foreign Office in 1917 for permission to use his poetry 'for propaganda in neutral countries'.[42]

Binyon's war poems were greeted as 'noble' in a review in the *Observer* by Alice Meynell, who at the deaths of Tennyson and Austin had twice had her advocates for the laureateship. The volume of poetry production generated by the Great War in England was extraordinary: the work of 2,225 English poets has been identified, of whom at least 532 were women.[43] The variety of this 'women's voice' is emphasized in the anthology edited by Catherine Reilly, ranging from jingo to protest verse and frequently reflecting heartfelt experience of service and bereavement. In many cases, too, the patriotic ideal and the religious ideal were linked; and Mrs Meynell was a high exponent of this kind.[44] She had cause to feel the significance of this sentiment personally, like millions more, when a loved one was killed in the fighting, in her case her daughter Madeline's husband, Percy Lucas. Mrs Meynell reached 70 years of age in 1917, the year her son Everard joined the Artists' Rifles—'the only corporal in the British army who has written a Life of Francis Thompson'. She redirected her proclivity for devotional verse towards the national service. 'Summer in England, 1914' ended by asserting that 'The soldier dying dies upon a kiss, | The very kiss of Christ'; and in 'To Conscripts' she inspirited the enlisted soldiers with St Luke's Gospel of 'compel them to come in'. Nor, as a feminist with daughters who were busy potting jams,

---

[40] See L. J. Collins, *Theatre at War, 1914–18* (1998).

[41] Douglas Sladen, who was a first-class shot, founded the Lord Mayor of London's Recruiting Bands; and he praised Kipling for his assistance in that work. See Sladen, *Long Life*, 223.

[42] Binyon to Sir Frederick Macmillan, 4 Apr. 1917, in Nowell-Smith (ed.), *Letters to Macmillan*, 309.

[43] Catherine W. Reilly, *English Poetry of the First World War: A Bibliography* (1978), p. xix.

[44] Catherine W. Reilly (ed.), *Scars upon my Heart: Women's Poetry and Verse of the First World War* (1981), 73–4, for Alice Meynell's 'Lord, I Owe Thee a Death', and 'Summer in England, 1914'.

did she overlook the women land-workers in 'The Girl on the Land'. As a pious Catholic, however, she had been troubled by the trend of pre-war foreign policy which brought her country into closer cooperation with the French Republic, deplorable to her on account of its anticlericalism. She had written to one of her daughters, 'You know that our *entente* with France (a real alliance, we all see now, kept secret from the nation) has been my horror and my dismay for the years it has lasted. An alliance with so much that I detest against so much that I respect!' Publication in *The Times* of the Notes exchanged between Sir Edward Grey and Berlin at the onset of war subsequently dispelled some doubt: 'Nothing could be more honourable to us. I do think there is such a thing as distinctively English honour.' But she would not be induced to progress from that conviction into a wholesale condemnation of the enemy. Her youngest son, Francis, was a conscientious objector, a co-founder in 1916 of the Guild of the Pope's Peace. When her friend G. K. Chesterton wrote a panegyric of her and a denunciation of Germany in 'Mrs. Meynell and the Destruction of Louvain' for the *New Witness*, she remarked: 'It is delightful about me, but too wrong-headed about the Germans. He must have no music in him when he says they have created nothing—music being the one creative art, and German music the greatest that is or, surely, can be.'[45]

The German contribution to civilization was also conspicuous by omission from *The Spirit of Man*, a best-selling anthology of prose and verse compiled by the Poet Laureate Robert Bridges and dedicated to the King in 1915. Bridges had spent eight months in Germany in the 1860s, after going down from Oxford; and Heine's lyrics, among his favourite reading, had influenced his own poetry. But there was no place for them in *The Spirit of Man*. When war broke out, Bridges was aged 70; nonetheless, he drilled with a regiment of Oxford dons and townsmen over military age.[46] First published by Longmans, Green & Co. in January 1916, simultaneously in ordinary and India paper editions, *The Spirit of Man* was reprinted four times in that year and twice more in both 1917 and 1918. Its portability was one factor that weighed with Herbert Read in making up his soldier's trousseau for the trenches: *The Spirit of Man* joined *Don Quixote*, Plato's *Republic*, and Christina Rossetti's poems in his pack.[47] Bridges's purpose was to emphasize that 'spirituality is the basis and foundation of human life—in so far as our life is a worthy subject for ideal philosophy and pure aesthetic—rather than the apex or final attainment of it'. The more lusty appetites—'sexual passion and mirth'—were, therefore, excluded, though the ageing Prime Minister, Asquith, who had appointed Bridges, was in the habit of giving *The Spirit of Man* to his younger lady friends, inscribing the copy with a suggestive quotation of his own (from *All's Well That Ends Well*): 'Let me not live, after my flame lacks oil, to be

---

[45] Quotations from Meynell, *Alice Meynell*, ch. xviii. On Francis, later Sir Francis, Meynell (1891–1975), see *DNB 1971–1980*, 567–9. Churchill's secretary, Eddie Marsh, testified before the military service tribunal to Francis Meynell's 'unimpeachable courage and complete sincerity'; see John Rae, *Conscience and Politics* (Oxford, 1970), 80, 100.   [46] Thompson, *Bridges*, 6, 85, 120.

[47] Diary, 8 and 22 May 1917, in Read, *Contrary Experiences*, 92, 96.

the snuff of younger spirits.'[48] Bridges anthologized chiefly British and French authors—the French were published untranslated—and they were buttressed by a strong supporting cast of classical Greek and Latin authors and Christian writers in the Neoplatonist tradition, with allied support from sundry Americans (Thoreau, Lincoln), Russians (Tolstoy, Dostoevsky) and Asians (Tagore, and from the Chinese). Given Bridges' remit, the spirit of man, it seemed perverse to exclude Robert Browning because, as C. A. Alington wrote on behalf of Browningites everywhere, 'there was no subject with which Browning so constantly, and to my mind so successfully, dealt';[49] but Bridges considered Browning's verses both unbeautiful and illustrative of 'a *perfectly confused* mind'.[50] This was the most singular of Bridges' many omissions: there was no Kipling naturally, but no Hardy, Francis Thompson, Alice Meynell, or any Rossetti.[51] Above all, there was no place for any German. Bridges drew up the charge sheet in justification of that decision:

The progress of mankind on the path of liberty and humanity has been suddenly arrested and its promise discredited by the apostasy of a great people, who, casting off as a disguise their professions of Honour, now openly avow that the ultimate faith of their hearts is in material force . . . two things stand out clearly, and they are above question or debate. The first is that Prussia's scheme for the destruction of her neighbours was long-laid, and scientifically elaborated to the smallest detail: the second is that she will shrink from no crime that may further its execution. How far the various Teutonic states that have been subjugated by Prussia are infected or morally enslaved by the machinery that overlords them, how far they are deluded or tempted by a vision of world-empire, how far their intellectual teachers willingly connive at the contradictory falsehoods officially imposed upon their assent, and what their social awakening will be, we can only surmise . . . but we now see them all united in a wild enthusiasm for the great scheme of tyranny, as unscrupulous in their means as in their motives, and obedient to military regulations for cruelty, terrorism, and devastation.

Douglas Goldring, pacifist and socialist, inevitably thought that he detected in the Poet Laureate's presentation 'signs of marked discomfort at the realisation of the part he was expected to play'.[52] Certainly, Bridges allowed that some fault might lie on the British side, also that the state of the nation required some reconstruction. Nonetheless, he was confident that

our country is called of God to stand for the truth of man's hope, and that it has not shrunk from the call . . . for truly it is the hope of man's great desire, the desire for brotherhood and universal peace to men of good-will, that is at stake in this struggle.

[48] Kennet, *Self-Portrait*, 134 (1 Feb. 1916).
[49] C. A. Alington, *A Dean's Apology: A Semi-Religious Autobiography* (1952), 149. Alington (1872–1955) was headmaster of Shrewsbury and Eton, before becoming Dean of Durham in 1917.
[50] Thompson, *Bridges*, 86, 120.
[51] The best represented among British authors were Shakespeare, Shelley, Milton, Keats, Blake, Coleridge, Wordsworth, Dixon, Yeats, Herbert, and Hopkins. Stevenson managed five entries, Rupert Brooke three (the same as Tennyson), and Meredith one.
[52] Goldring, *Reputations*, 112. Goldring's pacifist novel *The Fortune* (1917) targeted, *inter alia*, Government incompetence and war-profiteering: it sold only 300–400 copies but grew in reputation during the 1920s. See Alec Waugh's Preface to Douglas Goldring, *Life Interests* (1948) pp. vii–viii; and the notice of Goldring (1887–1960) by George Malcolm Johnson, in *Oxford DNB*.

Britons have ever fought well for their country, and their country's Cause is the high Cause of Freedom and Honour. That fairest earthly fame, the fame of Freedom, is inseparable from the names of Albion, Britain, England: it has gone out to America and the Antipodes, hallowing the names of Canada, Australia, and New Zealand; it has found a new home in Africa: and this heritage is our glory and happiness. We can therefore be happy in our sorrows, happy even in the death of our beloved who fall in the fight; for they die nobly, as heroes and saints die, with hearts and hands unstained by hatred or wrong.[53]

In 1920 Bridges collected his war poems—'Hell and Hate', 'The Chivalry of the Seas', 'British Graves in France', and (on the surrender of the German fleet) 'Der Tag'—in *October and Other Poems*; but he was denounced by *The Times* in that same year for organizing a letter, signed by many leading academics and sent to the heads of German universities, that called for the restoration of intellectual ties.[54]

IV

Contrasting passions had moved others. In 1911, anticipating a new dimension to the terrors of war, Galsworthy had petitioned through *The Times* for the proscription of the deployment of aeroplanes in wartime. Through the International Arbitration League he endeavoured to enrol leading European names from the arts, sciences, and religion in this cause. He secured 220 signatures but none from France or Germany.[55] Come 4 August 1914, Galsworthy was downcast with anguish when war was joined: 'The horror of the thing keeps coming over one in waves; and all happiness has gone out of life. I can't keep still, and I can't work.'[56] His strongest feeling was for the fighting to end; nevertheless, he believed that the 'cynical trampling force' of the German ruling class which started the war had to be defeated. He was convinced that 'France, England and America are the only hope and stronghold of these ideas' (what he termed 'the principles of Liberty, Democracy, and Humanism'), and that 'France and England had to fight for them, and to fight for them tooth and nail—hence, such misfortunes as our Conscription Act.'[57] Like many, he tormented himself that he lacked the moral and physical courage to do his duty by enlisting. In July 1918 he was examined for the Army Reserve and discharged as 'permanently and totally unfit for any form of Military Service'; it was his defective eyesight, he thought, though he was a month shy of his fifty-first birthday.[58] He and his wife had previously done volunteer nursing—Galsworthy as a masseur—at a hospital for wounded soldiers in France, November 1916–March 1917; otherwise, he had occupied himself by writing on behalf of, and liberally subscribing to, war charities and relief funds. He gave away 'perhaps three-quarters of his income' in this manner.[59] He would not stoop to war fever, unlike Sir Owen Seaman, the editor of *Punch*, who put

[53] Robert Bridges (ed.), *The Spirit of Man* (1916), preface. The volume contains no pagination.
[54] Thompson, *Bridges*, 89, 92.   [55] Marrot, *Galsworthy*, 320.   [56] Ibid. 396.
[57] Galsworthy to Edward Garnett, 17 Mar. 1916, in Garnett (ed.), *Galsworthy Letters*, 225–6.
[58] Discharge certificate reproduced in Marrot, *Galsworthy*, opp. p. 443.   [59] Marrot, *Galsworthy*, 448.

humour on the back burner and served up a ditty, 'I hate all Huns'.[60] Arthur Benson, who became Master of Magdalene in 1915, was equally disgusted by another of Seaman's poems, which spurred soldiers returning to Oxford and Cambridge to 'duck' those dons who had not joined up: 'Elderly non-combatants denouncing shirkers seem to me a generation of vipers indeed—fit for hell, and wholly unfit for heaven.'[61]

German atrocities much exercised Conan Doyle.[62] He drew these lessons: 'that the Prussian military system is and always has been cruel, and that they have now moulded all the rest of Germany to their own image'.[63] The atrocities complained of covered many forms—the destruction, rapine, and slaughter perpetrated in occupied territories; the maltreatment and murder of prisoners of war; the air raids designed to terrorize and kill civilians; and the submarine torpedoing of passenger and mercantile shipping[64]—and Doyle found it a thorny problem to decide how Britain should respond. While it was vital to advertise to (as yet) neutral countries such as the United States what crimes were being committed by 'these European Red Indians', it was probably useless to plead with the enemy directly: 'All appeals to good feeling are unavailing, for the average German has no more understanding of chivalry than a cow has of mathematics.'[65] Condign justice would be served by an official statement that the Kaiser and others in authority must be tried for their lives at the war's end, and neutral countries warned 'to be careful whom they may accept as guests, since we shall certainly

---

[60] Gardiner, *Leaves in the Wind*, 182. Cf. Owen Seaman's scornful response to Alfred Noyes's poem 'To England in 1907: a Prayer that she might Speak for Peace' (published in *Forty Singing Seamen, and Other Poems* (1907)), which Noyes wrote in sympathy with the ideals of the Disarmament Conference held at The Hague. Seaman's riposte, 'To England in 1908', derided such 'waste words ... based on a general funk', and instead cried

> ... Build *Dreadnoughts* two to one;
> And let your children, every mother's son,
> Shoulder the rifle, prime the rakish gun,
> And fling this shattering message o'er the sea:—
> ' 'Tis ours to stamp the world with Freedom's brand!
> Love us, or we will blow you out of hand
> Into the *Ewigkeit*. So understand,
> We mean, this way or that, to make you free!'
>
> (*Punch*, 1 Jan. 1908, 2)

[61] Newsome, *Edge of Paradise*, 335. Cf. Seaman's poem 'To the Shirker', *Punch*, 11 Nov. 1914, 390. To be fair, he also penned appeals for numerous war charities; for instance, for the Red Cross, in *Punch*, 9 Sept. 1914, 214.

[62] Conan Doyle offered himself for military service in 1914 but, aged 55, was rejected and had to content himself with drilling and patrolling in a civil defence unit, of which system he had been a leading advocate before the war. His daughter Mary worked in a munitions factory and his son Kingsley, invalided out of the Hampshires after being wounded at the Somme in 1916, died in the influenza epidemic of 1918. Booth, *Doyle*, 296–7, 311.

[63] Letter to the *New York Times*, 6 Feb. 1915, in Gibson and Green (eds.), *Unknown Conan Doyle*, 217.

[64] For a recent reassessment, John Horne and Alan Kramer, *German Atrocities, 1914: A History of Denial* (New Haven, 2001); John Horne, 'German Atrocities, 1914: Fact, Fantasy or Fabrication?', *History Today* (Apr. 2002), 47–53.

[65] Letter to *The Times*, 13 Apr. 1915, in Gibson and Green (eds.), *Unknown Conan Doyle*, 219.

not recognize any rights of asylum from those whom we regard as murderers'.[66] Until then a policy of keener defence and selective reprisals was sensible.

In the first category, Doyle's reputation both as a man of medical science and as the author of ingenious solutions in his detective stories meant that his urgent call for life-saving appliances was answered by a torrent of letters from inventors. These included a trident on the bow of boats to deflect or explode sea-mines, collapsible canvas lifeboats and inflatable collars or waistcoats ('the swimming bladder') for crews and passengers, and body armour and metal shields as worn by the Australian outlaw Ned Kelly to protect soldiers against machine-gun fire. German officers should also be carried on board hospital ships as hostages against attack, and German prisoners of war positioned in districts of London where air raids were thought likely.[67] But reprisals were also necessary, because 'The Hun is only formidable when he thinks that he can be frightful with impunity. "Blood and Iron" is his doctrine so long as it is his iron and some one else's blood.'[68] The naval blockade of Germany was right, but the Government must also broadcast that 'every [air] raid upon an open town in Great Britain would automatically and remorselessly cause three similar raids on German towns'.[69] For this he wanted the construction of more airfields, in eastern France especially. He did not suggest targeting German civilians specifically:

The proposal is that we attack Cologne, Coblentz, and the other Rhine towns, most of which are actual fortresses and all of them places on the lines of communications with railways and bridges of strategic importance. If, however, in these military operations civilians get hurt, the Germans will realize what we feel and will probably reconsider their murderous tactics.[70]

Doyle had no patience with ecclesiastical and other critics of such policies, though his animus against the Church establishment was not new, having been formed in the pre-war years by his campaign for divorce law reform and by his movement towards spiritualism.

Doyle enjoyed government and service contacts, but he would not accept an invitation to direct a Home Office propaganda department. This again was consistent with his pre-war view that serving the patriotic and party cause was not one and the same, although coalition nominally operated in wartime. Doyle divided from the government line in several important respects. He placed more emphasis on volunteer regiments and Civilian Reserve units than politicians, in spite of their rousing calls, were inclined to do; and he did not care for conscription. He still rode hobby-horses, among them the Channel Tunnel idea, which he had pressed since the Agadir incident in 1911, when, in his view, 'war

[66] Letters to *The Times*, 8 Oct. and 12 Nov. 1918, ibid. 268–9.
[67] Letters to the *Daily Chronicle*, 22 Jan. 1915; *The Times*, 27 July 1915, 28 July and 4 Aug. 1916; and *Observer*, 20 Aug. 1916, ibid. 214–15, 222–3, 239–43; Booth, *Conan Doyle*, 297–8, 300.
[68] Letter to *The Times*, 18 Jan. 1916, in Gibson and Green (eds.), *Unknown Conan Doyle*, 230.
[69] Letter to *The Times*, 15 Oct. 1915, ibid. 226.
[70] Letter to the *Saturday Review*, 26 Feb. 1916, ibid. 233.

with Germany became more probable'.[71] More notable still, he contributed £700 towards the legal expenses of Sir Roger Casement, on trial for traitorous collaboration with the enemy to abet Irish independence. This sum amounted to almost half of Casement's costs. Doyle further organized a petition to spare him the death penalty when he was found guilty. Arnold Bennett, G. K. Chesterton, John Drinkwater, John Galsworthy, Jerome K. Jerome, John Masefield, and Israel Zangwill, all lent their signatures to this, whereas Bernard Shaw mounted his own campaign and Kipling and H. G. Wells refused to subscribe to either. Doyle did not contest Casement's guilt; but justice in this case was rendered almost impossible by reference to so-called *Black Diaries* which detailed Casement's homosexual couplings and pornographic fantasies. Doyle was made privy to their content, as the Home Office and Special Branch sought to destroy sympathy for Casement both in Britain and in the United States, where the poet Alfred Noyes, then Professor of Modern English Literature at Princeton, acted as a conduit for their circulation.[72] Doyle did not abandon Casement. The 'diaries' he regarded as abhorrent but irrelevant to the charge of treason; indeed, they rather confirmed Doyle's belief that Casement was 'a sick man...worn by tropical hardships...[and] not in a normal state of mind'. Like several signatories to his petition, Doyle admired Casement's part in exposing the atrocities committed against native labour in the Congo and Peru before the war, when he had shown himself to be 'a man of fine character'.[73]

Doyle decided differently when it came to the participants in the 1916 Easter Rising in Ireland. He understood the danger of making political martyrs, yet he did not oppose their execution. Policemen and others had been killed in the Dublin fighting; hence those responsible 'should be tried not for rebellion, which might put a halo round their memories, but for most cowardly murder'.[74] As a convert to Home Rule before the war, Doyle was disgusted by Sinn Fein: 'It has, so far as it could, thrown away the fruits of fifty years of patient Constitutional reform.'[75] In advising how to retrieve the situation Doyle responded entirely in character: he had none of the guile of the politician for whom principles were means to an end. He believed in the efficacy of frank statements of truth and honour as he saw them. He was unabashed about hating the Germans; indeed, he

[71] Letter to the *Glasgow Herald*, 23 June 1916, ibid. 239.
[72] Saunders and Taylor, *British Propaganda*, 174–6. In the 1930s, having been execrated by W. B. Yeats for his part in the campaign, Noyes came to think that the Black Diaries were forgeries; see Angus Mitchell, 'Forgery or Genuine Document?', *History Today* (Mar. 2001), 16–18; and *DNB 1951–1960*, 776–8, for Noyes (1880–1958). Forensic testing has finally established the diaries' authenticity 'beyond all reasonable doubt'; (*The Times*, 13, 16 Mar. 2002; *Sunday Times*, 10 Mar. 2002).
[73] Letter to *Daily Chronicle*, 30 Nov. 1914, in Gibson and Green (eds.), *Unknown Conan Doyle*, 213; Booth, *Conan Doyle*, 306–7. Cf. T. P. O'Connor's view, recorded by the editor of the *Manchester Guardian*, C. P. Scott, on 27 November 1914: that Casement was ' "both mad and bad" and he was open to prosecution on either score should he venture again on English or Irish soil...' (Trevor Wilson (ed.), *The Political Diaries of C. P. Scott 1911–1928* (1970), 114).
[74] Letter to *Daily Chronicle*, 9 May 1916, in Gibson and Green (eds.), *Unknown Conan Doyle*, 237.
[75] Letter to the *Belfast Evening Telegraph*, 17 July 1917, ibid. 251.

thought it right because of the things they had done. Hence his puzzlement about wartime dissidents, who included the pacifists of the Union of Democratic Control and socialist subversives who fomented strikes in shipyards and munitions industries, as well as Sinn Feiners. They could only be behaving in this way, Doyle presumed, because the message had failed to get through to them about the nature of the enemy. His answer, therefore, was to step up the propaganda about German atrocities, multiplying picture posters and other forms of communication:

Let them be hung in every shop . . . The bestiality of the German nation has given us a driving power which we are not using, and which would be very valuable in this stage of the war. Scatter the facts. Put them in red-hot fashion [and] spread the propaganda wherever there are signs of enemy intrigues, on the Tyne, the Clyde, in the Midlands, above all in Ireland and in French Canada. Let us pay no attention to platitudinous Bishops or gloomy Deans, or any other superior people who preach against retaliation or whole-hearted warfare. We have to win, and we can only win by keeping up the spirit and resolution of our own people.[76]

Doyle devoted every waking moment to advance his country's cause. He was not passive while sleeping either. On 4 April 1917 he arose from bed with a message, 'Piave! Piave!', ringing in his head. He had visited the Italian front, also the Western Front, to make an assessment for the Foreign Office in 1916,[77] but he could not remember having crossed the Piave, whose location he now ascertained in an atlas; nor could he think why it should assume significance because in April 1917 it was 50 miles to the rear of the Italian line. Continuing uneasy, Doyle sent a sealed letter about it to the Society for Psychical Research; next year everything became clear when, on 17 June 1918, at the depths of the Allies' fortunes, the turning point of the war on the Italian front was secured on the Piave. Doyle's letter was opened on 20 November 1918 and, in addition to the Allies' victory, Doyle was now able to register a triumphant vindication of spiritualism: 'the only possible explanation is that my friends on the other side, knowing how much I worried over the situation, were giving me comfort and knowledge'.[78]

V

A more conventional form of communication directed towards Italy during the war was composed by G. K. Chesterton, whose *Letters to an Old Garibaldian* (1915) were placed in the Italian newspaper *Il Secolo*. Anthony Hope also wrote

---

[76] Letter to *The Times*, 26 Dec. 1917, ibid. 257. Not all Conan Doyle's commissioned letters directed at munitions workers were thought to hit the right note; for instance, when he chastised labour on the subject of drink. See A. D. Harvey, 'On the Literary Front', *TLS.*, 14 Jan. 2005, 12.

[77] Booth, *Conan Doyle*, 302–4.

[78] Letter to the *Journal of the Society for Psychical Research*, Jan. 1919, in Gibson and Green (eds.), *Unknown Conan Doyle*, 270–1, where there is also reproduced Conan Doyle's sealed letter of 4 November 1917.

pamphlets putting the allied case to and for the Italians;[79] but it was the winning
of American opinion that chiefly occupied the authorities and authors. Among
those whom this duty animated was Douglas Sladen. He met the future president
Herbert Hoover, who, while visiting London, expressed concern about the
spread of German propaganda in his country, especially a booklet entitled
Truth about Germany: Facts about the War. Sladen devised a counter: *The Secret
White Paper.* GERMANY'S GREAT LIE. *The Official German Justification of the War.
Exposed and Criticised*. This reprinted the original, paragraph, by paragraph
followed by Sladen's riposte; 50,000 copies were distributed.[80] American tours
were arranged for a number of authors, including J. M. Barrie. He, like many
celebrities, was also invited to pay visits to soldiers serving on the Western Front,
not just British forces but Dominion and colonial troops and Americans too. The
invitation to the American lines in 1918 was engineered by his secretary, Lady
Cynthia Asquith, and came from General Pershing himself. This Barrie moodily
accepted. He still had the painful recollection of his visit to America itself when
admirers gushed about how much they loved his *Prisoner of Zenda*.[81] That visit, in
the early months of the war and accompanied by A. E. W. Mason, had been a flop
which pointed up the want of proper planning in the British propaganda drive,
especially the failure to coordinate the activities of Wellington House and the
Foreign Office. Apparently, Masterman and Parker had not even informed the
British Ambassador, Sir Cecil Spring-Rice, about the Barrie–Mason tour until they
were within thirty-six hours of landing at New York. Spring-Rice had their boat
met and told them that he did not want them making speeches about the war,
whereupon Mason turned round for home. Barrie stayed on for three weeks,
ostensibly as a guest of the theatre impresario Charles Frohman. He then tried to
make light of their failure, though the visit had been designed to allay American
susceptibilities over the interception or sinking of merchant trips supplying
Germany, if not to bring America into the war. He told George Llewelyn Davies,
who was then serving at the front, that America 'has some ships, of course, and
an army so small that I came to the conclusion after my talk with Roosevelt that it
consisted of him and his four sons . . . Italy would be of more practical help.'[82]

  Authors had to learn not to rush into situations whose political complexity
they had not sufficiently studied or grasped. HM Foreign Office was prone to be
stand-offish about authors (as about every other living soul not diplomatically
accredited). The situation was different in the United States, where, though the

  [79] Mallet, *Hope*, 219–20, 226. According to the British Ambassador in Rome, the foreign book trade in
Italy was practically monopolized by Germany, and efforts made by a committee in London, chaired by
Sir Henry Newbolt, were unavailing; Sir James Rennell Rodd, *Social and Diplomatic Memories, 1902–1919*
(1925), 309–10.   [80] Sladen, *Long Life*, 95–6.
  [81] Asquith, *Diaries*, 473, 475 (11 and 18 Sept. 1918); Kennet, *Self-Portrait*, 252 (29 Nov. 1926); Asquith,
Barrie, 21–2. *The Prisoner of Zenda* was, of course, written by Anthony Hope in 1894.
  [82] Dunbar, *Barrie*, 208–9. See also Barrie's letter to Nan Herbert, 22 Sept. 1914, in Meynell (ed.), *Barrie
Letters*, 110. For an appreciation of Parker's direction of propaganda in America, see Saunders and Taylor,
British Propaganda, ch. 5. Parker remained in charge until early 1917.

State Department may have been no more enthusiastic, the patronage system exercised by presidents and political parties had in the past promoted various scholars and authors to represent their country in embassies and legations. This list included not just distinguished historians such as J. L. Motley, who had been American Minister to Austria (1861–7) and to Britain (1869–70), but the poet and literary critic James Russell Lowell, who was American Minister to Spain (1877–80) and to Britain (1880–5). A predecessor in both Lowell's postings was Washington Irving; Nathaniel Hawthorne had also undertaken consular duties in Liverpool (1853–7). It was consistent with this tradition, therefore, that Colonel House, President Wilson's representative in Europe, should suggest Barrie's name as a possible Ambassador to Washington in 1919. The very notion struck even Barrie's friends as 'wonderfully comic';[83] but it had been a subject debated off and on for half a century, since William Hepworth Dixon, editor of the *Athenaeum*, had asked in 1869 why Dickens should not be appointed to the Washington embassy.[84] Anthony Hope had also grumbled, at a banquet in response to a toast to Literature: 'in America they took their literary men seriously. They made them Ambassadors. Nothing of that sort happened over here'. 'He was not airing a personal grievance,' he concluded limply, 'merely representing his trade.'[85] But the standing of authors, especially authors of fiction, was not such as to command these exalted spheres in British public life, although it appeared pardonable to compose poetry: the actual Ambassador in Washington during the war, Spring-Rice, was one of several career diplomats, together with Sir Rennell Rodd (HM Ambassador in Rome, 1908–19), who were also poets.[86] Spring-Rice's friendship with Theodore Roosevelt made for difficulties in his relations with President Wilson and acted to compound a character already prone to nervous strain; nevertheless, he believed that a common literary tradition, together with the Bible, made for a natural alliance of sympathy between Britain and America. In 1918, while morosely awaiting recall, he responded to Senator Bryan's 'Heart to Heart Appeal' by composing his enduring poem 'I vow to thee, my country . . . .'.[87]

---

[83] Kennet, *Self-Portrait*, 177 (27 July 1919).

[84] At the banquet to honour Dickens in St George's Hall, Liverpool, on 10 April 1869, in Fielding, *Dickens's Speeches*, 390.   [85] Richards, *John Bull and Jonathan*, 225.

[86] A friend of Wilde at Oxford, Rodd published a book of poetry called *Songs of the South* in 1881. When in America, Wilde took pains to publish an 'aesthetic' edition of Rodd's book, retitled *Rose Leaf and Apple Leaf*; and he added a preface and a dedication to himself as Rodd's 'Heart's Brother'. Rodd had inscribed this sentiment in the personal copy of the English edition which he had presented to Wilde; but, fearful of jeopardizing his prospects of a diplomatic career, he was now appalled and required the dedication to be removed from unsold copies. Wilde referred to him subsequently as 'the true poet, and the false friend'. (letter to R. H. Sherard, Apr. 1883, in Hart-Davis (ed.), *Wilde's Letters*, 50–1, and 45 n. 2; Ellman, *Wilde*, 165–6, 188–90, 200–1). During the long vacancy of the laureateship following Tennyson's death in 1892, Queen Victoria's daughter the Empress Frederick even 'tried to get Rennell Rodd appointed'. So, at any rate, Lord Cromer told Wilfrid Blunt; see Blunt, *Diaries*, i. 212 (5 Jan. 1896). Blunt's own view was that Rodd had 'a small talent for verse, but no great originality'.

[87] Stephen Gwynn, *The Letters and Friendships of Sir Cecil Spring-Rice* (1929), i. 94–5, ii. 166–7, 426–33. On Vaughan Williams's suggestion, Spring-Rice's poem was combined with the Jupiter theme from Gustav

A. E. W. Mason's American tour had been aborted in 1914 but, like Compton Mackenzie and Somerset Maugham, he was afterwards engaged in intelligence operations which involved bizarre duties in sometimes outlandish places: in Spain, Morocco, and Mexico for Mason, in the Aegean for Mackenzie, and Switzerland, the South Seas, and Russia for Maugham.[88] This globe-trotting tended to bear out the Victorian pacifist John Bright's apophthegm that the only thing to be said for war was that it educated people in geography.[89] Aged 49 in 1914, Mason was a bachelor who relished adventure in real life as in novels: his recreations were exploring, mountaineering, and sailing. As a Liberal MP 1906–10, he had intrigued with Viscount Esher, sharing his concerns about military and naval preparedness and about the future of India.[90] Commissioned as a captain in the Manchester Regiment in 1915, he was promoted to major in the Royal Marine Light Infantry and became a General Staff Officer in 1917. After the war Mason enthralled Arnold Bennett at the Garrick Club with stories of his exploits in Mexico, where he had spied on the German Embassy and followed German trade movements by using the guise of a lepidopterist—a ruse borrowed from Conan Doyle's Stapleton, the scheming villain in *The Hound of the Baskervilles* (1902). He particularly entertained Bennett by saying that 'practically all the German spies . . . carried a packet of obscene photographs on their persons'. Mason's view was that the German secret service was incompetent and expensive; by contrast, Bennett judged Mason to have had 'a great gift for secret service, though he said he began as an amateur'.[91]

Somerset Maugham was much less well equipped either for active service or for intelligence or political duty. He served initially in Flanders with a Red Cross ambulance unit before being adopted for intelligence work, as a go-between linking spies in the field with their London controllers. He turned out to be as useless as any German agent, although concealment was practically second nature to him owing to his troubled private life: 'I was a quarter normal and three-quarters queer, but I tried to persuade myself that it was the other way round.' In 1915 he fathered a child and, while he married the mother in 1917, having been cited in her divorce, he was already involved in a homosexual affair with his male secretary. So far as the intelligence services were concerned, Maugham's being a professional writer was thought ideal cover to explain why he should suddenly pop up in odd spots. Maugham so far entered into the spirit of things as to lay the basis for his *Ashenden* (1928) stories while in Switzerland and for *Rain* (1921) while in the Pacific. He also picked up a Gauguin for next to

Holst's Planet Suite for public singing in 1921; see Michael Short, *Gustav Holst: The Man and his Music* (Oxford, 1990), 197.

[88] On Mackenzie's adventures, see *My Life and Times: Octave Five 1915–1923* (1966), 13–146.

[89] Quoted in Gardiner, *Leaves in the Wind*, 231.

[90] Brett, *Esher*, ii. 261–2, 285 (21, 22 Nov. 1907, 14 Feb. 1908). Esher sent Mason's novel *The Broken Road* (1907) to the Secretary of State for India, Morley, believing that it summed up the problem of Indian government. [91] Flower (ed.), *Bennett Journals*, ii. 247 (entry for 5 Mar. 1919).

nothing when in Tahiti, and began to conceive of a novel based on the painter's life, *The Moon and Sixpence* (1919). In Russia in 1917 he was officially acting as correspondent for the *Daily Telegraph*; in fact, with substantial funds at his disposal, jointly contributed by British and American governments, 'I was supposed to help the Mensheviks buy arms and finance newspapers so as to keep Russia in the war and to prevent the Bolsheviks from seizing power.' To stop the Russian Revolution was a tall order for any one-man job. Maugham failed to convince intelligence chiefs that he was not the man. Later, he explained the ludicrous consequences to his nephew:

you can have no idea what a disadvantage my stammer was to me when I was a secret agent. One morning in the autumn Kerensky sent for me and gave me a message for Lloyd George. It was so secret that he wouldn't put it in writing. But when I got back to London I wrote the message down because I knew that when I came to tell it to the Prime Minister I'd begin to stammer. Lloyd George was in a hurry when I met him, so I just handed him what I'd written out. And he only glanced at the note. If I'd read the memo out to him it might have made all the difference. And perhaps the world today might be a very different place. But I made a hash of the whole business.[92]

John Masefield was another writer who first saw service with the Red Cross before being taken up by the Ministry of Information. In his case the new duty was more in keeping with his lurid imagination and capacity to deliver. He was at Gallipoli briefly with the Red Cross, whereupon, encouraged by the authorities, he turned the disaster of the Dardanelles into a tragic romance. His *Gallipoli* (1916) sold 'like wildfire' and deflected public odium from the director of military operations, General Sir Ian Hamilton. The relish with which Masefield mixed up blood and flowers in his descriptions amused those who were familiar with Masefield's style; still, it was 'a very remarkable book—a work of genius'.[93] Viscount Esher considered it a prose achievement 'on a level with Tennyson's "Charge of the Light Brigade" ',[94] and with his encouragement Field Marshal Haig invited Masefield to undertake the same exercise for the Somme; but, though the intrinsic implausibility of this task might have deterred most, it was Whitehall bureaucracy rather than any reluctance on Masefield's part that reduced the eventual product.[95]

Masefield's epical treatment was only a grander version of a common product issuing from the Ministry of Information. Keble Howard, widely known for his light fiction and popular sketches, was charged with the task of romancing the Zeebrugge raid, and given facilities to interview the surviving officers. His resultant text, *The Glory of Zeebrugge*, over which Anthony Hope passed an approving eye at Wellington House before it went into print, sold in 'vast quantities' in Britain and the Empire and in North America, where the United

---

[92] Maugham, *Somerset*, 207–8. See also Morgan, *Maugham*, 199–232.
[93] Barbellion [B. F. Cummings], *Journal of a Disappointed Man*, 307.
[94] Harvey, 'On the Literary Front', *TLS*, 14 Jan. 2005, 12.   [95] Smith, *Masefield*, pt. III.

States and Canada produced their own editions. Howard's first commission had been to write about maltreatment of British prisoners of war: 'All the facts were contained in a Government White Paper, but they were dull reading in that official shape. I did my best to put them into narrative form, and called the pamphlet, "The Quality of Mercy". It made my blood boil, and I hope it had the same effect on other people in neutral countries.'[96] Howard's final assignment was to extol the contributions made by different classes of worker on the home front: miners, fishermen, land girls, and all. Afterwards he collected in book form wartime articles he had written. He called it *An Author in Wonderland* (1919).[97]

VI

The wonderland of the romantic imagination was a familiar habitation for the novelist and socialite Elinor Glyn. During the war she worked not for British but for French propaganda agencies. She was initially commissioned to produce articles about Hun devastations for publication in America and, as she put it with splendid ingenuousness, she 'went to stay at the Ritz Hotel in Paris, feeling sure that I would see more of the kaleidoscope of events from there than from anywhere else'.[98] This was in 1915; and, while waiting for the necessary permits, she started her researches by taking flowers and cigarettes to British soldiers lying wounded in the Trianon Palace Hotel at Versailles, then converted to a hospital. She was both shocked by their suffering and struck by their fortitude and cheerfulness; incidentally, she 'used to pick out the regular soldiers from the Territorials by their dirty and bad teeth'. 'Toothbrush drill must have been unknown in the British Army before the war,' she added. She was little advanced in her work before being recalled to London by her dissolute husband's final illness. She salved her own state of depression by joining the midnight shift at a canteen in Grosvenor Gardens, serving hot meals to soldiers passing through Victoria station. 'I was never a good waitress, always stupid and muddling,' she admitted, 'but I could sweep and clean nicely, and finally became one of the most expert of the washing-up staff!' This satisfaction survived her rough treatment by 'the hard-faced professional canteen manager from Woolwich, who loved to show her authority by humiliating the voluntary workers'.[99] Glyn's war in London did not lack glamour and drama, however. She published two new romances, *The Man and the Moment* (1915) and *The Career of Katherine Bush* (1917),

---

[96] Howard, *Motley Life*, 255.
[97] Howard joined the Ministry of Information in 1917. He had applied for an Army commission in 1914 but was over the age limit, and had had to be contented with serving as an equipment officer for the Air Force. He also drilled with the United Arts, a volunteer corps of writers, actors, artists, and musicians, along with Granville Barker and Frank Benson. The principal theme of *An Author in Wonderland* was that it was 'the absolutely dauntless nature of the British Character' that brought about the defeat of Germany (p. 3).   [98] Glyn, *Romantic Adventure*, 225.
[99] Ibid. 226–8.

and her reflections on life—at least, on the triplice of truth, common-sense, and happiness—*Three Things* (1915).

The year 1917 brought the famous million-copy cheap edition of Glyn's novels. Previously her publisher Duckworth never issued her at less than 2s. 6d.; this shilling imprint, marketed by Jonathan Cape (as Jonathan Page & Co.), greatly enlarged her public and yielded copious fan mail from ordinary soldiers and their wives and lovers.[100] Glyn herself sought to rekindle two old flames, the former proconsuls now Cabinet ministers, Lords Curzon and Milner. The first effort was snuffed out in shocking fashion, *The Times* bearing to her breakfast table notice of Curzon's engagement to be married. He had given her no warning, nor did explanation follow; and they never met or communicated again. An incineration of his near 500 letters to her, written over a period of eight and a half years, ritualized the extinction of their passion.[101] Glyn's friendship with Milner, never so heated on her part, persisted. They dined together on several occasions and discussed affairs of state, that well-known aphrodisiac: 'I left him at the Majestic at midnight. I have never looked so well or so young for 20 years. He is flabbergasted at me, he says it is some magic.'[102] This high-level contact proved invaluable when she returned to the Paris Ritz in April 1917 to fulfil her original commission. This involved visits to French and American forces at the front, and she heard enough first-hand of German atrocities to be convinced that these were not inventions of allied propaganda. Appointed vice-president of Secours Franco-Americain, which assisted refugees to resettle in the recaptured zones, Glyn also engaged in practical philanthropy. She remained in Paris throughout the German air raids and artillery bombardments of the spring of 1918, right to the war's end, and eventually covered the Peace Conference for various magazines and newspapers including the *Ladies' Field* and *News of the World*. The upshot of her experiences ran entirely contrary to her purposed mission. She was revolted by 'the extraordinary narrowness and ingratitude' she found, particularly in the French upper classes, towards their British and American allies. She was disgusted too by the vice she saw rampant in Paris and by the panic evacuations.[103] Glyn's admiration of French culture and civilization was irretrievably dashed.

Before the war few English authors were so familiar with French ways as Arnold Bennett, who had lived there for several years and acquired a French wife. His war was largely spent in England, yet Bennett was to give exceptional literary service to the allied cause. In common with many, he had not foreseen that war might occur. This was especially dismaying for Bennett, who prided himself on his realism. He had believed that wars between nations, like religious wars, were things of the past. Once in the war, Bennett also believed it would not last: in February 1915 he was thinking that it would end in June or July.[104] As war persisted, Bennett behaved in character, with thoroughness and generosity.

---

[100] Glyn, *Elinor Glyn*, 244.   [101] Ibid. 226–8.   [102] Ibid. 258.   [103] Ibid., chs. xxi–xxv.
[104] Lowndes, *Diaries and Letters*, 52 (17 Feb. 1915).

His large house, Comarques, at Thorpe-le-Soken, Essex, which had been expensively refurbished to an American standard of central heating, electric lighting, and plumbing, became a kind of grand hotel for military officers, not all of whom were convalescent; and the contents of his (and his wife's) wardrobe were consigned to aid Belgian refugees, together with weekly hampers of produce from their fruit and vegetable garden. Fat cheques were directed to the Refugees Association, and to the English and French Red Cross; and Bennett's yacht *Velsa*, whose purchase had fulfilled 'the dream of his life', was turned over to the Admiralty.[105] Bennett's own first commission, following Masterman's 'eminent authors' conference on 2 September 1914, was to produce a booklet, *Liberty: A Statement of the British Case*, which was published simultaneously in London, New York, and Toronto. It was a plain exposition of how Sir Edward Grey's strivings for peace since 1908 had been frustrated. It was 'absolutely certain', Bennett wrote, 'that Germany and Austria desired war'; and foremost he blamed the German 'military caste' because 'at the final moment Austria quailed'.[106] The calendar of crucial events leading up to the war as set out by Bennett followed the conventional Foreign Office line—from the unprecedented severity of the Austrian ultimatum to Serbia to the 'shameless violation' of Belgian neutrality by Germany—but the thesis was given a keen democratic spin for the audience in the New World, in Bennett's asides such as his description of Archduke Franz Ferdinand as 'an out-and-out royalist and military reactionary animated by one idea, namely that the earth exists in order that the ruling classes may rule it'.[107] Cleverly, he turned an appreciation of the German advance since unification in 1870 into an indictment, in much the same way as the Germany military caste 'and the sinister Krupp family' had done when it

discovered what a marvellous instrument it possessed in the German people—a people docile, ingenuous, studious, industrious, idealistic, and thorough; but above all docile and thorough. German commerce increased astoundingly; the energy of the race seemed illimitable; its achievements in sheer civilisation became brilliant; for example, the municipal government of cities such as Frankfort is of a quality unequalled in the world. The autocracy availed itself of all the talents shown, and in particular it exploited German docility so ruthlessly . . .[108]

The British case Bennett put simply enough: a question of honour, to uphold a treaty protecting Belgian neutrality and independence; an ideal of liberty, to defend 'the right of every individual to call his soul his own' instead of kneeling as a slave to military tyranny; and a matter of national self-preservation. He painted in the darkest colours the Germans' planning and prosecution of a new concept of war, unscrupulous and atrocious and directed against civilian buildings and unarmed people as much as against opposing forces; and he brought it directly

---

[105] Bennett, *My Arnold Bennett*, 118–29, 150, 152.
[106] Arnold Bennett, *Liberty: A Statement of the British Case* (1914), 37.   [107] Ibid. 8.
[108] Ibid. 20–1.

into the American reckoning by arguing that, were it to conquer the European allies, Germany would shortly target the United States:

Thus, in New York, the new City Hall, the Metropolitan Museum, and the Pennsylvania Railway Station, not to mention the Metropolitan Tower, would go the way of Louvain, while New York business men would gather in Wall Street humbly to hand over the dollars amid the delightful strains of 'The Watch on the Rhine' and the applause of Professor Munsterburg.[109]

Bennett's gifts as a writer of a clear, pointed prose, with a disciplined popular didacticism, of the kind that had issued *How to Live on Twenty-Four Hours a Day*, and *How to Make the Best of Life*, were ideal for propaganda purposes. So was his fluency in French, in which, possibly because he spoke it slowly and deliberately, he stammered more seldom than in English. Arrangements were made for him to visit the trenches in 1915, where he was received by General Joffre and his staff. He brought back some shattered stained glass from Rheims Cathedral, photographs of battlefields, and disturbing visions which excited his neuralgia. Thereafter he slept with a loaded revolver in the drawer by his bed, which his worried wife clandestinely disarmed. His pen remained prolific, however, and he published over 400 articles in the press relating to the war during its course. He knocked off at the same time two plays and three novels and was halfway through a fourth by November 1918, thus reducing his own literary output to the level which 'an ordinary writer might have produced in ordinary times'.[110] Throughout he maintained a close interest in the Government and was drawn into the web woven by Max Aitken, Lord Beaverbrook, owner of the *Daily Express* and high political intriguer. In May 1918 he joined him at the Ministry of Information, as head of its French department, though Bennett waived a salary for his work and even took with him his own secretary, the devoted Miss Winifred Nerney, who served him from 1912 until his death in 1931.[111]

VII

It would be too innocent to suppose that authors showed no concern to project themselves as well as the national cause. Bennett was upset a few months into the war by the collapse in the price of literary stock brought about by zealous overproduction for American outlets:

Last week I learnt that, owing to the glut of English authors' 'distinguished copy' in U.S.A. offered practically for nothing either in order to get it published quickly, or because American copyright had been sacrificed to instant publication in England, there

[109] Ibid. 28–9.   [110] Hepburn (ed.), *Bennett Letters*, i. 211–12.
[111] Bennett, *My Arnold Bennett*, 40, 127–35, 147–8. On Bennett's position at the Ministry, and dismay about his resources for use of propaganda in France being dwarfed by American spending, see Harvey, 'On the Literary Front', *TLS*, 14 Jan. 2005, 13.

was no longer any market for such copy in U.S.A., American editors, with characteristic foolishness, setting down as valueless that which they could get cheap. I was told that they now adopted a patronising smile towards all English war-'copy' other than news. Thus our literary patriotism has cost us authors' money and done no good. Personally, a contract for 10 articles for £1,000 was practically arranged for me, and then called off. This was for American use of *Daily News* article, so it was a clear net loss.[112]

For Mrs Humphry Ward the war revived her flagging literary fortunes. It was a long-standing admirer, ex-President Roosevelt, who in December 1915 invited her to put the British case to American readers. A bargain had then to be struck with Masterman and Parker at Wellington House, because Mrs Ward's financial position at this juncture was awkward. She faced an income tax demand for £1,250, her husband owed a substantial sum to the picture-dealers Agnew, and her wastrel son the MP Arnold Ward drained away money by his gambling. She also sought Treasury grants to fund the children's play centres and facilities for crippled children at the Passmore Edwards Settlement, with which she was connected. Once Mrs Ward's conditions were met, the resources of the State were mobilized to assist her propaganda. She had an interview with the Foreign Secretary, Sir Edward Grey, and she was privileged to tour munitions factories, review the battle fleet, and visit the front in France. Scrutinized by Wellington House, Mrs Ward's 'letters to an American friend' were syndicated in American newspapers in April 1916 and published in book form as *England's Effort* in May–June with separate American and English prefaces written by, respectively, the former American Ambassador in London Joseph Choate and the former Prime Minister Lord Rosebery. Similar arrangements were made for a sequel, *Towards the Goal*, in 1917. By these productions, Mrs Ward gained a renewed literary prominence, which boosted the sales of her war-novel *Missing* (1917). This sold more rapidly than any of her last five years' fiction. It was also the first of her books to which film rights were sold.[113]

Writers were not mere hirelings, however. Where individual conscience and the greater cause combined, well and good; but that this combination was adventitious may be evidenced by the antics of that queer mongrel the Chesterbelloc. Both G. K. Chesterton and Hilaire Belloc had resolutely opposed (as they saw it) the British bully in the Boer War. Since they were dedicated anti-Puritans, this was not because they were attracted by Kruger and his kind. Nor were they pacifists. Chesterton included among his battle honours a punch-up with 'an Imperialist clerk outside the Queen's Hall, and giving and receiving a bloody nose', although he magnanimously allowed that his sacrifice for a cause

---

[112] Flower (ed.), *Bennett Journals*, ii. 106, 109 (9 Oct., 5 Nov. 1914). Cf. the position six months later, if Mrs Belloc Lowndes's diary record is accurate: 'Bennett told me of the vast sums he was making: a hundred pounds for a 1,500 word article in the new Sunday paper. He gets two hundred pounds from American papers for each article he writes of the same length and £3,500 for serial rights of a novel. He has fixed up three serials for £10,000 with an American paper' (Lowndes (ed.), *Lowndes Diaries and Letters*, 60 (24 Mar. 1915)).   [113] Sutherland, *Mrs Ward*, ch. 29.

did not deserve to be ranked with martyrdom in a Roman amphitheatre or at the stake in Smithfield.[114] Chesterton and Belloc were anti-imperialist patriots, and it was more their suspicion of the Stock Exchange than approval of Boerdom that fuelled their dissent. Their anti-Semitism was clumsy: concerning 'the modern Anglo-Judaic plutocracy under which we live' (Belloc's parliamentary speech on the Address in 1910), Chesterton commented, 'their names were symbolic as their noses'. Chesterton and Belloc pursued an unorthodox political line throughout the Edwardian period and after, hammering out their crusading philosophy of 'distributism' against the counter-contentions of Shaw's Fabian Socialism and Arthur Penty's Guild Socialism in the columns of the *New Age*.[115] Though Belloc served as a Liberal MP in 1906–10 and even (grotesquely) believed he might be offered a peerage or place in a new government during the constitutional crisis, he like Chesterton was anti-capitalist as well as anti-socialist.[116] Central to their philosophy was individual independence, for the attainment of spiritual dignity and moral worth; and this they would foster through extensive popular proprietorship. It reflected Catholic social teaching with its mistrust of the giantisms of plutocratic capitalism and revolutionary communism, both of which showed a propensity to manipulate the State apparatus in order to standardize and coerce the mass of people and to extinguish a concern for the individual soul.[117] Belloc inveighed against the bogusness of the party system and mistrusted the emerging welfare state, as a new species of slavery;[118] and, as well as issuing books and articles on these subjects, he participated in public debates, famously against Bernard Shaw.[119] When he stood down as MP in December 1910, he was reported as stating that he had quit parliament 'perhaps because the bribes were not large enough; but probably because he was getting sick of the vilest and dirtiest society in which he had ever mixed in his life'.[120]

The Great War caused Belloc and Chesterton not to renounce past opinions, rather to reorder priorities. Chesterton periodically continued their long-standing quarrel with Shaw's political philosophy; but it was Belloc, recently widowed, who initially made most of the running because Chesterton suffered a nervous breakdown for several months in late 1914 and early 1915. Sales of Belloc's weekly paper *Land and Water* rose over the 100,000 mark, Belloc falling victim to his own propaganda by proving to his own satisfaction that the Central Powers must soon

---

[114] Chesterton, *All Things Considered*, 109. [115] Ward, *Return to Chesterton*, 55–63.

[116] Blunt, *Diaries*, ii. 284–5, 290 (5 Dec. 1909, 23 Jan., 19 Feb. 1910).

[117] Dermot Quinn, 'Distributism as Movement and Ideal', *Chesterton Review* (May 1993), 157–73. I am grateful to Professor Quinn for sending me a copy of his article.

[118] See *The Party System* (1911) written jointly by Belloc and Cecil Chesterton; also Belloc's *The Servile State* (1912) and, 'The Change in Politics', *Fortnightly Review* (Jan. 1911), 33–45; Blunt, *Diaries*, ii. 405 (24 Nov. 1912).

[119] Arnold Bennett attended that at the Queen's Hall, on the connection between private property and servitude; Flower (ed.), *Journals*, ii. 57–8 (28 Jan. 1913).

[120] Quoted in Gardiner, *Pillars of Society*, 314. The subject of the corruption of politicians was sure to animate Belloc whenever raised; Asquith, *Diaries*, 48 (26 June 1915).

collapse from manpower shortages.[121] Soldiers were not so easily convinced. Gilbert Frankau, who, while serving at Loos, Ypres, and the Somme, wrote poetry that was published in *Land and Water*, noted that Hilaire Belloc was 'affectionately known to the front line as "Hilarious Bolux" '.[122] Before his collapse Chesterton had briskly turned out what he called 'my very bellicose essay', *The Barbarism of Berlin* (1914). 'I have always thought that there was in Prussia an evil will,' he explained to Bernard Shaw.[123] Chesterton was disgruntled by the attitude shown to authors by the infighting bureaucracies of the War Office and Foreign Office, yet full of admiration for the wiles of Masterman's department, which distributed his pamphlet throughout Europe, from Sweden to Spain. That Chesterton himself had not changed his spots was bizarrely illustrated by *The Crimes of England* (1915), in which he put paradox into propaganda service by arguing that all the past sins of British imperialism should be attributed to a tendency to imitate Prussian examples. The German Empire, he concluded, was by far the worst development.[124]

Belloc's literary service in the Great War should also be qualified by his pre-war record as prophet when, on almost every question that mattered in international relations and human rights, he was completely wrong. The editor of the *Daily News*, A. G. Gardiner, catalogued Belloc's bombast across a decade, from France to Africa to Spain: 'When the conspiracy against Dreyfus was exposed, his voice rose like a hurricane in defence of the anti-Dreyfusards. When the Congo horrors shocked the world, he braved the storm on behalf of the wretched Leopold. When Ferrer was shot after a secret trial for an offence he did not commit, it was he who justified the shooting.'[125] As for the Balkans policy of the Foreign Secretary, Grey, Belloc predicted in 1911 that it would 'bring about a rapprochement between France and Germany, and the uniting of all Europe against us'.[126] With the same dash, having paid a couple of visits to Germany in 1910–11, he was 'more than ever certain that in the next war the French will beat the Germans'. Yet on the whole, believing 'the French army to be better than the German', Belloc was confident that 'Germany will not dare go to war.'[127] With Armageddon only days away, on 29 July 1914 Belloc insisted that 'Germany is afraid of fighting, being unprepared for war.' The privileged recipient of these breezy confidences, Wilfrid Scawen Blunt, here demurred and instead opined 'that it is Russia that is unprepared, and that the fatal year 1913 having passed by,

---

[121] One enthusiastic reader of *Land and Water* was the poet James Elroy Flecker, who, in the process of dying in a Swiss sanatorium, requested his parents to take out a subscription to the paper for him. Flecker was now very Chestertonian in Christianity and Chesterbellocian in politics. His view of the war was that it was justified by German wickedness and, had he been fit, he would have joined up like his brother Oswald; but he was scornful of the notion that Britain entered the war to fulfil treaty obligations to Belgium: 'The Belgian business served as a useful ultimatum to Germany, who we knew twenty years ago had decided on that route—and a sop to a populace wanting something to drivel about' (letter to his mother, Sept. 1914, in Hodgson, *Flecker*, 218–20).   [122] Frankau, *Self-Portrait*, 222.

[123] Letter, 12 June 1915, in Ward, *Gilbert Keith Chesterton*, 332.

[124] Chesterton, *Autobiography*, chs. v, xi.   [125] Gardiner, *Pillars of Society*, 317.

[126] Blunt, *Diaries*, ii. 343 (19 Mar. 1911).   [127] Ibid. 346 (1 and 6 May 1911).

Kaiser Wilhelm thinks he may try his luck at last, and means to stand his ground with Austria against the Franco-Russian Entente, England being practically negligible just now'. Not that Blunt himself monitored the final collapse into war with pinpoint precision. His perception too was clouded by a fervid anti-imperialism. He did not fear war as a European conflict: that he would almost welcome if it spelled the end of the industrialized society he loathed and did not understand. What he feared was a war that would spread over into the Middle East, Africa, and Asia, and complete that devastation of traditional societies which European imperialism had started. Still, Blunt's judgement was sounder than Belloc's, who, on 31 July, when Belgrade was being bombarded, remained 'convinced that France is stronger than Germany. I [Blunt] am not.' On 1 August Germany declared war on Russia, the French mobilised, and the Italian Government announced its neutrality. Belloc and Blunt dined together on the following night, bringing their differences to a head:

We had another great argument, whether to join in the war or not. Belloc is for it, I against. He looks upon Prussia as a 'nation of atheists', who, if they beat the French, will destroy Christianity, whereas if the French beat them, 'Prussia would be hamstrung'. Russia, he thinks, will never be a danger to Western Europe. If we do not side with France now we shall be left without a friend. England will cease to be a great Power. My view is a very simple one. It seems to me that having no army of any value it would be ridiculous to fight, and would only hasten our discomfiture. Between France and Germany one seems to me as atheistical as the other, and Russia worse than either. England is in no condition to fight any but a naval war, and France does not need us at sea. Grey...will hardly be fool enough now to send a twopenny-halfpenny Army Corps to the Continent where he can effect nothing. No. Asquith will announce neutrality to-morrow, not perhaps a very *beau rôle*, but less absurd than the other.[128]

Nevertheless, Belloc got his war, though hardly as he had imagined it. His eldest son, Louis, was killed shortly before the Armistice.

VIII

The idiosyncratic independence of the writer and, from the authorities' point of view, his unreliability were also demonstrated by Jerome K. Jerome. In his memoirs he related that 'a member of the Cabinet'—Masterman, probably—suggested that he might go to America to assist in British propaganda. On the surface Jerome was an excellent choice. He had made two pre-war tours of America; better still, he knew Germany, having lived there for four years, and during his editorship of *To-day* in 1893 he had 'constantly attacked Kaiser Wilhelm II and warned his readers to beware of his over-weening ambition'.[129] Jerome held no brief for Prussian militarism and would have enlisted at the start of war

[128] Ibid. 429–31 (28, 31 July, 2 Aug. 1914).
[129] See his friend and associate George Burgin's notice in *DNB 1922–1930*, 455.

had his age (then 54) allowed it. However, by 1915, when he embarked for America, he was rethinking his position. The cause was the Atrocity campaign by Wellington House and Fleet Street: 'If I knew and hated the German military machine, so likewise I knew, and could not bring myself to hate, the German people . . . I knew them to be a homely, kind, good-humoured folk . . . This attempt to make them out a nation of fiends seemed to me as silly as it was wicked. It was not clean fighting.'[130] Such scrupulosity rather set Jerome apart. The essayist Charles Whibley was especially robust when arguing about German atrocities with Beb Asquith, who had been wounded in the war and who was a barrister by training: 'When Beb was judiciously trying to disentangle the evidence and be fair, Whibley exclaimed, "But I don't want 'truth'; I'm not looking for Truth—I'm looking for Malice." '[131] It was the involvement of reputable authors in (to his mind) a disreputable campaign that so disturbed Jerome. Douglas Goldring—a conscientious objector by 1916—echoed this dismay about their 'deliberate poisoning of the wells of human feeling, that organised campaign of lying and incitement to hatred', in which 'some of the most influential novelists and imaginative writers have engaged with all the energy and skill at their command . . . Had these men possessed sufficient moral courage they could soon have made the Censorship unworkable.' Instead, the 'national sense of decency' was dulled, the opportunity of achieving 'a clear and democratic settlement' through a negotiated peace was lost, and the country was urged to press on to deliver the 'knock-out blow', which Goldring translated as meaning allowing an 'irresponsible Government to murder millions of poor people by a misuse of the Blockade'.[132]

Such indignation supposed (at worst) malignancy and (at best) gullibility on the part of authors who penned this propaganda. Each no doubt existed but altogether appear less common than their being genuinely moved to outrage by accounts of atrocities committed in the Germans' sweep through Belgium in 1914; and, while their reading may have been rushed and selective, their indictment of the ideologies that they believed to have inspired the German war machine was driven by a sense of mission to save not just their own country but all civilization from its beastliness. William Archer, for one, regarded the war as a 'nightmare' and 'a pain unspeakable'; but 'though war is thus torturing to my temperament as it is abhorrent to my intellect, I have never for a moment dreamt of wishing that my country had made another choice than that which she made in August, 1914—if, indeed, she can be said to have had any choice after Germany had crossed the Belgian frontier'. So he wrote in a twopenny pamphlet, *Colour-Blind*

---

[130] Jerome, *Life and Times*, 213. Cf. Harvey, 'On the Literary Front', *TLS*, 14 Jan. 2005, 12: 'By June 1915, Wellington House had distributed 2.5 million books and pamphlets in seventeen languages, plus editions of the Bryce Report, on German atrocities, in thirty languages.'

[131] Asquith, *Diaries*, 389 (4 Jan. 1918).

[132] Goldring, *Reputations*, 82–4. Goldring thought that the British public and writers so easily slipped into this mode of thinking because they habitually swallowed justifications for atrocities committed under imperial rule. He was writing in 1920, in the shadow of the Amritsar massacre.

Neutrality: An Open Letter to Dr. George Brandes, in 1916. Brandes was the most influential proponent of modernism in European literature in the late nineteenth and early twentieth centuries, author of a six-volume general study as well as of individual treatments of Ibsen and Bjørnson; and he was among the first to signal the importance of Nietzsche. Archer, Britain's leading Ibsenite, saluted Brandes as 'my dear Master';[133] he had also translated Brandes' brother Edvard's social drama *Et Besøg* (1882) as *A Visit* (1892). Now, Archer vehemently dissented from Brandes' appeal to the belligerents to negotiate an armistice. He reminded Brandes of his previous championship of freedom of thought and detestation of political tyranny; and he accused Brandes and his country, Denmark, of adopting not neutrality but colour-blindness, unable to distinguish black from white. For Archer, the issue was clear-cut: Britain was fighting a war of defence. He reviewed the history of the first fourteen years of the new century, including a detailed account of the final thirteen days before 4 August 1914, to demonstrate 'one long record of German menace and aggression'.[134] Atrocities were the natural outcome of a philosophy of ruthless race supremacy: 'May we not remember that . . . your friend Nietzsche (whose "Zarathustra" the cultured German soldier is said to carry in his knapsack) has glorified the ideal of the conquering "blond beast"?'[135] Archer was far from being an automatic Germanophobe; before the war he had extolled the superiority of German theatre. Now, however, 'I find it impossible to reconcile the German spirit of to-day with my memories of Germany and of many German friends. But—again yielding to evidence—I cannot doubt that the spirit of callous brutality is not peculiar to the military forces, but has in some degree permeated the civil population.' Archer thought it would be 'hard—terribly hard—to resume human relations with the German people'.[136]

Archer continued to publish in the same vein. His *501 Gems of German Thought* was issued in 1917, Archer's introduction being dated 6 December 1916. This anthology of quotations from German books, pamphlets, and press amounted to an 'amazing outburst of tribal arrogance, unrestrained and unashamed', not from nobodies but from 'men of world-wide reputation', all exuding 'racial vanity' and a 'craving for aggrandisement'.[137] The most numerous contributions were from a trinity—'Trietschke is the prophet of tribalism, Nietzsche of ruthlessness, Bernhardi of ambition'—though Archer also found space for the Germanized race theorist 'Herr Houston Stewart Chamberlain' because Germans placed such high value on his writings.[138] The old rationalist in Archer could not be stilled, as he 'noted that many of the wildest shrieks of self-glorification and ferocity proceed from clerics and theologians', asserting the Germans' 'special relation to God, the

---

[133] William Archer, *Colour-Blind Neutrality: An Open Letter to Dr. George Brandes* (1916), 52.

[134] Ibid. 19.

[135] Ibid. 34. In *501 Gems of German Thought* (1917), p. xxiv, Archer explained this allusion: 'Gerhart Hauptmann, near the beginning of the war, averred that the cultured German soldier carried *Zarathustra*, along with *Faust* and the Bible, in his knapsack.'   [136] Archer, *Colour-Blind Neutrality*, 36–7.

[137] Archer, *501 Gems*, pp. xvi–xix.   [138] Ibid., pp. xxiv, xxvi.

claims to the status of a Chosen People, and the comparisons, direct and indirect, between Germany and Christ'.[139] *The Pirate's Progress: A Short History of the U-Boat*, a sixpenny paperback published in 1918, rounded off Archer's indictment. Here he recounted how German submarine warfare had degenerated from attacks on the Royal Navy to the sinking of British merchant ships, passenger liners, hospital and relief ships, and neutral vessels—'sufficient to show to what depths of infamy she has been dragged down by a false philosophy playing into the hands of an overweening national egoism', yet another reference to Nietzscheanism. 'It is an appalling picture,' he concluded, 'and one well calculated to give the final touch of bitterness to that loathing of the German idol—War— with which Germany has made it her business to inspire all reasonable men.'[140]

Archer eventually embraced League of Nations ideals; but the principal themes and sentiments he expressed in these wartime tracts were little different from a plethora of polemic produced by prominent British authors during the emergency. Anthony Hope, based in Wellington House itself, which he daily attended (unpaid) as official Literary Adviser, turned out *The New (German) Testament*, exposing General von Bernhardi's doctrines; *Paper Bulwarks*, highlighting the German disregard of pledges to uphold Belgian neutrality; *The Will to Power and the Will to Freedom*, rejecting 'the austere and grim features of Prussian bureaucracy'; and *Militarism—German and British*, contrasting the reasons for the two countries' great navies, the one to ensure food and survival, the other for domination. These and many similar works were designed for American as much as home consumption, very deliberately so in the case of *Great Britain's Blunder*, in which Hope dwelt on Bernhardi's thesis that Britain had 'unhappily and stupidly' missed its chance of backing the South against the North in the American civil war and thus of dismembering the Union and emasculating the power of the republic.[141] Yet, in framing the charge against Germany's cynical abuse of power, Hope did not neglect to set out an alternative ideal. 'The State is a trustee for its citizens', he avowed; and, while it must protect and promote their rights and interests foremost, it should also pay 'due regard to the rights and legitimate interests of other nations. It is to observe not only international law, but international morals—and even international manners. It is to respect the national life and the freedom of its neighbours. Though vigilant in its own cause, it is yet to be a good member of the community of nations.'[142]

Jerome K. Jerome did not perceive the belligerents' positions to be so plainly established at the polar points of a moral scale. Taking his troubled thoughts to America in 1915, he met President Wilson, who stressed America's desire to intervene only as peacemaker, and a group of German businessmen, who assured him that Germany would welcome a peace conference, perhaps in Washington itself. From reactions to his lectures, Jerome gathered that Britain's blockade

---

[139] Archer, *501 Gems*, pp. xvii, xxvii.
[140] William Archer, *The Pirate's Progress:- A Short History of the U-Boat* (1918), pp. vi, 71.
[141] Mallet, *Hope*, 222.   [142] Ibid. 223.

strategy was causing indignation; the only note that uniformly elicited a sympathetic response was any reference he made to a 'just and lasting' peace that must follow the war. All this Jerome dutifully reported home, without effect. He thus looked for an alternative to propaganda work, which in conscience he could no longer pursue. He was accepted by the YMCA as an entertainer to the troops, but a War Office representative refused him a permit for the front because, according to Jerome's laconic account, 'half the British army were making notes for future books'.[143] He was offered work in the Army Clothing Department at Pimlico; instead, by a series of quirks, he became a volunteer driver with the French Ambulance Unit, around Verdun. He endured a long winter, and returned 'cured of any sneaking regard I may have ever had for war'.[144] His final war service, therefore, was to join the peace platform of Ramsay MacDonald, E. D. Morel, Philip Snowden, and others; and he welcomed the Lansdowne Letter in 1917, which called for a negotiated peace. Jerome's loathing of the war and mounting antipathy to the Lloyd George Government had the further consequence of completing his disenchantment with politics. He was born a Radical: his father, a failed colliery owner who moved from Walsall to begin an equally unsuccessful ironmongery business in London's East End, had been a Nonconformist lay preacher and, at his death in 1872, when Jerome was 12, he was president of the Poplar branch of the International Peace Association. By his mid-twenties, Jerome himself was a 'die-hard Tory' from which, he later wrote, he 'passed on naturally to Socialism'. This ignored his Liberal Radical phase. An outspoken critic of the Turks' Armenian atrocities and then of the Boer War, he was certainly a member of the National Liberal Club, recording that dignity in *Who's Who* in 1905; and his biographer states that he was once invited to become a Liberal parliamentary candidate. Jerome joined the Fabian Society in 1907, and Oxford undergraduates made him honorary vice-president of their Labour Club; but after the war he seems to have abjured all party allegiance, reflecting that 'the future of mankind does not depend upon any party, but upon natural laws, shaping us to their ends quite independently of governments and politics'.[145]

IX

Where such as Jerome wavered, it was not to be expected that Rudyard Kipling should be other than ramrod rigid. In 1903 *T.P.'s Weekly* judged that Kipling—'whose name stands for action and magnetism'—appealed predominantly to the martial sort:

Mr. Kipling is not essentially a woman's writer . . . The many women who do appreciate him do so because their minds are more than ordinarily strong and flexible, and they have

---

[143] Jerome, *Life and Times*, 214.   [144] Ibid. 227.
[145] Ibid. 102–3, 149, 209; Joseph Connolly, *Jerome K. Jerome* (1982), 126–7.

the ability to travel beyond themselves into the world and thoughts of the virile, fighting, empire-building man. Such women are increasing in numbers every year.[146]

The *Manchester Guardian* was generally no friend to Kipling, yet it understood the centrality of his voice in the debates of the day; and Methuen's catalogue for November 1900 seized on its declaration that in Kipling 'The Empire has found a singer; it is no depreciation of the songs to say that statesmen may have, one way or other, to take account of them.'[147] During the Boer War, Kipling's 'Absent-Minded Beggar' monologue, appearing in the *Daily Mail*, provided the masthead for a charity that amassed £340,000, including the gift of a 66-acre site for a hospital at Alton in Hampshire. Much of the money was raised from recitals of the verses by stage celebrities such as Maud Tree at the Palace Theatre. All round the country Kipling's appeal was heard. Cecil Roberts recalled as a boy being taken to the Empire Music Hall in Nottingham: 'The curtain rose revealing a portly woman dressed as Britannia, with shield and spear.' Towards the end of her rendering 'she put on a protective gilt mask and covered herself with a shield, and as she sang the final "Pay-pay-pay!" a rain of coins fell on the stage from all over the house. I was given a penny to throw. It was a long way from the gallery to the stage and probably hit someone in the stalls.'[148] Kipling was not particularly proud of the piece, *qua* poetry. He excluded 'The Absent-Minded Beggar' from his collected Boer War verses, *The Five Nations* (1903), remarking 'I would shoot the man who wrote it if it would not be suicide.'[149] Kipling's self-deprecation was otiose when Robert Buchanan was available to chastise him. A generation earlier, in the *Contemporary Review* 1871, Buchanan had reviled Rossetti as the headmaster of 'The Fleshly School of Poetry'; now, in 1899 in the same journal, he lambasted Kipling as 'The Voice of the Hooligan'. For Buchanan, Kipling personified 'the present relapse back to barbarism of our public life'.[150]

Other authors and critics protested against this misrepresentation. Walter Besant ranked Kipling with Scott and Dickens as a spellbinding storyteller; more than that, Kipling was a teacher, and his sense of imperial destiny was complex, not simple. 'What Seeley taught scholars', asserted Besant, 'Kipling has taught the multitude.' The 'White Man's Burden' and the 'Recessional' were not hooligan hymns. Rather they spoke of 'the heavy harness' that weighed on those who sought to administer the Empire justly, and the sin of hubris, which might bring imperial decay, 'one with Nineveh and Tyre'. Both Besant and Edward Dowden expatiated on this quasi-religious, prophetic mood of Kipling's poetry of empire,

---

[146] *T.P.'s Weekly*, 28 Aug. 1903, 395; and ibid., 11 Sept. 1903, 459, for letters from women on the subject. Max Beerbohm, loathing Kipling's parade of virility, naturally supposed that 'Rudyard Kipling' was a woman writer's pseudonym. See also 'P. C., X 36', his Kipling parody, salivating over a police constable's thuggish arrest of Santa Claus for burglary; *Christmas Garland*, 13–20

[147] Advertisement for Kipling's *The Seven Seas* (1896), Methuen's catalogue (Nov. 1900), 13.

[148] Cecil Roberts, *Growing Boy*, 73.

[149] M. van Wyk Smith, *Drummer Hodge: The Poetry of the Anglo-Boer War 1899–1902* (Oxford, 1978), 105.

[150] Robert Buchanan, 'The Voice of the Hooligan', *Contemporary Review* (Dec. 1899), 774–89, in Roger Lancelyn Green (ed.), *Kipling: The Critical Heritage* (1971), 233–49; quotation from p. 236.

with its warnings against mere 'lust of territory or empty pride of power'.[151] This was a proper riposte, but Kipling appeared far too close to Cecil Rhodes; and it was hardly calculated to allay Liberals' suspicion when Besant endorsed what he took to be Kipling's philosophy: that

there are worse evils than war . . . The poisonous weeds that grow rank in times of peace corrupt the national blood; they deaden the sense of honour; they encourage the ruthless company promoter who trades upon the ignorance of the helpless; they lower the standards of honour; they enlarge the slough of indulgence and the unclean life. War does not kill these things, but it may restore the sense of duty, sacrifice, patriotism; it may bring back the nobler ideals . . .[152]

Liberals were unconvinced. In 1911 E. M. Forster read 'with mingled joy and disgust' *A School History of England*, which Kipling and C. R. L. Fletcher had just published:

It's a fine conception, but oh is it necessary to build character on a psychological untruth? In other words to teach the young citizen that he is absolutely unlike the young German or the young Bashahri—that foreigners are envious and treacherous, Englishmen, through some freak of God, never—?[153]

J. K. Stephen had best expressed the Liberals' revulsion in verse in 1891, when he apostrophized Kipling and his supposed sidekick of literary imperialism Rider Haggard, looking forward to the time

> When there stands a muzzled stripling,
> Mute, beside a muzzled bore:
> When the Rudyards cease from kipling
> And the Haggards ride no more.[154]

Kipling could always dish out more than he received. Stephen's stanzas 'I would have given much to have written myself', he wrote admiringly; above all, he was delighted to possess the gift of provoking the very people he most disliked.[155] A mock biography published in 1901 appreciated his extraordinary stature:

KIPLING, RUDYARD, Poet Laureate and Recruiting Sergeant was born all over the world some eighteen years ago. After a lurid infancy at Westward Ho! in the company of Stalky & Co., he emigrated to India at the age of six and swallowed it whole. In the following year the British Empire was placed in his charge, and it is still there. A misgiving that England may have gone too far in the matter of self-esteem having struck him in 1897, he

---

[151] For Dowden's defence, 'The Poetry of Mr. Kipling', *New Liberal Review* (Feb. 1901), see Green (ed.), *Kipling*, 259–68. Dowden was Professor of English at Trinity College, Dublin, and well-known as a critical authority on Shakespeare.

[152] Besant in Green (ed.), *Kipling*, 258. On Besant's enthusiasm for Kipling; Nicoll, *Bookman's Letters*, 150. Besant told Nicoll that no sooner had he read *The Light that Failed* (1891) on a long train journey than he started it again and read it through a second time.

[153] To Malcolm Darling, 29 July 1911, in Lago and Furbank (eds.), *Forster's Letters*, i. 123.

[154] The lines formed part of a parody of Browning, were published in the *Cambridge Review* (Feb. 1891), and were included in Stephen's *Lapsus Calami*, collected posthumously in 1896.

[155] Kipling, *Something of Myself*, 55–6.

wrote 'The Recessional', but there are signs that he has since forgotten it . . . His stories have great popularity, and his poems are in the repertory of every volunteer; but it is by his masterly lyric, 'Pay, pay, pay', that he holds his place in the great heart of the people, who are still paying and seem likely to continue to do so.[156]

The real Kipling was better displayed as the scourge of mountebank patriots such as the 'Jelly-bellied Flag-flapper' who so offends Stalky & Co. with the revelation that 'life was not . . . all marbles'.[157] During the Boer War, Kipling did a tour of duty in South Africa, visiting the front and military hospitals. Indignant about the authorities' incompetence and about Liberal Party equivocations, Kipling celebrated the common soldier—in this, anticipating the trench poets of the Great War. Kipling did not glorify war; rather, he believed that just causes were worth fighting for, and he therefore sung those brave enough to fight them. He had been unflinching in conviction that the suppression of the Boer republics was essential for the good of the Empire and mankind. Eventual victory in that war did not exculpate the nation's leaders from a charge of negligence or absolve them from an obligation to prepare for further tests. 'It's a first-class dress-parade for Armageddon,' says the General in 'The Captive' (1902).[158] Kipling exercised vigilance about the need for moral and military rearmament throughout the Edwardian period, and he supported both the National Service League and the Boy Scout movement. Vaticination was Kipling's trademark as an author. He was able to joke about it in later life, telling the Brazilian Academy of Letters in 1927: 'I am a man of short views. I rarely look beyond two or three hundred years.'[159] During the last decade of the nineteenth century and the first two of the twentieth, Kipling conducted his mission as seer with high seriousness and without impairment of popularity. It was the imperial spirit, not war, that enthused him. Uplifted by the presence of dominion and colonial troops fighting alongside British soldiers in South Africa, he believed that the world also would heed the lesson that 'when one of our community was in distress Canada went to her aid, as Australia went, as New Zealand went, as the Crown colonies went, without one thought of present interests, or politics, or pocket'. Countries of the Empire, Kipling declared, faced five great problems of development—'I prefer to call them Points of Fellowship—Education, Immigration, Transportation, Irrigation, and Administration'—yet through cooperation they would overcome these.[160] Kipling was inspired by a sense of responsibility for this cause. 'I *have*', he confessed simply in Canada in 1907,

done my best for about twenty years to make all the men of the sister nations within the Empire interested in each other . . . And if, through any good fortune, any work of mine

---

[156] Stephen and Lee (eds.), *Lives of the 'Lustrious*, 49.
[157] Rudyard Kipling, *Stalky & Co.* (1962), 182–5.
[158] Kipling, 'The Captive' (1902), in Kipling, *Traffics and Discoveries* (Bombay, 1914), 21.
[159] 'The Spirit of the Latin' (1927), in Rudyard Kipling, *A Book of Words* (1928), 292.
[160] 'Imperial Relations', delivered at the Canadian Club, Toronto, Oct. 1907, ibid. 25–30. See also Richmond, *Twenty-Six Years*, 194, for Kipling's encouragement of a member of Milner's kindergarten.

has helped to make the men all over the world understand each other a little bit—I won't say, understand—to keep them more interested in each other, then great is my reward.[161]

Kipling was a potent name with the public. The sales of his books, released by his principal publisher, Macmillan's, in 1910, showed him approaching the million mark.[162] Most progressives rued that popularity and explained it as a consequence of Kipling's imperial braggadocio, although John Galsworthy was an exception: 'There is to my mind no doubt that his real importance, even his actual position, is more due to his actual power over words and his vision, than to his imperialism . . .'.[163] Come the Great War and Kipling threw himself into making recruiting speeches, promoting military bands, raising funds for soldiers' benefits, and visiting the troops in Picardy and Flanders and in Italy.[164] He also took a close interest in methods of propaganda for the home front; for instance, writing for Lord Beaverbrook at the Ministry of Information in 1918 a memorandum specifically directed at munitions workers in which, characteristically, he showed a keen awareness of the value of films, adding

Almost as important as the cinema is the lecturer who accompanies, and here it seems to me use could be made of the sound non-conformist preacher who has either been at the front or had in his time worked in a factory. The munition workers listen best to a person they consider of their own class. That is why a personally commissioned Government Lecturer *above a certain line of culture* might be regarded with suspicion. Ignorance and suspicion is the trouble which is being exploited.[165]

Kipling had previously waived his royalty on *If*, which was reproduced in tens of thousands as a leaflet or on printed cards for men going off to the front; and the sales generally of his works increased during the war.[166]

---

[161] 'Growth and Responsibility', delivered at the Canadian Club, Winnipeg, Oct. 1907, in Kipling, *Book of Words*, 33–7.

[162]

Jungle Book (1894)	99,000	*Stalky & Co.* (1899)	47,000
Kim (1901)	79,000	*Captains Courageous* (1897)	38,000
The Day's Work (1898)	73,000	*Traffics and Discoveries* (1904)	37,000
Plain Tales from the Hills (1888)	65,000	*Puck of Pook's Hill* (1906)	34,000
The Light that Failed (1891)	64,000	*Actions and Reactions* (1909)	34,000
Just So Stories (1902)	62,000	*Soldiers Three* (1888)	34,000
The Second Jungle Book (1895)	61,000	*Wee Willie Winkie* (1888)	30,000
Life's Handicap (1891)	54,000	*From Sea to Sea* (1899)	22,000
Many Inventions (1893)	51,000	*The Naulahka* (1892)	19,000

(*T.P.'s Weekly*, Nov. 1910, 594). Very probably, Kipling had easily passed the million sales, because this catalogue does not include his books published by Methuen, notably *Departmental Ditties* (1886), *Barrack-Room Ballads* (1892), *The Seven Seas* (1896), and *The Five Nations* (1903). Methuen's catalogue for November 1900, for instance, was advertising *Barrack-Room Ballads* in its 68th thousand, and *The Seven Seas* in its 57th thousand; and in 1908 Methuen published a uniform edition of the poems. For Kipling's relations with this firm, see Duffy, *Methuen*, 5–6, 37. As for the total audience reached by his stories and poetry through magazines and other outlets, that was uncountably huge.

[163] Galsworthy to Garnett, 17 Oct. 1903, in Garnett (ed.), *Galsworthy Letters*, 52.

[164] Birkenhead, *Kipling*, ch. xvii; and *The Times*, 28 Jan. 1915, for Kipling's speech on behalf of the Recruiting Bands Committee.   [165] Harvey, 'On the Literary Front', *TLS*, 14 Jan. 2005, 13.

[166] Nowell-Smith (ed.), *Letters to Macmillan*, 277–9.

Kipling's literary reputation did not rise with his sales, and he failed to convert his pre-war critics. His Great War poetry, according to Douglas Goldring, 'exhibited the bankruptcy of his point of view in several archaic bleats, so feeble in thought and style that a practical joker was easily able to hoax one of the leading newspapers into publishing a burlesque of them'.[167] The odium in which Kipling was held by Liberals had been manifested at the highest levels. During a Cabinet meeting on 14 September 1914 notes flew across the table between the Foreign Secretary, Grey, and the Chancellor of the Duchy of Lancaster, Masterman, who was now in charge of propaganda. Grey was so disturbed by a report that Kipling intended to visit the United States that he threatened resignation unless he was in a position officially to discountenance the visit, which he believed would nullify his efforts to cultivate American goodwill. Grey's preference, indeed, was to acquire powers to lock up Kipling 'as a danger to the state'.[168] Equally unforgiving was the attitude of E. F. Benson, author of the *Dodo* novels which teased 1890s Society. He charged that Kipling had complained during the Boer War when there had been 'no satisfactory killing' for several months. He added nastily that Kipling 'was not likely to be disappointed again', during the Great War.[169] Hun-hatred became personal for Kipling after his son John was killed in the battle of Loos, on 27 September 1915. John had celebrated his seventeenth birthday shortly after the outbreak of war. He was initially rejected as unfit for service because of myopia, a trait he shared with his famous father. Kipling then used his influence with Field Marshal Lord Roberts, with whom he had been associated in the National Service League, to enable John nonetheless to serve. His loss was devastating; for over a year Kipling refused to accept that he was dead rather than wounded and missing.[170] In his addresses to young men about to enlist, Kipling not only reverenced their sense of duty and readiness to sacrifice themselves but also directed their gaze to the post-bellum challenge: 'For then the work will begin of reconstructing, not only England and the Empire, but the whole world— on a scale which outruns imagination.'[171] He also assuaged his private sorrow by undertaking in 1917 the history of his son's regiment, the Irish Guards, and by serving on the Imperial War Graves Commission. It was Kipling's inscription that dignified the headstones over the graves of unidentified remains: 'A soldier of the Great War known unto God'.[172] He was also called upon to polish the letter of sympathy sent by the King and Queen to the families of all who were killed in the war.[173] But the death of his son permanently marked Kipling and no amount of public work could remove the pain. In his desolation Kipling was a figure representative of millions. War subverted the natural order when parents

---

[167] Goldring, *Reputations*, 112.   [168] Masterman, *Masterman*, 277.
[169] E. F. Benson, *As we Are* (1932), 49.
[170] Kipling's correspondence with the authorities is contained among over 216,000 personal files relating to soldiers of the Great War, released by the Public Record Office in 1998; see *The Times*, 3 Feb. 1998.   [171] Address at Winchester College, Dec. 1915, in Kipling, *Book of Words*, 123–7.
[172] Birkenhead, *Kipling*, ch. xvii.   [173] Harvey, 'On the Literary Front', *TLS.*, 14 Jan. 2005, 12.

outlasted children. Literary men and women who suffered that common grief became closer to their readers than perhaps ever before or since.

X

Among the non-combatant literary men who pressed their pens in the patriotic cause, many had been far from content or uncritical about proceedings. Given H. G. Wells's bumptiousness, it is no shock to discover that he held individual views about politics and strategy. In his novel *The New Machiavelli* (1911), as well as in formal statements of his scientific credo, he had indicted the 'muddle' of laissez-faire individualism that engendered such inefficiencies on all sides: overseas in the incompetent prosecution of the Boer War, and pervasive at home in the planless mess of Britain's urban industrialization that was so inimical to healthy living. This lambasting style did not make Wells any less of a patriot. A story of his had happily sat companion during the Boer War with others by Kipling, Walter Besant, S. R. Crockett, A. E. W. Mason, Max Pemberton, and Mrs B. M. Croker, in a collection edited by C. J. Cutcliffe Hyne and entitled *For Britain's Soldiers*, the proceeds of which went to the War Fund.[174] It was Wells who in 1914 coined the phrase about 'The War that will end War';[175] but historians should not place a more utopian gloss on this than Wells originally intended. It is true that his radicalism made him urge comprehensive political and social reform and that his idealism eventually drew him towards a League of Nations system; but Wells's League of Nations would have initially excluded Germany from membership.[176] Wells's first inclination in 1914 had not been to canvass for the banishment of war for ever, rather for the extermination of German militarism, as the means of ridding the world of nationalism. The methods he advocated were only nominally consistent with the British liberal tradition of voluntarism; in effect, he demanded the mobilization of all subjects in total war. At the outset of war he had articulated his furious plan in a letter to *The Times*, calling 'for the enrolment of all that surplus of manhood and patriotic feeling which remains after every man available for systematic military operations has been taken'. His 'idea was that comparatively undrilled boys and older men, not sound enough for campaigning, armed with rifles, able to shoot straight with them, and using local means of transport, bicycles, cars, and so forth, would be a quite effective check upon an enemy's scouting, a danger to his supplies, and even a force capable of holding up a raiding advance'. Wells believed that 'the mere enrolment and arming of the population would have a powerful educational effect in steadying and unifying the spirit of our people'; and he had been dismayed when his

---

[174] The publisher was Methuen; see Methuen's catalogue (Nov. 1900), 8.

[175] In an article, then published as a pamphlet, in September 1914. *Punch*'s editor, Sir Owen Seaman, coined a similar phrase, 'a war against war', in August; Thwaite, *Milne*, 162–3.

[176] For an account of the row caused by Wells at the annual meeting of the League of Nations Society, see Bell (ed.), *Woolf Diary*, 157 (17 June 1918).

'proposals were received with what seemed even a forced amusement by the "experts"'. But he was only momentarily knocked off his stride, and on 31 October 1914, he returned to the subject with renewed vigour:

In the first place, let the expert have no illusions as to what we ordinary people are going to do if we find German soldiers in England one morning. We are going to fight. If we cannot fight with rifles, we shall fight with shot guns, and if we cannot fight according to Rules of War we will fight according to our inner light.

Many men, and not a few women, will turn out to shoot Germans . . . If the experts attempt any pedantic interference, we will shoot the experts. And if the raiders . . . are so badly advised as to try terror-striking reprisals on the Belgian pattern, we irregulars will, of course, massacre every German straggler we can put a gun to. We shall hang the officers and shoot the men. A German raid to England will in fact not be fought—it will be lynched.[177]

Summarized with some sarcasm by Douglas Goldring, Wells's plan amounted to 'urging all the middle-aged gentlemen living in the country to clean their rook-rifles so that, when the Hun invaded, they might lurk behind hedges and bag at least a victim apiece before their women were raped'. Moreover, Wells appeared to have overlooked a catch; namely, that, 'according to those laws of warfare which we observed so faithfully in South Africa [during the Boer War], such a proceeding would have justified the Germans in burning every village they entered'.[178] Arnold Bennett also thought Wells's idea absurd. When serving as military representative on the Thorpe Division Emergency Committee to make preparations against an invasion in Essex, Bennett found that the area commander, Major-General H. N. C. Heath, was keen to ascertain where he stood on the Wells line.[179] Within the War Office, attitudes continued to be scornful. Edward Heron-Allen, seconded to its propaganda section for his linguistic ability, in 1918 groaned: 'We have been suffering in our department from the interference and cock-sureness of H. G. Wells, who is—or thinks himself—a "Sir Oracle" in all matters concerning the psychology of the war.'[180] Wells indeed was then still banging his drum, firing off a 'Memorandum on the General Principles of Propaganda' to Lord Beaverbrook at his new Ministry of Information, in which he boomed that Germany must be compelled to choose between Peace and 'Judgement and Death'. This message should be driven home, 'over and over again, in various forms, to German women, to German sentimentalists, to civilized and reasonable Germans, to fearful Germans'.[181] At the new Department of Enemy Propaganda at Crewe House, presided over by Lord Northcliffe, Wells was included in its advisory committee, which debated overall policy, and in May 1918

---

[177] Letter in *The Times*, 31 Oct. 1914.   [178] Goldring, *Reputations*, 90.
[179] Flower (ed.), Bennett, *Journals*, ii. 111, 117 (16 Nov., 12 Dec. 1914). Bennett in any case believed that 'the chance of an invasion was nil'. See also his letters to *The Times* and *East Anglia Daily Times*, 3 Dec. 1914, in Hepburn (ed.), *Bennett Letters*, i. 216–17.
[180] Harvey and Fitzgerald (ed.), *Allen's Journal*, 201 (20 July 1918).
[181] Harvey, 'On the Literary Front', *TLS*, 14 Jan. 2005, 13.

he had been made head of its anti-German branch. It could not last. On 17 July he resigned, having fallen out with Northcliffe's line. That Germany must suffer total defeat was the cardinal objective they both shared, but Wells was now wanting to give more emphasis to the need to effect a transformation and reformation of Germany and to the creation of 'a practical League of Free Nations . . . to assure the freedom of all on a basis of self-determination to be exercised under definite guarantees of justice and fair play'.[182] This naturally created consternation in the Foreign Office and in government circles generally, that maverick propagandists like Wells were seeking to determine war aims and to shape post-war foreign policy.

From the start of the war Wells had not required persuasion to place patriotic articles in the press. He was not designed by nature to be patient. In May 1915 he was telling Bennett that 'he knew that French [Sir John, then commanding British forces] believed the war would be over in June'; unfazed, in December 1916 he 'offered to bet 2 to 1 that the war would be over by August next'.[183] Wells threw off sparks in all directions. From another letter of his to *The Times*, in June 1916, originated the fashion of decreeing Thursdays to be a meatless day.[184] Wells even discovered God in a quaintly English kind of revelation, *Mr. Britling Sees it Through*. This sold out thirteen printings between publication in October and Christmas 1916.[185] Its popularity with the troops was guaranteed once it was known that Wells had described them as 'stupidly led';[186] but its principal theme lay elsewhere. The eponymous Britling, a previously lax sort of liberal humanist, is rocked when war discloses the force of evil in the world. He gradually reviews his easy assumptions about democratic progress along the path of reason and goodness. His views on the enemy vacillate. After Zeppelin bombs kill his aunt, he mentally composes an 'Anatomy of Hate' before exclaiming of the German airmen, 'Father, forgive them, for they know not what they do.' And his own son's death is followed by news of the death of his German tutor, whereupon he writes to his tutor's parents from 'England bereaved to Germany bereaved'. The God he comes to believe in is one of personal suffering.

The sculptress Kathleen Bruce, widow of the Arctic explorer Captain Scott, found an otherwise tedious dinner party in 1916 become absorbing when she 'talked for an hour to H. G. Wells about God'.[187] Not that she herself was persuaded to start believing in 'a personal God' or in life after death, and she

---

[182] Saunders and Taylor, *British Propaganda*, 91–2, 235–8.

[183] Flower (ed.) *Bennett Journals*, ii. 130, 179 (13 May 1915, 7 Dec. 1916).

[184] Flower, *Just as it Happened*, 171–2.

[185] Lovat Dickson, *H. G. Wells* (Harmondsworth, 1972), 310. R. D. Blumenfeld, a neighbour of Wells in Essex, recorded several accounts of the making of *Mr. Britling*; Blumenfeld, *All in a Lifetime*, 70, 83–4, 92, 173–8, 188–9. Wells told his publisher at Cassell's that he had written *Mr. Britling* in late 1914-early 1915, thinking the war would be over by the end of 1915; Flower, *Just as it Happened*, 170.

[186] Paul Fussell, *The Great War and Modern Memory* (Oxford, 1977), 164.

[187] Kennet, *Self-Portrait*, 144 (June 1916).

became positively scornful when she read Wells's *God the Invisible King* in 1917;[188] but the prospect of Wells's 'conversion' or, at least, his publicist's power being linked to the evangel, had excited the Church establishment. The Regius Professor of Divinity at Oxford, Henry Scott Holland, wrote to Mrs Drew, daughter of the former Prime Minister Gladstone, on 31 October 1916: 'About Britling. Everything sounds thrilling. But I have clamoured in vain to the library to send it to me. So I have not yet read it. Gore showed me the noble ending. I should *love* it. There is nothing like Wells, when he is at his best.'[189] Sermons on *Britling* were preached from pulpits but, as usual, no sooner had Wells raised expectations than he dashed them. In 1917 the same Charles Gore, Bishop of Oxford, who had so enthused about *Britling* felt obliged to mount a defence of the Church of England's ministrations and message, in order to rebut the ridicule that Wells in his latest pronouncement was heaping on it.[190]

By offending the Churches, Wells finally appeared to have his finger on the popular pulse. According to E. F. Benson—whose father had been Archbishop of Canterbury—the indifferentism towards religion that had risen as a tidal wave in the late nineteenth century was now superseded among many serving soldiers by a more open hostility. Christianity could not be patched up any longer. It was impossible to reconcile with daily horrors. As a guide to life and a consolation in death, the Christian tradition appeared near exhaustion. Many young men concluded that they 'had a bone to pick with God'.[191] This was extreme. It might not have been orthodox Christianity that was practised at the front, but men under fire still summoned the supernatural to protect them, be it by pressing the Bible to their chests and praying to some Deity or by wearing amulets and following superstitious rituals. Yet Church leaders were also lumped with the politicians and generals who, by sermon or speech, all spouted bull. These were 'They':

> The Bishop tells us: 'When the boys come back
> They will not be the same; for they'll have fought
> In a just cause: they lead the last attack
> On Anti-Christ; their comrades' blood has bought
> New right to breed an honourable race,
> They have challenged Death and dared him face to face.'
>
> 'We're none of us the same!' the boys reply.
> 'For George lost both his legs; and Bill's stone blind;
> Poor Jim's shot through the lungs and like to die;
> And Bert's gone syphilitic: you'll not find
> A chap who's served that hasn't found some change.'
> And the Bishop said: 'The ways of God are strange!'[192]

---

[188] Kennet, *Self-Portrait*, 155 (20 May 1917).   [189] Ollard (ed.), *A Forty Years' Friendship*, 233.

[190] G. L. Prestige, *The Life of Charles Gore: A Great Englishman* (1935), 406.

[191] Benson, *As we Are*, 63–7.

[192] Sassoon's poem 'They', in Dennis Silk, *Siegfried Sassoon and the Great War: The Making of a Poet* (1998) 17–18.

When the popular novelist George A. Birmingham (the Revd J. O. Hannay) arrived as army chaplain at a troop camp in Boulogne, he was told, 'We want no bloody parsons here.'[193]

Not that Wells's 'new hocus-pocus' satisfied inveterate opponents of religion. Again, there was a sense of betrayal in the air: William Archer had assumed that Wells stood alongside him and the Rationalist Press Association. The best defence Archer could now make for his friend was that in *God the Invisible King* Wells deluded himself into thinking he was serving humanity and striving for social betterment by it, hoping that a new world order would arise 'if only some malignant spell could be lifted from the spirit of man...He foresees that Christianity will come bankrupt out of the War, and yet that the huge, shattering experience will throw the minds of men open to spiritual influences'. Panicked by this prospect, Wells had simply given a new 'glow of supernaturalism, of the worship of a personal God, to the good old Religion of Humanity'.[194] By unhappy irony, Archer's own rationalist confidence shortly afterwards disintegrated when his only son was killed in 1918; and Archer himself turned to spiritualism to fill the emotional void.

XI

By 1917 the war appeared a very different sort of thing, compared with that to which almost universal support had been committed in 1914. No institution escaped upheaval meanwhile. Within Whitehall the intrusions by writers naturally made hackles rise. This, and wartime politics, account for various movements in and out of favour. Charles Masterman, who had recruited authors in the first place, was one such casualty. He was forced out of the Cabinet in February 1915, having for the past year been without a parliamentary seat and exhausted the Prime Minister's patience, Asquith considering him 'quite clever but strangely unattractive'. Still, with the connivance of his Foreign Secretary, Grey, Asquith arranged to 'find him out of Secret Service a salary to go on supervising American & other press work'.[195] Wellington House, Masterman's organization, was progressively disciplined, eventually subsumed within a new Department of Information in February 1917, though Masterman kept his place as manager of its Literary Branch, still supported by Anthony Hope. The Director of the

---

[193] Brook, *Writers' Gallery*, 23. For a more sympathetic and rounded assessment, Alan Wilkinson, *The Church of England and the First World War* (1978). George Lyttelton recalled that of all the countless sermons he heard at Eton the best was from George Birmingham: Hart-Davis (ed.), *Lyttelton Hart-Davis Letters*, 81 (15 Feb. 1956).

[194] William Archer, *God and Mr. Wells: A Critical Examination of 'God the Invisible King'* (1917), 96–7.

[195] M. G. and Eleanor Brock (eds.), *H. H. Asquith: Letters to Venetia Stanley* (Oxford, 1982), 341, 398–9. Cf. John Buchan's 'tribute to one of the most brilliant, misunderstood, and tragically fated men of our time. Charles Masterman began by being overestimated, or rather estimated on the wrong lines, and he ended by being most unjustly decried...When we worked together during the War I found his judgment shrewd and bold and his mastery of detail impeccable' (Buchan, *Memory*, 170–1).

Department of Information was John Buchan, whose thriller *The Thirty-Nine Steps* came out in October 1915 and sold 25,000 by that year's end. Blackwood's had published it in a one-shilling edition, on which he received 12 ½ per cent royalty; these high-flying sales enabled him then to screw a 30 per cent royalty out of Hodder & Stoughton, which issued *Greenmantle* in a six-shilling edition in November 1916. This also took off, and 34,000 copies were bought by March 1917. Both stories had been serialized in magazines before book publication; there were American and overseas sales in addition, and by 1919 his annual income from writing was £4,000–5,000.[196]

Buchan's rise to popularity on the back of these stories was sudden, therefore. He had not qualified for invitation to Masterman's inaugural conference of supposed important and influential authors on 2 September 1914, yet here he was, some two and a half years later, sitting on top of the tree, directing government propaganda. How had he done that? He was talented, of course; and as a director of Nelson's, he had extensive knowledge of and contacts in the world of publishing. From February 1915 the *Nelson History of the War* appeared in instalments, largely penned by Buchan and with a preface by the former Prime Minister Rosebery. This sold hugely and its profits benefited war charities and the families of Nelson's employees who had joined up: it also brought invitations for Buchan to present lectures on the war and in May 1915 for him to cover the second battle of Ypres as correspondent for *The Times*. By October he was a lieutenant in the Intelligence Corps and during the course of 1916 he speedily gained further promotions to major and lieutenant-colonel as he compiled communiqués from GHQ on the Western Front for the Foreign and War Offices and digests for use by the press and Wellington House. An offshoot of this was *The Battle of the Somme: First Phase*, issued in November 1916, principally for deployment on the Continent, where it was translated into Danish, Dutch, Spanish, and Swedish. Buchan further advised on propaganda in eastern Europe, for Romania and Russia. In all this Buchan's path was smoothed by social connections with the political and military establishment. His father-in-law was first cousin to the Duke of Westminster; Field Marshal Haig was a Brasenose man like Buchan himself; and he had long known top brass such as Sir Henry Wilson, Sir John French, and General Byng, the last since South Africa, where Buchan as a member of the High Commissioner Milner's staff during the Boer War had been placed in charge of land settlement.

Lloyd George's ousting of Asquith as Prime Minister in December 1916 was the prelude to a shake-up of the propaganda drive, in common with the war effort generally. He straight away commissioned the editor of the *Daily Chronicle*, Robert Donald, who criticized deficiencies and want of coordination.[197] The directorship of the resultant new Department of Information was first offered to others, including several MPs;[198] but Buchan's champions were led by Curzon

---

[196] Smith, *Buchan*, 293–7.   [197] H. A. Taylor, *Robert Donald* (1934), 154–6.
[198] Saunders and Taylor, *British Propaganda*, 59–63.

and Milner, respectively Lord President and Minister without Portfolio in Lloyd George's War Cabinet, and by Leo Amery, political secretary to the War Cabinet, who had originally recommended Buchan to Milner in South Africa. Amery was struck by Buchan's acuity and facility, thinking his articles in *The Times* in 1915 'excellent': 'He is a born journalist in the very best sense of the word—he can sense a situation quickly and can with the minimum of effort make a vivid story out of it.'[199] Now, in January 1917, Amery was invited to address the Cabinet on the merits of Buchan, 'whereupon I delivered an eloquent oration which Lloyd George told me afterwards had impressed him considerably'.[201].

Buchan's appointment, at a handsome £1,000 a year, represented a pay cut from what he had been getting from Nelson's.[201] In other respects too he suffered. His youngest brother, Alastair, was killed at Arras on Easter Monday 1917; he was plagued by an ulcer; and his department drew persistent sniping from inside and outside the Government. Some of it was just, much of it not, and in part the result of Buchan having risen too high too fast. Military men were always sensitive about rank and did not like theirs being handed out as bon-bons. Buchan was now ensconced as lieutenant-colonel; it was thus easier to keep down an author such as John Masefield who, as temporary second lieutenant, wanted promotion in order to strut about the United States in uniform during a propaganda tour there. From the War Office came the chilly response that 'he had far better stand on his own well known literary merits than seek to pose as a military man which he is not & which he will soon prove. America is full of titular Colonels and Captains who are native to the soil, & I hardly think that it is desirable to add to their number by manufacturing them for lecturing purposes.'[202] Buchan's department's requests for release of information met characteristic obstruction from the service ministries and equally practised obtuseness from the Foreign Office, though Buchan's press critics painted him as a Foreign Office creature. Nor were belligerent sections of the press happy about Buchan's scrupulousness when in May 1917 his department would not exploit an atrocity rumour reported in *The Times* about a German factory for boiling down human body parts. A Propaganda Committee was then appointed by Lloyd George 'to control Buchan and his whole rather extensive department of war propaganda in neutral, allied and enemy countries'. So wrote the editor of the *Manchester Guardian*, C. P. Scott, in his diary in June, after its second meeting comprising 'Lord Northcliffe [of *The Times*] (in his absence in America, Lord Beaverbrook [of the *Daily Express*]), Lord Burnham [of the *Daily Telegraph*], Donald of the "Chronicle" and myself'.[203] Buchan considered this superintendence by

---

[199] Barnes and Nicholson (eds.), *Amery Diaries*, i. 117 (7 June 1915).

[200] Ibid. 140 (26 Jan. 1917). This diary entry notes that Lloyd George beforehand had thought that 'Buchan was too purely a literary man' and, though converted by Amery, still felt obliged to consider Ramsay Muir, first Professor of Modern History at Manchester, whose claims were being pressed by the Labour Party's representative in the War Cabinet, Arthur Henderson.

[201] Smith, *Buchan*, 200, 206.   [202] Harvey, 'On the Literary Front', *TLS*, 14 Jan. 2005, 12.

[203] Wilson (ed.), *C. P. Scott Diaries*, 293 (21 June 1917).

13 July 1918, drew a dismissive response from the authorities, a letter from the Deputy Director of Military Intelligence, Brigadier-General George Cockerill, telling readers of that journal that Sassoon's poetry demonstrated that 'his mind is still in chaos and that he is not fit to be trusted with men's lives'.[211]

Sassoon's was the most memorable protest, but doubts about the probity of the Allied cause and German war-guilt were voiced openly in liberal intellectual circles in Cambridge and Bloomsbury, among whom John Masefield singled out 'Goldie and those other eunuchs [who] with their messy points of view simply make me sick'.[212] This was a reference to the pacifist Goldsworthy Lowes Dickinson, a humanist and political scientist, homosexual and boot fetishist. Before the war Cambridge undergraduates, when in their cups, liked to yell at him across the quad, 'Dirty Dick' and 'That's the Don who goes in for Free Love.'[213] Masefield's abuse was in the same vein, on the base assumption that sexual deviancy, being pernicious and unmanly, must naturally make for traitors. There was much more accomplishment, and courage in the face of public hostility, about Lowes Dickinson, Lytton Strachey, and their circle than Masefield allowed, although their promotion of League of Nations ideology and pacifism was often combined with pitiless social observation. Virginia Woolf was one of the worst offenders. Her periodic descents into insanity did not make her more sympathetic towards the permanently afflicted, such as the 'long line of imbeciles' whom she met shuffling along the Thames towpath outside Richmond in 1915: 'They should certainly be killed.'[214] A eugenics programme fitted snugly into a social philosophy which held that 'the poor have no chance; no manners or self control to protect themselves with; we have a monopoly of all the generous feelings—(I dare say this isn't quite true; but there's some meaning [in] it. Poverty degrades, as Gissing said)'.[215] When her brother Adrian Stephen reported 'how it positively frightened him to see peoples' faces on the Heath "like gorillas, like orang-outangs—perfectly inhuman—frightful" & he poked his mouth out like an ape', she was encouraged to reflect how the greater intermingling of social classes during the war was highlighting their differences: 'Perhaps the horrible sense of community which the war produces, as we all sat in a third class railway carriage together, draws one's attention to the animal human being more closely.'[216]

Bernard Shaw was also in the anti-war camp; indeed his *Common Sense about the War* (1914) was one of the most exaggerated defiances. In it he equated British and German militarism and accused Britain's warmongers of cynically exploiting the plight of 'little Belgium'. As a check against any repetition of this, he advocated 'open diplomacy'; for the present, he invited troops everywhere to shoot their

---

[211] Quoted in *Sunday Times*, 11 Jan. 1998, on the release after eighty years of government documents relating to the Sassoon case among 216,000 other personal service records. See also *The Times*, 3 Feb. 1998.
[212] Smith, *Masefield*, 128.
[213] Newsome, *On the Edge of Paradise*, 246; and ibid. 335 for Benson's revulsion at the abuse directed against Lowes Dickinson during the war: 'so undeserved by one who has always sought for peace and beauty'.   [214] Bell (ed.), *Woolf Diaries*, 13 (9 Jan. 1915).
[215] Ibid. 91 (13 Dec. 1917).   [216] Ibid. 153 (7 June 1918). Cf. ibid. 199 (7 Oct. 1918).

officers and return home. Arnold Bennett, normally tolerant of Shaw's standard mix of insights and barminess, calculated the 'unusual percentage' here of 'perverseness, waywardness, and harlequinading'; and, reckoning it 'may do some harm', instantly countered it by 'The Nonsense about Belgium', an article that appeared simultaneously in the *Daily News* and *New York Times*. He placed such importance on its appearing quickly in the United States that he instructed his agent Pinker not to fuss 'whether I am paid for it'.[217] Bennett's reaction was almost equable compared to Henry James, who exclaimed that he 'made several attempts' to read Shaw's broadside, 'but his horrible flippancy revolts me. To think of a man deliberately descending into the arena at the present crisis and playing the clown!'[218] James's Liberal sympathies had become more ardent with age, and it was his loathing of the Central Powers' aggression that provided the final spur to his application for British nationality in 1915 as a symbolic commitment to the survival of the values he most cherished. John Bailey had visited James in October 1914 and recorded this in his diary: 'He is passionately English and says it is almost good that we were so little prepared, as it makes our moral position so splendid. He almost wept as he spoke.'[219]

As the war developed, Shaw's position wavered. He did not oppose conscription and he began to believe that Germany should be beaten. Still, his initial stand, and his continued declarations that war and Britain's part in it represented a failure of civilization, arrested his previously rising literary reputation. Drafting Sir Roger Casement's defence speech against the charge of high treason in 1916 hardly improved matters. Newspapers turned down Shaw's essays and epistles; his plays were little staged; his books went unsold in shops and unread in libraries; an attack by his erstwhile friend Henry Arthur Jones compelled his resignation from the Dramatists' Club; and he withdrew from the management committees of both the *New Statesman* and the Society of Authors.[220] Shaw could put up with this obloquy, however wounding. Less bearable was to be ranked with the trivial or judged irrelevant amid world-shattering events, such as B. F. Cummings contemptuously observed in his journal in 1916: 'Mr. Shaw and his Scintillations . . . revolving like haggard windmills in a devastated landscape!'[221] Shaw's continued gyrations took the form of pamphlets, not plays. Though he started on *Heartbreak House*, he issued no new dramatic work during the war. Afterwards he explained that abstention:

Why, it may be asked, did I not write two plays about the war instead of two pamphlets on it? The answer is significant. You cannot make war on war and on your neighbour at the same time. War cannot bear the terrible castigation of comedy, the ruthless light of

[217] To J. B. Pinker, 15 Nov. 1914, in Hepburn (ed.), *Bennett Letters*, i. 215.
[218] Reported by Bennett to Pinker, 2 Dec. 1914, ibid. 217. See also the vituperative verses addressed 'To Mr. Bernard Jaw', *Punch*, 25 Nov. 1914, 430, and 2 Dec. 1914, 458.
[219] Bailey (ed.), *Bailey Letters and Diaries*, 152 (11 Oct. 1914).
[220] Michael Holroyd, *Bernard Shaw: The Pursuit of Power* (1989); also Ervine, *Shaw* 461–71.
[221] Barbellion [B. F. Cummings], *Journal of a Disappointed Man*, 287.

laughter that glares on the stage. When men are heroically dying for their country, it is not the time to shew their lovers and wives and fathers and mothers how they are being sacrificed to the blunders of boobies, the cupidity of capitalists, the ambition of conquerors, the electioneering of demagogues, the Pharisaism of patriots, the lusts and lies and rancours and bloodthirsts that love war because it opens their prison doors, and sets them in the thrones of power and popularity . . . And though there may be better things to reveal, it may not, and indeed cannot, be militarily expedient to reveal them whilst the issue is still in the balance.[222]

It was thus no ordinary war that was capable of making Shaw, however fleetingly, see things in perspective.

[222] Preface to *Heartbreak House* (1919), in G. B Shaw, *Prefaces* (1934), 397.

27

Pricking Censorship

Just now authors, an interesting class, are displaying a great deal of uneasiness about their goods: whether they are to be in one volume or in three, how the profits (if any) are to be divided, what their books should be about, and how far the laws of decency should be observed in their construction.

(Augustine Birrell, 1898, in *Self-Selected Essays*)

If I had to begin again . . . I believe I should try to honour Sex more religiously. The worst of our education is that Christianity does not recognize and hallow Sex . . . Well, it is so; I cannot be wiser than my generation.

(Robert Louis Stevenson, 1894, in Margaret Mackay, *The Violent Friend*)

One great folly of modern culture, typically English, is the veil which has been cast over the natural functions of man. The scroll *decency forbids* is placarded not only on stray walls and corners, but on the very soul of Englishmen, so that numbers of harmless, necessary acts have acquired a tone which is almost pornographic.

(Somerset Maugham, 1902, in *A Writer's Notebook*)

I am not surprised at the veto of the Censor. I always feel that there is in the world, especially the English world, a sort of crusade against everything that is real or true; a hushing up, an insincerity & boggling about quite harmless things.

(Mrs Bontine to Edward Garnett, 1904)

I am not at all sure that the reign of narrowness in dogma is over as you seem to assume; if it does not exist in an Evangelical direction it goes on in others—in that of conventional morality for instance, where artificial, clumsy, & ineffectual laws are regarded as sacred.

(Thomas Hardy to Edmund Gosse, 3 Nov. 1907)

Apropos of the agitation for abolishing the Censor in England, it occurred to me that not even the advocates of freedom seek to justify the free treatment of sexual matters in any other than a high moral-pointing vein. The notion that sexual themes might allowably be treated in the mere aim of amusement does not seem to have occurred to anybody at all.

(Arnold Bennett, *Journals*, ed. Newman Flower, 31 Oct. 1907)

I

The sex gospel as a means of human fulfilment, still less as a device for titillation and entertainment, could not be preached with impunity. *Sons and Lovers* (1913) first presented D. H. Lawrence's case for frankness about the Oedipal frustrations of a claustrophobic working-class family. This, even in its bowdlerized published form, was banned by libraries;[1] *The Rainbow* (1915) was prosecuted as an obscene publication and withdrawn from circulation until 1926; and *Women in Love*, completed in 1916, was not published in England until 1921. In the year before the Great War, Lawrence earned £450; by 1917–18, as an outlaw, he was reduced to a quarter of that and supporters were appealing on his behalf to the Royal Literary Fund for alms. Yet several such supporters shared the common aversion. Charles Whibley told Lady Cynthia Asquith in March 1918 that he remained 'against publication of *Women in Love* and, though 'he could probably get him £100 from the Literary Fund . . . he thought there should in that case be a tacit understanding that he should write something—and that, not inevitably censorable'.[2]

This was easier said than done. Only a few months before, Lawrence told Lady Cynthia that 'all the money he has in the world is the *prospect* of eighteen pounds for the publication of some poems all about bellies and breasts'.[3] Even other authors who were leading irregular lives tended to think Lawrence excessive in his focus. Katherine Mansfield, who with her lover, John Middleton Murry, cohabited in bruising proximity to the Lawrences during a part of the Great War, found this sex fixation of Lawrence repellent. It led to a rare agreement with Lawrence's wife, Frieda, when Mansfield proposed that Lawrence ought to rename his house The Phallus.[4] Ironically, Murry (like Lawrence, medically unfit for military service) ended the war as Chief Censor, though in regard to political intelligence for the War Office, not the nation's literary morals. To later tastes, until *Lady Chatterley's Lover* (1928), Lawrence's published writing was not pornographic in language or incident; but the contemporary verdict was otherwise. It seemed to *The Times*'s obituarist of Lawrence in 1930 inevitable that he should have come into conflict with the law—'He confused decency with hypocrisy, and honesty with the free and public use of vulgar words.'[5] Sexuality in the lives of his characters was plainly addressed. In the first chapter of *The Rainbow* the reader is told of Tom Brangwen's visit to a prostitute and how 'He was tormented with sex desire, his imagination reverted always to lustful scenes.' Lady Cynthia found

---

[1] The editing for publication by Duckworth was done by Edward Garnett, who excised about 100 pages. Lawrence was so desperate for the £100 advance that he not only submitted to the cuts but dedicated the book to Garnett. The restored version, with annotations by Helen and Carl Baron, was published by Cambridge University Press in 1992.

[2] Asquith, *Diaries*, 418 (6 Mar. 1918). Reading the manuscript of *Women in Love*, Lady Cynthia was shocked by its 'nightmarish', 'fantastic', 'unpleasant', and 'morbid' qualities: 'Surely he is delirious—a man whose temperature is 103?' (ibid. 424 (24 Mar. 1918)).   [3] Ibid. 356 (16 Oct. 1917).

[4] Lea, *Murry*, 52.   [5] *The Times*, 4 Mar. 1930.

The Rainbow a 'strange, bewildering, disturbing book. It is full of his obsessions about sex conflict (all the lovers hate one another) and the "amorphousness" of actual life. Excellent bits of writing, but still too much over-emphasis and brutality. One cannot count how often and how gratuitously he employs the word "belly".'[6] This sort of thing, and the complications subsequently resulting from Ursula Brangwen's awakening sexual consciousness, were unacceptably strong for the Public Morality Council, which indicted the book as 'a mass of obscenity of thought, idea and action throughout'.[7]

By contrast, the suffragist Helena Swanwick, who reviewed *The Rainbow* for the *Manchester Guardian*, 'praised many of the qualities of the book very highly and only protested mildly at the boring obsession of sex'. She agreed with a theory propounded by her husband, a mathematician at Manchester University, that the expression of a lust for domination becomes 'more shrill as the physical means of domination decline', and that there was 'immensely magnified... in him [Lawrence] what lies hidden in the hearts of many weak men'. Still, she had been surprised when the police suppressed *The Rainbow*.[8] As for Douglas Goldring, he was more disgusted by the spineless response of the London literary claque who previously, on the publication of *The White Peacock* (1911), proclaimed Lawrence's genius and nominated him 'the white hope of English letters':

Not one of Mr Lawrence's fervent boosters ventured into print to defend him; not one of his brother authors (save only Mr Arnold Bennett, to whom all honour is due) took up the cudgels on his behalf. English novelists are proverbially lacking in *esprit de corps*, but surely they were never so badly shown up as when they tolerated this persecution of a distinguished confrère without making a collective protest. But our intelligentsia has always been more fickle and cowardly than the man in the street whom it so dearly loves to deride.[9]

II

Whether Robertson Nicoll merited classification as a member of the intelligentsia Goldring and others might dispute, but the name of this prolific literary critic, periodical editor, and publishers' reader was one that carried weight with sections of the public, particularly Nonconformists. Nicoll, who now boasted a knighthood, had treated readers of the *Daily Express* to his views in 1913. He opened up

---

[6] Asquith, *Diaries*, 86 (11 Oct. 1915). On 18 October she recorded how 'The Rainbow is causing an explosion on account of its "belly", etc., motif. His incidental "foulness" is a great pity, because he will be read flippantly for that only—the last thing he would wish. People will read him *for* it, instead of *in spite* of it.'

[7] Richard Aldington, Introduction to the Phoenix edition (1955) of D. H. Lawrence, *The Rainbow*; and James T. Boulton and Andrew Robertson (eds.), *The Letters of D. H. Lawrence*, iii: *1916–21* (Cambridge, 1984). [8] Swanwick, *I have been Young*, 168–70.

[9] Goldring, *Reputations*, 70–1; id., *Life Interests*, 103. For a private protest against the suppression of *The Rainbow*, see E. M. Forster (though he had not read it) to Sir Henry Newbolt, 7 Nov. 1915, in Lago and Furbank (eds.), *Forster's Letters*, i. 231.

promisingly enough, with a thumping platitude, delivered in bluff, man-of-the-world manner: 'sex, deny it as much as we will must, after all, be considered a part of life'. He then ruled that what mattered was 'the author's treatment of his theme and the spirit in which a book is written', deciding that there were authors

who deliberately put coarse passages into their novels with a view to attract certain readers and you know it. I know it, and the average man and woman in the street outside knows it too!

Such authors are, not to put too fine a point on it, vermin, and they should be caught, cracked and exterminated!

Let one of the societies which exist for the suppression of this sort of thing obtain that which it considers after taking proper advice, a clear case against an author and prosecute.

I would trust a British jury, guided perhaps a little by a broad-minded judge, to decide definitely the question whether a book is offensive or not.

The effect of a conviction in such a case it would be difficult to over-estimate.

It would be felt among offending authors everywhere.

I venture to believe that there is not much subtlety required to discover whether a book is impure or not, and that the jurymen would be fully equal to their task.[10]

Nicoll wrote this at a time when not only Lawrence's *Sons and Lovers* but also Hall Caine's *The Woman Thou Gavest Me* (1913), Compton Mackenzie's *Youth's Encounter* (1913; being the first volume of *Sinister Street*) and W. B. Maxwell's *The Devil's Garden* (1913) were placed under restriction by the Libraries Association, either banned altogether or removed from shelves and available only on request by subscribers. Nicoll was no isolated voice among influential literary critics of the day. The editor of the *Sphere*, Clement Shorter, while repudiating the idea of state censorship, responded to Maxwell's letter to *The Times* protesting about the circulating libraries' ban. Shorter objected to the scene in *The Devil's Garden*, in which William Dale, who has murdered his wife's seducer, fantasizes about dancing naked in a stream with a young servant girl. Maxwell's rejoinder, that Shorter was taking this scene out of context, and that Dale was unhinged and never fulfilled his fantasy, apparently did not satisfy.[11]

Lawrence, therefore, was hardly the first author to suffer attack on the 'morality question'. In Samuel Butler's satire *Erewhon* (1872) its faraway inhabitants worship the fearsome deity Ydgrun (a confused Mrs Grundy), when her reign was far from exhausted at home. The 1880s and 1890s had seen the issue of propriety debated in response to the work of two quite antithetical schools of writing, by so-called 'realist' or 'naturalistic' writers and 'aesthetes' or 'decadents'. Rough treatment was meted out by reviewers, who (honestly or otherwise) defended a moral code. This could be taken on the chin and even, as the years

---

[10] Quoted in McMillan, *Way we Were*, 268.
[11] Kemp *et al.* (eds.), *Edwardian Fiction*, 98–9, where Maxwell's letter to *The Times* is given as 9 September. 1913.

passed, laughed at, as George Moore did about Edmund Yates's reception of his *Pagan Poems* (1881). Yates, he recollected forty years on, had then run *The World*, 'a mighty organ of public opinion', and he reviewed Moore's work under the headline, 'A Bestial Bard', recommending that 'The book ought to be burnt by the common hangman, and the author whipped at a cartwheel.' 'Poor little book!', Moore mused.[12] At the time Moore's humour had failed him, and he was not forgiving when he pondered how much censorship was exercised unofficially. This provoked him famously to protest against the circulating library Mudie's, which blacklisted his first two novels. *A Modern Love* (1883) was withdrawn when two women subscribers objected to the seductions achieved by the hero, an artist, and in particular to a scene in which one of his conquests models *déshabillé* for a Venus ('"Naked"', Moore commented, 'is using a word that nobody of taste would think of using'). On the strength of this reputation, Moore's second novel, *A Mummer's Wife* (1885), was rejected as outré. Moore's fury against 'the censorship of a tradesman' was extreme:

I hate you [Mudie] because you dare question the sacred right of the artist to obey the impulses of his temperament; I hate you because you are the great purveyor of the worthless, the false and the commonplace; I hate you because you are a fetter about the ankles of those who would press forward towards the light of truth; I hate you because you feel not the spirit of scientific inquiry that is bearing our age along; I hate you because you pander to the intellectual sloth of to-day; I hate you because you would mould ideas to fit the narrow limits in which your own turn; I hate you because you impede the free development of our literature.[13]

Moore's public explosion ventilated a frustration felt by many writers against the tyranny of the circulating library system, which had included dictation of format and price as well as supervision of morals. Wilkie Collins was much put out in 1873 during the serialization of *The New Magdalen* when Mudie demanded that his publisher Bentley change the title: 'His proposal would be an impertinence if he was not an old fool . . . this ignorant fanatic holds my circulation in his pious hands. What remedy have we? What remedy have his subscribers?' Collins refused: he even went ahead and staged a play of the story, keeping the same title—the Examiner of Plays quibbled only about using a biblical quotation in the publicity—before the novel was published. With a theatre success behind him, Collins was confident that 'that fanatical old fool Mudie will be obliged to increase his order'; but it was not to be, for the Mudie disapproval dampened sales in England, by contrast with the United States, where *The New Magdalen* sold

---

[12] Goodwin, *Moore*, 239–40.

[13] George Moore, *Literature at Nurse; or, Circulating Morals*, ed. P. Coustillas (Hassocks, 1976), p. 111, 16–17. Moore subsequently claimed that it was his assault on the Mudie and Smith circulating library system broke their monopoly; thus 'it was I [who] established the six-shilling novel, so that people who were inclined to reading, may read' (Goodwin, *Moore*, 88). This is a large claim for what was no more than an indirect contributing cause.

strongly. Collins was so disillusioned that he threatened to stop writing stories for the home market 'as long as the Mudie system obtains'.[14]

Neither Wilkie Collins nor George Moore was to know it but they were soon to be in saintly company. Mudie's *Index Prohibitorum* by 1890 also included the founder of the Salvation Army, 'General' William Booth's study of and proposed solution to Britain's demoralized poor, *In Darkest England and the Way Out*. It was reported in the *Review of the Reviews* that Mudie, 'after ordering some copies of the book at first, countermanded the order and refused to put it into circulation'.[15] This hardly slowed down the General's bandwagon: his book was an instant best-seller, with six editions and 200,000 sales within a year of publication. In this light, it was easy to mock Mudie. Derision came easily to Bernard Shaw, who took the measure of current fiction from that which came his way as a reviewer for the *Pall Mall Gazette*, 1885–8. 'The most dangerous public house in London is at the corner of Oxford Street,' he once informed an audience, referring to Mudie's. The reason was that Mudie's circulated only a make-believe romantic literature containing a falsely idealized picture of society and personal relationships. Such bad novels make a bad nation, Shaw declared, which argument then licensed his explanation of the fundamental cause:

At the centre of this vicious circle, we find the root of all evil—bad economic conditions . . . [producing] a general hypocrisy of the most searching kind, under the influence of which everyone dreads the truth, and agrees to stigmatize all efforts to expose it as indecent. Hence springs up a false morality which seeks to establish dignity, refinement, education, social importance, wealth, power and magnificence, on a hidden foundation of idleness, dishonesty, sensuality, hypocrisy, tyranny, rapacity, cruelty, and scorn. When the novelist comes to build his imaginary castle, he builds on the same foundation, but adds heroism, beauty, romance, and above all, possibility of exquisite happiness to the superstructure, thereby making it more beautiful to the ignorant, and more monstrous to the initiated.[16]

In fact, neither Shaw nor Moore in their respective rants was being fair to Mudie and the other circulating libraries. The custodians of free municipal libraries were equally neurotic; nor was the propensity for sanctimonious utterance and action confined to staid English shores. Kipling's *Plain Tales from the Hills* (1888) was banned as indecent by Melbourne's public library, on the strength of which a local newspaper invited him to report the country's premier horse race when he briefly visited Australia in 1891.[17] Mudie and his like may have appeared as complacent prudes and irresponsible censors, but they were responding to

---

[14] Peters, *Collins*, 340, 345; Taylor, *Secret Theatre of Home*, 210. The play *The New Magdalen* opened at the Olympic Theatre on 19 May 1873.

[15] *Review of Reviews* (Dec. 1890), 651. The editor, W. T. Stead, was in the best position to know since he ghosted much of *In Darkest England*. Stead and Booth died within a few months of each other in 1912. In a posthumously published article, 'General Booth', *Fortnightly Review* (Dec. 1912), 1042–50, Stead nominated Booth as 'the most remarkable man' in the world.   [16] Holroyd, *Shaw*, i. 207–8.

[17] Nowell-Smith, (ed.), *Letters to Macmillan*, 213.

outside pressure from their subscribers and (apropos W. H. Smith's bookstall trade) from railway companies who were anxious about their legal position concerning the circulation of indecent literature.[18] There was a profusion of moral reform societies in the Victorian period. Measured by subscription lists many appeared puny. Thus the Pure Literature Society (established in 1854) counted only 1,048 subscribers, and the National Vigilance Association (established in 1885) only 228 in 1885; but they reflected wide concern, were extremely energetic and were unafraid to instigate legal proceedings wherever possible. Moreover, they involved a quantity of women at every level of organization, and this mobilization of an opinion that symbolized the sanctity of home and marriage as the bulwark of social virtue and stability could not be lightly disregarded.[19] In 1909, the big six circulating libraries—Mudie, W. H. Smith, Boots, Day's, Cawthorn & Hutt, and the *Times* Book Club—briefly combined as the Circulating Libraries Association and issued this proclamation:

In order to protect our interests, and also, as far as possible, to satisfy the wishes of our clients, we have determined in future that we will not place in circulation any book which, by reason of the personally scandalous, libellous, immoral, or otherwise disagreeable nature of its contents, is in our opinion likely to prove offensive to any considerable section of our subscribers.[20]

Operating much like a varsity Final Honour School, the circulating libraries proposed dividing books into three classes of degree: satisfactory, doubtful, and objectionable. The satisfactory would be stocked, as also the doubtful though for restricted circulation, lent out only on direct application; the objectionable would be prohibited.

This essayed censorship precipitated the resignation of the *Times* Book Club's librarian, Janet Hogarth, who was already disenchanted with its management after the Northcliffe takeover of *The Times* in 1908. She protested 'both in the interests of freedom and in the interests of art', because the rules by which the circulating libraries now bound themselves de facto ceded judgement about a book to ignorant readers in-house or to a veto of a mere three fussed subscribers.[21] When writing her memoirs in 1926, having meanwhile become Mrs W. L. Courtney, wife of the editor of the *Fortnightly Review*, she had by her

---

[18] Charles Wilson, *First with the News: The History of W. H. Smith, 1792–1972* (1985), 101–9, 365–88.

[19] F. K. Prochaska, *Women and Philanthropy in Nineteenth-Century England* (Oxford, 1980), 233, 242, for the subscription lists of the Pure Literature Society and the National Vigilance Association, of which women comprised 43 and 45 per cent respectively.

[20] Quoted in Philip Ziegler, 'Bad Banners', *TLS*, 18 Dec. 1992. Ziegler was citing a paper by Nicholas Hiley, collected in Robin Myers and Michael Harris (eds.), *Censorship and the Control of Print in England and France 1600–1910* (Winchester, 1992), which made a further point about the economics of the business. The circulating libraries apparently found that books of dubious reputation, while in great demand for borrowing, did poorly when the time came to sell them second-hand. This was another argument against stocking them, therefore, to avoid being left with a heap of unsaleable books. The publishers, by contrast, having been deprived of the sure sales to circulating libraries, would issue cheap editions of these books to the general public. Thus, the 'censorship' failed in its purpose of limiting the audience for this class of literature. [21] Courtney, *Recollected in Tranquillity*, 194–5.

side the first list which the libraries compiled—though never publicized—of books to be rejected and restricted. The rejected, she considered, contained 'no books of literary merit' except George Moore's *Memoirs of my Dead Life* (1906); but the restricted included H. G. Wells, *Ann Veronica* (1909), H. H. Richardson, *Maurice Guest* (1908), Dion Calthrop, *Everybody's Secret* (1909), Netta Syrett, *A Child of Promise* (1907), E. Temple Thurston, *Sally Bishop* (1908), and Mrs Havelock Ellis, *Kit's Woman* (1907).[22] Their common denominator was some treatment of extramarital relationships and illegitimacy, but invariably their manner was that commended by the *Observer* in reviewing another of the novels on the restricted list, Stanley Hyatt's *Black Sheep* (1909): 'written so pleasantly and with such freedom from sordidness, because Mr. Hyatt knows exactly what to put in or leave out'.[23] It was to the *Observer* that Janet Hogarth wrote to alert the public to the circulating libraries' resolution. The press took up the controversy, and she was widely supported, particularly keenly by Arnold Bennett, writing as Jacob Tonson in the *New Age*. According to Hogarth, the libraries then panicked in the resultant storm and, without repudiating the policy, little implemented it thereafter. The essayed coordinated action in 1913 over Hall Caine's *The Woman Thou Gavest Me*, W. B. Maxwell's *The Devil's Garden*, and the first volume of Compton Mackenzie's *Sinister Street* was therefore exceptional and met with another outcry. *Punch*'s response can be reckoned as a gauge of professional middle-class opinion on the subject. It found the situation farcical, poked fun at the busybodies and faddists who fired off letters to the press, and cheerfully invented an authors' strike, with picketing against the libraries.[24] Its reviews of the books in question conspicuously failed to register disgust concerning their morals. *Sinister Street* it found 'difficult to overpraise', indeed a 'masterpiece' which confirmed the emergence of an exceptionally talented author, following the promise Mackenzie had shown with *Carnival* (1911).[25] *The Devil's Garden* was criticized, but on grounds of composition, it containing seemingly irrelevant and meandering passages; yet these details ultimately added up to 'a very masterly analysis of character' and it was 'a book to be read twice'.[26] Predictably, *The Woman Thou Gavest Me* was poorly received; this was because Hall Caine had served as the butt of *Punch*'s jokes for nigh on two decades, on account of his self-advertisement. Still, *Punch* reproduced Caine's own announcement that his novel had been commended by the Archdeacon of Westminster and other worthies.[27] This want of support for the circulating libraries' action signalled defeat. After 1913 intermittent cases occurred of one or two libraries taking against a particular book, but 'nothing very general'.[28]

---

[22] See Kemp *et al.* (eds.), *Edwardian Fiction*, for identification of these authors and a summary of several of these works.   [23] Courtney, *Recollected in Tranquillity*, 197.

[24] *Punch*, 17 Sept. 1913, 240, and 24 Sept. 1913, 266.

[25] Ibid., 3 Sept. 1913, 217; and similar praise for volume ii of *Sinister Street*, ibid., 18 Nov. 1914, 427.

[26] Ibid., 24 Sept. 1913, 277–8.   [27] Ibid., 20 Aug. 1913, 161 and 180.

[28] Courtney, *Recollected in Tranquillity*, 198.

It is tempting, amid all this kerfuffle, to imagine the prim attitudes of the circulating libraries' subscribers. In 1917 Virginia Woolf described an encounter with a typical Mudie's borrower—'a stout widow [who] chose 10 novels; taking them from the hand of Mudie's man, like a lapdog, only stipulating that she wanted no vulgarity, not much description, but plenty of incident'—typical, that is, if we forget that Virginia Woolf was a Mudie's subscriber too.[29] During the controversy over the banning of Wells's *Ann Veronica*, Arnold Bennett triumphantly published a letter from one irate Mudie's subscriber who asserted *his* right to be supplied with what reading he wanted: 'I didn't pay my subscription in order to have my choice of books limited to such books as some frock-coated personage in Oxford Street thought good for me. I've spent forty years in learning to know what I like in literature, and I don't want anybody to teach me. I'm not a young girl, I'm a middle-aged man . . . '.[30] Still, it was an elementary point to grasp about the circulating library system that safety first must rule. For it to be suspended there must be a special cause. Samuel Butler, riding his own hobby-horse about religion, once cynically mused how the Psalms were, 'for the most part, querulous, spiteful and introspective into the bargain. Mudie would not take thirteen copies of the lot if they were to appear now for the first time—unless indeed their royal authorship were to arouse an adventitious interest in them, or unless the author were a rich man who played his cards judiciously with the reviewers.'[31]

'I wonder', George Moore ruminated, 'why murder is considered less immoral than fornication in literature.' The point was fairly made, but Moore's position was not straightforward. Moore liked to scandalize. During the Great War, when he heard that the Royal Hospital in Chelsea had been bombed, he was upbraided for expressing concern only that a fine building, and not people, might have been lost; but he stood his ground, saying, 'as for human life, any kitchenmaid and any scullion can produce it in five minutes'.[32] Moore postured about both art and sex. Having consorted with notable painters during his bohemian Paris period, he thereafter set up as an authority on art, promoting its value above ordinary morality—'What matters the slaughter of ten thousand virgins if they provide Delacroix with a masterpiece?' Moore's conversation was unusually free with accounts of his conquests, which were understood to be more numerous in fancy than in fact; hence, the taunt that Moore was a man who told but did not kiss. He was naturally the hunted rather than the hunter in all these affairs, and responded heroically, such as his parting shot to Pearl Craigie, booting her behind—'or at least on the bustle'.[33] Poetry, he asserted, must have rules if only for the pleasure

---

[29] Bell (ed.), *Woolf Diary*, 61 (17 Oct. 1917).

[30] *New Age*, 30 Dec. 1909, in Bennett, *Books and Persons*, 174.

[31] Jones (ed.), *Notebooks of Samuel Butler*, 202.   [32] Goodwin, *Moore*, 163.

[33] Hart-Davis (ed.), *Lyttelton Hart-Davis Letters*, 300 (15 May 1957). It is improbable that their relationship was physical, Craigie having been infected with syphilis by her former husband and taken a vow of celibacy on her conversion to Catholicism in 1892.

of breaking them, in the same way that women must be clothed if only for the pleasure of stripping them.[34] But it would be wrong to underrate Moore's serious intellectual concerns or his fighting spirit. His struggle to release the corsets that confined literature embraced the drama too. He lent support to the Independent Theatre Club, which was started by J. T. Grein and C. W. Jarvis in 1890–1 and was modelled upon André Antoine's Théâtre Libre established in Paris in 1887. Moore served on the Independent Theatre Club Committee, together with a miscellany of strange and unorthodox talents such as Frank Harris and Julia Frankau (the novelist Frank Danby);[35] moreover, in collaboration with Teixeira de Mattos, he translated Zola's *Thérèse Raquin* for performance in October 1891, and he was involved, as director or writer, in the production of three other works for that theatre.[36] Regarding the censorship of plays, however, Moore advocated not outright abolition but 'an intelligent censorship [which] will preserve the artist against folly, ignorance, and pruriency'. Published books were different, and their censorship on the ground that they were liable to deprave the reader he compared to the superstition that witches fly through the air on broomsticks: 'Two centuries hence the belief that books can corrupt the mind will be as dead as the latter is to-day. Argument is of no immediate avail; time alone can cure.'[37]

In his own novels Moore was far from being uninhibited. Bernard Shaw reviewed *A Mere Accident* (1887) for the *Pall Mall Gazette* and noted Moore's 'commendable reticence' in drawing a veil over the unpleasantness of a rape, an evasion which, in Shaw's view, 'might have been taken further, even to the point of not writing the book'.[38] And in *Evelyn Innes* (1898) Moore described how Sir Owen Asher and Evelyn became lovers, with modest periphrasis: 'it was not until the third night that they entered into the full possession of their delight'.[39] This sort of thing did not prevent the conservative editor of the *St James's Gazette* and *Anti-Jacobin*, Frederick Greenwood, from expressing his disgust for 'Moore's Zolaesqueries'.[40] Unlike Lawrence later, who elevated sexual congress into a kind of naturalist sacrament, Moore initially saw himself primarily as a scientific observer studying humanity in terms of environment and heredity who was

---

[34] Goodwin, *Moore*, 15. Max Beerbohm parodied Moore's salaciousness in *Christmas Garland*, 183–4.

[35] For Julia Frankau's association, see her sister's memoir: Mrs Aria, *My Sentimental Self* (1922), 57–9.

[36] Gerber, *Moore in Transition*, 62–3.

[37] George Moore, 'The Dramatic Censorship', *New Review* (Oct. 1890), *Review of Reviews* (Oct. 1890), 360. Moore's phrase about books corrupting the mind is a clear allusion to Lord Chief Justice Cockburn's authoritative judgment in 1868, in applying the Obscene Publications Act 1857: 'The test of obscenity', he opined, was 'whether the tendency of the matter charged' was 'to deprave and corrupt those whose minds are open to such immoral influences, and into whose hands a publication of this sort may fall'.

[38] Holroyd, *Shaw*, i. 210.

[39] George Moore, *Evelyn Innes* (1898), 113. The American edition was still more expurgated, owing to the insistence of George William Sheldon, the American publisher Appleton's representative. On Sheldon's ludicrous objections to particular phrases, which Moore (possibly with the help of Edmund Gosse) obliged by removing, see Gerber, *Moore*, 156–9.

[40] Scott, *Pall Mall Gazette*, 303. Sent a copy of the *News of the World* by its proprietor, George Riddell, Greenwood first put it in the bin, then, thinking 'if I leave it there the cook may read it', he burnt it. Ibid. 417.

obliged, if he was to be faithful to reality, to depict all aspects of man's natural history. Musing about the possibility of enticing Evelyn to Paris, Asher reckons,

She was a clever girl, and knew as well as he how such adventures must end . . . She was a religious girl, a devout Catholic, and as he had himself been brought up in that religion, he knew how it restrained the sexual passion or fashioned it in the mould of its dogma. But we are animals first, we are religious animals afterwards.[41]

Indeed, Moore observed, just as the sex urge is stronger than the religious, so instinct generally is more powerful than reason: 'Our actions obey an unknown law, implicit in ourselves, but which does not conform to our logic.'[42] Every human incident, therefore—whether a seduction, an illegitimate birth or whatever—was not moral or immoral, noble or ignoble but natural and mundane. In *Esther Waters* (1894) the eponymous heroine, a God-fearing, illiterate servant girl, becomes pregnant as a result of her first sexual encounter. This occurs after she is tipsy with drink; she is not used to alcohol but she is celebrating the race victory of a horse at the stables where she works, and she is in love with her seducer, William Latch, a fellow servant who has made money by betting on the horse. Esther leaves her employment, struggles to bring up their son on her own, and does not meet William again for another eight years, when he is an unhappily married albeit prosperous publican–bookmaker and she is engaged to the worthy, religious Fred Parsons, a stationer's foreman. William now asks Esther to part from Fred and to live with him, promising to divorce his wife and to marry her. As Moore describes it, the fact that William is the father of her child strongly influences her; so does his physical attraction and, as they go upstairs to bed, she 'tried to think of Fred, but William's great square shoulders had come between her and this meagre little man. She sighed, and felt once again that her will was overborne by a force which she could not control or understand.'[43]

Esther Waters was blacklisted by W. H. Smith's circulating library, apparently after objection was taken to the scene (chapter 16) in the lying-in hospital, where Esther has her baby; but there was an additional fuss made because of the novel's other leading theme, gambling. Moore included lavish descriptions of the crowds drawn to the Epsom Derby; more particularly, he depicted the pervasiveness of betting among all social classes, giving strong indications that much crookedness obtained, with race-fixing taking place and stable-information influencing the betting. Above all, he exposed the inequity of the law that declared on-course betting legal and off-course betting illegal, a situation that discriminated heavily against the lower classes, whose bookmakers ran the risk of prosecution. When William Latch is set up and induced to accept a bet from a plain-clothes policeman, Moore revels in describing his appearance in court before a judge who inveighs against the social evils of drinking and gambling after he has had a pint of claret with his lunch and previously downed a magnum of champagne to dull the

---

[41] Moore, *Evelyn Innes*, 64.   [42] Ibid. 94.   [43] Moore, *Esther Waters*, 219.

pain of his own lost wager on the Cesarewitch. 'It was the old story,' thinks William; 'one law for the rich, another for the poor.'[44] The Prime Minister, Gladstone, was much moved by this and, ignoring the question of Esther's 'immorality', he interpreted the novel as a treatise showing the deleterious effects of betting. Gladstone sent Moore an 'approving postcard'.[45] This, when publicized, did much to counteract the ban imposed by W. H. Smith's, and the novel was into its eleventh thousand only a month after publication. Conan Doyle had also taken up the cudgels on Moore's behalf, acting as spokesman for the Society of Authors, which initially contemplated taking action against Smith's until advised by counsel that there was no prospect of legal redress. Instead, Doyle fired off letters to the *Daily Chronicle*, making much the same point as Gladstone: 'It is the greatest sermon against gambling that has ever been preached . . .'.[46]

Gratifying though it was for Moore to find the great and the good now ranged on his side against W. H. Smith's, it need hardly be remarked that sermon production had not been his intention in writing his novel. It was a matter, as Moore put it in his dedication of *Esther Waters* to T. W. Rolleston, of 'holding the mirror up to Nature'.[47] This was the philosophy of Zola, whose disciple Moore was assumed to be. Indeed, Ibsen's champion William Archer had been so excited by Moore's *A Mummer's Wife* that he 'proclaimed his discovery of an English Zola who was greater than Zola'. That was to jump to the wrong conclusion, as Bernard Shaw, the recipient of Archer's enthusiasm, was quick to point out: 'I laughed him to scorn and assured him that George, ex-painter and ex-poet, was incapable of writing a presentable advertisement for a lost dog.'[48] Equally under misapprehension was Mrs J. R. Green, who wrote to Will Rothenstein: 'I am told Esther Waters proves that Mr George Moore has found a soul. Will that set the world's crazy balance straight again?'[49] Moore was not placated. He was outraged by the insult to his artistic purpose, by the injury to his pocket, and by what he saw as the selectiveness of W. H. Smith's action. In his protest against Mudie's in 1885 he had cited extracts from Mrs Campbell Praed's *Nadine* (1882), W. H. Mallock's *A Romance of the Nineteenth Century* (1881), Robert Buchanan's *Foxglove Manor* (1884), Ouida's *Puck* (1870) and *Moths* (1880), and Florence Marryat's fiction, all of which contained scenes of seduction and yet were freely circulated by Mudie's.[50] Nor was it only lovemaking in the ordinary sense that was written about. There was frequently an admixture of cruelty in the passionate romances of the period. Sidney Dark in 1925 condemned as 'a novelist's illusion' and 'an ancient and stubborn superstition that women adore strong, masculine and rather brutal men'. He added, 'One of the most popular

---

[44] Moore, *Esther Waters*, 305.   [45] See Walter Allen's Introduction to Moore, *Esther Waters*, p. v.
[46] Gibson and Green (eds.), *Unknown Conan Doyle*, 43–5, 351–2.   [47] Moore, *Esther Waters*, 1.
[48] Letter to Geraint Goodwin, 5 Mar. 1934, in Goodwin, *Moore*, 18. Moore did approach Zola to write a preface; this, however, was ill-timed, as his *Confessions of a Young Man*, which poked fun at Zola's want of style and his journalist's method and banality, was then running in a French periodical.
[49] Rothenstein, *Men and Memories, 1872–1900*, 202.   [50] Moore, *Literature at Nurse*, 7–15.

contemporary novelists always makes her heroes thrash her heroines with a whip. And they love them for it'[51]—a probable reference to Ethel M. Dell, whose best-selling career began with *The Way of an Eagle* (1912).

The prevailing standard of female submission to an assertive male easily acquired a sadomasochistic coating. In 1920 Elinor Glyn published a collection of extracts from her best-selling novels of the previous two decades, because, she claimed in the preface, 'my friends have often told me that they wished that they could have the parts they liked in all my works brought together in one volume, just to dip into from time to time'. These were arranged according to subject, beginning with 'Man', 'Woman', and 'Love'. The first established that 'Man is a hunter—a hunter always' and that

man was meant to be strong. He was not designed in the scheme of things to be a soft, silky-voiced creature—talking gossip and handing tea-cups; he was just intended to be a fierce, great hunter, rushing round killing his food and capturing his mate; and women have remained such primitive, unspoilt darlings, they can still be dominated by these lovely qualities—when they have a chance to see them! But, alas! half the men have become so awfully civilized, they haven't a scrap of this delightful aboriginal force left![52]

Naturally, when Glyn turned to 'Woman', she averred that 'Woman is as willing to be ruled as ever she was—she always adores a master';[53] and, when it came to 'Love', that

A woman will stand almost anything from a passionate lover. He may beat her and pain her soft flesh; he may shut her up and deprive her of all other friends—*while the motive is raging love and interest in herself on his part*, it only makes her love him the more. The reason why women become unfaithful is because the man grows casual, and having awakened a taste for passionate joys, he no longer gratifies them—so she yawns and turns elsewhere.[54]

It was Glyn's *Three Weeks* (1907), about an infatuation between an upper-class Englishman and a Balkan queen, that originally alerted the public to the passionate possibilities of tiger-skin rugs. 'The impropriety of the book was cleverly boomed beforehand' by her publisher Duckworth, noted *Punch*'s reviewer, who sniffily judged it 'not likely to do much harm in drawing-rooms... though it might possibly damage the moral fibre of some callow tweenie in the servants'-hall—its natural destination'.[55] Arnold Bennett too considered it 'merely infantile and absurd' rather than 'an awful example of female licentiousness'; but Glyn's *His Hour* (1910), which included a rape fantasy at the heart of a tempestuous affair between a well-bred English widow and a part-Cossack Russian prince, bothered Bennett more. Above all, he pondered why it had passed the censorship of the circulating libraries. He found the answer in the novel's dedication, fulsomely

---

[51] Dark, *Mainly about Other People*, 218.   [52] Elinor Glyn, *Points of View* (1920), 9.
[53] Ibid. 14.   [54] Ibid. 22–3.   [55] *Punch*, 26 June 1907, 463–4.

presented by Glyn 'with grateful homage and devotion...to Her Imperial
Highness The Grand Duchess Vladimir of Russia'. If only other authors who
upset the libraries had had the savvy to dedicate their 'wretched provincial'
stories to the Queen of Montenegro or some such sublime, they too would have
escaped trouble, Bennett mused.[56]

Moore, then, had genuine cause for complaint that he was blacklisted for
attempting to portray 'real' life while 'romantic' novelists were apparently able
with impunity to philosophize in their work about primitive sexual urges. This
inequity rather amused Oscar Wilde's set, who revelled in the 'artless impropriety' of Ouida and her sort and speculated whether Moore had not been
boycotted by W. H. Smith's on account of his want of style.[57] George Gissing, no
stranger to low life in fact and fiction, reacted similarly: 'Gloomy day. Read
"Esther Waters". Some pathos and power in latter part, but miserable writing.
The dialogue often grotesquely phrased.'[58] In his old age Moore allowed his
bitterness and jealousy to become more pronounced as he complained that he
had never made pots of money out of his books—'£1,500 or so out of *Esther
Waters*', he told Arnold Bennett in 1917—and equally had not established himself
as a 'classic' author. He specialized in coining the dismissive phrase about more
esteemed writers, speaking of 'Hardy the Villager, Conrad the Sailor, etc.' and,
best of all, calling Bernard Shaw 'the funny man in a Bloomsbury boarding-
house'.[59] Previously Moore had sneered at Rider Haggard as a plagiarist; but, if he
had coolly weighed Haggard's talent, he might have acknowledged that he at
least found a way of purveying sexual glamour without calling upon himself the
wrath of the authorities. It was possible for best-selling novels to be suffused with
sexuality, and even adorned with illustrations of naked beauties, where the
females were 'natives' or 'savages'. Haggard's stroke of genius in *She* (1887) was to
make Ayesha not merely the most beautiful woman in the world, an ageless
queen–goddess, but also, inexplicably for an African, white-skinned.[60] It was a
formula Haggard repeated for other climes and centuries. Thomas Hardy, to
whom Haggard sent his Norse adventure *Eric Brighteyes* (1891), was roused by 'a
wild illustration' to start reading a chapter nearer the end than the beginning, the
likely illustration 'showing a huge sword impaled between a woman's naked
breasts'.[61] A similar tactic was deployed for the serialization in the *Illustrated
London News* of Hall Caine's Moroccan melodrama *The Scapegoat* (1891), which
included drawings of bare-breasted women.[62]

[56] *New Age*, 9 May 1908 and 10 Nov. 1910, in Bennett, *Books and Persons*, 10, 276–7.
[57] Hichens, *Green Carnation*, 120, 131.   [58] Coustillas (ed.), *Gissing's Diary*, 356 (9 Dec. 1894).
[59] See Shaw's letter on this, 5 Mar. 1934, in Goodwin, *Moore*, 18. For the other jibes, see Goodwin,
Moore, 75–6, 218–21, and Flower (ed.), *Bennett Journals*, ii. 197, 285, 289 (11 May 1917, 10 Jan. and 22 May 1921).
Bennett remained an admirer of Moore's writing, for instance, rereading *Esther Waters* in 1915 and finding
it 'still vigorously lives' (ibid. 149 (30 Dec. 1915)).   [60] Higgins, *Haggard*, 94–106, 112.
[61] Hardy to H. Rider Haggard, [May 1891?], in Purdy and Millgate (eds.), *Hardy Letters*, i. 235, where the
artist is identified as Lancelot Speed.   [62] Sutherland, *Companion*, 317.

III

There was no law to regulate taste. Bernard Shaw recognized that in the right key you can say anything, in the wrong key nothing. In 1929, together with Bertrand Russell, he spoke in the Wigmore Hall, London, at the grandly titled International Congress of the World's League for Sexual Reform, which passed a resolution calling for an end to 'all kinds of censorship on sex subjects in literature, scientific publications, pictures and other representations'. The Congress justified this position on the ground that 'obscenity and impropriety are matters too subjective and indefinite to serve as a basis for laws'; and it proposed as a more civilized alternative to legal intervention and penalty a rational system of sex education through schools. This would ensure that people grew up without unhealthy ignorance and inhibitions and could decide for themselves what to avoid; but sex education then, even in fundamental aspects such as birth control, was often subject to prosecution where it employed ordinary and commonly understood language rather than scientifically complex and technical terms. The monitoring of literature was also incongruous: 'Experience showed that frankly salacious works evaded the law, and that serious works were sacrificed to censorships.' When paradoxes were flying about, it was usual to find Shaw in the thick of them. Now he added another, treating the Congress to his verdict that as women had become more skimpily dressed and 'taken a very large step towards nudity', so 'sex appeal had vanished'. Apparently, Victorian ladies, whose every voluptuous contour was upholstered and emphasized, were masterpieces of sex appeal; therefore, modern women, if they had any sense, ought to put on more clothes.[63]

There was wisdom in such observations in so far as they bore the message that each culture and generation tend to express sexuality differently. Yet it remained questionable how much subscription was paid to such sets of norms, for within each culture and generation there always existed divergent opinion and behaviour, involving sometimes sizeable dissentient minorities. In the late Victorian and Edwardian period authors who wrote for the stage had been aggrieved that in this particular they were compelled to conform to the more conservative rather than liberal standards of their day. The best-seller Hall Caine represented them before the parliamentary Joint Select Committee on Censorship in 1909 and, whatever might be said about the defective literary quality of Caine's work, he proved an impressive witness, knowledgeable about the law and its application (he was a magistrate), incisive in argument, and resolute under cross-examination. Without pretending to be 'an advanced author' like Shaw, Caine cogently pressed the case that the 'scope of the theatre should be enlarged . . . to draw from material which is now forbidden to it'.[64] There was even drama in Caine's

---

[63] *The Times*, 14 Sept. 1929.
[64] Joint Select Committee on Stage Plays (Censorship), *PP* (1909), vol viii, no. 451, Q. 5663.

testimony, because he substantially revised the position he had adopted in a written submission for the Select Committee. Previously, he appeared prepared to accept the Lord Chamberlain system by which an official, the Examiner, licensed plays for public performance on the basis of having read the script. That, 'however unwelcome' to authors, seemingly conferred a general good by providing theatre managers and actors with some security for their investment. Now he wanted the powers granted to the Lord Chamberlain under the 1843 Act to be transferred to the courts, substituting a 'judgment according to the law for one official who would use his own opinion'.[65] Conscious that theatre management feared uncertainty arising from umpteen local magistrates' rulings, Caine countered this by arguing for a new form of central direction. The lead would be taken by the Public Prosecutor on behalf of the Attorney-General, who, acting on a complaint or where there was ground to suspect a play of having an 'immoral or seditious or blasphemous tendency', would consider whether to bring a charge before a court with judge and jury. The play's production might be suspended meanwhile; this was temporary authority, not summary power of suppression without appeal such as the Lord Chamberlain enjoyed. Asked whether he thought that 'unless a play is bad enough to be prosecuted and convicted, it ought not to be censored', Caine replied: 'I very strongly feel that. We cannot consider questions of taste in that relation—at least, the law cannot.'[66]

Caine studiously avoided criticism of the current Examiner of Plays; indeed, he went out of his way to laud him—'Mr. Redford is better than the law . . . Too good for his place'—because he had passed a number of so-called 'problem plays' which dealt with serious moral issues.[67] This obviated a suspicion that Caine's position derived principally from personal injury, because two of his own plays— a projected play about Muhammad in 1890 and now his adaptation of *The White Prophet* in 1909—had not reached the stage. They were never formally refused a licence; instead, their producers, respectively Henry Irving and Beerbohm Tree, succumbed to anxieties that the plays might get into trouble because of press rumours or winks emanating from the Lord Chamberlain's office. This was plainly unsatisfactory; but Caine argued that the current system was illogical as well as inequitable. At the heart of it was the fallacy that a play was simply a manuscript that could be vetted, whereas 'a play is not a play until it has been performed . . . There are three collaborators—the author, the actor, and the audience, each of whom . . . contributes something.' Thus expressions could easily be twisted by actor or audience, and a 'word that is innocent in London may have a very foul interpretation in New York'.[68] What also mattered was spirit and purpose: an author 'may paint vice in order to condemn it', but the 'Censor can take no account of tendency. He sees bad people, and he sees bad scenes in a play, and he is therefore compelled to censor it. He cannot enter into any argument with the author as to the moral tendency of his play.'[69] Caine's

---

[65] Q. 5597.   [66] Q. 5580.   [67] Qs. 5519, 5545–6.   [68] Qs. 5526–7.   [69] Q. 5531.

examples were calculated to warm Bernard Shaw's heart. *Ghosts*, by 1909 the only one of Ibsen's plays still not to have been licensed, Caine called 'the most distinctively moral of all his dramas';[70] and lest Shaw was still not roused, Caine described his disgust when, as it happened, he was staying in a hotel opposite the Garrick Theatre in New York and saw the police move in to stop the production of *Mrs. Warren's Profession*, 'that drama by one of the most distinguished of living literary men'.[71]

Caine made other telling observations. It was erroneous to think that public morality was a fixed standard and that it was the function of the theatre to reflect it. 'Morality is a fluid thing,'[72] as different today from yesterday as it would be different again in future, Caine adding that, judged by the criteria that were imposed on present-day dramatists, 'Shakespeare is nothing better than a chartered libertine. No play of Shakespeare is ever produced as Shakespeare wrote it; it is always censored by managers and actors.'[73] Such intervention rendered the Censor superfluous; and for the same reason, he thought the Censor 'helpless to control the morality of the plays of the present'.[74] What decidedly turned Caine against the Lord Chamberlain system was the defence of it by previous witnesses before the Select Committee: chiefly George Edwardes, manager of the Gaiety and the Empire, who appeared brutally anti-intellectual, emphatic that the theatre should provide only light entertainment (including, Caine argued, prurient material that yet evaded the Censor's vigilance); George Alexander, actor–manager of the St James's, who thought the Censor essential to prevent blasphemy, obscenity, and the production of political plays; W. S. Gilbert, librettist of the Savoy operas, who argued that the stage was no place to debate 'delicate moral problems'; and the playwright Comyns Carr, who declared that the theatre 'ought not to be a pulpit'. Caine's riposte was direct and forceful:

I hold that it [the drama] should have, and always has had, a much higher purpose . . . [and] that to say that the theatre ought not to be a pulpit, a platform for the discussion of moral, political, and religious questions, such as Ibsen is constantly dealing with, is to insult the memory of nearly all the great dramatists. The moral conscience is written all over the great dramas of the past in all ages and in every country.[75]

Caine also slapped down A. B. Walkley, the influential drama critic of *The Times*, whose judgement given to the Select Committee was that writers would be dissatisfied 'with anything in the nature of interference with their views, with the freedom of their art'. Caine regarded that as untrue and unfair: 'authors desire to obey the law'.[76] Within that limitation, he saw no reason why current political questions should be prohibited: 'Living statesmen are dealt with in the newspapers every day; they are caricatured in "Punch", and . . . I can see no conceivable difference between the treatment of living statesmen in Parliament in the newspapers, on the platform, and in the pulpit also, and the treatment of them on

---

[70] Q. 5542.   [71] Q. 5577.   [72] Q. 5524.   [73] Q. 5521.   [74] Q. 5526.
[75] Qs. 5539, 5543.   [76] Qs. 5671–2.

the stage.'[77] Likewise, moral issues: 'How can there be any difficulty when we
have Divorce Courts discussing delicate questions in public and allowing the
proceedings to be reported?'[78] For himself, Caine particularly wanted freedom to
write plays about scriptural characters. He refused to be drawn as to whether he
would include the Divine, stressing instead that the 'stories of David and Bathsheba, of Eli and his sons, of Joseph and his brethren, and the Apostles of our
Lord, which are all forbidden to us on the stage, are among the finest material
which the dramatist has at his hand'.[79] Such characters not being divine, a charge
of blasphemy could not hold; as for the representation of individuals in holy
orders causing offence to people, Caine boldly acknowledged that certain sorts
would object, but not those whom the Select Committee might suppose.
He cited a play of his own—he did not name it, but it was *The Eternal City*—in
which 'I had the temerity to introduce the Pope.' He was amazed, he said, that
the Examiner passed it. Again, this allowed him to remark that 'Mr. Redford was
so much better than his job.' Before having a London performance, the play was
tested in the provinces. He was warned off Dublin by a manager worried that his
theatre would be torn down by a hostile audience; but it proceeded, and 'when
the Pope entered . . . instead of there being a riot . . . the whole house rose and
cheered for a solid five minutes, from which I judge that the fear of disturbance
arising out of religious plays is generally a bogey'. An unconvinced member of the
Select Committee queried if the play had been taken to Belfast. It had, said Caine;
'and the same thing occurred'. Catholics not only did not mind the representation
of the Pope, 'on the contrary, they made the fortune of our play by coming in
great numbers to see it'. Asked who did object, Caine replied: 'Atheists for the
most part, and people who apparently cared nothing about religion . . . It was not
the religious people who objected?—No. That I am perfectly certain of.'[80]

   Caine's final argument against the current censorship concerned the greater
scope allowed to the novel, a subject on which he could speak authoritatively
because most of his plays were adaptations from his novels. He used the comparison to underpin a contention that the censorship tended to conventionalize
and to stereotype the drama when all the while mores were quietly shifting:
'No Examiner of Plays would have dared to allow Hetty Sorrel [from George
Eliot's *Adam Bede* (1859)] or Jane Eyre [from Charlotte Brontë's *Jane Eyre* (1847)] to
appear on the stage in their day, but we have now hundreds of them. The Adelphi
drama is built up of them.'[81] In sum, Caine sounded a clarion for freedom from
the present system, to permit the theatre to present plays which openly engaged
in political, religious, and moral debate. He did not attempt to shuffle off the
charge that this would court controversy: 'the morality which is just ahead of the
time does threaten the public peace'. But, he maintained,

the theatre is not like a parish church to which people must go or do without their
spiritual nourishment. It is not like a chapel in which they pay their pew rents, but it is an

---

[77] Q. 5572.   [78] Q. 5602.   [79] Q. 5551.   [80] Qs. 5566–8, 5673–5.   [81] Q. 5538.

independent place. There are many theatres and the public is at liberty to choose the theatre which it likes best. If it does not like the fare at one theatre, it can go to another. There is no excuse for its not knowing what is being played at the theatre.[82]

In the end, it was not topic so much as tone and treatment that mattered. *Overruled* (1912), Shaw's study of marital infidelity, is a case in point: he claimed to be the first playwright to have staged sexual intercourse. This was so successfully done, no one else seemed to have noticed.[83] The Victorian idealization of the family was both a social and religious construct which affirmed sexual sin as a predominantly female crime. Accordingly, it required a counterpoint to strengthen its purpose. 'Fallen women' were part of the stock of Victorian literature and theatre, their role being invoked in the *Saturday Review* in 1862:

The fast man makes love to them; the slow man discusses them; the fashionable young lady copies their dress; the Evangelical clergyman gives them tea, toast and touching talks at midnight; and the devout young woman gives herself up to the task of tending them . . . while they are resting between the acts of their exhausting lives.[84]

In 1886 Samuel Butler enjoyed embarrassing a stuffy Richard Garnett, the keeper of books at the British Museum and man of letters, when he told him that he was contemplating writing an oratorio on some sacred subject. And what in particular? 'The Woman Taken in Adultery', replied Butler 'demurely', who ended his journal account thus: 'Garnett did not quite like this.'[85]

Yet we should not forget that, in its own eyes, each age is 'modern' and apt both to rail about its falling standards and to congratulate itself on its maturity. Women writers were much to blame for the degradation of the literary profession which offered them such opportunities. This was the opinion of one of them, Mrs Amelia E. Barr, given in 'The Relations of Literature to Society' in the *North American Review*, July 1891. Mrs Barr, now aged 60, hailed originally from the Lake District, where her father was a clergyman whose private wealth was dissipated through a friend's financial fraud; Amelia herself, having married a Glasgow merchant who also became bankrupt, migrated to America, eventually settling in the new state of Texas, where she lost her husband and three children to yellow fever in 1867. Thereafter she maintained herself by authorship, writing novels set either in northern England or in the United States, the most memorable today being *Remember the Alamo* (1888), which John Wayne made into a film, epitomizing patriot civic virtue, in 1960.[86] Mrs Barr's indictment of her sister writers consisted of this:

They do hasty and slip-shod work, inaccurate and sentimental, overloaded with adjectives, frescoed all over with purple passages of what they consider fine writing. But this is

---

[82] Qs. 5548–9.
[83] Holroyd, *Shaw*, ii. 276–8. *Overruled* had its first performance at the Duke of York's Theatre on, 14 October 1912.   [84] Quoted in Peters, *Collins*, 338.
[85] Jones, *Butler: A Memoir*, ii. 38.
[86] On Amelia Barr (1831–1919), see Sutherland, *Companion*, 45–6.

a venial fault; where they chiefly offend is in making love the all-important and absorbing passion of life. Their stories teach too often that a girl has an absolute right to the fool of her choice, though she has to break every holy domestic tie to gratify herself.

Mrs Barr added further, on the authority of Florence Layard, that women were also 'translators of the lowest and most sensual French novels, though they gain by this dirty work only the smallest and most precarious of incomes'.[87] The same concatenation of causes was identified by R. B. Haldane, keen student of German philosophy and educational systems, in a letter to Constance Flower, a salon hostess who enjoyed friendships with numerous intellectuals and literary people:

I feel the force of what you say about the French Novelists. It is a great evil in literature and in life too that one passion and the sins connected with it should bulk so largely in the imagination. I think that people exaggerate grossly the importance of both. The passion of love is one important spring of action in life, but certainly not the most important, nor of the highest quality. And the sin of immorality, although like all sin, bad and black and importing the complete temporary negative of what is highest, is not more bad and black, more completely this negative, than many other sins which men and women commit with social impunity . . . I think that the education of women, as it has been of late, has something to do with all this exaggeration. Marriage means too much for them.[88]

So spoke a future Lord Chancellor and eternal bachelor. Rhoda Broughton was perhaps better placed to monitor developments. Her output of best-selling fiction began in 1867 when '*Cometh up as a Flower* impressed the hall and the parsonage with a vague sense that it was dreadfully improper.' This was Herbert Paul's sardonic verdict in 1897, adding:

The imputation of impropriety without the reality is an invaluable asset for an English novelist. It is not, of course, Miss Broughton's sole capital. The 'rough and cynical reader', always rather given to crying over cheap sentimentalism, has shed many a tear over *Good-bye, Sweetheart* [1872], and *Not Wisely but too Well* [1867]. The very names are lachrymatory. Then, Miss Broughton is witty as well as tragic. She first discovered the possibilities of humour which had so long been latent in family prayers.[89]

This was the right combination with which to treat the challenges posed to conventional virtue by romantic attachments. 'Innocent and yet racy' was Mary Gladstone's satisfied conclusion after finishing Broughton's *Second Thoughts* (1880), although her assessment of *Red as a Rose is She* (1870) contained a characteristic Gladstonian tut-tut: 'well written but flippant to excess'.[90] Broughton continued to produce novels through the Edwardian period, now adding the country-house story to her repertoire.[91] She was famously outspoken in company. Her old-fashioned, quasi-aristocratic directness delighted Henry James.

---

[87] *Review of Reviews* (Aug. 1891), 179.
[88] Haldane to Mrs Flower, 5 Sept. 1890, in Cohen, *Rothschild*, 229–30.
[89] Herbert Paul, 'The Victorian Novel', *Nineteenth Century*, (May 1897), in Paul, *Men and Letters*, 154.
[90] Masterman (ed.), *Mary Gladstone*, 53, 207 (7 May 1870, 17 Aug. 1880).
[91] On Rhoda Broughton (1840–1920), see *DNB 1912–1921*, 69–70, and Sutherland, *Companion*, 88–9, 143.

They frequently attended the theatre together, 'Miss Broughton always militantly paying for her own ticket'.[92] In fact, James became so fond of her, he never reviewed her novels. Before that happy relationship was formed, he had lambasted *Joan* (1876) for its 'puerility and nastiness, inanity and vulgarity ... What immaturity and crudity of art, what coarseness of sentiment and vacuity of thought.'[93] It was commonly remarked that Broughton's directness and wit smacked of the eighteenth century, of which she was a devotee: Pope and Dr Johnson were favourites of hers, and she was collaterally connected to the Sheridans.[94] She summarized her own odyssey thus: 'I began my career as Zola, I finish it as Miss Yonge; it's not I that have changed, it's my fellow-countrymen.' She enjoyed telling Asquith how at Newcastle station bookstall she came across a collection of her novels, second-hand and bound together with string, boasting a label: 'Rhoda Broughton—soiled and cheap'.[95] With origins much the same as Mrs Barr, Broughton was one of those clergymen's daughters—like Eliza Lynn Linton and Mary Cholmondeley also—who succeeded in scandalizing the straitlaced by their highly coloured boldness in tackling Victorian orthodoxies about religion and family, love and marriage. As the opening line of a review of *Red Pottage* (1899) protested, 'Murder and adultery are nothing to Miss Cholmondeley.' Broughton herself declared with finality: 'When an elderly vestal sets out to be improper, she can give points to Silenus.'[96]

In 1892 the novelist Julia Wedgwood, herself approaching 60, wrote of the new liberty in contemporary fiction where social questions were debated without reserve: 'Girls in the schoolroom are ready to discuss matters which their mothers shrink from recognizing, and their grandmothers did not understand; and a representative novel of the hour must touch on ground which a generation ago would have excluded it from popular perusal'.[97] Still, it was plain that not all inhibition was cast aside. In 1913 the parameters of prudery were debated by Mary Cholmondeley, Ellen Thorneycroft Fowler, and Marie Belloc Lowndes, who met over lunch; especially they considered

how hard it is that while a novelist can allow unmarried lovers in a novel do anything— *The Rosary* was the novel in question—you must not let a man hold a married woman's hand without the average reader being shocked. We went on talking of *The Rosary* and

---

[92] Edel (ed.), *James Letters*, iii. 248.   [93] Edel, *James*, ii. 378–80.
[94] See the appreciation of her for *The Bookman* by Walter Sichel, in part reproduced in Sichel, *Sands of Time*, 221–3; and, for a dig at her by the aesthetic set, see Hichens, *Green Carnation*, 121.
[95] Asquith, *Memories*, i. 217 n. 2.
[96] Percy Lubbock, *Mary Cholmondeley* (1928), 24–5. Broughton was an old friend of the Cholmondeleys: ibid. 33–43.
[97] Julia Wedgwood, 'Fiction and Faith', *Contemporary Review* (Aug. 1892), 222. On Wedgwood (1833–1913), see Sutherland, *Companion*, 664–5. A descendant of the pottery manufacturer and connected to the Darwins, Miss Wedgwood was handicapped by deafness, 'severely repressed by the evangelical atmosphere of her upbringing' and unhappily wont to attach herself to 'dominant men, older than herself', including Robert Browning when a widower. Twenty-nine letters of Browning and forty-four of Wedgwood, part of the Halsted B. Vander Poel collection of English Literature, were auctioned by Christie's in London in 2004; fetching £83,650; see *The Times*, 24 Feb., 3 and 4 Mar. 2004.

its wonderful success, and I said I felt sure this was owing to the suggestiveness of certain scenes.[98]

The Women Writers' Committee was not notably liberated on this question. Ostensibly, it confined its disapproval to an author's writing and refused to judge personal behaviour, as described by Mrs Belloc Lowndes:

There was a curious discussion as to professional ethics. Someone wanted a young girl asked to the dinner who had written *Letters From a Flapper at the Durbar*. A distinguished woman journalist on the Committee said she would not go to it if this girl were asked, though she did not know her, so there was no personal prejudice. I upheld her on the point that any woman who has disgraced herself professionally should not be asked by us. What a person does in private life seems to me to be none of our business; this was proved by the fact that we are asking half a dozen women who have been very notorious in the last year, but I do not think we ought to ask a novelist who writes pornographic work or a journalist who does work against the whole feeling of what is decent in the profession.[99]

An important test case arose when the complex scandal of Ford Madox Ford's cohabitation with Violet Hunt became public knowledge. Ford's wife, though separated from him since 1909, would not divorce him, and Ford himself had become a Catholic convert. He then attempted to circumvent these obstacles by taking out German citizenship (his father was German) and securing a divorce and remarriage in Germany. This was unrecognized in Britain, and the original Mrs Ford in 1912–13 successfully sued a journal which, carrying a publicity paragraph about the novel *The Governess*, described Hunt as Ford's wife.[100] Hunt was a member of the Women Writers' Committee, who were well aware of her relationship with Ford; but, following the court case, the advice given to her by her friends on the Committee—who included fellow novelists Marie Belloc Lowndes, Mrs W. K. Clifford, and May Sinclair—was not only to keep away from the Committee's functions but also to go abroad and stay there for however long it took. Hunt herself, like May Sinclair and several more, was a suffragist; but this counted for nothing. May Sinclair was—according to Virginia Stephen, who met her in 1909—'a woman of obtrusive, and medicinal morality; and prodded it home with little round eyes bright as steel'.[101] Hunt was mortified with disappointment: 'I expected all my friends to treat the attack with contempt and not

---

[98] Lowndes (ed.), *Lowndes Diaries and Letters*, 42 (7 Jan. 1913). *The Rosary* (1911) was Florence Barclay's best-seller, on which, see above, Ch. 20.

[99] Lowndes (ed.), *Lowndes Diaries and Letters*, 35 (22 May 1912).

[100] *The Governess* (1912) was largely written by Violet Hunt's mother, Mrs Alfred Hunt (Averil Beaumont), but completed by Violet following her mother's death and published with a preface by Ford. See Sutherland, *Companion*, 314.

[101] Virginia Stephen to Lady Robert Cecil, 12 Apr. 1909, in Nicolson and Bank (eds.), *Flight of the Mind*, 390. For a more sympathetic account of May Sinclair's response to the Ford–Hunt scandal, Raitt, *Sinclair*, 147. Her suffragist position cooled before the Great War, because of suffragette violence and party politicking. Her primary concern was for female employment; Raitt, *Sinclair*, 110–13, 149 n. 8, 171–4.

help . . . to make it impossible for me to live in England.'[102] Ford himself—'rather a fly blown man of letters',[103] in E. M. Forster's description—edited the *English Review*, which had quickly assumed a dubious reputation. When Leonard Woolf was looking to place his story 'Pearls and Swine', Forster advised with a flourish: 'Try the English Review—I know of no other magazine that will pay for erections and excrement.'[104] Later Ford perceived the essence of the fuss about his relationship with Hunt in *No More Parades* (1925), part of his Tietjens trilogy: 'English people of good position consider that the basis of all marital unions or disunions is the maxim: No scenes. Obviously for the sake of the servants—who are the same thing as the public. No scenes, then, for the sake of the public.'[105]

Writers and publishers policed themselves as much as they were policed by librarians and vigilantes. Thus, Frederic Chapman, of the publishers Chapman & Hall, had exhorted Olive Schreiner, when she submitted *The Story of an African Farm* (1883), to include a couple of sentences which would suggest that Lyndall and her Stranger had contracted a secret marriage, otherwise 'the British public would think it wicked, and Smiths, the railway booksellers, would not put it on their stalls'.[106] Chapman backed down when Schreiner threatened to take her book elsewhere; but not all first-time authors were so spirited. Somerset Maugham substituted 'stomach' for 'belly' in the manuscript of *Liza of Lambeth* (1897) because his publisher Fisher Unwin instructed that this would be less offensive; he was equally ready to alter *Mrs Craddock* (1902), his Flaubert-influenced novel, for Heinemann, although he subsequently noted that 'the propriety of the book seems almost painful'.[107] Where a magazine contract was involved, the author had no alternative. Thomas Hardy agreed to remove or rewrite offending passages when bargaining for the serialization of his fiction in order to win Tillotson's syndication or to comply with Leslie Stephen's judgement of what the *Cornhill*'s readers would find acceptable. The *Cornhill* under Stephen's editorship (1871–82) serialized 'with gingerly treatment' *Far from the Madding Crowd* (1874) but declined *The Return of the Native* (1878). Stephen scolded Hardy for letting his heroines marry the wrong man. Hardy protested that women mostly did, to which Stephen replied: 'Not in magazines.'[108] By 1894, when Hardy

---

[102] Goldring, *South Lodge*, 88–115. On Mrs W. K. Clifford (1853–1929), see Sutherland, *Companion*, 132. Maurice Hewlett dedicated his best-seller *The Forest Lovers* (1898) to her. Note also Henry James's reaction: he withdrew an invitation to Ford and Hunt to visit him in 1909. Ford's most recent and comprehensive biographer emphasizes that James did not do so out of censoriousness: he would not pronounce about their relationship, which was none of his business, but he did not wish to become embroiled in any scandal that might result from litigation. Max Saunders, *Ford Madox Ford* (Oxford, 1996), i. 294–6.

[103] To Alice Clara Forster, 22 July 1914, in Lago and Furbank (eds.), *Forster's Letters*, i. 211.

[104] To Leonard Woolf, *c*.24 May 1912, ibid. 135.   [105] Quoted in Goldring, *South Lodge*, 75.

[106] Quoted in Ruth First and Ann Scott, *Olive Schreiner* (New York, 1980), 119. *The Story of an African Farm* was first published under a male pseudonym, Ralph Iron.   [107] Morgan, *Maugham*, 63, 88–9.

[108] Millgate, *Hardy*, 211. The habit of families reading aloud serialized fiction made for constraints, although practice was variable. Having accepted that he must bow to an editor's censorship if he was to market his stories in periodicals, Hardy wrote to Clement Shorter on 28 March 1893, sending him 'Master John Horseleigh, Knight' for the *Illustrated London News*: 'If you don't like the word "bastard" which I have used you are kindly welcome to *dele* it.' But Shorter did publish it: Purdy and Millgate (eds.), *Hardy*

deleted a passage from 'An Imaginative Woman' for publication in the *Pall Mall
Magazine*, he was telling the editor, Sir Douglas Straight, not only that he did so
'quite willingly' but also that he 'may as well say once for all—in case I shd write
again for you—that I always give editors *carte blanche* in these matters...'.[109]
The need to place work in the American market also made publishers wary.
Chapman & Hall declined George Sturt's first fictional effort, *A Year's Exile*, in
1896 following a report from John Buchan, who, among other criticisms and
some applause, noted 'sickly descriptions of sensuous passion'. The manuscript
then went to John Lane of the Bodley Head. Lane had a reputation as a
womanizer, being nicknamed 'Petticoat Lane', though it was an appeal lost on
Edith Wharton, who though him 'a fat white slug'. He also had a reputation for
publishing risqué work—the *Yellow Book* and the Keynote series—and Wells
would find him willing to take on *The New Machiavelli* in 1911 after Macmillan,
Heinemann, Chapman & Hall, and more, all rejected it.[110] Yet Lane was no anti-
Grundy crusader who ignored commercial calculations; and he also hesitated
about accepting Sturt's manuscript (as Arnold Bennett put it) 'on the score that it
was *seksy* and America didn't want no seks-problems and he was determined to
please America'.[111]

Enthusiasts of convention easily outnumbered those enlisting to subvert it. So
J. A. Spender was gratified to discover in 1895 when he wrote a series of slashing
articles in the *Westminster Gazette* attacking 'a certain school of novelists for their
exploitation of the decadent and the sexual'. These articles were then published as
a pamphlet, *The New Fiction: A Protest against Sex-Mania* (1895), 'in a flaming red
cover embellished with a vigorous drawing of a frantic young woman by Mr.
Arthur Rackham'. A former Balliol classicist, Spender remained loyal to 'the
masterpieces of English literature', in poetry chiefly Wordsworth, then Tennyson, Matthew Arnold, and Browning, and in fiction Scott and Austen, then
George Eliot and Thackeray, before tackling Meredith and the early Hardy,
lightened by a little Dickens. Harrison Ainsworth and Wilkie Collins had satisfied
his generation's 'appetite for shockers', and Spender was determined to halt the
slide into lower depths. According to John Lane, he succeeded. He told Spender
in later years that his intervention 'killed the *Yellow Book* and spoilt the sales
of some of his favourite writers', one of whom accused Spender of 'literary

---

Letters, ii. 6. The editor of *Harper's Magazine*, which published a bowdlerized *Jude the Obscure* told Hardy:
'Our rule is that the Magazine must contain nothing which could not be read aloud in any family circle'
(quoted in Cox (ed.), *Hardy*, p. xxxii). Another sufferer from his publishers' insistence on happy endings
was George Gissing; see Jacob Korg's Introduction to *The Unclassed* (Brighton, 1976), p. xiii; Pierre
Coustillas's Introduction to *A Life's Morning* (Brighton, 1984), p. xvi; Nash, *Life*, 54–5.

[109] Hardy to Sir Douglas Straight, 20 Jan. 1894, in Purdy and Millgate (eds.), *Hardy Letters*, ii. 48.
[110] Lambert and Ratcliffe, *Bodley Head*, 96, 150, 152.
[111] Arnold Bennett to George Sturt, 16 May 1896, in Hepburn (ed.), *Bennett Letters*, ii. 50. Lane
eventually published the novel (in 1898) having read the manuscript himself and received Bennett's
assurances that there was nothing in it he would not publish in his magazine *Woman* and that in any case
he could freely amend any such passages if found.

homicide'.[112] That was to exaggerate Spender's part, ignoring as it did the impact of the Wilde trials; still, in 1896 Lane actually proclaimed that 'the sex novel was played out'.[113] His may be reckoned a spectacular misjudgement in the long run, but publishers were operating in current and short-term market conditions and conscious of general public taste as well as fast-moving fashions. Moreover, they had the overall reputation of their house to consider. When the literary agent Michael Joseph, who had previously worked for Hutchinson's, inquired of over forty publishers what kinds of book they were seeking for their lists, and reported their replies *in extenso* in *The Commercial Side of Literature* (1925), 'the sex novel' was mentioned only as an anathema. 'We are tired of sex novels,' said Newman Flower on behalf of Cassell's. 'Novelists who devote themselves to the minute analysis of sexual emotions would probably save time if they sent their MSS to other firms,' wrote Methuen; and John Murray attested, 'As regards fiction, I regard the more pronounced type of "problem novels" as bad in every way—bad in art, execution and influence. Such eminent writers as Sir Walter Scott, Dickens and George Eliot never condescended to such meretricious methods.' George Harrap too stated, 'I have little time for literature whose only merit is sensationalism or which appeals solely to the senses.' The recurrent note was best caught by Murray: 'Of course, every publisher wants to bring out books that pay their way—and something more—but like all who desire to uphold the dignity and good name of our craft—I want to bring out books which have a permanent value and are of use to mankind.' These replies may be discounted as so much flannel, what is now called the corporate mission statement; and perhaps John Lane's declaration that the Bodley Head 'has always been particularly noted for its introduction of original and enterprising talent to the public' should be read with a wink as an amusing code. Yet, there are no real grounds for thinking that commercial publishers, Lane included, were deliberately touting for licentious literature.[114]

Publishers' and editors' circumspection about the law regarding indecent publications and about offending their readership was predictable. What was less so was the attitude of writers themselves about what constituted proper reticence or artistic validity in the sex question.[115] The humorist Jerome K. Jerome turned all solemn on this subject:

The only suggestion I can make is that the writers of our stories should harp less upon sexuality: though at present there appears no sign of their doing so: and that among older men there should be less lewdness of talk and jest. In my schooltime, quite little boys would whisper to each other 'smutty' stories: they must have heard them from their elders. I do not speak as a prude. Some of the best and kindest men I have met have been

[112] Spender, *Life, Journalism and Politics*, i. 12–14, 58.
[113] Joseph, *Commercial Side of Literature*, 36.   [114] Ibid., ch. xii: 'What Publishers Want'.
[115] For a glimpse of the similar debate in the United States, see W. D. Howell's reply to critics of his own fiction and of his championship of Tolstoy and Zola, in his column 'The Editor's Study', *Harper's Monthly* (June 1889), repr. in Cady (ed.), *W. D. Howells as Critic*, 147–56.

grave sinners in this respect. But knowing how hard put to it a young man is to keep his thoughts from being obsessed by sexual lust, to the detriment of his body and his mind, I would that all men of good-feeling treated this deep mystery of our nature with more reverence.[116]

John Galsworthy held no such superstition. He admired sections of Lawrence's *Sons and Lovers*, especially those dealing with Paul Morel's relations with his parents; but he disliked others, notably 'the love part'. He wrote to Edward Garnett, who edited *Sons and Lovers* for publication:

that kind of revelling in the shades of sex emotions seems to me anaemic. Contrasted with Maupassant's—a frank sensualist—dealing with such emotions, it has a queer indecency; it doesn't see the essentials; it revels in the inessentials. It's not good enough to spend time and ink in describing the penultimate sensations and physical movements of people getting into a state of rut; we all know them too well . . . The body's never worth while, and the sooner Lawrence recognizes that the better—the men we swear by, Tolstoy, Turgenev, Tchekov, Maupassant, Flaubert, France, knew that great truth; they only use the body, and that sparingly, to reveal the soul.[117]

This reaction was significant coming from one who, in *The Man of Property* (1906), hardly shirked a strong subject: the hypocrisies of bourgeois marriage, where wives were acquired as decorative articles. Galsworthy had not spared the reader painful scenes as he dissected a loveless marriage. He even included a reference to marital rape where Soames forces himself on Irene, possessed by 'his over-mastering hunger'. About this, Galsworthy commented with cool irony: 'Soames asserted his rights and acted like a man.'[118] What mattered for Galsworthy was to expose the cant that enveloped the social institution of marriage and to illuminate the sufferings of individuals trapped within it. Thomas Hardy, who had held similar concerns a decade before, now privately deplored Galsworthy's treatment. Galsworthy sent Hardy a presentation copy of *The Man of Property* and,

---

[116] Jerome, *Life and Times*, 40.

[117] Galsworthy to Garnett, 13 Apr. 1914, in Garnett (ed.), *Galsworthy Letters*, 218. The response of Galsworthy's friend the naturalist W. H. Hudson is equally interesting. In *The Crystal Age* (1887), his futurist fantasy, he argued that peace in human affairs would come only with the slackening of the male sex urge; now, reading *Sons and Lovers*, he judged it a 'very good book indeed except in that portion where he relapses into the old sty—the neck-sucking and wallowing-in-sweating-flesh'. Lawrence's 'obsession' with sex, he argued, led to debased art and insincere literature, unlike the bawdy of Chaucer or Smollett. See Tomalin, *W. H. Hudson* (Oxford, 1984), 213.

[118] John Galsworthy, *The Man of Property* (Harmondsworth, 1951), 264. For Galsworthy's justification for having selected the husband's insistence on his 'conjugal rights' as the point of marital breakdown, 'that last and most violent degradation of the spirit', both between Soames and Irene in *The Man of Property*, and between George and Clare Desmond in his play *The Fugitive* (first staged in a matinée at the Court Theatre on 16 September 1913), see his letter, 20 Sept. 1913, in *Glimpses and Reflections*, 267–8. Arnold Bennett, impressed by *The Man of Property* as a 'really distinguished, passionate, truly romantic universal book', judged that 'the erotic parts—and there are plenty of them—were done under the influence of George Moore. If Galsworthy had never read and admired George Moore, the similarity is extremely remarkable' (Flower (ed.), *Bennett Journals*, i. 368–9 (30 May, 4 June 1910)). *The Fugitive* by contrast fell flat, a didactic story unrelieved by interest in character or plot: see the scathing review by Desmond Mac-Carthy, 27 Sept. 1913 (when the play had been transferred to the Prince of Wales Theatre), in MacCarthy, *Drama*, 194–9.

Hardy told Florence Henniker, 'I began it, but found the people too materialistic & sordid to be interesting.'[119]

Galsworthy, however, was decidedly no Lawrence. He did not denounce the God of Property in order to light a candle on the altar of physical love. Sexual frustration was a symptom but sexual satisfaction was not a solution. He would not elevate the sex instinct and reject the intellect and the spirit. Further:

to write grossly of sex, to labour in a story the physical side of love is to err aesthetically— to over-paint; for the imagination of readers requires little stimulus in that direction, and the sex impulse is so strong that any emphatic physical description pulls the picture out of perspective. A naïve or fanatical novelist may think that by thoroughly exploring sex he can reform the human attitude to it; but a man might as well enter the bowels of the earth with the intention of coming out on the other side. If it were not for the physical side of love we should none of us be here, and the least sophisticated of us knows intuitively so much about it that to tell us more, except in scientific treatises, is to carry coals to Newcastle. But the atmosphere and psychology of passion are other matters; and the trackless maze in which the average reader wanders where his feelings are concerned is none the worse for a night-light or two. In every artist, moreover, who is not a freak there is a sensibility to the scent and colour of the Dark Flower, to its fascination, and the fates lurking within its lure, which demands a vent. And though—especially in England and America—many novelists deliberately stifle this sensibility, and treat of passion exclusively as the prelude to wedding-bells, they do so at the expense of truth and their stature as artists . . .

But whatever explanation biologists may offer of the puritanical streak in Anglo-Saxon blood will leave the artist unconsoled and open to the attacks of a particularly virulent type of intolerance, which in turn produces a spirit of revolt, often expressing itself in terms of sexual exaggeration equally undesirable. The artist is better advised to pay no attention, but to tell the truth as delicately and decently as he can. *L'excès est toujours un mal*, whether in Puritan or his victim.[120]

Galsworthy was thus disinclined to mistake for artistic genius a medical report about the gymnastics involved in sexual intercourse.

---

[119] Hardy to John Galsworthy, 8 Apr. 1906, and to Florence Henniker, 12 Sept. 1906, in Purdy and Millgate (eds.), *Hardy Letters*, iii. 201, 225.

[120] Galsworthy, 'Faith of a Novelist' (1926), in Galsworthy, *Castles in Spain*, 184–6. Galsworthy published *The Dark Flower* in 1912.

28

Theology versus Sociology and Psychology

I

Provincial–metropolitan tensions in English culture were nothing new, but they became acute as a result of intellectual, political, and social transformations developing since the 1860s, when Matthew Arnold gave vent to an impassioned Hellenism and Anglicanism. For Arnold, culture meant the poetic spirit in pursuit of 'a harmonious perfection'. It could flourish only in an environment of 'sweetness and light', the antithesis of a provincialism defined as vulgar materialism and philistine Nonconformity. How, Arnold asked, could a provincial politician persist 'with his glorifying of the great towns' and not see the ugliness, misery, and ignorance which urban industrialization had generated; above all, 'how do you propose to cure it with such a religion as yours? How is the ideal of a life so unlovely, so unattractive, so incomplete, so narrow, so far removed from a true and satisfying ideal of human perfection, to conquer and transform all this vice and hideousness?'[1] To cultivate the poetic spirit in national literature was essential, as a means of disseminating 'beauty', not scientific 'truth' or theological dogma. Arnold predicted that increasingly men would 'have to turn to poetry to interpret life for us, to console us, to sustain us. Without poetry our science will appear incomplete; and most of what now passes for religion and philosophy will be replaced by poetry.'[2]

This was not a course of action that commended itself to the leader of the English Positivists, Frederic Harrison, for whom Christianity was destined to develop into the Religion of Humanity. He was not prepared to allow Literature, still less one branch of it, to throw that desirable evolution off course. Poets were no match for Positivists. Poetry, he proclaimed, 'is one thing, Science, Action,

---

[1] Matthew Arnold, *Culture and Anarchy*, ed. J. Dover Wilson (Cambridge, 1932), 18, 58. The first question was asked of John Bright, the second of the *Nonconformist* journal.

[2] Arnold, 'The Study of Poetry', quoted in L. E. Elliott-Binns, *English Thought 1860–1900: The Theological Aspect* (1956), 297. This was in line with Carlyle's prediction in 1831: 'Literature is but a branch of Religion, and always participates in its character: however, in our time, it is the only branch that still shows any greenness; and, as some think, must one day become the main stem' ('Characteristics', *Edinburgh Review*, no. 108 (1831), in Carlyle, *Critical and Miscellaneous Essays*, iv. 20).

Life, Religion are far other—all much wider and more continuous. Poetry is but one mode of Art, and Art is but *one* side of *one* of the elements of Human Nature.' Hence, 'poets are not (for all some people say) the guides of life: their business is to beautify life'.[3] It was also rather rich of Arnold to have blamed provincial Nonconformity for an attenuated culture when the educational establishment of Oxbridge formally excluded its followers, as many a Nonconformist did not fail to rejoinder.[4] 'A dandy Isaiah' was what George Meredith called him.[5] Nevertheless, the literary treatment of Nonconformity frequently echoed Arnold and was disparaging. For every acknowledgement of the warmth, fellowship, and ideal of chapel life, there were more indictments of its meanness, coldness, jealousy, repressiveness, and obscurantism. Even after the turn of the twentieth century there were still to be found Nonconformists who shunned novel-reading in the belief that works of the imagination drew people away from God and into mischief—the very notion which Carlyle indexed in his *Critical and Miscellaneous Essays*: 'Fiction, and its kinship to lying'.[6] When Florence Murray married in 1902, her husband, a Colne valley woollen manufacturer, was a widower with a young son in poor health who was looked after by an aged housekeeper. This house-keeper was 'an extra particular Baptist'; hence, 'many channels of conversation were closed by reason of her persuasion'. No mention to her, therefore, of the newly-weds' dancing and playing cards, or of their visit to the theatre and shopping exploits during a stay in London. However, one wet afternoon Florence 'took David Copperfield from the bookshelf and boldly began to read it aloud to her while she knitted. She disapproved of novels, but I represented it as Dickens' life. It was such a treat after the everlasting sermons, her usual literature, that the old lady was greatly interested and amused and she remembered every detail.'[7]

Novelists generally showed as little sympathy to Nonconformists as they received from them. Dickens had given currency to the worst stereotypes, Stiggins in *Pickwick Papers* (1837) and Chadband in *Bleak House* (1852–3); and George Eliot's Bulstrode in *Middlemarch* (1871—2) further enforced an image of Nonconformist pious pretence and commercial sharp practice, at best canting humbugs, at worst cheating hypocrites. George Moore's cameo of a Non-conformist shopkeeping family in *Esther Waters* (1894) was modelled to the point of caricature: 'the Bingleys were Dissenters who exacted the uttermost farthing from their customers and their workpeople. Mrs Bingley spoke in a sour, resolute voice, when she came down in a wrapper to superintend the cooking, but on

---

[3] Vogeler, *Harrison*, 289.

[4] Cunningham, *Everywhere Spoken Against*, 18–22. Following the repeal of university religious tests in 1871, Oxford contained some 100–200 Nonconformist undergraduates by the early 1880s, and sundry Nonconformist dons; by 1900 the number was about 500. Total undergraduate numbers were rising meanwhile, from 2,000 to 3,000 in the early 20th century, among whom sons (and daughters) of Anglican clergy remained well represented. See Brock and Curthoys (eds.), *Nineteenth Century Oxford*, 103–4, 578.

[5] Lady Battersea's journal, 2 Sept. 1897, in Cohen, *Rothschild and her Daughters*, 256.

[6] Carlyle, *Critical and Miscellaneous Essays*, vii. 267.

[7] Mrs Josiah Lockwood, *An Ordinary Life 1861–1924* (1932), 107–8.

Sundays she wore a black satin, fastened with a cameo brooch, and then her manners were lofty.' Esther is employed by them as 'general servant, with wages fixed at sixteen pounds a year; and for seventeen long hours every day, for two hundred and thirty hours every fortnight, she washed, she scrubbed, she cooked, she ran errands, with never a moment that she might call her own'.[8] The Bingleys' pasty-faced son spies on her and, predictably, seeks to entrap her by leaving a half-crown on the floor. Then there is Fred Parsons, whom Moore introduces with mocking distaste. He is physically unattractive: meagre build, sloping shoulders, pointed face, with a voice into which 'no trace of doubt ever seemed to come, and his mind was neatly packed with a few religious and political ideas . . . He had been in business in the West End, but an unrestrained desire to ask every customer if he were sure he believed in the second coming of Christ had been the cause of his dismissal.'[9] Fred, however, becomes a more appealing character in Moore's hands. He proposes marriage to Esther in full knowledge that she has an illegitimate child; moreover, after his rejection by Esther, who goes to live with the child's father, William Latch, he tips her off that there is to be a police raid on the public house where William conducts an illegal bookmaking business. In none of this is Fred Parsons seen to abrogate his principles. His theology remains basic, and he disapproves of novels. He believes in the existence of sin and the need to suppress sin, which in his view includes betting; but he also believes in the forgiveness of sin for those who truly repent, and he behaves with generosity to Esther and without hypocrisy to the world. What explains this more sympathetic portrayal? The clue is found in the description of Fred when he comes into the bar of the King's Head to warn Esther:

He wore the cap and jersey of the Salvation Army; he was now Captain Parsons . . . 'Oh, it is you, Fred', and she stood looking at him, surprised by his uniform. 'So you are in the Army?' 'Yes, I've joined up', he answered; 'but I was always in it in spirit from the beginning, as I think you know.'[10]

Moore was prepared to make an exception in favour of the Salvation Army, not because he subscribed to its credo but because, however wrong-headed they might be, its members demonstrated moral courage in proclaiming their faith at large and acting upon it by giving succour to the fallen.[11]

It was the by now established and institutionalized Nonconformist sects that Moore, in common with other self-consciously modern writers of radical or progressive opinions, could not abide. Even (or especially) those who had been brought up in the Dissenting tradition, such as Mark Rutherford, by the 1880s were disparaging the theological narrowness, social gracelessness, and moral deceptions of chapel-going Nonconformity. Mark Rutherford was born in Bedford like his hero John Bunyan, but disillusionment drove him to conclude that religious Dissent

---

[8] Moore, *Esther Waters*, 150.   [9] Ibid. 174.   [10] Ibid. 277.
[11] Walter Besant made the same exception in his *Autobiography*.

was now devitalized. What remained was a petrified small-mindedness, with mechanical 'conversion' experiences and prefabricated homilies. The 'emptiness' and 'worldliness' of fellow Dissenting ministers plunges Mark Rutherford into melancholia, from which only a reading of Wordsworth's *Lyrical Ballads* rescues him: 'his real God is not the God of the Church, but the God of the hills, the abstraction Nature, and to this my reverence was transferred'.[12] There was no lyricism at all in Hubert Henry Davies, only a smouldering resentment against a censorious Welsh Nonconformist father who threatened to turn him out of the family home when he learned that he had gone to the theatre to see Henry Irving and Ellen Terry in *The Merchant of Venice*. Davies emigrated to America and returned to become one of Edwardian England's most fashionable playwrights. In *Lady Epping's Lawsuit*, which played at the Criterion in 1908, Davies includes the Revd Dr Gull as an unlovely representation of the Nonconformist divine. For the purposes of the play, he is Scottish not Welsh—the Eppings have invited him down to their London home from their Scots estate—but all the common characteristics are intact. Gull denounces any sort of recreation on Sundays (*'emphasising his words with uncouth gesture*: The Sawbath is the Sawbath, my lord, whether ye be in Scotland or whether ye be in England. The Sawbath is the Sawbath'); and he blows his top when he discovers that Lady Epping herself is writing a play for 'the theayter' (*'bringing his fist heavily down on the tea tray and shouting*: . . . I thought I were in England, but I see that I'm e'en in the city of Babylon'). Lady Epping begins to repent of the invitation, though her daughter demurs, cherishing the man entirely as a figure of derision:

LADY EPPING. Oh, look at my poor husband talking to that dreadful Dr. Gull. I
    thought I was so fortunate to secure the Caledonian Missionary for one of my
    parties, but he's such an awful bore.
LUCY. Oh, but he's so funny when he eats fish.

Table entertainment aside, Dr Gull is pronounced fit only to lead the servants in hymn-singing, which Lucy encourages their other house guests to look in on— 'Dr. Gull is *sure* to beat time with his arms and legs. So *sweet!*'[13]

II

This was a jaundiced picture of Nonconformity; however, what is striking as the nineteenth century waned is not that so many novelists and dramatists broadly registered this impression but how the whole question of religious truth within

---

[12] [William Hale White], *The Autobiography of Mark Rutherford*, ed. William S. Peterson (Oxford, 1990), 22. Hale White (1831–1913) followed up the *Autobiography* with *Mark Rutherford's Deliverance* (1885), *The Revolution in Tanner's Lane* (1887), *Miriam's Schooling* (1890), *Catherine Furze* (1893), and *Clara Hopgood* (1896). He wrote a Life of Bunyan in 1905. On Hale White, see Sutherland, *Companion*, 669–70; and Flower (ed.), *Bennett Journals*, ii. 83 (19 Feb. 1914) on reading the *Autobiography* and *Deliverance*.
[13] Davies, *Plays*, i. 162–7.

the Christian tradition ceased to occupy their attention. Theosophy, tapping Hindu and Buddhist mysticism, and experiment in the occult were preferred; otherwise, intellectual and social progress came to be associated with detachment from religious scruples. Paganism was lustily proclaimed, as by followers of Whitman, for whom the appeal of animals was that they 'do not make me sick discussing their duty to God'.[14] Alternatively, the further advance of mankind would arise from the application of scientific understanding, such as the laws of eugenics as promulgated by Francis Galton or of civics as enunciated by Patrick Geddes. There was admittedly need for additional research in these areas, which was why Galton endowed a post at London University for 'the study of the agencies under social control that may improve or impair the racial qualities of future generations either physically or mentally'.[15] For eugenics to become accepted social policy there were

three stages to be passed through. *Firstly* it must be made familiar as an academic question, until its exact importance has been understood and accepted as fact; *Secondly* it must be recognised as a subject whose practical development deserves serious consideration; and *Thirdly* it must be introduced into the national conscience, like a new religion. It has, indeed, strong claims to become an orthodox religious tenet of the future, for Eugenics co-operate with the workings of Nature by securing that humanity shall be represented by the fittest races.[16]

Too many people, authors in the van, reached stage three without awaiting the completion of stage one. Zola was identified by several medical critics as responsible for diffusing a 'totally false conception as to what the laws of heredity are, and as to how they work out in the human race. He supposes that since the parents have certain mental and moral peculiarities the children will reproduce them with variations.'[17] Bernard Shaw jumped the gun too: 'nothing but a eugenic religion can save our civilisation from the fate that has overtaken all previous civilisations', he declared:

What we must fight for is freedom to breed the race without being hampered by the mass of irrelevant conditions implied in the institution of marriage . . . What we need is freedom for people who have never seen each other before and never intend to see one another again to produce children under certain definite public conditions, without loss of honour.[18]

H. G. Wells was another writer to be excited by eugenics. In 1904 he acknowledged that Galton had modified his position since his original statement (in his Huxley

---

[14] Hart-Davis, *Lyttelton Hart-Davis Letters*, 303 (21 May 1957).

[15] Francis Galton, 'A Eugenic Investigation', in Galton *et al., Sociological Papers* (1905), 89.

[16] Galton, 'Eugenics: Its Definition, Scope and Aims', ibid. 50.

[17] Dr C. A. Mercier in the discussion following Galton's paper at the meeting of the Sociological Society on 16 May 1904, ibid. 55. Dr C. W. Saleeby, 'Eugenics: The New Scientific Patriotism', *The World's Work* (Dec. 1904), made the same criticism of Zola; ibid. 83. Mercier was a physician specializing in mental illnesses at Charing Cross Hospital; Saleeby was an obstetrician, who married a daughter of the poet Alice Meynell.

[18] Shaw in the discussion following Galton's paper, 16 May 1904, *Sociological Papers* (1905), 74–5.

Lecture in 1901). Thus the simple proposition that 'superior persons must mate with superior persons' was untenable. Wells indeed was

inclined to believe that a large proportion of our present-day criminals are the brightest and boldest members of families living under impossible conditions, and that in many desirable qualities the average criminal is above the average of the law-abiding poor, and probably of the average respectable person. Many eminent criminals appear to me to be persons superior in many respects, in intelligence, initiative, originality, to the average judge. I will confess I have never known either,

he added coyly. However, Wells was convinced that the inverse proposition still held, namely, 'inferior persons must not have offspring at all'; and this should be made public policy. It fitted with our understanding of evolution,

that in the all-round result the inferior usually perish, and the average of the species rises, but not that any exceptionally favourable variations get together and reproduce . . . The way of Nature has always been to slay the hindmost, and there is still no other way, unless we can prevent those who would become the hindmost being born. It is in the sterilisation of failures, and not in the selection of successes for breeding, that the possibility of an improvement of the human stock lies.[19]

Wells liked to think of himself as applying science to social problems; but science did not suffuse every part of him. When in *A Modern Utopia* (1905) he presented his idea of a new samurai, a sort of secular priesthood of scientifically trained experts, Arnold Bennett scornfully riposted: 'Why should the Samurai have any religion? I hope you aren't going to defend that worn out platitude to the effect that religion is a necessity of man's nature. Because it isn't. Religion is done for—any sort of religion.'[20] Bennett added in a letter of 23 November 1908, 'I myself have never, at any rate for 25 years, had the slightest movement towards worship or anything resembling worship.'[21] Bennett dabbled in rather than systematically explored other options. In 1917 he participated in a séance with W. B. Yeats and Roger Fry, and appeared quite impressed;[22] but, Bennett's wife insisted, though he wrote a story called *The Ghost* (1907), he did not believe in ghosts either.[23] Wells was not so definite about things. When the Rationalist Press wanted to issue a sixpenny edition of *Anticipations* (1901), it was pointed out to him that 'God' was mentioned several times in the book and their subscribers would not like this. Of course, the Rationalist Press noted helpfully, they knew

[19] Wells in the discussion following Galton's paper, 16 May 1904, ibid. 58–60. Cf. Max Beerbohm's parody of Wells—'Perkins and Mankind'—which contains the description of General Cessation Day, when citizens of the future, who have reached the legal age limit, cheerfully present themselves for extermination at the Municipal Lethal Chamber; *Christmas Garland*, 33–47.

[20] Bennett to Wells, 18 Apr. 1905, in Hepburn (ed.), *Bennett Letters*, ii. 196.   [21] Ibid. 230.

[22] Flower (ed.), *Bennett Journals*, ii. 185–6 (8 Feb. 1917).

[23] Bennett, *My Arnold Bennett*, 99. *The Ghost* was actually a reworking of the first serial Bennett sold to Tillotson's in the late 1890s, for £75. It underwent several changes of title, *The Curse of Love*, then *For Love and Life*. As *The Ghost*, it sold poorly and Bennett blushed about both its quality and its sales; Drabble, *Bennett*, 79, 82.

that Wells only used the word figuratively; to which Wells replied, 'Not so figuratively as all that.'[24] Wells's principal objections to the Christian religion concerned its established, institutional form. As a teacher wanting employment he had bridled at schools whose statutes obliged its staff to be Anglican communicants, seeing such a test as a barrier to meritocracy. Again, the Churches' resistance to, or incomplete acceptance of, scientific doctrines of evolution led Wells to deride sacerdotal authority; he was equally plainly at odds with orthodox ethical teaching about marriage and sexual freedom. Wells was very much the modern man in wanting instant results. As a child he had implored God for assistance and enlightenment in answering an examination paper; but when God did not deliver on cue, Wells thereafter did not set much store by prayer.[25] Nonetheless, there remained a religious side to Wells, and the Great War years saw him develop it more.[26] It was erratic and idiosyncratic; all the same, it was a religious streak. As the editor of the *Church Times* recognized: 'He is religious, but he has preferred to invent a religion for himself.'[27]

Here, ironically, Henry James showed himself more 'advanced' than Wells. James's 'passion for research', Desmond MacCarthy noted, was confined exclusively to the social side of human nature. He was fascinated by what was 'hidden, ambiguous, illusive and hard to understand' in human emotions and in their 'complex, shifting relations'. This was an interest in the obscure, not the mystical. Both Nature and God were not so much written off as written out of James's work: 'The universe and religion are as completely excluded from his books as if he had been an eighteenth-century writer. The sky above his people, the earth beneath them, contains no mysteries for them. He is careful never to permit them to interrogate these.'[28] James was, as Joseph Conrad styled him, 'the historian of fine consciences'; but this was as an observer of social phenomena, and 'the mass of weaknesses, vacillations, secondary motives and false steps and compromises which make up the sum of our activity' did not include theological perplexities.[29] As the proprietor of Lamb House, one of the historic houses of Rye, James enjoyed the privilege of having his own 'immemorial pew' in the church nearby; but he entered it once only. Sundays usually found James dictating to his typist with a glance through the window to observe the church congregation 'go in to their righteousness and come out to their dinners'.[30] James's so-called supernatural tales, notably *The Turn of the Screw* (1898), he styled 'a trap for the unwary'. Unlike that band of psychical researchers who included his brother William, the Harvard sage, Henry James was not interested in verifying or explaining ghostly phenomena. He abstained from

---

[24] Flower (ed.), *Bennett Journals*, i. 190 (31 July 1904).   [25] Wells, *Autobiography*, i. 96–7.
[26] On this, see above, Ch. 26.   [27] Dark, *Mainly about Other People*, 168.
[28] MacCarthy, *Portraits*, i. 159.
[29] 'Henry James: An Appreciation', *North American Review* (1905), in Conrad, *Notes on Life and Letters*, 13–23.   [30] Edel, *James*, ii. 372.

'specifications' in these stories in order to heighten the power of imagination, in particular to convey the awful plasticity of children's imagination: 'So long as the events are veiled the imagination will run riot and depict all sorts of horrors, but as soon as the veil is lifted, all mystery disappears and with it the sense of terror.'[31]

Religion, unmentionable by James, was unavoidable for Bennett if he was going to render a true picture of provincial culture in his fiction. In spite of his own decided irreligion, Bennett kept the Bible at his bedside and read it. He perceived it as 'probably the finest treasury in existence, east or west', of 'purely mystical emotion'. He thought, further, that 'many religious people, and many readers of the Bible, seem to be insensible to mysticism, and are thus deprived of what is perhaps the deepest source of private comfort'.[32] Nevertheless, Bennett was unqualified to handle the subject of religious feeling and practice. He knew nothing first-hand about the metaphysics and ritual of the Established Church. He recorded as an event in his journal in 1918 'the first morning Church of England service I ever (I think) attended in my life';[33] and his fictional treatment of Methodism in the life of the Potteries was more anthropological than theological. When he conceived of the novel that was to become *Anna of the Five Towns* (1902) in 1896, he stated in his journal that it was to be 'a study of paternal authority'.[34] Religion could not be left out because it made for tribal organization; but what really mattered was money and mastery, and the story of Anna Tellwright is essentially about escape from the agglutinated, joyless respectability of provincial society, as personified by her father, Ephraim, the Wesleyan circuit treasurer. Religion was the lever by which he became 'a man of great wealth, having few rivals in the entire region of the Five Towns':

he expounded the mystery of the Atonement in village conventicles and grew garrulous with God at prayer-meetings in the big Bethesda chapel; but he did these things as routine, without skill and without enthusiasm, because they gave him an unassailable position within the central group of the society. He was not, in fact, much smitten with either the doctrinal or the spiritual side of Methodism. His chief interest lay in those fiscal schemes of organization without whose aid no religious propaganda can possibly succeed. It was in the finance of salvation that he rose supreme—the interminable alternation of debt-raising and new liability which provides a lasting excitement for Nonconformists. In the negotiation of mortgages, the artful arrangement of appeals, the planning of anniversaries, and of mighty revivals, he was an undisputed leader . . . The minister by his pleading might bring sinners to the penitent form, but it was Ephraim Tellwright who reduced the cost per head of souls saved, and so widened the frontiers of the Kingdom of Heaven.[35]

---

[31] Ibid. 254–6.   [32] Bennett, *Journal 1929*, 158, 164.
[33] Flower (ed.), *Bennett Journal*, ii. 223 (18 Mar. 1918).   [34] Ibid. i. 15 (29 Sept. 1896).
[35] Arnold Bennett, *Anna of the Five Towns* (Harmondsworth, 1936), 32.

III

Arnold Bennett's materialist and instrumental interpretation of the role of religion was common among many Edwardian novelists.[36] In this they both reflected and hastened a public disenchantment with theological discussion. That may be measured also by the output of new publications. In 1885–9 some 14 per cent of new books were classified as theological, but fewer than 8 per cent could be placed in this category by 1911–14.[37] Juvenile and adult fiction, poetry and drama, together made up over a quarter to a third of all books; but such figures convey the impression of a speedily spreading secularity that is misleading. Works of formal theology may have been in relative decline, but the quantity of fiction whose tone or theme was religious remained considerable. This included many best-sellers. Historians would be unwise to underestimate the influence in the fiction market exerted by the church- and chapel-going public.

That the Christian message was now being commonly transmitted through works of fiction and mixed up with adventure and romance was naturally deplored by the older generation, whose habits were more austere. The leading Congregationalist divine Dr R. W. Dale complained in the 1890s that even Nonconformist ministers now derived their sermons from novels. He added, 'I hear very discouraging things sometimes—things showing the most melancholy indifference, on the part of very good men, to exegesis and to the whole range of theological inquiry.'[38] Others were more sanguine. When the thousandth number of the *British Weekly* was issued on 28 December 1905, its editor, Robertson Nicoll, trumpeted that 'Nonconformity as a religious force has conspicuously advanced.' *Inter alia*, he acknowledged that the 'signal feature in literature is the increasing power and predominance of fiction'. But he did not see this as necessarily a mark of irreligion or cause for Churchmen to despair. On the contrary, this widening market of readers spelled opportunity; and he believed, as his biographer put it, 'that there will yet arise some great modern novelist as a chief apostle of God'.[39] It is not evident that Nicoll had any particular novelist in mind for that mission. Rather, he gave encouragement to a wide variety of authors whose work, while even critical of the shortcomings of Nonconformity such as Mark Rutherford or Ellen Thorneycroft Fowler, he believed fundamentally healthy and Christian in spirit. He was especially keen to promote Ian Maclaren, S. R. Crockett, Joseph Hocking, and Annie S. Swan.[40] Moreover,

---

[36] The Fabian J. H. Harley, who had been ordained a Congregationalist minister, criticized Bennett on this very point, as a serious shortcoming in his quality as a novelist. For Harley's paper, and the divided opinions it aroused in debate at the Rainbow Circle in 1918, see Freeden (ed.), *Minutes of the Rainbow Circle*, 281.

[37] See Jonathan Rose, *The Edwardian Temperament, 1895–1919* (Athens, Ohio, 1986), app. The war years 1914–18 brought a minor revival.

[38] R. W. Dale to E. A. Lawrence, 16 Aug. 1894, in A. W. W. Dale, *The Life of R. W. Dale of Birmingham* (1898), 680.   [39] Darlow, *Nicoll*, 190, 271.

[40] Ibid. 331–3.

Nicoll's positive attitude towards fiction was increasingly adopted by Churchmen of all stripes, and pulpits almost routinely rang with some reference to the talked-about novel of the moment. This was not surprising, given the state of affairs described by the Revd B. J. Johns, who exposed 'the traffic in sermons' in the *Fortnightly Review* in 1892. He denounced most preaching as dry, dreary, and platitudinous failures, because clergy were resorting to hacks who had an ample stock of sermons, at anything from 9*d*. to a guinea, or job lots at 10*s*. per quarter.[41] Little wonder many a clergyman reached for a novel in order to supply some fizz to a routine sermon. For their authors, this publicity oxygenated sales.

There was no more striking instance than Guy Thorne's *When it was Dark* (1903). Published by Greening & Co., at 20 Cecil Court, off Charing Cross Road, London, the novel was in its 175th thousand after a year, by which time a cheap popular edition was available. By 1908 Greening's catalogue offered a variety of editions to suit the pocket: six shillings, 1*s*. 6*d*., and sixpenny, and proclaimed the '310th Thousand'.[42] Boomed as 'The most daring and original novel of the century'—the reading public may have needed pinching to recall that the century was only a few years old—it was lauded by a gaggle of leading clergymen: the Dean of Durham and the Bishop of Exeter, Father Ignatius and the proponent of the New Theology the Revd R. J. Campbell. The publisher's advertisement also included a sizeable paragraph about the book from a Westminster Abbey sermon by the Bishop of London. There was space, too, for plaudits from the *Pall Mall Gazette* and *Daily News*; and, so sensational was *When it was Dark*, a rejoinder followed—*When it was Light* (1906), published by John Long, with whom Guy Thorne had placed his next popular success, *A Lost Cause*. The writer of *When it was Light* was masked: the title page stated only that it was 'By A Well-known Author', though it was attributed to Andrew Lang.[43] The author of *When it was Dark* also wore disguise: 'Guy Thorne' was the pseudonym of Cyril Arthur Edward Ranger Gull, aged 27 and educated at Manchester Grammar School, Denstone College, and (he liked to claim in *Who's Who*) Oxford.[44] He was on the literary staff of the *Saturday Review*, 1897–8, writing also for *The Bookman* and *The Academy*; he was editor of *London Life*, 1899, then on the *Daily Mail* before moving to the *Daily Express* and, while contributing to the gossip weekly *Society*, mostly giving up journalism for novel-writing. His first novel was *The Hypocrite: A Modern Novel of Oxford and London Life* (1898), published anonymously at first, though listed under his name in Greening's 1908 catalogue when it was in its

---

[41] The Revd B. J. Johns, 'The Traffic in Sermons', *Fortnightly Review* (Feb. 1892), *Review of Reviews* (Feb. 1892), 181.

[42] Greening & Co., 1908 catalogue, 52. Greening's had moved premises, now based at 51 Charing Cross Mansions, and 91 St Martin's Lane, London.

[43] This is not included in the bibliography of Lang's works compiled by Roger Lancelyn Green, *Andrew Lang* (Leicester, 1946).

[44] *Who's Who* (1905), 1329. Ranger Gull (1875–1923) now has a notice, by Caroline Zilboorg, in the *Oxford DNB*. This has him matriculating at Oxford in 1894 as a non-affiliated student and leaving within a year. Charles Bernard Ranger Gull (his younger brother) matriculated at St Edmund Hall in 1897 and received his BA in 1903.

seventh impression, at 2s. 6d., and in a popular sixpenny. The hypocrite—or cynic—appears well to capture Ranger Gull's relaunch as a supposed guardian of Christianity. He was a drinker on a heroic scale, who used to soak up the stuff in the louche company of Ernest Dowson, Reggie Turner, and Leonard Smithers. When in Cornwall, he planted whisky bottles all over Bodmin Moor so that while out strolling he was buoyed by knowing that he was never far away from a tipple.[45]

When it was Dark was subtitled 'The Story of a Great Conspiracy'. It is difficult now to summarize that plot without risibility; but it underlines the distance that separates us from the turn of the twentieth-century best-seller.[46] *When it was Dark* involves a conspiracy to forge an inscription in the Holy Land which, when discovered, will read: 'I, Joseph of Arimathœa, took the body of Jesus, the Nazarene, from the tomb where it was first laid and hid it in this place.' The readers of 1903 would instantly recognize that if Joseph had removed and concealed Jesus' corpse, then the disciples who believed Jesus rose from the dead had been duped or else were trying to deceive the world. Thus, the Resurrection did not take place, and Christianity was founded on a hoax or a lie. In 1896 Coulson Kernahan also had had a best-seller with *The Child, the Wise Man and the Devil*: this too involved the discovery of Christ's body and the questioning of his divinity. In 1898 that was being marketed in cheap editions, with the announcement 'the fiftieth thousand now ready' and the endorsement of two glowing reviews from prominent clergymen:

It is powerfully conceived, and thrills with passion, but its chief value is its exposure of the hopelessness and impossibility of the goal to which modern infidelity would conduct us. It will arrest and convince thousands.

(Revd F. B. Meyer)

No laboured apology for Christianity will go so far or accomplish so much as this impassioned utterance, this poem in prose, this thought of the years distilled in one pearl-drop of purest water.

(Revd Dr R. F. Horton)[47]

---

[45] Mackenzie, *Life and Times*, iii. 12. The present author, living also on Bodmin Moor, has unhappily not located any of these—a tribute to Ranger Gull's memory retrieval and/or thirst.

[46] Written before the best-selling success of Dan Brown's *The Da Vinci Code* (2004), with its lurid premiss that Jesus avoided a crucified death, cleared off to the south of France, married Mary Magdalene, and sired children. This tapped into centuries of hokum concerning the Knights Templar, myriad secret societies, and heterodox religious orders; see Bill Putnam and John Edwin Wood, 'Unravelling the Da Vinci Code', *History Today* (Jan. 2005), 18–20; Bernard Hamilton, 'Puzzling Success: Specious History, Religious Bigotry and the Power of Symbols in *The Da Vinci Code*', *TLS*, 10 June 2005.

[47] Advertisement contained in Charles Garvice, *Just a Girl* (1898). The publisher was James Bowden, manager of Ward, Lock & Bowden, for whom Kernahan acted as reader. Meyer was a leading Baptist, Horton a leading Congregationalist. Kernahan's publications enjoyed large sales, although there is some discrepancy between Sutherland, *Companion*, 350, where *The Child, the Wise Man and the Devil* 'is estimated to have sold upward of a quarter of a million copies', and Kemp *et al.* (eds.), *Edwardian Fiction*, 223, where it is said that Kernahan's 'religious works, *God and the Ant* (1895) and *The Child, The Wise Man And The Devil* (1896) had combined sales exceeding 100,000'.

Both Kernahan's and Ranger Gull's novels rested on the assumption that all civilized life depended upon the validity of Christian faith—and that their readership would endorse that precondition. In *When it was Dark*, when news of the inscription is flashed across the wires, hard-boiled reporters tremble and faint, non-Christian India rises against its discredited imperial masters, the Turks mount even more terrible Balkan massacres, Russia mobilizes, and throughout the once civilized world—which, following the author's criteria, means Britain, America, and Australia—anarchy and crime obtain: the Stock Market crashes, communal sanctions disintegrate, women are raped, mayhem takes over.

Who are the architects of this global destruction? It is the fell scheme of a corrupt media tycoon, a Jew, Constantine Schuabe, in league with the director of the Palestine department of the British Museum, Professor Sir Robert Llewellyn, who owes Schuabe a vast sum of money, borrowed to finance his immoral living. And who are the eventual saviours of the world, after darkness has reigned for a full six months? The principals are a High Church curate, Basil Gortre, who 'had private means of his own, and belonged to an old west country family', and Harold Spence, a former university extension lecturer, now a leader-writer for the *Daily Wire*, who 'was at Merton [College, Oxford] with me, you know, lived on the same staircase in "Stubbins", and is just one of the best fellows in the world.'[48] Harold is 'a great friend of the Pusey House people at Oxford'.[49] They share bachelor rooms in Lincoln's Inn with a largely absentee third tenant, Cyril Hands, a young Cambridge professor of archaeology who is the unwitting means of introducing to the world the devastating inscription. Happily, when the fraud is uncovered Llewellyn is torn apart by a righteously indignant mob and Schuabe ends his days as a gibbering idiot in an asylum, where he provides entertainment for visiting parties of young ladies.

The grotesquerie of the plot, the snobbishness of the characterization, and the extreme nastiness of the stereotypes will strike the modern reader. To the author, an apparent concern of *When it was Dark* is to detail the obstacles in the way of bringing religious truth to a north-country urban parish whose inhabitants are largely 'contemptuous of all that was not tangible and material'.[50] We first meet Basil when he is about to move to a prosperous parish in London's Bloomsbury after four futile years as curate at St Thomas's in an industrial conurbation, styled Walktown in the story. He is engaged to the daughter of St Thomas's vicar, Ambrose Byars, who is isolated in his ministry because of the strength of Dissent, and especially Unitarianism, in the district. Byars is unshakeable in his beliefs:

He held that, even scientifically, historically and materially the evidence for the Resurrection was too strong to be ever overthrown. And beyond these intellectual evidences he knew that Christ must have risen from the dead, because he himself had found Christ and was found in him.[51]

[48] Thorne, *When it was Dark*, 13.   [49] Ibid. 15.
[50] Ibid. 8. Ranger Gull's father served as vicar of such parishes, Pendleton near Manchester and Rainhill near Liverpool.   [51] Ibid. 9.

But Byars has to contend with the tiresome objections of such as Baxter, owner of an engineering firm, who

never came to church on what he called 'principle', but spent his Sundays in bed with a sporting paper, [and] was one of those half-educated people who condemn Christianity by ridiculing the Old Testament stories.

They walked home together, Baxter quoting the *Origin of Species*, which he knew from a cheap epitomised handbook.

'Do you really think, Mr Byars,' he had said, 'do you really believe, after Darwin's discovery, that we were made by a sort of conjuring trick by a Supreme Power? Seven days of cooking, so to speak, and then a world! Why, it's childish to expect thinking people to believe it. We are simply evolved by scientific evolution out of the primaeval protoplasm.'

'Very possibly,' said the vicar; 'and who made the protoplasm, Mr Baxter?'[52]

If Byars finds the going hard, this was nothing compared with Basil, who, the vicar muses, will 'be far happier in London, in more congenial environment. He would never be a great success in Walktown. He has tried nobly, but the people won't understand him. They would never like him; he's too much of a gentleman. How they all hate breeding in Walktown!' Having advertised for a replacement but able to offer a stipend of only £120 per year, Byars is resigned to appointing 'an inferior man' as he sifts through the applications: 'they were a weary lot'. He reaches the end of the pile:

A non-collegiate student from Oxford with a second class in Theology, a Manchester Grammar-School boy, whose father lived at Higher Broughton, seemed to promise the best. He would be able to get on with the people, probably. 'I suppose I must have him, accent and all,' the vicar said with a sigh, 'though I suppose it's prejudice to dislike the lessons read with the Lancashire broad "a" and short "o". St Paul probably spoke with a terrible local twang! And yet, I don't know, he was too great to be vulgar; one doesn't like to think that—'

The problem was clear:

The best men would not come to the North. Men of family with decent degrees, Oxford men, Cambridge men, accustomed to decent society and intellectual friends, knew far too much to accept a title in the Manchester district.[53]

When it was Dark concludes with an epilogue, advancing the action five years after the dastardly plot to discredit the Resurrection has been exposed and civilization restored, whereupon Basil, now happily married, preaches about the Resurrection to a responsive congregation in a no longer drab and dismal St Thomas's. The routing of unbelief and indifferentism, the rejection too of Low Church chill and the errors of Nonconformity, and the assertion of Christian authority in its High Anglican form as the proper foundation for moral order in

---

[52] Thorne, *When it was Dark*, 9–10.   [53] Ibid. 11–12.

society, these were the leitmotifs of the book. Such explicit sectarian credentials doubtless confined the keenest appeal of *When it was Dark* to a particular clerical party; but it was not only they who were moved by its message. In 1970, on radio, Field Marshal Montgomery said that reading *When it was Dark* had been a turning point in his life.[54] Over half a million copies were sold by the time of its author's death in 1923.

Preaching prelates did not restrict their attentions to the overtly religious thriller of this kind. It took not just a laudatory review in *The Times* but a sermon in St Paul's Cathedral to launch the success of Robert Louis Stevenson's *Dr Jekyll and Mr Hyde* in 1886.[55] There was not a little irony about this clerical adoption of authors who were otherwise godless. Somerset Maugham, for example, decisively resisted his uncle and guardian's ambition that he follow him into the Church; nonetheless, Bishop Wilberforce employed Maugham's first novel, *Liza of Lambeth* (1897), as the subject of a sermon in Westminster Abbey.[56] Publicity given to a pulpit condemnation of Mary Cholmondeley's *Red Pottage* (1899) also satisfactorily speeded sales of that novel, all 8,000 copies of the first impression being cleared out in a fortnight.[57] Not only were clergymen taking their cue from novels, clergymen and ex-clergymen made their appearance in the lists of best-selling novelists. Silas Hocking, S. R. Crockett, and Ian Maclaren were among the most popular story tellers of the late nineteenth and early twentieth centuries. The gospel message was also being rewritten to read like a novel. F. W. Farrar's *Life of Christ* was planned by the publishers Cassell's just like any other best-seller. They wanted a 'book which would make Christ a human being to the man in the street'; hence the 'directors surveyed the names of all the greatest preachers of the time. At length they decided on Farrar. They asked him if he would go to Palestine, walk in the steps of Jesus, and write His life. All expenses would be paid, and he would be given £500 for the copyright of the book.'

Farrar made his trip to Palestine in 1870 and published his *Life of Christ* in 1874. Twelve editions sold out in the first year and thirty in England alone by the time of Farrar's death in 1903. It was comprehensively pirated in America and translated widely throughout Europe, also into Russian and even Japanese. Wherever they could, Cassell's 'hammered it home... The sales became prodigious.'[58] It was

---

[54] Cockburn, *Bestseller*, 2.

[55] Mackay, *Violent Friend*, 145; and Colvin (ed.), *Stevenson's Letters*, ii. 3: 'Jekyll and Hyde, after threatening for the first week or two to fall flat, in no long time caught the attention of all classes of reader, was quoted from a hundred pulpits, and made the writer's name familiar to multitudes both in England and America whom it had never reached before.' See also Brookfield, *Reminiscences*, 51, for his recollection of the fervour with which a 'celebrated preacher at Trinity Church, Sloane Street ... dilated upon the two natures that exist in everyone', basing his sermon on the text of Stevenson's fable.

[56] Maugham, *Somerset*, 141–3. Cf. Maugham, *A Writer's Notebook*, 26: 'I do not believe in God. I see no need of such an idea' (entry dated 1894). E. F. Wilberforce (1840–1907) was Bishop of Chichester from 1895 and chairman of the Church of England Temperance Society.

[57] See Kate Flint's notice of Cholmondeley (1859–1925) in *Oxford DNB*.

[58] Flower, *Just as it Happened*, 78–9. Cassells voluntarily paid Farrar a royalty, the sales were so vast, though they had bought the copyright outright for £500. Farrar, however, was not appeased as Cassells reputedly made £50,000 to his £2,000; see Farrar, *Frederic William Farrar*, 196; Hepburn, *Author's Empty Pusse*, 77.

precisely this sort of commercialism that so offended both the apostles of pure religion and the apostles of pure literature. In 1894, the year of his conversion to Catholicism, Robert Ross developed his friend Oscar Wilde's contention that books were neither moral nor immoral, only well or badly written:

I do not know what an immoral book is and I have read a good many. I know what a pornographic book is. I think many books badly written. If that is what is meant by immoral, Archdeacon Farrar's irreligious novel *The Life of Christ* is a very immoral book. It is I think the most deleterious reading, not excepting Miss Marie Corelli, that I am acquainted with.[59]

Ross's expostulation should not be read as deliberate absurdity. This was a time when all best-selling novelists seemed seized with the idea that a Life of Christ would serve as a suitable crown to their careers: Mrs Humphry Ward and M. P. Shiel had this thought, Marie Corelli was invited to write one, and Hall Caine eventually did so.[60] It had also been a 'fixed intention' of Oliver Schreiner to write such a Life and, though this lapsed during the early 1880s, her free-thinking involved a mystical element, and New Testament morality remained central to her attitudes.[61] Frank Harris's spirit was altogether more (to put it generously) humanist but he too, having tackled Shakespeare, then considered taking on Jesus.[62] The reduction in the number of theological and religious publications and the declining public interest in literature with a religious theme can easily be exaggerated, therefore. Eric Parker, whose chief interest was not in religion but in naturalism and field sports, adventitiously tapped into this market with his first novel, published in 1901, which to his surprise was twice reprinted in the first three months and went on selling for another twenty-four years. It was called *The Sinner and the Problem* and was actually about two schoolboys but, as one of Parker's daughters explained, the public 'think the book's about what the title says, and it's bought every year by religious maniacs'.[63]

IV

The Churches had proved far from unenterprising in their response to new forms of communication in the late nineteenth century. The Church Missionary Society

---

[59] Borland, *Ross*, 38. Robert Hichens picked up the hostility of Wilde's circle to Farrar in *The Green Carnation*, 51. The Dean of Canterbury (1895–1903), Farrar was also a *bête noire* of William Morris and the Society for the Protection of Ancient Buildings, being 'bent on scraping and destroying all that has hitherto escaped' at Canterbury Cathedral; Blunt, *Diaries*, i. 232 (12 July 1896). Farrar's ambition of becoming a bishop was not helped by his rejection of the doctrine of eternal punishment in hell, a position he had derived from F. D. Maurice, who taught him at King's College London. As a housemaster at Harrow, when he had written the best-selling school story *Eric; or, Little by Little* (1858), he had also deplored 'the scandalous neglect of science' in the curriculum of schools. A friend of Darwin, Farrar was elected to the Royal Society for his work on philology.

[60] Trevelyan, *Mrs. Ward*, 182; *Oxford DNB* for Shiel (1865–1947); and above, Chs. 21 and 22, for Caine and Corelli.   [61] First and Scott, *Schreiner*, 52.

[62] Harris, *Life and Loves*, 880–9.   [63] Parker, *Memory Looks Forward*, 33.

had acquired seventy-two magic lanterns by 1891 and, in the year ending 30 September, lent out their slides 808 times, calculating that altogether these lectures with pictures brought their work before 200,000 people.[64] To close the gap between the Churches and the poor, all sorts of Christian social programmes were advanced to counter the class spirit, to deal with labour issues, to press for housing reform and old age pensions, and to remove the evils of drink, crime, and prostitution. There were also strategies to make the parish a more flexible Christianizing influence, an attractive centre for communal participation, with kindergartens and night schools as well as ordinary schools, and with sports and other recreational activity. The principal literary means of getting across the Christian message to the mass of people was via journals, pamphlets, and printed sermons, not books. 'General' Booth told W. T. Stead that the Salvation Army, had thirty-two different versions of its journal *War Cry* and that in 1889 alone it distributed 30 million tracts throughout the world, most of which were paid for by those to whom they were directed.[65] Again, Spurgeon's tracts and sermons sold by the millions (and totalled over sixty volumes). There were nonetheless peculiarities about the position occupied by the Churches in the media world. The *Reporters' Magazine* in 1890 drew attention to one: why, it asked, when the circulation of the religious weeklies was enormous and the advertising revenue they generated made them among the most lucrative of properties, was there no religious daily? This was puzzling because pulpits rang with denunciations of the wicked influence wielded by the secular press in pandering to a low public appetite for sensationalism and for every form of gambling, from the racetrack to the Stock Exchange. The speculative answer was that their subdivisions into innumerable sects, each jealous that another party would gain paramountcy, prevented their combination to propagate daily a common Christian message.[66]

Religious publications, though declining as a percentage, remained plentiful. Their quality did not pass Balliol examination. Jowett, the Master, contemptuous especially of narrow evangelicalism, wrote: 'And what trash this religious literature is! Either formalisms or sentimentalisms about the atonement, or denunciations of rational religion, or prophecies of the end of the world, explanations of the Man of Sin, the little Horn, and the number of the Beast—even these last are no inconsiderable part of English literature'.[67] Still, individual works of theology could rouse great fuss. *Lux Mundi*, which was rejected by Oxford University Press and published by John Murray in November 1889, collected twelve essays by priests of the Liberal Catholic wing of the High Church party, and was edited by Charles Gore, then Principal of Pusey House, Oxford. Their stated purpose, in the preface, was to place religion in proper relation to modern intellectual and moral problems.[68] The book quickly entered into a fourth

---

[64] 'The Magic Lantern Mission', *Review of Reviews* (Dec. 1890), 561–7; *Church Missionary Intelligencer, Review of Reviews* (Feb. 1892), 177.   [65] *Review of Reviews* (Mar. 1890), 210.
[66] *Review of Reviews* (Nov. 1890), 486.   [67] Faber, *Jowett*, 46.
[68] Prestige, *Charles Gore*, ch. vi.

edition, whereupon the *Review of Reviews* in May 1890 responded to it as to a best-selling novel. The *Review*'s editor, Stead, called it a 'sensation', made it his book of the month, and issued a ten-page précis of its contents: 'Everybody who is anybody is reading it; and as there are a great multitude of nobodies who can neither afford time nor money to buy the book and read it for themselves, I have decided to give the substance of it in place of the customary novel.' Stead also interviewed leading clergymen, and trawled the religious press, to stir the pot further. No doubt, he entertained his readers by recording the verdict of the Bishop of Lincoln, Edward King, and the Dean of St Paul's, Canon Liddon, who both wished that the whole subject could be discussed in Latin; but there seemed no doubt that the book was the sensation he called it. The leading Nonconformist minister Price Hughes reported in the *Methodist Times*, 'If you enter the shop of any bookseller of repute just now, you are likely to see a good substantial pile of *Lux Mundi*. The bookseller will tell you, by way of business, "This is the book that is all the go now"'—a telling comment about a volume priced at 14s.[69] Altogether, it was the most significant theological work, judged by the reaction of other Churchmen, since *Essays and Reviews* (1860), that symposium of essays by Broad Church writers which endeavoured to revise traditional doctrines in response to historical and scientific scholarship, much as the *Lux Mundi* authors were now doing for the Catholic school of the Anglican Church. Of course, as with many another best-seller, public interest was liable to wane. Frederick Rogers's autobiography in 1913, making passing mention of *Essays and Reviews*, did so with the observation that that once notorious book was now forgotten; but *Lux Mundi* had entered its fifteenth edition in 1904, by which date its editor, Gore, was promoted bishop.[70]

In the intervening years there were worrying signs of a falling-off of faith. A. F. Winnington-Ingram, Bishop of Stepney and soon-to-be Bishop of London, greeted the new century by lamenting, 'The cry of modern life is: I want to be myself: I want to live my own life.'[71] As for churchgoing, Bernard Shaw gleefully proclaimed that the *Daily News*' 1902–3 census of Sunday worshippers in London proved it to have been largely replaced by playgoing. The theatre was now more important than the Church, 'as important as the Church was in the Middle Ages'.[72] A head-on collision was avoided because (unlike the cinemas) theatres and music halls remained closed on Sundays. Speaking for the Actors' Association, which debated this question in 1912, Ben Webster thought that the profession's continued resistance to Sunday opening was largely a practical matter—the

---

[69] *Review of Reviews* (May 1890), 434–44.   [70] Rogers, *Labour, Life and Literature*, 26.

[71] McMillan, *Way we Were*, 129, quoting the *Daily Express*.

[72] Shaw made a phrase of it, but the sentiment was commonly voiced. When T. P. O'Connor descanted on the moral influence wielded by the theatre, this drew corroboration from ordinary readers of *T.P.'s Weekly*, with, however, an obeisance towards the press as supreme over all: 'For good or for evil, the Drama is a potent influence in the life of a people, an influence greater, more direct, more wide-spread, though less ostentatious than that of the Pulpit—an influence second only to that of the Press' (*T.P.'s Weekly*, 24 July 1903, 250).

numbers employed in cinemas were still few compared to theatres and music halls—but Beerbohm Tree, who presided at the meeting, did not neglect the opportunity to score the significance which the theatre now occupied in national life. He declared that ' "uplift" and beauty were not to be found exclusively in the churches'; 'the stage . . . had a great power for good . . . [and] today preached the wider religion of humanity. The English Sunday had undergone a very considerable change during the last quarter of a century and had become a day not only of rest, but of healthy recreation.'[73]

Since the 1890s, according to Shaw, the new Theatre of Ideas had treated religion in a notably liberated and unorthodox way, in the mission to have the theatre taken seriously as 'a factory of thought, a prompter of conscience, an elucidator of social conduct, an armory against despair and dullness, and a temple of the Ascent of Man'.[74] This was characteristic of Shaw, who was struck when reading St Paul's Epistles by their 'inveterate crookedness of mind'. He admitted to having used the Lord's Prayer once or twice when a child as a protective spell against Irish thunderstorms; otherwise he had concentrated on becoming healthily heathen and on 'the sport of making fun of the accessories and legends of religion'.[75] But Shaw's materialism was short-lived; instead, he became 'a most vehement anti-Rationalist'. He read the Bible all through; and he was much affected by Bunyan's *Pilgrim's Progress*. One of the first things Shaw wrote, at the age of 21, was a passion play. He never completed it, and his was a profane version;[76] yet, Shaw was overflowing with moral passion, and no amount of intellectual investment in the sciences of evolution and eugenics, psychology and sociology, in the philosophy of vitalism and in the politics of Fabian Socialism, could compensate for or answer the quest for religious salvation or resolve the mystery of life. Having presented his post-Christian vision at its most confident in *Man and Superman* in 1901–3 ('Beware of the man whose god is in the skies'), and having incurred the censorship of the Lord Chamberlain by attempting to put God on stage in *The Shewing-Up of Blanco Posnet* in 1909 ('I am a specialist in immoral and heretical plays'), Shaw went on to compose several plays, prefaces, and other pieces which he classified as religious, beginning with *Androcles and the Lion* (play 1912, preface 1916).[77] 'Why do you want to break men's spirits for?', Shaw asked Henry James after reading his one-act play *The Saloon* in 1909. 'Surely George Eliot did as much of that as is needed,' he added. Shaw denounced 'that useless, dispiriting, discouraging fatalism which broke out so horribly in the 1860s at the word of Darwin, and persuaded people in spite of their own teeth and claws that Man is the will-slave and victim of his environment'. As a socialist, Shaw credited environmentalism with an 'enormous power', but he abjured

[73] *The Times*, 11 Sept. 1912.   [74] 'Our Theatres in the Nineties' (1906), in Shaw, *Prefaces*, 742–3.
[75] 'Immaturity' (1930), ibid. 625–48.   [76] Holroyd, *Shaw*, i. 71–2, 96, 291.
[77] *Back to Methuselah* (play 1920, preface 1921), *Saint Joan* (play 1923, preface 1924), and *The Adventures of the Black Girl in her Search for God* (1932); Shaw, *Prefaces*, 479–622. See also W. R. Inge, 'Shaw as Theologian', in S. Winsten (ed.), *G.B.S. 90: Aspects of Bernard Shaw's Life and Work* (1946), 110–21; and 'What is my Religious Faith?', in Shaw, *Sixteen Self Sketches*, 73–9.

determinism and asseverated: 'we can change it; we must change it; there is absolutely no other sense in life than the work of changing it'.[78] Later, when asked whether he wanted the disestablishment and disendowment of the Church of England, Shaw answered: 'No. We need much more establishment and endowment, not less.' He favoured the Free Churches being able to use Anglican cathedrals and parish churches for their services, but he did not object to the Church of England continuing to control its own schools—subject, of course, to State inspection of their efficiency and sanitation—and he strongly affirmed the proposition that religion be taught in schools. 'The only question is *what shall be taught in the name of religion,*' Shaw concluded cryptically.[79]

Outside of Shaw's cosmology, religious themes appeared to hold few attractions for modern dramatists. In large part this was due to a 300-year tradition which prevented the direct representation of biblical characters on the stage. It was possible to circumvent this; but plays 'pointedly adapted from or taken from the Scriptures' stood no chance. 'I do not even read them,' the Lord Chamberlain's Examiner of Plays, George Redford, told the parliamentary Joint Select Committee inquiring into the censorship in 1909. 'If they are obviously scriptural, I point out the fact and the play goes back to the person who submitted it.'[80] Redford acknowledged that this was convention, not law; but he banned public performances of Laurence Housman's nativity play *Bethlehem* (1902) for this reason—'it traversed the custom'.[81] Redford also, just like Smyth Pigott, his predecessor as Examiner before 1895, made it clear to the impresario of Drury Lane, Sir Augustus Harris, that his ambition of bringing the Oberammergau Passion Play to London would not be allowed. 'Religious feeling would be outraged at seeing the Crucifixion . . . enacted on a public stage in a theatre'[82] was the official view. Pigott similarly banned Wilde's *Salomé* (1892) for its featuring John the Baptist, though it probably also trespassed against his sense of decency.[83] The Joint Select Committee heard powerful testimony from upset authors such as Hall Caine who bridled under this restraint;[84] and in its recommendations the Committee was inclined to relax the ban on characters from the Scriptures appearing on the stage, while upholding the Lord Chamberlain's prerogative to refuse to license plays which 'it may be reasonably held . . . to do violence to the sentiment of religious reverence'.[85]

Fear of an interdict from the Censor had not been the sole reason for playwrights' avoidance of religious subjects. The fact was that orthodox Christian religion had ceased to interest the intellectual classes; but this indifference or animosity shown to simple religion by most advanced authors meant that they forfeited and cut themselves off from a sizeable audience, a move which the

---

[78] Edel, *James,* ii. 666.   [79] Interview with Shaw, in Brook, *Writers' Gallery,* 140.
[80] Joint Select Committee on the Stage Plays (Censorship), *PP* (1909), vol. viii, no. 451, Qs. 222–3.
[81] Ibid. 526–34.   [82] Ibid. 254.
[83] Wilde first wrote it in French and had it published and performed in Paris; Ellmann, *Wilde,* 351–2.
[84] See above, Ch. 27.   [85] Joint Select Committee on Stage Plays, Report, p. xi.

best-sellers took care not to imitate. One who understood this was the actor-manager Wilson Barrett, whose forte was melodrama. This made him a joke figure among the aesthetic and cerebral classes. In *The Green Carnation* (1894) the epicene Lord Reggie recalls once spending a week with a colonel: 'Soldiers are never original. They think it is unmanly ... I never heard the same remarks so often in all my life ... I know I tried to be manly. I talked about Wilson Barrett. What more could I do? To talk about Wilson Barrett is generally to show your appreciation of the heroic age. Of course nobody thinks about him now.'[86] Barrett was prematurely written off. In 1895–6 he recouped his flagging fortunes with his own play, *The Sign of the Cross*. As the *Saturday Review*'s critic, Bernard Shaw thought it a travesty: 'if Mr Wilson Barrett writes to the papers to assure us, in the usual terms, that so far from his having taken his play from the Bible, he has never even read that volume, I am quite prepared to believe him'.[87] *The Times* too deplored the play as 'a sensational and crude exploitation of religious sentiment'; yet, it also noted that it 'succeeded in making theatre-goers of a large number of people who had till then regarded the stage as an immoral and pernicious influence'.[88] In Ernest Raymond, still a boy and living with his guardian, 'Aunt' Emily Calder in West Kensington, it ignited all kinds of fires:

Aunt, missing no excitement that was the talk of the day, had hastened to see Wilson Barrett and Maud Jeffries in *The Sign of the Cross* and had wept so generously when Wilson Barrett as the Roman officer approached the Christian girl to seize and rape her and she whipped a cross from her breast, held it on high (while Heaven's lightning flashed around it) and cried out (the lovely girl) 'Thou cans't not harm me now'—then, I say, Aunt was so damp with tears, and exalted, that she decided, 'The children must see this' ...

I wept quite as gulpingly, and more openly, when at last the Roman officer, giving himself to Maud Jeffries's beauty, walked with her, hand-in-hand, to the lions. For weeks afterwards, as I walked homeward from school, I was a Christian martyr walking, head erect, not to Gledstanes Road, but to the Colosseum gates and the waiting lions. Sometimes I walked hand-in-hand with a Christian girl giving to her, a weaker vessel, something of my strength.[89]

The American-born Mrs T. P. O'Connor was not one who shunned the theatre—she had ambitions both to write plays and to perform—and she encouraged her housemaid, an Irish convent girl, Agnes Vale, to see *The Sign of the Cross*. Afterwards, Agnes declared that 'she felt more "at home" in it than any play she ever saw. When I asked her why, she said it reminded her so much of the life of St Agnes.' Mrs O'Connor's own response was possibly even more startling:

---

[86] Hichens, *Green Carnation*, 53.   [87] *Saturday Review*, 11 Jan. 1896, in Shaw, *Plays and Players*, 64–6.
[88] *The Times*, 23 July 1904. T. P. O'Connor observed in *M.A.P.*, 30 July 1904, 121–3: 'Bishops, ministers, stern Nonconformists, who had held always aloof from the theatre, were at last brought within its walls; they found at last a play in which the poignant emotions of faith and charity were embodied.' Likewise, A. M. Thompson, who collaborated in writing a play (unstaged) with Barrett, stated that *The Sign of the Cross* 'did more to popularize the stage amongst people who had never entered a theatre before, than the loftiest of intellectual plays' (Thompson, *Here I Lie*, 286).
[89] Raymond, *Story of my Days*, 30.

'I actually soaked a handkerchief with tears, and as I left the theatre, put the wet little wad in an envelope, and wrote "My tribute" upon it, and sent it around to the stage door.'[90] T. P. O'Connor himself reckoned: 'Rarely, if ever has there been such a success. Seven companies played it simultaneously; the seats were all booked months beforehand on its third visit; in the United States the success was even more overwhelming.'[91] Barrett was both delighted and awed by the responses he awakened, because people 'came in the same spirit as they went to church'. At the Theatre Royal, Brighton, he had peeped out before the play began to see old ladies leaning forward 'with their heads in their hands on the ledge of the circle, and engaged in silent prayer. They then sat back, with faces full of calm spiritual satisfaction, and enjoyed the drama to the full.'[92] There was, it seemed clear, a potentially vast audience of religious-minded people anxious to attend the staging of dramas that would affirm, not question, their faith.

Biblical as well as classical subjects were embraced in the pretentious poetic drama of Stephen Phillips, the son of a clergyman. He also had to disguise his intent. The theatre critic William Archer related how Phillips, wanting to write a play about David and Bathsheba and knowing that the Censor would refuse it, transposed the action to the English civil war period.[93] This play, *The Sin of David*, failed;[94] otherwise it was remarkable how (as the poet Roy Flecker contemptuously put it) Phillips's 'rather meretricious wonders impressed the London mob'.[95] Phillips's meteoric rise and fall is one of the strangest episodes in modern English literature. His eminence was such that James Knowles, editor of the leading monthly *Nineteenth Century*, accepted a Phillips poem, 'Midnight—The 31st of December 1900', to usher in the new epoch for the first issue of *Nineteenth Century and After*.[96] Phillips's *Herod* (1900)—followed by *Ulysses* (1902), *Nero* (1906), and *Faust* (1908)—was staged by Beerbohm Tree at His Majesty's and ran for 100 performances. Sidney Colvin and many more hailed Phillips as a successor to Sophocles, Shakespeare, Dante, Milton, and the elder Dumas; yet, soon, all that was left of him was a walk-on part in Anthony Hope's joke about Barrie's *Peter Pan*, 'Oh for an hour of Herod!'[97]

---

[90] O'Connor, *I Myself*, 301–2. Barrett's response to the tear-stained tribute, written from the Lyric Theatre and dated 21 January 1896, is provided on the same pages.

[91] *M.A.P.*, 30 July 1904. For accounts of the play's provincial success when Barrett took it on tour, see Trewin, *Edwardian Theatre*, 5; Harvey Crane, *Playbill: A History of the Theatre in the West Country* (Plymouth, 1980), 162.   [92] Preston, *Memories*, 227–8.

[93] Joint Select Committee on Stage Plays, Report, Q. 701.

[94] Published in 1904, *The Sin of David* was not staged for another decade, opening at the Savoy on 9 July 1914; Nicoll, *English Drama*, 885.   [95] Flecker, *Collected Prose*, 218.

[96] Knowles did, however, remove some of the sorriest lines from the poem in proof; see Metcalf, *Knowles*, 349.

[97] On Phillips (1864–1915), see J. P. Wearing's notice in *Oxford DNB*; Pearson, *Tree*, 134–9, 163; Nicoll, *English Drama*, 283–94; Blumenfeld, *R.D.B.'s Diary*, 100, 113. Some indication of the vogue for Phillips at the turn of the century is gained from the size of the imprints by his publisher John Lane: *Poems* (1897) was in its 10th thousand, *Paolo and Francesca* (1899–1900) 19th thousand, and *Herod* (1900–1) 25th thousand, in 1901. His stage performance royalties reached £150 per week in 1902, although Viscount Esher, who saw *Paolo* on 30 June, considered it 'a poor weak play in spite of the fine subject . . . The play is tedious, and Phillips is far

Barrett and Phillips aside, it was rare for a play with a religious theme to achieve a successful staging; but Jerome K. Jerome did just that, with a dramatization in 1908 of his own short story, 'The Passing of the Third Floor Back'. Perhaps quasi-religious is the better description. There was no straightforward Christianity about its author, who wrote of his Nonconformist upbringing: 'When I was a boy, a material hell was still by most pious folks accepted as fact. The suffering caused to an imaginative child can hardly be exaggerated. It caused me to hate God, and later on, when my growing intelligence rejected the conception as an absurdity, to despise the religion that had taught it.' Having been brought up to believe that the theatre was the gateway to hell, it gave Jerome extra satisfaction then to become a popular playwright; and having discarded formal religion, he went on to think that 'the Christ spirit is in all men'.[98] This immanentist faith was embodied in *The Passing of the Third Floor Back*, in the Christ-like character known only as The Stranger, who pricks the consciences of the rest of the cast—and of the audience. Jerome never resolved the enigma of The Stranger's identity. It was this mystery that accounted for the play's success, together with the acting of Johnston Forbes-Robertson, with his 'golden voice' and 'high seriousness'. This was the judgement of the *Daily News*'s editor, A. G. Gardiner, who, talking to Jerome and Forbes-Robertson one Sunday afternoon at the home of W. T. Stead, discussed 'the problem of the Better Self. I found both the author and the actor full of this means of regenerating humanity.'[99] This chimed with the opinion of those who recognized that 'the real Jerome is more faithfully expressed in *The Passing of the Third Floor Back* than in *Three Men in a Boat*', and that he was a writer of serious purpose and only incidentally a humorist;[100] but the play was deemed by hostile critics to have no artistic merit. 'Twaddle and vulgarity' and 'vilely stupid' was Max Beerbohm's verdict in the *Saturday Review*. He added for good measure, 'Well, I suppose blasphemy pays.'[101] Clergy were divided about it; but, the 'appeal of the play and actor to religious sentiment was irresistible. People for whom the theatre had normally no message flocked to see the piece in both England and

from being Shakespeare. The play leaves one unmoved. How different from Maeterlinck' (Brett, *Esher*, i. 336–7). His *Ulysses* was known to the stagehands at His Majesty's as 'Useless' (Pearson, *Tree*, 139). Davies, *Later Days*, 140, credited Arthur Symons with exploding the bubble of Phillips's reputation. Symons criticized Phillips in the *Academy*, 15 Mar. 1902, and the criticism was repeated in Symons's *Studies in Prose and Verse* (1904). Phillips's *Poems* won the first prize of 100 guineas awarded by the *Academy* in 1898 for the work of most signal merit produced in the preceding year, against competition from such as Conrad's *Nigger of the 'Narcissus'* and Henry James's *What Maisie Knew*. Max Beerbohm linked Phillips's brief glory with that of Le Gallienne in the previous decade: Le Gallienne had then moved to America and, asked how long he intended to stay there, Max replied, 'He is waiting for Stephen Phillips to blow over' (Rothenstein, *Memories 1872–1900*, 283). Thomas Hardy also rumbled Phillips from the start: his *Poems* 'was strongly recommended to me, & I bought him, but with every wish to discover a new bard I am bound to say that I was woefully disappointed on reading his book' (Hardy to Sir George Douglas, 3 Mar. 1898, in Purdy and Millgate (eds.), *Hardy Letters*, ii. 188). See also above, p. 159.

[98] Jerome, *Life and Times*, 17, 34, 238.

[99] Gardiner, *Pillars of Society*, 118; Jerome, *Life and Times*, 122–5.   [100] Gribble, *Seen in Passing*, 133.

[101] Connolly, *Jerome*, 148. On the other hand, see the guarded welcome of the review in *Punch*, 9 Sept. 1908, 186.

America.'[102] The play had a long run in the West End in 1908; it was revived there in 1913, played in provincial repertories, and was first filmed (with Forbes-Robertson again in the starring role) in 1918.

All this was not necessarily encouraging to the nation's Christian leaders; but the late nineteenth century had seen a movement started among Churchmen and Nonconformists to abandon their old condemnation and to employ the theatre as a moral force; as the Church and Stage Guild put it, 'to promote religious and social sympathy between the members of the Church and Stage'.[103] Some even came to appreciate the value of presenting dramatizations of their own, by extending welcome to William Poel's and Mabel Dearmer's adaptations of medieval mystery cycles and Tudor morality plays.[104] The best-known of these was the sixteenth-century *Everyman*, in which God was personified on the stage. Having been discovered in a cathedral muniment chest, it was not required to be submitted for the Censor's examination. Just like Shakespeare and most other old plays, it was deemed already licensed—a technical evasion whose inconsistency was seized on by critics of the Lord Chamberlain system.[105] Poel first produced it at the Charterhouse in 1901, because the authorities at Westminster Abbey and Canterbury Cathedral would not permit its performance on their premises. The experiment was repeated in 1902 when *Everyman* was staged by Ben Greet at the St George's Hall. This proved so successful that it was transferred to the Imperial Theatre for matinee performances through the summer. Edith Mathison's acting in the lead role was singled out for its 'restraint, simplicity and real religious fervour'; and the impact of the piece gained from its being 'staged practically without modern accessories'. This compounded 'the air of strangeness and novelty which pervaded the theatre.'[106] Dent's Everyman Library published *Everyman with Other Interludes, including Eight Miracle Plays* in 1909; it was reprinted four times before the conclusion of the Great War, in 1910, 1912, 1914, and 1917. Not all its audience was charmed as well as curious. Wilfrid Blunt, who attended the 1902 production during Lent, was particularly scornful:

a terribly dreary business, which more than half reconciled me to having been born in the nineteenth century. These ancient plays . . . are worse than the worst comic parts of Shakespeare, which is saying a great deal, crude, childish, long-winded. The mediaeval idea of life in Christian Europe with death and hell as a perpetual background of all pleasure, is repellent, when put nakedly before us in action.[107]

---

[102] *DNB 1931–1940*, 938 (entry for Forbes-Robertson). See also Nicoll, *English Drama*, 234–5, 332–6, on this and for the dramatic device of introducing disruptive strangers into ordinary settings.

[103] Nicoll, *Late Nineteenth Century Drama*, i. 17.

[104] Nicoll, *English Drama*, 228–40. On Poel (1852–1934), *DNB 1931–1940*, 708–9; Mabel Dearmer, wife of the Christian Socialist Percy Dearmer (1867–1936), ibid. 216–17.

[105] Joint Select Committee on Stage Plays, Report, Qs. 225–35.

[106] *Annual Register for 1902* (1903), pt. II, 93.

[107] Blunt, *Diaries*, ii. 21 (24 Mar. 1902). The memory of this painful experience was revived in 1903 when Blunt saw the Irish Literary Society's production of Yeats's play, 'a terrible infliction, called "The Hour Glass" . . . a stupid imitation of that dull old morality, "Everyman", which bored me so much last year' (ibid. 53 (2 May 1903)).

V

The theatre remained generally under-exploited by religious bodies. Another approach to audiences was through accounts of the lives of notable clerics; these still held fascination, but as much for their public life as for their search for religious truth. The centre of gravity was moving from doctrine to experience, from theology to biography. Notoriously, Edmund Purcell's *Life of Cardinal Manning* (1896) provoked a storm of criticism because of its secular interpretation; but Purcell was strongly conscious of a public movement away from ecclesiastical debate:

Strange as it may sound in the ears of our somewhat cynical generation, the religious world in that day consisted not only of bishops and clergy, but included well-known statesmen and lawyers and men of letters. Not merely religious papers like the *Guardian* and the *Record,* but newspapers like the *Times* in 1850 discussed the Gorham case and Tractarianism, Cardinal Wiseman's famous 'Letter out of the Flaminian Gate', and 'Papal Aggression', with as much fierceness or ferocity as Home Rule and Mr Gladstone—though with far more truth and justice—are denounced to-day.[108]

The furore that Purcell's biography aroused would seem to give the lie to that belief; but his instinct was not wrong, only imprudent in the directness of its expression. Three years previously, in 1893, Rowland Prothero had published his *Life and Correspondence of Arthur Penrhyn Stanley, Late Dean of Westminster,* in two volumes, which, he later recalled, was 'the success of the publishing year. It passed in less than twelve months into a fifth edition.' His exposition of the theological controversies that had engaged Stanley was extensive and, Prothero felt, 'in itself constituted a strong popular appeal. Twenty-two years later, the change of feeling was recognized. In 1915, when an abridged edition of the *Life* was published in Nelson's Popular Series, the discussion of these questions was either shortened or wholly omitted.'[109]

What remained was Stanley's stressing the need for the Church of England to fulfil its mission as a National Church, to achieve comprehensiveness through toleration, against the rancorous dogmatics of both Low and High persuasion:

One aspect of his mission was the attempt to vindicate the sanctity of the secular world; to maintain that the sacred seal which is set on one side of life is the pledge of the sacredness of the whole; to find the same law in things earthly and things heavenly; to claim for every natural opportunity of doing good or turning from evil a channel of Divine grace; to break down the limits within which ecclesiastical parties confine the

---

[108] E. S. Purcell, *Life of Cardinal Manning, Archbishop of Westminster* (1896), i. 528. Controversy about Purcell's treatment of Manning erupted soon after the Cardinal's death, when Purcell published in the *Dublin Review* an account of Manning's Anglican period and extracts from the diary Manning kept when in Rome in 1847–8; see *Review of Reviews* (May 1892), 484.

[109] Lord Ernle, *Whippingham to Westminster* (1938), 163–5. Prothero's memory for dates may have been at fault: Nelson's popular edition has a preface dated 13 September 1909.

exclusive operations of spiritual influences; to show that all history, and not one branch of history only, contains the record of God's dealings with mankind. Another aspect of the same mission was the effort to lay bare the deep basis of morality on which theology rested; to bring sacred thought out of the shadowy region of abstraction; to humanise conventional forms and to make them living instruments of moral education; to propagate Christianity as a life, rather than to hand it down as a system, a thesis, or a philosophy . . . The danger that he dreaded was, not the intolerance of science, but the intolerance of the dominant orthodoxy, which was seeking to crush the advocates of free critical inquiry.[110]

It was with this conviction that Stanley fancied, according to Augustus Hare, that 'he could make the Abbey the great temple of reconciliation' by inviting 'the most heterogeneous preachers . . . to make use of its pulpit—preachers from the very north and south and east and west of opinion'.[111] But shortly before his death in 1881 Stanley had been oppressed by a sense of failure: 'This generation is lost; it is either plunged in dogmatism or agnosticism. I look forward to the generation which is to come.'[112]

Joseph Dent's Everyman Library endeavoured to cater for the religious-minded section of that next generation, but in a way that expressed the new emphases: not as an assertion of Christian dogmas, but as an exploration of comparative cultures, appropriate for free historical, scientific, and psychological inquiry:

we have made a great speciality in all kinds of religious books, books which will teach the people religion in its widest and most human sense. For instance, I have produced a special edition of the *Koran*. We printed it with great trembling, hoping that it might be the beginning of a great series of religious books. It caught the public fancy in an astonishing manner, and I get two hundred orders for it at a time. Above all, we have issued the New Testament arranged in the order in which the books came to the Christians of the first century. This has been done by Principal Lindsay in a masterly way, and becomes quite a new book for students. We have also issued Seeley's *Ecce Homo*, with an introduction by Sir Oliver Lodge. Latimer's Sermons, in all their quaintness, with the sermon preached on the game of whist. Robertson's Sermons are extremely popular, and Law's *Serious Call to a Devout and Holy Life* proves that there is a great public even for mystical religious books. We have already issued *St. Augustine's Confessions* and Swedenborg's *Heaven and Hell*, and we are hoping to add in the coming issue in September *Thomas à Kempis*, and probably Taylor's *Holy Living and Holy Dying*.[113]

[110] Rowland Prothero, *Life and Letters of Dean Stanley* (n.d.), 368–72.

[111] Augustus J. C. Hare, *Biographical Sketches* (1895), quoted in Metcalf, *Knowles*, 194.

[112] Prothero, *Stanley*, 290. Stanley himself had first achieved celebrity as the author of the *Life of Dr Arnold* (1844)—Thomas Arnold of Rugby—although it did not find approval with Arnold's granddaughter, the novelist Mrs Humphry Ward, who 'spoke of the tiresome habit which now prevails of writing a man's life by the simple process of throwing his letters at your head . . . She said that she never could see why people praised so much Arthur Stanley's biography of her grandfather, never having been able to form from that book any definite idea of what he was like' (Grant Duff, *Diary, 1896 to 1901*, i. 24–5 (27 Feb. 1896)).

[113] Joseph Dent, quoted in Raymond Blathwayt, 'England's Taste in Literature', *Fortnightly Review* (Jan. 1912), 168.

How specialized this interest had become was underlined by Butler Wood, librarian of the Bradford Public Library:

The ordinary 'man in the street' does not read religious books with avidity. This class is mainly consulted by ministers, Sunday-school teachers and others actively connected with the religious organisations in the city. If, however, a striking book appears in this class, *e.g.*, Drummond's *Natural Law in the Spiritual World*, there is sure to be a 'run' upon it by the general public. Apart from such works, the usage of religious books is largely confined to the people I have mentioned.[114]

Further evidence came from Hatchard's bookshop, Piccadilly, which for over a century had supplied the upper classes with their reading: 'Hatchard's used to have a special stand set apart for the latest theological work, but theology is now a drug in the market.'[115]

Symbolic of the changing times was the death in 1901 of the novelist Charlotte M. Yonge. The daughter of an ex-army officer and small landowner, and the granddaughter of clergymen, she lived all her life at Otterbourne, near Winchester. When she published her first book, *Abbey Church; or, Self-Control and Self-Conceit* (1844), a family council had followed and the decision made 'that she would not take money herself for it, but that it would be used for some good work—it being thought unladylike to benefit by one's own writings'.[116] Yonge was greatly influenced by the Tractarians: Keble was vicar of Hursley, which was joined to Otterbourne, and it was he who encouraged her fiction-writing. In Guy Morville in *The Heir of Redclyffe* (1853) and Ethel May in *The Daisy Chain* (1856) Yonge produced a fictional hero and heroine who held readers spellbound. This upset Oscar Wilde. During his American tour in 1882, when he visited a convict awaiting execution and discovered that he was reading *The Heir of Redclyffe*, he despaired: 'it's perhaps as well to let the law take its course'.[117] Wilde notwithstanding, Yonge succeeded in making goodness interesting while pressing moral lessons about the danger of worldly ambition. All profits from *The Heir of Redclyffe*, which entered a twenty-second edition in 1876, were donated to the Melanesian Mission. This was designed to continue the work of her kinsman John Coleridge Patteson, the first bishop in Melanesia, whose purpose had been simply to Christianize the natives, not to Anglicize them by insisting that they adopt English clothes and customs. Alas, Patteson's mission was misunderstood and he was murdered in 1871 by natives in reprisal for the 'black-birding' practices of traders, the kidnapping of natives for forced labour in Fiji and Queensland. Yonge wrote a Life of Patteson (1873), and the £2,000 accruing from *The Daisy Chain* also supported a missionary college at Auckland, New Zealand. *Pro ecclesia et Deo* was Yonge's favourite maxim. Her fiction, her historical studies, her editorship for

---

[114] Ibid. 171.   [115] Ibid. 161.
[116] Christabel Coleridge, *Charlotte M. Yonge: Her Life and Letters* (1903), 153 n. 1. Coleridge further related how 'until the necessities of the trade forced it on her, she never wrote stories in Lent' (ibid. 234).
[117] Ellmann, *Wilde*, 191.

thirty-eight years of a girls' shilling magazine (ingenuously entitled the *Monthly Packet*): all this was designed to encourage young people in High Church ritual and in parochial work and missions. The appeal of her writing derived from its focus on village life and family relationships, idealized within a frame bounded by honest squires, devoted clergy, and refined ladies. Religious belief and social duty were fundamental, not optional. Yonge herself daily taught scripture in the village school but, her sympathetic biographer noted, her stories gradually lost their attraction to a new public and 'did not really represent . . . the girl of the eighties and nineties'.[118]

T.P.'s Weekly, reviewing Christabel Coleridge's biography of Yonge in 1903, came to the same conclusion: Yonge's 'literary manner and literary outlook belong to the past'. Yet, it added, though the current religious and social ideals were different, she had exercised an enormous influence on the makers of the modern age.[119] *The Heir of Redclyffe* was the first book greatly to impress William Morris, according to Canon Dixon, one of Morris's Pre-Raphaelite set at Oxford in the 1850s. Morris's biographer explained this to a possibly doubting readership in 1896:

The young hero of the novel, with his overstrained conscientiousness, his chivalrous courtesy, his intense earnestness, his eagerness for all such social reforms as might be effected from above downwards, his high-strung notions of love, friendship, and honour, his premature gravity, his almost deliquescent piety, was adopted . . . as a pattern for actual life; and more strongly perhaps by Morris . . . from his own greater wealth and more aristocratic temper.[120]

Others among the senior generation remained devoted. The Liberal MP Robert Farquharson, who was born in 1837 and who became a medical officer with a guards' regiment, was not ashamed to admit in his memoirs in 1911 that he had 'a feminine corner in my heart'. Proof of this was that as a boy 'I would never venture to read aloud' *The Heir of Redclyffe*, presumably for fear of breaking down.[121] D. G. Rossetti had been entranced, like William Morris; tears filled his eyes as he read about Guy Morville's death in *The Heir of Redclyffe*. More flowed from Charles Kingsley over *Heartsease* (1854): he told the publisher that it was 'the most delightful and wholesome novel I ever read . . . and I found myself wiping my eyes a dozen times before I got through it'.[122] Miss Yonge, disapproving of Kingsley's religious position, did not reciprocate: she refused to read him. Cambridge philosophy also fell at her feet. Henry Sidgwick, having been smitten by *The Heir of Redclyffe*, then glowed over *The Trial: More Links of the Daisy Chain* (1864). 'I can't get *The Trial* out of my head,' he wrote, contrasting it with Flaubert's *Madame Bovary* (1857): the latter 'describes how the terrible ennui of mean French rural domestic life drags down the soul of an ambitious woman, whereas Miss Yonge makes one feel how full of interest the narrowest sphere of

---

[118] Coleridge, *Yonge*, 275.   [119] *T.P.'s Weekly*, 17 Apr. 1903, 729.   [120] Mackail, *Morris*, i. 43.
[121] Farquharson, *In and Out of Parliament*, 123.
[122] Quoted in Battiscombe, *Charlotte Mary Yonge*, 87.

life is. I think her religion is charming, and it mellows with age, the *âpre* Puseyism wears off.'[123] Finally, it was reported about the Bishop of London Frederick Temple that he 'could stand an examination in Miss Yonge's books, and, on one occasion [in the late 1880s], he was heard keenly discussing with Lord Rosebery the careers of the May family, in the *Daisy Chain*, as though they were living acquaintances'.[124] On Miss Yonge's seventieth birthday, 13 August 1893, she was presented with an 'album, its back powdered with daisies, and inside the signatures of some ten thousand of her admirers, photographs sent by the Queen of Spain and the Queen of Italy, and a cheque for £200'.[125] She used the money characteristically, to provide a lych-gate for her church. Six years later, at the suggestion of Sir Walter Besant, the Charlotte Yonge Scholarship was founded from a fund of £1,900 which was subscribed by donors from Britain, the Empire, and America, to enable every alternate year a girl from Winchester High School to go to university.

Miss Yonge was not oblivious of the different generations. Her article in the *Monthly Packet* of January 1891, 'Nous Avons Changé Tout Cela', contrasts the girl of the 1890s with that of the 1850s, noting the enhanced personal freedom and speed of communication, the increased opportunities of independent work outside the home, and a greater demand for trained social workers now that voluntary associations were organized in national networks. A new series of the magazine had been launched in 1890, its scope now widened to include articles on employment for women 'by persons writing with authority'.[126] It survived only until 1895, but the new female generation did not prove impervious to the appeal of *The Heir of Redclyffe* as many supposed. The Prime Minister's daughter Violet Asquith read it seven times 'from cover to cover—never failing to cry at the end', though later she was presented with the dismaying news that the new King, George V, 'never really *cared* for Miss Yonge and even the Queen spoke coldly of the *Heir of Redclyffe*'.[127] The pronouncements of those who considered Miss Yonge's books a spent force in the twentieth century were constantly being belied, however. The popular inter-war novelist E. M. Delafield, author of *The Diary of a Provincial Lady* (1930), remained one such admirer and, in her introduction to Georgina Battiscombe's biography of Yonge in 1943, she noted that her public still existed, 'vigorously and independently of fashion'. In the first year of the Second World War a feature-writer in *The Times* recommended Yonge's novels as 'escape literature', upon which Delafield wrote to correct errors in the article and to advise about the order in which the novels should be read:

The result was an avalanche of letters, the number of enquiries eventually totalling between four and five hundred . . . It may be relevant to add here that the Yonge novels

---

[123] Letter to Roden Noel, 1864, in Sidgwick and Sidgwick, *Henry Sidgwick*, 109.
[124] E. G. Sandford (ed.), *Memoirs of Archbishop Temple* (1906), ii. 21.
[125] Battiscombe, *Yonge*, 159–63. [126] *Review of Reviews* (Jan. 1891), 80.
[127] Bonham Carter and Pottle (eds.), *Lantern Slides*, 50 n. 2; Augustine Birrell to Violet Asquith, 7 Sept. 1911, ibid. 283.

are frequently taken out of the London Library fiction shelves, and that the largest second-hand bookshop in London always places any of her works in the window, on the grounds that they never remain unbought, and are usually sold within twenty-four hours.[128]

VI

Although she believed in the inherent inferiority of women and recommended self-denial as woman's best course, Yonge had been a supporter of Lady Margaret Hall, the Tractarians' response to the non-denominational Somerville: these were the first two colleges founded at Oxford in 1878–9 to provide higher education for women. Matthew Arnold's niece Mary was involved in these ventures, as secretary of the Association for the Education of Women, which led to the foundation of Somerville; and she had once been part of Yonge's circle. One of her first attempts at fiction, 'A Westmorland Story', was published in the *Churchman's Companion*, edited by Yonge, although another was rejected for the *Monthly Packet*, it being judged too passionate.[129] Mrs Humphry Ward, as Mary Arnold became, was to fare better with her second novel, *Robert Elsmere* (1888). This was a *succès fou*, in eighteen months selling about 40,000 copies in England and 200,000 in America. By 1911, Mrs Ward herself estimated, nearly a million copies had been sold in the English-speaking world and it had been translated into many languages.[130] It recounted the struggle for the soul of an earnest, questioning clergyman, Robert Elsmere, who is torn between polar points represented by Squire Wendover, an atheist slowly succumbing to hereditary lunacy, and Elsmere's wife, Catherine, whose faith was formed by narrow north-country fundamentalism. Elsmere himself is a product of doubting Oxford, still feeling the ferment caused by the Tractarian insurgence of the 1830s and 1840s but now susceptible to new approaches developed in the intervening decades, including positivist social inquiry, historical criticism of the Bible, liberal scepticism about miracles, and philosophical idealism. Questions of conscience and citizenship are resolved by Elsmere's renunciation of his ministry and foundation of a humanistic New Brotherhood of Christ, a settlement for post-Christian ethical enthusiasts to engage in social work among the London needy. Mrs Ward subsequently explained her purpose: 'I wanted to show how a man of sensitive and noble character, born for religion, comes to throw off the orthodoxies of his day and

---

[128] E. M. Delafield, Introduction to Battiscombe, *Yonge*, 11. See also Violet Powell, *The Life of a Provincial Lady: A Study of E. M. Delafield and her Works* (1988), 124, 141–2, 163, 180–1; and the centenary appreciation of 'The Heir of Redclyffe', a BBC Third Programme talk by Kathleen Tillotson, Jan. 1953, in Geoffrey and Kathleen Tillotson, *Mid-Victorian Studies* (1965), 49–55.

[129] Trevelyan, *Mrs. Ward*, 25, 30; Sutherland, *Mrs Ward*, 38–9.

[130] Mrs Humphry Ward, *Robert Elsmere*, ed. and introd. P. Rosemary Ashton, World's Classics (Oxford, 1987), vii. For the European receptions of *Elsmere*, see *Review of Reviews* (Jan. 1890), 61–2 (France); (May 1890), 397 (Germany); (June 1890), 490 (Norway); (Aug. 1890), 233 (Holland).

moment, and to go out into the wilderness where all is experiment, and spiritual life begins again.'[131] Contracting tuberculosis, Elsmere dies in a state of physical, intellectual, and spiritual exhaustion; yet, 'an ecstasy of joy was on his face'.

The novel was laboriously long and ponderously plotted. Poor Henry James was more contorted than ever when, in correspondence with Mrs Ward, he endeavoured to point out her failings of characterization without supplying offence.[132] He soon came to accept that advice was futile, because 'a finer "case" of serene, sublime and imperturbable self-complacency' than Mrs Ward was impossible to conceive.[133] Macmillan's had originally turned down *Elsmere*, believing the subject unlikely to interest the public; and George Smith, of Smith, Elder & Co., who did take it, did so largely on account of Mrs Ward being Matthew Arnold's niece. Subsequently, A. G. Gardiner weighed her achievement. It was 'an unparalleled triumph over natural disadvantages', for she had 'every disqualification for the rôle of a successful novelist', being without humour, genuine feeling, or charm in the composition of her books. He proposed putting Mrs Ward's novels to a simple test: 'Name one character from them that moves you with happy memories or even painful memories. You will find it as difficult as it is to quote a line from the poetry of Mr Alfred Austin.'[134] The éclat which *Robert Elsmere* generated was not caused by its artistic distinction, therefore. While wrestling with his review of it, Gladstone wrote to his friend the Liberal Catholic historian Lord Acton, on 1 April 1888: 'You perhaps have not heard of *Robert Elsmere*, for I find without surprise, that it makes its way slowly into public notice. It is not far from twice the length of an ordinary novel; and the labour and effort of reading it all, I should say, sixfold....'.[135]

Wilde captioned *Robert Elsmere* as 'simply Arnold's *Literature and Dogma* with the literature left out'.[136] The last words of Arnold's 1883 preface to *Literature and Dogma* (1873) were 'miracles do not happen'. In part *Elsmere*'s success derived from the element of *roman-à-clef*: the intelligentsia were intrigued to detect traces of the likes of T. H. Huxley, J. R. Green, T. H. Green, Mark Pattison, Benjamin Jowett, Arthur Clough, and the author's uncle and father among the cast. From the fashionable world, the sisters Laura and Margot Tennant (who married the politicians Alfred Lyttelton and H. H. Asquith, respectively) were also supposedly

---

[131] *Ward, A Writer's Recollections*, 230.

[132] To Mrs Humphry Ward, 3 July 1888, in Edel (ed.), *James Letters*, iii. 234–7.

[133] To Grace Norton, 12 Mar. 1890, ibid. 271.   [134] Gardiner, *Pillars of Society*, 263.

[135] Letter, 1 Apr. 1888, in Morley, *Gladstone*, ii. 597. Charitably, Mrs Ward's friend Dean Inge, who preached at her funeral in 1920, noted that 'there is something *soigné* about her style which will not conduce to popularity. It may be that after a period of undeserved neglect her novels may be recognized as giving an accurate picture of the life of the upper and upper-middle class in the last generation of their prosperity' (W. R. Inge, *Diary of a Dean, St Paul's 1911–1934* (1949), 54 (28 Mar. 1920)).

[136] Quoted in Ashton, Introduction to Ward, *Elsmere*, p. xvii. Wilde further called *Elsmere* 'a masterpiece of the *genre ennuyeux*, the one form of literature that the English people seem to thoroughly enjoy ... it reminded him of the sort of conversation that goes on at a meat tea in the house of a serious Nonconformist family...'. Hart-Davis (ed.), *Wilde's Letters*, 77, quoting Wilde's 'The Decay of Lying', *Nineteenth Century* (Jan. 1889).

portrayed as Catherine and Rose. Laura Lyttleton, who had died during childbirth in 1886, was one of two dedicatees of *Robert Elsmere*: the other was T. H. Green, Professor of Moral Philosophy at Oxford, who had died in 1882. The Master of Balliol, Jowett, reassured Margot Asquith, however: 'All the portraits are about equally unlike the originals.' He added that the book's success was 'really due to its saying what everybody is thinking. I am astonished at her knowing so much about German theology—she is a real scholar and takes up things of the right sort. I do not believe that Mrs Ward ever said "She had pulverized Christianity". These things are invented about people by the orthodox, i.e. the infidel world, in the hope that they will do them harm.'[137] Two representatives of 'the infidel world' among men of letters, Frederic Harrison and Thomas Hardy, who might be dubbed the leaders of the Positivist and Pessimist parties, were taken aback by the stir which the book made. They pondered whether to exercise their right of reply and in what style. 'Satire, I suppose, is bad as a rule,' wrote Hardy to Harrison, 'but surely the New Christians (or whatever they are) who, to use Morley's words "have hit their final climax in the doctrine that everything is both true & false at the same time" are very tempting game—I mean the "Robert Elsmere" school.'[138] However, the agnostic party, personified by Professor T. H. Huxley, was compromised by personal connection: Huxley's son Leonard and Mrs Ward's sister Julia had married in 1885. The Professor's criticism of *Robert Elsmere* was mostly token and, for the rest, almost simpering:

As an observer of the human ant-hill, quite impartial by this time, I think your picture of one of the deeper aspects of our troubled times admirable. You are very hard on the philosophers . . . If I may say so, I think the picture of Catherine is the gem of the book. She reminds me of her namesake of Siena—and would as little have failed in any duty, however gruesome.[139]

Mrs Ward placed her work in the tradition of J. H. Newman's *Loss and Gain* (1848), J. A. Froude's *Nemesis of Faith* (1849), and Charles Kingsley's *Alton Locke* (1850), semi-autobiographical novels that dealt painfully with crises of faith and

---

[137] See Jowett's letters to Margot Tennant, 28 Nov. 1888 and 11 Mar. 1889, in Asquith, *Autobiography*, i 119–23. For all his dislike of denominationalism and of the ecclesiastical establishment's discouragement of liberal thought, Jowett was unsympathetic to the course taken by Mrs Ward's Elsmere, that is, to found a new church. As he wrote to Florence Nightingale on 10 February 1889, 'We must almost always begin with the organization which is nearest—unless it be essentially bad and immoral. You & I would be foolish in trying to make a new one, like Robert Ellesmere [*sic*] or Mr Stopford Brook [*sic*]'. E. V. Quinn and J. M. Prest (eds.), *Dear Miss Nightingale: A Selection of Benjamin Jowett's Letters to Florence Nightingale 1860–1893* (Oxford, 1987), 310. Stopford Brooke (1832–1916) had seceded from the Church of England in 1880, ministering to his own congregation at the Bedford chapel, Bloomsbury. Jowett also wrote to Mrs Ward herself: 'It seems to me that the world is growing rather tired of German criticism, having got out of it nearly all that it is capable of giving . . . We must give up doctrine and teach by the lives of men, beginning with the life of Christ instead. And the best words of men, beginning with the Gospels and the prophets, will be our Bible' (letter, 29 Aug. 1892, in Evelyn Abbott and Lewis Campbell, *The Life and Letters of Benjamin Jowett* (1897), ii. 454). See also Grant Duff, *Diary, 1896 to 1901*, ii. 30–1 (27 June 1898) for Mrs Ward's readiness to discourse about German historicist theology.

[138] Hardy to Frederic Harrison, 17 May 1888, in Purdy and Millgate (eds.), *Hardy Letters*, i. 176.

[139] Trevelyan, *Mrs. Ward*, 68.

civic duty. These had been written a generation earlier, a point made by several reviewers now who chided Mrs Ward's curiously old-fashioned preoccupations. When Wilfrid Blunt subsequently reread *Loss and Gain* he was struck how 'Newman's mind . . . seems never to have faced the real issues of belief and unbelief, those which have to be fought out with materialism . . . What a gulf separates us from that time, the epoch of undoubting belief in the literal inspiration of the Holy Scriptures.'[140] Mrs Ward, however, believed that she was confronting this, 'the *second* religious battle of the nineteenth century', which was the struggle between dogmatic religion of all kinds and liberalism, modernism, and evolutionary scientific progress, as means towards individual fulfilment and social improvement. For her, the tradition of 'the novel of religious or social propaganda' was not superannuated. Indeed,

it seemed to me that the novel was capable of holding and shaping real experience of any kind, as it affects the lives of men and women. It is the most elastic, the most adaptable of forms. No one has a right to set limits to its range. There is only one final test. Does it interest? -does it appeal? Personally, I should add another. Does it make in the long run for *beauty*? Beauty taken in the largest and most generous sense, and especially as including discord, the harsh and jangled notes which enrich the rest—but still Beauty—as Tolstoy was a master of it.[141]

Mrs Ward was, therefore, conscious of continuing a distinguished line of novels that dealt seriously with issues of faith; and this was how *Robert Elsmere* was received. The retired Governor of Madras Sir Mountstuart Grant Duff, to whom Mrs Ward read extracts from *Robert Elsmere* before it was published, was arrested by the novel's passages of 'extraordinary power', and his diary musings illustrate that its themes were central concerns for the troubled intellectual of the times, Grant Duff asking,

When will Christianity have disengaged itself from the mass of doubtful history, blundered chronology, manifest myths, equally manifest legends, stories invented for national glorification, stories invented for political or class purposes, stories for edification, amidst which any one who is chiefly occupied, as I am at present, in studying the past of this country, must perforce spend his time?[142]

E. S. Talbot, the first Warden of Keble College, Oxford, a Tractarian foundation, was equally shaken:

Robert Elsmere has been rather a cloud upon the holiday. It is a book to take a great deal out of one. I would certainly not advise a person unnecessarily to read it, beautiful though I think it is in parts. I have seldom met a book more 'unsettling', and there are some large assumptions or generalizations which an ordinary person would have difficulty in testing.[143]

---

[140] Blunt, *Diaries*, ii. 233 (1 Mar. 1909).

[141] Ward, *Recollections*, 229–30. The admiration was mutual: 'Tolstoy concurred in ranking Mrs. Ward as England's greatest artist in fiction—England's Tolstoy' (Sutherland, *Mrs Ward*, 260).

[142] Grant Duff, *Diary, 1886–1888*, ii. 26 (10 Feb. 1888); also ibid. i. 197–8 (9 Oct. 1887), ii. 73, 107–9 (30 Mar. 27 and 30 May 1888).   [143] Stephenson, *Edward Stuart Talbot*, 52–3.

past Gladstone had on occasions been taken in;[156] but the refrain in Gladstone's diaries, in his notes on the many controversial works of fiction he read, from Hardy to Zola, was his moral anxiety that a society without a Christian framework would lose its ethical bearings.[157] Religion permeated Gladstone's thoughts and actions. Kitchen was no different from cathedral: 'Engaged a cook', ran an entry in Mrs Gladstone's journal, 'after a long conversation on *religious matters, chiefly between her and William.*'[158] Authors who dealt with religious issues in a serious and reflective manner could be sure of the statesman's attention. Edna Lyall, who sent a copy of *Donovan* (1882) to Gladstone at a time when his mind was troubled by the Bradlaugh case, was favoured by a letter in which the premier confessed:

I cannot but admire the fidelity with which, while it avoids being didactic, it conveys true & deep knowledge: & combines a thorough equity & clarity [*sic*] towards an atheist with a not less thorough homage to the authority of truth. Let me presume to add my poor tribute especially to the first volume as a very delicate & refined work of art.[159]

In 1884, when staying in Oxford as a guest of the Warden of Merton, Gladstone 'gave our house-party a short *résumé* of *Joshua Davidson* (which he greatly admired), with so much fervour and pathos as to reveal the secret of his influence over large audiences'.[160] *The True History of Joshua Davidson, Christian and Communist*, by the freethinking Eliza Lynn Linton, was first published in 1872: it translated Christ's story to contemporary England in order to pose the question 'Is practical Christianity impossible?'[161]

Gladstone's excited response to *Joshua Davidson*, *Donovan*, and *John Inglesant* was as nothing compared to his reaction to *Robert Elsmere*. He was shaken by what he took to be a message of quack theism in the book and cross-examined the author thoroughly before issuing a 10,000 word exhalation, 'Robert Elsmere and the Battle of Belief', in the *Nineteenth Century*, May 1888, to which Mrs Ward rejoindered in March 1889 with 'The New Reformation: A Dialogue'.[162] This was

---

[156] St Helier, *Memories*, 251–2, recounts that Gladstone wrote 'a most effusive critique' about an anonymously published book of letters, entitled *An Author's Love*, supposing the author to be Prosper Mérimée, and was 'exceedingly annoyed—in fact, very angry' when it emerged that they were a hoax, composed 'by an American lady of great literary ability, then well known in English society'. It should be remembered, however, that Lady St Helier, as a Conservative, took pleasure in tales told against Gladstone. The author of *An Author's Love: The Unpublished Letters of Prosper Mérimée's 'Inconnue'* (1889) was Elizabeth Balch.   [157] Matthew (ed.), *Gladstone Diaries*, introd. to vols. xii–xiii, p. lxxxiii.

[158] Drew, *Catherine Gladstone*, 57 (n.d. [c.1843]).

[159] Letter, 27 Apr. 1883, in Matthew (ed.), *Gladstone Diaries*, x. 438. My addition of '*sic*': probably, 'clarity' is a misprint for 'charity'. On Edna Lyall (Ada Ellen Bayly, 1857–1903), see above, Ch. 24. The Bradlaugh case concerned the freethinker who in 1880 had been elected MP for Northampton and disallowed from taking his seat when he claimed the right to affirm rather than swear the oath. See Walter L. Arnstein, *The Bradlaugh Case* (Oxford, 1965).

[160] Brodrick, *Memories and Impressions*, 228.

[161] Sutherland, *Companion*, 341; and Anderson, *Woman against Women*, 145–9, and pp. 180, 189, 193–4 for Linton's differences with Gladstone.

[162] Matthew (ed.), *Gladstone Diaries*, xii, 106, 110–11; Trevelyan, *Mrs. Ward*, ch. iv; Morley, *Gladstone*, ii. 596–601. See also Drew, *Catherine Gladstone*, 109–10, for Mrs Gladstone's opinion of *Robert Elsmere* and her husband's review.

a chastening experience for Gladstone, who, thereafter, did not like to be drawn out by Mrs Ward again. He was disappointed by her successor novel, *The History of David Grieve* (1892), though he read it all, recorded Stuart Rendel, who admitted that was 'a thing I could not do. He consulted me most gravely, as to whether my daughters should read it, and gave me the incriminated portion to read.'[163] With Mrs Ward herself, Gladstone now kept his own counsel. In August 1893 Lord Rothschild invited Mrs Ward to dine at Tring when the Gladstones were among his house guests but, Reginald Brett reported to the Duchess of Sutherland, while Gladstone talked to her, he 'carefully avoided her novels. He thinks *them* quite hopeless—although he admires her intellectually and quite apart from her powers of invention.'[164]

Gladstone's intervention, then, had helped launch Mrs Ward as a literary celebrity of the first rank (though the influential *British Weekly*, edited by Robertson Nicoll, had devoted a leader to the novel and its author—'The Woman of Feeling'—on 9 March 1888, two months before Gladstone's article).[165] Another kind of intervention came from *Punch*, which naturally judged it fair game for a parody, and thought as little of Mrs Ward's literary ability as of her theological agonizing. The long-windedness of 'Bob Sillimere' by 'Mrs Humphry John Ward Preacher' was curbed by numerous editorial interventions—'[Two pages of fancy writing are omitted. Ed.]'—but enough remained to make a joyous farce of it all. Catherine is described thus:

Cold, with the delicate but austere firmness of a Westmoreland daisy, gifted with fatally sharp lines about the chin and mouth, and habitually wearing loose grey gowns, with bodices to match, she was admirably calculated, with her narrow meat-tea proclivities, to embitter the amiable Sillimere's existence, and to produce, in conjunction with him, that storm and stress, that perpetual clashing of two estimates without which no modern religious novel could be written, and which not even her pale virginal grace of look and form could subdue.

Sillimere is eventually confounded by the ogre Squire's remorseless logic:

'Pronounce the word "testimony" twice, slowly. Think of a number, multiply by four, subtract the Thirty-nine Articles, add a Sunday School and a packet of buns. Result, you're a freethinker.' And with that he bowed Bob out of the room.

A terrible storm was raging in the Rector's breast as he strode, regardless of the cold, along the verdant lanes of Wendover. 'Fool that I was!' he muttered, pressing both hands convulsively to his sides. 'Why did I not pay more attention to arithmetic at school?'- ...[The] thought of Catherine knitting quietly at home, while she read Fox's *Book of Martyrs*, with a tender smile on her thin lips, unmanned him. He sobbed bitterly ... The

---

[163] Rendel, *Personal Papers*, 99 (29 Feb. 1892).

[164] Brett, *Esher*, i. 174 (27 Aug. 1893). Laura Lyttelton, one of the dedicatees of *Robert Elsmere*, was a niece of Gladstone's wife, Catherine.

[165] Darlow, *Nicoll*, 86, where this is identified as 'the first serious criticism' of *Robert Elsmere*, and where a letter to Nicoll from Mrs Ward in 1911 is quoted, in which she wrote: 'I remember the fair and kindly review.'

Dowson preceded him, converting in 1891, following a period of agonizing pre-
cipitated by his unrequited love for an under-age girl. In March 1889, having read
Robert Elsmere, he was full of admiration. Though prolix and with other 'enormous faults', it was nonetheless 'a great book'.[177] Yet the more he pondered
medieval and modern theological writers and their critics, the less viable he
considered Mrs Ward's line. By May 1889 he had narrowed the field: 'Agnosticism—not of course à la Mrs. H. Ward—but a reasonable Huxleian agnosticism is
logical and consistent—but when you come to forms of belief—there is only
Pessimism & Catholicism. They are the only respectable "isms". Theism strikes
me as about the worst kind of balderdash that I have yet come across except
perhaps Positivism.'[178] Two years later Dowson affirmed his choice, imitating
Newman and believing that it was 'the deliberate conclusion of a logical process,
and not at all emotional' to reject 'the flimsy and local claims of Anglicanismus
& the Protestant sects . . . I am so tired of Anglican condescension and Latitudi-
narian superiority; where Rome is in question. That, and the vulgarity of the
dogmatic atheists, and the fatuous sentimentality of the Elesmere [*sic*] people et
hoc genus omne!'[179] But it would be wrong to suppose that Mrs Ward gained no
adherents to her position. There were a good many in Victorian England, lapsed
from one faith or another, who found mere doubt and agnosticism unfulfilling,
and who yearned for something more purposeful and uplifting. Lady Battersea,
a Rothschild before marriage to the Liberal politician Cyril Flower, was a lapsed
Jew who sought new bearings to compensate for those she had sundered; and in
1893 she wrote in her journal: 'The society I live in, Cyril's political friends, are
thoroughly agnostic and unbelieving, neither Jews nor Christians; in Mrs. Ward
alone I seem to be finding a kindred spirit who in reverent, free thought still
acknowledges the power of the Unseen and the Great Ideal . . .'.[180]

Robert Elsmere and *David Grieve* were received generally with high seriousness,
therefore; yet, the overall evaluation of their quality was a low one, and such
debates were almost the last of their kind. Theology largely departed from the
agenda of most novelists. Where an epiphanic element remained, it was invariably
unorthodox. Mrs Ward herself provoked a certain curiosity in 1898 with *Helbeck
of Bannisdale*, a Gothic tale which dealt with the incompatibility of Catholicism
and rationalism and which revived family agonies about her father's Catholic
conversion, apostasy, and reconversion. However, it is important to notice how
The Case of Richard Meynell (1911), her essayed sequel to *Robert Elsmere*, backfired.
Astute bargaining brought her £11,000 in British, American, and foreign publication
and serial rights; but her publishers soon discovered that they had burnt their
fingers. An expensive advertising campaign moved the sales figures towards the
40,000 mark, but this was insufficient to recoup their investment. Mrs Ward
and, with her, the novel of theological discussion were demoted from best-seller

---

[177] To Arthur Moore, 17 Mar. 1889, in Flower and Maas (eds.), *Dowson's Letters*, 51–2.
[178] To Arthur Moore, 26 May 1889, ibid. 81.   [179] To Arthur Moore, 10 May 1891, ibid. 198.
[180] Cohen, *Rothschild and her Daughters*, 238.

status.[181] Between *Robert Elsmere* and *Richard Meynell* Mrs Ward's career developed in other directions. Her fiction meanwhile turned to topics of more pressing secular interest: challenges to the landed and political establishment made by radical and socialist agitations in *Marcella* (1894), the politics of reform of the sweated trades in *Sir George Tressady* (1896), and so into her Edwardian phase, in which she tackled, *inter alia*, suffragism and divorce. Mrs Ward's public activity registered these commitments. Her foundation of the Passmore Edwards Settlement (which subsequently took her name) and work in the cause of children's play centres furnished models for the treatment of the physically handicapped which influenced the London County Council to set up similar schools. Her support for the admission of women into higher education was also strong.

Less appreciated in the progressive camp was Mrs Ward's opposition to women acquiring the parliamentary franchise. She had been a prominent signatory of the famous anti-suffrage appeal, orchestrated by Frederic Harrison, which was published in the *Nineteenth Century* in June 1889;[182] and she was a co-founder of the Women's National Anti-Suffrage League established in 1908, and a mainstay of the *Anti-Suffrage Review*.[183] Quite why she was so antagonistic to the extension of the parliamentary franchise to her own sex was a great puzzle to many Edwardian progressives, who were familiar with her philanthropic work; who were aware of her canvassing to secure the election of her spendthrift son as a Conservative MP; above all, who knew of her contribution to the National Union of Women's Workers (1888) and her foundation of the Local Government Advancement Committee (1911), which aimed to introduce more women onto public bodies and to network their activities. Part of the answer to this paradox may be found in Mrs Ward's essentially static conceptualization of what was the appropriate sphere for women; and the business of the imperial parliament, involving larger portfolios and divisive party politics, threatened the inherent virtue of women's nature and propriety of their ideal social conduct.[184] But this could not be the whole answer in Mrs Ward's case, and A. G. Gardiner believed that he discovered the true explanation of her hostility in her intellectual frigidity and social hauteur: that Mrs Ward's

ideal is of a small governing class of exquisite souls who would behave nicely to the poor, make just laws for them, and generally keep them in their proper station with a firm but gentle hand. In a word, she is against democracy.[185]

---

[181] Sutherland, *Mrs Ward*, 316–17.

[182] The petitioners protested against female suffrage as 'distasteful to the great majority of women of the country—unnecessary and mischievous both to themselves and the state'. Christina Rossetti was another signatory, on whose view, see Marsh, *Rossetti*, 553–5.

[183] On Mrs Ward's activities, see Brian Harrison, *Separate Spheres: The Opposition to Women's Suffrage in Britain* (1978). See also Vogeler, *Harrison*, 211–14; and, for a supporter of Mrs Ward's views before the Great War, Markham, *Return Passage*, ch. xii.

[184] See Mrs Ward's letter to *The Times*, 6 Aug. 1912, blaming suffragette violence for the prejudice against the admission of qualified women in local government; also Trevelyan, *Mrs. Ward*, ch. xii.

[185] Gardiner, *Pillars of Society*, 266–7.

'why, if people must have a religion, they didn't all become Roman Catholics'[200] because it was so colourful—at a stroke thus sweeping aside England's
Reformation Protestant creed, so crucial to an understanding of the country's
history and culture. Religion is a joke, the sort of thing that only crazy, malevolent, and frustrated spinster aunts take seriously. Terence Hewet, the writer
who forms a relationship with Rachel and who is an amalgam of Woolf's own
husband, Leonard, and her brother-in-law Clive Bell, remarks how he has an
aunt, by coincidence also called Rachel, 'who put the life of Father Damien into
verse. She is a religious fanatic—the result of the way she was brought up in
Northamptonshire, never seeing a soul.' To which Rachel confesses that she
lives with her aunts in Richmond: 'They are small, rather pale women, very
clean...They have an old dog, too, who will only eat the marrow out of
bones...They are always going to church. They tidy their drawers a good
deal.'[201] Hirst also has a spinster aunt and thinks that, like Charles Kingsley, she
is 'now obsolete'. This aunt 'spends her life in East Lambeth among the
degraded poor...[and] is inclined to persecute people she calls "intellectual"',
he says, before rounding off with an outburst—'Oh, you Christians! You're the
most conceited, patronizing, hypocritical set of old humbugs in the kingdom!'[202] Hirst is a Fellow of King's College, Cambridge, and 'one of the three,
or is it five, most distinguished men in England'.[203] His father is actually an
Anglican clergyman, a country parson in Norfolk; but Gibbon is a favourite
author of Hirst, as also of Mrs Flushing, who is of aristocratic stock and
associates Gibbon 'with some of the happiest hours of my life. We used to lie
in bed and read Gibbon—about the massacres of the Christians, I remember—
when we were supposed to be asleep.'[204]

This brings us to the set piece in chapter xvii, Sunday service for the
expatriates in the hotel—a converted monastery. Rachel naturally troops along:
she 'still went to church, because she had never, according to Helen, taken the
trouble to think about it'.[205] Others conform more cynically: '"I've been every
Sunday of my life ever since I can remember," Mrs. Flushing chuckled, as
though that were a reason by itself.'[206] The service is conducted by a Mr Bax:
many of Woolf's readers would enjoy this sly allusion to Ernest Belfort Bax, a
particularly eccentric and noisy Fabian advocate of communism, republicanism,
and atheism.[207] The Mr Bax of her story, with his smooth, eggshell face,
sermonizes like 'a leading article upon topics of general interest in the weekly
newspapers',[208] such as responsibility for the natives, while giving especial
emphasis to women's duties. As she listens to this, the prayers, and the lessons,

---

[200] Virginia Woolf, *The Voyage Out* (1957), 109.   [201] Ibid. 165.   [202] Ibid. 238–9.
[203] Ibid. 168.   [204] Ibid. 236.
[205] Ibid. 274; and p. 168 for a previous aggressive questioning of Rachel's Christian assumptions by
Hewet, Hirst, and Helen Ambrose.   [206] Ibid. 284.
[207] See Ernest Belfort Bax, *Reminiscences and Reflexions of a Mid and Late Victorian* (1918).
[208] Woolf, *Voyage Out*, 281.

Rachel is progressively struck by the irrelevance and incomprehensibility of Christ's gospel for modern lives:

All around her were people pretending to feel what they did not feel, while somewhere above her floated the idea which they could none of them grasp, which they pretended to grasp, always escaping out of reach, a beautiful idea, an idea like a butterfly. One after another, vast and hard and cold, appeared to her the churches all over the world where this blundering effort and misunderstanding were perpetually going on, great buildings, filled with innumerable men and women, not seeing clearly, who finally gave up the effort to see, and relapsed tamely into praise and acquiescence, half-shutting their eyes and pursing their lips.[209]

Amid the sheeplike baaing responses of the congregation, Rachel's eye fixes on the one person,

a hospital nurse, whose expression of devout attention seemed to prove that she was at any rate receiving satisfaction. But looking at her carefully she came to the conclusion that the hospital nurse was only slavishly acquiescent, and that the look of satisfaction was produced by no splendid conception of God within her. How, indeed, could she conceive anything far outside her own experience, a woman with a commonplace face like hers, a little round red face, upon which trivial duties and trivial spites had drawn lines, whose weak blue eyes saw without intensity or individuality, whose features were blurred, insensitive, and callous? She was adoring something shallow and smug, clinging to it, so the obstinate mouth witnessed, with the assiduity of a limpet; nothing would tear her from her demure belief in her own virtue and the virtues of her religion. She was a limpet, with the sensitive side of her stuck to a rock, for ever dead to the rush of fresh and beautiful things past her. The face of this single worshipper became printed on Rachel's mind with an impression of keen horror, and she had it suddenly revealed to her what Helen meant and St. John meant when they proclaimed their hatred of Christianity. With the violence that now marked her feelings, she rejected all that she had implicitly believed.[210]

Significantly, this nurse, Nurse McInnis, will fail to save Helen when she is dying from tropical fever. Meanwhile Hirst has been reading during the service, instead of the Prayer Book, Sappho's 'Hymn to Aphrodite' together with Swinburne's translation. Mrs Flushing takes over his book and greedily devours it, while Hirst himself concentrates on Mr Bax's utterances in order to work up some verses he has in mind about God. Later, he discloses to Mrs Ambrose that

He had lain awake all night thinking, and when it was light enough to see, he had written twenty lines of his poem on God, and the awful thing was that he'd practically proved the fact that God did exist. He did not see that he was teasing her, and he went on to wonder what would happen if God did exist—'an old gentleman in a beard and a long blue dressing-gown, extremely testy and disagreeable as he's bound to be? Can you suggest a rhyme? God, rod, sod—all used; any others?'[211]

[209] Ibid. 278. [210] Ibid. 279. [211] Ibid. 340–1.

Here is a classic counter-epiphanic moment in modern literature; and it is complemented when another of the hotel guests, Miss Allan, careworn 'after fifteen years of punctual lecturing and correcting essays upon English Literature... observed reflectively that going to church abroad always made her feel as if she had been to a sailor's funeral'.[212]

In *The Voyage Out* Virginia Woolf thus discarded Mrs Humphry Ward's matter as well as her method. It marks the chasm between the pre-Great War best-seller and the modern (though Woolf would sell sluggishly before her work was deemed canonical by university literature departments): a shift involving not just new practices of composition but ushering in entirely different outlooks. Authors who had no religion conspicuously failed to grasp a significant source of inspiration in others. More than that, this carelessness cut them off from the past.

[212] Woolf, *Voyage Out*, 210, 291.

BIBLIOGRAPHY

Place of publication is London, unless otherwise stated.

ABBOTT, EVELYN, and CAMPBELL, LEWIS, *The Life and Letters of Benjamin Jowett*, 2 vols. (1897).

AGATE, JAMES, *A Shorter Ego* (1945, 1946).

AINGER, ALFRED, *Lectures and Essays*, 2 vols. (1905).

ALCORN, JOHN, *The Nature Novel from Hardy to Lawrence* (1977).

ALINGTON, C. A., *A Dean's Apology: A Semi-Religious Autobiography* (1952).

ALLEN, GRANT, *Post-Prandial Philosophy* (1894).

ALLEN, VIVIEN, *Hall Caine: Portrait of a Victorian Romancer* (Sheffield, 1997).

ALPERS, ANTONY, *The Life of Katherine Mansfield* (Oxford, 1980; paperback edn., 1982).

ALTICK, RICHARD D., *The English Common Reader: A Social History of the Mass Reading Public 1800–1900* (Chicago, 1957; paperback edn., 1963).

ANDERSON, NANCY FIX, *Woman against Women in Victorian England: A Life of Eliza Lynn Linton* (Bloomington, Ind., 1987).

ANDERSON, PATRICIA J., and ROSE, JONATHAN (eds.), *British Literary Publishing Houses, 1820–1880, Dictionary of Literary Biography*, 106 (1991).

ANDREWS, C. F. (ed.), *Rabindranath Tagore: Letters to a Friend* (1928).

ANESKO, MICHAEL, *Friction with the Market: Henry James and the Profession of Authorship* (Oxford, 1987).

ANGELL, NORMAN, *After All* (1951).

ANNAN, NOEL, *Leslie Stephen: The Godless Victorian* (1984).

Annual Register (1880–1918).

ARIA, MRS., *Woman and the Motor Car* (1906).

—— *My Sentimental Self* (1922).

ARCHER, WILLIAM, *America To-day: Observations and Reflections* (1900).

—— *Real Conversations* (1904).

—— *Through Afro-America: An English Reading of the Race Problem* (1910).

—— *The Life, Trial, and Death of Francisco Ferrer* (1911).

—— *Colour-Blind Neutrality: An Open Letter to Dr. George Brandes* (1916).

—— *501 Gems of German Thought* (1917).

—— *God and Mr. Wells: A Critical Examination of 'God the Invisible King'* (1917).

—— *The Pirate's Progress: A Short History of the U-Boat* (1918).

[Arnim, Countess von], *Elizabeth and her German Garden* (1898, 1931).

ARNOLD, BRUCE, *Orpen: Mirror to an Age* (1981).

ARNOLD, GUY, *Held Fast for England: G. A. Henty, Imperialist Boys' Writer* (1980).

ARNOLD, MATTHEW, *Culture and Anarchy* (1869), ed. J. Dover Wilson (Cambridge, 1932).

—— *Literature and Dogma* (1873, popular edn., 1897).

—— *Discourses in America* (1885).

ARNOLD-FORSTER, MARY, *The Right Honourable Hugh Oakeley Arnold-Forster: A Memoir* (1910).

ARNSTEIN, WALTER L., *The Bradlaugh Case* (Oxford, 1965).

ASHBY, M. K., *Joseph Ashby of Tysoe, 1859–1919* (Cambridge, 1961; London, 1974).

ASQUITH, Earl of Oxford and, *Memories and Reflections 1852–1927*, 2 vols. (1928).

ASQUITH, LADY CYNTHIA, *Remember and Be Glad* (1952).

—— *Portrait of Barrie* (1954).

—— *Diaries 1915–1918* (1968, 1987).

ASQUITH, RT. HON. H. H., *Occasional Addresses 1893–1916* (1918).

ASQUITH, MARGOT, *Autobiography*, 2 vols. (1920).

AUSTIN, ALFRED, *Alfred the Great, England's Darling* (1896, 1901).

The Autobiography of Alfred Austin Poet Laureate 1835–1910, 2 vols. (1911).

AVEBURY, LORD [Sir John Lubbock], *The Pleasures of Life, Part I* (1887, 1913).

—— *The Use of Life* (1894, 1900).

AYERST, DAVID, *Garvin of the Observer* (1985).

BAILEY, MRS S. K. (ed.), *John Bailey, 1864–1931: Letters and Diaries* (1935).

BAILY, R. E. H. (ed.), *Ruth Bourne Diaries: A Victorian Memoir* (Colchester: privately printed, 1973).

BALDICK, CHRIS, *The Social Mission of English Criticism 1848–1932* (Oxford, 1983).

BALFOUR, LADY FRANCES, *Ne Obliviscaris*, 2 vols. (1930).

BANCROFTS, THE, *Recollections of Sixty Years* (1909).

BARBELLION, W. N. P. [B. F. Cummings], *The Journal of a Disappointed Man* (1919; Harmondsworth, 1948).

—— *Enjoying Life, and Other Literary Remains* (1919).

BARCLAY, FLORENCE *The Rosary* (1909; complete popular edn., 1925).

—— *The Following of the Star: A Romance* (1911).

—— *Through the Postern Gate* (1912; popular edn., n.d.).

—— *In Hoc Vince* (1915).

—— *The White Ladies of Worcester* (1917).

BARING, MAURICE, *Landmarks in Russian Literature* (1910; new edn., 1960)

—— *Diminutive Dramas* (1911, 1919).

—— *The Puppet Show of Memory* (1922).

BARKER, SIR ERNEST, *Father of the Man: Memories of Cheshire, Lancashire, and Oxford, 1874–1898* (1948).

BARNES, J. H., *Forty Years on the Stage: Others (Principally) and Myself* (1914).

BARNES, JOHN, and NICHOLSON, DAVID (eds.), *The Leo Amery Diaries*, i: *1896–1929* (1980).

BARRIE, J. M., *Two of Them* (1893).

—— *Margaret Ogilvy* (1896).

—— *Echoes of the War* (1918).

—— *Courage* (1922).

—— *The Plays* (1928).

—— *The Greenwood Hat* (1937).

BARTRIP, P. W. J., *Mirror of Medicine: A History of the British Medical Journal* (Oxford, 1990).

BATTISCOMBE, GEORGINA, *Charlotte Mary Yonge: The Story of an Uneventful Life* (1943).

BAX, ERNEST BELFORT, *Reminiscences and Reflexions of a Mid and Late Victorian* (1918).

BECKSON, KARL, *Arthur Symons* (Oxford, 1987).

—— *London in the 1890s: A Cultural History* (1992).

BEDFORD, SYBILLE, *Aldous Huxley* (1973; New York, 1974).

[BEECHING, H. C.], *Pages from a Private Diary* (1898).

BEERBOHM, MAX, *A Christmas Garland* (1912), introd. N. John Hall (New Haven, 1993).

BEGBIE, HAROLD, *The Life of General William Booth, the Founder of the Salvation Army*, 2 vols. (1920).

BEHRMAN, S. N., *Conversation with Max* (1960).

BELL, ANN OLIVIER (ed.), *The Diary of Virginia Woolf*, i: *1915–1919* (1977; Harmondsworth, 1979).

BELL, E. H. C. MOBERLY, *The Life and Letters of C. F. Moberly Bell* (1927).

BELL, LADY, *At the Works: A Study of a Manufacturing Town (Middlesbrough)* (1907; Newton Abbot, 1969).

BELL, R. S. WARREN, 'The Houses of Celebrated People', *Windsor Magazine*, 2 (July 1895).

BELLAMY, JOYCE M., and SAVILLE, JOHN (eds.), *Dictionary of Labour Biography*, i (1972–).

BELLAMY, WILLIAM, *The Novels of Wells, Bennett and Galsworthy: 1890–1910* (1971).

BELLOC, HILAIRE, *On Everything* (1909, 1926).

—— *The Servile State* (1912).

—— and CHESTERTON, CECIL, *The Party System* (1911).

BENFEY, CHRISTOPHER, *The Double Life of Stephen Crane* (1992, 1994).

BENKOVITZ, MIRIAM J., *Frederick Rolfe, Baron Corvo* (1977).

BENNETT, ARNOLD, *The Grand Babylon Hotel* (1902; Harmondsworth, 1938).

—— *Anna of the Five Towns* (1902; Harmondsworth, 1936).

—— *Literary Taste* (1909).

—— *Paris Nights and Other Impressions of Places and People* (New York, 1913).

—— *Liberty: A Statement of the British Case* (1914).

—— *The Price of Love* (1914).

—— *Books and Persons: Being Comments on a Past Epoch 1908–1911* (1917).

—— *The Title* (1918).

—— *Things that have Interested Me*, 2nd ser. (1923).

—— *Journal 1929* (1930).

—— *The Journals of Arnold Bennett*, ed. Newman Flower, i: *1896–1910*, ii: *1911–1920* (1932).

—— *The Journals of Arnold Bennett*, ed. Frank Swinnerton (1954).

BENNETT, E. A., *Fame and Fiction: An Enquiry into Certain Popularities* (1901).

BENNETT, MARGUERITE, *My Arnold Bennett* (1931).

BENSON, A. C., *From a College Window* (1906).

—— *Father Payne* (1915, 1917).

BENSON. E. F., *As We Are* (1932).

BENTLEY, NICHOLAS, SLATER, MICHAEL, and BURGIS, NINA, *The Dickens Index* (Oxford, 1990).

BENZIE, WILLIAM, *Dr. F. J. Furnivall: Victorian Scholar Adventurer* (Norman, Okla., 1983).

BERDOE, EDWARD, *The Browning Cyclopaedia* (1892).

BESANT, SIR WALTER, *The City of Refuge* (new edn., 1897).

—— *Autobiography* (ed. S. Squire Sprigge) (1902).

—— *As We Are and As We May Be* (1903).

BILLSON, CHARLES JAMES, 'The English Novel', *Westminster Review*, 138 (Dec. 1892).

BIRCH, DINAH (ed.), *Ruskin and the Dawn of the Modern* (Oxford, 1999).

BIRD, JOHN, *Percy Grainger* (1976, 1982).

BIRKENHEAD, LORD, *Rudyard Kipling* (1978).

BIRRELL, AUGUSTINE, *Obiter Dicta* (1884).

BIRRELL, AUGUSTINE, *Essays about Men, Women and Books* (1894, 1907).

—— *Miscellanies* (1901).

—— *Self-Selected Essays: A Second Series* (1916).

—— *Things Past Redress* (1937).

BLACK, CLEMENTINA (ed.), *Married Women's Work* (1915), introd. Ellen F. Mappen (1983).

BLATCHFORD, ROBERT, *My Eighty Years* (1931).

BLUMENFELD, R. D., *R.D.B.'s Diary* (1930).

—— *All in a Lifetime* (1931).

BLUNT, FANNY, LADY, *My Reminiscences* (1918).

BLUNT, WILFRID, *'England's Michelangelo': A Biography of George Frederic Watts* (1975).

BLUNT, WILFRID SCAWEN, *My Diaries, Being a Personal Narrative of Events 1888–1914*, 2 vols. (1921; New York, 1980).

BONHAM CARTER, MARK, and POTTLE, MARK (eds.), *Lantern Slides: The Diaries and Letters of Violet Bonham Carter, 1904–1914* (1996).

BONHAM-CARTER, VICTOR, *Authors by Profession* (1978).

BOOTH, BRADFORD ALLEN (ed.), *The Letters of Anthony Trollope* (Oxford, 1951).

BOOTH, MARTIN, *The Doctor, the Detective and Arthur Conan Doyle: A Biography of Arthur Conan Doyle* (1997).

BOOTHBY, GUY, *The Red Rat's Daughter* (1899).

BORLAND, MAUREEN, *Wilde's Devoted Friend: A Life of Robert Ross, 1869–1918* (Oxford, 1990).

BOULTON, JAMES T. (ed.), *The Letters of D. H. Lawrence*, i: *Sept. 1901–May 1913* (Cambridge, 1979).

—— and ROBERTSON, ANDREW (eds.), *The Letters of D. H. Lawrence*, iii: *1916–21* (Cambridge, 1984).

BOWYER, FREDERIC, and SPRANGE, W. E., *The New Barmaid* (n.d. [1897]).

BRADY, L. W., *T. P. O'Connor and the Liverpool Irish* (1983).

BRAIN, RUSSELL, *Tea with Walter de la Mare* (1957).

BRALEY, EVELYN FOLEY (ed.), *Letters of Herbert Hensley Henson* (1950).

BRENDON, PIERS, *Thomas Cook: 150 Years of Popular Tourism* (1991).

BRETT, MAURICE V. (ed.), *Journals and Letters of Reginald, Viscount Esher*, i: *1870–1903*, ii: *1903–1910* (1934).

BRIGGS, ASA, *Victorian People* (1954; paperback edn., 1965).

—— *Victorian Things* (1988; paperback edn., 1990).

—— and MACARTNEY, ANNE, *Toynbee Hall: The First Hundred Years* (1984).

BRETT, SIMON (ed.), *The Faber Book of Parodies* (1984).

BRIDGES, ROBERT (ed.), *The Spirit of Man* (1916).

BRIGGS, JULIA, *A Woman of Passion: The Life of E. Nesbit 1858–1924* (1987; Oxford, 1989).

BRITAIN, IAN, *Fabianism and Culture: A Study in British Socialism and the Arts c.1884–1918* (Cambridge, 1982).

BRITTAIN, VERA, *Pethick-Lawrence: A Portrait* (1963).

BROADBENT, R. J., *Annals of the Liverpool Stage* (Liverpool, 1908).

BROCK, M. G. and ELEANOR (eds.), *H. H. Asquith: Letters to Venetia Stanley* (Oxford, 1982).

—— and CURTHOYS, M. C. (eds.), *The History of the University of Oxford*, vii: *Nineteenth Century Oxford*, pt. 2 (Oxford, 2002).

BROCKWAY, FENNER, *Socialism over 60 Years* (1946).

BRODRICK, HON. GEORGE CHARLES, *Memories and Impressions, 1831–1900* (1900).

BROGAN, HUGH, *The Life of Arthur Ransome* (1984).

BROMLEY, J., *The Man of Ten Talents: A Portrait of Richard Chevenix Trench, 1807–86: Philologist, Poet, Theologian, Archbishop* (1959).

BROOK, DONALD, *Writers' Gallery* (1944, 1970).

BROOKE, STOPFORD A., *The Poetry of Robert Browning* (1902).

BROOKFIELD, CHARLES H. E., *Random Reminiscences* (1902; popular edn., 1911).

BROWN, LUCY, *Victorian News and Newspapers* (Oxford, 1985).

BROWNE, G. F., *The Recollections of a Bishop* (1915).

BROWNE, J. H. BALFOUR, *Recollections Literary and Political* (1917).

BROWNING, D. C., and COUSIN, JOHN W. (eds.), *Everyman's Dictionary of Literary Biography, English and American* (1958).

BUCHAN, ANNA [O. DOUGLAS], *Unforgettable, Unforgotten* (1945).

BUCHAN, JOHN, *Memory Hold-the-Door* (1940).

BUCKLE, G. E. (ed.), *The Letters of Queen Victoria*, 3rd ser., vol. i: *1886–1890* (1930).

BUNDOCK, CLEMENT J., *The National Union of Journalists: A Jubilee History 1907–1957* (Oxford, 1957).

BURKE, THOMAS, *Son of London* (1947, 1948).

BURNAND, SIR FRANCIS C., *Records and Reminiscences, Personal and General*, 2 vols. (1904).

CADY, EDWIN H. (ed.), *W. D. Howells as Critic* (1973).

CAINE, T. H. HALL, *Politics and Art: A Lecture Delivered at the Royal Institution, Liverpool* (Liverpool, 1880).

—— *Cobwebs of Criticism* (1883; 2nd edn., with new preface, 1908).

—— *The Shadow of a Crime* (1885, 1905).

—— *The Deemster* (1887, 1921).

—— *Drink: A Love Story on a Great Question* (n.d [1908].

— *My Story* (1908).

—— *Letters to the Author from the Friends to Whom Copies of the Privately-Printed Edition of 'The Master of Man' Were Sent* (privately printed, 1921).

CAMPBELL, R. J., *Christianity and the Social Order* (1907).

CAMROSE, VISCOUNT, *British Newspapers and their Controllers* (1947).

CANNADINE, DAVID, *G. M. Trevelyan: A Life in History* (1992; Harmondsworth, 1997).

CARDUS, NEVILLE, *Autobiography* (1947).

CAREY, JOHN, *The Intellectuals and the Masses: Pride and Prejudice among the Literary Intelligentsia, 1880–1939* (1992).

CARLYLE, THOMAS, *Heroes, Hero-Worship, and the Heroic in History* (1840), lectures iii, v.

—— *Past and Present* (1843, n.d.).

—— *Critical and Miscellaneous Essays*, 7 vols. (1872).

CARPENTER, EDWARD, *My Days and Dreams* (1916).

CARPENTER, HUMPHREY, *O.U.D.S.: A Centenary History of the Oxford University Dramatic Society 1885–1985* (Oxford, 1985).

—— *Secret Gardens: The Golden Age of Children's Literature* (1985).

CARR, KENT, *Miss Marie Corelli* (1901).

CARR, RAYMOND, *English Fox Hunting: A History* (1976; rev., 1986).

CARROLL, LEWIS, *Alice's Adventures in Wonderland and Through the Looking-Glass*, World's Classics (Oxford, 1982).

CECIL, DAVID, *Max* (1964).

CHAMPNEYS, BASIL, *Memoirs and Correspondence of Coventry Patmore*, 2 vols. (1900).

CHARLES KINGSLEY: His Letters and Memories of the Life, ed. his wife, 2 vols. (1877).

CHATURVEDI, BENARSIDAS, and SYKES, MARJORIE (eds.), *Charles Freer Andrews*, foreword M. K. Gandhi (1949).

CHESTERTON, G. K., *Leo Tolstoy* (1903), in *Collected Works*, xviii (San Francisco, 1991).

—— *Charles Dickens* (1906).

—— *All Things Considered* (1908).

—— *Autobiography* (1936).

CHITTY, SUSAN, *The Beast and the Monk: A Life of Charles Kingsley* (1974).

CHURCHILL, RANDOLPH S., *Winston S. Churchill*, i: *Youth 1874–1900* (1966).

—— *Winston S. Churchill*, ii: *Young Statesman 1901–1914* (1967).

—— *Winston S. Churchill, Companion vol. ii/pt. 1: 1901–1907* (1969).

—— *Winston S. Churchill, Companion vol. ii/pt. 2: 1907–1911* (1969).

CHURCHILL, WINSTON S., *My Early Life* (1930, 1959).

—— *Lord Randolph Churchill*, i (1906).

CLARK, ALAN (ed.), *'A Good Innings': The Private Papers of Viscount Lee of Fareham* (1974).

CLARK, LEONARD, *Alfred Williams: His Life and Work* (Bristol, 1945).

CLEGG, JAMES, *The Directory of Second-Hand Booksellers* (1891).

CLINE, C. L. (ed.), *The Collected Letters of George Meredith*, 3 vols (Oxford, 1970).

COATES, THOMAS F. G., and BELL, R. S. WARREN, *Marie Corelli: The Writer and the Woman* (1903).

COBURN, ALVIN LANGDON, *More Men of Mark* (1922).

—— *An Autobiography*, ed. Helmut and Alison Gernsheim (1966, 1978).

COCKBURN, CLAUD, *Bestseller: The Books that Everyone Read, 1900–1939* (1972).

COHEN, J. M. (ed.), *Letters of Edward FitzGerald* (1960).

COHEN, LUCY, *Lady de Rothschild and her Daughters, 1821–1931* (1935).

COHEN, MORTON N., *Lewis Carroll: A Biography* (New York, 1995, 1996).

COHEN, STUART A., *English Zionists and British Jews: The Communal Politics of Anglo-Jewry, 1895–1920* (Princeton, 1982).

COLERIDGE, CHRISTABEL, *Charlotte M. Yonge: Her Life and Letters* (1903).

COLLIE, MICHAEL, *George Borrow: Eccentric* (Cambridge, 1982).

COLLINGWOOD, STUART DODGSON, *The Life and Letters of Lewis Carroll* (1898, n.d.).

COLLINS, DOROTHY (ed.), *Selected Essays of G. K. Chesterton* (1949).

COLLINS, HORACE, *My Best Riches: Story of a Stone Rolling Round the World and the Stage* (1941).

COLLIS, MAURICE, *Nancy Astor* (1960).

—— *Somerville and Ross* (1968).

COLLS, ROBERT, and DODD, PHILIP (eds.), *Englishness: Politics and Culture 1880–1920* (1986).

COLVIN, SIDNEY (ed.), *Vailima Letters* (1895; 3rd edn., 1901).

—— (ed.), *The Letters of Robert Louis Stevenson to his Family and Friends*, 2 vols. (1899; 5th edn., 1901).

—— *Memories and Notes of Persons and Places 1852–1912* (1921).

CONAN DOYLE, ARTHUR, *The Great Boer War* (complete edn., 1902).

CONNELL, JOHN, *W. E. Henley* (1947; New York, 1972).

CONNOLLY, JOSEPH, *Jerome K. Jerome: A Critical Biography* (1982).

CONRAD, JOSEPH, *Nostromo: A Tale of the Seaboard* (1904; Harmondsworth, 1963).

——*A Personal Record* (1912).

——*Chance (1914)* introd., Ray Martin, World's Classics (Oxford, 1988).

——*Notes on Life and Letters* (1921).

——*Collected Works* (1925–8; repr. 1995), ix.

COOK, SIR EDWARD, *Literary Recreations* (1918).

——*More Literary Recreations* (1919).

COOKE, WILLIAM, *Edward Thomas: A Critical Biography, 1878–1917* (1970).

COOPER, LADY DIANA, *The Rainbow Comes and Goes* (1958; Harmondsworth, 1961).

COOPER, DUFF, *Haig* (1935).

CORELLI, MARIE, *Thelma: A Norwegian Princess* (1887, 1896).

——*The Soul of Lilith* (1892, 1897).

——*The Sorrows of Satan* (1895; Oxford, 1996).

——*Cameos* (1896, 1919).

——*God's Good Man: A Simple Love Story* (1904).

——*Free Opinions, Freely Expressed on Certain Phases of Modern Social Life and Conduct* (1905).

COURTNEY, JANET E., *Recollected in Tranquillity* (1926).

——*The Making of an Editor: W. L. Courtney 1850–1928* (1930).

COUSTILLAS, PIERRE (ed.), *London and the Life of Literature in Late Victorian England: The Diary of George Gissing, Novelist* (Hassocks, 1978).

[COWELL, F. R.], *The Athenaeum: Club and Social Life in London 1824–1974* (1975).

COX, R. G. (ed.), *Thomas Hardy: The Critical Heritage* (1970).

COXHEAD, ELIZABETH, *Lady Gregory: A Literary Portrait.* (1961; rev 1966).

CRANE, HARVEY, *Playbill: A History of the Theatre in the West Country* (Plymouth, 1980).

CRAWFORD, ELIZABETH, *The Women's Suffrage Movement: A Reference Guide 1866–1928* (1999, 2001).

CREIGHTON, LOUISE, *Life and Letters of Mandell Creighton*, 2 vols. (1904).

——*Life and Letters of Thomas Hodgkin* (1917; 2nd edn., 1918).

CUMBERLEGE, G. F. J. (ed.), *Essays Mainly on the Nineteenth Century Presented to Sir Humphrey Milford* (Oxford, 1948).

CUNNINGHAM, VALENTINE, *Everywhere Spoken Against: Dissent in the Victorian Novel* (Oxford, 1975).

DALE, A. W. W., *The Life of R. W. Dale of Birmingham* (1898).

DANSON, LAWRENCE, *Max Beerbohm and the Act of Writing* (Oxford, 1989, 1991).

DARK, SIDNEY, *The Life of Sir Arthur Pearson Bt., G.B.E.* (n.d.).

——*Mainly about Other People* (1925).

DARLOW, T. H., *William Robertson Nicoll: Life and Letters* (1925).

DAUNTON, M. J., *House and Home in the Victorian City: Working-Class Housing 1850–1914* (1983).

DAVID, EDWARD (ed.), *Inside Asquith's Cabinet: From the Diaries of Charles Hobhouse* (1977).

DAVIES, HUBERT HENRY, *Plays*, introd. Hugh Walpole, 2 vols. (1921).

DAVIES, W. H., *Later Days* (1925, 1927).

——*Young Emma*, foreword C. V. Wedgwood (1980).

DAVIS, JOHN, *Reforming London: The London Government Problem, 1855–1900* (Oxford, 1988).

DEANE, ANTHONY C., *Time Remembered* (1945).

DELANY, PAUL, *The Neo-Pagans: Friendship and Love in the Rupert Brooke Circle* (1987).

DENT, ALAN (ed.), *Bernard Shaw and Mrs Patrick Campbell: Their Correspondence* (1952).

HUEFFER [FORD], FORD MADOX, *Ancient Lights and Certain New Reflections, Being the Memories of a Young Man* (1911).

HUGHES, WINIFRED, *The Maniac in the Cellar: Sensation Novels of the 1860s* (Princeton, 1981).

HUMPHRIES, STEPHEN, *Hooligans or Rebels? An Oral History of Working-Class Childhood and Youth 1889–1939* (Oxford, 1981).

HURD, MICHAEL, *The Ordeal of Ivor Gurney* (Oxford, 1978).

HURT, J. S., *Elementary Schooling and the Working Classes 1860–1918* (1979).

HUTCHINSON, HORACE G., *Life of Sir John Lubbock*, 2 vols. (1914).

——(ed.), *Private Diaries of the Rt. Hon. Sir Algernon West, G.C.B.* (1922).

HUXLEY, GERVAS, *Both Hands: An Autobiography* (1970).

HUXLEY, JULIAN, *Memories* (1970).

HYDE, H. MONTGOMERY, *Oscar Wilde* (1976; paperback edn., 1982).

HYNDMAN, H. M., *The Record of an Adventurous Life* (1911).

INGE, W. R., *Diary of a Dean, St Paul's 1911–1934* (1949).

IRVING, LAURENCE, *Henry Irving: The Actor and his World* (1951; paperback edn., 1989).

JACKS, LAWRENCE PEARSALL, *Life and Letters of Stopford Brooke*, 2 vols. (1917).

JACKSON, HOLBROOK, *The Eighteen Nineties* (1913; Harmondsworth, 1939).

——*Southward Ho! And Other Essays* (1914).

JACOBS, ARTHUR, *Arthur Sullivan: A Victorian Musician* (Oxford, 1984; paperback edn., 1986).

JACOBS, W. W., *Many Cargoes* (1896, 1912).

JAMES, HENRY, *Notes on Novelists, with Some Other Notes* (New York, 1914, 1969).

JAMES, ROBERT RHODES, *Rosebery* (1963).

JAY, ELIZABETH (ed.), *The Autobiography of Margaret Oliphant* (Oxford, 1990).

JEPSON, EDGAR, *Memories of a Victorian* (1933).

——*Memories of an Edwardian and Neo-Georgian* (1937).

JEROME, JEROME K., *The Idle Thoughts of an Idle Fellow: A Book for an Idle Holiday* (1886).

——*My Life and Times* (1926, 1983).

JERROLD, DOUGLAS, *Georgian Adventure* (1937, 1938).

JOHN, ANGELA V., *Elizabeth Robins: Staging a Life, 1862–1952* (1995).

——and EUSTANCE, CLAIRE (eds.), *The Men's Share? Masculinities, Male Support and Women's Suffrage in Britain, 1890–1920* (1997).

JOHNSON, EDGAR, *Charles Dickens*, 2 vols. (1953).

JOLLIFFE, JOHN (ed.), *Raymond Asquith: Life and Letters* (1980).

JONES, HENRY FESTING, *Samuel Butler, Author of Erewhon (1835–1902): A Memoir*, 2 vols. (1919)

——(ed.), *The Notebooks of Samuel Butler* (1912) introd. P. N. Furbank (1985).

JONES, JOHN, *Balliol College: A History 1263–1939* (Oxford, 1988).

JORDAN, JOHN O., and PATTEN, ROBERT L. (eds.), *Literature in the Marketplace: Nineteenth-Century British Publishing and Reading Practices* (Cambridge, 1995).

JOSEPH, MICHAEL, *The Commercial Side of Literature* (n.d. [1925]).

JOYCE, JAMES, *Ulysses* (1922; Harmondsworth, 1968).

JOYCE, PATRICK, *Visions of the People* (Cambridge, 1991).

KADISH, ALON, *Apostle Arnold: The Life and Death of Arnold Toynbee, 1852–1883* (Chapel Hill, NC, 1986).

—— 'University Extension and the Working Classes: The Case of the Northumberland Miners', *Historical Research* (June 1987).

KARL, FREDERICK R., *Joseph Conrad: The Three Lives* (New York, 1979).

—— and DAVIES, LAURENCE (eds.), *The Collected Letters of Joseph Conrad*, i. *1861–1897* (Cambridge, 1983).

—— —— (eds.), *The Collected Letters of Joseph Conrad*, ii: *1898–1902 (Cambridge, 1986).*

—— —— (eds.), *The Collected Letters of Joseph Conrad*, iii: *1903–1907 (Cambridge, 1988).*

—— —— (eds.), *The Collected Letters of Joseph Conrad*, iv: *1908–1911 (Cambridge, 1990).*

KARPELES, MAUD, *Cecil Sharp: His Life and Work* (1967).

KEATING, PETER, *The Haunted Study: A Social History of the English Novel 1875–1914* (1989).

KEDLESTON, EARL CURZON OF, *Modern Parliamentary Eloquence* (1913).

KEIR, DAVID, *The House of Collins: The Story of a Scottish Family of Publishers from 1789 to the Present Day* (1952).

KELLY, JOHN S., *A W. B. Yeats Chronology* (Basingstoke, 2005).

—— and SCHUCHARD, RONALD (eds.), *The Collected Letters of W. B. Yeats* iii: *1901–1904* (Oxford, 1994), *iv: 1905–1907* (Oxford, 2005).

KELLY, THOMAS, *A History of Public Libraries in Great Britain, 1845–1975* (1977).

KEMP, PETER (ed.), *The Oxford Dictionary of Literary Quotations* (Oxford, 1997).

KEMP, SANDRA, MITCHELL, CHARLOTTE, and TROTTER, DAVID (eds.), *Edwardian Fiction: An Oxford Companion* (Oxford, 1997).

KENNEDY, MICHAEL, *Portrait of Elgar*, 2nd edn. (Oxford, 1982).

KENNET, LADY, *Self-Portrait of an Artist* (1949).

KENYON, C. FRED, *Hall Caine: The Man and the Novelist* (1901).

KENYON, FREDERIC G. (ed.), *The Letters of Elizabeth Barrett Browning*, 2 vols. (1897).

KETTLE, MICHAEL, *Salomé's Last Veil* (1977).

KEYNES, SIR GEOFFREY (ed.), *The Letters of Rupert Brooke* (1968).

—— *The Gates of Memory* (1981).

KINGSLEY, CHARLES, *Yeast: A Problem* (1851, 1888).

KINGSMILL, HUGH, *Frank Harris* (1932, 1949).

KIPLING, RUDYARD, *Mrs. Bathurst and Other Stories*, introd. John Bayley, World's Classics (Oxford 1991).

—— *Stalky & Co.* (1899, 1962).

—— *Traffics and Discoveries* (1904, 1914)

—— *A Book of Words: Selections from Speeches and Addresses Delivered between 1906 and 1927* (1928).

—— *Something of Myself*, ed. Thomas Pinney (Cambridge, 1990, 1991).

KITTON, FRED G., *Dickensiana: A Bibliography of the Literature Relating to Charles Dickens and his Writings* (1886).

KNIGHT, WILLIAM (ed.), *The Robert Browning Centenary Celebration* (1912).

KORG, JACOB, *George Gissing: A Critical Biography* (1963).

KOSS, STEPHEN, *Fleet Street Radical: A. G. Gardiner and the Daily News* (1973).

—— *Nonconformity in Modern British Politics* (1975).

KRIPALANI, KRISHNA, *Tagore A Life* (Oxford, 1961, 1971).

KUNITZ, STANLEY J. (ed.), *Twentieth Century Authors: First Supplement* (New York, 1955).

LAGO, MARY (ed.), *Men and Memories: Recollections 1872–1938 of William Rothenstein* (1978).

—— and FURBANK, P. N. (eds.), *Selected Letters of E. M. Forster*, i: *1879–1920* (1983, 1985).

—— (ed.), *Mary Gladstone (Mrs. Drew): Her Diaries and Letters* (1930).

MASTERMAN, NEVILLE, *The Forerunner: The Dilemmas of Tom Ellis, 1859–1899* (Swansea, 1972).

MASTERS, BRIAN, *Now Barabbas was a Rotter: The Extraordinary Life of Marie Corelli* (1978).

MASTERS, EDGAR LEE, *Whitman* (1937).

MATHEW, DAVID, *Acton: The Formative Years* (1946).

MATTHEW, H.C.G. (ed.), *The Gladstone Diaries, with Cabinet Minutes and Prime-Ministerial Correspondence*, iv–xiii (Oxford, 1974–94).

—— *Gladstone 1809–1874* (Oxford, 1986).

MAUDE, AYLMER, *The Life of Tolstóy*, ii (1910; World's Classics, Oxford, 1930).

MAUGHAM, ROBIN, *Somerset and All the Maughams* (1966).

MAUGHAM, W. SOMERSET, *Cakes and Ale* (1930, 1979).

—— *The Summing Up* (1938, 1940).

—— *A Writer's Notebook* (1949; Harmondsworth, 1967).

MEIXNER, JOHN A., *Ford Madox Ford's Novels* (Minneapolis, 1962).

METCALF, PRISCILLA, *James Knowles: Victorian Editor and Architect* (Oxford, 1980).

MEYER, MICHAEL, *Henrik Ibsen*, iii: *The Top of a Cold Mountain 1883–1906* (1971).

—— *Strindberg* (1985; paperback edn., Oxford, 1987).

MEYNELL, ALICE, *The Second Person Singular and Other Essays* (Oxford, n.d. [1921]).

MEYNELL, VIOLA, *Alice Meynell: A Memoir* (1929, 1947).

—— *Francis Thompson and Wilfrid Meynell* (1952).

—— (ed.), *Letters of J. M. Barrie* (1942).

MILLER, BETTY, *Robert Browning* (1952).

MILLER, JAMES E., JR. (ed.), *Theory of Fiction: Henry James* (Lincoln, Nebr., 1972).

MILLER, WILLIAM, *The Dickens Student and Collector: A List of Writings Relating to Charles Dickens and his Works 1836–1945* (1946).

MILLGATE, JANE, *Scott's Last Edition: A Study in Publishing History* (Edinburgh, 1989).

MILLGATE, MICHAEL, *Thomas Hardy: A Biography* (1982; paperback edn., Oxford, 1985).

—— *Testamentary Acts: Browning, Tennyson, James, Hardy* (Oxford, 1992; paperback edn., 1995).

—— (ed.), *Letters of Emma and Florence Hardy* (Oxford, 1996).

MILLS, J. SAXON, *Sir Edward Cook K. B. E.* (1921).

MILNE, A. A., *First Plays* (1919, 1924).

—— *Autobiography* (1939).

MITCHELL, B. R. and DEANE, P., *Abstract of British Historical Statistics* (Cambridge, 1962).

MITCHELL, DAVID, *Queen Christabel: A Biography of Christabel Pankhurst* (1977).

MITCHELL, LESLIE, *Bulwer Lytton: The Rise and Fall of a Victorian Man of Letters* (2003).

MITFORD, NANCY (ed.), *Noblesse Oblige* (1956; Oxford, 1989).

MIZENER, ARTHUR, *The Saddest Story: A Biography of Ford Madox Ford* (1971; paperback edn., New York, 1985).

MONTGOMERY, MAUREEN E., *Gilded Prostitution: Status, Money, and Transatlantic Marriages 1870–1914* (1989).

MONYPENNY, W. F., and BUCKLE, G. E., *The Life of Benjamin Disraeli, Earl of Beaconsfield*, 6 vols. (1910–20).

MOON, G. WASHINGTON, *Men and Women of the Time: A Dictionary of Contemporaries*, 13th edn. (1891).

MOORE, A. W., *A History of the Isle of Man*, 2 vols. (1900).

Moore, Doris Langley, *E. Nesbit: A Biography* (Philadelphia, 1966).

Moore, George, *Literature at Nurse; or, Circulating Morals* (1885), ed. P. Coustillas (Hassocks, 1976).

—— *Confessions of a Young Man* (1886, rev. 1904, 1916; Travellers' Library ed. 1928).

—— *Esther Waters* (1894; Everyman edn., 1962).

—— *Evelyn Innes* (1898).

—— *Memoirs of my Dead Life* (1906, 1915).

—— *Hail and Farewell! A Trilogy*: i: *Ave* (1911); ii: *Salve* (1912); iii: *Vale* (1914).

Moore, John, *The Life and Letters of Edward Thomas* (1939; paperback edn., Gloucester, 1983).

Moorman, Mary, *George Macaulay Trevelyan* (1980).

Morgan, Charles, *Epitaph on George Moore* (1935).

—— *The House of Macmillan* (1943).

Morgan, K. O. (ed.), *Lloyd George, Family Letters 1885–1936* (1973).

Morgan, Ted, *Somerset Maugham* (1980).

Morley, John, *Studies in Literature* (1890, 1907).

—— *The Life of William Ewart Gladstone* (1903; 2 vols., 1911)

—— *Recollections*, 2 vols. (1917).

Morrison Arthur, *A Child of the Jago* (1896), introd. P. J. Keating (1969).

Mosley, Leonard, *Curzon: The End of an Epoch* (1960, 1961).

Mosley, Nicholas, *Julian Grenfell: His Life and the Times of his Death 1888–1915* (New York, 1976).

Muddock, J. E. (ed.), *The Savage Club Papers* (1897).

Munro, Hector Hugh, *The Complete Stories of Saki* (Ware, 1993).

Murray, Nicholas, *A Life of Matthew Arnold* (1996).

Murry, J. Middleton, *Fyodor Dostoevsky: A Critical Study* (1916).

Nash, Eveleigh, *I Liked the Life I Lived* (1941).

Naylor, L. E., *The Irrepressible Victorian: The Story of Thomas Gibson Bowles* (1965).

Nesbit, E., *The Railway Children* (1906; Oxford, 1991).

Nevill, Ralph (ed.), *The Reminiscences of Lady Dorothy Nevill* (1906, n.d. [1910]).

Nevinson, Henry W., *More Change, More Chances* (1925).

—— *Fire of Life* (1935).

Newbolt, Henry, *Collected Poems, 1897–1907* (n.d.).

Newsome, David, *On the Edge of Paradise: A. C. Benson, the Diarist* (1980).

Nicholas, H. G. (ed.), *To the Hustings: Election Scenes from English Fiction* (1956).

Nicoll, Allardyce, *A History of Late Nineteenth Century Drama 1850–1900*, 2 vols. (Cambridge, 1946).

—— *English Drama 1900–1930* (Cambridge, 1973).

Nicoll, Mildred Robertson (ed.), *The Letters of Annie S. Swan* (1945).

Nicoll, W. Robertson, *'Ian Maclaren': Life of the Rev. John Watson* (1908).

—— *A Bookman's Letters* (1913).

Nicholls, C. S. (ed.), *The Dictionary of National Biography: Missing Persons* (Oxford, 1993).

Nichols, Beverley, *Twenty-Five: Being a Young Man's Candid Recollections of his Elders and Betters* (1926, 1930).

Nicolson, Harold, *Helen's Tower* (1937).

QUILLER-COUCH, SIR ARTHUR, *Oxford Book of English Verse* (Oxford, 1900; new edn., 1939).

QUINAULT, ROLAND, 'The Cult of the Centenary, *c*.1784–1914', *Historical Research*, 71/176 (Oct. 1998).

QUINN, E. V., and Prest, J. M. (eds.), *Dear Miss Nightingale: A Selection of Benjamin Jowett's Letters to Florence Nightingale 1860–1893* (Oxford, 1987).

RAE, JOHN, *Conscience and Politics: The British Government and the Conscientious Objector to Military Service, 1916–1919* (Oxford, 1970).

RAEPER, WILLIAM, *George MacDonald* (1987).

RAITT, SUZANNE, *May Sinclair: A Modern Victorian* (Oxford, 2000).

RALEIGH, LADY (ed.), *The Letters of Sir Walter Raleigh (1879–1922)*, 2 vols. (1926).

RALEIGH, WALTER, *Robert Louis Stevenson* (1919).

RAMM, AGATHA (ed.), *Beloved and Darling Child: Last Letters between Queen Victoria and her Eldest Daughter 1886–1901* (1990).

RANSOM, TERESA, *The Mysterious Miss Marie Corelli: Queen of Victorian Bestsellers* (Stroud, 1999).

RANSOME, ARTHUR, *Bohemia in London* (1907; Oxford, 1984).

RAWNSLEY REVD. H. D., *Memories of the Tennysons* (Glasgow, 1900).

RAYMOND, ERNEST, *The Story of my Days: An Autobiography 1888–1922* (1968).

READ, HERBERT, *The Contrary Experience: Autobiographies* (1963, 1973).

REILLY, C. H., *Scaffolding in the Sky: A Semi-Architectural Autobiography* (1938).

REILLY, CATHERINE W., *English Poetry of the First World War: A Bibliography* (1978).

—— *Late Victorian Poetry, 1880–1899: An Annotated Bibliography* (1994).

—— (ed.), *Scars upon my Heart: Women's Poetry and Verse of the First World War* (1981).

RENDEL, LORD, *Personal Papers* (1931).

REYNOLDS, AIDAN, and CHARLTON, WILLIAM, *Arthur Machen* (Philadelphia, 1964).

REYNOLDS, QUENTIN, *The Fiction Factory* (New York, 1955).

REYNOLDS, STEPHEN, and WOOLLEY, BOB and TOM, *Seems So! A Working-Class View of Politics* (1911, 1913).

RHYS, ERNEST, and VAUGHAN, LLOYD (eds.), *A Century of English Essays* (1913).

RICHARDS, JOHN MORGAN, *With John Bull and Jonathan: Reminiscences of Sixty Years of an American Life in England and the United States* (1905).

—— *The Life of John Oliver Hobbes, Told in her Correspondence with Numerous Friends* (1911).

RICHARDS, THOMAS, *The Commodity Culture of Victorian England: Advertising and Spectacle 1851–1914* (Stanford, Calif., 1990).

RICHMOND, SIR ARTHUR, *Twenty-Six Years, 1879–1905* (1961).

RIDDELL, LORD, *More Pages from my Diary 1908–1914* (1934).

RIDLEY, JANE, and PERCY, CLAYRE (eds.), *The Letters of Arthur Balfour and Lady Elcho* (1992).

RIEWALD, J. G. (ed.), *Beerbohm's Literary Caricatures* (1977).

ROBERTS, CECIL, *The Growing Boy: Being the First Book of an Autobiography, 1892–1908* (1967).

—— *The Years of Promise: Being the Second Book of an Autobiography, 1908–1919* (1968).

ROBERTS, ELIZABETH, *A Woman's Place: An Oral History of Working-Class Women, 1890–1940* (Oxford, 1984).

—— *Women's Work 1840–1940* (1988).

ROBERTS, ROBERT, *The Classic Slum: Salford Life in the First Quarter of the Century* (Manchester, 1971).

—— *A Ragged Schooling: Growing Up in the Classic Slum* (Manchester, 1976; Glasgow, 1978).

ROBERTSON, W. GRAHAM, *Time Was* (1931, 1955).

ROBINSON, DAVID, *World Cinema: A Short History* (1973; rev. 1981).

—— *Chaplin: His Life and Art* (1985).

RODD, SIR JAMES RENNELL, *Social and Diplomatic Memories, 1902–1919* (1925).

ROGERS, FREDERICK, *Labour, Life and Literature* (1913); new edn., ed. David Rubinstein (Brighton, 1973).

ROGERS, NEVILLE (ed.), *The Complete Poetical Works of Percy Bysshe Shelley* (Oxford, 1972).

ROGERS, TIMOTHY (ed.), *Georgian Poetry 1911–1922: The Critical Heritage* (1977).

ROLFE, FR. [Frederick Baron Corvo], *Hadrian the VII* (1904; Ware, 1993).

ROLPH, C. H., *Kingsley: The Life, Letters and Diaries of Kingsley Martin* (1973).

—— [C.R. HEWITT], *London Particulars* (Oxford, 1980; paperback edn., 1982).

ROSE, JONATHAN, *The Edwardian Temperament, 1895–1919* (Athens, Ohio, 1986).

—— *The Intellectual Life of the British Working Class* (New Haven, 2001).

—— and ANDERSON, PATRICIA J. (eds.), *British Literary Publishing Houses, 1881–1965, Dictionary of Literary Biography*, 112 (1991).

ROSE, KENNETH, *King George V* (1983).

ROSEBERY, LORD, *Miscellanies, Literary and Historical*, 2 vols. (1921).

ROSENBERG, JOHN, *Dorothy Richardson: The Genius they Forgot* (1973).

ROTHENSTEIN, WILLIAM, *Men and Memories, 1872–1900* (1931; new edn., 1934).

—— *Men and Memories, 1900–1922* (1932; new edn., 1934).

ROVER, CONSTANCE, *Love, Morals and the Feminists* (1970).

ROWELL, GEORGE, *The Victorian Theatre 1792–1914* (2nd edn., Cambridge, 1978).

—— (ed.), *Later Victorian Plays 1890–1914* (Oxford, 1968; 2nd rev. edn., 1972).

—— (ed.), *Nineteenth Century Plays*, (2nd edn., Oxford, 1972).

ROWSE, A. L., *A Cornish Childhood* (1942; 1975).

ROY, BRANDON [Florence Barclay], *Guy Mervyn*, 3 vols. (1891).

RUSKIN, JOHN, *Praeterita* (1899; paperback edn., Oxford, 1978).

RUSSELL, CHARLES E. B., *Social Problems of the North* (1913).

RUSSELL, SIR EDWARD, *Arrested Fugitives* (1912).

RUSSELL, G. W. E., *Collections and Recollections: Series II* (1902, 1909).

—— (ed.), *Sir Wilfrid Lawson: A Memoir* (1910).

—— *One Look Back* (1911).

ST HELIER, LADY [Mary Jeune], *Memories of Fifty Years* (1909).

ST JOHN, CHRISTOPHER (ed.), *Ellen Terry and Bernard Shaw: A Correspondence* (1931, 1949).

SAINTSBURY, GEORGE, *The Earl of Derby* (1892).

—— *Corrected Impressions*, 2nd edn. (1895).

—— *A Short History of English Literature* (1898).

—— *A History of Criticism and Literary Taste in Europe*, i (1900).

—— *A Scrap Book* (1922).

—— *A Second Scrap Book* (1923).

—— *Collected Essays and Papers 1895–1920*, 3 vols. (1923).

—— *A Last Scrap Book* (1924).

—— *Prefaces and Essays* (1933).

SALMON, ERIC, *Granville Barker: A Secret Life* (1983).

STEPHEN, SIDNEY, and LEE, LESLIE (eds.), *Lives of the 'Lustrious: A Dictionary of Irrational Biography* (1901).

STEPHENSON, GWENDOLEN, *Edward Stuart Talbot 1844–1934* (1936).

STEVENSON, LIONEL, *The Ordeal of George Meredith* (New York, 1953, 1967).

STEVENSON, ROBERT LOUIS, *Familiar Studies of Men and Books* (1882, 1925).

—— *Memories and Portraits* (1887).

STOREY, GRAHAM, TILLOTSON, KATHLEEN, and EASSON, ANGUS (eds.), *The Letters of Charles Dickens*, vii: *1853–1855* (Oxford, 1993).

STRACHEY, JOHN ST LOE, *The Adventure of Living: A Subjective Autobiography* (1922).

SULLIVAN, ALVIN (ed.), *British Literary Magazines: The Victorian and Edwardian Age, 1837–1913* (1984).

—— (ed.), *British Literary Magazines: The Modern Age, 1914–1984* (1986).

SUTCLIFFE, PETER, *The Oxford University Press: An Informal History* (Oxford, 1978).

SUTHERLAND, JAMES (ed.), *The Oxford Book of English Talk* (Oxford, 1953).

—— (ed.), *The Oxford Book of Literary Anecdotes* (Oxford, 1975).

SUTHERLAND, JOHN, *Fiction and the Fiction Industry* (1978).

—— *The Longman Companion to Victorian Fiction* (1988).

—— *Mrs Humphry Ward: Eminent Victorian, Pre-eminent Edwardian* (Oxford, 1990).

SUTRO, ALFRED, *The Cave of Illusion*, introd. Maurice Maeterlinck (1900).

—— *Celebrities and Simple Souls* (1933).

SWAN, ANNIE S., *My Life: An Autobiography* (1934).

SWANWICK, H. M., *I have been Young* (1935).

SWINBURNE, ALGERNON CHARLES, *Studies in Prose and Poetry* (1915).

SWINNERTON, FRANK, *The Georgian Literary Scene* (1935; rev. 1938).

—— *Arnold Bennett: A Last Word* (New York, 1978).

—— (ed.), *The Journals of Arnold Bennett* (1954).

SYMONDS, RICHARD, *Oxford and Empire: The Last Lost Cause?* (1986).

SYMONS, A. J. A., *The Quest for Corvo* (1934; Harmondsworth, 1940).

SYMONS, JULIAN, *Horatio Bottomley* (1955).

TAIT, HUGH, and WALKER, RICHARD, *The Athenaeum Collection* (2000).

TAYLOR, D. J., *Thackeray* (1999; paperback edn., 2000).

TAYLOR, F., and SIMPSON, W. G., *The John Rylands University Library of Manchester*, brochure (1982).

TAYLOR, H. A., *Robert Donald* (1934).

TAYLOR, JENNY BOURNE, *In the Secret Theatre of Home: Wilkie Collins, Sensation Narrative, and Nineteenth-Century Psychology* (1988).

TAYLOR, JUDY (ed.), *Beatrix Potter's Letters* (1989).

TELLAR, MARK, *A Young Man's Passage* (1952).

TEMPLE, WILLIAM, *Life of Bishop Percival* (1921).

TENNYSON, SIR CHARLES, *Stars and Markets* (1957).

TENNYSON, HALLAM, *Alfred Lord Tennyson* (2 vols., 1897; 1-vol. edn., 1899).

TERRY, R. C. (ed.), *Robert Louis Stevenson: Interviews and Recollections* (1996).

THOMAS, EDWARD, *Richard Jefferies* (1909, 1978).

THOMPSON, ALEX M., *Here I Lie: The Memorial of an Old Journalist* (1937).

THOMPSON, EDWARD, *Robert Bridges 1844–1930* (Oxford, 1944).

THOMPSON, E. P., *William Morris: Romantic to Revolutionary* (1955; rev. 1977).

THOMPSON, FLORA, *Lark Rise to Candleford* (Oxford, 1945, 1947).

——*A Country Calendar and Other Writings*, ed. Margaret Lane (Oxford, 1979; paperback edn., 1984).

THOMPSON, FRANCIS, *Works*, 3 vols. (1913).

THOMSON, SIR J. J., *Recollections and Reflections* (1936).

THORNE, GUY [Cyril Arthur Edward Ranger Gull], *When It Was Dark* (1903; popular edn., 1904).

THWAITE, ANN, *Waiting for the Party: The Life of Frances Hodgson Burnett, 1849–1924* (1974; paperback edn., 1994).

——*Edmund Gosse: A Literary Landscape 1849–1928* (Oxford, 1984; paperback edn., 1985).

——*A. A. Milne: His Life* (1990).

——*Emily Tennyson: The Poet's Wife* (1996).

TILLETT, BEN, *Memories and Reflections* (1931).

TILLOTSON, GEOFFREY and KATHLEEN, *Mid-Victorian Studies* (1965).

TOLLEMACHE, HON. LIONEL A., *Talks with Mr. Gladstone* (1898).

TOLSTOY, LEO, *What I Believe ('My Religion')*, ed. V. Tchertkoff and A. C. Fifield (Christchurch, 1902).

TOMALIN, CLAIRE, *The Invisible Woman: The Story of Nelly Ternan and Charles Dickens* (1990, 1991).

TOMALIN, RUTH, *W. H. Hudson: A Biography* (1982 Oxford; paperback edn., 1984).

TORR, DONA, *Tom Mann and his Times*, i: *1856–1890* (1956).

TOWNSEND, JOHN ROWE, *Written for Children: An Outline of English-Language Children's Literature*, rev. edn. (1974; Harmondsworth, 1976).

TRANTER, N. L., *Population and Society, 1750–1940* (1985).

TREE, (SIR) HERBERT BEERBOHM, *Thoughts and Afterthoughts* (1913; popular edn., 1915).

TREVELYAN, G. M., *Recreations of an Historian* (1919).

——*Sir George Otto Trevelyan* (1932).

——*An Autobiography and Other Essays* (1949).

TREVELYAN, JANET PENROSE, *The Life of Mrs. Humphry Ward* (1923).

TREWIN, WENDY, *All on Stage: Charles Wyndham and the Alberys* (1980).

TROLLOPE, ANTHONY, *North America* (1862; Harmondsworth, 1968).

——*An Autobiography* (1883, 1946).

TROYAT, HENRI, *Tolstoy*, trans. Nancy Amphoux (1965; Harmondswoth, 1970).

TSUZUKI, CHUSCHICHI, *Edward Carpenter 1844–1929: Prophet of Human Fellowship* (Cambridge, 1980).

TWEEDSMUIR, LADY (ed.), *John Buchan by his Wife and Friends* (1947).

UNWIN, SIR STANLEY, *The Truth about Publishing* (1926; rev. 1946).

VANBRUGH, IRENE, *To Tell my Story* (1948).

VICINUS, MARTHA, *The Industrial Muse* (1974).

VILJOEN, HELEN GILL (ed.), *The Brantwood Diary of John Ruskin* (New Haven, 1971).

VINCENT, BENJAMIN, *Haydn's Dictionary of Dates and Universal Information*, 22nd edn. (1898).

VINCENT, DAVID, *The Culture of Secrecy: Britain, 1832–1998* (Oxford, 1998).

VINCENT, JOHN (ed.), *The Later Derby Diaries* (Bristol: privately printed, 1981).

——(ed.), *The Crawford Papers: The Journals of David Lindsay, Twenty-Seventh Earl of Crawford and the Tenth Earl of Balcarres* (Manchester, 1984).

VOGELER, MARTHA S., *Frederic Harrison: The Vocations of a Positivist* (Oxford, 1984).

VYVER, BERTHA, *Memoirs of Marie Corelli* (1930).

WADE, ALLAN (ed.), *The Letters of W. B. Yeats* (1954).

WAIN, JOHN (ed.), *The Oxford Library of Short Novels* (Oxford, 1990).

WALKLEY, A. B., *Frames of Mind* (1899).

WALLER, P. J., *Democracy and Sectarianism: A Political and Social History of Liverpool 1868–1939* (Liverpool, 1981).

—— *Town, City and Nation: England 1850–1914* (Oxford, 1983).

—— (ed.), *Politics and Social Change in Modern Britain: Essays Presented to A. F. Thompson* (Hassocks, 1987).

WALTON, ALAN HULL (ed.), *The Perfumed Garden*, translated by Sir Richard Burton (1963).

WALTON, JAMES (ed.), *The Faber Book of Smoking* (2000).

WARD, A. C. (ed.), *Specimens of English Dramatic Criticism*, XVII–XX *Centuries* (Oxford, 1945).

WARD, MRS HUMPHRY, *A Writer's Recollections* (1918).

—— *Robert Elsmere* (1888), ed. and introd. Rosemary Ashton, World's Classics, (Oxford, 1987).

WARD, MAISIE, *Gilbert Keith Chesterton* (1944).

—— *Return to Chesterton* (1952).

WASSERSTEIN, BERNARD, *Herbert Samuel: A Political Life* (Oxford, 1992).

WATSON, AARON, *A Great Labour Leader, Being a Life of the Right Hon. Thomas Burt M.P.* (1908).

WATTS, CEDRIC, and DAVIES, LAURENCE, *Cunninghame Graham* (Cambridge, 1979).

WATTS-DUNTON, THEODORE, *Old Familiar Faces* (1916).

WEBB, BEATRICE, *Our Partnership*, ed. Barbara Drake and Margaret Cole (1948).

WEINTRAUB, STANLEY, *The London Yankees: Portraits of American Writers and Artists in England 1894–1914* (New York, 1979).

WELLS, G. P. (ed.), *H. G. Wells in Love: Postscript to an Experiment in Autobiography* (1984).

WELLS, H. G., *Tono-Bungay* (1909, 1911).

—— *The New Machiavelli* (1911; Harmondsworth, 1946).

—— *Experiment in Autobiography*, 2 vols. (1934; paperback edn., 1969).

WEST, ANTHONY, *H. G. Wells: Aspects of a Life* (1984; Harmondsworth, 1985).

WEST, REBECCA, *The Strange Necessity: Essays and Reviews* (1928, 1987).

WEST, SIR ALGERNON, *Recollections, 1832 to 1886* (1899, n.d.).

WESTCOTT, ARTHUR, *Life and Letters of Brooke Foss Westcott*, 2 vols. (1903).

[WHITE, WILLAM HALE], *The Autobiography of Mark Rutherford* (1881), ed. William S. Peterson, World's Classics (Oxford, 1990).

WHITEHOUSE, J. HOWARD, *The Solitary Warrior: New Letters by Ruskin* (1929).

—— (ed.), *Ruskin the Prophet and Other Centenary Studies* (1920).

WHITWORTH, GEOFFREY, *The Making of a National Theatre* (1951).

WILDE, OSCAR, *Plays* (1954).

—— *Plays, Prose Writings, and Poems*, introd. Hesketh Pearson (1930, 1962).

WILKINSON, ALAN, *The Church of England and the First World War* (1978).

WILLETT, JOHN, *Art in a City* (1967).

WILLIAMS, ALFRED, *Life in a Railway Factory* (1915; Newton Abbot, 1969).

WILLIAMSON, C. N. and A. M., *The Lightning Conductor* (1902, n.d.).

WILSON, CHARLES, *First with the News: The History of W. H. Smith, 1792–1972* (1985).

WILSON, JEAN MOORCROFT, *Siegfried Sassoon: The Making of a War Poet, 1886–1918* (1998, 2002).

WILSON, TREVOR (ed.), *The Political Diaries of C. P. Scott 1911–1928* (1970).

WINSTEN, S. (ed.), *G.B.S. 90: Aspects of Bernard Shaw's Life and Work* (1946).

WOODWARD, E. L., *Short Journey* (1942).

WOOLF, VIRGINIA, *The Voyage Out* (1915, 1957).

WORTHEN, JOHN, *D. H. Lawrence: The Early Years, 1885–1912* (Cambridge, 1991).

WRENCH, JOHN EVELYN, *Geoffrey Dawson and our Times* (1955).

YATES, EDMUND, *His Recollections and Experiences*, 2 vols. (1884).

YEATS, W. B., *Autobiographies* (1955).

YOUNG, JESSICA BRETT, *Francis Brett Young: A Biography* (1962).

ZANGWILL, ISRAEL, *Without Prejudice* (1896).

—— *Ghetto Comedies* (1907).

—— 'The Awkward Age of the Women's Movement', *Fortnightly Review*, 92 (Nov. 1912).

ZATLIN, LINDA GERTNER, *Aubrey Beardsley and Victorian Sexual Politics* (Oxford, 1990).

ZYTARUK, GEORGE J., and BOULTON, JAMES T. (eds.), *The Letters of D. H. Lawrence*, ii: *June 1913–October 1916* (Cambridge, 1982).

INDEX OF BOOK, ESSAY, PAMPHLET, PLAY, POEM AND SHORT STORY TITLES